Black Sea

Caspian Sea

Aral Sea

Toros Dağlari

Cyprus

Kuhha-ye Zagros

Reshteh-ye Alborz

Aras River

Amu Darya (Oxus River)

Hindu Kush

Mesopotamia

Tigris River

Euphrates River

Dasht-e Kavor (Salt Desert)

Iranian Plateau

Syrian Desert

Jordan River

Dead Sea

Sinai

Nafud

Dasht-e Lut (Sand Desert)

Persian Gulf

Nile River

al-Hijaz

Najd

Red Sea

Gulf of Oman

Nubian Desert

Arabian Peninsula

al-Rub al-Khali

Athara River

Arabian Sea

Blue Nile River

Gulf of Aden

Socotra

Nile River

INDIAN OCEAN

N

0   200   400 mi.

0   200   400 km

For Reference

Not to be taken from this room

ENCYCLOPEDIA OF THE
MODERN
MIDDLE EAST &
NORTH AFRICA
SECOND EDITION

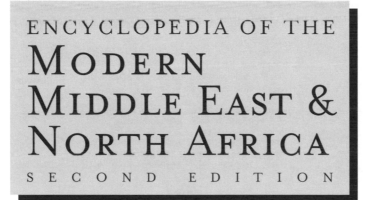

ENCYCLOPEDIA OF THE

MODERN MIDDLE EAST & NORTH AFRICA

SECOND EDITION

VOLUME 3

Laabi – Shamlu

Philip Mattar

EDITOR IN CHIEF

MACMILLAN REFERENCE USA

An imprint of Thomson Gale, a part of The Thomson Corporation

THOMSON

GALE

Detroit • New York • San Francisco • San Diego • New Haven, Conn. • Waterville, Maine • London • Munich

The Encyclopedia of the Modern Middle East and North Africa, 2nd Edition

Philip Mattar

For permission to use material from this product, submit your request via Web at http://www.gale-edit.com/permissions, or you may download our Permissions Request form and sumbit your request by fax or mail to:

Thomson Gale
27500 Drake Rd.
Farmington Hills, MI 48331-3535
Permissions Hotline:
248-699-8006 or 800-877-4253, ext. 8006
Fax: 248-699-8074 or 800-762-4058

Cover photographs reproduced by permission of Corbis, and AP/Wide World Photos.

Since this page cannot legibly accommodate all copyright notices, the acknowledgements constitute an extension of the copyright notice.

While every effort has been made to ensure the reliability of the information presented in this publication, Thomson Gale does not guarantee the accuracy of the data contained herein. Thomson Gale accepts no payment for listing; and inclusion in the publication of any organization, agency, institution, publication, service, or individual does not imply endorsement of the editors or publisher. Errors brought to the attention of the publisher and verified to the satisfaction of the publisher will be corrected in future editions.

LIBRARY OF CONGRESS CATALOGING-IN-PUBLICATION DATA

Encyclopedia of the modern Middle East and North Africa / edited by Philip Mattar.— 2nd ed.
   p. cm.
     Includes bibliographical references and index.
     ISBN 0-02-865769-1 (set : alk. paper) — ISBN 0-02-865770-5 (v. 1 : alk. paper) — ISBN 0-02-865771-3 (v. 2 : alk. paper) — ISBN 0-02-865772-1 (v. 3 : alk. paper) — ISBN 0-02-865773-X (v. 4 : alk. paper)
     1. Middle East—Encyclopedias. 2. Africa, North—Encyclopedias. I. Mattar, Philip, 1944-

DS43.E53 2004
956'.003—dc22   2004005650

This title is also avalable as an e-book.
ISBN 0-02-865987-2 (set)
Contact your Gale sales representative for ordering information.

Printed in the United States of America
10 9 8 7 6 5 4 3

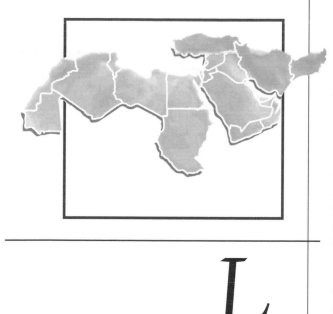

L

LAABI, ABDELLATIF
[1942–]

Moroccan poet and novelist.

Abdellatif Laabi was born in Fez, Morocco, to a Muslim family. He obtained a B.A. in French literature and taught French at the Lycée Mulay Idris. He founded the journal *Souffles* (Breaths) with Mohammed Khair-Eddine and Mustafa Nissaboury in 1966; the Arabic version of this journal was called *Anfas*. Laabi was imprisoned in 1972 and released on 18 July 1980. He has lived in France since 1985.

Laabi received strong support from friends and intellectuals all over the world while in prison. He continued to write poetry during this period and received many literary prizes. He describes his prison years in a series of poems and letters titled *Chroniques de la citadelle d'exil* (1983; Chronicles of the citadel of banishment).

Laabi seeks to eliminate the dividing lines between literary genres, but he is primarily a poet with an impressive number of poetry collections, including *Le règne de barbarie, et d'autres poèmes* (1980; The cruel rule and other poems), which marks the beginning of his poetic and literary writings. His most recent publications are *Le spleen de Casablanca* (1997; The spleen of Casablanca) and the illustrated collection *Petit musé portatif* (2002; A small portable museum). Laabi's success with poetry led him to write plays, including *Le baptême chacaliste* (1987; Jackalian baptism), *Exercices de tolérance* (1993; Drills in tolerance), and *Rimbaud et Shéhérazade* (2000; Rimbaud and Scheherazade). He also published four novels. *L'oeil de la nuit* (1969; The eye of the night), *Les rides du lion* (1989; The wrinkles of the lion), and *Le chemin des ordalies* (1982; The road of ordeals), re-edited in 2000 as *Le fou d'espoir* (Crazy with hope), relate his painful years in prison. His *Le fond de la jarre* (2002; The bottom of the jug) evokes the traditional life in Fez during the colonial period.

Laabi has translated extensively from Arabic into French: the poems of the Moroccan Abdallah Zrika, published as *Rires de l'arbre à palabre* (1982; Laughter of the palaver tree); an anthology of Palestinian poetry, *La poésie palestinienne de combat* (1970;

Palestinian struggle poetry); Mahmud Darwish's poetry, as *Rien qu'une autre année* (1983; It is only another year); *Soleil en instance* (1986; Sun in process), by the Syrian novelist Hanna Mina; a collection of poetry by the Iraqi Abd al-Wahhab al-Bayati, *Autobiographie du voleur de feu* (1987; Autobiography of the fire thief); and a collection of poems by the Palestinian Samih al-Qassim, *Je t'aime au gré de la mort* (1988; I love you at the pleasure of death).

Laabi's works reveal an interest in the human being and a strong commitment to the Palestinian cause. Much of his writing can be described as revolutionary. His long-term goal was to sever the strong link to Western culture in order to end the cultural alienation of the Maghribi writer. Yet he also sought renewal through the elimination of antiquated and unsuitable traditions. His pre-prison poetry was characterized by a violent anger provoked by the repressive policy of the time. The writings published in *Souffles* reflect a similar attitude. His post-prison poetry shows signs of greater wisdom, maturity, and depth of reflection.

Laabi explained his positions, ideology, and prison experience in a series of conversations with Jacques Alessandra published under the title *La brûlure des interrogations* (1985; The scald of interrogations). He provided in the same book a useful assessment of the literary scene in Morocco and an insight into his writings and thought.

See also LITERATURE: ARABIC, NORTH AFRICAN.

Bibliography

Abdel-Jaouad, Hédi. *Encyclopedia of African Literature.* London: Routledge, 2003.

AIDA A. BAMIA

LAAYOUNE

The largest city in Western Sahara.

Laayoune (also El-Aaiun, El-Ayoun, al-Ayun) is both the largest city in Western Sahara and the capital of one of the three provinces that Morocco established in the territory. The discovery of potable water at the site resulted in the establishment of a Spanish military garrison in 1938, marking the beginning of the town. It was made the capital of Spain's new Sahara province in 1958. The Spanish authorities subsequently established a port on the Atlantic coast 18 miles from the town, along with facilities for the export of newly discovered phosphates. The European population when the Spanish withdrew in 1976 was approximately 10,000; the local Sahrawi population was around 30,000, a considerable number of whom were living in tents or makeshift structures on the edge of town. Many of the Sahrawis fled to Algeria with Polisario forces in 1975 and 1976. Since then, the population has grown to 175,000. Morocco has sought to consolidate its control of the territory by launching large-scale infrastructure projects such as the construction of hospitals, schools, and a football stadium and the expansion of drinking water facilities, and it has given incentives to Moroccan professionals to work there.

In 1991 Morocco orchestrated the entry of around 35,000 persons of Sahrawi origin in order to expand the list of eligible voters for the proposed UN referendum on the future of the western Sahara. Most of them were housed in tents in so-called unity camps. Fall 1999 witnessed major socioeconomic protests, with Sahrawis complaining of poor employment and housing conditions and discrimination in favor of Moroccans from the north. The unrest occasioned a harsh police crackdown in the city, aided by vigilante action by "northerners." The events shook the Moroccan regime headed by newly installed King Muhammad VI and contributed to the deposal of longtime interior minister Driss Basri. The government declared a new policy emphasizing regional development in order to win the hearts and minds of the population in advance of the proposed UN referendum. This new strategy was highlighted by three visits to the region by the king between October 2001 and February 2002, when he presided over a mass ceremony of allegiance to the throne.

See also GREEN MARCH; HASSAN II; MOROCCO; MUHAMMAD VI; TINDOUF; WESTERN SAHARA.

Bibliography

Pazzanita, Anthony G., and Hodges, Tony. *Historical Dictionary of the Western Sahara.* Metuchen, NJ: Scarecrow Press, 1982.

BRUCE MADDY-WEITZMAN

LABOR AND LABOR UNIONS

Depending on the country, trade unions in the Middle East are nonexistent (in some cases, illegal), state-controlled, or independent, but they rarely represent many workers effectively.

There are also an increasing number of socioeconomic problems (from child labor to the situation of migrant labor to widespread adult unemployment) that they can do little to address although these problems have been worsened by the impact of globalization on much of the region.

Formal trade-union structures in the Middle East grew out of European imperialism and colonialism—especially from the extension of capitalist markets and the introduction of mechanized production. From a relatively undeveloped division of labor with a guild form of collective action, the labor force now comprises a clearly articulated division of labor, new means of production, and workers who own nothing but their labor power. This process occurred relatively quickly in each locality but at very different times. The critical period was from the beginning of the twentieth century until shortly before World War I. After World War II, Middle Eastern economies became relatively closed, socialist, or quasi-socialist. Trade unions played secondary roles and have often been subordinated to state policies.

During the late years of the Ottoman Empire (in Anatolia and the Arab provinces) and the Qajar dynasty (in Iran), peasant production predominated. Urban areas accounted for little more than 15 percent of the economy. Industry was largely artisanal (skilled manual labor), based on simple instruments of production. The division of labor within productive enterprises was slight. Competition from European production often forced domestic artisanal and craft producers out of old sectors and into new ones and new government structures reduced the effective support of the state for their associations. In Iran and Egypt, integration into the world capitalist market reduced the role of artisans and craftsmen in textile production and animal transport even as it opened up some new sectors of the economy. Something similar occurred in Tunisia, although there foreign domination began in the late 1800s.

Direct colonial control, where it existed, transformed property rights to allow the creation of capitalist corporations and also the political power European and local entrepreneurs needed to affect tariff regulations and local costs to ensure their success. Trade unions arose in the context of European colonial domination and thus invariably engaged not only in local social conflict but in the political struggles over control of the various states.

Foreign capitalists used access to political power and to external sources of capital to take advantage of cheap local raw materials and labor in most of the Arab world (but this was somewhat less true of the relatively more independent states of Turkey and Iran). In Palestine, the Arabs were gradually dominated by the European-backed Jewish settlers. In Tunisia, French control allowed the Europeans to command both the agricultural and the mineral sectors. In Iran and Iraq, foreigners (Europeans and Americans) provided the capital for developing the petroleum industry, and intense conflict over the role of the state occurred repeatedly.

European capitalists often introduced foreign (European) labor into the region at higher wages than local laborers could command. They also brought in local workers from various sections of the countryside to work in factories; their employees thus had little in common and were easily manipulated. In Palestine, this interplay of nationalist politics and social conflict was particularly acute because the socialist institutions of the Zionist labor movement often acted to exclude Palestinian Arabs from particular labor markets; the General Federation of Labor in Eretz Yisrael (Histadrut)—unlike Arab, Turkish, or Persian trade unions—created the foundations of a labor economy to support Zionist nationalism as well as to protect the rights of workers. Exceptionally, Histadrut thus had a dual role, as investor as well as trade union, insofar as Histadrut controls the Hevrat ha-Ovedim firm with its many subordinate companies. Elsewhere, the struggle of workers against capital was often perceived as a national struggle and was co-opted into the struggle of nationalist politicians.

Two important political currents guided the early labor movement. Marxist intellectuals from outside the working class brought the ideas of class struggle and "scientific socialism" into the working class and often (but not always) also recruited workers into Leninist political parties. Workers hostile to the dominance of the liberal professionals in their movement also created their own independent unions.

In the Maghrib (North Africa), and especially in Tunis, the struggle for independence reached a heroic climax with the creation of a separate labor-union structure, the Union Générale des Travailleurs Tunisiens (General Union of Tunisian Workers; UGTT). It was led by Ferhat Hached rather than French communists in 1946. Elsewhere in the Arab world, leaders of the trade-union movement associated with the nationalist left allied themselves with political elites. After gaining independence, they extended the power of the state over the economy by nationalizing firms and creating a corporate trade-union structure. State investments created large public sectors in most countries, and it is the workers in the public sector who usually make up the bulk of trade-union members.

Those countries in the Middle East with unions generally have a single, often compulsory, trade-union structure. Countries with single-, state-, or ruling-party–controlled federations are Djibouti, Kuwait, Libya, Mauritania, Somalia, Syria, and Yemen. Iraq's public-sector employees were part of the state-controlled union federation until 1987, when the law was changed to exclude them so the state could cut its public-sector wage bill. Foreign nationals there, mainly Egyptians, are reported to be underpaid and mistreated. In these countries and in Egypt (where the Egyptian Trade Union Federation is formally separate from the state and the ruling National Democratic party), strikes by public-sector employees are illegal, and collective bargaining between workers and employers as equals is absent. The mid-1980s saw a renewal of protests and strikes in Egypt, especially in the public sector, as the government retreated from its social-welfare commitments. In many countries in the region, strikes are illegal and workers have few ways of challenging the power of the state or private employers.

The bulk of child labor in the region remains in agriculture but these children often work in export-intensive agriculture. By some estimates, there may be as many as two million children who work in Egypt. Most of them work in the fields, but they also play a role in urban small-scale production. Child labor is a problem on its own but it also in-

hibits the acquisition of literacy by substantial sections of the population.

Israel's Histadrut, although founded in 1920 in British-mandated Palestine, now controls significant economic resources through its associate institutions—thus remaining the state's sole trade union. Since 1953, Israeli Arabs have been accepted as members. Palestinians in the West Bank and Gaza Strip lack strong unions; both the Israeli government and the Palestinian nationalist movement are uncertain about the long-term effects of unions, and, in the pre-1993 Israel-Palestine Liberation Organization (PLO) accord atmosphere, union creation was difficult. In Lebanon and Jordan, autonomous and plural trade-union federations exist—in Lebanon, they continued to operate during the civil war.

In Tunisia, an independent trade-union federation with historic links to the ruling Neo-Destour party has operated independently and sometimes in antagonism to the state. The union federation was engaged in a massive wave of strikes in January 1977. In Morocco and Algeria, multiple trade-union federations exist independently of the state, and high unemployment coupled with low economic growth has produced labor unrest.

In Bahrain (where worker arbitration committees exist), Oman, Qatar, Saudi Arabia, and the United Arab Emirates, trade unions are illegal. Persistent reports exist of the arrests and executions of workers attempting to form unions in the eastern oil-rich provinces of Saudi Arabia, which also have large Shi'ite populations. Because a large part of the workforce in many of the countries of the Arabian peninsula are migrant laborers from elsewhere in the Arab world or from non-Arab Muslim countries, the absence of unions intensifies their liability to mistreatment. These workers, who in some cases make up a majority of the workforce, have no political rights and can be easily deported if they appear troublesome to their employers.

In Turkey, the trade-union movement was not integrated into the state, and plural union movements remained, the most important of which is the Confederation of Turkish Trade Unions (Türk Iş). Although dominant, Türk Iş faces competition from several other trade unions, notably DISK (The Confederation of Revolutionary Trade Unions, which was banned after the 1980 coup) and Islamic and Turkish nationalist confederations (Haqq Iş and MISK, respectively).

Trade unions in Iran have infrequently functioned freely since the 1950s. Between the 1953 coup and the 1979 Iranian revolution, the state actively intervened in trade-union affairs. After the revolution, there was (in addition to unions) an experiment in a broader form of workers' councils, known as *shura*. In 1983, the labor minister of the Islamic Republic of Iran failed to win passage of a restrictive new law. Most unions and the *shura* system were dissolved in 1985, and the government appears to have accepted the principle that workers and owners enter into individual contracts rather than collective agreements.

In the precolonial period, unions were often weak but provided workers with some independent voice in regard to the state and firm owners; in the post-colonial period, the material conditions of workers and their families have been more profoundly affected by decisions of central political authorities than by union struggles. If privatization continues to increase in Middle Eastern economies, "wildcat" struggles by workers are likely to increase. Privatized industries frequently attempt to increase profits by decreasing the size of the work force, thereby setting the stage for conflicts with unions (where they exist) and with sections of government that fear the impact of growing unemployment.

See also CONFEDERATION OF TURKISH TRADE UNIONS; HISTADRUT; LABOR ZIONISM; UNION GÉNÉRALE DES TRAVAILLEURS TUNISIENS (UGTT).

Bibliography

Batatu, Hanna. *The Old Social Classes and the Revolutionary Movements of Iraq.* Princeton, NJ: Princeton University Press, 1978.

Bayat, Assef. *Workers and Revolution in Iran.* London and Atlantic Highlands, NJ: Zed Press, 1987.

Economic Research Forum. *Economic Trends in the MENA Region.* Cairo: The Forum, 1998.

Goldberg, Ellis. *The Social History of Labor in the Middle East.* Boulder, CO: Westview, 1996.

Lockman, Zachary. *Workers and Working Classes in the Middle East.* Albany: State University of New York Press, 1994.

United Nations Development Programme, Regional Bureau for Arab States. *Arab Human Development Report 2002: Creating Opportunities for Future Generations.* New York: Author, 2002.

ELLIS GOLDBERG

LABOR ZIONISM

One of the main ideologies and political currents within the Zionist movement.

From the beginning of the twentieth century, Labor Zionism dominated the political philosophy of the Jews who went to resettle in Palestine, both during the British Mandate and then as the philosophical banner of the dominant political party in the new State of Israel until the parliamentary elections of 1977. Its leaders are considered the founding fathers of the Jewish state, the architects of its most distinctive social and economic institutions.

Origins of Labor Zionism

Two powerful ideologies of the nineteenth century—nationalism and socialism—were synthesized into several Labor Zionist expressions. Even before the establishment of the first Zionist organizations, Moses Hess published in 1862 *Rome and Jerusalem,* which advocated a socialist Jewish commonwealth in Palestine as the only solution to the plight of the Jewish masses in the diaspora, especially those of Russia, Eastern Europe, and the Middle East. As a member of the League of Communists, along with Karl Marx and Friedrich Engels, Hess became one of the first Jewish writers to discuss the collective existence of the dispersed Jews in terms of the socioeconomic conditions of capitalism and to put forth the idea of a political and economic revolution as the solution to the so-called Jewish problem.

For Labor Zionists, the core of the Jewish problem was not that Jews existed in Christian and Islamic host countries, but that only a small proportion of Jews were farmers or workers in the mainstream of their adopted societies. Most were scholars and teachers of Jewish studies or merchants and traders

In the early 1900s, over forty thousand Jews fled to Palestine to escape brutal Russian pogroms. The first Labor Zionist leader to actually reside in Palestine, Aaron David Gordon, believed that only through physical labor and a return to the land could the Jews truly form their own nation. © HULTON-DEUTSCH COLLECTION/CORBIS. REPRODUCED BY PERMISSION.

on a small or large scale. The explanation for this distorted occupational structure was rooted in modern European history, with its legislation that excluded Jews in most countries from joining guild-dominated trades or from owning land (the Austro-Hungarian Empire was an exception). According to Labor Zionist views, most Jews had been denied the opportunity of engaging in productive labor, and therefore their socioeconomic structure was fatally distorted. Although there were Jewish artisans, merchants, and farmers throughout the diaspora, Labor Zionism assumed there were too few to create an agricultural and craft base for a new Jewish society. For that reason, the framework of ordinary class analysis had to be reworked to account for the plight of European Jewry. In socialist doctrine, class struggle arises from the relations of production, but Jewish socialists saw that most Jews needed to gain access to "the conditions of production,"—to land, natural resources, and channels of trade.

Without a country of their own, Jews had to acquiesce to those with economic and political power;

consequently, they were also forced to discharge functions that other groups refused. In Russia, for example, Jews were routinely called upon to fill pioneering roles in new territories of the Pale and to develop economies there, but they were evicted by edict when the economies matured and competitors for their positions emerged from the national majority. Not only did such circumstances produce uncertainty, they also posed enormous dangers. Each expulsion was accompanied by an ideology of degradation that justified the destruction of Jewish property and lives. The ideology of Jew hatred became so internalized that Jews in these circumstances came to accept their powerlessness as natural and unchangeable. Antisemitism thus affected their economic options, political position, social status, and self-conception. Since socialism postulated class struggle as the means to final and full human liberation, Jews, who were unable to participate in the process, could not expect to benefit from the outcome.

Labor Zionism in Palestine

In the nineteenth century the educated youth of Russia and Eastern Europe proved a receptive audience for socialism. Educated and assimilated Jewish youth also became socialists, but some were Jewish nationalists as well, and they became Labor Zionists. In 1905 two small Zionist labor parties were founded by Eastern European Jewish youths who went to Palestine. They both advanced the idea of socioeconomic normalization and emphasized that in their own national society Jews would assume all economic roles, not just the restricted and vulnerable occupations of the diaspora. Although the ultimate aim was to create in Palestine a Jewish working class, the immediate concern was to find or create employment in a land that had no industrial base. The only jobs at first were on farms owned by Jews—earlier immigrants or those from the religious community of Jerusalem—whose own economic base was insecure, sustained by philanthropic external financial aid. On these farms Jews had to compete with local Palestinians who were willing to work for low wages. Jewish farmers first had to be convinced to employ Jews instead of Palestinians, even if costs were higher and profits lower. The immigrant Jews themselves had to be persuaded to work for lower wages than they might have expected.

One of the political parties, Po'alei Zion (Workers of Zion), tried to organize craftsmen into unions and initiated strikes in protest against the conditions of employment in the Jewish farming colonies. A small group from this party also turned its energies toward self-defense. Some Labor Zionists had founded guard units in Eastern Europe to protect Jewish communities there during pogroms. They and their defense concepts were transported to Palestine and expanded; their members were hired as guards on Jewish farms.

The second labor party, ha-Po'el ha-Tza'ir (The Young Worker), was formed just weeks before Po'alei Zion. Assuming a capitalist development in Palestine, ha-Po'el ha-Tza'ir nevertheless traced its intellectual roots to Russian populism (rather than Marxism), rejected most of the socialist doctrine, and shunned the very word socialism. It had no ties to the international workers' movement, opposed strike actions, and rejected the utility of class struggle. It romanticized the idea of labor, but called on Jews to return to the soil, to drain swamps, to build roads. It also established the first kibbutz, Deganya, and was involved with the founding of the first *moshav* (agricultural cooperative), Nahalal.

The political changes triggered by the Russian Revolution and the end of World War I facilitated the spread of Labor Zionism from 1917 to the early 1920s. The dissolution of the Ottoman Empire and the changed boundaries of Austria-Hungary and Russia stimulated many Jews to leave for the new British Mandate territory of Palestine, where the Labor Zionists pressed for the rapid immigration and settlement of Jewish workers. Many adherents, taking matters into their own hands, crossed war-torn borders to enter Palestine without regard to the established policies of either the World Zionist Organization (WZO) or Palestine's Mandate government. Coming of age in the midst of the traumatic conditions of war, revolution, and counterrevolution in Eastern Europe, these Labor Zionists also experienced the postwar pogroms that were unleashed by the Ukrainians and the Poles.

Economic and political circumstances in Palestine forced both political parties to readjust their strategies and activities. The proposals for cooperative settlement on the land that were advanced by

One of the biggest stumbling blocks the Labor Zionism movement faced was the fact that Jews had little experience with physical labor, since in most countries they were banned from owning land or seeking certain guild-dominated occupations. © HULTON-DEUTSCH COLLECTION/CORBIS. REPRODUCED BY PERMISSION.

the leadership of the WZO provided plans for employment, but the new agricultural settlements challenged the socialist emphasis on industrial development. Both parties also had to find ways to justify their cooperation with the bourgeois Zionist leadership and their policies. After World War I, there were powerful incentives to unify the labor movement. In 1920 the Histadrut (General Federation of Labor) was founded, bringing into a unified framework all Labor Zionist political parties and undertaking, on their behalf, a broad range of political, economic, and cultural activities. One segment of the Labor Zionist movement founded in Vienna (1916) was ha-Shomer ha-Tza'ir (The Young Guard). Its members were youths educated for kibbutz life in Palestine, and it retained its distinctive structure and ideology, although it also joined the Histadrut. It founded agricultural collectives, and its vision of liberation owed as much to Sigmund Freud as to Marx.

For the settlers in Palestine, the careful balancing between Labor Zionist ideology and practicality—the need to revise policies because of changing circumstances—often involved a deviation from socialist principles. Many Labor Zionists, concluding that such adjustments foreclosed all hope for realizing socialism in their time, left their political parties, and some even left Palestine. The evolving political parties were sometimes fractured by the strains of accommodating political reality. Sometimes, however, circumstances generated strong impulses to unity. In 1930, the MAPAI political party was founded, unifying Ahdut ha-Avodah and ha-Po'el ha-Tza'ir. MAPAI led the labor movement in Palestine on a course of constructive socialism, seeking class goals plus a democratic Jewish nation. It also cooperated with the nonsocialist movements that accepted some social-democratic principles. These principles had been promoted by Berl Katznelson, but their implementation was executed by the party's pragmatic leader, David Ben-Gurion. Those who did not accept Ben-Gurion's pragmatism in dealing with the British Mandate authorities in 1935 joined Vladimir Ze'ev Jabotinsky and formed the Revisionist movement. Other disagreements led to the formation of other parties, but Ben-Gurion of MAPAI proclaimed the new State of Israel in 1948, and MAPAI provided all but one of the early prime ministers, Histadrut secretaries-general, and Knesset (legislature) speakers, and presidents.

See also AHDUT HA-AVODAH; DIASPORA; HISTADRUT; KIBBUTZ; MOSHAV; NATIONALISM; WORLD ZIONIST ORGANIZATION (WZO); ZIONIST REVISIONIST MOVEMENT.

Bibliography

Avineri, Shlomo. *The Making of Modern Zionism.* New York: Basic Books, 1981.

Frankel, Jonathan. *Prophesy and Politics: Socialism, Nationalism, and the Russian Jews, 1862–1914.* Cambridge, U.K.: Cambridge University Press, 1981.

Halpern, Ben, and Reinharz, Jehuda. *Zionism and the Creation of a New Society.* Oxford, U.K.: Oxford University Press, 1998.

Segev, Tom. *One Palestine, Complete: Jews and Arabs under the British Mandate.* New York: Metropolitan Books, 2000.

Shlaim, Avi. *The Iron Wall.* New York: W. W. Norton, 2000.

Sternhell, Ze'ev. *The Founding Myths of Israel.* Princeton, NJ: Princeton University Press, 1998.

DONNA ROBINSON DIVINE

LACHERAF, MOSTEFA
[1917–]

Algerian intellectual, minister, and ambassador.

Mostefa Lacheraf was born in Sidi Aissa in northern Algeria. His father was a Muslim magistrate. Lacheraf was educated at the lycée in Mostaganem and then at Paris's prestigious Lycée Louis-le-Grand. He joined Messali Hadj's Mouvement pour le Triomphe des Libertés Démocratiques (MTLD) but left it in 1952. Subsequently, as a member of the Front de Libération Nationale (FLN), he was seized along with the "historic chiefs" of the Algerian War of Independence—Ahmed Ben Bella, Hocine Ait Ahmed, Mohamed Khider, and Mohamed Boudiaf—in the infamous French skyjacking of an Air Maroc airplane in October 1956. Lacheraf was imprisoned from 1956 to 1961. After Algeria's independence, he helped to draft the Tripoli Programme (1962). He later served as ambassador to Argentina and Mexico. He was an adviser to Colonel Houari Boumédienne, who appointed Lacheraf as minister of national education (April 1977). Lacheraf's ministry was very controversial because he questioned the pragmatism of official Arabization policies—he urged a bilingual approach. In 1982 Lacheraf became Algeria's permanent delegate to UNESCO. He was appointed to the Conseil Consultatif National in 1992. He is an opponent of Islamism and has defended the army against its critics—notably in a petition that he signed with other intellectuals in March 2001. His most famous works are *L'Algérie, nation et société* (1965, 1978; Algeria: Nation and society) and, coauthored with Abdelkader Djeghloul, *Histoire, culture et société* (1986; History, culture, and society).

See also ALGERIAN WAR OF INDEPENDENCE; FRONT DE LIBÉRATION NATIONALE (FLN); MOUVEMENT POUR LE TRIOMPHE DES LIBERTÉS DÉMOCRATIQUES.

Bibliography

Naylor, Phillip C. *Historical Dictionary of Algeria,* 3d edition. Lanham, MD: Scarecrow Press (forthcoming), 2005.

PHILLIP C. NAYLOR

LACOSTE, ROBERT
[1898–1989]

Resident minister of Algeria from 1956 to 1958.

Robert Lacoste was a socialist who served as resident minister during the Algerian War of Independence under the Mollet, Bourgès-Maunoury, and Gaillard Fourth Republic governments. He supported repression, which included torture, thereby eroding civilian control, in order to keep Algeria under French control. Lacoste also promoted accelerated social and economic programs, highlighted by his efforts to "Algerianize" the administration. He increased Algeria's departments (to twelve) and drafted the Loi Cadre (enabling or framework law) designed to enhance internal autonomy and Muslim representation. He was a fervent advocate of France's involvement in the Suez War of October 1956. Lacoste later served in the French senate from 1971 to 1980.

See also ALGERIA: OVERVIEW; ALGERIAN WAR OF INDEPENDENCE; LOI CADRE.

Bibliography

Horne, Alistair. *A Savage War of Peace: Algeria, 1954–1962,* 2d edition. New York: Penguin, 1987.

PHILLIP C. NAYLOR

LADINO

Various forms of Judeo-Spanish spoken and written by the Sephardim—Jews who came to the Ottoman Empire and the Maghrib (North Africa) after their expulsion from Spain in 1492.

Ladino is also called Spanyol or Judezmo; in Northern Morocco, it is called Haketía. It is at base Old Castilian (Spanish, a Romance language). Like all Diaspora Jewish languages, it is written in Hebrew characters and has a significant Hebrew and Aramaic vocabulary. It also—depending upon the region—has assimilated loanwords from Arabic, Greek, Turkish, Italian, and French.

Ladino was the language of Jewish merchants throughout much of the Islamic Mediterranean region from the sixteenth through nineteenth centuries. Except for folk songs and ballads (*cantigas* and *romances*) and some rabbinical writings, there was only a limited Ladino literature until 1730, when Jacob Culi published his popular encyclopedic *Me'am Lo'ez* in Istanbul. In the nineteenth and early twentieth centuries, Ladino became the primary medium of modern learning among Jews in the Ot-

toman Empire. Hundreds of novels and plays were translated from French, Hebrew, and Yiddish writers. There was a flourishing Ladino press in Turkey, Greece, the Balkans, Palestine, and Egypt.

The language policies of the post–World War I Republic of Turkey, the destruction of much of Balkan Jewry during World War II, and the migration of most of North African and Levantine Jews to Spain, South America, France, and Israel has led to the near disappearance of Ladino as a living language.

Bibliography

Lida, Denah. "Ladino Language and Literature." In *Jewish Languages: Theme and Variations,* edited by Herbert H. Paper. Cambridge, MA: Association for Jewish Studies, 1978.

NORMAN STILLMAN

LADO ENCLAVE

Colonial territory in Sudan, connecting the Congo and Nile rivers.

The Lado Enclave was a remnant of the ambitions of King Leopold of Belgium to link his personal empire (the Congro Free State) with the Nile, whose waters flowed to the Mediterranean Sea. He appeared to have achieved his goal in 1894 when Great Britain ceded to him the Bahr al-Ghazal, which gave access to the Nile, in a futile attempt to prevent French encroachment on the vital Nile waters. Leopold yielded to French pressure to abandon the Bahr al-Ghazal but demanded his rights under a treaty with Great Britain to retain a small enclave called Lado, which would connect the two great waterways of Africa, the Congo and Nile rivers. Because the Congo Free State and the Lado Enclave were the personal fiefs of King Leopold and not of Belgium, whose government had no desire to acquire the enclave at the expense of Britain's hostility, they passed into history upon the death of Leopold on 17 December 1909. By a treaty signed between Belgium and Great Britain in 1906, the enclave was incorporated into the Anglo-Egyptian Condominium.

See also BAHR AL-GHAZAL.

ROBERT O. COLLINS

LAHAD, ANTOINE
[1929–]

Lebanese leader of the Israeli-backed South Lebanon Army.

A Christian from Dayr al-Qamar, Antoine Lahad graduated from the Lebanese Military Academy in 1952. He eventually reached the rank of major general in the Lebanese army. In January 1984, following the death of Sa'd Haddad, the founder and leader of the Israeli-funded, -equipped, and -trained South Lebanon Army, Lahad was enticed by Israel out of retirement to become the new head of the militia. Under his leadership, the militia was expanded and upgraded, and its dependence upon Israeli support intensified. Lahad and his "army," which had a negative reputation in South Lebanon, ended their role in 2000 when Israel withdrew from South Lebanon due to the escalation of the resistance movement against its troops. Lahad and his associates sought asylum in Israel. In 2003 the Israeli press reported that Lahad had opened a Middle Eastern restaurant called Byblos, and he was nicknamed "General Hummus" by journalists.

See also HADDAD, SA'D; SOUTH LEBANON ARMY.

Bibliography

Hiro, Dilip. *Lebanon: Fire and Embers: A History of the Lebanese Civil War.* New York: St. Martin's Press, 1992.

GUILAIN P. DENOEUX
UPDATED BY AS'AD ABUKHALIL

LAHHUD, EMILE
[1936–]

President of Lebanon, 1998–.

Emile Lahhud was born in 1936 to a Maronite family that had a long tradition of serving in the Lebanese army. Lahhud joined the military academy in 1956 and rose through the ranks thereafter. His family was known for avoiding sectarian politics, and Lahhud did not side with any of the warring factions during his military career. His father was one of the founders of the Lebanese army, and later served in the Lebanese parliament as a moderate, pro-Arab parliamentarian. Emile attended military courses and received training in the United States and Britain; he became a symbol of the new nonsectarian Lebanese army that was reformed after the end of the Lebanese Civil War in 1989.

Lahhud was appointed commander in chief of the Lebanese Army in 1989, and he was credited with infusing the new army with ideas of national unity and Arab identity. Lahhud worked very closely with the Syrian government, and was one of Syria's allies in Lebanon. He insisted on a very large budget for the new Lebanese army, which reinstituted compulsory military service for Lebanese males. The role of the army and the intelligence apparatus increased with the expansion of the ranks and size of the military-intelligence apparatus of the government, which reduced the heavy-handed involvement of the Syrian military in Lebanese affairs, although the Syrian government still exercised great political influence in Lebanon thereafter. As commander in chief, Lahhud closely coordinated with the Hizbullah-led Lebanese resistance in south Lebanon (during the Israeli occupation of southern Lebanon from 1982–2000), providing logistical and political support for Hizbullah.

Lahhud was elected president in 1998, and his inaugural speech promised wide-ranging political and economic reforms. His blueprint for government included a promise to fight corruption, but his administration has so far avoided attacking the powerful symbols of corruption in government. His administration was also marred by an acute conflict with prime minister Rafiq Hariri.

See also HARIRI, RAFIQ BAHA'UDDIN AL–; HIZBULLAH.

AS'AD ABUKHALIL

LAHIJI, SHAHLA
[1942–]

Women's rights activist and publisher in Iran.

Shahla Lahiji started writing for newspapers at age fifteen and was admitted to the Association of Women Writers and Journalists at age sixteen. The first female publisher in Iran, she founded in 1984 and is director of Roshangaran Publishing, a prominent publishing house of women's books. She also established the Women's Studies Center, a private research institute devoted to women's issues.

Lahiji has written several books, including *Portraits of Women in the Work of Bahram Beizaie, Filmmaker and*

Scriptwriter in 1989 and *The Quest for Identity: The Image of Iranian Women in Prehistory and History* with Mehrangiz Kar in 1992.

In 2000 she was arrested with eighteen other Iranians who had participated in a conference in Germany on the future of Iran. She was charged with acting against internal security of the state and sentenced to four years' imprisonment, but she was released after two months. Over the years she has maintained her critical, secular stance, always promoting the right to free speech and advocating equality between men and women in Iranian culture, law, and society. She received the Women in Publishing Award in 2000, after which she continued to live and work in Iran.

See also GENDER: GENDER AND LAW.

CHERIE TARAGHI

LAHOUEL, HOCINE
[1917–]

Algerian nationalist.

Born in the Constantine region, Hocine Lahouel joined Messali al-Hadj's Etoile Nord-Africaine (North African Star) in 1930. He was a leader in the Parti du Peuple Algérien (Algerian People's Party) and an editor of *El Ouma*. Together with al-Hadj, he was imprisoned by the French in 1937. In 1946, Lahouel participated in the Oran elections as a candidate for the Mouvement pour le Triomphe des Libertés Démocratiques (Movement of the Triumph of Democratic Liberties), becoming its secretary-general in 1950. A leading centrist within the movement, Lahouel was torn between supporting the paramilitary operations of the Organisation Spéciale (Special Organization) or the imperfect electoral process after World War II. In the late 1940s, Lahouel took a harsh stance against the Berberist members within the nationalist movement. Together with A. Kiouane, he founded La Nation Algérienne (The Algerian Nation), an organization opposed to L'Algérie Libre (Free Algeria). He joined the Front de Libération Nationale (National Liberation Front) in 1955 and represented it in Indonesia and Pakistan. In 1965, he became president of the National Textile Society. Together with Ben Youssef Ben Khedda, Ferhat Abbas, and Mohamed Kheireddine, Lahouel was

placed under house arrest from 1976 until 1977 after cosigning an antigovernment manifesto entitled "New Appeal to the Algerian People." They were deemed "reactionary elements" by the Algerian government, and Lahouel lost his post in the National Textile Society.

See also BEN KHEDDA, BEN YOUSSEF; FRONT DE LIBÉRATION NATIONALE (FLN); HADJ, MESSALI AL-; MOUVEMENT POUR LE TRIOMPHE DES LIBERTÉS DÉMOCRATIQUES; PARTI DU PEUPLE ALGÉRIEN (PPA).

PHILLIP C. NAYLOR
UPDATED BY VANESA CASANOVA-FERNANDEZ

LAMARI, MOHAMED
[1939–]

Lieutenant-general and chief of staff of Algeria's People's National Army.

Born in 1939 in Algiers, Mohamed Lamari is the strongman of the Algerian army and security services. He has a reputation as an absolute opponent of the armed Islamist movement. Trained in the cavalry at Saumur War School in France, he joined the National Liberation Army in 1961. After independence, he studied at the military academy in Moscow and then at the war school in Paris.

After holding several positions in the Algerian military hierarchy, he commanded the regional military staff (1970–1976) and was attached to the operations office of the national military staff until 1988, after which he became head of the fifth military region and was then promoted to the rank of land forces commander.

In January 1992, along with other generals, he demanded the resignation of President Chadli Bendjedid. In mid-1992 Lamari was appointed head of the special antiterrorist units at the Defense Ministry. Ten months later he was promoted to chief of staff of the armed forces when Liamine Zeroual replaced General Khaled Nezzar as defense minister. Lamari vigorously opposed the plan for reconciliation with the opposition parties, including the Islamists, proposed by Zeroual and his supporters. His promotion in 1994 to the rank of lieutenant-general at the moment when President Zeroual announced the failure of the dialogue with the opposition parties signaled that the eradicators were in the ascendant and that Lamari had become the most powerful man in Algeria. From mid-1994 on, he ordered a vigorous military campaign against the armed groups and intensive bombardments of Islamists. He was delegated by President Zeroual to sign all acts and decisions, including decrees on mobilizing reservists, the creation of popular militias, the treatment of security information addressed to the national press, and the creation of areas in southern Algeria to preserve gas sites and oil fields.

In addition to his determination to eradicate Islamism, Lamari is known for initiating the army's professionalization project and for being the architect of military cooperation agreements between Algeria and its foreign partners, including the United States, the North Atlantic Treaty Organization, and Turkey.

See also ALGERIA; BENDJEDID, CHADLI.

Bibliography

Lahouari, Addi. "Algeria's Army, Algeria's Agony." *Foreign Affairs* 77 (July–August 1998): 44–53.

Willis, Michael. *The Islamist Challenge in Algeria: A Political History.* New York: New York University Press, 1997.

AZZEDINE G. MANSOUR

LA MARSA CONVENTION

The document that formally established the French protectorate over Tunisia.

The La Marsa Convention was signed in June 1883 and ratified by the French Chamber of Deputies in April 1884. The force behind the convention was Paul Cambon, resident general in Tunisia from 1882 to 1886. The convention provided for a French loan to the bey, allowing him to settle his debts to other European states and thereby bringing an end to the International Financial Commission. With these measures, France won control over the Tunisian economy and, with the protectorate in place, the political affairs of Tunis as well.

Bibliography

Abun-Nasr, Jamil M. *A History of the Maghrib in the Islamic Period.* Cambridge, U.K., and New York: Cambridge University Press, 1987.

MATTHEW S. GORDON

LAMRANI, MUHAMMAD KARIM
[1919–]

Moroccan politician and business leader.

Educated in Morocco and France with a degree in economics, Muhammad Karim Lamrani served as an economic adviser to Hassan II in the 1960s. Lamrani went on to various prominent offices, including vice chairman, then president, of the Casablanca Chamber of Commerce; director of the national airline, Royal Air Maroc; and director general of the Sharifian Office of Phosphates. Hassan II appointed Lamrani as prime minister on six occasions—in 1971, 1972, 1983, 1985, 1992, and 1993. Unaffiliated with any major political group, Lamrani effectively served as a mediator between the crown and opposition parties. As prime minister, Lamrani was a champion of the private sector of the Moroccan economy.

In the early 1990s Lamrani led a government formed mainly by technocrats to guide the country through a difficult period of economic liberalization reforms. Renewed activism by Moroccan labor unions and Lamrani's failure to rally the opposition parties' support proved to be a major obstacle for the prime minister's policies in an atmosphere of social discontent. King Hassan II replaced him with Abdellatif Filali in 1994. Lamrani remains one of the wealthiest and most influential businessmen in Morocco.

Bibliography

Zartman, I. William, ed. *The Political Economy of Morocco.* New York: Praeger, 1987.

MATTHEW S. GORDON
UPDATED BY ANA TORRES-GARCIA

LAND CODE OF 1858

Extension of Tanzimat reforms to agricultural property and taxation.

The Ottoman Land Code of 1858 (Turkish, *Arazi Kanunnamesi*) was an extension of the Tanzimat reforms to the areas of agricultural property and taxation. Aimed at increasing tax revenues while replacing local rule by notables with centralized administration, the code reaffirmed prior laws pertaining to land, updated some old terminology, and introduced two major innovations that, by permitting individuals to possess large areas of land, completely transformed the relationship of people to land in many parts of the Ottoman Empire during the last half of the nineteenth century.

Land Ownership and Taxation prior to 1858

Classical Ottoman land-tenure legislation made a fundamental distinction between the right to cultivate land (*tasarruf*) and the absolute ownership of land (*raqaba*). The two main categories of land were *mülk* and *miri*. The owners of *mulk* land combined the right to cultivate with absolute ownership; this land was largely confined to orchards adjacent to villages and constituted a small proportion of land in the empire. *Mülk* land comes closest to private property as understood in the West. *Miri* land was owned by the state; the actual cultivators of the land were essentially tenants of the state, although they were entitled to pass on the right of cultivation to their heirs. *Miri* land consisted of arable land upon which crops were sown and constituted the vast majority of agricultural land in the empire.

Taxes on agricultural lands were a primary source of income for the Ottoman state. By the late fourteenth century, a system of revenue collection was established called the *timar* system. Large grants of land were given to military officers who collected the land tax and used it to procure and equip military forces to fight the empire's wars. Until the 1800s, this system was gradually replaced by one called *iltizam* (tax farming). Wealthy individuals, often government officials, would bid at open auction for the right to collect taxes. An agreed-upon proportion of taxes would be transferred to the government, and the tax farmer could keep the rest. While initially tax farms were granted for limited periods of time, in a further development, they were granted for life, and even became inheritable. These grants were known as *malikane*. A consequence of *malikane* was that tax farmers increased their autonomy from the state and often became local rulers (*ayan*). The *ayan* did not challenge the state's claim to ownership of land, but they did prevent the state from collecting taxes, enhancing their own power. In the early nineteenth century, *ayan* from the western provinces of the empire were briefly able to impose their will on the sultan. But this supremacy was short-lived, and by 1815, Sultan Mahmud II had reestablished the dominant position of the central state.

Mahmud II's successful campaign to reassert state control over the *ayan* created a need for a new system to administer the state's vast tracts of land while preventing reemergence of the *ayan* political challenge. Land Reform was taking place throughout the Middle East. The distinguished historian Ahmed Cevdet Paşa, who served on the commission that drafted the code, stated that the radical administrative and financial changes created by the Tanzimat reforms of the first half of the century produced the need for new regulations of landed property. In addition, the growing need of the state for revenue demanded new forms of land tenure and taxation that would enhance cultivation of existing lands and encourage the reclamation of dead lands, while guaranteeing state collection of tax revenues. Finally, both merchants and farmers inside the empire and European countries were pressuring the sultan to pass reforms that would rationalize the government. Part of this rationalization would be accomplished by guaranteeing the property rights of the sultan's subjects. The 1858 Land Code was a response to these multiple needs.

The passage of the code was preceded by several reforms. In 1846, a ministry of agriculture was established to stimulate agricultural production. Efforts were made to sedentarize nomadic tribes, both to provide laborers for the cultivation of cotton and to subject them to taxation. Tax exemptions offered villages for performing public services such as road building were abolished; new state agencies would perform these services. The agricultural tax, which previously had fluctuated between 10 and 50 percent of the product was fixed at 10 percent; this tax was called the *üşür*. In 1847, the government prepared a system of land registration; land would be registered in a centralized government office, the *defterhane*, and owners would be given deeds of ownership.

Land Ownership and Taxation following the 1858 Land Code

The Land Code was characterized by marked continuity with the classical fifteenth- and sixteenth-century *qanuns* regulating agrarian property rights. The fundamental distinction between *tasarruf* and *raqaba* was retained, and land continued to be divided into five categories: *mülk, miri,* waqf (tax-exempt land devoted to supporting religious establishments), *metruk* (land designated for the public activities of villages, such as the village threshing floor), and *mevat* (dead and unclaimed land). The preponderance of land continued to be owned by the state. The Land Code reiterated basic legal doctrine on the means of acquiring land through possession and cultivation of land for a ten-year period, the condition that land uncultivated for a three-year period became *mahlul* (lapsed ownership), and the means of inheriting land. The code liberalized the right of bequeathing land, in the hope that keeping land within one family would lead to greater efforts to improve land.

Despite its conservative nature, the Land Code did contain two crucial innovations that would alter the nature of land ownership in much of the Middle East. The first innovation was the obligation of landowners to register their land with the government and receive formal deed to the land. This measure was not designed to prevent absentee ownership; indeed, the code specifically stated that legal ownership of land took precedence over actual occupation and cultivation. Thus, whereas previously the *ayan* had possessed the right to collect taxes, now those who did not cultivate land could still possess land and become taxpayers. The code was thus concerned with determining the legal status of the taxpayer, suggesting that the drafters of the code perceived the new legislation as a revenue-raising instrument. The code did, however, prohibit any individual or several individuals from gaining title to occupied villages in their entirety. Nevertheless, the second innovation found in the code permitted individuals to own vast tracts of land; beginning in 1858, the state could issue deeds to formerly unoccupied lands. This was designed to increase the area of land under cultivation. When these two innovations were combined, it meant that individuals could now on paper own very large tracts of land.

The major consequence of the 1858 Land Code was the separation of the taxpayer/owner from the cultivator in many parts of the empire. Before the code's passage, peasants had leased land from the state, and powerful individuals had acted as intermediaries who collected taxes from the actual cultivator; after the code's passage, powerful individuals could legally own land that they leased to peasants. It is frequently asserted that this outcome was precisely the opposite of what was intended by the Ottoman government. Inefficient administration of the law, it is contended, allowed powerful individuals to register in their own names lands previously held by peasants. This occurred because peasants depended on local notables for protection; because peasants were afraid that registration of land would be followed by conscription or increased tax burdens; because peasant indebtedness to moneylenders led to forfeiture of deeds to land; because peasants were too ignorant to comprehend land registration; or because bedouin *shaykhs* used their authority within the tribe to usurp all the land of their tribesmen.

More recent scholarship has contested this view, arguing that the consequences of the Land Code differed from region to region in the empire and that peasants were willing to participate in and benefit from the new system. In Palestine, for example, in the hilly country surrounding Jerusalem, peasants did register land in their own names, and a survey of property records did not find a single case of a city notable or moneylender registering land. On the coastal plains, however, city notables were able to take advantage of the government's new policy of selling deeds to unclaimed lands. Large-scale landlords took possession of vast tracts of land, still mostly unoccupied or unclaimed. Similarly, in Anatolia large estates were formed on wasteland, often located in swampy plains and in the Kurds' tribal lands to the east. In areas of established peasant settlements in central Anatolia and on the coasts, peasant ownership continued to be the predominant form of land tenure.

In other regions, large estates were created. In Mesopotamia (now Iraq), Ottoman governors, seeking the cooperation of tribal shaykhs, permitted them to register tribal lands as their personal property, creating large estates. In Syria, powerful local families had obtained *malikane* grants and ruled almost unchecked from the eighteenth century. By 1858, the distinction between *mülk* and *miri* land had been considerably blurred. Thus, the Land Code seems to have accelerated, not caused, the creation of large estates. The major mechanism for estate formation in Syria seems to have been peasant indebtedness and default to moneylenders. As a result, by the start of the twentieth century, large landholdings had been created and many peasants reduced to the status of tenant farmer or share-cropper. In Syria, as in other regions of the empire where peasants lost ownership of land, estate formation did not mean the creation of unified, plantation-like farms; instead, absentee landowners negotiated arrangements with individual peasants, who continued to farm small plots of land.

Although a great deal of research remains to be done, these divergent consequences of the Land Code mitigate against drawing any overly generalized conclusions about its results. If in Syria and Iraq urban notables and tribal *shaykhs* were able to wrest ownership of land from peasants, in Palestine and Anatolia large estates were created primarily through the sale by the state of wasteland that needed to be reclaimed. The capacity of peasants in parts of Palestine and Anatolia to obtain legal possession of their land suggests that peasants were not automatically unwilling to register their land; it would seem to be the case that in many regions, they were unable to do so.

It is not clear that the creation of large estates constitutes the failure of the 1858 Land Code. If a primary purpose of the code was to raise state revenues, it was a success: Between 1887 and 1910, a period when the territory of the empire was shrinking, the revenue collected from the agricultural tax increased from 426 million to 718 million piastres.

See also LAND REFORM; MAHMUD II; QANUN; TANZIMAT; WAQF.

Bibliography

Baer, Gabriel. "The Evolution of Private Landownership in Egypt and the Fertile Crescent." In *The Economic History of the Middle East, 1800–1914,* edited by Charles Issawi. Chicago: University of Chicago Press, 1966.

Gerber, Haim. *The Social Origins of the Modern Middle East.* Boulder, CO: L. Rienner, 1988.

Haider, Salah. "Land Problems of Iraq." In *The Economic History of the Middle East, 1800–1914,* edited by Charles Issawi. Chicago: University of Chicago Press, 1966.

Karpat, Kemal H. "The Land Regime, Social Structure, and Modernization in the Ottoman Empire." In *Beginnings of Modernization in the Middle East: The Nineteenth Century,* edited by William R. Polk and Richard L. Chambers. Chicago: University of Chicago Press, 1968.

Sluglett, Peter, and Farouk-Sluglett, Marion. "The Application of the 1858 Land Code in Greater Syria: Some Preliminary Observations." In *Land Tenure and Social Transformation in the Middle East,* edited by Tarif Khalidi. Beirut: American University of Beirut, 1984.

Warriner, Doreen. "Land Tenure in the Fertile Crescent." In *The Economic History of the Middle East, 1800–1914,* edited by Charles Issawi. Chicago: University of Chicago Press, 1966.

DAVID WALDNER

LAND DAY

Strike by Palestinians to protest confiscation of Arab land in Israel (30 March 1976).

After Israel's government announced plans to confiscate Arab land in February 1976, the National Committee for the Defense of Arab Lands, the first political organization claiming to represent the entire Palestinian population of Israel, called for a strike and named it Land Day. In the Galilee region, where the appropriations were to take place, villagers clashed with Israel's troops, leading to six Arab deaths, and numerous arrests and injuries. These incidents were similar to demonstrations at Kafr Qasim twenty years before.

The strike demonstrated the political strength of Rakah, the Communist party of Israel, which had organized the demonstrations and had created the committee. Land Day was declared a Palestinian national holiday in 1992 and is celebrated annually with demonstrations and a general strike by Palestinians residing in Israel, the West Bank, and the Gaza Strip.

See also KAFR QASIM.

Bibliography

Kimmerling, Baruch, and Migdal, Joel S. *Palestinians: The Making of a People.* New York: Free Press, 1993.

LAWRENCE TAL

LAND REFORM

Land tenure refers to the relationships, rules, and institutions that define rights of ownership in, and access to, landed property.

Officials in Egypt survey land in the Fayum oasis. A land reform program in the country during the 1950s limited ownership size, controlled rents, and ceded property rights to tenants. © HULTON-DEUTSCH COLLECTION/CORBIS. REPRODUCED BY PERMISSION.

Land reform generally denotes government measures designed for a relatively equitable redistribution of agricultural land, but actual reform measures can reflect a range of ideological positions. The political nature of reform is difficult to avoid given the effect of changes in land tenure arrangements on the social relations and hierarchies they embody.

The distribution of property rights is a key indicator of the relationship between state and society, as well as a fundamental determinant of production and distribution. While a wide range of land tenure systems have worked themselves out across the modern Middle East, three phases in the changing relationship between state and society can usefully be highlighted where landed property is concerned. The early phase begins during the nineteenth century when centralizing state structures, colonial rule, and the emergence of global capitalism and market forces often concentrated property rights in relatively few hands. A second phase emerged in the post–World War II period when governments, often coming to power as anticolonial national independence movements, implemented ambitious programs to develop agriculture, redistribute land to middle-class or smaller farmers, and substitute state-supervised cooperatives and monopolies for private marketing networks. A third phase may be discerned in which states have, since the 1980s, repositioned themselves in the economy and, under local and international pressure, retreated to various degrees from direct intervention in agriculture.

In pursuit of fiscal and administrative goals toward which modern states typically aspire, the Ottoman state and its successors, the European-dominated colonial administrations in the Middle East, were determined to make more legible the complexity of local, often communal, landholding patterns and to pursue the standardization and individualization of title to land. The land register and the cadastral map were the instruments that best reflected the new centralized, unmediated reality officially sought by the state. Utilitarian arguments in favor of private property were commonly put forth. For example, in societies that were overwhelmingly agricultural and where land was the principal factor of production, tax collection could be facilitated by the individualization of rights. Further, it was widely assumed that unless individual users knew they would capture the benefits of investment and conservation, degradation and overuse of resources would ensue. As a wealth-creating institution, the promise of individualized property rights, particularly in the colonial period, was that resources would naturally find their way through the market into the hands of those individuals who value them most. In colonies of settlement—Algeria, Morocco, Tunisia, Libya, and Palestine—a market in land also obviously facilitated the transfer of native property to European immigrants who mainly accumulated large estates. Moreover, by asserting in philosophical terms that private property constituted the basis of civilization, European colonial officials could point to the evidence of communally or tribally held property in a colonized territory as demonstration of the necessity of imperial rule.

Subject to such pressures and interests, a variety of landholding patterns emerged. The critical variables appear to have been the considerable ecological diversity and the will or the capacity of the state to control relations at the local level. For example, in the Ottoman Empire during the nineteenth century, in Thrace and those areas of Anatolia close to

Istanbul, small-scale farming became the norm. By contrast, in the more remote areas of the empire, such as Eastern Anatolia or Syria, the need to rely on local intermediaries for administration created a highly skewed distribution of land. In some cases, the local governor played a central role: Across the provinces of Baghdad, Mosul, and Basra, Midhat Paşa initiated a process whereby cultivators of land were granted title deeds that secured virtually complete rights of ownership (although, in tribal areas, cultivators were often turned into tenant farmers when the name of the most powerful individual was placed on the title deed). In Ottoman Palestine large estates came into being once new land laws and modern registration procedures created the opportunity to benefit from the increasing foreign demand for agricultural products by purchasing vast tracts of land on paper.

European colonialism could have a profound impact on land tenure patterns. In Algeria, the best farmland was seized by French colonists, who forced the indigenous population onto marginal land or dispossessed them. This pattern of concentration under colonialism prevailed elsewhere. In Egypt a highly unequal distribution of ownership placed tremendous political and economic power into the hands of those few families who dominated rural areas. During the British mandate over Iraq, the administration came to rely heavily on intermediaries and, rather than seek direct contacts with all landowners, in fact strengthened the position of large landowners vis-à-vis small owners and tenant farmers: By 1932 only 10 percent of government revenues were derived from land taxes (as compared to 25 percent in 1921). In Iraq one of the region's (and the world's) most unequal land distributions was thereby created: By 1953, 1.7 percent of the landholders had 63 percent of the land; 75 percent of the population was landless. The impact of European imperialism on land tenure relationships varied, however, across the Middle East, the transformation often being dependent on the role played by local power structures and interests. In Transjordan British efforts to settle individual title to land overlapped with patterns on the ground.

Sharecropping was the most common method of farming, though estates in Egypt and the Maghrib relied on more direct management by the landowner or his representative. During the first half of

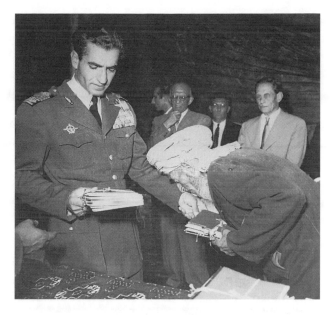

Mohammad Reza Shah Pahlavi of Iran grants a land deed to a grateful new owner. Beginning in 1962, Iran went through a series of land reform measures, many of which were unpopular with clerical leaders and the poorer classes. © BETTMANN/CORBIS. REPRODUCED BY PERMISSION.

the twentieth century, rural conditions deteriorated and landlessness was implicated in a number of problems: urbanization, high birth rates, low productivity, and lack of purchasing power. Meanwhile, large landlords enjoyed wide powers under the direct or indirect influence of European powers. In the post–World War II period, land reform—responding generally to the widespread call, "land to the tiller"—was adopted by newly independent governments to tackle socioeconomic inequities. While improvements flowing from land reform have been difficult to measure, the political goal of eliminating the power of large landowners has generally been regarded as successful. Countries experiencing significant land reforms during this phase include Egypt, Syria, Iraq, Algeria, Tunisia, Iran, and the People's Democratic Republic of Yemen.

Egypt

The pioneering attempts at land reform here progressively lowered the legal limitation of ownership size from 200 feddans (1.038 acres) in 1952 to 50 in 1969. Those who received land, whether through reform or "distress sales" of the wealthy, were rarely the poorest rural people. Direct beneficiaries were either the year-round workers of the estates—not the landless seasonal workers—or members of the rural middle class who could afford to purchase land made available. The reforms also controlled rents and, by making it nearly impossible to evict tenants, ceded property rights to them. Remarkably, output did not fall: The government created a system of supervised agricultural cooperatives that allowed for economies of scale, took over marketing functions, and facilitated the application of inputs such as improved seed and credit. These cooperatives were also used by government to extract part of the agricultural surplus by manipulating the terms of trade. Egypt was in this way transformed into a country of predominantly small farms. Farms under five feddans covered roughly 66 percent of the land area in 1975, but by the early 1980s the share of small farms had fallen to 52 percent, largely as a result of the consolidation of the very smallest farms.

Syria and Iraq

Both countries attempted to follow the Egyptian model despite the very different conditions prevailing. Much larger areas of land were appropriated than in Egypt, the agroecologies were enormously varied (again, in contrast to Egypt where virtually all land was irrigated), stronger resistance was met, and there were far fewer trained officials. Output fell considerably. Although the Syrian and Iraqi governments found it relatively easy to expropriate land, they found it difficult to redistribute it and to take over the marketing functions. Only in the 1970s were Ba'thist governments able to redistribute land and to create fully functioning cooperatives.

Algeria

When European colonial farmers hastily abandoned large farms at the time of independence (1962), employees on many estates tried to manage them collectively. So-called *autogestion* was immediately championed by politicians, but eventually proved economically counterproductive. Pressure grew and in 1972 the government began attempts to expropriate all private farmland that exceeded the area a family could directly exploit. Agrarian reform encountered considerable resistance and evasion. By 1980, about 13 percent of the arable land had moved into the reform sector, but economic growth was disappointing compared to private farm production.

Tunisia

Reform here went through three stages. From 1956 to 1960 holders of usufruct rights (legal rights to use and profit from property owned by another) were transformed into owners. In 1961 the state began to acquire land formerly held by European colonialists, and a "cooperativization" program was launched, aimed at incorporating the surrounding small farms. Local resistance, poor investment policies, the cessation of World Bank funding, social conflict, and uncertainty about property rights all took their toll on agricultural production. By the end of 1969, cooperativization was abandoned, and the private sector was increasingly relied upon.

Iran

Beginning in 1962 landlords were required to sell to the government any land in excess of "one village." A second phase gave landlords options, such as forming "corporations" with their former tenants and distributing shares rather than land, leasing land for cash, and so on. The "farm corporation" concept, however, was unpopular with peasants; it often led to small farmers selling out to larger ones. Further, landless agricultural workers were excluded from the reform, and many, perhaps most, of the recipients of land received too little to support a family. The reforms also adversely affected the land and water rights of Islamic charities. During the 1970s the shah's government became increasingly obsessed with promoting large farms and agribusinesses. These were mostly unsuccessful and survived only thanks to massive state subsidies. After the Iranian Revolution (1979), in the early days of the Islamic republic, considerable amounts of land changed hands as Pahlavi officials were expropriated, peasants occupied land, and local religious officials took advantage of opportunities. A long debate in the *majles* (legislature) has since ensued about the legality and the desirability of further land reform, but Muslim jurists have reached competing conclusions regarding the compatibility of such measures with the basic principles of *shari'a*.

(Former) People's Democratic Republic of Yemen

In 1968 land reform was implemented after independence. Previously, most farmers were tenants; the rulers, merchants, and religious institutions owned most of the land. Land was redistributed to private farmers, some 65 percent of whom were organized into cooperatives. About 23 percent of all cropped land was held as state farms.

Since the 1980s governments have increasingly withdrawn from direct management of agriculture. Expanding reliance on the private sector in both farm production and marketing, as well as on reduced regulation of farm prices, is visible today in many of the countries in the region. In Egypt, for example, landowners are for the first time since 1952 permitted to evict tenants. In large part, such liberalization measures have resulted from unhappiness with the sluggish performance of state farming and from the prevailing conventional wisdom in favor of foreign direct investment and international trade. However, social inequities can be expected to grow, at least in the short run, and free-market reforms will likely require various forms of political repression as increased levels of popular opposition are confronted.

Bibliography

Fischbach, Michael. State, Society, and Land in Jordan. Boston and Leiden, Neth.: Brill, 2000.

Gerber, Haim. The Social Origins of the Modern Middle East. Boulder, CO: Lynne Rienner; London: Mansell, 1987.

Mitchell, Timothy. Rule of Experts: Egypt, Techno-politics, Modernity. Berkeley: University of California Press, 2002.

Mundy, Martha. "Village Land and Individual Title: Musha and Ottoman Land Registration in the Ajlun District." In Village, Steppe and State: The Social Origins of Modern Jordan, edited by Eugene L. Rogan and Tariq Tell. New York and London: British Academic Press, 1994.

Owen, Roger, and Pamuk, Sevket. A History of Middle East Economies in the Twentieth Century. Cambridge, MA: Harvard University Press, 1998.

Ruedy, John. Modern Algeria: The Origins and Development of a Nation. Bloomington: Indiana University Press, 1992.

Warriner, Doreen. Land Reform and Development in the Middle East: A Study of Egypt, Syria and Iraq; Issued Under the Auspices of the Royal Institute of International Affairs, 2d edition. London: Oxford University Press, 1962.

ALAN R. RICHARDS
UPDATED BY MARTIN BUNTON

LANDSMANNSCHAFTEN

Jewish immigrant benevolent associations.

These groups were formed by Jews in North and South America and Israel according to place of origin of members, to assist their persecuted *landsleit* (hometown brethren) overseas and to ease their emigration and immigration. In the New World, such groups multiplied exponentially until World War I, began to decline after 1930, and largely disappeared by the 1960s. In Israel such organizations developed welfare institutions, mutual aid societies, and even several short-lived political parties.

ZEV MAGHEN

LANGER, FELICIA
[1930–]

Israeli human rights attorney; defender of Palestinian rights.

Born in Poland in 1930, Felicia Langer emigrated to Israel with her husband, Moshe Langer, a Holocaust survivor, in 1950 to be with her mother. Langer became a member of the anti-Zionist Israeli Communist Party. She became disenchanted with the new state of Israel for its treatment of Palestinians. Trained as a lawyer, after the 1967 war she devoted her entire practice to assisting Palestinian political prisoners. She worked for more than two decades in defense of Palestinian rights, often taking her cases to the Supreme Court, charging violations of the Geneva Convention, to which Israel is a signatory.

Langer faced social ostracism, physical assaults, and death threats for her defense of Palestinians. During the first Palestinian *intifada* (uprising) of 1987 through 1991, she was overwhelmed by the impossibility of adequately representing her clients in the Israeli courts. "I felt I could not address the judge as 'your honor' as a gesture of protest I closed my Jerusalem office and left the country."

Langer resettled in Tübingen, Germany, and continued to criticize the Israeli treatment of Palestinians in Israel and the Occupied Territories. She is a member of the Israeli League for Human Rights and received the Right Livelihood Award for human rights in 1990. She is the author of several books documenting human rights violations in Palestine, including her best-known work *With My Own Eyes* (1975), *These Are My Brothers* (1979), *An Age of Stone* (1987), and an autobiography, *The Epoch of Stones, and Rage, and Hope.*

See also COMMUNISM IN THE MIDDLE EAST; INTIFADA (1987–1991); PALESTINIAN CITIZENS OF ISRAEL.

Bibliography

Rady, Faiza. "A Portrait of Felicia Langer." *Al-Ahram Weekly,* 1998. Available from <http://weekly.ahram.org.eg/1998/1948/402_flci.htm>.

CAROLYN FLUEHR-LOBBAN

LANSDOWNE, HENRY CHARLES KEITH PETTY FITZMAURICE
[1845–1927]

British politician.

Becoming fifth marquess in 1866, Henry Charles Keith Petty Fitzmaurice Lansdowne, or Lord Lansdowne, held posts in various Liberal administrations in Britain and was governor-general in Canada (1883–1888) and viceroy in India (1888–1894). As war secretary (1895–1900) and foreign secretary (1900–1905) under prime ministers Lord Salisbury, Arthur Balfour, and Henry Campbell-Bannerman, Lansdowne negotiated the Anglo-French Entente of 1904, which, among other things, settled Anglo-French differences over Egypt and Morocco. In Morocco's crisis of 1905, Lansdowne acknowledged French supremacy in that country and supported France against Germany. Involved in the diplomatic intrigues surrounding the proposed Baghdad Railway, Lansdowne, Balfour, and many Cabinet members were in favor of supplying funding for the project, but in the face of anti-German public opinion, they were forced to drop the proposal.

Bibliography

Anderson, M. S. *The Eastern Question, 1774–1923: A Study in International Relations.* London: Macmillan; and New York: St. Martin's, 1966.

Taylor, A. J. P. *The Struggle for Mastery in Europe.* New York: Oxford University Press, 1971.

ZACHARY KARABELL

LARAKI, AHMAD
[1931–]

Moroccan diplomat and minister.

Ahmad Laraki earned a medical degree in Paris and in 1957/58 joined the ministry of foreign affairs in Morocco. He served as permanent representative to the United Nations from 1957 to 1959 and as ambassador to Spain, Switzerland, and the United States from 1962 to 1967. Appointed as prime minister in 1969, Laraki weathered rising discontent in Morocco, particularly over economic problems and government corruption, as well as an attempt on the life of Hassan II in 1971. In August 1971, Laraki was replaced by Muhammad Karim Lamrani. From 1971 to 1974, he headed the ministry in charge of medical affairs. In 1974 Laraki was appointed to head the ministry of foreign affairs, an office he held until 1977.

Bibliography

Nelson, Harold D., ed. *Morocco: A Country Study,* 5th edition. Washington, DC: U.S. Government Printing Office, 1985.

MATTHEW S. GORDON

LATA'IF AL-MUSAWWARA MAGAZINE

Trendsetting Egyptian weekly magazine.

Al-Lata'if al-Musawwara (Illustrated witticisms) was a pictorial compilation of current events, politics, famous people, social organizations, sporting events, fashion, and social criticism. It was founded by Iskandar Shahin Makarius, whose family was also involved with the publication of *al-Lata'if, al-Muqtataf,* and *al-Muqattam.* The journal began in 1915, at a time when pictures of any sort were rare in Egyptian publications. Nevertheless, by the final year of its publication in 1941, many other journals began to copy and surpass its style, and its original readership was drained perhaps by its own offshoots: *al-Awlad* (Children), *al-Arusa* (Bride), and *al-Fan al-Sinema'i* (Cinematic art).

Since early twentieth century, Egypt was a place in which even urban literacy rates were low, a journal with large pictures and easy-to-read text was a welcome innovation. Makarius invited readers to submit their own photographs of unusual occurrences, crimes, sporting events, celebrities, oddities, and children, as well as political cartoons or caricatures. Promoting photography was typical of the magazine's support of new styles of consumption, as was its advanced advertising. Advertisements promoted local (non-Western) products, stores, and industries, often utilizing nationalist iconography. Ads appealed to women through the use of indigenous models, feminine forms of address, and products for the modern Egyptian home. Although these techniques became common in the early 1920s, in 1915 they were innovative. The emphasis on advertising demonstrated a shift from the limited press of the late nineteenth and early twentieth centuries, which had depended upon subventions and subscriptions. Makarius promoted his advertising department, boasting immediate results in a 1920 advertisement and claiming a circulation of 40,000. While this figure is probably close to double the true circulation, the magazine had appeal to readers of Arabic as far away as Brazil.

See also ART; GENDER: GENDER AND EDUCATION; NEWSPAPERS AND PRINT MEDIA: ARAB COUNTRIES.

MONA RUSSELL

LATAKIA

Major Syrian seaport.

On the Mediterranean Sea, Latakia was known in Greek as Laodicea after the name of the mother of Seleucus Nicator (301–281 C.E.), who built it. A fertile coastal plain stretches around Latakia (Arabic, *al-Ladhaqiyya*). According to the 1982 administrative divisions of Syria, the province of Latakia included 4 *mintaqas* (sections) based on Latakia, Jabala, al-Haffa, and al-Qardaha, 13 *nahiyas* (subdivisions) based on 13 towns, 501 villages, and 590 farms. The population of Latakia province in 2002 was 1 million; the city population was about 345,000.

ABDUL-KARIM RAFEQ

LATIFE

See NEWSPAPERS AND PRINT MEDIA: TURKEY

LA TUNISIE MARTYRE

Manifesto of the Tunisian nationalist movement.

Written by two leading Tunisian nationalists, Abd al-Aziz Thaalbi, the founder of the Destour political party, and Ahmad Sakkah, this manifesto was published in Paris in 1921. It presented the key demands and premises of the fledgling Tunisian movement for nationalism. At its heart was the claim that, prior to the French occupation (1881), a viable Tunisian state had been in place, complete with its own constitution, representative assembly, open press, and healthy economy. On the basis of those earlier institutions, a new and independent Tunisia would be established.

See also THAALBI, ABD AL-AZIZ.

Bibliography

Micaud, Charles. *Tunisia: The Politics of Modernization.* New York: Praeger, 1964.

MATTHEW S. GORDON

LAUSANNE CONFERENCE (1949)

United Nations–sponsored international conference to resolve the Arab–Israeli conflict.

The United Nations Conciliation Commission for Palestine (UNCCP) was created by UN General Assembly Resolution 194 (III) of December 1948 with the lofty goal of mediating among the warring parties after the Arab–Israel War of 1948. The UNCCP's first major initiative in this direction was to hold a conference in Lausanne, Switzerland, from 27 April to 12 September 1949, at which it hoped to bridge the differences among Arabs and Israelis.

Israel, Jordan, Egypt, Lebanon, and Syria sent delegations; Iraq refused. Various delegations claiming to represent Palestinian refugees were also present. Among these were the Arab Higher Committee and the General Refugee Congress, represented by Muhammad Nimr al-Hawwari and Aziz Shehadeh. Other Palestinians representing large landowners like Shukri al-Taji al-Faruqi and Sa'id Baydas arrived later to work with al-Hawwari.

The conferees never met in a general session. Rather, the UNCCP held separate meetings with the

Arabs and Israelis over many months. Informal meetings were held, but the formal procedures produced little. One document that emerged was the Lausanne Protocol that dealt with territorial and boundary issues. Almost immediately after signing it, the warring parties sparred over its implementation.

The conference discussed other issues as well, especially relating to Palestinian refugees. Israel offered to repatriate 100,000 of them in the context of a final settlement. The refugees' abandoned property also emerged as a major issue. In June 1949 the UNCCP created its first subcommittee, the Technical Committee, to investigate practical ways of resolving refugee issues. The conference also produced the United Nations Economic Survey Mission for the Middle East (the Clapp Mission), established by the UNCCP in late August to explore economic solutions to the refugee problem.

Bibliography

Caplan, Neil. *The Lausanne Conference, 1949: A Case Study in Middle East Peacemaking.* Tel Aviv: Tel Aviv University, 1993.

Fischbach, Michael R. *Records of Dispossession: Palestinian Refugee Property and the Arab-Israeli Conflict.* New York: Columbia University Press, 2003.

MICHAEL R. FISCHBACH

LAUSANNE, TREATY OF (1923)

Renegotiation of treaties ending World War I resulting in more favorable treatment of Turkey.

Defeat in World War I resulted in a harsh peace treaty for the Ottoman Empire. The Treaty of Sèvres (1920) stripped Turkey of all its European territory except for a small area around Constantinople (now Istanbul); demilitarized the straits between the Black and Mediterranean seas, opened them to ships of all nations, and placed them under an international commission; established an independent Armenia and an autonomous Kurdistan in eastern Anatolia; turned over the region around İzmir to the Greeks; restored the capitulations; and placed Turkish finances under foreign control. By separate agreement, some parts of Turkey left to the Turks were assigned to France and Italy as spheres of influence.

Unlike the other nations on the losing side in World War I, Turkey was able to renegotiate its treaty terms. This was the result of the decline of the sultan's power, the rise of the nationalists under Mustafa Kemal Atatürk, and the defeat of the Greeks' attempt to expand their power in Turkey. The latter development placed Turkish forces near British troops in the area of the straits and led to an armistice at Mudanya in October 1922 at which the Allied powers restored Constantinople and the straits to Turkish authority and called for a peace convention to renegotiate the terms laid down at Sèvres. The Allies invited both of the contesting powers in Turkey—the sultan's government and the nationalists under Kemal—to a conference at Lausanne, Switzerland. This precipitated Kemal's decision to separate the positions of sultan and caliph, abolishing the former, exiling Mehmet VI and giving the residual powers of caliph to his cousin, Abdülmecit II. Thus, when the conference at Lausanne began in November 1922, Kemal's Ankara government was the sole representative of Turkey.

İsmet Paşa, later İsmet İnönü in honor of his two victories over the Greeks at İnönü, led the Turkish delegation as the newly appointed foreign minister. He was determined to reestablish Turkish sovereignty and negotiate as an equal with the British, French, and Italians at the conference. However, İsmet found himself treated as a supplicant rather than the representative of a government with recent victories. Unable to compete with the sophisticated debate of the Allied diplomats, İsmet responded with his own unique tactics. He feigned deafness, contested every point however minor, read long prepared statements, delayed debate by consultations with his colleagues, and periodically insisted on deferring discussion pending instructions from Ankara. These tactics led to a break of negotiations for two months beginning in February 1923.

The Lausanne conference resulted in seventeen diplomatic instruments. Turkey recognized the loss of its Arab provinces, but plans for an independent Armenia and an autonomous Kurdistan were abandoned. The European powers no longer demanded capitulation, and although Turkey agreed to minor financial burdens and tariff restrictions, there were to be no war reparations. The Greeks lost their zone around İzmir, and no other powers retained zones of influence. Turkish territory in Europe expanded, but control over Mosul in Iraq and Alexandretta in Syria remained with the British and French respectively. Finally, the conference recognized Turkish sovereignty over the straits, although there were some concessions in the form of a demilitarized zone and an international commission to supervise transit through the straits. In short, İsmet achieved virtually all that nationalist Turkey under Kemal's leadership desired.

See also SÈVRES, TREATY OF (1920).

Bibliography

Ahmad, Feroz. *The Making of Modern Turkey.* New York: Routledge, 1993.

Howard, Harry N. *The Partition of Turkey: A Diplomatic History, 1913–1923.* New York: Ferig, 1966.

DANIEL E. SPECTOR
UPDATED BY ERIC HOOGLUND

LAVON AFFAIR

1960s political crisis in Israel sparked by the security "mishap" of 1954.

The Lavon Affair was a dramatic and divisive political crisis that shook the entire Israeli political system, led to the resignation of prime minister David Ben-Gurion in July 1963, and caused major shifts in political alignments in the state. Its roots lay in what the Israeli press nicknamed *Esek ha-Bish* (the "Mishap"). A dormant group of Israeli-trained Egyptian Jews who were prepared for missions of espionage and sabotage in the event of war were ill-advisedly activated in June 1954 under orders from Colonel Benjamin Gibli (Givly), the head of the Intelligence Division of the Israeli Defense Forces. They were instructed to detonate firebombs in a few U.S. and British cultural institutions in Cairo and Alexandria in order to disrupt the negotiations, which were nearing conclusion, on the evacuation of British troops from bases along the Suez Canal. The group was captured by Egyptian security services. Two of the leading saboteurs were sentenced and hanged, an Israeli spy committed suicide in prison, and the others were sentenced to long terms of imprisonment.

Colonel Gibli maintained that he had received orders from Pinhas Lavon, who at the time was re-

placing Ben-Gurion as minister of defense. A secret inquiry committee appointed by the government of Moshe Sharett could not reach a clear judgment, and both Gibli and Lavon were obliged to resign their respective posts.

Four years later the commander of the special unit in charge of the operation in Egypt disclosed that one of the documents presented to the 1954 cabinet inquiry committee was forged. The attorney general was asked by Ben-Gurion to look into these allegations. Colonel Gibli admitted the forgery but continued to claim that he had received the order orally from Lavon, and that he had been compelled to forge the document when he realized that Lavon was trying to put all the blame on him. Lavon, who was then serving as secretary-general of the Histadrut, Israel's powerful trade-union umbrella organization, demanded a public exoneration from Ben-Gurion, who declined to give it, insisting that the affair had to be subjected to a judicial investigation.

Despite strict censorship, the incident became known under different euphemisms and code names to the general public, stirring up a political crisis within and outside of the Labor Party. The entire country was divided between those who supported Ben-Gurion's position and those who opposed him. The aging prime minister had angered the second generation of party leaders by promoting a group of still younger people such as Moshe Dayan and Shimon Peres to important posts in the government, jumping over the heads of his erstwhile loyal lieutenants. For his part, Ben-Gurion was enraged that Lavon had brought his grievances to different forums outside of the party and had mobilized pressure by parties and newspapers that sought to weaken Labor's long-standing political dominance.

In order to quiet things down, the minister of finance, Levi Eshkol, by then the most powerful political figure besides Ben-Gurion, asked the minister of justice, Pinhas Rosen, to lead a ministerial committee of seven to determine how to deal with Lavon's demand for exhonoration and to bring the crisis to an end. This committee ruled that Lavon had not given the order for the sabotage action and that the document was indeed a forgery. But Ben-Gurion was indignant and threatened to resign if Lavon did not quit his post at the Histadrut. Ben-Gurion, the "Old Man," was still powerful enough to impose his will on the party's central committee, but the entire affair weakened his standing among most of his party's elite. Eshkol refused to retract the committee's exonerating verdict and Ben-Gurion continued to demand a judicial inquiry. Additional friction ensued between Ben-Gurion and the party elite, led by Golda Meir, minister of foreign affairs, who until then had been a long-time loyal supporter of Ben-Gurion. These frictions included a bitter controversy over Israel's relations with West Germany and over the development of the Israeli nuclear option.

The tired and embittered seventy-seven-year-old Ben-Gurion resigned in June 1963. Levi Eshkol replaced him as prime minister and minister of defense. In the 1965 elections Ben-Gurion and some of his supporters in the Lavon Affair split from the Labor Party and formed a new party, Rafi (List of Israeli Workers). This effectively marked the end of Ben-Gurion's political career.

See also BEN-GURION, DAVID; ISRAEL: POLITICAL PARTIES IN; LAVON, PINHAS.

Bibliography

Lucas, Noah. *The Modern History of Israel.* London: Weidenfeld and Nicolson, 1974.

Sachar, Howard. *A History of Israel from the Rise of Zionism to Our Time.* New York: Knopf, 1988.

Teveth, Shabtai. *Ben-Gurion's Spy: The Story of the Political Scandal that Shaped Modern Israel.* New York: Columbia University Press, 1996.

MORDECHAI BAR-ON

LAVON, PINHAS
[1904–1976]

Israeli labor leader and politician.

Born in Galicia, Poland, Pinhas Lavon was active in a Zionist socialist youth movement and was one of the founders of the Gordonia-Pioneer Youth Movement. After immigrating to Mandatory Palestine in 1929, he was active in the Kibbutz movement and became one of the ideologists of MAPAI, whose secretary-general he was in 1938 and 1939. Elected to the Histadrut Executive Committee, he became its secretary-general from 1948 to 1951. Elected to the Knesset in 1949, a year later he joined the cabinet as minister without portfolio, minister of agriculture, and from 1954 to 1955, minister of defense. In that position Lavon sought to reform the Defense Ministry, thereby angering many of its top officials and senior echelons of the Israel Defense Force (IDF). In 1954 his name was linked to a failed operation in Egypt, in which a cell of young Egyptian Jews, activated by the IDF, placed explosives in American facilities in Cairo, with the intent of souring relations between Egypt and the West in order to delay the British withdrawal from Egypt, thus removing a buffer between Egypt and Israel. Lavon argued that he did not give the order to carry out these operations. The director of Military Intelligence claimed he had.

Lavon was forced to resign his post as defense minister when the leadership of MAPAI felt his erratic behavior and hawkish policies were not acceptable. They persuaded David Ben-Gurion to return from his self-imposed retirement. Lavon was reappointed secretary-general of the Histadrut (1956–1961). In 1959, with new evidence in his hands, Lavon demanded the re-opening of the investigation of the 1954 affair in order to clear his name. In the process he accused senior IDF officers and Defense Ministry officials of perjury. Ben-Gurion demanded Lavon's ouster from the Histadrut. In 1964 he left the MAPAI party. The Lavon Affair led to a split in the ruling MAPAI Party and to Ben-Gurion's resignation in 1963. To his dying day Lavon continued to demand that his name be cleared. New research suggests that he knew of the operation but did not necessarily sanction it.

Bibliography

Bar-Zohar, Michael. *Ben-Gurion: A Biography,* translated by Peretz Kidron. New York: Adama Books, 1978.

Teveth, Shabtai. *Ben-Gurion's Spy: The Story of the Political Scandal That Shaped Modern Israel.* New York: Columbia University Press, 1996.

REEVA S. SIMON
UPDATED BY MERON MEDZINI

LAW IN THE SERVICE OF MAN
See HAQ, AL-

LAW, MODERN

Varieties of legal systems in Middle Eastern countries.

Modernization of law in the Middle East has entailed converting to civil law systems (generally based directly or indirectly on the French model) and, in the process, restricting and transforming the heritage of Islamic law (*shariʿa*) as set forth in juristic treatises.

Centralized legal systems, in which lawmaking is monopolized by governments of nation-states and uniform law applies throughout the national territory, are now in place throughout the Middle East, though the process remains incomplete in parts of the Arabian Peninsula. The adoption of modern legal systems has led to the marginalization or suppression of formerly vital local and customary legal systems. Modernization of legal systems has also eliminated special, extraterritorial status for members of powerful foreign communities who had succeeded in getting exemptions from the premodern legal systems of Middle Eastern countries.

The Role of *Shariʿa*

In its early stages, modernization of Middle Eastern law involved a large degree of Westernization, since the models for the new laws were European and the lawyers and other legal professionals who staffed the modernized legal systems were trained either in Europe or along European lines. Westernizing reforms were most often imposed from above by members of ruling elites or under the auspices of European powers. The process was initially slow and involved establishing new systems that operated alongside of—rather than replaced—the older, *shariʿa*-based systems. Gradually, the scope of the new legal systems widened, and the *shariʿa*-based system was increasingly confined (generally to matters of personal status, such as marriage, divorce, and inheritance). Over time, many states reined in the autonomy of this remnant of the *shariʿa*-based system, sometimes even folding its courts into the newer structures. However, only Turkey completely secularized its law.

The reaction against these trends was slow in coming. In the middle of the twentieth century, some outside of the systems of religious law and education began to complain that Middle Eastern so-cieties were abandoning their Islamic nature. In the 1960s and 1970s, this argument took a particularly radical turn, as movements arose claiming that the failure of existing governments to implement Islamic law rendered them un-Islamic and therefore illegitimate. Although in most countries those calling for revolution in the name of defending Islamic law were a minority, the denunciation of the marginalization of the *shariʿa* had great resonance.

Some countries therefore worked to move their legal system in an Islamic direction, and many pledged in their constitutions to make the principles of the *shariʿa* a (or even the) main source of law. Yet this vague promise provoked new problems. The *shariʿa* as traditionally understood was not a legal code with easily identifiable rules but a broad intellectual tradition. Introducing elements of Islamic law into the legal system raised questions of what interpretation should be used and who had the authority to interpret law. Further, training in Islamic legal sciences had atrophied in some locations. The result was that secularly trained legal personnel often bore primary responsibility for applying the law. This did not stop attempts to integrate elements of the Islamic legal tradition in various fields of law. This solution has proved controversial in many societies, but only a few countries have resisted the general trend.

Political and Other Pressures on Legal Development

Besides the conflict over the role of Islamic law, three other conflicting pressures have operated over time. First, many Middle Eastern states attempted to build socialist economic systems through law in the 1950s through the 1970s. This effort often led them to use law as a means to restructure property rights (through measures like land reform and rent controls). Since the 1980s these states have faced international pressure to liberalize their economic and legal frameworks.

Second, the general political environment has deeply affected legal development, most obviously (but not exclusively) in constitutional law. Early constitutional efforts in the nineteenth century seem fairly modest in retrospect, focusing on establishing clear political structures and chains of command. Some tried but failed to constrain the authority of the ruler. In the twentieth century, constitutions became markers of sovereignty and were generally issued after independence. After midcentury, with the rise of revolutionary ideologies, Middle Eastern governments often experimented with attempts to transform the social order through the constitutional and legal order. In addition, the spread of authoritarianism made it common to construct special court systems and emergency laws to solidify existing regimes. But Middle Eastern governments have faced demands for political liberalization and enhanced guarantees for the rule of law, the independence of the judiciary, and respect for international human rights principles.

Finally, international factors have fluctuated in importance over time. Middle Eastern countries have varied in the degree to which they sought integration in the increasingly internationalized post–World War II legal environment. For example, they followed differing policies regarding submission to dispute-resolution institutions such as the International Court of Justice and international arbitration, and they also have disparate records of ratifying major international treaties. In general, however, the trend has been in favor of closer integration in the internationalized legal order.

As a result of these pressures, modernization of law—which started as a top-down reform process in the nineteenth century—had become an extremely sensitive and highly politicized topic by the beginning of the twenty-first.

British and French Influences

Leaving aside their occasional Islamic components, modern laws in the Middle East have been shaped by the same forces that led to the adoption of the civil law systems of continental Europe in almost all countries around the world. The primary, and partial, exceptions are those that were dominated by Britain. British colonization or the exercise of British mandatory or protectorate authority in the Middle East led to some transplants from the common law in areas like Aden (later part of South Yemen), Bahrain, Sudan, and Oman. Nevertheless, the common law had little long-term impact on the legal systems of many countries that fell under British rule, such as Egypt, Iraq, Jordan, and Kuwait. Thus civil law, mostly of French derivation, now predominates throughout the Middle East, and the oc-

casional remnants of common law seem unlikely to survive. For example, in 1987 Bahrain broke from British tradition, choosing to enact a commercial code derived from Egyptian and Kuwaiti models, which were themselves French in inspiration.

The contemporary legal systems of Middle Eastern countries thus share the basic features of French law, such as relying on comprehensive and systematic statements of the law in codes as formal sources of law, maintaining a sharp distinction between public and private law and between commercial and private law, and using the inquisitorial mode of procedure in criminal cases. Characteristics of the French judicial system such as separate administrative court hierarchies and the parquet/prosecutor's office are also found. French law codes have also been influential, sometimes directly and sometimes through the intervening influence of Egyptian law (which adopted and adapted much French law). However, parts of the substantive legal provisions in Middle Eastern codes often have no counterparts in continental European law, corresponding instead to governmental policies, local custom, or Islamic principles. Various codifications of *shariʿa* law were enacted into law, especially in matters of personal status, and many secular codes refer to principles of Islamic law or custom as supplementary sources of law.

The Progress of Reform

Although a few states substantially reformed their legal and judicial systems in the nineteenth century, in most areas of the Middle East change did not begin in earnest until the early twentieth century. It was delayed in countries like Afghanistan, Bahrain, Kuwait, Oman, Saudi Arabia, the states comprising the United Arab Emirates, and Yemen until the middle of the twentieth century. Newer legal systems generally initially focused on constitutions, criminal law, procedural rules, and matters involving contracts and commerce. The longest-enduring control of *shariʿa* law was over personal status matters, although even in this area it was for the most part ultimately reformed or systemized in codes. Saudi Arabia has remained the most resistant to this trend, never having made a formal break with the preexisting Islamic system of jurists' law but instead following a steady course of supplementing juristic

Merve Kavakci, a newly elected member of Turkey's Parliament, was asked to leave the swearing-in session when she arrived for the ceremony wearing an Islamic head scarf. The scarves are a controversial issue in Turkey, seen as representing an Islamic threat to the secular constitution, and public servants are forbidden to wear them. © AP/WIDE WORLD PHOTOS. REPRODUCED BY PERMISSION.

treatises by gradually introducing governmental "regulations" in areas important for administration and economic development.

The Ottoman Empire began comprehensive legal reform in the mid-1800s, undertaking many codification projects, some of which remained influential long after its collapse. Modernization began with attempts to codify Islamic criminal laws in 1840 and 1851, which were followed by the adoption of two French-inspired codes, a penal code in 1858 and a penal procedure code in 1879. An Ottoman constitution was adopted in 1876 (though it was quickly suspended); it was amended and restored in 1909. Inspired by French models, a commercial code (later borrowed by Saudi Arabia in 1931) was enacted in 1850, and commercial proce-

dure codes were enacted in 1861 and 1880. The most famous monument of the Ottoman legal modernization process was the Majalla (Mecelle), issued between 1869 and 1876. This was an attempt to develop a codified version of Islamic law by relying on principles found in treatises of jurists of the Hanafi school, the official school of law in the Ottoman domains. In addition to substantive rules on civil and commercial transactions and on procedures and evidence, the Majalla was composed of statements and general principles of law designed to guide the application and interpretation of its provisions.

After the collapse of the Ottoman Empire, the Majalla survived in some of its former territories, though most eventually turned to French-based codes, as occurred in Iraq in 1951, in Jordan in 1966,

Ehud Barak, former prime minister of Israel, prepares to testify in front of Israel's Supreme Court. The Supreme Court interprets the law, as well as the statutes of the Knesset, Israel's parliament. © AP/WIDE WORLD PHOTOS. REPRODUCED BY PERMISSION.

in Kuwait in 1980, in Lebanon in 1932, in Libya in 1954, and in Syria in 1949. The substantive provisions of the Majalla still exert an influence, inspiring many provisions of the 1951 Civil Code of Iraq and the 1985 Code of Civil Transactions of the United Arab Emirates. The Ottoman Family Law of 1917 was another historical experiment with crafting a modern statute out of *shariʿa* rules, using the innovative technique of combining principles of family law from different Sunni schools of law.

Egypt, which during the nineteenth century became largely independent of Ottoman control, began legal reform in the mid-nineteenth century. Initially, legal reform proceeded on two tracks. For cases involving Egyptians, Ottoman models were initially used before the legal system converted to a French model in the 1880s. For cases in which a foreigner was involved, Egypt constructed Mixed Courts that were more purely French from the beginning. In 1937, however, Egypt secured international agreement for the unification of its legal system and began to draw up a new set of comprehensive codes. Much of this work was overseen by the Egyptian jurist Abd al-Razzaq al-Sanhuri (1895–1971). An expert in European and Islamic law, he played a major role in drafting the influential Egyptian Civil Code of 1948 (effective in 1949). This essentially French code, which allowed the *shariʿa* to be used as a supplementary source of law, provided the model for the civil codes subsequently adopted in Iraq, Jordan, Kuwait, Libya, and Syria and indirectly influenced the 1984 Sudanese Civil Transactions Act. Italian law shaped Egypt's 1937 criminal code.

As a result of long-standing French political domination of North Africa, French legal culture spread through the region. During the time that Algeria was a French colony, from 1830 to 1962, it was integrated into the French legal system. Algeria enacted new codes after independence in which

French influence persisted. In 1984 it adopted a code of family law reinstating *shariʿa* rules and reinforcing the patriarchal structure of the family. Faced with popular pressures for legal reform, in 1989 Algeria adopted a new constitution that diluted the militant socialist character of the 1976 constitution and reflected demands both for strengthened human rights guarantees and for changes that would give the constitution a more Islamic character. In 1861 Tunisia had become the first Middle Eastern country to enact a constitution. As a French protectorate, from 1881 to 1956, Tunisia enacted in 1906 a code of obligations and contracts that combined elements of French and Islamic law, and in 1913 it adopted a penal code. After independence Tunisia amended old codes and enacted new ones, the most significant being its 1956 Personal Status Code, constituting the most progressive interpretation in Arab law of Islamic legal requirements in the area of family law. Morocco, a French protectorate from 1912 to 1956, enacted in 1913 its Code of Obligations and Contracts, which was similar to the 1906 Tunisian code. Morocco enacted some French-inspired codes after independence, but it retained many rules of traditional *shariʿa* law in its 1958 Personal Status Code and incorporated aspects of Islamic criminal law in provisions of its 1962 Penal Code.

Distinctive Paths of Legal Development

Some Middle Eastern countries followed distinctive paths of legal development. For example, Iran adopted a constitution in 1906 and 1907. An Iranian Civil Code was enacted in the period from 1927 to 1937 that combined elements of Twelver Shiʿi law with French and Swiss law. French law provided the models for other codifications undertaken by Iran in the 1930s. The progressive Iranian Family Protection Act of 1967, amended in 1975, was abrogated after the Islamic revolution of 1978–1979. Since the revolution, Iran has officially endorsed Islamization, adopting a constitution in 1979 that placed an Islamic jurist at the apex of the scheme of government and established Islamic principles as the supreme law of the land. Westernized legal professionals and Western-style legal training were replaced; Shiʿa clerics and Shiʿi jurisprudence were given a preeminent role in the legal system. However, there was no return to the old system of jurists' law: Iran's parliament retained its lawmaking

authority, and French legal influences were not obliterated.

Turkey was reconstituted in 1921 as a nation-state after the collapse of the Ottoman Empire. Under Kemal Atatürk (1881–1938), the military leader who became the first president, Turkey pursued a program of complete secularization of law, which led to the abandonment of Islamic law even in personal status matters. In 1928 Islam lost its status as the state religion. Turkey imported European codes in the 1920s that were variously taken from German, Italian, and Swiss sources. The Turkish constitutions of 1921, 1924, 1961, and 1982 have differed in many respects, but Turkey's governments have continued to uphold the principle of secularism.

Israel emerged in 1948 as a Jewish state with a legal system in which there coexisted elements deriving from the Ottoman law of prepartition Palestine, Jewish law, and Western law, the latter being an unusual hybrid of common law and civil law elements. As with almost all other Middle Eastern countries, however, personal status law retains a religious basis.

Upon achieving independence in 1951, Libya largely divested itself of Italian law, which had been imposed after it was colonized by Italy in 1912. Egyptian influences on the new legal system were initially strong, but after the 1969 revolution Libya pursued a separate course of radical legal changes that were dictated by the theories of its leader, Muammar al-Qaddafi.

Bibliography

Brown, Nathan J. *Constitutions in a Nonconstitutional World: Arab Basic Laws and the Prospects for Accountable Government.* Albany, NY: State University Press, 2001.

Centre of Islamic and Middle Eastern Law. *Yearbook of Islamic and Middle Eastern Law.* Dordrecht, Netherlands, 1994–.

Liebesny, Herbert J. *The Law of the Near and Middle East: Readings, Cases, and Materials.* Albany, NY: State University Press, 1975.

Mayer, Ann Elizabeth. *Islam and Human Rights: Tradition and Politics.* Boulder, CO: Westview, 1998.

Sonbal, Amira, ed. *Women, the Family, and Divorce Laws in Islamic History.* Syracuse, NY: Syracuse University Press, 1996.

Vogel, Frank E. *Islamic Law and Legal System: Studies of Saudi Arabia.* Leiden, Netherlands: E. J. Brill, 2000.

ANN E. MAYER
UPDATED BY NATHAN J. BROWN

LAW OF RETURN

Law that allows Jews to immigrate to Israel and become Israeli citizens.

The Law of Return (*Hok ha-Shvut*) was passed by the Knesset on 5 July 1950. In accordance with the notion that Israel is a Jewish state and the state of the Jews, the law provides that any Jew is entitled to immigrate to Israel and acquire a certificate and status of *oleh,* an immigrant with automatic citizenship. The law was amended in 1954 to exclude individuals with a criminal past that might endanger public welfare. An amendment in 1970 extended citizenship rights to non-Jewish spouses and children of Jews.

Some Orthodox leaders have called for an amendment to the law that would narrowly define a Jew as one born of a Jewish mother or one who converted according to Orthodox tradition. To many, this proposed amendment makes the debate over Jewish identity so volatile that it threatens the fabric of worldwide Jewish unity. It has sparked passionate debate both in Israel and the Diaspora over definitions of Jewish identity, and has aroused strong opposition from the Jewish Reform and Conservative movements. There have been periodic calls for repeal of the law by some non-Zionists and others who view it as discriminatory. From their perspective, Israel should be a state like any other modern state, without laws that discriminate on the basis of religion or ethnicity.

See also ISRAEL: OVERVIEW.

Bibliography

Ben-Rafael, Eliezer. *Jewish Identities: Fifty Intellectuals Answer Ben-Gurion.* Leiden, Netherlands: Brill, 2002.

Landau, David. *Who Is a Jew? A Case Study of American Jewish Influence on Israeli Policy.* New York: American Jewish Committee, Institute on American Jewish-Israel Relations, 1996.

Schochet, Jacob Immanuel. *Who Is a Jew?: 30 Questions and Answers About this Controversial and Divisive Issue.* New York: Shofar Association of America, 1987.

Shachar, Ayelet. "Citizenship and Membership in the Israeli Polity." In *From Migrants to Citizens: Membership in a Changing World,* edited by T. Alexander Aleinikoff and Douglas Klusmeyer. Washington, DC: Brookings Institution Press, 2000.

CHAIM I. WAXMAN

LAWRENCE, T. E.
[1888–1935]

British soldier and adventurer, known as Lawrence of Arabia.

Thomas Edward Lawrence was born on 15 August 1888 in Tremadoc, Wales, and was educated at the University of Oxford, where he graduated with a thesis on the military architecture of the Crusades. Having developed an interest in archaeology and Arab culture, he toured the Crusader castles in Greater Syria when the region was in its last years under Ottoman rule. At the outbreak of World War I, disgusted by the hypocrisy of his own society's values, Lawrence turned from an adventurer into a secret agent, becoming the famed Lawrence of Arabia. From the British Military Intelligence Service in Cairo, which he joined in 1914, he was dispatched to the Hijaz, where the Hashimites acted as the Ottoman sultan's representatives of the two holy cities of Mecca and Medina. Lawrence's mission was to help organize the Arab tribes into a national movement that ultimately was to serve British imperialism. The Arab national movement, in which Lawrence himself came to believe, turned into a military success, and in 1918 Lawrence and Hashimite prince Faisal (later King Faisal I ibn Hussein of Iraq) entered Damascus before the arrival of the British army so as to avoid a Muslim backlash.

In spite of the success of the so-called Arab Revolt of 1916 to 1918, Lawrence, who narrated his adventures in *Seven Pillars of Wisdom* (1926), thought that his battle for an "Arab cause" was "lost" because "the old men came out again and took from us our victory" in order to "re-make [the world] in the likeness of the former world they knew" (Introduction to the first edition, 1926; passage omitted from later editions). Unable to cope with his fractured self and with the historical necessities of British imperialism, Lawrence ultimately stopped believing in a meaningful Arab national movement, which he thought was only "necessary in its time and place" (*Letters,* in

1930, p. 693). He rejoined the air force in 1925 and served as an enlisted man until 1935. On 19 May of that year, shortly after his discharge, he was killed in a motorbike accident in Dorset.

See also ARAB REVOLT (1916); HASHIMITE HOUSE (HOUSE OF HASHIM).

Bibliography

Lawrence, T. E. *The Letters of T. E. Lawrence,* edited by David Garnett. New York: Doubleday, Doran, 1939.

Thomas, Lowell. *With Lawrence in Arabia.* New York and London: Century, 1924.

Wilson, Jeremy. *Lawrence of Arabia.* Stroud, U.K.: Sutton, 1998.

BENJAMIN BRAUDE
UPDATED BY ZOUHAIR GHAZZAL

LAZ

See GLOSSARY

LAZMA

See GLOSSARY

LEAGUE OF ARAB STATES

This foremost pan-Arab organization provides the institutional expression for the aspiration of Arab unity.

The League of Arab States, also known as the Arab League, is composed of twenty-two independent Arab states that have signed the Pact of the League of Arab States. Palestine, represented by the Palestinian Authority, is included as an independent state. The multipurpose League of Arab States seeks to promote Arab interests in general, but especially economic and security interests. It also works to resolve disputes among members and between member states and nonmember states. It has the image of unity in the protection of Arab independence and sovereignty. It promotes political, military, economic, social, cultural, and developmental cooperation among its members.

The league is an international governmental organization with permanent headquarters in Cairo, Egypt. From 1979 to 1990 its headquarters were in Tunis. It maintains delegations at United Nations

Secretary-General Amr Mousa of the League of Arab States speaks at the United Nations in 2003. Mousa, a career diplomat, also served as the foreign minister of Egypt after 1991. © AP/WIDE WORLD PHOTOS. REPRODUCED BY PERMISSION.

facilities in New York and Geneva, and at the Organization of African Unity in Addis Ababa, Ethiopia. It also has offices in such key cities as Washington, D.C., London, Moscow, Paris, Bonn, Beijing, Brussels, Vienna, Madrid, Rome, and New Delhi. The league has not realized the perfect Arab unity desired by some Arab nationalists. From its inception some states emphasized state sovereignty in accordance with the league's pact and rejected federalist or unionist proposals. The league not only serves the mutual interests of its members, but also reflects the differences. The league members agreed to an Arab Charter on Human Rights in 1994 and to the Arab Convention for the Suppression of Terrorism in 1998.

History

The League of Arab States was founded on 22 March 1945 with the signing of the pact by seven Arab states. Sixteen additional states joined, but in 1990 Yemen (Aden) and Yemen (San'a) merged to form the Republic of Yemen, bringing the total to twenty-two.

Although the league was formed after World War II, the process that led to its creation is a function of the development of Arab nationalism, which predated the twentieth century but grew dramatically after World War II. Egyptian prime minister

The League of Arab States meets in Bludan in 1946. Formed in 1945, the league is a voluntary association of independent countries whose main purposes are to strengthen ties among member and nonmember states, coordinate their policies, and promote their common interests. © BETTMANN/CORBIS. REPRODUCED BY PERMISSION.

Mustafa al-Nahhas, Iraqi prime minister Nuri al-Sa'id, and Transjordan's King Abdullah I ibn Hussein are credited with being early architects of the league in the 1940s. The British initiated, in part, the preparatory talks leading to its creation. In the fall of 1944, seven Arab states met in Alexandria, Egypt, to discuss the creation of a "Commonwealth of Arab States." On 7 October 1944 Egypt, Iraq, Lebanon, Syria, and Transjordan signed the Alexandria Protocol, which envisioned a league of independent states, rather than a union or federation. The main points of the protocol were subsequently incorporated into the league, as was an appendix stressing Palestinian independence. The league's initial members were Egypt, Iraq, Lebanon, Saudi Arabia, Syria, Transjordan (now Jordan), and Yemen (Sanaa).

The league's general structure has remained intact since its formation, but the scope of its activities has expanded dramatically, especially in nonpolitical fields. The organization consists of a council, special committees, and a secretariat-general. In addition, the league has become an umbrella organization responsible for the numerous specialized agencies, unions, and other institutions created to promote Arab interests.

Organization

The pact established a council as the league's principal organ. It is composed of representatives of each member state, with each state having one vote. Unanimous decisions of the council are binding on all members. Majority decisions are binding only on those members that accepted them, except that majority decisions are enforceable on all members for certain specific matters relating to personnel, the budget, administrative regulations, and adjournment. The council implements league policies and pursues league goals. It meets twice a year, in March and September, but extraordinary meetings can be called at the request of two members.

Special committees have been established to support and represent the council. The league's committees have included the Political Committee, Culture Committee, Communications Committee, Social Committee, Legal Committee, Arab Oil Experts Committee, Information Committee, Health Committee, Human Rights Committee, Permanent Committee for Administration and Financial Affairs, Permanent Committee for Meteorology, Committee of Arab Experts on Cooperation, Arab Women's Committee, Organization of Youth Welfare, and Conference of Liaison Officers.

The secretariat-general consists of the secretary-general, assistant secretaries-general, and other principal officials of the league. It is responsible for administrative and financial activities. The council, with the approval of a two-thirds majority of the league's members, appoints the secretary-general to a renewable five-year term. The secretary-general has the rank of ambassador.

The office of the secretary-general was held by Egyptians during the first three decades of the league: Abd al-Rahman al-Azzam (1945–1952); Abd al-Khaliq Hassuna (1952–1972); and Mahmud Riyad (1972–1979). A Tunisian, Chadli Klibi, held the post from 1979 until 1990. He resigned during the controversy surrounding the Gulf Crisis. Ahmad Ismat Abd al-Majid, an Egyptian, served as secretary-general from May 1991 to 2001. He was followed in 2001 by the popular Egyptian foreign minister Amr Moussa (also Musa).

In 1950 the Treaty of Joint Defense and Economic Cooperation complemented the league pact and provided for the establishment of the Joint Defense Council and the Permanent Military Commission. An Economic Council was set up under the treaty in 1953. An Arab Unified Military Command was formed in 1964. In 1976 an Arab Deterrent Force was sent to Lebanon under league auspices.

Financing

The League of Arab States is financed by an assessment of charges made to each member. The secretary-general prepares a draft budget and submits it to the council for approval before the beginning of each fiscal year. The council then fixes the share of the expenses or dues to be paid by each member state. This share may be reconsidered if necessary.

The league experienced significant difficulties in the collection of member-state dues in the aftermath of the Gulf Crisis (1990–1991) and subsequently. Its 1991 budget was over $27 million, with the largest share being assessed to Saudi Arabia (14%), Kuwait (14%), Libya (12%), Iraq (10%), Egypt (8.5%), Algeria (8%), the United Arab Emirates (6.5%), and Morocco (5%). Bahrain, Kuwait, Libya, Morocco, and Yemen had reservations concerning their share of the league budget. The 1999 budget was set at $26.5 million, but when Amr Moussa took office in 2001, it was estimated at $50 million. Also, late dues reportedly had reached $100 million, with some states more than a decade in arrears. According to Article 15 of the league's bylaws, approved in 1973, members can be denied

Issues at Arab League summits

No.	Date and location	Resolutions, outcomes
1st	January 1964, Cairo	Agreed to oppose "the robbery of the waters of Jordan by Israel."
2nd	September 1964, Alexandria	Supported the establishment of the Palestine Liberation Organization (PLO) in its effort to liberate Palestine from the Zionists.
3rd	September 1965, Casablanca	Opposed "intra-Arab hostile propaganda."
4th	29 August–1 September 1967, Khartoum	Held post-1967 Arab-Israeli War, which ended with crushing Israeli victory; declared three "no's": "no negotiation with Israel, no treaty, no recognition of Israel."
5th	December 1969, Rabat	Called for the mobilization of member countries against Israel.
6th	November 1973, Algiers	Held in the wake of the 1973 Arab-Israeli War, it set strict guidelines for dialogue with Israel.
7th	30 October–2 November 1974, Rabat	Declared the PLO to be "the sole and legitimate representative of the Palestinian people," who had "the right to establish the independent state of Palestine on any liberated territory."
8th	October 1976, Cairo	Approved the establishment of a peacekeeping force (Arab Deterrent Force) for the Lebanese Civil War.
9th	November 1978, Baghdad	Condemned the Camp David Peace Accords between Egypt and Israel, and threatened Egypt with sanctions, including the suspension of its membership if Egypt signed a treaty with Israel.
10th	November 1979, Tunis	Held in the wake of Israel's invasion of Lebanon in 1978, it discussed Israel's occupation of southern Lebanon.
11th	November 1980, Amman	Formulated a strategy for economic development among League members until 2000.
12th	November 1981/September 1982, Fez	Meeting was suspended due to resistance to a peace plan drafted by Saudi crown prince Fahd, which implied de facto recognition of the Jewish state. In September 1982 at Fez, the meeting reconvened to adopt a modified version of the Fahd Plan, called the Fez Plan.
13th	August 1985, Casablanca	Failed to back a PLO-Jordanian agreement that envisaged talks with Israel about Palestinian rights. Summit boycotted by five member states.
14th	November 1987, Amman	Supported UN Security Council Resolution 508 regarding cease-fire in the Iran-Iraq War. Also declared that individual member states could decide to resume diplomatic ties with Egypt.
15th	June 1988, Casablanca	Decided to financially support the PLO in sustaining the Intifada in the occupied territories.
16th	May 1989, Casablanca	Readmitted Egypt into Arab League, and set up Tripartite Committee to secure a cease-fire in the Lebanese Civil War and re-establish a constitutional government in Lebanon.
17th	May 1990, Baghdad	Denounced recent increase of Soviet Jewish immigration to Israel.
18th	August 1990, Cairo	12 out of 20 members present condemned Iraq for invading and annexing Kuwait. Agreed to deploy troops to assist Saudi and other Gulf states' armed forces.
19th	June 1995, Cairo	Held after a hiatus of five years. Iraq not invited.
20th	October 2000, Cairo	Set up funds to help the Palestinians' Second Intifada against the Israeli occupation, and called on its members to freeze their relations with Israel. Iraq was invited.
21st	March 2001, Amman	Held after the election of Ariel Sharon as Israel's prime minister, it appointed Egypt's Amr Mousa as the Arab League's new secretary-general.
22nd	March 2002, Beirut	Adopted the Saudi Peace Plan of Crown Prince Abdullah, which offered Israel total peace in exchange for total Israeli withdrawal from Arab territories conquered in the 1967 war. Opposed the use of force against Iraq.
23rd	March 2003, Sharm al-Sheikh, Egypt	Agreed not to participate in the U.S.-led attack on Iraq, but allowed the United States to use military bases in some of their countries.

TABLE BY GGS INFORMATION SERVICES, THE GALE GROUP.

voting rights if their delinquent dues total more than their total assessment of the current year and the two preceding years.

Policy

The League of Arab States has had a significant impact on the Middle East and on its members. Although it has not been a stepping-stone to Arab political unity, it has fostered Arab cooperation in many fields. Cooperation on political questions, however, has been difficult. In fact, political conflicts in the Arab world are frequently reflected in the league. Governmental diversity is protected in the league pact, which requires each member to respect the systems of government of other members. The pact also requires states to abstain from action calculated to change the systems of government in other members.

The Cold War served to draw political lines within the league between clients of the United States and those of the Soviet Union. Despite the wealth of some of its members, the league is more closely aligned to the South in the North-South conflict, sometimes acting as a bloc for the South in the United Nations.

The league has actively sought to bolster Arab security, but its efforts are limited by inter-Arab rivalries. It has facilitated the peaceful settlement of disputes between its members, as between Morocco and Mauritania; between groups within member states, as in Lebanon or Somalia; and between members and outside parties, as between Libya and the United States. The league has acted as a regional alternative to the United Nations in this regard.

The league has been united in its support for Palestine vis-à-vis Israel, but has come under increasing criticism in recent years for failing to do enough for the Palestinians and for Iraq. Egypt's treaty with Israel (the 1978 Camp David Accords) resulted in its suspension from the league from 1979 to 1989. Members were also divided over the Fahd Plan (1981); over the leadership of the Palestine Liberation Organization (PLO); and over the Iran-Iraq War (1980–1988). Iraq's invasion of Kuwait and the first Gulf War (1991) prompted additional controversy. The U.S. move against Iraq in 2003 brought strong and united condemnation of "American-

British aggression against Iraq." The league also emphasized its cooperation with the United Nations.

Membership

League members are: Algeria, Bahrain, Comoros, Djibouti, Egypt, Iraq, Jordan, Kuwait, Lebanon, Libya, Mauritania, Morocco, Oman, Palestine, Qatar, Saudi Arabia, Somalia, Sudan, Syria, Tunisia, United Arab Emirates, and Yemen. In November 2002 Libya asked to withdraw its membership. Any independent Arab state is theoretically entitled to become a member, but a request for membership must be made through the permanent secretariat-general of the league and submitted to the council. Eritrea assumed an observer status in January 2003.

Satellite Organizations

Numerous specialized organizations and other institutions that promote Arab cooperation and protect Arab interests in a wide array of fields fall under the league umbrella. These include, among others: the Academy of Arab Music; Administrative Tribunal of the Arab League; Arab Bank for Economic Development in Africa; Arab Bureau of Narcotics; Arab Bureau for Prevention of Crime; Arab Bureau of Criminal Police; Arab Center for the Study of Arid Zones and Dry Lands; Arab Civil Aviation Council; Arab Fund for Economic and Social Development; Arab Fund for Technical Assistance to Africa and Arab Countries; Arab Industrial Development Organization; Arab Labour Organization; Arab League Educational, Cultural, and Scientific Organization; Arab Maritime Transport Academy; Arab Monetary Fund; Arab Organization for Agricultural Development; Arab Organization for Standardization and Metrology; Arab Organization of Administrative Sciences; Arab Postal Union; Arab Satellite Communications Organization; Arab States Broadcasting Union; Arab Telecommunications Union; Council of Arab Economic Unity; Council of Arab Ministers of the Interior; Inter-Arab Investment Guarantee Corporation; Organization of Arab Petroleum Exporting Countries; and the Special Bureau for Boycotting Israel.

Prospects

After the second Persian Gulf war in 2003, relations between member states of the league remained uncertain. Amr Moussa moved to reunify the Arab ranks and worked through the United Nations. The uncertainties unleashed in the gulf spawned new dangers aimed at regimes friendly to the United States. The crisis offers new challenges to Arab leadership that could enhance the role of the Arab League. The league's aspiration of Arab unity will be central to the creation of a new world order, as will the inevitable divisions in the Arab ranks. Arab cooperation in nonpolitical areas will continue under the league's aegis and will promote not only improved relations among Arabs, but also between Arabs and outside states and organizations.

> See also ABDULLAH I IBN HUSSEIN; ARAB BOYCOTT; CAMP DAVID ACCORDS (1978); FAHD PLAN (1981); GULF CRISIS (1990–1991); NAHHAS, MUSTAFA AL-; ORGANIZATION OF ARAB PETROLEUM EXPORTING COUNTRIES (OAPEC); PALESTINE LIBERATION ORGANIZATION (PLO).

Bibliography

Arab League. Available from <http://www.arableagueonline.org/arableague>.

Burdett, Anita, ed. *The Arab League: British Documentary Sources, 1943–1963.* Slough, U.K.: Archive Editions, 1995.

Hasou, Tawfiq Y. *The Struggle for the Arab World: Egypt's Nasser and the Arab League.* Boston: Routledge and Kegan Paul, 1985.

Hassouna, Hussein A. *The League of Arab States and Regional Disputes: A Study in Middle East Conflicts.* Dobbs Ferry, NY: Oceana Publications, 1975.

MacDonald, Robert W. *The League of Arab States: A Study in the Dynamics of Regional Organization.* Princeton, NJ: Princeton University Press, 1965.

Pogany, Istvan S. *The Arab League and Peacekeeping in the Lebanon.* New York: St. Martin's Press, 1988.

Riad, Mahmoud. *The Struggle for Peace in the Middle East.* New York: Quartet Books, 1981.

Zamzami, Sirag G. "The Origins of the League of Arab States and Its Activities within the Member States: 1942–1970." Ph.D. diss., Claremont Graduate School, 1978.

CHARLES G. MACDONALD

LEBANESE ARAB ARMY

Muslim military group in Lebanon.

The Lebanese Arab Army was formed in 1975 by a group of Muslim officers and soldiers who defected from the army of Lebanon and accused its Maronite leadership of collaboration with Maronite rightwing militias. Supported by the Palestine Liberation Organization (PLO; the al-Fatah movement in particular), it succeeded in overrunning military barracks controlled by the army of Lebanon. The Lebanese Arab Army's role came to an end in the spring and early summer of 1976, when its forces (along with PLO forces and forces loyal to the Lebanese National Movement) clashed with the army of Syria, which was supporting the coalition of Maronite-oriented right-wing militias.

> See also FATAH, AL-; PALESTINE LIBERATION ORGANIZATION (PLO).

AS'AD ABUKHALIL

LEBANESE CIVIL WAR (1958)

Uprising against the government.

Fifteen years after Lebanon became officially free of French mandatory control, it assumed its role as an independent republic on the basis of an unwritten national pact, whose symbolic and practical importance is difficult to exaggerate. In May 1958, the nation of 1.1 million people, whose political institutions reflected the balance of power between its confessional communities, exploded in civil war.

Rooted in a series of interlocking factors of domestic, regional, and international origin, the primary causes of the war were domestic in nature. They were shaped by the policies of the presidential regime of Camille Chamoun (1952–1958), whose personal ambitions capped a domestic politics and foreign policy that greatly exacerbated existing divisions in a state whose civil and national consciousness were less developed than its successful mercantile character.

President Chamoun's ambition to succeed himself in office contributed to the existing political tensions and was widely viewed as one of the major catalysts of civil strife. The Lebanese government claimed that civil insurrection was a function of external intervention organized by Egypt and Syria, in the United Arab Republic (UAR). But the war that

Women belonging to the Phalanges Libanaises party demonstrate during the Lebanese civil war. © Bettmann/Corbis. Reproduced by permission.

was sparked by the assassination of the journalist Nasib Matni, on 8 May 1958, was rooted in pre-existing grievances that involved questions of political access; confessionalism and class; group identity and national consensus; and the major discontent of political elites displaced by corrupt elections in 1957, as well as the dissatisfaction of those constituencies deprived of significant representation.

Opposition groups that included an array of established political figures, some of whom would come to office in the post–Chamoun regime for the first time, opposed the president's perpetuation in office, and, in some instances, his foreign policy as well.

Under the Chamoun regime, Lebanon threw its support to the conservative Arab coalition and became a staunch advocate of U.S. policy and the Eisenhower Doctrine of 1957. That stance identified Lebanon with the anti-Nasserist and anti-Arab nationalist forces in the region. The intensification of domestic tensions exploded with the Nasib Matni assassination, and President Chamoun was challenged by the opposition. The Lebanese government's response was to blame civil strife on interference by the UAR and to charge it with the attempt to undermine Chamoun regime and state. These charges came before the League of Arab States (Arab League) and the United Nations, which assigned a task force to investigate charges of massive infiltration by foreign forces in Lebanon. It was on the basis of this same charge that President Chamoun had requested assistance from the United States. With the military coup in Iraq on 14 July, an event that shook the Western powers, the United States responded on 15 July with military intervention in Lebanon, while Great Britain gave protective cover to the Jordanian regime. The United States remained in Lebanon overseeing the election of a new president, Fu'ad Chehab, an event which marked the beginning of a new phase in the nation's development. Many would argue, however, that the fundamental roots of this first civil war had not been satisfactorily resolved.

See also CHAMOUN, CAMILLE; CHEHAB, FU'AD; UNITED ARAB REPUBLIC (UAR).

Bibliography

Agwani, M. S., ed. *The Lebanese Crisis, 1958: A Documentary Study.* New York: Asia Publishing House, 1965.

Qubain, Fahim. *Crisis in Lebanon.* Washington, DC: Middle East Institute, 1961.

IRENE GENDZIER

LEBANESE CIVIL WAR (1975–1990)

Domestic conflict in Lebanon.

There is no consensus among scholars and researchers on what triggered the Lebanese Civil War. The strike of fishermen at Sidon in February 1975 could be considered the first important episode that set off the outbreak of hostilities. That event involved a specific issue: the attempt of former President Camille Chamoun (also head of the Maronite-oriented National Liberal Party) to monopolize fishing along the coast of Lebanon. The injustices perceived by the fishermen evoked sympathy from many Lebanese and reinforced the resentment and antipathy that were widely felt against the state and the economic monopolies. The demonstrations against the fishing company were quickly transformed into a political action supported by the political left and their allies in the Palestine Liberation Organization (PLO). The state tried to suppress the demonstrators, and a government sniper reportedly killed a popular figure in the city, Ma'ruf Sa'd, who was known for his opposition to the government and his support for the Palestinians.

The events in Sidon were not contained for long. The government began to lose control of the situation in April 1975, when a bus carrying Palestinians was ambushed by gunmen belonging to the Phalange party. The party claimed that earlier its headquarters had been targeted by unknown gunmen. The attack against the bus in Ayn al-Rummana marked the official beginning of the Lebanese Civil War. Initially, the war pitted Maronite-oriented right-wing militias (most notably the Phalange party and the National Liberal party) against leftist and Muslim-oriented militias (grouped together in the Lebanese National Movement) supported by the PLO. The eruption of military hostilities produced a heated political debate on whether the army of Lebanon, led by a right-wing Maronite commander, should be deployed to end the fighting. Most Muslims and leftists opposed any use of the army, which was seen as anti-Palestinian; most right-wingers called for its immediate deployment.

The characterizations of the combatants in the civil war often obscure the nature of the conflict. Many Lebanese still see the civil war as the product of a conspiracy hatched by outsiders who were jealous of "Lebanese democracy and prosperity." The civil war should be viewed as a multidimensional conflict that at its roots is a classical civil strife with the domestic parties determining the course but rarely the outcome of the fighting. Over the course of Lebanese history external parties have insisted on preventing the Lebanese from proceeding unrestrained in their civil strife. Had the Lebanese been allowed to continue fighting without external restraints, some sects in Lebanon would have been eliminated long ago. This is not to say that the external parties—notably Syria, Iraq, Iran, and Israel—have not contributed to the intensification of the conflict whenever it suited their interests. All of these states have had proxy militias operating in Lebanon.

The roots of the civil war are a set of issues, some having to do with domestic politics and others with foreign policy. It is fair to say that the system of sectarian distribution of power that had been

The controversial military figure Ariel Sharon (b. 1928), pictured left, has served as both defense minister and prime minister of Israel. Sharon is most widely known for his lengthy occupation of Lebanon from 1982 to 1985, and for his continuing conflict with Palestinian leader Yasir Arafat. © AP/WIDE WORLD PHOTOS. REPRODUCED BY PERMISSION.

sponsored by France since 1920 led to the increasing frustration of Muslims, who grew demographically but not politically. In 1975 the political system continued to assume that the figures of the 1932 census—the only census in Lebanon's history—which showed the Maronites to be the single largest sect in the country, had not changed. However, it was widely known that the Shiʿa had long been the single largest sect, although their political representation was small. The ceremonial post of speaker of Parliament was reserved for the Shiʿa, whereas the presidency was reserved for Maronites, and the prime ministership for Sunnis. The Shiʿa included a disproportionate number of poor people, and, to add to their misery, predominated in the area of southern Lebanon that in the 1960s became an arena for Israel-Palestinian conflict. The state of Lebanon, which always avoided provoking Israel,

simply abandoned southern Lebanon. Many of the people there migrated to the suburbs of Beirut which are known as "poverty belts." The young Shiʿite migrants, who had not participated in the prosperity of prewar Beirut, joined many Lebanese and Palestinian organizations.

The Sunnis had grievances, too. The office of the prime minister was marginalized by the strong presidency of Sulayman Franjiyya, who was elected in 1970. In 1973, when Prime Minister Saʾib Salam could not fire the commander in chief of the army after a commando raid launched from Israel that targeted three high-ranking PLO leaders, the issue of the powers of the prime minister emerged as a symbol of the sectarian/political imbalance in the country. Socioeconomic dissatisfaction plus political resentment produced an unstable political system.

The presence of Palestinians in Lebanon was another thorny issue. The state decided to crack down on their armed presence in Lebanon while right-wing militias were being armed and financed by the army. Many leftists and Muslims wanted the state to support the Palestinians and to send the army to protect southern Lebanon against raids from Israel. The PLO, on the other hand, was tempted to take advantage of the domestic turmoil to shore up support for its cause and to undermine the military power of the Army, which had long harassed Palestinians.

The first phase of the Lebanese Civil War did not end; it merely came to a temporary halt as a result of regional and international consensus. When it was becoming clear that the PLO and its Lebanese allies were about to overrun predominantly Christian areas, Syria intervened militarily in Lebanon and, with support from Israel, the United States, and France, fought the Palestinians and their Lebanese allies. The fighting stopped for a while, although southern Lebanon continued to be an arena for the conflict between Israel and the Palestinians, as well as the armed militias, who were present throughout Lebanon. By 1978, Syria's relations with Maronite-oriented parties had worsened, and the rise of Bashir Jumayyil as head of the Lebanese Forces—the coalition of right-wing fighting groups—caused a change in the course of the civil war. Israel became a close ally of the Lebanese Forces, and Syria's regime decided to sponsor the leftist-Palestinian coalition. In the spring of 1978, Israel's army invaded Lebanon in order to end any military presence in southern Lebanon, except that of the pro-Israel militia. Although international opprobrium forced Israel southward, and although UN forces were deployed in southern Lebanon to pacify the region, Israel continued to occupy part of southern Lebanon, calling the strip of land "the security zone."

The civil war took another turn in 1982, when Israel invaded Lebanon again; this time Israeli's forces reached Beirut. Israel took advantage of the deteriorating security situation throughout the country and expected that popular frustration with the misconduct of members of the PLO, and Syrian and Lebanese troops, would provide positive climate for its all-out military intervention. The invasion claimed the lives of some 20,000 Lebanese and Palestinians. Israel also wanted to influence the 1982 presidential election; Bashir Jumayyil was elected president but was assassinated a few days later. His assassination was the pretext that the Lebanese Forces gave for their mass killing of Palestinian civilians in the Sabra and Shatila refugee camps.

Amin Jumayyil, the next president, supported the signing of an Israel-Lebanon peace treaty in May 1983. Lebanon's opposition, coupled with Syria's rejection on the pro-Israel, pro-United States orientation of Jumayyil, resulted in the eruption of hostilities throughout the latter's administration. When Jamayyil's term ended in the summer of 1988, he appointed the Maronite commander in chief of the army, Gen. Michel Aoun, as interim president. His appointment was rejected by many Lebanese, and Aoun launched a "war of national liberation" against Syria's army in Lebanon. His shells, however, fell on innocent Lebanese living in areas under Syria's control.

The beginning of the end of the civil war came in October 1989, when Lebanese deputies gathered in the city of Ta'if in Saudi Arabia. The meeting produced a document of national accord. It was impossible to implement, however, until General Aoun's forces were defeated in October 1990, when Syria's troops attacked his headquarters and he was forced to seek refuge in France. President Ilyas al-Hirawi was elected in 1989, and the territorial integrity of Lebanon has been partially restored.

See also AOUN, MICHEL; CHAMOUN, CAMILLE; FRANJIYYA, SULAYMAN; JUMAYYIL, BASHIR; LEBANESE FORCES; PHALANGE; SABRA AND SHATILA MASSACRES; SALAM FAMILY.

AS 'AD ABUKHALIL

LEBANESE CRISES OF THE 1840s

Druze versus Christian sectarian violence.

The London Treaty of 1840 ended the Egyptian occupation of Mount Lebanon (1831–1840). Soon afterwards the Ottomans dismissed the local governor, Bashir II, whose collusion with the Egyptian ruler Muhammad Ali had discredited him with the local population. The years of Egyptian manipulation of sectarian politics produced a backlash under the Ottomans in the Druze versus Christian conflicts at Dayr al-Qamar in 1841. Bashir III, the last Chehab amir, was replaced in 1842 by a direct governor, Umar Pasha al-Nimsawi (the Austrian). Continued civil strife and European pressure led the Ottomans to establish a system of two sub-governorates in Mount Lebanon (qa'im maqamiyatayn) divided on religious lines. Despite further sectarian clashes in 1845 at Mukhtara, Jazzin, and Dayr al-Qamar, the tottering new system survived until 1860 when the mutasarrif system finally ended Mount Lebanon's autonomy.

Bibliography

Khalaf, Samir. *Persistence and Change in Nineteenth Century Lebanon: A Sociological Essay.* Beirut: American University of Beirut, 1979.

TAYEB EL-HIBRI

LEBANESE FORCES

Lebanese political-military organization.

The Lebanese Forces (LF) emerged in 1976 under the leadership of Bashir Jumayyil. At that time various Lebanese Christian militias had joined forces to destroy the Palestinian Tall al-Za'tar Refugee Camp. In August 1976 a joint command council was established to integrate those militias formally and to achieve a degree of political independence from the traditional Maronite Catholic (Christian) political leaders. Jumayyil took control of the military wing of his father's Phalange Party and then proceeded to incorporate other Christian militias. Those that resisted were forcibly integrated. In 1978 Jumayyil subjugated the Marada Brigade, the militia of the Franjiyya family and former president Sulayman Franjiyya, killing his son Tony Franjiyya in the process. In 1980 the Tigers militia of Camille Chamoun was absorbed.

By the early 1980s, the LF controlled East Beirut and parts of Mount Lebanon, and Jumayyil became its "commander." He did not confine the LF to combat; he also created committees within its structure responsible for health, information, foreign policy, education, and other matters of public concern. Jumayyil established links with Israel, and

he consistently battled with Syrian forces. The LF began to decline in 1982, when President-elect Bashir Jumayyil was assassinated. After numerous succession struggles, including the brief tenure of Fu'ad Abu Nadir as head of the forces, Elie Hobeyka—notorious for his role in the 1982 bloodshed in the Sabra and Shatila refugee camps—assumed the leadership of the LF. After Hobeyka signed the Syrian-sponsored Tripartite Declaration in December 1985, against the wishes of president Amin Jumayyil, LF chief of staff Samir Geagea launched an attack on Hobeyka early in 1986 and took over the LF. Although Geagea was able to take advantage of the mood of frustration and despair among the Christian masses, Israel, his chief backer, was less interested in his cause than it had been—although it continued to supply his forces with money and arms.

After the appointment of General Michel Aoun as interim president by Amin Jumayyil, Lebanon's army tried to disarm the LF but failed to eliminate its political and military power. The defeat of Aoun by Syrian troops in 1990 led Geagea to try to impose himself as the overall Maronite leader. His attempt to become president of the Phalange Party failed, and George Saade remained the head of that predominantly Maronite party.

Geagea promised to allow Lebanon's army to confiscate weapons and ammunition belonging to his militia, according to the terms of the Ta'if accord. He promised to transform his militia into a political party and obtained a license toward that end. Lebanon's army, however, accused his forces of obstruction and discovered large amounts of hidden supplies and weapons. In early 1994, when a bomb exploded in a church in East Beirut, Lebanese authorities uncovered a terrorist ring that answered to Geagea personally. The government found evidence linking him to a series of bombs, car bombs, and assassinations. He was arrested and has been in prison since 1994.

See also AOUN, MICHEL; CHAMOUN, CAMILLE; FRANJIYYA FAMILY; GEAGEA, SAMIR; HOBEIKA, ELIE; JUMAYYIL, AMIN; JUMAYYIL, BASHIR; PHALANGE.

Bibliography

Abukhalil, As'ad. *Historical Dictionary of Lebanon.* Lanham, MD: Scarecrow Press, 1998.

Abukhalil, As'ad. "Lebanon." In *Political Parties of the Middle East and North Africa,* edited by Frank Tachau. Westport, CT: Greenwood Press, 1994.

As'ad AbuKhalil
Updated by Michael R. Fischbach

LEBANESE FRONT

A coalition of major Christian conservative parties, which became an important player in the 1975 civil war in Lebanon.

Established in 1976, the Lebanese Front included the National Liberal Party of the former president, Camille Chamoun; Sulayman Franjiyya, the president of Lebanon when the Lebanese Civil War began in 1975; Pierre Jumayyil, head of the Phalange—the front's major military power; the Guardians of Cedars; the Permanent Congress of the Lebanese Orders of Monks; al-Tanzim of Dr. Fuad Shemali; the Maronite League headed by Shakir Abu Sulayman; and other independent personalities such as Dr. Charles Malik, Fu'ad Bustani, and Edward Honein.

In August 1976, the coalition established a military branch, known as the Lebanese Forces, which could mobilize 30,000 troops. At the beginning of 1978, Franjiyya became critical of the open collaboration between Israeli government officials and front leaders Chamoun and Jumayyil. Franjiyya was also against the Camp David peace accord negotiations between Egypt and Israel (approved by other front members) but championed a close relationship with Syria. In May 1978, Franjiyya resigned from the front. It was subsequently wracked with dissent and disintegrated.

The Lebanese Front charter had stressed the need to maintain the unity of Lebanon, to reestablish the authority of the law, and to respect private enterprise in the economic sector.

See also Franjiyya, Sulayman; Jumayyil, Pierre; Lebanese Forces; National Liberal Party.

Bibliography

Al-Montada Reports. *The Lebanese Conflict, 1975–1979* (Dossier 2). Beirut, 1979.

George E. Irani

LEBANESE NATIONAL MOVEMENT (LNM)

A coalition of Islamic and leftist Lebanese parties and groups.

Established in 1975, the Lebanese National Movement (LNM) advocated, among other objectives, the solidarity of Lebanon with the Palestinians, the adoption of a proportional system of elections, and the elimination of political and administrative sectarianism. During the Lebanese Civil War, the LNM joined forces with the Palestine Liberation Organization (PLO) and was headed by Kamal Jumblatt. After his assassination in 1977, his son Walid Jumblatt took over and, in October 1982, announced the dissolution of the LNM.

See also Jumblatt, Kamal; Jumblatt, Walid.

Bibliography

Khalidi, Walid. *Conflict and Violence in Lebanon: Confrontation in the Middle East.* Reprint, Cambridge, MA: Center for International Affairs, Harvard University, 1983.

George E. Irani

LEBANESE UNIVERSITY

University located in Beirut.

The Lebanese University, established in 1952, is under the jurisdiction of the ministry of education. It was founded to allow Lebanese from lower-income groups to receive a university education, which for decades had been the monopoly of those who could afford private universities. It has two branches—one in East Beirut and the other in West Beirut—and smaller branches in the provinces of the north, the south, and the Biqa valley. University faculties (departments) include law, political science and management, engineering, literature and humanities, education, social sciences, fine arts, journalism and advertising, business administration, and agriculture. The language of instruction is Arabic; study of one foreign language is required by all faculties.

Although the Lebanese University has filled a gap and has catered to a sector of the population that had been virtually left out of the private educational system, holders of degrees from the Lebanese

University are regarded as inferior job applicants, compared with holders of degrees from the American University of Beirut or Saint Joseph University. The state apparatus also favors graduates of the two private universities. The Lebanese University's lack of endowment forces it to be totally dependent on state funding, which is not always forthcoming. Classes are overcrowded, and there are no admissions standards. Staff and faculty are underpaid, which forces many of them to seek outside employment as well. Furthermore, the large student body enables some students to show up only for final exams.

Like other institutions, the university was affected by the Lebanese Civil War of 1975. Many professors were forced to take a political stance, and some were pressured by armed students to change their grades. Some of the buildings of the university were occupied by militias, and others were heavily damaged.

See also AMERICAN UNIVERSITY OF BEIRUT (AUB); SAINT JOSEPH UNIVERSITY.

Bibliography

Collelo, Thomas, ed. *Lebanon: A Country Study,* 3d edition. Washington, DC: Dept. of the Army, 1989.

AS'AD ABUKHALIL
UPDATED BY MICHAEL R. FISCHBACH

LEBANESE WOMEN'S COUNCIL

Association of Lebanese women's and human rights organizations.

The Lebanese Women's Council (LWC), or Lebanese Council of Women, is an umbrella association encompassing over 140 women's and human rights organizations, including welfare, religious, academic, political, and feminist organizations. It has been a key advocate for women's rights in Lebanon since its establishment in 1952 by Lebanese feminists Ibtihaj Qaddurah and Laure Moghaizel. At its inception, the LWC focused on furthering political rights for Lebanese women and on encouraging women to run for public office.

Today the goals of the LWC have broadened to include supporting women's rights in education, health, and employment. The organization also ad-

vocates for women's legal rights (for example, the right of women to pass citizenship to their children). In addition, it continues to work to support women political candidates; in 2003 there were only three women in the Lebanese parliament.

The LWC participates in numerous local and international coalitions. Most notably, it took part in the 1995 UN Fourth World Conference on Women in Beijing as well as in Beijing +5, the five-year assessment of the Beijing Conference, held during a special session of the UN General Assembly in New York City in 2000. The LWC was one of the drafters of the subsequent report of the Non-Governmental Committee for the Follow-Up of Woman Issues. It also was instrumental in attaining Lebanon's ratification (with reservations) of the Convention on the Elimination of all forms of Discrimination against Women (CEDAW) in 1996. CEDAW is a human-rights treaty focused on women's rights that was adopted by the UN General Assembly in 1979. As one of the major women's rights organizations in Lebanon, The LWC continues to work toward the institutional and legal implementation of CEDAW.

See also GENDER: GENDER AND LAW; GENDER: GENDER AND POLITICS; LEBANESE CIVIL WAR (1958); LEBANESE CIVIL WAR (1975–1990); LEBANON; MOGHAIZEL, LAURE.

Bibliography

AbuKhalil, As'ad. "Feminism." In *Historical Dictionary of Lebanon.* London, U.K., and Lanham, MD: Scarecrow, 1998.

Joseph and Laure Moghaizel Foundation. Available from <http://www.kleudge.com/moghaizelfoundation>.

Lebanese NGO Forum. Available from <http://www.lnf.org.lb>.

LARA Z. DEEB

LEBANON

Independent Arab country located on the eastern end of the Mediterranean Sea.

A small country of 10,632 square kilometers (4,105 square miles), with a maximum length (north to south) of 217 kilometers (135 miles), Lebanon is bordered by Syria and Israel. There is no current

A mountain range in Aqura, Lebanon. © ROGER WOOD/CORBIS. REPRODUCED BY PERMISSION.

reliable census of Lebanon's population (the last official census was conducted in 1932); in 1994 the country's population was estimated to be around 3 million. The sectarian composition of the population remains a contentious issue because political power has been distributed according to a formula that favors the Maronites (Catholic Christians), who in the 1932 census reportedly constituted the largest religious group in the country. The demographic profile of the population has changed dramatically since 1932, with the Shi'ite Muslims becoming more prominent because of their high birth rate. Some estimates put the Shi'a at 45 percent of the population, and most authorities agree that Muslims (including all sects) are now the majority, constituting some 70 percent of the overall population.

The historical myth of Lebanon, which has been challenged by the Lebanese historian Kamal Salibi, among others, is predicated on the belief that Lebanon has always been a haven for persecuted minorities, its rugged mountains providing shelter for hetero-dox groups from throughout the Middle East. Lebanonese ultranationalists claim that Lebanon has been in existence since before Phoenician times. The late Princeton University historian Philip Hitti suggested that people have been residing in what is today Lebanon for thousands of years. Lebanon as a political entity is a twentieth-century phenomenon, the product of the division between Britain and France of the spoils of World War 1. Central Lebanon, known as Mount Lebanon, was occupied by Maronites, Druze, and Shi'a. Those groups have lived together yet apart, separated by geographic lines of demarcation and by fear and suspicion. Lebanon cannot, and may not, continue to exist as a political entity in the absence of the minimum degree of social-national cohesion.

Lebanon under the Ottoman Empire

For much of the period between 1516 and 1918, Lebanon was only quasi-independent. This relative autonomy is exaggerated by those who claim that the

Lebanese state has been in continuous existence for thousands of years. The region in question, Mount Lebanon, was governed by a local prince (from the Ma'nid and, later, from the Chehab dynasties) who was in turn under the jurisdiction of a sultan of the Ottoman Empire. The political independence of the local ruler depended on the relative power of the government in Istanbul at a given time, and on the degree of external intervention in Lebanese affairs. During the earlier part of the period in question, the Druzes were the politically ascendant group. In the nineteenth century, however, the ruling Chehabi dynasty converted (originally secretively) to Maronite Christianity, and the Maronites began moving into areas that had been exclusively Druze-inhabited. The power of the Maronite Church, which was taking advantage of the consequences of Tanzimat, was also increasing.

In 1840 Mount Lebanon was divided into a southern district (Druze) and a northern district (Maronite). Druze–Maronite clashes occurred throughout the century, and a major conflict in 1860 left the Druzes militarily victorious and the Maronites politically victorious (due to support by European powers). The war resulted in the establishment of a European commission to oversee the situation. After negotiation with the Ottoman government, it was decided that Lebanon should be ruled by a non-Maronite, non-Lebanese Christian citizen of the Ottoman Empire. The governor (*mutasarrif* in Turkish, and later in Arabic too) would be assisted by a council of representatives from the various sects, with the Maronites constituting the largest group. The regime established in 1861 continued until World War I.

Lebanon Under French Mandate

During World War I, Lebanese and Syrians of all religions were executed for anti-Turkish activities. After the war, France would not allow the "protected" Maronites, who called France al-Umm al-Hanun (the Tender Mother), to be placed in an inferior position in Lebanon. Before the beginning of the French mandate system, Lebanese Maronites launched a strong propaganda campaign, characterized by Christian evangelical zeal, in Egypt (where members of the Maronite elite resided) and in France. The campaign led to the creation of Greater Lebanon, which included Mount Lebanon, southern Lebanon, Tripoli and the North, the Biqa region, and the Beirut region. The addition of those areas was motivated not by considerations of national harmony but by calculations of economic viability and French calculations. The predominantly Muslim population of the annexed areas was not consulted, and many staunchly opposed what appeared to be a Western-engineered attempt to sever ties between Lebanon and the larger, surrounding Muslim Arab nations.

In 1926 the French mandate authorities urged the elected Lebanese representatives to draft a new constitution. The constitution affirmed the political, diplomatic, economic, and legal supremacy of the French government and their ally the president, who was to be a Christian. Article 95 confirmed the sectarian foundation of Lebanese politics by stipulating that governmental posts shall be distributed "equitably" between the sects. This in effect established a system that had as its basic unit not the individual citizen but the sect. The highly controversial 1932 census revealed that the Maronites were the most numerous sect; consequently, the highest government posts were reserved for them.

Independence and Nationhood, 1943–1975

Although official and quasi-official Lebanese historiography claims there was an "independence movement" in the country, British–French rivalries in the Levant helped to bring about the independence of Lebanon in 1943. Bishara al-Khuri, the foremost Maronite politician and first president after independence, and Riyad al-Sulh, the foremost Sunni politician and first prime minister after independence, were the architects of Lebanon's National Pact. This unwritten document became, in the words of Maronite Phalange leader Pierre Jumayyil, more important than the written laws of the country. It stipulated that the Christians (for whom the Maronites spoke, according to the agreement) would not seek protection or alliance with France, and the Muslims (for whom the Sunnis spoke) would respect the sovereignty of Lebanon and renounce dreams of unity with Syria or any other Arab country. The National Pact also decreed that the presidency of Lebanon would be held by a Maronite, the weak speakership of parliament by a Shi'ite, and the prime ministership by a Sunni. It is still regarded as a social contract, though most Lebanese were not consulted about its provisions.

The country was governed by a small group of wealthy politicians who monopolized power within their sects. Political competition, when it occurred, was between members of the economic/political elite and not between average citizens. The first president, Bishara al-Khuri (1943–1952), disregarded the minimum standards of honesty and integrity. His cronies and relatives enriched themselves, and he had the parliament (which was chosen in the scandalously fraudulent 1947 election) amend the constitution so that he could have a second term as president. In 1952 a large bloc of parties and politicians formed a front to force his ouster. After his resignation, Camille Chamoun was elected president.

The rule of Chamoun was marked by what many considered to be violations of the National Pact. Although early in his career he had been identified with pan-Arab politics, he closely aligned Lebanon with the West during his presidency, particularly on anticommunism and anti-Nasserism. His opposi-

The Roman Temple of Bacchus stands in ruins in Ba'albak, Lebanon. © CARMEN REDONDO/CORBIS. REPRODUCED BY PERMISSION.

tion to Gamal Abdel Nasser, the president of Egypt, provoked many Lebanese who admired the Egyptian leader. Following the example of his predecessor, Chamoun flagrantly rigged the 1957 elections to ensure a subservient parliament that would allow him a second term, and thus ousted most of his rivals from parliament. In 1958 the Lebanese civil war (still known in Lebanon as the "1958 Revolution") broke out, and the United States dispatched the marines to protect the Chamoun regime.

The most important politician in contemporary Lebanese history was president Fu'ad Chehab (1958–1964). This former commander in chief of the Lebanese army remains the only politician in the history of Lebanon to have an "ism" associated with his name. Chehabism, the ideology of limited political and economic reforms, was based on the realization that the social and political unrest in Lebanon had socioeconomic roots. Chehab worked to reorganize the Lebanese administrative structure in an attempt to stem the corruption that had been rampant since independence. His regime, however, did not go far enough in its reforms, and Chehab, who distrusted the politicians, ruled through his trusted military aides and his ruthless Intelligence Apparatus (Deuxième Bureau). Rule by the military establishment was inconsistent with the constitution's promises of freedom; the army used heavy-handed tactics against all who opposed the regime.

Chehab was succeeded by his follower Charles Hilu (1964–1970). Hilu quickly disillusioned his former mentor and associated himself with the right-wing factions such as the Phalange Party, of which he was a founder. He preserved the rule of the Deuxième Bureau (military intelligence) because he lacked a political power base. His weak response to internal instability led to the election of Sulayman Franjiyya (1970–1976), a semiliterate ultranationalist who favored strong support for the army in light of the growing power of the Palestine Liberation Organization (PLO) in Lebanon. Franjiyya sought to use the army to crush the PLO as King Hussein did in Jordan. The army was too weak to succeed, and Israel was increasingly exposing Lebanon's impotence against their continued military actions in Lebanon, which did not distinguish between Lebanese and Palestinian targets, or between civilian and military targets. Franjiyya urged the army to arm and train members of the right-wing Maronite militias in Lebanon, which he wanted to use in his war against the Palestinians. During his presidency there were numerous clashes between the PLO and the Lebanese army aided by right-wing militias. Franjiyya's autocratic rule brought calls for a more meaningful partnership between the president and the prime minister.

Civil War, 1975–1990

Much has been written about the civil war, but there is no consensus about its origins. Lebanese often emphasize the external causes of what befell the country; they seem reluctant to place any blame for the protracted conflict on themselves. The civil war allowed various external forces to intervene openly in Lebanese affairs. Syria and Israel both exploited the conflict for their own purposes. In 1976 Syria intervened in the war to save the right-wing militias from what seemed an inevitable defeat by the leftist-PLO alliance. It did not want Lebanon to turn into a radical arena that could drag Syria into an unwanted confrontation with Israel.

The presence of Syrian forces in Lebanon made possible the election of Ilyas Sarkis as president in 1976, and Israel began its de facto occupation of part of southern Lebanon. The relationship of the PLO and its Lebanese allies with Syria began to improve as soon as right-wing militia leader Bashir Jumayyil (then commander of the Lebanese Forces) solidified his alliance with Israel and initiated a campaign against Syria's forces in Lebanon. The lat-

ter responded with heavy bombardment of East Beirut, the site of Lebanese Forces' headquarters. In the south, Israel formed a surrogate militia to further its goals. In 1978 Israel launched a full-scale invasion of Lebanon, and was later forced to withdraw to a narrow strip that it called its Security Zone. The United Nations dispatched troops to serve as a buffer between the PLO forces and Israel's forces.

In 1982 Israel launched its biggest invasion ever. Its forces advanced all the way to Beirut and brought about the election of Bashir Jumayyil as president. The invasion resulted in the deaths of some 20,000 Lebanese and Palestinians, mostly civilians. The PLO came under pressure to withdraw its forces from Lebanon. Jumayyil was assassinated before he officially assumed his responsibilities, and pro-Israel forces killed the Palestinians and Lebanese in the Sabra and Shatila refugee camps in revenge for Jumayyil's assassination. Amin Jumayyil (1982–1988) succeeded his brother Bashir as president and began a rule by the Phalange Party. In 1983 the security situation deteriorated further when Druze and Maronite militias engaged in one of the most ferocious battles of the Lebanese civil war. The Druze militia was able to evict Christians from areas under its control.

The rule of Amin Jumayyil divided the country more sharply than ever before, and most Muslims boycotted his government. In 1988, minutes before the expiration of his term, he appointed General Michel Aoun (the Maronite commander in chief of the army) as interim president. Aoun cracked down on the Lebanese Forces and declared a war of "national liberation" against Syria's forces in Lebanon. The war did not bear political fruits for him, although it did generate enthusiasm among the Maronite masses. In 1990, when world attention was focused on Iraq's invasion of Kuwait, Syria's forces entered Lebanon and destroyed the force commanded by Aoun, who fled to France.

The civil war theoretically ended with the defeat of Aoun and the establishment of the authority of the government of President Ilyas al-Hirawi. The support of Syria and Saudi Arabia for the new administration revived hopes for badly needed financial aid to wartorn Lebanon. President Hirawi and Prime Minister Rafiq Baha'uddin al-Hariri solidified the rule of the Lebanese government and disarmed the militias in the country except for the Party of God, which continues to wage a war of national resistance against Israel's occupation of southern Lebanon. Whether the war has ended completely or whether a truce at last prevails in Lebanon is a question that requires knowledge of the future. Hirawi was succeeded in 1998 by commander in chief Emile Lahhud, who—like his predecessor—enjoyed strong Syrian support. Lahhud's relationship with Hariri was tense, and he preferred Salim al-Hoss as his prime minister. But Hariri was able to utilize his enormous financial powers, and his regional connection, to replace Hoss after a two-year term as prime minister. Hariri and Lahhud continue to express disagreements on a range of issues, from privatization to election laws.

See also AOUN, MICHEL; BEIRUT; CHAMOUN, CAMILLE; CHEHAB, FU'AD; DRUZE; FRANJIYYA, SULAYMAN; HARIRI, RAFIQ BAHA'UDDIN AL-; HILU, CHARLES; JUMAYYIL, AMIN; JUMAYYIL, BASHIR; JUMAYYIL, PIERRE; KHURI, BISHARA AL-; LEBANESE ARAB ARMY; LEBANESE CIVIL WAR (1958); LEBANESE CIVIL WAR (1975–1990); LEBANESE CRISES OF THE 1840s; LEBANESE FORCES; LEBANESE FRONT; LEBANESE NATIONAL MOVEMENT (LNM); LEBANON, MOUNT; MANDATE SYSTEM; MARONITES; PALESTINE LIBERATION ORGANIZATION (PLO); PHALANGE; SABRA AND SHATILA MASSACRES; SARKIS, ILYAS; SHI'ISM; SULH, RIYAD AL-; TANZIMAT.

Bibliography

AbuKhalil, As'ad. *Historical Dictionary of Lebanon.* Lanham, MD: Scarecrow Press, 1998.

Ajami, Fouad. *The Vanished Imam: Musa al Sadr and the Shi'a of Lebanon.* Ithaca, NY: Cornell University Press, 1986.

Collelo, Thomas, ed. *Lebanon: A Country Study,* 3d edition. Washington, DC: Library of Congress, 1989.

Halawi, Majed. *A Lebanon Defied: Musa al-Sadr and the Shi'ia Community.* Boulder, CO: Westview Press, 1992.

Keddie, Nikki, and Cole, Juan R. I., eds. *Shi'ism and Social Protest.* New Haven, CT: Yale University Press, 1986.

Kramer, Martin. *The Moral Logic of Hizballah.* Tel Aviv: Tel Aviv University, 1987.

Norton, A. R. *Amal and the Shi'a: Struggle for the Soul of Lebanon.* Austin: University of Texas Press, 1987.

AS'AD ABUKHALIL

LEBANON, MOUNT

A rugged mountain range that constitutes the geographical core around which modern-day Lebanon was established in 1920.

Mount Lebanon extends from the hinterland of Tripoli in the north to that of Sidon in the south. Because of its geographical isolation and rugged landscape, it historically attracted minorities in search of a haven from persecution. Maronites moved into the area in the seventh century, and they continue to this day to form the majority of its population. South of the Beirut-Damascus highway, Mount Lebanon is predominantly populated by Druze. Smaller Greek Orthodox and Greek Catholic communities also inhabit the area.

Over the centuries, Mount Lebanon developed its own traditions and a distinct identity. Under Ottoman rule (1516–1916), it enjoyed considerable political autonomy. Governance of the area was in the hands of an indigenous amir, who paid nominal allegiance to the Ottoman sultan and oversaw a political structure dominated by a few powerful local families. Following intercommunal hostilities and the mass killing of Christians by Druze in 1860, European countries, particularly France, pressured the authorities in Istanbul to formally grant the area autonomous status in the Ottoman Empire. The so-called Règlement Organique of 1861, guaranteed by the Great Powers, thus established Mount Lebanon as a self-governing province headed by a Christian governor. This development paved the way for the subsequent creation of the modern state of Lebanon in 1920, when the French mandatory power added parts of Greater Syria to Mount Lebanon. Today Mount Lebanon refers to one of the five administrative provinces (governorates) into which Lebanon is divided.

See also DRUZE; GREATER SYRIA; MARONITES.

Bibliography

Zamir, Meir. *The Formation of Modern Lebanon.* Ithaca, NY: Cornell University Press, 1988.

GUILAIN P. DENOEUX

LEBANON NEWS AGENCY

See NEWSPAPERS AND PRINT MEDIA: ARAB COUNTRIES

LEFF

See GLOSSARY

LEGISLATIVE COUNCIL (PALESTINE)

A 1922–1923 British proposal, never implemented, for a limited form of self-government in Palestine.

The League of Nations entrusted Palestine to Great Britain—which conquered the territory in December 1917—as a mandate, one of whose terms called for the "development of self-governing institutions." As a first step in that direction, the high commissioner of Palestine, Sir Herbert Louis Samuel, formally proposed in August 1922 to the country's Muslim, Christian, and Jewish communities the establishment of a legislative council. The council was to be composed of twenty-three members: the high commissioner, ten appointed British members; and twelve elected members—ten Palestinians (eight Muslims and two Christians) and two Jews. However, the British denied the council legislative authority over such central issues as Jewish immigration and land purchases in order to safeguard its Balfour policy of support for the Jewish national home. To allay Palestinian concerns regarding Jewish immigration, the elected members were to form a standing committee to advise the Palestine government on immigration issues.

Palestinian leaders argued that participation in the council would be tantamount to acceptance of the British mandate and Balfour policy, which they opposed. They considered unfair the allocation of only 43 percent of the seats to Palestinians, who constituted 88 percent of the population. And they objected to the limitations placed on the power of the council. A campaign against the proposed council by the Palestine Arab Executive and the Supreme Muslim Council was a potent factor in the Palestinian boycott of the council elections in February 1923. The Jews accepted the proposal despite their objections to the allocation of only two seats to Jews, which, they argued, would have reduced them to a minority role and would have meant that the concerns of the Jewish people as a whole would have been ignored. The poor election turnout caused the high commissioner to shelve the proposal.

The idea was revived repeatedly from 1923 until 1936. It was discussed, for example, in 1928 when a new high commissioner, Sir John Chancellor, took over, but it was derailed by the Western (or Wailing) Wall disturbances of 1929, only to reemerge as a proposal in the Passfield White Papers of 1930. Although the new proposal was similar to the 1922 proposal, the Palestinians this time did not oppose it, but the Jews rejected their minority role in the council and sought a parity formula that would recognize the numbers and the economic role of world Jewry. Intermittent discussions continued until 1935. By then the proposed composition of the council had expanded to twenty-eight, of whom fourteen were to be Muslims and Christians (five nominated), eight Jews (five nominated), five British officials, and one a nominee representing commercial interests. The Palestinians were divided over the proposal, and the Jews were strongly opposed to it. This opposition prompted the British government to once again suspend its implementation, and the concept finally died with the start of the Arab Revolt of 1936 to 1939.

The Legislative Council was probably a missed opportunity for the Palestinians because it could have improved their political and socioeconomic conditions. It could have given them an opportunity to help draft legislation and to participate in formulating expenditure allocations and Jewish immigration quotas. It could have also provided them with a platform to criticize British policy and to appeal for the support of the British public and the League of Nations. Most of all, it could have put them in a position to ask for more.

See also BALFOUR DECLARATION (1917); MANDATE SYSTEM; SAMUEL, HERBERT LOUIS; WESTERN WALL DISTURBANCES; WHITE PAPERS ON PALESTINE.

Bibliography

Caplan, Neil. *Futile Diplomacy: Early Arab–Zionist Negotiation Attempts, 1913–1931,* vol. I. London: Frank Cass, 1983.

Lesch, Ann M. *Arab Politics in Palestine, 1917–1939: The Frustrations of a Nationalist Movement.* Ithaca, NY: Cornell University Press, 1979.

Porath, Y. *The Emergence of the Palestinian–Arab Nationalist Movement, 1918–1929.* London: Frank Cass, 1974.

Porath, Y. *The Palestinian Arab National Movement: From Riots to Rebellion, 1929–1939,* vol. 2. London: Frank Cass, 1977.

Wasserstein, Bernard. *The British in Palestine: The Mandatory Government and the Arab-Jewish Conflict, 1917–1929.* London: Royal Historical Society, 1978.

PHILIP MATTAR

LEIBOWITZ, YESHAYAHU
[1903–1994]

Israeli chemist, philosopher, and social critic.

Yeshayahu Leibowitz was born in Riga, Latvia, and educated at the University of Berlin and Basel University. He was professor of biochemistry at Hebrew University and editor of the *Hebrew Encyclopedia,* and was widely known for his iconoclastic views and outspoken opinions. As a philosopher, he is best known as an interpreter of Maimonides, whom Leibowitz staunchly portrayed as an ardent theocentrist. As a rationalist and an opponent of mysticism, Leibowitz denied any sacred character to the State of Israel and its agencies. He was a religiously observant Jew who adamantly insisted on the separation of religion and state, including the dissolution of the government-supported rabbinate. He believed that Halakhah, Jewish religious law, developed before there was a Jewish state and has become so firmly set that it cannot be adapted to the new circumstance of statehood. He was loudly critical of the tendency to mystify the 1967 Arab-Israel War, and he totally opposed Israel's occupation and administration policies in Palestine. His rationalism also served as the basis of his opposition to viewing the Western Wall as a holy Jewish shrine.

Leibowitz wrote more than a dozen books (in Hebrew). At least eight books of conversations with him have been published, and more than a half-dozen books about him and his thought have been published.

See also HALAKHAH.

Bibliography

Leibowitz, Yeshayahu. *The Faith of Maimonides,* translated by John Glucker. New York: Adama Books, 1987.

Leibowitz, Yeshayahu. *Judaism, Human Values, and the Jewish State,* edited by Eliezer Goldman. Cambridge, MA: Harvard University Press, 1992.

Newton, Adam Zachary. *The Fence and the Neighbor: Emmanuel Levinas, Yeshayahu Leibowitz, and Israel Among the Nations.* Albany: State University of New York Press, 2001.

CHAIM I. WAXMAN

LE JOURNAL D'ÉGYPTE

See NEWSPAPERS AND PRINT MEDIA: ARAB COUNTRIES

LEMSINE, AICHA
[1942–]

Pseudonym for Aicha Laidi, an Algerian novelist and essay writer.

Aicha Lemsine was born in the Nemencha, Algeria, to a Muslim family. As of 2004 she was living in Algeria and was active in women's literary organizations, in addition to contributing newspaper articles on the political and ethnic situation in her country. Her first novel, *La chrysalide* (1976; The chrysalis), is a romantic account of women of two generations; the elder battles polygamy and the younger displays her emancipation by becoming pregnant out of wedlock. *Ciel de porphyre* (1978; Porphyry sky), set during the Algerian War of Independence, tells the story of the initiation of a young woman into the Resistance. Lemsine's third book, *Ordalie des voix* (1983; Voices of tribulations), consists of interviews with Arab women on their role in society and their struggle to achieve emancipation.

See also LITERATURE: ARABIC, NORTH AFRICAN.

Bibliography

Graebner, Seth. *Encyclopedia of African Literature.* New York and London: Routledge, 2003.

Jack, Belinda. *Francophone Literatures: An Introductory Survey.* New York: Oxford University Press, 1996.

AIDA A. BAMIA

LEND-LEASE PROGRAM
Provided U.S. military aid to the Allies in World War II.

Lend-lease was a program that, from 1940, enabled President Franklin D. Roosevelt to extend aid to any country whose fate he felt was vital to U.S. defense—for the sake of national security. Not until March 1941 did the U.S. Congress pass the Lend-Lease Act. It provided for military aid to the World War II Allies, under the condition that equipment extended would be returned or paid for after the war. In practice, lend-lease became the main wartime U.S. aid program of the Roosevelt administration.

Little was returned, and even less was paid for. Coordinated first by Harry Hopkins and then by Edward Stettinius, the lend-lease programs conveyed the equivalent of some $3 billion in aid to the Middle East and the countries of the Mediterranean.

Lend-lease for the Middle East was administered primarily through Cairo, Egypt, and Tehran, Iran. Both Egypt and Iran were occupied by the Allies—Iran from the autumn of 1941 to 1945. In 1942, the United States supplied its ally, the U.S.S.R., via the Persian/Arabian Gulf and Iran; therefore, Iran became eligible for lend-lease. Although lend-lease was supposed to aid only democratic countries in the struggle against the Axis, petroleum-rich Saudi Arabia was also included in the program by February 1943. The lend-lease program was terminated in August 1945.

Bibliography

Rubin, Barry. *Paved with Good Intentions: The American Experience and Iran.* New York: Oxford University Press, 1980.

Yergin, Daniel. *The Prize: The Epic Quest for Oil, Money, and Power.* New York: Simon and Schuster, 1991.

ZACHARY KARABELL

LESKOFCALI GALIP
[1829–1867]

Ottoman poet.

Born in Nicosia (Levkosia), Cyprus, Leskofcali Galip was the son of an exiled Rumelian *ayan.* He came to Constantinople (now Istanbul) in 1846 and by 1851 had entered the civil service. He composed in a classical style similar to his contemporaries, Naili and Fehim. A collection of his works, *Divan,* was published in 1916.

DAVID WALDNER

LESSEPS, FERDINAND DE
[1805–1894]

French entrepreneur and promoter of building a canal to connect the Mediterranean and the Red seas.

After consular service for France at Lisbon and Tunis, Ferdinand de Lesseps became the French consul in Alexandria, Egypt, where he befriended Muhammad Ali Pasha's son, Sa'id. De Lesseps was appointed consul at Cairo from 1833 to 1837 and, after serving in other countries, resigned from diplomatic service in opposition to the Second Republic of France. In 1854, when Sa'id became *khedive* (ruler), de Lesseps returned to Egypt. Despite the findings of scientists who accompanied Napoléon Bonaparte during his occupation of Egypt (1798–1801) that a canal could not be built from the Mediterranean Sea to the Red Sea, de Lesseps (not an engineer) had become convinced of the feasibility of the project. He hoped to use his friendship with Sa'id to promote his plan. De Lesseps quickly convinced Sa'id to back him, in part by persuading Sa'id that his name would be immortalized as the builder of the Suez Canal. In 1856, de Lesseps organized an international commission to study the technical aspects of the project. He also set up a company that would be financed by selling shares to the Egyptian and European governments. The Egyptian government provided labor through conscription, and construction took from 1859 to 1869. De Lesseps is remembered as the inspired leader who did whatever was necessary to get the canal built.

See also SA'ID PASHA; SUEZ CANAL.

Bibliography

Goldschmidt, Arthur, Jr. *Modern Egypt: The Formation of a Nation-State.* Boulder, CO: Westview Press, 1988.

DAVID WALDNER

LE TUNISIEN

See NEWSPAPERS AND PRINT MEDIA: ARAB COUNTRIES

LEVANTINE

Noun or adjective that defines the non-Muslim populations and cultures of the modern Middle East.

The term *levantine* is French in origin—*levantin*—and implies a geographic reference to the sun rising—*soleil levant*—in the east, or *levant.* The French coined the term because France, in the sixteenth century, was the first Christian national state to exchange diplomatic recognition with the Ottoman Empire located in the eastern Mediterranean littoral. By the early 1800s, English travel literature referred to the lands of the Ottoman Empire as the Levant. Indeed, in the 1990s the London-published international business weekly the *Economist* still refers to their reporters based in Cyprus as their Levant correspondents.

The Rise of a Levantine Bourgeoisie

From the 1500s to the 1850s, Levantine traditionally meant a European resident of the Levant involved in European–Ottoman trade. By the end of the nineteenth century, the label was significantly broadened to include a European born in the Levant whose parentage included Greek or Armenian blood. Moreover, Levantine was by then applied to Syro-Lebanese Christians, Sephardic Jews, Maltese, Cypriots, Armenians, and Greeks, all minorities in the Muslim East living and doing business in the large trading centers of the Ottoman Empire. The term almost always indicated an urbanized commercial bourgeoisie whose members were usually rich and influential merchants and who were different, due to their Westernized education and culture, from the petit bourgeoisie in the provincial towns and the villages of the hinterland.

Historically, the development of a Levantine bourgeoisie was the result of significant trade with Europe and reflected the growing cultural interaction that both preceded and paralleled imperial ties between Europe and the lands of the Ottoman Empire. The Westernization of Levantines was the result of commerce, travel, emigration, and attendance at the foreign missions' schools that dotted the eastern Mediterranean by the mid-1800s. Believing in progress, Levantines saw Europe as the leader of a progressive world, and easily accepted its values. They formed a mercantile elite whose cultural anchors transcended local and regional boundaries, and whose perspective was fixed on Europe. Consequently, there arose a natural affinity between these modernizing groups, regardless of their ethnonational backgrounds, in different parts of the Middle East. Levantines were individuals who were never Muslims nor usually Arab Christians, whose origins were somewhere in the eastern Mediterranean, and whose primary language and culture,

except for Syro-Lebanese Christians, were not Arabic. Because Levantines were conversant in a number of foreign languages and local dialects, many became the indispensable interpreters and translators of the foreign consulates throughout the Levant.

As non-Muslims, members of these minorities usually acquired the protection of European powers in order to benefit from the privileges afforded foreigners under the Capitulations. Centuries of insecurity under Mamluk or Ottoman rule had conditioned them to try to obtain the protection of European powers who, in most cases, were only too willing to extend it. This phenomenon had begun as early as the seventeenth century in Lebanon with the Maronite Christians, who received French protection inside the Ottoman Empire.

Twentieth-Century Evolution of the Term

By the 1900s *Levantine* had acquired a negative moral coloration. Sir Evelyn Baring, British agent and consul-general in Egypt from 1883 to 1907, adhered to the traditional definition, but emphasized the southern European origin of those to whom the term applied. He further included a pejorative nuance that had recently been attached to the term: "Levantines . . . suffer in reputation by reason of qualities which are displayed by only a small minority of their class . . . among this minority are to be found individuals who are tainted with a remarkable degree of moral obliquity." Other writers were more specific and referred to Greek or Armenian money lenders or to "sellers of strong waters to Muslims in most cities of Western Asia."

The pejorative implication gained ground. An impressive publication that served as a guide to British investors in Egypt, in discussing Alexandria as a summer resort, informed its readers that the city became the temporary home of "businessmen from the capital unable to get over to Europe and a certain class of Levantines who invariably return to Cairo richer than they left." Thus, the term *Levantine* evolved to encompass both ethnocultural identity as well as moral judgment. From applying to a European born and living in the eastern Mediterranean, it came to include either an Eastern Christian or another member of a non-Arab minority whose business dealings were ethically tainted to the point of implementing the profit motive even while on vacation.

The metamorphosis of the term probably reflected a change in the attitudes of Europeans toward the East. By the end of the nineteenth century, European Arabists believed that Eastern civilization was "purer, more spiritual and more wholesome" than Western civilization, and that European greed and viciousness were destroying the Arab East. To such Europeans, Levantines were the carriers of Western and European greed and viciousness, since it was through them—Christian brothers of the Europeans and, to a lesser extent, Jews—that it flowed into Eastern and Arab society.

By the 1920s *Levantine* and *Levantinism* had also acquired political nuances commensurate with the seismic effects of World War I on the region. Various authors used the terms to describe the political crisis affecting Turkish society; the expression ascribed Turkey's defeat in World War I to the fact that Turks from Istanbul had "become Levantiny." Writing in the postcolonial mid-1950s, Elie Kedourie, an Iraqi Jew by birth and an incisive student of Middle Eastern politics and society, maintained that by the 1940s the Levant was perceived as much a region of the spirit as a region of the globe, and that the spread of Levantinism was the characteristic malady of Islamic and Arab society.

Albert Hourani, an Arab Christian and a perceptive student of Middle East history, writing shortly after World War II, maintained that Levantinism was a symbol of national and ethnocultural dispossession. He further ascribed to it philosophical aspects of the human condition, a sort of postwar mal de siècle, by stating: ". . . to be a Levantine is to live in two worlds or more at once without belonging to either; to be able to go through the external forms which indicate the possession of a certain nationality, religion or culture without actually possessing it. It is no longer to have a standard of one's own, not to be able to create but only able to imitate. . . . It is to belong to no community and to possess nothing of one's own. It reveals itself in lostness, pretentiousness, cynicism and Despair" (Hourani, 1947). Undoubtedly affected by the postwar atmosphere of frustrated nationalist self-assertion, Hourani cast Levantines as a group adrift without the contemporary concerns of national self-realization. However, his alarm underlines the concerns of Arab Christian minorities caught in the dilemma of decolonization: the fear of rejection by the Arab Muslim majority.

The twentieth-century political definitions of Levantinism encompass the notion that people and cultures can be divided into genuine and hybrid, with the implication that the former are clearly superior to and more desirable than the latter. They present an arbitrary division of historical phenomena driven by ideology and containing ahistorical value judgments. To apply this perspective to the Middle East overlooks the fact that the area has historically absorbed a number of vastly diverse cultures, languages, customs, and values. Although some of these cultures had a stronger influence than others, they all contributed to the region's heterogeneity. Thus, an understanding of Middle East history must include an assessment untainted by ideological prisms, but comprising a perspective that includes the experience and the contributions of its diverse populations.

See also CAPITULATIONS; MARONITES; OTTOMAN EMPIRE: OVERVIEW.

Bibliography

Cromer, Lord. *Modern Egypt*. London: Macmillan, 1908.

Hourani, Albert. *Minorities in the Arab World*. Oxford, U.K.: Oxford University Press, 1947.

Kedourie, Elie. *England and the Middle East: The Destruction of the Ottoman Empire, 1914–1921*. London: Bowes and Bowes, 1956.

Oppenheim, Jean-Marc Ran. "Twilight of a Colonial Ethos: The Alexandria Sporting Club, 1890–1956." Ph.D. diss., Columbia University, 1991.

JEAN-MARC R. OPPENHEIM

LEVINGER, MOSHE
[1935–]

Spiritual leader of Gush Emunim and Hebron settlers.

Moshe Levinger was born in Jerusalem in 1935 to highly educated German-Jewish immigrant parents. After completing his army service, he studied in Yeshivat Merkas ha-Rav, where he was strongly influenced by its head, Rabbi Zvi Yehuda Kook, who is widely viewed as the spiritual father of Gush Emunim. It was, apparently, there that Levinger developed his strong belief that he is obligated by the Torah to help re-establish the kingdom of Israel in all of Eretz Yisrael. After his ordination, he lived in a kibbutz in the Upper Galilee. He married an American immigrant, Miriam, who was a nurse.

In April 1968 Levinger led a group of Jews who rented a hotel in Hebron to celebrate the Passover and subsequently refused to leave. They were supported by the Eretz Yisrael ha-Shelema (Whole Land of Israel) movement, and several weeks later they moved to an Israeli military compound nearby. Within a few months, they began the construction of Kiryat Arba on confiscated land. Levinger was the ideological leader of Gush Emunim and, in a 1987 poll undertaken by an Israeli weekly, was voted, along with Menachem Begin, as the "person . . . who has [had] the greatest effect on Israeli society in the last twenty years." On the other hand, he was named "Israel's foremost religious fascist" by *The New Republic*.

Levinger and his family live in the Jewish quarter of Hebron. Along with his wife, he asserted that Judea and Samaria (the West Bank) cannot again be left *Judenrein,* and he announced his intention to live with the local Arab community, to work with them to provide education and health, but to remove those who would harm Jews. He was arrested and imprisoned for killing a Palestinian after his car was attacked in 1989. His rigid personality has lost him many followers even among supporters of the ideology of Gush Emunim, but he still remains the spiritual leader of the Jewish community in Hebron.

See also GUSH EMUNIM; HEBRON; ISRAELI SETTLEMENTS; KOOK, ZVI YEHUDA.

DAVID NEWMAN

LEVIN, HANOCH
[1943–1999]

Israeli playwright and storyteller.

Hanoch Levin was born and grew up in a poor section of Tel Aviv. He began writing satirical plays while still a student. Levin's work is avant-garde,

minimalist, and controversial. His *Malkat ha-Ambatya* (Queen of the bathtub, 1970), a satire on Israeli society after the Arab–Israel War of 1967, created an uproar, and performances had to be canceled.

Levin's plays ridicule many of Israel's national myths: the ideals of its youth culture, family life, and the exuberance following the military victory in 1967. His work stresses the dull parochialism of people's lives. His plays include *Solomon Grup* (1969), *Hefetz* (1972), and *Ya'akobi ve-Ledental* (1972). The latter was widely performed both in Israel and abroad. Many of his plays were first staged at the Cameri, Tel Aviv's municipal theater, and in 1988 Levin was appointed its in-house playwright.

Bibliography

Abramson, Glenda. *Drama and Ideology in Modern Israel.* New York: Cambridge University Press, 1998.

Brenner, Rachel Feldhay. "A Symposium on Hanoch Levin's Play, *Murder. . .*" *Hebrew Studies* 43 (2002).

ANN KAHN
UPDATED BY DONNA ROBINSON DIVINE

LEVIN, SHMARYAHU
[1867–1935]

Zionist orator, propagandist, and advocate.

After serving in the Duma (Russian parliament), in 1906, Shmaryahu Levin left Russia. In Germany, he gained support for founding the Haifa Technion (1908). During World War I he mobilized the support of American Jews for the Zionist cause. A strong supporter of Chaim Weizmann within the Zionist movement, Levin settled in Palestine in 1924.

MARTIN MALIN

LEVIN, YIZHAK MEIR
[1894–1971]

Merchant, banker, Jewish leader, and communal activist.

Yizhak Meir Levin was born in Poland and descended from a family of Gerer Hasidim. He was a leader of and active participant in Agudat Israel, a worldwide Orthodox Jewish organization and a political party in Israel, from its inception in Poland following World War I. Levin was elected to the organization's world presidium in 1929 and headed its delegation to Palestine in 1935.

Escaping Nazi-occupied Poland, he reached Palestine in 1940, where he worked for the rescue of Jews stranded in Europe. In 1947, he was placed in charge of the Israeli branch of Agudat Israel. As a party member, he was elected to the first Knesset (parliament), serving as minister of social welfare until 1952, when he resigned over the issue of drafting women into the army, to which he was thoroughly opposed. He remained a member of the Knesset until his death.

See also AGUDAT ISRAEL.

ANN KAHN

LEVONTIN, ZALMAN
[1856–1940]

Zionist leader.

Born and educated in Russia, Zalman Levontin later became a businessman and banker. Levontin was a close associate of Theodor Herzl and a founding member of the Zionist settlement of Rishon le-Zion. Levontin was the director of the Jewish Colonial Trust in 1901; he moved to Palestine, where he founded the Anglo-Palestine Bank (which later became the Bank Leumi L'Yisrael).

See also BANKING.

BRYAN DAVES

LEVY, DAVID
[1937–]

Israeli political leader.

Born in Morocco, David Levy has held either an elected or an appointed office in Israel's government since 1965. He was one of the first North African immigrants to rise to national political prominence. Since 1969 he has been a member of the Israeli Knesset. From 1977 to 1998 he served as a government minister—as minister of immigration and absorption (1977–1979), minister of housing and construction (1979–1980; 1981–1984), and min-

ister of foreign affairs (1990–1992; 1996–1998). He made a bid for the Likud leadership in the 1992 election, suggesting that the leadership of the party was guilty of anti-Sephardic racism, but he eventually lost to Benjamin (Binyamin, or Bibi) Netanyahu. Afterwards, he left the Likud Party and helped form the Gesher ("Bridge") Party, only to realign with Netanyahu just before the 1996 election. Although Levy joined the coalition of Prime Minister Ehud Barak following the election of 1999, serving as foreign minister, he resigned from the coalition in August of 2000 in protest to Barak's willingness to make concessions to the Palestinians in the peace negotiations. In April 2002, in the government of Prime Minister Ariel Sharon, Levy was appointed minister without portfolio—a member of the Cabinet with the right to attend Cabinet meetings and advise the prime minister but without responsibility for a division of government bureaucracy (as are the Ministry of Housing, Ministry of Labor, Ministry of Foreign Affairs, etc.). Levy resigned from this position in July of the same year.

Bibliography

American-Israeli Cooperative Enterprise. "David Levy." In *Jewish Virtual Library*. Available from <http://www.us-israel.org/jsource/biography>.

Gilbert, Martin. *Israel: A History*. New York: Morrow, 1998.

State of Israel Ministry of Foreign Affairs. "David Levy." In *Personalities*. Available from <http://www.mfa.gov.il/mfa>.

BRYAN DAVES
UPDATED BY GREGORY MAHLER

LIBERAL CONSTITUTIONALIST PARTY

Egyptian political party founded by former Prime Minister Adli Yakan (October 1922).

Members of the party, mainly landowners and intellectuals, were former members of the Wafd who came to oppose Saʿd Zaghlul because of his intransigence and demagogery. The program of the party, written by Ahmad Lutfi al-Sayyid, called for an independent Egypt, constitutional rule, the protection of civil rights and free speech, and social justice. The party defended the 1922 declaration of independence granted by Britain, which many nationalists considered inadequate, and supported the 1923 constitution, which it had helped to draft. In the late 1920s and early 1930s, the party alternated between allying with the Wafd against Britain and joining with Britain in forming anti-Wafd governments. The newspaper of the party was *al-Siyasa* (Politics). The party was banned by the Revolutionary Command Council in 1953.

See also WAFD.

Bibliography

Goldschmidt, Arthur, Jr. *Modern Egypt: The Formation of a Nation-State.* Boulder, CO: Westview Press, 1988.

Sayyid-Marsot, Afaf Lutfi al-. *Egypt's Liberal Experiment, 1922–1936.* Berkeley: University of California Press, 1977.

DAVID WALDNER

LIBERATION RALLY

Political party formed by Egypt's Revolutionary Command Council following the January 1953 ban on all existing political parties.

The Liberation Rally was intended to mobilize popular support for the new regime—the Free Officers who had overthrown the government of King Farouk in a military coup in 1952—by co-opting student leaders and workers. The Liberation Rally called for the unconditional withdrawal of the British from the Suez Canal zone, self-determination for Sudan, the establishment of a socialist welfare state, pan-Arabism, and the installation of a constitution guaranteeing civic liberties. The rally became associated with Gamal Abdel Nasser in his struggle for supremacy with General Muhammad Naguib, who was supported by the Muslim Brotherhood. Following a clash between the Liberation Rally and the Muslim Brotherhood on the campus of Cairo University in January 1954, Nasser began to mobilize his support in the Rally against Naguib. After Naguib and his supporters were purged from the government, the Liberation Rally was dissolved.

See also FAROUK; FREE OFFICERS, EGYPT; MUSLIM BROTHERHOOD; NAGUIB, MUHAMMAD; NASSER, GAMAL ABDEL; PANARABISM.

Bibliography

Goldschmidt, Arthur, Jr. *Modern Egypt: The Formation of a Nation-State.* Boulder, CO: Westview, 1988.

DAVID WALDNER

LIBERTY, USS

U.S. ship attacked by Israel.

On 8 June 1967 the electronic surveillance ship USS *Liberty* was 14 nautical miles north of al-Arish, Egypt, gathering intelligence data when it was attacked by three Israeli combat aircraft, and later by three torpedo boats, one of which launched a torpedo that demolished the *Liberty*'s communications room and killed twenty-five technicians. A Mayday message from the ship drew rescue aircraft from the carrier USS *America,* and Israel halted the attack. In all, 34 crew members were killed and 171 wounded.

Israel's attack has never been satisfactorily explained. The *Liberty* was displaying the U.S. flag very prominently and the attack continued after the ship had been identified by Israeli pilots whose conversations were monitored by a U.S. surveillance aircraft. Israel swiftly apologized for what it called "a tragic error." Although a U.S. inquiry found no evidence that the attack was premeditated, military experts concluded that it could not reasonably be attributed to error, and that Israel must have felt that the information being gathered by the *Liberty* could be so damaging that it accepted the risk of incurring the anger of the United States. Two possible explanations are (a) that Israel was "cooking" (intercepting and altering) messages between Egypt and Jordan in hopes of drawing Jordan into the war so that Israel could occupy the West Bank, and (b) that Israel wanted to conceal the true extent of its dramatic victory over Egypt in order to delay the imposition of a cease-fire. Israel paid $7 million in damages to the families of the U.S. crewmen but never admitted culpability. Controversy about the incident, which was frequently cited in the propaganda war between Israel and its critics, continued to rage for decades afterwards.

Bibliography

Bamford, James. *Body of Secrets: Anatomy of the Ultra-Secret National Security Agency: From the Cold War through the Dawn of a New Century.* New York: Doubleday, 2001.

Dupuy, Trevor N. *Elusive Victory: The Arab–Israeli Wars, 1947–1974.* New York: Harper and Row, 1978.

Ennes, James M., Jr. *Assault on the* Liberty: *The True Story of the Israeli Attack on an American Intelligence Ship.* New York: Random House, 1979.

JENAB TUTUNJI
UPDATED BY IAN BLACK

LIBYA

In theory, a jamahiriyya *(state governed by the masses); in reality, the Socialist People's Libyan Arab Jamahiriyya is ruled by Muammar al-Qaddafi.*

In 2002 Libya's population was about 5.4 million, distributed over 686,000 square miles on the northern coast of Africa, bordered to the north by the Mediterranean Sea, to the west by Tunisia and Algeria, to the south by Niger and Chad, and to the east by Sudan and Egypt. The capital city, Tripoli, and the other principal urban centers, Misurata, Benghazi, and Derna (or Darnah) are on the coast; several large oases, including Sabha (or Sebha), provincial capital of the southern region of Fezzan, and Kufrah, in the southeast, were major trading centers of the trans-Saharan caravan trade, but they are now principally administrative centers. The population clusters along the coast, where two ranges of hills—Jabal al-Gharb in the western province, Tripolitania, and Jabal al-Akhdar in Cyrenaica, the eastern region—divide the narrow coastal plain from the arid plateaus and deserts to the south.

Climate and Resources

Except along the coast, Libya's climate is severe, with wide extremes of temperature, particularly in the mountains and deserts. There is scanty rainfall; even along the coast, the timing of the annual average of 8 inches of rain is unpredictable. As a result, less than 2 percent of the country's surface is arable, and only another 4 to 5 percent is suitable for raising livestock. Historically, much of the country's wealth derived from animal husbandry and from trans-Saharan and coastal trade rather than from agriculture. During the late 1950s, large quantities of petroleum were discovered and by 1968 oil exports accounted for more than 50 percent of gross domestic product (GDP). Since then, oil revenues have generally represented one-half to one-third of GDP. In 2002, Libya had one of the highest per capita incomes in Africa, $7,600, and a relatively high population growth rate at 2.4 percent. Thanks to oil, the government provides generous welfare benefits to Libyan citizens and the economy relies heavily on foreign workers; in the 1980s and 1990s, more than half a million foreign nationals, mostly Africans, have found employment there.

Population and Culture

Libya has a largely homogeneous population, both ethnically and religiously. Virtually all the citizens are Arabs practicing Sunni Islam. Small communities of Berbers, many of whom are followers of Ibadi Islam, still reside in the western hill villages, but nothing remains of the once substantial Jewish community, most of which moved to Israel. Libya is not home to any major educational or cultural institutions; apart from some locally venerated saintly families, the people of the area traditionally looked to Tunisia and Egypt for their religious teachers and legal authorities. Despite the contemporary urbanization of the country—over two-thirds of the population live in Tripoli and Benghazi alone—the importance of pastoral nomadism in recent history is evident in the continued social and political significance of kinship and tribal ties. Although women are being educated in increasingly large numbers, they ordinarily marry while in their late teens and are not expected to work outside the home.

Government

The Libyan government structure was designed by Muammar al-Qaddafi (also Muʿammar al-Qadhdhafi), who holds no formal position of authority but serves as head of state. As he conceives it, Libyans rule themselves, without the intervention of elections, politicians, or political parties, through a system of local and national committees and congresses that deliberate, administer, and supervise the affairs of the country on their behalf. By most accounts, the basic people's congresses and committees do fulfill governmental functions at local levels, but in national, particularly foreign, policymaking, Qaddafi and his immediate advisers are believed to make virtually all important decisions.

History

At the beginning of the nineteenth century, today's Libya was three loosely administered provinces of

An oil rig in the Libyan desert. Large deposits of petroleum were discovered in the late 1950s, and oil is now the country's principle resource, accounting for 95 percent of Libya's export trade. © BETTMANN/CORBIS. REPRODUCED BY PERMISSION.

the Ottoman Empire, ruled by the local Qaramanli dynasty in Tripoli. In 1835, disturbed by local unrest, the Ottoman central government overthrew the dynasty and thereafter Libya was ruled directly from Istanbul.

Although never a rich province, Libya prospered during the second Ottoman era. As the Ottoman order spread throughout the territory, many nomads settled in coastal villages; local agricultural production and trade increased. The Sanusiyya, a religious brotherhood with political aspirations, saw its substantial trading interests flourish in Cyrenaica and the Sahara.

By the beginning of the twentieth century, Italy had established Libya as a sphere of influence, and in 1911 Rome launched its long-anticipated invasion. The Ottoman government mounted a major war effort to oppose the Italian encroachment but was soon forced to withdraw, preoccupied by unrest and nationalism in the Balkans. Local Libyan leaders took up the cause of resistance, however, and the Italians faced an armed insurgency until well into the 1930s, only to lose the province a decade later in the North African campaigns of World War II. Libya was then governed by British and French military administrations until the country was granted independence by the United Nations at the end of 1951.

The upheavals occasioned by the precipitous withdrawal of the Ottoman administration, the protracted Italian conquest, and the devastating battles

Residents in Tripoli celebrate as drinking water reaches their city as part of the Great Man-Made River project. Conceived to ease the country's water shortage, the GMMR is a vast pipeline that draws water from the aquifers of oases in the Sahara and transports it to Libyan cities and agricultural regions along the Mediterranean coast. © AP/WIDE WORLD PHOTOS. REPRODUCED BY PERMISSION.

for control during World War II left Libya one of the poorest countries in the Middle East. The population had been nearly halved by famine, war casualties, and emigration. At independence, illiteracy rates were well over 80 percent, and the per capita income was no more than $25 a year; the country's major export was scrap metal scavenged from World War II battlefields.

The leader of the Sanusiyya brotherhood, Idris al-Sayyid Muhammad al-Sanusi, had spent the years between the world wars in exile in Cairo, where he came to know the British authorities, who sponsored him as the king of the new country. Despite qualms in Tripoli about Idris's partiality for Cyrenaica, provincial leaders acquiesced in his accession to ensure the country's unity and independence. In the early years, the British subsidized Libya's operating budget while the king's clientele and local tribesmen staffed the administration.

The export of commercial quantities of oil during the early 1960s coincided with the heyday of Arab nationalism. A new generation of politically active Libyans argued that the monarchy's close ties with Britain and the United States were now both economically unnecessary and politically undesirable. Moreover, the administration proved unequal to the task of allocating the new wealth, and the government foundered in corruption and mismanagement. On 1 September 1969, a twenty-seven-year-old captain, Muammar al-Qaddafi, and a small group of his friends and fellow military officers engineered a bloodless coup; the king abdicated as his government collapsed.

At the outset, the new regime appeared to be a typical Arab nationalist military government, with an additional Islamic coloring, reflecting both Qaddafi's personal piety and the regime's efforts to appeal to the followers of the deposed Sanusi leader.

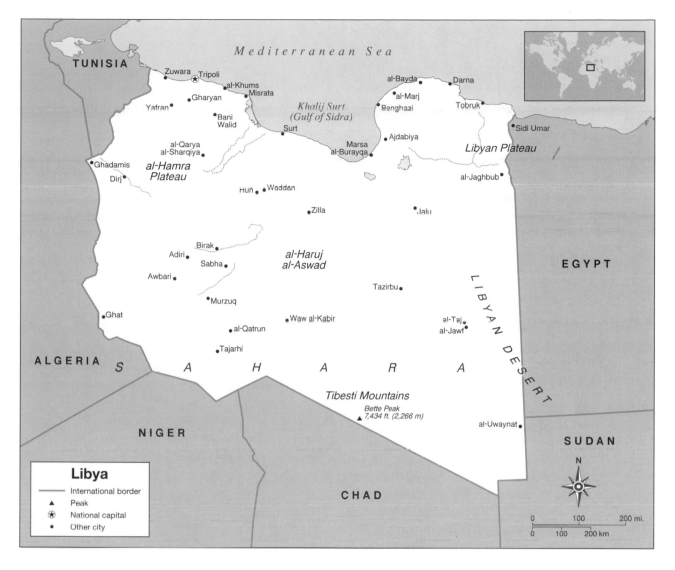

MAP BY XNR PRODUCTIONS, INC. THE GALE GROUP.

The British and U.S. military bases were closed, the remaining Italian residents were expelled, alcohol was forbidden, nightclubs and churches were closed, and Qaddafi called his fellow rulers to join him in establishing a unified Arab state.

By the mid-1970s, however, with the publication of the first volume of Qaddafi's Green Book, the Libyan regime began to develop its distinctive profile. Disappointed with the failure of other Arab rulers to heed his calls for immediate and unconditional unity and with the average Libyan's apparent lack of revolutionary fervor, Qaddafi concentrated on domestic affairs, proclaiming a cultural revolution at home. The Declaration of the Establishment of the People's Authority, issued on 2 March 1977,

stated that direct popular authority would now be the basis for the Libyan political system. It also changed the official name of the country from Libya to the Socialist People's Libyan Arab Jamahiriyya. A newly coined Arabic word, *jamahiriyya* was translated unofficially as "state of the masses." Under the new system, the people exercised authority through people's committees, people's congresses, unions, and the General People's Congress (GPC). Qaddafi was designated GPC general secretary and the remaining members of the now defunct Revolutionary Command Council (RCC) composed the GPC general secretariat.

In part because of accompanying economic reforms—retail trade was abolished as exploitative;

In 1977, eight years after seizing power in a bloodless coup, Libyan head of state Muammar al-Qaddafi declared the country's political system would be based on direct popular authority, declaring Libya a "state of the masses." In 1979 he relinquished all formal administrative posts, but remained the country's unquestioned leader. © UPI/CORBIS-BETTMANN. REPRODUCED BY PERMISSION.

wage earners were declared partners in their enterprises; rent was outlawed and houses given to their occupants—opposition to the new edicts grew quickly. The regime reacted harshly. During the early 1980s, "revolutionary committees" were established to ensure the revolutionary enthusiasm of the Libyan people, and it was these committees that carried out the assassination of Libyan opposition figures abroad.

By then the regime had grown disenchanted with Arab leaders and devoted itself to exporting the Libyan revolution throughout the world. As a result, Qaddafi found himself in disputes not only with his neighbors but with the Western powers, particularly the United States. Accusing Qaddafi of having harbored terrorists and sponsored terrorism throughout the world, the administration of Ronald Reagan bombed Tripoli and Benghazi in April 1986 in hopes of reforming (if not removing) the Libyan leader. Despite its international isolation and the economic difficulties precipitated by the fall of oil prices during the mid-1980s, it was not until the implosion of its international patron, the Soviet Union, at the end of the decade, that the Qaddafi regime began to show signs of moderating its opposition to the international status quo.

Domestically, a period of economic and political liberalization, called green perestroika by some observers, marked the late 1980s. Often molding economic and political decisions into a single package, the liberalization program implemented by Qaddafi initially proved popular with the Libyan people. An increased emphasis on human rights and political reform accompanied some liberalization of the economy. The merger of economic and political reforms rolled necessary but painful austerity measures into a generally popular reform package, including curbs on the revolutionary committees, amnesty for political prisoners, and increased tolerance of the exiles constituting the bulk of regime's opposition. Economic components of green perestroika included the legalization of private ownership of shops, small businesses, and farms, together with increased private retail trade incentives. Unfortunately, the program failed to attract long-anticipated, and much desired, foreign investment, largely because modest attempts to create an internal market were not accompanied by the reversal of the political experiments begun in 1969.

Accused of complicity in the December 1988 terrorist bombing of a transatlantic flight, Pan Am 103, Libya was subjected to United Nations (UN)-sponsored economic sanctions in 1991 for failing to extradite the two men indicted for the action. Alleged Libyan involvement in the terrorist bombing of UTA flight 772 over Niger in September 1989 further complicated Libyan external relations in this period. Libya remained under the yoke of UN-sponsored sanctions until 1998, when it accepted a proposal to try the suspects in the Pan Am 103 bombing in the Netherlands under Scottish law. Successful in thwarting opposition on several fronts in the second half of the 1990s, Qaddafi enjoyed a strengthened domestic position at the time, enabling him to remand the two suspects with minimal concern for domestic repercussions.

Following suspension of the UN sanctions, Libya initiated an aggressive international campaign to end its commercial and diplomatic isolation. Initially focused on Africa, Qaddafi launched a series of bilateral and multilateral initiatives, beginning in February 1998 with the creation of the Community of Sahel-Saharan States (COMESSA), which linked poor, land-locked African states with oil-rich Libya. In August 1999, he called for the creation of a United States of Africa, including an African central bank. He later added the goal of a pan-African parliament with lawmaking powers. A measure of Libya's improved standing in Africa was the support it received, in the face of determined opposition from the United States and human rights groups, for chairing the UN Human Rights Commission in 2002. In addition to regional initiatives, the Qaddafi regime also aggressively pursued expanded bilateral ties with a number of African states.

At the same time, Libya moved to strengthen economic and political relations with key European states like Britain, Italy, and Russia. The Libyan economy, adversely affected by low oil prices throughout much of the previous decade, stood to benefit from the expanded European trade and investment essential to the revitalization of the petroleum sector. The Qaddafi regime also worked to expand its political options in Europe, increasing its dialogue with bodies like the European Union and the Euro-Mediterranean Partnership and promoting Libya as a natural bridge between Europe and Africa.

After the special court sitting in the Netherlands found one of the two Pan Am 103 defendants guilty in January 2001, the Qaddafi regime expanded its efforts at global rehabilitation to include the U.S. government. In the aftermath of the 11 September 2001 terrorist attacks on New York and Washington, Libya actively cooperated with the United States and its allies in the war on terrorism. In return, Qaddafi sought Washington's support for a permanent lifting of the UN sanctions, together with the bilateral sanctions progressively imposed by the United States after 1986.

In the longer term, the Qaddafi regime hoped to achieve a restoration of full commercial and diplomatic ties with the United States. Libya took several steps that affected its relations with the United States and the world. In September 2003 Libya agreed to pay $2.7 billion to the families of the victims of Pan Am 103, after which the UN Security Council permanently lifted its sanctions regime. In December 2003 Libya renounced its unconventional weapons programs, agreeing to in-

ternational inspections to verify compliance. And in January 2004 Libya also reached a final settlement in the UTA 772 case, in which it agreed to pay the families of victims $170 million.

See also BASIC PEOPLE'S CONGRESSES; BENGHAZI; FEZZAN; GREEN BOOK; IDRIS AL-SAYYID MUHAMMAD AL-SANUSI; JABAL AL-AKHDAR, LIBYA; QADDAFI, MUAMMAR AL-; QARAMANLI DYNASTY; TRIPOLI.

Bibliography

Davis, John. *Libyan Politics: Tribe and Revolution: An Account of the Zuwaya and Their Government.* Berkeley: University of California Press; London: I. B. Tauris, 1987.

Khadduri, Majid. *Modern Libya: A Study in Political Development.* Baltimore, MD: Johns Hopkins Press, 1963.

El-Kikhia, Mansour O. *Libya's Qaddafi: The Politics of Contradiction.* Gainesville: University Press of Florida, 1997.

Obeidi, Amal. *Political Culture in Libya.* Richmond, U.K.: Curzon Press, 2001.

St John, Ronald Bruce. *Historical Dictionary of Libya*, 3d edition. Lanham, MD: Scarecrow Press, 1998.

St John, Ronald Bruce. *Libya and the United States: Two Centuries of Strife.* Philadelphia: University of Pennsylvania Press, 2002.

Vandewalle, Dirk. *Libya since Independence: Oil and State-Building.* Ithaca, NY: Cornell University Press, 1998.

Vandewalle, Dirk, ed. *Qadhafi's Libya, 1969–1994.* New York: St. Martin's Press, 1995.

Vikor, Knut S. *Sufi and Scholar on the Desert Edge: Muhammad b. Ali al-Sanusi and His Brotherhood.* Evanston, IL: Northwestern University Press, 1995.

Wright, John. *Libya: A Modern History.* Baltimore, MD: Johns Hopkins University Press, 1982.

LISA ANDERSON
UPDATED BY RONALD BRUCE ST JOHN

LICA

The abbreviation for the League against German Anti-Semitism, Association Formed by all Jewish Works and Institutions in Egypt.

LICA (Ligue contre l'Antisémitisme Allemand, Association Formée par Toutes les Oeuvres et Institutions Juives en Egypte) was founded in April 1933 as part of the mass protests organized by the Cairo B'nai B'rith against rising German antisemitism.

Among the leading founders was Léon Castro, lawyer, journalist, and Wafd party activist. In September 1933, the organization joined the International League against German Anti-Semitism (also abbreviated as LICA), which had recently been formed in Amsterdam, the Netherlands, with Castro as its vice-president. About the same time, a youth section, LISCA (Ligue Internationale Scolaire contre l'Antisémitisme; International Student League against Anti-Semitism) was founded in Egypt. By 1935, LICA counted about 1,500 members, and LISCA had about 650.

LICA organized an active campaign in Egypt's Hebrew- and European-language press. It also undertook a boycott of German goods and films. The boycott was most successful in barring German films from Egyptian theaters and in affecting the sale of a number of German products. Egyptian and British officials fearing possible disorders and financial repercussions, however, intervened to halt the boycott, which continued unofficially thereafter on an individual level.

Bibliography

Krämer, Gudrun. *The Jews in Modern Egypt, 1914–1952.* Seattle: University of Washington Press, 1989.

NORMAN STILLMAN

LIGUE TUNISIENNE POUR LA DÉFENSE DES DROITS DE L'HOMME (LTDH)

Tunisian human rights organization.

The Tunisian League for the Defense of Human Rights (LTDH) was officially recognized in May 1977, thus being the oldest politically independent human rights organization in North Africa. All major political groups were represented on its executive committee, with most being dissidents of the Parti Socialiste Destourien (Destourian Socialist Party; PSD). During its first decade of existence the league proved to be an active and independent organization that increasingly gained popular support. By 1982 the LTDH had 1,000 members in 24 local chapters. By 1985 it had 3,000 members in 33 chapters, and four years later it had 4,000 members in 40 chapters.

In 1985 the LTDH elaborated a charter to define precisely what it stood for. Members decided that the United Nations Universal Declaration of Human Rights (UDHR) would be adopted as the model but modified to fit Tunisian conditions. Internal debates focused on adaptations of the articles on the rights to change one's religion and to marry a non-Muslim, and the rights of illegitimate children.

After President Zayn al-Abidine Ben Ali came to power in 1987, part of its leadership joined ranks with the government. Controversial statements made by the league's president, Moncef Marzouki, during the Gulf War, against adopting an unconditional pro-Iraqi stance, further eroded popular support and deepened dissent within the organization. In June 1991 the league issued a critical statement on arrest and detention procedures that eventually attracted international attention. This incident aggravated the league's relations with the government.

In March 1992 the National Assembly passed a law that sought to tame the LTDH and bring it under Democratic Constitutional Rally (RCD) control or effect its dissolution by 15 June. Refusing to comply, the LTDH dissolved itself. The ensuing international outcry led the regime to reconsider the law. On 26 March 1993, under pressure from President Ben Ali, the court authorized temporary resumption of the league's operations.

In 2000, at the league's fifth national congress, Mokhtar Trifi was elected its new president. Since then, the new outspoken leadership of the organization has faced strained relations with the regime, even enduring the suspension of its new executive and the disruption of its activities.

Bibliography

Amnesty International. *Tunisia: Annual Report.* 2003.

Dwyer, Kevin. *Arab Voices: The Human Rights Debate in the Middle East.* Berkeley: University of California Press, 1991.

Waltz, Susan. *Human Rights and Reform: Changing the Face of North African Politics.* Berkeley: University of California Press, 1995.

LARRY A. BARRIE
UPDATED BY ANA TORRES-GARCIA

LIKUD

An Israeli electoral bloc established in 1973.

Originally, Likud consisted of several independent parties: the Herut Party, the Liberal Party, the Free

Center, State List, and part of the Land of Israel Movement. Much of the emphasis of its program has been on extension of Israeli sovereignty to the territories conquered in the Arab–Israel War of 1967. It also called for improvement of the social and economic conditions of disadvantaged communities known as Oriental Jews (Edot ha-Mizrah).

Taking advantage of public disenchantment with the Labor Party in 1977, Likud won forty-three Knesset seats and formed a coalition government led by Menachem Begin, which continued until 1984. In that year, neither Likud nor the Labor Alignment bloc won enough to form a coalition without the other. The two joined in a National Unity Government in which Likud leader Yitzhak Shamir held the office of prime minister for half of the electoral period, and the blocs divided other government offices. In 1988, Likud and other right-wing and religious parties improved their showing, and Shamir again led the government until the Labor victory of 1992.

During its years in power, Likud strongly resisted surrendering sovereignty over the Palestinian territories and made little progress in reducing the role of the government in the economy. One of Likud's problems has been the presence in it of several strong individuals and their factions, including Shamir, former Chief of Staff Ariel Sharon, and Moroccan leader David Levy—all of whom have tried vigorously to become dominant. In 1993, the Likud chairmanship was won by Benjamin Netanyahu, former ambassador to the United Nations and brother to the hero of the Israeli raid on Entebbe. He defeated his former rivals as well as younger figures like Ze'ev Begin, with a spirited campaign based on American-style politics and effective use of the media, even though it was an election confined to party members.

See also ARAB–ISRAEL WAR (1967); ISRAEL: POLITICAL PARTIES IN; MIZRAHI MOVEMENT.

WALTER F. WEIKER

LILIENBLUM, MOSES LEIB
[1843–1910]

Russian Zionist writer and philosopher.

Moses Leib Lilienblum received an Orthodox education and was a recognized scholar of the Talmud.

His major activity was as a publicist and social critic. For most of his early career, he advocated normalization of Jewish life in Russia and closer association with that country's non-Jews, as well as an evolutionary concept of religious practice, in the spirit of Haskalah (enlightenment). As political difficulties increased in Russia, he also demanded equal rights. After the pogroms in the late 1870s, however, he became an ardent Zionist and one of the first Russian writers to campaign for the return of Jews to Palestine. One of his main associations was the Hibbat Zion movement. In addition to these political activities, Lilienblum was a renowned literary critic. His approach has been described as anti-aesthetic pragmatism, stressing the usefulness of art to society and that "the Jewish people wanted to live for the sake of life and not for any purpose beyond life." His influence was based on the great simplicity as well as the logic of his writings.

See also HASKALAH; HIBBAT ZION.

WALTER F. WEIKER

LIRA

See GLOSSARY

LISAN AL-HAL

See NEWSPAPERS AND PRINT MEDIA: ARAB COUNTRIES

LITANI OPERATION (1978)

Israeli invasion of Lebanon in 1978.

Following a Palestine Liberation Organization (PLO) assault on a civilian bus traveling Israel's Haifa–Tel Aviv highway that killed thirty-seven Israelis, in March 1978 20,000 troops of the Israel Defense Forces (IDF) invaded Lebanon to the Litani River. The operation's goal was to destroy PLO bases and staging areas south of the Litani and to drive PLO guerrillas beyond the range of the Israeli-Lebanese border. The invasion caused an estimated 1,000 Lebanese and Palestinian casualties and prompted UN Security Council Resolution 425, which called for a cease-fire, an Israeli withdrawal, the dispatch of Lebanese army units to the area, and the creation of a United Nations Interim Force in Lebanon (UNIFIL) peacekeeping force. Israel objected to the resolution's failure to censure anti-Israeli PLO activity in and stemming from Lebanon. The IDF occupied a stretch of Lebanese territory 37 miles long and 3 to 6 miles deep, ceding it after three months as a buffer zone to UNIFIL and to an Israeli-supported local Lebanese militia headed by Sa'd Haddad. Over the next four years the PLO reinfiltrated south Lebanon, and the Litani Operation's failure to secure Israel's northern border figured in the larger scope of Israel's 1982 invasion of Lebanon.

See also HADDAD, SA'D; UNITED NATIONS INTERIM FORCE IN LEBANON.

Bibliography

Evron, Yair. *War and Intervention in Lebanon: The Israeli–Syrian Deterrence Dialogue.* London: Croom Helm, 1987.

Fisk, Robert. *Pity the Nation: The Abduction of Lebanon.* New York: Maxwell Macmillan International, 1990.

Haley, P. Edward, and Snider, Lewis W., eds. *Lebanon in Crisis: Participants and Issues.* Syracuse, NY: Syracuse University Press, 1979.

ELIZABETH THOMPSON
UPDATED BY LAURIE Z. EISENBERG

LITANI RIVER

River in Lebanon.

MAP BY XNR PRODUCTIONS, INC. THE GALE GROUP.

Flowing entirely within Lebanon, the Litani rises in the Biqa valley and flows south between the Lebanon mountains to the west and the anti-Lebanon mountains to the east until Nabatiya, where it turns sharply to the west crosses Lebanon and empties into the Mediterranean Sea.

The major Litani development plan, initiated in the 1950s, was concluded in 1966; it includes the Qar'un reservoir and the Awali hydroelectric power station, which utilizes the water diverted via a tunnel. Hydropower and domestic use receive priority over irrigation, and Shi'a farmers in the south resent this, fearing diversion of all the water to the north.

After 1971, the growth in southern Lebanon of the Palestine Liberation Organization (PLO)—by refugees from the Jordanian Civil War—resulted in a rise in hostilities in that border area with Israel. These led in 1978 to Operation Litani by Israel and the 1982 Arab–Israel War. The fear exists in Lebanon that Israel will divert the Litani to join the Jordan River system, but Israel has replied that this is politically unfeasible.

See also ARAB–ISRAEL WAR (1982).

Bibliography

Naff, Thomas, and Matson, Ruth C., eds. *Water in the Middle East, Conflict or Cooperation?* Boulder, CO: Westview Press, 1984.

SARA RIGUER

LITERARY SOCIETY

See MUNTADA AL-ADABI, AL-

LITERATURE

This entry consists of the following articles:

LITERATURE: ARABIC
LITERATURE: ARABIC, NORTH AFRICAN
LITERATURE: HEBREW
LITERATURE: PERSIAN
LITERATURE: TURKISH

LITERATURE: ARABIC

Arabic literature of the nineteenth and twentieth centuries diverged substantially from inherited practices.

Arabic literature has its roots in pre-Islamic odes, enshrining prosodic and thematic conventions that remained unchallenged centuries after the ethos of desert life had ceased to be widely applicable. The emergence of historic Islam in the seventh century C.E., together with the dogma that the Qur'an is the actual word of God and that its superhuman eloquence is the miracle that proves the genuineness of the Prophet's mission, gave the language of that period an all but hallowed character that was perpetuated in formal writing but displaced by local uninflected vernaculars in everyday Arabic speech.

The literary tradition was therefore tinged with a conservative and puristic quality that gave it uncommon homogeneity and continuity. Its conservativeness also insulated it from daily concerns, so that the uneducated majority turned instead to regional folk literatures that were ignored or even despised by the establishment. Nevertheless, changes did occur. One was a growing taste for verbal ornaments, such as the pun and the double entendre. What modern Arabs inherited from the immediate past, therefore, was the literature of a conservative elite in which correctness, convention, and linguistic virtuosity were prized above content or originality.

By the 1800s, the encroachments of Europe brought new perceptions to Arab intellectuals, who came to admire the very power that the colonialists used against them and sought the knowledge that made it possible. By the 1870s, especially in Egypt and the Levant, a new westward-looking elite had emerged. From it came the producers and consumers of the new literature.

New Direction

The conscious adaptation of literary standards to changed conditions was gradual. The earliest Arab intellectuals with extensive opportunity to get to know Europe, such as the perceptive Rifaʿa Rafi al-Tahtawi (1801–1871) and the more mercurial Faris (later, Ahmad Faris) al-Shidyaq (1804–1887), were aware that Europeans had different concepts of literature than Arabs did, but they deemed them inferior. And yet a new form of writing was coming into being, which was evident wherever there was a need to convey information (as in the books of Shidyaq and Tahtawi). It was fostered in transla-

tions, even nonliterary ones, where Arabic had to accommodate notions never before expressed; and it was important to a new Middle Eastern profession born of an imported technology: journalism.

The new direction was strikingly illustrated in the career of Abdullah al-Nadim (1845–1896), the fiery orator of the Urabi rebellion. He was well established as a master of finely bejeweled rhymed prose, but when he took to journalism, he faced up to the need to reach a wide public. He experimented, briefly, with writing an occasional piece entirely in the vernacular, but the choice he deliberately made was to use a vocabulary as close as possible to that of everyday speech without deviating from the rules of classical Arabic grammar. Others have since wrestled with the strains and anomalies of writing in the Arabic idiom that no one speaks and, indeed, the colloquial has gained a large measure of acceptance in the theater and a more grudging one in the dialogue of novels and short stories. But al-Nadim's practice has prevailed among prose writers for at least eighty years, with only a few in the last generation allowing themselves liberties with the syntax as well.

The transformation was not merely stylistic; by the 1870s, admiration of Europe's successes in science and technology was extended, by a loose association, to political, social, and philosophic endeavors as well. The adoption of European aesthetic norms could not lag far behind. By the turn of the twentieth century, direct and unadorned prose was widely recognized as not only functional but also literarily desirable. Because the learned were few, the principal medium of dissemination was the periodical press, so some major literary works were serialized before appearing in book form.

With little to encourage specialization in any one genre, the recognized stylists found their main vehicle in short prose pieces, such as the moralistic essays and tearful narratives of Mustafa Lutfi al-Manfaluti (1876–1924). Indeed, the first half of the twentieth century was dominated by immensely prolific and versatile writers, among whom were Taha Husayn (1889–1973) and Abbas Mahmud al-Aqqad (1889–1964). They were virtually all secularist and liberal sociopolitically, and romantic in their literary inclinations. Although few set out their aesthetic

The 1988 Nobel Prize for literature went to Najib Mahfuz of Egypt. Mahfuz is the author of over thirty novels and thirty-two books of poetry, many of which have been adapted for theatre, film, and television. © VERNIER JEAN BERNARD/CORBIS SYGMA. REPRODUCED BY PERMISSION.

principles systematically, they accustomed their generation to seek neither formalism nor virtuosity in literature but sincerity and emotion. Experience and maturity, the events of World War II, the subsequent decline of Britain and France, and above all, the challenges of independence in tandem with the turmoil of the Palestinians caused the next generation to turn away from romanticism. The keynote of postwar Arabic writing has been political commitment and realism, strongly tinged with socialism.

Prose

The prose style of the West fostered genres previously unknown in Arabic literature. In particular, narratives were discredited as no more than folk art, and the only form to have gained the critics' acceptance as serious literature was the *maqama,* pioneered by Badi al-Zaman al-Hamadhani (968–1008). It was a short piece that usually recounted, in highly ornate prose, some petty fraud perpetrated by an amiable rogue. By the end of the nineteenth century there was growing public demand for short stories and novels of the European type. The demand was readily met by translations, adaptations, or imitations. The short story proved particularly suitable to the needs of journals and an excellent medium for the piecemeal propagation of new ideas and perceptions. In its Arabic garb, it was brought to a high level of sophistication as early as the 1920s by such authors as Mahmud Taymur (1894–1973).

The novel was a more difficult form, especially in the absence of an Arabic tradition. Translations and adaptations aside, a pioneering attempt at a long narrative was made by Muhammad al-Muwaylihi (1858–1930) in *Hadith Isa ibn Hisham* (The Discourse of Isa ibn Hisham), in which a resurrected pasha had a series of adventures that offered opportunities to comment on social changes. The fact that it borrowed the name of the narrator and, in places, the style of (al-Hamadhani), caused it to be labeled an extended *maqama,* but the purpose it served was different, and its link to the novel form was tenuous.

Jurji Zaydan (1861–1914), the indefatigable owner and editor of the journal *al-Hilal,* published more than a score of romances, each twined around some episode of Islamic history—but invention in them is minimal. The first novel of recognized merit rooted in contemporary Arab life was *Zaynab,* the story of a village girl married against her will; it was written by Muhammad Husayn Haykal (1888–1956) in 1910/11 and first published anonymously. No others of consequence were published until the 1930s, when several writers with already established reputations, such as Taha Husayn, Mahmud Taymur, and Ibrahim Abd al-Qadir al-Mazini (1890–1949), turned to the novel. Greater progress was made under the banner of realism, notably by Najib Mahfuz (b. 1911), the first Arab to devote most of his energies to one genre. His abundant, varied, and highly competent production earned him the Nobel Prize for literature in 1988.

Theater

Even more than the novel, dramatic literature was hindered by the absence of any regional precedent, except as folk art, and by resistance to the use of the Arabic colloquial—even between unlearned characters and before mixed audiences. Yet drama made a comparatively early start; the first performance was *The Miser,* a play which, although not a translation of Molière's play, owed a great deal to the great French comedic playwright (1622–1673). It was produced in Beirut (Lebanon) in 1847 by Marun al-Naqqash (1818–1855). His company, and several others that branched out of it or imitated it, found acceptance in Egypt, but their activities were looked upon as mere entertainment. In fact, although some writers established in other genres also tried to write plays, no Arab acquired a reputation as a playwright until the 1930s, when Tawfiq al-Hakim (1898–1987), who had had experience as a hack writer for a theatrical company, returned from a period of study in Paris determined to give drama a recognized place among literary arts. His long career, marked by productivity and versatility even into old age, brought him fame and inspired an impressive group of new playwrights.

Poetry

In contrast to the newly imported genres, Arabic poetry has a long and rich tradition. In the first three-quarters of the nineteenth century, poets perpetuated the highly ornate style of their immediate predecessors. When the times called for a less ornamental and more purposeful poetry, the practice of the most talented turned not to European models but to the example of early poets from an equally dynamic age. By the turn of the century, a school now known as the neoclassical quickly attained a high level of accomplishment, emulating the grandiloquent odes of Abbasid poets but addressing the public issues of the day. Its leading exponents were Ahmad Shawqi (1868–1932) and Muhammad Hafiz Ibrahim (c. 1872–1932).

Resonant as they were, their voices were not the only ones to be heard. Others favored more radical initiatives and the expression of more personal emotions. From outside the Arab heartlands, Syrian Christian émigrés to the Americas headed by Kahlil Gibran (1883–1931) echoed a type of poetry

Kahlil Gibran was a Lebanese poet, philosopher, and artist who immigrated to the United States. *The Prophet,* perhaps his most famous work, is a book of twenty-six poetic essays which has been translated into over twenty languages. © E.O. HOPPE/ CORBIS. REPRODUCED BY PERMISSION.

long accepted in the West. Not least influential were the leading critics al-Aqqad and Taha Husayn, who harried the neoclassicists for not equaling the subtleties of the British poet Percy Bysshe Shelley (1792–1822) or the French poet Alphonse de Lamartine (1790–1869). The leanings of these various groups were unmistakable, and after the death of Ahmad Shawqi and Hafiz Ibrahim, the romanticism already evident in prose became evident in poetry as well.

Another new note was sounded in 1949 when two Iraqis, Badr Shakir al-Sayyab (1926–1964) and Nazik al-Mala'ika (b. 1923), almost simultaneously published their first experiments with free verse. The adoption of lines of uneven length with muted rhymes irregularly arranged, or with no rhymes at all, was the most radical departure ever from classical Arabic poetry. No less significant is that the movement grew—and has continued to grow—out of perceptions shared with Western poets of international stature, especially T. S. Eliot (1888–1965). Most revolutionary of all has been its purpose; for it has given rise to a host of committed poets often able to give voice to their predicaments as individuals and, at the same time, as Arabs and as humanists.

All Genres

All along, Arab writers have given expression to the fervor and then to the disappointments and antagonisms generated by the succession of Western ideologies embraced by the elite. This expression has to some extent been tinged by the prestige of the world power most closely associated with each ism. In the second half of the twentieth century, following growing disappointment in the way the liberalism and secularism associated with Western Europe had worked out, the dominant doctrine has been socialism, but the collapse of the Soviet Union undermined confidence in its forthcoming triumph. Very few carry their disillusion to the extent implied in a short story by Mahmud al-Rimawi (b. 1948) titled "The Train" and included in his *Liqa lam yatimm* (2002). In it, a train running to an unknown destination and stopping only at deserted stations is packed with people who have been on it long enough for a baby girl to be born to one of them, and the name she is given is Palestine. More confidently, contributors to all literary genres view themselves as individuals sharing a distinctive experience but informed by a universal consciousness, and dealing with issues that have a humanistic as well as an Arab dimension.

> *See also* GIBRAN, KAHLIL; HAKIM, TAWFIQ AL-; HUSAYN, TAHA; IBRAHIM, MUHAMMAD HAFIZ; MAHFUZ, NAJIB; MALA'IKA, NAZIK AL-; SAYYAB, BADR SHAKIR AL-; SHAWQI, AHMAD; SHIDYAQ, AHMAD FARIS AL-; TAHTAWI, RIFA'A AL-RAFI AL-; ZAYDAN, JURJI.

Bibliography

Badawi, Mustafa, ed. *Modern Arabic Literature*. Cambridge, U.K.: Cambridge University Press, 1992.

Cachia, Pierre. *Arabic Literature—An Overview*. London: Routledge Curzon, 2002.

Starkey, Paul. *Modern Arabic Literature*. Edinburgh, U.K.: Edinburgh University Press, 2003.

PIERRE CACHIA

LITERATURE: ARABIC, NORTH AFRICAN

North African writers convey their ideas in French and Arabic in a variety of literary genres.

The three countries of the Maghrib—Algeria, Morocco, and Tunisia—share more than common geographic boundaries. They all succumbed to foreign invasions in the past and fell victim to the same colonial power: France. Colonial rule in the countries of the Maghrib differed only in its strength and its duration, Algeria having endured the longest and most traumatizing occupation. The French army landed on the coast of Algeria in 1830 and completed its occupation of the country in 1881. Tunisia was conquered in 1880, and in 1912 Morocco was colonized. Algeria was a French province from 1848 until it achieved independence in 1962; the other two countries remained French protectorates until 1956.

In Algeria, Arabic lost its efficacy long before it was declared a foreign language in 1938. Algerians conceded the fact that the language of the colonizer was the language of bread, but because it is the language of Islam, Arabic maintained its place in the lives of the people, even the Berbers, who spoke various Berber dialects. It became primarily the language of religious teaching and practice. Culturally, Morocco and Tunisia experienced French colonialism in a more subdued manner because they had centers of Arabic learning—the two mosque universities, al-Qarawiyyin in Fez and the Zaytuna in Tunis—that safeguarded and continued an existing cultural tradition. Many schools opted for bilingual instruction, so Arabic was on a par with French. The linguistic situation in the Maghrib has provoked heated polemics between the partisans of French and those of Arabic, particularly in Algeria. Although it remains an issue to the present day due to the growing number of writers expressing themselves in French, it has lost its political connotation.

The three countries of the Maghrib are similar in the role assumed by traditional Muslim centers,

Abdelwahhab Meddeb, a Tunisian poet and scholar, often draws upon his Arab Islamic history and heritage in his writings, which include novels, poetry volumes, translations, and essays. © AP/WIDE WORLD PHOTOS. REPRODUCED BY PERMISSION.

the *zawiyas*. Jealous of their power over the population and intent on playing a role in the political arena, some Zawiya leaders placed themselves in an ambiguous position when they cooperated with French colonial authorities The French used them to legitimize their presence and gain the support of the local population. Aided by widespread illiteracy, the *zawiyas* maintained their control until they were challenged by the reformists of the Salafiyya movement, who were increasingly alarmed by the interference of the colonial administration in the religious affairs of their countries. The Algerian Reda Huhu ridiculed the official imams appointed by the colonial authorities and even spoke of an "official Islam," in contrast to the "people's Islam" in his *Ma Himar al-Hakim* (Conversations with al-Hakim's donkey).

Following in the footsteps of the Salafiyya of the Mashreq, Maghribi intellectuals such as Allal al-Fasi (1910–1974) in Morocco, Abd al-Hamid Ben Badis (1889–1940) in Algeria, and Mohammad al-Fadel Ben Ashour (1909–1970) and Mohammad al-Taher Ben Ashour (1879–1973) in Tunisia confronted the leaders of the *zawiyas*. Their aim was to prove the compatibility of Islam and modernity, and the absence of a contradiction between progress, even in a Western context, and Islam. Their position appealed to the Maghribi youth. Opening up to the West, however, did not occur without a price, even for the French-educated Maghribis. The clash of the two civilizations was successfully dramatized by the Moroccan Driss Chraibi in *Succession ouverte* (1962; Heirs to the past) and *Le passe simple* (1983; The simple past), the Algerian Mouloud Mammeri (1917–1989) in his novel *Le sommeil du juste* (1955; The sleep of the just), and the Tunisian Albert Memmi (b. 1920). Memmi endured hardships as a Tunisian Jew caught between family traditions, colonial policy, and Nazi ideology, which he related in his novel *La statue de sel* (1953; The statue of salt).

Moroccan author Mubarak Rabi belongs to the country's first generation of contemporary writers. His works include short stories, plays, novels, children's books, and psychological studies of childhood socialization processes. COURTESY OF AIDA BAMIA.

Maghribi writers writing in French are finally reconciled with their native culture and at ease in their setting. Some, such as the Algerian Habib Tengour (b. 1947), the Tunisian Abdelwahhab Meddeb (b. 1946), and the Moroccan Taher Ben Jelloun (b. 1944), dug into their Arab Islamic history and their folk heritage in search of subject matter for their works. Independence has, in a certain way, liberated the writers from guilt vis-à-vis their adoption of the French language.

The 1980s witnessed an explosion of production in the Maghrib in various literary genres, in prose and in verse, and in Arabic and French. Particularly prominent in this trend are the women writers. They are slowly filling a space that for many years was dominated by the lone presence of the Algerian novelist Assia Djebar (b. 1936). Approaching the women's world from a feminist angle, her writings shed much of their traditionally romantic outlook on gender relations and with *L'amour, la fantasia* (1985; Fantasia: An Algerian Cavalcade) and *Ombre sultane* (1987; A sister to Scheherazade), she achieved a new depth by mixing history and fiction.

Although Djebar has given a voice to Algerian women through films and plays, her greatest contribution is in fiction. Her latest novel, *La femme sans sepulture* (2002; Woman without a shroud) is a somewhat fictionalized biography of an Algerian woman who fought during the war of independence. Algeria's now long list of other women writing in French includes established names such as Leila Sebbar (b. 1941), Aicha Lemsine (b. 1942), and Anna Greki (1931–1966), and new names such as Hawa Djabali (b. 1949), Miriam Ben (b. 1928) and, more recently, Nina Bouraoui (b. 1967).

Women writing in Arabic, on the other hand, have relied more on poetry to express themselves. One of the early poets, Ahlam Mustaghanmi (b. 1953), has recently turned to fiction, publishing two novels, *Dhakirat al-jasad* (1996; Memory of the flesh) and its sequel *Fawda al-Hawas* (1998; The chaos of the senses). In Tunisia, Hélé Béji (b. 1948) contrasted traditional and modern cultures in her first novel, *L'oeil du jour* (1985; The eye of day). Women writing in Arabic who preceded her include Hind Azzouz (b. 1926), Nadjia Thamer (b. 1926), Arusiyya Naluti (b. 1950), and the poet Zoubeida Béchir (b. 1938). Contributing to the feminist debate in the Arab world, Zahra al-Jlasi (b. 1950) published *al-Nas al-Muʾannath* (2000; The feminine text). In Morocco, Khanatha Bannounah (b. 1940) has contributed four collections of short stories and two novels, *al-Nar wa al-Ikhtiyar* (1968; Fire and choice) and *al-Ghad wa al-Ghadab* (1981; The future and the fury). A new generation of women novelists is slowly making headway but many have not published more than a single novel.

The boundaries of the Maghribi writers have expanded tremendously, both geographically and culturally. Consequently, it is impossible to ignore the growing presence of Maghribi literature outside the countries of the Maghrib, both in Europe and in the Americas. Many writers live and work outside the Maghrib, and come into contact with various cultures. The Tunisian Mustafa Tlili brings his experience in the United States to his novels, and the writings of a Tunisian residing in Canada, Hédi Bouraoui (b. 1932), reveal a rich canvas on which multiple Western cultures intertwine with Maghribi folklore. Majid el-Houssi bridges Italian and Tunisian cultures in his poetry and fiction.

It is important to mention the role that private publishing houses in the Maghrib have played in the promotion of Maghribi literature. Although they impose a financial burden on aspiring young writers who publish their works at their own expense, they nevertheless provide them with greater freedom of expression and accelerate the publication process with the elimination of bureaucracy.

The writings of the Maghribis have echoed during the last two decades the concerns of the population and the social ills in Morocco that contribute to clandestine immigration, as dramatized in Youssouf Amin Elalamy's *Les clandestins* (2000; The clandestines). The rejection of both the Islamists and the government in power in Algeria has fallen on the shoulders of women novelists struggling to secure their rights in a society where they are constantly victimized. Many of the more political writers have so far been the authors of a single work, so it is difficult to assess their literary future.

Whereas more writers in Algeria are resorting to the French language as their medium of expression, the scene in Morocco seems well balanced between Arabic and French, with the scale tilting in favor of Arabic. New fiction works of great literary value are being published, among them Ahmad al-Tawfiq's novels in which he reconciles Arab and Berber traditions, Izz ed-dine Tazi's huge literary production, and the numerous works of Mohammad Shukri, Mubarak Rabi, and Bensalem Himmish. The change in leadership in Morocco after 1999 led to the release of many prisoners who published books describing their experiences in what came to be called prison literature. In contrast, francophone literature in present-day Tunisia is not a strong trend and offers no clear direction. Except for Hélé Béji (b.1948) and to a lesser extent Moncef Ghachem (b. 1947), few have established a reputation beyond Tunisia's borders.

Algeria

To counteract the impact of French culture, the Association of Algerian Muslim Ulama (AUMA) was founded in 1931 by Abd al-Hamid Ben Badis (1889–1940). Its motto was "Algeria is my country, Islam is my religion, and Arabic is my language." The AUMA contributed to the revival of the Arabic language and the launching of a significant literary

Algerian author Assia Djebar is one of North Africa's most acclaimed writers. Djebar is best known for her fictional works, which frequently address feminist issues and focus on themes of social emancipation. © AP/WIDE WORLD PHOTOS. REPRODUCED BY PERMISSION.

movement through its schools and its press. Well-known literary figures such as Ahmad Reda Huhu (1911–1956) and Zuhur Wanisi (b. 1936) either taught in the schools of the AUMA or studied there. Both fiction and poetry were published in the AUMA's two papers, *al-Shihab* (1925–1939) and *al-Basa'ir* (1935–1956). It is fair to say that modern Arabic literature in Algeria was born in the shadow of the AUMA.

While fiction in Arabic was in an early stage and limited to short stories, Algerian fiction in French made its first appearance in the period between the two world wars. However, the most significant novel, *Le fils du pauvre* (The pauper's son), by Mouloud Feraoun (1913–1962), was not published until 1950. Its author stated that his motivation to write it was his desire to present a true portrait of the Algerian people, in reaction to Albert Camus's novels dealing with life in Algeria. Algeria's earlier novels were mostly ethnographic, but they became increasingly political as most writers set out to define and defend their national cause. They voiced the people's aspiration to freedom, described social ills, and condemned France's repressive colonial policy. The nascent literary movement coincided with the political consciousness of the Algerians heightened by their participation in the Etoile Nord Africaine, a party established in 1925 by Maghribis in France.

The Algerian War of Independence (1954–1962) was another literary catalyst. It became the topic of choice for novelists, short-story writers, poets, and playwrights, especially after independence. Few, however, succeeded in reproducing the tragic and momentous events of the struggle without writing documentary-type works. The most original novel on the subject is Mohammed Dib's (1920–2003) *Qui se souvient de la mer* (1962; Who remembers the sea). Writers dwelt on the war years, using incidents mainly to incriminate the parasites and the false nationalists who exploited the ideals of the revolution and the memory of the martyrs. Rachid Boudjedra (b. 1941) pointed the finger at the new leadership and their coconspirators, the religious authorities, in his novel *La fépudiation* (1969; Repudiation). Al-Taher Wattar's *al-laz* (1974; The ace) stresses the tragic fate of the martyrs of the war who were quickly forgotten after independence.

The French Algerian literature gained momentum following independence while Arabic writing lagged behind for more than a decade. In view of Algeria's Arabization policy, the French language was not expected to survive for long in postindependence Algeria; although the prediction did not materialize, the advocates of the two languages engaged in heated polemics on the merits of one over the other. The debates subsided in virulence, and the linguistic choice of the Maghribi writers is still a subject of contention. The only writer to cross the language barrier in Algeria is, so far, Rachid Boudjedra. With his novel *al-Tafakkuk* (1982; The dismantling) he began the trend of writing novels in Arabic and translating them into French, a process that continues to the present day. It is doubtful, however, that readers view Boudjedra as an Arab-language writer.

After the war of independence, writers' interests shifted to other social, personal, and philo-sophical themes. Minority groups such as the Berbers used their writings to promote their heritage. The most committed writer of the postindependence period was Mouloud Mammeri (1917–1989). Meaningful works also were published by the novelist Nabile Farès (b. 1940). Before them, the Amrouche family—Jean el-Mouhouv (1906–1962); his mother, Fadhma At Mansour (1882–1967); and his sister, Mary Louise Amrouche (1913–1976)—endeavored to safeguard the Berber folk heritage.

One of Algeria's most prolific and greatest writers, Mohammed Dib, shifted his attention from politics to other topics following independence. Between his well-known trilogy, Algeria, which included *La grande maison*, (1952; The big house), *L'incendie* (1954; The fire), and *Le métier à tisser* (1957; The loom), and his latest novel, *L'Infante maure* (1994; The Moorish Infanta), the author traversed a path that led him from a direct approach and straightforward style to the depths of abstraction. He remains attuned to events in Algeria in his collection of short stories, *La nuit sauvage* (1995; The savage night), which depicts violence in his country and in the rest of the world. Dib was among those who believed that the role of the writer as an advocate for the national cause was finished when their country achieved independence. Another who began writing in the colonial period and continued long after independence is the poet Noureddine Aba (1921–1996). After Algeria's independence he dedicated his efforts to other Arab causes, particularly to the Palestinian problem, which figures in two of his poetic plays, *Montjoie Palestine* (1970; Palestine, my joy) and *Tel El-Zaatar s'est tu à la tombée de la nuit* (1981; Tel El-Zaatar fell silent at night). Many younger poets writing in Arabic have also expressed a great affinity with the ordeal of the Palestinian people.

The younger generation of writers who did not experience the war years have manifested a particular concern with their leadership's handling of the political, financial, and social affairs of the country. Writers such as Taher Djaout (1954–1993), Rachid Mimouni (1945–1995), and the poet Hamid Skif (b. 1951) have not minced their words in criticizing the government. In the 1990s the dissent was aimed at the government and the Muslim fundamentalists, in Boudjedra's *FIS de la Haine* (1992), Mimouni's *La malediction* (1993; The malediction), and

Djebar's *Le blanc de l'Algérie* (1995; The white of Algeria) and *Oran, langue morte* (1997; Oran, a dead language), in which the author mourns the assassinations of Algerian writers and intellectuals, including Taher Djaout. Most of the works dealing with violence in Algeria reveal the difficulty of reproducing the magnitude of the tragedy in fiction. Unable to distance themselves from events they endured daily, writers provided testimonies rather than fictional accounts of reality, a trend observed in Leila Aslawi's *Survivre comme l'espoir* (1994; To survive like hope), Latifa Ben Mansour's *La prière de la peur* (1997; The prayer of fear), and Nina Hayat's *La nuit tombe sur Alger la blanche* (1995; Night falls on white Algiers). In Arabic, Laraj Wasini wrote *Sayyidat al-Maqam* (The mistress of the abode), relating the events in the framework of a love story, while Wattar used his traditional Sufi approach in *al-Wali al-Tahir ya'udu ila makamihi al-zaki* (2000; The chaste Wali returns to pure his tomb).

Other angry voices heard around the Mediterranean in the mid-1980s were those of the second generation of Maghribi immigrants, mainly Algerians living in France (and in Belgium), known as Beurs. They decried their feelings of loss and their search for identity in violent texts that reflected deep frustration, some of which have achieved notoriety: Farida Belghoul's (b. 1958) *Georgette* (1986), Sakina Boukhedenna's (b. 1959) *Journal and "nationalité: immigré(e)"* (1987; Nationality: Immigrant), and Mehdi Charef's (b. 1952) *Le thé au harem d'Archi Ahmed* (1983; Tea in the harem). Their movement is significant for its global nature. One writer, Azouz Begag, who attracted the attention of the critics with his first novel, *Le gone du chaâba* (1986; The lad of the alley), has established himself as a spokesperson for the Beur with a prolific literary production. Begag shows the human face of the immigrant in quietly humorous works such as *Dis Oualla* (1997; Say, by God) and *Le passport* (200; The passport) where Arabic terms abound.

Morocco

Morocco's modern literary history is in many aspects similar to Tunisia's, but its proximity to the Iberian Peninsula has added an extra dimension to its culture. The Arab Islamic heritage of Andalusia and the flight of many Muslims and Jewish Andalusians to Morocco upon the reconquest of Spain has linked Morocco to Europe historically and cultur-

Tahar Ben Jelloun, one of North Africa's most successful post-colonial authors, was born in Morocco in 1944 but immigrated to France in 1971. A practicing psychologist as well as a writer, Ben Jelloun produced many works of poetry, prose, and criticism, frequently touching on themes of racism and alienation. © RUSSELL CHRISTOPHE/CORBIS KIYA. REPRODUCED BY PERMISSION.

ally. Because French occupation came late to Morocco and as a result of the political organization of the territory, French culture did not deeply or easily infiltrate the educational foundations of the country. It was also counteracted by the Arab Islamic cultural activities centered in Fez.

The two writers who dominated the colonial period and wrote in French, Driss Chraibi and Ahmed Sefrioui, did not promote French ideals. Chraibi denounced the traumatic impact of Western civilization and the hardships of the emigrant workers in France, and in his latest novels has become an advocate of the Berber cause. Sefrioui, on the other hand, revived the folk literature of his country, thus drawing the line between his world and the Western world. Another writer, Mohammad Khair Eddine (b. 1941–1995), has shown strong connections with his country in spite of his vagabond life and the many years he spent outside Morocco. A younger novelist, Taher Benjelloun (Taher ben Jelloun; b. 1944), well known for his innovative style and form, won the Prix Goncourt for *La nuit sacrée* (1987; The sacred night).

Parallel to an important literary movement in French, Morocco counts an impressive array of distinguished writers expressing themselves in Arabic, including Mohammad Ezzeddine Tazi (b. 1948) and Mohammad Zafzaf (1946–2001). Many among them, such as al-Miloudi Shaghmoum (b. 1947) and Abdessalam al-Boqqali (b. 1932), are bilingual and have used their multiculturalism to produce original works reflecting new trends in the European novel. A few, such as Mohammad Aziz al-Habbabi (1922–1993), write in both Arabic and French. Many of the Moroccan novels written in the middle of the twentieth century were historical, stressing the authors' pride in the country's past. Bensalem Himmish's (b. 1949) *Majnun al-Hukm* (1990; Power crazy) and Lotfi Akaley's (b. 1943) *Ibn Battuta* (1998; Ibn Battuta, the well-known Arab traveler) found in Arab culture and history a rich source of material for their fiction works.

Poetry is a particularly popular genre in Morocco among those writing in Arabic and in French. The imprisonment of Abdellatif Laabi for his daring critical works shows the efficacy of this literary genre. Poety is celebrated on a national and official level in Morocco. It occupies a major place in the yearly Rabat cultural festival. Moroccan poetry has a permanent center known as Bayt al-shiʿr (The house of poetry), under the presidency of the poet Muhammad Bannis. Among Moroccan women poets, Malika al-Asimi is exceptionally outspoken, discussing intimate topics and contesting society's restrictions, in her two collections *Kitabat Kharij Aswar al-Alam* (1988; Writings outside the walls of the world) and *Aswat Hanjara Mayyita* (1988; Voices from a dead throat). An equally bold attitude can be observed in Siham Benchkroun's *A toi* (2000; To you).

Traditional in form and patriotic in content at the beginning of the twentieth century, Moroccan literature has taken a more personal and philosophical trend since the mid-1970s, with a tendency for renewal and experimentation in form and style.

Tunisia

Tunisia's cultural history is quite different from that of its neighbor, Algeria. Tunisia benefited from the activities of the *Zaytuna* mosque-university and the Sadiqi college; both were instrumental in preserving and promoting Arabic culture. The country's close contacts with the Mashriq in opposition to the term *maghrib* (referring to North Africa) designates the Egypt and the Levant were another asset in its rich literary activities. As Tunisian writers contributed to the *nahda,* the literary revival in the Arab world, the most significant input came from the poet Abu al-Qasim al-Shabbi (1909–1934).

Most Tunisian writers expressed themselves in Arabic. Between the two world wars the journal *al-Alam al-Adabi* (1930–1952; The literary world) encouraged writers of the young generation, including members of the most famous literary group of this period, Jamaʿat Taht al-Sur (Below the wall group), which counted such established authors as Ali al-Duʿaji (1909–1949) and Mahmoud al-Mesʿadi (b. 1911). A similar role was assumed by the journal *Al-Fikr* (1955–1986; The thinking, or The thought) in the second half of the twentieth century.

Tunisia had very few writers in French during the colonial period. The best known among them was Albert Memmi, who now lives in France. Surprisingly, their numbers have soared in the last two decades. Although they write in French, they borrow heavily from their Arab Islamic heritage. A few, such as Salah Garmadi (1933–1982) and Taher Bakri (b. 1951), are bilingual poets.

Arabic literature in Tunisia, especially fiction, continues to flourish. It is a field for innovation and experimentation both in style and in form. The nationalist and patriotic works of the early period, the period of the French protectorate, gave way to a broader variety of subjects; the tone also became less moralizing. It is not unusual to find writers contributing to more than one literary genre, producing novels, short stories, and plays. The theater, too, has had a revival in Tunisia thanks to the efforts of Izziddin al-Madani (b. 1938). Because of the numerous cultural festivals held in Tunisia, many plays are performed.

Of the three countries of the Maghrib, Tunisia has the largest number of women writing in Arabic.

Although the mere fact of their writing is a reflection of change in society, the women do not always promote complete emancipation. Slowly but progressively their tone has become more daring. Raising certain questions is in itself a revolutionary stance: Subjects such as birth control and abortion, discussed by Hind Azzouz (b. 1926) in *Fi al-Darb al-Tawil* (1969; On the long road), are a novelty. Some, such as Fatima Slim (b. 1942), observe the loss of the old values in a changing society. The most uninhibited is Laila Ben Mami (b. 1944), author of *Sawma'a Tahtariq* (1968; The burning hermitage), who believes in sexual freedom for the artist.

The image of the modern woman also is defined by male writers. Generally, most novelists of the late 1960s and the 1970s called for a bigger role for women in society. In the novel *Wa Nasibi min al-Ufuq* (1970; My share of the horizon), Abdel Qader Ben Shaikh (b. 1929) calls for the emancipation of women, the easing of parents' control, and the relaxing of social traditions. Mustafa al-Farsi (b. 1931) takes a similar position in *al-Mun'araj* (1969; The curve). As reflected in literature, Tunisian women suffered from a changing society and the consequences of their efforts to balance the claims of a traditional upbringing with those of the modern world in which they wanted to prove themselves. The situation claimed some victims in the period of transition—for example, the characters drawn by Natila al-Tabayniyy (b. 1949) in *Shay'un fi Nafsika* (1970; Something within yourself) but an irreversible trend was set for future generations.

Some contemporary writers have achieved recognition for their innovative techniques and timely topics while remaining close to the people's problems. Such is the case of Mohammad al-Hadi Ben Saleh (b. 1945), who portrayed the bread riots in his novel *Sifr al-Naqla wa al-Tasawwur* (1988; The book of transfer and imagination). Poetry, too, responded to the people's concerns, as shown in the work of Mohammad al-Habib al-Zanad (b. 1946) in his collection *al-Majzum bi lam* (1970; The form tense). Fadila al-Shabi (b. 1946) believes in the free expression of the poet in her work, without outside guidance. Another poet, Samira al-Kasrawi (b. 1957), is preoccupied with the political situation in the Arab world, as is obvious in her books *Balagha Shi'riyya fi al-Rafd wa al-Huriyya wa al-Rasas* (1982; Poetic

eloquence in rejection, freedom, and bullets) and *Malhamat al-Mawt wa al-Milad fi Sha'bi* (1983; The epic of death and life for my people). Tunisian poetry maintains a constant connection with the problems of the Arab world and especially those of Palestine. Writers reacted to the Gulf War of 1991 in a spirit of Arab solidarity; one example is Aroussia Nalouti (b. 1950), who incorporates the war into her novel *Tamas* (1995; Tengance).

Some writers, poets, and novelists seek an escape from life's constraints in love, sexual adventures, and exile, but few find solace, which explains Ridha Kéfi's (b.1955) pessimism in his poetic collection *Mariya al-Mayyita* (1981; Dead Mary) and his novel *al-Qina Taht al-jild* (1990; The masque under the skin). Similar sentiments prevail in Nefla Dahab's (b. 1947) third novella, *Samt* (1993; Silence).

Though many writers have authored only a single book or are still searching for the most suitable form for their ideas, it is possible to trace a general trend in Tunisian literature: There is a growing sense of melancholy and disappointment in the most recent writings, which has led to introversion. This is manifested in a fashion for autobiographical novels, an example of which is Hassouna Misbahi's (b. 1950) *Kitab al-Tih* (1997; The book of the maze).

See also AMROUCHE, FADHMA AT MANSOUR; AMROUCHE, JEAN; AMROUCHE, MARY LOUISE (A.K.A. MARGUERITE TAOS); ASSOCIATION OF ALGERIAN MUSLIM ULAMA (AUMA); BEN BADIS, ABD AL-HAMID; BOUDJEDRA, RACHID; CHRAIBI, DRISS; DIB, MOHAMMED; DJAOUT, TAHER; DJEBAR, ASSIA; FARÈS, NABILE; FASI, ALLAL AL-; FERAOUN, MOULOUD; LAABI, ABDELLATIF; LEMSINE, AICHA; MAGHRIB; MEDDEB, ABDELWAHHAB; MEMMI, ALBERT; MIMOUNI, RACHID; RABI, MUBARAK; SEBBAR, LEILA; SEFRIOUI, AHMED; SHUKRI, MOHAMMAD; TLILI, MUSTAFA; WATTAR, AL-TAHER.

Bibliography

Berger, Anne-Emmanuelle, ed. *Algeria in Others' Languages.* Ithaca, NY, and London: Cornell University Press, 2002.

Cox, Debbie. *Politics, Language, and Gender in the Algerian Arabic Novel.* New York: The Edwin Mellen Press, 2002.

Mortimer, Mildred, ed. *Maghrebian Mosaic. A Literature in Transition.* Boulder CO: Lynne Reinner, 2001.

AIDA A. BAMIA

LITERATURE: HEBREW

A long and varied tradition that includes innovative techniques and more conventional approaches, a focus on the individual as well as on nationalist concerns.

Modern Hebrew literature began in late eighteenth-century Prussia, surrounded by Yiddish and German. It developed and came of age in central and eastern Europe, centuries after Hebrew ceased being a spoken language. Only after World War I and the destruction of many Jewish cultural centers in Europe did Palestine and later Israel become the focus for Hebrew *belles lettres*, this time in a Hebrew-speaking milieu.

Haskalah Era

The year 1784, when *Ha-Me'asef*, the first Hebrew periodical, appeared, serves as a period marker for the beginning of modern Hebrew literature. Its founder, Moses Mendelssohn, a German Enlightenment philosopher, was the leader of the Jewish Enlightenment, or Haskalah, which advocated the modernization of Jewish religious and social life. The writers of the Haskalah chose to write in Hebrew not only because it was known to many readers, but also because Hebrew was the only remnant of Jewish independence.

For almost a century, Hebrew literature was committed to the Haskalah movement. From Germany, it spread to Polish Galicia and later to Russia. Poetry was the dominant genre until the mid-nineteenth century. While romanticism was raging in Europe, Hebrew poetry was neoclassical, universalistic, and mimetic. It didactically reinterpreted biblical stories, failing to develop a genuinely poetic idiom. Nevertheless, Haskalah literature revolutionized culture by extracting the literary creation from its religious and communal framework and revived, despite its limitations, the poetic language and universal themes of the Hebrew Bible.

This poetry's most powerful voice was Judah Leib Gordon, who retold biblical and historical stories with dramatic intensity, satirized Jewish life with wit, and empathized with the plight of Jewish women. Micah Joseph Lebensohn's highly charged romantic poems were more individualistic.

The first popular novel was *Ahabat Zion* (Love of Zion; 1853) by Abraham Mapu. Its pastoral view of nature and biblical theme and language reflect Haskalash taste. In 1865, Mapu attempted to depict contemporary life, but not until the work of Mendele Mokher Sefarim later in the century did the form mature and acquire new literary and linguistic models. Mendele stands at the crossroads between Haskalah and the period of nationalism and social realism. He manipulated postbiblical materials—Mishnah, the Talmud, and prayer—to create an innovative prose style.

Hibbat Zion Era

The year 1881, with its wave of pogroms in Russia, marks the shift from Haskalah assimilationism to the Zionist credo of auto-emancipation. The newly established school of Hibbat Zion (Love of Zion) produced national poetry, replete with sentimental and hyperbolical avowals of love for mother Zion and her miserable children, the Jewish people, as well as romantic poetry.

The philosopher of the new nationalist movement and the editor of its periodical, *Ha-Shiloach,* was Ahad Ha-Am, who saw Zion as the future spiritual and cultural center of the Jewish people. He believed that the nonspoken Hebrew of his time could articulate concepts, not emotions, and that the literature should concentrate on Jewish issues exclusively. The challenge to both Ahad Ha-Am's stifling prescription and Mendele's realism and style came from Isaac Leib Peretz, David Frischmann, and the neoromantic Micah Joseph Berdyczewski who all maintained that Hebrew literature was like all others. The individual's subterranean energies motivate Berdyczewski's works of lyrical prose and his style. He believed that national renaissance and vitality would come only with releasing the irrational creative spark and rejecting the restraint of traditional Judaism's intellectualism.

Bialik, Agnon, and the Modernist Era

Modern consciousness burst into Hebrew literature in the 1890s through Berdyczewski's fiction and Hayyim Nahman Bialik's verse. Writers began experimenting with modernist techniques. With Bialik, for the first time in Hebrew literature, the "I" of the individual became the central entity, and poetry became the arena of the self. Bialik's verse, like that of the Bible, is both a powerful lyrical expression and a rich essence of the Jewish culture that produced it. From 1892 to 1917, Bialik was dedicated to the idea of national revival. He searched for a meaningful Jewish identity while anguished by a loss of faith.

Saul Tchernichovsky expanded the horizons of Hebrew poetry through his admiration of Hellenic beauty and mastery of classical form. Like Berdyczewski, he broke the constricting bounds of Hebrew literature and the Jewish framework and aspired to express the totality of existence.

Many of the writers of this period started in Europe and continued in Ottoman-ruled Eretz Yisrael, or Palestine. Works of this second Aliyah period (1904–1914) were often dominated by questions of identity and by the pendulum of despair and hope reflecting the crisis of immigration. Yosef Hayyim Brenner's seemingly fragmented, unrefined prose reflects the tortured inner worlds of his intellectual, uprooted, antiheroes and their existential struggles. In his quest for truth and realism, he improvised a semblance of spoken Hebrew and slang. Uri Nissan Gnessin's novellas of alienation and uprootedness, written in a lyrical, figurative prose, are among the first stream-of-consciousness narratives in world literature.

But the towering figure of Hebrew fiction was Shmuel Yosef Agnon, the 1966 Nobel laureate. Zionist philosophy was only one component of Agnon's complex artistic and spiritual oeuvre, which merges Jewish sources with European traditions. Agnon tells the story of the Jews in the modern age: faith and heresy, exile and redemption, Holocaust, uprootedness and belonging. But the Jewish condition is also a reflection of the human condition: tragic fate; nightmarish, at times surrealistic existence; social disintegration; and loss of identity. Like Agnon, Hayyim Hazaz, the expressionist, wrote in a style different from the spoken language about Jewish life in Europe and Eretz Yisrael.

Shlonsky Era

At the heart of Hebrew literary activity at the time of the British mandate was poetry. With Bialik's

Famed Hebrew poet Avraham Shlonsky (1900–1973). Best known for his contributions to modern Hebrew poetry, Shlonsky is also credited with translating many classic works, including *Hamlet* and *King Lear*, into Hebrew. © PHOTOGRAPH BY ZOLTAN KLUGER. GOVERNMENT PRESS OFFICE (GPO) OF ISRAEL. REPRODUCED BY PERMISSION.

hegemony challenged in the 1920s, minor, deviant voices were heard: Rachel, whose lean, intimate diction, musical lyricism, and unfulfilled pioneer and personal dreams won her the public's unmatched love; Esther Raab, the poetically untamed individualist; David Vogel, the lyrical minimalist; and Avraham Ben Yizhak.

The most vocal revolutionary was Avraham Shlonsky, the editor of *Ktubim* and later *Turim*. Classicist style, layered language, and nationalist preoccupations were overthrown by Russian and French symbolism and postsymbolism, futurism, and German neoromanticism and expressionism as modernism swept through Hebrew verse. Shlonsky's symbolist poetics, subconsciously motivated images and *melos* (tune) abound with intellectual insight. With linguistic virtuosity, he articulated his war-weary generation's despair, exposing urban alienation or describing, like his fellow pioneers Isaac Lamdan, Rachel, and Uri Zvi Greenberg, the struggle and infatuation with a new landscape.

In Shlonsky's close leftist circle were Natan Alterman and Leah Goldberg. Alterman's maiden collection, *Stars Outside* (1938), nourished more than a generation of poets with its captivating rhythms, carnivalesque imagist world, and oxymoronic metaphors. He later wrote engaged poetry but strictly separated his lyrical and public verse. An unofficial national spokesman, Alterman wrote a column in the labor daily *Davar* in which he took active part in the struggle for independence and for Jewish immigration against British rule. Goldberg refused to write ideological poetry. Well versed in world literature, she often used complex traditional forms to create her own modernist verse.

In his poetics of form, Yonatan Ratosh favored Shlonsky's school, but ideologically he belonged to Vladimir Zeʾev Jabotinsky's nationalist camp. Believing in a shared cultural heritage for the entire Middle East, Ratosh founded the Canaanite movement and created idiosyncratic verse suffused with prebiblical mythology and vocabulary.

Expressionism shone through the poetry of Greenberg, the ultranationalist who prophesied the Holocaust and Jewish sovereignty. Drawing from personal and national landscapes and vocabularies, his Whitman-like verse captures raw feeling and pain, messianic and historical visions.

Dor Ba-Arez

While European Jewry was approaching its demise, the first generation of native Hebrew speakers was coming of age in Eretz Yisrael. Its writers, nicknamed Dor Ba-Arez (A Generation in the Land), made their debut in 1938 with a story by S. Yizhar. They were associated with Zionist socialism and its aspirations, and their realist-positivist works reflect the collective experiences of the new Jew: kibbutz, youth movement, Haganah, and the War of Independence in 1948. The individual character and inner turmoil and the shadow side of society are often neglected or suppressed in short stories and novels by Nathan Shaham, Aharon Meged, Moshe Shamin, and Yigal Mossinsohn. But their readers, awed with heroism and struck by the idea of national re-

demption, received them warmly. Yizhar's introspective, lyrical prose is distinguished in its depiction of mood and contemplation, its renditions of sensory impressions and landscape, and its narrator's wartime ethics and empathy for the Arabs.

Poets of the time, such as Haim Guri, Ayin Hillel, and Nathan Yonathan, expressed an intimate, physical attachment to their local space. They adopted Alterman's poetics, and the values landed in his poems—loyalty, friendship, and the eternal bond between the dead and the living—helped them integrate the traumas of the 1948 battles. Poems from Guri's *Flowers of Fire* became sacred texts, read alongside Alterman's in memorials for the fallen in war. Somewhat different from this generation's unified voice were Abba Kovner and Amir Gilboa who lamented their destroyed European homes.

With the establishment of the state and the waves of immigrants changing the land's character, some writers wrestled with their disillusion through historical novels with reference to present discontent. Others, like Benyamin Tammuz and David Schachar, nostalgically depicted childhood and bygone days.

Generation of the State poets of the 1950s and 1960s unbridled the nationalist agenda's long hold on Hebrew literature. Free, ironic poetics, influenced by modernist English, American, and German works usurped symbolist poetics and nationalist norms. This group believed that poetry ought to focus on the individual's experience not the collective; it rejected pathos and transcendentalism in favor of the concrete and existential and lowered the diction in favor of everyday discourse and freer form. Natan Zach, the spokesman of this school, attacked Alterman and his disciples and foregrounded previously marginalized poets like Vogel and the American Hebrew imagist Gabriel Preil. With poetic genius and originality, Zach's critically acclaimed free verse realized the new principles. Yet, his friend Yehuda Amichai's poetry was more easily accepted, due in part to Amichai's ability to merge poetic and linguistic traditions. Amichai's antiwar lines such as "I want to die in my bed" expressed this generation's yearnings, while his conceitlike metaphors and whimsical combinations of colloquial and classical Hebrew revolutionized Hebrew verse. David Avidan's linguistic inventiveness was at the forefront of this school. Dan Pagis, who survived a concentration camp, conveyed a sense of horror in his enigmatic verse. Dahlia Ravikovitch delved into the psyche's depths. Her intense, at times desperate, verse elegantly reintroduced archaisms and myths to the poetry without surrendering spoken language and syntax.

Fiction of the 1950s and 1960s followed poetry's lead in its challenge to Zionist prescriptions. It focused on the individual's psychological world or on universal, existential themes. The confessional, erotic novel *Life as a Fable* (1958) by Pinhas Sadeh reflected the turn inward and away from realism. Early stories by Amos Oz and Avraham B. Yehoshua are metaphorical and allegorical. Amichai's surrealist novel, *Not of This Time, Not of This Place,* uncovers suppressed wishes for an alternative existence. Amalia Kahana-Carmon's works explore life's mysteries and delve into intense, personal analysis reminiscent of Virginia Woolf. Aharon Appelfeld's characters wander through inner and outer nightmares of the Holocaust.

Post–1973 Era

After the Arab–Israel War of 1973, the myth of the new Jew was shattered. Hebrew literature's role as the arena for examining the national state of affairs was partly reinstated: Collective tensions were again realized through individual destinies. Post-1973 literature depicts the Israeli condition in relation to changes in social values, the Arabs, immigration and absorption, Jewish roots, the Diaspora, and the Holocaust. Questions of Jewish and Israeli existence occupy late works of veteran 1948 authors, but also others. The Generation of the State abandoned its abstract, schematic universalism and returned to concrete Israeli life, understanding symbolic layers of its texts. Yehoshua's late family novels, for example, are rich with realistic detail and make original and unpopular political, national, and historical philosophical statements. Oz lowered his diction and substituted fantasy with realistic, semiautobiographical works. The renewed interest in the tangible brought late blooming to Yizhak Ben Ner, Yeshayahu Koren, Yehudit Hendel, Shulamit Hareven, Yaacov Shabtai, and Yehoshua Kenaz. Shabtai painstakingly forges the decline of his pioneer parents' Tel Aviv milieu. His *Past Continuous* follows the protagonist's stream of associations in a style unprecedented in Hebrew literature. Kenaz's

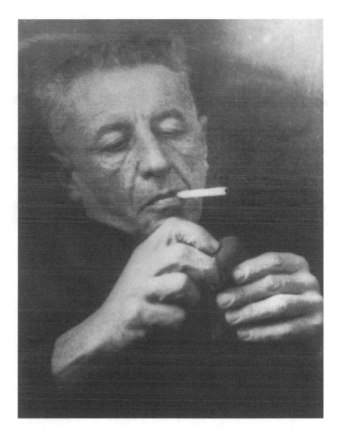

Natan Alterman (1910–1970), an Israeli writer known for his poetry lamenting the themes of life and independence, won the Israel Prize in 1968. Because of his Jewish nationalistic views, some of his early writings were seen as contentious and were censored by the British colonizers of Palestine. Aside from his poetry, he has also written both children's books and journalistic contributions. © PHOTOGRAPH BY MOSHE MILNER. GOVERNMENT PRESS OFFICE (GPO) OF ISRAEL. REPRODUCED BY PERMISSION.

patient, almost painful realism depicts social and psychological states with authenticity and linguistic mastery. Longing for a declining Eretz Yisrael translates into a bittersweet return to childhood for Ben Ner, Shabtai, and Meir Shalev. Others, like Kenaz, Ruth Almog, and David Grossman, look back with anger. In many of their works, however, the pained personal story is loaded with social and national meaning.

The many writers active in the 1970s and 1980s belong, then, to a number of literary generations. But despite the supposed centrality of male-authored works wrestling with the Zionist undertaking and all its reverberations, subversive narratives crystallized. Although only a few novels and short stories by women had been published previously, in the 1980s there was a proliferation of woman authors. Kahana-Carmon argued that mainstream Hebrew literature, an offspring of synagogue culture, indoctrinated Jewish readers to expect a male national spokesman, while intimate matters of the soul were relegated to the women's gallery of the synagogue, or rather the margins of literature. Dvora Baron was the only woman whose prose won critical acclaim before the 1950s. Hendel, Hareven, Naomi Frenkel, Rachel Eytan, Kahana-Carmon, and later Almog broke through in the interim. But the female voice, often undermining conventional conceptions of women and family institutions, conquered a well-deserved place only in the 1980s.

Prose fiction of the late 1980s and early 1990s was characterized by postmodernist pluralism. Opposing styles coexisted: conventional artistic measures; buds of religious or mystical writing; self-referential experiments with genre, language, theme, and typography. Orli Castel-Bloom's stories and novels shatter myth, reality, and text with lean language as she undermines any existence of truth. Yuval Shimoni internalized fiction and the connections between signifier and signified, while Yoel Hoffman's unpaged works in numbered paragraphs, surrounded by empty spaces or miniature pictures, are dotted with German, translated in the margins. He blends Far Eastern with Western philosophy and blurs the boundaries between languages, sexes, the self, and the universe.

Unlike prose, poetry opened itself to a wide prism of possibilities in the 1970s, but its public role was diminished. In the spirit of poststructuralism, this generation of poets had no use for common poetics. Yair Hurvitz wrote romantic symbolist verse, with high diction, and strove to unite opposites. Meir Wieseltier's modernist poetry is biting, almost vulgar, with social, political, and existential emphases. Yona Wallach smashed all borders of psyche and language, theme and form. Her poetry "unravels the unconscious like a fan" and allows words to flow without social, cultural, or literary inhibitions or taboos. Older poets who became central were Zelda and Avoth Yeshurun, whose poetry dismembers reality. Aharon Shabtai created a personal mythology drawn from Greek classics. In her "Data Processing" series, Maya Bejerano drowns chaos in a psychic, rhythmical associative stream.

The war in Lebanon and the Intifada in the late 1980s led to a reawakened interest in political and protest poems. Various contemporary issues—including erotic and homosexual themes, and imagery drawn from the modern media—came to prominence in the 1990s.

See also AGNON, SHMUEL YOSEF; AHAD HA-AM; ALTERMAN, NATAN; AMICHAI, YEHUDA; APPELFELD, AHARON; BARON, DVORA; BEJERANO, MAYA; BIALIK, HAYYIM NAHMAN; BRENNER, YOSEF HAYYIM; FRISCHMANN, DAVID; GOLDBERG, LEAH; GREENBERG, URI ZVI; GURI, CHAIM; HAREVEN, SHULAMIT; HASKALAH; HAZAZ, HAYYIM; HOFFMAN, YOEL; JABOTINSKY, VLADIMIR ZE'EV; KENAZ, YEHOSHUA; KOVNER, ABBA; MEGED, AHARON; OZ, AMOS; PAGIS, DAN; RAAB, ESTHER; RATOSH, YONATAN; SHLONSKY, AVRAHAM; TAMMUZ, BENYAMIN; TCHERNICHOVSKY, SAUL; WALLACH, YONA; YEHOSHUA, AVRAHAM B.; YIZHAR, S.; ZACH, NATAN.

Bibliography

Alter, Robert. *Hebrew and Modernity.* Bloomington: Indiana University Press, 1994.

Cohen, Joseph. *Voices of Israel: Essays on and Interviews with Yehuda Amichai, A. B. Yehoshua, T. Carmi, Aharon Appelfeld, and Amos Oz.* Albany: State University of New York Press, 1990.

Fuchs, Esther. *Encounters with Israeli Authors.* Marblehead, MA: Micah, 1982.

On Jerusalem: Selections in Prose and Verse. Jerusalem, 1979.

Wirth-Nesher, Hana. *What Is Jewish Literature?* Philadelphia: Jewish Publication Society, 1994.

Yudkin, Leon I. *Escape into Siege: A Survey of Israeli Literature Today.* London and Boston: Routledge and K. Paul, 1974.

NILI GOLD

LITERATURE: PERSIAN

Since the Iranian Revolution, Persian literature has become more and more relevant to contemporary politics, society, and day-to-day living.

The first nine centuries of imaginative literature in the Persian language constituted an aesthetically rich tradition. Modern Persian literature emerged at the beginning of the twentieth century and arguably has constituted an equally exciting chapter in the development of the Persian literary tradition. Modern imaginative literature emerged from a history of court patronage, Sufi brotherhoods, and Twelver Shiʿite environs to address a general Iranian audience. Iranian writers began to comprise a new class of intellectuals, independent of crown or turban.

Prose

Prose developed more quickly than verse during the twentieth century, starting with journalistic writing by leaders of the Constitutional Revolution, such as that by Ali Akbar Dehkhoda (1879–1956). In a preface to *Once upon a Time* (1922), the first collection of Persian short stories ever, Mohammad Ali Jamalzadeh argued that literature in straightforward, living prose was a key to education and enlightenment for Iranians. His six stories in that volume introduced realism, local color, and popular language into one genre of Persian writing.

During the 1920s, Nima Yushij (1895–1960) began experimenting with traditional forms and content in Persian poetry. He experimented with individuating the lyric speaker and eschewed didactic intent; his quatrain sequence poem "Legend" (1922) and other poems in the 1920s heralded the new sensibility.

The 1930s marked the first age of the preeminence of prose in Persian literature, a situation that held true to the end of the century. Sadegh Hedayat (1903–1951) played the chief role in this development. His four collections of short stories from 1930 to 1942 and his enigmatic, surrealistic novella, *The Blind Owl* (1937, 1941), demonstrated how a new Persian literary language could create atmosphere and voice surrealism.

The Short Story and the Novel

The Iranian short story grew to maturity in the 1940s and thereafter. During the period beginning with the 1941 Allied occupation of Iran and the abdication and exile of Reza Shah Pahlavi (r. 1925–1941) and ending with the American-orchestrated coup d'état that brought down the short-lived government of Mohammad Mossadegh (1882–1967) in August 1953, no government censorship interfered with or controlled literary expression. However, beginning in 1885, when Naser al-Din Shah Qajar (r. 1848–1896) established an office of censorship, and throughout most of the twentieth century, Persian literary artists labored under the constraints of censorship. There were exceptions: the first two years of the constitution (1906–1908); the so-called "Twelve Years of Freedom" (1941–1953); and the revolution years (1977–1979). This has meant that, except during the period from 1941 to 1953 period, Iranian prose fiction, lyric verse, and drama have had to resort to indirection and symbolism when dealing critically with the Iranian present.

During the 1940s, Sadeq Chubak (1916–1995), Ebrahim Golestan (1922–), Jalal Al-e Ahmad (1923–1969), and others joined Hedayat and Bozorg Alavi (1904–), who had published his first collection of short stories in 1934, providing Iranian audiences with fiction written in various styles, including realist, naturalist, and social realist, paving the way for later generations of short-story writers who contributed to magazines and collections of stories to the end of the century. Chief among them was the prolific Gholamhossein Saʿedi (1935–1985).

During the 1950s the Iranian novel likewise gained a foothold and led to mature works in the 1960s and after. Alavi's *Her Eyes* (1952), Behʿazin's *The Serf's Daughter* (1952), and Al-e Ahmad's *The School Principal* (1958) dealt critically with the Reza Shah Pahlavi and early Mohammad Reza Pahlavi eras.

From the 1960s on, Iranian novels became central to Iranian literary life. Chubak published *Tangsir* (1963) and *The Patient Stone* (1966). Houshang Golshiri (1937–2000) published *Prince Ehtejab* (1969), with a stream-of-consciousness narration and a condemnation of monarchy and aristocracy, which some critics think is Iran's best novel. In 1969, Simin Daneshvar (1921–), who in 1948 became the first Iranian woman to publish a collection of short stories with the *The Extinguished Fire*, published *Savushun* (The mourners of Siyavosh), which became Iran's best-selling novel of all time, reportedly selling more than 150,000 copies by the 1990s.

Poetry

The 1940s and 1950s also witnessed the blossoming of new or modernist Persian verse. Nima began publishing verse again in 1938, and his experiments and achievements with untraditional verse forms attracted the attention of Ahmad Shamlu (1925–), Mehdi Akhavan-Saless (1928–1990), and other major figures in the next generation of modernist poets. In response, traditionalists maintained their devotion to classical forms, diction, and didacticism, but used them to write about contemporary issues. Conservative readers still outnumbered those receptive to modernist verse; they pointed to the achievements of traditional poets Mohammad Taqi Bahar (1886–1955) and Parvin E'tesami (1907–1941), or accepted the moderate modernism of Faridun Tavallali (1919–1985) and others who maintained quatrain sequence forms and traditional imagery and figures of speech while hinting at modern issues. By the 1970s, however, the traditionalists were in retreat or in the minority, although the debate over traditionalism and change in Persian poetry remains alive in Iranian literary circles.

In the 1950s and 1960s, modernist Persian poetry achieved great things. Shamlu approached free verse in forceful works supporting his causes. Akhavan-Saless breathed fresh air into traditional meters, using Iranian myths and history as texture for his poetry. From the mid-1950s to the end of 1966, Forugh Farrokhzad (c. 1934–1967) added a dimension and voice to modern Persian poetry that Persian literature previously had lacked: a female speaker and female concerns. Her verse, dealing with a lyric speaker's growth and concerns as an individual, as a poet, and as a woman, represents a culmination of Nima's modernism. Another trend appears in the poetry of Sohrab Sepehri (1928–1980), that of the nature poet with, in his case, neo-Sufic or pantheistic implications.

By the mid-1970s, modernist Persian poetry had come to a standstill. Although a new generation of poets had begun to publish and modernist poetry was produced in abundance into the 2000s, no new poets joined the highest ranks or fully replaced the earlier poets. Nader Naderpur (1929–), a popular poet from the mid-1950s and the most prominent moderate modernist, crossed the moderate line in the 1980s after opting for self-exile in Paris and then Los Angeles. Voicing the alienation and anger of Iranians abroad who opposed the Islamic Republic, Naderpur's characterizations of life in Iran of the 1980s and 1990s, and of the Iranian exile's lack of integration in the life of the West, strike familiar chords for many Iranians. Another poet in exile, Esma'il Kho'i (1938–), who had been an almost first-rank modernist before the revolution, seemed to gain poetic timbre through his suffering in exile in London.

Censorship and Writers Abroad

Circumstances and censorship during the Pahlavi era muted or silenced literary voices. During the first two decades of the Islamic Republic, establishment pressure and censorship seemed designed merely to coerce writers to avoid sexual imagery and direct questioning of Islam but not to silence them. In consequence, and also because of a decrease in other entertainment after the revolution and an increase in the reading public due to a mass literacy campaign in the early 1980s, Persian literary activity, especially in prose fiction, became a profession for self-employed writers for the first time in Iranian history. Novelists, short-story writers, and some essayists became able to support themselves through writing as of the 1980s. Moreover, Iranian novels began to compete for readership for the first time with Western novels in translation.

Among landmark works in Iranian prose fiction after the revolution are: Esma'il Fasih's *Sorayya in a Coma* (1984), Shahnush Parsipur's *Tuba and the Meaning of Night* (1989) and *Women without Men* (1990), and Reza Baraheni's *Song of the Slain* (1983) and *Secrets of My Land* (1987). With their negative depictions of Iranian SAVAK (secret police) and American intelligence and military figures, Baraheni's fictions signal a post-Pahlavi literary trend denouncing life under the U.S.-supported Pahlavi regime. Fiction that presented similarly negative depictions of life under the Islamic Republic, such as Golshiri's *King of the Benighted* (1990), were banned in Iran, although in the case of Golshiri, manuscripts of his explicitly critical novels and short stories were smuggled out of the country and published in Europe and the United States.

One novel stands by itself: Mahmoud Dowlatabadi's *Klidar* (1983), a tragic saga of mid-twentieth century tribal and village life in 3,700 pages, which brought its author recognition as the leading writer of fiction in the Islamic Republic period. Just as Ali Mohammad Afghani's *Ahu Khanom's Husband* (1961) earlier had encouraged Iranians to think that the Persian language had the resources to serve as the vehicle for any sort or length of prose fiction, Dowlatabadi's *Klidar*—the title refers to a Kurdish village area in Khorasan—convinced readers of the richness of the everyday rural Iranian experience and of descriptive Persian prose, even though Dowlatabadi attempts nothing experimental in his story.

Of all pre-revolution genres, Iranian drama suffered most in the 1980s. Although it was still a new medium in the late Pahlavi period, or a medium to which few Iranians had direct exposure, it had grown by leaps and bounds, with the prolific Sa'edi the best-known playwright. Stage dramas been had turned into television dramas and became screenplays for the New Wave cinema of the 1970s, as had several important short stories and novels. By the mid-1980s Iranian cinema was thriving again, but without the plots, themes, and texture that romantic love stories and women in anything other than traditional Islamic garb would provide. Iranian stage drama began to regain status in the 1990s, with the government supporting theaters in provincial cities. Persian drama also flourished in the West, where local Iranian communities in major cities enthusiastically supported touring companies. Prominent among them was that of Parviz Sayyad in Los Angeles. Through the 1980s, Sayyad staged plays featuring his earlier folk character Samad, who first went to the Iran–Iraq war and then came back from the front. Another play presented an imaginary trial stemming from the 1978 torching of Abadan's Rex Cinema, which killed hundreds of patrons who were locked inside. Sayyad's one-man show in the early 1990s, presenting himself and Samad in witty conversation, one on video and the other live, provided sophisticated, culture-specific entertainment and introspection into the nature of modern Iranian artistic expression.

The Persian literary essay survived the revolution, both at home and abroad. Originally Western in inspiration, it is socially and politically involved. It came of age in the first four decades of the twentieth century. Writers exhibited signature styles and concerns that were a far cry from those at the beginning of the century, when a florid, Arabic-laden style and a rhetorical eye to the past prevailed.

Shahrokh Meskoob's conversational style in *Iranian Nationality and the Persian Language* (1981) and Al-e Ahmad's brusque and sometimes angry voice in *West-struckness* (1962, 1964), *Lost in the Crowd* (1966), and *A Stone on a Grave* (1964, not published until 1981) are more recent examples.

See also AKHAVAN-SALESS, MEHDI; ALAVI, BOZORG; BAHAR, MOHAMMAD TAQI; BARAHENI, REZA; CHUBAK, SADEQ; CONSTITUTIONAL REVOLUTION; DANESHVAR, SIMIN; DEHKHODA, ALI AKBAR; DOWLATABADI, MAHMOUD; FARROKHZAD, FORUGH; GOLESTAN, EBRAHIM; GOLSHIRI, HOUSHANG; HEDAYAT, SADEGH; JAMALZADEH, MOHAMMAD ALI; MOSSADEGH, MOHAMMAD; NASER al-DIN SHAH; PAHLAVI, MOHAMMAD REZA; PAHLAVI, REZA; PARSIPUR, SHAHRNUSH; SEPEHRI, SOHRAB; SHAMLU, AHMAD.

Bibliography

Ghanoonparvar, M. R., and Green, John, eds. *Iranian Drama: An Anthology.* Costa Mesa, CA: Mazdâ, 1989.

Javadi, Hasan. *Satire in Persian Literature.* Rutherford, NJ: Fairleigh Dickinson University Press, 1988.

Karimi-Hakkak, Ahmad, ed. *An Anthology of Modern Persian Poetry.* Boulder, CO: Westview, 1978.

Moayyad, Heshmat, ed. *Stories from Iran: A Chicago Anthology 1921–1991.* Washington, DC: Mage Publishers, 1991.

Southgate, Minoo S., ed. and trans. *Modern Persian Short Stories.* Washington, DC: Three Continents Press, 1980.

Sullivan, Soraya Paknazar, ed. and trans. *Stories by Iranian Women since the Revolution.* Austin: University of Texas at Austin, 1991.

Yavari, Houra, et al. "Fiction." In *Encyclopedia Iranica*, Vol. IX, edited by Ehsan Yarshater. New York: Bibliotheca Persica.

MICHAEL C. HILLMANN
UPDATED BY ERIC HOOGLUND

LITERATURE: TURKISH

National literature that began during the Tanzimat period of the Ottoman Empire.

Halide Edip Adivar, Nazim Hikmet, Sait Faik Abasiyanik, Fazil Hüsnü Dağlarca, Nüsret Aziz Nesin, Yaşar Kemal, and, more recently, Orhan Pamuk are writers whose works are known outside of Turkey.

Orhan Pamuk, one of Turkey's most famous novelists, at his home in Istanbul, December 1998. This photograph was taken just days before Pamuk rejected the title of "State Artist," one of Turkey's most coveted prizes, in protest against the country's restrictive policies on freedom of the press. © AFP/CORBIS. REPRODUCED BY PERMISSION.

As more translations appear—the latest is a postmodernist novel titled *Gece* (Night), by Bilge Karasu—an increasing number of works are being recognized as having universal appeal. The literature represented evolved in the second half of the nineteenth century with a group of writers who were members of the bureaucratic intelligentsia. Committed to the Tanzimat reforms, they sought to bring change to literature as well, making it a vehicle for influencing sociopolitical thinking and culture in general. At its inception, therefore, modern Turkish literature has set both didactic and aesthetic goals: to be an art form and source of enjoyment, but also to be engaged.

The pioneers of modernism—İbrahim Şinasi (1826–1871), Namik Kemal (1840–1888), and Ziya Paşa (1825–1880)—were familiar with European literatures and had lived in Europe. They witnessed the central role literature played there, a role lacking in Turkey, where two distinct literary traditions (elitist and popular) split society. The first, following Arab-Persian classical Islamic tradition and seeking artistic perfection rather than social reality, gave priority to poetry *(divan şiiri)*; was rigid in verse form, meter, and rhyme patterns, highly sophisticated in rhetoric and imagery; and employed language saturated with Arabic and Persian loanwords largely unintelligible to the masses. The second was based on Turkish folk traditions of form, content, and style in both poetry and prose, and linked the Turks to their Central Asian heritage. In general it was denigrated by the small, educated class. Religiously inspired works, many of them mystic, were important in both traditions.

In the 1860s the Şinasi-Namik Kemal-Ziya Paşa school took the first steps toward modernity. Through translation and adaptation (primarily from French), then original composition, they introduced Western-style poetry and fiction, and wrote the first Turkish plays designed for the modern stage. They also turned to journalism—the *Tasvir-i Efkar* (Description of ideas) was the principal forum for introducing their works—and accustomed readers to editorials, essays, and literary criticism propagating such concepts as fatherland, patriotism, nation, justice, freedom, and constitutional government. They did not completely reject the past, but gave old poetic forms new elements of content and style, using language more comprehensible to the expanding, middle-class reading public. This movement surged again under the republic, resulting in the romanization of the alphabet and measures to produce an *öz türkçe* (pure Turkish), both of which had a great effect on literature.

These writers lauded proreform statesmen and satirized traditionalists. They targeted social customs like arranged marriages and moralized against the harem system, marital infidelity, prostitution, and inhuman treatment of slaves. Namik Kemal's play *Vatan yahut Silistre* (Fatherland or Silistria, 1873) caused antiregime demonstrations, and he spent many years in exile as a result. He and his colleagues put reform before creative art, and in articles and prefaces to their works stressed the didactic and social role of literature. Abdülhak Hamit Tarhan (1852–1939) and Recaizade Mahmud Ekrem (1847–1914), in contrast, showed increasing concern with aesthetics. Ekrem, a teacher, published his lectures, which displayed his knowledge of Western literature and concern for liberating Ottoman poetic style, and was led into a literary battle with Muallim Naci, represented (somewhat unjustly) as the prime defender of the old style. Ekrem also influenced the literary school that flourished in the 1890s, the Edebiyat-i Cedide (New Literature) or Servet-i Fünun (Wealth of Sciences), the latter the title of the journal serving as its main platform. Its leading poets, Tevfik Fikret (1867–1916) and Cenap Sehabettin (1870–1934), spoke lyrically of love and nature in a Turkish inspired by the language of the *divan* poets. Fikret also wrote very provocative antiregime poems.

In fiction, building on the pioneer efforts of Ahmet (1844–1912), the leading prose writer, Halit Ziya Uşhakliğil (1866–1945), brought to his novels a more developed literary realism and psychological analysis. His two collections of prose poems show an inclination for artistry that set a trend followed by his contemporary Mehmet Rauf (1875–1931), and still finds the occasional follower today.

Although the 1908 constitutional period brought hope to writers after the repressive control of Abdülhamit II, further Ottoman decline and Europe's antagonism engendered permission and anti-Western outbursts among writers of the Fecr-i Ati (Dawn of the Future) group that formed in 1909. Meanwhile, a current of Nationalism gained strength, poets such as Mehmet Emin Yurdakul (1869–1944) proclaiming pride in being a Turk and turning to the folk tradition for verse form, meter, and language. The presence in the empire of émigré Turks from Russia fanned consciousness of belonging to a wider "Turanian" nation, and groups of scholars and writers, including Yusuf Akçuroğlu (1876–1935), Mehmet Fuat Köprülü (1890–1966), and Ziya Gökalp (1876–1924), promoted study of the early history and culture of the Turks. The most important group was Genç Kalemler (Young Pens), formed in 1910, which stressed language reform. Despite strong romanticism, the short stories of its leader, Ömer Seyfettin, represent a breakthrough in the strongest in modern Turkish literature.

World War I and the War of Independence, culminating in the demise of the Ottoman Empire and the founding of the Turkish Republic, presented writers with a fresh panorama of people, places, and events to observe and depict, even greater possibilities for artistic choice through emphasis on Westernization, and an ever-increasing array of readers. Novelists of the older generation, such as Halide Edip Adivar (1884–1964), the first important activist woman writer; Yakup Kadri Karaosmanoğlu (1889–1974) and Reşat Nuri Güntekin (1889–1956), represent an important advance in both narrative and character analysis, their works depicting the weaknesses of late Ottoman society, the inner conflicts of its people, the surge of patriotism during the War of Independence, and the new roles of women.

In poetry, three prominent poets adhered to the classical meter and verse form: Yahya Kemal Beyath (1884–1958), a neoclassicist who expressed his nationalism by nostalgically recalling Ottoman splendors; Ahmet Haşim (1885–1933), a symbolist steadfast in an art for art's sake approach, painting dreamlike vignettes of nature in its most tranquil moments; and Mehmet Akif Ersoy (1873–1936), who, although also choosing the classical traditions, wrote in a language very close to prose and spoken Turkish.

Of the many ideologies to which the Turks were exposed from the early days of the Republic, communism captivated Nazim Hikmet (1902–1963), the major poet of the century. Having been imprisoned for many years, he fled Turkey in 1951 and spent his remaining years behind the Iron Curtain. He fashioned Turkish free verse, and his works (prison poetry, love lyrics, social or political declamation, long narrative verse) display a striking fluidity of language and a new depth of human understanding. Only Fazil Hüsnü Dağlarca (b. 1914), with the breadth of his aesthetic view and intellectual delving into the metaphysical, approaches his stature.

Of prime importance has been the development of realist village literature. Urban-born nineteenth-century and early-twentieth-century writers seldom focused on Anatolia and its rural population. With the center of government moved to Anatolia, and especially after the introduction of a two-party system, the villager became a focus of attention for fiction writers, who now included those born in villages or closely familar with village life. Yaşar Kemal writes of the plight of the peasants in the Taurus Mountains and Çukurova Plain. Other writers have followed the villagers in their migration to country towns or big cities. In recent years an increasing number of works have drawn attention to the problems facing Turks who have migrated to Germany and other European countries since the late 1960s. Among other writers who depict the "little man" with deep understanding are Nüsret Aziz Nesin (b. 1915) and Sait Faik Abasiyanik, who has over 100 short stories set in Istanbul, nearly half of them on the island of Burgaz, revealing the life of the fisherfolk on the Sea of Marmara.

Poets also turned to the "common man." In 1941, Ornan Veli (1914–1950), Oktay Rifat (1914–1988), and Melih Cevdet Anday (b. 1915) published a collection of poems, *Garip* (Strange), calling for poetic realism untrammeled by rules and dictates, unadorned and in colloquial speech, concerned with and attempting to communicate with the man in the street. In the mid-1950s Anday joined the Second New Movement, a group including Ilhan Berk (b. 1916), Cemal Süreya (1931–1990), and Edip Cansever (1928–1986), who turned to obscurantism, writing poetry that was abstract and abtruse, in some cases almost totally incomprehensible.

Women were rarely mentioned among the writers of the Ottoman Empire before the nineteenth century. Their number increased after the Tanzimat, when a new generation of well-educated women emerged who understood French and were familiar with the works of both the French Romantics and the new Ottoman writers. Best known is Fatma Aliye Hanim (1862–1936), elder daughter of Ahmed Cevdet Paşa. The first Turkish woman novelist, her publications also included translations of French, articles, works on history, and a newspaper for women. Halide Edip Adivar served as a model for women from the early days of the Republic, both as a writer and as an activist. Women have turned to fiction rather than poetry. Güiten Akin (b. 1933), for example, a poet who has won many awards, is the only women represented in *The Penguin Book of Turkish Verse*. In contrast, the surge of enthusiasm for the short story in the 1970s, the Füruzan phenomenon, is credited to the stories published by Füruzan (Selçuk; b. 1935), a young writer of village background who deals especially with the exploitation of villagers in the cities.

In the 1990s women continue to participate fully on the Turkish literary scene. Both male and female writers continue to explore the wealth of their heritage and new avenues of expression.

See also ABASIYANIK, SAIT SAIK; ADIVAR, HALIDE EDIP; DAĞLARCA, FAZIL HÜSNÜ; ERSOY, MEHMET AKIF; GÖKALP, ZIYA; KOPRÜLÜ, MEHMET FUAT; NAMIK KEMAL; NESIN, NÜSRET AZIZ; RECAIZADE MAHMUD EKREM; ŞINASI, İBRAHIM; TEVFIK FIKRET; UŞAKLIĞIL, HALIT ZIYA; YURDAKUL, MEHMET EMIN.

Bibliography

Evin, Ahmet Ö. *Origins and Development of the Turkish Novel.* Minneapolis, MN: Bibliotheca Islamica, 1983.

Halman, Talat Said. *Contemporary Turkish Literature: Fiction and Poetry.* Rutherford, NJ: Fairleigh Dickinson University Press, 1982.

Halman, Talat Said. "Turkish Literature: Modes of Modernity." *Literature East and West* 17, no. 1 (March 1973).

Halman, Talat Said, ed. *Modern Turkish Drama.* Minneapolis, MN: Bibliotheca Islamica, 1976.

Menemencioğlu, Nermin, and İz, Fahir, eds. *The Penguin Book of Turkish Verse.* New York: Penguin, 1978.

Rathburn, Carole. *The Village in the Turkish Novel and Short Story, 1920–1950.* The Hague: Mouton, 1972.

Reddy, Nilüfer Mizanoğlu, trans. *Twenty Stories by Turkish Women Writers.* Bloomington: Indiana University Press, 1988.

KATHLEEN R. F. BURRILL

LIVNAT, LIMOR
[1950–]

Israeli politician and government minister.

Born in Haifa, and after graduating from high school, Limor Livnat served in the Israeli army's 7th Armoured Brigade as an education and welfare sergeant. Later she studied Hebrew literature at Tel Aviv University. During her student days she became active in Likud student politics and was also involved in women's rights as a member of the Women's Lobby. Her views accorded with the hawkish side of Likud. Livnat vehemently opposed the Oslo Peace Process and campaigned for the rights of Jews to live anywhere in the State of Israel. She also consistently opposed the establishment of a Palestinian state and later the Road Map, a three-part phased peace plan presented to Israel and the Palestinian Authority in March 2003 by the Quartet (United States, United Nations, European Union, and Russia) that calls for a two-state solution, or a Palestinian state alongside Israel.

First elected to the Knesset in 1992, she attracted attention by diligence, quick grasp of issues, and close attention to detail. In the 1996 elections she headed the Likud's Information Office and actively supported the candidacy of Benjamin Netanyahu. He rewarded her with the post of communications minister in his cabinet (1996–1999). Livnat was responsible for the growing communications market in Israel, supervising the licensing of cable television channels, and administering the Broadcasting Law. Between 1999 and 2001 she served on the Knesset's Education and Culture Committee and the Committee for the Advancement of Women. In 2001 Prime Minister Ariel Sharon appointed her as minister of education, and reappointed her two years later. In this post she paid special attention to educational programs instilling nationalist values and Jewish themes, arguing that Israeli school children were not sufficiently exposed to Jewish history and heritage.

See also ISRAEL: POLITICAL PARTIES IN; KNESSET.

Bibliography

Livnat, Limor. *Straight to the Point!: The Leading Woman in Israeli Politics Speaks Her Mind.* Jerusalem, Israel, and New York: Gefen Publishing House, 1999.

MERON MEDZINI

LIWA

See GLOSSARY

LIWA, AL-

See NEWSPAPERS AND PRINT MEDIA: ARAB COUNTRIES

LLOYD GEORGE, DAVID
[1863–1945]

British statesman; prime minister of Great Britain during World War I.

Of Welsh ancestry, David Lloyd George, first earl of Dwyfor, was born in Manchester, England, and became a solicitor. He was a Liberal member of parliament from 1890, and during World War I served as minister of munitions (1915–1916) and secretary of state for war (1916). In December 1916 he replaced H. H. Asquith as prime minister. As head of a coalition government from 1916 to 1922, he directed Britain's war policies to victory in 1918 and played a leading role in the peace settlements.

Lloyd George's governments made a number of fateful decisions regarding the Middle East. The most momentous was the Balfour Declaration (November 1917), which promised British support for a Jewish national home in Palestine. Lloyd George strongly supported Zionism; he later said that his intention had been to lay the foundation for a future Jewish state. In December 1917 British troops entered Jerusalem—this was Lloyd George's "Christmas present to the British nation." His government issued a number of statements designed to reassure Arab nationalists, France, and others apprehensive about British intentions in Palestine. But as he put it: "We shall be there by conquest and shall remain, we being of no particular faith and the only Power fit to rule Mohammedans, Jews, Roman Catholics, and all religions."

At the 1919 Paris peace conference he secured agreement on a partition of the former Ottoman territories of the central Middle East between Britain and France. France was to be granted mandates over Syria and Lebanon, Britain over Mesopotamia (henceforth known as Iraq) and Palestine (subsequently expanded to include Transjordan). In Palestine Lloyd George appointed Sir Herbert Samuel as the first high commissioner, charged with implementing the Balfour Declaration. He also approved the decision by Samuel, supported by the colonial secretary, Winston Churchill, to annex Transjordan to Palestine—without, however, extending the Jewish national home east of the Jordan. Following the French ouster in July 1920 of the amir Faisal from Damascus, where his supporters had declared him king of Syria, the British arranged for Faisal's accession to the throne of Iraq.

Lloyd George's downfall came as a result of his ill-judged support for Greece in its attempt to conquer western Anatolia. The military defeat of the Greeks by Mustafa Kemal (later Atatürk) doomed this effort. The Chanak crisis of October 1922, when British occupation forces in Constantinople were threatened by advancing Turkish troops, led the Conservative Party, on whom Lloyd George depended for his majority in the House of Commons, to withdraw their support. In the ensuing general election, he suffered a humiliating defeat. Lloyd George never held office again.

See also ATATÜRK, MUSTAFA KEMAL; BALFOUR DECLARATION (1917); CHURCHILL, WINSTON S.; PALESTINE; PARIS PEACE SETTLEMENTS (1918–1923); SAMUEL, HERBERT LOUIS; VERSAILLES, TREATY OF (1920).

Bibliography

Fromkin, David. *A Peace to End All Peace: The Fall of the Ottoman Empire and the Creation of the Modern Middle East.* New York: Avon Books, 1989.

Lloyd George, David. *War Memoirs.* Vol. 1, London: Odhams, 1933; Vol. 2, London: I. Nicholson and Watson, 1936.

BERNARD WASSERSTEIN

LOHAMEI HERUT YISRAEL

Zionist underground militia whose name translates as "fighters for the freedom of Israel," abbreviated as LEHI.

Lohamei Herut Yisrael, or LEHI, also known as the Stern Gang, was founded on 26 June 1940 by Abraham (Ya'ir) Stern in a split with the Irgun Zva'i Le'umi (IZL) over ideology and tactics. It would always remain small, ranging from 200 to 800 members. Stern and his followers viewed Britain as the foremost enemy of the Jewish people and of Zionism and rejected the Irgun's declared truce with Britain for the duration of the Second World War. LEHI's ideology was an evolving blend of fascist, Bolshevik, and messianic nationalist elements, which led the organization in its early years to see Nazi Germany and Fascist Italy, and later the Soviet Union, as potential allies in the "anti-imperialist" armed struggle against Britain.

In 1941 the group tried to reach an agreement with Nazi Germany in the hope of ousting Britain from Palestine. From 1940 to 1944, while the other Zionist underground groups, including the Irgun, were cooperating with Britain in the war effort,

LEHI carried out an anti-British campaign of propaganda and terror attacks, setting off bombs, killing soldiers and police officers, and robbing banks to fund their activities. On 9 January 1942, LEHI members accidentally killed two Jewish bystanders in an attempted robbery of a Histadrut bank in Tel Aviv. The Zionist leadership and the majority in the Yishuv opposed LEHI's methods; LEHI was widely regarded by both Jews and the British as a terrorist underground and was often ostracized and persecuted as such. In the early months of 1942, members of Haganah intelligence and the Palmah began kidnapping LEHI fighters, a policy that would continue on and off until the group's final demise in 1948.

Abraham Stern (1907–1942), a native of Poland, emigrated to Palestine in 1925, where he later joined the militant organization Irgun to fight for Jewish independence. He saw the British presence in Palestine to be more of a threat to Jewish nationalism than the Arabs. COURTESY OF THE JABOSTINSKY INSTITUTE IN ISRAEL.

LEHI entered a crisis period when Stern was killed by members of the British Criminal Investigation Division (CID) on 12 February 1942. By 1943 the organization had been reconstructed under the leadership of Natan Yellin-Mor, Israel Eldad, and Yitzhak Shamir. Ideologically, LEHI moved to the left after Stern's death, openly embracing the Soviet Union and class struggle in addition to anti-imperialism. It would always remain marginal ideologically but at various times would cooperate organizationally with the other underground groups. When the Irgun began its armed revolt against Britain in February 1944, LEHI joined in. In coordination with the Irgun, LEHI attacked or bombed British military and administrative sites in Palestine, including police and radio stations and CID headquarters.

On 6 November 1944, LEHI members assassinated Walter Edward Guinness, Lord Moyne, the senior British minister in Cairo. The assassination led the Yishuv leadership to initiate operations known as "the Saison" to liquidate the dissident underground organizations. In 1945 and 1946, LEHI was an active member of the Hebrew Resistance Movement, an ad hoc framework that coordinated anti-British operations among all the Jewish undergrounds. In April 1948 LEHI participated with the Irgun in the attack on the Arab village Dayr Yasin. On 17 September 1948 LEHI members assassinated the United Nations mediator, Count Folke Bernadotte, in Jerusalem. Following this incident David Ben-Gurion declared the organization illegal and it was forcibly dismantled. Its members established a political party, the Fighters Party, which won only one seat (and 1.22 percent of the vote) in the elections for the first Knesset in 1949.

LEHI members became divided along ideological lines, with Yellin-Mor taking a strong leftist position advocating class struggle, a pro-Soviet foreign policy, and support for proletarian movements in Arab countries. Eldad led the right-wing faction that embraced positions in line with Revisionist maximalism, while Shamir took a less ideological and more pragmatic stance. The split ultimately proved irreconcilable, and the Fighters Party did not survive to the second Knesset elections in 1951. Some members drifted to MAPAM or the Israeli Communist Party, while others joined Menachem Begin's Herut.

See also BERNADOTTE, FOLKE; DAYR YASIN; GUINNESS, WALTER EDWARD; IRGUN ZVA'I LE'UMI (IZL); SHAMIR, YITZHAK; STERN, ABRAHAM; YELLIN-MOR, NATAN.

Bibliography

Bell, J. Bowyer. *Terror out of Zion: The Fight for Israeli Independence.* New Brunswick, NJ: Transaction Publishers, 1996.

Heller, Joseph. *The Stern Gang: Ideology, Politics, and Terror, 1940–1949.* Portland, OR; London: Frank Cass, 1995.

Sofer, Sasson. *Zionism and the Foundations of Israeli Diplomacy,* translated by Dorothea Shefet-Vanson. New York and Cambridge, U.K.: Cambridge University Press, 1998.

PIERRE M. ATLAS

LOI CADRE

French legislative initiative (1957–1958) during Algerian war of independence (1954–1962).

Premier Maurice Bourgès-Maunoury staked his government's political life on the Loi Cadre, which attempted to resolve the contradiction of acknowledging Algeria's "personality" while keeping it integral to France. The French government charged Resident Minister Robert Lacoste with the task of drafting the document for administrative reform. Its provisions divided Algeria into eight to ten autonomous territories linked by a federal organ. The single electoral college increased Muslim political participation but also recognized ethnic interests (e.g., the Kabylia). The Loi Cadre aimed to sap the strength of Algerian nationalism. The *pieds-noirs* (European settlers in Algeria) viewed it suspiciously. The National Assembly repudiated the reform and Bourgès-Maunoury's ministry. Though a redrafted Loi Cadre eventually passed during Félix Gaillard's ministry, the extension of *pied-noir* power in the planned territorial assemblies impaired its reforming intent. When Charles de Gaulle came to power, his government discarded this initiative, though it supported the concept of a single electoral college before eventually pursuing an agonizing decolonization.

See also DE GAULLE, CHARLES; KABYLIA; LACOSTE, ROBERT.

Bibliography

Horne, Alistair. *A Savage War of Peace: Algeria, 1954–1962,* 2nd edition. New York: Penguin, 1987.

PHILLIP C. NAYLOR

LONDON CONFERENCE (1956)

Two conferences convened in August and September 1956 in London to handle the crisis triggered by President Nasser's nationalization of the Suez Canal Company.

In response to Egypt's nationalization of the Suez Canal Company in late July 1956, the United States, Britain, and France convened two conferences to which certain maritime states were invited to consider the proper reaction to the crisis. The first London Conference met from 18 to 23 August 1956. The invitation was sent to all states signatory to the 1888 Constantinople Convention, which regulated the administration and supervision of the Suez Canal, plus states that shipped considerable cargo through the Canal. Egypt declined to attend but the Soviet Union and the representative of India tried to represent the views and the rights of Egypt. During the conference Selwyn Lloyd, Britain's minister of foreign affairs, managed to induce eighteen states, including the United States, to sign a formal declaration demanding the establishment of a new international agency, representing the interests of the Canal users, to take over the administration of the Canal affairs.

The expected failure of a delegation, headed by Australian prime minister Robert Menzies, to convince Nasser to accept the London Conference decisions and the growing signs of an imminent Franco-British military operation moved John Foster Dulles, the U.S. secretary of state, to call for a second conference, which convened in London on 19 September. The eighteen states that had signed the first declaration adopted Dulles's proposal to establish a Suez Canal Users Association (SCUA), which was mandated to deal with matters of finance and administration of the Canal on a practical level and thus enforce the users' rights. But, as Anthony Eden later said, the new association was "stillborn." The new Egyptian management continued to operate the Canal successfully, leaving the SCUA unable to enforce its own agenda.

There was nothing illegal in Egypt's nationalization of the Suez Canal, but the British and French governments considered it a severe blow to their standing in the Middle East and North Africa. The London conferences were part of a larger campaign to mobilize international pressure to make Nasser revoke his action. As it later became clear, these two Western powers were less interested in annulment of the nationalization as in a clear rebuff to the Egyptian president and perhaps his ouster as leader of both Egypt and the Arab world. Indeed, even while they were drumming up international diplomatic support, their chiefs of staff were busy planning and preparing a military attack on Egypt, code-named "Musketeer." To a large degree the London conferences were little more than an attempt to go through the motions in order to prove that only a military response could solve the problem. Following a last-minute failed attempt by UN secretary-general Dag Hammarskjöld to mediate a compromise, the British and French, in collusion with Israel, decided to opt for a military solution, leading to the Suez war (Israel's "Sinai Campaign") in late October 1956.

See also SUEZ CANAL; SUEZ CRISIS (1956–1957).

Bibliography

Kyle, Keith. *Suez.* New York: St. Martin's Press, 1991.

Lloyd, Selwyn. *Suez 1956: A Personal Account.* London: Cape, 1978.

Love, Kennett. *Suez: The Twice-Fought War.* New York: McGraw-Hill, 1969.

Murphy, Robert. *Diplomat among Warriors.* Garden City, New York: Doubleday, 1964.

MORDECHAI BAR-ON

LONDON CONVENTION

International agreement to keep warships out of the Bosporus.

On 15 July 1840, British Foreign Secretary Lord Palmerston obtained the adherence of the Ottoman Empire, Prussia, Russia, and Austria to a treaty redefining the international status of the Straits of the Bosporus and the Dardanelles. Under its terms, no foreign warships, except small vessels on diplomatic missions, were to pass the straits while the Ottoman Empire was at peace.

In a separate protocol, a graduated series of penalties was laid out if Muhammad Ali, viceroy of Egypt, and his son, Ibrahim Pasha, refused to retreat from Syria. Consequently, Britain's navy bombarded Beirut and Acre, landing troops. This threat to cut off Egyptian supply lines forced the Egyptians to retreat south of the Sinai. On 13 July 1841, the 1840 London Convention was reaffirmed, this time with French adherence. As France had been Muhammad Ali's patron, this second London Convention was a clear defeat for France. Muhammad Ali lost everything for which he had gambled, retaining only the hereditary viceroyship of Egypt, south of the Sinai desert.

Bibliography

Webster, Sir Charles. *The Foreign Policy of Palmerston, 1830–1841: Britain, the Liberal Movement, and the Eastern Question.* 2 vols. New York: Humanities Press, 1969.

ARNOLD BLUMBERG

LONDON (ROUNDTABLE) CONFERENCE (1939)

Conference convened at St. James's Palace (London) to consider the future of Palestine.

In late 1938, as fears of a European war loomed, Britain sought ways of pacifying growing Arab displeasure over her pro-Zionist policy in Palestine. On 7 November 1938 the British Cabinet proposed convening a conference that would bring together Jews and Arabs in "separate parallel discussions between His Majesty's Government and the Arabs, and His Majesty's Government and the Jews."

The Palestinian position heading into the conference called for the establishment of an Arab national government in Palestine; the cessation of all Jewish immigration; the prohibition of further land sales to Jews; and the granting of minority rights to Jews. Representatives of several Arab states met in Cairo in January 1939 and agreed on a joint position. During the days leading up to the opening session, Jewish Agency Chairman David Ben-Gurion advocated the following four guidelines for the Zionist negotiation strategy: no concessions on immigration; no Arab state, but a regime based on parity in Palestine; cantonization might be acceptable if the Jewish area was not less than that recommended by the Peel Report and if control over immigration were in Jewish hands; and a Jewish state would be willing to belong to a future Middle Eastern confederation.

The conference opened at St. James's Palace on 7 February 1939. Representatives of Egypt, Iraq, Saudi Arabia, Transjordan, Yemen, and the Palestinians (led by Jamal al-Husayni, George Antonius, and Musa al-Alami) met with British officials, who held parallel discussions with members of the Jewish delegation. Colonial Secretary Malcolm MacDonald served as host and go-between. Because of the Arab refusal to meet directly with the Jewish delegation, the British managed to convene only two informal meetings between several representatives from the Arab states and Jewish delegates.

During the lengthy discussions, the Arabs presented their position as formulated in Cairo, demanding an end to the Mandate and insisting on the creation of an independent Arab state in Palestine. They also argued that the Husayn–McMahon Correspondence (1915–1916), which they interpreted as including Palestine within the areas of promised Arab independence, took precedence over the 1917 Balfour Declaration, which committed Britain to promote a Jewish national home in Palestine. The Jews, for their part, would not budge from their insistence on large-scale immigration into Palestine, becoming even more adamant in light of Adolf Hitler's escalating anti-Jewish policies and the recent annexation of Austria.

Faced with no prospect of mutual agreement after some three dozen sessions with the parties, on 15 March 1939 Malcolm MacDonald outlined Britain's proposals: After ten years, a Palestinian state would be created, possibly a federation with Arab and Jewish cantons. Since the Arabs would have a majority in the assembly, legal guarantees would be included for the Jewish minority and its national home. During the coming five years, 75,000 Jewish immigrants (of whom 25,000 would be refugees) would be admitted into Palestine. Subsequent immigration would depend on Arab consent.

The conference officially ended on 17 March. Chaim Weizmann informed MacDonald that the Zionists were unable to accept Britain's terms. British officials in Cairo resumed contact with representatives of the Arab states, leading to some modifications of MacDonald's provisions in an effort to gain fuller Arab acceptance of the proposed new British policy. Finally, on 17 May 1939, Britain published the MacDonald White Paper, the end result of the London conference's failure to reach an Arab–Zionist agreement. Its terms—admittedly "disappointing to both Jews and Arabs"—would govern Britain's official Palestine policy for the coming war years, although little was implemented on the ground, with both Arab and Zionist leaders continuing their efforts to obtain changes favorable to their respective causes.

See also BALFOUR DECLARATION (1917); HUSAYN–MCMAHON CORRESPONDENCE (1915–1916); MACDONALD, MALCOLM; WHITE PAPERS ON PALESTINE.

Bibliography

Caplan, Neil. *Futile Diplomacy*, Vol. 2: *Arab-Zionist Negotiations and the End of the Mandate, 1931–1948*. Totowa, NJ; London: Frank Cass, 1986.

Lesch, Ann Mosely. *Arab Politics in Palestine, 1917–1939: The Frustration of a Nationalist Movement*. Ithaca, NY: Cornell University Press, 1979.

Porath, Yehoshua. *The Palestinian Arab National Movement: From Riots to Rebellion*, vol. 2, *1929–1939*. Totowa, NJ; London: Frank Cass, 1977.

Rose, Norman A. *The Gentile Zionists: A Study in Anglo-Zionist Diplomacy, 1929–1939*. London: Frank Cass, 1973.

NEIL CAPLAN

LONDON, TREATY OF (1871)

Pact restoring Russian access to the Black Sea.

Articles XI–XIII of the 1856 Peace of Paris restricted Russian access to the Turkish Straits and forced a demilitarization of the Black Sea. Czar Alexander II (1855–1881) never accepted this defeat of Russian interests, and in 1870, he finally found an opportunity to amend the galling Black Sea clauses. With the French faring badly in the Franco-Prussian War, in October 1870 Alexander instructed his foreign minister, Prince Aleksandr Gorchakov, to announce that Russia no longer wished to abide by Articles XI–XIII. The French agreed to an international conference to discuss the proposed Russian

revision. The conference opened in London in January 1871, and an agreement was reached by March. The Treaty of London annulled the Black Sea naval rearmament. However, in compensation, the sultan of the Ottoman Empire was given greater latitude to close the straits in times of war.

Bibliography

Anderson, M. S. *The Eastern Question, 1774–1923: A Study in International Relations*. London: Macmillan, and New York: St. Martin's, 1966.

Hurewitz, J. C., ed. *The Middle East and North Africa in World Politics: A Documentary Record*, 2nd edition. 2 vols. New Haven, CT: Yale University Press, 1975–1979.

ZACHARY KARABELL

LONDON, TREATY OF (1913)

Pact securing Italian claims in the Middle East.

Signed on 26 April, this treaty paved the way for Italy's entry into World War I on the side of the Entente (France and Britain). In return for its support, Italy was promised territory in the Balkans and Anatolia as well as the right to annex Libya, which it had occupied in 1914, and the Dodecanese Islands, part of Greece and formerly, when taken by Italy in 1912, part of the Ottoman Empire.

Bibliography

Anderson, M. S. *The Eastern Question, 1774–1923: A Study in International Relations*. London: Macmillan; and New York: St. Martin's, 1966.

Hurewitz, J. C., ed. *The Middle East and North Africa in World Politics: A Documentary Record*, 2nd edition. 2 vols. New Haven, CT: Yale University Press, 1975–1979.

ZACHARY KARABELL

L'ORIENT

See NEWSPAPERS AND PRINT MEDIA: ARAB COUNTRIES

LOTZ, WOLFGANG
[1921–1993]

Israeli espionage agent in Egypt, 1960–1965; dubbed "the champagne spy" for his extravagance.

Born in Mannheim, Germany, Wolfgang Lotz moved with his mother to Palestine after Hitler's rise to power, changed his name to Ze'ev Gur-Aryeh, and fought in the Haganah and Israel Defense Forces (IDF). Sent to infiltrate Egypt's military and political circles posing as an ex-Nazi and race-horse breeder, Lotz befriended high-echelon officers and transmitted invaluable information, until caught in 1965 and sentenced to life in prison. Freed in a POW exchange after the Arab–Israel War (1967), Lotz eventually tired of civilian life in Israel and moved to West Germany, then to California.

ZEV MAGHEN

LUKE, HARRY
[1884–1969]

British civil servant in the Middle East.

Harry Luke was British chief commissioner in Georgia, Armenia, and Azerbaijan, then assistant governor of Jerusalem (1920–1924). He served on the commission investigating the Jaffa Riots in 1921 and was chief secretary in Palestine (1928–1930). In August 1929, as acting high commissioner, Luke permitted activist Jewish youth to march to the Western Wall. Jews were attacked, and riots broke out a few days later. Unable to restore order, Luke asked for reinforcements from Jordan and Egypt and turned public security over to the Royal Air Force. He served as lieutenant governor of Malta (1930–1938), then as governor of Fiji and high commissioner of the western Pacific (1938–1942). Among his published books are *A Handbook of Palestine* (1922) and *The Handbook of Palestine and Trans-Jordan* (1934).

JENAB TUTUNJI

LURS

Luri-speaking people of western Iran.

Lurs are found primarily in three provinces in and adjoining the Zagros Mountains of western Iran: Luristan in the west, Chahar Mahall Bakhtiari in the center, and Boir Ahmad/Kuhgiluyeh in the south. Lurs also comprise a majority of the population of Ilam, to the west of Luristan, and many Lurs live in northern Khuzistan province. Lurs speak Luri, a nonwritten language closely related to Persian. During the nineteenth century, most Lurs were organized

as tribal groups and practiced pastoral nomadism, although there were some Luri agricultural villages in the fertile plains of Luristan. The largest Luri tribe was the Bakhtiari. Other important tribes included the Boir Ahmadi, the Kuhgiluyeh, and the Mamasani. During the reign of Reza Shah Pahlavi, the Luri tribes, as well as others, were forcibly disarmed and settled. Although many tribal groups returned to pastoral nomadism after 1941, the economic changes in Iran before and since that date have made this way of life less and less appealing. By the early 2000s, the majority of Lurs lived in cities, including the major industrial centers of Borujerd and Khorramabad in Luristan, and did not identify with any tribal group. About one-third of Lurs lived in villages, and only 10 percent continued to practice seasonal migrations organized by livestock-herding tribes. The overwhelming majority of Lurs are Shiᶜa Muslims, although a small number are Ahl-e Haqq.

See also PERSIAN.

Bibliography

Black-Michaud, Jacob. *Sheep and Land: The Economics of Power in a Tribal Society.* New York and Cambridge, U.K.: Cambridge University Press, 1986.

ERIC HOOGLUND

LUTI

See GLOSSARY

LUXOR

Upper Egyptian commercial and tourist center.

This town on the east bank of the Nile in Upper Egypt is called al-Uqsur in Arabic. It is noted for its ancient temple and its proximity to Karnak, Thebes, and the tombs of the pharaohs, queens, and nobles on the opposite (west) bank of the Nile. It is the site of numerous Coptic churches and monasteries. With the coming of Islam, it became the site of mosques, notably that of al-Hajjaj, built above the Temple of Luxor. After the discovery of King Tut's tomb in 1922, the area became one of Egypt's premiere tourist attractions, and to this day the local economy is strongly dependent on tourism.

See also NILE RIVER.

Bibliography

Shaw, Ian. *Exploring Ancient Egypt.* Oxford: Oxford University Press, 2003.

ARTHUR GOLDSCHMIDT
UPDATED BY PAUL S. ROWE

LUZ, KADISH
[1895–1972]

Israeli labor leader and third speaker of the Knesset.

Born in Bobruisk, Byelorussia, Kadish Luz studied economics, agriculture, and sciences at Russian and Estonian universities. Luz served in the Russian army during World War I. After the Bolshevik revolution, he assisted Joseph Trumpeldor in founding the Hehalutz Zionist youth movement, then immigrated to Palestine where he worked at land reclamation and road building. He became a leader of the kibbutz movement and the Histadrut, and from 1951 was a MAPAI member of the Knesset, Israel's parliament. Luz was minister of agriculture (1955–1959) and speaker of the Knesset (1959–1969).

ZEV MAGHEN

LYAUTEY, LOUIS-HUBERT GONZALVE
[1854–1934]

French officer and colonial governor of Morocco during the French protectorate, 1912–1925.

Born in Nancy, France, Louis-Hubert Gonzalve Lyautey was one of the generation of army officers who had been affected by Germany's defeat of France in the Franco-Prussian War (1870–1871). As did many others, he tried to compensate through the colonial adventure. First in Tonkin (French Indochina), then in Madagascar, under General Joseph S. Gallieni's command, he experimented with a doctrine of colonization after the British model—which respected the culture and institutions of the colonized populations more than the French system had.

At the beginning of the twentieth century, when he served in Algeria, first in the southern territories and then as chief of the division based in Oran, he drew a negative image from the colonial system as it was instituted there. Above all, he wanted to keep the original Algerian model from extending into Morocco when that country came under French control. Since the conquest of Morocco was not easy, his theses became attractive to the French government at the beginning of the French protectorate in 1912; they were already preparing for the oncoming conflict with Germany, now called World War I (1914–1918), and wanted to maintain their resources and troops in Europe.

After Lyautey's appointment to Morocco in 1912, he succeeded in freeing the commercial and religious center of Fez from the *makhzen* (mercenary) system of the tribal peoples. He regained the lowlands and the main cities, which traditionally were under their control. Then he had to get Sultan Mulay Hafid, who would not cooperate, to abdicate and put his brother Mulay Youssef on the throne.

Lyautey was a monarchist, and he admired Napoléon Bonaparte's methods of administration in early nineteenth-century Egypt. He wanted to follow them and to get the support of a legitimizing authority, which would help him subdue Morocco without his own submission to strict controls from Paris. Therefore he tried to maintain the Moroccan monarchy while making sure that it would not present a source of future problems. Under such conditions, the new sultan was allowed to keep the major Islamic prerogatives of Moroccan sovereignty: to be a caliph and an imam.

On 30 March 1912, when Lyautey signed the Fes Treaty, establishing the French protectorate over Morocco, which was going to define the relationships between the two countries until 1956, he was given the mission to reform the structure of the colonial administration. He would succeed in doing so by joining to the traditional services of the makhzen at the central and local levels a parallel French hierarchy. Without any resistance on the part of the sultan, Lyautey would create the laws and regulations by edict, which would guarantee the "administrative legal, educational, economic, financial and military reforms the French government will judge have to be introduced on Moroccan territory" (Article I of the Fes Treaty). Lyautey would then be able to establish a quick modernization, using only a few competent civil servants. At the beginning, this plan was widely accepted. He would also be able to place most of the country under the formal author-

Resident general of Morocco Louis-Hubert Gonzalve Lyautey (1854–1934; seated, third from left) dining at the table of Sultan Mulai Yussef, Morocco, ca. 1925. © HULTON-DEUTSCH COLLECTION/CORBIS. REPRODUCED BY PERMISSION.

ity of the *makhzen* by using traditional ways of negotiating with the tribes and by limiting his need for force.

His opposition to both parliamentary and political control by France led him to preserve the autonomy of Morocco so that, in the long run, he might exert a larger hidden power. The romantic idea of a feudal system constituted the basis for his debatable policy. As a tolerant Roman Catholic, he was open toward and respectful of Islam; since he was attracted to marginal people (those living neither within one system nor the other), he thought they might help him understand this country's essence—outside official circles. Adept at understanding cultural differences and hierarchical controls, he came to consider the possible development of two distinct but parallel societies that might save old cities and architecture but also lead in education. It was a separated system (akin to a "mild" apartheid) because he refused to introduce into Morocco the French system that prevailed in Alge-

ria, based on colonization by poor whites. He then had to turn to private bankers, especially the Banque de Paris et des Pay-Bas, but he was unable or unwilling to avoid the expropriation of the richest, most fertile lands for the benefit of French settlers. Although he cared about the sultan's interests, he did not or could not prevent the basic elements of a future berber policy to take root.

Under the authority of the protectorate, Lyautey practiced a direct administration policy and benefited from it, because of the fiction of Moroccan sovereignty. In keeping the sultan, he confined him to an outdated traditionalism. Meanwhile, Lyautey's colonial *officiers des affaires indigènes* (officers in charge of native affairs) had been taught his ruling philosophy, and they used the pashas and the Arab shaykhs as intermediaries, to keep things under control. His system did not leave much space for the development of a Moroccan elite, which he became aware of toward the end of his mission. From 1920, he worried about the future of the country and considered formulas that would allow an easy withdrawal of French control.

His authority was shaken by the beginning of the rebellion of Rif leader Abd al-Karim, who in 1921 began fighting against the Spanish in their sector of Morocco. By April of 1925, Abd al-Karim had turned to fight the French. A French-Spanish force was organized against him in July and in September, under World War I hero French Marshal Henri-Philippe Pétain; the Rifians were driven back. Toward the end of September, Lyautey resigned, and he left Morocco for France in October. He was replaced by a civilian resident and by Marshal Pétain as the military leader. Lyautey left as the legendary leader who had safeguarded the sultan's monarchy, the reputation of the country in international affairs, and its resources and finances through development of its phosphate mining company. He left as the launcher of its modernization.

He ended his life in France as an anti-republican, supporting the extreme right—an admirer of Italian dictator Benito Mussolini. He was suspected, not long before his death, to have encouraged the aborted coup against the French parliament on 6 February 1934, launched by the Croix de Feu (Cross of Fire, a French fascist organization).

See also FES, TREATY OF (1912).

RÉMY LEVEAU

LYDDA

Town in Israel (in Hebrew, Lod; *in Arabic,* al-Lidd).

An ancient biblical town, Lydda was known through the nineteenth century as an intermediate center for caravans and for its magnificent Byzantine basilica over the tomb of St. George. Under Ottoman rule, it was an Arab town that was part of the Jerusalem *sanjak* (district) and an important center for soap and olive oil manufacture. During the 1930s, it became one of the most important railroad junctions in the Middle East, with lines connecting Jaffa, Jerusalem, and Cairo. Lydda sustained human and material losses in the 1927 earthquake. During the bloody events of 1936 to 1939, the Jews left the town and it became a base of operations for Palestinian Arabs who were attacking Jewish towns. Most of the town's more than ten thousand Palestinian Arabs escaped or were forcibly evacuated by the Israel Defense Force during the 1948 Arab–Israel War.

Lydda is located northeast of Ramla, south of Ben Gurion Airport (originally opened in 1937). It is also the center of Israel's aircraft industry. Both the airport and the industry constitute important sources of income for the town's population. At the end of 2002 the population numbered 66,500, including more than 4,000 Muslim and Christian Palestinian citizens.

ELIZABETH THOMPSON
UPDATED BY YEHUDA GRADUS

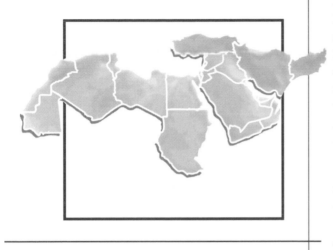

M

MA AL-AYNAYN
[1840–1910]

Important figure in the religio-political history of Mauritania and southern Morocco.

Ma al-Aynayn (also known as Shaykh Muhammad Mustafa ibn Muhammad Fadil al-Qalqami) was the son of Muhammad Fadil, founder of the Fadiliyya Sufi brotherhood, a religious scholar and leader among the nomadic populations of northern Mauritania. Like his father, Ma al-Aynayn was head of the Fadiliyya, a noted scholar, and political leader. A prolific author, he is credited with over 140 books on a wide variety of topics.

A close ally and adviser of the sultans of Morocco from 1859, Ma al-Aynayn cooperated in the extension of Moroccan authority into the Western Sahara. Under Sultan Hassan I and his successor Abd al-Aziz, he organized resistance to imperialist incursions into the western Sahara by France and Spain.

At his death in 1910 he was succeeded by his son Ahmad Hibat Allah, known as "El Hiba."

See also AHMAD HIBAT ALLAH; HASSAN I; MAURITANIA.

Bibliography

Martin, Bradford G. *Muslim Brotherhoods in Nineteenth-Century Africa.* Cambridge, U.K., and New York: Cambridge University Press, 1976.

EDMUND BURKE III

MA'ALOT

Urban community in Upper Galilee, Israel.

Founded in 1956 to replace two *ma'abarot* (temporary housing communities) of mostly North African Jewish immigrants, Ma'alot is situated some 6 miles south of the Lebanese border, in the heart of the Western Galilee, on hilly terrain at an elevation of 1,970 feet, with a commanding view of Wadi Koren. In 1963 the town united with the nearby Palestinian village of Tarshiha. The town's population, totaling some 20,000 in 2002, works mainly in industry.

On 15 May 1974 three Arab terrorists from Nayif Hawatma's Democratic Front for the Liberation of Palestine, disguised in Israeli uniforms, entered Ma'alot, overpowered and killed a guard posted outside, and took control of a school building, where a group of ninety children on a field trip slept on the floor. Some of the children were killed on the spot, but others escaped by jumping out of a window on the second floor. The terrorists demanded the release of Arab guerrillas from Israeli prisons by 6:00 P.M. and threatened to kill the hostage children if the demands were not met. At 5:45 P.M. a unit of the Israeli army's elite Golani Brigade stormed the building, killing the three terrorists, but not before the terrorists killed sixteen children and wounded seventy.

See also HAWATMA, NAYIF.

ZEV MAGHEN
UPDATED BY YEHUDA GRADUS

MA'ARIV

Daily newspaper published in Tel Aviv.

Ma'ariv was founded in 1948 by a group of journalists as an afternoon paper, following their departure from another newspaper, *Yedi'ot Aharonot.* The splinter group was headed by Ezriel Carlebach, who became the paper's first editor.

For many years, *Ma'ariv* garnered the largest readership of any paper in Israel. Over the years its fortunes have waned considerably. Under its editor, Dan Margalit, *Ma'ariv* defines itself as broad based, apolitical, and with an appeal to both secular and religious Israelis.

ANN KAHN

MA'BARAH

Residential transit camps for immigrants in Israel established in the early 1950s.

In the years 1950 to 1952, when Israel was unprepared for mass immigration, about 250,000 immigrants (many of them from Iraq and Romania) lived in about 110 *ma'barot* (plural of *ma'barah*). Con-

ditions were dismal: Housing was in canvas shacks and tents, or at best in tin huts; infrastructure, sanitation, and water supply were deplorable; health and education facilities were inadequate. But in comparison with the immigrant camps of 1948 to 1949, people were less dependent upon public officials, and there were more employment opportunities. *Ma'barot* were spread throughout the country, particularly near agricultural locations, and the government undertook massive relief-work projects. Many *ma'barot* residents put down roots in their localities and stayed on to live in permanent housing that was eventually erected nearby by the government. Most residents obtained housing within two to three years, but some remained in temporary housing for close to ten years. Beginning in 1953 immigrants were moved to newly built houses, ending the *ma'abarot* stage of absorption.

The bitterness of the *ma'barot* experience, particularly among *adot ha-mizrah* (Israeli Middle-Easterners), had wide ramifications in Israeli politics and culture. It figures in Israeli literature, particularly in the writings of major authors of Iraqi origin such as Sami Michael, Shimon Balas, and Eli Amir. In their earlier writings the authors presented realistic descriptions of the assertiveness of *ma'barot* residents striving to become established Israelis. In their later writings some of the authors depicted social uprootedness and alienation, and some evinced nostalgia for the Jewish life of their countries of origin.

See also ADOT HA-MIZRAH; REFUGEES: JEWISH.

Bibliography

Berg, Nancy E. "Transit Camp Literature: Literature of Transition." In *Critical Essay on Israeli Society, Religion, and Government: Books on Israel,* Vol. 4, edited by Kevin Avruch and Walter P. Zenner. Albany: State University of New York Press, 1997.

Bernstein, Deborah. "Immigrant Transit Camps: The Formation of Dependent Relations in Israeli Society." *Ethnic and Racial Studies* 4, no. 1(1981): 26–43.

SHLOMO DESHEN

MABARRAT MUHAMMAD ALI

Egyptian women's organization.

The Mabarrat Muhammad Ali, or the Muhammad Ali Benevolent Society, was founded in 1909 by

Princess Ayn al-Hayat Ahmad, a member of Egypt's royal family and a noted philanthropist. She called on other members of the royal family to donate funds to establish a small clinic in one of the poor quarters of Cairo. The Mabarrat was formed to run the clinic and quickly expanded into an organization of women from prominent political families. Hidaya Afifi Barakat (1899–1969), an Egyptian Muslim, and Mary Kahil (1889–1979), a Syrian Christian, were for many years the driving forces in the organization.

In subsequent decades members of the Mabarrat held concerts and other fund-raising events to support medical relief for Egypt's poor. Eventually it established and administered a network of hospitals and outpatient clinics throughout Egypt. During the severe malaria and cholera epidemics of the 1940s, the Mabarrat distributed emergency relief and administered vaccination programs.

The Wafdist Ministry of Health, which was locked in a power struggle with the palace, saw the Mabarrat as a rival. Following the Free Officers' coup of 1952, all independent charitable societies came under direct governmental supervision. In its first half-century, the Mabarrat hospitals and clinics had served hundreds of thousands of people. Barakat continued to volunteer under the new regime. In 1969, on the last day of her life, the state awarded her its First Class Order of Merit for public service. Kahil was similarly recognized in 1972.

NANCY GALLAGHER

MACCABI

International Jewish sports organizations.

Named for the Judean heroes who fought Antiochus in the second century B.C.E., the Maccabi World Union began in 1895 with the formation of clubs like the Israel Gymnastics Club in Istanbul and others in Bucharest, Berlin, and Saint Petersburg. By World War I, membership in the Turkish Maccabi was two thousand.

Although not ideologically a Zionist movement, the Maccabi was part of the phenomenon of a rising Jewish national consciousness during the late nineteenth and first half of the twentieth centuries. Maccabi clubs became important institutions in British-mandated Palestine, Egypt, Lebanon, Syria, and Libya. There was a popular Maccabi club in Baghdad during the late 1920s, but it ceased to be officially active as anti-Zionist Arab nationalism turned virulent. Along with groups such as the Union Universelle de la Jeunesse Juive (Universal Union of Jewish Youth), Jewish Scouts, cultural associations, and modern Hebrew-language schools, the Maccabi helped to foster a feeling of solidarity among Middle Eastern and North African Jewry with their coreligionists worldwide, as well as sympathy for Zionism.

Bibliography

Stillman, Norman A. *The Jews of Arab Lands in Modern Times.* Philadelphia: Jewish Publication Society, 1991.

NORMAN STILLMAN

MACDONALD LETTER

See MACDONALD, RAMSAY

MACDONALD, MALCOLM

[1901–1981]

British politician who played a central role in the decolonization of the British Empire.

The son of the first British socialist prime minister, Ramsay MacDonald, Malcolm MacDonald was the link between the Jewish Agency and Britain's cabinet following the publication of Passfield's White Paper of 1930 that restricted Jewish immigration to Palestine. Between 1931 and 1935 he was parliamentary undersecretary of state for dominion affairs. In the first months of 1935 and from 1938 to 1940 he served as colonial secretary, and between 1935 and 1938, as secretary of state for dominion affairs.

When MacDonald became colonial secretary for the second time, in view of the deterioration of law and order due to the rebellion of Palestinian Arabs (1936–1939) and the looming threat of a world war, he tried to stabilize the situation by placating the Arab states. Opposing the proposed partition of Palestine, he envisaged, initiated, and organized the London (Roundtable) Conference of early 1939, in which representatives of Arab states participated along with the Palestinian Arabs, and a Jewish delegation from abroad joined the Palestinian Jewish delegation. The failure of the conference resulted in the formulation of a new British policy on Palestine embodied in MacDonald's White Paper of May 1939. This document set limits on Jewish immigration and land sales, and held out the promise of an independent state in Palestine.

> See also LONDON (ROUNDTABLE) CONFERENCE (1939); MACDONALD, RAMSAY; WHITE PAPERS ON PALESTINE.

Bibliography

Bill, James, and Leiden, Carl. *Politics in the Middle East.* Boston: Little, Brown, 1979.

Sanger, Clyde. *Malcolm MacDonald: Bringing an End to Empire.* Liverpool, U.K.: Liverpool University Press, 1995.

JENAB TUTUNJI
UPDATED BY JOSEPH NEVO

MACDONALD, RAMSAY

[1866–1937]

Prime minister of Great Britain (1924, 1929–1935).

Ramsay MacDonald is best known in connection with the Middle East as the author of the MacDonald Letter (1931), sent to Chaim Weizmann, which overrode the white paper of 1930 and served as the legal basis for administering Palestine until the white paper of 1939.

From January to October 1924, MacDonald was Britain's first Labour prime minister. He again became prime minister in 1929. The onset of the Great Depression precipitated a crisis in 1931, and MacDonald was persuaded to head an all-party national government until 1935. In that year he was replaced by Stanley Baldwin.

The white paper of October 1930 presented the findings of two commissions. The Shaw Commission report of 1930 concerned the investigation of an outbreak of violence between Arabs and Jews in 1929, and the mass killing of Jews in Hebron and Safed. It found that the deeper cause of the violence was the uprooting of Arab villagers from the lands they had cultivated for generations, as a result of land sales to Jews.

The Hope-Simpson Commission was appointed to study the matter. Its report, completed in October 1930, found that a significant portion of the Arab rural population was on the verge of destitution. It recommended that the immigration of Jews should be assessed not only in terms of the absorptive capacity of the Yishuv but also in terms of its economic impact on the Arab rural population. It recommended a land development scheme primarily to aid displaced Arab farmers and suggested greater controls on immigration.

The Zionists were outraged, perceiving this as undermining the terms of the mandate. Weizmann maintained that the obligation of the mandatory power was to the Jewish people as a whole, not just the 170,000 Jews already in Palestine. To protest, on 20 October, Weizmann resigned the presidency of the Jewish Agency, which served as a liaison with Britain's government.

The government came under very strong pressure from Zionists, as well as from established British political figures and political parties. To placate Weizmann, MacDonald issued a letter addressed to him as head of the Jewish Agency, and submitted it to the Council of the League of Nations. The letter was also recorded as an official document and dispatched to the high commissioner of Palestine as an instruction of the cabinet.

While reiterating the principle that Britain's mandate involved a double undertaking to the Jewish as well as the non-Jewish population of Palestine, the letter reaffirmed responsibility for establishing a national home for the Jewish people in Palestine. It spoke in positive terms of the obligations of the government to facilitate Jewish immigration under suitable terms, subject to the abstract proviso that "no prejudice should result to the rights and position of the non-Jewish community." The negative impact of immigration on Arab farmers was displaced from the central position it had occupied. No reference was made to the proposed development scheme or to another proposal for the creation of a Legislative Council.

MacDonald's letter also precipitated an Arab rebellion during the years 1936 to 1939, an outcome the authors of the Shaw and Hope-Simpson reports had been trying to avoid.

> See also HOPE-SIMPSON COMMISSION (1930); JEWISH AGENCY FOR PALESTINE; SHAW COM-

MISSION; WEIZMANN, CHAIM; WHITE PAPERS ON PALESTINE; YISHUV.

Bibliography

Geddes, Charles L., ed. *A Documentary History of the Arab-Israeli Conflict*. New York: Praeger, 1991.

Hirst, David. *The Gun and the Olive Branch: The Roots of Violence in the Middle East*, 2nd edition. London and Boston: Faber and Faber, 1984.

Porath, Yehoshua. *The Palestinian Arab National Movement: From Riots to Rebellion*. Vol. 2: *1929–1939*. London: Cass, 1977.

Rose, Norman A. *The Gentile Zionists: A Study in Anglo-Zionist Diplomacy, 1929–1939*. London: Frank Cass, 1973.

JENAB TUTUNJI

MACMICHAEL, HAROLD
[1882–1969]

High commissioner of Palestine (1938–1944).

Harold MacMichael favored abandoning the Peel Commission's partition plan, temporary suspension of land sales to Jews, and limiting immigration of Jews for a few years. He initially opposed implementing the provisions of the White Paper for gradual Palestinian Arab self-government, then shifted his position.

MacMichael recommended that Britain terminate the mandate and the Jewish Agency, and under various scenarios, set up either a small, independent Jewish state or one with dominion status, and allowing local autonomy for an Arab state while Britain retained control over the holy places. His recommendations were not accepted.

When there was a controversy about establishing a Jewish army, MacMichael recommended that the recruitment program for the Jewish settlement police and special constabulary be expanded; he feared, however, that a Jewish army in Palestine could be turned against the mandate or used to back up postwar Zionist demands. In August 1944, MacMichael was the target of an unsuccessful assassination attempt by Jewish extremists.

See also JEWISH AGENCY FOR PALESTINE; PEEL COMMISSION REPORT (1937); WHITE PAPERS ON PALESTINE.

Bibliography

Lenczowski, George. *The Middle East in World Affairs*, 4th edition. Ithaca, NY: Cornell University Press, 1980.

JENAB TUTUNJI

MADANI, ABASSI AL-
[1931–]

Algerian founder and president of the Islamic Salvation Front (Front Islamique du Salut; FIS), a major opposition political movement.

Born in Sidi Okba in southeast Algeria, son of a rural imam, Abassi (often referred to by his last name, Madani) had a dual education in Qur'anic and French schools. An early recruit to the nationalist movement, he was arrested by the French authorities in 1955 for placing a bomb at Radio Algiers. He spent the remainder of the Algerian War of Independence in prison.

Upon the country's independence, Madani became a schoolteacher while simultaneously pursuing a *licence* degree in philosophy at the University of Algiers. Influenced by the Islamic philosopher Malek Bennabi, he became active in *Al-Qiyam* (Values), an association that popularized the ideas of Middle Eastern fundamentalist thinkers. Yet he remained within the conservative "Arabist" wing of the National Liberation Front (FLN), and was elected to the Algiers departmental assembly in 1971. While studying for a doctorate in London in the mid-1970s, he became acquainted with international Islamist circles. Appointed professor of education at the University of Algiers, he began preaching in various mosques around the city. For his participation in violent anti-regime demonstrations, he returned to prison in December 1982, serving sixteen months of a two-year sentence.

Madani quickly capitalized upon the liberalization of the regime after the October 1988 riots by founding the FIS in February 1989. In this he worked closely with a younger firebrand preacher, Ali Ben Hadj. Emerging as the strategist of the Algerian Islamist movement, he organized an effective electoral machine, which rode to an unanticipated victory in the municipal elections of June 1990. The FIS captured 54 percent of the popular vote and won control of some 850 city councils including those of Algiers, Oran, Constantine, and Annaba. Heady with victory, Madani called for national parliamentary elections, then declared a general strike in May 1991 to protest the gerrymandering electoral law under which the government proposed to hold the election. The strike led to violence, Madani was reported to have threatened jihad against the army, and once again—on 30 June 1991—the Islamist militant was arrested on charges of conspiracy against the state.

Imprisoned once again and his party officially dissolved, Madani nevertheless remained a significant interlocutor for the government during the civil war of the 1990s. In 1997, he was released from jail but kept under house arrest. In July 2003, he completed his twelve-year sentence; in failing health and his party still banned, he remained a controversial symbol of political protest in Algeria.

ROBERT MORTIMER

MADANI, ABDULLAH AL-

Journalist and member of both the Constitutional Assembly and the National Assembly in Bahrain.

A religiously trained Shi'ite, Abdullah al-Madani represented a rural district in Bahrain. He was elected to the Constitutional Assembly in 1972 and 1973. In both assemblies, he was the leader of the conservative (Shi'a) religious bloc—the other two blocs being the bourgeois nationalists and the reformists (leftists). During his service, he started a weekly magazine, *al-Mawaqif*, which he edited and published. He was conservative on social-Islamic issues but liberal on political issues. His editorials in *al-Mawaqif* probably made him some enemies; he was assassinated in the late 1970s.

See also BAHRAIN.

Bibliography

Nakhleh, Emile A. *Bahrain: Political Development in a Modernizing Society.* Lexington, MA: Lexington Books, 1976.

EMILE A. NAKHLEH

MADANI, TAWFIQ AL-

[1899–1983]

Secretary-general of the Algerian Association of Reformist Ulama, ambassador, and historian.

Born in Tunis, Tawfiq al-Madani studied at Zaytuna University and became a cofounder of the Destour Party. His pro-nationalism activities provoked his expulsion from Tunisia to Algeria where he contributed profoundly toward reviving Arabic study and a national identity. His works include *Book of Algeria* (1931), an introduction to the country for youth that was implicitly nationalist, and *The War of Three Hundred Years Between Algeria and Spain* (1968). He wrote the play *Hannibal* and was editor-in-chief of *al-Basa'ir*.

Besides his cultural role, Madani also played an important political role. In 1952 he became secretary general of the Algerian Association of Reformist Ulama (body of *mullahs*) and integrated that organization within the revolutionary Front de Libération Nationale (FLN). He was later chosen minister of cultural affairs (1958) in the *Gouvernement Provisoire de la République Algérienne (GPRA)*. He became minister for *habous* (religious foundations) in Ahmed Ben Bella's first two governments. He later served as ambassador to Iraq and Pakistan. He retired in order to devote time to his scholarship, which included editorial work for the Centre National D'Etudes Historiques (National Center for Historic Studies) and its journal *al-Tarikh* (History).

See also FRONT DE LIBÉRATION NATIONALE.

PHILLIP C. NAYLOR

MADKOUR, IBRAHIM

[1902–1995]

Egyptian scholar.

Born in Abu al-Numrus, Giza, Ibrahim Madkour gained worldwide recognition for his efforts to promote the recovery and publication of the texts fundamental to Arabic and Islamic culture. Following studies at Dar al-Ulum, Madkour was sent to Paris, where he received a Ph.D. in 1934. The two required dissertations, "La place d'al-Farabi dans l'école philosophique musulmane" (Al-Farabi's place in the Muslim philosophical school) and "L'Organon d'Aristote dans le monde arabe" (Aristotle's organon in the Arab world), both published in the same year, remain fundamental texts for the history of Islam. Returning to Egypt, he was appointed professor of philosophy at the Fu'ad I University (later, University of Cairo) in 1934. Named minister of social affairs prior to the 1952 revolution, Madkour had his greatest influence on Arabic culture through his work with the Academy of Arabic Language (member 1946–1959, general secretary 1959–1974, and president 1974–1995), the Union of Academies of Arabic Language, and the Supreme Council of Culture in Egypt.

He launched the projects of editing Avicenna's great multivolume work the *Kitab al-Shifa* (Healing) in 1949; the Mu'tazilite theological summa of Abd al-Jabbar, *al-Mughn* (Sufficer); and Ibn al-Arabi's massive *al-Futuhat al-Makiyya* (Mekkan contributions). In addition, he facilitated the publication of several of Averroes's works and encouraged Georges Chehata Anawati in his translation of Avicenna's *Metaphysics* as well as Daniel Gimaret, Jean Jolivet, and Georges Monnot in their translation of al-Shahrastani's *Kitab al-Milal wa al-Nihal* (Book of religious communities and of sects).

In his constant encouragement of scholars to recover the rich medieval Arabic and Islamic patrimony, then to present it in critical, scientific editions and sound translations, Ibrahim Madkour made this heritage known throughout the world. He died in Cairo in 1995.

See also ANAWATI, GEORGES CHEHATA.

CHARLES BUTTERWORTH

MADRASA

Arabic word for an Islamic college and, more specifically, a center for religious and legal studies.

The madrasa originated in Eastern Iran in the tenth century and spread to major urban centers throughout the Middle East by the late eleventh century. The architect of the madrasa as a state-sponsored institution of higher education was Nizam al-Mulk (died 1092 C.E.), the prime minister of the Seljuk empire. These residential colleges were designed by the ruling elite both as a training ground for state bureaucrats and as a Sunni Islam response to the propaganda of Ismaili Shi'ism already being generated at al-Azhar, the theological learning center founded by the Fatimid dynasty in Cairo in 969 C.E. As part of a Sunni Muslim religio-political agenda, the madrasa spread throughout the Islamic world. The madrasa system augmented already extant mosque-centered training sites for the study of religion and

law. Unlike these centers, the madrasa forged links between the *ulama,* the religious scholars who directed Islamic education, and the ruling government authorities whose financial support made their control of the madrasa possible.

The madrasa system of education was linked to the mosque, which traditionally had been the place of instruction for Muslims in the Qur'an and in the Hadith—the traditions that preserved the words and deeds of the Prophet Muhammad. The madrasa combined the site for education with student residences. Libraries and sometimes hospitals would adjoin the madrasa. Financial support for the educational institution was generated by the state in the form of a charitable endowment called *waqf.* The revenue on these endowments paid for the maintenance of the buildings, student stipends, and instructors' fees.

The course of instruction at a madrasa included the Qur'an, tradition, Arabic language, theology, arithmetic, geometry, astronomy and, often, medicine; however, the study of Islamic law (*shari'a*) provided the core of the madrasa's rigorous curriculum. Initially, madrasas were founded to provide specialized instruction in one of the four Sunni legal schools. In time, legal instruction in one or more of the Sunni legal schools might be offered in a single madrasa.

The method of instruction relied heavily on memorization—of the Qur'an and as many traditions as possible. Once these preliminaries were accomplished, students were trained in the technicalities of the law, divergent legal opinions, and the disputed questions that distinguished their law school from the other Sunni legal schools. After four or more years of study, an instructor determined whether an individual student could be licensed to teach law and given a diploma, a signed certificate called an *ijaza.* Any Muslim male could join a madrasa, but the number of students per teacher was usually limited to twenty. Only male students studied at madrasas; Muslim women were not allowed to study Islamic law. Major Sunni madrasas were founded at Medina, Cairo, Tunis, and Fez. Al-Azhar remains the most famous Sunni theological center in the Arab world; it underwent a series of curriculum reforms in the early twentieth century that made the director of that institution the prime link between the Egyptian government and the country's traditional religious elite. Shiʿite madrasas in Iran include those of Mashhad and Qom and, in Iraq, al-Najaf, and Karbala.

In the nineteenth century, the Ottoman Empire founded schools influenced by European models to train their military officers, bureaucrats, and doctors. Similar professional schools were also created in Egypt and Tunisia during this period to offer instruction to those Muslims in government service forced to contend with the European colonial presence in the Middle East. These non-Islamic educational institutions created new urban nationalist elites. In the twentieth century, the breakup of the Ottoman Empire and the formation of Arab states hastened educational reform; secular schools of higher education undermined the madrasa system in the Sunni Muslim world. State-sponsored higher education throughout the Middle East promoted new secular avenues of social mobility and professional prestige for male and female Muslim students in areas such as medicine and engineering. Shiʿite madrasas flourish in Iran since the Ayatollah Ruhollah Khomeini's Iranian Revolution of 1979 reestablished Islamic rule.

See also ARABIC; AZHAR, AL-; HADITH; IRANIAN REVOLUTION (1979); MOSQUE; QURʾAN; *SHARIʿA;* SHIʿISM; SUNNI ISLAM; *ULAMA;* WAQF.

Bibliography

Husayn, Taha. *The Stream of Days: A Student at the Azhar,* 2d edition, translated by Hilary Wayment. London and New York: Longmans, Green, 1948.

Makdisi, George. *The Rise of Colleges: Institutions of Learning in Islam and the West.* Edinburgh: Edinburgh University Press, 1981.

Mottahedeh, Roy. *The Mantle of the Prophet: Religion and Politics in Iran.* New York: Pantheon, 1986.

DENISE A. SPELLBERG

MADRID CONFERENCE (1991)

Middle East peace conference, 30 October–1 November 1991.

Convened in 1991, the three-day Madrid Middle East Peace Conference was a historic breakthrough in Arab–Israeli diplomacy. It became a link between the end of the 1991 Gulf War and the signing of the 1993 Oslo Accord. It broke the taboo against Arab states, Palestinians, and Israelis meeting in public. In the years after the conference, bilateral and multilateral talks ensued, agreements were reached, and countries other than the United States became overtly engaged in managing the conflict.

A series of factors made the Madrid Conference possible. With the end of the Cold War, no patron could provide military assistance to sustain support for an Arab military option against Israel. Otherwise reluctant Arab states that had vilified Egypt for her separate peace with Israel during the 1970s were willing to accept Israel as a fact, primarily because the United States had, in defeating Saddam Hussein's aggression against Kuwait, secured the territorial integrity, sovereignty, and political independence of Arab Gulf states. Extensive pre-negotiations over several years had outlined the conference's procedures, content, and representation issues. Since the conference validated its earlier peace treaty with Israel, Egypt warmly endorsed the conference's convocation. Tirelessly, after the Gulf War's conclusion, in eight diplomatic shuttle missions, U.S. secretary of state James A. Baker III persevered in convincing reluctant Israeli and Arab neighbors to meet in Madrid on 30 October 1991.

Historically, Israel had shunned conference diplomacy, where it feared that Arab states could align themselves uniformly against it and impose unwanted solutions. Israel accepted this conference's format because bilateral talks were to emerge immediately from the ceremonial opening, with a U.S. assurance that the conference would not dictate solutions. While Moscow and Washington officially convened the conference, both Israel and the Arab world again placed their faith almost exclusively in U.S. diplomacy to push negotiations forward. For Israel, the United States remained its most dependable ally. After much hesitation, the Syrian leadership attended the Madrid Conference because it was conceptually based on Security Council Resolutions 242 and 338, which called for an exchange of territory for peace through direct negotiations between the parties. The Palestinian representation issue, which bedeviled the conference's preparations, was solved with creation of a

Jordanian-Palestinian delegation. Israel refused to attend a conference with the Palestine Liberation Organization (PLO) as a separate negotiating entity. While Yasir Arafat's PLO was not seated at the conference, indirect PLO participation ensured his containment of, if not control over, Palestinian leaders in the West Bank and Gaza who were emerging as a political alternative to the PLO's leadership. Grudging support for the conference also helped refurbish the Palestinians' tarnished international image due to their earlier ringing endorsement of Hussein's invasion of Kuwait.

No real negotiations were carried out at the conference; each delegation head used the podium to make political points to audiences listening at home. Political and regional issues, not military matters, were the main items on the negotiating agendas that flowed from the conference's opening. In the years that followed the conference, Palestinian–Israeli and Syrian–Israeli negotiations evolved, some of which led to detailed discussions and agreements during the 1990s. For several years after Madrid, multilateral talks were conducted in different world venues where issues of arms control, economic development, the environment, refugees, and water were discussed. While the United States continued to catalyze the diplomatic process in the 1990s, the Madrid Conference officially made the conflict's resolution and management a multilateral undertaking, thereafter engaging advocacy and financial support from individual European states, the European Union, Canada, Japan, Saudi Arabia, and others.

See also BAKER, JAMES A.; OSLO ACCORD (1993).

KENNETH W. STEIN

MAGEN DAVID ADOM (MDA)

The national emergency medical, ambulance, blood, and disaster service of Israel.

Magen David Adom (MDA; "red shield of David" in Hebrew) was founded on 7 June 1930 as a first-aid society for the city of Tel Aviv with about twenty volunteers, an ambulance, and a first-aid hut. Seventy years later, MDA served the entire population of Israel with 9,000 volunteers, 1,000 paid employees (including physicians, medics and para-medics, ambulance emergency medical technicians, and blood bank and fractionation experts and technicians), and 600 ambulances.

MDA supplies all of the blood used for transfusions by Israel's armed forces and more than 85 percent of the country's blood requirements. It also provides first-aid instruction.

In 1950 MDA's duties and responsibilities were legally defined in the Magen David Adom Law, in which MDA was recognized as the organization entrusted to carry out in Israel the functions assigned to a National Red Cross Society under the Geneva Conventions. MDA failed, however, to gain recognition from the League of Red Cross Societies (which accepts the Red Crescent Society based in Muslim countries and the Red Lion and Sun Society based in Iran) because of Arab and Communist-bloc objections. The issue remains unresolved despite support from the American Red Cross for MDA's inclusion. Some progress was evident in mid-2003 with the signing of the first bilateral cooperation agreement between the MDA and the International Committee of the Red Cross.

See also MEDICINE AND PUBLIC HEALTH; RED CRESCENT SOCIETY.

Bibliography

Magen David Adom U.S.A. web site. Available from <http://www.magendavidadom.org/>.

MIRIAM SIMON
UPDATED BY NEIL CAPLAN

MAGHRIB

Arabic term for northwest Africa in general, and for Morocco in particular.

In its broadest meaning, the Maghrib (also Maghreb) refers to Morocco, Algeria, Tunisia, Tripolitania, and, occasionally, Libya. The region is characterized by fertile plains and the Atlas mountain range near the Mediterranean and Atlantic coasts, and sweeping desert in its hinterland.

The term *maghrib* comes from the Arabic word meaning "west" or "place of sunset." The Arabs conquered the region between 643 and 711 C.E., and ruled it through semiautonomous kingdoms and tribes. From the ninth to the fourteenth century, the Maghrib produced impressive Islamic realms with robust trade economies tied to Saharan caravan routes. In the sixteenth century, the Ottoman Empire conquered the coasts of present-day Tunisia and Algeria, while the interior desert regions and Morocco remained autonomous, free from imperial rule.

France colonized the Maghrib between 1830 and 1912, and from that period, French was commonly spoken in addition to Berber and Arabic. Morocco and Tunisia achieved independence with little violence in 1956, while Algeria fought the bitter Algerian War of Independence from 1954 until 1962 to achieve its freedom. Libya, once a colony of Italy, was next governed by France and Britain, and became independent in 1951.

See also ALGERIAN WAR OF INDEPENDENCE.

Bibliography

Laroui, Abdullah. *The History of the Maghrib: An Interpretive Essay.* Princeton, NJ: Princeton University Press, 1977.

ELIZABETH THOMPSON

MAGIC CARPET OPERATION

Airlift of Jews to the new State of Israel from the southern Arabian Peninsula.

Operation Magic Carpet was the popular name given to Operation on Wings of Eagles, the airlift that, between 16 December 1948 and 24 September 1950, brought most of the ancient Jewish communities of the southern Arabian peninsula to the new State of Israel. The evacuees included about 43,000 Yemenites, more than 3,000 Adenis, and nearly 1,000 Habbanis (from Hadramawt).

This dramatic operation was run by the Jewish Agency with assistance from the American Joint Distribution Committee. The planes for the airlift came from a specially formed U.S. charter airline, the Near East Air Transport Company. During the height of this exodus, in the fall of 1949, as many as eleven planes flying around the clock carried people from the departure point in the British protectorate of Aden to Lod Airport in Israel. Many of the Yemenite refugees trekked hundreds of miles over rough terrain, in many cases entirely on foot, to reach the Hashid transit camp in Aden to await evacuation.

See also HADRAMAWT; JEWISH AGENCY FOR PALESTINE.

Bibliography

Ahroni, Reuben. *Jewish Emigration from the Yemen, 1951–98: Carpet without Magic.* Richmond, U.K.: Curzon, 2001.

Barer, Shlomo. *The Magic Carpet.* New York: Harper, 1952.

Parfitt, Tudor. *The Road to Redemption: The Jews of the Yemen, 1900–1950.* Leiden, Netherlands, and New York: Brill, 1996.

NORMAN STILLMAN

MAGNES, JUDAH
[1877–1948]

U.S. Reform rabbi, founder and first president of the Hebrew University of Jerusalem.

Judah Magnes was born in San Francisco, and received rabbinic ordination at Hebrew Union College in 1900 and a doctorate in philosophy at the University of Berlin and University of Heidelberg. He served as rabbi of New York's Temple Emanuel from 1906 to 1910, when he was forced to resign because he was viewed as too traditional. He then served as rabbi of New York's Conservative Congregation B'nai Jeshurun from 1911 to 1912. He was one of the founders of the American Jewish Committee and president of New York's organized Jewish community (the *Kehilla*) from 1908 to 1922, and he helped to found the Yiddish daily newspaper *Der Tag*, the American Civil Liberties Union, and the American-Jewish Joint Distribution Committee. He was a delegate to the Zionist Congress in 1905, and served as secretary of the Federation of American Zionists from 1905 to 1908.

Magnes immigrated to Palestine in 1922 and became the first president of the Hebrew University of Jerusalem in 1925. He rejected the dominant Zionist notion of "the negation of the Diaspora" and continued to believe that both Zion and the diaspora were of equal importance in Jewish life. His personal contacts and political discussions with Harry St. John Philby, Musa al-Alami, George Antonius, and Nuri Saʿid periodically put him at loggerheads with the official Zionist leadership. He was one of the leaders of the Ihud (unity) movement, a small group of intellectuals who opposed the establishment of a Jewish state in Palestine and argued instead for a binational state. Among his colleagues were such notables as Martin Buber, Hans Kohn, Arthur Ruppin, Samuel Hugo Bergman, and Gershom Scholem. A confirmed pacifist for much of his life, Magnes modified his views after Hitler's rise to power. Following the creation of the Jewish state and the outbreak of war in early 1948, Magnes continued to lobby, during the few remaining months of his life, for a confederation of Middle Eastern states and for a conciliatory and humanitarian approach to the conflict.

See also AMERICAN JEWISH COMMITTEE; ANTONIUS, GEORGE; BUBER, MARTIN; HEBREW UNIVERSITY OF JERUSALEM; PHILBY, HARRY ST. JOHN; RUPPIN, ARTHUR.

Bibliography

Brinner, William M., and Rischin, Moses, eds. *Like All the Nations?: The Life and Legacy of Judah L. Magnes.* Albany: State University of New York Press, 1987.

Goren, Arthur A. *Dissenter in Zion: From the Writings of Judah L. Magnes.* Cambridge, MA: Harvard University Press, 1982.

Magnes, Judah Leon. *The Magnes–Philby Negotiations, 1929: The Historical Record.* Jerusalem: Magnes Press, Hebrew University, 1998.

BRYAN DAVES
UPDATED BY NEIL CAPLAN
UPDATED BY CHAIM I. WAXMAN

MAHALLA AL-KUBRA, AL-

Egyptian city in the Nile delta.

Mahalla al-Kubra is a city (pop. 395,000 in 1996) located near the center of the Nile delta, some sixty miles (96.5 km) north of Cairo, in the province of Gharbiya. The climate is, like much of Egypt along the Mediterranean, relatively wetter than that of Cairo, with humidity averaging about 60 percent. Winter temperatures range from 43–66F° (6–19C°), while summer ranges from 63–88F° (17–31C°).

The delta is the great cotton-growing area of Egypt, and the principal industry of Mahalla is cotton-

textile production, as it was for much of the twentieth century. Mahalla is, in fact, the center of the Egyptian textile industry, but rice and flour mills are also important. The area has been associated with textiles for a long time, since silk weaving became important there in the Middle Ages. In 1927, Egypt's Bank Misr created the Misr Spinning and Weaving Company there—a giant modern industrial plant and one of the three largest industrial undertakings in Egypt (the other two being a sugar refinery in Giza province and a textile firm in Alexandria). As of 2002, textile production accounted for about a quarter of Egypt's industrial revenues.

Bibliography

Davis, Eric. *Challenging Colonialism: Bank Misr and Egyptian Industrialization, 1920–1941.* Princeton, NJ: Princeton University Press, 1983.

Goldberg, Ellis. *Tinker, Tailor, and Textile Worker: Class and Politics in Egypt, 1930–1952.* Berkeley: University of California Press, 1986.

ELLIS GOLDBERG

MAHALLE SCHOOLS

Provincial schools in the Ottoman Empire.

Most of the public schools in the Ottoman Empire were built and funded by local governments. These governments often organized councils to build the schools, hoping that they would stimulate economic development. Most *mahalle* schools offered elementary level education, although curricula varied. With the 1869 Regulation for Public Instruction, the central government organized provincial councils to distribute state funds and encourage standardization of curricula and examinations at the local schools.

The number of students in mahalle schools rose from 242,017 boys and 126,454 girls in 1867 to 640,721 boys and 253,349 girls in 1895, roughly one-third of all children of elementary school age. There were only 35,731 students in the Ruşdiye schools (funded by the central government), and nearly 400,000 in foreign and Millet System elementary schools.

See also MILLET SYSTEM; OTTOMAN EMPIRE; RUŞDIYE SCHOOLS.

Bibliography

Shaw, Stanford J., and Shaw, Ezel Kural. *History of the Ottoman Empire and Modern Turkey.* Vol. 2: *Reform, Revolution, and Republic, 1808–1975.* Cambridge, U.K., and New York: Cambridge University Press, 1977.

ELIZABETH THOMPSON

MAHDAWI, FADIL ABBAS AL-
[1915–1963]

Iraqi army colonel with a bachelor's degree in law; a cousin of Prime Minister Abd al-Karim Qasim.

Fadil Abbas al-Mahdawi was born in Baghdad to a poor family. He became known for his role as head of the special military court, commonly called the people's court. Established by Abd al-Karim Qasim, the court was infamous for its unorthodox and demagogic procedures. From 1958 to 1962, the court tried leaders of Iraq's monarchical regime (1958–1959), members of the Baʿth party who had tried to assassinate Qasim (1959), and army officers who attempted a coup against Qasim (1959). Mahdawi was executed, along with Qasim, by the officers who staged a successful coup against his regime in February 1963.

See also BAʿTH, AL-; QASIM, ABD AL-KARIM.

Bibliography

Khadduri, Majid. *Republican Iraq: A Study in Iraqi Politics since the Revolution of 1958.* London and New York: Oxford University Press, 1969.

LOUAY BAHRY

MAHD-E ULYA, MALEK JAHAN KHANUM
[1805–1873]

Wife of Mohammad Shah Qajar, third monarch of Persia's Qajar dynasty, and mother of Naser al-Din Shah, the fourth monarch. She became known as Mahd-e Ulya upon her son's accession to the throne in 1848.

Malek Jahan Khanum Mahd-e Ulya was the daughter of Soleyman Khan E'tezad al-Dowleh Qajar Qovanlu; her mother was the daughter of Fath Ali Shah, second monarch of Persia's Qajar Dynasty. Her marriage to Mohammad Shah, third monarch of the Qajar dynasty, in 1819 united the two branches of the Qajar tribe, as decreed by Agha Mohammad Qajar, the founder of the dynasty. In addition to her son, she had a daughter, Malekzadeh Khanum, who married Mirza Taqi Khan Amir Kabir, who later became premier for her brother the shah. Mahd-e Ulya was well educated, knew Arabic, was an accomplished calligraphist, and was well versed in literature.

Mahd-e Ulya was entrusted with the affairs of state at the end of her husband's life, until the crown prince could reach the palace in Tehran from Tabriz, the traditional seat of the heir to the throne. She had ruled successfully and continued to be involved in politics after her son became shah but was displeased by her daughter's husband, Amir Kabir, who was trying to enact modern reforms as premier. Court intrigues caused Amir Kabir to lose the trust of the young shah, and he was dismissed, then exiled, and later put to death.

Mahd-e Ulya has been blamed for this action and remains an unpopular historical figure because of her association with the death of one of Persia's most remarkable ministers.

See also AMIR KABIR, MIRZA TAQI KHAN; FATH ALI SHAH QAJAR; QAJAR, AGHA MOHAMMAD; QAJAR DYNASTY.

Bibliography

Avery, Peter. *Modern Iran.* New York: Praeger, 1965.

Watson, R. G. *A History of Persia from the Beginning of the Nineteenth Century to the Year 1858.* London: Smith, Elder, 1866.

MANSOUREH ETTEHADIEH

MAHDI

Arabic term for the redeemer or messiah.

In Arabic, the term *al-mahdi* means "the guided one." For Islam, the term developed through medieval Shiʿite thought into a concept charged with genealogical, eschatological (referring to the end of the world), and political significance. By the eighth century, the *mahdi* would be characterized as a descendant of the prophet Muhammad, whose appearance as the redeemer, or messiah (from Hebrew *mashiah,* the anointed), presaged the end of the world and all earthly political and religious corruption.

Today, in Iraq and Iran, and in portions of Arabia and the gulf, the Shiʿa branch of Islam is represented by Twelver Shiʿites, who believe in the return of the hidden twelfth descendant of Muhammad as the *mahdi*. Until he reappears, Twelver Shiʿites believe that only their *mujtahids* (an elite group among their religious learned) have the power as the *mahdi*'s intermediaries to interpret the faith.

The concept of the *mahdi* is not central to the beliefs of Sunni Islam, but it has popular appeal. In 1881, Muhammad Ahmad (d. 1885) claimed to be the *mahdi* and led an uprising in the Sudan that outlasted him and was not put down by the British until 1898. *Mahdism* inspired unrest during the nineteenth century in both West and North Africa. In 1849, Bu Zian led a revolt in Algeria against taxation and the French occupation in the name of the *mahdi*.

See also AHMAD, MUHAMMAD; SHIʿISM; SUNNI ISLAM.

Bibliography

Sachedina, Abdulaziz Abdulhussein. *Islamic Messianism: The Idea of Mahdī in Twelver Shīʿism.* Albany: State University of New York Press, 1981.

DENISE A. SPELLBERG

MAHDIST STATE

Independent government formed in the northern Sudan from 1885 to 1898.

The Mahdist state was established in the Sudan in January 1885 by Muhammad Ahmad ibn Abdullah, the self-declared *mahdi* (the expected divine leader of Islam), after he routed the Turko-Egyptian government and armed forces. He died 22 June 1885 and was succeeded by Muhammad Turshain Abdullahi, who ruled as Khalifat al-Mahdi (successor of the Mahdi) until 1898. Abdullahi, the Mahdi's closest lieutenant since 1881, commanded the army, treasury, and daily administration during the rebellion. A member of the Taʿaysha tribe, he led the troops of the *baqqara* (cattle-herding) nomads of the western provinces of Kordofan and Darfur.

Khalifa Abdullahi transformed a tribally based, religious-nationalist uprising into a centralized bureaucratic state that controlled most of the northern Sudan. From 1885 to 1891, his rule was contested by the Ashraf (relatives of the Mahdi) and their supporters in the tribes that originated in the Nile valley *(awlad al-balad)*. The Khalifa, whose troops controlled the capital of Omdurman and the corn-growing Gezira, prevented the Mahdi's kinsman Khalifa Muhammad Sharif ibn Hamid from being named ruler and deposed most of the military and administrative leaders of the awlad al-balad army. The Khalifa also feared losing control over the baqqara forces and even his Taʿaysha tribe and therefore, in March 1888, ordered them to march to the capital and serve as his standing army. There, the Taʿaysha had to be placated by massive supplies of food and gold, and their presence exacerbated the Khalifa's rift with the *awlad al-balad*. When the Ashraf attempted a final rebellion in November 1891, the Khalifa destroyed their military and bureaucratic power.

Natural calamities in 1889/90 led to famine and epidemics, which were exacerbated by the limited administrative capacities of the government and the food requirements of the troops. The exodus of the tribal forces also reduced grain and cattle production in the west while overburdening the Nile valley. Meanwhile, the Khalifa regularized the operations of the state treasury and reintroduced the taxes and administrative methods of the Turko-Egyptian period. Moreover, he organized a 9,000-person bodyguard, commanded by his son Uthman Shaykh al-Din. Called the Mulazimiyya, that half-slave force superseded the Taʿaysha tribe as the principal military support for the regime. The Khalifa thus isolated and destroyed any alternative power centers and consolidated his control over the state apparatus.

The territorial limits of the Mahdist state encompassed most of today's northern Sudan. Its control of the Nile river route through the south was tenuous: it only ruled Bahr al-Ghazal in 1885/86, and Belgian and French expeditions began to penetrate the south in the mid-1890s. The Khalifa controlled Darfur from 1887 to 1889, but the border region with Ethiopia remained contested and British troops controlled Suwakin port on the Red Sea. Seesaw battles with Ethiopia helped to open the way for Italy to consolidate control over Eritrea and to capture grain-rich Kassallah, and for Britain to capture the Tukar region south of Suwakin.

The Mahdi had envisioned that his revolution would spread throughout the Muslim world. But the Khalifa's effort to march on Egypt was crushed at the battle near Tushki on the Egyptian frontier, 3 August 1889. (The Khalifa had sent messages inviting Britain's Queen Victoria, the sultan of the Ottoman Empire, and the khedive of Egypt to submit to the Mahdiyya.) The Khalifa then focused on consolidating his administration at home, rather than attempting to spread the message abroad.

The Mahdist state fell in 1898, not as a result of internal disintegration, but at the hands of the superior power of the Anglo-Egyptian army led by Lord Horatio Herbert Kitchener. His forces entered the Sudan in early 1896 from Egypt and constructed a railway system as they moved south. In April 1898, three thousand Sudanese died in the battle at Atbara; eleven thousand died in the battle of Karari, north of Omdurman, on 2 September 1898, which marked the end of the Mahdist state. The Khalifa escaped to the west, dying in the battle of Umma Diwaykarat, near Kosti, 24 November 1899.

The Mahdist movement was based on a blend of religion, social discontent, and antiforeign sentiment. In its short time span, the Mahdist state became bureaucratized and lost its religious aura. Although the tribes resented taxes and the controls imposed by government, the increasingly complex administration and judiciary stabilized the regime and enabled it to rule over wide expanses for its thirteen years.

See also ABDULLAHI, MUHAMMAD TURSHAIN; AHMAD, MUHAMMAD; ANSAR, AL-; KASSALLAH; KHARTOUM; KITCHENER, HORATIO HERBERT; SUDAN.

Bibliography

Holt, P. M., and Daly, M. W. *The History of the Sudan: From the Coming of Islam the Present Day,* 5th edition. Harlow, U.K., and New York: Longman, 2000.

Shebeika, Mekki. *The Independent Sudan.* New York: Speller, 1959.

ANN M. LESCH

MAHFUZ, NAJIB
[1911–]

Egyptian author; winner of the Nobel Prize for Literature, 1988.

Najib Mahfuz (also Naguib Mahfouz) was born in the Jamaliyya district of Cairo in 1911 and began writing at the age of seventeen. He studied philosophy at Cairo University, and is said to have been influenced by Balzac, Zola, Camus, Tolstoy, Dostoevsky, and Proust. He has written nearly forty novels as well as some fourteen volumes of short stories, many of which have been translated and published in English. The first Arab writer to have devoted most of his energies to one literary genre, he excels at the experimental novel, most notably in *al-Liss wa al-Kilab* (1961; *The Thief and the Dogs*), in which he employs modern techniques such as stream-of-consciousness. He has freely acknowledged his indebtedness to the early Fabian socialist Salama Musa, and although he later showed some skepticism about the sufficiency of reason as the arbiter of human affairs, there are no indications that he favors the revival of the traditional values of Islam, or that he has ever departed from a broad humanism. Mahfuz is as much a social historian or anthropologist as a writer who, like a fly on the wall, captures an unadulterated picture of daily life among Cairo's urban masses. He recreates a world he is intimately familiar with, lending a story of his creation to a space that is ethnographic. His novels are also highly political and historic. In *Miramar* to the *Cairo Trilogy,* he weaves a political history of Egypt between the wars, and yet his objective narration and use of a polyphonic narrative (in *Miramar*) prevents them from being one-sided. However, after translating James Baikie's *Ancient Egypt* into Arabic in 1932, Mahfuz was inspired to write a series of historical novels set in pharaonic times. One of them, *Radubis* (1943), which concerned a young pharaoh who loses the support of his people, was interpreted as an attack on Egypt's King Farouk. It was not until 1959, when he published *Children of Gebalawi* (also known as *Children of the Alley*), that his work was denounced—by religious leaders as blasphemous. It was banned in Egypt, and later published in Beirut. In 1994 Mahfuz was stabbed in the neck, presumably by religious extremists angered by his unorthodox depictions of religious prophets. Najib Mahfuz has more than fifty titles to his credit, more than a dozen of which are available in translation. He was awarded the Nobel Prize for literature in 1988.

See also LITERATURE: ARABIC; MUSA, SALAMA.

Bibliography

Peled, Mattityahu. *Religion, My Own: The Literary Works of Najib Mahfuz.* Fredericton, NJ: Transactions Books, 1983.

Somekh, Sasson. *The Changing Rhythm: A Study of Najib Mahfuz's Novels.* Leiden, Netherlands: Brill, 1973.

PIERRE CACHIA
UPDATED BY ROXANNE VARZI

MAHIR, AHMAD

[c. 1886–1945]

Egyptian politician; prime minister, 1944–1945.

Ahmad Mahir was one of the most important figures in the early history of the Wafd party in Egypt, which under the leadership of Saʿd Zaghlul came to prominence in Egyptian politics after World War I and the Egyptian Revolution of 1919. Son of Muhammad Mahir, Egypt's under-secretary of state for war, and brother of Ali Pasha Mahir, he attended Cairo University for a doctoral degree in law and economics.

Implicated in the November 1924 assassination of Sir Lee Stack, the British governor-general of the Sudan, but acquitted of all charges, Mahir occupied several ministerial positions in Wafd governments before being expelled from the party in January 1938, along with Mahmud Fahmi al-Nuqrashi, as a result of an internal party dispute. The two then founded the Saʿdist party (named for Saʿd Zaghlul). Mahir served as prime minister of Egypt from October 1944 to February 1945. During the preliminaries to the San Francisco conference at which the United Nations was to be founded, Mahir, believing that Egypt's future interests lay in participation, advocated a declaration of war against the Axis. On 24 February 1945 he was assassinated while presenting this proposal to the Egyptian parliament.

See also STACK, LEE; WAFD; ZAGHLUL, SAʿD.

Bibliography

Deeb, Marius. *Party Politics in Egypt: The Wafd and Its Rivals 1919–1939.* London: Ithaca Press, 1979.

ROGER ALLEN

MAHIR, ALI

[1882–1960]

Egyptian politician.

While Ali Mahir and his younger brother, Ahmad Mahir, were both prominently involved in the politics of Egypt during the turbulent years between the two world wars, their careers took quite different paths. Ali was educated in the law and an early associate of Saʿd Zaghlul and the Wafd (Egyptian independence party) in the years following Egypt's anticolonial uprising in 1919 (Egypt had become a British protectorate). Following the squabble between Zaghlul and Adli Pasha in 1921, Mahir dissociated himself from the Wafd. In 1922, Britain had been forced to declare Egypt a sovereign state but reserved rights to the Suez Canal and to defend Egypt. With a Machiavellian instinct for political intrigue and survival, Mahir managed to occupy a large number of political positions in the ensuing decades, including service on three occasions as prime minister of Egypt.

Mahir was closely associated with the palace, being appointed chief of the royal cabinet in 1935. His services were always at the king's disposal whenever there was a need to express royal displeasure at outside pressure, most especially when the British were involved. Mahir's terms as prime minister were short. He served in the post for a few months in 1936 but was dismissed during the constitutional discussions that followed the death of King Fuʾad and the succession of King Farouk. Equally brief was his premiership from 1939 until June 1940, when his palace affiliations and King Farouk's preference for the Axis powers (Germany and its allies) led to British demands that Mahir be dismissed.

Following World War II, Ali Mahir continued to play his role as one of the éminences grises of Egyptian political life. It was hardly surprising that, following the uprisings in Cairo in January 1952, Mahir was one of several politicians asked to serve as prime minister in the period leading up to the July Revolution. It was Mahir who conveyed to King Farouk the command of the Revolutionary Council (chaired by General Muhammad Naguib) that the king abdicate. Following Farouk's abdication and departure for Italy in June 1953, Mahir continued to play a role as chairman of a constitutional commission. Its work was never completed, being overtaken by the rapid developments of the ensuing months—the abolition of the monarchy and the proclamation of a republic under General Naguib, who turned it over to Gamal Abdel Nasser.

See also ADLI; FAROUK; FU'AD; MAHIR, AH-MAD; NAGUIB, MUHAMMAD; NASSER, GAMAL ABDEL; WAFD; ZAGHLUL, SA'D.

Bibliography

Deeb, Marius. *Party Politics in Egypt: The Wafd and Its Rivals, 1919–1939.* London: Ithaca Press for the Middle East Centre, St. Antony's College, Oxford, 1979.

ROGER ALLEN

MAHMUD II
[1785–1839]

Ottoman sultan, 1808–1839.

Mahmud, the youngest of twelve sons of Sultan Ab-dülhamit I, ascended the throne of the Ottoman Empire on 28 July 1808. Demonstrating strong leadership and dedication to traditional values, he gradually assembled a coalition of religious and po-litical leaders who desired to reestablish orderly gov-ernment. During Mahmud's reign, the Ottoman Empire continued its decline in relation to the West: Its dependence on Europe increased, and it suffered military humiliation and territorial losses. But within the reduced confines of his realm, Mahmud's achievements were considerable. He resurrected the sultan's office and reformed and rejuvenated the central government. He arrested the disintegration of the state and initiated a process of consolidation. In spite of his intensive reform activities, Mahmud did not attempt to alter the basic fabric of Ottoman society, rather to strengthen it through modern means, and generally he succeeded in integrating the old elite into the new institutions. This was in keeping with his strong attachment to the ideal of justice in the traditional Ottoman sense. The so-briquet he selected for himself, "Adli" (Just, or Law-ful), is an indication of the cast of his mind. Although he may not have intended it, Mahmud's reforms produced basic change and launched Ot-toman society on the course of modernization in a final and irrevocable manner.

Wars with Russia (1806–1812, 1828–1829) re-sulted in the Ottomans ceding to Russia the area of Bessarabia (Treaty of Bucharest, 28 May 1812) and subsequently the Danube delta in Europe and the province of Akhaltsikhe (Ahisha) in Asia (Treaty of Adrianople, 14 September 1829). The latter treaty also required the Ottomans to pay Russia a sizable indemnity and to recognize the autonomy of Ser-bia, Moldavia, Wallachia, and Greece under Russ-ian protection. Later, as a result of negotiations among the European powers, Greece became an in-dependent monarchy (July 1832).

During his efforts to quell the rebellion in Greece (1821–1828), Mahmud appealed to Muham-mad Ali, his governor of Egypt, for assistance. Al-though Egypt's newly formed, European-style army initially was successful (1825–1827), the plight of the Greeks elicited European intervention. Britain, France, and Russia sent their fleets to Greece, and on 20 October 1827, inside the harbor of Navarino, they destroyed an Ottoman-Egyptian fleet. Muham-mad Ali sought compensation for his losses in Greece and demanded that Mahmud cede to him the governorship of Syria. When this request was re-jected, Egypt's army invaded Syria (October 1831), defeated three Ottoman armies, marched into Ana-tolia, occupied Kütahya (2 February 1833), and was poised to march on Constantinople. Mahmud sought help from the great powers, but only Russia dis-patched a naval force to defend Constantinople (February 1833). This induced Britain and France to offer mediation that resulted in the Peace of Kü-tahya (8 April), which conferred on Muhammad Ali the governorship of Syria and the province of Adana.

Despite military disasters, Mahmud proceeded with his reform measures, continuing to focus on centralization of government and greater efficiency in its work. Since early in his reign, he had intro-duced significant improvements in the military, es-pecially in the artillery and the navy. In the spring of 1826, with his authority restored at the capital and in many provinces, Mahmud decided to reor-ganize part of the janissary corps as an elite unit of active soldiers called Eşkinciyan. Mahmud enlisted the support of the religious and bureaucratic elite as well as the janissary officers themselves. Never-theless, on the night of 14 June the janissaries rose up in arms. Mahmud mustered loyal troops, and on 15 June the rebellion was crushed with considerable bloodshed. Two days later an imperial decree abolished the janissary corps.

The suppression of the janissaries had an enormous impact on Ottoman society and also in Europe, where the Janissary Corps had been viewed for five centuries as the military strength of the Ottoman Empire. In an effort to gain universal approval, the regime called the incident "the Beneficial Affair" (*Vaka-i Hayriye*). The Eşkinciyan project was abandoned in favor of a more ambitious plan calling for the formation of an entirely new army organized and trained according to Western models. Military defeats and the apparent failure of the government's attempts to reform the army rekindled unrest and rebellion in far-flung provinces, especially in Bosnia, Albania, eastern Anatolia, and Baghdad. The government was generally successful in suppressing these uprisings by employing the newly disciplined troops, who proved effective at coercion and centralization.

In 1835 Mahmud reconstituted the entire government into three independent branches: the civil bureaucracy, the religious-judicial hierarchy, and the military. Their respective heads were considered equal and were responsible directly to the sultan. The aggrandizement of the court, now the seat of all power, was mainly at the expense of the grand vizier's office. To underscore the reduction of his authority, in 1838 the grand vizier's title officially was changed to prime minister. At the same time, his chief assistants were given the title of minister. Consultative councils were established to supervise military and civil matters and to propose new legislation. The highest of these, the Supreme Council for Judicial Ordinances (*Meclis-i Vala-yi Ahkam-i Adliye*), established in 1838, acted as an advisory council to the sultan.

The military, which during Mahmud's last years was allocated about 70 percent of the state's revenues, continued to be the focal point of reform. Most significant was the gradual extension of the authority of the commander-in-chief. His office came to combine the roles of a ministry of war and general staff, and was in charge of all land forces. The navy continued to operate independently under the grand admiral, whose administration comprised a separate ministry.

Mahmud II came to power in 1808, after the deposition and murder of his brother, Mustafa IV. His most notable achievement was the destruction of the janissaries, an elite Ottoman fighting corps that had become inefficient and rebellious. © GETTY IMAGES. REPRODUCED BY PERMISSION.

In May 1835 an Ottoman expeditionary force occupied Tripoli in Africa, claiming it back for the sultan. In the following years, Ottoman fleets appeared several times before Tunis, but were turned back by the French navy. In the spring of 1839, believing that his army had sufficiently recovered and that a general uprising in Syria against Egypt's rule was imminent, Mahmud precipitated another crisis. On 24 June the Egyptians decisively routed the Ottoman army at Nizip. Mahmud died on 1 July, probably before learning of his army's defeat.

See also JANISSARIES; MUHAMMAD ALI; VAKA-I HAYRIYE.

Bibliography

Berkes, Niyazi. *The Development of Secularism in Turkey.* Montreal: McGill University Press, 1964.

Levy, Avigdor. "The Officer Corps in Sultan Mahmud II's New Ottoman Army, 1826–1839." *International Journal of Middle East Studies* 2 (1971): 21–39.

Levy, Avigdor. "Ottoman Attitudes to the Rise of Balkan Nationalism." In *War and Society in East Central Europe*, Vol. 1, edited by Bela K. Kiraly and G. E. Rothenberg. New York: Brooklyn College Press, 1979.

Levy, Avigdor. "The Ottoman Ulema and the Military Reforms of Sultan Mahmud II." *Asian and African Studies* 7 (1971): 13–39.

Shaw, Stanford J., and Shaw, Ezel Kural. *History of the Ottoman Empire and Modern Turkey*. Vol. 2. Cambridge, U.K.: Cambridge University Press, 1977.

AVIGDOR LEVY
UPDATED BY ERIC HOOGLUND

MAHMUD DURRANI
[1765–1829]

Amir of Afghanistan, 1800–1803, 1809–1818.

Mahmud Durrani was one of twenty-one sons of Afghan Amir Timur Shah (1773–1793) and the second oldest. Mahmud was governor of Herat, and in 1800 he successfully fought his half brother Zaman Shah for the Kabul throne. Content to leave the governing to Barakzai ministers, Mahmud was ousted by another half brother, Shah Shuja, the seventh son of Timur. Mahmud was imprisoned but escaped to Kandahar in 1809 and regained the Kabul throne in 1813. Once again driven from power in 1819, he retired to Herat, where he died in 1829; according to some reports the cause of death was malaria, but others suggest that he was poisoned by his ambitious son Kamran.

Mahmud's reign marked the beginning of internal conflict and civil war, which was to continue throughout the nineteenth century, until the reign of Abdur Rahman (1880–1901). During this period, much of the territory originally belonging to Afghanistan was lost. Mahmud was a weak leader who preferred to enjoy the perquisites of royalty rather than tending to affairs of state.

See also BARAKZAI DYNASTY.

Bibliography

Fletcher, Arnold. *Afghanistan: Highway of Conquest*. Ithaca, NY: Cornell University Press, 1965.

GRANT FARR

MAHMUDIYYA CANAL

Artificial waterway in Egypt.

Built between 1817 and 1820 at the command of Muhammad Ali, viceroy of Egypt, this navigation canal connected Alexandria with the delta village of al-Atf and hence with Bulaq, the port city of Cairo. Its construction cost 35,000 purses (7.5 million French francs). Possibly as many as 300,000 peasants were conscripted to dig it during the period of concentrated work in 1819, costing between 12,000 and 100,000 casualties. Owing to the Nile floods, the canal has been dredged often, and annual improvements have been made since its construction. It also provided some summer irrigation and some of Alexandria's drinking water supply.

See also MUHAMMAD ALI.

Bibliography

Rivlin, Helen Anne B. *The Agricultural Policy of Muhammad Ali in Egypt*. Cambridge, MA: Harvard University Press, 1961.

ARTHUR GOLDSCHMIDT

MAHMUD, MUHAMMAD
[1877–1941]

Egyptian politician and prime minister.

Born into a family of wealthy landowners in Upper Egypt and educated at Oxford University in England, Muhammad Mahmud was one of the original members of the Wafd. Along with Sa'd Zaghlul and two other Egyptian leaders, he was banished by the British to Malta during the anticolonial uprising in March 1919. In 1922, after Britain declared Egypt's independence, he split from the Wafd and became a leader in the Liberal Constitutionalist Party. King Fuad appointed him prime minister in June 1928, and he ruled without a parliament for eighteen months under a "law and order" slogan. During the 1930s he and his party steered a middle course between the royalist government of Isma'il Sidqi and the popular Wafd Party.

In 1937, when young King Farouk dismissed the Wafdist cabinet of Mustafa al-Nahhas, Mahmud again became prime minister, heading a cabinet made up of minority parties that excluded the Wafd. His resignation in August 1939 was attributed to ill health but was, in fact, due to Ali Mahir's political intrigues and the king's partiality toward Germany at the onset of World War II.

See also LIBERAL CONSTITUTIONALIST PARTY; MAHIR, ALI; NAHHAS, MUSTAFA AL-; SIDQI, ISMA'IL; WAFD; ZAGHLUL, SA'D.

Bibliography

Deeb, Marius. *Party Politics in Egypt: The Wafd and Its Rivals, 1919–1939.* London: Ithaca Press for the Middle East Centre; Oxford: St. Antony's College, 1979.

Goldschmidt, Arthur. *Biographical Dictionary of Modern Egypt.* Boulder, CO: L. Rienner, 1999.

Sayyid-Marsot, Afaf Lutfi al-. *Egypt's Liberal Experiment, 1922–1936.* Berkeley: University of California Press, 1977.

ROGER ALLEN
UPDATED BY ARTHUR GOLDSCHMIDT

MAHMUD, MUSTAFA
[1921–]

Muslim physician, author, philanthropist, and television personality.

Born and raised in Tanta, Mustafa Mahmud studied at the Faculty of Medicine at Cairo University. He practiced medicine from 1952 to 1966 and wrote a book, *Allah wa al-insan* (God and the human being), that was banned by a state court during the Nasser era for its materialism. After several years of adherence to leftist, secular, and materialistic values, he gave up his medical practice to write books, including a commentary on the Qur'an, and he gradually became a convinced Muslim, as described in his autobiography, *Rihlati min al-shakk ila al-iman* (My journey from doubt to belief), first published in 1972. Concurrently he began to host a television series called *Al-Ilm wa al-Iman* (Science and faith), portraying the phenomena and the creatures of the natural world and proving God to be their primary cause. The series became immensely popular with Egypt's educated middle class. Dissatisfied with the efficacy of doctors and hospitals in caring for sick people, he raised the funds necessary to build a mosque in the upscale Muhandisin district of Cairo with an attached charitable association, including a hospital and polyclinic, in 1975. This organization

now includes an aquarium, library, observatory, geological museum, and seminar hall. While managing this complex of religious institutions, he has continued to write and to speak on television. Among his publications are two books that have been translated into English, *Marxism and Islam* and *Dialogue with an Atheist.* Drawing on charitable contributions by Egyptians and by Arabs from the Gulf states, he has successfully provided generous benefits to a large professional staff and low-cost health care for thousands of patients, independent of the Egyptian government. He has successfully avoided any involvement in revolutionary Islamist movements and forthrightly condemns terrorism. Although not a member of the *ulama*, Mustafa Mahmud has become one of Egypt's most influential and respected authorities on Islamic beliefs and institutions because of his reconciliation of science and faith in terms understandable to modernized Egyptians.

Bibliography

Mahmud, Mustafa. *Dialogue with an Atheist,* translated by Mohamed Yehia. London: Dar al-Taqwa, 1994.

Mahmud, Mustafa. *Marxism and Islam,* translated by M. M. Enani. Cairo, 1984.

Murphy, Caryle. *Passion for Islam: Shaping the Modern Middle East—The Egyptian Experience.* New York: Scribner, 2002.

Rubin, Barry. *Islamic Fundamentalism in Egyptian Politics.* Updated ed. New York: Palgrave Macmillan, 2002.

Salvatore, Armando. "Social Differentiation, Moral Authority, and Public Islam in Egypt: The Path of Mustafa Mahmud." *Anthropology Today* 16, no. 2 (2000): 12–15.

Sullivan, Denis J. *Private Voluntary Organizations in Egypt: Islamic Development, Private Initiative, and State Control.* Gainesville: University Press of Florida, 1994.

ARTHUR GOLDSCHMIDT

MAHMUD OF SULAYMANIYA
[1878–1956]

Kurdish leader.

Born to a prestigious family of Islamic shaykhs in Barzinja (Ottoman Kurdistan, later Iraq), Mahmud Barzinji became the main adversary of Britain's efforts to integrate the Kurds of the *vilayet* (province) of Mosul into Iraq. Proclaiming himself king of Kurdistan in the city of Sulaymaniya, he led several revolts from 1918 to 1930—first against the British then against the new Iraqi monarchy.

See also KURDS.

Bibliography

Edmonds, C. J. *Kurds, Turks, and Arabs: Politics, Travel, and Research in North-Eastern Iraq, 1919–1925.* London and New York: Oxford University Press, 1957.

CHRIS KUTSCHERA

MAIMON, YEHUDAH LEIB HACOHEN
[1875–1962]

Religious Zionist leader, author, and first Israeli minister of religious affairs.

Yehudah Leib Hacohen Maimon was born in Markuleshti, Bessarabia, Russia. His parents supported the Lovers of Zion (Horevei Zion; also Hibbat Zion) movement and he was exposed to classic religious Zionist writing from an early age. He studied in the yeshivas (Jewish religious schools) of Lithuania, developing extensive ties with other religious Zionists. One of his associations was with Rabbi Isaac Jacob Reines, founder of the Mizrahi party within the World Zionist Organization, and Maimon rose to leadership there. He immigrated to Palestine in 1913, was arrested and imprisoned, then expelled by the Turks in 1915. He returned to Palestine in 1919, by permission of the British, after spending some years in the United States.

Along with Rabbi A. I. Kook, Maimon established the chief rabbinate in Palestine. In 1935, he was elected Mizrahi representative to the executive of the Jewish Agency. Maimon then founded the Mossad Harav Kook educational institute and publishing house, where he edited the periodical *Sinai*. As Israel's first minister of religious affairs, 1948–1951, he set policy regarding a number of major public religious issues. Maimon also authored many books on religious Zionism and major rabbinic figures.

See also HIBBAT ZION; KOOK, ABRAHAM ISAAC HACOHEN; MIZRAHI MOVEMENT.

CHAIM I. WAXMAN

MAJALI FAMILY

Prominent Jordanian political family.

The Majali family has been one of two leading Sunni Muslim families in the town of al-Karak in south-central Jordan (the other being the al-Tarawina family). Family members have long served both the Ottoman Turks and the Hashimite family that has ruled Jordan since 1921 and have occupied senior positions in the government and military.

Rufayfan (d. 1945) was decorated by the Ottomans during World War I. He later headed the self-described "Arab Government of Moab" in al-Karak, with British assistance, from 1920 to 1921. After the establishment of Transjordan, he became a significant figure in the socioeconomic and political life of south-central Jordan. He founded the Moderate Liberal Party in 1930 and sat in the Transjordanian legislative council from 1931 until his death in 1945.

Habis (1910–2001) joined the Jordanian Arab Legion in 1932. In the Arab–Israel War of 1948, he commanded the legion's fourth battalion, which defeated the Israelis at Latrun. Thereafter, Majali headed the Royal Guards unit of the army and was aide-de-camp to King Abdullah I ibn Hussein from 1949 to 1951. In 1956 he was appointed assistant chief of staff of the army following the failed coup led by Ali Abu Nuwwar. Majali was chief of staff from 1957 to 1965 and chairman of the joint chiefs of staff from 1965 to 1967. He was appointed defense minister after the Arab–Israel War of 1967, but returned to his post as chief of staff during the Black September crisis of 1970. He was later appointed to the Jordanian senate, and died in April 2001.

Hazza (1916–1960) served as minister of agriculture (1950–1951), justice (1951 and 1954–1955), and interior (1953–1954 and 1955). A rising young star on the political scene, he first served as prime minister in 1955 when King Hussein tried to join the Baghdad Pact, but quickly resigned following popular protests. He served both as prime minister and foreign minister starting in May 1959, but was assassinated in August 1960 in a bomb attack generally believed to have been carried out by agents of the Egyptian-Syrian United Arab Republic. His daughter, Taghrid (1950–), married Prince Muhammad ibn Talal, brother of King Hussein, in 1981.

Abd al-Salam (1925–) received his medical degree from the Syrian University in 1949. He was director of medical services for the Jordanian armed forces, president of Jordan University (1971–1976), and minister of health (1969–1970 and 1970–1971). He served as advisor to King Hussein starting in the late 1980s. Majali was prime minister from 1993 to 1995, during which time he signed the 1994 Jordanian-Israeli peace treaty. He later was prime minister from 1997 to 1998, after which he was appointed to the Jordanian senate.

Abd al-Hadi (1934–) was chief of staff of the Jordanian army from 1979 to 1981, after which he served as ambassador to the United States from 1981 to 1983. Al-Majali returned to Jordan to direct the Public Security Directorate (police) from 1985 to 1989. In 1990 al-Majali formed the Jordanian Covenant Party (Hizb al-Ahd al-Urdunni) to express pro-regime, East Bank nationalist feeling in opposition to leftist and Palestinian-oriented parties. He served in parliament from 1993 to 1997 and was minister of public works from 1996 to 1997. In 1997 his party merged with eight other centrist parties to form the National Constitutional Party. Al-Majali was speaker of the house of delegates in 1997.

See also KARAK, AL-; MAJALI, HAZZA AL-.

Bibliography

Salibi, Kamal. *The Modern History of Jordan.* New York: St. Martin's Press, 1992.

Wilson, Mary. *King Abdullah, Britain, and the Making of Jordan.* Cambridge, U.K., and New York: Cambridge University Press, 1987.

MICHAEL R. FISCHBACH

MAJALI, HAZZA AL-
[1918–1960]

Jordanian prime minister.

As a member of a very influential clan from the Karak area of southern Jordan, Hazza al-Majali had a strong popular base in Jordan but was viewed as a threat by Palestinians. He was asked by King Hussein ibn Talal to form a government in December 1955 that would push through Jordan's participation in the Baghdad Pact. He was forced to resign, however, a few days later as a consequence of violent demonstrations against joining. He was known

to be strongly pro-regime and encouraged cooperation with the West, particularly the United States, Britain, and Germany, who were supporting Jordan at the time both financially and technically. Yet Majali was considered to be progressive for his times because of his activism in parliament. As a member of parliament in 1953, he helped found the National Socialist Party, consisting of thirteen members of parliament. He led them in lively opposition to then Prime Minister Tawfiq Abu al-Huda, forcing him to call for new elections in 1954 rather than face a no confidence vote. He quit the party, however, after Sulayman al-Nabulsi had joined and transformed it into a left-leaning, pro-Nasser party. Majali was assassinated on 29 August 1960, fifteen months into his term as prime minister. During his term, he had earned a reputation for taking firm measures against communism and subversive activities. He was killed by a bomb placed in his office; it was widely assumed to have been the work of agents of the United Arab Republic.

See also ABU AL-HUDA, TAWFIQ; BAGHDAD PACT (1955); HUSSEIN IBN TALAL; NABULSI, SULAYMAN AL-; UNITED ARAB REPUBLIC.

JENAB TUTUNJI

MAJLES

See GLOSSARY

MAJLES AL-SHURA

National assembly of Iran.

The history of a representative, elected assembly in Iran dates to the Constitutional Revolution, when the Majles was stipulated as the legislative branch of government in the constitution. The first elections were held in the summer of 1906, and the new Majles convened in October. Except for a brief period from its inception to the end of World War I, and again from 1941 to 1953, the Majles in monarchical Iran did not enjoy a significant degree of autonomy, and it exercised little initiative in the nation's political life. Women gained suffrage in 1963, and twenty-four assemblies met from 1906 to 1978.

After the Iranian Revolution of 1979, the Majles al-Shura-ye Melli (National Assembly) was renamed the Majles al-Shura-ye Islami (Islamic Assembly), and it has played a prominent role in political affairs. The first postrevolutionary Majles opened on 28 May 1980 and elected Ali Akbar Hashemi Rafsanjani as its speaker. Its most significant act was the impeachment of the Islamic Republic's first president, Abolhasan Bani Sadr, in June 1981. After Rafsanjani became president in 1989, Mehdi Karrubi succeeded him as speaker of the Majles, a position he held until 1992, when he failed to win a seat in that year's elections. Ali Akbar Nateq-e Nuri then served as speaker until he was defeated in the 2000 Majles elections. Karrubi returned to the Majles in those elections and again was elected as speaker.

See also Bani Sadr, Abolhasan; Constitutional Revolution; Iranian Revolution (1979); Rafsanjani, Ali Akbar Hashemi.

Bibliography

Abrahamian, Ervand. *Iran between Two Revolutions.* Princeton, NJ: Princeton University Press, 1982.

Moslem, Mehdi. *Factional Politics in Post-Khomeini Iran.* Syracuse, NY: Syracuse University Press, 2002.

Neguin Yavari
Updated by Eric Hooglund

MAJLIS SHURA AL-NUWWAB

Egypt's first quasi-representative assembly.

Established in 1866 by a decree from Khedive Isma'il of Egypt, the *majlis* was intended to be a consultative council that would advise him on administrative matters. But he may have been driven by his growing financial straits to co-opt the landowning notables to raise taxes. Its seventy-five members, barred from government posts while they held office, were elected for three-year terms. Timid at first, they grew more assertive as they gained experience and often passed resolutions for administrative reforms. Nevertheless, they met for only three months at a time and were not even convened in 1872, 1874, and 1875.

While its role was subordinated to the other deliberative bodies, the Privy Council and the Council of Justice, which were smaller and made up of powerful government officials, the *majlis* emerged as one of the standard-bearers of Egyptian national-

ism in the era of the Urabi revolution. In part, this happened because the Egyptian landowners were, along with the peasants, victims of Isma'il's mismanagement and the financial stringencies adopted by Khedive Tawfiq and the Dual Control.

See also Dual Control; Isma'il ibn Ibrahim; Urabi, Ahmad.

Bibliography

Hunter, F. Robert. *Egypt under the Khedives, 1805–1879.* Pittsburgh, PA: University of Pittsburgh Press, 1984.

Landau, Jacob M. *Parliaments and Parties in Egypt.* New York: Praeger, 1954.

Schölch, Alexander. *Egypt for the Egyptians!* London: Ithaca Press, for the Middle East Centre, St. Antony's College, Oxford, 1981.

Arthur Goldschmidt

MAKDASHI, HESNA

Lebanese publisher and activist.

Originally from Lebanon, Hesna Makdashi has been active in the Egyptian publishing world since the late 1970s. In Cairo in 1992, together with four other Arab women, Makdashi founded Nour, the first publishing house to specialize in works by and about Arab women. In a publication issued by Nour in 1996, Makdashi reviewed the aims of the publishing house. She stated that the magazine should encourage women's literary and critical production, and also serve as a venue for the announcement of books by women and what is written about them. According to Makdashi, a third aim of the Nour publishing house was to organize an Arab women's book fair every two years that would serve as a platform for discussing the situation of Arab women and featuring their intellectual and creative achievement. Nour publishing house raised the funds to sponsor the first such exhibition in November 1995. The exhibit was held in the prominent Hanager Cultural Center in Cairo and attracted publishers from all over the Middle East. Makdashi served as managing editor of the magazine *Nour,* which featured articles on women writers, announcements and reviews of their literary and scholarly work, and published papers and responses emanating from the book fairs it sponsored.

See also EGYPT; GENDER: GENDER AND EDUCATION; NEWSPAPERS AND PRINT MEDIA: ARAB COUNTRIES.

Bibliography

Fernea, Elizabeth. "A Woman's Book Fair in Cairo!" In *The Middle East Women's Studies Review* 11, no. 1 (March 1996) 1–3.

Makdashi, Hesna. "Al-Nashr fi dar mutakhasisa li-kutub al-mar'a" (Publishing in an institution specializing in women's books). In *Al-Mar'a al-'arabiyya fi muwajahat al-'asr* (The Arab woman facing the epoch). Cairo: Nur- Dar al-mar'a al-'arabiyya lil-nashr, 1996.

CAROLINE SEYMOUR-JORN

MAKHMALBAF FAMILY

An Iranian family of film directors, screenplay writers, and producers.

One of Iran's internationally acclaimed film directors in the post-revolutionary period is Mohsen Makhmalbaf. His films are deeply social and deal with issues as diverse as an attack on police in the autobiographical *Bread and the Alley,* where he introduced innovations to the neorealist genre by having the original police officer play himself; to jail in *Boycott;* to the aftermath of war in *The Marriage of the Blessed;* to the situation of Afghan refugees in Iran in *The Bicycle Run;* to film itself in *Saalam Cinema.* He has also made art-house films, including *Once upon a Time Cinema.* He was the subject of a film by a fellow film director, Abbas Kiarostami; *Close-up* is the true story of an ordinary man who impersonated Makhmalbaf to gain access to a wealthy Tehran family. Makhmalbaf caught international attention with his colorful film *Gabbeh,* after which he took a break from filmmaking (in 1996) to start the Makhmalbaf film house, where his wife and children have learned the arts of filmmaking, photography, and writing, and excelled in them. Samira Makhmalbaf, his oldest daughter, became at eighteen the youngest filmmaker ever to enter a film in the Cannes Film Festival with *The Apple.* His wife Marziyeh Meshkini won international acclaim for her film, *The Day I Became Woman.* His son, Maysem, is a photographer and has produced the stills for the family's films as well as a book on his father's film *Silence* and a documentary on Samira's film *The Blackboards.* Makhmalbaf's youngest daughter, Hana, born

in 1988, has already made two films and published poetry. Her documentary on Afghanistan debuted at the Cannes Film Festival in 2003.

See also IRANIAN REVOLUTION (1979).

Bibliography

Stardust Striken. Directed by Houshang Golmakani. 1996.

ROXANNE VARZI

MAKHMALBAF, MOHSEN
[1957–]

Major Iranian filmmaker of the post-1979 era.

Mohsen Makhmalbaf's career as a filmmaker has never veered far from his career as a political activist and writer—only the genres and the political ideologies have changed over time. Born in Tehran, at the age of fifteen he began an Islamic militia organization. Later, he wounded a police officer in the shah's regime, for which he was imprisoned in 1974 and released with the Iranian Revolution of 1979. Many of his films blur the lines of social realism, fiction, and his own life story: *Boycott* (1985) is based on his experience in prison; *Moment of Innocence* (1995), on the wounding of a police officer (the real police officer plays a role in the film). Makhmalbaf is an innovator of the Iranian new wave, as seen in his films *Gabbeh* (1995) and *Salaam Cinema* (1994). He is also a visual activist concerned with domestic social issues such as the failing economy, as seen in *The Peddler* (1986); Afghans in Iran and abroad, as seen in *The Cyclist* (1987), *Kandehar* (2000), and *Afghan Alphabet* (2002) (as well as in his writings about and activism in Afghanistan); and the aftermath of the Iran-Iraq War, as seen in *Marriage of the Blessed* (1988). He is also an innovator of art-house cinema, as evidenced in films such as *Images from the Qujar Dynasty* (1992). In 1996 he began the Makhmalbaf Film House in Tehran, where he is educating his two daughters, son, and wife in the art of filmmaking and social awareness.

Bibliography

Dabashi, Hamid. *Close-up: Iranian Cinema, Past, Present, and Future.* London: Verso, 2001.

Makhmalbaf Film House web site. Available from <www.makhmalbaf.com>.

Stardust Striken. Directed by Houshang Golmakani. 1996.

ROXANNE VARZI

MAKKI, HASAN MUHAMMAD
[c. 1935–]

Yemeni government official.

Born in the mid-1930s, Hasan Muhammad Makki came from a prominent merchant family from the port of Hodeida on the Red Sea; he was a member of the Famous Forty—the boys sent abroad for education by Imam Yahya in 1947—and received his secondary and university education in Egypt and Italy, respectively. Makki held high government office in the Yemen Arab Republic, in each of its five regimes after the 1962 revolution, as well as in the Republic of Yemen after the unification of the two Yemens in 1990; he did so despite his relatively advanced and leftist political views and reputation. In the Yemen Arab Republic he was prime minister during a turbulent time in 1974, president of San'a University from 1975 to 1976, and deputy prime minister or foreign minister on several occasions between the mid-1960s and the mid-1980s. He was first deputy prime minister during the first years of the Republic of Yemen, after Yemeni unification in mid-1990; and in 1994, after the brief civil war, he was appointed adviser to the president. Seriously wounded in the Siege of San'a in 1968 and the victim an assassination attempt during the politically tumultuous spring of 1994, he has been in ill health much of the time since the mid-1990s.

See also SAN'A UNIVERSITY; YEMEN ARAB REPUBLIC.

Bibliography

Burrowes, Robert D. *The Yemen Arab Republic: The Politics of Development, 1962–1986.* Boulder, CO: Westview; London: Croon Helm, 1987.

Dresch, Paul. *A History of Modern Yemen.* New York and Cambridge, U.K.: Cambridge University Press, 2000.

ROBERT D. BURROWES

MAKSOUD, CLOVIS
[1928–]

Lebanese lawyer, journalist, and diplomat.

Clovis Maksoud (also Maqsud) was born in 1928 into a Christian family. He completed his graduate studies at the American University of Beirut. Afterwards, he obtained a J.D. from George Washington University and did postgraduate studies at Oxford University. Between 1961 and 1966 Maksoud was the League of Arab States' chief representative in India. Following his diplomatic stint Maksoud went back to journalism, and from 1967 to 1979 he served as the senior editor of the Egyptian newspaper *al-Ahram* and chief editor of the Lebanon-based *al-Nahar Weekly.* Maksoud has authored several articles and books on the Middle East, including: "The Meaning of Non-Alignment," "The Crisis of the Arab Left," "Reflections on Afro-Asianism," and the "Arab Image." Currently, Maksoud is professor of international relations at American University in Washington, D.C., where he also is director of the Center for the Global South. He is also a member of the advisory group of the United Nations Development Program (UNDP).

See also SALAM FAMILY.

GEORGE IRANI

MAKTUM FAMILY, AL-

Head of Al Bu Falasa tribe and a member of the Banu Yas federation, the ruling family of the Dubai emirate.

The founder, Maktum ibn Buti, seceded from Abu Dhabi in 1833 and established himself independently in Dubai. The rulers of the family were well known for their skill in diplomacy and their interest in trade. The most prominent of them were Rashid ibn Maktum (1886–1894) and Maktum ibn Hashr (1894–1906), during whose reign the Dubai port flourished, particularly in 1902, after the British-Indian Steam Navigation Company made it a port of call. As a result of his encouragement, the rich immigrant merchants from the Lingeh port on the Persian coast came to reside in Dubai. In 1938, because of a reform movement in the emirate, the Dubai municipality was established during the rule of Sa'id ibn Maktum (1912–1958). His son Rashid created and ruled (1958–1990) modern Dubai, becoming vice-president of the United Arab Emirates when it was formed in 1971 and prime minister in 1979.

See also DUBAI; UNITED ARAB EMIRATES.

Bibliography

Heard-Bey, Frauke. *From Trucial States to United Arab Emirates: A Society in Transition.* London and New York: Longman, 1982.

Reich, Bernard, ed. *Political Leaders of the Contemporary Middle East and North Africa: A Biographical Dictionary.* New York: Greenwood Press, 1990.

M. MORSY ABDULLAH

MALA'IKA, NAZIK AL-
[1923–]

Iraqi poet and critic.

Nazik al-Mala'ika was born in 1923 in Baghdad, and is one of the greatest Arab poets of the twentieth century. One of the earliest creators and advocates of what is known in the Arab world as modern free poetry, this Iraqi woman influenced the course of contemporary Arabic poetry. Al-Mala'ika's mother was a poet, and her father wrote a twenty-volume encyclopedia on Arabic grammar and literature. In her youth, al-Mala'ika was influenced by the modern poetry of Mahmud Hasan Isma'il, Badawi al-Jabal, Amjad al-Tarabulsi, Umar Abu Risha, and Bishara al-Kuli, and also by the contemporary music of Umm Kulthum and Mohammed Abdul Wahab. In 1947 she broke free from the constraints of traditional Arabic poetry and composed the poem "Cholera" in lines of unequal length. Only in this new nonclassical form, she would write, could her emotions be expressed.

Al-Mala'ika has been primarily a poet of blank verse, although she has not strayed entirely from traditional poetic forms. In 1949, her second collection of poems, *Sparks of Ashes,* was published, including a controversial introduction explaining her new poetic theories. Her work was widely read and criticized across the Arab world, altering the debate on Arabic poetry. She became a regular contributor to leading poetry and critical journals in Egypt, Lebanon, and Syria, and soon numerous poems using the same form were in print, many dedicated to al-Mala'ika herself. In 1954 she wrote one of many essays dealing with the repression of women in Arab patriarchal society. Her essay, "Women between the Extremes of Passivity and Ethical Choice," is considered a feminist classic.

A significant event in al-Mala'ika's life was the 1958 Iraqi revolution, which she commemorated with joyous poetry comparing Iraq to an orphan now in a "paternal embrace." The revolution, however, did not yield what it promised, and al-Mala'ika fled to Beirut. When she later returned to Iraq, she and her husband founded a university in Basra where she taught and wrote. She continued to publish for decades, living in Iraq, Kuwait, and Egypt. Her poetry continued to evolve, securing her a place in the canon of Arabic literature.

See also GENDER: GENDER AND EDUCATION; LITERATURE: ARABIC; NEWSPAPERS AND PRINT MEDIA: ARAB COUNTRIES.

Bibliography

Handel, Nathalie. *The Poetry of Arab Women: A Contemporary Anthology.* New York: Interlink, 2001.

Mala'ika, Nazik al-. *Yugaer Alwanhu Al-Bahr.* Cairo, Egypt: 1998.

ELISE SALEM

MALIK

See GLOSSARY

MALIK, CHARLES HABIB
[1906–1987]

Lebanese academic, philosopher, and diplomat.

Born 11 February 1906 to a Greek Orthodox family from Kura in Lebanon, Malik was schooled at the American Tripoli Boys' High School, then attended the American University of Beirut (AUB), Harvard University, and the University of Freiburg. Throughout his academic career, Malik taught philosophy, mathematics, and physics at AUB, where he was also dean. During the 1958 Lebanese Civil War, Malik was president of the 13th session of the General Assembly of the United Nations. Foreign minister (1956–1958) during the presidency of Camille Chamoun, Malik alienated many Lebanese politicians because of his pro–United States and pro-Western stands. He accused Egypt, Syria, and the Palestinians of fomenting trouble in the Land of Cedars.

During the Lebanese Civil War of 1975–76, Malik joined a coalition of conservative Christian leaders known as the Lebanese Front. In several statements and publications, Malik expressed his full awareness of the tragedy of the Palestinian people, but he was very distrustful of the intentions of Muslim leaders in Lebanon. Malik feared that

Lebanon as a land of Christian-Muslim coexistence was bound to be destroyed by outside interference, mainly from Syria and radical Palestinian forces. Malik authored several books and publications and was awarded honorific titles and degrees.

Bibliography

Helmick, Raymond G. "Internal Lebanese Politics: The Lebanese Front and Forces." In *Toward a Viable Lebanon,* edited by Halim Barakat. Washington, DC: Center for Contemporary Arab Studies, 1988.

Hudson, Michael C. *The Precarious Republic: Political Modernization in Lebanon.* New York: Random House, 1968.

Petran, Tabitha. *The Struggle over Lebanon.* New York: Monthly Review Press, 1987.

GEORGE E. IRANI
UPDATED BY MICHAEL R. FISCHBACH

MALIKI SCHOOL OF LAW

One of the four approaches (called schools) to Sunni Muslim law.

The Maliki school of law was named after the traditionalist and lawyer Malik ibn Anas (died 795) of Medina (in today's Saudi Arabia). Malik's active career fell at a time when the prophetic sunna (record of the utterances and deeds of the Prophet) had not yet become a material source of the law on equal footing with the Qur'an and when *hadith* (prophetic traditions) were still relatively limited in number. In his legal reasoning, therefore, Malik made little reference to prophetic traditions and more often resorted to the *amal* (normative practice) of Medina in justification of his doctrines. As expressed in his *Muwatta,* in which he recorded the customary Medinese doctrine, Malik's reliance on traditions as well as his technical legal thought lagged behind those of the Iraqis.

Once the transition from the geographical to the personal schools took place, Malik became the eponym of the former Hijazi or Medinan school. This may be explained by the fact that Malik's writings represented the average doctrine of that geographical area, coupled perhaps with the high esteem in which he was held as a scholar.

Like the namesake of the Hanafi school of law, but unlike the founder of the Shafi'i school of law, Malik did not provide his school with a developed body of legal doctrine. It was left for his successors, chiefly in the ninth and tenth centuries, to articulate a legal system particular to the school. Among the most important positive law works of the school are: *al-Mudawwana al-Kubra* by Sahnun (died 854); *al-Risala* by Ibn Abi Zayd al-Qayrawani (died 996); al-Tahdhib, an authoritative synopsis of *al-Mudawwana,* by Abu Sa'id al-Baradhi'i (died probably after 1039); *al-Bayan,* a commentary by Ibn Rushd (died 1126) on *al-Utbiyya* of al-Utbi (died 869); *Bidaya al-Mujtahid wa Nihaya al-Muqtasid* by Ibn Rushd al-Hafid (died 1189); *al-Mukhtasar* by Sidi Khalil (died 1365); *al-Mi'yar al-Mughrib wa al-Jami al-Mu'rib* by al-Wansharisi (died 1508), one of the most important *fatwa* collections in the school. Further, in writing on legal theory *(usul al-fiqh),* the Malikis were not as prolific as their Hanafi and Shafi'i counterparts. Three of their most distinguished legal theoreticians are: Ibn Khalaf al-Baji (died 1081), the author of *Ihkam al-Fusul*; al-Qarafi (died 1285), whose main work on the subject is *Sharh Tanqih al-Fusul,* a commentary on the work of the Shafi'i jurist and theologian Fakhr al-Din al-Razi; and Abu Ishaq al-Shatibi (died 1388), who elaborated in his *Muwafaqat* one of the most innovative legal theories that is highly regarded by modern legal reformers.

Since early medieval Islam, Malikism succeeded in spreading mainly in the Maghrib (North Africa) and Muslim Spain, being now the dominant doctrine in all Muslim African countries. In Egypt, it has traditionally shared influence with Shafi'ism. Maliki presence may also be found today in Bahrain and Kuwait.

See also FATWA; HANAFI SCHOOL OF LAW; HANBALI SCHOOL OF LAW; SHAFI'I SCHOOL OF LAW.

WAEL B. HALLAQ

MALKOM KHAN, MIRZA
[1833–1908]

Persian diplomat, political philosopher, and advocate of modernization.

The son of Mirza Ya'qub, an Armenian from Jolfa who had converted to Islam, Mirza Malkom (also Malkam, Malkum) Khan studied in Paris, where he became familiar with French social and political theories, especially those of Auguste Comte. On his return to Persia, he was employed as a translator for the European teachers of the Dar al-Fonun, the modern school of higher learning inaugurated in 1851 by Persia's modernizing premier, Amir Kabir.

In 1857, Malkom wrote the first of his many pamphlets, entitled *Ketabcheh-ye Ghaybi* (The invisible booklet), in which he discussed the urgent need for modern reforms for Persia, if it were to survive as an independent nation. He also organized the Faramush-Khaneh (House of oblivion), a pseudo-masonic (secret) organization, which incurred the suspicion of the Naser al-Din Shah. Malkom was exiled in 1861 and went to Baghdad. There he was befriended by Mirza Hoseyn Khan, the Persian ambassador to the Ottoman Empire, who agreed with him about modernization and reforms and who obtained his pardon from the shah. Malkom was then made a counselor in the Persian embassy in Istanbul in 1864, during the early modernization period of Ottoman Turkey, called the Tanzimat. In 1871, Mirza Hoseyn was recalled to Tehran and appointed minister of justice, then prime minister. Malkom was appointed minister to Britain.

From London, Malkom continually addressed the shah and his ministers about the need for modernization reforms. His arguments were not always original, but they were simply argued, easily understood, and effective—he criticized the government, but spared the shah. Some of his suggestions were attempted, but the experiment did not last, since the shah grew tired of the complications of change and the ongoing rivalry at court. He lost interest in all this and became more tyrannical toward the end of his reign.

While Malkom was in London, the shah took three trips to Europe, visiting London each time, where several important concessions were granted to European and British companies. Malkom was involved in their transactions and had the opportunity to benefit financially each time. In 1889, the shah granted a lottery concession to an English company, which came under attack when he returned to Persia, and the concession was canceled. Malkom, however, who knew this, did not reveal the cancellation until he had sold out his own shares.

This unethical situation cost him his position, his title, and his salary. In 1890, he began to pub-

lish a pamphlet entitled *Qanun* (The law) in London. In it his arguments turned to criticism, then outright attack, not even sparing the shah. He also mentioned secret societies that were working for reform and suggested that the natural leaders of the people were by right the *ulama* (body of mollas), and that they should lead the movement. It has since been suggested that these secret societies were not actually organized but that Malkom was saying they should be. *Qanun* was smuggled into the country and enjoyed a widespread popularity, making its mark on a generation that was soon to become involved in the Constitutional Revolution.

After the assassination of Naser al-Din Shah in 1896, Malkom was restored to favor and was appointed minister to Italy. He lived to see the beginning of the Constitutional Revolution in 1906. Despite a lifetime of argument in favor of reform, his role in the lottery concession continues to sully his name. Notwithstanding such criticism, his influence on the shah, the politicians of his day, and the modernization of Persia cannot be denied.

See also AMIR KABIR, MIRZA TAQI KHAN; CONSTITUTIONAL REVOLUTION; TANZIMAT.

Bibliography

Algar, Hamid. *Mirza Malkum Khan: A Study in the History of Iranian Modernism.* Berkeley: University of California Press, 1973.

Bakhash, Shaul. *Iran: Monarchy, Bureaucracy, and Reform under the Qajars, 1858–1896.* London: Ithaca Press, 1978.

MANSOUREH ETTEHADIEH

MA'LOUF, AMIN
[1949–]

Prominent Lebanese novelist and journalist now living in and a citizen of France.

Amin Ma'louf (also Ma'luf) was born in Beirut in a Catholic family of journalists and writers. His father, Rushdi Ma'louf, was and is still considered one of Lebanon's major publicists. Following his schooling, Ma'louf joined *al-Nahar,* a major Lebanese daily, and traveled to several countries. In 1977, because of the violence brought by the Lebanese Civil War, Ma'louf fled with his family to Paris. Ma'louf is a prolific novelist and writer, and most of his fiction is based on historical events. His books have been translated into more than twenty languages. His first book, *The Crusades through Arab Eyes,* has become an important reference, especially after the terrorist attacks of 11 September 2001. Among his other novels are *The Gardens of Light* (1991) and *Leo the African* (1986), a narrative of the life and travels of a geographer who lived in sixteenth-century Spain and who, after roaming Africa and the Mediterranean, ended by living in Fez, Morocco. In 1993, Ma'louf was awarded the prestigious French literary award Le Prix Goncourt for *The Rock of Tanios.* In this book, based in nineteenth-century Lebanon, Ma'louf details the lives of a Lebanese *shaykh* and his out-of-wedlock son. The novel is filled with local myths, romance, international intrigues, and political games. His more recent novels include *The First Century after Beatrice* (1992) and *Balthasar's Odyssey* (2000). In 1998, Ma'louf published an essay entitled *Les identités meurtrieres* (translated as *On Identity*), which draws on his multilayered identity to explain how fluid identities have become in the age of globalization. In 2000, he wrote an opera libretto, *L'amour de loin* (*Love from Afar*) based on a twelfth-century love story set in Tripoli (Lebanon) during the Crusades. The opera was performed in Salzburg (2000) and Paris (2001); the music was composed by the Finnish composer Kaija Saariaho.

See also LEBANESE CIVIL WAR (1975–1990).

GEORGE IRANI

MAMLUKS

Rulers in Baghdad from 1749 to 1831.

The Mamluks emerged under Hasan Pasha (1704–1724) and his son Ahmad Pasha (1724–1747), both *wali* (provincial governor) of Baghdad. Hasan Pasha's intent was to strengthen his personal base of power by creating a group of disciplined military and civil functionaries committed uniquely to him and not to the government at Istanbul or the Arabs of Baghdad. A page corps was formed, originally recruited from local families but later composed almost exclusively of slaves (mamluks) imported from the Caucasus and Georgia. These slaves were instructed in reading and writing, but also horsemanship and swimming, a combination of martial and bureaucratic virtues making them superior to Turks and Iraqis as civil servants. Their training emphasized a sense of interdependence and "esprit de corps." They were made to feel that they owed their privilege to their master and to the Mamluk institution. They dominated the power elite, but as an alien force, and were merciless to any suspected rival to their authority. A close disciplined fraternity, and the only effective civil and military organization within the country, the Mamluks provided their pashas with the power of an independent monarch. Nevertheless, Mamluk pashas at no time renounced allegiance to the sultan of the Ottoman Empire. They defended Iraq from the Wahhabis and Persians but did not war on neighbors within the empire.

The first Mamluk pasha, Sulayman Abu Layla (1750–1762), came to power two years after the death of Ahmad Pasha, following an unsuccessful attempt by the Sublime Porte (the Ottoman government) to check Mamluk power by naming non-local candidates as pasha of Baghdad. He was followed by Ali Agha (1762–1764) whose obscure Persian birth may have contributed to his fall. The reign of Umar Pasha (1764–1775), while peaceful, was feeble and characterized by ever-lessening authority. His deposition by the sultan introduced in interregnum (1775–1780) during which a number of mostly alien pashas (Abdi Pasha, 1775; Abdullah Pasha, 1775–1777; Hasan Pasha 1778–1780) reigned briefly and without much influence. Sulayman Agha (1780–1802), known as "the Great," restored the dominance and institutions of the Mamluks with such success that his period is known as the zenith of the Mamluk era. His immediate successors, Ali Pasha (1802–1807), Sulayman the Little (1808–1810), Abdallah Pasha (1810–1813), and Sa'id Pasha (1813–1817), all died violently after brief reigns. The last of the Mamluk rulers, Da'ud Pasha (1817–1831), confronted Ottoman resolve, ignited by his failure to provide suitable remissions in the desperate circumstances of the sultan's war with Russia, to end the century-long independence of Iraq and to bring the province once again firmly into the imperial fold. Plague and flooding helped weaken the Mamluk regime and Da'ud ultimately capitulated to the sultan in 1831. He and his family were exiled to Bursa. He was subsequently recalled to service and held a number of important posts throughout the empire before dying in 1851.

Bibliography

Longrigg, Stephen Hemsley. *Four Centuries of Modern Iraq.* Oxford: Clarendon Press, 1925.

Nieuwenhuis, Tom. *Politics and Society in Early Modern Iraq: Mamluk Pashas, Tribal Shaykhs and Local Rule between 1802 and 1831.* The Hague and Boston: M. Nijhoff, 1982.

ALBERTINE JWAIDEH

MANAMA

Capital and largest city of the State of Bahrain.

Located on the north coast of Bahrain's main island and connected by causeway to Muharraq, Manama was a commercial and pearling center coveted by the Sassanids, Omanis, and Safavids. In 1782, it fell to the Al Khalifa family, under whose control it grew into a key transshipment point for trade between India and the Persian Gulf. After the 1820 General Treaty of Peace with Britain, the city's merchants flourished. By the early twentieth century, Manama was a cosmopolitan center, with large Iranian, Indian, and Gulf Arab communities; in 1946, it became home to the British Resident in the Gulf. Greater Manama houses more than 50 percent of Bahrain's inhabitants. The city's population in 2001 was about 156,000—some 70 percent larger than at independence in 1971. Bahrain's largest port, Mina Sulman, lies at the southern end of the city, next to the former British naval base at al-Jufayr, which now serves as headquarters for the United States Navy's Fifth Fleet.

See also AL KHALIFA FAMILY; BAHRAIN.

Bibliography

Clarke, Angela. *The Islands of Bahrain: An Illustrated Guide to Their Heritage.* Manama: Bahrain Historical and Archaeological Society, 1981.

FRED H. LAWSON

MANDAEANS

Gnostic baptist community based in Iraq and Iran.

The Mandaeans of today live as their ancestors did, along the rivers and waterways of southern Iraq and Khuzistan, Iran. The Mandaeans (from *manda,* knowledge) practice a religion that has affinities with Judaism and Christianity. Known by their neighbors as *Subbi* (baptizers), they perform repeated baptism *(masbuta)* on Sundays and special festival days. Two small rites of ablution that require no priest,

rishama and *tamasha,* are performed by individual Mandaeans. All rituals take place on the riverbank.

MAMOON A. ZAKI

MANDATE SYSTEM

The system established after World War I to administer former territories of the German and Ottoman empires.

Until World War I, the victors of most European wars took control of conquered territories as the spoils of victory. This was especially true of the colonial territories of defeated European powers, as the victors sought to expand their own empires. World War I marked a significant break in this tradition. While Britain, France, Italy, and Japan still retained imperial aspirations, other forces tempered these goals. The United States emerged as a world power committed to an anti-imperial policy, one that sought to consider the national aspirations of indigenous peoples as well as the imperial agendas of the victors. The 5 November 1918 pre-armistice statement of the Allies, moreover, affirmed that annexation of territory was not their aim for ending the war.

The result was the mandate system of the League of Nations, established by the treaties ending World War I. Under this system, the victors of World War I were given responsibility for governing former German and Ottoman territories as mandates from the League. The ultimate goal was development of each mandate toward eventual independence. This goal was tempered, some would argue, by the fact that mandates were awarded with full consideration of both public and secret agreements made during the war. For the Middle East, the Sykes–Picot Agreement of 1916 and the Balfour Declaration of 1917 helped structure the division of Ottoman territories between France and Britain.

Article 22 of the League's covenant required that the conditions of mandates vary with the character of each territory. This resulted in the establishment of three classes of mandate. Class A mandates were those to be provisionally recognized as independent until they proved able to stand on their own. Class B mandates were those further from qualifying for independence and for which the mandatory powers took on full responsibility for administration and promotion of the material and moral welfare of the inhabitants. Class C mandates were those whose best interests were to be served by integration into the territories of the mandatory power, with due consideration being given to the interests of the inhabitants.

The Ottoman territories in the Middle East became Class A mandates. Based on World War I agreements, Britain was given responsibility for Iraq and Palestine (later Palestine and Transjordan); France got Syria (later Syria and Lebanon). These were to be supervised by the Permanent Mandates Commission consisting originally of members from Belgium, Britain, the Netherlands, France, Italy, Japan, Portugal, Spain, and Sweden, to which representatives from Switzerland and Germany were later added, and a representative from Norway took the place of the Swedish representative. Although the non-mandatory powers constituted a majority, the commission never followed an aggressive policy against the interests of the mandatory powers. This was manifest by the fact that Britain and France restructured their mandates by the time the formal system came into place in 1924. Britain split the Palestinian mandate into Palestine and Transjordan, giving a special role in the latter to Sharif Husayn's son, Abdullah, as amir of Transjordan to deter his further pursuit of territorial goals in Syria. France split its mandate in Syria into Syria and Lebanon to enhance the position of Uniate Christians in Lebanon and as part of its overall strategy of sponsoring communal differences to solidify its position of eventual arbiter of all disputes in the area. The British mandate for Iraq remained intact, despite the fact that its population diversity invited similar divisions.

Although few would have predicted it in the early 1920s, all of the Class A mandates achieved independence as provided under the conditions of the mandates. The first was Iraq in 1932, although Britain retained significant diplomatic and military concessions. Syria and Lebanon followed in 1941 as World War II was getting under way. In March 1946, just before the formal dissolution of the League of Nations and transfer of its assets to the United Nations, the Treaty of London granted independence to Transjordan as the Hashemite Kingdom of Jordan. Only Palestine was left to the United Nations under its trusteeship program, and in 1947, Britain

presented this thorny problem to the UN General Assembly for resolution. The result was approval of a plan for the partition of Palestine into two Arab and Jewish states and an international city of Jerusalem. Subsequent events precluded implementation of this plan, but since 1949, Israel has been a member of the United Nations.

See also BALFOUR DECLARATION (1917); SYKES–PICOT AGREEMENT (1916).

Bibliography

Lenczowski, George. *The Middle East in World Affairs,* 4th edition. Ithaca, NY: Cornell University Press, 1980.

Walters, F. P. *A History of the League of Nations.* London and New York: Oxford University Press, 1952.

DANIEL E. SPECTOR

MANIFESTO OF THE ALGERIAN MUSLIM PEOPLE

Document that urged Algerian autonomy within the French Union.

Ferhat Abbas, in collaboration with other Algerian leaders, drafted the Manifesto of the Algerian Muslim People during February and March 1943. It contains an analysis of the Algerian condition followed by a program of reform that marks a major stage in the progression of Algerian protest from assimilationism to separatism.

See also ABBAS, FERHAT.

JOHN RUEDY

MANSAF

See FOOD: MANSAF

MANSURA, AL-

Egyptian delta city.

Al-Mansura is located near Damietta, Egypt, in the delta. Founded by the Ayyubid dynasty as a fortified camp in 1219, it served as a buttress against Crusader expansion in 1221 and again in 1250, when the Mamluks scored a significant victory over Louis IX of France. It has been the administrative capital of Daqhaliyya province since 1526. Although predominantly Muslim, there have been some Copts in the city since the seventeenth century. Its population was estimated at 441,700 in 2004.

ARTHUR GOLDSCHMIDT

MANSURE ARMY

Ottoman army organized in 1826.

Established by the same proclamation that abolished the Janissary Corps, the new army's formal name translated as the Trained Victorious Soldiers of Muhammad. It soon recruited 12,000 troops, initially organized largely along the lines of the former Nizam-i Cedit and headed by a commander called serasker. The Mansure army was headquartered at a palace in Bayezit (Istanbul), combining the functions of military headquarters and war ministry until the end of the empire. As serasker, Mehmet Paşa Koja Husrev introduced French military organization into the Mansure and by 1830 expanded it to 27,000 troops, including the former cavalry. All remaining Ottoman fighting corps were incorporated into the Mansure in 1838, when the army's name was changed to the Ordered Troops.

Bibliography

Shaw, Stanford J., and Shaw, Ezel Kural. *History of the Ottoman Empire and Modern Turkey.* Vol. 2: *Reform, Revolution, and Republic, 1808–1975.* Cambridge, U.K., and New York: Cambridge University Press, 1977.

ELIZABETH THOMPSON

MANUFACTURES

Goods made from raw materials, originally by hand; also those made by machinery.

In antiquity and into the Byzantine Empire, the Middle East was the center of Western civilization and the region from which a wide variety of goods were first made and traded. The settled farming society allowed time for handicrafts, between crop work, and for market days and market towns. Regional trade became established by land caravan, by riverboats, and by coastal vessels that sailed the Mediterranean, the east coast of Africa, and beyond Arabia, into the Indian Ocean.

Pre-1900

The ancient Near East was the seat of civilizations that traded with one another—luxury goods for the urban elite and utilitarian items for both urban dwellers and for rural agricultural, herding, and artisan folk. Specialty products included textiles, metals, glassware, pottery, chemicals, and, later, sugar and paper. By the fourteenth and fifteenth centuries, however, Europe had progressed to the point that it was exporting to the Middle East not only high technology goods, such as clocks and spectacles, but refined types of textiles, glassware, and metals. During the following centuries the flow from Europe to the Middle East increased; by the nineteenth century, Europe overwhelmed the region with goods produced cheaply and abundantly by the machinery of the Industrial Revolution, including the railroads and steamships that transported them. The Anglo–Ottoman treaty of 1838 (called the Convention of Balta Liman) fixed import duties to the Ottoman Empire at a low 8 percent. These factors drove thousands of Middle Eastern craftsmen and artisans out of business, but some managed to retain their shops and others found employment in the new textile factories of the late nineteenth century.

1900–1945

World War I exposed the region's lack of industry and, with the achievement of total or partial independence, the various governments began to take measures to encourage development. Around 1930, the Commercial and Navigation Treaties regulating tariffs lapsed, and most countries regained full fiscal autonomy. They immediately raised tariffs to favor local industry. They also promoted manufacturing in various other ways, such as encouraging people to buy national goods and giving such goods preference for government purchases. Moreover, they set up special banking, such as the Sümer and Eti banks in Turkey and the Agricultural and Industrial banks of Iran and Iraq, to promote manufacturing and mining; they also channeled credit through existing banks, such as Bank Misr in Egypt. Local entrepreneurs also became more active in the economic field, including manufacturing. In Egypt, the Misr and Abboud groups set up various industries, and in Turkey, the İş Bank promoted development. In Palestine, where some European and Russian

A Mercedes-Benz plant in Egypt, 1990s. The car manufacturer's origins in Egypt date back to the 1950s, but it was not until 1997 that the company started manufacturing vehicles there, at its 6th of October City factory. © BOJAN BRECELJ/CORBIS. REPRODUCED BY PERMISSION.

Jewish immigrants brought with them both capital and skills, some set up factories or workshops in a wide variety of fields.

It is difficult to estimate the rate of industrial growth: In Turkey, between 1929 and 1938, net manufacturing production increased at 7.5 percent a year and mining advanced at about the same pace. In Egypt, the rate of growth was slightly lower and in the Jewish sector of Palestine distinctly higher. In Iran, between 1926 and 1940, some 150 factories were established with a paid-up capital of about US$150 million and employing 35,000 persons. Nevertheless, industry still played a minor role in the basically agricultural Middle Eastern economy. By 1939, employment in manufacturing and mining was everywhere less than 10 percent of the labor force, and in most of the countries it was closer to 5 percent. Industry's contribution to gross domestic product (GDP) was put at 8 percent in Egypt, 12

in Turkey, and 20 in the Jewish sector of Palestine; in the other countries it was lower. Industry still depended on imports of machinery, spare parts, raw materials, and technicians—and there were no exports of manufactured goods. A wide range of light industries, including textiles, food processing, building materials, and simple chemicals, had developed in Egypt, Turkey, Iran, Palestine, and, to a smaller extent, in Lebanon, Syria, and Iraq. In addition, Turkey had the beginnings of heavy industry—iron, steel, and coal. Petroleum production and refining had become important to Iran, Bahrain, and Iraq. Several countries were meeting most of their requirements of such basic consumer goods as textiles, refined sugar, shoes, matches, and cement.

Post–1945

World War II gave great stimulus to Middle Eastern industry. Imports were drastically reduced and Allied troops provided a huge market for many goods. The Anglo–American Middle East Supply Center helped by providing parts, materials, and technical assistance. By 1945, total output had increased by some 50 percent. With the resumption of trade, from 1946 to 1950, many firms were hit by foreign competition, but the governments gave them tariff and other protection, so output continued to grow at about 10 percent per annum from 1946 to 1953. This rate was maintained, and in some countries (like Iran) exceeded through the 1970s, but in the 1980s it fell off sharply because of such factors as the Iran–Iraq War, the Sudanese and Lebanese civil wars, and the 1980s fall in oil prices.

Table 1 shows a breakdown of the structure of Middle Eastern industry. The main industries are still textiles (including garments); food processing (sugar refining, dough products, confectionery, soft drinks, beer); tobacco; building materials (cement, bricks, glass, sanitary ware); and assembly plants for automobiles, refrigerators, radio and television sets, and so forth, with some of the components produced locally. Important new industries have also developed—notably chemicals—including basic products, fertilizers, and various kinds of plastics; basic metals and metal products; and many types of machinery. A particularly rapidly growing branch is petrochemicals, using gases produced in the oil fields or in refineries. Only in petrochemicals, textiles, and food processing does the region's share approach or exceed 5 percent of world output. Similarly, only in phosphates and chromium is the region's share of mineral production significant.

Israel, however, has a large diamond-cutting industry and is a significant exporter of precision instruments. It is also a large exporter of arms, as is Egypt; in the late 1980s each country exported more than US$1 billion worth of weapons; they ranked third and fourth, respectively, among exporters from developing countries, and twelfth and fifteenth, among world exporters of arms. The Arab boycott has, of course, restricted some of Israel's economic pursuits within the region as well as with some international trade.

Today, manufacturing plays an important part in the Middle East's economy, accounting in many countries for 15 to 20 percent of GDP. Industry,

Manufacturing Industry in 1970, 1983, 1987

Value Added (millions of U.S. dollars)

	1970	1983	1987
Egypt	—	8,950	—
Iran	1,501	11,596	—
Iraq	325	—	—
Israel	—	—	—
Jordan	32	—	552
Kuwait	120	—	1,902
Oman	—	—	464
Saudi Arabia	372	—	6,068
Syria	—	—	2,341
Turkey	1,930	—	15,863
United Arab Emirates	—	—	2,155
North Yemen	10	—	578

Distribution of Value Added (percent)

	Food Beverages Tobacco	Textiles Clothing	Machinery & Transport Equipment
Egypt	20	26	13
Iran	12	21	15
Iraq	14	9	10
Israel	12	8	32
Jordan	22	3	1
Kuwait	10	7	4
Oman	—	—	—
Saudi Arabia	—	—	—
Syria	24	10	3
Turkey	17	15	15
United Arab Emirates	14	1	—
North Yemen	—	—	—

Distribution of Value Added (percent)

	Chemicals	Other
Egypt	9	32
Iran	4	48
Iraq	16	50
Isreal	8	39
Jordan	7	67
Kuwait	6	73
Oman	—	
Saudi Arabia	—	—
Syria	15	48
Turkey	11	43
United Arab Emirates	—	84
North Yemen	—	—

SOURCE: World Bank. *World Development Report*, 1990, Table 6. *World Development Report*, 1986, Table 7.

TABLE BY GGS INFORMATION SERVICES, THE GALE GROUP.

in the broader sense, which includes mining (and therefore oil), construction, electricity, water, and gas as well as manufacturing, generally constitutes over 30 percent of GDP. In the major oil nations it is 60 percent or more, usually employing 20 to

30 percent of the labor force (including immigrant labor).

Factors for Low Productivity

With rare exceptions, industries still export very little and survive through government protection. Productivity is low; for example, gross annual value added in 1974 was only worth US$4,000 to US$5,000 in most countries (compared to $20,000 in West Germany). This is particularly marked in the more capital-intensive industries, such as steel, automobiles, and aircraft. In the late 1970s, in the Turkish state-owned steel mill in Iskenderun, a ton of steel took 72 worker-hours, compared with 5 in the United States and 7 in Europe; in Egypt, annual output per worker in the automobile industry was one car, compared with 30 to 50 in leading Japanese firms. In the more labor intensive industries, such as textiles, however, physical output per worker is about 30 to 50 percent of European output. Here, very low wages offset low productivity and enable the Middle East to compete. In 1980, hourly wages in the textile industry were equal to US$1 in Syria and Turkey and 40 cents in Egypt, compared to US$8.25 in Western Europe.

Low productivity in the Middle East is caused by many factors. First, capital investment per employee is low, although governments have poured large amounts into industry; in the late 1970s the share of manufacturing, mining (including oil), and energy was over 40 percent of total investment in Egypt, Iraq, and Syria, and 30 percent in Iran. In the Gulf region's petrochemical industry, however, capital intensity is high and up-to-date machinery is used. Second, industry is greatly overstaffed; many governments compel firms to take on more workers—to relieve unemployment or for other political purposes. Third, the poor health, education, and housing of workers adversely affect their productivity—but conditions are improving. Fourth, there has been much bad planning, with factories being located far from suitable raw materials or good transport.

General conditions are also unfavorable for industrial development. The region is, on the whole, poor in raw materials. Wood and water have become very scarce. Minerals are generally sparse, remote, and often low grade. Most agricultural raw materials are of poor quality, lacking the uniformity required for industrial processes. The protection given to manufacturers of producers' goods (e.g., metals, chemicals, sugar) creates a handicap for industries that use their products. The main exceptions are natural and refinery gas, which are available almost free of cost, and raw cotton, which is of fine quality. The small size of the local market makes it impossible to set up factories of optimum size and the general underdevelopment of industries prevents profitable linkages among industries; both factors raise unit costs. Although the infrastructure has greatly improved, it still does not serve manufacturing adequately; for example, the frequency of power failures led many firms to install their own generators and transport costs remain high. A dependence on imported machinery, spare parts, and raw materials, although declining, is still great— hence, when a shortage of foreign exchange curtails imports, factories work below capacity, further raising unit costs.

Middle East industry also suffers from a lack of competition. Because of the small size of the local market and the high degree of protection, firms often enjoy a quasi monopoly—and behave accordingly. Finally, a great shortage of industrial skills exists at both the supervisory and foreperson levels. Even more serious is the shortage of managers; this is compounded where the government has nationalized the bulk of industry—as in Egypt, Iran, Iraq, Sudan, and Syria. Here market discipline has been replaced by bureaucratic control, so efficiency has been sharply reduced.

On the whole, then, manufacturing does not make the contribution to the Middle East's economy commensurate with either the efforts or the capital invested in it. Conditions may be expected to improve, however, as the society and the economy continue to develop and as some measure of peace takes hold.

See also ARAB BOYCOTT; BALTA LIMAN, CONVENTION OF (1838); COMMERCIAL AND NAVIGATION TREATIES; TRADE.

Bibliography

Aliboni, Robert, ed. *Arab Industrialization and Economic Integration.* London: St. Martin's, 1979.

Economist Intelligence Unit. *Industrialization in the Arab World.* London, 1986.

Hershlag, Z. Y. *Contemporary Turkish Economy*. London and New York: Routledge, 1988.

Issawi, Charles. *An Economic History of the Middle East and North Africa*. New York: Columbia University Press, 1982.

Turner, Louis, and Bedore, James. *Middle East Industrialization*. Fainborough, U.K., 1979.

United Nations. *The Development of Manufacturing in Egypt, Israel, and Turkey*. New York, 1958.

CHARLES ISSAWI

MAPAI

See ISRAEL: POLITICAL PARTIES IN

MAPAM

See ISRAEL: POLITICAL PARTIES IN

MA'PILIM

See GLOSSARY

MAQARIN DAM

Dam on the Yarmuk river.

Proposed in 1953, the Maqarin (colloquially, Magarin) dam was to span the Yarmuk River between Syria and Jordan. No action was taken toward its construction, however, until 1988, when the two governments decided upon a joint project. Renamed Sadd al-Wahda (the Unity Dam), it will hold some 300 million cubic yards (225 million cu. m) of water. Jordan will pay for construction while Syria will gain use of much of the resulting electricity that is generated. In 1988, when Israel and Jordan held discussions on partitioning the waters of the Yarmuk, Syria refused to participate. Jordan and Syria finally agreed, in April 2003, to go forward with the project. A scheduled inauguration of the project in November 2003 was postponed, however.

See also YARMUK RIVER.

Bibliography

Metz, Helen Chapin, ed. *Jordan: A Country Study*, 4th edition. Washington, DC: U.S. Government Printing Office, 1991.

MICHAEL R. FISCHBACH

MARABOUT

A Muslim saint or holy person in North Africa.

Marabout (Arabic *murabit*, literally, "the tied one") refers in North Africa to saints or holy persons, living or dead, reputed to serve as intermediaries in securing Allah's blessings (Arabic *baraka*) for their clients and supporters. The term also refers to their shrines. In earlier centuries, marabouts "tied" tribes to Islam and mediated disputes. Although *marabout* remains current in French usage, most North Africans today use the term *salih*, "the pious one," which does not imply that Allah has intermediaries, a notion at odds with Qur'anic doctrine. Unlike Roman Catholicism, Muslims have no formal procedures for recognizing saints, although North African Muslims associate specific "pious ones" with particular regions, towns, tribes, and descent groups. Many shrines are the site for local pilgrimages and annual festivals. Jewish communities in Morocco and Israel have similar practices, calling such a holy person *tzaddik* (or *saddiq*).

Bibliography

Eickelman, Dale F. *Moroccan Islam: Tradition and Society in a Pilgrimage Center*. Austin: University of Texas Press, 1976.

Weingrod, Alex. "Saints and Shrines, Politics, and Culture: A Morocco-Israel Comparison." In *Muslim Travellers: Pilgrimage, Migration, and the Religious Imagination*, edited by Dale F. Eickelman and James Piscatori. Berkeley: University of California Press, 1990.

DALE F. EICKELMAN

MARATGHI, MUSTAFA AL-
[1881–1945]

Egyptian religious leader and politician.

Mustafa al-Maratghi served as head of al-Azhar in 1928/29 and from 1935 until his death in 1945. A supporter of the Muslim reformer Muhammad Abduh, al-Maratghi used his post at al-Azhar to defend the political institutions of Islam and fight against secular nationalist leaders.

Al-Maratghi had played a pivotal role in the Cairo Caliphate Congress of May 1926. The congress discussed the restoration of the caliphate, the office of political and spiritual leader of the Muslim world, which had been abolished by Mustafa Kemal (Atatürk) in 1924. Al-Maratghi supported the candidacy of Egypt's King Farouk for the caliphate but was opposed by forty teachers from al-Azhar, who argued that the caliphate could not be brought to Egypt as long as the country was occupied by Britain. Meanwhile, Egyptian public opinion was more concerned with the parliamentary elections taking place that month. The congress produced no results. In 1930, al-Maratghi participated in efforts to forge a coalition between the Wafd and the Liberal Constitutionalist parties in opposition to the government of Isma'il Sidqi, the prime minister.

See also ABDUH, MUHAMMAD; SIDQI, ISMA'IL.

Bibliography

Gershoni, Israel, and Jankowski, James P. *Egypt, Islam, and the Arabs: The Search for Egyptian Nationhood, 1900–1930.* New York: Oxford University Press, 1986.

Sayyid-Marsot, Afaf Lutfi al-. *Egypt's Liberal Experiment, 1922–1936.* Berkeley: University of California Press, 1977.

Wucher King, Joan. *Historical Dictionary of Egypt.* Metuchen, NJ: Scarecrow Press, 1984.

DAVID WALDNER

MARDAM, JAMIL
[1894–1960]

Syrian politician.

Born in Damascus to a landowning bureaucratic Sunni Muslim family, Jamil Mardam was active in the Arab national movement from its beginnings in late Ottoman days. He helped to organize al-Fatat and the first Arab Nationalist Congress and was a member of a Syrian Arab delegation to the Paris Peace Conference of 1919. When the Great Syrian Revolt (1925–1927) erupted, Mardam took part in it, seeking, like other Damascene and Druze leaders, not the overturn of the French-controlled system of rule but the modification and relaxation of that rule in a manner that would restore the influence of Syrian notables over local politics. The French had already undercut that influence in various towns as well as in the Jabal Druze. In this regard, Mardam was the principal strategist of the policy of "honorable cooperation" with the French, which stated that popular opposition to French presence should not be allowed to disrupt the delicate negotiations between the French and the leadership of Syria's independence movements.

This policy tarnished the reputation of Mardam and his supporters and forced them to look beyond Syria's frontiers for political support. In an attempt to rehabilitate their reputation and Pan-Arabism, they turned their attention to Palestine, creating in 1934 the Bureau for National Propaganda, a political body devoted to the dissemination of information on Palestine and other critical Arab issues.

Mardam was a founder of the National Bloc, a broad-based group established in 1927 to spearhead the independence struggle in Syria. He also was one of its most active members at the leadership level in Damascus, where the Bloc's headquarters were based. During the French mandate, Mardam was elected a deputy in Syria's National Assembly in 1932, 1936, and 1943 and served as minister from 1932 to 1933, 1936 to 1939, and 1943 to 1945. After full independence was achieved, he served as prime minister from December 1946 to December 1948, as well as minister of the interior in 1947 and minister of defense in 1948.

The growth of action-oriented political organizations in Syria after the Arab-Israel War of 1948 (the Communists, the Muslim Brotherhood, and Ba'th), damaged the prospects of the National Bloc (renamed the National Party in 1943) in the new local and inter-Arab rivalries that governed political life in Syria throughout the 1950s. In the end, the discrediting of the old guard who led the National Bloc rendered the political fortunes of Mardam bleaker and bleaker, thus forcing him out of politics.

See also ARAB-ISRAEL WAR (1948); BA'TH, AL-; FATAT, AL-; JABAL DRUZE; MUSLIM BROTHERHOOD; NATIONAL BLOC; NATIONAL PARTY (SYRIA); PALESTINE; PAN-ARABISM.

Bibliography

Khoury, Philip S. *Syria and the French Mandate: The Politics of Arab Nationalism, 1920–1945.* Princeton, NJ: Princeton University Press, 1989.

MUHAMMAD MUSLIH

MARDOM PARTY

A government-sponsored political party, created in Iran in 1957 as an opposition party.

As a result of pressure for democracy and in the hope of giving the appearance of a two-party system, the Mardom party was established as an "opposition" party under Mohammad Reza Shah Pahlavi's rule in Iran in 1957. Its founder, Amir Asadollah Alam, was a large landlord, a former prime minister, and a close associate and confidant of the shah. The party's official platform included such issues as raising the standard of living for farmers, workers, and government officials, as well as facilitating the acquisition of land by the farmers. Together with the "official" government party, the Nationalist party or Hezb-e Melliyun, however, the Mardom party came to have a reputation for being a government organ, the Nationalist being known as the "yes" party and the Mardom as the "yes, sir" party. In 1975, the Mardom party was dissolved when the shah decided to revert to a one-party system and started the Rastakhiz party. Many people point to the establishment and dissolution of the Mardom party, both government-inspired, as indications of Mohammad Reza Shah Pahlavi's failure in developing Iran's political system.

See also ALAM, AMIR ASADOLLAH.

Bibliography

Abrahamian, Ervand. *Iran between Two Revolutions.* Princeton, NJ: Princeton University Press, 1982.

Wilber, Donald N. *Iran: Past and Present: From Monarchy to Islamic Republic,* 9th edition. Princeton, NJ: Princeton University Press, 1981.

PARVANEH POURSHARIATI

MARETH LINE

A defensive position in Tunisia.

The Mareth Line was designed by the French to protect Tunisia's southeastern flank against an Italian invasion from Libya. Twenty-two miles (35 km) long, it was named for Mareth, a small town southeast of Gabès. In November 1942, following the defeat of Gen. Erwin Rommel's Afrika Korps at al-Alamayn by British forces under Field Marshal Bernard Montgomery, the Germans rushed reinforcements and equipment to Tunisia. The Mareth Line was the southern key to German defenses.

Breaking through the Mareth Line became a major objective of Allied forces. In March 1943, the British Eighth Army—together with forces from France and New Zealand—assaulted the Mareth Line. An outflanking maneuver by New Zealand troops forced General Jürgen von Armin to withdraw his forces to Enfidaville, near the Cape Bon peninsula.

Bibliography

Nelson, Harold D., ed. *Tunisia: A Country Study,* 3d edition. Washington, DC: U.S. Government Printing Office, 1988.

LARRY A. BARRIE

MARGUERITE TAOS KABYLE

See AMROUCHE, MARY LOUISE

MA'RIB

Ancient town of North Yemen, enjoying new life because of oil.

Ma'rib was, until the 1980s, the small government center and garrison of the large, sparsely populated Yemeni province of the same name. The town is located about a hundred miles east of San'a, on the edge of the desert. For centuries before the Common Era, Ma'rib was the capital of the trading kingdom of Saba, once ruled by Bilqis, the Queen of Saba (or Sheba). The fabled Ma'rib dam is nearby, and its monumental remains and those of the vast associated irrigation system are still in evidence. The gradual collapse of these works early in the Common Era forced the depopulation of the region; in the 1960s, the sleepy town that remained was all but abandoned after bombardment during the Yemen Civil War. Since the mid-1980s, however, the town has undergone a major renewal as the center closest to the important oil operations in the Ma'rib/al-Jawf basin; major natural gas reserves also have been discovered. The construction of a new dam in the 1980s, financed by Abu Dhabi, made possible the revival of major irrigated agriculture. All this has also given the area new military significance, especially since much of the province is tribal and beyond the effective control of the state.

See also SAN˓A; YEMEN CIVIL WAR.

Bibliography

Dresch, Paul. *A History of Modern Yemen.* New York and Cambridge, U.K.: Cambridge University Press, 2000.

Stookey, Robert W. *Yemen: The Politics of the Yemen Arab Republic.* Boulder, CO: Westview, 1978.

ROBERT D. BURROWES

MARIETTE, AUGUSTE
[1821–1881]

French Egyptologist.

Auguste Mariette founded the Egyptian Antiquities Service in 1858 and the Egyptian Museum, thereby slowing the indiscriminate destruction and export of pharaonic antiquities to Europe. His workers in archaeology excavated scores of monuments: the Serapeum of the Apis bulls at Saqqara was his most famous discovery. French control of the Antiquities Service was to last until 1952, when the Egyptian monarchy and colonialism ended and a republic was declared.

See also EGYPTIAN MUSEUM.

Bibliography

Dawson, Warren R., and Uphill, Eric P. *Who Was Who in Egyptology,* 2d edition. London: Egypt Exploration Society, 1972.

DONALD MALCOLM REID

MAR˓I, MARIAM
[1945–]

Palestinian activist; a founder of Dar al-Tifl al-Arabi.

Mariam (also Maryam) Mar˓i was born in Acre (now in northern Israel but then in the British Mandate of Palestine). She received a bachelor of arts degree in counseling education and art from Haifa University in 1975 and a master of arts degree in counseling education from Michigan State University in 1977. She received her doctorate in international education from Michigan State University in 1983. Mar˓i worked as an elementary school teacher in Acre from 1966 to 1967 and as an instructor in the Arab Teacher Training College in Haifa from 1973 to 1977. She also directed the Acre branch of the Arab Teacher Training College from 1993 to 1997. She was the founder and director general of Dar al-Tifl al-Arabi (Early Childhood Educational Center) in Acre between 1984 and 1997. She was also the founder and first president of the Acre Arab Women's Association in 1975, and the founder and first president of the Galilee Social Research Center in Nazareth in 1987. Mar˓i's activities and publications focus on early childhood education and development, the status of Palestinian women in Israel, and dialogue between Arab and Jewish peace groups. Mar˓i received the Rotfield Prize for Education for Peace in 1989, and she serves on the boards of various national and international organizations.

ISIS NUSAIR

MARINE BARRACKS BOMBING (LEBANON)

A bombing that caused the deaths of 241 U.S. Marines in the Lebanese Civil War.

Following the Israeli invasion of Lebanon in 1982 and the massacre by the Phalange militia of Palestinians in the Sabra and Shatila refugee camps on the outskirts of Beirut, the administration of President Ronald Reagan dispatched peacekeeping troops to Lebanon in the framework of the Multinational Force (MNF). The MNF was composed of U.S., French, British, and Italian contingents tasked with shoring up the regime of President Amin Jumayyil, brother of the assassinated Bashir Jumayyil. The presence of U.S. Marines in West Beirut polarized animosities between Christians and Muslims in Lebanon, and the American contingent became the target of hatred and distrust.

Lebanese Muslims, especially Shi˓ites living in the slums of West Beirut and around the airport—where the marines were headquartered—saw the MNF not as a peacekeeping force but as another faction in the Lebanese war. U.S. troops particularly were seen as perpetuating Maronite Catholic rule over Lebanon. Muslim feelings against the American presence were exacerbated when missiles lobbed by the U.S. Sixth Fleet hit innocent by-standers in the Druze-dominated Shuf mountains. On 20 October 1983, a Shiʿite Islamic Jihad member drove a truck loaded with 12,000 pounds of TNT into the lobby where the U.S. contingent was stationed and blew himself up, thereby killing 241 servicemen. In 1984, the Reagan administration withdrew the U.S. contingent from Lebanon.

See also REAGAN, RONALD.

Bibliography

Friedman, Thomas L. *From Beirut to Jerusalem.* New York: Farrar Straus Giroux, 1989.

Pintak, Larry. *Beirut Outtakes: A TV Correspondent's Portrait of America's Encounter with Terror.* Lexington, MA: Lexington Books, 1988.

GEORGE E. IRANI

MARITIME PEACE IN PERPETUITY, TREATY OF (1853)

Treaty between Great Britain and the rulers of the lower Persian Gulf shaykhdoms.

After crushing local opposition to its claim of hegemony over the Persian Gulf portion of its economically important route to India, Britain sought to maintain its prerogatives and influence over the region's rulers and their subjects through a number of general treaties. The first of these was signed in 1820 and called for general disarmament and an end to attacks on British shipping. The treaty did not prohibit declared maritime warfare among local tribes, so this continued unabated, often disrupting the harvesting of pearls, an important source of income for merchants and rulers. In order to prevent attacks during the six-month pearling season, the ruler of Sharjah and Raʾs al-Khaymah suggested to the British that they oversee a truce. The British did so reluctantly, and a maritime truce was signed in 1835 and renewed annually until 1843, when a ten-year truce was signed. Reflecting Britain's willingness to expand its military and political commitments in the Persian Gulf, the 1853 Treaty of Maritime Peace in Perpetuity was meant to make the provisions of the 1843 treaty "lasting and invio-

lable," and called on the rulers to bring about a complete cessation of hostilities, to punish any of their subjects who attacked subjects of another treaty signatory, and to refrain from retaliating if they were victims of aggression and instead inform the British authorities, who promised to obtain reparations for any injury or damage. The emirates whose rulers signed the treaty were known afterward by English speakers as the Trucial States.

Bibliography

Metz, Helen Chapin. *Persian Gulf States: Country Studies,* 3d edition. Washington, DC: Library of Congress, 1994.

Peck, Malcolm C. *The United Arab Emirates: A Venture in Unity.* Boulder, CO: Westview; London: Croon Helm, 1986.

Tuson, Penelope, and Quick, Emma, eds. *Arabian Treaties, 1600–1960,* vol. 2. Slough, England: Archives Editions, 1992.

ANTHONY B. TOTH

MARJA AL-TAQLID

Senior clergy of Shiʿism whom faithful are supposed to follow in religious matters.

Marja al-taqlid, or authority appointed to be emulated by believers, is one of the main pillars of Twelve Imam Shiʿism during the period of the occultation of the twelfth imam, the last of the faith's infallible leaders. Twelver Shiʿism holds that the Twelfth Imam, Hasan al-Askari, left earth in 873 C.E., beginning a period of occultation in which Shiʿites are left without a member of the progeny of the first imam, Ali ibn Abi Talib, son-in-law and nephew of the prophet Muhammad, to rule over them. Before his major occultation, the Twelfth Imam appointed four special assistants, the last of whom died in 939 C.E. Shiʿite biographical compilations generally take Abu Jaʿfar Mohammad Koleyni (d. 940), one of the first compilers of Shiʿite traditions, to be the first *marja al-taqlid* after the occultation. In the medieval period, however, the office was not well defined. That task was undertaken by Shaykh Mohammad Hasan Esfahani Najafi, known as Sahb al-Javaher (d. 1849). In all, seventy-seven *marja al-taqlid* were recognized from 940 to 1995 (different sources provide slightly different tabulations), forty-nine of whom were Iranians and the rest Arabs.

The *marja al-taqlid* is regarded as one of the highest *ulama* (clergy) in Shi'ism; his words and deeds serve as a guide for those members of the community unable to exert independent judgment *(ijtihad)*. As such, holders of the position have come to enjoy substantial political clout in the modern period, especially because believers throughout the world provide the *marja al-taqlid* with considerable donations in the form of religious tithes. In fact, one of the qualifications of a *marja* is his ability to attract donations and raise enough money to finance the education of religious students. There are six conditions for the *marja al-taqlid* that are accepted unanimously by Shi'ite theologians, namely maturity *(bulugh)*, reasonableness *(aql)*, being of the male sex *(dhukurrat)*, faith *(iman)*, justice *(edalat)*, and legitimacy of birth. (These are general principles for the selection of a *marja al-taqlid*, and no specific process has ever been formalized.) Except for a brief period of centralization in nineteenth-century Iran engineered by Shaykh Morteza Ansari (d. 1864), clerical decentralization is an integral part of the Shi'ite hierarchy. Another defining characteristic of the *marja al-taqlid*, which again distances it from the papacy, is that designation to the position is entirely at the discretion of the believers themselves. The *marja al-taqlid* is not appointed by an official body resembling a council of *ulama*.

The sanctity of the office has increased in political clout in the modern period. In 1963, when Ayatollah Ruhollah Khomeini was arrested by the government of Mohammad Reza Pahlavi, the entire Shi'ite world rallied behind him and pressured the shah into releasing him. With the Iranian Revolution of 1979 and the establishment of the governance of the jurist *(velayat-e faqih)*, which designates a single leader *(vali-ye faqih)* for Shi'ites, the office of *marja al-taqlid* has acquired an ambiguous position, somewhat rivaling that of the *vali-ye faqih*. Since the death of Khomeini, no single ayatollah has emerged as a sole, authoritative *marja al-taqlid*; rather, several ayatollahs are recognized as sharing relatively equal status as *marja al-taqlids*.

See also IRANIAN REVOLUTION (1979); KHOMEINI, RUHOLLAH; PAHLAVI, REZA; SHI'ISM; VELAYAT-E FAQIH.

Bibliography

Momen, Moojan. *An Introduction to Shi'i Islam: The History and Doctrines of Twelver Shi'ism*. New Haven, CT: Yale University Press, 1985.

NEGUIN YAVARI
UPDATED BY ERIC HOOGLUND

MARK VIII

108th Coptic patriarch of Egypt serving from 1796 to 1809.

The papacy of Mark VIII is remembered more for the great historic event that occurred during his tenure—the Napoleonic expedition to Egypt (1798–1801)—than for his accomplishments. The prosperity enjoyed by the Coptic laity throughout Mark's career resulted from individual ambition not from the patriarch's initiative. Even construction of the Cathedral of St. Mark (dedicated to the archbishop's namesake) at al-Azbakiyya was the work of two influential citizens, not the patriarch.

Likewise, a Coptic military unit was more effective than Mark in dealing with Muslim tensions. Under the French, many Copts held high political and military positions and were handsomely rewarded for their loyalty. The Islamic majority could not tolerate the double disgrace of so many European Christians descending upon Egypt and their subsequent favoritism shown not only to the Copts but also to all other non-Muslims living in Cairo (Syrians, Greeks, and Jews). Several brutal assaults on the Copts in Cairo occurred during the French occupation and even thereafter. The famous Coptic Legion commanded by the illustrious General Ya'qub was created to counter this persecution.

In spiritual matters Mark achieved some distinction. He maintained an active correspondence with the Coptic parishes throughout Egypt and sent an important pastoral letter to Ethiopia. Because the church of St. Mark in "Babylon," the Coptic quarter of Cairo, had been destroyed during the Islamic rampages, the patriarch built a new church dedicated to his namesake.

See also COPTS.

DONALD SPANEL

MARMARA UNIVERSITY

Public university in Istanbul, Turkey.

Marmara University was founded as a vocational school in 1883 under the name of Hamidiye Higher School of Business. Until the 1960s, it comprised three separate divisions (secondary, high school, and college). Its title was changed first to Istanbul Academy of Economics and Business Administration in 1959 and later, in 1982, to Marmara University, after the Sea of Marmara, on which it is located. Today, the university has thirteen faculties (education; communications; dentistry; divinity; economics and administrative sciences; engineering; fine arts; health education; law; medicine; pharmacology; science and letters; and technical education), nine vocational schools, and eleven research institutes. It has twelve separate campuses and is one of the most prestigious universities in Turkey.

English is the language of instruction in medicine and in some branches of engineering and social sciences, whereas French is used in the program of public administration. Turkish constitutes the medium of instruction in the rest of the academic units. During the 1998–1999 academic year, the university had 2,539 faculty members and 51,024 students. Its 2003 budget amounted to 93,747 billion Turkish lire, 99 percent of which came directly from state funds.

Bibliography

Marmara University. Available at <http://www.marmara.edu.tr/Genel/?id=3>. (The university does not have an English web site, but brief information about the school can be found at <http://www.worldmedline.8k.com/contact.html>.)

I. METIN KUNT
UPDATED BY BURÇAK KESKIN-KOZAT

MARONITES

An indigenous church of Lebanon and Lebanon's largest Eastern-rite church.

The communion between the Maronite church and the Roman Catholic church was established in 1182, broken thereafter, and then reestablished in the sixteenth century. The union allowed the Maronites to retain their own rites and canon laws and to use Arabic and Aramaic in their liturgy, as well as the Karashuni script with old Syriac letters. The origins of the Maronites are a subject of continuing debate. Some historians trace them to Yuhanna Marun of Antioch in the seventh century; others trace them to the Yuhanna Marun who was a monk of Homs in the late fourth and early fifth centuries. In Syriac, the word *maron,* or *marun,* means small lord.

In the late seventh century, following persecution by other Christians for their heterodox views and rituals, the Maronites migrated from the coastal regions into the mountainous areas of Lebanon and Syria. During the Ottoman era, the Maronites remained isolated and relatively autonomous in these areas, although in recent times this autonomy has been greatly exaggerated for ideological and national reasons and made into a national myth. The Maronite community underwent socioeconomic changes in the nineteenth century, when the Maronite Church wielded tremendous economic and political power and the peasants within the community grew increasingly dissatisfied with the uneven distribution of the community's wealth and with the rigid social hierarchy that placed the patriarchate at the top. In 1858, the peasants revolted against the large land-owning families, but the church quickly engaged them in sectarian agitation. The revolt soon degenerated into a communal war between Druze and Maronites. This conflict came to characterize much of the history of nineteenth-century Lebanon, as the ruling families of the two communities split over the credibility of the Chehabi dynasty and over other political and economic issues. Land ownership, distribution of political power, and the question of safe passage of one community's members in the territory of the other remained thorny issues in their relationship. The conflict was internationalized in 1860, when France, historically the ostensible protector of the Maronites, sent a military expedition to the area.

The relationship of the two groups was not decisively settled in 1920 with the establishment of the mandate system, but the carnage of the previous century seemed to have ended. The Druze, however, despite their apparent military victory, only seemed to accept the political dominance of the Maronites, who were favored by the French authorities. Their dissatisfaction centered on their desire for a continuous, albeit inferior, political representation.

The Maronite sect has been directed and administered by the Patriarch of Antioch and the East. Bishops are generally nominated by a church synod from among the graduates of the Maronite College in Rome. In 2004, Mar Nasrallah Butrus Sfeir (also Sufayr) was the Maronite patriarch.

In addition to the Beirut archdiocese, nine other archdioceses and dioceses are located in the Middle East: Aleppo, Ba'albak, Cairo, Cyprus, Damascus, the Jubayl al-Batrun area, Sidon, Tripoli, and Tyre. Parishes and independent dioceses are also found wherever Maronites reside in large enough numbers: in Argentina, Brazil, Venezuela, the United States, Canada, Mexico, the Ivory Coast, and Senegal. Lebanon has four minor seminaries (al-Batrun, Ghazir, Ayn Sa'ada, and Tripoli) and a faculty of theology at Holy Spirit University at al-Kaslik, which is run by the Maronite monastic order. The patriarch is elected in a secret ceremony by a synod of bishops and confirmed by the pope in Rome.

An estimated 416,000 Maronites live in Lebanon, although the number is exaggerated by Lebanese ultranationalists, including an unknown number abroad. Maronites make up 16 percent of Lebanon's population. Historically, most Maronites have been rural people, like the Druze, although, unlike the Druze, they are scattered throughout the country, with a heavy concentration in Mount Lebanon. Urbanized Maronites reside in East Beirut and its suburbs. The Maronite sect has been traditionally awarded—thanks to French support—the highest posts in government, and its status within the socioeconomic hierarchy of Lebanon has been, in general, higher than that of other sects. Lebanese nationalism has been associated over the years with Maronite sectarian ideologies, so much so that most non-Maronite Lebanese tend to feel uneasy with the notion of Lebanese nationalism because it has come to signify the Lebanese political system with its Maronite dominance.

The Maronites, like other sects in Lebanon, have suffered from the civil war and its consequences. Although many Maronites were combatants, much of the Maronite civilian population paid a price—as did all civilians in Lebanon—for the recklessness of the warring factions. Many Maronites were displaced, especially from the Shuf Mountains, as a result of battles and forced expulsions. Many (no reliable figures exist) chose to emigrate, going to Europe, the United States, Canada, and Australia in search of peace and prosperity. Maronite leaders continue to warn of the dangers of diminishing Maronite demographic weight due to immigration. The Lebanese political reforms of Ta'if in 1989 did not necessarily undermine the political dominance of the Maronite community, since the presidency, the Central Bank, and command of the Lebanese Army remained in Maronite hands. In fact, the sectarian designation of governmental seats was solidified by the reforms, and the presidency was kept exclusively for Maronites. Nevertheless, the increased powers of the council of ministers curtailed some of the previous arbitrary powers of the president. But the implementation depended, and will continue to depend, on the personal and political impact of politicians, in terms of both their popularity within their own communities and the external support they receive from various regional and international powers. The political nervousness of the Maronite community in 2004, due to the exile of General Michel Aoun and the imprisonment of former Lebanese Forces commander Samir Geagea, has propelled the Maronite patriarch Nasrallah Sfeir into a position of unprecedented political and religious authority.

See also DRUZE; LEBANESE CIVIL WAR (1975–1990); LEBANON; LEBANON, MOUNT; MANDATE SYSTEM; SFEIR, NASRALLAH.

Bibliography

Moosa, Matti. *The Maronites in History*. Syracuse, NY: Syracuse University Press, 1986.

Salibi, Kamal S. *Maronite Historians of Medieval Lebanon*. New York: AMS Press, 1959.

AS'AD ABUKHALIL

MARRAKECH

Second largest city in Morocco; one of the four imperial cities of precolonial Morocco, established about 1060 C.E.

Located in the Hawz, an agricultural plain bounded to the south and east by the High Atlas mountains, and watered by the Tansift river, Marrakech is situated in a natural site of great potential. In opposition to Fez, the Arab capital of Morocco, Marrakech is a Berber metropolis, which drew population from the Berber-speaking groups of the nearby central High Altas mountains. The city was founded by Yusuf ibn Tashfin (1060–1106), first ruler of the Almoravid dynasty (1055–1157), under whom Marrakech became the base for the conquest of Morocco, portions of the Maghrib, and Andalusia. Extensive irrigation works were undertaken at this time, but little remains of the architecture of the Almoravid period.

Conquered by the Almohads (1130–1269) in 1147, Marrakech became the capital of an empire that at its height extended from Tunisia to the Atlantic, and from the Sahara to Andalusia. The Almohads were the effective builders of the city, constructing the Kutubiya mosque, one of the finest examples of Hispano-Moorish architecture, together with the ramparts, a fortress complex, and extensive bazaars and gardens. The celebrated philosopher, doctor, and savant Ibn Rushd (known in the West as Averroes, 1126–1198) lived in Marrakech, where he wrote several of his best-known works.

Marrakech went into a prolonged decline during the reign of the Marinids (1244–1578), whose capital was at Fez. Under the Saʿdians (1510–1603), who made it their capital in 1554, Marrakech once again became an imperial city. Numerous important palaces were constructed at this time, and the irrigation system of the surrounding Hawz plain was revived. The Alawi dynasty (1603–present) has continued this tradition. The city continued to benefit from its position as a crossroad of trade between the mountains, the pre-Saharan steppe, and the fertile plains of central Morocco. Under Sultan Hassan I and his successors Abd al-Aziz ibn al-Hassan and Abd al-Hafid, Marrakech was drawn increasingly into the world capitalist market. In the period of the Moroccan question (1900–1912), European business interests in collaboration with local urban notables and Berber lords based in the city began to acquire substantial holdings in the Hawz plain and the surrounding area.

Under the French protectorate (1912–1956), effective authority was conceded to Madani and Tuhami al-Glawi, who ruled much of southern Morocco as pashas of Marrakech and imperial viceroys. In this period, the city became a major agricultural entrepôt and center of light manufacturing. There was considerable investment in irrigation technologies and agriculture, and the population of the city increased from 70,000 in 1912 to 145,000 in 1921 to 215,000 in 1952.

Since Moroccan independence in 1956, Marrakech has continued to grow. Its population in 1994 was about 673,000 people. It is a center of tourism and an agricultural marketplace for southern Morocco, with a university and important cultural installations.

Bibliography

Julien, Charles-André. *History of North Africa: Tunisia, Algeria, Morocco,* translated by John Petrie. New York: Praeger, 1970.

Pascon, Paul. *Capitalism and Agriculture in the Haouz of Marrakech,* translated by C. Edwin Vaughan and Veronique Ingman. London and New York: KPI, 1986.

EDMUND BURKE III

MARRIAGE AND FAMILY

The institutions, patterns, and practices of marriage and the family play a key role in Middle Eastern society.

Marriage and family form the heart of Middle Eastern society, which is structured around the extended family system. Familial loyalty takes precedence over loyalty to work, friends, the law, and the nation. The institutions and practices of marriage are enforced by kinship networks to form reliable alliances. Hence, marriages between families serve important social, economic, and political functions by bringing together families in an expanding network of relationships, which extends membership rights and duties to relatives and their spouses. Each nuclear or extended family arranges different kinds of marriage alliances to accomplish both general and specific purposes. Membership in an influential family may be the only necessary criterion for success.

The Middle Eastern family is unequivocally patriarchal. The male is recognized as the head of his family, and his role is overt, whereas the female's

A Yemenite bride and groom sit in ceremonial attire in front of the traditional feast. In Yemen, marriages are arranged, then finalized with a contract. Islam permits a man to marry as many as four wives, but only if he can treat all as equals. In practice, polygamy is rare. © RICHARD T. NOWITZ/CORBIS. REPRODUCED BY PERMISSION.

role is more covert. Patriarchy also connotes obeying and respecting the decisions of elders. Respect for elders is held as the highest family duty, and disagreements with patriarchs are considered sinful. Hence, age and bearing children increase an individual's status in the family.

Bonds of obligation and trust unite people, and relationships within families are often multidimensional and intense. Families and kin groups are brought together to witness births, marriages, deaths, religious and other rituals, and the affairs of daily life. In-group cohesion is a sign of a strong family, and individuals may count on family members for unconditional support. Even at times of antipathy among relatives, they defend each other's honor and display group cohesion. Religion plays an important role in dictating family life and law; it is an integral part of the inherited social identity, rather than a matter of choice or personal conviction.

Most family relations, however, are constrained by tradition rather than religion. While traditions provide support for family members, they also constrain their personal freedom and privacy. For instance, it is a common practice for single adults (male and female) to live with their family until

marriage. They are governed by their elders and seek their permission regarding personal decisions. Traditions also play an important role in selecting a spouse, proposing a marriage and deciding its various logistics. Marriages are built based on financial security, social status, and child-bearing potentials rather than on love and romance.

Marriages are often arranged by women and are initiated with an official request from an elder in the groom's family to an elder in the bride's family. And elaborate engagement celebration is then held as a public announcement permitting the groom and bride to appear in public together prior to marriage. Engagements usually are short unless economic hardships prevent the couple from securing a residence. Marriage ceremonies are almost always large, expensive, and joyous affairs involving the groom and bride's wider kinship and residential groups.

Children are important elements of a successful marriage. No marriage is considered complete unless it produces many children. The average family size in the Middle East is over six members, including the parents. Desiring large families is common, but sons are often preferred to daughters because sons carry the name of the family, and remain with their parents after marriage in this patrilineal society. Nonetheless, daughters are desired as caregivers of aging parents, while sons are obliged to provide financial security.

Boys' education and work begin at a very early age and are usually mediated by various adult male relatives. Girls' domestic training starts early as well and is transmitted by various female relatives. Overall, relatives, neighbors, and friends participate in raising children and teaching them family values and morals. Young adults are given duties and responsibilities within the family setting, against which they rarely rebel. They are also encouraged to maintain and pass on social values from one generation to another. Disciplining children is an acceptable practice that may be carried out by any relative, neighbor, or friend.

The Middle Eastern family is neither unique nor constant nor uniform. Changes happen at all levels at all times. For instance, while, the bride and the groom often live with the groom's family in more traditional and rural settings, the trend for the urban middle and upper classes is for a new, separate residence to be established. The groom and bride's families remain in close contact and visit frequently. Similarly, more rural and traditional settings tend to favor marriage at a very young age for both males and females as a tool of social control. However, in modern urban settings, new marriage laws and new opportunities in education and employment have raised the age of marriage for both sexes.

Although polygamy is accepted as a lesser evil than divorce, it is outlawed in Tunisia, Turkey, Israel, and Iraq and is subject to court approval in Morocco, Syria, Jordan, and Yemen. Moreover, polygamy rates have always been low, and they are decreasing rapidly almost everywhere, primarily for economic and social reasons. Alternatively, while divorce is considered a social stigma for both men and women, its rates vary widely across the region and are increasing overall, in tune with rapid social change and economic pressures. In the case of divorce or widowhood, Islamic laws grant women the custody of children until age seven for boys and nine for girls. Divorce is much more difficult for Jews and Christians in the region. Among the Druze, a husband and wife who divorce are forbidden from remarrying, unlike in Islam.

Familial honor is another social asset and stigma. The reputation of any family member influences the reputation of the entire family. However, women who bring dishonor to their families because of presumed sexual indiscretions are forced to pay a terrible price at the hands of male family members. The problem of "honor killings" throughout the Middle East is manifested in the legal safeguards protecting men by granting them special legal exemptions and reduced sentences in cases of conviction.

The Middle East experienced rapid changes and challenges in the twentieth century. While women continue gaining access to formal education and careers, they continue to face societal restrictions concerning their contacts outside the home and beyond their kinship groups. Widespread economic change, especially trends toward modernization and Westernization vis-à-vis reactionary and Islamist

A Palestinian family in the West Bank. © PETER TURNLEY/ CORBIS. REPRODUCED BY PERMISSION.

movements, have affected customary notions of marriage and the family.

See also POLYGAMY.

Bibliography

Doumani, Beshara. *Family History in the Middle East: Household, Property, and Gender.* New York: State University of New York Press, 2003.

Esposito, John L., and DeLong-Bas, Nanata. J. *Women in Muslim Family Law.* Syracuse, NY: Syracuse University Press, 2001.

Fernea, Elizabeth W. *Women and the Family in the Middle East: New Voices of Change.* Austin: University of Texas Press, 1985.

Hale, Sondra. "Gender and Economics: Islam and Polygamy—A Question of Causality." *Feminist Economics* 1 (1995): 67–79.

King-Irani, Laurie. "Kinship, Ethnicity, and Social Class." In *Understanding the Contemporary Middle East,* 2d edition, edited by D. Gerner and J. Schwedler. Boulder, CO: Lynne Rienner, 2003.

Lopata, Helena Z. *Widows: The Middle East, Asia and the Pacific.* Durham, NC: Duke University Press, 1987.

Moghadam, Valentine M. "Gender, National Identity and Citizenship: Reflections on the Middle East and North Africa." *Comparative Studies of South Asia, Africa and the Middle East* 19 (1999): 137–157.

Obermeyer, Carla. M. *Family, Gender, and Population in the Middle East: Policies in Context.* Cairo: American University in Cairo Press, 1995.

Prothro, Edwin T., and Diab, Lutfi. N. *Changing Family Patterns in the Arab East.* Beirut: American University of Beirut, 1974.

Sonbol, Amira El Azhary. *Women, the Family, and Divorce Laws in Islamic History.* Syracuse, NY: Syracuse University Press, 1996.

RITA STEPHAN

MARSH ARABS

Inhabitants of the vast marshlands in southern Iraq.

The Marsh Arabs lived in one of the great marsh areas of the world, a 20,000-square-mile (52,000 sq. km) area triangulated by Kut on the Tigris, al-Kifl on the Euphrates, and Basra on the Shatt al-Arab. A significant number may be non-Semitic in origin, perhaps descendants of the ancient Sumerians, although they have mixed with other peoples through time. Called Marsh Arabs by some owing to their language, social structures, and religion, others designate them Ma'dan to reflect that their way of life is dependent on the water buffalo. Nomads of the marshes, relying on a variety of canoes for transport, they follow buffalo herds as their desert counterparts follow camels or sheep. Most are cultivators, reed gatherers, or buffalo breeders. Traditionally they lived in villages in island settlements, on floating platforms, or on man-made reed islands. Today, their structures are of brick and concrete. Roads and causeways connect major settlements facilitating social improvements, especially in education and health.

Bibliography

Thesiger, Wilfred. *The Marsh Arabs.* New York: Dutton, 1964.

ALBERTINE JWAIDEH

MA'RUFI, ABBAS

[1957–]

Iranian writer and editor.

Abbas Ma'rufi was born in Tehran and graduated from Tehran University's Faculty of Fine Arts with a degree in dramatic arts. His novels and short stories experiment with psychoanalytic techniques, incorporating them into a clear and flowing narrative style. He published several collections of short stories in the 1980s and his first and most famous novel, *Samfoni-ye Mordegan* (Symphony of the dead), in 1989. Subsequent novels include *Sal-e Bala* (Year of catastrophes, 1992) and *Peykar-e Farhad* (Statute of Farhad, 1995). Ma'rufi edited the literary journal *Gardoon* in Tehran, but after the publication was closed by the government for "offending religious sensibilities," he left Iran for exile abroad. Since 1996, he has edited *Gardoon* in Europe.

See also LITERATURE: PERSIAN.

Bibliography

Yavari, Houra. "Discourse in Psychoanalysis and Literature and Post-Revolutionary Iran: A Case of *The Symphony of the Dead* by Abbas Ma'rufi." *Critique* 7 (fall 1995): 101–111.

PARDIS MINUCHEHR
UPDATED BY ERIC HOOGLUND

MARZOUKI, MONCEF

[1945–]

Tunisian opposition leader, human-rights activist, writer, physician.

Moncef Marzouki, a Tunisian neurological and public-health specialist trained in France (1973), became a human-rights advocate after observing medical experiments on patients. He returned to Tunisia in 1979 and founded the Center for Community Medicine in the slums of Sousse, south of Tunis. Marzouki cofounded the African Network for Prevention of Child Abuse (1981) and joined the Tunisian League for Human Rights (LTDH), becoming its vice president (1987) and president (1989–1994).

In 1991 his opposition to Iraq's invasion of Kuwait drew Western praise, but the Tunisian government retaliated by neutering the LTDH in 1992. In 1993 Marzouki and seventeen others launched the National Committee for the Defense of Prisoners of Conscience. They were arrested, and he resigned after it was taken over by supporters of the regime.

In 1994 he ran for the presidency even though there was no provision for unapproved candidates, accusing the regime of human-rights violations and arguing that its experiment with democracy and the anti-Islamist crackdown were excuses for deposing Habib Bourguiba. Without human rights, the ideological vacuum in which secularist and Islamist extremisms flourished would persist. He was imprisoned for propagating false news.

Released after four months, Marzouki was thrice rearrested (in 1996 following a LTDH human-rights report, in 1999 at election time, and in 2000 after allying with exiled Islamists) and twice imprisoned. In 1998 he was founding spokesperson for the National Committee for Liberties (CNLT) and president of the Arab Commission of Human Rights. He subsequently established the Congress for the Republic (CPR), uniting democratic secularists and Islamists against President Ben Ali's "constitutional putsch." From 2002, he ran the CPR from France.

See also BEN ALI, ZAYN AL-ABIDINE; HUMAN RIGHTS; TUNISIA: POLITICAL PARTIES IN.

Bibliography

Marzouki, Moncef. *Second Independence, or For a Democratic Arab State.* Beirut, Lebanon: Dar al-Kunuz al-Adabiyah, 1996.

Moncef Marzouki web site. Available from <http://www.globalprevention.com/news.htm>.

                                        GEORGE R. WILKES

MASADA

Site of Jewish revolt and martyrdom, 74 C.E.

An isolated mountain on the western shore of the Dead Sea, Masada was turned by King Herod the Great of Judea (37–34 B.C.E.) into a major stronghold. In 66 C.E., at the onset of the Jewish revolt against Rome, the extremist *Sicarii* ("dagger-men") captured Masada; after the revolt's suppression, it remained the last Jewish fortress to hold out. When the Romans were about to storm its walls in the spring of 74 C.E., the defenders, preferring death to slavery, decided to commit collective suicide. Men slew their women and children, then killed one another—thus relates Flavius Josephus, the only historian to describe these events. The story of the mass suicide is supported by comparable occurrences in the Greco-Roman world.

In traditional Judaism, Masada went largely unmentioned for centuries. Only with the advent of Zionism did it gain prominence, with the defenders portrayed as freedom-loving heroes and their stance hailed as an example to live by. In Yitzhak Lamdan's influential poem of 1927, Masada came to symbolize the entire Zionist enterprise, with the most famous line announcing, "Masada shall not fall again." From the 1940s, Masada became the goal of ritual treks organized by Zionist youth movements; from the 1950s, recruits of Israel's army swore their oath of allegiance in ceremonies atop Masada. The excavation of the fortress in the 1960s enhanced still further its salience in Israeli consciousness.

The veneration of Masada was never total; for instance, in 1946 David Ben-Gurion coined the slogan "Neither Masada nor Vichy." From the 1970s onward, the Masada myth repeatedly came under attack. The credibility of Josephus's account was questioned; the cruelty of Masada's "dagger-men" toward other Jews was emphasized; and the portrayal of the perpetrators of a group suicide as national heroes was decried as incongruent with Judaism's teachings and educationally misguided. Hard-line Israeli leaders were accused of being possessed by a "Masada complex"—that is, of so identifying with Masada's desperate situation that they were no longer reacting to the reality of their own times.

In 2002 the United Nations Educational, Scientific and Cultural Organization's (UNESCO) proclamation of Masada as a World Heritage Site entailed another round of exchanges between Masada's admirers and detractors.

Bibliography

Ben-Yehuda, Nachman. *The Masada Myth: Collective Memory and Mythmaking in Israel.* Madison, WI: The University of Wisconsin Press, 1995.

Josephus, Flavius. *The Jewish War,* translated by H. St. John Thackeray. Cambridge, MA: Harvard University Press, 1979.

Kedar, Benjamin Z. "Masada: The Myth and the Complex." *The Jerusalem Quarterly* 24 (1982): 57–63.

Yadin, Yigael. *Masada: Herod's Fortress and the Zealots' Last Stand.* London: Weidenfeld and Nicolson, 1966.

                                        BENJAMIN KEDAR

MAS'ADI, MAHMOUD AL-
[1911–]

Tunisian essayist, playwright, and politician.

Mahmoud al-Mas'adi was born in Tazerka, Tunisia. He obtained his *agrégation* in Arabic literature from the Sorbonne in 1947, and was a teacher and educational administrator until 1958. He subsequently held various posts in Tunisia's cabinet and was named the nation's representative to the United Nations Educational, Scientific and Cultural Organization (UNESCO). He was editor of the journal *al-Mabahith* from 1944 to 1947. In 1979 he published his editorials from *al-Mabahith* in a book titled *Ta'silan likayan* (The grounding of the human being).

Although he is bilingual in Arabic and French, al-Mas'adi writes only in Arabic. He occupies a unique place in modern Tunisian literature. His writings are characterized by a hermetic style that is strongly reminiscent of the language of the Qur'an. He is deeply influenced by European existentialism and culture as well as by Arab Islamic culture. According to him, existentialism and commitment are strongly linked. His deeply philosophical writings are primarily concerned with a person's role in life and the significance of existence. His play *al-Sudd* (1955; The dam) is an expression of his philosophical outlook on man and his destiny, whereas his novel *Haddatha Abu Hurayra, Qala . . .* (1923; Abu Hurayra said . . .) transposes this philosophical inclination into an Islamic framework. The collection of short stories titled *Mawlid al-Nisyan* (1974; The birth of forgetfulness) portrays the struggle between good and evil in the human being.

See also LITERATURE: ARABIC, NORTH AFRICAN.

AIDA A. BAMIA

MASHHAD

Major city of northeast Iran and capital of Khorasan Province.

Mashhad originally developed as a pilgrimage center after the eighth Shi'ite Islamic imam, Reza, died and was buried (ninth century C.E.) in what then was a small village containing the tomb of Caliph Harun al-Rashid. The village began to develop as a trade center renamed *Mashhad,* or "place of the martyr," during the fourteenth century, after the Mongols had destroyed the ancient city of Tus, located

15 miles to the northwest of what is now central Mashhad. Its growth was slowed, however, by the general insecurity that prevailed in this region until the nineteenth century. After 1850, Mashhad developed as a major transshipment center for the overland trade between Iran and Russia and Iran and British India. The Qajar dynasty shahs expended funds on the embellishment and expansion of the shrine to Imam Reza (originally built during the early fifteenth century), including its affiliated seminary and other religious institutions. During the reign of Reza Shah Pahlavi the city was rebuilt with a ring road around the shrine and wide avenues.

Mashhad began to develop as an important industrial center during the 1930s, initially with carpet and textile manufacturing; by the end of the 1990s, food processing, chemicals, and pharmaceuticals also were significant industries. Its importance as a transportation center is enhanced by air, rail, and road connections to Tehran and the rest of Iran. In 1996 the railway to Turkmenistan was inaugurated; this connected to the main railroad system through the Central Asian republics. Ferdowsi University, established in 1947, provides undergraduate and graduate education in agriculture, art, economics, law, medicine, social sciences, and technology. The Imam Reza shrine continues to be the major tourist site in Iran, attracting several hundred thousand visitors annually. Mashhad is now the second largest city in the country, having grown from a medium-sized city of 147,000 in 1947 to a metropolis of 1,887,405 in 1996.

See also PAHLAVI, REZA; QAJAR DYNASTY.

Bibliography

Mashhad web site. Available from <http://www.farsinet.com/mashhad>.

CYRUS MOSHAVER
UPDATED BY ERIC HOOGLUND

MASIRA ISLAND

A strategically important island in the Arabian Sea off the south coast of Oman.

Masira Island's rocky hills have made it inhospitable for agriculture, and historically its small population has subsisted on the sea, exporting such products as fish, turtle shells, and shark fins. During World War

II, the British built an air base and a powerful radio transmitter on the island. When Oman attained independence, Sultan Qabus, the ruler, funded the construction of modern housing, schools, and a clinic. The United States signed a ten-year lease for the military facilities on the island in 1980. It was from here that the abortive mission to rescue U.S. hostages in Iran was launched. The island's facilities also were used by coalition forces during the 1990–1991 Gulf War. The United States has spent hundreds of millions of dollars on its military facilities on the island. In the late 1990s the island had about 8,000 inhabitants and hosted one of the largest group of nesting loggerhead turtles in the world.

See also OMAN.

Bibliography

DeGaury, Gerald. "A Note on Masirah Island." *Geographical Journal* 123 (1957): 499–502.

ROBERT G. LANDEN
UPDATED BY ANTHONY B. TOTH

MASMOUDI, MUHAMMAD
[1925–]

Tunisian diplomat.

Muhammad Masmoudi was educated in Tunis and at the law faculty in Paris. As representative of the Neo-Destour Party in France, Masmoudi was one of the party leaders who headed the official talks with France between September 1954 and May 1955 that led to independence. In 1956, he took part in the Tunisian delegation that signed the protocols formalizing independence from France (which had held a protectorate from 1881). Despite uneven relations with President Habib Bourguiba, he held various government posts, including ambassador to France (1965–1969). As minister of foreign affairs (1970–1974), he led an effort to forge ties with Libya, which culminated in a short-lived merger in 1974. With its collapse, Masmoudi was removed from office; shortly thereafter he went into exile, returning in 1977. His ties to Libya put him at the center of controversy in 1984, when he briefly accepted a United Nations post from Libya, from which Bourguiba forced him to withdraw. Masmoudi has also been an important diplomatic mediator between Tunisia and Saudi Arabia. Following his withdrawal from the diplomatic scene, Masmoudi has participated in numerous conferences throughout the Arab world, working for the promotion of scientific research, and has collaborated with the Temimi Foundation for Scientific Research and Information (Tunisia).

See also BOURGUIBA, HABIB; TUNISIA.

Bibliography

Hahn, Lorna. *North Africa: Nationalism to Nationhood.* Washington, DC: Public Affairs Press, 1960.

Perkins, Kenneth J. *Tunisia: Crossroads of the Islamic and European Worlds.* Boulder, CO: Westview Press; London: Croom Helm, 1986.

MATTHEW S. GORDON
UPDATED BY VANESA CASANOVA-FERNANDEZ

MASPÉRO, GASTON
[1846–1916]

French Egyptologist.

Gaston Maspéro studied at the École Normale, Paris. He succeeded Auguste Mariette as professor of Egyptian Philology and Archaeology at the Collège de France. Upon Mariette's death in 1881, Maspéro followed him as director of the Egyptian Antiquities Service and the Egyptian Museum in Cairo. Maspéro served as director from 1881 to 1886 and from 1899 to 1914, overseeing archaeology throughout Egypt. He published the pyramid texts he discovered at Saqqara, initiated the systematic clearing of the temple of Karnak, and coordinated the publication of the immense catalog of the Egyptian Museum. Maspéro may have published more than any other Egyptologist.

See also ARCHAEOLOGY IN THE MIDDLE EAST; EGYPTIAN MUSEUM; MARIETTE, AUGUSTE.

Bibliography

Bierbrier, M. L., ed. *Who Was Who in Egyptology,* 3d edition. London: Egypt Exploration Society, 1995.

DONALD MALCOLM REID

MASRI, MAI
[1959–]

Filmmaker, director, and producer.

Mai Masri was born in Jordan in 1959 to an American mother from Texas and a Palestinian father from the Masri family of Nablus. She developed an interest in film and photography during her high school years in Beirut, traveling to the United States to pursue her university education in 1977, where she received her bachelor's degree in film from San Francisco State University in 1981. Masri has directed and produced several award-winning films that provide a fine-grained view of women's and children's lives in situations marked by conflict, uncertainty, and crisis. Her films have been broadcast in the Arab world, Europe, the United Kingdom, and North America and have received ten international awards, including Best Documentary at the Institut du Monde Arabe Film Festival in Paris. She has also directed *Children of Fire* (1990) and *Children of Shatila* (1998), which won Best Director and Best Camera awards at the Arab Screen Festival in London.

During the later years of the Lebanese Civil War, Masri and her husband, Lebanese filmmaker and producer Jean Khalil Chamoun, filmed Lebanese and Palestinian civilians attempting to live and work under bombardments in Beirut and in South Lebanon, turning their copious footage of the war years into award-winning films such as *Under the Rubble* (1983), *Wild Flowers* (1987), *War Generation-Beirut* (1989), and *Suspended Dreams* (1992). All of these films show the costs of war and displacement, but also the strength of the human spirit and the importance of creative expression in the midst of large-scale destruction. In 1995 Masri directed a portrait of Hanan Ashrawi for BBC television, entitled *A Woman of Her Time*. She has also produced *Hostage of Time* (1994) and the feature film *In the Shadows of the City* (2000), which won the Cannes Junior Award. Masri currently lives in Beirut with her husband and their two daughters.

LAURIE KING-IRANI

MATAWIRAH TRIBE

See TRIBES AND TRIBALISM: MATAWIRAH TRIBE

MATRAH

Port city of Oman.

Originally a fishing village, after the sixteenth century Matrah became the hub of Oman's domestic commerce and home of a cosmopolitan merchant community. Today the site of Oman's largest port, Matrah lies adjacent to Muscat, the sultanate's capital. It is essentially being absorbed into the burgeoning capital urban complex.

See also MUSCAT.

Bibliography

Hawley, Sir Donald. *Oman and Its Renaissance,* 4th revised edition. London: Stacey International, 1987.

ROBERT G. LANDEN

MATZPEN

Israeli leftist, anti-Zionist group.

Israel's most vilified anti-Zionist group from 1967 to 1972, Matzpen (Hebrew, "compass," also known as the Israeli Socialist Organization) was the first leftist organization to identify Jewish colonization and Palestinian dispossession as the basis of the Arab–Israel conflict. The group, formed by students in 1962, broke with the Communist Party over its acceptance of the Israeli state. Harassed and often hounded out of jobs, a number of members moved abroad, created a European support network, and established contacts with Palestinian leftists there.

Never more than a few dozen strong, Matzpen came to public attention for protesting Israel's occupation of the West Bank in 1967; this was viewed as treachery by those who saw the occupation as a defensive necessity. Most Matzpen members favored a binational state. In their first dialogues at Bir Zeit University, and in subsequent dialogues with the Palestine Liberation Organization and Democratic Front for the Liberation of Palestine representatives, they argued that Jews should enjoy national rights in a future Palestinian state, whereas their Palestinian interlocutors insisted that Jews should have simply cultural and religious rights.

Matzpen attracted further hostility in Israel in the early 1970s, when it encouraged Black Panther protests in Israel and supported Palestinian resistance in the Territories. Its members were accused of supporting foreign espionage, and in 1972 one of them, Ehud "Udi" Adiv, was arrested and later imprisoned, for contacting Syrian authorities. The group split over ideological affiliation in 1972 and nearly dissolved after the Oslo Accord (1993). But the influence of former members—including Moshe Machover, Akiva Orr, Haim Hanegbi, Michel Warschawski, and Leah Tsemel—among leftists engaged in Israeli–Palestinian dialogue and opposed to human rights abuses in the occupied territories grew enormously. By the 1990s, its assertion that Jewish colonization was the primary cause of the Israel–Arab conflict was also a common feature of post-Zionism.

> *See also* ARAB–ISRAEL CONFLICT; ARAB–ISRAEL WAR (1967); ISRAEL: MILITARY AND POLITICS; OSLO ACCORD (1993); PALESTINE LIBERATION ORGANIZATION (PLO); TSEMEL, LEAH; WEST BANK.

Bibliography

Bober, Arie, ed. *The Other Israel: The Radical Case against Zionism.* Garden City, NY: Doubleday Anchor, 1972.

Matzpen: Anti-Zionist Israelis. Directed by Eran Torbiner. Matar Plus, 2003.

Schnall, David. "Anti-Zionism, Marxism, and Matzpen: Ideology and the Israeli Socialist Organization." *Asian Profile* 6, no. 4 (1978): 381–393.

Sprinzak, Ehud. *Brother against Brother: Violence and Extremism in Israeli Politics from Altalena to the Rabin Assassination.* New York: Free Press, 1999.

GEORGE R. WILKES

MAUDE, FREDERICK STANLEY
[1864–1917]

British soldier.

Frederick Stanley Maude entered the military in 1884, fought in the South African wars (1899–1902), and became commander of the 13th Division at the Dardanelles in 1915 after the outbreak of World War I. He was ordered to take his troops to Mesopotamia (the area between the Tigris and Euphrates rivers) to relieve the Anglo-Indian forces in the Mesopotamia Campaign besieged at Kut al-Amara. On 22 February 1917 he drove the Ottoman army from the town and then planned the advance that culminated in the fall of Baghdad on 11 March 1917. Shortly after this, the so-called Maude Declaration (actually written by Sir Mark Sykes) announced to the people of Baghdad that Britain intended to grant them self-determination. Maude died of cholera in 1917.

> *See also* MESOPOTAMIA CAMPAIGN (1914–1918); SYKES, MARK.

Bibliography

Fromkin, David. *A Peace to End All Peace: The Fall of the Ottoman Empire and the Creation of the Modern Middle East.* New York: Avon, 1990.

ZACHARY KARABELL

MAURITANIA

Constitutional republic located in northwest Africa.

The Islamic Republic of Mauritania covers an area of 398,000 square miles and is bordered by Western Sahara and Algeria on the north, Mali on the east, Mali and Senegal on the south, and the Atlantic Ocean on the west. The population in 2002 was about 2.6 million people (United Nations estimate). Nouakchott, the capital and largest city, has more than 800,000 people. The second largest city is Nouadhibou, a maritime commercial center in the northwest, with a population of about 100,000.

Due to endemic drought in Mauritania, some 500,000 displaced nomads and oasis dwellers were forced into sprawling shanty towns that surround the capital city of Nouakchott. © YANN ARTHUS-BERTRAND/CORBIS. REPRODUCED BY PERMISSION.

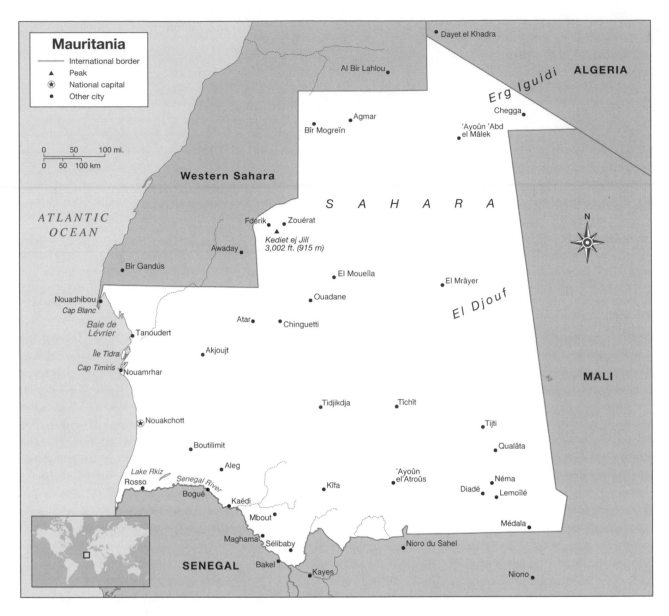

Mauritania

— International border
▲ Peak
✪ National capital
• Other city

0   50   100 mi.
0   50   100 km

Dayet el Khadra

Al Bir Lahlou

Erg Iguidi   **ALGERIA**

Agmar

Bîr Mogreïn

Chegga

'Ayoûn 'Abd el Mâlek

Western Sahara

S   A   H   A   R   A

ATLANTIC OCEAN

Fdérik   Zouérat

Kediet ej Jill
3,002 ft. (915 m)

Awaday

El Moueïla

El Mrâyer

Bir Gandús

Ouadane

El Djouf

Nouadhibou
Cap Blanc

Atar   Chinguetti

Baie de Lévrier   Tanoudert

Île Tidra

Akjoujt

Cap Timiris   Nouamrhar

MALI

Tidjikdja   Tîchît

Tijti

✪ Nouakchott

Qualâta

Boutilimit

Aleg

Néma

Lake Rkiz

'Ayoûn el'Atroûs

Rosso   *Senegal River*

Kîfa

Diadé   Lemoïlé

Bogué   Kaédi

Mbout

Médala

Maghama   Sélibaby

Nioro du Sahel

SENEGAL   Bakel

Kayes

Niono

Map by XNR Productions, Inc. The Gale Group.

Mauritania has twelve administrative regions plus the district of Nouakchott.

Climate and Resources

Mauritania has three major geographic and climatic areas. The northern Sahara region is more than 65 percent of the country. Covered by arid plains, plateaus, and sand dunes, it receives almost no rainfall and is subject to severe fluctuations in temperature. To its south is the Sahel, a wide area consisting of steppes and meadows. On Mauritania's southern border is the Senegal River region, a narrow strip of cooler temperatures and higher rainfall that supports considerable plant life.

The national economy has suffered from a lack of natural resources. Climatic conditions limit agriculture to the Senegal River region, where millet, sorghum, rice, and dates are grown. In the Sahel, livestock raising supports much of the rural population. Oil was discovered in 2001 56 miles southwest off the coast of Nouakchott, and although findings were modest, Mauritania's economy can expect a large boost when it acquires the means to extract and export its oil.

To date, however, iron ore, gypsum, and copper constitute the only major mineral exports. Mauritanian waters are considered to be among the richest fishing areas in the world. In the 1980s offshore fishing grew rapidly, making fish the country's chief export. The small manufacturing sector is based largely on fish processing. Food and capital goods account for the bulk of imports.

Population and Culture

Mauritania boasts a unique mixture of North African and West African culture, and it struggles to unite them. Approximately 66 percent of the population are Maures of Arab, Berber, and black African descent who speak Hassaniya, a dialect of Arabic and one of the two official languages of Mauritania. The remaining population is ethnically black African, composed of Halpulaar, Fulbe, Soninké, and Wolof (speakers of Pulaar, Soninké, and Wolof). French is the other official language of Mauritania, spoken in the marketplace as a common second language. Almost all Mauritanians are Sunni Muslims.

History

In the early 1800s amirs and Islamic religious leaders controlled the area that is now Mauritania. France gradually expanded its military and economic presence from Senegal into Maure areas. Between 1901 and 1912 France gained control of all major regions of Mauritania and declared it a protectorate, ruling indirectly through traditional leaders. After World War II, nationalist parties became active. Under the leadership of Mokhtar Ould Daddah and his Mauritanian Regroupment Party, Mauritania declared its independence from France in 1960. Since independence, Mauritania has faced severe problems with national unity, desertification (enlargement of desert areas), and economic stability. In 2000 the Heavily Indebted Poor Country Initiative qualified Mauritania for debt relief programs. In 2002 Mauritanians wrestled with a severe drought that led to food shortages and the slaughtering of livestock.

Mauritania also faced disputes with its neighbors to the north and south at the end of the twentieth century. In August 1976 the armed POLISARIO Front of Western Sahara invaded Mauritania and forced it to give up its claims to one-third of Western Saharan territory. Morocco quickly took over the land as Mauritanian forces withdrew.

A conflict between Senegal and Mauritania in 1989 intensified to a near-war situation as tens of thousands of Senegalese in Mauritania were expelled or killed, and more than 200,000 white Mauritanians in Senegal were forced to return to Mauritania. In 1991 Senegal and Mauritania resolved their differences and resumed their diplomatic relationship.

In 2000 Mauritania withdrew from ECOWAS (the Economic Community of West Africa) and aligned itself more with the Arab Maghreb Union.

Based on the 1991 constitution, the government is headed by a president elected by universal suffrage, who appoints a prime minister and a constitutional council. The legislature is composed of the National Assembly with seventy-nine members and the Senate with fifty-six members. The constitution guarantees the right of political parties to form. The government is controlled by the Parti Républicain Démocratique et Social (PRDS), whose leader Maaouya Ould Sid Ahmed Taya has been the president since his self-appointment in 1984. Amid claims of election fraud Taya was elected to the presidency in 1992 and again in 1997. Mauritania's 2001 legislative elections were internationally recognized as free and open.

See also ARAB MAGHREB UNION; DADDAH, MOKHTAR OULD; OULD SID'AHMED TAYA, MA'OUIYA; POLISARIO; WESTERN SAHARA WAR.

Bibliography

U.S. Library of Congress Federal Research Division. *Mauritania: A Country Study*, 2d edition, edited by Robert E. Handloff. Washington, DC: Author, 1990.

BRADFORD DILLMAN
UPDATED BY NAOMI ZEFF

MAWDUDI, ABU AL-A'LA, AL-
[1903–1979]

Founder and leader of Jama'at-i-Islami, one of the most important Muslim parties in Pakistan.

Abu al-Aʿla al-Mawdudi was born in India under British colonial rule. A journalist by profession, he was mostly self-taught although very well read in Islamic sciences and Western thought. He devoted himself first to founding the state of Pakistan and then to the Jamaʿat, which advocated the establishment of an Islamic state in Pakistan. Mawdudi's stance is similar to that of the founders of Egypt's Muslim Brotherhood and was shaped by the same forces: the violent disruption of the traditional economic, social, and political structures in the Muslim world by colonial powers. Their goal was to fight Western intervention and adapt Islamic thought to the needs of the modern world. Mawdudi responded to orientalists' contemptuous descriptions of Islam as a backward and inferior religion with an equally contemptuous denunciation of the self-serving colonialism, nationalism, materialism, atheism, and moral laxity of Western culture.

A prolific writer, Mawdudi attempted to show that Islam is a comprehensive system that encompasses all aspects of life, whether social, political, or economic. He did not advocate a mindless return to the Prophet's time but rather urged Muslims to restore the true Islamic spirit that had been overshadowed by cultural traditions, the *taqlid* (imitation) practice of the theologians, as well as the passive otherworldliness of Sufism. His own commentary on the Qurʾan, which is his best-known work, is such an attempt. His followers tend to be well-educated professionals dedicated to freeing their country from Western political institutions and cultural encroachment and to the restoration of Islamic law. The Jamaʿat is politically active and was suppressed at times because of its opposition to government policies. Shunned as a reformer by conservatives and criticized as too conservative by liberals, Mawdudi can be faulted mostly for calling for new institutions without being able to produce a blueprint for a modern Islamic state.

See also PAKISTAN AND THE MIDDLE EAST.

Bibliography

Ahmad, Khurshid, and Ansari, Z.I. eds. *Islamic Perspectives: Studies in Honour of Mawlana Sayyid Abul A'la Mawdudi.* Leicester, U.K.: The Islamic Foundation, 1979.

MAYSAM J. AL FARUQI

MAYSALUN

Site of armed combat between French and Arab forces immediately prior to the French mandate over Syria.

Khan Maysalun, a quiet market town on the highway between Beirut and Damascus just east of Alayh, won notoriety as the site of the 24 July 1920 clash between French troops and the armed forces of the Arab government in Damascus. The outcome eventuated in France's taking control of Syria for the ensuing quarter century.

British imperial troops occupied the cities of central Syria as soon as the Ottoman garrisons evacuated them in September 1918. With British acquiescence, an Arab government quickly established itself in Damascus, and Arab nationalists announced the creation of a similar administration in Beirut on 1 October. But when British forces entered Beirut a week later, the nationalist government was disbanded and French military governors took charge of Beirut, Sidon, and Tyre in the name of implementing the League of Nations mandate. The Arab leader in Damascus, Faisal I ibn Hussein, nevertheless toured Lebanon the following month and received an enthusiastic welcome from the populace in each city he visited. On 21 November, he returned to Beirut on his way to the Versailles peace conference.

While Faisal was in Europe, Britain and France negotiated the boundaries separating their respective zones of control in Syria, according to the terms of the wartime Sykes-Picot agreement. The division of Syria into British and French zones was confirmed at Versailles, over strenuous objections from the United States. By the next summer, it was clear that Britain intended to withdraw its troops from central Syria, prompting Faisal to press the British government to take over the mandate for the region. Britain refused to do this, and on 1 November 1919, while the amir was once again in Europe, British commanders in the Syrian interior turned over their positions to forces loyal to Faisal, while those in Lebanon relinquished their garrisons to French units. In the Biqa valley, Lebanese Christians attacked Syrian outposts, providing French commanders with a pretext to move into the area in force at the end of the month.

Faisal returned to Syria in mid-January 1920 and attempted to salvage his reputation, which had been badly tarnished during the months of fruitless negotiations with the French. He acquiesced in the General Syrian Congress's decision to declare Syria independent that March and accepted the title of monarch of the new unified kingdom of Syria. Not only did Britain, France, and the United States refuse to recognize Syrian sovereignty, but the authorities in Beirut responded to the declaration by proclaiming Lebanese independence under the mandatory authority of the French. Syria then set up a ministry of war under the leadership of Yusuf al-Azma, and King Faisal delivered a series of strongly worded speeches reaffirming the country's independence. Meanwhile, French troops pulled out of Cilicia and took up positions along the Lebanon-Syria border.

On 9 July 1920, the French military command in Beirut issued an ultimatum to the Arab government in Damascus, demanding immediate acceptance of the mandate throughout central Syria. Publication of the ultimatum sparked rioting in Damascus and Aleppo, but the Syrian cabinet reluctantly agreed to its terms on 20 July and dispatched a telegram to inform the French of its decision. The next morning, the Third Division of the Armée du Levant, made up of Senegalese, Moroccan, and Algerian battalions, advanced from Shtura and Zahiya toward Damascus and on 23 July encamped outside Khan Maysalun. An Arab force of some six hundred regular troops and two thousand volunteers led by al-Azma attacked the encampment at dawn the following day and were routed before noon. The Third Division pursued the retreating Arabs and marched into Damascus unopposed on 25 July. Three days later, the French commander ordered Faisal to leave for British-controlled Palestine, and the mandate era began. Maysalun became a symbol of heroic Arab resistance, in the face of insurmountable odds, to European domination.

See also FAISAL I IBN HUSSEIN; SYKES–PICOT AGREEMENT (1916).

Bibliography

Al-Husri, Abu Khaldun Sati. *The Day of Maysalun: A Page from the Modern History of the Arabs,* translated by Sidney Glazer. Washington, DC: Middle East Institute, 1966.

FRED H. LAWSON

MAZAR-E SHARIF

Northern Afghan city.

Mazar-e Sharif is a city in northern Afghanistan and the provincial capital of Balkh Province. *Mazar-e Sharif* means "holy tomb"; locals believe that Caliph Ali (656–661) is buried there, although al-Najaf, Iraq, is generally accepted as Ali's actual burial place. Mazar-e Sharif is Afghanistan's largest northern city and a major marketing and trading center for the northern area. The official population taken in 1988 was about 150,000, but with an influx of internally displaced persons, the population in 2003 was thought to be over 600,000. The people in the area are largely Uzbek, but the city contains major Tajik, Turkoman, and Hazara populations as well. During the resistance war (1978–1992) the city was a major stronghold of the Marxist government because of its close proximity to the Soviet Union and its flat terrain, which made it easy to defend against guerrilla activities. After the Marxist government fell in 1992, the city saw fighting between the Tajiks led by Ahmad Shah Mas'ud and the Uzbeks under the command of General Abd al-Rashid Doestam.

Mazar-e Sharif became an important city in the resistance against the Taliban. The city changed hands several times between 1997 and 1998, resulting in the killing of several thousand civilians. After the ouster of the Taliban, the forces of General Doestam and General Ata Mohammad fought for control of Mazar-e Sharif.

Bibliography

Adamec, Ludwig. *Historical Dictionary of Afghanistan.* 2d edition. Lanham, MD: Scarecrow, 1997.

Rubin, Barnett. *The Fragmentation of Afghanistan.* New Haven, CT: Yale University Press, 2002.

GRANT FARR

MAZIQ, HUSAYN
[1916–?]

Libyan politician, prime minister.

With a limited formal education, Husayn Maziq acquired his political skills through extensive practical experience. Head of the Barassa tribe and a long-time Cyrenaican politician, he began his extensive government service in 1943 when the British administration named him secretary of the interior. He became *wali* (governor) of Cyrenaica in 1953 and also served as foreign minister under the premiership of Mahmud Bey Muntasir (1951–1954). Appointed prime minister in March 1965, his administration focused on maintaining order and stability in Libya. Maziq was forced to resign in 1967 when his government proved unable to cope with public disorder in the aftermath of the June 1967 Arab–Israel War. With the overthrow of the monarchy in September 1969, Maziq was eventually forced into exile by the Muammar al-Qaddafi regime, accused of participating in an abortive July 1970 coup attempt against the new government.

Bibliography

Khadduri, Majid. *Modern Libya: A Study in Political Development.* Baltimore, MD: Johns Hopkins Press, 1963.

St John, Ronald Bruce. *Historical Dictionary of Libya,* 3d edition. Lanham, MD: Scarecrow Press, 1998.

RONALD BRUCE ST JOHN

MAZZA

See FOOD: MAZZA

MCMAHON, HENRY
[1862–1949]

Britain's high commissioner in Egypt, 1914–1916.

During Sir Henry McMahon's tenure as high commissioner, he was responsible for mobilizing war matériel from Egypt for Britain's efforts in World War I. McMahon is best known for his role in the negotiations with Sharif Husayn of Mecca that led to the 1916 Arab Revolt against the Ottoman Empire. These negotiations are contained in the Husayn–McMahon correspondence. The extent of the territorial concessions that McMahon pledged for an independent Arab state continues to be a subject of debate.

See also HUSAYN–MCMAHON CORRESPONDENCE (1915–1916).

Bibliography

Wucher King, Joan. *Historical Dictionary of Egypt.* Metuchen, NJ: Scarecrow Press, 1984.

DAVID WALDNER

MEAH SHE'ARIM

A section of Jerusalem established in 1874 as an Orthodox quarter outside the Old City.

Inhabited almost exclusively by ultra-Orthodox Jews, Meah She'arim is one of the most densely populated neighborhoods in Jerusalem and is characterized by a very high birth rate. In 1995 its population numbered 29,214. It houses hundreds of yeshivas and synagogues, and is also the center of Orthodox anti-Zionist ideology and activity. The neighborhood is highly picturesque, and upon crossing into it, one senses having entered the domain of an almost autonomous ethnoreligious culture. Many of its inhabitants view the neighborhood as their own turf, and some view all strangers with suspicion. Its streets are closed to vehicular traffic on the Jewish Sabbath; breaches of that closure are occasionally met with violent reactions. Women are enjoined to dress modestly.

See also JERUSALEM.

Bibliography

Heilman, Samuel C. *Defenders of the Faith: Inside Ultra-Orthodox Jewry.* New York: Schocken, 1992.

CHAIM I. WAXMAN

MECCA

Islam's holiest city and the third largest city in Saudi Arabia.

Situated about 45 miles east of the Red Sea port of Jeddah in the rocky foothills of the Hijaz Mountains, Mecca has a hot, arid climate, and lack of water and other resources have kept its population and economic fortunes heavily dependent on outside factors. The estimated two million pilgrims who visit the city each year during the hajj season have a vital impact on the local economy. Many of Mecca's inhabitants work in the large service industry that caters to the hajjis, providing transport, security, food, lodging, medical care, and other services. Because many pilgrims from around the world have settled in the city, its population is the most ethnically varied in Saudi Arabia. According to a 2000 estimate there were 1.3 million inhabitants. Non-Muslims are not permitted to enter the city and its environs.

In the sixth century C.E. Mecca became an important market town and stopping point along the caravan routes connecting Yemen with Syria. A square stone structure called the Ka'ba, believed to have been built by Ibrahim (Abraham), also gave the city religious importance. The city is paramount in the history of Islam because it was the birthplace of the prophet Muhammad, the site of many of his revelations from God, the focal point of daily prayer and the main center of pilgrimage. The Ka'ba became the center of the Islamic pilgrimage ritual, and the Grand Mosque eventually was built up around it. The sacred precinct of Mecca extends as far as 14 miles outward from the Ka'ba in an irregular circle. Inside it, a number of prohibitions apply, including bans on fighting, cursing, hunting, and uprooting plants.

Despite its continuing religious significance, Mecca lost its political importance in the seventh century (the first century of Islam) when the capital of the caliphate moved first to Medina and later outside Arabia altogether. Thus Mecca became a provincial backwater ruled by governors appointed from afar. But as central authority weakened, local sharifs claiming descent from the prophet Muhammad were able to assert their control and remain substantially in power from about 965 to 1924, but never with full independence. From 1517, the sharifs fell under the suzerainty of the Ottoman Empire but remained effective local rulers, sharing power with the Turkish governors of Jidda. From 1916 to 1924, Mecca was part of the short-lived Kingdom of the Hijaz proclaimed by the last sharif, but then was conquered and incorporated into Saudi Arabia.

See also HIJAZ; ISLAM; KA'BA; MUHAMMAD; QUR'AN.

Bibliography

De Gaury, Gerald. *Rulers of Mecca.* London: Harrap, 1951.

Peters, F. E. *The Hajj: The Muslim Pilgrimage to Mecca and the Holy Places.* Princeton, NJ: Princeton University Press, 1994.

Peters, F. E. *Mecca: A Literary History of the Muslim Holy City.* Princeton, NJ: Princeton University Press, 1994.

Sabini, John. *Armies in the Sand: The Struggle for Mecca and Medina.* New York; London: Thames and Hudson, 1981.

Wolfe, Michael, ed. *One Thousand Roads to Mecca: Ten Centuries of Travelers Writing about the Muslim Pilgrimage.* New York: Grove Press, 1997.

KHALID Y. BLANKINSHIP
UPDATED BY ANTHONY B. TOTH

MEDDEB, ABDELWAHHAB
[1946–]

Tunisian novelist and poet.

Abdelwahhab Meddeb was born in Tunis and studied literature, art history, and archaeology in Tunisia and Paris. He subsequently taught history of architecture at the École des Beaux Arts in Paris. Although he writes in French, his books are rich with references to Arabic texts and contain many quotations in Arabic, revealing not only his knowledge of the language but also his familiarity with Arabic literature and civilization. Meddeb's first novel, *Talismano* (1979), shows his constant concern with the past and his reaction to his Arab-Islamic culture.

The interest of Meddeb's writings lies, to a large extent, in his original handling of language and his experimentation with words. His point of departure is the bilingual situation in the Maghrib, which gives the writer access to two cultures and languages and an opportunity to juggle them and, possibly, combine them. The starting point in his novel *Phantasia* (1989; Fantasia) is the human body. Meddeb conceives of writing as an act of perpetual creation, the result of an inner inspiration. The book revolves around the Muslim mystic Ibn al-Arabi, about whom Meddeb later wrote a collection of poems, *Tombeau d'ibn Arabi* (1988; The tomb of Ibn Arabi). The classical Arabic religious and cultural heritage inspired Meddeb's latest book, *Suhrawardi, Chihab al-Din Yahya: Récits de l'exil occidental* (1993; Suhrawardi Shihab al-Din Yahya: narratives of western exile).

See also LITERATURE: ARABIC, NORTH AFRICAN.

Bibliography

Mortimer, Mildred, ed. *Maghrebian Mosaic.* Boulder, CO, and London: Lynne Rienner, 2001.

AIDA A. BAMIA

MEDIA

See NEWSPAPERS AND PRINT MEDIA

MEDICINE AND PUBLIC HEALTH

An improving field based on a combination of traditional and modern practices.

The largest populations, comprising 52 percent of the Middle East, are in Egypt, Turkey, and Iran. About half of the Middle East population is urban. Because of public health advances, a Middle Eastern child born in 1990 can expect to live for seventy years, thirteen years longer than his or her parents. Death rates have fallen faster than birthrates, and at the current pace the population will double in twenty-nine years. Cultural traditions, including Islam, shape some curative options, but socioeconomic factors prevail. Local beliefs in breast feeding and birth spacing enhance maternal and child health. Access to health services, quality of environment, and labor opportunities remain uneven. Israel's comprehensive, Western-style healthcare system and developed economy exclude it from many generalizations here.

Typhoid fever, cholera (on the decrease because of better sanitation and improved water sources), typhus, leishmaniasis, trachoma, and gastroenteritis are characteristic of the area. Increased irrigation has raised the incidence of malaria and schistosomiasis. Smallpox was eliminated by the 1970s through systematic vaccination, but measles remains a problem in some countries. Tuberculosis, which replaced smallpox as the illness of crowded cities, decreased after a 1950s World Health Organization (WHO) and UNICEF immunization program but could resurge if AIDS expands. Ministries of health have combated AIDS, which is seen as the scourge of Western decadence, with frank public health campaigns.

Curative Options: Humoral, Prophetic, Local, and Cosmopolitan

Health care resonates with curative resources and one's life situation. Most people self-prescribe for mild symptoms, whether by taking vitamin C or consulting the local herbalist. Middle Easterners pick eclectically from a repertoire that includes humoral, prophetic, local-practice, and cosmopolitan (modern or Western) cures. Western medicine was introduced in the nineteenth century in medical schools in Cairo, Tunis, and Istanbul, and by the 1920s most governments required practitioners to be licensed.

Humoral medicine, predicated on the balance of the four humors, as in the allopathic, Galenic tradition, is important for herbal pharmacists (*attarin*) who provide such household remedies as ginger for sore throats.

Prophetic medicine (*al-tibb al-nabawi*) is based on sayings of the Prophet Muhammad, such as the *Sahih* by al-Bukhari (d. 870). The *Sahih* contains eighty paragraphs (2.3% of the entire collection) concerned with medical issues, including the ever-popular "God did not send down an illness without also sending down a cure."

In the twentieth century, prophetic medicine has assumed two forms: popular literature, which intermingles standard collections of prophetic sayings with local wisdom, including humoral principles of balanced, normal bodily functions; and formal medical practice, or Islamic medicine, advocated by such groups as the Islamic Medical Organization (IMO). Founded in Kuwait in the 1970s, the IMO administers a hospital that treats patients by the tenets of Islamic medicine and tests Prophetic cures under controlled, laboratory conditions. The experiments concentrate on symptoms ambiguous in etiology and cure, such as renal failure and eczema. The IMO ethical code critiques Western medicine's origin in a "spiritualess" civilization and adjures the Islamic physician to include the patient's therapy managers in the treatment. Other Middle Eastern physicians who consider themselves Islamic practice cosmopolitan medicine but within an Islamic-medicine moral context, such as Islamic benevolent association clinics.

Local and Cosmopolitan medicine frequently overlap. Local practitioners, a trusted first recourse, cooperate with cosmopolitan practitioners. For instance, the traditional birth attendant may encourage the mother through delivery but call the licensed midwife to cut the umbilical cord and provide postnatal care. Training by the ministries of health targets socially accepted but technically inadequate midwives, herbalists, and self-made nurses.

Such local practices as amulets against the evil eye or shrine visitation to enhance fertility, which is forbidden by official Islam, are part of a complex

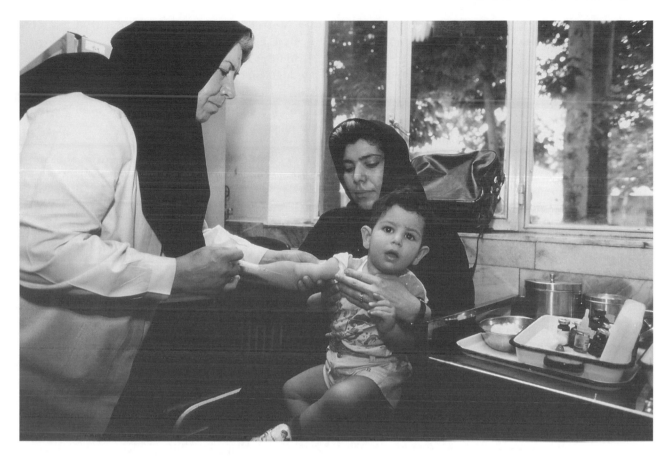

A child receives immunization shots, Tehran, Iran, 1995. Led by organizations such as WHO and UNICEF, massive immunization campaigns have helped protect thousands of children throughout the world from contracting easily preventable diseases such as polio and measles. © SHEPARD SHERBELL/CORBIS SABA. REPRODUCED BY PERMISSION.

curative strategy. Caretakers calibrate symptom severity: They make a vow for a sickly child but rush a fevered child to the hospital. Western, cosmopolitan medicine may be construed in local terms. Traditional Egyptian physiology speaks of circulation of microbes that bombard a patient, much as black magic does, and are neutralized by the injection of a powerful agent, or exorciser. Western medicine may be well understood but not used. For instance, agriculturalists will return to snail-infested irrigation canals to cultivate, though they know doing so means reinfection with schistosomiasis.

Public Health: Child Survival and Maternal Health

Major public health problems among infants and children are dehydration from diarrhea; malaria and immunizable diseases; acute respiratory infections; and injuries from war. Among women, ma-

ternal mortality and morbidity from inadequate prenatal, delivery, and postpartum care are often problems. Infant mortality rates (deaths per one thousand live births) dropped in the period 1960–1995 from 214 to 109 in Yemen, 139 to 62 in Iraq, and 89 to 12 in Kuwait.

With oral rehydration solution widely available to parents, mortality from dehydration is no longer a major threat to infants. Nevertheless, early childhood acute diarrhea—exacerbated by nonpotable water, poor sanitation, and malnutrition—may cause more than fifty deaths per one thousand per year in pre-school children. Public health programs consider local perceptions of diarrhea and dehydration and teach mothers the warning signs of dehydration and home recipes for oral rehydration solutions in case mothers cannot obtain commercial packets. Given the synergy between malnutrition and diarrhea, these programs have promoted supplements based on such local dietary practices as Egypt's seven grains, which has been marketed as Supramin.

The percentage of children who are fully vaccinated ranges from 88 percent in Jordan and 85 percent in Morocco, to 45 percent in Yemen. Full-immunization rates have fallen in recent years, most notably in Iraq, after a decline in support from UN agencies previously leading this worldwide effort. While tuberculosis has subsided, acute respiratory infection remains a significant problem, in part because there is no vaccine to prevent it. In most Middle Eastern countries, it has replaced acute diarrhea as the number-one cause of infant mortality.

War exerts a heavy price on women and children, including death from military operations; starvation; orphaning; disruption of services that protect health, such as water, sewer, irrigation works, and health services; rape and sodomy; and separation of children from their families. For political reasons, there are no accurate data on children killed or maimed in Middle Eastern wars. Estimates are as high as two million killed and five million disabled.

The long conflict in Lebanon severely damaged the quantity and quality of drinking water. One 1990 study found that 66 percent of urban Lebanese water sources were contaminated and that one-third of urban communities were using cesspools for sewage disposal. It is more difficult to assess war's psychic trauma for children than its physical wounds. Civil strife in the Levant, West Bank, Gaza, and Israel has created a generation of children with dead parents and siblings, lost limbs, and nightmares of bombs and mines. Women and children pay much of the human price after several years of sanctions against Iraq. The food-rationing system provides less than 60 percent of the required daily calorie intake, and the water and sanitation systems are in a state of collapse. During the Gulf War, Iraq laid multitudes of mines; the allies also laid some one million land mines along the Iraq–Kuwait border. These pose serious threats to life and limb.

Countries are just beginning to recognize at the policy level the importance of maternal health to the health of a nation. Very few have as yet provided adequate resources. Reproductive morbidity—illness related to the reproductive process—remains rela-

tively unstudied but critical. Over half of a sample of rural Egyptian women had such gynecological morbidities as reproductive-tract infections and anemia. Maternal mortality—fewer than 30 per 100,000 births in developed countries—remains high. Morocco averaged 332 in the late 1980s; an Egyptian province, 126 in the 1990s.

Poor maternal health and nutrition, too-short birth intervals, prematurity, and low birth weight underlie 40 to 60 percent of all infant and child deaths. In 1992, Egypt reported 26 percent of children from zero to thirty-five months with stunted growth, while Jordan and Tunisia reported 18 percent.

Public Health: The Politics of Population, Body, and Food

Women have always sought to control their fertility, first with folk remedies, such as aspirin vaginal suppositories, and now with largely safer, modern technology. Women obtain abortions in private clinics and also try such folk remedies as drinking boiled onion leaves. While birth-control pills, and more recently implants, have been widely used, IUDs (intrauterine device) have been popular in places such as Syria, Egypt, and Jordan. In 1994, 63 percent of Turkish, 47 percent of Egyptian, and 50 percent of Tunisian married women used contraceptives. Side effects or a pregnancy history with at least one infant death often prompt a woman to abandon the birth-control pill.

With population (as with all public health), local custom and socioeconomic context play a more critical role than what Islamic culture allows. For example, fertility rates have dropped in poor Islamic countries, such as Tunisia and Morocco, and remained higher in oil-rich Islamic countries where governments have until recently subsidized child rearing and de-emphasized female education, which is often associated with smaller families.

The Egyptian shaykh al-Azhar has in the past given *fatwas* (religious pronouncements) in support of family planning. The Qur'an is silent on birth control, but jurisprudence texts record the use of *azl* (coitus interruptus). Muslim promotion of population control waxes and wanes for political and economic, more than religious, reasons. In Pahlavi

Iran, the regime legalized abortion, but the Islamic revolution promptly condemned family planning as a Western imperialist plot. Population skyrocketed and threatened economic growth. In the mid-1980s, Friday sermons in Iran took a 180-degree turn and began to advocate family planning.

Child-survival and maternal-health programs are an integral part of family planning. While the population of the Middle East is growing at 2.7 per cent a year, the labor force is growing at 3.3 percent. Jobs for forty-seven million new entrants to the labor force must be found by 2011. The Cairo conference on population in 1994 and the Beijing women's conference in 1995 hotly debated such issues as gender equity, employment and economic development, and a woman's right to control her body. Some Muslim *ulama* (theologians) united with Roman Catholics to oppose a platform seen as threatening family values.

Female excision—a non-Islamic custom practiced locally in Egypt, Sudan, and parts of Africa—is vehemently critiqued by Western feminists. In the Middle East, folk beliefs link excision and fertility; in traditional areas of Egypt, a recently excised girl who crosses before another woman is believed able to strike that woman with infertility. While Egypt outlawed female excision in the mid-1950s, the practice, referred to in the Western press as "female genital mutilation," continues in traditional areas. Middle Easterners criticize Western feminists for seeking to impose their standards cross-culturally.

The politics of medicine includes not only issues of population and cross-cultural judgments, but also such issues as access to food and health facilities. The Sudanese famine of the late 1980s was not a problem of food, because the harvests had been ample; rather, it was an issue of the logistics of food placement during civil strive. Finally a quick review of public health cannot cover specialized treatment and scientific advances in Middle Eastern hospitals and research centers in such fields as oncology and cardiology.

Bibliography

Burgel, J. Christoph. "Secular and Religious Features of Medieval Arabic Medicine." In *Asian Medical Systems: A Comparative Study*, edited by Charles Leslie. Berkeley: University of California Press, 1977.

Early, Evelyn A. "The Baladi Curative System of Cairo, Egypt." *Culture, Medicine, and Psychiatry* 12, no. 1 (1988): 65–85.

Kuhnke, Laverne. "Disease Ecologies of the Middle East and North Africa." In *The Cambridge World History of Human Disease,* edited by Kenneth F. Kiple. Cambridge, U.K., and New York: Cambridge University Press, 1993.

The State of the World's Children. UNICEF, 1996.

Claiming the Future: Choosing Prosperity in the Middle East and North Africa. World Bank, 1995.

EVELYN A. EARLY

MEDINA

City in Saudi Arabia, second to Mecca as a holy site to Muslims.

Located in Hijaz, about 100 miles from the Red Sea and 215 miles north of Mecca, Medina is revered by Muslims as the prophet Muhammad's destination after his emigration (*hijra* in Arabic) from Mecca in 622 C.E., and as the site of his tomb. Although it is not mandatory, many pilgrims to Mecca also visit Medina. The city became the southern terminus of the Ottomans' Hijaz Railway upon its completion in 1908. The site of a major Ottoman garrison during World War I, Medina and the rest of Hijaz came under Hashimite rule after the empire's defeat. The city's high walls were the last refuge of the Hashimites, and Medina was the last city in Hijaz to fall to the attacking forces of Abd al-Aziz ibn Abd al-Rahman Al Sa'ud in 1926, after which many of the city's historical monuments and tombs were destroyed because the conservative religious allies of Abd al-Aziz found them offensive.

Relatively abundant water has enabled Medina to have an important agricultural hinterland, with dates the main crop. However, the growth of the city during the oil era and diversion of water to other uses has caused agriculture to suffer. The annual pilgrimage provides an important source of income, as do trade and the provision of services. Long a center of Islamic learning, the city now hosts the Islamic University of Medina. A 2000 estimate put the city's population at 891,000.

See also ISLAM; MECCA; MUHAMMAD.

Bibliography

Makki, Mohamed S. *Medina, Saudi Arabia: A Geographic Analysis of the City and the Region.* New York: Prometheus Books, 1984; Aversham, U.K.: Avebury, 1982.

Watt, W. M., and Winder, R. B. "Al-Madina." In *Encyclopedia of Islam, New Edition,* vol. 5, edited by C. E. Bosworth, E. van Donzel, B. Lewis, and C. Pellat. Leiden, Neth.: Brill, 1986.

ANTHONY B. TOTH

MEDITERRANEAN SEA

Sea between Europe, Africa, and Asia.

The Mediterranean Sea is about 2,400 miles long, covers an area of about 965,000 square miles, and is ringed by a winding coastline of peninsulas and mountains. The sea opens to the Atlantic Ocean through the Strait of Gibraltar, to the Black Sea through the Dardanelles, and to the Red Sea through the Suez Canal.

Since antiquity, the Mediterranean has been an important waterway for trade and has fostered great civilizations on its shores. The sea's strategic significance declined after the sixteenth century as trade routes shifted to the Atlantic but increased again with the 1869 opening of the Suez Canal and its subsequent use for oil shipping. The 1995 Declaration of Barcelona marked the beginning of political and economic collaboration between the European Union and countries on all shores of the Mediterranean.

The pollution of the sea remains a cause of concern for governments in the region, as reflected in the signing of two protocols for the protection of the Mediterranean Sea against pollution in 1980 and 1982. Land-based sources of pollution account for 80 percent of the total pollution. Participant countries in the convention for the protection of the Mediterranean Sea have made periodic commitments to reducing pollution, with mixed results.

Bibliography

Braudel, Fernand. *The Mediterranean and the Mediterranean World in the Age of Philip II,* translated by Siân Reynolds. New York: Harper and Row, 1972.

Cerutti, Furio, and Ragionieri, Rodolfo, eds. *Identities and Conflicts: The Mediterranean.* New York: Palgrave, 2001.

McNeill, J. R. *The Mountains of the Mediterranean World: An Environmental History.* New York and Cambridge, U.K.: Cambridge University Press, 1992.

ELIZABETH THOMPSON
UPDATED BY VANESA CASANOVA-FERNANDEZ

MEGED, AHARON
[1920–]

Israeli writer and dramatist.

Born in Włocławek (Poland), Meged emigrated to Palestine in 1926. A member of kibbutz Sedot Yom from 1938, Meged left in 1950 for Tel Aviv. He was an editor of the journal *ba-Sha'ar,* founded the literary biweekly *Massa,* and was literary editor of the *Lamerhav* newspaper before becoming a columnist for *Davar* in 1971. From 1960 to 1971, he was Israel's cultural attaché to London.

Because his writing spans such a long period, it is difficult to class him simply—as he often is classed—as a writer of the "1948 generation." Over the years, his works have been increasingly critical of patriotic exuberance while at the same time firmly focused on a faithful expression of the highest Zionist ideals. Meged's prize-winning works often have autobiographical content, and the anti-hero, as an outsider, is prominent in his writings. In his most notable opus, *ha-Hai Al ha-Met* (1965, translated as *The Living on the Dead,* 1970), he criticizes Israeli society for abandoning the Zionist ideals of the early *halutzim* (pioneers). Among his plays are *Hannah Szenes, Genesis,* and *I Like Mike,* a comedy. Meged's works have been translated into several languages, including English.

A former member of the Peace Now movement, Meged took issue with what he saw as the movement's focus on criticizing Israeli governments, rather than reaching out to Arabs. By 2000, Meged was a leading figure in the left-wing reaction against post-Zionist or revisionist intellectuals, contending that they mounted a fundamental attack on Judaism and Israeli morality and identity, and that their work was based on a fundamental misreading of the readiness of Israel's Arab neighbors for peace.

Bibliography

Giniewski, Paul. "Arabs and Other Problems: A Conversation with Aharon Mehgged." *Midstream* 45, no. 3 (1 April 1999): 29.

Nash, Stanley. "Patterns of Failed Return in Aharon Megged's Work: Revisiting the Jewish-Christian Nexus." *Modern Judaism* 19, no. 3 (1999): 277–292.

Ramras-Rauch, Gila. *The Arab in Israeli Literature.* Bloomington: Indiana University Press, 1989.

ANN KAHN
UPDATED BY GEORGE R. WILKES

MEHMET RAUF

[1874–1932]

Ottoman Turkish writer.

Mehmet Rauf was born and died in Constantinople (now Istanbul). He graduated from the Naval Academy and became an officer. In the 1890s, he was a member of the group that published *Servet-i Fünün*. In 1901, he published his most famous novel, *Eylul* (September), which is considered the first Turkish example of the psychological novel. Among the ten novels Mehmet Rauf wrote are *Genç Kiz Kalbi* (1914; A young girl's heart), *Karanfil ve Yasemen* (1924), *Son Yildiz* (1927; The last star), and *Halas* (1929). In addition to his novels, he wrote poetry, some of which was collected in a volume entitled *Siyah Inciler* (1900; Black pearls); plays, including *Cidal* (1922), *Sansar* (1920), and *Ceriha* (1923); and dozens of short stories. Mehmet Rauf also published two women's magazines, *Mehasin* (1909) and *Süs* (1923).

DAVID WALDNER

MEHMET V REŞAT

[1844–1918]

Ottoman sultan, 1909–1918.

A brother of Sultan Abdülhamit II, Mehmet V was sixty-five years old in April 1909 when he was chosen by the Young Turks to succeed his deposed sibling as sultan of the Ottoman Empire. Mehmet V is usually seen as a weak ruler who functioned mostly as a figurehead for the Young Turks and the Committee for Union and Progress (CUP). His powers were severely circumscribed by the constitution, which had been restored in 1908. He could not nominate his own ministers without the approval of parliament and the CUP. He remained sultan during World War I, but his influence on policy was negligible, as the war was conducted by the Young Turk triumvirate headed by Enver Paşa. Mehmet V did not command an independent base of support.

He died of natural causes on 28 June 1918, before Istanbul was occupied by the Allies, and was succeeded by his younger brother Mehmet VI Vahidettin.

See also ABDÜLHAMIT II; COMMITTEE FOR UNION AND PROGRESS; ENVER PAŞA; YOUNG TURKS.

Bibliography

Shaw, Stanford J., and Shaw, Ezel Kural. *History of the Ottoman Empire and Modern Turkey*, Vol. 2: *Reform, Revolution, and Republic: The Rise of Modern Turkey, 1808–1975.* Cambridge, U.K., and New York: Cambridge University Press, 1977.

ZACHARY KARABELL
UPDATED BY ERIC HOOGLUND

MEIR, GOLDA

[1898–1978]

Labor-Zionist politician; fourth prime minister of Israel, 1969–1974.

Golda Meir, née Goldie Mabovitch, was born in Kiev, Russia. Her family moved in 1906 to Milwaukee, Wisconsin, where she spent her early years and became active in the Milwaukee Labor Zionist Party, later serving as its leader. In 1921 she and her husband, Morris Myerson, emigrated to Palestine and joined Kibbutz Merhavia. Goldie Myerson represented the kibbutz movement in the Histadrut (Labor Federation) and served as secretary of Histadrut's Women's Labor Council (1928–1932). In 1934 she was elected to the Histadrut's Executive Committee. In the years prior to Israel's independence, Myerson was the acting director of the Jewish Agency's Political Department under Moshe Sharett. In this capacity she took an active part in the negotiations with King Abdullah that resulted in long-term, strategic understandings between Israel and Jordan.

When the State of Israel was declared on 14 May 1948, Myerson was one of the signatories to the Declaration of Independence, and she subsequently became Israel's first ambassador to the Soviet Union. Elected to the first Knesset in 1949, Myerson remained a Knesset member until her resignation from the office of prime minister in 1974. As minister of labor (1949–1956) she was credited with initiating major housing and road programs. During

Once described by former Israeli prime minister David Ben-Gurion as "the only man in the cabinet," the tenacious Golda Meir served as foreign minister of the country from 1956 to 1965 on Ben-Gurion's appointment, and herself held the prime ministry from 1969 to 1974. © AP/WIDE WORLD PHOTOS. REPRODUCED BY PERMISSION.

the crisis that led to the Sinai–Suez war of 1956, Myerson, a Ben-Gurion loyalist, replaced Sharett as foreign minister and Hebraicized her name to Meir. In the aftermath of the war, Meir played a major role in formulating the framework of relations between Israel, Egypt, the United States, and the United Nations. This framework called for Israel's withdrawal from Sinai and Gaza under U.S. and UN pressure; the stationing of a United Nations Emergency Force (UNEF) in Sinai; and negotiating U.S. assurances of Israel's right of free passage through the Strait of Tiran.

During the early 1960s Meir's main focus as foreign minister was the building of close ties be-

tween Israel and newly independent African states. At the same time, Meir energetically consolidated her political power base. Together with other leaders in MAPAI (Labor Party), she led an opposition front against several of Prime Minister David Ben-Gurion's policies, especially Israel's relations with Germany. Ben-Gurion gradually found himself in political isolation within his party and consequently was forced to resign from office in June 1963. Under Levi Eshkol's premiership, Meir strengthened her political position. During Eshkol's tenure, she served as foreign minister, and from 1966 to 1968 as MAPAI's secretary-general. In this role she strove to unite Israel's socialist parties and establish the Israel Labor Party. Prior to the 1967 war, Meir strongly opposed the popular demand for a national unity government that would include the right-wing party and Ben-Gurion's faction. In particular, she rejected the call to appoint Moshe Dayan defense minister in place of Levi Eshkol. Eventually, she was compelled to yield on both counts.

Following Eshkol's death in February 1969, Meir became prime minister. During her tenure she had to deal with growing military tension in the region, especially the war of attrition being fought along the Suez Canal. Increasingly faced with severe internal and external criticism for her "uncompromising positions," Meir refused to accept the authenticity of any specifically Palestinian national attachment to the land that became Israel. Furthermore, her government turned down some offers for partial settlements with Egypt that might have prevented the outbreak of the Yom Kippur War. Her policy as prime minister was based on the following principles: Israel's goal was to conclude formal peace treaties with the Arab states; Israel would make territorial concessions only within the framework of comprehensive peace treaties; and as long as no peace treaties existed, Israel was fully justified in building and fortifying Jewish settlements in the occupied territories.

The Arab–Israel War that erupted on 6 October 1973 caught Israel in a strategic surprise that resulted in heavy losses and forced Israel to ask the United States for emergency military equipment and financial aid. Though broadly admired for her self-restraint during the fighting, Meir could not withstand the accusations that she bore the overall responsibility for the war and its consequences.

Thus, she was obliged to resign from office, though not before laying the foundations for interim agreements between Israel and Egypt, which eventually led to the formal peace treaty between the two countries. Golda Meir died in Jerusalem on 8 December 1978.

See also BEN-GURION, DAVID; ESHKOL, LEVI; ISRAEL: POLITICAL PARTIES IN.

Bibliography

Mann, Peggy. *Golda: The Life of Israel's Prime Minister.* New York: Coward, McCann, and Geoghegan, 1971.

Meir, Golda. *My Life.* New York: Dell, 1975.

Perla, Shoshana. *Golda Meir: Prime Minister of Israel.* New York: 1972.

Sachar, Howard M. *A History of Israel: From the Rise of Zionism to Our Time,* 2d edition, revised and updated. New York: Knopf, 1996.

Shlaim, Avi. *The Iron Wall: Israel and the Arab World.* New York: Penguin, 2000.

Syrkin, Marie. *Golda Meir: Israel's Leader.* New York: G. P. Putnam's Sons, 1969.

GREGORY S. MAHLER
UPDATED BY ZAKI SHALOM

MEKNES

A city of northern Morocco.

Meknes is situated 40 miles (60 km) west of Fez and 90 miles (140 km) east of Rabat and is surrounded by Arab and Berber tribes. Its population was estimated in 1994 as 460,000 inhabitants. Close to the fertile plain of Sais, Meknes benefits from its rich agriculture.

Meknes (or Miknas al-Zaytun) is one of the oldest Moroccan cities. The gathering of one faction of the Miknasa tribes (tenth century) seems to be the beginning of the founding of the city, which flourished later under different dynasties that ruled the Maghrib. Meknes gained prestige in the seventeenth, eighteenth, and nineteenth centuries when it became a *makhzaniya* city. Sultan Mulay Isma'il built palaces and made this city the capital of his kingdom.

Numerous religious groups—such as the Hamadish Brotherhood and the Isawiyya Brotherhood—consider Meknes to be sacred and hold celebrations there. The most important occurs in the month of Mulud and honors Shaykh al-Kamil.

RAHMA BOURQIA

MEKNES, TREATY OF (1836)

The second treaty between Morocco and the United States, signed at Meknes on 16 September 1836.

With two exceptions (a final clause continuing the treaty beyond its fifty years validity until it was actually cancelled by one of the parties and an addendum concerning protection of U.S. ships in Moroccan ports against third-party enemies), the Meknes treaty precisely mirrored the first U.S.-Moroccan treaty, signed in Marrakech on 28 June 1786. Both treaties focused on two concerns: the protection of U.S. shipping against pirate attacks by Moroccan ships and the enhancement of commercial relations. The question of pirates, or corsairs, was indeed an important issue in 1786, but by 1836 it was no longer relevant: the Moroccan corsairing fleet existed only on paper. Moreover, U.S. commerce with Morocco was insubstantial, and U.S. interest in the country minimal. The consul who signed the treaty, James Leib, left the conduct of negotiations to the vice consul and his interpreter.

The importance of the treaty lay in its symbolic value: it deeply worried the British consul general, E. W. A. Drummond-Hay, and the authorities in London. They believed, quite unjustifiably, that it marked the beginnings of an attempt by the United States to occupy physically a position on the Mediterranean coast of Morocco that would be used to expand U.S. influence. At this time Britain was easily Morocco's largest trading partner, particularly through the garrison colony of Gibraltar, and dominated Morocco's foreign relations. Drummond-Hay tried to steer a path that would open Morocco to foreign—especially British—commerce, while ensuring that other powers—especially France—would not extend their influence too much. The supposed agreement about a U.S. base on the coast would undercut British predominance. In fact nothing of the sort happened; British predominance was sealed by the Moroccan-British treaty of 1856, which paved the way for the real opening of Morocco to international commerce.

See also CORSAIRS.

Bibliography

Hall, Luella J. *The United States and Morocco, 1776–1956.* Metuchen, NJ: Scarecrow Press, 1971.

Parry, Clive, ed. *The Consolidated Treaty Series.* Vols. 50 (1786 treaty) and 86 (1836 treaty). Dobbs Ferry, NY: Oceana Publications, 1969–1981.

C. R. PENNELL

MELILLA

Spanish enclave on Morocco's northeast coast.

One of Spain's two remaining footholds on the African continent, the enclave of Mellila occupies approximately 7 square miles on the Guelaia Peninsula, near the city of Nador on Morocco's northeast Mediterranean coast. In addition to the town, there are also two groups of adjacent islands. A majority of the population of 69,000 are ethnically Spanish and Catholic; a substantial minority—about 40 percent—are Berber Muslims, most of whom have Spanish citizenship. In recent years, Melilla, like its companion Spanish enclave Ceuta, has attracted both Moroccans and black Africans seeking to immigrate illegally into Europe.

Founded by the Phoenecians in the third century B.C.E., Melilla was occupied by Spain in 1497, one of several presidios established to protect the Spanish mainland. More territory was added to it after the 1860 war, and in 1861 it was made a free port. Morocco has never ceased to insist on the return of Melilla and Ceuta, but the two countries agreed in 1976 to shelve the dispute as part of their agreement on Western Sahara. In the mid-1990s, as Moroccan political life slowly revived, the status of Mellila and Ceuta became a prime national issue for the country's political parties. The Spanish parliament's approval of statutes of autonomy for the two enclaves in 1995 irked the Moroccans considerably.

The five hundredth anniversary of Spain's control of Melilla was marked in September 1997 in a low-key manner, as Muslim residents complained of socioeconomic difficulties and discrimination. One outcome of the difficulties was the election of a Muslim mayor in 1999. While Morocco's prime minister Abderrahmane Youssoufi suggested in 1999 that Macao and Hong Kong could serve as possible models for a resolution of the dispute, Spain reiterated that no foreign sovereignty claims would be considered, and Spanish prime minister Jose Maria Aznar visited Melilla and Ceuta in January 2000, stressing the "Spanishness" of the two cities. By the end of the century, both cities had become jumping-off points for illegal immigration into Europe and for smugglers of European goods, with potential immigrants from all over the African continent seeking entry. Morocco's assertion of authority over an unoccupied rock outcropping off the Moroccan coast in the summer of 2002 nearly boiled over into an international crisis, as Spain treated it as a Moroccan test of its intentions. Spanish troops evicted the small Moroccan contingent, the status quo was restored, and Spain reinforced its presence in both Melilla and Ceuta and tightened its borders. Moroccans from the neighboring areas are allowed into the towns for work.

See also CEUTA; MOROCCO; SPAIN AND THE MIDDLE EAST; SPANISH MOROCCO.

Bibliography

Gold, Peter. *Europe or Africa? A Contemporary Study of the Spanish North African Enclaves of Ceuta and Melilla.* Liverpool, U.K.: Liverpool University Press, 2000.

BRUCE MADDY-WEITZMAN

MELLAH

See GLOSSARY

MEMMI, ALBERT
[1920–]

Tunisian Jew; émigré; French novelist and sociologist.

Albert Memmi was raised in a poor Jewish quarter in Tunis; however, his evident abilities enabled him to be educated at an elite French colonial secondary school. After university studies in Algiers and Paris, he returned to Tunis, where he taught philosophy at a lycée. Following Tunisia's independence in 1956, he emigrated to France, where he became a professor of sociology at the University of Paris in 1970. The alienation he felt growing up—belonging to neither the Muslim nor European cultures and removed from his traditional Jewish background through French education, yet snubbed by his wealthier European classmates—was a powerful influence on the themes of his work. Memmi is best known for two types of works: his largely autobiographical novels of alienation and his essays exploring the social psychology of colonization and Jewish identity. These works include his first novel, *La statue de sel* (1953; published as *Pillar of Salt* in 1955), and the influential essay "Portrait du colonisé;" (1957; published as the "Colonizer and the Colonized" in 1965). Racism and the various forms of dependency are significant themes in his later works. Memmi has also edited anthologies of North African francophone literature and in 1990 he published a poetry collection, *Le mirliton du ciel.*

Bibliography

Wakeman, John, ed. *World Authors, 1950–1970: A Companion Volume to Twentieth-Century Authors.* New York: Wilson, 1975.

WILL D. SWEARINGEN
UPDATED BY STEFANIE K. WICHHART

MENDERES, ADNAN
[1899–1961]

Turkish politician.

Adnan Menderes was born in İzmir and educated at the American College in İzmir and the Law Faculty of Ankara University. He was elected to the Turkish Grand National Assembly in 1930 as a member of the Republican People's Party (RPP), which had been founded by Mustafa Kemal Atatürk. In 1945, he was one of the deputies who introduced a bill calling for the introduction of multiparty politics and other political rights specified in the United Nations Charter. In 1946 he resigned from the RPP and with Celal Bayar cofounded the Democrat Party, which subsequently challenged RPP policies. In 1950, after the Democrat Party won a majority of seats in the assembly, Menderes became prime minister, a position he held for ten years. His policies aroused considerable opposition on the part of the RPP, and in May 1960 Menderes was ousted by a military coup d'état, charged with corruption and abuse of power, and, along with 600 other former government officials, tried on the island of Yassiada. Menderes and fourteen colleagues were convicted and sentenced to death; he was executed by hanging in 1961.

See also ATATÜRK, MUSTAFA KEMAL; BAYAR, CELAL; DEMOCRAT PARTY.

Bibliography

Weiker, Walter F. *The Turkish Revolution 1960–1961: Aspects of Military Politics.* Washington, DC: Brookings Institution, 1963. Reprint, Westport, CT: Greenwood Press, 1980.

WALTER F. WEIKER
UPDATED BY ERIC HOOGLUND

MENOU, JACQUES FRANÇOIS
[1750–1810]

French military officer; governor of Egypt, 1800–1801.

The last leader of the French forces that occupied Egypt from 1798 to 1801, Jacques François Menou succeeded General Kléber as Napoléon Bonaparte's governor of Egypt in July of 1800. He converted to Islam in order to marry an Egyptian and changed his name to Abdullah. Believing that French occupation of Egypt would continue for a long time, Menou drafted proposals to encourage Egyptian agriculture, commerce, and industry. When Menou began to survey land-holdings in preparation for the assessment of new land taxes to pay for these reforms, Egyptians of all social classes, already alienated by Menou's declaration of Egypt as a colony of France, opposed him.

In March of 1801, a joint Anglo-Ottoman force occupied the Nile river delta. Leaving the defense of Cairo, the capital, to General Belliard, Menou led his troops to Alexandria. When Belliard surrendered, Menou, isolated in Alexandria, was forced to surrender. French forces left Egypt in October of 1801.

Bibliography

Goldschmidt, Arthur, Jr. *Modern Egypt: The Formation of a Nation-State.* Boulder, CO: Westview Press, 1988.

Wucher King, Joan. *Historical Dictionary of Egypt.* Metuchen, NJ: Scarecrow Press, 1984.

DAVID WALDNER

MENZIES MISSION
See SUEZ CRISIS (1956–1957)

MERETZ

See ISRAEL: POLITICAL PARTIES IN

MERNISSI, FATEMA
[1940–]

Moroccan sociologist, author, and feminist Qur'anic scholar.

Born in Fez, Morocco, Fatema Mernissi studied at Muhammad V University in Rabat, where she received a degree in political science. She continued her studies at the Sorbonne in Paris, where she earned a degree in sociology. Her doctorate in sociology is from Brandeis University (1973). She is currently professor of sociology with a research appointment at the Institut Universitaire de Recherche Scientifique, Muhammad V University in Rabat.

Working at the intersection of gender, religion, and sociopolitical organization, Mernissi has taken on some of the most contentious issues of her time, such as pointing out the inconsistencies inherent in basing Morocco's *moudawana* (code of personal status) on religious law while the constitution and penal code are based on civil law, or claiming to establish a democratic polity while denying Moroccan women full and equal political rights. Mernissi has entered difficult religious debates, attributing the betrayal of women's political agency, for example, to misogynistic, patriarchal interpretations of the *hadith*. Mernissi envisions a pluralist, Islamic civil society in which women and the poor would exercise their full rights as citizens.

Widely translated, her work has moved from the study of sexual dynamics in Muslim society in *The Veil and the Male Elite* (1975), to examinations of sexual inequality as experienced by marginalized and silenced women in *Doing Daily Battle* (1983), to the recovery of women's Islamic history in *Forgotten Queens of Islam* (1990). Mernissi next turned her attention to contemporary Islam, looking at the question of fundamentalism in *Islam and Democracy* (1992), at the role of the state and Islamic thought in setting the parameters of women's position in *Women's Rebellion and Islamic Memory* (1993), and at her own memories of growing up Muslim, Moroccan, and female in *Dreams of Trespass* (1994) and *Harem Days* (1999).

Her description of the empowerment of remote villagers in the High Atlas as they worked through a nongovernmental organization (NGO) to solve their own problems concerning water in *Les Aït-Débrouille* (1997) marked Mernissi's shift in focus. She introduced a cross-cultural examination of the production and reception of representations of Middle Eastern women in *Scheherazade Goes West* (2001), and began to invest her energies in local action and democratization through two projects. In Civic Synergy, begun in 1995, Mernissi facilitates writing workshops to enhance the communication skills of NGO members, and in return they provide material for her research on the connection between access to new technologies and growing membership in NGOs. The Civic Caravan is a series of workshops designed to teach young NGO members the arts of dialogue and networking. The thread that runs through all Mernissi's work is the belief in the power of communication to create agency. The female storyteller Scheherazade embodies the intellect, humor, wisdom, and wit that Mernissi associates with active community building, be it in the harem of her childhood where women dream of far horizons, or in the workshops where activists work to build a better community with their own energies and ideas.

See also MOUDAWANA, AL-.

Bibliography

Abu-Lughod, Lila. "Orientalism and Middle East Feminist Studies." *Feminist Studies* 27, no. 1 (Spring 2001): 101–112.

"Fatema Mernissi Web Site." Available from <http://www.mernissi.net/index.html>.

LAURA RICE

MESOPOTAMIA CAMPAIGN (1914–1918)

World War I British military campaign in part of the Ottoman Empire.

In November 1914, within days of the British declaration of war on the Ottoman Empire (which was allied with Germany in World War I), the British landed an Indian Expeditionary Force (IEP) at Basra in Mesopotamia (present-day Iraq). Meeting scant resistance from the Ottoman Turks, the IEF moved north and, in April 1915, Sir John Nixon took command. Nixon ordered his lieutenant, Sir Charles Townshend, to advance north—up the river

Tigris toward Baghdad. By November 1915, Townshend succeeded in advancing to Ctesiphon, just south of Baghdad, but his supply lines were stretched thin, and he was repulsed by the newly invigorated Ottoman armies under the command of German General Kolmar von der Goltz. Townshend retreated south to Kut al-Amara, where he was trapped by the Ottoman Turks.

The British failed to reinforce Townshend, and after a 146-day siege, he surrendered his entire force on 29 April 1916. Lacking men and matériel, the Turks were unable to take advantage of the victory. Under the command of Sir Frederick Maude, the British again advanced north, retook Kut on 22 February 1917 and entered Baghdad on 11 March. By September, the British were in control of central Iraq, and by the war's end in 1918, they had occupied all of Mesopotamia south of the city of Mosul.

Bibliography

Barker, A. J. *The Bastard War: The Mesopotamian Campaign of 1914–1918.* New York: Dial Press, 1967.

Fromkin, David. *A Peace to End All Peace: The Fall of the Ottoman Empire and the Creation of the Modern Middle East.* New York: Avon, 1990.

Shaw, Stanford, and Shaw, Ezel Kural. *History of the Ottoman Empire and Modern Turkey.* 2 vols. Cambridge, U.K., and New York: Cambridge University Press, 1976–1977.

Sluglett, Peter. *Britain in Iraq 1914–1932.* London: Ithaca Press, 1976.

ZACHARY KARABELL

MESSAOUDI, KHALIDA

See TOUMI, KHALIDA

MESSIANISM

The expectation that a prophet will arrive at the end of time to usher in the divine kingdom.

Messianism is common to all three of the major Middle Eastern religions. The word *messiah* is derived from the Hebrew Old Testament, where it was used to refer to actual kings who were anointed

(*mashiah*) with oil. In the intertestamental period, the term was applied to the future king who would restore the Kingdom of Israel and deliver the people from evil. In Christianity, Jewish ideas about the *messiah* were applied to Jesus. The word messiah was translated into Greek as *Christos,* or Christ, thereby identifying Jesus with Jewish messianic expectations. Though Christianity builds on Jewish messianic precedents, it adds the idea that Christ has already fulfilled messianic expectations in person and that he will return to bring these expectations to their final fulfillment. Comparable ideas are found in Islam in the person of the *Mahdi* (the rightly guided one), a person who will come at the end of time to defeat the enemies of Islam and thus create a just world. Islamic messianism does not, however, deal strictly or solely with the end of the world; it has played a role in various reformist and revivalist movements.

See also MAHDI.

DAVID WALDNER

MESTIRI, AHMAD
[1925–]

Tunisian political opposition leader, formerly an important figure in the Neo-Destour (later the Socialist Destour) Party (PSD).

Ahmad Mestiri, from an upper-middle-class family, was trained as a lawyer and achieved prominence within the Neo-Destour Party in the early 1950s. While the party was outlawed (1952–1954), he served on its clandestine Political Bureau. Mestiri was rewarded for his party services by being appointed minister of justice in 1956 and minister of finance and commerce in 1959. In the meantime, Neo-Destour leader Habib Bourguiba had appointed Mestiri to the Political Bureau in 1957; he was elected to it in 1959. Mestiri also was elected a National Assembly deputy. Additionally, from 1960 to 1966 he was ambassador to Moscow, Cairo, and Algiers.

During the 1960s Mestiri became disenchanted with the unrestrained power exercised by Bourguiba as both president and party leader. He and other opponents of the economic strategies of planning minister Ahmed Ben Salah were particularly critical of Bourguiba for refusing to remove Ben Salah from his post, even when the weight of evidence indicated the failure of his policies. As a result, Mestiri broke with the PSD in 1968. Following Ben Salah's disgrace in 1969, Mestiri resumed his affiliation with the party. Although widely acknowledged as the leader of a liberal current within the PSD, he was appointed minister of the interior and, in 1971, was elected to the party's Central Committee. Mestiri initiated a campaign to open important party business to broader participation by advocating the direct election of Political Bureau members. He also called for the establishment of institutional constraints on the president. Bourguiba responded by dismissing Mestiri and, in 1972, ordering his expulsion from the party.

By the mid-1970s, Bourguiba became president for life, and opposition elements within the PSD were pushed outside the party, later originating the Mouvement des Démocrates Sociales (MDS) led by Mestiri. The MDS was denied official acceptance as a political party, but he was recognized as the leader of a loyal opposition and was permitted to publish a newspaper, al-Ra'i.

The appointment of Mohammed Mzali as prime minister in 1980 inaugurated a more open political era. The PSD again rehabilitated Mestiri, even giving him a minor cabinet post. He accepted the government's invitation to opposition political groups to participate in the 1981 National Assembly elections, but the MDS list failed to gain the 5 percent of the total vote needed to be sanctioned as a political party. During the 1980s, however, the regime moved closer toward the secular opposition to counter emerging Islamist tendencies. Finally, in 1983 Mestiri's MDS was granted formal recognition.

Prior to the 1986 elections, Mestiri was imprisoned for organizing a demonstration protesting the U.S. bombing of Tripoli in April. The MDS therefore boycotted the elections. Relations with the government remained poor until the removal of Bourguiba from the presidency in 1987. Thereafter, Mestiri consulted with President Zayn al-Abidine Ben Ali about implementing an effective system of political pluralism. Nevertheless, the MDS repeated poor results in the 1989 elections. Disappointed with what he considered a fraudulent scrutiny, Mestiri resigned and retired from political life in 1989. His successor at the head of the MDS was Mohamed Moadda.

Bibliography

Murphy, Emma. *Economic and Political Change in Tunisia: From Bourguiba to Ben Ali.* New York: St. Martin's in association with University of Durham, 1999.

Ruf, Wener. "Tunisia: Contemporary Politics." In *North Africa: Contemporary Politics and Economic Development,* edited by Richard Lawless and Allan Findlay. New York: St. Martin's, 1984.

Stone, Russell. "Tunisia: A Single Party System Holds Change in Abeyance." In *Political Elites in Arab North Africa,* edited by I. William Zartman. New York: Longman, 1982.

KENNETH J. PERKINS
UPDATED BY ANA TORRES-GARCIA

MEUSHI, PAUL PETER
[1894–1975]

Maronite patriarch who worked to preserve peaceful Christian–Muslim relations in Lebanon.

Paul Peter Meushi was born 1 April 1894 in the town of Jazzin (southern Lebanon) to a Maronite Christian family. He completed his elementary and secondary education in Lebanon, then left for Rome to join the Gregorian University, where he completed a degree in philosophy and theology. In 1917, Meushi was ordained a priest in Rome and, at the end of World War I, he came back to Lebanon. From then until 1934, when he was nominated to be bishop for the city of Tyre, Meushi served as a priest for two Maronite parishes in the United States (New Bedford, Massachusetts, and Los Angeles, California). In May 1955, by papal decree, Meushi was appointed Maronite patriarch of Antioch and all the East.

In 1958, Lebanon plunged into civil war, the partisans of then-President Camille Chamoun pitted against the opposition—led mostly by Muslims and Christians. Meushi opposed the Chamoun policy of aligning Lebanon with the West, thus alienating the country's Muslim population. Chamoun, however, suspected the patriarch of wanting to reassert religious authority in Lebanon's political affairs, but Meushi was concerned about the fate of Christianity in the Middle East and the preservation of Christian–Muslim coexistence in Lebanon. Cardinal Meushi died 11 January 1975.

See also CHAMOUN, CAMILLE; LEBANESE CIVIL WAR (1958).

Bibliography

Kerr, David. "The Temporal Authority of the Maronite Patriarchate, 1920–1958: A Study in the Relationship of Religious and Secular Power." Ph.D. diss., Oxford University, 1973.

GEORGE E. IRANI

MEVLEVI BROTHERHOOD

A Sufi order.

The Mevlevi Brotherhood is a style of Anatolian Sufism founded by Mevlana Celalledina (also Jalal al-Din) Rumi (1207–1273), a Central Asian mystic and poet. He developed the sama'a, a rite of communal recitation, which consists of a call to Allah, performance of the zikr (the divine ceremony of remembrance that signifies an attempt to connect and give thanks for the primordial moment of creation),—dancing, and meditating. The sama'a evokes a dialogue with nature; members methodically join in an individual, synchronized, whirling dance that emulates the movement of the planets on their journey of spiritual fulfillment. Rumi's son and grandson developed the order into a community of followers, which flourished during the Ottoman era.

The Mevlevis played an important role in Turkey's social and intellectual development, and the order served as a conduit for the common people. Mustafa Kemal Atatürk and his secular colleagues who established the Republic of Turkey distrusted the Mevelvis on account of their influence among the masses and forcibly disbanded the order in 1925. The Mevlevi monastery in Konya was converted into a museum in 1927 and the members were banned from using it. Even though the monastery remains a museum, it serves de facto as a shrine that thousands of pilgrims visit each year. Despite its suppression in Turkey, the Mevlevis spread to other countries and today their centers exist in more than seventy-five cities worldwide.

See also ATATÜRK, MUSTAFA KEMAL; KONYA; OTTOMAN EMPIRE; SUFISM AND THE SUFI ORDERS.

Bibliography

Friedlander, Shems. *Rumi and the Whirling Dervishes: Being an Account of the Sufi Order Known as the Mevlevis and Its Founder the Poet and Mystic.* New York: Parabola Books, 2003.

"The Whirling Dervishes." The Rumi Society. Available from <http://www.rumisociety.org/WhirlingDervishes.html>.

TAYEB EL-HIBRI
UPDATED BY RITA STEPHAN

MI-6

Branch of the British government responsible for the collection and analysis of foreign intelligence.

The function of this government service is primarily espionage, the obtaining of accurate information from the enemy by means of spies or agents; double agents generally work for MI-5, the British internal security agency. Cooperation between both services was necessary when working with enemy spies who were uncovered in Great Britain and persuaded to work for the British from then on, thus double-crossing their original masters. Other agencies included primarily the Admiralty, the Air Force, the Home Office, and the Foreign Office; in both World War I and World War II, university faculty members and special professions were inducted into the intelligence services. After the last war, MI-6 continued to work in the Middle East, as did the U.S. Central Intelligence Agency (CIA).

Bibliography

Masterman, J. C. *The Double-Cross System in the War of 1939 to 1945.* New Haven, CT: Yale University Press, 1972.

Roosevelt, Kermit. *Countercoup: The Struggle for the Control of Iran.* New York: McGraw-Hill, 1979.

Stevenson, William. *A Man Called Intrepid: The Secret War.* New York: Harcourt Brace, 1976; reprint, New York: Lyons Press, 2000.

West, Nigel. *MI6: British Secret Intelligence Service Operations 1909–45.* New York: Random House, 1983.

ZACHARY KARABELL

MICHAEL, SAMI
[1926–]

Israeli author.

Michael Sami was born in Baghdad, Iraq. Due to his involvement in the communist underground, he was forced to leave his homeland in 1947 and arrived in Israel in 1948. He has published numerous novels for adults and young adults. He is best known for his literary representation of women, Middle Eastern Jews, and Arabs, and their political and ethnic struggles and cultural systems.

His first novel, published in English as *Equal and More Equal* (1974), depicts the socioeconomic and cultural frustrations of Jewish immigrants from Arab countries as they arrive in Israel. In *Refuge* (1977), also translated into English, Sami shows the personal and political strife of a group of young Jews and Arabs in the Israeli Communist Party during the 1973 Arab-Israel War. His writing reached its height in his later books and eventually brought him both popular and literary acclaim with the best-selling *Victoria* (1993), a novel based on his mother's life. It shows the traditions and customs of the Baghdad Jewish quarter in great detail, focusing particularly on its male domination, its lack of privacy, and the intensity of sexual motivation. It ends in Israel, where the men are disempowered by their cultural clash with a new reality and hierarchy. Victoria, as her name implies, is the ultimate winner, seasoned by her experience of self-denial and accommodation. Michael's novel *Water Kissing Water* (2001) draws on his background in hydrology, revisiting Little Israel of the 1950s.

See also ADOT HA-MIZRAH.

Bibliography

Michael, Sami. *Refuge,* translated by Edward Grossman. Philadelphia: JPS, 1985.

Michael, Sami. *A Trumpet in the Wadi.* New York: Simon and Schuster, 2003.

Michael, Sami. *Victoria.* Translated by Dalya Bilu. London: MacMillan, 1995.

Michael, Sami, and Arad, Shlomo. *Bedouins: The Sinai Nomads,* translated by Shoshana Rothschild. Ramat Gan, Israel: Massada, 1984.

ZVIA GINOR
UPDATED BY NANCY BERG

MIDDLE EAST

Regional name with various usages and meanings.

The usage and meaning of "Middle East" have been a source of heated debate. As early as 1949, when other terms, particularly "Near East," were still used, Winston Churchill said: "I had always felt that the name 'Middle East' for Egypt, the Levant, Syria, and Turkey was ill-chosen. This was the Near East. Persia and Iraq were the Middle East." Despite the tacit acceptance of the term by most scholars, journalists, and politicians, few specialists would deny a lingering discomfort with the two words.

Regional geographic names based upon directions are always problematic. They necessarily imply a perspective—in this case, obviously that of "the West." "The East" brings to mind the "Eastern Question" that had plagued Europe since the eighteenth century. Earlier, Europeans had used "the Levant," from the French *lever* (to rise), meaning the place where the sun rises: the eastern coast of the Mediterranean (or of Spain). In the Middle Ages, the favored term was *outremer* (overseas).

"The East," and its adjectival form "oriental," connoted in the European mind more than just a geographic locale. It evoked a world of strange customs, religious fanaticism, exotic sexual practices, and sybaritic culture. As travels and colonial activity made India, and then China, familiar, the need arose to define "East" further. By the late nineteenth century the Ottoman realm was the "Near East" in contradistinction to China and Japan, the "Far East."

It is generally accepted that the earliest reference to "Middle East" occurs in Alfred Thayer Mahan's "The Persian Gulf and International Relations," in the September 1902 issue of the *National Review* (London). Popularization of the new usage is credited to Valentine Chirol, Tehran correspondent for *The Times* who, in the title of the first in a series of articles, "The Middle Eastern Question," dated 14 October 1902, retrieved the term from Mahan's text. An additional factor in its popularization was the shifting balance of power from mainland Europe to the American side of the Atlantic. From an American point of view, everything on the European side of the Atlantic is, geographically, east. Thus, the further reaches occupied by Arabs, Turks, and Persians plausibly seemed more "middle" than "near."

Since the 1950s "the Middle East" has been the favored American term for newly founded academic institutes, programs, and professional associations, though use of "Near East" has persisted in archaeological circles and academic departments founded before World War II. The U.S. Department of State compromised with a division for "Near and Middle East" affairs.

Today "the Middle East" encompasses the lands that stretch from Egypt to Turkey and Iraq, including the Arabian peninsula, usually Iran, and, somewhat less frequently, Morocco, Algeria, Tunisia, Libya, and Sudan.

The term is in no way coterminous with "the Muslim (or Islamic) world." The majority of the world's Muslims live outside "the Middle East," by any definition. It has been suggested that "the Middle East" is best considered a purely geographical term that encompasses roughly the area of the earliest wave of Muslim conquests, stretching from Morocco to Afghanistan and Pakistan, with the later inclusion of Anatolia (modern Turkey). Others disagree, saying that such a historical definition would also include parts of Europe (such as Spain and Sicily) and central Asia.

Bibliography

Davison, Roderic H. "Where Is the Middle East?" *Foreign Affairs* 38, no. 4 (July 1960): 665–675.

Keddie, Nikki R. "Is There a Middle East?" *International Journal of Middle East Studies* 4 (1973): 255–271.

KAREN PINTO

MIDDLE EAST DEFENSE ORGANIZATION (MEDO)

U.S.-proposed group for military security in the Middle East; never formed.

The beginning of 1952 saw riots in Egypt and a continuing erosion of Britain's position in the Middle East. The U.S. foreign policy establishment considered plans to replace Britain as the preeminent power in the Middle East. Paul Nitze, then head of the U.S. Policy Planning Staff, proposed the creation of a Middle East Defense Organization that would protect the Suez Canal and provide military security to the petroleum-producing regions and to the Northern Tier countries of Iran, Pakistan, and Turkey. Cosponsored by Turkey, MEDO was not endorsed by Egypt's President Gamal Abdel Nasser, who viewed MEDO as a tool of American imperialism.

Although both U.S. President Harry Truman and Secretary of State Dean Acheson were committed to MEDO, Egypt's resistance and the generally lukewarm reaction of other Arab states made the realization of MEDO impossible. In 1953, Truman left the White House, and MEDO became defunct. The ideal of a NATO-like security arrangement for the Middle East remained alive, however, and aspects of MEDO were included in the Baghdad Pact.

See also BAGHDAD PACT (1955).

Bibliography

Hurewitz, J. C., ed. *The Middle East and North Africa in World Politics: A Documentary Record,* 2d edition. 2 vols. New Haven, CT: Yale University Press, 1975-79.

Leffler, Melvin. *A Preponderance of Power: National Security, the Truman Administration, and the Cold War.* Stanford, CA: Stanford University Press, 1992.

Lenczowski, George. *The Middle East in World Affairs,* 4th edition. Ithaca, NY: Cornell University Press, 1980.

ZACHARY KARABELL

MIDDLE EAST SUPPLY CENTER (MESC)

World War II agency in Cairo set up to coordinate supply and transport problems of the Middle East.

The economic strength of the Middle Eastern countries was necessary to the success of the Allied war effort. A multitude of agencies—British and American, military and civilian—had roles in ensuring that Middle Eastern economies remained viable and strong. In April 1941, the British established the Middle East Supply Center (MESC) as a clearinghouse for all matters of civilian supply in the Middle East; it reported directly to the ministry of war transport in London. The goal was to regulate and control shipping and commerce among the countries of the Middle East, to eliminate nonessential shipping and trade, and to avoid the political and military hazards posed by populations made hostile because of hunger, unemployment, and the other problems of disorganized economies.

The U.S. Lend-Lease Act of 1941 sent massive amounts of American-made matériel, and after May 1942, the United States joined the British in the MESC, using it to coordinate the American war effort in the Middle East.

Bibliography

Motter, T. H. Vail. *The Persian Corridor and Aid to Russia.* Washington, DC: Office of the Chief of Military History, Dept. of the Army, 1952.

DANIEL E. SPECTOR

MIDDLE EAST TECHNICAL UNIVERSITY

Public university in Ankara, Turkey.

Founded in 1959 as a joint project between the Turkish government and the United Nations, Middle East Technical University (METU) was the first English-language university in Turkey. It comprises faculties of economics and administrative sciences, architecture, education, engineering, and arts and sciences; it also has the School of Foreign Languages and the Institute of Marine Sciences. In 2002 it had a teaching staff of 1,600 and 19,154 students (about 37 percent female).

METU was envisaged as bringing to Turkey American methods of education and organization rather than the European methods practiced at the older Istanbul University and Ankara University. Instruction in English was expected to provide excellent language training for local students and also to enable students from other countries of the region to attend the university. In its early development, it received considerable financial support from the U.S. Agency for International Development, the Ford Foundation, the Organization for Economic Cooperation and Development, and the Central Treaty Organization. Its governance, too, resembled that of an American state university, unlike the other universities where a board of trustees, appointed by the Turkish government, appointed the university president and the deans.

See also ANKARA UNIVERSITY; ISTANBUL UNIVERSITY.

Bibliography

Higher Education in Turkey. UNESCO, European Centre for Higher Education. December 1990.

The World of Learning, 2000. Available at <http://www.worldoflearning.com>.

I. METIN KUNT
UPDATED BY ERIC HOOGLUND

MIDFA'I, JAMIL AL-
[1890–1959]

Iraqi soldier, politician, and businessman.

Jamil al-Midfa'i was born in Mosul in what is today northern Iraq. He fought in the Ottoman army in World War I but subsequently joined the Arab Revolt. He became minister of interior in the first cabinet of Nuri al-Sa'id in 1930, holding the post until November 1933. He was prime minister of Iraq seven times between 1933 and 1953.

See also ARAB REVOLT (1916).

PETER SLUGLETT

MIDHAT PAŞA
[1822–1884]

Ottoman provincial governor, grand vizier, and father of the first written Ottoman constitution.

Midhat Paşa (also called Ahmet Şefik) was born into an Ottoman Turkish family in Istanbul. His father, a native of Rusçuk on the Danube, held judgeships in Muslim courts. In his youth, Midhat studied Arabic and Persian in mosque schools, while employed from the age of twelve in offices of the Ottoman Empire's central government at the Sublime Porte. He began to learn French when he was about thirty-five; in 1858, he spent six months on leave in Europe, improving his French.

Midhat was on the payroll of the Supreme Council of Judicial Ordinances from the 1840s to 1861, but was often sent out of Istanbul as inspector or trouble-shooter on short-term missions that took him to Damascus, Konya, Kastamonu, Edirne, Bursa, Silistre, and Vidin. In 1861 he achieved the rank of vizier when appointed governor of the *eyalet* (province) of Niş, where he proved successful as a provincial administrator. In 1864 he was brought back to Istanbul to help the grand vizier, Mehmet Fuad Paşa, draft a law recasting provincial government in larger units (the *vilayet*). Midhat then became governor of the Tuna (Danube) *vilayet,* the first one created, a Bulgarian area with its capital at Rusçuk. Midhat's reputation as an effective provincial governor continued to grow as he built roads and bridges, curbed banditry, settled refugees, and started small factories. He established the first official provincial newspaper in the empire, and created agricultural credit cooperatives that evolved into modern Turkey's Agricultural Bank (Ziraat Bankasi). He tried to incorporate Bulgarians into the government councils, but he repressed Bulgarian nationalists.

In 1868 Midhat was appointed head of the new Council of State, created to draft laws, in Istanbul. But friction with Grand Vizier Mehmed Emin Ali Paşa led to his transfer in 1869 to the governorship of the Baghdad *vilayet,* together with command of the Sixth Army. Midhat used his civil and military powers with partial success to settle tribes, to collect taxes, and to institute conscription. Thereafter, Iraqi nomads declined in numbers, and cultivators increased. Midhat's application of the 1858 Ottoman land code furnished tapu (title) deeds to individual cultivators, but principally tribal *shaykhs,* city merchants, and former tax farmers took advantage of the law. In the city of Baghdad, Midhat introduced municipal improvements including street lighting and paving, a bridge over the Tigris, schools, and a horse-car tramway line to a suburb. Here also he established the first Iraqi newspaper, the *Zawra,* a semi-weekly in Turkish and Arabic. In the Baghdad *vilayet,* he established government schools—a technical school and two secondary schools, one preparing students for the military and one for the civil service, with free tuition. Disagreements with the grand vizier, Mahmud Nedim Paşa, caused Midhat's resignation in 1872.

Returning to Istanbul, Midhat persuaded Sultan Abdülaziz to appoint him grand vizier, on 31 July 1872. But political opponents, backed by the Khedive Isma'il of Egypt and the Russian ambassador, managed his dismissal on 18 October. He had been impolitic, too outspoken. During this time, Midhat had begun to think about a constitution for the empire. Such thoughts occupied him during the next three years, when he had two brief terms as minister of justice, one as governor of Salonika, and periods out of office. By the spring of 1876, Midhat was a key member of a group that sought to bring change to an Ottoman government perceived as ineffectual in the face of financial bankruptcy and of revolts in Bosnia and Herzegovina.

Midhat and others used popular discontent to force the dismissal of Grand Vizier Mahmud Nedim, and then engineered the bloodless deposi-

tion of Sultan Abdülaziz on 30 May. Sultan Murat V succeeded. Midhat became president of the Council of State again, and began pressing for a constitution. When Murat V suffered a nervous breakdown, following the deposed Abdülaziz's suicide, Midhat and the ministers deposed Murat in turn for his younger brother. Abdülhamit II succeeded on 31 August 1876 after promising Midhat that he would speedily promulgate a constitution.

Midhat chaired a commission in the fall of 1876 that drafted a constitution providing for an elected chamber of deputies. The sultan accepted it only after his own powers were augmented to include the power of exiling. On 19 December Abdülhamit appointed Midhat grand vizier, and on 23 December promulgated the constitution. At the same time, representatives of the European great powers were meeting in Istanbul to devise reformed administration for the Balkan provinces of the Ottoman Empire. Midhat's hopes that Europe would accept the constitution as the fundamental reform were deceived. An Ottoman consultative council, convened by Midhat, in turn rejected the powers' proposals. The stand-off eventually led to Russia's invasion in April 1877 and the Russian-Ottoman Wars of 1877/78.

Meanwhile, Midhat seemed to act less like a grand vizier responsible to the sultan, and more like a prime minister responsible to the nation. Abdülhamit, who feared Midhat also as a sultan-deposer, exiled him to Europe on 5 February 1877. In late 1878, Midhat was allowed to return, but not to Istanbul. He became governor of the Syrian *vilayet.* In Damascus he was almost as vigorous as in Rusçuk and Baghdad but was refused the broader military power he requested. Abdülhamit transferred Midhat in August 1880 to İzmir as governor, apparently to keep a closer eye on him. There Midhat was arrested on 18 May 1881, taken to Istanbul, tried on trumped-up charges of having participated in the murder of former Sultan Abdülaziz, and convicted. Abdülhamit converted his death sentence to life banishment. Midhat was transported to a prison in al-Ta'if in Arabia. On 8 May 1884 he was strangled by soldiers, presumably on Abdülhamit's order.

As administrator, especially as provincial governor, Midhat achieved much, although some of his innovations were superficial. He was known for his energy, his fairness, his honesty, his Ottoman patriotism, his secular-mindedness, and his zeal for borrowing Western techniques and institutions. Midhat was also known for his blunt speech and his haste to act, qualities that helped terminate his two short grand vizierates. But without him, there would have been no 1876 constitution.

See also ABDÜLAZIZ; ABDÜLHAMIT II; RUSSIAN–OTTOMAN WARS.

Bibliography

Ali Haydar Midhat. *The Life of Midhat Pasha* (1903). New York: Arno Press, 1973.

Davison, Roderic H. *Reform in the Ottoman Empire, 1856–1876.* Princeton, NJ: Princeton University Press, 1963.

Devereux, Robert. *The First Ottoman Constitutional Period: A Study of the Midhat Constitution and Parliament.* Baltimore, MD: Johns Hopkins Press, 1963.

Midhat Pasha. "The Past, Present, and Future of Turkey." *Nineteenth Century* 3, no. 18 (June 1878): 981–993.

RODERIC H. DAVISON

MIHRAB

An indicator of the direction toward which Muslims face in prayer.

While the etymology of the word is the subject of some debate, *mihrab* (pl. *maharib*) is the Arabic term used to refer to any object, marking, or architectural feature that indicates the direction Muslims must face (that is, toward Mecca) in the performance of the five daily prayers. Since the *mihrab* commonly takes the form of a distinctive recess in the wall of a mosque, the word is often translated as "prayer niche." Traditionally crafted in stucco, marble, or tile and adorned with calligraphic scriptural inscriptions, the *mihrab* is usually the most elaborately decorated piece of architecture in a mosque and in some simpler settings may be the only ornamented part of a mosque's interior.

SCOTT ALEXANDER

MILANI, TAHMINEH
[1960–]

Iranian filmmaker.

Tahmineh Milani was born in Tabriz in 1960 and educated as an architect in Tehran. In 1989, after attending a screenwriting workshop and assisting in making films, she wrote and directed her first feature film, *Children of Divorce*. This marked the beginning of her career as a writer and director concerned with social issues, such as the effects of divorce, in middle-class Tehran. Her films focus on strong women protagonists. Her works gained momentum in the 1990s, culminating in two films that address the universal issue of women's rights through the specific problems of women in Islamic Iran. With *Two Women* (1999) Milani earned international recognition and a reputation as a feminist activist in Iran. Her next film, *The Hidden Half* (2001), deals with more personal material from her own past as a left-wing college student opposed to the shah's regime. She was jailed for a short period for suggesting in this film that those like her who were active in the Islamic Revolution were later suppressed by the very regime they helped to bring to power.

See also ART; GENDER: GENDER AND EDUCATION; IRAN; IRANIAN REVOLUTION (1979).

Bibliography

Friendly Persuasion: Iranian Cinema after the 1979 Revolution, directed by Jamsheed Akrami. Documentary, United States, 2000.

ROXANNE VARZI

MILITARY AND POLITICS
See MILITARY IN THE MIDDLE EAST

MILITARY IN THE MIDDLE EAST

Internal security and external conflict have heightened the importance of the military in most Middle Eastern countries.

The use of force and weaponry, including weapons of mass destruction, continues to play a large role in the Middle East. Aggravated by conflicts between and among Middle Eastern nations and their populations, military considerations are paramount in diverse situations ranging from the Israeli–Palestinian conflict to various international terrorist threats, such as that posed by the al-Qaʿida movement, to the fear that various "rogue" states will either use weapons of mass destruction to further their goals or provide them to terrorist movements.

Iraqi deputy commander-in-chief of the armed forces Izzat Ibrahim (sixth from left) with his staff on Army Day in 1991. During the Gulf War, the Iraqi military was composed of three divisions: the Special Republican Guard (responsible for internal defense), the Republican Guard, and a regular army. © FRANCOISE DE MULDER/CORBIS. REPRODUCED BY PERMISSION.

The history of the military and the quest for security in the modern Middle East can be examined on three often interlocking levels: internal, regional, and international. The history of each nation reveals a variety of religious, ethnic, tribal, ideological, social, and economic conflicts that often result in violence and therefore also result in a prominent role for the military in internal security. At the regional level, the quest for hegemony by one state has often led to wars among Middle Eastern states, as well as to the exploitation of the internal problems of rival nations. Finally, the Middle East has been an important arena in the international rivalries of the great powers.

Military Organization

European nations and the United States have had a great impact on the training, organizing, and equipping of the military in the Middle East. This accelerated during the nineteenth century, largely due to rivalries among European countries. The result has been a tendency for Middle Eastern nations to organize their militaries along Western lines. More traditional tribal armies, such as that led by Amir Faisal (Faisal I, who later became King of Iraq) and T. E. Lawrence in World War I, continued to play a role but decreasingly so as they were eclipsed by modern forces. For instance, the Ottoman army had significant successes, including the decisive defeat of 200,000 Allied troops at Gallipoli in 1915, the surrender of an entire British army in Mesopotamia in 1916, and continued occupation of Medina throughout the war. The legacy of the Ottomans continued long after the end of the empire in the contributions of trained officers, Arab as well as Turkish, to the emerging nations of the Middle East. Foremost among these was Atatürk, but many Arab leaders, such as Iraq's Nuri al-Saʿid, were graduates of Ottoman military colleges and learned from Ottoman officers.

Active force levels

Country	1955 or 1956			1965			1969			1975		
	Popula-tion in million	Force level in thou-sands	Force as percent-age of population	Popula-tion in millions	Force level in thou-sands	Force as percent-age of population	Popula-tion in millions	Force level in thou-sands	Force as percent-age of population	Popula-tion in millions	Force level in thou-sands	Force as percent-age of population
Afghanistan	—	—	—	12	90	0.75	15.8	110	0.70	19.1	88	0.46
Algeria	—	—	—	11.7	65	0.55	12.6	66.5	0.53	16.9	63	0.37
Bahrain	—	—	—	—	—	—	—	—	—	—	—	—
Egypt	22.9	80	0.35	29.6	180	0.61	31.5	216	0.68	37.5	322.5	0.86
Iran	18.5	135	0.73	23.4	185	0.79	26.3	236	0.90	33.1	250	0.75
Iraq	6	40	0.68	7.4	82	1.11	8.5	92	1.08	11.1	135	1.21
Israel	1.8	250	13.88	2.6	375	14.42	2.8	280	10.18	3.4	156	4.59
Jordan	1.4	23	1.64	2	45	2.25	2.1	55	2.62	2.7	80.3	2.97
Kuwait	—	—	—	0.4	7	1.50	0.6	7.5	1.37	1.2	10.2	0.84
Lebanon	1.7	6.2	0.35	2.4	13	0.54	2.6	15.5	0.60	3.2	15.3	0.47
Libya	—	—	—	1.6	18.2	1.13	1.8	7	0.40	2.3	32	1.39
Morocco	10.6	30	0.28	13	42	0.32	14.2	78.3	0.55	17.3	61	0.35
Oman	—	—	—	—	—	—	0.8	2.8	0.37	0.8	14.1	1.85
Qatar	—	—	—	—	—	—	—	—	—	—	—	—
Saudi Arabia	—	—	—	3.2	45	1.41	6	56	0.93	8.9	63	0.71
Sudan	10.2	5	0.05	13.5	18.5	1.37	14.4	30	0.21	17.9	48.6	0.27
Syria	5.8	40	0.69	5.6	60	1.07	5.7	67.9	1.20	7.4	177.5	2.40
Tunisia	3.8	1.3	0.03	4.6	17.5	0.38	4.7	23	0.49	5.8	24	0.42
Turkey	24.8	400	1.61	31.4	480	1.52	33	534	1.62	39.9	453	1.14
United Arab Emirates	—	—	—	—	—	—	0.4	6	1.50	—	—	—
Yemen, North	—	—	—	—	—	—	5	60	1.20	6.5	32	0.49
Yemen, South	—	—	—	—	—	—	1.3	10.5	0.84	1.7	18	0.23

[continued]

TABLE 1 BY GGS INFORMATION SERVICES, THE GALE GROUP.

This trend toward Westernization of the military has continued to the point that most Middle Eastern militaries are mirror images of one or more Western models. The model chosen is normally a function of which of the great powers has provided the most support to a nation. Turkey, as part of the North Atlantic Treaty Organization (NATO), organizes its forces along American lines, with doctrine, training, and equipment closely paralleling that of the U.S. military. Iraq, since the 1958 revolution, has traditionally looked to the Soviet Union for support, and its military has reflected this. It has often been said that the success of the United States and its European allies in the 1991 Gulf War stemmed from their fighting an enemy they had been training to fight for decades: the Soviet military organization. Political alliances with Cold War rivals have changed, often rapidly, but change in the military comes more slowly. The result was often a hybrid military.

Israel presents a unique case. At first glance, its military appears to be much like those of the NATO nations from which much of its equipment comes. Some factors, however, make Israel different. Much of its equipment is captured, and imported equipment is often dramatically modified; how else could World War II–vintage Sherman tanks have been successful in the Arab–Israel War of 1973? The successes of the Israeli military affect doctrine and organization, not only in Israel but in other nations whose militaries study those successes and in turn contribute to the Israeli military. Finally, the organization of the Israeli military is more reminiscent of the Swiss citizen army than of the armies of other countries. While most militaries have a reserve system, few have one as extensive as Israel's. Almost all males and many females of military age are in the reserves, on active duty at least thirty consecutive days annually, and available for mobilization in seventy-two hours.

Active force levels [CONTINUED]

Country	1979 Population in million	Force level in thousands	Force as percentage of population	1991 Population in millions	Force level in thousands	Force as percentage of population	1995/1996 Population in millions	Force level in thousands	Force as percentage of population	2000/2001 Population in millions	Force level in thousands	Force as percentage of population
Afghanistan[a,b]	21.3	90	0.42	20.8	45	0.22	a	a	a	b	b	b
Algeria	19.1	88.8	0.46	26.3	125.5	0.48	28.8	123.7	0.43	32.1	124.0	0.39
Bahrain	0.4	2.3	0.65	0.5	7.5	1.49	.588	11	1.88	.626	11.0	1.76
Egypt	40.5	395	0.98	56	420	0.75	58.7	440	0.75	70.6	443.0	0.63
Iran	39.3	415	1.05	53.8	528	0.98	66.8	513	0.79	68.3	513.0	0.76
Iraq	12.7	22.2	0.17	19.9	382.5	1.93	21.7	382.5	1.76	22.3	424.0	1.90
Israel	3.8	165.6	4.33	4.8	141	2.92	5.7	175	3.07	6.3	163.5	2.6
Jordan	3	67.2	2.20	4.3	101.3	2.36	4.6	98.6	2.14	6.9	100.2	1.45
Kuwait	1.2	11.1	0.92	2.1	8.2	0.39	1.6	15.3	0.96	2.1	15.5	0.74
Lebanon	2.7	8.8	0.33	2.7	17.5	0.65	4.1	48.9	1.19	3.1	71.8	2.32
Libya	2.9	42	1.46	4.8	55	1.15	5.6	65	1.16	5.6	76.0	1.36
Morocco	19.3	98	0.51	25.4	195.5	0.77	28.3	194	0.69	28.5	198.5	0.70
Oman	0.9	19.2	2.21	1.5	34.1	2.21	2.0	43.5	2.18	2.7	43.4	1.61
Qatar	0.2	4.7	2.23	0.4	7.5	1.71	0.55	11.8	2.15	.610	12.3	2.01
Saudi Arabia	8	64.5	0.81	10.6	131.5	1.24	19.3	162.5	0.84	22.2	201.5	0.91
Sudan	20.9	62.9	0.30	26.1	71.5	0.27	29.6	89.0	0.30	29.6	117.0	0.40
Syria	8.4	227.5	2.72	12.8	404	3.16	14.8	421.0	2.84	16.5	321.0	1.95
Tunisia	6.4	22.3	0.35	8.2	35	0.43	9.23	35.0	0.38	9.7	35.0	0.36
Turkey	44.4	566	1.27	57	579.2	1.02	62.3	639.0	1.02	67.7	515.1	0.76
United Arab Emirates	0.9	25.1	2.78	1.7	44	2.57	1.86	64.5	3.47	2.6	65.0	2.50
Yemen, North	7.5	36.6	0.49	11.5	65	0.56	14.8	42.0	0.28	18.9	54.0	0.29
Yemen, South	1.9	20.8	1.11	—	—	—	—	—	—	—	—	—

[a]Numbers very problematic because of revolution and refugees
[b]Numbers very problematic because of overthrow of the Taliban by U.S. and Afghan forces
Note: Figures for Yemen after unification of North and South Yemen are reported in the line item for Yemen, North.

SOURCE: J. C. Hurewitz, *Middle East Politics: The Military Dimension* (1969); T. N. Dupuy, *The Almanac of World Military Power* (1970); and annual issues of *The Military Balance*, published by the International Institute for Strategic Studies (London: Oxford University Press).

Table 1 on active-force levels shows the impact of the military in the Middle East since the Sinai/Suez war of 1956. These figures reflect the many conflicts with which nations in the area have been involved. The figures for Israel are illustrative. In excess of 10 percent of the population was in the military through the 1960s because the military included citizen-armies. The figures after 1969 reflect only those reservists on active duty, but even here Israel has maintained the highest percentage of the population in the military of any Middle Eastern nation. This is a heavy burden but reflects the price that Israel has had to pay for the protracted Arab–Israel conflict. Arab nations around Israel have also maintained large military establishments. Egypt, for example, had almost 1 percent of its population in the military at the end of the 1970s, and both Jordan and Syria had more than 2 percent. By comparison, in 1990 the United States had 0.68 percent of its population on active military duty, with global force projection objectives far greater than any Middle Eastern nation.

Any reduction of force levels would have long-term benefits, including the minimization of the potential for conflict and of the destruction of lives and property that results from conflict. It would also free manpower for more productive activities. Table 2 on defense costs as a percentage of gross national product (GNP) or gross domestic product (GDP) illustrates the amount of fiscal resources that could be put to other uses. An example of this may be seen in the figures for Iran. As war with Iraq loomed, and as a carryover of the shah's perceived role as policeman of the Persian Gulf, Iran spent 13.24 percent of its GNP on defense in 1979. After the end

Defense costs as percentage of Gross National or Gross Domestic Product

Country	1965 GNP (billions of U.S. $)	1965 Defense (% of GNP)	1969 GNP (billions of U.S. $)	1969 Defense (% of GNP)	1975 GNP (billions of U.S. $)	1975 Defense (% of GNP)	1979 GDP (billions of U.S. $)	1979 Defense (% of GNP)	1991 GDP (billions of U.S. $)	1991 Defense (% of GDP)	1995/1996 GDP (billions of U.S. $)	1995/1996 Defense (% of GDP)	2000/2001 GDP (billions of U.S. $)	2000/2001 Defense (% of GDP)
Afghanistan[a]	1.25	1.8	1.50	1	1.6	2.81	2.30	2.65	3.70	7.74	[a]	[a]	[a]	[a]
Algeria	2.63	3.8	2.80	6.20	8.8	3.24	15.90	3.81	45.43	1.99	49.0	2.8	44.2	6.79
Bahrain	—	—	—	—	—	—	1.70	5.76	4.01	5.04	5.0	5.3	6.9	6.43
Egypt	5.06	9.1	5.10	13.50	17.9	34.10	18.10	11.99	39.45	3.98	56	4.29	90	3.22
Iran	5.83	5.4	7.60	6.44	35.6	20.20	75.10	13.24	59.49	6.34	62.5	4.0	99	7.58
Iraq	1.92	12.7	2.30	10.90	5.6	14.30	15.50	13.03	40.78	21.11	18.3	14.75	15.4	9.91
Israel	3.40	9.3	3.93	16	11.7	29.90	10.50	15.43	51.22	12.03	78	9.23	107	8.88
Jordan	0.50	12	0.50	16.20	1	15.50	1.85	20.59	3.87	14.76	6.6	6.67	7.6	6.84
Kuwait	1.71	4.2	1.87	2.94	5.4	3	11.90	2.82	25.31	5.94	26.7	11.6	33.4	9.88
Lebanon	0.89	3.3	1.20	3.70	3.7	3.90	3.40	6.91	3.37	4.15	7.7	5.3	16	3.53
Libya	1.20	5.1	1.73	1.62	5.9	3.44	19	2.36	24.38	6.19	25	5.6	38	3.16
Morocco	2.60	3.9	2.90	5.17	6	3.17	9.50	9.64	25.36	5.28	31.5	4.13	33	5.15
Oman	—	—	0.16	—	—	—	2.55	26.98	8.40	16.55	12.2	14.75	17.7	9.60
Qatar	—	—	—	—	—	—	1	6.10	7.05	13.25	7.4	4.41	12.4	11.29
Saudi Arabia	1.52	8.6	2.40	13.40	12	52.90	64.20	22.09	87.97	36.22	125	10.56	185	10.11
Sudan	1.35	4.4	1.63	3.30	2.8	3.46	6.15	3.97	11.03	4.18	9.1	4.27	9.5	6.11
Syria	1.08	8.8	1.35	10.20	2.9	23.03	7.10	28.73	17.41	9.30	30	6.67	13.8	5.62
Tunisia	0.88	1.6	0.94	1.50	3.6	1.56	5.83	2.49	12.42	3.23	18.2	2.03	21	1.70
Turkey	8.78	5	10.60	4.45	31.9	6.82	45.30	5.72	80.93	2.59	—	—	—	—
United Arab Emirates	—	—	0.49	—	—	—	12	6.25	33.67	7.69	39	4.87	58	5.86
Yemen, North	—	—	0.52	2.70	—	—	1.50	5.27	7.98	12.53	9	3.83	6.4	7.78
Yemen, South	—	—	0.23	14.60	0.5	5.20	0.50	11.20	—	—	—	—	—	—

[a]Because of the revolution, the ascendancy of the Taliban, its subsequent overthrow by U.S. Forces and Northern Alliance and the difficulties in establishing national control, any figures for Afghanistan are very problematic.

Note: Figures for Yemen after unification of North and South Yemen are reported in the line item for Yemen, North.

SOURCE: J.C. Hurewitz, *Middle East Politics: The Military Dimension* (1969); T. N. Dupuy, *The Almanac of World Military Power* (1970); and annual issues of *The Military Balance*, published by the International Institute for Strategic Studies. (London: Oxford University Press).

TABLE 2 BY GGS INFORMATION SERVICES, THE GALE GROUP.

of the war with Iraq and the subsequent weakening of Iraq after the 1991 Gulf War, that percentage went down to 6.34.

The high force levels in the Middle East reflect more than the conflict between Israel and its neighbors. Internal conflicts tend to drive up the levels as well. The figures for Iraq illustrate this tendency. The Kurdish minority in the north was in a state of rebellion when the Ba'th came to power in 1968, forcing a growth in the force level from 0.68 percent of the population in 1955 to more than 1 percent in 1965, 1969, and 1975. The temporary end of the revolt in 1975 may have contributed to the force level reduction in 1979.

However, the relatively low force levels for strife-torn Lebanon may be deceptive since they do not reflect sectarian militias or the presence of Israeli and Syrian troops; if these were factored in, the Lebanese force levels would probably be much higher and more reflective of the level of civil unrest. The same could be said of any number of Middle Eastern conflicts, from the internal unrest in Iraq as it relates to Kurdish populations outside Iraq, who may look toward Iraqi Kurds as the vanguard of a Kurdish nation incorporating Kurdish populations in neighboring countries—a source of Middle Eastern tension that may well rival that between Arabs and Israelis—to the desires of Shi'ite Muslims in Iraq and elsewhere who resent domina-

Syrian president Bashshar al-Assad (right) attends military training games with his army chief of staff Ali Aslan. Syria's armed forces have suffered a decline since the days of former president Hafez al-Assad's and his goal of military parity with Israel, but Bashshar has undertaken a program to modernize and revitalize the system since taking office in 2000. © AP/WIDE WORLD PHOTOS. REPRODUCED BY PERMISSION.

tion by Sunni minorities. These conflicts, and others, although perhaps not as well known in the West, will probably continue to foster an elevated level of military and paramilitary investment on the part of Middle Eastern nations.

Military involvement in the internal affairs of other nations also requires an increase in the force level; Egypt's dispatching almost 70,000 troops to Yemen by 1965 to support the military revolt there partially accounts for the increase in Egypt's level from 0.35 percent in 1955 to 0.61 percent in 1965. Conflicts among nations in the Middle East also tend to drive up force levels. This can be seen not only in the figures for Israel and its immediate

neighbors but also for Iran and Iraq. After the fall of the shah in 1979, and before the long war between Iraq and Iran and the Gulf War of 1991, the force levels for Iraq increased dramatically.

Finally, the potential for conflict outside the Middle East has an impact on force levels. Turkey has maintained relatively high force levels because of its commitments to NATO and because of the dispute between the Greek and Turkish populations in Cyprus. The NATO commitment dates to the Cold War and the end of that conflict may change the force level requirements. Any change will, however, depend on the role of NATO in the future, and the troop levels that role requires. The conflict

Force structure: active and reserve troops in thousands (Army, Air Force, and Navy only)

Country	1969 Army Active	1969 Army Reserves	1969 Air Force Active	1969 Air Force Reserves	1969 Navy Active	1969 Navy Reserves	1975 Army Active	1975 Army Reserves	1975 Air Force Active	1975 Air Force Reserves	1975 Navy Active	1975 Navy Reserves	1979 Army Active	1979 Army Reserves	1979 Air Force Active	1979 Air Force Reserves	1979 Navy Active	1979 Navy Reserves
Afghanistan	84	200	5	—	—	—	80	150	8	12	—	—	80	150	10	12	—	—
Algeria	55	100	2	—	1.5	—	55	50	4.5	—	3.5	—	7.8	100	7	—	3.8	—
Bahrain	—	—	—	—	—	—	—	—	—	—	—	—	2.3	—	—	—	0.2	—
Egypt	180	70	20	4	12	5	275	500	30	20	17.5	15	350	500	25	—	20	15
Iran	175	—	15	—	6	—	175	300	60	—	15	—	285	300	100	—	30	—
Iraq	70	—	10	—	2	—	120	250	12	—	3	—	190	250	28	—	4	—
Israel	60	200	8	6	3	3	135	240	16	4	4	2	138	267	21	6	6.6	3.4
Jordan	55	35	0.2	—	0.25	—	75	30	5	—	0.25	—	60	30	7	—	0.2	—
Kuwait	4.5	2.5	0.5	—	0.035	—	8	—	2	—	0.2	—	9	—	1.9	—	0.2	—
Lebanon	11	—	0.8	—	0.20	—	14	—	1	—	0.3	—	8	—	0.5	—	0.25	—
Libya	6	—	0.8	—	0.20	—	25	—	5	—	2	—	35	—	4	—	3	—
Morocco	50	—	3	—	1	—	55	—	4	—	2	—	90	—	6	—	2	—
Oman	2.8	—	—	—	—	—	12.9	—	1	—	0.2	—	16.2	3.3	2.1	—	0.9	—
Qatar	—	—	—	—	—	—	—	—	—	—	—	—	4	—	0.3	—	0.4	—
Saudi Arabia	30	20	5	—	1	—	40	16	5.5	—	1.5	—	35	20	8	—	1.5	—
Sudan	24	—	0.5	—	0.50	—	45	3.5	3	—	0.6	—	60	3.5	1.5	—	1.4	—
Syria	50	40	9	—	1.5	—	150	100	25	—	2.5	2.5	200	100	25	—	2.5	2.5
Tunisia	17	—	0.5	—	0.50	—	20	9	2	—	2	—	18	2.5	1.7	—	2.6	—
Turkey	425	500	5	—	39	70	365	750	48	—	40	25	470	400	51	—	45	25
United Arab Emirates	6	—	—	—	—	—	—	—	—	—	—	—	23.5	—	0.75	—	0.9	—
Yemen, North	10	20	—	—	—	—	30	20	1.7	—	0.3	—	35	20	1	—	0.6	—
Yemen, South	10	—	0.35	—	0.15	—	15.2	—	2.5	—	0.3	—	19	—	1.3	—	0.5	—
[continued]																		

TABLE 3 BY GGS INFORMATION SERVICES, THE GALE GROUP.

Force structure: active and reserve troops in thousands (Army, Air Force, and Navy only) [CONTINUED]

Country	1991 Army Active	1991 Army Reserves	1991 Air Force Active	1991 Air Force Reserves	1991 Navy Active	1991 Navy Reserves	1995/1996 Army Active	1995/1996 Army Reserves	1995/1996 Air Force Active	1995/1996 Air Force Reserves	1995/1996 Navy Active	1995/1996 Navy Reserves	2000/2001 Army Active	2000/2001 Army Reserves	2000/2001 Air Force Active	2000/2001 Air Force Reserves	2000/2001 Navy Active	2000/2001 Navy Reserves
Afghanistan[a]	40	—	5	—	—	—	[a]	[a]	[a]	[a]	[a]	[a]	[a]	[a]	[a]	[a]	[a]	[a]
Algeria	107	150	12	—	6.5	—	123.7	150.0	10.0	—	6.7	—	107.0	150.0	10.0	—	7.0	—
Bahrain	6	—	0.45	—	1	—	8.5	—	1.5	—	1.0	—	8.5	—	.5	—	1.0	—
Egypt	290	500	30	20	20	14	310.0	150.0	30.0	20.0	20.0	14.0	320.0	150.0	29.0	20.0	19.0	14.0
Iran	305	350	35	—	18	—	345.0	350.0	30.0	—	18.0	—	325.0	350.0	45.0	—	18.0	—
Iraq	350	—	30	—	2.5	—	350.0	650.0	30.0	—	2.5	—	375.0	650.0	30.0	—	30.0	—
Israel	104	494	28	9	9	1	134.0	365.0	32.0	55.0	9.0	10.0	120.0	400.0	37.0	20.0	6.5	5.0
Jordan	90	30	11	—	0.3	—	90.0	30.0	8.0	—	0.7	—	84.7	33.0	15.0	—	0.54	—
Kuwait	7	—	1	—	0.2	—	11.0	23.7	2.5	—	1.8	—	11.0	23.7	2.5	—	2.0	—
Lebanon	17.5	—	0.8	—	0.5	—	47.5	—	0.8	—	0.6	—	70.0	—	.0	—	0.83	—
Libya	55	40	22	—	8	—	35.0	40.0	22.0	—	8.0	—	45.0	43.0	23.0	—	8.0	—
Morocco	175	100	13.5	—	7	—	175.0	150.0	13.0	—	6.0	—	175.0	150.0	13.5	—	10.0	—
Oman	20	4	3	—	3.4	—	25.0	—	4.1	—	4.2	—	25.0	—	4.1	—	4.2	—
Qatar	6	—	0.8	—	0.7	—	8.5	—	1.5	—	1.8	—	8.5	—	2.1	—	1.7	—
Saudi Arabia	45	55	18	—	9.5	—	70.0	—	18.0	—	13.5	—	75.0	—	20.0	—	15.5	—
Sudan	65	—	6	—	0.5	—	85.0	—	3.0	—	1.0	—	112.5	—	3.0	—	1.5	—
Syria	300	392	40	—	4	8	315.0	400.0	40.00	92.0	6.0	8.0	215.0	280.0	40.0	4.0	6.0	4.0
Tunisia	27	—	3.5	—	4.5	—	27.0	—	3.5	—	4.5	—	27.0	—	3.5	—	4.5	—
Turkey	—	—	—	—	—	—	525.0	260.0	63.0	65.0	51.0	55.0	402.0	258.7	60.1	65.0	53.0	55.0
United Arab Emirates	40	—	2.5	—	1.5	—	59.0	—	4.0	—	1.5	—	59.0	—	4.0	—	2.0	—
Yemen, North	60	40	2	—	3	—	37.0	40.0	3.5	—	1.5	—	49.0	40.0	3.5	—	1.5	—
Yemen, South	—	—	—	—	—	—	—	—	—	—	—	—	—	—	—	—	—	—

[a]Due to instability in the area reliable figures are not available

Note: Figures for Yemen after unification of North and South Yemen are reported in the line item for Yemen, North. Force totals may not match Table 1 because of differences in force structures regarding air defense, marines, coast guard, paramilitary forces, etc.

SOURCE: T. N. Dupuy, *The Almanac of World Military Power* (1970); and annual issues of *The Military Balance*, published by the International Institute for Strategic Studies (London: Oxford University Press).

Defense equipment

Country	1969 Medium and Heavy Tanks	1969 Combat Aircraft	1969 Navel Vessels	1975 Medium and Heavy Tanks	1975 Combat Aircraft	1975 Navel Vessels	1979 Medium and Heavy Tanks	1979 Combat Aircraft	1979 Navel Vessels	1991 Medium and Heavy Tanks	1991 Combat Aircraft	1991 Navel Vessels	1995/1996 Medium and Heavy Tanks	1995/1996 Combat Aircraft	1995/1996 Navel Vessels	2000/2001 Medium and Heavy Tanks	2000/2001 Combat Aircraft	2000/2001 Navel Vessels
Afghanistan[a]	200	130	0	150	160	0	800	169	0	800	253	0	[a]	[a]	[a]	[a]	[a]	[a]
Algeria	400	150	25	400	186	26	500	260	47	960	241	35	960	180	76	1,087	239	28
Bahrain	—	—	—	—	—	—	—	—	11	81	24	13	106	48	14	106	74	20
Egypt	630	450	159	1,945	500	96	1,600	563	109	3,190	495	94	3,650	670	91	3,860	709	104
Iran	—	186	28	1,160	238	52	1,735	447	47	700	213	63	1,520	295	95	1,645	283	100
Iraq	535	213	30	1,290	247	29	1,800	339	49	2,300	261	13	2,700	316	15	2,200	316	11
Israel	975	295	32	2,700	461	66	3,050	576	63	4,488	591	120	4,300	815	58	3,930	829	52
Jordan	230	36	5	440	42	12	500	73	9	1,131	113	1	1,069	121	5	1,077	121	6
Kuwait	—	16	2	100	32	29	280	50	31	36	34	2	215	92	2	385	102	10
Lebanon	40	37	6	85	24	6	—	16	5	175	3	17	330	7	16	363	—	9
Libya	—	10	7	345	92	17	2,000	201	21	2,150	409	109	2,210	472	65	2,025	413	38
Morocco	130	46	6	145	60	5	140	72	19	284	90	34	624	136	35	844	119	36
Oman	—	12	1	—	47	6	—	35	18	82	57	17	128	46	17	154	40	18
Qatar	—	—	—	—	—	—	12	4	35	24	18	10	24	32	8	35	37	7
Saudi Arabia	18	44	23	175	95	4	350	178	134	700	253	43	1,055	313	59	1,255	348	56
Sudan	—	35	4	130	43	15	160	36	18	230	51	4	350	65	14	300	45	8
Syria	400	150	30	2,100	400	16	3,600	389	26	4,350	651	42	4,600	679	45	4,700	676	32
Tunisia	0	14	8	30	24	18	30	14	22	84	53	21	139	51	24	138	58	21
Turkey	—	520	202	1,500	292	183	3,500	303	187	3,783	530	152	4,280	434	145	4,205	505	144
United Arab Emirates	—	—	3	—	—	—	—	52	9	131	100	21	201	141	26	486	150	25
Yemen, North	30	24	—	30	12	5	232	11	10	1,275	101	39	1,125	111	22	910	119	18
Yemen, South	—	18	3	50	27	9	260	109	16	—	—	—	—	—	—	—	—	—

[a]We need the same generic statement for all tables to the effect that Civil War, brief Taliban control, US/Northern Alliance control, continued disruptions, etc., make numbers unreliable

SOURCE: T.N. Dupuy, *The Almanac of World Military Power* (1960); and annual issues of *The Military Balance*, published by the International Institute for Strategic Studies (London: Oxford University Press).

TABLE 4 BY GGS INFORMATION SERVICES, THE GALE GROUP.

in Cyprus remains a stalemate, with no progress being made in United Nations—led talks between the two sides since January 2002.

Tables 3 and 4 on force structure and defense equipment reflect the increasing modernization of the military in the Middle East. With the exception of Turkey, naval forces are modest. Turkey's commitment to NATO has resulted in the largest navy in the area by far, not only in the number of ships but in their size. Egypt, Israel, and Libya have large numbers of naval vessels, but most of these are small and include patrol craft, which are more defensive than offensive.

Most area nations rely heavily on ground and air forces. For example, Israel in 2000 had 120,000 in its active army, 37,000 active air force, and only 6,500 active navy; Syria's figures were 280,000, 40,000, and 6,000, respectively. The equipment of the ground and air forces reflects modern force structures. Ground forces are heavily mechanized, as the figures for heavy and medium tanks show. Accompanying these tanks are large numbers of tracked armored personnel carriers for mechanized infantry, tracked artillery pieces, and modern rocket artillery. Most of this is imported, but an increasing amount is available from local industries. The Israelis have displayed ingenuity in weapons development with the Merkava main battle tank; reactive armor; small-arms weaponry, such as the Uzi submachine gun and Galil assault rifle; and a purported nuclear capability. Other nations have vigorous domestic programs aimed at producing weapons or upgrading imported weapons. Iraq not only tried to develop nuclear weapons, a program set back by the pre-emptive Israeli strike on the Osirak reactor in 1981, but also had a program for an ultra-long-range artillery tube. Iraq also was developing range improvements for its ballistic missiles before the invasion in 2003. Iran's nuclear program aroused alarm in the United States, fueled by its reticence to allow international inspection of its programs. Both Iran and Iraq have had vigorous chemical and biological weapons programs, and it is likely that other nations have done the same.

The Middle East has developed a modern, lethal military capability to wage war on the ground, including sophisticated air defense forces. Matching this modern capability to wage war on the ground is an equally modern air capability. A number of Middle Eastern air forces have fielded the latest American and Soviet aircraft and avionics, all of which are capable of destroying opposing aircraft and supporting ground forces.

A wide variety of weapons systems from an equally wide variety of sources gives the forces in the Middle East, at least theoretically, highly lethal capabilities. Training, maintenance, and supply issues do, however, temper that capability. Some examples of the weapons systems proliferating in the Middle East provide an illustration of the potential effectiveness of the forces. In 1996, well after the Gulf War, Iraq reportedly retained significant numbers of Soviet-bloc surface-to-air missiles (SAMs), ranging from the heavy SA 2, 3, and 6 to the lighter SA 7, 8, 9, 13, 14, and 16, giving it a capability of air defense from fixed-site SAMs, mobile SAMs, and hand-held SAMs. A wide variety also exists in surface-to-surface and air-to-surface missile capability. Iran used about 100 Scud B missiles in its war with Iraq. This missile, which is also in the inventories of Afghanistan, Egypt, Libya, Syria, the United Arab Emirates, and possibly Iraq and Yemen, has a payload of 1,760 pounds (800 kg) of high explosives and a range of 186 miles (300 km). Saudi Arabia has the Chinese-produced CSS-2 missile, which has a range of 1,740 miles (2,800 km) and a payload of 4,730 pounds (2,150 km).

One must also factor in nontraditional military forces when evaluating this aspect of the Middle East. These include the role of terrorist groups and paramilitary organizations that have no parallel in Western militaries. Tribal and ethnic organizations with military arms can also have a great impact. The recent conflict against the Taliban regime in Afghanistan, in which the United States allied itself with tribal paramilitaries normally called the Northern Alliance, illustrates that conflict in the Middle East does not necessarily follow patterns familiar to the Western military. Because of this, the numbers in the various tables of this article cannot adequately reflect the role of nontraditional military forces; they can only roughly measure the order of magnitude of forces from a Western point of view and offer calculations that are useful mainly in estimating the results of conventional conflict.

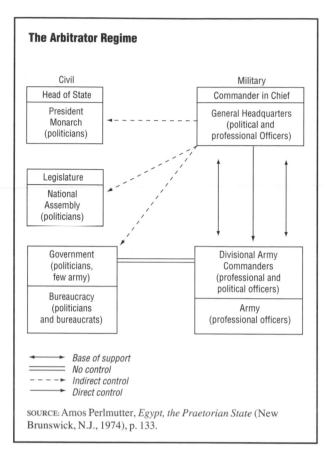

The Arbitrator Regime

SOURCE: Amos Perlmutter, *Egypt, the Praetorian State* (New Brunswick, N.J., 1974), p. 133.

FIGURE 1 BY GGS INFORMATION SERVICES, THE GALE GROUP.

Internal Conflicts

Middle Eastern military forces have been often been involved in internal conflicts such as domestic unrest, revolutions, and coups d'état. All Middle Eastern countries have police forces dedicated to internal security. Civil strife, however, has often overwhelmed the police forces of many nations. In such cases, the military has assisted in maintaining internal security. Success has been mixed. In Lebanon, the weak state-run army has usually been unable to guarantee domestic peace. This has led to the creation of militias by sectarian rivals, which have the role of maintaining order in their respective areas. Israeli (1982–2000) and Syrian armed forces have also assumed a role in maintaining internal security in parts of Lebanon, with mixed results.

Turkish, Iranian, and Iraqi Kurdish groups seeking increased autonomy or independence have presented internal security problems for those regimes, resulting in the use of the military to restore order.

Turkey and Iran have usually been able to achieve a modicum of order through normal police powers and the occasional use of the military. Iraq, by the mid-1970s, had also restored order through military force, but this broke down during the war with Iran and again after the Gulf War (1991).

During its first months of independence, the newly consolidated Israel Defense Force (IDF) under David Ben-Gurion resorted to force to disarm rival Revisionist Zionist terrorist groups such as the Irgun Zvaʾi Leʾumi and the Stern Gang and to ensure their loyalty to a single command. From 1948 to 1965, the army was responsible for administering security and other restrictions on the Palestinian Arab minority in Israel. After the 1967 war, the IDF used military force to maintain security in the occupied territories, but the Israeli police forces have that responsibility within Israel proper. One branch of the Israel National Police is the border guard, which is deployed throughout Israel and the occupied territories. This branch, called the Mishmar ha-Gvul, is organized along IDF military lines and is available to augment the IDF as necessary. This organization is staffed by significant numbers of Druze, Circassians, Bedouin, and other minorities and is open to eighteen-year-old recruits who can choose service with the border guard instead of the IDF. Many commentators predict that military force may have to be used in the event of a peace settlement to control Jewish militants who oppose returning any territory to Arab authority, as was the case during the evacuation of the Jewish settlement of Yamit during the 1982 Israeli evacuation of Sinai, in conformity with the Israeli–Egyptian peace treaty of 1979.

Since World War II, Middle Eastern military establishments have differed from those of Europe and North America in the extent of their participation in revolutions and coups d'état. Some countries have experienced relatively few military coups. Iran has faced two changes of power since World War II—the temporary assumption of power by Mohammad Mossadegh in the early 1950s and the overthrow of the shah in 1979—but the military did not play a major role in either. In Lebanon, the central government has never been strong enough to develop a powerful military, and no coup by a government military has been feasible. Saudi Arabia, the Gulf states, Jordan, and Morocco are monarchies that have shown remarkable stability in a tumultuous area, and none has faced a serious political threat from its military. The use of tribal levies loyal to the monarch to form large parts of the military may explain this. Tunisia also has not faced a military revolt, although its president, Habib Bourguiba, was deposed by a general serving as prime minister in 1987. Presumably, the military approved.

The experience of other Middle Eastern states has been different. Turkey, long viewed as a paragon of stability in the area, has had three military coups since World War II: in 1960, 1971, and 1980. In all three cases, however, power was eventually returned to civilian politicians. Elsewhere, military coups have resulted in governments run by military leaders, some retaining their uniforms, some shedding them for civilian garb but still relying on the military for their power. King Farouk of Egypt was overthrown in 1952 by a group of military officers led by Muhammad Naguib and Gamal Abdel Nasser. Since that time, Egypt has been ruled by a succession of former military officers: Nasser, Anwar al-Sadat, and Husni Mubarak. Algeria achieved independence from France through military revolt in 1962, and the Algerian military has played a primary role in governing the nation since that time. In 1965, led by Colonel Houari Boumédienne, it overthrew the government of Ahmed Ben Bella; in 1991 it obtained the resignation of President Chadli Bendjedid after elections appeared to presage a turn to Islamic fundamentalism. Syria, Iraq, and Libya have all had similar experiences with their militaries taking control of the government.

Conflict between States

Violence between countries is not uncommon in the Middle East. The Israeli declaration of independence in May 1948 triggered an invasion of Palestine by armies from Egypt, Jordan, Syria, and Iraq, with volunteers from elsewhere. These were repulsed by an Israeli military that was at the time, and has been since, underrated in terms of numbers and equipment. Since 1948, Israel and its Arab neighbors have fought a succession of wars. The first, in 1956, was fought in collusion with two aging empires—Britain and France—and began with an Israeli quasi-blitzkrieg campaign in the Sinai. The 1967 war followed the pattern of the 1956 Sinai campaign,

with a surprise attack and dramatic gains by Israel on three fronts, but without the collusion of European powers or the subsequent international pressure to withdraw from territories Israel won from Egypt, Jordan, and Syria.

After 1967, Israeli military successes were not nearly so spectacular. Caught by surprise in the war of 1973, the Israelis fell victim to their 1967 success. Ignoring some of the lessons of combined-arms warfare that led to a quick victory in the earlier war, particularly the need for infantry support of armor and the critical role artillery plays, Israel was eventually able to repulse the Egyptians and Syrians. The humbling of the Israeli military and the aura of Arab success created conditions that helped produce a peace treaty between Israel and Egypt in 1979. The lesson might be that a military force does not have to win to achieve political success, but the problem is how to engineer a loss that leads to success.

The Israeli experience in Lebanon in 1982 is also instructive. Israel has not faced a military coup since it was established, but the role of Defense Minister Ariel Sharon in this operation came close to being a coup. Sharon directed operations far beyond those envisioned by the cabinet headed by Menachem Begin, but was restrained by both international and domestic pressures. Given the potential power of the Israeli right, one cannot exclude the possibility that a militant general might one day become a threat to an elected Israeli government, much like the majors and colonels who have overthrown numerous Arab governments since World War II.

While Arab–Israel wars have captured international headlines over the years, they were not the only wars fought between nations in the Middle East. There have been several mini-wars, mostly border skirmishes between Egypt and Libya, Syria and Jordan, Morocco and the former Spanish Sahara, and others. During the 1960s, Egypt became involved in a protracted campaign in Yemen in support of a revolutionary regime against a royal counterrevolution. This involved thousands of troops, the use of chemical weapons, and the weakening of the Egyptian military to the point that it could not cope with the Israeli surprise attack in June 1967.

The most protracted military encounter was that between Iraq and Iran from 1980 to 1988. The causes of this war included disputes over the border between Iran and Iraq, exploitation of minority and sectarian unrest, particularly among the Kurds and Shi'a, and the question of which nation would be the primary force in the Persian Gulf. The border dispute centered on the Shatt al-Arab and dated back to Ottoman times. The fall of the shah of Iran in 1979 gave Iraq an opportunity to assert primacy in the Gulf. This, along with the threat that Iran would export its Islamic revolution and the continued subversion of dissident groups in each country, led to an escalation of fighting along the border, and on 17 September 1980 Iraq declared the Shatt al-Arab to be a totally Iraqi waterway. The war that followed was costly. The cost to Iran was about $206 billion, while Iraqi costs were around $147 billion. Firm casualty figures may never be established, but Iranian casualties are estimated at between 1 million and 2 million and Iraqi casualties at between 500,000 and 1 million. Of these, the number of dead ranges from 450,000 to 730,000 for Iran and 150,000 to 340,000 for Iraq. The failure of both sides to force a decision may have been as much political as ideological in nature. In both countries, loyalty to the regime is a valued commodity for the leadership, and military promotions depend as much on loyalty as on military skill. In Iran, the fall of the shah was followed by the decimation of the officer corps and a reliance on religious fanaticism, which led to mass attacks by poorly trained soldiers and militia, with horrendous casualties. Finally, the war was controlled from Baghdad and Tehran with relatively little freedom of action for the commanders on the scene. It may be that victory was associated with a higher level of discretion by local commanders and defeat with strategic and tactical decisions made by the political or ideological leadership in the capitals.

The high cost of the Iran–Iraq War, and the failure of either side to win a decisive victory in spite of the extensive use of chemical weapons, led to the cease-fire of 8 August 1988, brokered by the United Nations with heavy pressure from the United States, European nations, and Iraq's Arab neighbors. Both sides set about rebuilding their military establishments, embarking on ambitious programs to increase their chemical warfare potential and to develop nu-clear weapons. There were also efforts to improve artillery and missile-delivery capabilities to provide a more accurate means of projecting munitions.

It was not long before one side felt strong enough to again challenge its neighbors. Less than two years after the cease-fire between Iran and Iraq, on 2 August 1990, Iraq invaded Kuwait, precipitating American and international involvement in the form of operations Desert Shield and Desert Storm—the Gulf War of 1991. Within hours, an Iraqi force that eventually numbered 140,000, with 1,800 tanks, dispatched a Kuwaiti military of 16,000 troops and occupied the nation. Iraq began the invasion able to field an army of 1 million, seasoned by eight hard years of fighting with Iran. Iraq's potential enemies were initially not well situated. Kuwait's ability to fight had been destroyed. Saudi Arabia, viewed by many as Iraq's next target, had a force of only 70,000 troops, 550 tanks, and 850 artillery pieces, far smaller than Iraq's force. The Saudis did have a credible air-defense capability and 155 F-15 and F-5 fighter aircraft. The other Gulf states had some forces but not nearly enough to match Iraq's. Without outside intervention, Iraq had every expectation of retaining Kuwait and possibly threatening Saudi Arabia and other Gulf states.

Contrary to Iraqi expectations, the building of that outside force began within hours of the invasion. The United States decided to implement Plan 1002–90, designed to defend Saudi Arabia. Within a week, the United States deployed 122 F-15s and F-16s to augment the air cover available to the Saudis. By the middle of September, almost 700 aircraft were in place. As the weeks rolled by, the United States, operating under the authority of the United Nations, set about building a coalition force to defend Saudi Arabia and expel Iraq from Kuwait. By January 1991, the coalition force included contingents from the Persian Gulf states, Egypt, Syria, the United States, and several European countries, including some from the old Warsaw Pact bloc. The numbers deployed were impressive—almost 800,000.

At the beginning of the ground war, Iraq had about 250,000 troops in the Kuwaiti theater of operations. These were backed by 4,000 tanks, 3,000 pieces of artillery, and 3,000 armored personnel carriers. Iraq also had Scud missiles capable of reaching Israel and chemical warfare capability. The

Iraqi navy, however, was negligible, and the air force, although sizable, was not a factor after substantial numbers of American aircraft arrived in the area.

On 16 January 1991 (Washington time; 17 January in Iraq), Operation Desert Storm began with an intensive air campaign of four phases. The land war began on 24 February and lasted only 100 hours. The success of the air campaign may be seen in the numbers of tanks, armored vehicles, and artillery pieces remaining on 24 February. Of an estimated 4,280 tanks, 1,772 were out of operation. Iraq had only 53 percent of its prewar artillery and just 67 percent of its armored vehicles. The ground campaign was even more brutal. Total Iraqi losses in January and February were 3,847 tanks, 1,450 armored vehicles, and 2,917 artillery pieces. Although no firm numbers exist on Iraqi casualties and the original estimates of 100,000 killed were exaggerated, a total of 35,000 is not unlikely. This compares with 240 deaths for coalition forces.

Arab states, which had heretofore been notably weak in coalition warfare (as shown by their wars with Israel), were able to derive satisfaction from their successful performance against Iraq, under the tutelage of the United States, in 1991. The experience of the Gulf War may instill a confidence that can be transferred via the noncommissioned officer corps and the officer corps to younger soldiers. The status of the military in those Arab countries, especially the mechanized ground forces and the air forces, has been enhanced. As these are the most modern components of the forces, this may result in a more favorable view of modernization in Arab nations. If the prospects for peace in the area improve and the numbers in the military decrease, then more military personnel with this modern experience will return to civilian life.

Operation Desert Storm ended with the total military defeat of Iraq and its ejection from Kuwait. It left Saddam Hussein in power with considerable military forces at his command. In 2000 he had over 400,000 in his active force structure, with 600,000 reserves, over 2,000 tanks, and 300 aircraft. There were no-fly zones in southern and northern Iraq, enforced by coalition forces, but only for fixed-wing flights. Saddam was able to sup-

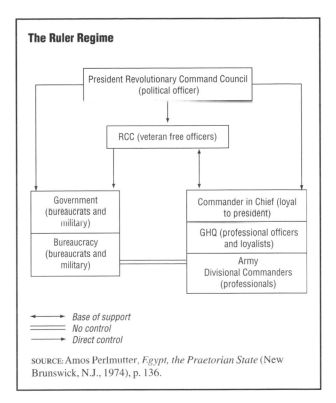

FIGURE 2 BY GGS INFORMATION SERVICES, THE GALE GROUP.

press revolts by Iraqi Kurds and Shi'a with ground forces and rotary-wing aircraft.

The defeat of Iraq did lead to the destruction of large amounts of chemical weapons and for several years UN inspections precluded the development of weapons of mass destruction (WMD)—chemical, biological, and nuclear. These inspections were suspended for a time but resumed in 2002 because of pressure from the United States, which believed that Iraq had an active program to develop WMD, had secreted significant amounts of such weapons, and was improving its missiles for delivery of such weapons.

The inspection regime was cut short in 2003 when the United States and the United Kingdom attacked, acting on intelligence indicating the possession of chemical and biological weapons and a vigorous program to develop and field nuclear weapons. The United Nations withdrew its inspectors, and the United States and United Kingdom formed a coalition outside the aegis of the United Nations to topple Saddam's regime and destroy its WMD capability.

The coalition consisted of fifty-seven nations, but the United States and United Kingdom provided the overwhelming bulk of forces. The scope of the coalition can be assessed by the fact that it included Micronesia, the Marshall Islands, and Palau, but did not include China, France, Germany, or Russia.

The coalition launched military action against Iraq on 19 March 2003 and declared victory on 1 May. The campaign included simultaneous operations by special operations units, mobile land forces, and air strikes. By 5 April, U.S. forces were in Baghdad, and Saddam's home base of Tikrit fell on 14 April. For the most part, the Iraqi military surrendered en masse or went home. Hussein and his top leadership went underground; several surrendered or were caught or killed over the next few months. Hussein was finally captured by American troops in December 2003.

The military campaign resulted in minimal coalition casualties: fewer than 400 coalition deaths during the campaign and the six months of occupation after 1 May. Use of precision weapons, the surrender of large numbers of the Iraqi military, and the defection of thousands more minimized Iraqi military and civilian casualties, although precise figures were not available at the time of publication.

The successful military campaign gave way to a torturous period of occupation and reconstruction after 1 May. Many of Saddam's military continued to resist the coalition through guerrilla warfare that included attacks on coalition personnel and sabotage of reconstruction efforts. These guerrilla activities were reportedly augmented by terrorist groups from outside Iraq, encouraged by al-Qaʿida and other groups. The failure of the coalition to find WMD or verify the WMD programs that prewar intelligence had indicated presented problems in gaining broader international support and eroded public support in the United States and United Kingdom.

Considerable criticism has been leveled at the intelligence upon which the coalition attack was based. The intelligence does appear to have led to a quick military victory. The criticism, however, centers on the actual threat Iraq posed with its alleged WMD, the ability of the Iraqi military and paramilitary forces to wage guerrilla war after coalition victory, and what would be necessary and actually available to reconstruct the country.

Conflicts with and among the Great Powers

In addition to internal conflicts and wars among area nations, the military in the Middle East has also been involved in conflicts with and among the great powers. In some cases, the local military has had to repulse the incursions of the great powers. They were not generally successful, but there are notable exceptions. The Afghans were formidable foes of the British during the nineteenth century and of the Soviets after 1979. Such success enhanced the status of those under arms and led to greater participation of the military in political decision making. The numerous conflicts in which the Ottoman Empire was involved until the end of World War I led to the increased power of the military in political life and effective control of the government by such military leaders as Enver Paşa. This pattern continued after World War I, with political leadership in the Middle East often devolving on military heroes. During both world wars, the military in the Middle East gained a great deal of experience. Many Arabs remained loyal to the Ottoman Empire and fought in its armies, while others joined forces with Britain against the Turks. French North African divisions fought in the trenches of the western front in World War I. Other European nations had levies of colonial troops in both world wars, and Jews from Palestine served with the Jewish Mule Corps at Gallipoli in World War I and with the Jewish Brigade in Italy in World War II. The experiences of these veterans were critical to the revolutionary movements that ousted Europeans from the Middle East after World War II, and many assumed leadership roles in the new governments.

The Role of the Military

Because of the level of conflict in the Middle East, the role of the military looms large. This is because large portions of the population and much of the national wealth are devoted to military establishments. One way of understanding the Middle Eastern military is in terms of the homogeneity or heterogeneity of the state. In a homogeneous state, such as Egypt, the military serves as a mechanism of upward mobility for the lower middle classes, as is seen in the careers of Nasser and Sadat. In a heterogeneous state, such as Iraq or Syria, the military serves as a way for a minority, such as the Syrian Alawites or Iraqi Sunnis, to achieve power.

Much as been made of the function of the military as the school of the nation. The military has been increasingly a modern segment of Middle Eastern society, and many believe that this modernization carries over into societies in general. This may be true, but it should not be exaggerated. As the military becomes more career oriented, fewer officers return to civilian life to influence society with their modern skills. Enlisted personnel may learn to operate sophisticated equipment, but if they do not have such devices when they return to their villages, that skill may be of little use. The experience of Israel—a heterogeneous society populated by peoples from all over the world, speaking different languages—is instructive. From 1948 on, the formative common experience of Israelis was their military training and service, during which they learned to share a common language and common values, emphasizing the need to unite in defending the existence of their state. This model could be instructive for other Middle Eastern nations with diverse populations. Whether it is, however, will depend on internal developments within the societies of the Arab, Turkish, and Iranian nations of the area. Whether it will continue to be the pattern in Israel is also questionable. In recent years, Israel has incorporated a large number of graduates from religious Zionist military academies into its military establishment. Not sharing the common experience of other, secularized Israelis in the military, these recruits may cause the military to become less of a school of the nation than it traditionally has been.

The Future

What does the future hold for the role of the military in the Middle East? As long as internal and international strife continue in the area, the military will continue to play a large role. National resources will be devoted to military affairs, and a large portion of the populations will serve. Economic and technological spin-offs will continue, sometimes beneficial but not without negative aspects. The end of the Cold War during the early 1990s seemed to hold out some hope for greater stability and a reduced role for the military in this volatile area. Yet,

although there is no longer the intense rivalry between the United States and its allies and one hand the Soviet Union and its allies on the other, the economic resources of the region, not the least of which is oil, continue to result in nations outside the region pursuing their own economic goals and using the continuing regional conflicts to enhance their positions.

Other factors also point to a continuing preeminent role for the military in the Middle East: the eruption and duration of the al Aqsa Intifada since September 2000, the American destruction of the Taliban regime in Afghanistan following the al-Qaʿida terrorist attack of 11 September 2001, continuing sectarian strife throughout the area, and the rise of radical Islamic fundamentalism, with violent terrorist acts extending far from the borders of the Middle East. All these serve to remind us that the region remains one with more than its fair share of unresolved, protracted conflict and instability—and one in which we may expect a continuing prominent role for the military.

See also AQSA INTIFADA, AL-; ARAB–ISRAEL WAR (1948); ARAB ISRAEL WAR (1956); ARAB–ISRAEL WAR (1967); ARAB–ISRAEL WAR (1973); ARAB–ISRAEL WAR (1982); GULF WAR (1991); IRAN–IRAQ WAR (1980–1988); KURDISH REVOLTS; OTTOMAN MILITARY; WAR IN IRAQ (2003); YEMEN CIVIL WAR.

Bibliography

Abdulghani, J. M. *Iraq and Iran: The Years of Crisis.* Baltimore, MD: Johns Hopkins University Press, 1984.

Aruri, Naseer H., ed. *Middle East Crucible: Studies on the Arab–Israeli War of October 1973.* Wilmette, IL: Medina University Press International, 1975.

Asher, Jerry, and Hammel, Eric. *Duel for the Golan: The 100-Hour Battle that Saved Israel.* New York: Morrow, 1987.

Bar-Siman-Tov, Yaacov. *The Israeli–Egyptian War of Attrition, 1969–1970: A Case-Study of Limited Local War.* New York: Columbia University Press, 1980.

Beeri, Eliezer. *Army Officers in Arab Politics and Society,* translated by Dov Ben-Abba. New York: Praeger, 1969.

Cordesman, Anthony H. *Iran and Iraq: The Threat from the Northern Gulf.* Boulder, CO: Westview Press, 1994.

Cordesman, Anthony H., and Wagner, Abraham R. *The Lessons of Modern War,* Vol 2: *Iran-Iraq War,* and Vol. 3:

The Afghan and Falklands Conflicts. Boulder, CO: Westview Press, 1990–1996.

Dayan, Moshe. Diary of the Sinai Campaign. Jerusalem: Steimatzy's, 1966.

Fisher, Sydney Nettleton, ed. The Military in the Middle East: Problems in Society and Government. Columbus: Ohio State University Press, 1963.

Freedman, Lawrence, and Karsh, Efraim. The Gulf Conflict, 1990–1991: Diplomacy and War in the New World Order. Princeton, NJ: Princeton University Press, 1993.

Friedman, Norman. Desert Victory: The War for Kuwait. Annapolis, MD: Naval Institute Press 1991.

Haykal, Mohamed H. Cutting the Lion's Tail: Suez through Egyptian Eyes. London: A. Deutsch, 1986.

Hurewitz, J. C. Middle East Politics: The Military Dimension. New York: Praeger, published for the Council on Foreign Relations, 1969.

Joffe, Lawrence. "Research Guide: The Military in the Middle East." Middle East Review of International Affairs at Bar-Ilan University. Available from <http://meria.idc.ac.il/research-g/military.html>.

Karsh, Efraim, ed. The Iran–Iraq War: Impact and Implications. New York: St. Martin's Press, 1989; Basingstoke, U.K.: Macmillan, in association with the Jaffee Center for Strategic Studies, Tel-Aviv University, 1987.

Khalaf, Samir. Lebanon's Predicament. New York: Columbia University Press, 1987.

Khalidi, Walid. Conflict and Violence in Lebanon: Confrontation in the Middle East. Cambridge, MA: Center for International Affairs, Harvard University, 1979.

Kimche, David, and Bawly, Dan. The Sandstorm: The Arab–Israeli War of June 1967: Prelude and Aftermath. New York: Stein and Day; London: Secker and Warburg, 1968.

Kurzman, Dan. Genesis 1948: The First Arab–Israeli War. New York: World Publishing, 1970.

Larkin, Margaret. The Six Days of Yad Mordechai. Tel Aviv: Ma'arachoth, 1965.

Lorch, Netanel. Shield of Zion: The Israeli Defense Forces. Charlottesville, VA: Howell Press, 1991.

Macleish, Roderick. The Sun Stood Still: Israel and the Arabs at War. New York: Atheneum, 1967.

Marshall, S. L. A. Sinai Victory: Command Decisions in History's Shortest War: Israel's Hundred-Hour Conquest of Egypt East of Suez, Autumn, 1956. New York: Morrow, 1958.

"Middle East." In A Dictionary of Military History and the Art of War, edited by André Corvisier and John Childs.

Cambridge, MA, and Oxford, U.K.: Blackwell, 1994.

Mohamedou, Mohammad-Mahmoud. Iraq and the Second Gulf War: State Building and Regime Security. San Francisco: Austin and Winfield, 1998.

O'Ballance, Edgar. No Victor, No Vanquished: The Yom Kippur War. London: Barrie and Jenkins, 1979.

Pelletiere, Stephen C.; Johnson, Douglas V., II; and Rosenberger, Leif R. Iraqi Power and U.S. Security in the Middle East. Carlisle Barracks, PA: Strategic Studies Institute, U.S. Army War College, 1990.

Pollack, Kenneth M. Arabs at War: Military Effectiveness, 1948–1991. Lincoln: University of Nebraska Press, 2002.

Robertson, Terence. Crisis: The Inside Story of the Suez Conspiracy. New York: Atheneum; London: Hutchinson, 1964.

Scales, Robert H., Jr. Certain Victory: The U.S. Army in the Gulf War. Washington, DC: Office of the Chief of Staff, U.S. Army, 1993.

Schiff, Ze'ev. A History of the Israeli Army: 1874 to the Present. New York: Macmillan, 1985.

Schiff, Ze'ev, and Ya'ari, Ehud. Israel's Lebanon War, translated by Ina Friedman. New York: Simon and Schuster, 1984.

Schmidt, Dana Adams. Yemen: The Unknown War. New York: Holt, Reinhart, and Winston; London: Bodley Head, 1968.

Schubert, Frank N., and Kraus, Theresa L., eds. The Whirlwind War: The United States Army in Operations Desert Shield and Desert Storm. Washington, DC: Center of Military History, U.S. Army, 1994.

Schwarzkopf, H. Norman. It Doesn't Take a Hero: H. Norman Schwarzkopf, The Autobiography. New York: Bantam, 1992.

Sifry, Micah L., and Cerf, Christopher, eds. The Gulf War Reader: History, Documents, Opinions. New York: Times Books, 1991.

Thomas, Hugh. Suez. New York: Harper and Row, 1967.

Troen, Selwyn Ilan, and Shemesh, Moshe. The Suez–Sinai Crisis, 1956: Retrospective and Reappraisal. New York: Columbia University Press; London: F. Cass, 1990.

Watson, Bruce W., et al. Military Lessons of the Gulf War. Novato, CA: Presidio Press; London: Greenhill Books, 1991.

Wells, Samuel F., Jr., and Bruzonsky, Mark A., eds. Security in the Middle East: Regional Change and Great Power Strategies. Boulder, CO: Westview Press, 1987.

Westwood, J. N. *The History of the Middle East Wars.* New York; London: Hamlyn. 1984.

Wiegele, Thomas C. *The Clandestine Building of Libya's Chemical Weapons Factory: A Study in International Collusion.* Carbondale: Southern Illinois University Press, 1992.

DANIEL E. SPECTOR

MILLET SYSTEM

The term commonly used to describe the institutional framework governing relations between the Ottoman state and its large and varied non-Muslim population.

Although recent research has challenged both the systemic quality and the traditional origins of the arrangements under the millet system, the term, for want of a better one, remains in use.

Fifteen–Seventeenth Century

According to the traditional accounts, the Ottoman sultan. Mehmet II, upon his conquest of Constantinople (now Istanbul) in 1453, granted extensive autonomy to the Greek, Jewish, and Armenian millets—that is, religiously defined communities of the empire—through, respectively, Gennadios Scholarios, the then-reigning patriarch of the Greek Orthodox church in the capital; Moses Capsali, a leading rabbi; and Joachim, a bishop of the Armenian church. They and their successors thereby became titular heads of their coreligionists throughout the land. The traditional accounts, furthermore, claim that the state did not deal with Christians and Jews as individuals, but only as members of their respective communities. Correspondingly, non-Muslims dealt with the state only through the titular heads of their community. Lastly, in matters of taxation—specifically the *jizya*, the poll tax required of non-Muslim heads of household—once the state determined the amount, its apportionment between individuals was left to the community leader, who supervised its collection and was responsible for its payment. Subsequent research has challenged these claims by noting that they are in no way confirmed by contemporary Ottoman sources and that the non-Muslim chronicles on which they were based were compiled centuries after the events they claim to describe.

What the traditional story does accurately represent, however, is the Ottomans' relative indifference to (and to that degree, tolerance of) much of the activities of their non-Muslim subjects before the nineteenth century. They allowed them much autonomy, particularly in matters of religious observance, education, and personal status (birth, marriage, death and inheritance). The sphere of internal communal control, however, was far more limited than that claimed by the traditional accounts, and the opportunities for direct contact between the individual non-Muslim and the Ottoman Muslim state and society were far greater, extending even into the realm of personal status. Thus recent research in Ottoman records has revealed that Christians and Jews regularly had recourse to Muslim courts, in addition to their own courts, even in questions of divorce, inheritance, and other supposedly internal communal matters. Furthermore, the claim by the traditional accounts of hierarchical centralization under the patriarch or chief rabbi in Constantinople is contradicted by the abundant evidence of local arrangements, often under lay control, and often independent of the capital, as well as by the differing structural traditions of each community. Jewish communal organization, unlike that of the Orthodox church, was not pyramidal, and even the Orthodox patriarch of Constantinople (unlike the bishop of Rome) was merely first among equals. As for the Armenian church, it had long been divided by competing centers of hierarchical authority. Certainly no empirewide fiscal administrative systems existed under the control of the so-called millets, and the term itself was not consistently used to designate the communities. Thus in the classical age of Ottoman rule, during the sixteenth and seventeenth centuries, there were neither millets nor a millet system, although there was a considerable, but by no means absolute, degree of local communal autonomy. In this age, from time to time the clerical leaders in Constantinople did assert claims of empirewide authority, but they were rarely successful.

This complex Ottoman practice was by no means an innovation but reflected ancient Near Eastern and Islamic administrative practices (*dhimma*), as well as contemporary reality and communal traditions. In the aftermath of war, conquest, and dynastic turmoil, religious institutions often were the only institutions to survive. Individuals were most comfortable identifying and organizing themselves according to religion, so the state, even a new one, had no interest in defying them.

Eighteenth–Nineteenth Century

The situation began to change, however, late in the seventeenth century. The Ottoman state's indifference to its non-Muslim subjects diminished when the great powers made their status a stick with which to beat the Turks. As the empire became weaker, European rivals started to vigorously push claims for the protection of the rights and privileges of their coreligionists and other non-Muslims. The Hapsburgs protected the Catholics, particularly those strategically located in what is now Slovenia and Croatia. More aggressive were the Romanovs, who laid claim to the huge Orthodox population conveniently concentrated in provinces adjacent to Russia's frontier. The French asserted an interest in the welfare of the Catholics of the Levant, particularly those in Syria and Lebanon. The British, who had few coreligionists in the region, opposed the claims of their rivals while they protected the few Protestants there and, at times, the Jews. The process of protection was often the first stage of invasion and territorial annexation. The Ottomans proved too weak on the battlefield to confront these challenges directly, and so they were forced to respond with diplomatic maneuverings, administrative accommodation, and, ultimately, commitments to reform. This program for reform in the nineteenth century (the Tanzimat) formally defined and, to a large degree, created the millet system, as it has conventionally come to be understood. For the first time, an attempt was made to impose uniform administrative systems upon all non-Muslim communities throughout the empire. The attempt was consistent with a guiding element of the Tanzimat, the drive toward centralization of all spheres of governance.

The creation of the formal millet system and the consequent abandonment of local autonomy, noninterference, and flexibility, which were the hallmarks of the traditional nonsystem, forced the communities themselves and the Ottoman government to become increasingly embroiled in religious-diplomatic entanglements, which in turn were resolved by the creation of yet more millets. The religious imperialism of Catholic and Protestant missions, which sought to win souls from the indigenous Orthodox and Monophysite churches, as well as other, smaller, churches of the East, complicated the process further. Since these missions were fully supported by the Western powers (i.e., by France, the Hapsburgs, and Great Britain respectively), religious quarrels easily escalated into international crises. The pattern was repeated throughout the nineteenth century.

The Armenian community was the first to succumb to these difficulties. Catholic missions had been very successful in winning converts to Rome from among Monophysite Armenians. Accustomed to the formal hierarchical structure of the Roman church, Catholics repeatedly pressed to replace the traditional lack of system in the relations between Muslims and non-Muslims with a formalized set of institutions. During the late 1820s, they got their opportunity when the Ottomans, desperately in need of foreign support with which to resist the Greek revolt and a Russian invasion, acceded to French pressure to improve the conditions of these converts by establishing a Catholic millet, which was formally recognized in 1831. Since the Ottoman and Roman criteria and procedures for selecting the head of the millet were at odds, however, the millet itself became a source of tension. Furthermore, many important communities within the Ottoman Empire that supposedly came under the jurisdiction of this new institution—notably the wealthy Armenian Catholics of Aleppo, the influential Melkite Catholics (converts from Eastern Orthodoxy), and the numerous Maronites of Mount Lebanon—either resented or ignored it. In 1848 the Melkites obtained their own millet status. In 1850 Protestants followed suit. Other millets were formed: the Bulgarian Uniates in 1861 and the Bulgarian exarchate in 1870. Despite the proliferation of these communal-religious structures, many of the oldest and most deeply rooted Christian churches in the East—the Copts (the indigenous Monophysite church in Egypt), the Jacobites (the indigenous Monophysite church in Syria), and the Nestorians (based in Iraq and southeastern Anatolia) never sought millet status.

The major communities of the empire—Greek Orthodox, Armenian Gregorian, and Jewish—never sought formal millet status in the nineteenth century, since by accepted tradition (the complex historical reality notwithstanding), they had always had it. The reforms of this era nevertheless had a drastic effect upon them as well. The most far-reaching effect derived from the Reform Decree of 1856, which laid the foundation for formal constitutional arrangements reducing the power of the clergy and increasing lay influence. Although Ottoman leaders sponsored these changes in the hope that they might lead to a greater, supracommunal sense of Ottoman patriotic loyalty, the result was often the opposite. Lay leaders, stirred to political activity by the new opportunities that the constitutions now offered, devoted their energies to agitation on behalf of their communities, which increasingly defined themselves as nation-states in the making.

See also DHIMMA; JIZYA; TANZIMAT.

Bibliography

Braude, Benjamin, and Lewis, Bernard, eds. *Christians and Jews in the Ottoman Empire: The Functioning of a Plural Society.* 2 vols. New York: Holmes and Meier, 1982.

Davison, Roderic H. *Reform in the Ottoman Empire, 1856–1876.* Princeton, NJ: Princeton University Press, 1963.

BENJAMIN BRAUDE

MILLI GÖRÜS HAREKETI

Movement in Turkey that advocated religious education and industrialization.

Milli Görüs Hareketi (National Outlook Movement) was founded by Necmeddin Erbakan and his supporters in the early 1970s. The movement promoted a program of cultural renewal, industrialization, social justice, and moral development as a remedy to social problems caused by secularization and Westernization. It reconstructed Ottoman history to demonstrate the major contribution of the Turks to Islamic civilization and attributed its decline to Westernization. It called for the restoration of Muslim and Turkish national values. The movement stressed religious education and became the defender of Imam Hatip schools, in which religious courses are taught along with other topics. Under the leadership of Erbakan, the National Outlook Movement formed a succession of political parties and participated in three coalition governments in the 1970s; it was the senior partner in the coalition government formed by Erbakan in 1996. The National Outlook Movement also maintains close contacts with Turkish workers in Germany.

See also ERBAKAN, NECMEDDIN.

Bibliography

Yavuz, M. Hakan. *Islamic Political Identity in Turkey.* Oxford, U.K.: Oxford University Press, 2003.

NERMIN ABADAN-UNAT
UPDATED BY M. HAKAN YAVUZ

MILLI İSTIHBARAT TEŞKILATI

The Turkish government's intelligence bureau, referred to as MIT.

MIT was organized in 1965, as the reformulation of the older National Security Organization of Turkey. At the time, its 4,000 personnel, linked directly to the prime minister, were to track conspiracies within the armed forces and among radical leftist groups. In later years, officials of the Turkish National Security Council sat on MIT's board.

In the 1970s, MIT was criticized for inefficient intelligence on urban guerrilla groups and for subversive infiltration of leftist and Kurdish groups. It did not inform the government, intentionally or out of ignorance, of secret meetings among generals before the 1980 coup. Officials blamed MIT's inefficiency on understaffing—it had only 390 officers in 1979—and a small budget (equivalent to about $30 million in 1983).

Bibliography

Ahmad, Feroz. *The Turkish Experiment in Democracy 1950–1975.* Boulder, CO: Westview Press, 1977.

Birand, Mehmet Ali. *The Generals' Coup in Turkey,* translated by M. A. Dikerdem. Washington, DC: Brassey's Defence Publishers, 1987.

ELIZABETH THOMPSON

MILLIYET

See NEWSPAPERS AND PRINT MEDIA

MILLSPAUGH, ARTHUR
[1883–1955]

American political scientist.

Arthur Chester Millspaugh was born in Augusta, Michigan, on 1 March 1883. He received degrees from Albion College in 1908, the University of Illinois in 1910, and Johns Hopkins University in 1916. After teaching political science at Johns Hopkins in 1917 and 1918, Millspaugh joined the U.S. State Department in 1918, serving as a petroleum specialist from 1920 to 1922.

In 1922, he was appointed financial adviser to the Persian government, then dominated by Reza Khan Pahlavi (Reza Shah after 1925) and just after that government had annulled the Anglo-Persian Agreement and canceled all debts due to Russia. Millspaugh set about increasing revenues and affecting economies, improving the credit of the Persian government, and balancing the budget by requiring that the *Majles* (legislature) increase taxes when increasing expenditures. His measures, although initially supported by Reza Khan, met some opposition toward the end of his tenure in 1927.

As his contract neared its end, the Persian government tried to reduce his authority by insisting that any difference between Millspaugh and the minister of finance would be referred to the Council of Ministers or the Majles. Millspaugh argued that his contract left it to the Majles to resolve any problems, a position the government refused to honor. At this point, the government decided to employ German and Swiss financial advisers whose powers were more limited. Millspaugh then went on to work with the government of Haiti with its financial problems and with the Brookings Institute.

During World War II, he returned to Iran in 1942 as an economic adviser, virtually the country's economic czar. Iran had matured and developed a technical bureaucracy that resented the more rigid Millspaugh and his assistants. This mission was not a success, and Millspaugh found himself at odds with both the Iranian government and press as well as the American embassy. In 1945 he returned to the United States to work with the Brookings Institute. He died 24 September 1955.

Bibliography

Millspaugh, Arthur C. *Americans in Persia*. Washington, DC: Brookings Institution, 1946.

DANIEL E. SPECTOR

MILNER MISSION

Official British Foreign Office commission sent to Egypt to ascertain Egypt's political aspirations "within the framework of the Protectorate" during the 1919 revolution.

Formation of the commission, headed by Colonial Secretary Alfred Milner, was announced eight months before its arrival in Egypt, weakening its effectiveness. The Wafd organized a nationwide boycott of the Milner Mission to show that the Egyptian people would oppose any extension of Britain's rule. Muslim *ulama* (religious scholars), Coptic priests, students, and women aided the boycott. The Mission was able to meet only King Fu'ad, the ministers, and a few notables. Milner's final report admitted that most Egyptians wanted independence and greatly influenced later British thinking on Egypt. Milner resigned his post in 1921, when the British Cabinet rejected his proposal for giving modified independence to Egypt.

See also WAFD.

Bibliography

Marlowe, John. *Anglo-Egyptian Relations, 1800–1956*, 2d edition. London: F. Cass, 1965.

Mcintyre, John D., Jr. *The Boycott of the Milner Mission: A Study in Egyptian Nationalism*. New York: P. Lang, 1985.

ARTHUR GOLDSCHMIDT

MIMOUNA FESTIVAL

Moroccan and Jewish celebration of spring.

Mimouna is a springtime celebration marked by Jews in Morocco and elsewhere in North Africa. It begins on the evening that Passover ends and continues into the next day. Women set tables adorned with green stalks and filled with dried fruits and nuts, fava beans, wheat, honey, sweets, milk, a fish, and a crêpe prepared after Passover ended. Families visit each other throughout the night, with greetings expressing the beginning of a year full of merit and blessing. The following day, they go outdoors, picnicking in fields or near water.

In North Africa Mimouna entailed the cooperation of local Muslims who gave or sold green stalks and wheat to the Jews in the evening, sometimes loaned clothes to young people who would dress up in Muslim garb, and invited Jews to picnic on their land. From the mid-1960s, Moroccan Jews in Israel began celebrating the Mimouna picnic in mass gatherings that grew as large as 100,000 people by the end of the decade. The celebration expressed a desire to recognize their integration into the society, and the value of their traditions within it. It became a symbolic bridge between Moroccan Jews, by then the largest country-of-origin group in Israel, and other sectors of the country's population. Mimouna is now a standard part of Israeli society's standard cycle of festivals.

Bibliography

Goldberg, Harvey E. "The Mimuna and Minority Status of Moroccan Jews." *Ethnology* 17 (1978): 75–87.

HARVEY E. GOLDBERG

MIMOUNI, RACHID
[1945–1995]

Algerian writer.

Rachid Mimouni was born in the small village of Boudouaou, near Sctif, into a poor peasant family. A professor of economics in Algiers, he has, more than other writers of his generation, expressed his disappointment with Algeria's evolution since independence. Among his ten novels, the most acclaimed are *Le fleuve détourné* (1982), *Tombéza* (1984), *L'honneur de la Tribu* (1989, translated as *Honor of the Tribe*), and *La malédiction* (1993, Académie Française Award, 1994). After an essay, *De la barbarie en général et de l'intégrisme en particulier* (1992), violently criticizing the Islamist movement, he had to leave Algeria and settled in Tangier, Morocco.

See also ALGERIA: OVERVIEW.

PHILLIP C. NAYLOR
UPDATED BY RABIA BEKKAR

MINARET

Tower associated with a mosque.

The minaret has been used for centuries by *muezzins* (Arabic *mu'adhdhinun*, Muslim criers) for the call to daily prayers, but its original use is unclear. The earliest mosques in Arabia had no minaret, and the first towers in seventh-century Cairo (Egypt) and Damascus (Syria) may not have been built expressly for the call.

Minarets have been designed in many styles over time and space. Early ones were often square or octagonal, some with winding exterior staircases, while the sixteenth-century Ottomans built needle-thin, cylindrical minarets with conical peaks. Today, the muezzin does not always climb the minaret to call for prayers; minarets are often outfitted with loudspeakers.

ELIZABETH THOMPSON

MINORITIES

Subdominant or subordinate groups.

The term minorities is misleading and inappropriate when discussing subdominant or subordinate groups in Middle Eastern history and society. It is a term rooted in the naive assumption of Western social scientists that minor demographic groups can wield only minor political and economic power. In the states of the Middle East, demographic minorities have exercised considerable—even dominant—political and economic power. In the past, an ethnically distinctive minority, Muslims from the Caucasus, ruled the Arabic-speaking majority for centuries (the Mamluk dynasty of Syria [1250–1516] and Egypt [1250–1517]). During the twentieth century, in Iraq and Lebanon, the only two Arab states where Sunni Muslim Arabs are a minority, the traditional dominance of Sunni Islam has given its adherents disproportionate—in Iraq, dominant—power. The internal disorders that have torn these polities apart are due in no small part to the contradiction between the majoritarian democratic principles to which all pay lip service and the very different realpolitik.

Furthermore, the bases—religious, ethnic, or linguistic—by which one defines such groups are inconsistent over time and place. In addition, the very existence of such groups and the markers that define them have become a controversial political and intellectual issue. A given group might be considered part of the majority by one criterion in one century; in the next, by very different criteria, it might be considered or—more significantly—might consider itself an oppressed minority. The process also may be reversed so that an oppressed minority may attempt to join the formerly oppressing majority.

Religion

Groups in the Islamic Middle East have been defined largely by religion. The traditional minorities—or, more accurately, subdominant groups—have been Christian and Jewish. Within these there have been further divisions by virtue of dogma, rite, and ethnic-linguistic identity. The Ottoman Empire, which dominated the Middle East and North Africa into the twentieth century, recognized most such groups as components of the so-called Millet System. The traditional states of Morocco and Iran followed practices that reflected their different social and religious needs. Because in Morocco, unlike the Ottoman Empire, the Jews were the only significant indigenous non-Muslim group, the institutional arrangements governing them were less elaborate, and their status tended to vary with the reigning Alawite dynasty (1654–). The most significant Christian and Jewish groups in Iran under Qajar rule (1795–1925) were the Armenians, with small groups of Jews and Nestorians, as well as Zoroastrians. Because of the hostile attitude of Iranian Twelver Shi`ism toward non-Muslims, the opportunities of such groups have been much more restricted than in the Sunni world. However, because of their larger number and economic importance, Armenians in Iran on the whole have fared better than other non-Muslims.

In addition to Christians and Jews, there was another religiously defined subdominant category, Muslim sectarians. For the Ottomans these were Shi`ites. In Iran, in addition to Sunni Muslims, there arose a messianic syncretistic offshoot of Shi`ism, the Baha`i faith. Such groups, unlike Christians and Jews, presented a unique threat to Muslim states because they articulated claims to power based on a similar religious discourse. Unlike Christians and Jews, who had been conditioned by more than a millennium of Muslim rule to accept the principle of status quo, religiously dissenting Muslims had to be retaught that principle from time to time.

Shi`ism represented a significant challenge to Ottoman authority in the sixteenth and seventeenth centuries when the rival Safavid dynasty in Iran attempted to use its Shi`a coreligionists in eastern Anatolia as a fifth column in the Persian-Turkish wars. As this conflict diminished, both Ottoman Sunni rulers and Shi`ite subjects pretended that their differences did not really exist. This process was hastened by the Shi`ite application of the Islamic principle of *taqiyya* (caution), a doctrine of dispensation that justifies concealing one's true beliefs lest they antagonize the authorities. In the mid-nineteenth century an offshoot of Shi`ism, the Druze of Syria and Lebanon, emerged as a short-lived irritant to Ottoman rule in the region when they helped precipitate a conflict with a rival sectarian group, the Christian Maronites. However, it was only in the last quarter of the twentieth century, decades after the collapse of the Ottoman Empire, that Shi`a became a force in the Arab world. In Lebanon, as a result of the urbanization of previously rural populations and emigration of the Christian elite brought on by years of civil war and foreign invasions, the poor and ignored Shi`ite community of southern Lebanon became a majority that could no longer be ignored. In Iraq, despite comparable upheaval, a Shi`ite community nearly as large, in relative terms, failed to gain comparable influence.

By the nineteenth century in Iran, as a result of the Safavids' successful campaign to convert the country to Twelver Shi`ism centuries earlier, Sunni Islam was reduced to the unaccustomed status of a statistically insignificant religion largely limited to the rural Kurdish community, and thus trebly marginalized. There was also a smaller Sevener Shi`ite community. A far more dangerous religious challenge arose from within Twelver Shi`ism. At first it manifested itself in the Bab movement, which arose in open rebellion to proclaim a new scripture superseding the Qur`an. Once defeated, it reemerged nonviolently as the Baha`i religion, whose tolerant outlook proved attractive in the twentieth century. However, Shi`ite religious authorities regard it as heresy.

Ethnicity and Linguistics

In the twentieth century, recognized markers of group identity became newly significant in political terms, with extremely disruptive consequences. Ethno-linguistic-regional identity, as it was called, tried to superimpose itself on strong religious affiliations. The quality of being Aleppine, Arab, Azeri, Berber, Cairene, Damascene, Egyptian, Hijazi, Khorasani, Kurdish, Jerusalemite, Najdi, Persian, Syrian, Turkish, and so forth had always existed. Traditionally such identities had been sources of group feeling, of ethnic pride and humor, of poetry, of distinctive cuisine and speech; but they had not been the basis for political organization, power, and sovereignty. Muslims (whether Arabic-speaking or Turkish-speaking or whatever) ruled non-Muslims (whether Arabic-speaking or Turkish-speaking or whatever). Although the latter might on occasion have wealth and exercise political influence, it was always behind the scenes and under the table. Modeling themselves on the newly dominant European notions of national political sovereignty, in the wake of the collapse of the traditional Islamic polities during and after World War I, Middle Eastern peoples attempted to fit the round peg of their traditional religious communal identities into the square hole of ethno-linguistic politics. This seemed to change the basis for determining dominant versus subdominant roles. And it required a number of uneasily and inconsistently reached decisions, none of which were—or are—self-evident. What were the new identities to be? Egyptian, Syrian, or Arab? Turkish or Turanian? Azeri, Turcoman, or Persian? These are merely samples of the host of complex questions that had to be answered for new nations and states to emerge.

In the new nation-states of the Arab world all speakers of Arabic—Christian, Jew, and Muslim (both Sunnis and Shi'a)—were to be equal; there no longer were to be religious minorities. But that theory hardly described the far more complex and tortured reality. Different Christian groups chose different responses to these opportunities. By and large the Orthodox of Syria and Lebanon identified themselves with their traditional allies, Sunni Muslims, and attempted to support the cause of Arab nationalism. The Maronites, by contrast, preferred the independence of Lebanese identity. Although individual Copts had played a notable role in the rise of Egyptian nationalism, they grew marginalized as it increasingly transformed into Arab nationalism. Even less than Christians, some individual Jews participated in the early stage of Egyptian and Syr-

ian nationalism; but the rise of Zionism and the conflict over Palestine, along with strong religious discrimination, excluded them from any lasting role. There has, however, been one political success story in the politics of religious minorities: the Alawites who dominate Syria's ruling elite, a small Shi'ite sect so extreme that some Muslims deny they are part of Islam. Two factors explain their unique achievement. During the colonial period the French recruited them for military service, so that by the 1960s they were overrepresented in the Syrian officer corps, the country's only electorate. They also denied their sectarian traditions and flocked to the Ba'th party, a bastion of secular Arab nationalism.

The smaller ethnic groups of the Muslim world that lost in the game of national musical chairs—notably the Kurds of western Asia and the Berbers of North Africa, who previously had some claim to power and dominant status by virtue of their Sunni identity—are now ignored and suppressed minorities within new political boundaries. During the 1920s Mustafa Kemal Atatürk and his Turkish Republic, through war and diplomacy, rid Anatolia of most of its Armenians and Greeks—though a large proportion of them in fact spoke Turkish as their first language—and then tried to redefine the only non-Turkish group remaining, the Kurds, as Mountain Turks. Iran has been more successful than most states in the Middle East in welding its varied subdominant groups—Turkic-speaking Azeris, Turcomans, Qashqa'is, as well as the Arabs of Khuzistan and the Sunnis—into a relatively coherent polity. Although Persian speakers constitute a bare majority—if that—they have successfully used the appeal of Shi'ite Islam, to which 90 percent of the population adheres, to maintain the country's unity.

The redrawing of the map of the Middle East and North Africa after World War I created new sub-dominant groups without abolishing the old. In short, the region suffers from the worst of both worlds: it is riven both by the old confessional loyalties and by the new political demands of ethnic nationalism.

See also Baha'i Faith; Christians in the Middle East; Druze; Jews in the Middle East; Maronites; Millet System; Shi'ism; Sunni Islam; Zionism.

Bibliography

Braude, Benjamin, and Lewis, Bernard, eds. *Christians and Jews in the Ottoman Empire: The Functioning of a Plural Society.* 2 vols. New York: Holmes and Meier, 1982.

BENJAMIN BRAUDE

MINZ, BENJAMIN
[1903–1961]

A leader and founder of the Po'alei Agudat Israel, a religious Zionist labor movement and political party in Israel.

Benjamin Minz was born in Lodz, Poland, and immigrated to Palestine in 1925. Under his leadership, the political party was established in Tel Aviv in 1933, and in 1946 Minz became its head. He served as chairman of the World Union of Po'alei Agudat Israel. Unlike leaders of Agudat Israel, he advocated close cooperation with the Zionist Yishuv (Jewish community of Jerusalem) and its institutions. During World War II, he was active in rescuing Jews from the Holocaust. In 1948 Minz was a member of the Provisional State Council of Israel and served as deputy speaker of the second and third Knessets. In 1960 and 1961, he served as postmaster general. He wrote numerous books on topics relating to the beliefs and practices of the Hasidim.

See also AGUDAT ISRAEL; HASIDIM; HOLOCAUST; YISHUV.

Bibliography

Gitelman, Zvi, ed. *The Emergence of Modern Jewish Politics: Bundism and Zionism in Eastern Europe.* Pittsburgh, PA: University of Pittsburgh Press, 2003.

ANN KAHN

MISRI, AZIZ ALI AL-
[1879–1965]

Egyptian officer and Arab nationalist politician.

Born in Cairo, of mixed Arab and Circassian parentage, Aziz Ali al-Misri (also Masri) was trained at the Istanbul Military Academy and was commissioned as an Ottoman army officer in 1901. He joined the Committee for Union and Progress (CUP) (Young Turks), but after the Young Turks seized power in 1908, he turned against the organization and became an Arab nationalist. It is often alleged that Misri's change of heart occurred because of a personal quarrel that erupted between him and CUP leader Enver while both were serving in the Ottoman army during the Libyan war. Misri formed secret Arab societies called al-Qahtaniyya in 1909 and al-AHD (Covenant) in 1913. He was arrested by the Ottoman government, tried for treason, and condemned to death, but the Turks let him go to Egypt instead. When the Arab Revolt broke out in 1916, he served briefly as Sharif Husayn's chief of staff. After World War I, he joined several Egyptian fringe groups committed to Arab nationalism. He directed the Cairo Police Academy from 1927 to 1936 and was inspector general of the Egyptian army in 1938. In 1939, Premier Ali Mahir named him chief of staff, but he was dismissed from that post in 1940 at Britain's insistence. He deserted the Egyptian army and tried to reach the Axis forces in the Libyan desert but was caught and court-martialed in 1941. After Aziz Ali had helped the Free Officers prepare for the revolution of 1952, they named him ambassador to Moscow in 1953 and considered making him president in place of Muhammad Naguib, but he retired in 1954. Fiercely nationalistic, Azi Ali was hampered in his career by his political idealism, which got the better of his discretion.

See also COMMITTEE FOR UNION AND PROGRESS.

Bibliography

Khadduri, Majid. *Arab Contemporaries: The Role of Personalities in Politics.* Baltimore, MD: Johns Hopkins University Press, 1973.

ARTHUR GOLDSCHMIDT

MISSIONARY SCHOOLS

Primary and secondary schools, colleges, and universities established by Christians to do charitable work and promote conversion.

In the Middle East, Christian missionary schools were founded in the wake of the extension of Western power and influence in the Ottoman Empire during the seventeenth, eighteenth, and nineteenth centuries. With the demise of the empire, the Eu-

A missionary school under construction. © AUB ARCHIVES. REPRODUCED BY PERMISSION.

ropean domination of the region, and then the European mandates over the post–World War I successor states, a variety of motives led both lay and religious organizations to aid in the educational enterprise of modernizing the peoples of the region.

Muhammad Ali in Egypt and his son Ibrahim Pasha in Syria facilitated the entry of such groups; the Ottoman millet system—which granted limited autonomy to the various Christian communities—allowed Christians to bring in missionaries to staff new schools and train teachers in the sciences, which were considered the secret of Western power and prestige. Practically all Western nations sent missionaries at some time, but the most sustained efforts were those of the American Board of Christian Missions (ABCM) and the Arabian Mission (both U.S. Protestant), the North African Mission (French Protestant), the Church Missionary Society (British Anglican), and a variety of Roman Catholic orders and congregations.

Until almost the end of the twentieth century, the desire of Westerners to bring education and enlightenment to the peoples of the Middle East coincided with the peoples' desire for learning and was considered a service rather than a cultural intrusion. Moreover, the schools registered a presence and an influence that were not considered religious per se. Christian missionary schools were, in fact, religiously motivated, but the sensitivity of the dominant Muslim population was respected, since Islam opposed any attempts at direct conversion or proselytization. Christian religious efforts remained within the faith—with Roman Catholics trying to attract Christians separated from Rome and with Protestants trying to convert Roman Catholics and Eastern Orthodox Christians. Many Roman Catholic educational efforts began as seminaries that trained local clergy for the Eastern churches.

Several missionary schools developed into notable institutions and have become landmarks in the history of the region: the American University of Beirut, Saint Joseph University of Beirut, Aleppo College, Baghdad College (now Baghdad University), Robert College of Istanbul (now Boğaziçi University), and the American University in Cairo. Undoubtedly, the widespread elementary schools in Lebanon and Syria had the broadest impact. In 1894, for example, the Jesuits (Society of Jesus) had 192 primary schools in the region with students numbering some 8,000 boys and 3,000 girls, and the American Protestant Mission had 130 primary schools with more than 7,000 students. Today, the teaching orders of men, of women, and of dedicated Christian lay teachers—all citizens of Middle Eastern countries—still direct primary and secondary schools that were formerly mission operations.

After the demise of the Ottoman Empire, during the European-dominated years of the first half of the twentieth century, only a limited opposition to these schools existed, mostly in Islamic religious circles. The national governments produced by the post-World War II revolutions of the 1950s and 1960s, however, tightened controls over all education—limiting not only missionary schools but all private education—as in Syria in 1967 and Iraq in 1969. In North Africa the new governments also limited private schools, and then in the 1970s, an Islamic religious dimension was added to the growing regional preoccupation with national cultural identities—culminating in a growing Islamist political movement and the successful Iranian Revolution of 1979, which set out to eliminate all non-Islamic cultural influences. Since that time, a new set of forces, both social and political, has been in the making throughout the region.

See also AMERICAN UNIVERSITY IN CAIRO (AUC); AMERICAN UNIVERSITY OF BEIRUT (AUB); BAGHDAD UNIVERSITY; BOĞAZIÇI (BOSPORUS) UNIVERSITY; SAINT JOSEPH UNIVERSITY.

JOHN J. DONOHUE

MISSION CIVILISATRICE

French term for "civilizing mission," describing the essence of French colonial policy.

As the primary rationalization for colonialism, the "civilizing mission" signified France's attempt to convert its colonial subjects into French people. Whereas the British tended to reject the notion that an Indian, for example, might become British, the French believed that if properly taught French values and the French language, Algerians and Vietnamese alike would slowly evolve and become French. Hence the term *evolué*, which was used to refer to those who had adapted to French culture. There was also a moral component to the civilizing mission, in that some French held that it was their duty as a more enlightened race to elevate the ignorant masses of the non-Western world.

Bibliography

Fieldhouse, D. K. *Economics and Empire, 1830–1914.* London: Macmillan, 1984.

Hobsbawm, E. J. *The Age of Empire, 1875–1914.* New York: Pantheon, 1987.

ZACHARY KARABELL

MIXED ARMISTICE COMMISSIONS

Four tripartite committees established in accordance with the Israel-Egypt, Israel-Jordan, Israel-Lebanon, and Israel-Syria General Armistice Agreements (GAAs) of 1949.

Equal numbers of military delegates met periodically under the chairmanship of the chief of staff of the United Nations Truce Supervision Organization (UNTSO) or his authorized representative. Informal civilian advisers often assisted the official military personnel. Their purpose was to provide for the implementation and supervision of the various articles of the GAAs. As hopes for political negotiations in other forums faded after 1949, the Mixed Armistice Commissions (MACs) also became, by default, one of the last channels through which Arabs and Israelis could communicate directly with each other—although not always with the result of relieving tensions or contributing to a positive atmosphere.

In dealing with a growing number of complaints, the commissions took on quasi-judicial functions, quickly becoming (in the words of one critic) "courts and scoreboards." In the early 1950s, the MACs proved unable to meet their peacekeeping functions effectively when faced with an increase of infiltrations, expulsions, cross-border raids, and reprisals. As time went on, both Arab and Israeli authorities made the tasks of MAC observers and investigators increasingly difficult. Offering lip service rather than true cooperation, the parties—Israel, Egypt, Jordan, Lebanon, and Syria—became skilled at manipulating the MACs for the purpose of scoring political and propaganda points. The effectiveness of the MACs as organs for conflict management also suffered from periodic walkouts and boycotts, by one party or the other, and from recurring challenges to the impartiality and integrity of various UN officials who served as chairmen.

After the 1956 Arab-Israel War, the truce supervisory machinery was further weakened, with some MACs virtually inoperative. The MACs ceased to exist following the June 1967 Arab-Israel war. In 1974, Israel officially declared the four General Armistice Agreements, which had provided the legal basis for the MACs, to be null and void. During the 1970s and 1980s, the UNTSO (with a staff of 220 military observers and offices in Jerusalem, Amman, Beirut, and Gaza) continued to monitor Arab-Israeli frontier incidents.

Bibliography

Berger, Earl. *The Covenant and the Sword: Arab-Israeli Relations, 1948–1956.* London: Routledge and K. Paul, 1965.

Burns, E. L. M. *Between Arab and Israeli.* New York: I. Obolensky, 1963.

Morris, Benny. *Israel's Border Wars, 1949–1956: Arab Infiltration, Israeli Retaliation, and the Countdown to the Suez War.* Oxford: Clarendon, and New York: Oxford University Press, 1993.

Pelcovits, Nathan A. *The Long Armistice: UN Peacekeeping and the Arab-Israeli Conflict, 1948–1960.* Boulder, CO: Westview Press, 1993.

NEIL CAPLAN

MIXED COURTS

Egyptian courts that tried commercial and civil cases from 1875 to 1949.

Although they had analogues in the Ottoman Empire and elsewhere, mixed courts achieved their classic form in Egypt between 1875 and 1949. As premier of Egypt, Nubar Pasha negotiated European treaties that approved the courts for Egypt's Khedive Isma'il; he promptly fell victim to their de-

cisions in favor of his foreign creditors and was forced to sell his Suez Canal shares to Britain in 1875.

Western and Egyptian mixed court judges heard the commercial and civil cases involving Westerners, but criminal cases remained under consular courts. The mixed courts used French law codes, and their working language was French. After 1882, British administrators often saw these courts as an impediment to their own plans for reform and political control. From the 1920s on, Egyptian nationalists campaigned for the abolition of any institution that infringed on Egyptian sovereignty. The Anglo-Egyptian Treaty of 1936 paved the way for the Montreux Convention of 1936, which provided for ending the mixed courts and the capitulations by 1949. The example of the mixed courts' bar association, law codes, structure, and procedures had a significant influence on Egypt's other court systems—the National (*Ahliyya*) and *shariʿa* (Islamic law) courts.

See also MONTREUX CONVENTION (1936); SHARIʿA.

Bibliography

Brinton, Jasper Yeates. *The Mixed Courts of Egypt*, 2d edition. New Haven, CT: Yale University Press, 1968.

Cannon, Byron. *Politics of Law and the Courts in Nineteenth-Century Egypt.* Salt Lake City: University of Utah Press, 1988.

DONALD MALCOLM REID

MIZRAHI MOVEMENT

Orthodox Zionist organization, founded in Europe in early 1902.

Mizrahi was founded by Rabbi Isaac Jacob Reines as the religious Zionist organization within the World Zionist Organization (WZO), after the fifth Zionist Congress of 1901 resolved to enter the educational sphere. Since many members of the WZO believed secular nationalism to be antithetical to Judaism, they could not agree to a program of secular Zionist education.

They founded the Mizrahi organization, an acronym for *merkaz ruhani* (spiritual center), under the banner "The Land of Israel for the people of

Israel according to the Torah of Israel." In 1904, a world conference of Mizrahi was convened in Bratislava, Czechoslavakia (then Pressburg, Hungary), and the Mizrahi World Organization was founded with the objective of educating and promoting religious Zionism. The first convention of the American Mizrahi organization was convened in 1914, under the influence of Rabbi Meir Bar-Ilan, then general secretary, who had recently toured the United States.

After World War I, Ha-Po'el Ha-Mizrahi (Mizrahi Labor) was founded, which established a group of religious kibbutz and moshav settlements in Palestine. Although Ha-Po'el Ha-Mizrahi worked very closely with Mizrahi, the two were separate and autonomous and remained so as new political parties in the Israeli Knesset (parliament), until they merged in 1956, becoming the National Religious party (NRP). From 1951 to 1977, they occupied ten to twelve seats in the Knesset. Although the Mizrahi-Ha-Po'el Ha-Mizrahi movement played a major role in establishing the public religious character of Israel in its initial decades of nationhood, the party's power and prestige declined by the 1980s. Always they struggled to establish the Sabbath rest and *kashrut* (dietary laws) in all national institutions, settlements, and organizations, so that a state constitution should be based on *Halakhah* (Jewish religious law).

Since 1981, the number of NRP Knesset seats declined by more than 50 percent. This has been attributed to the perceived accommodative stance of the majority party, Likud, to religious tradition; to ideological confusion, stagnation, and an absence of NRP leadership development; and to a move by NRP to the religious right, which led many former Mizrahi loyalists into the more sectarian religious parties, such as Agudat Israel and SHAS.

Bibliography

Friedman, Menachem. "The NRP in Transition—Behind the Party's Electoral Decline." In *Politics and Society in Israel* (Studies in Israeli Society 3), edited by Ernest Krausz. New Brunswick, NJ: Transaction, 1984.

Liebman, Charles S., and Don-Yehiya, Eliezer. *Civil Religion in Israel: Traditional Judaism and Political Culture in the Jewish State.* Berkeley: University of California Press, 1983.

Luz, Ehud. *Parallels Meet: Religion and Nationalism in the Early Zionist Movement, 1882–1904,* translated by Lenn J. Schramm. Philadelphia: Jewish Publication Society, 1988.

Schiff, Gary S. *Tradition and Politics: The Religious Parties of Israel.* Detroit, MI: Wayne State University Press, 1977.

CHAIM I. WAXMAN

MOADDA, MOHAMED
[1939–]

Leader of Tunisia's main legal opposition party, the Movement of Socialist Democrats.

A university professor and a founding member of the Mouvement des Démocrates Socialistes (MDS), the first party to split from the ruling Socialist Destour Party at the end of the 1970s, Mohamed Moadda moved to the forefront of the party after 1988, when President Zayn al-Abidine Ben Ali announced a restricted political liberalization for bodies that signed the National Pact. In the early 1990s Moadda led the MDS through a period of "critical support" for the regime until 1995, when opposition parties won only six of four thousand seats in the municipal elections. An open letter that he wrote to the president provoked his arrest in October, and convicted of contacts with Libyan intelligence agents, he was imprisoned in 1996. Soon released under conditions dictating that serious political activity would lead to reincarceration, he was kept under supervision and then placed under house arrest after making contact with exiles from the Islamist Nahda Party in 1997 and 1998. In 1999 he announced his candidacy for the presidency, a symbolic protest against the lack of provision for unapproved candidates, made in the knowledge that it could lead to imprisonment. He was reincarcerated in 2001 after making a televised broadcast and participating in a joint manifesto with Nahda. The object of an international human-rights campaign, Moadda went on hunger strike, was pardoned in March 2002, and was reinstated as MDS president. The price of his freedom was his agreement to moderate criticism of the regime, and to effect a difficult reunification between those MDS supporters who had remained loyal to him and those who had been recognized by the government under Ismail Boulahia.

See also BEN ALI, ZAYN AL-ABIDINE; TUNISIA: POLITICAL PARTIES IN.

Bibliography

Borowiec, Andrew. *Modern Tunisia: A Democratic Apprenticeship.* Westport, CT: Praeger, 1998.

GEORGE R. WILKES

MODA'I, YITZHAK

[1926–1998]

Israeli military leader, politician.

Born in Tel Aviv, Moda'i (originally Madrovich) joined the Haganah in 1941 and the police force in 1943. He served in the Israel Defense Force, eventually becoming a lieutenant colonel. After serving as military attaché to London and heading committees for cease-fire agreements with Syria and Lebanon, he received chemical engineering and law degrees at Haifa Technion (1957) and Hebrew University (1959). From 1961 to 1977 Moda'i was chief executive officer of Revlon (Israel).

As a member of the Liberal Party's directorate (1965–1968) he advocated uniting with Menachem Begin's Herut Party to create the Likud. He was appointed military commander of Gaza after the 1967 Arab-Israel War and was elected to the Knesset in 1974. Moda'i was minister of energy and infrastructure in the Likud government of 1977 and was minister of communication and later minister without portfolio (a member of the Cabinet with the right to attend Cabinet meetings and advise the prime minister but without responsibility for a division of government bureaucracy, such as the Ministry of Housing, Ministry of Labor, Ministry of Foreign Affairs, etc.). He was finance minister in the National Unity government of 1984, working closely with Prime Minister Shimon Peres on the economic stabilization program, which was the initiative for which Moda'i was probably best known. Tension between him and Peres forced Moda'i to switch to the Ministry of Justice and finally to leave the government in 1986. When Yitzhak Shamir took over the premiership in 1986 in an arrangement for power-sharing that had been made between Peres and Shamir at the time of the 1984 election, Moda'i returned as minister without portfolio and served as minister for economy and planning.

Moda'i served as chairman of the Jubilee Celebrations Committee in 1998, celebrating Israel's fiftieth anniversary, but resigned because of disagreements with tourism minister Moshe Katsav, the minister responsible for the celebrations. In May 1998 Moda'i died at age 72.

Bibliography

Honig, Sarah. "Too Brilliant for Israeli Politics." *Jerusalem Post.* 15 May 1998.

"Yitzhak Moda'i Dies, 72." *Jerusalem Post.* 15 May 1998.

ZEV MAGHEN
UPDATED BY GREGORY S. MAHLER

MODERNIZATION

Process of sociocultural change in the Middle East that began about 1800 with European colonial expansion into the area.

Modernization is the term commonly used to denote the process of social change that the Middle East (and other parts of the world) has been experiencing for the last two hundred years. It may be traced to the Industrial Revolution and the impact of European industrial expansion and colonialism that was continually promoted by European agents—merchants, bankers, consuls, administrators, and missionaries. This process was embraced by early modernizing monarchs such as Selim III and Mahmud II of the Ottoman Empire and Muhammad Ali of Egypt. Five aspects may be distinguished: economic, political, social, intellectual, and psychological.

Economic Aspects

The Middle East has long been integrated in the world market. The region has mainly exported primary products, agricultural goods such as cotton, tobacco, fruits, and coffee; recently, it became the prime producer and exporter of petroleum. To facilitate both export and the importation of manufactured goods, certain raw materials, and foodstuffs, a network for mechanized transport was developed (railroads, seaports, river traffic, roads [with bridges and tunnels], airports), along with a banking and finance system. This entailed vast investments of foreign and, more recently, national capital. A large manufacturing sector has been established, and the region encompasses the world's most abundant petroleum deposits—exploited by a large production and exporting industry.

Political Aspects

Modernization here constitutes the emergence of centralized nation-states. In addition to the ruling bodies, large, and usually cumbrous, civil services administer the various countries and provide social services. Taxation has risen steadily as a proportion of Gross National Product. Suffrage often excludes women, but elections are held for presidents and parliaments (although in practice many countries are under a one-party dictatorship). The prevailing political ideology is nationalism—utilizing certain elements of socialism—mainly as the outcome of working toward independence from European imperialism during the twentieth century.

Social Aspects

Many changes have occurred because of the great increase in population; the sharp fall in death rates has not been matched by a decline in birthrates, so the population has increased at about 3 percent per annum (including both immigration and emigration). Cities have grown to the point where more than 50 percent of the population is urban. Family structure has consequently shown some changes; most young middle-class couples live on their own and make their own decisions, instead of following the practices and decisions of their patriarch. Social services have been greatly expanded; those that were provided by religious or private philanthropy are now usually provided by the state. Education is available to almost all boys of school age (and to the majority of girls), and the literacy rate has risen from an average 5 percent in the early nineteenth century to an average of more than 50 percent today (in Israel, more than 90 percent).

Intellectual/Psychological Aspects

Intellectual modernization meant, originally, the absorption by a small elite of the bulk of Western science, scholarship, literature, and to a smaller extent, the arts. This was achieved primarily through the French language, but British and American sources have been increasingly used. Diffusion of Western-style culture has resulted in the establishment of a vast network of Western-style schools, which are secular and therefore distinct from the traditional Muslim/Christian/Hebrew schools. They include many universities and technical and research institutes.

Although printing was available in the eighteenth century, it became significant only during the nineteenth century, when books and pamphlets were followed by newspapers and periodicals that reached the general reading public. Concurrently, the traditional written languages—mainly, Persian, Turkish, Arabic, and Hebrew—which were highly elaborate, formal, and remote from everyday speech, have been both simplified and enriched. New and hitherto unknown literary genres have developed, notably novels and plays, based on Western models. It is perhaps in them that one sees most clearly the psychological modernization that has occurred—the growing individualism, the weakening of traditional ways, and the participation in what may be called a world culture. The expanding fundamentalist tendencies in both Islam and Judaism may be explained by sociopolitical problems that continue to need attention, not by a growing traditionalism.

Bibliography

Berkes, Niyazi. *The Development of Secularism in Turkey.* Montreal: McGill University Press, 1964; reprint, New York: Routledge, 1998.

Black, Cyril E., and Brown, L. Carl, eds. *Modernization in the Middle East: The Ottoman Empire and Its Afro-Asian Successors.* Princeton, NJ: Darwin Press, 1992.

Hourani, Albert. *Arabic Thought in the Liberal Age, 1798–1939.* London and New York: Oxford University Press, 1962.

Hourani, Albert. *A History of the Arab Peoples.* Cambridge, MA: Belknap Press, 1991.

Issawi, Charles. *An Economic History of the Middle East and North Africa.* New York: Columbia University Press, 1982.

Lewis, Bernard. *The Emergence of Modern Turkey,* 3d edition. New York: Oxford University Press, 2002.

CHARLES ISSAWI

MOGANNAM, MATIEL
[c.1900–1992]

Leader of the Palestinian women's movement, 1920s–1930s.

Matiel Mogannam, a Christian, was born in Lebanon but was raised in the United States, where her family immigrated during her childhood. There, she met and married her husband, Mogannam Mogannam, a native of Jerusalem. During the early 1920s, the couple relocated to Jerusalem, where Matiel became active in the Palestinian women's movement. Mogannam Mogannam was an advocate and officer of the National Defense Party. In 1929 Matiel Mogannam was one of the two secretaries of the Arab Women's Executive (AWE), which founded the Arab Women's Association (AWA) and the Arab women's movement in Palestine, in which she was extremely active. In 1933, when Sir Edmund Allenby, commander-in-chief of the Allied Forces of Palestine during World War I, came to dedicate the Young Men's Christian Association (YMCA) building in Jerusalem, Mogannam delivered a nationalist speech from the minbar of the Mosque of Umar at the Haram al-Sharif. In autumn of the same year, she spoke from a balcony in Jaffa during turbulent nationalist demonstrations held in the cities of Mandatory Palestine. Her book, *The Arab Woman and the Palestine Problem,* and her contributions to the Palestinian press, are firsthand accounts of the Palestinian women's movement before 1948. She and her husband relocated in 1938 to Ramallah, where she was active in the women's movement for many years. She died in the United States in 1992.

See also ARAB WOMEN'S ASSOCIATION OF PALESTINE; ARAB WOMEN'S EXECUTIVE COMMITTEE; JERUSALEM.

Bibliography

Fleischmann, Ellen L. "Selective Memory, Gender and Nationalism: Palestinian Women Leaders in the British Mandate Period," *History Workshop Journal* 47 (1999): 141–158.

Mogannam, Matiel E. T. *The Arab Woman and the Palestine Problem.* London: Herbert Joseph, 1937.

ELLEN L. FLEISCHMANN

MOGHAIZEL, LAURE
[1929–1997]

Lebanese legal, women's, and human rights activist.

Laure Moghaizel (also Mughayzil) was a pioneer in the field of women's legal rights in Lebanon and the Arab world. Born into a middle-class Maronite family from South Lebanon, she distinguished herself early as an outspoken student and member of the Kata'ib (Phalangist) Youth Organization, which was originally established in 1936 as a Christian nationalist youth movement. Following Lebanese in-

dependence in 1943, it turned from a populist youth group into a formal political party. Moghaizel led efforts to equalize women's participation in this group as she studied for her law degree at Saint Joseph's University in Beirut. During the outbreak of confessional (civil and religious) unrest in Lebanon in 1958, Moghaizel's husband Joseph and then she herself broke with the Kata'ib, disappointed in its anti-Islamic rhetoric. From that time onward, she identified herself as a pro-democracy Lebanese woman with strong allegiances to human and family rights. In 1968 she was a founding member of the Democratic Party of Lebanon.

Moghaizel was instrumental in lobbying for basic laws that changed the lives of Lebanese women, such as a woman's right to vote (obtained in 1953) and the equalization of the law of inheritance of non-Muslims (obtained in 1959). She also fought to abolish discriminatory policies preventing a woman from leaving the country without her husband's permission. During the Lebanese civil war (1975–1990) she was a founding member of Bahithat, an association of women scholars opposed to confessionalism. She also played an active role in the broader Arab region and international arena, heading committees on Arab Women and Childhood Development and serving as vice president of the International Council for Women. Beside her political activism, she published widely on women and Lebanese legislation, women during the civil war, crimes of honor, women's labor, and Arab women and political laws.

Moghaizel's activism also extended to the related area of human rights. During the mid-1980s she was a founding member of the Lebanese Association for Human Rights and the Non-Violence Movement. She represented Lebanon and the Arab world in countless forums on the rights of women, children, families, and human beings generally, and published legal guides on human and women's rights. Her work as an attorney was matched by her passion for the recognition of human rights. She believed that Lebanon had an important role to play regarding improving freedom and human rights in the Arab world. Her service to Lebanon earned her the Order of the Cedar, rank of Commander.

In 1996, the Moghaizel Foundation was founded to "enhance and disseminate the thoughts and discipline" of Joseph and Laure Moghaizel, especially issues relating to human rights, democracy, modernization, national unity, Arabism, and secularism. As of 2003, the foundation issued publications, encouraged research, organized workshops and seminars, and maintained a public library.

See also GENDER: GENDER AND LAW; GENDER: GENDER AND POLITICS; LEBANESE CIVIL WAR (1958); LEBANESE CIVIL WAR (1975–1990); LEBANESE WOMEN'S COUNCIL; LEBANON.

Bibliography

Official web site for the Moghaizel Foundation. Available from <http://www.kleudge.com/moghaizelfoundation>.

ELISE SALEM

MOHAJERANI, ATAOLLAH
[1954–]

Iranian politician.

Born in 1954 in Arak, Ataollah Mohajerani received his degrees (B.A., M.A., and Ph.D.) in history from Isfahan, Shiraz, and the Teachers' Training universities. He was a student during the Iranian Revolution and entered politics by running for and serving in the first parliament in the Islamic Republic of Iran (1980–1984). After serving one year as the cultural ambassador to Pakistan, he became the deputy for legal and parliamentary affairs, first for the prime minister and later for the president (1985–1989). Shortly after serving as a spokesperson for the newly elected president Mohammad Khatami in 1997, Mohajerani was appointed minister of culture and Islamic guidance—a position he held until April 2000.

Mohajerani is a culturally progressive, politically pragmatic, and religiously liberal politician affiliated with the Executives of Construction Party, which was established in 1996 with the support of the president, Ali Akbar Hashemi Rafsanjani, as a counterforce to religious conservatives. Relative to his predecessors, Mohajerani was an extremely liberal and visionary culture minister. He was one of the driving forces behind Khatami's liberal policies after 1997. During Mohajerani's tenure, Iran experienced more press freedom; increased publication of books, magazines, and newspapers; and a resur-facing of the Iranian cinema in the international arena. Previously banned artists and writers were allowed to produce their works again.

Mohajerani's policies generated conflicting reactions. When Salman Rushdie wrote *Satanic Verses* and Ayatollah Ruhollah Khomeini issued a *fatva* [fatwa] that absolved any Muslim who might kill him, Mohajerani wrote a book in which he defended Khomeini's verdict and declared the Rushdie affair to be part of a recurring Western plot against Islam. The conservatives adored Mohajerani, but when he advocated direct negotiations with the United States in 1989, he angered Ali Khamenehi, the leader of the Islamic Republic, who denounced him and suspended any discussion of the issue. Some conservatives viewed Mohajerani's policies as an assault on their religious values, and accused him of being a CIA agent hired to undermine the values of the Islamic Revolution. Several high-ranking clerics denounced him and demanded his impeachment by the parliament or dismissal by the leader. In 1998, radical vigilantes physically attacked Mohajerani and Hojatoleslam Abdolah Nuri, the minister of the interior, during Friday prayers in Tehran University. In 1999 conservatives tried to impeach Mohajerani in the parliament, but his eloquent defense prevented his critics from gaining enough votes for his removal.

Pressure on Mohajerani mounted from allegations of financial impropriety and legal challenges to his decisions, and rumors of his resignation continued. Finally, in April 2000 Khatami accepted his fifty-page letter of resignation. In 2001 Khatami asked him to serve as the director of the International Centre for Dialogue Among Civilizations (ICDC). As head of ICDC, Mohajerani continues to travel, give speeches and interviews, and write books and articles. He is married to Jamileh Kadivar, a parliament deputy, and they have four children.

See also KHATAMI, MOHAMMAD; KHOMEINI, RUHOLLAH; RAFSANJANI, ALI AKBAR HASHEMI.

ALI AKBAR MAHDI

MOHAMMAD ALI SHAH QAJAR
[1872–1925]

Sixth ruler of the Qajar dynasty in Iran.

Mohammad Ali was the eldest son of Mozaffar al-Din Shah Qajar. His mother was the daughter of Mirza Mohammad Taqi Khan Amir Kabir, the reformist prime minister executed by Mohammad Ali's grandfather, Naser al-Din Shah, in 1852.

Mohammad Ali became commander of the troops in the Iranian province of Azerbaijan in 1892. Four years later, when his father succeeded to the throne, Mohammad Ali was proclaimed crown prince. In 1905, as he was regent while his father was visiting Europe, the merchants of Tehran closed the bazaars and took refuge in the shrine of Shah Abd al-Azim in Rayy to protest against the policies of the Belgian administrator of Iran's customs. The secret political societies that organized this incident subsequently forced his father to grant a constitution and establish a parliament (the Constitutional Revolution of 1906). Mohammad Ali believed that these measures threatened authority and even rule of the shah.

In January 1907 Mohammad Ali succeeded to the throne following the sudden death of his father. From the outset he opposed the constitutionalists, who dominated the new parliament (majles) and on several occasions asked him to pledge his allegiance to the constitution. In July 1908, after months of political conflict, he authorized the Russian-officered Cossack Brigade to bombard the parliament, then dissolved it, abrogated the constitution, closed down political societies, banned newspapers that had been criticizing his rule, and imposed military government in Tehran. Pro-constitution forces immediately rallied in Tabriz, where they expelled supporters of the shah and established a temporary national parliament. Pro-constitution societies organized secretly in several cities, eventually taking control of Isfahan, Mashhad, and Rasht. Leaders of the Bakhtiari tribal confederation joined the constitutionalists in 1909 and recruited a large armed force to march north on Tehran from Isfahan. A volunteer paramilitary force that marched south from Rasht joined up with the Bakhtiari contingent outside Tehran in July 1909. Mohammad Ali Shah sought refuge in the Russian legation; he was forced to abdicate in favor of his minor son, Ahmad Shah, and depart Iran.

While in exile, Mohammad Ali gathered his supporters and resources and in 1911 returned to Iran via the Caspian Sea on a chartered Russian steamer. He captured Astarabad in Mazandaran province,

but the constitutionalists assembled their forces and defeated him in September 1911. Subsequently, he sailed away into permanent exile, settling initially in Russia, where his hopes of obtaining political support from the government of the tsar went unfulfilled. Mohammad Ali Shah died in April 1925.

See also BAKHTIARI; CONSTITUTIONAL REVOLUTION; COSSACK BRIGADE; ISFAHAN; MOZAFFAR AL-DIN QAJAR; NASER AL-DIN SHAH; TABRIZ.

Bibliography

Lambton, Ann K. S. "Persian Political Societies, 1906–1911." In *St. Antony's Papers* no. 16, *Middle Eastern Affairs* no. 3, edited by Albert Hourani. Carbondale: Southern Illinois University Press, 1963.

NEGUIN YAVARI
UPDATED BY ERIC HOOGLUND

MOHAMMADI, MAULAWI MOHAMMAD NABI
[1920–2002]

Afghan resistance leader and Muslim cleric.

Maulawi Mohammad Nabi Mohammadi was an Afghan resistance leader and Islamic scholar. He was a Gilzai Ahmadzai Pushtun from Logar province and had large landholdings in Helmand province. He was the head of a *madrasa* (Islamic school) in Logar province. In 1965, he was elected to the Afghan parliament representing the traditional *Ulama*. He strongly opposed the Marxist movement in Afghanistan and in 1978 fled to Peshawar, Pakistan, where he formed the Islamic resistance party Harakat-e Inqilab-e Islami-e Afghanistan (Movement for the Islamic Revolution of Afghanistan). His followers were among the traditional Islamic clergy and Gilzai Ahmadzai tribes in the Logar regions.

Mohammadi's religious and political beliefs resembled those of the Taliban, advocating a return to strict Islamic law and Pushtun tribal values. Mullah Omar, the leader of the Taliban, had once been a commander in Mohammadi's party. In 1994, Mohammadi aligned himself with the Taliban and largely withdrew from political life. He died at the age of eighty-one on 22 April 2002.

See also AFGHANISTAN: ISLAMIC MOVEMENTS IN; TALIBAN; *ULAMA*.

Bibliography

Ewans, Martin. *Afghanistan: A New History.* Richmond, U.K.: Curzon, 2001.

Roy, Olivier. *Islam and Resistance in Afghanistan.* New York and Cambridge, U.K.: Cambridge University Press, 1986.

GRANT FARR

MOHILEVER, SAMUEL
[1824–1898]

Rabbi, early Zionist leader.

Born in Russia, Samuel Mohilever helped to organize Jewish emigration to Palestine in the 1880s and persuaded Baron Edmond de Rothschild to support Russian families settling there. In 1882, he founded the first Hovevei Zion (also Hibbat Zion) group, in Warsaw. In 1890, he was a founder of Rehovot in Palestine. As head of Hovevei Zion in Bialystok, he helped Theodor Herzl plan the First Zionist Congress (Basel, 1897).

See also HIBBAT ZION.

Bibliography

Hertzberg, Arthur, ed. *The Zionist Idea: A Historical Analysis and Reader.* Philadelphia: Jewish Publication Society, 1997.

MARTIN MALIN

MOJADDEDI, SEBGHATULLAH
[1925–]

Afghan resistance leader; Sufi pir; Afghan president, 1992–1993.

Born in Kabul in 1927 to a family of hereditary leaders of the Naqshbandi Sufi order, Sebghatullah Mojaddedi was educated at al-Azhar University in Cairo and at Kabul University. He fled Kabul in the 1970s and headed the Islamic center in Denmark from 1974 to 1978. After the Saur Revolution (1978), he went to Peshawar, Pakistan, where he formed the National Liberation Front of Afghanistan (Jebhe-ye Nejat-e Milli) and began an armed insurgency in Afghanistan against the Marxist government. He was elected president of the Afghan Interim Government, a government in exile, in Pakistan in 1989, and after the Najibullah government fell in 1992, he returned to Kabul. When the Taliban captured Kabul in 1996, Mojaddedi returned to exile in Pakistan, although he continued to visit Kabul, where he maintained a home. With the fall of the Taliban government in 2001, Mojaddedi returned to Kabul to participate in the new government of Hamid Karzai, although he holds no official positions.

Bibliography

Roy, Olivier. *Islam and Resistance in Afghanistan.* New York and Cambridge, U.K.: Cambridge University Press, 1986.

Rubin, Barnett R. *The Fragmentation of Afghanistan: State Formation and Collapse in the International System,* 2d edition. New Haven, CT: Yale University Press, 2002.

GRANT FARR

MOJAHEDIN

Afghan Islamic resistance fighters.

The Afghan resistance groups who took up the war against the Marxist government in 1978 called themselves *mojahedin* (fighters of the holy war), a derivative from the Arabic *jihad* (holy war). By using the appellation *mojahedin,* they invoked a number of Islamic beliefs associated with the concept of jihad, particularly that a person who dies in a jihad becomes a martyr *(shahid)* whose soul goes immediately to the side of God. Fighting mostly out of Peshawar, Pakistan, Afghan mojahedin militias organized into groups that represent the sectarian and ethnic divisions of Afghanistan. Seven main parties represented Sunni Afghans; three were led by traditional and moderate clergy, and four were led by Islamist and fundamental leaders. The moderate-traditional parties were Harakat-e Inqilab-e Islami (the Islamic Revolutionary Movement), led by Maulawi Mohammad Nabi Mohammadi; Jebhe-ye Nejat-e Milli (National Liberation Front), led by Sebghatullah Mojaddedi, a Sufi pir; and Mahaz-e Islami (Islamic Front), led by Pir Sayyed Ahmad Gailani, head of the Qadiri Sufi order. The Islamist groups were Hezb-e Islami (Islamic Party), led by Golbuddin

A mojahedin patrols a village graveyard in Achin, Afganistan, 1988. AP/WIDE WORLD PHOTOS. REPRODUCED BY PERMISSION.

Hekmatyar; Hezb-e Islami, led by Mohammad Unis Khalis; Jami'at-e Islami (Islamic Society), led by Burhanuddin Rabbani; and Ittihad-e Islami (Islamic Union), led by Abd al-Rasul Sayyaf.

In addition there were a number of Shi'ite parties (Shi'a Muslims constitute between 15 and 20 percent of the Afghan population). They included Shura-ye Ittifagh-e Islami (Islamic Union), led by Sayyed Beheshti; Harakat-e Islami (Islamic Movement), led by Shaykh Mohseni; and Hezb-e Wahadat (Unity Party), an alliance of eight Shi'ite groups.

Each mojahedin party depended on followers in Afghanistan and on other governments for support. During the resistance war, the mojahedin parties with the largest following were the Jami'at-e Islami, which was the only Sunni party with non-Pakhtun leadership and thus popular in the non-Pakhtun ar-

eas of Afghanistan (especially the north and west), and the Hezb-e Islami, led by Hekmatyar, which had the support of the Pakistani military and therefore received a lion's share of the weapons and arms. When the Marxist government of Najibullah fell in 1992, the mojahedin parties returned to Kabul to form a government, which was generally referred to as the mojahedin government. Their attempt at unity failed and they began fighting among themselves. As a result, much of Kabul was destroyed in the fighting, and in 1996 the Taliban captured Kabul. Several of the mojahedin parties, especially Jami'at-e Islami and Hezb-e Wahadat, retreated to the north of Afghanistan to fight against the Taliban. With the arrival of the Karzai interim government in 2001 many of the original mojahedin parties returned to Kabul to take part in the new government.

See also GAILANI, AHMAD; HEKMATYAR, GOL-BUDDIN; HEZB-E ISLAMI; JAMIʿAT-E ISLAMI; KHALIS, MOHAMMAD UNIS; MOHAMMADI, MAULAWI MOHAMMAD NABI; MOJADDEDI, SEBGHATULLAH; RABBANI, BURHANUDDIN; SUNNI ISLAM.

Bibliography

Farr, Grant. "The Failure of the Mujahedin." *Middle East International* 476 (1994): 19–20.

Roy, Olivier. *Islam and Resistance in Afghanistan.* Cambridge, U.K.: Cambridge University Press, 1986.

Rubin, Barnett. *The Fragmentation of Afghanistan.* New Haven, CT: Yale University Press, 2002.

GRANT FARR

MOJAHEDIN-E KHALQ

The main armed force challenging the Islamic Republic of Iran.

The Mojahedin (or the Sazman-e Mojahedin-e Khalq-e Iran; Holy Warrior Organization of the Iranian People) was formed in the mid-1960s by Tehran University students who tried to synthesize Islam with Marxism, interpreting the former to be the divine message of revolution and the latter to be the main analytical tool for understanding society, history, and politics. While influenced by these features of Marxism, they rejected the philosophy of dialectical materialism. They also adopted the strategy of guerrilla warfare from Che Guevara, the Vietminh, and Algeria's Front de Libération Nationale (National Liberation Front, FLN). Some of their founding leaders received guerrilla training from the Palestine Liberation Organization (PLO).

From 1971 until 1979, the Mojahedin tried to destabilize the regime of Mohammad Reza Pahlavi with a series of assassinations, bank robberies, and daring armed assaults. In the process, more than eighty of their members lost their lives. Most of these were engineers, teachers, and university students. The group was further weakened by factional infighting. In 1975, one faction denounced Islam as a "conservative petty bourgeois ideology" and declared itself a pure Marxist-Leninist organization. This faction later became known as the Paykar (Combat) organization. By the time of the Iranian Revolution of 1979, little remained of the Moja-hedin, and the surviving members had been imprisoned.

Despite this, the Mojahedin regrouped during the revolution and quickly grew to become a major threat to the Islamic Republic of Iran. Maʿsud Rajavi, one of the few survivors from the 1960s, took over the leadership. The Mojahedin grew rapidly in part because of its mystique of revolutionary martyrdom; in part because of its adherence to Shiʿism; in part because of its social radicalism; and in part because of its anticlericalism and opposition to the theocracy of the Ayatollah Ruhollah Khomeini. By 1981, its publication, *Mojahed,* was one of the country's most widely read newspapers; its parliamentary candidates were winning a substantial number of votes; and its rallies were drawing hundreds of thousands. The regime reacted by ordering a major crackdown. The Mojahedin, in turn, retaliated by launching an assassination campaign against the top figures of the Islamic republic.

In the aftermath of the 1981 crackdown, the Mojahedin moved its leadership abroad, created an umbrella organization named the National Council of Resistance, and, with an army of some 9,000, waged an armed struggle, based in Iraq, against the regime. By the end of the decade, however, the Mojahedin was a mere shadow of its former self. Its overt alliance with Iraq during the eight-year Iran-Iraq War (1980–1988) undermined its nationalistic credibility. Its stress on martyrdom had little appeal to the postrevolutionary generation of youth in Iran. Its own ranks within the country were decimated by executions and mass arrests. Moreover, its tactics and alliance with Saddam Hussein prompted both the United States and the European Union to categorize it as a "terrorist organization." What is more, the U.S. occupation of Iraq in 2003 eliminated the Mojahedin's main patron and placed the entire organization at the mercy of the United States. The Mojahedin hope to salvage something out of this disaster by persuading the United States that they can be a useful tool against the Islamic Republic.

See also IRANIAN REVOLUTION (1979); IRAN–IRAQ WAR (1980–1988).

Bibliography

Abrahamian, Ervand. *The Iranian Mojahedin.* New Haven, CT: Yale University Press, 1989.

Irfani, Suroosh. *Revolutionary Islam in Iran: Popular Liberation or Religious Dictatorship?* London: Zed Books, 1983.

ERVAND ABRAHAMIAN

MOJTAHED-SHABESTARI, MOHAMMAD
[1936–]

Influential intellectual among Iran's theologians.

Mohammad Mojtahed-Shabestari was born in Shabestar, which is a rural district near Tabriz in Azerbaijan, Iran. He received a traditional seminary education in Qom, where he lived from 1950 to 1968. From 1970 until the Iranian Revolution of 1979, he was the director of the Islamic Center in Hamburg, West Germany. He is fluent in German and well-versed in German theological and philosophical traditions of scholarship. During his eighteen years of residence in Qom, Mojtahed-Shabestari served on the editorial board of the *Maktab Islam*, a Shiʿite journal that addressed many of the social and political issue of the 1960s and 1970s in Iran. After the 1979 revolution, he published a journal called *Andish-e Islami* in Tehran. He was elected to the first Islamic Consultative Assembly, but since then he has devoted most of his time to teaching and writing as a professor of theology at Tehran University.

Mojtahed Shabestari's thought, especially since the establishment of the Islamic Republic, has evolved to address the question of modernity and Islam in his native land. He has attempted to demonstrate the compatibility of human agency and human empowerment, and the notion of Divine Sovereignty. He also has recognized, albeit implicitly, the individual as the carrier of human agency. In turn, these two principles in his thought have allowed him to posit certain modern precepts such as the freedom of consciousness, which, according to him, constitutes the foundation of other types of freedoms and lays the grounding of civil rights. Thus, Mojtahed-Shabestari's discourse can be a source of inspiration for defying the notion of *velayat-e faqih* (guardianship of the jurisprudent), although he has avoided a frontal attack on this notion.

See also VELAYAT-E FAQIH.

Bibliography

Boroujerdi, Mehrzad. *Iranian Intellectuals and the West: The Tormented Triumph of Nativism.* Syracuse, NY: Syracuse University Press, 1996.

Vahdat, Farzin. "Post-revolutionary Discourses of Mohammad Mojtahed Shabestari and Mohsen Kadivar: Reconciling the Terms of Mediated Subjectivity. Part I: Mojtahed Shabestari." *Critique: Journal for Critical Studies of the Middle East,* no. 16 (spring 2000).

FARZIN VAHDAT

MOLLA

See GLOSSARY

MOLLET, GUY
[1905–1975]

French socialist and statesman.

Head of the French Socialist party (1946–1969) and premier of France (February 1956–May 1957), Guy Alcide Mollet sought an end to the civil war in Algeria (the Algerian War of Independence, 1954–1962). In October 1956, he allowed the French military to hijack a plane carrying several Front de Libération Nationale (FLN) leaders, including Ahmad Ben Bella. Convinced that Egypt's President Nasser was aiding the FLN, Mollet authorized French participation in the Suez invasion of October-November 1956.

See also ALGERIAN WAR OF INDEPENDENCE.

Bibliography

Horne, Alistair. *A Savage War of Peace: Algeria, 1954–1962,* 2d edition. New York: Penguin, 1987.

ZACHARY KARABELL

MOLTKE, HELMUTH VON
[1800–1891]

Prussian military officer

As a young lieutenant, in the 1830s Helmuth von Moltke was sent to Turkey to help train the army of the Ottoman Empire. At the battle of Nezib (1839), the Ottoman commander rejected his advice, and the Ottoman forces were then routed by the Egyptian army of Ibrahim Pasha. From 1858 to 1888, von Moltke was chief of the General Staff in Berlin.

Bibliography

Shaw, Stanford J., and Shaw, Ezel Kural. *History of the Ottoman Empire and Modern Turkey.* 2 vols. Cambridge,

U.K., and New York: Cambridge University Press, 1976–1977.

ZACHARY KARABELL

MONASTIR

Seaport on the northeastern coast of Tunisia; center of the governorate of the same name.

Probably a Punic port before Islam, Monastir became the site of a well-known Arab Islamic *ribat* (fortified religious center), founded by the Muslim commander Harthama ibn A'yan in 796. The fortress, enlarged over the centuries, is today an important tourist site. To bolster the tourist trade, a large hotel and commercial complex was begun in the late 1980s.

Never a political center, it was a religious hub for several centuries in the medieval Islamic period. Two mosques of architectural importance were built at the turn of the eleventh century. Monastir was the hometown of Tunisia's President Habib Bourguiba. Under his government, an international airport was built in Monastir, used primarily for the tourist trade. In 2002, its population was estimated at 67,730.

Bibliography

Tunisia: A Country Survey. Washington, DC, 1988.

MATTHEW S. GORDON

MOND, ALFRED MORITZ
[1868–1930]

British industrialist and politician.

Son of a prominent German-Jewish industrialist, the Baron Alfred Moritz Mond was a Liberal member of Parliament (1906–1928). In 1926, he was one of the founders of ICI (Imperial Chemical Industry). An ardent promoter of Zionism, he visited Palestine in 1921 and contributed an estimated 100,000 British pounds to the Jewish Colonization Corporation.

ZACHARY KARABELL

MONTAZERI, HOSAYN ALI
[1920–]

Iranian religious scholar and political activist.

Born to a peasant family in Najafabad, central Iran, Hosayn Ali Montazeri began his formal religious studies at Isfahan at the age of fifteen, moving in his early twenties to Qom to benefit from the scholars teaching there. In 1944 he joined the circle of Ayatollah Hosayn Borujerdi, the principal religious leader of the time, and before long began assisting him in his classes on Shi'ite jurisprudence. Also in Qom, Montazeri became a close associate of Ruhollah Khomeini, whose views he shared. Among the most active of Khomeini's associates in the uprising of June 1963, Montazeri was detained in its aftermath. He was rearrested several times in the following years, most notably in 1975 when he was sentenced to ten years' imprisonment (cut short in October 1978), and he was banished several times to various remote parts of Iran.

After the success of the 1979 Iranian Revolution and the establishment of the Islamic republic, Montazeri held several important posts. He was a member of the council for reviewing the draft constitution, a consultant on the appointment of revolutionary judges, an adviser on land reform, and a leader of the Friday prayers, first in Tehran and then in Qom. His eminence among the associates of Khomeini was confirmed by his selection (in December 1983) as successor-designate to Khomeini as the paramount political-religious authority in the system of government based on *velayat-e faqih*. However, a letter from Montazeri to Khomeini in which Montazeri criticized the shortcomings of the revolutionary order led to his forced resignation as successor-designate in March 1989. Montazeri then retired to Qom, where he taught Islamic jurisprudence until 1997. An open letter in which he questioned the religious qualifications of Ali Khamenehi as a *faqih* led to his house arrest in November 1997 and to a ban on his teaching. The house arrest was politically controversial and finally lifted in January 2003; the following September, he was allowed to resume teaching theology, even though he continued to criticize the government, especially the judiciary, as un-Islamic.

See also BORUJERDI, HOSAYN; IRANIAN REVOLUTION (1979); KHAMENEHI, ALI; KHOMEINI, RUHOLLAH; QOM; VELAYAT-E FAQIH.

Bibliography

Akhavi, Shahrough. "Clerical Politics in Iran Since 1979." In *The Iranian Revolution and the Islamic Republic,* new edition, edited by Nikki R. Keddie and Eric Hooglund. Syracuse, NY: Syracuse University Press, 1986.

Moslem, Mehdi. *Factional Politics in Post-Khomeini Iran.* Syracuse, NY: Syracuse University Press, 2002.

HAMID ALGAR
UPDATED BY ERIC HOOGLUND

MONTEFIORE, MOSES
[1784–1885]

Philanthropist and Zionist.

Born in Italy, Sir Moses Haim Montefiore made a fortune in stockbroking in London and retired in 1824. He devoted the remainder of his life to Jewish philanthropy and the cause of Zionism. Between 1827 and 1875, he made numerous trips to Palestine to aid the Jewish community there, and in 1839 he developed a program to improve Palestine's agricultural and industrial output and sought to obtain autonomy for the Jewish community. Among his many philanthropic activities, he endowed a hospital and a school for girls in Jerusalem in 1855 and purchased land outside of the walled city. Montefiore was also involved with the plight of the Moroccan Jews, whose situation seriously deteriorated after expeditions by France to Morocco in the 1840s. At the urging of the Rothschilds, Montefiore went to Morocco in 1864 and met with Sultan Mulay Sidi Muhammad, who issued an edict easing restrictions and forbidding hostile acts against the Moroccan Jews. Montefiore traveled throughout the Mediterranean Muslim world and was treated as an important dignitary wherever he went.

Bibliography

Halpern, Ben. *The Idea of the Jewish State,* 2d edition. Cambridge, MA: Harvard University Press, 1969.

Patai, Raphael. *The Seed of Abraham: Jews and Arabs in Contact and Conflict.* New York: Scribner, 1987.

ZACHARY KARABELL

MONTGOMERY, BERNARD LAW
[1887–1976]

British soldier.

A Sandhurst graduate, Bernard Law Montgomery (first viscount of Alamein) became commander of the Eighth Army in North Africa in August 1942, after General Sir Claude Auchinleck had checked German General Erwin Rommel at the first Battle of al-Alamayn (also El Alameih). On Prime Minister Winston Churchill's urging, Montgomery attacked in late October and won a decisive victory at the second Battle of al-Alamayn, leading to a full-scale retreat of Rommel's forces. Montgomery was later commander in chief of the ground forces during the Normandy invasion.

Bibliography

Barnett, Correlli. *The Desert Generals,* 2d edition. Bloomington: Indiana University Press, 1982.

ZACHARY KARABELL

MONTREUX CONVENTION (1936)

Agreement of 1936 giving Turkey sovereignty over the Turkish Straits.

Under the Treaty of Lausanne (1923), the Turkish Straits (the Dardanelles, the Sea of Marmara, and the Bosporus) were demilitarized and placed under international control. This settlement infringed on Turkish sovereignty, and after repeated demands by Turkey to reform the relevant clauses of the Lausanne agreement, the Montreux Convention was signed on 20 July 1936. Under the terms of the convention, sovereignty of the Straits reverted to Turkey, and the Turks were permitted to remilitarize the Straits as they saw fit. Furthermore, passage of the Straits in times of war was to be restricted to non-belligerents. All of the Lausanne powers endorsed the convention, with the exception of Italy and the addition of the USSR. Britain was represented by Foreign Secretary Anthony Eden. Alarmed by the growing power of Nazi Germany, Eden and the other European signatories felt it expedient to mollify Turkey.

Bibliography

Lenczowski, George. *The Middle East in World Affairs,* 4th edition. Ithaca, NY: Cornell University Press, 1980.

Shimoni, Yaacov, and Levine, Evyatar, eds. *Political Dictionary of the Middle East in the Twentieth Century,* revised edition. New York: Quadrangle/New York Times, 1974.

ZACHARY KARABELL

MOPSY PARTY

See ISRAEL: POLITICAL PARTIES IN

MOROCCAN–ALGERIAN WAR

Conflict in October and early November 1963 along the northern frontier between the two countries.

The causes of the Moroccan-Algerian War were rooted in colonialism, decolonization, and nationalism. Morocco considered the border established by colonialists artificial. During the Algerian War of Independence (1954–1962), the Provisional Government of the Algerian republic (Gouvernement Provisional de la République Algérienne; GPRA) agreed in July 1961 to address the frontier question after the liberation struggle. Ahmed Ben Bella further put off this issue as he attempted to secure power in 1962–1963. A revolt in Kabylia in late September 1963 offered Morocco an opportunity to seize the contested land. This resulted in a brief conflict, with Algeria receiving the heavier blows (60 dead and 250 wounded according to the French newspaper *Le monde*). Mediation by the Organization of African Unity (OAU) produced a cease-fire in early November. In 1972 Morocco and Algeria signed conventions that delineated the frontier and agreed to the common exploitation of natural resources. Algeria ratified the agreements, but Morocco did not and subsequently engaged in its Western Sahara expansion (beginning with the Green March in 1975). The Western Sahara War included a brief engagement between Moroccan and Algerian troops in 1976. In the late 1980s, bilateral relations improved as demonstrated by Morocco's ratification of the 1972 conventions, the full restoration of diplomatic relations (1988), and the formation of the Arab Maghrib Union (1989).

See also GREEN MARCH; WESTERN SAHARA WAR.

Bibliography

Heggoy, Alf A. "Colonial Origins of the Algerian–Moroccan Border Conflict of October 1963." *African Studies Review* 13, no. 1 (April 1970): 17–21.

Hodges, Tony. *Western Sahara: The Roots of a Desert War.* Westport, CT: L. Hill, 1983.

PHILLIP C. NAYLOR

MOROCCAN FAMILY LEGAL CODE

See MOUDAWANA, AL-

MOROCCAN QUESTION

Name given to the final phase of European imperialist rivalries over Morocco, 1900–1912.

Morocco owed its continued independence into the twentieth century to its rugged topography and combative rural populations, as well as the ability of Moroccan diplomats to play off the European powers against one another. In 1900 the diplomatic stalemate was broken when France annexed territories claimed by Morocco.

Each of the chief European rivals for Morocco—France, Britain, Spain, Germany, and Italy—cited reasons why its claims on Morocco should be recognized. Each cited historic and material interests, as well as nationalist ones, in justification. None took any cognizance of Moroccan wishes in the matter.

Between 1900 and 1904, French Foreign Minister Théophile Delcassé persuaded Spain, Italy, and Britain to renounce claims to Morocco by a series of bilateral agreements. Germany was not consulted and sought to compel France to grant it comparable territories elsewhere, which it did in 1911. By the 1912 Treaty of FES, an independent Morocco ceased to exist. The Moroccan Question is generally portrayed as a chapter in the diplomatic history of Europe. But Moroccans also played a major role in both its unfolding and its ultimate resolution. Sultans Abd al-Aziz (1884–1908) and Abd al-Hafid (1908–1912) opposed French ambitions, but ended up acquiescing to the inevitable. Moroccan official pusillanimity and European troop landings between 1902 and 1912 were opposed by various popular rebellions, peasant revolts, and millenarian movements.

Bibliography

Andrew, Christopher. "The Entente Cordiale from Its Origins to the First World War." In *Troubled Neighbours: Franco–British Relations in the Twentieth Century,* edited by Neville Waites. London: Weidenfeld, 1971.

Burke, Edmund, III. *Prelude to Protectorate in Morocco: Precolonial Protest and Resistance, 1860–1912.* Chicago: University of Chicago Press, 1976.

EDMUND BURKE III

MOROCCO

This entry consists of the following articles:

MOROCCO: OVERVIEW

Arab kingdom in the extreme northwest corner of Africa.

Morocco is bounded on the west by the Atlantic Ocean, on the north by the Mediterranean Sea, on the east and southeast by Algeria, and on the south by Western Sahara (claimed by Morocco). Spain administers two urban enclaves in northern Morocco—Ceuta and Melilla—and the offshore islands of Alhucemas, Penon de Velez de la Gomera, and Chafarinas. Most of Morocco was a protectorate of France from 1912 until 1956; northern Morocco was administered by Spain during that period. An 1860 war between Spain and Morocco established Spain's claim to Ifni, a small strip of land on the Atlantic coast of southern Morocco. The district of Tarfaya, near Western Sahara, became Spanish with the 1912 Treaty of Fes. Spain ceded Tarfaya to Morocco in 1958 and returned Ifni in 1969. Muhammad VI has ruled Morocco since 1999.

Geography and Climate

Morocco has an area of 178,620 square miles (446,550 sq km). It is dominated by the Atlas Mountains, which run through the center of the country from southwest to northeast, and the Sahara Desert, which dominates its frontier with Algeria, Western Sahara, and Mauritania. The Atlas chain comprises the High, Middle, and Saharan ranges, as well as the Rif Mountains along Morocco's Mediterranean coast. The northern Atlantic coastal plains of the Gharb constitute the chief agricultural area. Others include the Tadla plain of the Oum al-Rbi'a (Mother of spring) River south of Casablanca, the Haouz plain of the Tensift River near Marrakech, and the Sous River valley in southwestern Morocco. These rivers, navigable only by small boats, provide water for irrigation. The Mediterranean and Atlantic coasts have relatively moist, mild winter, and hot, dry summers. Eastern and southern Morocco have semiarid climates governed by the Sahara's heat and winds. Higher elevations of the Atlas Mountains, particularly the High Atlas between Marrakech and Ouarzazate, can be bitterly cold, and remain snow-covered year round. Morocco's highest peak, Mount Tubkal, is easily accessible from Marrakech and is a popular skiing area.

People, Language, and Religion

Morocco has 26 million people according to the last available census (1994), but later estimates place the population at about 30 million. About 55 percent of Moroccans live in urban areas, primarily in Casablanca (2,941,000), Rabat (1,386,000; the nation's capital), and Fez (775,000). Other major towns include Marrakech (746,000), Oujda (679,000), Agadir (550,000) Meknes (530,000), Tangiers (526,000), Kenitra (449,000), Beni-Mellal (387,000) and Safi (376,000). The population growth rate is 1.9 percent. Nearly 48 percent of the population is under twenty-one. Life expectancy for males is sixty-six; for females, seventy. Morocco's illiteracy rates are among the highest in North Africa: 34.4 percent for men and 62.8 percent for women. Most Moroccans are engaged in agriculture and fisheries, but an increasingly large number are in tourism, the liberal professions, commerce, industry, and government.

Morocco's ethnic groups are Arabs, mixed Arab Berbers who identify as Arabs, and Berbers. "Berber," primarily a linguistic term, applies to about 35 percent of the population. The three primary Berber dialects are Tarrifit (spoken in the Rif), Tamazight (spoken in the Middle Atlas and the east), and Tachelhit (also called Chleuh, spoken in the High Atlas and the south). The Moroccan constitution does not recognize any of these dialects.

Morocco's national language is Arabic, but French is widespread in the media, commerce, education, diplomacy, and most government ministries. Moroccan Arabic differs from the Arabic of Algeria. It is characterized by an intense clipping of vowels and some vocabulary that is not understood outside of Morocco. Many Moroccans have a rudimentary understanding of the Egyptian dialect because films and television shows produced in Egypt are widely popular.

Islam is the state religion. Progovernment imams are appointed to all mosques under the direction of

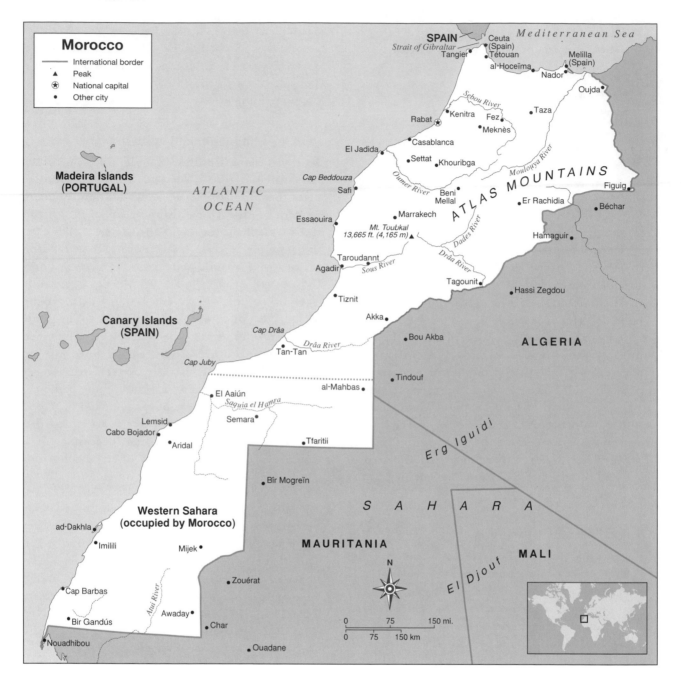

Morocco

International border
▲ Peak
⊛ National capital
• Other city

SPAIN
Strait of Gibraltar
Ceuta (Spain)
Tangier
Tétouan
al-Hoceïma
Melilla (Spain)
Nador
Oujda
Mediterranean Sea

Madeira Islands (PORTUGAL)

ATLANTIC OCEAN

Sebou River
Rabat ⊛
Kenitra
Fez
Taza
Meknès
Casablanca
El Jadida
Settat
Khouribga
Cap Beddouza
Safi
Beni Mellal
Oumer River
Moulouya River
Figuig
Er Rachidia
Béchar
ATLAS MOUNTAINS
Essaouira
Marrakech
Mt. Toubkal 13,665 ft. (4,165 m) ▲
Dades River
Hamaguir
Taroudannt
Agadir
Sous River
Drâa River
Tagounit
Tiznit
Hassi Zegdou
Akka

Canary Islands (SPAIN)

Cap Drâa
Tan-Tan
Drâa River
Bou Akba
ALGERIA
Cap Juby
Tindouf
al-Mahbas
El Aaiún
Saquia el Hamra
Lemsid
Semara
Cabo Bojador
Aridal
Tfaritii
Erg Iguidi

Bîr Mogreïn
SAHARA

Western Sahara (occupied by Morocco)
ad-Dakhla
Imilili
Mijek
MAURITANIA
MALI
El Djouf

Cap Barbas
Zouérat
Atui River
Bir Gandús
Awaday
Char
Nouadhibou
Ouadane

N

0   75   150 mi.
0   75   150 km

MAP BY XNR PRODUCTIONS, INC. THE GALE GROUP.

the ministry of religion. Important mosques, such as the Qarawiyin in Fez and the Kutubiyya in Marrakech, receive substantial endowments from the state. Most Moroccans profess Sunni Islam. A small Jewish community (estimates vary from 5,000 to 20,000) exists in Morocco and enjoys religious freedom and civil liberties. Following historical precedents, the monarch continues to include Jews within his circle of personal advisors. King Muhammad VI, as the symbol of Moroccan Islam, maintains the title *Amir al-Mu'minin* (Commander of the Faithful). He endeavors to buttress his religious legitimacy through ostensible piety, simplicity, and generosity. Closer to the masses than his father was, Muhammad VI is often referred to as the "king of the poor." His donations as well as his publicized visits to hospitals and crowded medinas have had a strong impact on the Moroccan population.

Islamism generally appears to be a growing force in Morocco. The Party of Justice and Development (PJD), a political party of Islamist base that gained legal status in 1997, is currently the third most powerful in the Chamber of Representatives. The most popular Islamic movement of the country—though still considered illegal—is al-Adl wa al-Ihsan (Justice and Benevolence). Its leader, Abdessalam Yacine, spent eleven years under house arrest until King Muhammad VI freed him in 2000. Events in the first years of the twenty-first century revealed the existence of Islamist armed groups in Morocco and their possible link to transnational Islamism. The terrorist attacks that killed forty-four people in Casablanca in May 2003 were attributed to al-Sirat al-Mustaqim (the Straight Path), a small Islamist group suspected of being loosely connected to al-Qaʿida.

Economy

Since 1992 Morocco has been dealing with recurrent droughts that have deeply affected the agricultural industry and, ultimately, the country's overall economic performance. About 40 percent of the labor force is engaged in agriculture (especially citrus and cereals), fishing, and raising livestock. These sectors of the economy contribute over 15 percent of gross domestic product. The decreasing fish stock in the Atlantic Ocean has led to diplomatic tensions with Spain and the European Union regarding the renewal of licenses to fish in Moroccan waters. Manufacturing is geared to phosphate production, but higher fuel costs have sparked inflation, and phosphate price declines have reduced export earnings. Tourism has been steadily growing since the 1980s and has become an important source of jobs and hard currency. Emigration is Morocco's safety valve for its unemployed population. About half a million to one million Moroccans reside in Europe as expatriate workers; their remittances are an important source of foreign exchange for Morocco. Among the country's most pressing economic problems are urban unemployment (which reached 20.2 percent in 2001) and the increasing foreign debt, which amounts to nearly eighteen billion dollars. In 1995 the privatization program supported by the International Monetary Fund (IMF) and the World Bank was extended to key state firms such as the Office Chérifien des

Phosphates and Royal Air Maroc. These privatizations were intended to attract foreign investment and to cover budget deficits. Yet the results are not fully satisfactory to the IMF because the Moroccan government maintains its expensive program of food subsidy.

History

Between 4,000 and 2,000 B.C.E., Berber peoples arrived from the Sahara and Southwest Asia. Most lowland Berber peoples eventually Arabized and Islamized. Beginning in the twelfth century B.C.E., Phoenicians began to explore the North African coastline. Their early coastal enclaves have been found in northern Morocco. By the late first century B.C.E., Rome's power had reached northern Morocco, and by the middle of the first century C.E., Morocco was the province of Mauretania Tingitana. The Vandals moved into North Africa in the 420s and ended Rome's presence. The Arabs' invasion of the late seventh and early eighth centuries transformed Morocco into an Islamic society with a powerful Arabic-speaking ruling class. Ruling dynasties were the Idrisids of Fez (early ninth century), the Almoravids and the Almohads of Marrakech (eleventh to thirteenth centuries), the Saʿadis (sixteenth century), and the Alawite dynasty (seventeenth century to the present).

Throughout the nineteenth century, Morocco integrated into the capitalist world economy on mostly unfavorable terms. The country also became the object of diplomatic rivalries among European powers. Britain pressured the sultans to open Morocco to commerce and free trade but preferred to keep a weak sultanate south of the Strait of Gibraltar. Military and administrative reforms failed to reinforce Morocco's position vis-à-vis European countries. Defeated by the Spanish armies in 1860 after a border conflict, Sultan Muhammad IV (r. 1859–1873) signed treaties that led his country to bankruptcy, financial subservience to Europe, and increasing foreign occupation.

France secured its preponderance in Morocco between 1900 and 1904 through various bilateral agreements with Italy, Spain, and Britain. Most of Morocco became a French unofficial protectorate until indigenous protests provided Paris with a

In the fourteenth century, the Marinid dynasty began construction of the Chella fortifications within the city of Rabat. The complex contains a mosque, zawiya (religious quarters), and numerous royal tombs. © ROBERT HOLMES/CORBIS. REPRODUCED BY PERMISSION.

pretext for further intervention. The 1912 Treaty of Fes officially divided Morocco into a protectorate under France over most of the country and a protectorate under Spain over the north, including the Rif Mountains. The country, however, was not yet conquered. Once the protectorates were established, the military forces of Spain and France became preoccupied with suppressing rebellion primarily among the highland Berbers of the Rif and the Atlas mountains. The troops of France began a long and systematic campaign of subjugating Atlas Berber rebels. Spanish troops, with assistance from France, finally broke the Rif rebellion of Abd al-Karim in the late 1920s and consolidated Spain's rule from the capital of Spanish Morocco at Tetuan. France's painstaking campaign, named "pacification," ended in 1934.

Moroccan nationalism gained momentum when both religious reformists and Westernized elites united to oppose the Berber *dahir* (decree) of 1930.

This divide-and-rule legislation intended to marginalize Berber Muslims by placing them under the jurisdiction of French rather than Islamic law. The nationalists founded the Istiqlal Party in 1944 and began asking for formal independence. Sultan Muhammad V tacitly supported their efforts, and as a result was exiled from 1953 to 1955. Morocco gained its independence in 1956, and the following year Muhammad V changed the Sultanate of Morocco to the Kingdom of Morocco. In the nationalist fervor that accompanied the first few years of independence, the king was able to push through a law making a one-party state illegal. This enabled the monarchy to break the power of Istiqlal by encouraging leftist elements to splinter off and create the National Union of Popular Forces (UNFP). The monarchy supported the fractionalization of political parties and the emergence of new ones in order to split the opposition. When Muhammad V died in 1961, Hassan II became king. Opposition to his personal rule and to the corruption within the

Morocco's port city of Tangiers is a popular tourist destination, due partly to its close proximity to Europe. The sunny city, with its large port, has always been an important commercial and strategic site. © PATRICK WARD/CORBIS. REPRODUCED BY PERMISSION.

system peaked in 1971 and 1972 with two failed coup attempts, one by army cadets and a second by air force personnel.

King Hassan's resolve to recover Western Sahara—a project that also aimed at bolstering his own position—led to a crisis with Spain when he ordered a Green March of 300,000 Moroccans in October 1975. His strategy bore almost immediate fruit, for in November Spain negotiated a withdrawal of its forces and the reversion of the area to Morocco and Mauritania. In February 1976 Morocco received the northern two-thirds and Mauritania gained the southern third.

In the meantime, indigenous inhabitants of Western Sahara (who call themselves Sahrawis, "Saharans") had undertaken a war of national liberation from Spain, establishing the Popular Front for the Liberation of Saqiya al-Hamra and Rio de Oro (POLISARIO), with a national government in ex-

ile (Saharan Arab Democratic Republic; SADR) in Algeria. As Morocco's forces replaced those of Spain in 1976, POLISARIO irregulars began a guerrilla war against Morocco that lasted until 1991. The long-delayed referendum on Saharan self-determination has still not taken place because of discrepancies concerning voter identification.

From 1992 onward, Hassan II embarked on a series of political reforms that gave opposition parties (including the Islamists) more participation in the government. After the legislative elections of 1997, the king invited the leader of the Socialist Union of Popular Forces (USFP), Abderrahmane Youssoufi, to become prime minister. The accession of Muhammad VI to the throne in July 1999 occurred peacefully. Although he continued to enforce the centrality and the inviolability of kingship, Muhammad VI furthered the political reforms. He removed several of his father's clients from office and freed more political prisoners.

Bibliography

Bourqia, Rahma, and Miller, Susan Gilson, eds. *In the Shadow of the Sultan: Culture, Power and Politics in Morocco.* Cambridge, MA: Harvard University Press, 1999.

Damis, John. *Conflict in Northwest Africa: The Western Sahara Dispute.* Stanford, CA: Hoover Institution Press, 1983.

Oussaid, Brick. *Mountains Forgotten by God: The Story of a Moroccan Berber Family,* translated by Ann E. Woollcombe. Washington, DC: Three Continents Press, 1989.

Pennell, C. Richard. *Morocco since 1830: A History.* New York: New York University Press, 2000.

Shahin, Emad Eldin. *Political Ascent: Contemporary Islamic Movements in North Africa.* Boulder, CO: Westview, 1997.

Spencer, William. *Historical Dictionary of Morocco.* Metuchen, NJ: Scarecrow Press, 1980.

Zartman, I. William, and Habeeb, William Mark, eds. *Polity and Society in Contemporary North Africa.* Boulder, CO: Westview, 1993.

LARRY A. BARRIE
UPDATED BY HENRI LAUZIÈRE

MOROCCO: CONSTITUTION

A series of constitutions, drafted in 1962, 1970, 1972, 1992, and 1996, that preserve the monarchical nature of the Moroccan regime.

The constitutional history of independent Morocco originated in a tug-of-war between the increasingly strong monarch and a heterogeneous group of nationalists. From 1956 onward, the once-united nationalists began to voice divergent views regarding the expected nature of the independent Moroccan polity. Amid their rivalries, King Muhammad V consolidated the monarchy and gradually reduced the hopes for parliamentary democracy. In return, he promised a written constitution and in 1960 appointed a constituent council to carry out this task. The first Moroccan constitution, however, did not originate from this body. King Hassan II, who succeeded his father in 1961, bypassed the council and asked French constitutional jurists to draft the constitution. Boycotted by the Union Nationale des Forces Populaires (UNFP), the first constitution was adopted by a majority of 97.86 percent in a national referendum in 1962. The secretive and unilateral origins of this document still constitute a thorny issue in Moroccan politics. The core of the 1962 constitution has remained unadulterated. The provisions concerning the monarchical nature of the regime and the basic prerogatives of the king have been carried over to the constitutions of 1970, 1972, 1992, and 1996. Therefore, legal analysts refer to these dates interchangeably as either the promulgation of new constitutions or mere constitutional revisions.

The constitution of 1962 was modeled after the French constitution of 1958 but granted even greater powers to the head of state. The document instituted hereditary monarchy (art. 20) and specified that the nature of the state could not be subject to constitutional revision (art. 108). The king was acknowledged as "commander of the faithful" (*amir al-mu'minin*) while his person was declared sacred and inviolable (art. 23). Among other prerogatives, the monarch gained the power to nominate and dismiss the prime minister and the ministers. The king also obtained the right to declare a state of emergency through the famous article 35, which he used in 1965 to dismiss representative institutions. Indeed, the constitution had created a bicameral parliament consisting of a chamber of representatives (two-thirds of which were directly elected) and a senatelike chamber of councillors nominated through electoral colleges. Theoretically, this parliament was relatively strong insofar as both chambers were to be consulted prior to the implementation of any royal legislative decree (art. 72). Yet the king had the capacity to dissolve the chamber of representatives (art. 27) and thus to paralyze the parliament. Hassan II held the upper hand at all levels.

The second constitution of 1970 was promulgated after a long hiatus of five years during which the king enforced a state of emergency. Repeatedly confronted by student strikes and protests, Hassan II attempted to solve the crisis by reviving the constitutional legitimacy of the kingdom. The new constitution was an authoritarian compromise. The bicameral system was abandoned and replaced by the creation of a single chamber of representatives whose composition was left unspecified (art. 43). In reality, only one-third of this new chamber would be directly elected by universal suffrage. Because the new constitution no longer specified a deadline for the establishment of the chamber, the elections could be postponed indefinitely. The reduced parliament was less powerful. Hassan II no longer needed to obtain the approbation of the chamber before issuing royal legislative decrees. He also became the sole person (art. 97) capable of initiating constitutional revisions—a privilege he had previously shared with the prime minister and the parliament.

After the attempted coup of 1971, however, it seemed unwise for the regime to base its legitimacy on constitutional monarchism while significantly undermining the role of the government and the chamber. To correct this flaw, a third constitution was submitted in 1972. It was less authoritarian than the second one, though less generous than the first one. The 1972 constitution granted more legislative powers to the chamber and the prime minister in the economic, social, and cultural realms. Also, the council of ministers was to be consulted on key issues such as a declaration of war, a declaration of the state of emergency, or a project of constitutional revision (art. 65). In principle, the new constitution allowed for more participatory democracy. Two-thirds of the chamber would be elected by universal suffrage (art. 43), as it was in 1962. Yet the elections expected for 1972 were delayed until 1976.

Besides two amendments voted in 1980 with respect to the regency council and the postponement of the elections, there was no major constitutional change until the early 1990s. Subject to increasing criticism from both Moroccan politicians and European human-rights activists, the king undertook a process of political liberalization. The fourth constitution of 1992 acquiesced to some of the opposition's demands. The preamble, for instance, addressed the kingdom's commitment to human rights. A constitutional council was created (title VI) to supervise the constitutionality of Moroccan politics and elections. In addition, both the king and the chamber were allowed to create temporary courts of inquiry (art. 40). The new constitution balanced the relationship between the government and the assembly. The prime minister obtained the right to nominate ministers, and the chamber gained the power to debate and vote the government's platform.

Morocco's last constitution was adopted by referendum in 1996. Hassan II, whose health was de-

clining, wished to hasten the process of political reform. New compromises were intended to convince the opposition parties (mainly the USFP and the Istiqlal) to participate in government. Thus the 1996 constitution reinstated the bicameral system of 1962 but changed the system of representation. All of the members of the chamber of representatives must now be elected by direct universal suffrage. The revived chamber of councillors is modeled after the German system of *länders*, its members, who are still indirectly elected, are supposed to represent the various regions of Morocco and the most important socioeconomic groups. Even though the king did not relinquish his key prerogatives (he can still dissolve both chambers separately), some new constitutional clauses are meant to reinvigorate parliamentary democracy. An important one states, for the first time, that sovereignty belongs to the nation (art. 2).

See also HASSAN II; ISTIQLAL PARTY: MOROCCO; MUHAMMAD V; UNION NATIONALE DES FORCES POPULAIRES (UNFP).

Bibliography

Leveau, Rémy. "The Moroccan Monarchy: A Political System in Quest of a New Equilibrium." In *Middle East Monarchies: The Challenge of Modernity*, edited by Joseph Kostiner. Boulder: Lynne Rienner, 2000.

HENRI LAUZIÈRE

MOROCCO: POLITICAL PARTIES IN

Political parties have been an integral part of Morocco since the early 1930s.

The severe constraints under which the parties have had to operate, the parliament's lack of real power vis-à-vis the monarch, and the fragmented nature of Morocco's society have combined to prevent political parties from establishing a basis of support beyond particularist, sectoral interests, and personal ties and have rendered them vulnerable to both manipulation and repression. Overall, Morocco's political parties have served a significant, albeit adjunct, function in what has been essentially a monarchy-dominated, traditional, patrimonial system of rule. This continued to be the case at the beginning of the twenty-first century, notwithstanding the increasing liberalization of public life during the

For the 1997 parlimentary elections in Morocco, vote turnout was higher than expected, with over 50 percent of the population casting ballots. © PARROT PASCAL/CORBIS SYGMA. REPRODUCED BY PERMISSION.

1990s, and particularly the establishment, with the king's blessing, of the *alternance* government in 1998, which was headed by longtime left-wing opposition leader Abderrahmane Youssoufi.

The Comité d'Action Marocaine (CAM) was established during the early 1930s to promote nationalist demands. A later incarnation, the Istiqlal Party, played a central role in the nationalist struggle during the decade before Morocco's independence in 1956. The Istiqlal and its offshoot, the Union Nationale des Forces Populaires (UNFP), led a vigorous challenge during the first decade of independence to the king's efforts to rule as well as reign. The result was an unmitigated triumph for the king. Opposition political parties were coopted and repressed. Methods of repression included bannings, arrests, imprisonments, and, in the case of the UNFP's Mehdi Ben Barka, assassination. In addition, the monarchy supported the establishment of the Mouvement Populaire (MP), the short-lived Front pour la Défense des Institutions Constitutionelles (FDIC), the Rassemblement National des Indépendants (RNI), and, in the 1980s, the Union Constitutionelle (UC), in order to counter the opposition.

From the mid-1960s until his death in 1999, King Hassan II governed with the assistance of the promonarchy groupings and parties. From the mid-1970s, he had considerable success in controlling

the pace of political change, including the holding of general elections at intervals suitable to his political requirements (1977, 1984, and 1993 and 1997), pushing through cosmetic constitutional reforms, and mobilizing nearly the entire political spectrum on behalf of his Western Sahara policies. Prior to the electoral reform of 1997, two-thirds of the members of parliament were elected by popular vote, and one-third indirectly, by various corporate and professional bodies. The system was heavily subject to manipulation.

The Istiqlal, the Union Socialiste des Forces Populaires (which had split in the early 1970s from the UNFP), and the Parti du Progres et du Socialisme (PPS) played the political game, to a large degree, according to the king's rules: Between 1977 and 1984, Istiqlal even participated in the ruling coalition. At the end of the 1980s Morocco's diplomatic and military successes in regard to Western Sahara, sustained macroeconomic gains, and successful restructuring of the external debt strengthened the regime's confidence in its ability to loosen its grip a bit. On the other hand, widespread poverty, Western pressure regarding human-rights issues, and the specter of increasing radical Islamic activism compelled the regime to broaden political participation. The most important Islamic grouping, Jami'at al-Adl wa al-Ihsan (the "Justice and Charity Group") is officially banned from political life but is tolerated by the regime. Its supreme guide, Shaykh Abdsalem Yasine, was held in custody for most of the last quarter of the twentieth century, and finally released in 2000 by King Muhammad VI.

In May 1992 the Istiqlal, the USFP, the PPS, the rump UNFP, and the splinter Marxist-Leninist Organisation pour l'Action Democratique et Populaire (OADP) formed the Democratic Bloc (*al-kutla*), a parliamentary group pressing for constitutional and electoral reform, and especially for enhancing the powers of parliament. Three of the center-right parties—the UC, the MP, and the Parti National Démocratique (PND)—formed the Entente Nationale. Both the Istiqlal and the USFP achieved gains in the 1993 parliamentary elections. Istiqlal won 43 seats in the direct balloting and the USFP won 48. Both suffered drops in the indirect balloting. Each had achieved 52 seats, making them roughly equal in size to the UC and MP as the largest parliamentary factions. King Hassan offered the *kutla* opposition a total of 19 ministerial positions in his proposed new cabinet, but reserved the key posts of prime minister and the interior, foreign, finance, and justice portfolios for his close associates. Both the Istiqlal and the USFP refused the terms and remained in the opposition. At first, the king established a government of nonparty technocrats. In early 1995 Hassan offered the prime ministership to Istiqlal head Muhammad Boucetta, but the continued presence of interior minister and regime strongman Driss Basri was the primary sticking point, and the offer was rejected. Subsequently, a new government was formed that included 20 representatives from the Entente "loyalist" parties.

The 1997 elections marked a watershed in Moroccan political life. Constitutional reform had resulted in the establishment of a second house of parliament, and the existing chamber of deputies would now be elected entirely by popular vote. Morocco's system of "authoritarian pluralism" was clearly modified, and the *kutla* parties had chosen to accept the path of incremental reform. In the 1997 elections the USFP won the most seats (56 out of 325) and the most votes (just under 14 percent) of any single party. The Istiqlal dropped to 32 seats, occasioning charges of voter fraud. Other leading parties in the election were the UC with 50 seats, the RNI with 46 seats, and the MP with 40. A primarily Islamist party, the Mouvement Populaire Démocratique et Constitutionnel (MPDC) won 10 seats. The regime's sanctioning of Islamist political activities was part of its time-honored efforts to divide and control the fragmented political system. The results of the elections allowed King Hassan to realize his program of democratic *alternance*, namely the rotation of political power between two major blocs. The new government, headed by the USFP's Abderrahmane Youssoufi, was formed in 1998, and included representatives from the Istiqlal, the centrist RNI, the Mouvement National Populaire, and smaller parties. A number of cabinet posts remained in the hands of the "king's men," including Interior Minister Driss Basri.

The Youssoufi *alternance* government began with high hopes for the genuine democratization and liberalization of political life and the promotion of greater equality and economic prosperity. By the end of its more than four years in office, the glow

had worn off; the pace of change remained slow, and public affairs were still dominated by the palace, with parliament having little influence. In the 2002 parliamentary elections the USFP dropped 7 seats, to 50, the Istiqlal gained 16 seats, to 48, the UC lost 34 seats, to 16, the RNI dropped 5 seats, to 41, and the MP lost 13 seats, to 27. Most noticeable was the leap forward by the moderate Islamist party, now called the Parti de la Justice et du Developpement (PJD), which became the third-largest party with 42 seats. King Muhammad VI designated his confidant and interior minister Driss Jettou (Basri had been removed in November 1999) as prime minister, and he formed a broad cabinet that included representatives from seven parties. The decision to appoint a prime minister who was not an elected party official confirmed anew the secondary status of Morocco's political parties, notwithstanding the regime's expressed commitment to liberalization.

See also BEN BARKA, MEHDI; BOUCETTA, MUHAMMAD; COMITÉ D'ACTION MAROCAINE (CAM); FRONT POUR LA DÉFENSE DES INSTITUTIONS CONSTITUTIONELLES (FDIC); HASSAN II; ISTIQLAL PARTY: MOROCCO; MOUVEMENT POPULAIRE (MP); PARTI NATIONAL DÉMOCRATIQUE (PND); RASSEMBLEMENT NATIONAL DES INDÉPENDANTS (RNI); UNION NATIONALE DES FORCES POPULAIRES (UNFP); UNION SOCIALISTE DES FORCES POPULAIRES (USFP); WESTERN SAHARA; YOUSSOUFI, ABDERRAHMANE.

Bibliography

Maddy-Weitzman, Bruce. "Morocco." Annual chapters in *Middle East Contemporary Survey*, 18–24, 1994–2000. Boulder, CO: Westview Press; Tel Aviv, Israel: Tel Aviv University, 1996–2002.

Mednicoff, David M. "Morocco." In *Political Parties of the Middle East and North Africa,* edited by Frank Tachau. Westport, CT: Greenwood Press, 1994.

BRUCE MADDY-WEITZMAN

MORRISON–GRADY PLAN (1946)

An Anglo-American report calling for the division of Palestine into semi-autonomous Arab and Jewish regions.

At the end of World War II, the British position in Palestine, its mandate, was becoming untenable.

With thousands of European Jewish refugees needing to immigrate to Palestine, Britain and the United States dispatched a commission of inquiry to that territory in April 1946. In July, headed by Herbert Morrison, representing Britain's Labour government, and Henry Grady, representing the United States, the commission drew up its report in London.

Called the Morrison-Grady Plan, the report suggested a division of Palestine into semi-autonomous Arab and Jewish regions, while the British high commissioner would remain in control of defense, foreign relations, customs, and immigration. The plan also called for a one-year quota of 100,000 Jewish refugees to enter Palestine, after which time the immigration quotas would be set by the British. Morrison-Grady would have meant an increase of British control over Palestine and was rejected by both the Arabs and the Jews.

Bibliography

Sachar, Howard. *Europe Leaves the Middle East, 1936–1954.* New York: Knopf, 1972.

Shimoni, Yaacov, and Levine, Evyatar, eds. *Political Dictionary of the Middle East in the Twentieth Century,* revised edition. New York: Quadrangle/New York Times, 1974.

Spiegel, Steven L. *The Other Arab-Israeli Conflict: Making America's Middle East Policy, from Truman to Reagan.* Chicago: University of Chicago Press, 1985.

ZACHARY KARABELL

MOSHAV

Collective village, based on agriculture, in Israel.

The moshav (plural, moshavim) is a collective village, of which there were 410 in 1991 with a combined population of 152,500. The collective provides agricultural inputs and marketing services to the families living there and the various moshav movements have national and regional organizations to provide these services. Land on the moshav is divided between the member families. In the early years, hired labor was banned and communal cultivation of some land prevailed. This changed in the 1960s and 1970s when Arab labor became an important part of the economy of many moshavim.

The moshavim have their own bank, savings and pension schemes, insurance company, and regional purchasing organizations.

The foundations of the moshav go back to 1919, when Eliezer Yaffe published a pamphlet suggesting the creation of moshavim on nationally owned land, with mutual aid, cooperative purchasing and marketing, and the family as the basic unit. Like the kibbutz, the moshav was to be a pioneering institution, emphasizing national and social rejuvenation for the Jewish people and the Land of Israel. The first moshav was founded at Merhavia in the Galilee. Yaffe's ideas were influential in the founding of the second moshav, Nahalal, in 1921, the model for future settlements of this kind. Between 1949 and 1956, 250 moshavim were set up to house and provide employment for immigrants mainly from North Africa and Asia, who were not attracted to the communal life of the kibbutz, but for whom agriculture was the only possible basis for employment. By 1970 the moshavim had a population of 100,000. They had, in terms of numbers of settlements and total population, become more important than the kibbutzim.

During the 1980s, many of the moshav movement's economic organizations, responsible for marketing and purchasing inputs, went bankrupt as a result of overexpansion and high interest rates. Many moshavim were badly affected, and the mutual guarantee, by which each member or family supported other members, fell into disfavor. During the 1980s, an increasing number of urban families moved to moshavim; they commute to towns and are not involved in agriculture.

Members of each moshav elect a management committee that organizes the provision of economic services as well as education and health services to the community. The moshavim are also affiliated with different political parties, the largest moshav is affiliated with the Labor Party. Others are affiliated to religious parties.

The *moshav shitufi* is a moshav with many of the characteristics of the kibbutz. In 1991 there were 46 *moshav shitufi* with a total population of 12,600. Production is organized communally and members' work is determined by an elected committee. Consumption is private, with families eating at home and providing their own domestic services, as on other moshavim and in contrast to the kibbutzim.

See also ISRAEL: POLITICAL PARTIES IN; KIBBUTZ; NAHALAL.

Bibliography

Eisenstadt, Shmuel Noah. *Israeli Society.* London: Weidenfeld and Nicolson; New York: Basic, 1967.

Viteles, H. *A History of the Co-operative Movement in Israel,* Vol. 4: *The Moshav Movement.* London: Vallentine, Mitchell, 1968.

PAUL RIVLIN

MOSQUE

Islamic place of worship.

Mosque is an anglicized French cognate for the Arabic word *masjid,* which literally means "place of prostration." In the most abstract sense, any private or public space properly prepared for the purposes of performing the five obligatory prayers of Islam (*salat*) constitutes a mosque. The term *mosque,* however, is most commonly used to refer to a space which has been permanently or semipermanently demarcated as a place of public Muslim worship.

While many mosques share such common features as a prayer niche (*mihrab*), pulpit (*minbar*), and area for performing ritual ablutions, the size, lay out, and architecture of any given mosque is usually particular to its own specific historical, social, and cultural context. In many well-established Muslim communities, the largest and most centrally located mosque will often function as the *masjid al-jami,* or central mosque, where a large number of worshippers gather for the Friday noon congregational prayer (*salat al-jumʿa*) and sermon (*khutba*). Not unlike their counterparts in other religious traditions, mosques and larger mosque complexes often serve as a primary locus for a variety of communal gatherings and activities, ranging from social-service programs and political rallies to Qurʾan study groups and scholarly lectures.

See also ISLAM; QURʾAN.

Bibliography

Creswell, K. A. C. *Early Muslim Architecture,* revised edition. 2 vols. Oxford: Clarendon, 1969; New York: reprint, Hacker Art Books, 1979.

Hoag, John D. *Islamic Architecture.* New York: Abrams, 1977; reprint, New York: Rizzoli, 1987.

SCOTT ALEXANDER

MOSSAD

Israel's Institute for Intelligence and Special Tasks.

The Mossad is Israel's central intelligence agency, responsible for intelligence collection, covert action, and counterterrorism outside the borders of the state. It was founded in 1951, under orders from Prime Minister David Ben-Gurion, by Reuven Shiloah, a senior member of Israel's diplomatic corps. It replaced a number of organizations, including the SHAI (Sherut Yediʿot), the intelligence service of the Haganah, and the political department of the Jewish Agency, which had been created by the political leadership of the Yishuv (Jewish community in Palestine).

Responsibilities and Leadership

The division of functions and the boundaries between the various intelligence agencies had for many years been unclear. The founding of the Mossad left all official and overt diplomatic activities to the Ministry of Foreign Affairs; military intelligence, intelligence analysis, and information assessment to the Intelligence Division (Aman) of the Israeli Defense Force (IDF); counterinsurgency and counterespionage inside the country to the Security Service (Shin Bet); and counter-criminal intelligence to the police. All covert activities and espionage abroad were assigned to the Mossad.

The head of the Mossad, whose identity was for many years kept secret, was directly responsible to the prime minister and served as chairman of the coordinating committee of all heads of Israel's intelligence services. In 1952, Shiloah was replaced by Isser Harel, until then the head of the Shin Bet, who went on to serve as director of the Mossad for more than a decade.

Despite formal definitions of the respective realms of activities, it took some years and some internecine struggles among the various services for the exact boundaries to be established. Thus, for example, military intelligence continued to keep a special unit that operated agents across the borders and was responsible for the ill-advised activation, in

Israel prime minister Ariel Sharon (center) toasts with recently appointed head of the Mossad spy agency Meir Dagan (left) and former head Ephraim Halevy, 30 October 2002. © REUTERS NEWMEDIA INC./CORBIS. REPRODUCED BY PERMISSION.

the summer of 1954, of its espionage ring in Egypt, which ended in a fiasco that later became known as the Lavon Affair. A public scandal erupted when it was discovered that Harel had ordered the planting of recording devices in the office of the leaders of the left-wing MAPAM Party, which followed a pro-Soviet line, under the false suspicion that MAPAM was implicated in subversive activities. On the other hand, Mossad agents managed in 1956 to obtain the full record of Nikita Khrushchev's famous speech at the Twentieth Congress of the Soviet Communist Party, in which some of the horrors of Stalin's rule were disclosed. This was shared with a grateful CIA in Washington.

Over the years Harel gained great personal influence over some key political leaders. He was also called upon to execute some unconventional and dramatic operations abroad. One such was the discovery and rescue of a boy who had been kidnapped by his ultra-orthodox grandfather, who hid the boy in France in order to bring him up according to strict Orthodox traditions. Harel's most famous operation was the kidnapping of Adolf Eichmann, the high-ranking Nazi SS commander who was responsible for organizing the extermination of many hundreds of thousands of European Jews during World War II. Eichmann was captured in his home in Buenos Aires, smuggled to Israel, tried in Jerusalem, and sentenced to death in 1962.

In 1963, Harel came under severe criticism by David Ben-Gurion for his disproportionate re-

sponse to the involvement of some ex-Nazi officers in unsuccessful Egyptian attempts to develop long-range missiles and unconventional weapons. He was obliged to resign in the spring of 1963.

Many subsequent heads of the Mossad were army generals who came from the ranks of the IDF. The man who replaced Harel was general Meir Amit, previously the director of military intelligence. Amit served as Mossad's chief from 1963 to 1968. Among his noteworthy activities was a trip to Washington to secure a cautious go-ahead from the Johnson administration before Israel launched its offensive in the June 1967 Arab–Israel War. Subsequent heads of the Mossad were Zvi Zamir (1968–1974), Yitzhak Hofi (1974–1982), Nahum Admoni (1982–1990), Shabtai Shavit (1990–1996), Dani Yatom (1996–1998), and Ephraim Halevy (1998–2003).

International Relationships and Operations

During the 1960s, the Mossad developed close relations with SAVAK, the intelligence service of Iran under the shah, and supported the Kurds in their rebellion against the officers' regime of Baghdad. Over the years, the Mossad managed to capitalize on its widespread image as one of the world's most efficient intelligence agencies and created close relationships with many other national agencies, not the least important of which was that with the CIA.

After the June 1967 war, the Mossad concentrated much of its resources on countering Palestinian terrorist activities. Thus, for example, it assassinated most of the al-Fatah operatives involved in the massacre of Israeli athletes at the 1972 Munich Olympics. Mossad agents also killed Khalil al-Wazir (Abu Jihad), Yasir Arafat's deputy in charge of military affairs, in his home in Tunis. Over the years, the Mossad also succeeded in placing its spies in a number of high positions in Arab capitals. Some of its successes may not be revealed for many years to come, but the spies who were eventually caught prove the point. The most important such was Eli Cohen, who established himself in Damascus, developed close relations with the Syrian elite, and reported invaluable information back to Israel before he was apprehended and hanged in 1965. Two more outstanding successes added to the towering prestige of the Mossad: the landing of a MiG-21 advanced Soviet combat plane from the Iraqi air force at an Israeli airport in 1966, and the January

1969 whisking away of three missile boats from the French port of Cherbourg, where they had been built for Israel but were being detained under an embargo declared by President Charles de Gaulle after the outbreak of the June 1967 Arab–Israel War.

The Mossad has also been involved in many nonintelligence operations, in particular with regard to clandestine political relations and endangered Jewish communities. Mossad agents undertook secret negotiations with Egyptian, Jordanian, Lebanese, and other Arab leaders long before the first peace treaty was concluded with Egypt in 1979. The Mossad also helped diaspora Jewish communities organize self-defense and was instrumental in the exodus of Ethiopian Jews via Sudan to Israel. It was also responsible for Israel's relations with Lebanese politicians and with Maronite militias, eventually paving the way for the IDF invasion of Lebanon in 1982.

On the eve of the October 1973 war, the Mossad gave the government an early warning of an imminent Egyptian offensive against the Bar-Lev Line, but military intelligence did not take the warning seriously. The failure of military intelligence to make the correct assessment during that war brought about changes in the mandate of Israel's various intelligence agencies. A unit for research and information assessment was added to the Mossad and to the Ministry of Foreign Affairs for the purpose of cross-assessment and verification.

The Mossad's main functions, and apparently also its main departments, are:

- information collection, utilizing a network of spies and other agents operating in stations around the world

- political action and intelligence liaison

- psychological warfare, propaganda, and disinformation

- research and assessment

- special operations, such as sabotage, assassination, and other activities, especially beyond Israel's borders.

A well-known example of special operations was the failed attempt to assassinate Khalid al-Mashʿal, head of the political bureau of HAMAS in Amman,

Jordan. On 4 October 1997, Mossad agents injected Mashʿal with a toxic substance, but his life was saved when, in response to heavy Jordanian and U.S. pressure, Prime Minister Benjamin Netanyahu sent a physician to administer an antidote to the poison. The affair caused not only a sharp deterioration in Israeli–Jordanian relations but also an uproar in Israeli political circles.

In what may signal a decline in its mythical infallibility, the Mossad has been faulted for failing to anticipate the outbreak of the al-Aqsa intifada in September 2000. On the other hand, in recent years senior Mossad officials have been intensively involved in the evolving peace process with the Palestinians. Mossad chiefs Ephraim Halevy and General Dani Yatom (along with Shin Bet's Israel Hasson) began to appear in the media in the unusual roles of unofficial peace negotiators. Since these activities exposed the head of the Mossad to public view, the government decided to make the names of past and future directors public. In 2002, Prime Minister Ariel Sharon nominated his longtime friend General Meir Dagan, who had served in the IDF under him, to replace Ephraim Halevy as Mossad's director.

See also AMIT, MEIR; AQSA INTIFADA, AL-; ARAB–ISRAEL WAR (1967); ARAB–ISRAEL WAR (1973); BEN-GURION, DAVID; HAGANAH; HAMAS; HAREL, ISSER; JEWISH AGENCY FOR PALESTINE; LAVON AFFAIR; SHILOAH, REUVEN; SHIN BET.

Bibliography

Bar-Zohar, Michael. *Spies in the Promised Land: Iser Harel and the Israeli Secret Service,* translated by Monroe Stearns. Boston: Houghton Mifflin, 1972.

Black, Ian, and Morris, Benny. *Israel's Secret Wars: A History of Israel's Intelligence Services,* London: Hamish Hamilton, 1991.

Eisenberg, Dennis; Dan, Uri; and Landau, Eli. *The Mossad: Israel's Secret Intelligence Service Inside Stories.* New York: Signet, 1978.

Eshed, Haggai. *Reuven Shiloah: The Man behind the Mossad,* translated by David and Leah Zinder. London: Frank Cass, 1997.

Raviv, Dan, and Melman, Yossi. *Every Spy a Prince: The Complete History of Israel's Intelligence Community.* Boston: Houghton Mifflin, 1990.

MORDECHAI BAR-ON

MOSSADEGH, MOHAMMAD
[1882–1967]

*Iranian politician and leading speaker for the national-
ist-democratic movement; prime minister, 1951–1953.*

Mirza Mohammad Khan, later called Mossadegh
(also Mosaddeq, Musaddiq) al-Saltaneh, was born
in Tehran in 1882, into a wealthy family connected
to the bureaucracy of the Qajar dynasty. His father,
Mirza Hedayatollah Vazir Daftar, belonged to the
Ashtiyani family, many of whom, such as Qavam
and Vosuq, became important public figures in
nineteenth- and twentieth-century Persia, now
Iran. His mother Najm al-Saltaneh (known as
Shahzadeh Khanom), was Prince Regent Abbas
Mirza's granddaughter. Mossadegh married at age
nineteen Khanom Zia al-Saltaneh, from an Islamic
clerical family.

When Mossadegh's father died, he inherited his
position as a chief *mostowfi* (representative of the state
treasury) in the province of Khurasan. In support
of the Constitutional Revolution (1905–1911),
Mossadegh joined, briefly, the Adamiyat and In-

Iranian premier Mohammed Mossadegh (1882–1967) speaks
before a UN Security Council hearing in New York, 13 October
1951. © BETTMANN/CORBIS. REPRODUCED BY PERMISSION.

saniyat societies. In 1909, he went to Europe but
returned because of an illness. On recovery, he returned to Europe in 1911, studied law at Neuchâtel
University in Switzerland, and completed his doctoral dissertation on the jurisprudence of Islam. He
returned home in 1914 and became known as Dr.
Mohammad Khan Mossadegh al-Saltaneh. During
World War I, from 1914 to 1918, he wrote essays on
legal and political matters, was active in the Democratic party (Hizb-i I'tidal), taught at the Tehran
School of Law and Political Science, and became the
deputy *(mo'avin)* of the ministry of finance.

In 1920, Mossadegh was appointed governor of
Fars, but he soon resigned when he refused to recognize the new government of Sayyed Zia Tabataba'i
that was formed following his and Reza Khan's coup
of February 1921. When Ahmad Qavam became
prime minister, Mossadegh was appointed minister
of finance. His attempts to reform the ministry were
blocked by the *majles* (parliament) and the royal
court, which led to the downfall of the cabinet. In
1922, Mossadegh was appointed governor of Azerbaijan and, in 1923, became foreign minister for
about four months—his last office until he became
prime minister in 1951.

Mossadegh's parliamentary activities began when
he was elected Tehran representative to the fifth
Majles. During his political career, Mossadegh increasingly personified Persia's nationalist and democratic aspirations. His first major move for
nationalism was opposition to the Anglo–Persian
Agreement of 1919. His commitment to democracy
was reflected in his vehement opposition to Reza
Khan's move to dethrone the Qajar dynasty to found
his own, the Pahlavi.

After Reza Khan became Reza Shah Pahlavi, in
1925, Mossadegh remained a major critic of the
regime, despite the shah's frequent efforts to co-
opt him. With the rise of Pahlavi's despotism, many
of Mossadegh's associates were exiled, jailed, or
killed. Being very cautious, he withdrew from politics, shutting himself away at his rural estate in Ah-
madabad, west of Tehran. (Meanwhile, in 1935,
Persia was renamed Iran.) In 1940, he was arrested
and imprisoned in Birjand. He was soon released,
because Reza Shah was ousted by the Allies (Britain
and the Soviet Union) in 1941 for being pro-Nazi;
the shah was succeeded by his son, Mohammad Reza
Pahlavi.

Mossadegh then returned to politics. In October 1949, he led a crowd of politicians, university students, and bazaaris into the shah's palace to protest voting fraud in Iran's fifteenth parliamentary elections. Once inside, the demonstrators elected a committee of twenty, headed by Mossadegh, which soon became the nucleus of the National Front. Under his leadership, the front was instrumental in pressuring the parliament to nationalize the British-run petroleum industry. On 30 April 1951, Mossadegh was elected prime minister by a large margin. The shah had no option but to ratify the oil-nationalization bill and, on 1 May the law went into effect. Although the United States initially supported the oil nationalization movement, it soon joined Britain in engineering the coup that overthrew Mossadegh in August 1953.

An aborted coup took place several days before the successful one. The shah fled the country after hearing that the coup had failed, but Mossadegh refused to have the shah arrested. Following the referendum that had given him the mandate in 1951, Mossadegh dissolved the parliament and had several military officers arrested for their roles in plotting against him. He continued to act constitutionally until he was removed by Fazlollah Zahedi, whom the shah named premier.

Mossadegh was subsequently tried and imprisoned by the shah's government. Mossadegh lived to age eighty-five and died while under house arrest on 5 March 1967.

See also CONSTITUTIONAL REVOLUTION; NATIONAL FRONT, IRAN; PAHLAVI, MOHAMMAD REZA; PAHLAVI, REZA; QAJAR DYNASTY.

Bibliography

Abrahamian, Ervand. *Iran between Two Revolutions.* Princeton, NJ: Princeton University Press, 1982.

Katouzian, Homa, ed. *Musaddiq's Memoirs,* translated by S. H. Amin and H. Katouzian. London: JEBHE, National Movement of Iran, 1988.

MANSOOR MOADDEL

MOSTAGHANEMI, AHLAM
[1953–]

Algerian writer.

Ahlam Mostaghanemi is acknowledged as the first woman writer of Arabic in Algeria, where she was born and raised and where she received a university education. Her first collection of poetry, *Ala marfa al-ayyam* (On the haven of days), was published in Algeria in 1973, and two more poetry collections followed. Before emigrating to France, Mostaghanemi also presented radio programs about poetry. In Paris, she completed her Ph.D. in sociology at the Sorbonne under the direction of Jacques Berque (1982). Her doctoral dissertation was published in 1985 as a book, *Algérie: Femmes et écritures* (Algeria: Women and writing). Mostaghanemi's novels brought her fame, especially *Dhakirat al-jasad* (1993). A first, quite literal, translation into English, *Memory in the Flesh* (2000), was revised and reissued in 2003 with the same title. Her second and third novels, *Fawda al-hawwass* (Chaos of the senses, 1998) and *Abir sarir* (Passing by a bed, 2003) have also attracted critical attention. *Memory in the Flesh* has won major literary prizes, including the Nur award for best literary work by a woman in Arabic (1996) and the Naguib Mahfouz medal for fiction (1998). The novel's insistence on the Arabic language—in its dedication to Malek Haddad and the author's father, who could neither read nor write Arabic—is central to its message and role as a postcolonial Algerian novel. *Memory in the Flesh* treats not only the ravages colonialism has exacted on its characters and country, but also Algeria's current problems. It is narrated by a man and poses questions about gender roles. Mostaghanemi's second novel uses characters from the first but replaces the male voice with a female narrator. Critics have commented extensively on the interplay between gender, language, and nation in these novels. Mostaghanemi lives in Beirut, where all of her novels have been published to consistent critical acclaim.

Bibliography

Bamia, Aïda A. "Dhakirat al-jasad (The Body's Memory): A New Outlook on Old Themes." *Research in African Literatures* 28.3 (1997): 85-93.

McLarney, Ellen. "Unlocking the Female in Ahlam Mustaghanami." *Journal of Arabic Literature* 33.1 (2003): 24-44

Mostaghanemi, Ahlam. *Memory in the Flesh.* Cairo: American University in Cairo Press, 2003.

MICHELLE HARTMAN

MOSTA'ZAFIN

See GLOSSARY

MOSUL

City in northern Iraq (Mesopotamia).

Mosul (also spelled Mawsil) is located on the west bank of the Tigris river opposite the ancient city of Nineveh. It was a significant center during the early Islamic period with a sizable Christian population. Destroyed by the Mongols, Mosul regained importance under the Ottoman Turks. Some of the older mosques and churches survived.

Located on the trade routes that led to eastern Anatolia and thence to the Black Sea, Syria, Lebanon, Iraq, and Iran to the south, goods from Mosul were shipped by raft down the Tigris to Baghdad or overland to Aleppo and Damascus or points north. The city was a center for regional and international trade: Grain export, the manufacture of cotton thread and fabric (whence the term *muslin*), and trafficking in sheep hides and wool were important activities.

The government at Istanbul regained administrative control of the city from local rulers in 1834; in 1879 it became a separate Ottoman province that included Kirkuk, Arbil, and Sulaymaniya, but real power remained in the hands of local families—Mustafa Çelebi Sabunci was virtual dictator from 1895 to 1911. The population of the mud-brick-walled city in the later nineteenth century was estimated at forty thousand, including seven thousand Christians and fifteen hundred Jews. By World War I the population of Mosul had risen to seventy thousand, and the city became the economic and administrative capital of the Ottoman province of Mosul, one of three (Baghdad, Basra, Mosul) that would make up modern Iraq.

With the breakup of the Ottoman Empire after World War I and the consequent protracted negotiations between Britain and Turkey for sovereignty over the city, Mosul became part of Iraq rather than Turkey. Though its stature as a center of trade waned as Baghdad became Iraq's capital, the city continued to expand. During the 1940s and 1950s many of the traditional families came to own much of the land and were instrumental, together with lo-cal Arab nationalists, in fomenting a rebellion against Abd al-Karim Qasim in 1959. With the discovery of oil nearby and the construction of a refinery, Mosul has retained its importance. It has rail links to Baghdad, Syria, and Turkey, a university, an airport, and a religiously diverse population. The population (estimated at 1,846,500 in 2004) is mainly Kurdish with a significant Christian minority and a Yazidi population that lives in the Sinjar mountains to the west of Mosul.

See also QASIM, ABD AL-KARIM.

Bibliography

Batatu, Hanna. *The Old Social Classes and the Revolutionary Movements of Iraq: A Study of Iraq's Old Landed and Commercial Classes and of Its Communists, Ba'thists, and Free Officers.* Princeton, NJ: Princeton University Press, 1978.

REEVA S. SIMON

MOSUL, ANGLO-TURKISH DISPUTE OVER

Dispute over oil deposits in Iraq, c. 1920–1928.

Mosul, a province in northern Iraq, is rich in oil deposits and serves as a transit center for trade with Turkey and Syria. Its population consists of Arab Sunni Muslims, a sizable Kurdish minority, and various Christian sects. In 1916, the Sykes-Picot Agreement between England and France designated Mosul as a French zone. In 1920, the San Remo Conference transferred Mosul to the British, with the stipulation that France would have a share in the Turkish Petroleum Company.

Mosul became a point of contention between Turkey and Britain in the early 1920s. Turkey claimed that Mosul was part of its territory because the majority of inhabitants were Ottoman non-Arabs and because Mosul had not been in the hands of Britain when the Mudros armistice pact was signed in 1918. Britain wanted Mosul to be part of Iraq for myriad reasons. It believed Mosul had substantial oil deposits and could be used as a bargaining chip with the newly established government of Iraq to extend Britain's mandated power over that country. Faisal I, the newly crowned king of Iraq, wanted Mosul to be part of his country in order to strengthen his authority and influence over nationalistic elements who opposed Britain's continued interference in Iraq's domestic affairs.

The dispute between Turkey and Britain continued for several years. The two countries failed to resolve their conflict when the Lausanne Peace Treaty of 1923 was signed by the Allies and Turkey, and again at the special conference convened at Istanbul in 1924. They finally agreed to settle the dispute through the League of Nations. The League appointed a fact-finding commission to visit Iraq, survey public opinion in Mosul, and meet with officials on both sides. On 16 July 1924, the commission's report to the League called for the inclusion of Mosul in Iraq, retaining the Brussels line as the border between the two countries. Additional conditions attached to the recommendation included (1) allowing Iraq to remain under the British mandate for twenty-five years; (2) recognizing the rights of the Kurds to use their language in educational institutions and administration of justice, and (3) encouraging the hiring of Kurds as administrators, judges, and teachers. Iraq welcomed the decision. Mosul was one of the few issues that united the full spectrum of public opinion.

Turkey rejected the recommendation of the League of Nations and vowed to use any means necessary, including military action, to stop the implementation of the resolution. On 5 June 1926, however, Turkey signed a tripartite agreement with Britain and Iraq confirming Mosul's inclusion in Iraq. Iraq agreed to give a 10 percent royalty on Mosul's oil deposits to Turkey for twenty-five years. On 19 January 1926, Iraq had signed a new treaty with Britain, despite opposition from nationalist elements, to extend the mandate period for twenty-five years, as stipulated by the League's resolution. This treaty was ratified in January 1928, on the condition that Britain would recommend Iraq for membership in the League of Nations at four-year intervals for the next twenty-five years. If admission was approved, the British mandate would end.

See also SAN REMO CONFERENCE (1920); SYKES–PICOT AGREEMENT (1916).

Bibliography

Longrigg, Stephen Hemsley. *Iraq, 1900–1950: A Political, Social and Economic History.* London and New York: Oxford University Press, 1958.

Shikara, Ahmad. *Iraq Politics, 1921–41: The Interaction between Domestic Politics and Foreign Policy.* London: LAAM, 1987.

AYAD AL-QAZZAZ

MOTAHHARI, MORTAZA
[1920–1979]

Iranian religious scholar and writer; a close associate of Ayatollah Khomeini, he fostered the intellectual developments that contributed to the Islamic revolution of 1978/79.

Born to a religious scholar who was also his first teacher, Motahhari (also Mutahhari) began his formal schooling in Mashhad at the age of twelve, swiftly discovering his fascination with philosophy and mysticism, which remained with him throughout his life. In 1937, he moved to Qom where he studied law and philosophy under teachers that came to include Ayatollah Ruhollah Khomeini. In 1952 he left for Tehran where, in addition to teaching philosophy at a traditional seminary, he accepted a position at the Faculty of Theology of Tehran University. He also collaborated with religiously inclined laymen in popularizing a view of Islam as a comprehensive and socially applicable ideology.

Briefly imprisoned after the uprising of June 1963, Motahhari remained in contact with Khomeini throughout the years of his exile in Iraq and participated in a series of clandestine religio-political organizations. Named to the Revolutionary Council established by Khomeini in the early weeks of 1979, after the success of the Iranian Revolution, he was assassinated on 1 May of the same year by members of Furqan, a group holding a radically modernist view of Shi‘ism that saw Motahhari as its chief intellectual opponent.

Motahhari's literary legacy is important, including works that express his passionate devotion to mysticism and philosophy as the ultimate core of Islam, as well as other works designed to present Islam as a fully coherent ideology, superior to all its numerous competitors.

See also IRANIAN REVOLUTION (1979); KHOMEINI, RUHOLLAH.

Bibliography

Mutahhari, Murtaza. *Fundamentals of Islamic Thought: God, Man, and the Universe,* translated by R. Campbell. Berkeley, CA: Mizan Press, 1985.

HAMID ALGAR

MOTHERLAND PARTY

Political party in Turkey formed in 1983 by Turgut Özal.

The Motherland Party (Anavatan Partisi, or ANAP) stood in the center-right of the political spectrum and governed Turkey from 1983 to 1991. The personality and worldview of Turgut Özal were instrumental to the party's success. Rejecting from the start the dichotomy between the state and society and Islam and modernity, the party tried to formulate a new synthesis. Its economic policies transformed Turkey during the 1980s, introducing free-market reforms and downsizing the public sector. The ANAP government also applied to join the European Union in 1987. Although Özal's policies produced an economic development boom, they also led to high inflation and charges of corruption.

Özal officially resigned as ANAP leader in 1989 to become president, but his influence—and that of his wife and brothers—continued in party affairs. For example, Özal handpicked his successor, Yildirim Akbulut. After Akbulut proved ineffective, both as party chair and as prime minister, Özal pressured him to resign in June 1991; in anticipation of the forthcoming parliamentary elections, Özal approved the younger and more dynamic Mesut Yilmaz as Akbulut's successor. Yilmaz faced the challenge of developing a new party identity that would appeal to a broader constituency; otherwise, ANAP would expend all its energies competing with the ideologically similar True Path Party. Although ANAP's policies and constituency were similar to those of the True Path Party, the intense personal rivalry between Süleyman Demirel and Özal precluded political cooperation between the two parties prior to Özal's death in 1993.

Since the 1991 elections, ANAP's position has declined steadily (in the 1987 elections it reached its peak by obtaining 65 percent of seats in the Turkish Grand National Assembly). It was forced to enter into a brief coalition government with the True Path Party in 1995, and then it supported the government of Bülent Ecevit from 1997 to 1998. ANAP was one of the big losers in the 1999 elections, declining to fourth place among Turkey's political parties when it won only 14 percent of total votes. Nevertheless, the proportional representation system that awarded parliamentary seats to parties that received at least 10 percent of the vote enabled ANAP to obtain 86 of the 450 seats in the parliament. In the 2002 general elections, however, ANAP won only 5.12 percent of the votes and thus could not qualify for any seats. While in opposition, ANAP has criticized the customs union with the European Union, arguing that its terms conflict with Turkey's interests.

See also DEMIREL, SÜLEYMAN; ECEVIT, BÜLENT; ÖZAL, TURGUT; TRUE PATH PARTY; TURKISH GRAND NATIONAL ASSEMBLY.

Bibliography

Zürcher, Erik J. *Turkey: A Modern History,* revised edition. London: I. B. Tauris, 1997.

FRANK TACHAU
UPDATED BY M. HAKAN YAVUZ

MOU'AWWAD, NAILA
[?–]

Lebanese female politician and advocate.

A member of parliament from the district of Zgharta in North Lebanon, Na'ila Mou'awwad (also Na'ila Mu'awwad) has been an important oppositional voice and a leader on issues relating to women and the disenfranchised. After the 1989 assassination of President René Mu'awwad, her husband, she took over his parliamentary seat, and since then has been one of a handful of women in the 128-seat Lebanese legislature.

In postwar Lebanon, Mou'awwad has been a constant voice for political reform and hence often in the opposition. She has defended Lebanese independence and cautioned against excessive Syrian control. She has actively argued for electoral reform, freedom of the press, and anticorruption policies.

Mou'awwad chairs the Parliamentary Committee for Women and Children's Affairs and has been active in social development. In 1996, she led efforts to raise the age of working children from eight to fourteen, and spearheaded legislation on compulsory education in 1998. She has argued for improved conditions in women's prisons. Indeed, Mou'awwad has lobbied consistently for women's rights in parliament, and has been trying to pass legislation allowing Lebanese women to bequeath their citizenship to their children.

In 1990, she established the René Mu'awwad Foundation with the objective to "create a dynamics of sustainable development and make social justice and education accessible to all. These two factors are crucial for the emergence of true democracy in Lebanon." As a result of her leadership, countless projects on health, agriculture, literacy, and employment have been conducted, especially in North Lebanon.

See also GENDER: GENDER AND EDUCATION; GENDER: GENDER AND LAW; GENDER: GENDER AND POLITICS; LEBANESE CIVIL WAR (1958); LEBANESE CIVIL WAR (1975–1990); LEBANON.

Bibliography

Rene Moawad Foundation. Available from <http://www .rmf.org.lb/>.

ELISE SALEM

MOUDAWANA, AL-

The set of laws dealing with personal status, family, and inheritance in Morocco.

The Moudawana, or Mudawanat al-Ahwal al-Shakhsiyya, is made up of six books issued in five *dahir* (decrees) between 22 November 1957 and 3 March 1958. The Moudawana refers back to one of the most important texts of Maliki law, al-Mudawana al-Kubra by Sahnun ben Saʿid (776/7–854) of Qairawan, although it follows French patterns of codification. Addressing those charged with promulgating the Code of Personal Status following Morocco's independence from France in 1956, King Muhammad V stated that Morocco's rich history meant that it did not need to have recourse to the legal codes of foreign powers. All that was needed to reveal this glorious heritage was to rid it of the sterile commentaries and aberrant customs that over time had become mixed in with the *shariʿa* (religious law) and had retarded the state's evolution and progress. The Moudawana today is influenced by three juridical sources: in addition to the legislation inspired by Islamic law (Fiqh) and the legislation inspired by French law, the Moudawana is affected by trends in comparative law and international conventions. Beyond these written texts, women's status in Morocco is also regulated by unwritten sources such as traditions and inherited customs. When laws are in conflict with normative traditions concerning family customs, women may find their lived experience does not equate with their constitutional rights and civil status.

In Morocco, as in the other states of the Middle East and North Africa, the family lies at the core of society, and women at the core of the family. The processes of modernization, the creation of Western-style nation-states following independence, and globalization and internationalization have constructed women as citizens in contradictory ways: women are at one and the same time universal subjects as reflected in state constitutions and international conventions, special subjects as reflected in family law codes such as the Moudawana where they are legal minors, and privileged bearers of national and cultural authenticity in the symbolic imaginary of nations.

While other legal texts promulgated after independence reflected a shift in emphasis from the extended to the nuclear family, and thus from collective to individual identities and rights, the Moudawana reinscribed principles of Islamic law and posited a patriarchal family model. Civil status, as embodied in the various Moroccan constitutions dating from 1962, is founded on the principle of equality between men and women: the Moroccan Constitution states "All Moroccans are equal before the law" (Article 5); men and women enjoy equally their political and civil rights (Article 8); and, the sexes are equal in exercise of public employment and in the conditions required (Article 12). These statements of equality for women contradicted the Moudawana, which constructed female citizens as minors unable to enter into marriage contracts on their own and needing to be represented by a *wali* (guardian or tutor) until their husbands take over. Women had no say in the event the husband decided to marry additional wives. Lacking autonomy, women had little control over their own lives or those of their children. These contradictions led to periodic movements to bring the Moudawana into harmony with other laws. A 1972 royal commission drafted some proposed changes, but this effort was soon halted. In 1979, two drafts for changing the Moudawana were submitted, but the Ministry of Justice went outside the Constitution, giving them to a group of *ulama* (religious scholars), and only a few initiatives passed. That same year, a royal commission of three magistrates proposed many minor changes and some major changes to the Moudawana, but they also met intense religious opposition.

Another campaign to liberalize the Moudawana began during the mid-1980s when Morocco suffered severe financial crises and underwent a process of structural adjustment. A series of economic reforms and human rights reforms followed as Parliament discussed a new constitution. Women at this time renewed their fight for equality, holding meetings and workshops, and sharing research on women's rights according to the Qur'an. In October 1990, the Union de l'Action Féminine (Union for Feminine Action), a group founded by professional and middle-class women, launched a campaign to gather a million signatures on a petition to reform the Moudawana. They came into increasingly bitter conflict with conservative religious groups. On 20 August 1992, in a national broadcast, Hassan II intervened, stating that the Moudawana was his responsibility as Commander of the Faithful (Amir al-Mu'minin) and that only he had the authority to amend it.

After meeting with the women to discuss the proposed reforms, Hassan II brought their suggestions before the Council of the Ulama, and in 1991 some reforms were passed, opening the door to change: a man now needed his wife's permission to take other wives; a religious judge's permission was required for a divorce; and a mother who is more than eighteen years of age would receive custody of their children if the father died. In 1999, pressure from various sources forced the government to create a National Plan of Action to integrate women into the economy. High on the agenda was protecting women from violence and raising levels of female literacy. Supporters of women's equality argued that the participation of women was essential to any process of modernization and to democracy, that there could be no true development without women, and that it was the women's movement that had opened space for a civil, democratic society.

See also AICHA, LALLA; HASSAN II; MERNISSI, FATEMA; MOROCCO; MUHAMMAD V; MUHAMMAD VI.

Bibliography

Brand, Laurie A. *Women, the State, and Political Liberalization: Middle Eastern and North African Experiences.* New York: Columbia University Press, 1998.

Charrad, Mounira M. *States and Women's Rights: The Making of Postcolonial Tunisia, Algeria, and Morocco.* Berkeley: University of California Press, 2001.

Esposito, John, and DeLong-Bas, Natana J. *Women in Muslim Family Law,* 2d edition. Syracuse, NY: Syracuse University Press, 2001.

Joseph, Suad, and Slyomovics, Susan, eds. *Women and Power in the Middle East.* Philadelphia: University of Pennsylvania Press, 2001.

Naciri, Rabéa. "Engaging the State: The Women's Movement and Political Discourse in Morocco." In *Missionaries and Mandarins: Feminist Engagement with Development Institutions,* edited by Carol Miller and Shahra Razavi. London: Intermediate Technology Publications in association with the United Nations Research Institute for Social Development, 1998.

LAURA RICE

MOUROU, ABDELFATTAH
[1942–]

A cofounder of the Islamic Tendency Movement in Tunisia.

Born in 1942, Abdelfattah Mourou is a cofounder of the Tunisian Islamic Tendency Movement, which adopted the name Harakat al-Nahda (Renaissance Movement) in 1989, and he was one of its influential leaders up to the early 1990s. A son of a small merchant, Mourou received his primary education at the celebrated Sadiki College, a bilingual high school established by Khayr Eddin Pasha in the nineteenth century to synthesize religious and modern education. Mourou then studied law and graduated from the University of Tunis in 1971. At an early stage of his life, he joined one of the esoteric Sufi orders, al-Madaniyya, a small order established in the beginning of the century and characterized by its rejection of any foreign presence in the country. He started his Islamist activities in the 1960s by delivering religious lectures and forming educational circles for secondary school and university students at the country's mosques.

Mourou, along with Rashid al-Ghannoushi, Hemida al-Naifar, and Salah Eddin al-Jurshi, founded the Islamic Tendency Movement in 1981. The regime denied legal recognition to the movement and engaged in a series of confrontations with its members. Mourou was arrested for his his part and spent two years in prison. The movement

MOUVEMENT NATIONAL ALGÉRIEN

nonetheless grew during the 1980s and 1990s to be the main Islamic opposition force to the Tunisian secular regime. Following an attack in 1991 on the state party's office, which was attributed to members of al-Nahda, Mourou was briefly detained. Following his release, he began to adopt a conciliatory approach and issued a statement in which he denounced violence, announced the suspension of his membership in the movement, and expressed his desire to form a legal political party. The regime, however, turned against Mourou and engineered a defamation campaign aiming to discredit his personal conduct. Mourou has resigned political activism and practices law in Tunis.

See also BEN ALI, ZAYN AL-ABIDINE; BOURGUIBA, HABIB; GHANNOUCHI, RACHED.

Bibliography

Shahin, Emad Eldin. *Political Ascent: Contemporary Islamic Movements in North Africa.* Boulder, CO: Westview Press, 1998.

EMAD ELDIN SHAHIN

MOUVEMENT DE L'UNITÉ POPULAIRE (MUP)

Tunisian political party in exile.

The Popular Unity Movement, formed by Ahmed Ben Salah in 1973, is ideologically socialist and personally hostile to former Tunisian president Habib Bourguiba. In the 1960s Ben Salah developed socialist planning as Tunisia's economic system. Disastrous attempts to collectivize agriculture led to his fall in 1969. Tried and imprisoned, he escaped from the country in 1973 and remains in exile. Little support exists for the party within Tunisia; most supporters are Tunisian expatriates living in Europe. The party still adheres to a staunchly socialist, state-managed economic program.

MUP attitudes toward the Bourguiba regime were highly personalized as a result of a contest of wills between Bourguiba and Ben Salah. The latter's refusal to participate in Tunisia's elections (which became somewhat more liberal after 1980) disillusioned many of the party's members, who consequently condoned a split in the party in 1981. A more flexible MUP emerged and renamed itself the Parti

d'Unité Populaire (Popular Unity Party [PUP]). Under Mohamed Belhaj Amor, the PUP retained its earlier socialist and nationalist orientation but ended Ben Salah's personal vendetta against Bourguiba. The party adopted a more flexible approach to participation in the political process. Following the 1988 political liberalization under President Zayn al-Abdine Ben Ali, PUP became one of seven legal parties in Tunisia.

From 1983 on the MUP had been trying to obtain legal recognition, but without success, given the regime's refusal to reintegrate Ben Salah into the Tunisian political scene. In 1990 some members of the party participated in the legislative elections as independent candidates.

See also BEN SALAH, AHMED; BOURGUIBA, HABIB; PARTI D'UNITÉ POPULAIRE (PUP).

Bibliography

Murphy, Emma. *Economic and Political Change in Tunisia: From Bourguiba to Ben Ali.* New York: St. Martin's in association with University of Durham, 1999.

Perkins, Kenneth J. *Historical Dictionary of Tunisia,* 2d edition. Lanham, MD: Scarecrow Press, 1997.

LARRY A. BARRIE
UPDATED BY ANA TORRES-GARCIA

MOUVEMENT NATIONAL ALGÉRIEN

An Algerian nationalist organization that rivaled, and eventually lost to, the FLN.

The Mouvement National Algérien (MNA; Algerian National Movement) was founded in Paris in December 1954 by Messali al-Hadj in reaction to the launching of the Front de Libération Nationale (FLN; National Liberation Front) by his revolutionary rivals in Algeria. It was a continuation of his branch of the Mouvement pour le Triomphe des Libertés Démocratiques (MTLD; Movement for the Triumph of Democratic Liberties) established at Hornu, Belgium, during the summer.

One element after another of the Algerian political spectrum rallied to the FLN during 1955 and 1956. Claiming that this demonstrated that the FLN contained too many moderates and reformists, Messali's MNA was, by June 1956, the only major party remaining outside the nationalist coalition.

Encyclopedia of THE MODERN MIDDLE EAST AND NORTH AFRICA

1587

Polarization led to bloody fighting between MNA and FLN factions within Algeria. Also, the FLN waged a concerted effort to win over the loyalties of the Algerian community in France, long commanded by Messali, and to tap its financial resources. Intracommunal fighting in France took many lives. The MNA lost in both arenas and, from 1958 onward, was of little political consequence, going formally out of existence on 19 June 1962.

See also FRONT DE LIBÉRATION NATIONALE; HADJ, MESSALI AL-; MOUVEMENT POUR LE TRIOMPHE DES LIBERTÉS DÉMOCRATIQUES.

JOHN RUEDY

MOUVEMENT POPULAIRE (MP)

Pro-monarchy, overwhelmingly Berber political party in Morocco.

The Mouvement Populaire (MP) was organized in 1956–1957 in the Rif. Its supporters were Berber notables and tribesmen, some of whom belonged to the Army of Liberation, and small landholders. It was founded to oppose the political domination of newly independent Morocco by the Istiqlal Party and to serve as a mechanism for Berber political participation in cooperation with the monarchy. At the same time, the MP sought to avoid being cast as a purely Berber party, and so became the voice of the rural masses neglected by the Istiqlal. Its founders were Abdelkarim Khatib, a former head of the Arab Liberation Army (and ethnically an Arab), and Majoub Ahardane, the governor of Rabat province. The Istiqlal-dominated government arrested its leaders in April 1958 and blocked its legalization. The MP was finally registered as a legal political party in February 1959.

The relationship between the monarchy and the MP was strengthened during the early 1960s, following the ascension to power of Hassan II and the split in the Istiqlal. In 1962–1963, the MP was the only organized group within the monarchist coalition, which ran in the 1963 elections under the banner of the Front pour la Défense des Institutions Constitutionelles (FDIC). It thus was able to take advantage of the boycott of the 1963 elections by Istiqlal and the Union Nationale des Forces Populaires (UNFP) and to fill many of the positions in provincial assemblies, chambers of commerce, and communal councils. Its base of economic and political power was strengthened by the regime's policy of Moroccanizing large tracts of land that had been controlled by the French administration and settlers.

In 1965 the defection from the ruling coalition of a single MP member deprived the government of its majority, sparking a constitutional crisis that led to King Hassan's assumption of emergency powers. In 1967 the MP split over personality differences between Ahardane and Khatib; the latter's breakaway faction took the name Mouvement Populaire Démocratique et Constitutionelle (MPDC), which in the 1990s served as the legal basis for a primarily Islamist party sanctioned by the authorities. Ahardane was expelled from the MP in 1985 for "authoritarian practices," and the party was taken over by Mohand Laenser. In July 1991 Ahardane cofounded the rival Mouvement National Populaire (MNP). In the 1993 parliamentary elections the MP, competing as part of the loyalist Entente/Wifaq bloc, won a total of fifty-one seats, a gain of four from the 1984 elections, and in the government reshuffle of January 1995, it attained three cabinet seats. In the 1997 elections the MP dropped to forty seats and was left out of the new, left-of-center government. In the 2002 elections there was a further drop, with the party winning twenty-seven seats. Still, the party did attain three cabinet posts in the newly formed government, with party head Laenser receiving the agriculture and rural development portfolio. How the MP and other Berber-based parties would be affected by the emergence of a more assertive Berber culture movement remained an open question.

See also AHARDANE, MAJOUB; ARAB LIBERATION ARMY; BERBER; FRONT POUR LA DÉFENSE DES INSTITUTIONS CONSTITUTIONELLES (FDIC); ISTIQLAL PARTY: MOROCCO; MOROCCO: POLITICAL PARTIES IN; RIF; UNION NATIONALE DES FORCES POPULAIRES (UNFP).

Bibliography

Ashford, Douglas E. *Political Change in Morocco*. Princeton, NJ: Princeton University Press, 1961.

Pennell, C. R. *Morocco Since 1830*. New York: New York University Press, 2000.

Waterbury, John. *The Commander of the Faithful.* London: Weidenfeld and Nicolson, 1970.

BRUCE MADDY-WEITZMAN

MOUVEMENT POUR LE TRIOMPHE DES LIBERTÉS DÉMOCRATIQUES

Algerian organization that sought to attain national rights through electoral participation.

The Mouvement pour le Triomphe des Libertés Démocratiques (MTLD; Movement for the Triumph of Democratic Liberties) was created in 1946 by Messali al-Hadj, leader of Algeria's clandestine Parti du Peuple Algérien (PPA; Party of the Algerian People), which colonial authorities had banned in 1939. Under French detention almost continuously since 1937, Messali urged his followers after World War II to boycott French elections. Released in 1946, he hastily organized the MTLD, however, to enter candidates in the elections to the first National Assembly of the Fourth Republic held in November. In spite of harassment by the authorities, the MTLD won five of the fifteen parliamentary seats reserved for Muslim Algerians. Major business of the National Assembly included drafting what became the 1947 Organic Law of Algeria. MTLD deputies regularly denied the competence of a French legislature to determine Algeria's status in any way. In the meantime, the MTLD became by far the most popular party in Algeria. But colonial authorities, fearful of a nationalist victory, openly rigged the Algerian legislative elections of 1948, and they tampered again with the elections of 1949, 1951, 1953, and 1954.

After years of urging Algerians to spurn the process, Messali's abrupt decision to present slates of candidates in 1946 confused many Algerians. They did not know whether the party was seeking national rights by direct action or through electoral participation. In fact, it was doing both. At a clandestine party congress in February 1947, delegates determined that the MTLD would pursue political strategies within the existing colonial framework, while a secret PPA would continue to press for independence by whatever means necessary. By the end of 1947, the PPA–MTLD leadership had, in fact, approved the creation of an Organisation Spéciale (OS), which conducted armed robberies and other acts of violence until broken up by the authorities in March 1950.

It appears that MTLD cohesiveness was constantly torn through these years by the partisans of direct action and those of political participation. The decision to pursue both strategies simultaneously reflected irreconcilable internal contradictions more than rationally chosen strategy. This fundamental conflict lay at the heart of a series of internal disputes that progressively sapped the party's effectiveness in the early 1950s. The weakening of the party was hastened by conflicts between the Central Committee and Messali Hadj, widely accused of authoritarianism and of attempting to establish a cult of personality. Banned from Algerian soil in 1952, Messali in 1954 called a party congress at Hornu, Belgium, that declared the Central Committee dissolved and elected him president for life. Since the Central Committee failed to recognize the authority of the Hornu Congress, the party was split down the middle.

In the spring of 1954, a group of militants—mainly veterans of or sympathizers with the OS—formed the Comité Révolutionnaire d'Unité et d'action (CRUA; Revolutionary Committee of Unity and Action). Disillusioned with the "politicals" and their failure to produce, they determined to launch an insurrection. By 1956, most of the MTLD centralists had rallied to the Front de Libération Nationale (FLN; National Liberation Front), which the CRUA had created. Messali, in Europe surrounded by the émigré loyalists who were his original base, refused to join. His wing of the MTLD became the Mouvement National Algérien (MNA; Algerian National Movement) entering into often violent conflict with the FLN both at home and in France.

See also ALGERIA; COMITÉ RÉVOLUTIONNAIRE D'UNITÉ ET D'ACTION (CRUA); FRONT DE LIBÉRATION NATIONALE (FLN); HADJ, MESSALI AL-; MOUVEMENT NATIONAL ALGÉRIEN; PARTI DU PEUPLE ALGÉRIEN (PPA).

Bibliography

Horne, Alistaire. *A Savage War of Peace: Algeria, 1954–1962.* London: Macmillan, 1977.

Ruedy, John. *Modern Algeria: The Origins and Development of a Nation.* Bloomington: Indiana University Press, 1992.

JOHN RUEDY

MOVEMENT FOR UNITY AND REFORM (MUR)

Moroccan Islamic movement.

The Movement for Unity and Reform (MUR) is the second largest Islamic movement in Morocco, after Abdelsalam Yassin's al-Adl wa al-Ihsan (Justice and Benevolence). Formerly the Movement of Reform and Renewal (HATM), the MUR was established in Morocco in 1996 following a merger of HATM and the Association of the Islamic Future. Though the MUR is not legally recognized, the Moroccan regime has tolerated the movement's activities since the 1980s.

Led by a group of moderate Islamists, the MUR has branches throughout the country and has issued newspapers and other publications (notably the daily *al-Tajdid* [Renewal] and the quarterly *al-Furqan* [Proof]), held general conferences, and participated in popular marches. The main objectives of the movement are reforming the conditions of Muslims at the individual and societal levels and renewing their understanding and commitment to Islam. On several occasions the leaders of the movement have expressed their commitment to the fundamental basis of the Moroccan regime: Islam, the constitutional monarchy, and the territorial integrity of the country. They also reconfirmed their willingness to participate in political life through legal means and to cooperate with other political groups.

A major transformation took place within the movement when a large number of its leaders and cadres joined the historic yet moribund Constitutional and Democratic Popular Movement (MPCD) in 1996. This federation revived the MPCD and provided the MUR with the opportunity to participate in politics through formal channels. Under the umbrella of the MPCD (which in 1998 changed its name to the Party of Justice and Development), the MUR contested the legislative elections of 1997 and 2002 and won 14 and 44 seats, respectively, of the parliament's 325 seats. The movement is popular among Morocco's youth, university students, secondary-school teachers, and middle-class professionals.

See also ADL WA AL-IHSAN, AL-; HASSAN II; MOROCCO: POLITICAL PARTIES IN; MUHAMMAD VI.

Bibliography

Al-Tajdid. Special Issue (December 2002).

Shahin, Emad Eldin. *Political Ascent: Contemporary Islamic Movements in North Africa.* Boulder, CO: Westview Press, 1998.

EMAD ELDIN SHAHIN

MOVEMENT OF RENEWAL

Formerly the Tunisian Communist Party.

Founded as an offshoot of the French Communist party in 1920, the Parti Communiste Tunisien (Tunisian Communist Party, PCT) broke with the French party in 1934. It remained legal after Tunisia gained its independence in 1956 but was banned by President Habib Bourguiba in 1963. In 1981, however, Bourguiba legalized the PCT in order to offset the growing influence of the Islamist movement, and in 1988 the party signed Zayn al-Abidine Ben Ali's National Pact. PCT influence remained marginal, and the party has never succeeded in capturing the imagination of Tunisia's young people.

The disintegration of the Soviet Union in 1991 dealt the PCT a heavy blow. General Secretary Mohammed Harmel (head of the party since 1981) sought to capitalize on the Ben Ali "regime of change" by renaming the PCT the Mouvement Ettajdid (Movement of Renewal; in Arabic, Harakat al-Tajdid) and emphasizing the party's reformist credentials during its tenth national congress on 23 April 1993. The publication of the party's tabloid, *al-Tariq al-Jadid* (The new path), was suspended between 1989 and 1993, when it re-emerged as a monthly magazine.

Currently, Ettajdid is one of the five opposition parties represented in the Tunisian parliament. In the 1999 elections, the party obtained 2.74 percent of the vote and five seats. That same year, Ettajdid supported Ben Ali's candidacy in the presidential elections. However, in 2002 it abstained from voting on a proposed referendum on constitutional reform, initially calling for nonparticipation and later asking for a "cleaning up of the political climate" and a general amnesty for political prisoners before the referendum. The February–March 2003 issue of al-Tariq al-Jadid was seized by authorities because it contained articles critical of the proposed constitutional reforms.

See also BEN ALI, ZAYN AL-ABIDINE; BOUR-GUIBA, HABIB; COMMUNISM IN THE MIDDLE EAST; TUNISIA: OVERVIEW.

Bibliography

Alexander, Christopher. "Back from the Democratic Brink: Authoritarianism and Civil Society in Tunisia." Middle East Report no. 205 (1997): 34–38.

Perkins, Kenneth J. Historical Dictionary of Tunisia. Metuchen, NJ: Scarecrow Press, 1989.

LARRY A. BARRIE
UPDATED BY VANESA CASANOVA-FERNANDEZ

MOYNE, LORD

See GUINNESS, WALTER EDWARD

MOZAFFAR AL-DIN QAJAR

[1853–1907]

Fifth monarch of Persia's Qajar dynasty.

Mozaffar al-Din became shah in 1897, after his father Naser al-Din Shah was slain by an assassin's bullet. Mozaffar had lived in Tabriz in Azerbaijan, the traditional seat of the heir to the throne. He was of a timid but kindly nature and had been overshadowed and humiliated by forceful *pishkars* (ministers of Azerbaijan), appointed by his father, so he had little experience of statecraft upon his accession. His father had radiated an aura of royalty, although he had become despotic and unpopular toward the end of his reign.

The courtiers who came with the new shah to Tehran were greedy for the spoils of office they had long awaited; politics and court intrigues undermined the shah's authority and prestige. Mozaffar al-Din Shah's reign began badly, since Anglo-Russian rivalry was at its worst, compromising Persia's independence both financially and politically.

A deep dissatisfaction among all the classes gave rise to widespread nationalism. The shah allowed some freedom of political discussion and activity, which soon resulted in the formation of political societies (anjomans), where reforms were discussed and contacts between various leaders were established. The printing and distribution of political tracts caused politics to be discussed and the government criticized.

Mozaffar al-Din Shah dismissed his father's unpopular minister, Amin al-Soltan, and appointed the liberal-minded Amin al-Dowleh, whose efforts to negotiate a much-needed loan from a neutral country failed. The shah recalled him and negotiated instead two loans from Russia at onerous terms. The monies were soon spent on trivialities during the shah's European trips in 1900, 1902, and 1905. These journeys were criticized and made him unpopular with the merchants, who resented the concessions granted to non-Persians; with the *ulama* (body of *mollas*), who were afraid of Western cultural influence; and with the liberals who feared a threat to Persia's independence. All the while, growing inflation and lawlessness weakened the central government. The dismissal of Amin al-Soltan and the appointment of the more autocratic Ayn al-Dowleh only exacerbated the situation.

Another cause of great resentment was the employment of Belgian customs officials at the borders, the proceeds of which were pledged as a guarantee against the loans from Russia and Britain. Naus, the director, was particularly hated; it was no coincidence that a photo of him, wearing the habit of a religious man to a costume party, was distributed with other propaganda by the opponents of the regime, to show the disrespect that foreigners had for the religious class. This was the spark that triggered the revolution in 1904. The first demands were for law and a House of Justice (Adalat-Khaneh), formulated by those merchants and *ulama* who took *bast* (sanctuary) in the Shrine of Shah Abd al-Azim in 1904. The shah agreed to their demands but took no real action; therefore a protest began that took the life of a religious student. As a result the *ulama* left Tehran in a body for Qom, and 14,000 merchants gathered at the British embassy. Their demands included the granting of a constitution and a national constituent assembly (a *majles-e shura-ye melli*). The shah reluctantly agreed, and the preparation of the constitutional laws and the promulgation of electoral laws were accomplished quickly. The elections were rushed since the shah was ill, and it was feared that his successor, Mohammad Ali Mirza, might not continue his father's new policies. The electoral law was so devised that Tehran was purposely to receive half the 120 seats. In fact, Mozaffar al-Din Shah died a few months after he made the October 1906 inaugural speech in the *majles*.

Since the events of the succeeding reign confirmed the fears of the people, Persia was to face a long period of political turmoil. Mozaffar al-Din is therefore remembered with reverence, and those who built the entrance to the majles adorned it with the motto: *"Adl-e Mozaffar"* (The justice of Mozaffar), which was left untouched even after the change of dynasty in 1925.

Bibliography

Avery, Peter. *Modern Iran.* New York: Praeger, 1965.

Browne, Edward G. *The Persian Revolution of 1905–1909* (1910). Washington, DC: Mage Publishers, 1995.

Kazemzadeh, F. *Russia and Britain in Persia, 1864–1914: A Study in Imperialism.* New Haven, CT: Yale University Press, 1968.

MANSOUREH ETTEHADIEH

M'RABET, FADELA
[?–]

Pseudonym of Fatma Abda, an Algerian journalist and essayist.

Fadela M'Rabet was born in Constantine, Algeria. She was a high-school teacher after Algeria gained its independence in 1962, then joined the staff of the newspaper *Alger-Républicain* and was in charge of a women's program on the radio. As of 2004 she lived in France.

M'Rabet's first book, *La femme algérienne* (Paris, 1964; The Algerian woman) was inspired by the correspondence she received while working as a journalist and radio commentator. Its tone is defiant, meant to shake the apathy of the reader and focus attention on women's suppressed rights. M'Rabet was critical of Islamic law, which granted a Muslim man the right to marry a non-Muslim woman while denying a Muslim woman the right to marry a non-Muslim man. Her second book, *Les Algériennes* (1967; Algerian women) is optimistic about the future as a result of women's greater access to education. M'Rabet echoes the concerns of a growing number of women to protect their rights, newly acquired as a result of their participation in the Algerian War of Independence.

A long period of silence followed the author's publication of *L'Algérie des illusions* (The Algeria of illusions), which she cowrote in 1972 with her husband Maurice T. Maschino, a French journalist. In 2003 she published an autobiographical novel, *Une enfance singulière* (An unusual childhood). The book is a nostalgic evocation of her childhood in Algeria during the colonial period and a reaction to the racism she experienced in France, where she lives and works.

See also ALGERIAN WAR OF INDEPENDENCE; GENDER: GENDER AND POLITICS; LITERATURE: ARABIC, NORTH AFRICAN; RADIO AND TELEVISION: ARAB COUNTRIES.

Bibliography

Gordon, David. *Women of Algeria: An Essay on Change.* Cambridge, MA: Harvard University Press, 1968.

AIDA A. BAMIA

MU'ALLA FAMILY, AL-

Ruling family of the emirate of Umm al-Qaywayn in the United Arab Emirates.

The first member of the Mu'alla dynasty was Majid Al Ali, who rose to power in 1775 as leader of the area's largest tribe, the Al Ali. During the early years of the twentieth century the emirate was ruled by Rashid ibn Ahmad (r. 1904–1922), a reputedly forceful leader who was successful in encouraging some tribes to seek his protection, thus expanding the territories of his emirate. His son, Ahmad bin Rashid al-Mu'alla, ruled from 1929 to 1981 and was known for his piety, support for modern education, and his membership in the Trucial States Rulers' Council in 1952. He also was honored as a Member of the British Empire. He was succeed by his son Rashid (b. 1930) in 1981.

See also UMM AL-QAYWAYN; UNITED ARAB EMIRATES.

Bibliography

Anthony, John Duke. *Arab States of the Lower Gulf: People, Politics, Petroleum.* Washington, DC: Middle East Institute, 1975.

Reich, Bernard, ed. *Political Leaders of the Contemporary Middle East and North Africa: A Biographical Dictionary.* Westport, CT: Greenwood Press, 1990.

ANTHONY B. TOTH

MUASHER, MARWAN
[1956–]

Jordanian diplomat.

Marwan Muasher (also Mu'ashshir) has remained one of the most important Jordanian diplomats working on the Jordanian–Israeli peace process since the inception of public bilateral talks in 1991. Born in Amman, he studied at the American University of Beirut from 1972 until 1975. He completed his B.A. at Purdue University in Indiana, eventually also receiving a doctorate in computer engineering from Purdue. After returning to Jordan, he worked in the private sector and wrote political columns for Jordan's English-language newspaper. Muasher first began working with the Jordanian government in 1985 in the ministry of planning, where he eventually directed the Socio-Economic Information Centre. In 1989, he was appointed press advisor for the prime minister.

Muasher's career advanced with the onset of Jordanian–Israeli peace talks in 1991. From 1991 to 1994, he utilized his fluent American-accented English as the spokesperson for the Jordanian delegation to the talks. He also served as head of the Jordanian embassy's Jordan Information Bureau in Washington. From April to November 1995, Muasher held the important post of Jordan's first ambassador to Israel, becoming the public face of the Jordanian government in that country. He was minister of information from February 1996 through March 1997, after which he held the important post of ambassador to the U.S. from September 1997 to January 2002. During Muasher's tenure as ambassador, Jordan and the U.S. signed the U.S.–Jordan Free Trade Agreement. He returned to Jordan to serve as foreign minister, serving at a time of tremendous change in the region as

a result of the U.S. invasion of Iraq and the resumption of Israeli–Palestinian peace talks.

MICHAEL R. FISCHBACH

MUBARAK, HUSNI
[1928–]

Egyptian officer and politician; president of Egypt since 1981.

Born in Minufiyya province to a middle-class family, Muhammad Husni Mubarak graduated from the Military Academy in 1949 and from the Air Force Academy the next year. After a brief stint as a fighter pilot, he served as an instructor at the Air Force Academy from 1954 to 1961. He spent the following academic year at the Soviet General Staff Academy. He was the commandant of the Air Force Academy from 1967 to 1969, air force chief of staff from 1969 to 1971, and then commander in chief from 1971 to 1974. He took charge of Egypt's aerial preparations for the Arab–Israel War in 1973. Because of his outstanding performance in the war, he was promoted to the rank of air marshal in 1974. President Anwar al-Sadat appointed him vice president in 1975, and Mubarak served him loyally for the next six years.

After Sadat was assassinated in October 1981, Mubarak quickly assumed the presidency, was officially nominated within a week by the National Democratic Party, and was confirmed without any opposition by a nationwide referendum. Upon taking over, he promised to address Egypt's economic and social problems, tried to curb the favoritism and corruption that had marred Sadat's final days, and released many of the political and religious leaders whom Sadat had sent to prison. Many of Sadat's henchmen were quietly removed from office.

Mubarak maintained Egypt's ties with the U.S. government, on whose economic aid it had become increasingly dependent. He did not break diplomatic relations with Israel (although he did recall Egypt's ambassador from Tel Aviv during Israel's invasion of Lebanon), and he slowly restored good relations with the other Arab governments and the Palestine Liberation Organization (PLO), which had withdrawn their ambassadors from Cairo upon Sadat's signing of the Egyptian-Israeli peace accord

Husni Mubarak became president of Egypt after the 1981 assassination of Anwar al-Sadat. Present during the attack, Mubarak himself was shot in the hand. A political moderate, Mubarak has worked hard to reestablish favorable relations with other Arab nations and curb extremist groups within his own country. © GETTY IMAGES. REPRODUCED BY PERMISSION.

in 1979. He hosts visits from Israeli leaders, but has seldom visited Israel since he became president. His government has played a prominent role in Israeli-Palestinian peace talks.

Although Mubarak's government encouraged Western and Arab investment in Egypt's economy, he curbed the operation of foreign multinational corporations within the country. He instituted a program of economic reform following a severe fiscal crisis in the late 1980s and also tried to form an economic union with Iraq, Yemen, and Jordan. His efforts to mediate the 1990 dispute between Iraq and Kuwait failed and instead became a precipitating factor in Saddam Hussein's decision to invade and occupy Kuwait. Although Mubarak initially hoped for an Arab solution to the problem, his government soon rallied behind Operation Desert Shield, sending 40,000 troops to join the allied coalition in Saudi Arabia. Egypt was later rewarded

by the cancellation of some $14 billion worth of accumulated foreign debt. Egypt's economy made impressive gains during the 1990s. He has been elected president, without opposition, for four six-year terms, making him the longest-serving Egyptian head of state since Muhammad Ali. He has not yet designated a successor.

The Mubarak government has been challenged by Islamist political movements, which attacked prominent government officials, secularists, Copts, and foreigners between 1992 and 1997, but has curbed such violence through arrests, detention, trials, and occasional executions. Mubarak himself was nearly assassinated while attending a meeting of the Organization of African Unity in 1995, an incident that increased his popularity within Egypt. The gap between rich and poor remains wide—a potential threat to the stability and survival of his regime. More self-effacing than either Nasser or Sadat, he inspires neither strong loyalty nor aversion among most Egyptians.

See also ARAB–ISRAEL WAR (1973); CAMP DAVID ACCORDS (1978); GULF WAR (1991); PALESTINE LIBERATION ORGANIZATION (PLO); SADAT, ANWAR AL-.

Bibliography

Baker, Raymond William. *Sadat and After: Struggles for Egypt's Political Soul.* Cambridge, MA: Harvard University Press, 1990.

Goldschmidt, Arthur. *Biographical Dictionary of Modern Egypt.* Boulder, CO: L. Rienner, 1999.

Ibrahim, Saad Eddin. *Egypt, Islam, and Democracy,* 2d edition. Cairo and New York: American University in Cairo Press, 2002.

Kienle, Eberhard. *A Grand Delusion: Democracy and Economic Reform in Egypt.* London and New York: I. B. Tauris, 2001.

Oweiss, Ibrahim M., ed. *The Political Economy of Contemporary Egypt.* Washington, DC: Center for Contemporary Arab Studies, Georgetown University, 1990.

Springborg, Robert. *Mubarak's Egypt: Fragmentation of the Political Order.* Boulder, CO: Westview, 1989.

Weaver, Many Anne. *A Portrait of Egypt: A Journey through the World of Militant Islam.* New York: Farrar Straus Giroux, 1999.

ARTHUR GOLDSCHMIDT

MUFIDE KADRI
[1889–1911]

One of the first modern Turkish women painters.

Although she had no formal art education, Mufide Kadri took lessons from Osman Hamdi Bey and Salvatore Velery, teachers at the Istanbul Fine Arts Academy, which for many years did not admit women. She was a prolific painter, and despite her death at an early age, forty of her works remain in existence today. Her oil paintings can be seen in the Istanbul Art Museum.

DAVID WALDNER

MUHAMMAD
[570–632]

The Prophet of Islam.

Muhammad is referred to by Muslims as *rusul allah* (the messenger of God) or *al-nabi* (the Prophet), an appellation that they always follow with the invocation *salla allah alayhi wa sallam* (May God's peace and blessing be upon him).

Early Life

He was born in Mecca in 570, the year of the Elephant, a fortuitous year in tradition, since Mecca in that year survived an Abyssinian invasion directed through Yemen. Although one of various pagan centers in Arabia, Mecca was considered the most important one on account of the Ka'ba, a cubical religious sanctuary revered since ancient times. A spiritual focal point for devotees, who came to it as pilgrims with sacrifices, Mecca provided a convenient meeting point for merchants who exchanged goods there and poets who displayed their literary talents and competed for the attention of its wealthy guests and residents. Authority over the city rested in a loose confederation of tribal groups largely dominated by the tribe of Quraysh. Muhammad was born to the clan of Banu Hashim (Hashimites), a branch within Quraysh that was known less for its wealth than for its religious prestige. The patriarch of the clan was traditionally entrusted with caring for the Ka'ba and maintenance of the pilgrimage facilities, such as the renowned well of *zamzam*, where Islamic tradition states that in ancient times Isma'il, abandoned with his mother Hagar by Abraham (Ibrahim), struck water in the desert and thereby attracted settlement in that spot. Because Mecca is situated on the overland route between Yemen and Syria, its importance as a station, market, and religious center grew with the increasing caravan trade in the region.

Muhammad grew up as an orphan, having lost both of his parents by the age of six. He was then cared for briefly by his grandfather, Abd al-Muttalib, the patriarch of his clan, and afterward by his uncle Abu Talib. In his adolescent years, Muhammad joined his uncle on trade journeys, the most notable of which were to Syria, and he noticed the effects of this commercial boom on his city. The growth of excessive competition in Mecca was gradually undermining traditional Arab tribal values that emphasized principles of solidarity, mutual help, and magnanimity *(muru'a)*, and leaving a pool of destitute and disenfranchised Meccans who were abandoned by a new, wealth-driven generation. In this troubled Arab milieu, Muhammad, who attracted attention in Mecca because of his fair dealing, honesty, and moral sensitivity, was commissioned by a wealthy widow, Khadija, to take charge of her caravan trade. Aged twenty-five, Muhammad married Khadija, fifteen years his senior; she bore him two sons (al-Qasim and Abdullah), who died in infancy, and four daughters (Zaynab, Ruqiyya, Umm Kulthum, and Fatima).

Beyond his distress about the social malaise in Mecca, Muhammad was dissatisfied with the pagan beliefs of the Meccans. The Ka'ba, surrounded by idols that catered to various pagan cults, had become a platform for profit making and opportunism.

Beginning of Islamic Religion

Seeking a full break with this society, Muhammad found solace in spiritual retreats that he undertook in a mountain cave, Hira, on the outskirts of Mecca. According to tradition, Muhammad spent long stretches of time alone in the cave, and it was on one of these occasions, in the year 610, that the angel Gabriel (Jabril) appeared to him and presented him with the words, "Recite in the name of thy Lord, the Creator" (Sura 96:1). Gabriel announced to Muhammad that he was to be the messenger of God and called on him to warn his people against polytheism and to lead them to the worship of the one God. The first words of the Qur'an came to light in the month of Ramadan—hence the religious importance of that month—and other verses followed in later years in various contexts over the course of Muhammad's life. Those closest to Muhammad—his wife, Khadija, his cousin Ali, his companion Abu Bakr, and his servant Zayd—were the first to hear the words of the Qur'an and to embrace the new message, Islam (meaning literally surrendering oneself to the will of God). After overcoming some initial hesitation, Muhammad grew confident in his sense of mission and took the message to the public arena of Mecca.

The earliest Qur'anic recitations of Muhammad emphasized the belief in absolute monotheism. Meccans were called on to cast aside all polytheism and to worship the one God, Allah, the creator of the universe. The Qur'an described the omniscience and omnipotence of God and invited the people (al-nas) to ponder the signs of creation. The Qur'an also admonished the Meccans for their exploitative business practices, involving usurious transactions and unfairness, and warned them of the existence of Judgment Day, when all would be rewarded or punished according to their deeds. This admonishment, together with Muhammad's public denigration of paganism, elicited the hostility of the leading Meccan merchants, who, in addition to feeling their pride offended, feared that the Islamic concept of one God would undermine the status of Mecca as a pagan center and an economic hub. Recognizing the significance of Hashimite solidarity, the Meccans at first attempted to make Muhammad abandon his attack on paganism by such methods as offering to make him king of Mecca, but when all failed, they declared a boycott against him and tried to extend it to all his clan.

In Mecca, Muhammad gained few Islamic converts (primarily young men, some from affluent families), and his attempt to preach in the neighboring town of Ta'if elicited even greater hostility than in Mecca. Finally, in 620, the prospects of the new religion began to change when Muhammad met six men from Medina who were visiting Mecca. This Medinese group, from the tribe of Khazraj, had long been familiar with messianic expectations that circulated in the discourse of Jews and Christians living in the region and proved receptive to the Islamic prophecy. The next year, this group held a larger meeting between Muhammad and seventy residents of Medina who pledged loyalty to the Prophet and invited him to their town. After years of rivalry in Medina between its two leading tribes, the Aws and the Khazraj, Muhammad's leadership offered the possibility of a neutral authority that could mediate disputes, administer the affairs of a diverse community, and contribute to its social recovery. As the hostility of the Meccans to the new religion and its adherents mounted, Muhammad finally decided to migrate, with Abu Bakr, to Medina in a secret journey that took place on 17 September 622. The trip, known in Arabic as *hijra* (migration), would later mark the beginning of the Islamic lunar calendar.

Rise of Islamic State

Once established in Medina, Muhammad set about organizing the nascent Islamic community and strengthening fraternalist ties between the Meccan emigrants (al-muhajirun) and the Medinese, known as the helpers (al-ansar). In a document referred to by scholars today as the Constitution of Medina, Muhammad declared the unity of the community (umma) of Medina under his leadership and stipulated that all matters of legal and political concern were to be referred to him. Medina's hosting of the new religion soon made it the target of Meccan hostility. In 624, mounting tension between the two cities finally led to the first military confrontation at the battle of Badr, where a small Muslim force succeeded in beating back a larger Meccan army. The significance of Badr was not so much military as political. Muhammad's victory strengthened his support in Medina, attracted the admiration of tribal leaders from around the Arabian peninsula, and undermined the prestige of the Meccan order. Between the years 624 and 628, Mecca engaged the Medinese in numerous military skirmishes and battles, the most famous of which was the battle of al-Khandaq (the Trench) in 626. In that year, Mecca assembled a massive confederation of neighboring tribes to invade Medina, but the campaign was forestalled by the Medinese strategy of digging a trench around Medina. The Meccan army, unprepared for a siege and composed of tribal groups that had united for a quick battle only, soon dispersed and retreated.

This last confrontation definitively turned Muhammad into the central leadership figure, and it was then only a matter of time before Mecca would itself become vulnerable to conquest. In 628, Muhammad set out to Mecca on pilgrimage with the new community, only to find his way blocked by the Meccans. At the peace of al-Hudaybiyya in that year, the Meccans called for a long-term truce, after which Muslims would be allowed access to Mecca for pilgrimage. Two years later, the treaty was violated by confederate tribesmen of Mecca, and this opened the way for the Islamic conquest of Mecca, which took place peacefully in 630. A year later, various Arab tribal chiefs from around the peninsula converged on Medina to pay homage or pledge allegiance to the Prophet. Whether nominal or effective, Muhammad's political authority had extended over the greater part of the peninsula, and texts of letters can be obtained from Islamic sources that Muhammad sent to neighboring kings of Persia and Byzantium, as well as various regional princes, inviting them to embrace Islam.

Medina continued its role as the capital of the Islamic state, although Mecca, after the destruction of the idols around the Ka'ba, became the spiritual center of Islam. In 632, soon after completing pilgrimage at Mecca and setting out again for Medina, Muhammad fell mortally ill from a fever. In his final days, he made no specific arrangements for succession. With illness preventing him from leading the prayers, the Prophet asked Abu Bakr to lead the community in prayers, and this gesture would later be interpreted in Sunni Islam as a recommendation for political succession. Shi'ite Islam, in contrast, turns toother traditions describing Muhammad's praise for Ali as a reflection of the Prophet's general designation of Ali as his successor. Ali was also, through his marriage to Fatima, the father of Muhammad's two grandchildren, al-Hasan and al-Husayn.

The life of Muhammad has long captivated the attention of Muslims and non-Muslims alike. Muslims look on him not only as a spiritual guide but also as an exemplar in social, ethical, and political terms. Islamic law grew not only from Qur'anic edicts but also from the Islamic understanding of Muhammad's day-to-day manner of handling all sorts of temporal issues. Oral tradition (hadith) transmitted through Muhammad's companions recounts in detail his instructions and how he lived. Outside observers, on the other hand, continue to weigh Muhammad's achievements in comparison with those of other spiritual masters. In his confrontation with polytheism and his experience of migration, he is compared to Abraham, whereas as promulgator of the rudiments of Islamic law, he evokes a connection with Moses; in his political leadership of the community, he evokes a connection with David. In the vast desert on the fringes of the urban and sophisticated empires of the time—those of the Byzantines and the Sassanians, each with long traditions of structured governmental institutions—Muhammad united both the nomadic and sedentary Arabs into a coherent social unit that would later conquer these powers. Although this political expansion took place under his successors, Muhammad had laid the foundation for an Islamic universalist social vision that was rooted in a unifying monotheistic belief. The memory of the prophetic experience of *hijra* between cities henceforth inspired its emulation on a grander scale outside Arabia.

See also KA'BA; MECCA; QUR'AN.

Bibliography

Cook, Michael. *Muhammad.* Oxford and New York: Oxford University Press, 1983.

Guillaume, Alfred. *The Life of Muhammad: A Translation of Ibn Ishaq's "Sirat Rasul Allah."* London, 1955.

Lings, Martin. *Muhammad: His Life Based on the Earliest Sources,* revised edition. Cambridge, U.K.: Islamic Texts Society, 2001.

Muir, Sir William. *The Life of Mohammad* (1912). New York: AMS Press, 1975.

Rodinson, Maxime. *Mohammed,* translated by Anne Carter. New York: Pantheon, 1971.

Watt, W. Montgomery. *Muhammad at Mecca.* Oxford: Clarendon, 1953.

Watt, W. Montgomery. *Muhammad at Medina.* Oxford: Clarendon, 1956.

Watt, W. Montgomery. *Muhammad: Prophet and Statesman.* London and New York: Oxford University Press, 1961; reprint 1974.

TAYEB EL-HIBRI

MUHAMMAD V
[1910–1961]

Sultan and king of Morocco from 1927 to 1961.

Sidi Muhammad Ben Yusuf was the third son of Mulay Yusuf, a colorless prince and brother of the

King Muhammad of Morocco (1910–1961; right) discusses state matters with his son, Mulay Hassan, 27 February 1961. © HULTON/ARCHIVE BY GETTY IMAGES. REPRODUCED BY PERMISSION.

sultan of Morocco, Mulay Hafid. Muhammad was born in Fez in 1910, at the beginning of the protectorate period; it seemed unlikely he would reign. Two years later, the French nominated his father to succeed the sultan, whom they had deposed because he refused to rule as they wanted. Muhammad V came to power after his father's death in 1927, because French authorities considered him to be more flexible and less ambitious than his brothers. Nevertheless, he used his popularity and his skills in international diplomacy to involve himself in a struggle, at first unequal, with the protectorate's authorities.

After the Berber *dahir* in 1930, which relieved Berber tribes from submitting to *shari'a* (Islamic law), Muhammad became more sensitive to Moroccan nationalism, which was just beginning to awaken. Without breaking off from the protectorate, he supported demonstrations by young traditional and modern intellectuals, such as Allal al-Fasi, Hassan El Ouezzani, and Ahmed Balafrej, which, in 1944, gave birth to the Istiqlal (Independence) Party. World War II presented the opportunity to persuade the protectorate to move toward a cooperative regime more faithful to the spirit of the original agreement between France and Morocco.

Muhammad opposed the French attempt to protect Moroccan Jews from persecution while he helped rebuild military forces to fight again with the Allies. The 1942 Casablanca meeting with U.S. President Franklin D. Roosevelt and Britain's Prime Minister Winston S. Churchill strengthened his resistance. From then on, he used a strategy of promoting gradual change to regain the sovereignty his country had lost in 1912. He approached French authorities directly to avoid the obstacles set up by both settlers and French civil servants, who opposed any change. But he did not succeed despite his good relationship with General Charles de Gaulle. At the local level, opposition to the French became more and more violent and led to the sultan's deposition and exile in Madagascar on 20 August 1953.

But France could not depose Muhammad in 1953 in the same way it deposed his uncle Mulay Hafid in 1912. The international environment was unfavorable to France, French public opinion accepted unwillingly the pro-consuls' plots, and, above all, Muhammad was the symbol of a very deep opposition movement, which mobilized Moroccan cities as well as the countryside. The nation could no longer be governed, and the French administration collapsed within two years in the face of the uprisings. Muhammad was called back to preserve the French economic and military presence, which, otherwise, could have been swept out by nationalistic currents far more radical than those represented by the king and the Moroccan bourgeoisie.

Once he regained his throne, in November 1955, Muhammad took on the role of spokesman for nationalism. He let the Istiqlal Party exert power without, however, becoming a prisoner of the nationalist movement. He continued to defend the monarchy's privileges. Muhammad kept his country out of the confrontation between France and the Algerian Front de Libération Nationale (FLN), which he supported. But, profoundly hurt by the 1956 hijacking of a Moroccan plane with FLN leaders on board, he then attempted to play an intermediary role in the Algerian conflict, hoping, in vain, that de Gaulle's return to power in 1958 would facilitate his reconciliation with France. The king would die without witnessing success. But, he was careful not to jeopardize his country's position within a new Maghrib that, already, some perceived as dominated by a revolutionary Algeria, the main heir of the former colonial power.

Having succeeded in reestablishing his country's independence on the international stage, Muhammad also consolidated the position of the monarchy within an institutional system, which was shaken by the 1953–1955 crisis. Some among the nationalists welcomed a king who reigned without governing. But Muhammad did not share that philosophy for himself or his son, Prince Mulay Hassan, his heir, whom he had gradually introduced to power since the end of World War II.

The support he gained by fighting with the Istiqlal against the protectorate helped him keep his authority over an important part of the nationalist movement. In that struggle, the monarchy recovered its powers that the Treaty of Fes (1912) had alienated and, added to that, the administrative means set up by the protectorate. The military and police forces were placed under monarchical authority, but other administrative sectors depended upon a government dominated by the Istiqlal. Without the help of the monarchy, it was not possible to ensure either the control of the resistance movement or the settlement of rural uprisings. A pluralist text related to public freedom rights allowed, in April 1958, the legalization of new political parties and soon favored the split of the Istiqlal Party, with a right wing remaining close to the king and a left wing following a moderate line. In May 1960, Muhammad took the reins of power by naming Mulay Hassan prime minister. The prince had been, at the beginning of independence, chief of staff in the Royal Armed Forces.

As Algeria's independence approached, the more anxious Muhammad became to grant his country a constitution and to organize its democratization under the monarchy's control. He died suddenly in March 1961 after surgery and left the country to the authority of his son, Hassan II.

During this thirty-two-year reign, Muhammad V listened to his country and took part in its evolution, which allowed it to recover its independence and to project itself into modernity. Chosen because of his apparent docility, he proved, in the long run, to be a cautious opponent, capable of appreciating the modernizing actions of such French resident generals as Auguste Nogues or Eric Labonne. They reciprocated by respecting his dignity. In extreme circumstances, he displayed firmness and in-tuitively anticipated the reactions of common Moroccan people. As far as the rivalry with the nationalist movement, which gradually replaced the common fight against the protectorate, is concerned, he knew how to take advantage of time, how to safeguard his best cards; he went on being attentive to the rural world and sometimes contributed to undermining the credit modern leaders were already losing. Thus, four years after his return, he regained all the power without having to share it. While favoring Algeria's independence, he feared Nasserist or Marxist influences, which could have come from that neighboring country and be exerted upon Morocco.

A man of tradition, Muhammad V was the symbol both of independence and modernity. That symbol continues today to stamp the monarchy's image and to give Morocco a strong identity highly differentiated from that of its neighbor countries.

See also ABD AL-HAFID IBN AL-HASSAN; BALAFREJ, AHMED; CHURCHILL, WINSTON S.; DE GAULLE, CHARLES; FES, TREATY OF (1912); FRONT DE LIBÉRATION NATIONALE (FLN); HASSAN II; ISTIQLAL PARTY: MOROCCO; MAGHRIB; ROOSEVELT, FRANKLIN DELANO.

Bibliography

Ashford, Douglas E. *Political Change in Morocco.* Princeton, NJ: Princeton University Press, 1961.

Waterbury, John. *Commander of the Faithful.* New York: Columbia University Press, 1970.

RÉMY LEVEAU

MUHAMMAD VI

[1963–]

King of Morocco since 1999.

Sidi Muhammad, the oldest son of King Hassan II, was born in Rabat on 21 August 1963. In 1985 he obtained a bachelor of arts degree in law from Muhammad V University, followed in 1987 by a master of arts degree in political science. In 1993 he earned a doctor in law degree from the Université de Nice Sophia Antipolis. Upon his father's death, on 23 July 1999, Sidi Muhammad ascended to the throne under the name Muhammad VI. He became the eighteenth king of the Alawite dynasty

Moroccan king Muhammad VI succeeded to the throne after the death of his father, Hassan II, in 1999. Muhammad VI's reign was initially quite popular with the public, but a slowdown in reforms lowered his support. © AP/WIDE WORLD PHOTOS. REPRODUCED BY PERMISSION.

bearing the title of Amir al-Mu'minin ("commander of the faithful"), befitting a monarch who claims descent from the Prophet.

From the outset, Muhammad VI distinguished himself by advocating religious tolerance, democracy, and human rights reforms. On religion and the state, he echoed his father's position when he asserted in 2000 that, although Islam is the state's official religion, there are also Jews who are an integral part of the Moroccan social fabric. The Amir al-Mu'minin is the leader of the Muslims but also of the Jewish minority still dwelling in the kingdom.

On democracy and human rights, Muhammad VI contended that his country must cultivate specific "homemade" democratic features and avoid blind emulation of Western political systems and advocacy organizations, which often seem irrelevant

to the local milieu. He soon released several thousand prisoners and reduced the prison terms of another 38,000, many of the latter affiliated with the Islamist Jama'at al-Adl wa al-Ihsan (Justice and Charity).

On 20 August 1999 the king broke a taboo by giving a speech in which he mentioned the "disappeared" and the victims of "arbitrary arrest." Simultaneously, emblematic political exiles, or their families, were permitted to return home. Such was the case with the Marxist activist Abraham Serfaty and the family of Mehdi Ben Barka, who had been eliminated in 1965 by the Moroccan secret service upon his arrival in Paris. On 12 November 1999 Muhammad VI dismissed Driss Basri, minister of the interior since 1979. Basri had been regarded as Hassan II's powerful right-hand man who, since the late 1970s, had exiled numerous political opponents or incarcerated them at the infamous Tazmamart prison colony. During the early and mid-1990s King Hassan II had himself set the stage for the reforms undertaken by his son, fearing that the suffering of his people could lead to chaos.

The new king faced major challenges. The population has expanded, despite an infant mortality rate of 57 per 1,000, from ten million in 1956 to thirty-one million in 2003 (an annual growth rate of 2.1 percent). The nation suffers from water scarcity. Unemployment, based on official figures, has reached 20 to 25 percent, but may well be much higher. An estimated 5.9 million people live at or near the poverty level. A major problem is the low access to education, mainly in rural areas. Some 53 percent of the population are illiterate (70 percent among women), while 93 percent receive no medical care.

Of further concern is the Sahara crisis. During the 1970s Hassan II captured large areas of the Western Sahara evacuated by Spain. With Algerian support, the POLISARIO, a Saharawi national liberation movement, sprang up in the Sahara and engaged in guerrilla activity against Morocco. The movement formed a phantom Saharan State in Algiers. Hassan ignored demands for territorial concessions. Muhammad VI pursued this policy despite international pressure to revise it. The policy has caused tensions between Morocco and Algeria.

Despite the proliferation of political parties, nongovernmental human rights organizations, and women's organizations, the struggle for democracy and the uprooting of bureaucratic corruption and inefficiency continues. His most significant effort to date in a drive toward democracy was his decision to convene legislative elections on 27 September 2002. These elections were a step toward a modern civil society. Until these elections, women were excluded from the political decision-making process. In parliament women's representation was only 0.6 percent of the 325 seats in the Moroccan house of representatives (lower house). Only one woman held a government position, that of minister-delegate, which was not a full-fledged portfolio. Since the convening of the newly elected lower house, there are thirty-five women MPs, or 10.8 percent of the total. However, the elections also enabled the Islamists and other opposition parties to fortify their position within Morocco's parliament.

Despite increased women's representation in politics, serious problems continue for the majority of women not represented in the political elite. Muhammad VI's endorsement of revising the religious *madawana* (family code pertaining to women's personal status) toward greater equality between men and women is progressing well but remains thus far in the embryonic stage. The king's "Plan of Action" includes the lifting of legal discrimination in marriage and divorce, the abolition of polygamy, and economic equality between the sexes. The Islamists vehemently oppose the Plan, having forced the government in past years to postpone reforms.

Whereas the Jama'at al-Adl wa al-Ihsan retained outsider status, because it questions the legitimacy of Muhammad VI's status as commander of the faithful, the legal Islamist party, al-Adala wa al-Tanmiya (Justice and Development), made vital electoral strides. It reached third place in the legislative elections, with forty-two seats as compared to the fifty seats won by the Union Socialiste des Forces Populaires (USFP) and forty-eight of the Istiqlal Party.

The attempt to form a new government in October 2002 revealed the shortcomings of Moroccan democracy. Neither the USFP nor Istiqlal, the dominant governmental partners, nor Muhammad VI wanted the Islamists to hold ministerial posts. Com-

mitted to the concept of a global economy and determined to privatize the public sector, the king feared that involving Islamists in government could stymie reforms and draw sharp criticism from the Moroccan business community as well as the European Union (EU). Moreover, after the 11 September 2001 terrorist attacks, the king thought such a move might irritate Washington. According to the 1996 constitution, the king appoints key members of the government and may, at his discretion, terminate the tenure of any minister or prevent any political party from participating in the ruling cabinet.

Owing to the more liberal atmosphere in Morocco after the death of Hassan II, both conservative Islamists and secular leftists leveled serious criticisms at the new king. They claimed that while Muhammad VI had placed, early in his reign, priority on technological advances aimed at supplying Morocco's rural areas with potable water, electricity, Internet access, and cellular phone service, it had soon became evident that the son was not all that different from the father. Thus the Islamists stepped in to provide some education and welfare services to communities as yet not benefiting from promised reforms and to organize effective mass protests against the government.

Also having grown more vocal, the Berber population demanded greater cultural recognition of their heritage. Berber leaders claim that 60 percent of the Moroccan population is of Berber heritage. It is almost impossible to verify the population figures; leading experts on Berber culture note that Morocco's Berber speakers (there are three Berber dialects as well as literary Berber) constitute 40 percent of the population, mostly in rural areas. The Berber associations protest against their youth being exposed generation after generation to the idea that Morocco is part of the Arab nation, making them Arabs in spite of themselves. Although Berbers were converted to Islam, their ethnic and linguistic purity has remained intact. Morocco, the Berbers argue, is Berber, Arab, and African. In March 2000 Berber leaders drafted a manifesto calling on the kingdom to recognize Berber as a national language, teach it in schools, license a Berber television station, and end restrictions on registering Berber names for their children. In a concession to the Berbers, in 2001 Muhammad VI created by royal decree an institute devoted to the conservation, dissemination, and teaching of the Berber language and culture of Morocco.

Until 2003 Muhammad VI had shown little interest in the Middle East. He declined a U.S.-Egyptian invitation to attend the June 2003 Sharm al-Shaykh meeting that preceded the U.S.-Israeli-Palestinian summit in Aqaba, and only grudgingly accepted his father's role as chairman of the al-Quds Committee, a body formulating Arab policies on Jerusalem. Unlike their political predecessors, Muhammad VI and the presidents of Tunisia and Algeria have chosen thus far to immerse themselves in domestic issues and ties with the EU.

See also HASSAN II; MAGHRIB; MOROCCO; POLISARIO.

Bibliography

Laskier, Michael M. "A Difficult Inheritance: Moroccan Society under Muhammad VI." *Middle East Review of International Affairs* 7, no. 3 (September 2003): 1–20.

Ramonet, Ignacio. "New Hope, Old Frustrations: Morocco—The Point of Change." *Le Monde Diplomatique* (July 2000): 18–26.

MICHAEL M. LASKIER

MUHAMMAD ALI

[1770–1849]

Ruler (pasha) of Egypt, 1805–1849.

Muhammad (also Mehmet) Ali Pasha was born to a military family in the Macedonian port city of Kavalla (in what is today Greece). He was apprenticed to the tobacco trade by his father, Ibrahim Agha, and took over the family business upon Ibrahim's death in 1790. He also succeeded his father as commander of the local militia, in which post he came to the attention of the Ottoman authorities in Istanbul, who assigned him a warship to protect the surrounding waters against pirates. He married a well-to-do widow, Amina, who bore him three sons, Ibrahim, Ahmad Tusun, and Isma'il, and two daughters, Tevhide and Nazli.

In 1801, Muhammad Ali was appointed second in command of the 300 troops from Kavalla ordered to take part in the Ottoman Empire's expedition to drive Napoléon's army from Egypt. Muhammad Ali took over the regiment when its commander hastily returned to Macedonia; his skill on the battlefield prompted the Ottoman general to promote him to the rank of *binbashi* during the first weeks of the campaign. After the evacuation of the French, the Kavallan regiment stayed on to assist the Ottomans in subduing the Mamluk commanders. When the new governor let their pay slide into arrears, Muhammad Ali led these irregulars in a demonstration demanding it and then collaborated with the Mamluks to overthrow Egypt's Ottoman governor, taking control of Cairo in 1804 with the support of the religious notability and rich merchants. In June 1805, he was confirmed as governor-general *(wali)* of Egypt by the Ottoman Porte (government).

During the next six years, he suppressed the Mamluks and confiscated their lands, disarmed the urban population, and established a regular fiscal administration. These steps set the stage for military campaigns in the Sudan and the Hijaz (Arabia) in 1810 and 1811, which were followed by expeditions to Crete and the Peloponnese (Greece) from 1820 to 1824 and an invasion of Palestine and Syria in 1831.

After reaching the gates of Istanbul at the end of 1832, his armies were gradually forced out of Anatolia through the intervention of the British and Russians. Repeated attempts to conciliate Britain failed, and in 1840 the London Convention was effected, with the Ottomans supported by Britain, Austria, Prussia, and Russia. British warships then bombarded Beirut and appeared off Alexandria (Egypt), forcing Muhammad Ali to agree to give up his empire in Syria, Arabia, and the Aegean in exchange for the hereditary right to rule Egypt. He traveled to the Ottoman capital in 1846 to confirm his family's succession, but he succumbed to dysentery and dementia on 2 August 1849. His descendants continued to rule Egypt, taking the titles of wali and khedive until 1952, when Farouk was ousted by a revolutionary government.

See also LONDON CONVENTION.

Bibliography

Dodwell, Henry. *The Founder of Modern Egypt: A Study of Muhammad Ali.* New York: AMS Press, 1977.

Lawson, Fred H. *The Social Origins of Egyptian Expansionism during the Muhammad 'Ali Period.* New York: Columbia University Press, 1992.

Sayyid-Marsot, Afaf Lutfi al-. *Egypt in the Reign of Muhammad Ali.* Cambridge, U.K., and New York: Cambridge University Press, 1986.

FRED H. LAWSON

MUHAMMAD ALI MOSQUE

Mosque commissioned by Muhammad Ali for Cairo's Citadel.

By its size and hilltop location, the Muhammad Ali Mosque at the Citadel dominates the Cairo skyline. As early as 1820, Muhammad Ali of Egypt asked French architect Pascal Coste to draw up plans for mosques in the Citadel and at Alexandria. Coste's plan was not used, however, when construction began in the early 1830s, just as Muhammad Ali was challenging his Ottoman overlord by invading Syria. Turning his back on local Mamluk-influenced architectural styles that had persisted through three centuries of rule by the Ottoman Empire, Muhammad Ali symbolized his ambitions by appropriating the style of great Ottoman mosques of Constantinople (now Istanbul). Sultan Ahmet's Blue Mosque, the Nuru Osmaniye, and the Yeni mosques have all been cited as influencing Yusuf Bushnaq, the Greek architect brought from Constantinople to construct the mosque. Its embellishments are in the baroque-rococo style in vogue in Constantinople in the eighteenth and early nineteenth centuries.

The mosque also symbolized Muhammad Ali's victory over the Mamluks, whom he had murdered in the Citadel in 1811. Dominating the citadel founded by Salah al-Din (known as Saladin [1137–1193]), it rose on the leveled ruins of the Qasr al-Ablaq (Striped Palace) of al-Nasir Muhammad, the Mamluk sultan whose mosque stands nearby.

The mosque is built of local Muqattam limestone, with columns and sheathing of alabaster—a stone softer than marble previously used mainly for vases and other small objects—from a quarry near Bani Suwayf. The mosque was completed in 1857 under Sa'id Pasha. Colonnades topped with small domes bound its open courtyard. The side opposite the great dome has a clock tower with an ornate timepiece presented by King Louis-Philippe of France; Muhammad Ali returned the favor with the obelisk now standing in the Place de la Concorde in Paris. Two slender Ottoman minarets rise 270 feet (82 m) on square bases only 10 feet (3 m) on a side. The great Byzantine Ottoman dome rests on four arches with four massive piers. Four half-domes lead out of the arches, four smaller domes fill in the corners, and a lower half-dome tops the *mihrab* (the niche at the east end of the mosque pointing to Mecca). Above the alabaster sheathing, the interior walls and domes are ornately painted. Muhammad Ali is buried beneath a marble monument to the right of the entrance, behind a bronze grill. Hundreds of lights hang from the ceiling on great chandeliers. Muhammad Ali's Jawhara (Bijou) Palace stands nearby.

The Muhammad Ali Mosque lacked local successors as well as local antecedents. In the second half of the nineteenth century, either Western or eclectic Mamluk-revival styles were preferred for major Egyptian buildings.

See also MUHAMMAD ALI; SULTAN AHMET MOSQUE.

Bibliography

Egypt. Blue Guide series. London: Benn, 1984.

DONALD MALCOLM REID

MUHAMMAD AL-SADIQ
[1814–1882]

Ruler of Tunisia, 1859–1882.

Muhammad al-Sadiq Bey was the son of Husayn Bey (ruler of Tunisia, 1824–1835) and the third Husaynid *mushir* (marshal). His reign saw Tunisia's first experiment with constitutionalism, parliamentary rule, and restrictions on the bey's authority; the unbridled control of Prime Minister Mustafa Khaznader; disastrous foreign loans; increased taxes; a bitter revolt; Europe's economic control; the reformist ministry of Khayr al-Din (1873–1877); and the imposition of a protectorate by France (1881).

From all reports, Muhammad al-Sadiq was a weak ruler who was easily influenced by his political entourage of Mamluks, especially Khaznader. Like his predecessor, Ahmad Bey, al-Sadiq evinced an early fascination with the military and showed some talent in that area. Soon after his accession, he sought to reconstitute the army and introduced a military code that provided for conscription of all able-bodied male adults for a period of eight years. An individual could send a proxy if he chose not to enter the army.

Upon assuming the throne in 1859, al-Sadiq declared that he would uphold the principles of the Fundamental Pact of 1857. He proclaimed a new constitution in April 1861. It included the principle of ministerial responsibility, financial control vested in the Grand Council, a strict budget controlled by the Grand Council, and a secular court system. Also provided was a "bill of rights" that included provisions for religious freedom and conversion from Islam.

Although the document appeared to guarantee constitutionalism and individual rights, it actually provided for a system that perpetuated the Turkish-Mamluk political elite and increased their power at the bey's expense. It was not, therefore, a parliamentary democracy that emerged, but a traditional elitist oligarchy. The limitations placed on the bey's authority by the constitution increased Khaznader's confidence and freedom of action. He used the constitution to eliminate his enemies on the Grand Council and install his close associates. He increased his financial exactions from the state treasury and more than doubled the national debt within one year. For this reason, he floated his first foreign loan in 1863. To pay for that loan, Khaznader increased the unpopular personal *majba* tax twofold. This led to the revolt of 1864.

From 1865 to 1869, Khaznader ran the state. In the latter year, after poor harvests, famines, and epidemics, al-Sadiq accepted the International Finance Commission, which aimed to ensure Tunisia's payment of its financial obligations. Khayr al-Din, Khaznader's son-in-law, represented Tunisia on the commission. In 1873 he persuaded the bey to remove Khaznader and install himself as prime minister.

Under Khayr al-Din's prime ministry, a number of reforms were instituted: regulation of the education at Zaytuna University, the founding of Sadiqi College, elimination of abuses in the administration of *hubus* (religious trust) properties,

reformation of the tax system, abolition of the *mahallas*, improvements in administrative accountability, introduction of protective tariffs on imports, and numerous public works projects. Sharp curtailment of public spending by the bey and support for Ottoman claims to sovereignty over Tunisia forced Khayr al-Din to resign in July 1877. Constraints on the bey's powers were lifted, and the weak Mustafa ibn Isma'il became prime minister.

Using the excuse of Tunisia's violations of its border with Algeria, France invaded Tunisia in 1881. On 12 May 1881, Muhammad al-Sadiq Bey signed the treaty, known as the Treaty of Bardo, officially establishing France's protectorate, which lasted until 1956. It was later repudiated by the bey, an action that forced the signature of a second treaty in July. Although this second treaty was never ratified, the La Marsa Convention of June 1883 (signed by Ali Bey, ruler of Tunisia from 1882 to 1900) confirmed the provisions of the Bardo treaty and France's imposition of a protectorate.

See also FUNDAMENTAL PACT; KHAYR AL-DIN; KHAZNADER, MUSTAFA; LA MARSA CONVENTION; MAHALLE SCHOOLS; MAMLUKS.

Bibliography

Anderson, Lisa. *The State and Social Transformation in Tunisia and Libya, 1830–1980.* Princeton, NJ: Princeton University Press, 1986.

Nelson, Harold D., ed. *Tunisia: A Country Study,* 3d edition. Washington, DC: U.S. Government Printing Office, 1988.

Perkins, Kenneth J. *Historical Dictionary of Tunisia,* 2d edition. Lanham, MD: Scarecrow Press, 1997.

LARRY A. BARRIE

MUHAMMAD, AZIZ
[1933–]

First secretary of the Communist Party of Iraq, 1963–1978.

A Kurd, born in Sulaymaniyya, Aziz Muhammad al-Hajj joined the Iraqi Communist Party in 1948. He was arrested the same year and jailed until the end of the monarchy in 1958. Soon after his release, he entered the Central Committee of the party and was appointed head of the Central Organizational Committee. From February 1963 to August 1965, he resided in Moscow, and in 1963 was elected first secretary of the party (in exile). Starting in 1978, following the rapprochement between the Soviet Union and the Ba'th regime in Iraq, Muhammad led the party to cooperation with the Ba'th. On 17 July 1978, Muhammad signed the National Action Charter with the president of Iraq and the secretary of the Ba'th party, which became a basis for strategic alliance between the communists and the Ba'th. By the time of the U.S. invasion of Iraq in 2003, real power in the party lay in the hands of Hamid Majid Musa.

Bibliography

Batatu, Hanna. *The Old Social Classes and Revolutionary Movements of Iraq.* Princeton, NJ: Princeton University Press, 1982.

MICHAEL EPPEL
UPDATED BY MICHAEL R. FISCHBACH

MUHAMMARA

See FOOD: MUHAMMARA

MUHARRAM

First month of the Islamic lunar calendar, containing thirty days.

The events that took place on the tenth of Muharram in the year 680 changed forever the character of this month by making it a month of mourning, at least for the Shi'a. On that date, Husayn—the grandson of the Prophet Muhammad and the third Imam of Shi'ite Islam—was brutally killed on the battlefield of Karbala. In this battle Husayn's sons, male relatives, and followers also perished. The women of his encampment were taken as captives to Caliph Yazid in Damascus. This tragic event overshadows any other event in that month. Husayn's ordeal started on the first of Muharram, when he and his party were intercepted by Yazid's troops, and continued even after his death, with the captivity of the Karbala survivors. Although the tenth of Muharram (known as *Ashura*), is the actual date of Husayn's death, the mourning has been extended to cover the whole month.

For the Shi'a, the Muharram tragedy of Husayn is the greatest act of suffering and redemption in history. It acquired a timeless quality, and, therefore, apart from the yearly Muharram observances, the Shi'a continually try to measure themselves against the principle of the paradigm of Husayn whenever they regard themselves as deprived, humiliated, or abused. In fact, one of the main slogans during the Islamic revolution in Iran (1978/79) chanted by the crowds or scribbled as graffiti on town and village walls was "Every day is Ashura; every place is Karbala; every month is Muharram." This same slogan was intoned on radio and television and was graphically depicted on posters and even postage stamps during Iran's eight-year (1980–1988) war against Iraq.

The Muharram commemoration of Husayn's passion and martyrdom is charged with unusual emotions throughout the world's Shi'a communities. Even the followers of Sunni Islam and the members of other religions who live among the Shi'a are greatly affected by these commemorative rituals. That participation in the annual observance of Husayn's suffering and death is considered an aid to salvation on the day of judgment provides an additional incentive for Shi'a to engage in the many mourning rituals. Elaborate Muharram observances were already carried out in the fourth Islamic century in Baghdad during the reign of Mu'izz al-Dawla of the Shi'ite Buyid dynasty. Many Muharram rituals have developed since, and although they may differ in form from one locality to another, passionate participation in them is universal.

These rituals may be divided into two categories, the ambulatory and the stationary. They are primarily performed during the first ten days of Muharram, with the greatest discharge of emotions and the greatest number of rituals occurring on the day of Ashura. The most common ambulatory rite is a procession, and the participants are divided into different groups of self-mortifiers—those who beat their chests with the palms of their hands; those who beat their backs with chains; and those who wound their foreheads with swords or knives. Some mortify themselves with stones, and others carry the *alam,* which signify the standard of Husayn at Karbala. In Iran, in some processions, floats with live tableaux representing the scenes from the Karbala tragedy can be seen, as well as Husayn's symbolic bier, called *nakhl* (date palm). Nakhl is carried because, according to tradition, Husayn's beheaded corpse was carried on a stretcher made of date palm branches. Some nakhl are so large that they require more than 150 people to carry them. Processions are accompanied by bands of martial and mournful music. The most characteristic features of Muharram on the Indo-Pakistani subcontinent are the huge artistic interpretations of Husayn's mausoleum carried or wheeled in the procession. At the end of Ashura day, these structures, called ta῾ziya, are either cremated or buried at the local cemetery, called Karbala, or are immersed in water.

The Muharram observances were brought as far as the Caribbean basin in the years 1845 to 1917, when indentured laborers from India went there. Muharram is still, after carnival, the most important event in Trinidad. Although the Muharram rituals in Trinidad have more of a festive than a mourning character, the main features continue to be processions. In this case, the processions are parades of colorful cenotaphs for Husayn, called tadja. In India, the Sunni and even the Hindus actively participate in many Muharram rituals. In Trinidad as well, this is a true ecumenical event.

To the stationary rituals belong majalis al-aza, recitation and singing of the story of Husayn at the Battle of Karbala. In Iran, this ritual is called rawda khwani. The storyteller (called rawda khwan) of the Shi῾ite martyrology sits above the assembled crowd on a minbar (pulpit) in a black tent, under an awning, or in a special edifice (Husayniyya or takiya in Iran; ashurkhanah or imambarah in India) and brings the audience to a state of frenzy with recitation, chanting, crying, sobbing, and body language. The most unusual stationary ritual is the ta῾ziya of Iran—the only serious drama and theater developed in the Islamic world depicting the martyrdom of Husayn and other Shi῾ite martyrs. Originally, it was performed in the month of Muharram, but now it is staged year round.

The Muharram processions actually served as prototypes for the massive demonstrations in Tehran and other Iranian cities during the 1978/79 revolutionary upheavals. The mixing of Muharram mourning slogans with political ones has been an old Muharram tradition. The Iranian Revolution utilized the Husayn Muharram paradigm and was carried out in accordance with the Islamic calendar. Ayatollah Ruhollah Khomeini's revolution started in Muharram on Ashura, 3 June 1963, when he delivered a speech at the Fayziya Madrasa in Qom, criticizing the internal and external policies of the shah, Mohammad Reza Pahlavi, and his government. In the article "Islamic Government," written while he taught in exile in Najaf, Khomeini states: "Make Islam known to the people, then . . . create something akin to Ashura and create out of it a wave of protest against the state of the government" (Islam and Revolution, p. 131). A few days before Muharram on 23 November 1978, in order to accelerate the revolution, Khomeini issued from Ncauphle-le-Château, France, a declaration called "Muharram: The triumph of blood over the sword," which was recorded in France and distributed in Iran through its network of mosques. The opening paragraph of the declaration reads as follows:

> With the approach of Muharram, we are about to begin the month of epic heroism and self sacrifice—the month in which blood triumphed over the sword, the month in which truth condemned falsehood for all eternity and branded the mark of disgrace upon the forehead of all oppressors and satanic governments; the month that has taught successive generations throughout history the path of victory over the bayonet. (Islam and Revolution, p. 242)

Less than two months later, the shah left Iran, enabling Khomeini to return from fourteen years of exile.

Muharram affects the entire Islamic community; however, it is primarily felt among Shi῾a. Muharram could be expressed both as a mourning depression and an exuberant agitation and will to act. These expressions of Muharram can be and have been converted into political actions.

Bibliography

Ayoub, Mahmoud. Redemptive Suffering in Islam: A Study of the Devotional Aspects of Ashura in Twelver Shi῾ism. The Hague: Mouton, 1978.

Canetti, Elias. "The Muharram Festival of the Shi῾ites." In Crowds and Power, translated by Carol Stewart. New York: Farrar Straus Giroux, 1984.

Chelkowski, Peter J., ed. Ta῾ziyeh: Ritual and Drama in Iran. New York: New York University Press, 1979.

Cole, J. R. I. *The Roots of North Indian Shiʿism in Iran and Iraq.* Berkeley: University of California Press, 1988.

Hollister, John Norman. *The Shiʿa of India.* London: Luzac, 1953.

Khomeini, Ruhollah. *Islam and Revolution: Writings and Declarations of Imam Khomeini,* translated by Hamid Algar. Berkeley, CA: Mizan Press, 1981; reprint, New York: Kegan Paul, 2002.

"Moharram in Two Cities, Lucknow and Delhi." *Census of India, 1961.* New Delhi, 1965.

Proceedings of the Imam Husayn Conference, July 1984, London. *Alserat* 12 (spring/autumn, 1986).

Rizvi, Saiyid Athar Abbas. *A Socio-Intellectual History of the Isna Ashari Shiʿis in India.* Canberra: Maʿrifat, 1986.

Saiyid, A. R. "Ideal and Reality in the Observance of Muharram." In *Ritual and Religion among Muslims of India.* New Delhi, 1981.

Von Grunebaum, G. E. *Muhammadan Festivals.* London: Abelard-Schuman, 1958.

PETER CHELKOWSKI

MUHARRAQ

The second-largest city in the Kingdom of Bahrain and the second-largest island of the archipelago in the Persian/Arabian Gulf.

During the early nineteenth century, Muharraq (also Moharek, al-Muharraq) was ruled by leaders of the Abdullah branch of the al-Khalifa (who rule Bahrain). They used it as a base for their long-standing rivalry with the Sulman branch, centered in Manama (the capital, on the main island of Bahrain, now across a short channel-bridge). More homogeneous in population than Manama, Muharraq has mainly Sunni Arabs and only two predominantly Shiʿite residential districts. During the 1950s and 1960s, both radical and Arab nationalist movements appealed to the city's people in an effort to remove the British. Muharraq was the site of the British air force and army bases during the later years of the British protectorate (1880–1971). It is also the site of the country's international airport. In 2001, the city's population was estimated at 74,000.

See also AL KHALIFA FAMILY.

Bibliography

Clarke, Angela. *The Islands of Bahrain.* Manama, Bahrain: Bahrain Historical and Archaeological Society, 1981.

FRED H. LAWSON

MUHSIN, ZUHAYR
[1936–1979]

Palestinian politician and guerrilla leader.

Born in Tulkarm in mandatory Palestine, Zuhayr Muhsin joined the Baʿth party at age seventeen and later became a teacher in Jordan. He was accused in 1957 of pro-Nasser subversion, and left to live briefly in Qatar and Kuwait, before finally settling in Damascus, Syria. In 1970, he became leader of Saʿiqa (Thunderbolt), the Syrian Baʿth party's Palestinian guerrilla organization. The following year, he was appointed to the Palestine Liberation Organization (PLO) executive committee as Saʿiqa's representative. Later, he became head of the PLO's military department.

Muhsin is believed to have led a battalion that attacked the Lebanese town of Damur in January 1976, where 582 people were killed. Saʿiqa also played a role in defending the Tal al-Zaʿtar Palestinian refugee camp in Lebanon under siege by the Phalange the following summer. At the 1977 Palestinian National Council meeting, Muhsin argued against partial, negotiated settlements on the Palestine question. He was assassinated by an unknown assailant on 15 July 1979 on a street in Cannes, France.

See also BAʿTH, AL-; PALESTINE LIBERATION ORGANIZATION (PLO); PHALANGE; SAʿIQA, AL-; TALL AL-ZAʿTAR REFUGEE CAMP.

Bibliography

Cobban, Helena. *The Palestinian Liberation Organisation: People, Power, and Politics.* Cambridge, U.K., and New York: Cambridge University Press, 1984.

Seale, Patrick. *Abu Nidal: A Gun for Hire.* New York: Random House, 1992.

ELIZABETH THOMPSON

MUHTAR, GAZI AHMET
[1839–1918]

Ottoman soldier and grand vizier.

One of the great Ottoman war heroes of the late nineteenth century, Gazi Ahmet Muhtar's first notable victory was his halt of Russian advances on the eastern front in the Turkish-Russian War (1877/78). In appreciation, Sultan Abdülhamit II awarded him the title of *gazi* and appointed him to head an imperial military inspection commission. From 1895 to 1906, Ahmet Muhtar served as the sultan's representative, or high commissioner, to Egypt.

During this time, Ahmet Muhtar became a prominent advocate of modernization and westernization and was loosely affiliated with the Committee for Union and Progress (CUP) and other groups. In July 1912, liberal officers opposed to the CUP's autocratic rule used military threats to bring down its grand vizier. They chose Ahmet Muhtar, then an elderly statesman considered above politics, to replace him. His government, known as "the great cabinet," consisted of several former grand viziers chosen to unite the empire in face of the Balkan crisis and Italian war. But Muhtar's government fell after only a few months, with the grave Ottoman losses at the outbreak of the Balkan War in October.

See also COMMITTEE FOR UNION AND PROGRESS.

ELIZABETH THOMPSON

MUHYI AL-DIN, KHALID
[1923–]

Egyptian politician.

A military officer from a well-to-do family, Khalid Muhyi al-Din received a degree in economics from the University of Cairo and the rank of major in the Egyptian army after graduating from the Royal Military Academy. He joined the clandestine Free Officers who toppled King Farouk in 1952. Although Muhyi al-Din was a member of the Revolutionary Command Council, he was eventually marginalized by Gamal Abdel Nasser, first for backing President Muhammad Naguib and later for being a communist in an Arab context that did not favor communism. He did, however, retain a position in the government overseeing the press. He opposed Anwar Sadat's pro-Western and pro-Israeli policies and in 1977 formed the National Progressive Unionist Party, over which he presided and which advocated a pan-Arab socialist ideology. He was elected to parliament in 1990.

See also ARAB SOCIALISM; FAROUK; FREE OFFICERS, EGYPT; NASSER, GAMAL ABDEL; NATIONAL PROGRESSIVE UNIONIST PARTY; SADAT, ANWAR AL-.

Bibliography

Muhyi al-Din, Khaled. *Memories of a Revolution: Egypt 1952.* Cairo: American University in Cairo Press, 1995.

MAYSAM J. AL-FARUQI

MUHYI AL-DIN, ZAKARIYYA
[1918–]

Egyptian military officer and politician.

Zakariyya Muhyi al-Din (or Mohieddin) came from a wealthy landowning family outside Mansura, Egypt. He was educated at the Military College and the Staff Officers College in Cairo, served in the Palestine War, and was an Army Staff College lecturer at the time of the revolution. An original member of the Free Officers and a key figure in the overthrow of King Farouk in 1952, he was appointed to the Revolutionary Command Council established to support Gamal Abdel Nasser in government. Muhyi al-Din subsequently served as interior minister (1953–1962), founded the General Intelligence Service, and then served as prime minister (1965–1966) and vice president (1967). After the 1967 war with Israel, Nasser resigned and named Muhyi al-Din his successor, a fact widely interpreted as acquiescence to U.S. influence, particularly since Muhyi al-Din supported economic liberalization throughout the 1960s. Public demonstrations encouraged Nasser to withdraw his decision, and Muhyi al-Din left public life in March 1968.

After Nasser's death in 1970, it was thought that conservatives were plotting to ensure that Muhyi al-Din succeeded as president, leading to a wave of "corrective" trials when Anwar al-Sadat secured the support of centrist and leftist camps. In 1972 Muhyi al-Din was again linked to a petition to Sadat by ministers and ex-officers opposed to Soviet influence, and in 1978 he publicly opposed Sadat's rapprochement with the United States and Israel. He has since refrained from making public interventions.

See also FREE OFFICERS, EGYPT; NASSER, GAMAL ABDEL; REVOLUTIONARY COMMAND COUNCIL (EGYPT).

Bibliography

Beattie, Kirk. *Egypt during the Sadat Years.* New York: Palgrave, 2000.

Mohi el Din, Khaled. *Memories of a Revolution: Egypt, 1952.* Cairo, Egypt: American University in Cairo Press, 1995.

Waterbury, John. *The Egypt of Nasser and Sadat: The Political Economy of Two Regimes.* Princeton, NJ: Princeton University Press, 1983.

DAVID WALDNER
UPDATED BY GEORGE R. WILKES

MUJADDARA

See FOOD: MUJADDARA

MUKHABARAT

See GLOSSARY

MUKHTAR

See GLOSSARY

MUKHTAR, UMAR AL-

[c. 1862–1931]

Preindependence Libyan guerrilla leader.

Umar al-Mukhtar was born into the Minifa tribe, which lives along the eastern Cyrenaican coast, otherwise known as Marmarica. His family was part of the Farhan lineage, itself part of the Braidan fraction. The Minifa were a client tribe of the al-Abaydat *sa'adi* tribe, to whom they paid dues as *marabtin al-sadqan* (clients for protection). Most of the tribe were seminomads, but some lineages were camel-herding nomads. The tribe had long been under Sanusi influence, with the closest *zawiya* (Islamic religious center) being located at Janzur, on the coast.

Umar al-Mukhtar's early education was provided at the Janzur *zawiya*. He then moved to the Sanusi order's headquarters at Jaghbub, 100 miles (160 km) inland, near the modern border between Libya and Egypt. He proved an adept pupil and a committed member of the Sanusi *ikhwan* (brotherhood), with the result that he was nominated shaykh of the al-Qasur *zawiya*, in the Abid tribe, just to the south of al-Marj in the Jabal al-Akhdar.

At the turn of the century, after only two years at al-Qasur, Umar al-Mukhtar was sent southward to the new Sanusi headquarters at al-Kufra, which had been created in 1895. From there he was sent to Wadai, to participate in the Sanusi resistance to French penetration into what today is central Chad. He returned to al-Qasur in 1906 and took a prominent role in the first Italo–Sanusi War, which followed on the Italian invasion and occupation of Darna and Tripoli in September 1911.

The war was brought to an end by the Treaty of Akrama in January 1917. The treaty was, in effect, a truce, enforced on the Sanusi by British pressure, which left the Italians in charge of the coastal areas, while the Sanusi controlled the hinterland. Sanusi armed forces were gathered into a series of camps running eastward along the southern slopes of the Jabal al-Akhdar from Ajidabiya to Akrama. The *badu* (bedouin) forces in these camps were controlled by Sanusi *ikhwan* and shaykhs. Umar al-Mukhtar was responsible for the camps at al-Abyar, due east of Banghazi and south of al-Marj, and Taknis, just southeast of al-Marj.

In November 1921, in accordance with the terms of the Accord of Bu Mariyam, four of these camps were transformed into *campi misti* (mixed camps), in which Italian and Sanusi units, under their own independent commands, were garrisoned side by side. Both the camps controlled by Umar al-Mukhtar were included in this bizarre experiment, which was designed to promote joint policing and security arrangements. The fascist march on Rome at the end of 1922 also marked the beginning of the end of this experiment in joint policing and, on 6 March 1923, Italian forces attacked the campi misti, thus ushering in the second Italo–Sanusi War.

Although the Sanusi family did not take direct charge of the new war—most of its members fled to Egypt for British protection—Sanusi *ikhwan* played a prominent role, alongside some of the younger members of the Sanusi family. Umar al-Mukhtar was to take charge of operations against the Italians. He took charge of all the guerrilla bands (*adwar*) on the plateau formed along the southern slopes of the Jabal al-Akhdar in Cyrenaica, as the *al-Na'ib al-Amm* (general representative) of the Sanusi.

According to E. E. Evans-Pritchard, the *adwar* were usually between 100 and 300 men, and each was the nominal responsibility of a particular tribe.

Its membership, however, was often heterogeneous, including members of other tribes, *ikhwan,* and sympathizers from the Sudan and Tripolitania. The overall numbers involved in the fighting were very small—around 600 to 700 toward the end of the war—simply because the terrain did not permit major movements of personnel. Umar al-Mukhtar's responsibilities were to determine strategy, to arrange logistics and to ensure discipline, particularly in terms of pillage and vendettas.

The guerrilla war obeyed few of the rules to which the Italians were accustomed. In a telling passage, Teruzzi, when governor of Cyrenaica, pointed out to the authorities in Rome that superiority in men and arms was "a vain illusion, because the struggle was not against an organized enemy, but against an enemy who had no consistency of form." It was difficult, for example, for the Italians to distinguish between friend and foe, because those tribes that were apparently submitted to Italian rule still provided material support to the guerrillas.

The strategy of al-Mukhtar was to hold the southern slopes of the plateau formed by the Jabal al-Akhdar to the south of the littoral escarpment. Although the Italian forces were able to establish themselves on the coast and to control the immediate hinterland of their major bases at Ajidabiya and al-Marj, they found it very difficult to ensure control of the land between. They were able to use air power to attack *badu* camps in the flatlands of the plateau, but could do little about the plateau itself. Even a line of permanent forts and outposts along the plateau of the Jabal did little to increase the effectiveness of Italian units, while an attempt to divert guerrilla activity by the capture of Jaghbub in 1926 proved to be irrelevant to the struggle.

Nonetheless, the constant military pressure severely depleted al-Mukhtar's forces; in 1928, both provinces of Libya were placed under a single administration. An offer of negotiations persuaded al-Mukhtar, his companion guerrilla leader, Sidi Fadil Bu Umar, and a young scion of the Sanusi family, Sayyid al-Hasan al-Rida, to accept a five-month truce. The negotiations broke up in disorder, however, with al-Mukhtar and his supporters rejecting the arrangements agreed to by Sayyid al-Hasan al-Rida. By late January 1930, al-Mukhtar was forced to back into his last redoubt, after his

forces were severely beaten at Wadi Mahajja; 800 men and 2,000 camels were lost during 1929, compared with Italian losses of only 114 men.

Command of the Italian campaign in Cyrenaica was then taken over by General Rodolfo Graziani, who applied a ruthless policy—providing Italian troops with great mobility, isolating the guerrilla bands from their logistics support base by herding the nomadic population of Cyrenaica into concentration camps, and cutting the guerrillas off from their Egyptian bases by a barbed-wire barricade.

On 11 September 1931, Sidi Umar al-Mukhtar was captured at Suluq and, five days later, was hanged before 20,000 Libyans in a demonstration of Italian power. The war was effectively over, even though 700 guerrillas had remained on the plateau. The last engagement was fought on 19 December 1931. The death of al-Mukhtar had destroyed the spirit of the Libyan resistance.

See also SANUSI ORDER.

Bibliography

Evans-Pritchard, E. E. *The Sanusi of Cyrenaica.* Oxford: Clarendon Press, 1947.

Hahn, Lorna. *Historical Dictionary of Libya.* Metuchen, NJ: Scarecrow, 1981.

Nelson, Harold D., ed. *Libya: A Country Study,* 3d edition. Washington, DC: U.S. Government Printing Office, 1979.

Wright, John. *Libya: A Modern History.* Baltimore, MD: Johns Hopkins University Press, 1982.

GEORGE JOFFE

MUKRANI FAMILY

Prominent family in preindependence Algeria.

During the late Ottoman period (c. 1800–1830), the Mukranis controlled a key section of the route between Algiers and Constantine. Under the French, Muhammad al-Mukrani was a regional commander until the military regime was weakened by Prussia's defeat of France in 1870. His revolt of 1871/72, supported by the Rahmaniyya brotherhood of Kabylia, was the largest and most harshly suppressed indigenous uprising prior to the War of Independence.

PETER VON SIVERS

MULAI

See GLOSSARY

MULUKHIYYA

See FOOD: MULUKHIYYA

MUNICH OLYMPICS

See TERRORISM

MUNIF, ABDEL RAHMAN

[1933–]

Saudi Arabian writer.

Abdel Rahman (also Abd al-Rahman) Munif, a prolific writer of novels and of autobiographical and political essays, was born in 1933 in Amman, Jordan, to a Saudi father and an Iraqi mother. He attended university in Baghdad and Cairo and earned a Ph.D. in oil economics from the University of Belgrade. Munif continued to visit Saudi Arabia until 1963, when the Saudi government stripped him of his citizenship because of his political activism. Munif held prominent positions in the oil industry and was editor in chief of the periodical *Oil and Development* in Baghdad. He published his first novel, *Al-ashjar wa ightiyal Marzuq* (The trees and Marzuq's assassination), in 1973. His 1978 novel, *Endings,* is distinguished from the many Arabic novels focused on urban life by its detailed portrayal of the culture and the harsh conditions of village life at the edge of the desert. His description of life, culture, and politics in the Arabian peninsula reaches its most elaborate expression in the five-book *Cities of Salt* series. The first volume, originally published as *Al-Tih* (The wilderness, 1984), presents a critical view of the development of a fictional Gulf emirate in the 1930s and explores the disruption of an oasis community as a result of the interaction between Americans and the local Bedouin community following the discovery of oil. Munif's devastating portrayal of government corruption and oppression in *Cities of Salt* and other novels has inspired censors in Saudi Arabia and Egypt to ban his books.

Bibliography

Allen, Roger. *The Arabic Novel: An Historical and Critical Introduction,* 2d edition. New York: Syracuse University Press, 1995.

Munif, Abdel Rahman. *Cities of Salt,* translated by Peter Theroux. New York: Random House, 1987.

Munif, Abdel Rahman. *Story of a City: A Childhood in Amman,* translated by Samira Kawar. London: Quartet Books, 1996.

CAROLINE SEYMOUR-JORN

MUNTADA AL-ADABI, AL-

A pro-Arab club founded in Istanbul in 1909; centered in Jerusalem after 1918.

Al-Muntada al-Adabi (Literary Society) was originally founded in Istanbul in 1909 by Abd al-Karim al-Khalil of Tyre, Lebanon, to act as a meeting place for Arab visitors and residents in the capital of the Ottoman Empire. The club played a role in the prewar reformist Arab movement in late Ottoman times. Membership of the club included politically conscious Lebanese, Palestinians, and Syrians. After the dissolution of the Ottoman state, the club reemerged in Jerusalem in November 1918 with new members and a new political program. It was largely dominated by prominent members of the Nashashibi family, most notably Is'af, a man of letters. Adopting a stance in favor of Arab nationalism, the club demanded complete Arab independence and Palestinian–Syrian unity. From its major center in Jerusalem, the club helped organize an anti-Zionist movement whose activities spread in Lebanon and Syria, where the club had branches. With the fall of the Syrian Arab government of Faisal I ibn Hussein (1920), the club lost a major source of support and was eclipsed by the emergence of the Arab Executive in 1920.

See also NASHASHIBI FAMILY.

Bibliography

Muslih, Muhammad. *The Origins of Palestinian Nationalism.* New York: Columbia University Press, 1988.

MUHAMMAD MUSLIH

MUNTAFIQ TRIBE

See TRIBES AND TRIBALISM: MUNTAFIQ TRIBE

MUNTASIR FAMILY

Prominent Tripolitanian Arab family in Libya.

The Muntasir family resided in the coastal town of Misurata. It collaborated with the Turkish administrators of Libya during the second Ottoman occupation, after 1835, but fell out with the Young Turk revolution of 1908, since one of its leading members was murdered, allegedly, at Young Turk instigation.

The Muntasirs switched support to Italy during Italy's entry into Libya, before the military occupation of 1911, and cautious support continued during the first Italo-Sanusi War that ensued.

When the United Nations took charge of Libya's transition to independence in 1950, Mahmud Bey Muntasir was made premier of the provisional government, a position that was confirmed upon independence until his resignation in 1954. As an intimate of the royal family, he became premier and interior minister again in 1964, during pro-Arab nationalist agitation in Tripoli. Since the Great September Revolution (1969), members of the family have acted in a ministerial capacity and Umar Muntasir has been seen as the leading light of the technocrat faction within the Jamahiriya.

Bibliography

Wright, John L. *Libya.* London: Benn; New York: Praeger, 1969.

GEORGE JOFFE

MURABITUN

Military arm of Harakat al-Nasiriyyin al-Mustaqillin (Independent Nasserite Movement); largest Sunni Muslim militia in west Beirut from the beginning of Lebanon's civil war of 1975 until the Arab–Israel War of 1982.

Founded by Ibrahim Qulaylat in early 1972, the Murabitun (Arabic for sentinels) of Lebanon maintained a close alliance with al-Fatah (of the Palestine Liberation Organization, PLO) and continuously replenished its arms stockpiles through the largesse of Libya. Qulaylat was a veteran of the Lebanese Civil War of 1958 and had cultivated a personal relationship with his hero, Egypt's President Gamal Abdel Nasser.

During the early stages of the Lebanese Civil War of 1975, the Murabitun expelled the Maronite Christian militias from the hotel district of downtown Beirut, and they maintained a sizable presence in the capital from then on. The dispersal of the PLO and the Murabitun's disarmament by Israel in 1982 greatly weakened the movement; in 1984, Syria's allies, the Shiʿite Amal and the Druze militias of the Progressive Socialist Party conducted a series of multiple strikes against Qulaylat, who increasingly advanced himself as the protector of the Sunni community. Qulaylat now lives in exile in France.

See also FATAH, AL-; LEBANESE CIVIL WAR (1958); NASSER, GAMAL ABDEL; PROGRESSIVE SOCIALIST PARTY.

Bibliography

Johnson, Michael. *Class and Client in Beirut: The Sunni Muslim Community and the Lebanese State, 1840–1985.* London: Ithaca Press, 1986.

Salibi, Kamal. *Cross Roads to Civil War: Lebanon, 1958–1976.* Delmar, NY: Caravan Books, 1976.

BASSAM NAMANI

MURRAH, AL

See TRIBES AND TRIBALISM: MURRAH, AL

MUSA DAGH

Mountain site of Armenian resistance to 1915 deportation orders in the Ottoman Empire.

Of the hundreds of villages, towns, and cities across the Ottoman Empire whose Armenian population was ordered removed to the Syrian desert, Musa Dagh was one of only four sites where Armenians organized a defense of their community against the deportation edicts issued by the Young Turk regime beginning in April 1915. By the time the Armenians of the six villages at the base of Musa Dagh were instructed to evict their homes, the inhabitants had grown suspicious of the government's ultimate intentions and chose instead to retreat up the mountain and to defy the evacuation order. Musa Dagh, or the Mountain of Moses, stood on the Mediterranean Sea south of the port city of Alexandretta and west of ancient Antioch.

With a few hundred rifles and the entire store of provisions from their villages, the Armenians on

Musa Dagh put up a fierce resistance against a number of attempts by the regular Turkish army to flush them out. Outnumbered and outgunned, the Armenians had little expectations of surviving the siege of the mountain when food stocks were depleted after a month. Their only hope was a chance rescue by an Allied vessel that might be roaming the coast of the Mediterranean. When two large banners hoisted by the Armenians were sighted by a passing French warship, swimmers went out to meet it. Eventually five Allied ships moved in to transport the entire population, more than four thousand in all.

The Armenians of Musa Dagh had endured for fifty-three days: from 21 July to 12 September 1915. They were disembarked at Port Saʿid in Egypt and remained in Allied refugee camps until the end of World War I when they returned to their homes. As part of the district of Alexandretta, or Hatay, Musa Dagh remained under French mandate until 1939. The Musa Dagh Armenians abandoned their villages for a second, and final, time when the area was incorporated in the Republic of Turkey.

In the face of the complete decimation of the Armenian communities of the Ottoman Empire, Musa Dagh became a symbol of the Armenian will to survive in the postwar years. Of the three other sites where Armenians defied the deportation orders, Shabin Karahissar, Urfa, and Van, only the Armenians of Van were rescued when the siege of their city was lifted by an advancing Russian army. The Armenians of Urfa and Shabin Karahissar were either murdered or deported to face starvation in the Syrian desert much as the rest of the Armenians of the Turkish empire. In what became known as the Armenian genocide, Musa Dagh stood as the sole instance where the Allies averted the death of an Armenian community. That story inspired the Prague-born Austrian writer, Franz Werfel, to write a novelized version of the events as *The Forty Days of Musa Dagh*. Published in 1933, the book became an instant best-seller, but with the rise of Hitler, Werfel himself fled Vienna that same year. *Forty Days of Musa Dagh* was eventually translated into eighteen languages, and Metro-Goldwyn-Mayer bought the rights to the book and announced plans for the production of a film version of the novel. The Turkish ambassador's protestations to the Department of State resulted in the intervention of the U.S. government in the matter. With a veiled threat to ban U.S.-made films from Turkey, MGM studios permanently shelved plans to produce the movie.

Bibliography

Minasian, Edward. "The Forty Years of Musa Dagh: The Film that Was Denied." *Journal of Armenian Studies* 2, no. 2 (1985/86): 63–73.

Walker, Christopher J. *Armenia: The Survival of a Nation*, revised 2d edition. New York: St. Martin's, 1990.

ROUBEN P. ADALIAN

MUSA KAZIM
[1858–1919]

Ottoman Turkish religious leader.

Musa Kazim was the Shaykh al-Islam of the Ottoman Empire after the deposition of Sultan Abdülhamit II in 1909. He was also a member of Talat's cabinet in 1917. Musa Kazim Efendi called for a return to the foundations of Islam as the only way to restore the empire to its former glory. He believed in an orthodox Islam based on the Qurʾan and the *shariʿa* (Islamic law) and not open to what he perceived to be the liberal interpretations of the educated elite. Though he urged the adoption of Western technology, he claimed that Western culture was incompatible with the *shariʿa*, and cultural Westernization was therefore forbidden to Muslims. He was a staunch defender of the institution of the caliphate, and he championed reforms in the teaching of religion. Musa Kazim was a Sufi (a Muslim mystic) though there is some dispute as to whether he was of the Naqshabandi or the Bektashi order.

See also SHAYKH AL-ISLAM.

Bibliography

Berkes, Niyazi. *The Development of Secularism in Turkey*. New York: Routledge, 1998.

Lewis, Bernard. *The Emergence of Modern Turkey*, 3d edition. New York: Oxford University Press, 2002.

Ramsaur, E. E. *The Young Turks: Prelude to the Revolution of 1908*. Princeton, NJ: Princeton University Press, 1957.

Shaw, Stanford J., and Shaw, Ezel Kural. *History of the Ottoman Empire and Modern Turkey*, Vol. 2: *Reform, Revolution,* and Republic: The Rise of Modern Turkey, 1808–1975. Cambridge, U.K., and New York: Cambridge University Press, 1977.

ZACHARY KARABELL

MUSA, NABAWIYYA
[1890–1951]

Early Egyptian feminist.

Nabawiyya Musa, often referred to as one of Egypt's first Muslim feminists, was a pioneer of girls' schooling, women's rights, women's journalism, and nationalist education. Musa graduated from, and then taught at, al-Saniyya teacher training institute for girls. She gained fame in 1907 as the first woman to sit for and pass the secondary-school certificate exam despite there being no secondary girls' school at the time. Consequently, she became the first female teacher to earn pay equal with that of her male counterparts, setting a precedent for postindependence Egypt. An outspoken critic of foreign education because of what she considered its dubious political and cultural influence, Musa stressed the importance of indigenous teachers and a nationalist curriculum. She advanced girls' schooling as teacher, administrator, inspector, author of a popular grammar text, and founder and director of two private girls' schools. Also an avid writer and public intellectual, she founded the journal *Majallat al-Fata* and in 1920 authored the groundbreaking feminist work *al-Mara'a wa al-Amal* (The woman and work). An honorary founder of the Egyptian Feminist Union (established in 1923) and a staunch nationalist, Musa believed that spreading women's education was an essential nationalist act with the greatest potential impact.

See also EGYPTIAN FEMINIST UNION; GENDER: GENDER AND EDUCATION; NEWSPAPERS AND PRINT MEDIA: ARAB COUNTRIES.

Bibliography

Badran, Margot. *Feminists, Islam, and Nation: Gender and the Making of Modern Egypt.* Princeton, NJ: Princeton University Press, 1995.

Baron, Beth. *The Women's Awakening in Egypt: Culture, Society, and the Press.* New Haven, CT, and London: Yale University Press, 1994.

LINDA HERRERA

MUSA, SALAMA
[1887–1958]

Egyptian socialist essayist.

Salama Musa was born into a Coptic, well-to-do, landed family in Zaqaziq, a town in Egypt's Nile delta. While still in high school, Musa left Egypt for Europe, where he studied in France and England. In England, he met and was influenced by several prominent members of the Fabian Society, including H. G. Wells and George Bernard Shaw. Fabianism was a doctrine that combined economic socialism with an emphasis on social and moral regeneration through the cultivation of traditional moral values such as culture, decency, and order.

Returning to Egypt, Musa sought to spread this doctrine, urging his readers to leave behind Asian civilization and to embrace European—specifically, British—civilization. Other themes he dealt with were the scientific spirit, the theory of evolution, and social democracy. He founded Egypt's Socialist Party in 1920 and established a journal, *al-Majalla al-Jadida* (The new magazine), a forum for radical critiques. In several of his works, Musa also developed the theme that the Coptic period was the apex of Egyptian civilization and that the Copts were the true present-day descendants of the ancient Egyptians.

See also COPTS.

Bibliography

Egger, Vernon. *A Fabian in Egypt: Salamah Musa and the Rise of the Professional Classes in Egypt, 1909–1939.* Lanham, MD: University Press of America, 1986.

DAVID WALDNER

MUSAVI-ARDEBILI, ABDOLKARIM
[1926–]

Politically active Iranian cleric.

Born in Ardebil in 1926, AbdolKarim Musavi-Ardebili began his religious career in 1942 in Qom, where he was a student of Ayatollahs Ruhollah Khomeini and Hosain Borujerdi. In 1948 he went to Najaf, Iraq, to pursue his education further, and he stayed there for nineteen months. In the 1960s in Qom he copublished the journal *Maktab-e Islam* (School of Islam), and also pursued political activities in his hometown of Ardebil. In 1971 he moved to Tehran to conduct sermons at a mosque. A founder, after the 1979 Iranian Revolution, of the now defunct Islamic Republican Party, Musavi-Ardebili also established the Bonyad-e Mostaz'afan (Foundation of the Oppressed). He was the prosecutor general from 1980 to 1981 and head of the supreme judicial council and the Supreme Court from 1981 to 1989. In 1988 he was appointed to the Expediency Council. Other positions held by Musavi-Ardebili include his appointment by Khomeini to the constitutional review panel in 1989 and his membership in the Supreme Council of the Cultural Revolution. Generally he has adopted moderate positions in the factional disputes among politicians since the early 1990s and has devoted his attention to a private high school that he founded.

See also BORUJERDI, HOSAYN; IRANIAN REVOLUTION (1979); KHOMEINI, RUHOLLAH.

Bibliography

Iran Research Group. *Iran 89/90.* Bonn, Germany: Author, 1989.

NEGUIN YAVARI
UPDATED BY ERIC HOOGLUND

MUSAVI, MIR-HOSAIN
[1941–]

Prime minister of Iran, 1981 to 1989.

Born in Khameneh in 1941, Mir-Hosain Musavi received a degree in architecture from the National University of Iran (now called Shahid Beheshti) in 1969. He was jailed in 1973 for anti-shah activities. Upon his release he left Iran for graduate studies in the United States, where he joined the Organization of Iranian Moslem Students. After the Iranian Revolution he joined the Islamic Republic Party and served as first deputy to the party's founder, Ayatollah Seyed Mohammad Hossein Beheshti (1929–1981).

A revolutionary favored by the left, he served as foreign minister in President Muhammad Ali Rajai's cabinet (1981). In October 1981, after a bomb attack had killed the president and the prime minister and a new election had resulted in the election of Hojatoleslam Seyed Ali Khamenehi as president, Musavi was appointed prime minister. He served in this position until 1989, when a constitutional

amendment abolished the post of prime minister in favor of a stronger presidential system. His departure from the office marked a change in both the international and domestic policies of the Islamic Republic.

Musavi's tenure involved major national and international challenges: the Islamization of the society, the consolidation of clerical power and elimination of secular opposition, the debilitating Iran–Iraq War (1980–1988), and economic sanctions imposed by the United States. During the 1980s Musavi tilted Iran toward the socialist bloc aligned with the former Soviet Union. When re-elected in 1985, President Khamenehi considered replacing him but was opposed by Ayatollah Khomeini, who saw Musavi as a counterbalance to the conservative faction. Musavi's premiership was overshadowed by a strong parliament presided over by Ali Akbar Hashemi Rafsanjani, and a president who did not favor his radical policies.

Musavi is a radical Islamic intellectual who supports a centralized and regulated economy, opposes the concentration of capital and land in private hands, and supports self-reliance over foreign investment and rapprochement with the United States. Despite his economic radicalism, he holds a relatively liberal attitude toward cultural policies.

After his premiership, he had a quiet life and assumed several nominal positions. Although both presidents Rafsanjani (1989–1997) and Mohammad Khatami (1997–present) appointed him as an adviser, he is rarely sought out. In 1987 Ayatollah Khomeini appointed him to the Expediency Council, but he has not been an active participant in recent years. Although he has a good relationship with the reformers, he is viewed as a radical member of the old guard. He remains a viable candidate for radical forces in the Islamic Republic, and during presidential elections his name often surfaces as a possible candidate.

He teaches at the Tarbiyat Modares University and is the chair of the Academy of Arts, the highest national institution overseeing national production of artistic works. He spends a good deal of his time on his own artistic works, which were shown in a 2003 exhibition in Tehran. He is married to Zahra Rahnavard, a sculptor and writer who is the chancellor of the all-women university, Al-Zahra, in Tehran. They have three daughters.

See also BEHESHTI, MOHAMMAD; IRANIAN REVOLUTION (1979); KHAMENEHI, ALI; KHOMEINI, RUHOLLAH; RAFSANJANI, ALI AKBAR HASHEMI; RAHNAVARD, ZAHRA.

Bibliography

Moslem, Mehdi. *Factional Politics in Post-Khomeini Iran.* Syracuse, NY: Syracuse University Press, 2002.

ALI AKBAR MAHDI

MUSCAT

Capital of Oman; formerly a Portuguese and later a British stronghold on the Oman coast.

Muscat's fine natural harbor has for centuries attracted local and foreign maritime powers. Otherwise, the city's location offers more challenges than benefits. Its climate is hot and humid most of the year, and the narrow, rocky strip of land upon which it lies is wedged tightly between the Indian Ocean and the steep flanks of the Hajjar Mountains. It is not known when Muscat was established, but the name first appears in written sources during the thirteenth century.

The port came into regional prominence during the sixteenth century, after Portugal seized control and built two massive forts that overlook the harbor to this day. Portugal ruled until the Ya'ariba imamate restored Omani rule in 1649. Although not Oman's capital, Muscat thrived under Ya'ariba patronage as a leading Indian Ocean emporium and shipping center and the hub of an expanding maritime empire. After a period of decline and Iranian rule, Muscat became one of the main ports and trading centers on the western Indian Ocean from the late eighteenth and early nineteenth century, controlled by the Al Bu Sa'id dynasty.

Muscat's prosperity began to decline in the 1830s, as Zanzibar became the region's premier commercial center. During the nineteenth century, British influence grew in Muscat, and the port became an important coaling station for ships plying routes between the empire's Indian possessions and the Middle East. By the early twentieth century, despite some arms smuggling, Muscat had become a sleepy steamer port. Its faltering business was conducted mainly by British-protected Indian merchants. Economic depression reduced the population in the early years of the twentieth century to just above 4,000 from about 30,000 in the mid-eighteenth century, before a revival began after the 1970 coup that installed Sultan Qabus ibn Sa'id al Bu Sa'id's modernizing regime.

As in other places on the Arabian Peninsula, oil revenues have been used to develop once-poor towns in Oman. Although lack of space has limited Muscat's growth, post-1970 improvements have included a sumptuous royal palace, restoration of historic structures, and a modern infrastructure. More extensive development has been possible in nearby towns because of the greater availability of land along the coastal strip between the capital and the international airport at Sib. Thus while Muscat had an estimated population of 55,000 in 2003, the nearby city of Ruwi had 112,000 inhabitants as well as much of the capital region's commercial, government, and residential development. Other towns in this region include Matrah, famous for its traditional *souk,* or market, Darsayt, Qurum, Mandinat Qabus, Ghubra, and Khuwayr.

See also AL BU SA'ID, QABUS IBN SA'ID; OMAN.

Bibliography

Hawley, Donald. *Oman and Its Renaissance,* revised edition. London: Stacey International, 1984.

Lorimer, J. G. "Masqat Bay and Town" and "Masqat District." In *Gazetteer of the Persian Gulf, Omān, and Central Arabia, Vol. 2B, Geographical and Statistical.* 1908–1915. Reprint, Farnsborough, U.K.: Gregg, 1970.

Scholz, Fred. "Muscat: Social Segregation and Comparative Poverty in the Expanding Capital." In *Population, Poverty and Politics in Middle East Cities,* edited by Michael E. Bonine. Gainesville: University Press of Florida, 1997.

Trench, Richard, ed. *Arab Gulf Cities: Muscat and Mattrah.* Slough, U.K.: Archive Editions, 1994.

Wilkinson, J.C. "Maskat." In *The Encyclopaedia of Islam,* vol. VI, new edition, edited by C.E. Bosworth et al. Leiden: Brill, 1991.

ROBERT G. LANDEN
UPDATED BY ANTHONY B. TOTH

MUSIC

Musicians in the Middle East have, over the centuries, produced a great classical tradition in a variety of regional forms.

Historically, Middle Eastern music has been predominantly melodic, drawing from a complicated system of modes called *maqam* in Arabic, *makam* in Turkish, and *mugam* in Azerbaijani. The melodic system of Iran is based on *dastgaha*, similar in principle if not in practice. These systems and their repertoires frequently have written histories—music theories that date back to the time of al-Farabi and earlier.

Sung poetry is fundamental to the musical art of the region. The elegant or clever text and the performance that highlights the affective phrase or the play on words often are highly valued by listeners.

Instrument types include long- and short-neck lutes, plucked and hammered dulcimers, end-blown reed flutes, hourglass drums, frame drums, and several sizes of double-reed wind instruments often played in concert with large field drums. These instruments have different names, shapes, and playing styles.

Overarching genres of performance occur throughout the region, often consisting of suites of instrumental and vocal music, both improvised and formally composed. They occur in devotional rituals, dance, neoclassical performance, and performances by folk musicians. Despite the disparate sounds, contexts, and audiences, these performances are often linked by listeners with their Arabic musical-poetic heritage (*turath*), which encompasses a broad range of religious, classical, and folk musics. Typologies common in the West that separate the religious and the secular, or the classical, the folk, and the popular, do not always apply to Middle Eastern repertoires. For instance, in Iran the classical *radif* stands in stark contrast to Kurdish folk songs but is colored by Iranian Sufi performance. By contrast, the Azerbaijani *mugam*, a classical genre, includes and arguably depends on Azeri folk music in its structure.

Regional Distinctions

Over the years these historic materials and aesthetics have yielded distinct styles, genres, and practices in different times and places. For example, the governments of Morocco and Tunisia and private agencies in Algeria have participated in the revitalization of local forms of *nawba,* a suite-like genre. It is believed to have originated in Andalusia and to have been carried from there to North Africa. What results, in the twentieth century, is "classical" music so emblematic of a particular region that it is really not possible to speak of "Algerian" classical music, let alone "Arab" classical music but rather the repertories of Tlemcen, Constantine, Algiers, Fez, Tunis, and so on. However in general, revitalization of these genes serves to mark cultures as "Arab" rather than Berber.

On the other hand, styles drawn from the peoples of southern Morocco, Algeria, Tunisia, and Libya have created distinctly North African popular genres exemplified by the Moroccan group Nas al-Ghiwan. Similiarly, Algerian *raʾi* offers an excellent example of a style rooted in local musical practice, transformed with imported electronic instruments and modern texts. These styles draw the historic aesthetic of the clever, sometimes stinging colloquial text and favorite local instruments into contact with the electronics, and sometimes the staging, of rock music. The result may or may not be considered "westernized" by local listeners.

Regional distinctions have long been part of *mashriq* performances. Microtonal intervals tend to be tuned slightly higher in Turkey and Syria than in Egypt and North Africa. The *buzuq* is an important part of Lebanese folk culture. The resurgence of "classical" repertoires has been discouraged in Turkey since the establishment of the republic (1923). The governments of Egypt, Iraq, and Lebanon have sponsored neoclassical ensembles that often give concerts in opera houses, with musicians in evening dress performing without the extemporization that is historically part of Middle Eastern traditions. In other words, Arab pieces of music are presented in the context of a Western concert.

Transformed classical and folk traditions have emerged in nongovernmental venues as well. Perhaps the best known are the plays by Fayruz and the Rahbani brothers, articulating local pride and local concerns by using distinctly Lebanese styles and a combination of local and Western instruments. The Western models of the musical play and film,

Kurdish folk dancers and musicians, eastern Turkey, ca. 1990–1996. © Chris Hellier/Corbis. Reproduced by permission.

popular in the Arab world, serve local purposes well. The best-known recent exponent of music from the *turath* is the Syrian Sabah Fakhri, who travels internationally, performing *muwashshahat, taqasim,* classical instrumental pieces, and newer songs in suite-like arrangements. Umm Kulthum and Muhammad ibn Abd al-Wahhab are well-known performers of "new" or "popular" music that has attracted a large audience throughout the Arab world. Abd al-Wahhab's style is the more innovative, creating a pastiche of Western and Arab musical styles in a single composition and establishing the free-form instrumental piece (*al-qitʿa al-musiqiyya*) as an important independent genre. Although both Umm Kulthum and Abd al-Wahhab sing complicated neoclassical works, Umm Kulthum has claimed this area as her own.

Instrumental improvisations (*taqasim*) and a historic suite-like genre, the Iraqi *maqam,* have persisted throughout the twentieth century, partly supported by the Arab diaspora. The performances of Munir Bashir, Nazim al-Ghazali, and Muhammad al-Qubbanji have been rereleased by firms in Paris and Baghdad. Iraq and the countries of the Arabian peninsula support rich traditions of singing and

dancing that have been documented by local musicologists and by folklore institutes such as that established in Oman.

Teaching and performing classical Persian music have formed part of musical life in Tehran throughout the twentieth century, especially among elites. The musical culture of Iran encompasses a range of folk and religious musics as well. Cabaret music also has become popular. Following the Iranian Revolution, the new government moved to suppress musical performance, including music at weddings. In the long run, the primary target was cabaret music, often associated with consumption of alcohol and prostitution. In recent years, *radif* recordings have become readily available, and performance of traditional music persists.

Israel presents a unique musical culture, consisting of a patchwork of musics from Europe, the former Soviet Union, the Arab world, and Africa, brought together in a small space over a relatively short period of time. A few syncretic repertoires have emerged, but musics more often persist as individual emblems of the immigrant communities.

Musical Occasions

Weddings and special occasions, often religious in nature, have long offered venues for musical performance. Starting the pilgrimage to Mecca, celebrating the birthday of Muhammad, remembering the martyrdom of Husayn, and the ceremonies of Sufi *dhikrs* have all involved music. During the nineteenth and twentieth centuries, urban nightclubs and cabarets often featured musical entertainment and dancing, as did tourist hotels. Generally speaking, there is a long history of professionalism in Middle Eastern music. In some areas, notably Iran, professional musicians tend to belong to minority groups; musical performance in the majority culture tends to be amateur.

These tendencies have persisted in the twentieth century. Often they have been transformed through the mass media, which quickly took hold throughout the Middle East and became very popular. Many would argue that the mass media have become primary patrons of musicians.

Commercial recording took hold in the first decade of the twentieth century, mainly in Algiers, Cairo, Beirut, Constantinople (now Istanbul), and Tehran. Radio became more popular than the phonograph in the 1930s. Television, beginning in the 1960s, and videocassettes in the 1970s, proliferated, especially among the middle and upper classes. This development is significant particularly because cassettes, which are inexpensive and portable, gave control over production to local artists, or at least to agencies that were closer to the artists than a national radio company or a European-based recording company. Artists were able to produce their own recordings and market them locally, circumventing those who select music for radio and television stations and the requirements of international production firms. In the 1990s, despite the opportunities for Middle Eastern artists to produce internationally marketed videos and compact disks, some of the most interesting performances are locally released cassettes.

Musical Processes and Issues

As a constituent of social life, musical performances in the Middle East have engaged local histories with the flow of new materials from other societies. Unsurprisingly, this engagement has fed debates on

Munir Bashir (1930–1997). Iraq's best-known musician, Bashir was famous for his mastery of the oud, a musical instrument of the lute family. © SHEPARD SHERBELL/CORBIS. REPRODUCED BY PERMISSION.

authenticity, music and sociocultural identity, modernity, and the proper nature of culture in the late twentieth century.

The development of mass media centered in urban areas has tended to promote the musics of those areas over others. Local musics from Morocco to Iraq have been dominated in the mass media by musics produced in Cairo and Beirut, for instance. Only in recent years, with the less expensive cassette and a recent interest in the musics of southern Morocco, Nubia, and the Gulf states, has this situation changed.

Contact with Europe and the United States has led some musicians to borrow, adapt, and integrate new sounds into local music. The accordion, cello, string bass, and electronic instruments have become widely popular and virtually consolidated with some local musics. Latin rhythms, disco, and nineteenth-century orchestral music (especially for film scores) have been borrowed outright. This vast array of sounds—ranging from religious chanting by a solo voice to improvisations on lutes, dueling songs, formally composed orchestral pieces, and special electronic effects—is being employed by musicians and their listeners to identify themselves and to suggest directions and affinities within their societies.

Boundaries are not always clear. The process of musical creation transforms past practices to contribute to the lively culture of Middle Eastern societies intent on maintaining an identity while responding to the challenges of the present.

See also ABD AL-WAHHAB, MUHAMMAD IBN; FAYRUZ; UMM KULTHUM.

Bibliography

Browning, Robert, ed. *Maqam: Music of the Islamic World and Its Influences.* New York: Alternative Museum, 1984.

During, Jean, et al. *The Art of Persian Music.* Washington, D.C.: Mage, 1991.

Farhat, Hormoz. *The Dastgah Concept in Persian Music.* Cambridge, U.K.: Cambridge University Press, 1990.

Al-Faruqi, Lois. "Music, Musicians, and Muslim Law." *Asian Music* 17, no. 1 (1985): 3–36.

Jenkins, Jean, and Olsen, Poul Rovsing. *Music and Musical Instruments in the World of Islam.* London: World of Islam Festival Publishing, 1976.

Nettl, Bruno. *The Radif of Persian Music: Studies of Structure and Cultural Context in the Classical Music of Iran,* 2d edition. Urbana, IL: Elephant & Cat, 1992.

Signell, Karl. *Makam: Modal Practice in Turkish Art Music.* Seattle, WA: Asian Music Publications, 1977.

VIRGINIA DANIELSON

MUSLIM BROTHERHOOD

Religious political organization that started in Egypt in 1928 and subsequently spread throughout most Muslim countries.

The founder of the Muslim Brotherhood (*Jam'iyyat al-ikhwan al-muslimin,* or the Society of Muslim Brothers) was Hasan al-Banna (1906–1949), the son of a modest but learned religious teacher, who received traditional as well as modern training at Dar al-Ulum in Cairo, where he was exposed to the prevailing Salafiyya ideology of Islamic revivalism preached in Egypt by Muhammad Abduh. It was in Isma'iliyya, a showcase of Egyptian poverty and European colonialist wealth and power where he was posted to teach Arabic in a primary school, that he founded the Muslim Brotherhood. In 1934 Banna moved back to Cairo, where his organization merged with the Society for Islamic Culture, which was headed by his brother, and the combined organization quickly became the largest grass-roots movement in Egypt. With more than half a million members drawn from the middle class as well as from labor groups, peasants, and the student population, and

with an efficient structure, hundreds of mosques and clubs throughout the country, and a printing press, in the 1940s the Brotherhood became a powerful organization intent on affecting the government's social policies and ridding Egypt of British occupation. Partly because of its mass power, and partly in order to play it against the other political parties, the Egyptian government in turn compromised with and fought the organization, jailing Banna intermittently on various charges and releasing him for fear of mass insurrection.

From the start, the Muslim Brotherhood exhibited the dual characteristics of an internal reform movement operating within the context of foreign occupation. Banna's early and primary concern, which molded the movement and provided it with its lasting method and policy, had been to bring about a return to the pristine sources of the faith and away from the distortions of popular religion. In that, it was the continuation of the powerful reform movement that spread throughout the Muslim world in the eighteenth century and became known in Egypt as the Salafiyya movement, although unlike the latter (but similar to earlier reform movements), the Muslim Brotherhood showed Banna's strong attachment to Sufi spirituality. Consistent with the pattern of Islamic reform movements in history, its ideology was translated into a praxis that sought to establish *shari'a* and to use Islam to combat corruption, moral laxity, economic exploitation, and oppression through the creation of a strong civil network centered around the mosque and providing for employment, education, welfare, clubs, health clinics, and other social services. In harmony with earlier reform movements and with orthodox Islamic doctrine, it advocated dialogue, preaching, and gradual reform rather than revolt.

But the Muslim Brotherhood was also operating in the context of Egypt's occupation by the British, who dictated government policy. Moving away from the Salafiyya, which had become concerned solely with a strict interpretation of the faith, the Brotherhood looked to fulfill popular aspirations such as Egyptian independence, and it used anti-imperialist rhetoric from the start. In order to keep its legal status and remain operational, the Brotherhood maintained a policy of nonconfrontation, but this was challenged by its followers. A major turning point came in 1936 with the eruption of riots in Palestine against the Zionist implantation. The Brotherhood, which already had offices in Palestine, helped to raise funds for the insurrection. In 1938 a meeting with the Palestinian mufti Muhammad Amin al-Husayni produced the decision that a military wing was needed to push back the territorial ambitions of the Zionists, and a secret order was created within the Brotherhood to repel Western colonialism. Thus, as part of the organization remained focused on reform and dialogue with a Muslim government, the other part took on jihad against the foreigners, and preachers and organizers were sent to Palestine to help in the Palestinian insurrection.

In 1939 Brotherhood members defected from the organization, claiming that its lack of action against British occupation was inconsistent with its stated ideology, and they started *Shabab Sayyiduna Muhammad,* the first of a number of radical Muslim political movements that advocated the use of force against a government that cooperates with Western occupation or with policies against the interests of the Muslim community. Banna had always opposed engaging in jihad against fellow Muslims. But to the military wing, largely formed in response to the defection of the disgruntled members, fighting the British occupation of Palestine was the same as fighting the occupation of Egypt. The partition of Palestine in 1948 led to uncontrollable riots and acts of violence against British and Jewish interests. The Muslim Brotherhood organized on the issue of partition, a major conference that was attended by foreign dignitaries and heads of state. This show of force led the Egyptian government to outlaw the Brotherhood, and to a wave of repression against its members. Although Banna tried to rein in his followers, some of them carried out assassinations of public figures, and as a result, Banna was assassinated by government officials in February 1949.

The Brotherhood after Banna

Under a new *murshid amm* ("supreme guide") and with the promise not to get involved in political activity, the Brotherhood was allowed to operate again in 1951. It had a large number of followers in the army, and it had even supplied arms to the stranded Egyptian soldiers in Palestine during the 1948 Arab–Israeli War. A liaison was established between the

Ma'mun al-Hudaybi, head of the Muslim Brotherhood from 2002–2004, speaks during an interview at the Brotherhood's headquarters in Cairo, 7 May 2003. Al-Hudaybi called for a jihad to expel foreign forces from Iraq. © REUTERS NEWMEDIA INC./CORBIS. REPRODUCED BY PERMISSION.

Brotherhood and the movement of the Free Officers who, in 1952, seized power in a coup that benefited from the mass support provided by the Brotherhood. As a result, the Brotherhood was the only organization not dissolved by the new regime dominated by Gamal Abdel Nasser, which quickly became a secular nationalist-socialist autocracy that banned any opposition to the state. An assassination attempt on Nasser in 1956 led to the dissolution of the movement, the jailing of hundreds of its members, and the execution of many of its leaders, including its chief ideologue, Sayyid Qutb.

Anwar al-Sadat became Egypt's president in 1970. Hoping to defuse the power of the followers of Nasser who opposed his policies of reconciliation with Israel, Sadat released from jail Umar al-Tilimsani, the leader of the Brotherhood, and allowed the Brotherhood to operate again (though without a legal status). The loss of the charismatic leadership of Nasser and the failure of the government's socialist policies helped the Brotherhood to regain its membership. Sadat promised to restore legal status to the Brotherhood if it supported his policy toward Israel, but it refused, and the leadership and hundreds of members were again thrown in jail. After the assassination of Sadat in 1981 by a member of one of the radical Muslim movements, the new president, Husni Mubarak, granted more freedom to the Brotherhood, which saw its membership soar. Because it had no legal status, it could not participate in political elections, so its members ran for parliamentary election by forming an alliance with the Wafd Party in 1984, and they won the majority of opposition seats. The same success was achieved in 1987, when the Brotherhood allied itself with the Socialist Labor Party and the Liberal Party, and included Coptic representatives. The Brotherhood's victories led to a massive crackdown by the government of Mubarak during the 1990s and an attempt to counter its ideology with strong government propaganda. But the Brotherhood retained its power, and in the parliamentary elections of November 2000, a majority of members of the Brotherhood were independently elected to parliament, thus making the Brotherhood, though officially banned, the largest holder of opposition seats in the parliament. The sixth leader of the Brotherhood, Ma'mun al-Hudaybi, who had assumed the leadership in 2002, died in January 2004, and Muhammad Mahdi Akif was elected the new guide-general for the Muslim Brotherhood.

The Muslim Brotherhood has offices throughout the Arab world, and a number of organizations emulating it have emerged in almost all Muslim countries. Its membership tends to be middle-class professionals and university graduates for whom the main goals are to oppose Western policies in the Muslim world in general and in Palestine in particular, and to bring about a social, economic, and political order in line with Islamic ideals. By avoiding theological discussion on the nature of law and state that could lead to divisiveness, taking a progressive stand on the rights of women (as demonstrated in the writings of Muhammad al-Ghazali), focusing on eliminating Western secular influences and ideologies (though accepting Western advances in technology, science, and education), and providing badly needed civic institutions, the Brotherhood has become the most important representative of the Egyptian masses.

See also BANNA, HASAN AL-; FREE OFFICERS, EGYPT; GHAZALI, MUHAMMAD AL-; MUBARAK, HUSNI; NASSER, GAMAL ABDEL; QUTB, SAYYID; SADAT, ANWAR AL-; SALAFIYYA MOVEMENT.

Bibliography

Lia, Brynjar. *The Society of the Muslim Brothers in Egypt.* Reading, PA: Ithaca Press, 1998.

Mitchell, Robert P. *The Society of the Muslim Street Brothers.* London: Oxford University Press, 1993.

Wickham, Carrie R. *Mobilizing Islam; Religion, Activism, and Political Change in Egypt.* New York: Columbia University Press, 2002.

MAYSAM J. AL FARUQI

MUSLIM-CHRISTIAN ASSOCIATION

See PALESTINE

MUSLIM SISTERS ORGANIZATION

Muslim women's group in Sudan.

The first woman recruited to the Muslim Brotherhood movement in Sudan was Fatima Talib, who joined the organization in 1949. Women from the al-Mahdi family joined her, and they formed the Society for Women's Development mainly to provide an alternative to the leftist Sudanese Women's Union. After the October 1964 popular revolution, the Muslim Brothers, which supported woman suffrage, launched a new women's organization called the Patriotic Women's Front. The small band of Muslim women's activists broke new ground in Sudanese politics by supporting the idea that women have a voice in religion as well as in politics.

The strength of the Muslim Brotherhood grew during the latter years of the military regime of Ja'far Numeiri, who moved the Sudan toward Islamization and Islamism. In 1983 *shari'a* was made the sole law in force in the nation. Hasan al-Turabi guided this process as attorney general under Numeiri; after Numeiri's popular overthrow in 1985, Turabi reinvented the Muslim Brotherhood as the National Islamic Front (NIF).

In 1973 Turabi had presented his ideas about the emancipation of women in Islamic societies in a pamphlet, *The Woman in Islamic Teachings.* The formation of the Muslim Sisters Organization was inspired by this pamphlet. Turabi's view states that women are equally responsible for heeding the call of God. Oppression of women in Muslim lands is not a proper reflection of Islamic principles, which should accept the full participation of women in public life. Islamists in all Muslim societies should seek to reform this situation, rejecting traditionalism, promoting the renaissance of women, and shielding them from exploitation by misguided Western groups. The acceptance of Turabi's arguments by the Muslim Brotherhood permitted the movement to adapt, making it part of the process of social modernization.

See also GENDER: GENDER AND LAW; GENDER: GENDER AND POLITICS; MUSLIM BROTHERHOOD; NUMEIRI, JA'FAR; SHARI'A; SUDAN; SUDANESE CIVIL WARS; SUDANESE WOMEN'S UNION; TURABI, HASAN AL-.

Bibliography

El-Affendi, Abdelwahab. *Turabi's Revolution, Islam and Power in Sudan.* London: Gray Seal, 1991.

CAROLYN FLUEHR-LOBBAN

MUSLIM WORLD LEAGUE

International Muslim organization.

The Muslim World League (in Arabic, Rabitat al-Alam al-Islami), headquartered in Mecca and funded by the government of Saudi Arabia, was founded under the auspices of King Faisal ibn Abd al-Aziz Al Sa'ud in 1966. The league promotes the cause of Islam throughout the world by holding conferences, distributing classical Islamic texts and modern religious publications, and paying the salaries of mosque preachers and missionaries.

KHALID Y. BLANKINSHIP

MUSTAFA FAZIL
[1829–1875]

Egyptian prince and supporter of Young Ottomans.

Prince Mustafa Fazil was the son of Ibrahim Pasha ibn Muhammad Ali and brother of the Egyptian Khedive Isma'il. In 1845, Mustafa Fazil traveled from Egypt to Constantinople (now Istanbul), where he took up politics. He served on the Council of Tanzimat from 1857 to 1862, and as minister of education in 1862 and 1863. In 1866, Isma'il secured a change in succession from Sultan Abdülaziz, thereby excluding Mustafa Fazil from the Egyptian

throne. Mustafa Fazil, apparently in revenge, bankrolled the movement of Young Ottomans, first in Constantinople, and later from Paris. His 1867 open letter to the sultan was widely reproduced for forty years as a manifesto for political reform.

See also YOUNG OTTOMANS.

Bibliography

Davison, Roderic H. *Reform in the Ottoman Empire 1856–1876.* Princeton, NJ: Princeton University Press, 1963.

ELIZABETH THOMPSON

MUSTAFA REŞID
[1800–1858]

Ottoman foreign minister, grand vizier, and reformer.

Mustafa Reşid is considered one of the major forces promoting the Tanzimat reforms that modernized the Ottoman Empire in the mid-nineteenth century. He was born in Constantinople (now Istanbul), the son of Mustafa Efendi, an administrator of religious foundations. Intending a career as a religious scholar, he studied at the *ilmiyye*, but at the age of ten his father died and he was forced to withdraw from school and live with his uncle, Ispartali Ali Paşa, a court chamberlain of Sultan Mahmud II. In 1816, Reşid accompanied Ali Paşa to the province of Morea, where the latter had been appointed governor. It was during Ali Paşa's second term as governor (1820–1821), that Reşid witnessed the rout of Ottoman forces by the European-supported Greek rebels and by the modernized army of Muhammad Ali, governor of Egypt, in the Greek War of Independence. Reşid learned two lessons from this experience: first, that reform of the basic institutions of the Empire was needed, and second, that diplomacy aimed at acquiring European support for the empire was as crucial as modernization of the army.

In 1826, with the help of an influential family friend, Mustafa Reşid entered the civil service as a clerk in the scribes bureau of the foreign minister, where he quickly rose to become assistant to the minister in charge of foreign affairs. From this position, Mustafa Reşid participated in negotiations with Muhammad Ali in 1830; the latter was so impressed with his talents that he offered him a high position in the Egyptian administration. In 1832, Reşid was appointed amedçi in the foreign ministry.

Between 1834 and 1836, he was ambassador to France, where he became acquainted with European statesmen, including the famous Austrian foreign minister, Prince Klemens von Metternich. In 1836, he was transferred to Britain as ambassador to the Court of Saint James, where he discussed reforms with Lord Palmerston. In 1837, Sultan Mahmud II, seeking a counterweight to Mehmet Koja Husrev, the leader of the conservative opposition to reform, appointed Mustafa Reşid, now a leading advocate of reform, foreign minister, giving him the title Paşa. For the next eighteen months, Reşid Paşa remained in London and Paris, while attempting to bolster Mahmud II's reform program and to convince the sultan to place his trust in the British. He returned to Constantinople only upon receiving news of the death of the sultan and of the ascension to the throne of his son, Abdülmecit I.

In 1839, Mustafa Reşid Paşa skillfully blended his mastery of domestic and foreign affairs to deter military disaster while advancing reform. As foreign minister and representative of the Sublime Porte in London, he had been unable to prevent his conservative rival Mehmet Koja Husrev Paşa from becoming grand vizier. But when Muhammad Ali, governor of Egypt, sent an army commanded by his son Ibrahim into Syria, Husrev Paşa responded by attempting to appease Muhammad Ali, offering to appoint him life-time governor not only of Egypt, but of Syria and Adana. Recognizing that this would result in a virtual dismemberment of the empire that would guarantee Russian domination, Mustafa Reşid Paşa negotiated with British foreign minister Lord Palmerston for the European support needed to counter the Egyptian advance. European, particularly British, military and diplomatic support, which was crucial in defusing the crisis, was linked to a commitment to support internal reform. Sultan Abdülmecit recognized the key role played by Reşid Paşa and rewarded him with a promise to advance the program of the reformers. On 3 November 1839 Sultan Abdülmecit initiated this reform program with the proclamation of the Imperial Rescript of Gülhane, a document which was composed by Mustafa Reşid and which is considered the opening salvo of the Tanzimat. Though the Tanzimat was initiated at a time of increased European involvement in the empire, it was promoted by Ottomans like Mustafa Reşid Paşa who recognized the need for continued reforms to remedy defects in the administration of the empire. Mustafa Reşid sought British support, but he was not acting under British pressure.

Mustafa Reşid Paşa's importance did not cease with the proclamation of the Tanzimat. He was one of the architects of a new commercial code, promulgated in 1841, that was based on French commercial law. When asked whether the new law was in comformity with Islamic law, he reportedly replied, "the Holy Law has nothing to do with it." Vociferous reaction from Islamic scholars led to suspension of the law and Mustafa Reşid's Paşa's dismissal. He served as ambassador to France until 1845, when he began a second period as leader of the reform movement. Over the next fifteen years, he served six times as grand vizier (28 September 1846 to 28 April 1848; 12 August 1848 to 26 January 1852; 5 March to 5 August 1852; 23 November 1854 to 2 May 1855; 1 November 1856 to 6 August 1857; and 22 October 1857 to 7 January 1858) and three times as foreign minister.

In addition, Reşid played a crucial role in recruiting and training a cadre of reform-minded bureaucrats who, under his leadership, became known as the "men of the Tanzimat" *(tanzimatcilar)*. In order to learn more about Islamic law, he retained Ahmet Cevdet as a tutor, subsequently hiring him as his personal scribe, and then appointing him to educational positions in the administration. The most well-known of his protégés were Mehmet Emin Ali Paşa, who served as Mustafa Reşid's translator and scribe in the embassy in London and later served as foreign minister and as grand vizier, and Mehmet Fuad Paşa, who became Mustafa Reşid's protégé in 1837. Mehmet Ali and Mehmet Fuad led the reform program during the last two decades of the Tanzimat. Whereas Mustafa Reşid had always sought alliance with Britain, his two protégés sought to orient empire politics toward an alliance with France. Partially as a result of this difference, the two eclipsed Mustafa Reşid Paşa in the early 1850s, though at the time of his death in 1858, Mustafa Reşid was once again grand vizier. After his death, his sons carried on the tradition of service to the empire, serving as ministers and ambassadors.

See also CEVDET, AHMET; MUHAMMAD ALI; TANZIMAT.

Bibliography

Baysun, Cavid. "Mustafa Reşid Paşa." In *Tanzimat.* Istanbul, 1940.

Shaw, Stanford J., and Shaw, Ezel Kural. *History of the Ottoman Empire and Modern Turkey,* Vol. 2: *Reform, Revolution, and Republic: The Rise of Modern Turkey, 1808–1975.* Cambridge, U.K., and New York: Cambridge University Press, 1977.

DAVID WALDNER

MUSTAFA SUPHI
[1883–1921]

Turkish communist leader.

The son of a district governor, Mustafa Suphi was born in the Giresun district on the Black Sea. He studied law in Constantinople (now Istanbul) in the late 1890s and then continued his education in Paris and Rome. A leftist thinker, Mustafa Suphi fled Ottoman police shortly before World War I and took up residence in Russia where he organized a communist movement among Turkish prisoners. He began publishing communist propaganda in Turkish, which was distributed in Anatolia. After the war, Suphi supported the nationalist movement against the sultan, although the Kemalists coldly received his small group of about two hundred communists. Suphi was arrested in January 1921, shortly after returning to Turkey. While being transported by boat to Erzurum for trial, he and several friends were assassinated by pro-Enver Paşa supporters who believed Suphi would discredit the former Committee for Union and Progress (CUP) leader.

See also COMMITTEE FOR UNION AND PROGRESS; ENVER PAŞA.

ELIZABETH THOMPSON

MUTASARRIF
See GLOSSARY

MUTAYR TRIBE
See TRIBES AND TRIBALISM: MUTAYR TRIBE

MUWAHHIDUN

Members of a reform movement that began in the eighteenth century to revive Orthodox Sunnism, stressing the Sunna, *or the ways of the Prophet Muhammad.*

The movement was started by a religious scholar from Najd (Saudi Arabia), Muhammad ibn Abd al-Wahhab (1703–1792), schooled by *ulama* (Islamic clergy) in what is now Iraq, Iran, and the Hijaz (western Arabia). He called for a return to the sources of Islam, stressing the absolute unity of Allah (*tawhid*) and strict obedience to the Qur'an (the sacred book of Islam) and the *hadith* (sayings and traditions attributed to the Prophet Muhammad). His understanding of *tawhid* was somewhat unique, following the teachings of Ahmad ibn Hanbal's (780–855) school of law (*madhhab*) and its later interpretation by Ibn Taymiyya (1263–1328). By 1736, his followers— often called the Muwahhidun (Unitarians), today known as Wahhabis—rejected religious innovation (*bid'a*) that promoted polytheism (*shirk*) and unbelief (*kufar*), and the tradition of *ziyaret,* or visits to saints believed to be intercessors between humans and Allah. Muwahhidun do not necessarily consider themselves members of a sect; rather, they reject esoterism on the basis of being people of tradition (Ahl al-Hadith).

The present-day structure of the Saudi government can be traced to the religious and political alliance sealed in 1744 between Ibn al-Wahhab with his marriage to the daughter of Muhammad ibn Sa'ud, ruler of the Dariyya near the modern city of Riyadh. Together they created the model of a state wherein allegiance to the *shari'a* (Islamic law), not tribal customs, reigned supreme. The movement spread rapidly, perhaps due to Abd al-Wahhab's introduction of firearms among Bedouin tribes accustomed to wielding the sword and lance. After his death, the Wahhabi forces had by 1806 sacked the Shi'ite shrines of Karbala (in southwestern Iraq), occupied the holy cities of Mecca and Medina where they destroyed the tombs of revered saints, and raided the Syrian interior.

Ottoman Turkish and Egyptian garrisons in the Hijaz were not able to prevent the emergence of the Wahhabi state in the twentieth century by the Al Sa'ud family in their capital, Riyadh. It began when their relations with the Al Rashid family, a Wahhabi clan governing the Shammar region, became strained and, in 1884, the Saudi family was forced to seek sanctuary with the Mubarak rulers of Kuwait. In 1901, Abd al-Aziz ibn Abd al-Rahman ibn Sa'ud, son of the last Saudi governor of Riyadh, led a daring raid that restored his family's power.

By 1912 a renewal in Wahhabi doctrine led to a consolidation of various tribes, or the Ikhwan (the brothers). In 1912 Abd al-Aziz (ibn Sa'ud) appealed to other Bedouins to join the Ikhwan and steadily enlarged his domains by creating militarized agricultural colonies (hujar) to transcend tribal loyalties. The Bedouin tribes posed a threat to the unification of the Saudi kingdom, and the colonies were an attempt to make farmers of seminomadic warriors. The hujar were built on the sacred principle of hijra (emigration or flight, referring to the Prophet Muhammad's flight to Medina when he was forced to leave Mecca). In 1921 Abd al-Aziz entered Ha'il, the capital of Shammar, overthrowing the Rashid family in the process. In 1924 he occupied the site of Islam's holiest cities and shrines and overthrew caliph Sharif Husayn ibn Ali.

An important shift occurred in the late 1920s. Abd al-Aziz deemed the ferocity of the Ikhwan and particularly their mutawwi'un (enforcers of obedience), Wahhabism's religious police, unfavorable to the modern Saudi state he wished to create. The Ikhwan wished to continue their advances into other areas under British protection only to be prohibited by Abd al-Aziz, who in 1926 had been proclaimed king of the Hijaz. The Ikhwan revolted in 1927 but were crushed with difficulty in 1929. However, their defeat did not mean the end of puritanical Wahhabism.

In 1932 Hijaz and Najd became a single country, which was officially named the Kingdom of Saudi Arabia, and fortunes of the Wahhabis became inextricably linked to it. King Abd al-Aziz strove to consolidate his power in those areas of the Arabian peninsula where he ruled. In alliance with the ulama, he strictly imposed the shari'a and paid careful attention to the services accorded to the hajj (pilgrimage to Mecca). He placated Hijazi opinion by allowing ijtihad (learned opinion) in the cases brought against the government before the mazalim courts. In dire financial straits, he signed a petroleum concession with a U.S. company in 1932, and oil was discovered in 1936. His famous 1945 meeting with U.S. president Franklin D. Roosevelt on the U.S. destroyer on the Suez Canal stressed the growing international importance of Saudi Arabia, and by the end of World War II, oil production began.

The Wahhabi model appealed to other Islamic reform movements, such as the Salafiyya movement in Egypt in the late nineteenth century and the fundamentalist Muslim Brotherhood (al-Ikhwan al-Muslimun) founded by Shaykh Hasan al-Banna in 1928. Like other Arab potentates, King Abd al-Aziz was greatly preoccupied with Palestine, and he sent a military contingent to participate in the Arab–Israel War of 1948, when Israel became a state. Wary of Western influence, Saudi Arabia joined Egypt and Syria in the 1950s in resisting a regional Middle East defense organization. The threat of a Nasser-type military coup brought Saudi Arabia's defection from that alliance and placed it more in line with the Hashimites.

As oil wealth began to permeate Saudi society in the early 1960s, the Wahhabi movement retained a profound influence on the social and economic development of Saudi Arabia. The mutawwi'un, a carryover from the Ikhwan, oversaw strict observance—challenging the melodious recitation of the Qur'an, excessive veneration at saints' tombs, desegregation of the sexes, and the appearance of the full (unveiled) female form on television.

In 1953, King Abd al-Aziz died. By the 1960s, King Faisal's call for an Islamic pact politically split the Arab world. It put him in hostile ideological conflict with the Egyptian Gamel Abdel Nasser's revolutionary, socialist and secular brand of nationalism. Egypt's swift defeat by Israel in the Arab–Israel War of 1967 seemed to vindicate King Faisal's position. Conversely, he successfully coordinated with Egypt's new president, Anwar al-Sadat, to achieve more attention to Islamic symbolism in the Arab–Israel War of 1973.

The 1973 Arab oil embargo and rise in OPEC's (Organization of Petroleum Exporting Countries) oil prices brought riches to Saudi Arabia. This wealth aided a Pan Islamic "revival" and the Wahhabi kingdom built mosques and provided aid throughout Muslim countries, contributing to the strengthening of Islamist fundamentalist political groups and parties worldwide. Different local varieties of Wahhabi philosophy exist today in such varied places as Burkina Faso, Chad, Egypt, Mali, Oman, Pakistan, Qatar, Uzbekistan, as well as some mosques in the United States.

The Islamic revolution in Iran (1979) and Israel's pursuit of the PLO (Palestine Liberation Organization) into Lebanon (1982), however, ushered in a new radical wave of politically motivated Islamic neo-fundamentalism that does not share either the Wahhabi doctrinal approach to Islam or Saudi Arabia's pro-American policy. In 1988, Saudi Arabia broke relations with Iran when Iranian pilgrims to Mecca rioted and the Iranian navy fired on Saudi vessels in the Gulf. Saudi aid given to anticommunist Mojahedin (holy warriors) in Afghanistan may be seen as keeping in line with the martial spirit of the early Wahhabi movement. During the Cold War, the U.S. supported the Mojahedin in an attempt to help Afghanistan overthrow Russian control. This support inadvertantly strengthened Mojahedin and Taliban forces in the area. Saddam Hussein's invasion of Kuwait in 1990 and the ensuing Gulf Crisis caused Saudi Arabia and Kuwait to align themselves with the U.S.–led United Nations Coalition.

Wahhabism has softened a great deal since its emergence in the eighteenth century. If Islamic neo-fundamentalism and Islamist political parties are perceived as anti-Western, it will be left to see how much the Wahhabiyya will influence the direction taken by the Islamic reformist movements.

See also MUSLIM BROTHERHOOD; SAUDI ARABIA.

Bibliography

Bourne, Kenneth, and Watt, D. Cameron, eds. *British Documents on Foreign Affairs: Reports and Papers from the Foreign Office Confidential Print; Part 2: From the First to the Second World War, Series B: Turkey, Iran, and the Middle East, 1918–1939*; Vol. 4: *The Expansion of Ibn Saud, 1922–1925.* Betheseda, MD: University Publications of America, 1986.

Hourani, Albert. *A History of the Arab Peoples.* Cambridge, MA: Harvard University Press, 1991.

Shaikh, Farzana. *Islam and Islamic Groups: A Worldwide Guide.* Essex: Longman Group, 1992.

Vitalis, Robert. "The Closing of the Arabian Oil Frontier and the Future of Saudi-America Relations." In *Middle East Research & Information Project*, no. 204, vol. 27. no. 3 (1997): 15–21.

BASSAM NAMANI
UPDATED BY MARIA F. CURTIS

MZAB

Berber-speaking area in the arid pre-Saharan hamada 360 miles (600 km) south of Algiers.

The five original towns—al-Ateuf, Bou Noura, Ghardaïa, Melika, and Beni Isguen—were founded in the eleventh century along the bed of the Wadi Mzab. Berriane and Guerrara were added outside the wadi in the seventeenth century. The people are mainly Kharidjite Ibadites, a sect of Islam dating from the schism at the time of the fourth caliph, Ali, that adheres to a doctrine of puritanical and egalitarian religious and social obligations. The Mzab is noted for its highly developed, essentially theocratic organization and the economic maintenance of strong communities through the extraordinary commitment and success of its people as tradesmen throughout Algeria.

THOMAS G. PENCHOEN

MZALI, MOHAMMED
[1925–]

Prime minister of Tunisia from 1980 to 1986.

Born in Monastir, the home village of Tunisia's first president, Habib Bourguiba, Mohammed Mzali began his professional life as a university professor of Arabic and Islamic philosophy. In 1980 he was named by Bourguiba to succeed Hedi Nouira, who had suffered a stroke, as Tunisia's prime minister and the president for life's designated successor. Mzali's accession was heralded at the time as marking a relaxation of the political authoritarianism associated with Nouira's tenure; he was younger, in closer contact with the country's young people, and associated with support for political liberalization. Under his aegis, in fact, the first contested elections for the national assembly were held in 1981. Although the results were widely believed to have been falsified in favor of the ruling party, several independents took seats, establishing that party membership was not necessary for assembly membership. Soon thereafter, some opposition political parties, including the Tunisian Communist Party and several social democratic parties, were legalized, and the decades-long monopoly on Tunisian political life held by the ruling Neo-Destour Party was broken.

Despite his success at initiating political reform, Mzali proved unable to solve the country's pressing economic problems, nor could he control the increasingly virulent political infighting among the Tunisian political elite. Even though Mzali had been designated by Bourguiba as his official successor, the Tunisian ruling elite openly jockeyed for position as the aging president's health began to deteriorate. In 1984 government-dictated consumer price increases touched off widespread rioting, prompting rescission of the increases. Mzali accused his rivals of deliberately encouraging the rioters to embarrass him.

In July 1986, worried that Mzali had lost the confidence of the government and the people, Bourguiba dismissed him in favor of the economist Rachid Sfar. A year and a half later, Bourguiba himself would be removed from the presidency by a Mzali appointment, General Zayn al-Abidine Ben Ali, the first military officer ever to sit in a Tunisian cabinet. Mzali himself was later accused of malfeasance and took exile in France, where he wrote a book, *Lettre ouverte à Habib Bourguiba* (1987), accusing many of his former political collaborators of corruption, mismanagement, and disloyalty. He remained an opposition leader in exile until he was allowed to return to Tunisia in 2002.

Additionally, since 1973 Mzali has held various positions at the International Olympic Committee; as of 2003 he is a member of the Commission for Culture and Olympic Education.

See also BEN ALI, ZAYN AL-ABIDINE.

Bibliography

Anderson, Lisa. "Democracy Frustrated: The Mzali Years in Tunisia." In *The Middle East and North Africa: Essays in Honor of J. C. Hurewitz,* edited by Reeva S. Simon. New York: Columbia University Press, 1990.

Murphy, Emma. *Economic and Political Change in Tunisia: From Bourguiba to Ben Ali.* New York: St. Martin's in association with University of Durham, 1999.

LISA ANDERSON
UPDATED BY ANA TORRES-GARCIA

N

NAʿAMAT

A Zionist women's organization active in Israel and the diaspora.

Naʿamat (the Hebrew acronym for the Movement of Working Women and Volunteers) was founded in 1921 by Rahel Yanait Ben-Zvi and a group of women in the United States who raised $500 to plant trees. Naʿamat U.S.A. was formed at the same time. Ben-Zvi and others founded Naʿamat in protest against a society in which women were relegated to the kitchens while men worked the land and built the country. It was the first feminist movement in Palestine and was affiliated with the Histadrut (General Confederation of Labor). Its work began with agricultural training schools and expanded into providing child care for children of working women and vocational training for women who wanted to work.

During the 1960s, Naʿamat established a fund enabling Israeli women to pursue higher education. The organization set up legal aid bureaus during the 1970s, and Status of Women departments were established in Israel. Since 1990 Naʿamat's agenda has grown to include working with immigrants, a support program for single-parent families, centers for the treatment and prevention of violence in the family, and a shelter for battered women.

The Naʿamat Israel elects a president and management every four years, along with the leadership of the Histadrut. The president elected in 2002 was Talia Livni.

See also BEN-ZVI, RAHEL YANAIT; GENDER: GENDER AND LAW; GENDER: GENDER AND POLITICS; GENDER: GENDER AND THE ECONOMY; HISTADRUT; ISRAEL: MILITARY AND POLITICS; ISRAEL: POLITICAL PARTIES IN; ZIONISM.

Bibliography

Naʿamat. <http://www.naamat.org>.

PAUL RIVLIN

NABAVI, BEHZAD
[1942–]

Iranian politician.

Born in Tehran in 1942, Behzad Nabavi has had a roller-coaster career in politics. A son of a historian closely affiliated with the shah's regime, he joined the secular National Front (NF) and participated in antishah activities at Tehran Polytechnic University (now Amir Kabir University), where he received a masters degree in electronics in 1964. In the late 1960s he left the NF and joined the new underground Organization of People's Mujahedin of Iran (OPMI), which mixed Marxism and Islam and advocated armed struggle against the Pahlavi regime. In 1971 he was arrested and jailed for his antigovernment activities. In 1975 the OPMI splintered and Nabavi joined a group of Muslim activists working closely with Ayatollah Ruhollah Khomeini against the shah's regime. When released from prison in 1978, he joined revolutionaries surrounding Khomeini and was assigned to oversee the transformation of the Iranian broadcasting system. He also founded the Organization of the Mujahedin of Islamic Revolution (OMIR), a semiclandestine paramilitary counterforce against the OPMI. With the outbreak of the Iran–Iraq War, internal disputes led to the closure of the OMIR; it re-emerged in 1994.

When the Iran–Iraq War began in 1980, Nabavi established the National Economic Mobilization Headquarters for rationing foods. In the government of Mohammad Ali Rajai, he was a spokesperson and a minister without portfolio for executive affairs. He was appointed minister of heavy industry in 1982—a post he held until 1989. He was also the government representative in the Iran–United States Claims Tribunal in the Hague, the Netherlands, a forum for dispute resolution set up in accordance with the Algiers Agreement of 1981 that ended the hostage crisis between Iran and the United States. Nabavi was one of the Iranian negotiators of that agreement. He had a major role in the centralized policies of Prime Minister Mir Hossein Mousavi's administration (1981–1989).

After the death of Khomeini in 1989, the conservative camp gained ascendancy and individuals such as Nabavi were pushed out of power. Nabavi and his associates restarted the OPMI and began the publication of the biweekly *Asre Ma* (Our times). This paper, along with the journal *Kian,* which was published by the supporters of Abdolkarim Soroush, transformed the religious discourse and kindled a reformist movement that culminated in the election

of Mohammad Khatami as Iran's president in 1997. This election brought the left back to power. In 2000 Nabavi was elected first deputy speaker of the sixth parliament.

This "old guerrilla," as his colleagues call Nabavi, is the most controversial revolutionary and political strategist in Iranian politics. The conservative faction views him with suspicion and has tried to bring him down politically, accusing him of embezzlement and financial corruption several times without any legal success. While a minister, he survived ten motions of no confidence initiated by the conservatives in the parliament. Nabavi's politics and economic views have changed tremendously. His current attitudes toward moderate privatization of markets and a rapprochement with the United States are the opposite of his views in the early 1980s.

ALI AKBAR MAHDI

NABI MUSA PILGRIMAGE

Annual Muslim pilgrimage to a shrine situated in the desert between Jerusalem and Jericho where, according to Muslim tradition, Moses is buried.

The Nabi Musa pilgrimage starts a week before the Greek Orthodox Good Friday. According to a widespread legend (not sustained by primary sources), it was established by Saladin after the conquest of Jerusalem in 1187 in order to outnumber Christian pilgrims during Easter. At the beginning of the twentieth century, especially during the British Mandate, the pilgrimage became a political event. In 1920, a crowd of pilgrims protesting for self-determination and against Zionism erupted into violence against Jews in Jerusalem. From 1921 to 1936 the pilgrimage was headed by Hajj Amin al-Husayni, the leader of the national movement. After the war of 1948 the pilgrimage was banned by the government of Jordan, which aimed to undermine the political influence of Hajj Amin in the West Bank. But worshipers, especially women, continued to go spontaneously to the shrine in order to perform rituals at the tomb. Between 1997 and 2000 the Palestinian Authority was closely involved in the organization of the pilgrimage, which once again became a great occasion for national celebration. Since the outbreak of the al-Aqsa intifada in 2000 the Israeli army has forbidden the celebrations.

See also AQSA INTIFADA, AL-; HUSAYNI, MUHAMMAD AMIN AL-.

Bibliography

Canaan, Tewfik. *Mohammedan Saints and Sanctuaries in Palestine.* Jerusalem: Ariel Publishing House, 1927.

Khalidi, Rashid. *Palestinian Identity: The Construction of Modern National Consciousness.* New York: Columbia University Press, 1997.

BENJAMIN JOSEPH
UPDATED BY EMMA AUBIN BOLTANSKI

NABI SALIH, AL-

Uninhabited island in the Bahrain archipelago of the Persian/Arabian Gulf.

Lying some two and one half miles (4 km) to the southeast of Bahrain's capital, Manama, al-Nabi Salih is situated midway between the island of al-Awal and the island of Sitra. Extensive date-palm gardens covered al-Nabi Salih in the eighteenth and nineteenth centuries. Sizable groves remain along the western and northern shores, watered by several natural springs. Bahraini Shiʿa revere the large pool at the center of the island, as well as the tomb of the local saint, Salih, from whom the island takes its name.

Bibliography

Cottrell, Alvin J., ed. *The Persian Gulf States: A General Survey.* Baltimore, MD: Johns Hopkins University Press, 1980.

FRED H. LAWSON

NABIZADE NAZIM

[1862–1893]

Ottoman Turkish writer.

Nabizade Nazim was born in Istanbul, where he graduated from military school. He served as an army officer, attaining the rank of captain. In the 1880s, his poetry appeared in a number of journals, but his reputation as a writer dates to the stories he published in *Servet-i Fünün* beginning in 1891; the first issue of the journal included his story "Seyyire-i Tesamüh." With his novel *Zehra* and his story "Kara Bibik," he established himself in the vanguard of Turkish literary realism; his later work was focused largely on the depiction of life in the villages of rural Turkey. His 1886 story "Yadigar-larm" told the story of his alcoholic father.

DAVID WALDNER

NABLUS

The largest West Bank city.

Nablus is 30 miles north of Jerusalem in a valley between Mount Ebal and Mount Gerizim. Known in the Bible as Shechem, it was the home of Jacob, Jacob's well, and the tomb of Joseph; it was the place of Jeroboam's rebellion and, as chief city of Samaria, became his capital of the kingdom of Israel. It was rebuilt and renamed Neapolis (from which the name Nablus derives) by the Roman emperor Vespasian, suffered damage in the Crusades, and became part of the Ottoman Empire. After the defeat and dismemberment of the Ottoman Empire in World War I, it became part of the British Mandate territory of Palestine. It became part of the Jordanian-occupied West Bank following the Arab–Israel War in 1948 and then part of the Israeli-occupied West Bank after June 1967. Israeli troops withdrew from the city in December 1995, after which it passed under the control of the Palestinian Authority. It was reoccupied by Israeli forces on several occasions since the start of the Al-Aqsa Intifada in late 2000.

Nablus has been a major economic, political, and cultural center for Palestinians. Several leading families in Palestinian history stem from Nablus, including the Tuqan Family and the Abd al-Hadi Family. It was long an important manufacturing city, particularly for textiles, food products, and olive oil soap. It has played an important role in Palestinian political history as well, especially as a center for Palestinian nationalism outside the family rivalries of Jerusalem. Home to al-Najah University (which obtained university status in 1977), the city has produced numerous writers, poets, and academicians. The population stood at 100,034 during the last official census in 1997.

See also ABD AL-HADI FAMILY; ARAB–ISRAEL WAR (1948); AQSA INTIFADA, AL-; PALESTINIAN AUTHORITY; TUQAN FAMILY; WEST BANK.

Bibliography

Doumani, Beshara. *Rediscovering Palestine: Merchants and Peasants in Jabal Nablus 1700–1900.* Berkeley: University of California Press, 1995.

Fischbach, Michael R. "Nablus." In *Encyclopedia of the Palestinians,* edited by Philip Mattar. New York: Facts On File, 2000.

Kimmerling, Baruch, and Migdal, Joel S. *The Palestinian People: A History.* Cambridge, MA: Harvard University Press, 2003.

Yaakov, Shimoni, and Levine, Evyatar, eds. *Political Dictionary of the Middle East in the 20th Century.* New York: Quadrangle, 1974.

BENJAMIN JOSEPH
UPDATED BY MICHAEL R. FISCHBACH

NABULSI, SULAYMAN AL-
[c. 1908–1976]

Prime minister of Jordan, 1956–1957.

Sulayman al-Nabulsi was the only prime minister in Jordan's history to be invited to form a government by virtue of his support in parliament and despite major policy differences with the king. He was prime minister of Jordan from October 1956 to April 1957 when he was suspected of participation in a conspiracy led by the chief of staff, General Ali Abu Nuwwar, to overthrow King Hussein ibn Talal.

Nabulsi was born in al-Salt in Jordan of a modest farming family, originally from the Nablus area in Palestine. He was an outspoken Arab nationalist, ideologically pro-Nasser, and a pan-Arabist. Active in politics since gaining a seat in parliament in 1948, he was constantly critical of the government. He published an article opposing Prime Minister Tawfiq Abu al-Huda's negotiations on the Anglo-Jordanian treaty, for which he was arrested and sent to prison for nine months.

Nabulsi then established the National Front party but was unable to obtain a license for it. Ironically, he ended up leading another political party, the National Socialist party, whose chairman had been Hazza al-Majali, a political rival and ideological adversary. Despite its name, analysts describe the party as principally Arab nationalist, social reformist, and pro-democracy. As with most political parties at the time in Jordan, this one would be more correctly described as a parliamentary bloc.

The party won eleven seats out of a total of forty in the October 1956 elections and was able to form a coalition government with Nabulsi as prime minister. It was comprised of seven National Socialists, one Ba'thist, one Communist, and two independents. This was the first "popular front" government of the Arab world and as such was dedicated to the struggle against domestic conservatism and Western influence.

Nabulsi negotiated with Britain to abrogate the Anglo-Jordanian treaty of 1948 and carried out negotiations with Saudi Arabia, Egypt, and Syria for financial aid to substitute for British subsidies. An agreement signed on 19 January 1957 included a promise from the three Arab states to pay Jordan 12.5 million Egyptian pounds over the next few years. An accord with Britain abrogating the Anglo-Jordanian treaty was signed on 13 February 1957. Both these moves had popular support, particularly as they came in the wake of the Suez Canal crisis and the anti-Western feelings it had created. In the meantime, King Hussein had negotiated with the United States for aid under the Eisenhower Doctrine (proclaimed in January 1957) to make up for the budgetary loss expected when Britain withdrew its subsidy. To ensure U.S. support, King Hussein played up his anti-communism position, while Nabulsi's government was purging government officials loyal to the monarch. King Hussein broadcast a message directed at Nabulsi on 2 February 1957, in which he claimed that communist doctrine had infiltrated the government. Nabulsi reacted indignantly, repudiating "alien creeds" and reasserting his Arab nationalism.

On 7 April 1957 a coup attempt was mounted by a group of Ba'thist and pro-Nasser officers, but it was foiled by loyal army troops who rallied to the king. By 13 April it had become clear that the coup attempt had been led by Abu Nuwwar, and the simultaneous antiroyalist purges and discordant relations between Nabulsi and the king led many to believe that Nabulsi was implicated. The government was asked to resign, but Nabulsi was asked to be a minister in a new cabinet headed by a conservative premier.

Despite Nabulsi's participation in the new cabinet, a wave of strikes and protests demanded the resignation of the government, the return of the "popular front" government, and the repudiation of the Eisenhower Doctrine. King Hussein responded by replacing the government with a cabinet made up entirely of ministers loyal to him, proclaiming martial law, abolishing political parties, suspending parliament, imposing a curfew, and placing security forces under army control. Nabulsi was placed under house arrest for the next four years. He never resumed political activity, although he was eventually pardoned by King Hussein and appointed to the Senate in 1971. Until his death, he remained virtually out of the public eye.

See also ABU NUWWAR, ALI; HUSSEIN IBN TALAL.

Bibliography

Dann, Uriel. *King Hussein and the Challenge of Arab Radicalism: Jordan, 1955–1967.* New York: Oxford University Press, 1989.

Lenczowski, George. *The Middle East in World Affairs,* 4th edition. Ithaca, NY: Cornell University Press, 1980.

Massad, Joseph Adoni. *Colonial Effects: The Making of National Identity in Jordan.* New York: Columbia University Press, 2001.

JENAB TUTUNJI

NADIR BARAKZAI, MOHAMMAD
[1883–1933]

King of Afghanistan, 1923–1933; known as Nadir Shah.

Mohammad Nadir Barazkai, known as Nadir Shah, was born to Sardar Mohammad Yusuf Khan from the Yahya Khel lineage of the Mohammadzai clan of the Barakzai branch of the Durrani Pushtun tribe. He was active in the court of Habibollah Khan but was arrested as a murder suspect when Habibollah was assassinated in 1919. He was freed by Amir Amanollah (reigned 1919–1929) and served briefly in his court. He left Afghanistan and spent some time in Paris before returning to India. In 1923, he led a revolt against Habibollah Kalakani and became king in 1929 but was assassinated in 1933 by a Hazara student who was the adopted son of Kalakani.

Bibliography

Adamec, Ludwig. *Historical Dictionary of Afghanistan,* 2d edition. Lanham, MD: Scarecrow Press, 1997.

GRANT FARR

NADI, YUNUS
[1880–1945]

Turkish nationalist, journalist, and publisher.

Yunus Nadi was born in Istanbul to the Abalioğlu family, although he dropped the use of the family name in later life. He studied at the Medrese-i Süleymaniye and Galatasaray and attended law school before taking his first newspaper job at the age of twenty. He became editor in 1910 of the Committee for Union and Progress newspaper in Salonika, *Rumeli,* and in 1918 established the *Yeni Gün* paper in Istanbul. During Turkey's war of independence, he moved the paper to Ankara and there befriended Atatürk. Returning to Istanbul after the war, in 1924 Nadi founded *Cumhuriyet,* known today as the *New York Times* of Turkey.

Nadi was a fervent nationalist. During the war of independence, he printed the headline "Greece must be destroyed" in his paper daily. He joined the Green Army, the most famous of the private armies in that war, but it was disbanded in 1921 by Atatürk because of its radical politics. Nadi wrote four books about the independence war, which were published post-humously in 1955. Nadir Nadi became publisher of *Cumhuriyet* when his father died.

See also COMMITTEE FOR UNION AND PROGRESS; NEWSPAPERS AND PRINT MEDIA.

Bibliography

Shaw, Stanford, and Shaw, Ezel Kural. *History of the Ottoman Empire and Modern Turkey,* Vol. 2: *Reform, Revolution, and Republic: The Rise of Modern Turkey, 1808–1975.* Cambridge, U.K., and New York: Cambridge University Press, 1977.

ELIZABETH THOMPSON

NAFUD DESERT

A desert in northern Saudi Arabia.

The Great Nafud desert of the Arabian peninsula extends over some 2,500 square miles (6,500 sq. km) of sand dunes, with elevations rising to 3,000 feet (915 m). Iron oxide in the sand gives the Nafud a unique reddish color. Winter rain produces grasses sufficient to support grazing in the winter and spring. The southeast portion of the Nafud is considered to be part of the tribal territory of the

Shammar bedouin, who make use of its wells and pastures.

ELEANOR ABDELLA DOUMATO

NAGUIB, MUHAMMAD
[1901–1984]

Egyptian military officer and politician.

Born in the Sudan to a professional family, Muhammad Naguib (also spelled Najib) was a graduate of Egypt's military academy. He served on the general staff during World War II and won respect from junior officers for his distinguished service in Palestine during the Arab-Israel War of 1948.

The Free Officers who overthrew King Farouk in 1952 decided to present Naguib as the head of the Revolutionary Command Council, to endow the revolution with his legitimacy. The monarchy was abolished in 1953 and Naguib took the posts of provisional president and premier, but he refused to be satisfied with a titular role. He favored a return to parliamentary government and, after a protracted struggle with Colonel Gamal Abdel Nasser, leader of the ruling military *junta*, Naguib was ousted in 1954. In 1955, Naguib published *Egypt's Destiny*. In 1956, Nasser was confirmed as president of Egypt by referendum.

See also ARAB–ISRAEL WAR (1948); REVOLUTIONARY COMMAND COUNCIL (EGYPT).

Bibliography

Waterbury, John. *The Egypt of Nasser and Sadat: The Political Economy of Two Regimes.* Princeton, NJ: Princeton University Press, 1983.

Wucher King, Joan. *Historical Dictionary of Egypt.* Metuchen, NJ: Scarecrow Press, 1984.

DAVID WALDNER

NAHAL

Acronym for Noar Halutzi Lohem (Fighting Pioneer Youth), a division of the Israel Defense Force integrating military training with agricultural labor and settlement.

Nahal was founded in 1948 at the urging of a delegation of kibbutz and youth-group representatives to Prime Minister David Ben-Gurion. Zionism's ideological notions of national redemption through work on the land coupled with the nascent state of Israel's pressing need for massive cultivation led to the institution of these units of "warrior-farmers." Nahal recruits entered the army in groups, under the joint command of a youth-movement instructor and Israel Defense Force (IDF) officer, and either reinforced existing kibbutzim and moshavim or, more significantly, established new "holding settlements" (*heakhzuyot*) on the country's vulnerable borders. Nahal paratroopers have been heavily involved in Israeli military operations since the 1950s.

The perception of Nahal as a restructured continuation of the recently defunct Palmah (dissolved in 1948), where informality, egalitarianism, and individual daring were the rule, led to persistent tension as military discipline was imposed on the rank and file. Nahal was opposed by much of the military establishment for attracting some of the most highly qualified recruits away from active combat duty. As the necessity for prolonged professional and specialized military training became more apparent to the IDF, increasing numbers of troops were diverted from Nahal, and agriculture figures less than previously in the unit's activities.

See also PALMAH.

ZEV MAGHEN

NAHALAL

First moshav, founded in the Jezreel valley in 1920.

Nahalal was a unique form of agricultural settlement in Palestine; called a moshav, it was based on cooperatively owned land, individual family farms, and homesteads with family labor—but mutual aid and a cooperative framework for purchasing and marketing. The majority of Nahalal's founders had been members of a kibbutz (an agricultural collective), who disagreed with the arrangements made for family life, child care, and education. They wished to preserve the integrity of the nuclear family within a cooperative community. The parents of Israeli soldier and statesman Moshe Dayan—who were among the founders of the first kibbutz, Degania—also helped establish Nahalal.

See also KIBBUTZ; MOSHAV.

Bibliography

Weintraub, D.; Lissak, M.; and Azmon, Y. *Moshava, Kib-butz, and Moshav: Patterns of Jewish Rural Settlement and Devel-opment in Palestine.* Ithaca, NY: Cornell University Press, 1969.

DONNA ROBINSON DIVINE

NAHAR, AL-

See NEWSPAPERS AND PRINT MEDIA

NAHDA, AL-

Algerian political party.

Al-Nahda party was at one time the third most pop-ular Islamic party in Algeria, after the Front Is-lamique du Salut (Islamic Salvation Front, FIS) and Hamas (Party for a Peaceful Society). It was founded in 1989 by Shaykh Abdallah Jaballah (b. 1956), fol-lowing constitutional amendments that allowed for pluralism and the formation of political parties. Al-Nahda's origins go back to the mid-1970s, when Jaballah, then a law student at the university in Con-stantine, formed a student group, al-Jama'a al-Islamiyya. Due to the group's secret nature, it had limited influence until the mid-1980s and was con-centrated in the eastern region of the country. Al-Nahda was influenced by the teachings and methods of the Egyptian Muslim Brotherhood and advocated education and gradualism as a means of social change. In 1987, as the political system in Algeria opened up, al-Jama'a became public, calling itself the Nahda Association for Social and Cultural Reform. In 1990 it became a political party that drew sup-port from students, teachers, and professionals. Following the cancellation of the 1991 legislative elections, al-Nahda opposed the military takeover, called for the government to respect the people's choice, and boycotted the 1995 presidential elec-tions. During the legislative elections of 1997, it won 34 seats out of 389 but refused to participate in a coalition government. The party experienced a major split in 1999, when its secretary general, Lah-bib Admi, supported the presidential candidacy of Abdelaziz Bouteflika instead of Jaballah's. Jaballah formed a new party, the National Reform Movement (MRN), which most of al-Nahda's members joined. In the May 2002 legislative elections, MRN came third, with 43 seats, after the National Liberation Front (FLN) and the Democratic National Rally (RND); al-Nahda lost all but one seat, probably ushering in the demise of that party. Shaykh Jabal-lah and the MRN have advocated reform, pluralism, national reconciliation, and the preservation of the country's cultural identity.

See also ALGERIA: POLITICAL PARTIES IN; FRONT ISLAMIQUE DU SALUT (FIS); HAMAS (MOVEMENT FOR A PEACEFUL SOCIETY).

Bibliography

Shahin, Emad Eldin. *Political Ascent: Contemporary Islamic Movements in North Africa.* Boulder, CO: Westview Press, 1997.

EMAD ELDIN SHAHIN

NAHHAS, MUSTAFA AL-
[1879–1965]

Egyptian politician.

After graduating from the Khedivial law school in 1900, Mustafa al-Nahhas worked as a lawyer and judge. He entered politics in 1919, joining the na-tionalist Wafd movement. British authorities exiled him to the Seychelles (1921–1923) in the wake of the 1919 revolution and anti-British nationalist agita-tion.

Nahhas became one of the most important and popular Egyptian politicians from the 1920s until the Free Officers' coup d'état in 1952. He was elected to the chamber of deputies in 1923 and as-sumed leadership of the Wafd following the death of Sa'd Zaghlul in 1927. As head of the most popu-lar party in Egypt, Nahhas served as prime minister, interior minister, and foreign minister on numer-ous occasions. His acceptance of the prime minis-ter's portfolio in February 1942 after an armed ultimatum delivered by the British to King Farouk, however, discredited the Wafd's nationalist creden-tials in the eyes of many Egyptians.

Nahhas exerted tremendous influence over Anglo-Egyptian relations. As prime minister, he represented Egypt in failed negotiations with the British in May 1930 over a proposed bilateral treaty. He headed the Egyptian delegation in talks that pro-duced the 1936 Anglo-Egyptian treaty, though he abrogated the treaty in October 1951 after negotiations over the future of British military bases in Egypt failed. Nahhas was also instrumental in the West's decision to abandon the capitulations at the 1939 Montreux Convention.

On the inter-Arab level, Nahhas brought together Arab leaders in October 1944 to sign the Alexandria Protocol, which laid the basis for formation of the League of Arab States. He was prime minister when the Free Officers' coup deposed Egypt's civilian government in July 1952. He was attacked for corruption afterward, though not imprisoned.

See also LEAGUE OF ARAB STATES; MONTREUX CONVENTION (1936); WAFD.

MICHAEL R. FISCHBACH

NAHNAH, MAHFOUD
[1942–2003]

Moderate Algerian Islamic leader and founder of Hamas (Movement for a Peaceful Society).

Born in 1942, Mahfoud Nahnah was the leader of the Movement for a Peaceful Society in Algeria. He was born in the city of Blida, southwest of Algiers, to a conservative family, and received his early education at one of the schools established by the nationalist movement. He graduated from the Algerian University in 1970 with a degree in Arabic language and literature and then worked at the university as a professor.

Nahnah was influenced by the ideas of the Muslim Brothers. In the mid-1960s he formed the organization al-Muwahhidun (Believers in One God) with the objective of establishing an Islamic state in Algeria. He opposed the socialist orientation of the regime and publicly criticized President Houari Boumédienne's proposed charter of 1976 as overemphasizing socialism at the expense of Islam. Nahnah was arrested for his political agitation in 1976 and sentenced to fifteen years imprisonment, but was released in 1980.

Nahnah remained politically active and focused on expanding his constituency. In 1989 he formed a social and cultural society, Jam'iyyat al-Irshad wa al-Islah (Association of Guidance and Reform), which after the adoption of a new constitution in 1989 permitting the formation of political associa-

tions became a party in November 1990 called Harakat al-Mujtama al-Islami (Movement of the Islamic Society) with the Arabic acronym HAMAS. The results of the 1991 legislative elections demonstrated that Nahnah's party enjoyed some degree of popularity, as it secured 450,000 votes. Nahnah ran as a candidate against President Liamine Zeroual in the 1995 elections and came in second with over 3 million votes. Nahnah is viewed as a moderate Islamic leader who on several occasions has condemned the escalation of violence in Algeria and defended the state and the military institutions. His critics charge him of exploiting the crackdown against the more popular Islamic party, the Islamic Salvation Front (FIS), and its leaders, to increase his own popularity. Under President Abdelaziz Boutefleka, Nahnah's party has participated in the cabinet with several ministerial positions. In June 2003, Shaykh Nahnah died of leukemia.

See also ALGERIA; BOUTEFLIKA, ABDELAZIZ; FRONT ISLAMIQUE DU SALUT (FIS); HAMAS; RASSEMBLEMENT NATIONAL DÉMOCRATIQUE (RND); ZEROUAL, LIAMINE.

Bibliography

Shahin, Emad Eldin. *Political Ascent: Contemporary Islamic Movements in North Africa.* Boulder, CO: Westview Press, 1998.

EMAD ELDIN SHAHIN

NAHUM, HALFALLAH
[1880–1963]

President of the Jewish community in Tripoli, Libya; industrialist and philanthropist.

Halfallah Nahum was born in Tripoli to a prominent, affluent Jewish family. He received his primary and advanced technical-business education in Italian schools in Tripoli and Manchester, England, where his uncle lived.

In 1917, after renouncing the Dutch citizenship held for generations by his family and becoming a naturalized Italian, he was elected the first president of the newly reconstituted Jewish community of Tripoli under the Italian occupation. Soon, his leadership was challenged by the young Zionists headed by E. Nhaisi. A power struggle ensued, but Nahum was reelected president from 1919 to 1924.

In 1943, after the Allies took Tripoli, Nahum was asked to head the Jewish community until 1945, when a British subject, Zachino Habib, took over. With the English branch of the family, Nahum built a commercial and industrial empire. He was known for his modesty and for aiding the needy. He was ambushed and killed one night by ten Arabs and one Maltese.

MAURICE M. ROUMANI

NAHUM, HAYYIM
[1873–1960]

Chief rabbi of Istanbul, 1901, and of Egypt, 1925–1960; Turkish representative to the post–World War I peace conferences and to Washington in the early 1920s; Egyptian senator, 1931.

Hayyim Nahum (called Nahum Effendi) was born in Manisa, Turkey, and studied law in Istanbul and at the Rabbinical College of Paris, where he also learned Oriental languages. He had ties with the Young Turks and their Committee for Union and Progress, and when he returned to Turkey following the Young Turks revolution, he was made chief rabbi *(haham bashi)* of Istanbul. In 1918/19, he joined the Turkish delegation for the armistice negotiations at The Hague and also served, unofficially, as Turkey's representative in Washington, D.C., during the early 1920s. In 1923, Nahum served as adviser to the Turkish delegation at the Lausanne Peace Conference.

When he moved to Egypt, King Fu'ad I made Nahum chief rabbi of Egypt in 1925, a position he held until his death in November 1960. Not only was he the most powerful figure of Egyptian Jewry vis-à-vis the Egyptian government, but in June 1931 the king appointed him a senator and in 1933 a member of the Egyptian Academy.

Bibliography

Krämer, Gudrun. *The Jews in Modern Egypt, 1914–1952.* Seattle: University of Washington Press, 1989.

Laskier, Michael M. *The Jews of Egypt, 1920–1970: In the Midst of Zionism, Anti-Semitism and the Middle East Conflict.* New York: New York University Press, 1992.

MICHAEL M. LASKIER

NAJAF, AL-

The capital of the Najaf Muhafaza (governorate) in central Iraq.

One of Iraq's two holy cities (the other is Karbala), al-Najaf (2003 pop. 500,000) lies on a ridge just west of the Euphrates River. The caliph Harun al-Rashid is reputed to have founded the city, whose growth occurred mostly in the tenth century, in 791 C.E. In the center of al-Najaf is one of Shi'ism's greatest shrines, the mosque containing the tomb of Ali ibn Abi Talib (c. 600–661), cousin and son-in-law of the prophet Muhammad, who was the fourth Muslim caliph (leader) and the spiritual founder of the Shi'ite sect. Al-Najaf also has schools and libraries that are valuable repositories of Islamic theology, especially Shi'ite jurisprudence.

Al-Najaf Muhafaza is a flat region extending over 10,615 square miles from the Euphrates River in the northeast to the Saudi Arabian border in the southeast. The governorate's population is concentrated near the river; the rest of the region is sparsely populated. Established in 1976, al-Najaf Muhafaza was formed from areas of the governorate of Qadisiyya in the east and the governorate of Karbala in the west.

Al-Najaf has long been a hotbed of Shi'ite resistance against the Sunni rulers in Baghdad, and in the twentieth century this resistance has been a source of tension between the Sunni-dominated government of Iraq and the Shi'ite government in Iran. The overthrow of Saddam Hussein by invading U.S. forces in April 2003 led to the return of open Shi'ite worship in the city, but the assassination of some of Iraqi Shi'ism's most important clerics, including the returned exile Ayatullah Muhammad Baqir al-Hakim (1939–2003), who was killed by a bomb in August 2003, marred the new era.

See also HUSSEIN, SADDAM; KARBALA; SHI'ISM; SUNNI ISLAM.

Bibliography

Batatu, Hanna. *The Old Social Classes and the Revolutionary Movements of Iraq.* Princeton, NJ: Princeton University Press, 1978.

MAMOON A. ZAKI
UPDATED BY MICHAEL R. FISCHBACH

NAJD

The central plateau region of Saudi Arabia.

A geographically isolated region of the Arabian peninsula, Najd (the Arabic word for plateau or highland) is bounded in the south by the great sand desert, the Rub al-Khali, and on the east by a long, narrow strip of sand desert known as al-Dahna. To the north lies another sand desert, the Nafud, and to the west, Najd is separated from the Red Sea coast by the mountains of Hijaz and Asir. The plateau is divided into three regions: southern Najd, the home of the eighteenth-century Wahhabi movement and the original home of the ruling Al Sa'ud family (main city, Riyadh); Qasim, an agricultural district in the center of Najd (main city, Unayza); and Jabal Shammar in the north (main city, Ha'il). Because of its geographic isolation, Najd, unlike other areas of the Gulf and Arabian Sea, was not subject to European colonialism. Most of the great camel-herding bedouin ranged at least part of the year in Najd, but the bulk of its permanent population were town dwellers and semi-nomadic oasis gardeners. Najd is today the central administrative district and home to the capital city of Saudi Arabia, Riyadh.

ELEANOR ABDELLA DOUMATO

NAJIBULLAH
[1947–1996]

President of Afghanistan from 1986 to 1992.

Najibullah was born in Kabul in 1947 into an Ahmadzai family of the Gilzai Pushtuns. He was educated at Habibia High School and studied medicine at Kabul University, graduating in 1975. He was active in politics at a young age and was a founding member of the People's Democratic Party of Afghanistan (PDPA) in 1965. When the PDPA split in 1967, he and Babrak Karmal became the leaders of the Parcham faction. After the Saur Revolution in 1978 Najibullah was named ambassador to Iran in an effort by the Khalq faction to send the Parchamis out of the country. He returned to Kabul in 1980, when Babrak Karmal was named president, and was made president of the Afghan secret police, Khad. In 1986 he became secretary-general of the PDPA and president of Afghanistan.

Najibullah was a powerful and ruthless leader, the strongest and most capable of the four PDPA presidents. He made a number of attempts to reunite the country and to subdue the Islamic resistance by modifying the Marxist ideology of the PDPA, by moving the country away from socialism, and by restoring the role of religion. However, he was un-able to overcome the PDPA's initial mistakes or to make himself acceptable to the mojahedin. In 1992, three years after the departure of the Soviet military, his government collapsed, and he fled to the United Nations compound in Kabul, where he sought sanctuary.

In September 1996 the Taliban captured Kabul. One of their first acts was to storm the United Nations compound, where they shot and killed Najibullah and his brother. His body was hung on a lamppost on the streets of Kabul.

See also MOJAHEDIN; PARCHAM; PEOPLE'S DEMOCRATIC PARTY OF AFGHANISTAN.

Bibliography

Adamec, Ludwig. *Historical Dictionary of Afghanistan*, 2d edition. Lanham, MD: Scarecrow Press, 1997.

Ewans, Martin. *Afghanistan: A Short History of Its People and Politics.* New York: HarperCollins, 2002.

GRANT FARR

NAJJADA, AL-

Name of several Arab paramilitary youth organizations.

A group called al-Najjada (Helpers) was formed in 1936 in Beirut by journalist Muhieddine Nsouli as a Sunni Muslim counterpart to the Christian Phalange party. In the 1950s, it emerged as a pro-Nasser party with about 10,000 members under the new leadership of Adnan al-Hakim; it clashed with the Phalangists in the 1958 Lebanese Civil War. It has since adopted an Islamist ideology.

Another group of the same name was established at Jaffa, Palestine, in 1945 by a Muslim lawyer, Muhammad Nimr al-Hawari, as a counterpart to the Jewish Haganah. The Palestinian group quickly grew to an estimated 6,000 members in at least ten cities. It played a prominent role in the 1947 Palestinian protests and the 1948 Arab–Israel War.

See also ARAB–ISRAEL WAR (1948); HAGANAH; HAKIM, ADNAN AL-; LEBANESE CIVIL WAR (1958); PHALANGE.

Bibliography

Hudson, Michael C. *The Precarious Republic: Political Modernization in Lebanon.* Boulder, CO: Westview, 1985.

Khalaf, Issa. *Politics in Palestine: Arab Factionalism and Social Disintegration, 1939–1948.* Albany: State University of New York Press, 1991.

ELIZABETH THOMPSON

NAKBA, AL-

Arabic term for the devastating consequences of the 1948 Arab–Israel War on the Palestinians.

Al-Nakba (in Arabic, disaster or catastrophe) refers to the flight and expulsion of the Palestinians during the 1947 to 1948 War, the confiscation of their property, massacres committed by Zionist (after 14 May 1948, Israeli) forces, the collapse of their society and, ultimately, the loss of their homeland. The term *al-Nakba* was widely used after a prominent Arab intellectual, Constantine Zurayk, wrote *Ma'na al-Nakba* (The meaning of the disaster) in 1948.

Of about 1,358,000 Palestinians living in Palestine in 1948, the United Nations (UN) estimated that some 726,000 became refugees during the two phases of the war: civil war after 29 November 1947, and the Arab–Israeli War after 14 May 1948. The exact number of Palestinians forced out is uncertain, but some scholars have estimated that about half of the refugees were expelled. Some of those who left did so after hearing of Zionist (later Israeli) attacks on Palestinians; according to one Israeli scholar, Benny Morris, there were about two dozen massacres in which 800 Palestinians were killed. More than 350 villages were abandoned or emptied, and most of these villages were destroyed—their homes were bulldozed or dynamited, their land was used to build Jewish settlements and house new Jewish immigrants, and the villages' names were removed from Israeli maps. A study by an American scholar, Michael R. Fischbach, of the archives of the United Nations Conciliation Commission for Palestine reveals that, in all, Palestinians lost some 6 to 8 million *dunums* (1.5 to 2 million acres), not including communal land farmed by villagers or state land. A Palestinian writer, Fayez Sayigh, estimated that 150,000 urban and rural homes were lost, as well as 23,000 shops, offices, and other buildings. To these losses must be added the human-capital losses of farmers, shopkeepers, laborers, and professionals and others who, within days, found themselves unemployed and destitute mostly in refugee camps in the West Bank, Gaza Strip, Jordan, Lebanon, and Syria.

Of the estimated 860,000 Palestinians who resided within the area that became Israel (which encompassed 78% of historic Palestine, about 23% more than the 1947 UN partition resolution allotted to the Jewish state), some 84 percent of the Palestinians were uprooted and displaced. In addition, about 20 percent of the 150,000 Palestinians who remained and became citizens of the Jewish state, were internally displaced persons, that is, refugees. There are many examples in modern times of mass transfer and human migration, but very few instances when most of the population has been substantially dispossessed and replaced by another, with its lands, homes and possession confiscated.

There are a number of long-term or fundamental causes of al-Nakba. Many Jews, seeking to escape antisemitic persecution and murderous pogroms in late-nineteenth-century Eastern Europe and Russia, became Zionists, dedicating themselves to establishing a state in their biblical homeland, Palestine, which they called Eretz-Yisrael. In 1917 the Balfour Declaration committed Great Britain to supporting the creation of a Jewish national home in Palestine, where, at the time, less than 10 percent of the population was Jewish. After conquering Palestine in late 1917, Britain—with the backing of the European powers and later the United States—gave the Jewish community time to grow, through Jewish immigration and land purchases, and to establish a quasi-government and military forces. The genocide of six million Jews during World War II generated considerable sympathy in the West for the Jews and their need for a state. In short, European antisemitism, Zionism, the Holocaust, and Western support for a Jewish state made the conflict, leading to al-Nakba, more likely.

An immediate cause of the disaster was Palestinian and Arab rejection of the 29 November 1947 United Nations General Assembly Resolution 181 (the partition resolution), which awarded the Zionists (who were one-third of the population and owned about 7% of the land) roughly 55 percent of Palestine. Inter-communal violence had preceded the UN resolution, and the Palestinians followed their rejection of it with more violent attacks, including massacres, on the Jewish community. Following the defeat of Palestinian and Arab irregular forces, and Israel's declaration of independence on 15 May 1948, five Arab armies entered Palestine. Three of these militaries invaded the nascent state of Israel, triggering the first Arab–Israeli War which produced more Palestinian refugees and cost the lives of 6,000 Jews, or 1 percent of the population, and approximately 13,000 to 16,000 Palestinians and 2,000 and 2,500 other Arabs.

Another immediate contributory cause of al-Nakba was a Zionist (later Israeli) policy of *cleansing,* a term used at the time, along with *transfer.* Many Zionist leaders believed, even before 1948, that in order to establish an ethnically Jewish state, and for the Palestinians to avoid becoming a fifth column within that state, it would be necessary to remove them. David Ben-Gurion, founding father of Israel and its first prime minister and defense minister, created a "consensus of transfer," according to Morris, and gave "transfer" instructions to his commanders who related them to their officers, sometimes in writing.

The legacy of al-Nakba—especially the nonresolution of the Palestinian refugee problem—has figured among the major causes of every Arab–Israeli war since 1948. Israel denies responsibility for the expulsion, claims that Arab leaders urged the Palestinians to leave, and looks to the Arab and the Western world to resolve the problem; Palestinians and other Arabs insist that Israel recognize its culpability and bear the burden of repatriating the refugees to their homes inside Israel or compensating them for their losses, consistent with international law.

The Israeli–Palestinian negotiators at Taba in January 2001 came close to resolving their conflict. The talks addressed Palestinian rights—including return and compensation—and the establishment of a Palestinian state in the West Bank and Gaza Strip. They also addressed Israel's security requirements and demographic fears. But time ran out on the negotiations and no serious effort has been made to resume them. Until Israel, the West (especially the United States), and the Arabs all take responsibility for failing to deal with the consequences of al-Nakba—particularly the continued dispossession and statelessness of the Palestinians—and until they are determined to solve the problem, the Arab-Israeli conflict is unlikely to end.

See also ARAB–ISRAEL WAR (1948); BALFOUR DECLARATION (1917); OSLO ACCORD (1993); PALESTINE; PALESTINIANS; REFUGEES: PALESTINIAN; TABA NEGOTIATIONS (1995, 2001).

Bibliography

Farsoun, Samih K., and Zacharia, Christina. *Palestine and the Palestinians.* Boulder, CO: Westview, 1996.

Fischbach, Michael R. *Records of Dispossession: Palestinian Refugee Property and the Arab-Israeli Conflict.* The Institute for Palestine Studies Series. New York: Columbia University Press, 2003.

Khalidi, Rashid. *The Palestinian Identity: The Construction of Modern National Consciousness.* New York: Columbia University Press, 1997.

Khalidi, Walid. *All That Remains: The Palestinian Villages Occupied and Depopulated by Israel in 1948.* Washington, DC: Institute for Palestine Studies, 1992.

Mattar, Philip, ed. *Encyclopedia of the Palestinians.* New York: Facts On File, 2000.

Morris, Benny. *The Birth of the Palestinian Refugee Problem Revisited.* Cambridge, U.K.: Cambridge University Press, 2004.

Pappe, Ilan. *A History of Modern Palestine: One Land, Two Peoples.* Cambridge, U.K.: Cambridge University Press, 2004.

Pappe, Ilan. *The Making of the Arab-Israeli Conflict, 1947–1951.* London: I. B. Tauris, 1994.

Rogan, Eugene L., and Shlaim, Avi, eds. *The War for Palestine: Rewriting the History of 1948.* Cambridge, U.K.: Cambridge University Press, 2001.

Shavit, Ari. "Survival of the Fittest" (interview with Benny Morris). *Ha'aretz,* 9 January 2004.

PHILIP MATTAR

NAMIK KEMAL
[1840–1888]

Turkish intellectual and a founder of the Young Ottoman movement.

The son of an Ottoman aristocrat, Namik Kemal was born in Tekirdağ. He entered the civil service in Istanbul when he was seventeen and began working with Ibrahim Şinasi on the Young Ottoman journal *Tasvir-i Efkar,* which among other things championed constitutionalism and parliamentary democracy. Namik Kemal's essays were read widely, and he left for Europe in 1867 to avoid persecution by the Ottoman authorities. He returned to Istanbul in 1871, and in 1873 he wrote *Vatan,* a play that dealt with the issue of fatherland and Ottomanism. After Sultan Abdülaziz was deposed in 1876, Kemal was one of the many framers of Midhat Paşa's 1876 constitution. After Sultan Abdülhamit II assumed power, Namik Kemal again went into exile and died on Chios in 1888. Kemal was one of the most important nineteenth-century Ottoman Turkish thinkers and reformers and a founder of the Young Ottoman movement. He wrote extensively about the meanings of *vatan* (fatherland), democracy, liberalism, and freedom in an Ottoman context. Although he was influenced by French philosophers, Kemal looked to Islam as the root of his ideas.

See also MIDHAT PAŞA; YOUNG OTTOMANS.

Bibliography

Hourani, Albert. *Arabic Thought in the Liberal Age, 1798–1939.* New York: Cambridge University Press, 1983.

ZACHARY KARABELL
UPDATED BY ERIC HOOGLUND

NAMIR, MORDEKHAI

[1897–1969]

Israeli Labor Party official and Knesset member.

Born in the Ukraine, Mordekhai Namir (originally Nemirovsky) settled in Palestine in 1924 after graduating from the University of Odessa. Beginning his political career as secretary of the Ahdut Ha-Avodah party, he served in the administrations of the Histadrut and the World Zionist Organization both before and after Israel's statehood. Namir joined the Haganah command from 1933 to 1948, and filled many foreign ministry positions in the Soviet Union and eastern Europe. He was elected to the Knesset (parliament) and appointed general secretary of the Histadrut in 1951, until becoming minister of labor and housing in 1956. From 1956 to 1969 he was mayor of Tel Aviv.

ZEV MAGHEN

NAMIR, ORAH

[1930–]

Israeli politician.

Born in Hadera, Israel, Orah Namir served in the Israel Defense Force as an officer during the 1948 Arab-Israel War. During the late 1950s she lived in New York, working for the Israeli delegation to the United Nations and attending Hunter College, from which she earned a B.A. in English literature and European civilization. Upon returning to Israel, she married Mordekhai Namir (1897–1975), a veteran Labor Party leader and a long-time mayor of Tel Aviv. After his death, she entered politics and served as secretary general of Na'amat. Elected to the Knesset on the Labor ticket in 1973, she specialized in social affairs and chaired the Education and Culture Committee (1974–1977) and the Labor and Social Affairs Committee (1977–1992). She also chaired the Committee on the Status of Women.

In 1992 Prime Minister Yitzhak Rabin appointed her minister for the environment and a year later minister of labor and social affairs. She held this latter position until 1996, when Prime Minister Shimon Peres appointed her Israel's ambassador to the People's Republic of China, a position she held until 2000. Her term of office in Beijing witnessed a strengthening of Israel-China relations, which was translated into a series of agreements on cultural, scientific, and economic matters.

See also ALONI, SHULAMIT; GENDER: GENDER AND LAW; GENDER: GENDER AND POLITICS; GROSSMAN, HAIKA; ISRAEL; NA'AMAT.

MERON MEDZINI

NAQSHBANDI

One of the major Sufi orders in the Islamic world.

The most distinctive characteristics of the Naqshbandi order are the tracing of the *silsila,* or initiatic chain, from the Prophet Muhammad to Abu Bakr al-Siddiq, a companion of the Prophet Muhammad; use of the silent invocation of God (*dhikr*); and a strong adherence to the *shari'a* or Islamic law. The first figure of importance in the history of the Naqshbandiya is Yusuf Hamadani (born 1048). In addition to providing four successors, he set down eight principles, or "sacred words," that provided the doctrinal framework of the order.

Although it is not possible to conclude that all branches or members of the Naqshbandiya were po-

Mas'ud al-Barzani, general secretary of the Kurdistan Democratic Party (KDP). The KDP was formed in 1946 under the leadership of Barzani's father, Mustafa. © BETTMANN/CORBIS. REPRODUCED BY PERMISSION.

litically active throughout the history of the order, the fervent belief in the adherence to the *shari'a* and the Sunna and a worldly attitude toward the role of Sufis in Islamic society contributed to the political participation of some Naqshbandi leaders. In the late medieval and premodern periods, it was not uncommon for Naqshbandi leaders to mediate in political disputes, pay taxes on behalf of a population, act in defense of popular sentiment, influence administrative policy, or control large tracts of land. In the regions of Khorasan and Transoxiana, in which Turko-Mongols ruled over predominantly Persian populations, Naqshbandi leaders at times played the role of defending Sunni Islam against Shi'ism and of thwarting the influence of Turko-Mongol nomadic customary law in favor of Islamic

law. The Naqshbandi order gained adherents among both the Turkic and Persian populations of Central Asia and was prevalent in both urban and rural areas. However, at the height of its power in Khorasan, the Naqshbandiya was firmly entrenched in the intellectual and cultural milieu of the capital city of Herat, enjoying great renown under the leadership of Sa'd al-Din Kashgari (died 1462) and then Abd al-Rahman Jami (died 1492).

Several separate branches of the Naqshbandi order developed, the main ones being the Yasavi, begun by Ahmad Yasavi (died 1167); the Mujaddidi, established first in India by one of the four successors of Hamadani, Shaykh Ahmad Sirhindi (born 1563); and the Khalidi, established by Mawlana Khalid Baghdadi (born 1776), the last branch of the Naqshbandi to achieve strong adherence throughout the Islamic world. There was an extraordinary diffusion of the different branches into regions as widespread as Ottoman Turkey, Kurdistan, Eastern Turkistan, Syria, Palestine, India, central Asia, and the Indonesian–Malaysian world.

A major renewal of the Naqshbandiya came through the leadership of Mawlana Khalid Baghdadi (died 1827), who founded the Khalidi branch that became particularly strong in Turkey and spread as far as Malaysia. His concern with the preservation of the *shari'a* was especially significant during a time when the Ottoman state was facing increasing challenges from the West. The Khalidi Sufi network spread throughout the Turkish, central Asian, and Arab world but was strongest in Anatolia and Kurdistan. The legacy of Naqshbandi activity is reflected today in the eminent position of established Naqshbandi families within Kurdish society, although over time most of those assumed political rather than spiritual leadership, one of the most well-known examples being that of the Barzani family.

In the modern period, particularly the nineteenth and twentieth centuries, Naqshbandis played a role in reformist and anticolonial resistance movements. Among the numerous examples are Shaykh Shamil's resistance to Russian imperialism in Daghestan in the nineteenth century, the active role of the Naqshbandiya in the mojahedin in the Soviet-Afghan war, the role of Shah Abd al-Aziz (died 1826) in the legal reform movement in India under British rule, and the role of Naqshbandi-led rebellions in China. Although it is difficult to ascertain the true extent of Naqshbandi activity in the new central Asian states today, there is particularly strong adherence in the regions of Dagestan and the Fergana valley, and Naqshbandi shrines continue to be popular places of pilgrimage. In other regions of the Islamic world, the Naqshbandiya maintains a following, particularly in Turkey, but also in Afghanistan, the Kurdish regions of Syria and Turkey, India, Indonesia, and China.

See also BARZANI FAMILY; *SHARIʿA*; SUFISM AND THE SUFI ORDERS; SUNNA.

Bibliography

Algar, Hamid. "A Brief History of the Naqshbandi Order." In *Naqshbandis: Cheminements et situation actuelle d'un ordre mystique musulman,* edited by Marc Gaborieau, Alexandre Popovic, and Thierry Zarcone. Istanbul and Paris: Editions Isis, 1990.

Algar, Hamid. "The Naqshbandi Order: A Preliminary Survey of Its History and Significance." *Studia Islamica* 44 (1976): 123–152.

JOANN GROSS

NARGHILA

See GLOSSARY

NASER AL-DIN SHAH

[1831–1896]

Fourth ruler of the Qajar dynasty in Iran.

Naser al-Din Shah was the son of Mohammad Shah Qajar (r. 1834–1848) and Malik Jahan Khanom (d. 1873). His father designated him crown prince in 1835, when Naser al-Din Shah was four. His accession to the throne upon the death of his father in 1848 was resisted, especially by a cousin in Khorasan, but by 1850 the new monarch had subdued all challenges to his authority.

Naser al-Din Shah's reign marked the beginning of national reforms that became known as modernization. His interest in modernization seems to have originated in the stories he had heard about the reforms his grandfather, Abbas Mirza, had undertaken while governor of the Iranian province of Azerbaijan during the 1820s and early 1830s. After his father sent him to Azerbaijan as governor in

Naser al-Din Shah of Iran began his rule displaying an interest in reform, but became wary of the potential of reforms to undermine his political authority and turned to conservatism. © BETTMANN/CORBIS. REPRODUCED BY PERMISSION.

1847, Naser al-Din Shah allied himself with Mirza Taqi Khan Farahani Amir Kabir, whom Abbas Mirza had sent as an envoy to Turkey. Amir Kabir was impressed by the Ottoman's Tanzimat reforms. Back in Iran, after Naser al-Din Shah appointed him chief of the army in 1848, Amir Kabir initiated, with the shah's support, wide-ranging reforms, including the establishment in 1851 of Iran's first secular school, the Dar al-Fonun. Amir Kabir's reforms, especially those related to rationalizing the tax system, alienated diverse Iranian interest groups and even disturbed Britain and Russia, which were trying to consolidate their own influence over Iran. The opponents of reform allied with Naser al-Din Shah's mother, who eventually persuaded Naser al-Din Shah to dismiss Amir Kabir in 1851.

Although Naser al-Din Shah did not support any major reform programs after the experience with Amir Kabir, he did not oppose all reforms and took a leading role in special projects such as the reconstruction of public areas in Tehran and the introduction of modern urban infrastructure for the capital. His interest in at least minimal reforms was encouraged by a foreign pilgrimage to the holy sites of Shi'ism in Iraq and by three extended tours of Europe.

Meanwhile, Iran's increasing economic and political involvement with Europe exposed an ever-larger percentage of the urban political elite to European ideas, especially those about representative government. A new intellectual class, dominated by such figures as Mirza Malkom Khan and Jamal al-Din al-Afghani, emerged and began to advocate wide-ranging reforms to protect Iran from foreign encroachment. Naser al-Din Shah initially was interested in their ideas and patronized both men, but when he perceived that their views about political reforms potentially threatened his rule he dismissed Malkom Khan as Iran's ambassador to London and banished al-Afghani to exile in Turkey.

Iran's strategic weakness relative to Europe was the main impetus for interest in reform. In 1856 and 1857, Naser al-Din Shah's efforts to restore Herat to Iranian sovereignty were blocked by Britain. Thereafter, both British and Russian influence in Iran increased yearly. The shah sought to counter their influence by granting them competitive economic concessions and by trying to involve third countries, such as France, in Iran. These economic concessions, however, angered the traditional bazaar merchants, who believed that manufactured imports were destroying local production and foreign monopolies were denying them profits. The merchants tended to be closely allied with the *ulama,* and their joint opposition (as well as that of Russia) to the Reuter Concession induced Naser al-Din Shah to cancel it in 1873. More serious politically, however, was his granting of a foreign monopoly concession for tobacco in 1890. This move led to Iran's first national political protest movement in 1891 and 1892. With a mass consumer boycott, bazaar strikes in all the major cities, and even members of the court and royal family refusing to smoke tobacco, Naser al-Din Shah was forced to cancel the concession. The experience apparently was upset-

ting for the shah, because he became increasingly autocratic, tried to repress any expressions of dissent, and ceased to support any type of reforms. Naser al-Din Shah was assassinated by a bankrupt merchant in 1896.

See also ABBAS MIRZA, NA'EB AL-SALTANEH; AFGHANI, JAMAL AL-DIN AL-; AMIR KABIR, MIRZA TAQI KHAN; AZERBAIJAN; BAZAARS AND BAZAAR MERCHANTS; HERAT; KHORASAN; MALKOM KHAN, MIRZA; QAJAR DYNASTY; SHI'ISM; TANZIMAT; TEHRAN; ULAMA.

Bibliography

Amanat, Abbas. "Nasir al-Din Shah." In *Encyclopedia of Islam,* 2d edition. Leiden: Brill, 1993.

Lambton, Ann K. S. *Qājār Persia: Eleven Studies.* Austin: University of Texas Press, 1987.

Ringer, Monica M. *Education, Religion, and the Discourse of Cultural Reform in Qajar Iran.* Costa Mesa, CA: Mazda, 2001.

ERIC HOOGLUND

NASHASHIBI FAMILY

Notable Muslim Palestinian family that established itself in Jerusalem during the fifteenth century.

The Nashashibi family is said to be of Circassian or Kurdish origin It gained prominence during the late nineteenth century when some of its senior members served in the administration of the Ottoman Empire. Uthman al-Nashashibi was elected to the Ottoman parliament as deputy of the Jerusalem *sanjak* (province) in 1912. Throughout the mandate years, the name Nashashibi denoted opposition to al-Hajj Muhammad Amin al-Husayni, a founder of Palestinian nationalism and the leader of the Palestine national movement until 1948. The leadership of the Nashashibi family was also well known for its advocacy of a policy of compromise with the Jewish Agency for Palestine and the British Mandate authorities. This position did not receive the same degree of support enjoyed by the Husayni program, which was based on the total rejection of the British government's Balfour policy. After 1948 the political influence of the Nashashibi family sharply declined, as did the influence of some other notable Palestinian families.

Raghib Nashashibi (1883–1951) was elected to the Ottoman parliament in 1914. During the British Mandate, Raghib became the most influential figure in the family and head of the anti-Husayni ("Opposition") camp. Ronald Storrs, governor of the Jerusalem district, appointed Raghib mayor of Jerusalem in 1920 as a reward for not participating in the anti-British demonstrations during the al-Nabi Musa celebrations in Jerusalem on 4 April 1920. Since the post had been occupied by Musa Kazim al-Husayni, who was dismissed for allegedly inciting the al-Nabi Musa celebrants, Raghib's acceptance of the mayoralty raised questions about his nationalism and exacerbated the Husayni-Nashashibi rivalry. Raghib helped form the Literary Society in 1918 and the Palestinian Arab National Party in 1928. In 1934, after he had lost his position as mayor to Dr. Husayn Fakhri al-Khalidi, Raghib formed the National Defense Party. Although the party's main source of support was the mayors and elites of the larger towns in Palestine, it was also able to reach the peasantry through the network of prominent families that supported the Nashashibi camp. He also served on the Arab Higher Committee from 1936 to 1937. After Israel became a state in 1948, Raghib served as minister in the Jordanian government, governor of the West Bank, and member of the Jordanian senate.

Raghib's nephew Fakhri Nashashibi (1899–1941) was a colorful and controversial political organizer and, from late 1920 until his assassination in Baghdad, the family's strong-arm man. After holding a number of posts in the mandate government, including aide-de-camp to High Commissioner Sir Herbert Samuel, he became Raghib's chief aide. Fakhri was a principal organizer of opposition to al-Hajj Amin and, at the peak of the Palestine Arab Revolt of 1936–1939, he organized the "Peace Bands," with help from the British military and the Zionist movement, to protect the Nashashibi camp from the campaign of intimidation launched against it at al-Hajj Amin's bidding. Fakhri favored a compromise settlement with the British and the Zionists.

Is'af Nashashibi (1882–1948), son of Uthman and a writer known throughout the Arab world, was described by contemporaries as an "Arabic dictionary that walks on two feet." Ali Nashashibi cofounded in 1912 a decentralization party for the

Muhammad Zuhdi Nashashibi (center) with other Palestinian officials attending the Syrian Trade Fair in 2001. Nashashibi, a senior political adviser to Yasir Arafat, also served as finance minister for several years. © AFP/CORBIS. REPRODUCED BY PERMISSION.

Arab provinces of the Ottoman Empire; in 1916, Cemal Paşa executed him on charges of treasonable political activities. Nasir al-Din Nashashibi (1924–), a journalist and political writer living mostly in Egypt, served for some time as League of Arab States representative in Europe. Muhammad Zuhdi Nashashibi (1925–), a politician, started his political career as a Ba'th party figure in Syria after 1960. He has occupied senior positions in the Palestine Liberation Organization, including membership on its Executive Committee, head of the Economics Department, and chair of the Palestine National Fund. He has also served the Palestinian Authority through membership in its Higher Council for Refugee Camps and as finance minister.

See also HUSAYNI, MUHAMMAD AMIN AL-; KHALIDI, HUSAYN FAKHRI AL-; PALESTINE ARAB REVOLT (1936–1939); PALESTINE LIBERATION ORGANIZATION (PLO); PALESTINIAN AUTHORITY.

Bibliography

Nashashibi, Nasser Eddin. *Jerusalem's Other Voice: Ragheb Nashashibi and Moderation in Palestinian Politics, 1920–1948.* Exeter, U.K.: Ithaca, 1990.

Porath, Y. *The Emergence of the Palestinian-Arab National Movement, 1918–1929.* London: Cass, 1974.

Porath, Yehoshua. *The Palestinian Arab National Movement: From Riots to Rebellion,* vol. 2, *1929–1939.* Totowa, NJ; London: Cass, 1977.

MUHAMMAD MUSLIH
UPDATED BY MICHAEL R. FISCHBACH

NASIR, AHMED SAYF AL-
[c. 1880–1960]

Libyan tribal and political leader.

Ahmed Sayf al-Nasir was a member of the Sayf al-Nasir family, hereditary shaykhs of the Awlad Slaiman tribe of the Sirtica and Fezzan regions of Libya. Ahmed Bey fought the Italian conquest of Libya from 1915, seeking exile in French Equatorial Africa (now Chad) toward its end in 1930. During World War II, he returned to Fezzan with Free French Forces advancing from Chad (1943) and became the chief instrument through which the French administered the territory. In February 1950, the French authorities set up a Fezzanese Representative Assembly that elected Ahmed Bey as *chef du territoire,* unopposed, and he headed a local administration under French supervision. Although associated with often unpopular French decisions, he promoted Fezzan's incorporation into a federal Libyan kingdom under Muhammad Idris al-Sanusi and thereby strengthened the hands of those who sought that form of independent Libyan state. After independence in 1951, Ahmed Bey became *wali* of Fezzan, the head of its provincial administration.

Bibliography

Wright, John L. *Libya.* London: Benn; New York: Praeger, 1969.

JOHN L. WRIGHT

NASIR, HANNA
[1936–]

Founding president of Bir Zeit University in the West Bank.

Born in Jaffa, Palestine, Nasir is a graduate of the American University of Beirut. In 1972 he became the founding president of Bir Zeit University, the leading Palestinian university in the West Bank. He was expelled by Israel to Lebanon in November 1974, charged with supporting the Palestine Liberation Organization (PLO). He remained in exile until May 1993. While in exile, Nasir remained president of Bir Zeit University. He was also an elected member of the Executive Committee of the PLO from 1981 to 1984.

JENAB TUTUNJI
UPDATED BY MICHAEL R. FISCHBACH

NASIR, NAJIB
[1865–1948]

Palestinian newspaper publisher and early anti-Zionist writer.

Born to a Greek Orthodox family in Tiberias, Najib al-Khuri Nasir converted to Protestantism while working for fifteen years in a hospital run by missionaries. He then worked briefly as a land sales agent for the Jewish Colonization Association before founding the daily newspaper *al-Karmil* in 1908 in Haifa. Nasir used his knowledge of land sales to Jews to write articles against Zionism and the first history of the Zionist movement in Arabic, *Zionism: Its History, Object and Importance.* Also, before World War I, he founded several activist organizations to limit Jewish immigration and land sales. *Al-Karmil* was closed permanently by court order in 1944. Nasir died in Nazareth.

See also JEWISH COLONIZATION ASSOCIATION.

Bibliography

Mandel, Neville J. *The Arabs and Zionism before World War I.* Berkeley: University of California Press, 1976.

Shafir, Gershon. *Land, Labor and the Origins of the Israeli–Palestinian Conflict,* revised edition. Berkeley: University of California Press, 1996.

ELIZABETH THOMPSON

NASRALLAH, EMILY
[1931–]

Lebanese fiction writer.

Emily (Abi Rashid) Nasrallah was born in South Lebanon in 1931 and writes popular Lebanese fiction, beginning with her award-winning 1962 *Tuyur Aylul* (Birds of September). The heroine, dismayed by village ignorance, moves to the city to study at the university. Her choices are difficult and not always liberating, and the novel ends on a sad and nostalgic note. For decades, Nasrallah has written novels and short fiction for adults and young readers and she is among the most regularly anthologized writers in the Lebanese educational curriculum. Her stories are usually set in a rural past and have served a role in recording and promoting folk culture.

Nasrallah has consistently centered her fiction on female characters and concerns, thereby serving as a pioneer in Arab women's literature. From her first novel to al-Jamr al-Ghafi (Sleeping embers; 1995), Nasrallah has focused on women's struggles for independence and self-expression. Repeatedly, she shows that access to knowledge should be the right of every human being. She has been a vocal and visible women's-rights activist.

Nasrallah remained prolific during the Lebanese Civil War (1975–1990) and wrote about the incomprehensible violence and the sudden fragmentation that leads to death, division, and forced emigration. Her 1981 al-Ikla Aks al-Zaman (Flight against time) is a haunting tale set during the war years. Nasrallah is the recipient of numerous awards, and many of her novels and short story collections have been translated into German, Danish, and English.

See also GENDER: GENDER AND EDUCATION; LEBANESE CIVIL WAR (1958); LEBANESE CIVIL WAR (1975–1990); LEBANON; LITERATURE: ARABIC.

Bibliography

Cooke, Miriam. War's Other Voices: Women Writers on the Lebanese Civil War. New York: Cambridge University Press, 1988.

Salem, Elise. Constructing Lebanon: A Century of Literary Narratives. Gainesville, FL: University Press of Florida, 2003.

ELISE SALEM

NASRALLAH, HASAN
[1960–]

Lebanese Hizbullah leader.

Hasan Nasrallah was born in 1960 in Qarantina, the eastern suburbs of Beirut, to a Shi'ite Muslim family. Hasan was religious at an early age. Because of the persecution of Shi'a in East Beirut by right wing militias, the family moved to the Tyre region. In his village of Bazuriyya, Nasrallah joined the ranks of the AMAL movement (founded by Imam Musa al-Sadr).

In the late 1970s Nasrallah moved to Najaf in Iraq to receive religious training at the renowned Shi'ite school. There he met and befriended Abbas al-Musawi, who would later lead Hizbullah. In 1978 the Iraqi government began harassing and persecuting Shi'ite religious students and leaders, and

Nasrallah returned to Lebanon, where he continued his religious training at a school established by his friend al-Musawi in Ba'albak. In 1982 Nasrallah was elected to the leadership of the AMAL movement in the Biqa region. After the Israeli invasion, AMAL leader Nabih Berri accepted the invitation of Lebanese president Ilyas Sarkis to join a "salvation committee" that included among its members the pro-Israeli right-wing militia leader Bashir Jumayyil. That decision by Berri alienated large segments of the movement and led to the creation of a splinter movement by Husayn al-Musawi, who founded the Islamic AMAL movement. Others gravitated toward a new group that would later become Hizbullah, or the Party of God. The group included people who formerly were leaders and members of the Iraqi Da'wa Party.

Nasrallah rose quickly in the Hizbullah ranks and became the leader of the Beirut region. In 1989, amid rumors of differences of opinion in party leadership, Nasrallah left Lebanon for Qom to complete his religious studies and training. In 1992 Israel assassinated Abbas al-Musawi, and Nasrallah was elected secretary-general of the party, even though he had not served as a deputy secretary-general. He was the youngest member of the Shura Council (the highest executive body of the party). Nasrallah quickly rose to become one of the most charismatic, most popular leaders in Lebanon and in the Arab world. His pictures are seen in demonstrations in places like Morocco and Gaza. Nasrallah's eldest son was killed by the Israelis in 1997, and his handling of the personal tragedy (refusing a special deal with Israel to receive his body) only increased his popularity. Nasrallah's popularity was boosted further in 2000, when Israeli troops withdrew from south Lebanon after years of Hizbullah resistance, managed in its last years by Nasrallah. Nasrallah led Hizbullah's transformation into a parliamentary party with extensive media and social services in Lebanon. The party also retained its security-military force, calling for Israel to withdraw from the Shab'a Farms, which are still occupied by Israel (which claims that they belong to Syria).

Bibliography

Saad-Ghorayeb, Amal. Hizbullah: Politics and Religion. London: Pluto Press, 2002.

AS'AD ABUKHALIL

NASRUDDIN HOCA

A well-loved character in the Turkish oral prose tradition; protagonist of humorous anecdotes told from the Balkans to central Asia.

Known as Nasr al-Din in Iran and as Juha in Arabia, Nasruddin Hoca appears in some stories as a wise folk philosopher or a witty if unconventional preacher. In others, he is naive and uninformed, the butt of youngsters' pranks, a figure of gentle ridicule who shows great resilience. However foolish he may seem, he survives all disasters and, having the last word, often turns the tables on those wielding power over or making fun of him. Although a village near Sivrihisar in central Anatolia is claimed as Nasruddin's birthplace and a mausoleum in Akşehir is said to be his 1284 burial place, a connection between the stories and any historical person is questionable.

The earliest Ottoman manuscript collections about Nasruddin Hoca are dated to the early sixteenth century and contain fewer than 100 stories. The first printed edition of 125 stories appeared in 1837; later publications present a body of several hundred items, and translations have appeared in many Western and Asian languages.

Bibliography

Başgöz, Ilhan, and Boratav, Pertev N. *I, Hoca Nasreddin, Never Shall I Die: A Thematic Analysis of Hoca Stories.* Bloomington: Indiana University Press, 1998.

Walker, Warren S., and Uysal, Ahmet E. *Tales Alive in Turkey.* Cambridge, MA: Harvard University Press, 1966.

KATHLEEN R. F. BURRILL
UPDATED BY BURÇAK KESKIN-KOZAT

NASSAR, SADHIJ
[c.1900–c.1970]

Palestinian women's activist.

Sadhij Nassar, of Iranian origin, grew up in Haifa, where she lived until 1948. She married Najib Nassar, editor of the newspaper *al-Karmil.* It was one of the few interfaith marriages during this period, and not without controversy. Najib Nassar, who was an Orthodox Christian, was also considerably older than his wife, who was the granddaughter of the founder of the Baha'i faith. Beginning in the 1920s, Sadhij Nassar contributed articles to the newspaper, translated articles from the foreign press, and was editor from 1941 to 1944, when the Mandate authorities refused to grant her a permit under the Emergency Defense Regulations. In 1930 she was a founding member and secretary of the Arab Women's Union in Haifa, which was one of the more militant branches of the women's movement during the Mandate period. In 1939 the British detained her for political reasons and held her without charges under the Emergency Defense Regulations in the women's prison in Bethlehem. She was released after an eleven-month imprisonment. She continued her activities in the women's movement until 1948. After 1948, when she became a refugee, she wrote for various publications in London and in Damascus, where she tried to open a branch of the Arab Women's Union. She is believed to have died in Damascus sometime during the 1970s.

See also BAHA'I FAITH; GENDER: GENDER AND LAW; GENDER: GENDER AND POLITICS; HAIFA; PALESTINE.

Bibliography

Fleischmann, Ellen L. *The Nation and Its "New" Women: The Palestinian Women's Movement, 1920–1948.* Berkeley: University of California Press, 2003.

ELLEN L. FLEISCHMANN

NASSER, GAMAL ABDEL
[1918–1970]

President of Egypt, 1956–1970.

Few Arab politicians rivaled the impact of Gamal Abdel Nasser (also known as Jamal Abd al-Nasir) on the Arab world in the twentieth century. His mid-century revolution and his rule of Egypt followed the corrupt monarchy of King Farouk and was fueled by nationalism. It held out the promise of socialism and Arab unity, stirring the imaginations of Arabic-speaking intellectuals and common people.

Born in Alexandria into the Muslim family of a modest postal clerk, Nasser received his primary education in the small Nile delta village of al-Khatatiba, to which his father had been assigned. After completing his secondary education in Cairo, where he lived with an uncle, Nasser attended law school for several months before gaining entry to the Royal Military Academy in 1936.

The military provided the vehicle for Nasser's rise to power. His historical role began as the leader of a military conspiracy, the Free Officers, who launched a coup d'état and seized power in July 1952, overthrowing King Farouk. A republic was proclaimed, 18 June 1953, under General Muhammad Naguib as both provisional president and premier; he gave up the premiership in 1954 to Nasser, then the leader of the ruling military junta. Naguib was deposed and Nasser was confirmed as president by referendum on 23 June 1956.

In the eyes of a trusted minister, "the Nasir revolution cohered around the ideas and principles of pan-Arabism, positive neutrality, and the social revolution." Nasser, as his ex-minister put it, "took the side of the poor, just as he took the side of development, democracy, Arab unity, and nonalignment." Such admirers believe that even with the changed conditions after Nasser's death, "these principles will undoubtedly take new forms; yet, the ideas are still alive and they still move people" (Baker 1990, p. 80).

Nasser's critics have emphasized his authoritarianism and his bitter defeats. Anwar al-Sadat, his successor as president, charged that Nasser's vaunted social revolution degenerated into "a huge, dark, and terrible pit, inspiring fear and hatred" and that Nasser's relentless hostility toward Israel had given Egypt only "years of defeat and pain," undermining prospects of achieving peace and prosperity while accomplishing little to realize Arab goals (Sadat, p. 20; and al-Ahram, 27 June 1977).

Early Domestic Affairs

Debate about the ultimate meaning of Nasser's rule does not preclude identification of key turning points that both supporters and detractors accept as decisive. A domestic power struggle and the necessity of coming to terms with the former British colonial power, which retained its base at Suez, gave early definition to the new regime. General Naguib, the figurehead for the Free Officers' movement, challenged Nasser's leadership from February to April 1954 by drawing support from the small middle class, the movement of the Muslim Brotherhood,

Former Egyptian president Gamal Abdel Nasser (1918–1970). Hailed by many Arabs as a champion of Arab interests, Nasser took power following a 1952 coup by the Free Officers revolutionary organization. © UNITED NATIONS. REPRODUCED BY PERMISSION.

and the former political parties who all opposed the authoritarian and plebeian thrust of the military regime. Rallying urban mass support through a newly created party called the Liberation Rally, Nasser relied on the military and police to defeat the middle- and upper class political forces arrayed against him. The formula worked, and the newly consolidated regime immediately launched an agrarian reform program that added peasant support and undermined the powerful landowning families that had backed the monarchy.

Early Foreign Relations

Regime priorities of power consolidation and domestic reform were reflected in moderation on the three major foreign-policy issues confronting Egypt—the Sudan, the British, and Israel. While an activist foreign policy later became the hallmark of

Nasserism, as a new ruler Nasser established himself as a moderate in foreign affairs. In 1954, Egypt signed a conciliatory agreement for a transitional period of self-government for the Sudan, which became an independent republic in 1956. Negotiations also produced an Anglo–Egyptian agreement in 1954 that provided for the gradual withdrawal of the British from their remaining Suez Canal zone base. Opponents, including the Muslim Brotherhood, charged that Nasser had compromised the national interest. An assassination attempt against Nasser in October 1954 justified the crushing of the Muslim Brotherhood; in fact, throughout Nasser's rule, the brotherhood suffered severe repression.

Nasser emerged only reluctantly as the champion of the Arab struggle against Israel. A few dangerous paramilitary actions had drawn Egypt into the conflict in the early to mid-1950s. Small bands of Palestinians, including some operating from the Egyptian-controlled Gaza Strip, launched raids against Israel. Israel immediately developed a policy of massive reprisal against the Arab states sheltering the raiders.

When the West failed to respond to Nasser's need for arms, he announced an arms agreement with Czechoslovakia (an intermediary for the Soviet Union). A dispute with the United States and Britain over their financing of a high dam project at Aswan accelerated the radicalization of Egypt's foreign policy in 1955 and 1956. The Egyptians looked to the electricity that the dam would provide to fulfill their dreams of industrialization. The Western powers, alarmed by Nasser's flirtation with the East, denied funds previously promised. In defiance, Nasser nationalized the Suez Canal Company on 26 July 1956. The response came swiftly.

In 1956, Egypt was invaded by Israel in October and by France and Great Britain in November. Militarily, the invading armies triumphed, but the Egyptians resisted fiercely under Nasser's inspiring leadership. They fought just long and well enough to give international opinion time to force the invaders to withdraw. Most dramatic were the Soviet missile threats against Europe and Israel, but U.S. diplomatic pressure actually proved effective in securing a cease-fire and the withdrawal of the invaders. Defeated militarily, Nasser triumphed politically;

he remained in power with the Suez Canal Company in Egyptian hands.

Union with Syria and Socialist Agenda

Buoyed by obtaining Suez, Nasser launched a bold bid for Egyptian leadership of the Arab world and laid the groundwork for an ambitious program of domestic change. On 1 February 1958, Syria voluntarily united with Egypt to form the United Arab Republic (UAR), which was later joined by Yemen. Although the union lasted only until 1961, it gave substance to the rhetoric of pan-Arabism. Nasser blamed the breakup of the UAR on reactionaries and responded by intensifying the revolution at home. A Charter of National Action then committed Egypt to socialism and announced the formation of a new mass political organization, the Arab Socialist Union.

Before he was forced to retreat, Nasser tried to realize a socialism for Egypt that had industrialization and improvement of mass welfare at its heart. The long-range goal was the creation of a heavy industrial base. Aziz Sidqi, Nasser's minister of industry, presided over a remarkable expansion of the nationalized public sector. Unfortunately, advances in agriculture did not match the industrial gains registered in the decade after Suez, which were diluted further by a rapidly expanding population. Still, Nasser did create the public sector and improvements in health and education reached even the rural countryside in limited ways. The issue of rural transformation was put on the national agenda.

The collapse of the union with Syria dealt a blow to Nasser's pan-Arab standing. He sought to regain momentum in the Arab arena by intervening in the Yemen Civil War in 1962, hoping that a victory by the republican side would give Egypt leverage on the strategic Arabian Peninsula. Instead, the intervention merely provoked conflict with the Saudi regime that supported the Yemeni royalists and with the Americans who stood behind the Saudis. Fearing Nasser's pan-Arabism as a destabilizing force, the Americans turned against the regime. Until this point, republican Egypt had earned impressive aid for its development effort from both the United States and the Soviet Union. After the intervention in Yemen, the United States cut off its aid to Egypt.

The period of growth and expansion at home and abroad was over by the mid-1960s.

1967 War with Israel

These reversals created a mood of desperation that culminated in Nasser's abandoning the heretofore cautious policy that he had pursued with Israel. In the Arab summit conferences of the 1960s, Nasser had consistently urged restraint. For ten years after Suez, Egypt lived in relative peace with Israel because the presence of a United Nations Emergency Force stationed on the Egyptian side of the border. Pressures mounted, however, as the Palestinians launched raids from Lebanon, Jordan, and especially Syria. Israel responded with deadly force. An outcry provoked by the response forced a weakened Nasser to act. Chided for hiding behind the United Nations (UN), Nasser requested the withdrawal of UN forces from the Sinai peninsula in 1967. The UN commander interpreted the order to mean the removal of his forces at the head of the Gulf of Aqaba. Egyptian troop replacements there meant closing the gulf to Israeli ships.

Israel viewed the closing of the Gulf of Aqaba as a cause for war. On 5 June 1967, Israel launched an attack, destroying the entire Egyptian air force in a matter of hours. In the course of the 1967 Arab–Israel War, Israel seized Jerusalem and the West Bank from Jordan and the Golan Heights from Syria, sweeping across Sinai and the Gaza Strip and routing the Egyptian army to leave an estimated ten thousand dead. On 9 June, Israel's forces reached the Suez Canal. On 10 June, a cease-fire was called by the UN; Egypt had lost the war, and Nasser then resigned.

In Cairo, Egyptians took to the streets to urge Nasser to remain as leader. For three more years Nasser ruled, refusing to accept an Israeli-dictated peace. In April 1969, he launched the so-called War of Attrition (1969–1970) in the canal zone that prolonged the Egyptian struggle against the Jewish state. At home, he announced a program that promised to revitalize the revolution. But Nasser's revolution never regained momentum. The exhausted Egyptian leader died on 28 September 1970 and was replaced by Anwar al-Sadat.

See also ARAB–ISRAEL WAR (1967); ARAB SOCIALIST UNION; FAROUK; FREE OFFICERS; EGYPT; LIBERATION RALLY; MUSLIM BROTHERHOOD; NAGUIB, MUHAMMAD; PAN-ARABISM; SADAT, ANWAR AL-; UNITED ARAB REPUBLIC (UAR); WAR OF ATTRITION (1969–1970); YEMEN CIVIL WAR.

Bibliography

Baker, Raymond William. *Egypt's Uncertain Revolution under Nasser and Sadat.* Cambridge, MA: Harvard University Press, 1978.

Baker, Raymond William. *Sadat and After: Struggles for Egypt's Political Soul.* Cambridge, MA: Harvard University Press, 1990.

Gorman, Anthony. *Historians, State and Politics in Twentieth Century Egypt: Contesting the Nation.* London and New York: Routledge Curzon, 2003.

Jankowski, James. *Nasser's Egypt, Arab Nationalism, and the United Arab Republic.* Boulder, CO: Lynne Rienner Publishers, 2002.

McNamara, Robert. *Britain, Nasser and the Balance of Power in the Middle East, 1952–1967: From the Egyptian Revolution to the Six Day War.* London and Portland, OR: F. Cass, 2003.

Nasser, Gamal Abdel. *The Philosophy of the Revolution.* Buffalo, NY: Smith, Keynes and Marshall, 1959.

Sadat, Anwar El-. *In Search of Identity: An Autobiography.* New York: Harper and Row, 1978.

Stephens, Robert. *Nasser: A Political Biography.* London: Allen Lane, 1971.

Waterbury, John. *The Egypt of Nasser and Sadat: The Political Economy of Two Regimes.* Princeton, NJ: Princeton University Press, 1983.

RAYMOND WILLIAM BAKER

NASSER, LAKE

A reservoir of the Nile located in southern Egypt and northern Sudan, created by the Aswan High Dam after 1971.

Lake Nasser, created by the construction of the High Dam at Aswan, is 298 miles long and 10 miles wide at its widest point, with a water capacity of 130 million acre-feet, of which 24 million acre-feet serve as dead storage for sediment and 73 million acre-feet as live storage. About one-quarter of all the Nile waters entering Lake Nasser are lost to evaporation and seepage. The largest man-made lake in the world, Lake Nasser has a major role in Egypt's fishing industry, yielding 15,000 to 25,000 tons per annum. Original hopes that Lake Nasser would also support agriculture in its vicinity, however, have yet to be realized.

In 1978 the Ministry of Irrigation authorized construction of the Tushka canal to carry away surplus water from Lake Nasser to the New Valley Project in the western desert in case a high flood upstream caused Lake Nasser's waters to pass over the spillway, leading to damage to barrages and bridge abutments downstream. This emergency canal was used for the first time in the late 1990s, at a time of unusually high Nile flows. At the beginning of the twenty-first century, the Tushka diversion was a source of international controversy in that the Egyptian government announced plans for routine diversions of lake water into the western desert to reclaim land. This came at a time when the ten riparian states of the Nile Basin were attempting to reach an accord on future uses of the limited waters of the river.

The lake is named for Egypt's president who held office at the time of the building of the dam, Gamal Abdel Nasser. The rising lake displaced over 100,000 Nubian inhabitants, and flooded sites of ancient Egyptian buildings such as Abu Simbel. Creation of the lake in the early 1970s led to an international rescue effort to save dynastic-era antiquities of the valley behind the dam.

See also ASWAN HIGH DAM; NILE RIVER.

Bibliography

Said, R. *The River Nile: Geology, Hydrology, and Utilization.* Oxford, U.K.: Pergamon, 1993.

Waterbury, John. *Hydropolitics of the Nile Valley.* Syracuse, NY: Syracuse University Press, 1979.

White, Gilbert F. "Environmental Effects of the High Dam at Aswan." *Environment* 30, no. 7 (1988): 34–41.

ARTHUR GOLDSCHMIDT
UPDATED BY GREGORY B. BAECHER

NASSIF, MALAK HIFNI
[1886–1918]

Egyptian writer.

An Egyptian Muslim, Malak Hifni Nassif (pseudonym, Bahithat al-Badiya) publicly advocated women's

advancement in the early twentieth century during the *al-nahda al-nisaʾiyya* (women's awakening). This was a period in which women were increasingly able to publish essays, stories, and letters in the nascent women's press and also in the general press. The women's press and the writers who contributed to it played an important role in the development of feminism and the reform of social institutions in a number of Middle Eastern countries. Nassif, along with other prominent figures such as May Ziadeh, were active in literary and social groups through which they contributed to the intellectual and public debate about nationalism and how to define Egyptian and Arab political and cultural identity under the British colonial government.

Nassif articulated one of the founding discourses of feminism that emerged in Egypt during the first third of the twentieth century. Her strain of feminism remained secondary to that embodied in the work of Huda al-Shaʿrawi (1882–1947) until the final decades of the twentieth century. In contrast to Shaʿrawi's secular and Western-oriented feminism, Nassif's feminism, expressed in her collection of talks and essays, *Al-nisaʾiyyat* (Women's affairs, 1910), de-emphasized Western values as it attempted to affirm and improve women's lives and experience through increased educational and work opportunities within a reformed Islamic context.

See also GENDER: GENDER AND EDUCATION; SHAʿRAWI, HUDA AL-; ZIADEH, MAY.

Bibliography

Ahmed, Leila. *Women and Gender in Islam: Historical Roots of a Modern Debate.* New Haven, CT: Yale University Press, 1992.

Badran, Margot. *Feminists, Islam, and Nation: Gender and the Making of Modern Egypt.* Princeton, NJ: Princeton University Press, 1995.

Baron, Beth. *The Women's Awakening in Egypt: Culture, Society, and the Press.* New Haven, CT: Yale University Press, 1994.

CAROLINE SEYMOUR-JORN

NATEQ-NURI, ALI AKBAR
[1943–]

Iranian cleric; speaker of the majles.

Ali Akbar Nateq-Nuri was born in Nur Mazandaran. His political activities before the revolution are said to have begun in 1963, against the Pahlavi regime. He lived briefly in Lebanon and Syria, and after the revolution in 1979, became Ayatollah Khomeini's representative in the Construction Crusade (Jihad-e Sazandegi). Nuri served as minister of the interior between December 1981 and August 1985. As of 1996, he was the speaker of Iran's parliament (majles).

FARHAD ARSHAD

NATIONAL BLOC

Lebanese political party headed by Emile and Raymond Eddé.

Established in 1934, the National Bloc became the political vehicle for Emile Eddé and his son Raymond Eddé. Originally from Jubayl (Byblos), the Eddé family played an important role in the history of Lebanon. Elected president of Lebanon in 1936, Emile Eddé was the first Maronite Catholic president to appoint a Muslim prime minister—thus establishing the tradition. In 1949 Emile Eddé died and was replaced as chairman of the National Bloc by Raymond.

As a member of the Lebanese parliament from 1953, Raymond, a firm believer in the free-enterprise system, introduced several important pieces of legislation—notably the 1956 law on bank secrecy, the law introducing the death penalty in 1959, and the joint banking account law in 1961. With the beginning of the Lebanese Civil War in 1975, Raymond Eddé kept the National Bloc from becoming a party of warlords. He was the first Lebanese politician to warn of the dangers of Lebanon becoming a hostage to her two neighbors: Syria and Israel. In 1969 Raymond Eddé and the National Bloc were the only group to vote down the Cairo Agreement between Lebanon and the Palestine Liberation Organization (PLO). In 1976, as a result of seven assassination attempts, Raymond Eddé opted for the relative safety of exile in Paris.

Since Raymond's death in May 2000, the bloc has been led by his nephew, Carlos Eddé, a businessman who had spent most of his life abroad. The National Bloc is no longer a major player on the Lebanese political scene.

See also EDDÉ, RAYMOND.

Bibliography

AbuKhalil, As'ad. *Historical Dictionary of Lebanon.* Lanham, MD: Scarecrow Press, 1998.

GEORGE E. IRANI
UPDATED BY MICHAEL R. FISCHBACH

NATIONAL CONGRESS PARTY

The principal opposition political party in Libya immediately after independence.

Government tampering in national assembly elections in 1952 deprived the National Congress party of its victory. Party stalwarts reacted violently, leading, first, to the expulsion of its founder, Libyan nationalist Bashir Bey Sadawi, from the country and then, soon thereafter, to the demise of party politics in Libya.

See also SADAWI, BASHIR.

Bibliography

Anderson, Lisa S. *The State and Social Transformation in Tunisia and Libya, 1930–1980.* Princeton, NJ: Princeton University Press, 1986.

Khadduri, Majid. *Modern Libya: A Study in Political Development.* Baltimore, MD: Johns Hopkins Press, 1963.

LISA ANDERSON

NATIONAL DEMOCRATIC FRONT (NDF)

Leftist movement in the Yemen Arab Republic.

The National Democratic Front (NDF) was an umbrella organization created in 1976 by six leftist opposition groups in the Yemen Arab Republic (YAR), which sought to move the YAR in a more radical direction and away from the republican-royalist reconciliation that ended the civil war in 1970. The roots of the NDF can be traced to the expulsion of the left from the YAR polity following the San'a Mutiny in 1968. In addition to an increasingly radical program of socioeconomic reform along socialist lines, the NDF sought to unify the YAR with the revolutionary South Yemen; to loosen ties of political dependency with Saudi Arabia; to curb the influence of tribal leaders; and to open up the closed political system of the YAR to popular participation. The NDF first sought through political means to pressure the government to accept it and its goals. Frustrated in this effort, during the late 1970s and early 1980s the NDF waged an armed rebellion against the YAR regime with the support of Marxist South Yemen; it played an important role in the 1979 border war between the two Yemens. The NDF rebellion was largely put down by force in 1982, and many NDF members accepted the regime's terms for reconciliation; almost all of the others reconciled on the occasion of Yemeni unification in 1990, effectively ending the NDF as an organized force in Yemeni politics. Many former NDF leaders ended up playing important political roles in unified Yemen, some in the ruling party of the president and most in the opposition. The NDF was virtually nonexistent by the time of the brief War of Secession in 1994 and hence played no role in it.

See also YEMEN; YEMEN ARAB REPUBLIC.

Bibliography

Burrowes, Robert D. *The Yemen Arab Republic: The Politics of Development, 1962–1986.* Boulder, CO: Westview Press; London: Croon Helm, 1987.

Carapico, Sheila. *Civil Society in Yemen: The Political Economy of Activism in Modern Arabia.* New York and Cambridge, U.K.: Cambridge University Press, 1998.

Dresch, Paul. *A History of Modern Yemen.* New York and Cambridge, U.K.: Cambridge University Press, 2000.

ROBERT D. BURROWES

NATIONAL DEMOCRATIC FRONT FOR THE LIBERATION OF OMAN AND THE ARAB GULF

Radical antigovernment organization (1970–1971), known as NDFLOAG.

NDFLOAG was formed in June 1970 by the merger of several small groups of foreign-educated Omanis. The front's members, fewer than a hundred, were united by shared antipathy for the reactionary sultan, Sa'id bin Taymur Al Bu Sa'id. Their aim was to carry out attacks on the government in northern Oman paralleling those that had been launched by the Popular Front for the Liberation of the Occupied Arabian Gulf (PFLOAG) in Dhufar in the south. Mortar assaults on garrisons at Nizwa and Izki failed, and most of the perpetrators were captured. The attacks, however, caused Omani supporters of the government, as well as its British protectors, to fear that rebellion could spread throughout the country. This fear led them to work with Sa'id's son, Qabus ibn Sa'id Al Bu Sa'id, to overthrow his father in July 1970. In December 1971 NDFLOAG, reduced to impotence, was absorbed by PFLOAG, which changed its name (but not its acronym) and became the Popular Front for the Liberation of Oman and the Arab Gulf.

See also POPULAR FRONT FOR THE LIBERATION OF THE OCCUPIED ARABIAN GULF.

Bibliography

Allen, Calvin H., Jr. *Oman: The Modernization of the Sultanate.* Boulder, CO: Westview Press; London: Croom Helm, 1987.

MALCOLM C. PECK

NATIONAL DEMOCRATIC PARTY (IRAQ)

A political party in Iraq, known as the NDP (Arabic, al-Hizb al-Watani al-Dimuqrati); licensed in 1946 under the leadership of Kamil Chadirchi.

An outgrowth of the old Ahali group, (People's Group) the party had semi-socialist views and attracted supporters from the wealthy, well-established families as well as from Shi'a and left-leaning middle-class people who believed in gradual change. In 1949 the party was banned along with the Iraqi Communist party. Even so, its members were involved in the strikes and riots that occurred in the early 1950s in opposition to the Anglo-Iraqi treaties. When free elections were held in 1954, the NDP won six seats but lost them when Prime Minister Nuri al-Sa'id suspended parliament and banned opposition parties. In 1956 the NDP applied for permission to form a party with Istiqlal (Independence party) the supported neutrality, an Arab federation, the liberation of Palestine, and political freedom. Denied, the Istiqlal, NDP, the Communist party, and the Ba'th party formed the United National Front, or United Popular Front.

Supporting the opposition to the monarchy, Chadirchi initially backed Abd al-Karim Qasim in his coup that overthrew the monarchy in June 1958. By 1961, Chadirchi opposed Qasim, even though Muhammad Hadid, second-in-command of the NDP, accepted the post of minister of finance in Qasim's government. As a protest to the antidemocratic nature of the regime, in October 1961

Chadirchi closed the NDP and ceased publishing *al-Ahali*.

See also AHALI GROUP.

Bibliography

Marr, Phebe. *The Modern History of Iraq*. Boulder, CO: Westview Press, 1985.

REEVA S. SIMON

NATIONAL FRONT FOR THE LIBERATION OF SOUTH YEMEN

An association opposed to Britain's role in South Yemen in the 1960s.

The National Front for the Liberation of South Yemen (NLF), an association of seven organizations, first met in San'a (capital of North Yemen) in 1963 to discuss strategies against the British position in South Yemen; three additional groupings joined later. Its intellectual and ideological origins lie primarily with the Arab national movement. It differed from other groups in two respects: its members agreed on the necessity of military action, and its primary popular base lay in the Protectorates rather than Aden. In 1967 the British turned over South Yemen to the NLF. In 1978 the NLF was recast as the Yemeni Socialist Party (YSP) and governed South Yemen (PDRY) until the merger with North Yemen in 1990. At that point, it became the second-most important party in the united state, and the major alternative and opposition party to the government of Ali Abdullah Salih. The frictions between the two constituent "regions" continue to be represented in the policies and personalities of their respective leaders and parties in the united state; the YSP continues to have its primary base of support in the old South.

Bibliography

Carapico, Sheila. *Civil Society in Yemen*. Cambridge and New York: Cambridge University Press, 1998.

Dresch, Paul. *A History of Modern Yemen*. Cambridge and New York: Cambridge University Press, 2000.

Gause, F. Gregory. *Saudi-Yemeni Relations, 1962–1982*. New York: Columbia University Press, 1990.

Halliday, Fred. *Revolution and Foreign Policy: The Case of South Yemen*. Cambridge and New York: Cambridge University Press, 1990.

Joffe, E. G. H., et al. *Yemen Today: Crisis and Solutions*. London: Caravel Press, 1997.

Mundy, Martha. *Domestic Government: Kinship, Community and Polity in North Yemen*. New York: St. Martin's Press, 1995.

Al-Suwaidi, Jamal, ed. *The Yemeni War of 1994*. London: Saqi Books, 1995.

Wenner, Manfred. *The Yemen Arab Republic: Development and Change in an Ancient Land*. Boulder, CO: Westview Press, 1991.

MANFRED W. WENNER

NATIONAL FRONT FOR THE SALVATION OF LIBYA

The principal opposition to Qaddafi's regime in Libya.

The National Front for the Salvation of Libya (NFSL) was established in 1981. Illegal in Libya, it operates in exile under the leadership of its secretary-general, Muhammad Yusuf al-Magarief, a former Libyan ambassador to India. Encompasing opponents of Muammar al-Qaddafi of a variety of political persuasions, many of whom served in early Qaddafi governments, the NFSL has broadcast radio programming into Libya, published several newspapers and magazines abroad, and is credited with having organized a 1984 attack on the military barracks at Bab al-Aziziyya, where Qaddafi often stayed. During the mid-1980s, at the height of the American confrontation with Libya, the NFSL denied widespread allegations that it received assistance from the United States. By the 1990s, leadership positions in the NFSL were being assumed by younger Libyans who had grown up in exile and lived most of their lives outside the country.

LISA ANDERSON

NATIONAL FRONT, IRAN

Coalition of nationalist parties and groups that became prominent in the early 1950s and advocated a constitutional regime and Iran's control of its oil resources.

The National Front was responsible for the nationalization of the British-owned Iranian oil industry in 1951. Its influence declined after the Anglo-American coup of 1953, which overthrew Mohammad Mossadegh and reinstalled Mohammad Reza Pahlavi as shah. The rise of the National Front was triggered by opposition to parliamentary election fraud. In October 1949 Mossadegh led a delegation to the shah's palace to protest the lack of free elections. A committee of twenty members was then formed to negotiate with the court minister, who promised to end electoral problems. The same committee later met at Mossadegh's house to form the National Front as a parliamentary faction. The front's diverse wings included social democrats, constitutional monarchists, and Islamists (led by clerics). Its social base consisted of bazaar merchants and craft guilds, members of the small industrial bourgeoisie, and urban professional middle classes. The front tried to enhance its political position by using the postwar rivalry between Britain and the United States for influence in Iran.

With opposition to foreign domination as its main goal, the National Front focused on ending British control of Iran's oil industry. The British rejected its demand for total Iranian control and equal profit-sharing with the Anglo-Iranian Oil Company. When the parliament nationalized Iranian oil, the shah delayed signing the bill, finally doing so in April 1950 when Mossadegh was elected prime minister.

Facing a British boycott of Iranian oil and increasing American hostility, Mossadegh's government encountered serious difficulties. The National Front's initial strength was its unification of disparate ideological and political currents under the banner of oil nationalization. But with the rapid polarization of Iranian politics in the early 1950s and under intense foreign pressure, the front began to unravel. Most significantly, its conservative and religious factions began opposing Mossadegh's defiant secular nationalism and defected to the monarchist and Anglo-American camp.

In August 1953, after a showdown with Mossadegh, the shah fled the country but was quickly returned to power through a CIA-engineered military coup. Mossadegh was overthrown and, along with many National Front leaders, ended up in prison. Some of his followers formed the National Resistance Movement but were unable to challenge the new regime effectively. In the early 1960s a Second National Front was organized by Mossadegh's former allies and played a leading role in another round of struggle for reform, but, like the Third National Front formed in 1965, was crushed by the regime.

Key personalities of the National Front emerged to lead the revival of popular opposition in 1977, but they soon were overtaken by Islamist forces. Still, the front's religious wing, led by Mehdi Bazargan, continued to be prominent. Following the fall of the monarchy in 1979, Bazargan became the prime minister of the provisional government. A few National Front old guards served in his cabinet; but they, along with Bazargan himself, were purged by the clerical Islamist forces close to Ayatollah Ruhollah Khomeini. Under the Islamic Republic, Bazargan continued to function as a loyal opposition figure, whereas most other National Front leaders were forced into exile.

See also BAZARGAN, MEHDI; KHOMEINI, RUHOLLAH; MOSSADEGH, MOHAMMAD; PAHLAVI, MOHAMMAD REZA.

Bibliography

Abrahamian, Ervand. *Iran between Two Revolutions.* Princeton, NJ: Princeton University Press, 1982.

Chehabi, H. E. *Iranian Politics and Religious Modernism: The Liberation Movement of Iran under the Shah and Khomeini.* Ithaca, NY: Cornell University Press, 1990.

Cottam, Richard W. *Nationalism in Iran,* 2d edition. Pittsburgh, PA: University of Pittsburgh Press, 1979.

AFSHIN MATIN-ASGARI

NATIONAL FRONT, LEBANON

Coalition of left-wing Lebanese and Arab political parties and forces formed in 1984.

In 1984 in Lebanon, the leftist-nationalist coalition known as the Lebanese National Movement was dissolved as a result of internecine battles. In Israel, elections led to the victory of the Likud under Yitzhak Shamir. In the United States, Ronald Reagan was on the brink of being reelected for a second term.

The National Front was created as a result of these events. This coalition included representatives of the Progressive Socialist Party, the Lebanese Communist Party, the Ba'th party, the Syrian Social Nationalist Party, the Arab Democratic Party, and the Arab Socialist Union. The platform of the National Front contained six principles: (1) consolidate the resistance to the Israeli occupation in south Lebanon, (2) stress the unity and integrity of

Lebanon in the struggle against partition plans, (3) emphasize the Arab identity of Lebanon, (4) adopt an independent foreign policy, (5) call for political reforms and the abolition of the confessional system, and (6) call for economic and social reform. The mainstream Shi'ite AMAL movement was later invited to join the coalition.

See also AMAL; ARAB SOCIALIST UNION; BA'TH, AL-; COMMUNISM IN THE MIDDLE EAST; LIKUD; PROGRESSIVE SOCIALIST PARTY; REAGAN, RONALD; SHAMIR, YITZHAK; SYRIAN SOCIAL NATIONALIST PARTY.

GEORGE E. IRANI

NATIONALISM

A people's sense of its political identity or a movement to achieve such identity.

The word *nationalism* refers to the feeling of political unity or of identity and patriotic sympathy that a people usually focuses on its own language or culture or on a land that it regards as its own. It also refers to that component of various political ideologies according to which this feeling is held to be essential to the existence of a state or to a political movement's aspirations to statehood. Finally, it is used in the arguments advanced by historians, ideologues, and politicians to justify actual or proposed actions on behalf of the people they see as embodying the nation.

Evidence of nationalism, in any of these related senses, is difficult to discern in the Middle East prior to the nineteenth century. Individuals often felt affinity with their coreligionists, but it was assumed that whatever the religion of the ruler might be, the state was not exclusively defined by religion. Tolerance of religious plurality was the norm, even though the ruler's coreligionists usually enjoyed greater official favor than people of a different religion. Language similarly served as a bond between people and as a dividing line between groups, but no state was linguistically homogeneous or disposed to regard language as the defining quality of a ruler's subjects. As for territory, strong feelings of identity with places of origin, particularly cities and their environs, were much in evidence in such guises as folk sayings, humor, and local traditions, but they were seldom accorded a political valuation.

As in most other parts of the world, the appearance of elements of national feeling in the Middle East preceded formal nationalist statements or political manifestos. Historians have debated the degree of indebtedness (certainly heavy) that various Middle Eastern nationalist writers and political leaders owed to European models in seeking to express their nationalism, but it would be an oversimplification to consider these models the sole source of nationalism in the region.

Greek Nationalism

The earliest nationalist movement manifested itself in the Greeks' war to obtain independence from the Ottoman Empire (between 1821 and 1832). The earlier revolt of the south Slavs (between 1804 and 1830) that culminated in the creation of an autonomous principality of Serbia had been a manifestation of widespread discontent with Ottoman maladministration and military disorder. Its leaders did not articulate nationalist positions, however, and the Slavs would presumably have been content with a return to competent Ottoman rule.

In Greece, however, despite a patchwork leadership ranging from bandit chiefs to Greek intellectuals educated in western Europe, a distinctly nationalist ideology came in time to be accepted as the best expression of the people's will. This ideology, however, was associated with a revolutionary organization called the Philike Hetairia that was based in Greek communities outside Greece (the most important one was in Odessa). Nationalist ideology followed rather than preceded the Greek rebellion, and many Greeks fought to escape Ottoman rule without being aware of any ideology. Many of the ideologues were more familiar with conditions and ideas in western Europe than in the Peloponnesus. Rhigas Pheraios, for example (who wrote in his immensely popular "War Hymn": "How long, my heroes, shall we live in bondage,/alone like lions on ridges, on peaks?/ . . . Better an hour of life that is free/than forty years in slavery!"), had a personal history of involvement with numerous revolutionary groups in western Europe dedicated to the ideals of the French Revolution.

Independent Greece not only fostered a revival of classical language and a glorification of ancient greatness—both common practices in later examples

The Shah of Iran places a crown on his wife, Queen Farah, after crowning himself in a lavish ceremony, Tehran, Iran, 26 October 1967. The Shah delayed his coronation for more than 25 years because he did not want to be crowned until he had accomplished a social revolution in Iran. © BETTMANN/CORBIS. REPRODUCED BY PERMISSION.

of Middle Eastern nationalism—but also developed the Megali Idea, an ideology that harked back to the Byzantine Empire and whose proponents visualized a broad Balkan realm extending to Istanbul (then Constantinople) in which people of various languages and ethnic groups would be led by Greeks. This approach to nationalism, manifesting a vision of the Greek people as a political entity rather than a geographical entity, reflects the thinking of Jean-Jacques Rousseau and other French ideologues rather than the German vision of complete identity of people and land. The concept of one people dominating others within a specified territory later becomes commonplace in Middle Eastern nationalism.

Turkish and Arab Nationalism

Although other nationalist stirrings in the nineteenth century were not consciously patterned on the Greek example, they had some common features. Many advocates of Turkish and Arab political and linguistic distinctiveness, for example, were educated in Europe or were familiar with European ideas. Namik Kemal, whose Turkish drama *Vatan* (Fatherland) helped establish that word (*watan* in Arabic) as an element of nationalism, spent three years in exile in Europe; and the Lebanese Christian Butrus al-Bustani, one of the most industrious advocates of a revived Arabic literary language, worked closely with American Protestant missionaries. Like the Greeks, the Turks and Arabs encountered difficulty in harmonizing their particularist views with a history of pluralistic empire. Just as adherents to the Megali Idea could visualize, on the Byzantine model, an ethnically plural state dominated by Greeks, the Arabs and Turks aspired mostly to a revival or assertion of ethno-linguistic identity within the pluralistic Ottoman Empire.

One difference between Greeks and other nineteenth-century nationalists was the association of religion with a people's identity. All Greeks were orthodox Christians, even though not all orthodox Christians were Greek, nor all Greek clergy nationalist in sympathy. By contrast, Christian Arabs were prominent in the protonationalist Arab literary revival, and the Turkish protonationalists supported the religiously plural Ottoman system. Therefore, even though the great majority of Turks and Arabs were Muslims, Islam did not from the outset become an integral element of nationalist thought.

Written expressions of nationalist views among Turks and Arabs circulated during the last decades of the nineteenth century. Religion, however, remained a problem. The foremost Turkish ideologue, Ziya Gökalp, concentrated his analysis of Turkish identity on language and folk customs and dismissed Islam as a transitory civilizational attribute that should not stand in the way of the adoption of European customs. The Arab Abd al-Rahman al-Kawakibi, on the other hand, called for a revival of the caliphate under an Arab of the prophet Muhammad's tribe, the Quraysh, instead of under the despotic Ottoman sultan Abdülhamit II.

Rise of Nationalism

The Committee for Union and Progress, a group of military officers that took control of the Ottoman Empire through a coup d'état in 1908, espoused Turkish nationalism and mandated the use of the Turkish language in certain administrative offices that had previously used local languages. Resentment against such Turkizing measures contributed to the formation of small Arab nationalist groups in Syria and Istanbul. Most of these Arab nationalists remained wedded to the concept of an Ottoman Empire, however, until the outbreak of World War I.

Ottoman defeat and the publicizing of Woodrow Wilson's advocacy of self-determination of peoples encouraged an outpouring of nationalist expressions throughout the Middle East. Kurds and Armenians, as well as Arabs whom Britain had encouraged in a nationalist revolt against the Ottomans during the war, tried to influence the peace negotiations in their favor. The most successful nationalist movement of the period, however, was that of an Ottoman army officer, Mustafa Kemal Atatürk, who established a Turkish republic that was ideologically rooted in the ideas of Gökalp. The new Turkish state expelled a Greek expeditionary force from western Anatolia; it also abolished the offices of sultan and caliph, and legislated the most strenuously secular form of nationalism known in the region.

Nationalism dominated Middle East politics from the end of World War II until the Iranian revolution of 1979. Arab nationalism flourished once the collapse of the Ottoman Empire resolved the question of whether or not to remain loyal to an ethnically plural state. Although some Muslims pushed for reestablishment of the caliphate, most nationalists were caught up in the tide of secularism, actually anticlericalism, that had engulfed Turkey. The Ba'th Party was founded in 1947 on a platform of Arab national unity and separation of religion from public affairs. Some other groups, such as the Syrian Socialist Nationalist Party, espoused an Arab nationalism based on a single country. The Arabic term qawmiyya (from qawm, group of people) distinguishes this type of nationalism from wataniyya, which calls for political unity of all the Arab peoples. Gamal Abdel Nasser, considered by many the most popular and effective Arab nationalist leader, strove for Arab unity but also inspired Egyptians with the feeling that Egypt was the center of the Arab world.

Zionism, a Jewish nationalist movement that originated in Europe and embodied many European ideas, came into bitter conflict with Arab nationalism, whose leaders viewed the Zionist community in Palestine as a manifestation of European colonialism. The basic elements important to Zionism— language, religion, land, and identity as a people— differed little from those that are important to Arab nationalism.

Being farther removed geographically from European cultural influence, Iran did not manifest a strong nationalist identity until the post–World War I period. Earlier anti-imperialist actions, such as the Tobacco Revolt of 1891 to 1893, engaged religious feelings as much as they did patriotic feelings. When the military commander Reza Khan assumed the throne as Reza Shah in 1925, he took the surname Pahlavi to indicate continuity with the pre-

Islamic imperial past, since the word is normally used to designate the form of the Persian language spoken at that time. The Pahlavi dynasty promoted a nationalist ideology focused on the person of the ruler and the historical sequence of imperial Iranian dynasties. It emphasized the dominant role of Persians and of the Persian language in a multiethnic kingdom.

In 1950, Prime Minister Mohammad Mossadegh became the focus of a strong nonroyal nationalist movement. Suppression of this movement on the shah's behalf by U.S. and British intelligence agencies detoured nationalist feelings in an antiroyal revolutionary direction. Thus the revolution that overthrew the monarchy in 1979 had a strong nationalist coloring along with its dominant religious ideology.

Some modern Muslim theorists maintain that nationalism can have no place in Islam because of the seamless unity of the *umma,* the community of Muslims. Observers of Middle Eastern politics often use the term *religious nationalism* to describe politically active Islamic movements. Proponents of current theories of nationalism often speak of the "peoples" for whom nationalist movements speak and act as "imagined communities." Rather than accepting nationalist myths proclaiming the unity of a particular tribal, ethnic, linguistic, or territorial group of people from time immemorial, these theorists emphasize that each factor adduced to explain or describe a group's national character is partly an invention of ideologues, a deliberate emphasis upon one or another characteristic that had not previously been considered so important. A new nationalism can thus develop whenever a community imagines itself as a unified entity deserving of special recognition. From this perspective, nationalism appears less as an immutable division of the human population into natural units than it does as an instrument for shaping and reshaping community identities and politics along varying lines. Consequently, the frequently posed question as to whether the new Middle Eastern states created after World War I would ever become genuine national communities (a question often answered in the affirmative in light of the loyal participation of Iraqi Shiʿa in Iraq's war with Shiʿite Iran) may be of little relevance in an unsettled region where communities of people may well reimagine their identities in future decades.

See also ABDÜLHAMIT II; ARAB NATIONALISM; ATATÜRK, MUSTAFA KEMAL; BAʿTH, AL-; COMMITTEE FOR UNION AND PROGRESS; GÖKALP, ZIYA; GREEK WAR OF INDEPENDENCE; IRANIAN REVOLUTION (1979); KAWAKIBI, ABD AL-RAHMAN AL-; MOSSADEGH, MOHAMMAD; NAMIK KEMAL; NASSER, GAMAL ABDEL; PAHLAVI, REZA; PAN-TURKISM; SYRIAN SOCIAL NATIONALIST PARTY; TOBACCO REVOLT; WILSON, WOODROW; ZIONISM.

Bibliography

Anderson, Benedict. *Imagined Communities: Reflections on the Origin and Spread of Nationalism,* revised edition. London and New York: Verso, 1991.

Cottam, Richard. *Nationalism in Iran: Updated through 1978,* revised edition. Pittsburgh, PA: University of Pittsburgh Press, 1979.

Dawn, C. Ernest. *From Ottomanism to Arabism: Essays on the Origins of Arab Nationalism.* Urbana: University of Illinois Press, 1973.

Gökalp, Ziya. *The Principles of Turkism,* translated by Robert Devereux. Leiden, Netherlands: E.J. Brill, 1968.

Haim, Sylvia, ed. *Arab Nationalism: An Anthology.* Berkeley: University of California Press, 1962.

Hourani, Albert. *Arabic Thought in the Liberal Age, 1798–1939.* Cambridge, U.K., and New York: Cambridge University Press, 1983.

Khalidi, R., et al., eds. *The Origins of Arab Nationalism.* New York: Columbia University Press, 1991.

Mardin, Serif. *The Genesis of Young Ottoman Thought: A Study in the Modernization of Turkish Political Ideas.* Princeton, NJ: Princeton University Press, 1962.

RICHARD W. BULLIET

NATIONALIST ACTION PARTY

Ultranationalist political party in Turkey in the 1970s and again in the 1990s.

The Nationalist Action Party (Milliyetci Hareket Partisi, or MHP) was originally known as the Republican Peasants Nation Party, but it adopted its current name in 1969. It developed during the 1970s under the leadership of Alparslan Türkes, a former military colonel. The party had a strong social and ideological base, combining militant nationalism and anticommunism with a strong emphasis on interventionist economic policies and the use of militia-style youth organizations. The Nine Lights of Türkes (nationalism, idealism, morality, corporatism, science, populism, progressivism, technology, and the defense of peasantry) became the ideological basis of the party. Popular support for the MHP was not widespread, but it was stable: The party won 12 percent of the parliamentary seats in 1961, 2 percent in 1965, 1 percent in 1973, and 4 percent in 1977. Throughout the 1970s the party was involved in right-wing violence against leftist groups. Following the 1980 military coup the government closed the MHP, but it reemerged in the 1990s, demonstrating its strength in the 1999 parliamentary elections by securing the second largest number of votes, after the Democratic Left Party of Bülent Ecevit. MHP's legislative representation rose to 23 percent of seats in the Turkish Grand National Assembly and its new leader, Devlet Bahçeli, became deputy prime minister in a coalition government formed by Ecevit. Since 1999 MHP has shifted its understanding of nationalism from ethnic to cultural nationalism.

See also ECEVIT, BÜLENT; TÜRKES, ALPARSLAN; TURKISH GRAND NATIONAL ASSEMBLY.

Bibliography

Yavuz, M. Hakan. "The Politics of Fear: The Rise of the Nationalist Action Party (MHP) in Turkey." *Middle East Journal* 56, no. 2 (Spring 2002): 200–221.

FRANK TACHAU
UPDATED BY M. HAKAN YAVUZ

NATIONAL LIBERAL PARTY

Lebanese political party established by and in support of the Chamoun family.

The National Liberal Party (NLP) was established by Camille Chamoun when he left the presidency of Lebanon in 1958. The NLP is a political vehicle used by the Chamoun family to reward its followers and partisans. While not having a defined political ideology, the NLP favored free enterprise and strong ties between Lebanon and the West, while at the same time it championed Maronite authority over Lebanon's politics. In the 1970s, the NLP claimed some 60,000 to 70,000 members, most of them from the Maronite Christian community, with some Shiʿite, Druze, and Greek Orthodox followers.

During the Lebanese Civil War of 1975, the NLP's militia, the Tigers (al-Numur), fought alongside the Phalange militias against the Islamic-Leftist coalition. In 1980, the Tigers were defeated, following an attack by the Lebanese Forces headed by Bashir Jumayyil. Following their defeat, the Tigers joined the Lebanese Forces and recognized Jumayyil as their leader. The NLP remains the party of Camille Chamoun, who used it to maintain his political power after leaving the presidency of Lebanon. Under his mandate, Lebanon was engulfed in a short civil war that ended with the 1982–1984 intervention of a multinational force composed of U.S. Marines and British, French, and Italian troops.

During the Cold War, Chamoun chose the anticommunist camp but created many enemies in Lebanon and the Arab world. In 1987, Camille Chamoun died and was replaced by his son Dany as the chair of the NLP. In 1990, Dany was assassinated and was replaced by his brother Dori.

See also CHAMOUN, CAMILLE; JUMAYYIL, BASHIR.

Bibliography

Suleiman, Michael W. *Political Parties in Lebanon: The Challenge of a Fragmented Political Culture.* Ithaca, NY: Cornell University Press, 1967.

GEORGE E. IRANI

NATIONAL LIBERATION FRONT (BAHRAIN)

Organization advocating political reform in Bahrain.

Following a general strike in Bahrain in the summer of 1954, liberal reformers from both the Shiʿite and Sunni communities organized a Higher Executive Committee (HEC) to press demands for an elected popular assembly, an appellate court, and the right to form trade unions. Protracted negotiations between the ruler, Shaykh Sulman bin Hamad Al Khalifa, and the HEC led to the official recognition of a Committee of National Unity in return for the HEC's agreement to stop calling for a parliament. Radical activists based in the industrial labor force responded by forming a succession of clandestine organizations, which called for more fundamental changes in Bahrain's political and economic structure.

Out of these groupings in the late 1960s emerged the Popular Front for the Liberation of Oman and the Arab Gulf, from which the Popular Front in Bahrain split off in 1974. More militant workers then formed the National Liberation Front (Bahrain) to press for the creation of a nonexploitative, egalitarian social order. Police cracked down on the organization after the National Assembly was dissolved in 1975. The National Liberation Front (Bahrain) was subsequently overshadowed by Bahrain's heterogeneous Islamist movement, although it continued to enjoy support among young professionals and intellectuals unsympathetic to the Islamists.

See also BAHRAIN; NATIONAL DEMOCRATIC FRONT FOR THE LIBERATION OF OMAN AND THE ARAB GULF.

Bibliography

Halliday, Fred. *Arabia without Sultans.* Baltimore, MD, and Harmondsworth, U.K.: Penguin, 1974.

Lawson, Fred H. *Bahrain: The Modernization of Autocracy.* Boulder, CO: Westview, 1989.

FRED H. LAWSON

NATIONAL OIL CORPORATION (LIBYA)

The state oil holdings of Libya.

In 1970, the government of Libya enacted Law 24, reorganizing its oil holdings as the Libyan National Petroleum Corporation, now the National Oil Corporation (NOC). This law directed future foreign investment in Libyan oil to be organized as a partnership with NOC. It also transferred to NOC concessions relinquished by foreign oil companies and oil properties acquired by nationalization. By September 1973, NOC owned a minimum of 51 percent of every oil operation in Libya.

Since then, NOC has expanded its operations, negotiating directly with foreign oil companies to set up new joint ventures. In response to the imposition of economic sanctions by the United States in 1986, NOC devised model exploration and production-sharing agreements (EPSAs) featuring terms highly favorable to foreign partners. These model EPSA contracts have allowed NOC to con-

tinue to attract new partners based outside the United States, despite the additional risks to foreign investors that U.S. and UN economic sanctions against Libya impose. Today NOC operates refineries, a petrochemical complex, and a tanker fleet.

Bibliography

Middle East Economic Survey. Nicosia, Cyprus: Middle East Petroleum and Economic Publications, 1957–.

Organization of Petroleum Exporting Countries. *OPEC National Oil Company Profiles.* Vienna: Author, 1981.

MARY ANN TÉTREAULT

NATIONAL PACT (LEBANON)

Agreement between Christian and Muslim communities in Lebanon.

The National Pact (al-Mithaq al-Watani), an unwritten agreement, came into being in the summer of 1943 as a result of numerous meetings between Bishara al-Khuri (a Maronite Christian), Lebanon's first president after independence, and the first prime minister, Riyad al-Sulh (a Sunni Muslim). At the heart of the negotiations was the Christians' fear of being dominated by the Muslim communities in Lebanon and the region, and the Muslims' fear of Western hegemony. In return for the Christians' promise not to seek foreign (i.e., French) protection and to accept the "Arab face of Lebanon," the Muslims agreed to recognize the country's independence and to accept the legitimacy of the 1920 boundaries. Muslims also were expected to renounce demands for unity with Syria. The National Pact was intended to reinforce the sectarian system of government by formalizing the confessional distribution of high-level posts in the government based on the results of the 1932 census, with Christians outnumbering Muslims by a ratio of six to five. Although some historians dispute the point, the terms of the National Pact are believed to have been incorporated in the statement of the first cabinet after independence (October 1943).

Specifically, the National Pact decreed that the presidency shall be reserved for a Maronite Christian, the prime ministership for a Sunni Muslim, and the speakership of parliament for a Shi'ite Muslim. Other top government posts—commander in chief of the army, head of military intelligence, head of internal security, and some important ambassadorships—were reserved for Maronites. It was agreed that the deputy prime minister should be a Greek Orthodox and that "minorities" (not one of the six major religious sects) should be occasionally represented in the cabinet and always in the parliament.

The confessional system outlined in the National Pact was a matter of expediency, an interim measure to overcome philosophical differences between Christian and Muslim leaders. It was hoped that once the business of governance got under way, and as national spirit grew, the importance of confessionalism in the political structure would diminish. Over the years, the frequent political disputes—the most notable of which were manifested in the Lebanese Civil Wars of 1958 and 1975, and the Palestinian controversies in the 1960s and 1970s have borne clear testimony to the failure of the National Pact to produce societal integration. Moreover, along with the system of *zuʿama* ("bosses") clientelism, it has guaranteed the maintenance of the status quo and the continuation of privilege for the sectarian elites.

The National Pact was affected by the Taʾif accord of 1989. Its weakness stems from the sectarian representation that was allowed to prevail in the 1940s. The Maronites were accepted as representatives of all Christians. Furthermore, nobody within either religious community assigned Khuri and al-Sulh the task of dividing the national government along sectarian lines. The Taʾif accord juridically legitimized the basic provisions of the National Pact but changed the representational formula. Muslims and Christians are now represented equally in parliament, although the top government posts will continue to be divided along the lines of the pact. The Taʾif accord constituted the first revision of the pact.

> See also KHURI, BISHARA AL-; LEBANESE CIVIL WAR (1958); LEBANESE CIVIL WAR (1975–1990); SULH, RIYAD AL-; TAʾIF ACCORD.

Bibliography

Abul-Husn, Latif. *The Lebanese Conflict: Looking Inward.* Boulder, CO: Lynne Rienner Publishers, 1998.

El-Khazen, Farid. *The Communal Pact of National Identities: The Making and Politics of the 1943 National Pact.* Oxford, U.K.: Centre for Lebanese Studies, 1991.

Picard, Elizabeth. *Lebanon, a Shattered Country: Myths and Realities of the Wars in Lebanon,* translated by Franklin Philip. New York: Holmes and Meier, 2002.

AS'AD ABUKHALIL

NATIONAL PARTY (EGYPT)

Egyptian nationalist movement and political party.

The National Party (al-Hizb al-Watani) is the name of two successive movements of Egyptian resistance against foreign economic or political control. The first emerged in November 1879, after Khedive Ismaʿil ibn Ibrahim's deposition. Although purportedly an Egyptian protest movement against the privileges of Turks and Circassians and against the Anglo-French Dual Financial Control, its initial patron was probably Prince Halim, who claimed that Ismaʿil had deprived him of the khedivate. Former Premier Muhammad Sharif, a constitutionalist, also claimed to have formed the party. During the Urabi revolt (1881–1882), it became associated with the most radical elements in the National Assembly and the officer corps, but it lacked a formal organization, and it is not easy to determine its role in the revolt. When British troops occupied Egypt in September 1882 to restore order, the party vanished.

The National Party was revived in 1893 as a secret society, under the aegis of Khedive Abbas Hilmi II and with strong ties to the government of the Ottoman Empire. Its leaders were Mustafa Kamil, Muhammad Farid, and several other professional men educated in Egyptian and European schools. In the 1890s the party disseminated propaganda in Europe against the British occupation of Egypt and among Egyptians to back the khedive against the British agent and consul general, Lord Cromer (Evelyn Baring). In 1900 Mustafa Kamil founded a daily newspaper, *al-Liwa* (The banner), which became the National Party's organ. The Nationalists broke with Abbas in 1904, but they became reconciled after the 1906 Dinshaway Incident. Mustafa Kamil publicized the party's existence in his long speech of 22 October 1907 and convened the first Nationalist assembly in December. Its main goals were to persuade the British by peaceful means to withdraw their occupying army from Egypt and to obtain a democratic constitution from Khedive Abbas.

Mustafa Kamil died two months later, and the Nationalists chose Muhammad Farid to succeed him. Farid tried to widen the party's appeal by circulating petitions demanding a constitution and by supporting the Young Turk revolution in Constantinople. It split, however, over whether to cooperate with the khedive in spite of his reconciliation with the British, whether to espouse pan-Islam even if doing so would alienate the Copts (Egyptian Orthodox Christians), and whether to seek Egypt's liberation by legal or by revolutionary means. Cromer's successors, Sir Eldon Gorst and Lord Herbert Horatio Kitchener, encouraged the khedive and his ministers to muzzle the press and, after a Nationalist killed Premier Butros Ghali in February 1910, passed special laws, banned or suspended newspapers, and jailed editors—even Farid—to intimidate and weaken the party. Farid's departure from Egypt in 1912 left the party leaderless and divided. During World War I, its emigré leaders sided against the British—that is, with the Ottoman Empire and Germany—but British security measures prevented them from inspiring an Egyptian uprising. The Nationalists aided the Wafd in the 1919 revolution and, when parliamentary rule was established in 1923, ran candidates for election. Led by Hafiz Ramadan, the National Party remained a small but vocal element in the fabric of Egyptian politics until the 1952 revolution, after which all political parties were abolished. Its name was incorporated by Anwar al-Sadat into his National Democratic Party, but the party itself was never revived.

See also ABBAS HILMI II; BARING, EVELYN; DINSHAWAY INCIDENT (1906); GORST, JOHN ELDON; ISMA'IL IBN IBRAHIM; KITCHENER, HORATIO HERBERT; WAFD; YOUNG TURKS.

Bibliography

Deeb, Marius. *Party Politics in Egypt: The Wafd and Its Rivals, 1919–1939.* London: Ithaca Press for the Middle East Centre; Oxford: St. Antony's College, 1979.

Gershoni, Israel, and Jankowski, James P. *Egypt, Islam, and the Arabs: The Search for Egyptian Nationhood, 1900–1930.* New York: Oxford University Press, 1986.

Goldschmidt, Arthur. "The Egyptian Nationalist Party, 1892–1919." In *Political and Social Change in Modern Egypt:*

Historical Studies from the Ottoman Conquest to the United Arab Republic, edited by P. M. Holt. London: Oxford University Press, 1968.

Schoch, Alexander. *Egypt for the Egyptians! The Socio-Political Crisis in Egypt, 1878–1882.* London: Ithaca Press for the Middle East Centre; Oxford: St. Antony's College, 1981.

ARTHUR GOLDSCHMIDT

NATIONAL PARTY (SYRIA)

Alliance of Syrian urban upper-class notables and politicians, formed in 1947 with Damascus as its center.

During the French mandate period in Syria (1920–1946), this alliance of notables and politicians had formed the Damascus branch of the National Bloc (al-Kutla al-Wataniyya), which had led Syria's nationalist political struggle against the French. The most prominent leaders of the National party (al-Hizb al-Watani) were Shukri al-Quwatli, Jamil Mardam, Faris al-Khuri, Lutfi al-Haffar, and Sabri al-Asali.

The National party did not have a modern political party structure—rather, it depended on its leaders, their loosely organized followings, and their extended family relations. Socially, the party represented industrial and merchant interests, which favored independence from France, in contrast to the largely more conservative landowning milieu, which was luke-warm toward such a prospect. The position of the National party together with the position of its Aleppo-based rival, the People's Party (Hizb al-Sha'b), was undermined in the late 1940s and early 1950s. This took place through the rise of more radical political parties like the Ba'th party and by the increased role of the military in Syria's politics during that period.

See also BA'TH, AL-; MARDAM, JAMIL; NATIONAL BLOC; QUWATLI, SHUKRI AL-.

Bibliography

Khoury, Philip. *Syria and the French Mandate: The Politics of Arab Nationalism, 1920–1945.* Princeton, NJ: Princeton University Press, 1987.

Seale, Patrick. *The Struggle for Syria: A Study of Post-War Arab Politics, 1945–1958.* New Haven, CT: Yale University Press, 1965.

MAHMOUD HADDAD

NATIONAL PROGRESSIVE FRONT (SYRIA)

Coalition of left-wing and progressive parties in Syria.

The National Progressive Front is a coalition of Syrian political parties established on 7 March 1972 after the Correction Movement led by President Hafiz al-Asad. It consists of six parties under the leadership of al-Ba'th Arab Socialist Party. The other parties are the Syrian Communist Party, the Arab Socialist Union, the Socialist Unionist Party, the Arab Socialists Party, and the Socialist Unionist Democratic Party. The charter of the coalition states that its central leadership is formed from a chairman (who is at the same time the president of the Republic and the secretary-general of the Ba'th Party), nine members of al-Ba'th, and two members of each of the other parties. With the exception of al-Ba'th, the parties that comprise the Front are not allowed to canvass for supporters in the army or the student unions. In December 2000 the Ba'th Party command allowed the six coalition parties to open provincial offices and issue newspapers publicly.

See also ASAD, HAFIZ AL-.

Bibliography

Seale, Patrick. *Asad of Syria: The Struggle for the Middle East.* Los Angeles: University of California Press, 1988.

KHALIL GEBARA

NATIONAL PROGRESSIVE UNIONIST PARTY

Originated as the left faction of the official Arab Socialist Union (ASU).

When Anwar al-Sadat dissolved the ASU in 1976, the National Progressive Unionist Party (NPUP) emerged as the official left opposition party. A coalition of leftist forces, including Nasserists and Marxists, the NPUP under the leadership of Khalid Muhyi al-Din, formerly a member of the Free Officers, has played the role of active and vocal opposition in the People's Assembly.

See also FREE OFFICERS, EGYPT.

RAYMOND WILLIAM BAKER

NATIONAL RELIGIOUS PARTY

See ISRAEL: POLITICAL PARTIES IN

NATIONAL SALVATION FRONT (LEBANON)

Lebanese nationalist group.

After the signing of the agreement between Amin Jumayyil's government and Israel on 17 May 1983, opposition groups and politicians met to commit themselves to aborting the accord. The three founders of the National Salvation Front were Sulayman Franjiyya, Rashid Karame, and Walid Jumblatt. Minor members of the Front were the Lebanese Communist Party and the Syrian Social Nationalist Party. All of these groups were loyal to the Syrian regime and opposed Jumayyil's government, which was then, with U.S. support, launching a war against the opposition. The Front wanted to annul the agreement with Israel, which amounted to a peace treaty, and to oppose the Phalangist takeover of the Lebanese government and administration under Jumayyil. The Front cooperated with Nabih Berri of the AMAL movement, and as a result of direct Syrian military and political support was able to pressure Jumayyil to nullify the agreement.

See also AMAL; BERRI, NABI, FRANJIYYA, SULAYMAN; JUMAYYIL, AMIN; JUMBLATT, WALID; KARAME, RASHID; SYRIAN SOCIAL NATIONALIST PARTY.

AS'AD ABUKHALIL

NATIONAL SALVATION PARTY

Political party in Turkey during the 1970s.

The National Salvation Party (Milli Selamet Partisi, or NSP) was formed in October 1972 as a successor to the National Order Party (NOP), which had been dissolved by Turkey's Constitutional Court following the March 1971 military coup d'état. Like the NOP, the NSP represented itself as a modern party inspired by and reflecting traditional Sunni Islamic ethical values. A key figure behind the formation of both parties was the Naqshbandi (Sufi order) leader Mehmet Zahid Kotku. The most prominent NOP/NSP politician, however, was Necmeddin Erbakan, who fled temporarily to Switzerland in 1971 to avoid arrest. In the election of 1973, the NSP received 11.8 percent of the vote and obtained eighty seats in the Turkish Grand National Assembly, thus becoming its third largest party. Erbakan returned to

Necmeddin Erbakan served as the prime minister of Turkey from 1996 to 1998 before being forced out of office for pursuing antisecularist policies. After Erbakan was banned from politics, his supporters founded the Islamic Virtue Party, which the government outlawed in 2001 on the grounds it was a center of fundamentalist activity and a threat to constitutional order. © REUTERS NEWMEDIA INC./CORBIS. REPRODUCED BY PERMISSION.

Turkey and became the NSP's leader in October, one week after the 1973 election.

In February 1974 the NSP joined the first coalition government formed by Bülent Ecevit of the Republican People's Party. The NSP held six cabinet positions during the seven-month tenure of this government. The most significant development in the period was the crisis in Cyprus, to which the coalition government dispatched troops to protect the Turkish minority living in the northern part of the island. The military intervention resulted in both Erbakan and Ecevit acquiring reputations as heroes, although this did not translate into electoral support for either man's party. Ecevit resigned in October 1974, thus ending the coalition.

The NSP next agreed to participate in the first National Front government under Süleyman Demirel of the Justice Party (April 1975 to July 1977). In the 1977 elections, however, the NSP's share of the national vote declined to 8.6 percent, and it lost half of its seats in the assembly. It participated in Demirel's brief second National Front government (July to December 1977) and in the minority government from November 1979 until the September 1980 military coup. All political parties were disbanded after the coup. The successor to the NSP

was the Refah Partisi, founded in July 1983. After the September 1987 referendum that reestablished the right of prominent former politicians to pursue political activities, Erbakan became chairman of Refah.

The strength of the NSP was in the small towns and rural areas of Anatolia. Religious groups such as the Naqshbandi, other Sufi orders, and the Nurcu generally supported the party. The NSP embraced industrialization and technological advancement but criticized what it termed blind imitation of European culture and lifestyles. Its main program was embodied in a document called the National Outlook (*Milli Görüş*), which called for the strengthening of culture, industrialization, social justice, and education. It was, in practice, a populist agenda based on respect for Turkey's Ottoman-Islamic heritage, conservative social values, and equal opportunities for the nonelite middle and lower classes.

See also ERBAKAN, NECMEDDIN; NAQSHBANDI; NURSI, SAID.

Bibliography

Landau, Jacob M. "The National Salvation Party in Turkey." *Asian and African Studies* 11, no. 1 (1976): 1–56.

Toprak, Binnaz. "Politicization of Islam in a Secular State: The NSP in Turkey." In *From Nationalism to Revolutionary Islam*, edited by Said Arjomand. Albany: State University of New York Press, 1984.

NERMIN ABADAN-UNAT
UPDATED BY ERIC HOOGLUND

NATIONAL SECURITY COUNCIL (TURKEY)

Political/military body that oversees the Turkish government.

Turkey's National Security Council (Milli Güvenlik Kurulu, or NSC), formed after the 1960 military coup d'état, consists of the president (the chair of the NSC); the prime minister; ministers of defense, foreign affairs, and the interior; the chief of the general staff; and commanders of the army, navy, air force, and gendarmerie. Its composition and duties are stipulated in Turkey's 1961 constitution. The function of the NSC is to maintain the military's position as guardian of the principles of Kemalism within the institutions of the state. Following the 1980 military coup, the new 1982 constitution not only retained the NSC but also enhanced its powers, stipulating, for example, that the cabinet must give priority to NSC recommendations. The military's influence on government has proved to be an impediment to Turkey's efforts to become a member of the European Union; in order to comply with criteria set forth by the European Union, constitutional amendments in 2001 curtailed the role of the military within the NSC. For example, the civilian members of the NSC have been increased, and the NSC no longer recommends policies to the cabinet, but rather conveys its views informally.

See also KEMALISM.

Bibliography

Zürcher, Erik J. *Turkey: A Modern History,* revised edition. London: I. B. Tauris, 1997.

M. HAKAN YAVUZ

NATIONAL UNION (EGYPT)

Founded in 1956 to succeed the Liberation Rally.

The National Union was the second of Egypt's official mobilization bodies, to be followed in its turn by the Arab Socialist Union. The National Union was an indirect outgrowth of the Tripartite Aggression of 1956, when Egypt was invaded by the colluding forces of the British, the French, and the Israelis. The Free Officers regime sought to consolidate the internal political front by creating a more effective mobilization vehicle for the solidification of patriotic sentiment behind the military regime.

The National Union structured a network of quasi-governmental intermediary organizations, such as a youth movement and women's organizations, that aimed to absorb and canalize popular energies in the service of regime goals. Though officially labeled a political party, the National Union, like its predecessors and successor, proved merely a bureaucratic extension of the authoritarian regime, failing to provide effective means of mass political participation.

See also ARAB SOCIALIST UNION; FREE OFFICERS, EGYPT; LIBERATION RALLY.

RAYMOND WILLIAM BAKER

NATIONAL UNITY COMMITTEE (TURKEY)

A group of military officers, commonly referred to as the NUC, who seized control of Turkey's government on 27 May 1960.

The National Unity Committee (in Turkish, Milli Birlik Komitesi) was a group of military officers, led by General Cemal Gürsel, that staged the revolution of 27 May 1960 and subsequently ruled Turkey through 20 November 1961. Although the coup was prepared by officers of middle and junior rank, it was the senior officers who took control of the National Unity Committee and the government. Serious divisions separated the two groups: junior members favored radical reform requiring longer-term retention of power by the military. Senior members supported an early return of elected civilian government. One of the first acts of the NUC was to convene a constitutional commission to draft a new constitution. On 12 June 1960 a provisional constitution granted sovereignty to the NUC until new elections could be held. The NUC exercised legislative power directly and executive power indirectly through a civilian council of ministers appointed and controlled by the NUC.

On 13 November 1960, in a move to rid the group of its more radical elements, thirteen of the original thirty-eight members of the committee were purged, including the ultranationalist Colonel Alparslan Türkes, paving the way for convocation of a civilian constituent assembly to draft a new constitution. The constitution was approved in a popular referendum on 8 July 1961, though a large negative vote was cast. On 15 October 1961 parliamentary elections produced indecisive results, leading to the election of the NUC leader, Cemal Gürsel, as president of the republic, and to the necessity of organizing coalition governments for the first time.

The NUC implemented some social and economic reforms designed to stabilize politics in Turkey. In addition, it abolished the Demokrat Parti and brought almost six hundred of its members to trial, three of whom were subsequently executed.

See also GÜRSEL, CEMAL.

Bibliography

Ahmad, Feroz. *The Turkish Experiment in Democracy, 1950–1975.* Boulder, CO: Westview Press, 1977.

Özbudun, E. *The Role of the Military in Recent Turkish Politics.* Cambridge, MA: Center for International Affairs, Harvard University, 1966.

Shaw, Stanford, and Shaw, Ezel Kural. *History of the Ottoman Empire and Modern Turkey,* Vol. 2: *Reform, Revolution, and Republic: The Rise of Modern Turkey, 1808–1975.* Cambridge, U.K., and New York: Cambridge University Press, 1977.

FRANK TACHAU

NATIONAL UNITY GOVERNMENT (ISRAEL)

See ISRAEL: POLITICAL PARTIES IN

NATIONAL WATER SYSTEM (ISRAEL)

Agency that oversees the planning and development of Israel's water resources.

With the establishment of the State of Israel in 1948, much effort was expended on drawing up an inventory of national water resources, defining growth objectives for the country, and planning methods of development. The first comprehensive water-development plan was adopted in 1950, stressing the maximum conservation of water. In 1952, Tahal, the Israel Water Planning Corporation, was set up to plan the water, sewage, and drainage systems and to supervise development. In 1959, Israel's Knesset (parliament) passed the Water Law, vesting all water rights in the state and giving the water commissioner in the ministry of agriculture the sole authority to fix tariffs, allocate water, and issue licenses for exploiting water resources.

All water development schemes are closely integrated with plans for agriculture and the realities of the scarcity of both land and water. The development plans must also take into account shortages of capital. The price of water is therefore high and, until recently, farmers paid the least, since preference was given to irrigation installations that facilitated control of the amounts of water used, minimized conveyance losses, and were economical in the use of labor.

Israel's climate is typically Mediterranean, with rainfall occurring only in the winter and decreasing from north to south. Rainfall in the north averages 39 inches (1,000 mm) yearly; in the central

A sweet-water reservoir flanks the Ruler road to Afula, in northern Israel. © HANAN ISACHAR/CORBIS. REPRODUCED BY PERMISSION.

coastal plain 19 inches (500 mm); in the extreme south only 1 inch (30 mm)—but there are yearly fluctuations. Its only major river running from north to south is the Jordan River. Its smaller rivers include the Yarkon, the Kishon, and the Sorek. They all empty into the Mediterranean Sea, along with more than a dozen major streams. National development projects aim at using groundwater, springs, storm runoff, and reclaimed wastewater. The largest project predated the Johnston Plan and was completed in the 1960s—the National Water Carrier—which conveys water from the northeast to the center and, at the same time, integrates all local and regional waterworks into one national water "grid," operated according to a national plan.

Israel claims that the integrated water sources available for the nation amount to about 370 million gallons (1,400 million cu m) per year. The majority of this water comes from the upper Jordan River and includes water from the springs around the Sea of Galilee (Lake Tiberias or Lake Kinneret), from the lake itself, and from coastal and foothill groundwater sources. A smaller amount of this water comes from the groundwater of the Galilee mountains, the Kishon river system, the Yarkon river system and the springs, storm runoff, and reclaimed waste of Israel's cities of Haifa and Tel Aviv.

Regulation is aided by the use of two main storage facilities: (1) the Sea of Galilee in the north, which is used for excess Jordan River waters during the rainy season, and (2) the aquifer under the central hills, which was integrated into the grid system after the 1967 Arab–Israel War.

A major priority in Israel's early decades was the expansion of irrigation, with domestic and industrial water supply taking second place. Priorities have now changed, and irrigation is being cut back as both population and industrialization have grown.

See also ARAB–ISRAEL WAR (1967); GALILEE, SEA OF; JOHNSTON PLAN (1953); JORDAN RIVER; KNESSET; WATER.

Bibliography

Blass, Simcha. *Water in Strife and Action.* Ramat Gan, Israel, 1973.

Wiener, Aaron. *The Role of Water in Development.* New York and London: McGraw-Hill, 1972.

SARA REGUER

NATIONAL WOMEN'S COMMITTEE (YEMEN)

The official women's organization of Yemen.

The National Women's Committee (NWC) is the official women's organization of the Yemen Republic, established in 1996 by a prime minister's act. Initially, the committee was established in 1993 to coordinate the official preparations for the Fourth World Conference of Women. In 2000 the committee was restructured to function under the Supreme Council for Women's Affairs headed by the prime minister. The NWC has consultative status with the Council of Ministers. The chairperson of the committee is nominated by presidential decree. NWC leaders have included such prominent women as Amat al-Alim al-Suswa, Rashida al-Hamdani, and Huriya Mashhur. The members of the committee include directors of women's departments in ministries and state institutions and coordinators in selected organizations and women's sections of political parties. The NWC has branches in all governorates with heads nominated by the governor of each province. The committee monitors state policies in regard to women's issues, carries out surveys (for example, *The Status of Woman in Yemen,* published in San'a in 1996), and launches campaigns for women's rights. Its branches organize seminars and training courses devoted to local leaders and grass roots ac-

tivists. Women's participation in elections and nomination in state offices have increased during the 1990s due to the joint activities of women's organizations. The NWC publishes the monthly newspaper *al-Yamaniyya* (Yemeni woman) and has a web page at <www.yemeni-women.org.ye>.

See also GENDER: GENDER AND LAW; YEMEN.

Bibliography

Republic of Yemen Women National Committee. *National Report on the Implementation Level of the Convention on Elimination of All Forms of Discrimination Against Women.* Sanaa, Yemen: Women's National Committee, 1999.

SUSANNE DAHLGREN

NATURAL GAS

This entry consists of the following articles:

ECONOMIC EXPLOITATION OF NATURAL GAS
MIDDLE EAST RESERVES OF NATURAL GAS

ECONOMIC EXPLOITATION OF NATURAL GAS

A mixture of hydrocarbons that are vapors at normal temperatures and below-normal pressures.

Methane (CH_4) is the primary component of natural gas; other components are ethane (C_2H_6), propane (C_3H_8), butane (C_4H_{10}) and pentane (C_5H_{12}); nonhydrocarbons, such as nitrogen, hydrogen, and water vapor; and traces of rare gases, such as helium. The heavier-than-methane hydrocarbons are collectively termed *natural gas liquids.*

Associated gas is gas dissolved in petroleum; it sometimes also appears as a gas cap over an oil-bearing formation. Associated gas is the primary source of the pressure forcing oil to the surface during production and also is a byproduct of this process. An estimated one-quarter of the world's natural gas reserves occurs as associated gas.

Natural gas is highly flammable, and the complexity and cost of the technology needed to recover and exploit it prompted oil companies at first to flare (burn) most of the natural gas they produced. During the 1920s, research into the production of petrochemicals led to the development of a number of commercial processes utilizing natural gas as a feedstock, but most of the natural gas produced as a byproduct of mining oil continued to be flared. At that time, the American Petroleum Institute commissioned a major study of the role of natural gas in oil production. Published in 1929—when industry leaders and government officials were worried about imminent fossil fuel depletion—the study produced the first empirical evidence of the relationship between gas pressure and recovery of oil reserves. In response to the study, the large, vertically integrated oil firms took the lead in changing traditional methods of oil production and processing so as to conserve natural gas.

Other modern uses of natural gas date back to the nineteenth century, when it was substituted for coal and wood in boilers located near oil fields. During the mid-nineteenth century, gas synthesized from coal was the chief source of illumination in urban areas, until it was displaced by the incandescent light bulb. During the first half of the twentieth century, gas gained a share of the home heating market and was used as a fuel in manufacturing. But the high cost of gas infrastructure, coupled with the larger profits from petroleum, made natural gas the stepchild of the oil industry.

The economic exploitation of natural gas depends on its commercial value, which in turn is a function of the size, quality, and location of the gas deposit; the projected rate of production; the price of natural gas; and the price of alternative fuels. The dependence of gas collection, transmission, and distribution on expensive infrastructure has historically been the biggest factor limiting the use of natural gas as a fuel. Oil-exporting countries in the Middle East have long protested the waste of their natural gas by flaring, but it was not until they could assume at least some of the cost of providing infrastructure that other than limited local uses for their natural gas became common.

Internationally, gas exporters have encountered resistance from importers with respect to the sharing of costs, particularly for pipeline construction and the expensive cryogenic facilities needed to liquefy and transport liquid natural gas. As long as the preponderance of natural gas is used for heating, demand is highly cyclical. As natural gas displaces other fuels, however, the load factor or average rate of capacity usage rises, making it more attractive.

The Organization of Petroleum Exporting Countries (OPEC)—which includes gas exporters such as Algeria, Qatar, Iran, and Libya—has had sharp pricing disputes with gas customers. Some led to interrupted deliveries, canceled contracts, and even the scrapping of entire projects. OPEC aspires to achieve a unified organizational position on natural gas pricing by developing formulas that link gas prices to crude oil prices. However, its efforts have been stymied by consumer resistance, by competition from non-OPEC gas sources (such as Russia) and nongas fuels (such as petroleum, which guarantees a built-in conflict of interest within OPEC itself), and by a long period of weakness in oil prices, which reduced producer incentives to link natural gas prices to crude oil prices.

Countering these drawbacks, improvements in transmission and storage technology and the growing global market for natural gas are positive economic signs. Although demand for natural gas in key industrial markets weakened in the 1980s as a result of recession, warmer winters, and conservation, the gas market has improved steadily for some years thanks to expansions in reserves (in 2000, proven reserves exceeded sixty times the rate of production); technical improvements in transmission, which is the most costly segment of the industry; marked improvements in load factors; and shifting priorities that make burning natural gas more attractive than oil and especially coal because gas produces lower levels of greenhouse gases and virtually no toxic pollutants.

Some OPEC countries see expanding internal consumption and manufacture of petrochemicals as superior alternatives to natural gas exports. However, neither the market for petrochemicals nor the domestic economies of most gas-rich members of OPEC can absorb the quantities of natural gas available. At the same time, antipollution regulations in fuel-importing countries make natural gas more attractive to developed-country consumers and lower its relative cost. Demand for natural gas is expected to top demand for coal by 2005, and it may approach demand for oil by 2025. Ongoing financial and regulatory changes in national and international markets support the continuation of these trends by improving security guarantees for producers as well as consumers.

See also ORGANIZATION OF PETROLEUM EXPORTING COUNTRIES (OPEC); PETROLEUM, OIL, AND NATURAL GAS.

Bibliography

Davis, Jerome D. *Blue Gold: The Political Economy of Natural Gas.* London: Allen and Unwin, 1984.

International Energy Agency. *Natural Gas: Prospects and Policies.* Paris: OECD/IEA, 1991.

Mitchell, John, et al. *The New Economy of Oil: Impacts on Business, Geopolitics, and Society.* London: Earthscan, 2001.

Mossavar-Rahmani, Bijan, and Mossavar-Rahmani, Sharmin. *The OPEC Natural Gas Dilemma.* Boulder, CO: Westview Press, 1986.

Stern, Jonathan P. *European Gas Markets: Challenge and Opportunity in the 1990s.* Brookfield, VT: Dartmouth, 1990.

MARY ANN TÉTREAULT

MIDDLE EAST RESERVES OF NATURAL GAS

The Middle East holds 36 percent of the world reserves of natural gas but generates only 9.3 percent of world production.

Natural gas must be transported by pipeline or liquefied by refrigeration in the form of liquid natural gas and transported on specially built ships. The liquefaction process is substantially more expensive. But since the main demand for gas from the Gulf has come from users in the Far East, Europe, and the United States, liquefaction has been the only option and has made the production of the main Gulf gas fields less competitive. Gas from Algeria—because it can be piped under the Mediterranean—has been extensively used in Europe.

Natural gas has become the major feedstock for petrochemicals. The development of the petrochemical industry in the Gulf region has given impetus to the development of the fields. Saudi Arabia uses most of its produced natural gas for firing desalination plants, running power plants, and producing 35 million tons per year of petrochemicals and fertilizers, which are exported worldwide.

In the mid-1990s some major projects were undertaken to develop fields and liquefaction plants for exports, mainly in Qatar and Oman. Because of

2001 Gas production and reserves in the Middle East and select African countries

Country	Gas Production*	Gas Reserves**
Bahrain	8.9	3.2
Iran	60.6	812.3
Iraq	—	109.8
Kuwait	9.5	52.7
Oman	13.4	29.3
Qatar	32.5	393.8
Saudia Arabia	53.7	213.8
United Arab Emirates	41.3	212.1
Yemen	—	16.9
Other Middle East	8.1	10.2
Total Middle East	228	1,974.6
% of World Total	9.3	36.1
Algeria	78.2	159.7
Egypt	21.0	35.2
Libya	5.4	46.4
Total	104.6	241.3
% of World Total	**4.3**	**4.3**

*In billion cubic meters
**In trillion cubic feet

SOURCE: British Petroleum Review of World Gas; United States Energy Information Administration.

TABLE BY GGS INFORMATION SERVICES, THE GALE GROUP.

this expansion of Qatari and Omani liquefied natural gas exports, the Middle East was the fastest-growing gas production region in 2001.

See also PETROCHEMICALS; PETROLEUM, OIL, AND NATURAL GAS.

JEAN-FRANÇOIS SEZNEC

NAVON, YIZHAK
[1921–]

Fifth president of Israel.

Yizhak Navon was born to a Jerusalem Sephardic family. Educated in religious schools and at the Hebrew University, from 1949 to 1950 he was a diplomat in Argentina and Uruguay, and served as political secretary first to Foreign Minister Moshe Sharett and then to Prime Minister David Ben-Gurion from 1951 to 1963. From 1963 to 1965, he was director of the Division of Culture and the Ministry of Education and Culture.

Navon was a member of the Knesset, first in the Rafi Party and later in the Labor Party. He chaired the important Knesset Foreign Affairs and Defense

Committee. From 1978 to 1983 Navon served as the fifth president of Israel, nominated by the opposition Labor Party and chosen over the Likud candidate. He was Israel's first "modern" president, departing from the "nonpolitical" role to take positions on controversial issues, most pointedly calling for an inquiry on the events in the Sabra and Shatila refugee camps in Lebanon, which were under Israeli control when Christian Phalangist forces massacred Palestinian refugees there. In 1984 he was reelected to the Knesset, serving as the minister of education and culture and as deputy prime minister in the government of Shimon Peres. Throughout his life, Navon has been a spokesman for the Sephardic community, serving as chairman of the National Authority for Ladino and as honorary chairman of the Abraham Fund promoting coexistence between Jews and Arabs.

Bibliography

American-Israeli Cooperative Enterprise. "Yitzhak Navon." In *Jewish Virtual Library*. Available from <http://www.us-israel.org/jsource/biography>.

State of Israel Ministry of Foreign Affairs. "Yitzhak Navon (b. 1921), Fifth President of the State of Israel 1978–1983." In *Personalities*. Available from <http://www.mfa.gov.il/mfa>.

MIRIAM SIMON
UPDATED BY GREGORY S. MAHLER

NAWFAL, HIND

[c. 1860–1920]

Writer and Lebanese immigrant to Egypt.

Nawfal Hind was the founder and editor of *al-Fatat* (1892–1894), the first Arabic-language periodical for and about women that published primarily female authors. She was the daughter of writers. Her mother, Maryam Nahhas Nawfal, was the author of what scholars assume to be the first Arabic-language biographical dictionary of women to be authored by an Arab woman. Her father, Nasim Nawfal, was a writer-publisher who helped launch *al-Fatat* in November 1892, as did Hind's sister Sara. Nawfal's family was Christian and from Tripoli (in present-day Lebanon) and was part of the nineteenth-century wave of writers emigrating to Egypt in search of opportunity and a freer publishing climate. She lived in Alexandria and published *al-Fatat* there un-

til her marriage to Habib Dabanam in March 1894, when the magazine published its fourteenth and final issue.

See also ANIS AL-JALIS MAGAZINE; GENDER: GENDER AND EDUCATION; *LATA'IF AL-MUSAWWARA* MAGAZINE.

Bibliography

Baron, Beth. *The Women's Awakening in Egypt: Culture, Society, and the Press.* New Haven, CT: Yale University Press, 1994.

Booth, Marilyn. *May Her Likes Be Multiplied: Biography and Gender Politics in Egypt.* Berkeley: University of California Press, 2001.

MARILYN BOOTH

NAZARETH

Historic market city and pilgrimage site in the Galilee region of Israel; the only all-Arab city in the State of Israel.

Nazareth (2001 population, 68,700) is located on the southernmost ridge of the hilly Galilee region of northern Israel, approximately 18 miles (30 km) southeast of the coastal city of Haifa. Its name in Arabic is al-Nasira, meaning "the one who grants victory." The city was conquered by Crusaders in 1099, taken by Saladin in 1187, and then retaken by Frederick II in 1229. Muslim forces led by Baybars, the Mamluk sultan of Egypt (1233–1277), recaptured Nazareth in 1263, massacring its Christian population. The city was virtually uninhabited for nearly three hundred years before being incorporated into the Ottoman Empire in 1517. The town gradually grew under the sponsorship of local and foreign Christian missions, attracting Christian Arab families from southern and coastal Palestine, the Hawran region of Syria, and what is now southern Lebanon.

Nazareth was an important administrative center during the British Mandate period (1922–1948) and was captured by Israel's pre-state military forces on 18 July 1948. Unlike in other Palestinian towns and cities, Nazareth's population was not displaced after 1948. The conscious policy of the Israeli military commanders in 1948 was to avoid violence and large-scale population displacements from this particular city. Immediately after the war, Nazareth's predominantly Christian population of 12,000 suddenly jumped to 18,000 with the arrival of more than 5,000 refugees, mostly Muslims, from neighboring Arab villages that had been destroyed during the hostilities. Overnight, Nazareth was transformed into the largest, densest, and most diverse concentration of Palestinians within the new state of Israel. Fifty-five years later, Nazareth's population had more than quintupled and Muslims greatly outnumbered Christians because of a higher Muslim birth rate and increasing Christian emigration.

The core of old Nazareth is situated in a long, bowl-like valley surrounded by several hills. Newer buildings and dense neighborhoods cover the hillsides above the old city, the elevation of which is approximately 1,200 feet (400 meters) above sea level. Well known throughout the Christian world as the home of Jesus, Mary, and Joseph, and as the scene of the Annunciation, Nazareth is a popular destination for tourists and pilgrims. The city boasts several churches, most notably the Roman Catholic Church of the Annunciation, completed in 1966, which is the largest church in the Middle East; the Greek Orthodox Church of the Annunciation (Gabriel's Church), constructed in the eighteenth century; and the Greek Catholic (Melkite) Synagogue Church. Nazareth is also a market town, a site of Arabic print media production, and home to several respected private primary and secondary schools administered by churches. It is known informally as the capital of the Arabs in Israel.

The municipality of Nazareth was founded in 1875. Until the mid-1990s, Nazareth housed the regional offices of state ministries and agencies, and the town's political life was dominated by a progressive political coalition, the Democratic Front for Peace and Equality (al-Jabba al-Dimuqratiyya lil-Salam wa al-Musawa), made up of the Nazareth branch of the Communist Party, the Committee of Merchants and Professionals, and the Association of Arab University Graduates. From the mid-1970s until the mid-1990s, Nazareth was a political base for left-wing, secularist, and Arab nationalist political currents among Palestinian citizens of Israel. Natzerat Illit, a Jewish development town founded on lands expropriated from Nazareth and other surrounding Arab localities in 1957 as part of a government campaign to Judaize the Galilee, has a population of 47,900, of whom approximately 11

percent are Arab. Since the mid-1990s, government offices formerly located in Nazareth have been relocated to the administratively separate although geographically adjacent Natzerat Illit. In the late 1990s, as Nazareth's municipality was undertaking Nazareth 2000, a multifaceted urban renewal program, with help from the Israeli government and Israeli businesses, to prepare the city for the millennial festivities and a tourism boom, hostilities erupted in the old city of Nazareth when a Muslim shrine was obstructed by construction crews. The ensuing conflict resulted in rioting and violence, polarized Muslims and Christians in Nazareth, halted the urban renewal project, paralyzed municipal governance, and involved the Vatican, the Israeli Ministry of Religious Affairs, and the Palestinian Authority. In October 2000, Nazareth was again the site of violence, this time occasioned by pogrom-like raids into Nazareth by Jewish mobs from Natzerat Illit one week after the outbreak of the second Intifada. Three Palestinian citizens of Israel were killed by police forces in the melée.

See also AQSA INTIFADA, AL-; PALESTINE; PALESTINIAN CITIZENS OF ISRAEL.

Bibliography

El-Asmar, Fouzi. *To Be an Arab in Israel.* Beirut: The Institute for Palestine Studies, 1978.

Emmet, Chad. *Beyond the Basilica: Christians and Muslims in Nazareth.* University of Chicago Geography Research Paper No. 237. Chicago: University of Chicago Press, 1995.

Rabinowitz, Dan. *Overlooking Nazareth: The Ethnography of Exclusion in the Galilee.* Cambridge, U.K.: Cambridge University Press, 1997.

BENJAMIN JOSEPH
UPDATED BY LAURIE KING-IRANI

NAZIF, SÜLEYMAN
[1869–1927]

Ottoman Turkish poet and writer.

The son of a historian, Süleyman Nazif was born and educated in Diyarbekir. While employed in the civil service, he began to write for the provincial press and, in 1897, was forced into exile in Paris. While in Paris, he contributed articles to Ahmet Riza's Meşveret. During the Constitutional period, he joined Ebüzziya Tevfik in producing *Tasvir-i Efkar.*

Süleyman Nazif's poetry, which was published in *Servet-i Fünun* under the name Ibrahim Cehdi, was strongly influenced by Namik Kemal. He published four volumes of poetry and numerous other literary and academic works.

DAVID WALDNER

NAZMI, ZIYA
[1881–1937]

Turkish painter.

The son of a financial official in the Ottoman Empire, Ziya Nazmi was born in the Aksaray quarter of Istanbul. Under the conservative influence of his father, he studied at the School of Political Science; but when his father died, he entered the Imperial Academy to study art and later went to France. While in France, Nazmi was influenced by Impressionism, and his landscapes depict people, buildings, and trees with pinks, greens, and yellows bathed in soft, diffuse light.

Upon his return to Istanbul, he taught art and held several exhibitions of his Impressionistic work. Nazmi and his generation of painters replaced the formal realism of nineteenth-century painters with informal and natural depictions of everyday life in cities and villages, including nude portraits. Nazmi was an enthusiastic follower of Mustafa Kemal Atatürk's cultural reforms, and he painted one of the best portraits of Atatürk, who was president of Turkey from 1923 to 1938.

See also ART; ATATÜRK, MUSTAFA KEMAL.

Bibliography

Renda, Günsel. "Modern Trends in Turkish Painting." In *The Transformation of Turkish Culture: The Atatürk Legacy,* edited by Günsel Renda and C. Max Kortepeter. Princeton, NJ: Kingston Press, 1986.

DAVID WALDNER

NE'EMAN, YUVAL
[1925–]

Israeli scientist and military and political leader.

Yuval Ne'eman was born in Palestine to an industrialist family in 1925. After early education in Egypt, he entered Herzeliya High School in Tel Aviv at the young age of eleven, matriculated at the age of fifteen, and entered the Technicion Institute in Haifa, from which he graduated as an engineer. From an early age he was a member of the Haganah, the Jewish clandestine paramilitary organization, and participated in several command courses. During the 1948 Arab–Israel War Ne'eman served as operation officer of the famous Giv'ati brigade; by the end of the war he was second in command. He remained in professional service to the Israel Defense Force (IDF) until 1961. After a year studying in the École d'État Major in Paris (1952), he fulfilled prominent positions in the IDF's General Staff, reaching the rank of colonel. In 1954 and 1955 he stood at the head of the strategic planning department, in which capacity he authored the "Lavie File," a comprehensive analysis of Israel's security problems and strategic and operative doctrines. The Lavie File was adopted by the IDF under the leadership of General Moshe Dayan as Chief of Staff (CoS), and it totally changed Israel's security policy from defensive to offensive. This strategy included options of pre-emptive strikes, which were implemented in 1956 and 1967. In 1955 Ne'eman was nominated deputy chief of the intelligence service, a post that involved him in the coordination of Israel's secret relations with the French military and intelligence services during the Suez War (1956).

While serving as Israel's military attaché in London from 1958 to 1960 he resumed his studies in nuclear physics, a field of research that he later pursued in the United States, where he developed the theory that explained the system of elementary particles and established theoretically the existence of a new particle, Omega Minus, which was later verified in laboratory experiments. These achievements gained him international recognition as a leading nuclear scientist. In the early 1970s he served as a professor at Tel Aviv University; from 1971 to 1975 he served as the university's president. In 1975 he was nominated as chief scientist of Israel's security system, but he resigned from this position in protest of the withdrawal from the western part of the Sinai. A superhawk, Ne'eman entered politics and with several colleagues founded ha-Tehiya, an extreme right-wing party that advocated full annexation and settlement of all territories conquered by Israel in 1967. He served three terms as a member of the Knesset (1981–1990) and was twice a member of the government, holding the portfolio of Science and

Technology from 1982 to 1984 and a double portfolio of Science and Technology and Energy and Infrastructure from 1990 to 1992. His party was defeated in the elections of 1992, and Ne'eman finally retired from politics and returned to his academic activities.

Bibliography

Aronoff, Myron. *Israeli Visions and Division: Cultural Change and Political Conflict.* New Brunswick, NJ: Transaction Books, 1990.

Etzioni-Halevy, Eva. *Political Culture in Israel: Cleavage and Integration among Israeli Jews.* New York: Praeger Publishers, 1977.

MORDECHAI BAR-ON

NEGEV

Desert region in southern half of Israel; northeastern extension of the Sinai Desert.

The Negev is a triangular area with a maximum elevation of 3,300 feet and includes more than half of Israel's land area. The Negev Hills are a series of ranges with gentle northwesterly and steep southeasterly slopes. Some craters were formed by the erosion of upward-folded strata; they are 6 to 19 miles long, up to 3 miles wide, and surrounded on all sides by precipitous slopes. On their eastern side is an opening through which they drain into the Aravah Valley. August temperatures average 79°F, but they reach 90°F in the southern area and in Aravah. January temperatures average 52°F, reaching 59°F in the south and in Elat. The gateway from the north is the Negev's largest city, Beersheba, with a population estimated at 181,500 in 2002. To the south, the Negev opens onto the Gulf of Aqaba at Elat. The Negev has been irrigated in the northwest for agriculture; it contains some mineral resources, such as copper, phosphates, bromine, and potash, as well as natural gas and petroleum.

Under the British Mandate (1922–1948), the Negev was inhabited mainly by Bedouin. A few Jewish settlements were established by 1946. Control of the desert was contested by Arabs and Jews in the various partition plans. In 1947, the United Nations General Assembly's partition recommendation assigned parts of the Negev to the proposed Jewish state. In May 1948, Egyptian forces entered Gaza and the Negev in the opening days of the Arab-Israel War. With the conclusion of that war by armistice agreement in 1949, the Negev remained part of Israel. The late 1940s and early 1950s brought hundreds of thousands of immigrants to Israel. With an aggressive settlement program, by 2000 the Negev reached a population of more than 300,000.

See also ARAB–ISRAEL WAR (1948).

Bibliography

Gradus, Yehuda, et al. *Atlas of the Negev.* Jerusalem: Ben Gurion University of the Negev, 1986.

Levinson, Ester, and Yehuda, Gradus. *Statistical Yearbook of the Negev.* Beersheba: Negev Center for Regional Development and Negev Development Authority, 2000.

ELIZABETH THOMPSON
UPDATED BY YEHUDA GRADUS

NERVAL, GÉRARD DE
[1808–1855]

A French romantic poet and novelist known for his writing about the Orient.

Gérard Nerval was born in Paris with the name Gérard Labrunie. His delicate, musical poetry (e.g., *Les chimères*, 1854) and prose (of which the short story "Sylvie" is the best known) earned him a respected place in French literature. His treatment of dreamlike topics and visions influenced the development of surrealism and his translation of Johann Wolfgang von Goethe's *Faust* (1828) was widely acclaimed. Like many of his contemporaries, he was swept by romantic depictions of the Orient. In 1842, he left for a trip to the Orient in search of the sources of religion and spirituality as well as the exotic horizons of the Arab and Muslim world. His travel account *Voyage en Orient* is considered among his finest works. His depiction of the Orient is more an occasion for introspective meditation on religious issues and criticism of his own culture and society than an objective social study. His friendly account, extolling the tolerance and openness of the cultures and religions he encountered, caused critics to accuse him of skepticism. The use of the Orient as a cover for self-criticism had been well established in literature, as seen in Montesquieu's *Lettres persanes* and Voltaire's *Zadig.* Like others before and after him

(Chateaubriand, Alphonse de Lamartine, Lord Byron, Thomas Moore, etc.), Nerval contributed to the movement of orientalism, which depicted the Orient in a romantic light, at times projecting onto it the negative characteristics and fears of Western culture. The distortion of reality in subjective arts was a normal cultural phenomenon; however, it contributed to the pseudoscientific discipline of orientalism, which was closely associated with colonialism and has in contemporary times been denounced for its lack of objectivity and its political motivations. Beset by mental illness, Nerval committed suicide in 1855.

Bibliography

Said, Edward W. *Orientalism.* New York: Pantheon Books. 1978.

Sharafuddin, Mohammed. *Islam and Romantic Orientalism: Literary Encounters with the Orient.* New York and London: Tauris, 1994.

MAYSAM J. AL FARUQI

NESHAT, SHIRIN
[1957–]

Iranian multimedia artist.

Shirin Neshat is a New York–based artist who works in the fields of video, video installation, and photography. She received her M.F.A. from the University of California in 1982 and did not return to Iran for some years because of the Islamic Revolution. In the 1990s Neshat became one of the most sought-after woman artists from the Middle East. She has won many awards and participated in major exhibitions in the United States and Europe. The majority of her work explores the male-female dynamic in Islam, as exemplified in the split-screen video installation *Rapture.* Later works, such as the trilogy *Passage, Pulse,* and *Possessed,* focus more specifically on both the limits and possibilities of women's experiences in Muslim societies. Neshat makes heavy use of allegory, mythic scenes, the imagery of the veil, and hypnotic music. Her work reflects her sense of displacement from her native Iran, the experience of living in an in-between state of self-imposed exile, and her attempts to come to terms with the massive social and religious changes in modern Iran.

Bibliography

Whitney Museum of American Art at Philip Morris, New York. *Shirin Neshat: Turbulent (1998–99).* Exhibition brochure, text by Neery Melkonian.

JESSICA WINEGAR

NESIN, NÜSRET AZIZ
[1915–]

Turkish playwright, novelist, short-story writer, and journalist.

Nesin was born in Istanbul, where he attended military high school and college until 1939. He worked as a journalist in Turkey in the 1940s, joining the leftist daily *Tan* in 1945, just before it was closed down by an anticommunist mob. He began writing novels and plays in the 1950s and quickly became known for his satirical style. He is considered by many the best Turkish humorist of recent years. He cofounded *Karikatür,* a humor magazine, in 1958. Since then, this prolific author has written dozens of short stories, several novels, and volumes of poetry, memoirs, and travel accounts. In the late 1980s, he served as chairman of the Turkish Writers Syndicate.

Nesin was an innovative playwright and was among the few to experiment with the theater of the absurd in the 1950s; he went on to write the leading plays of the 1970s. These included the antiwar play *The War between the Whistlers, Brushers,* and *Yasar, Neither Dead nor Alive.*

Bibliography

Şener, Sevda. "Contemporary Turkish Drama." In *The Transformation of Turkish Culture,* edited by Günsel Renda and C. Max Kortepeter. Princeton, NJ: Kingston Press, 1986.

ELIZABETH THOMPSON

NETANYAHU, BENJAMIN
[1949–]

Israeli politician; prime minister, 1996–1999.

Benjamin ("Bibi") Netanyahu was born in Tel Aviv in 1949 and spent his early childhood in Jerusalem. He graduated from high school in Philadelphia, where his father, Professor Benzion Netanyahu, taught history. Benzion, a major ideological influence, was a disciple of Vladimir Ze'ev Jabotinsky, the founder of the right-wing Zionist Revisionist movement. Netanyahu served in the elite Sayeret Matkal commandos from 1967 to 1972, reaching the rank of captain. Alongside another future prime minister, Ehud Barak, he stormed a hijacked Sabena airliner at Tel Aviv international airport in May 1972. After the army, he studied business administration at Massachusetts Institute of Technology (MIT), where he received his master's degree in 1976. That same year, Netanyahu's older brother, Yonatan, was killed while participating in the rescue of 98 Israeli and diaspora Jewish passengers aboard a hijacked Air France airplane in Entebbe, Uganda. Netanyahu worked as a management consultant in Boston from 1976 to 1978, then returned to Israel as marketing manager of a furniture company. In 1980 he founded the Jonathan Institute on terrorism, named after his brother. It established him as a public figure.

From 1982 to 1984 Netanyahu served as deputy to the Israeli ambassador in Washington, D.C., and then as the Israeli ambassador to the United Nations. He made his name as an eloquent advocate of Israel's cause. In 1988 he was elected to the Knesset on the Likud list and served as deputy foreign minister. In 1990 he was appointed deputy minister in the prime minister's office under Yitzhak Shamir. He was Israel's principal spokesman at the 1991 Madrid peace conference.

Netanyahu championed direct election of the prime minister. He was to become its first beneficiary, although the two-tier system was abolished for the 2003 elections after it failed to produce the stable governance he had promised. In March 1993 he succeeded Shamir as Likud leader, and he was an outspoken critic of the Oslo accords with the Palestinians. He was elected prime minister in May 1996 by barely 30,000 votes after a wave of bombings in Israeli cities undermined Shimon Peres's Labor administration. Under the new system, the electorate seized the chance to vote for a prime minister from a major party, but for the Knesset lists of special-interest parties (ethnic, religious, ideological). Netanyahu presided over a coalition of eight rightist and religious parties, each with its own agenda. The Oslo process had gone too far to be turned back, though Netanyahu insisted on Palestinian "reciprocity." In January 1997 he withdrew Israeli troops from 80

percent of Hebron, and at the Wye River conference in October 1998 he agreed to evacuate a further 13 percent of the West Bank. Within a year, he had lost the confidence of his own ministers, who accused him of manipulation and deceit. In May 1999 Ehud Barak defeated him in a bitterly fought election, and Netanyahu resigned the Likud leadership and his Knesset seat. He returned to parliament in January 2003. Ariel Sharon appointed him finance minister, and Netanyahu set out to implement the neoconservative economics he had learned at MIT.

Bibliography

Netanyahu, Benjamin. *A Place Among the Nations: Israel and the World.* New York: Bantam Books, 1993.

JULIE ZUCKERMAN
UPDATED BY ERIC SILVER

NETUREI KARTA

Group of ultra-Orthodox Jews living in Jerusalem and elsewhere who oppose Zionism prior to divine redemption.

Neturei Karta is Aramaic for "Guardians of the City." They are so named because their ideology rejects not only secular Zionism but all forms of Jewish sovereignty in Palestine prior to divine redemption. They deny all forms of cooperation with political Zionism, which they view as the hand-maiden of Satan. The Neturei Karta left the Orthodox political party, Agudat Israel, in 1938. They opposed the establishment of the State of Israel in 1948 and Israeli jurisdiction over Jerusalem.

Centered in the Meah She'arim district of Jerusalem, they do not recognize the validity of Israel's existence or participate in its political process. They maintain their own autonomous communal, religious, and educational structures and view themselves as the protectors of the religious nature of the city. The much larger Satmar Hassidic sect is highly supportive of Neturei Karta and often serves as its voice in Jewish communities outside Israel. Both groups have undertaken numerous public demonstrations against Zionism and the State of Israel.

Bibliography

Domb, I. *The Transformation: The Case of the Neturei Karta.* London, 1958.

Marmorstein, Emile. *Heaven at Bay: The Jewish Kulturkampf in the Holy Land.* London and New York: Oxford University Press, 1969.

CHAIM I. WAXMAN

NEUTRAL ZONE

An area shared by Iraq, Saudi Arabia, and Kuwait.

The neutral zone was originally devised because the boundary between Kuwait and Saudi Arabia, demarcated by the Anglo–Turkish Convention of 1913, was not ratified due to the outbreak of World War I. When the British government recognized the sovereignty of Ibn Sa'ud in 1915, a compromise was reached on the disputed boundary that involved the establishment of a 2,000-square-mile (5,180 sq. km) neutral zone. This was incorporated in the Uqayr Conference in 1922, which set up a similar neutral zone between Saudi Arabia and Iraq that abuts the Kuwaiti-Saudi neutral zone. The convention allowed the parties to explore, on an equal basis, the natural resources (presumably petroleum—oil and gas) of the neutral zone but did not address the question of sovereignty ("sharing equal economic rights" in the neutral zone does not necessarily mean that the two parties are co-sovereign in the zone). In fact, each of the two countries administers its part of the zone as if it were a part of its state, but both states share in the oil exploration in the zone. For years political sovereignty was not an issue, because the zone remained isolated and uninhabited. With the expansion of oil and gas exploration, both on-shore and offshore, divergent claims propelled the neutral zone to the forefront of regional politics.

Accepted practice has been that either Kuwait or Saudi Arabia could grant separate oil concessions to foreign companies for exploration in the neutral zone without prior approval from the other. Neither Kuwait nor Saudi Arabia can sign any binding agreement, however, regarding the entire zone without the other's approval. In July 1965, Kuwait and Saudi Arabia agreed to partition the neutral zone equally, with each state annexing its own part of the zone; however, the two states retained a shared sovereignty arrangement regarding the exploitation of natural resources. The status of the neutral zone did not change after the 1990 Gulf Crisis.

See also GULF CRISIS (1990–1991).

Bibliography

Baharna, Husain al-. *The Arabian Gulf States: Their Legal and Political Status and Their International Problems,* 2nd revised edition. Beirut: Librairie du Liban, 1975.

EMILE A. NAKHLEH

NEWSPAPERS AND PRINT MEDIA

This entry consists of the following articles:

ARAB COUNTRIES
IRAN
ISRAEL
TURKEY

ARAB COUNTRIES

Arab mass circulation print media, that is, newspapers and magazines that are intended for audiences in the Arab world.

Historical Development

The first printed periodical publication carrying news written by and for Arabs was *Jurnal al-Iraq*, which began appearing in Baghdad in Arabic and Turkish in the year 1816. Two Arab newspapers began publishing in Cairo in the 1820s, and these were followed by newspapers in Algeria in 1847, Beirut in 1858, Tunis, Damascus, and Tripoli Libya in the 1860s, San'a in 1879, Casablanca in 1889, and Mecca in 1908.

Lebanon and Egypt have been leading centers of print media, publishing important newspapers earlier than most Arab countries; they continue to hold leading positions in journalism into the twenty-first century. The first Arab daily newspaper appeared in Beirut in 1873, and *al-Ahram,* which still appears as a leading daily, started in Egypt in 1875. By the twenty-first century only Egypt had dailies with circulations over half a million copies. Its two leading "national" dailies, *al-Ahram* and *al-Akhbar,* each distributed over seven hundred thousand, and *al-Jumhuriyya* sold about four hundred thousand copies. During the last decades of the twentieth century, the oil-rich Arab states of the Persian Gulf quickly expanded their print media, to some extent benefiting from Arab talent they hired from such countries as Lebanon, Egypt, Jordan, and Palestine, and quality daily newspapers proliferated. Circula-

Palestinian and Israeli newspapers display coverage of an Israeli air raid in Gaza in 2002. The loyalist Palestinian press is frequently subjected to various kinds of controls by Israel and the Palestinian Authority. © AFP/CORBIS. REPRODUCED BY PERMISSION.

tions there remained small, however; for example, Qatar, Bahrain, and Oman have had successful dailies only since the 1970s, and their circulations have never exceeded a few tens of thousands.

Among the smaller Arab states on the Persian Gulf, Saudi Arabia has the oldest newspaper traditions, and some of its leading newspapers have relatively long traditions. In the Western region of Saudi Arabia, such newspapers as *al-Bilad* and *al-Madina* were flourishing as early as the 1930s, and the dailies *Ukaz* and *al-Nadwa* had appeared there by the 1960s. In the early 1960s, *Al-Jazira* and *al-Riyadh* dailies started in Riyadh, and *al Yawm* started in Dammam; as of 2003, all seven of these newspapers still existed. In Yemen, governments in the south and the north have published daily papers since the 1960s, but they were of limited circulation and generally of poor quality.

The United Nations Educational, Scientific, and Cultural Organization (UNESCO) has established a minimum standard of one hundred copies of daily newspapers per one thousand inhabitants, but by the year 1966 only Lebanon and four Gulf states, namely Bahrain, Kuwait, Oman, and the United Arab Emirates, had passed it (worldbank.org, March 2003). By the twenty-first century, five Arab countries had dailies with more than one hundred thousand in circulation. Assuming multiple readers of each copy, an estimated thirty million Arabs, or more than 10 percent of the total Arab population, are regular readers of dailies.

Common Characteristics

There are significant differences among Arab countries in the use and structure of print media, reflecting underlying differences in wealth, population, literacy, political systems, and cultural conditions. The following characteristics generally prevail, although variations and exceptions occur throughout the region.

First, most Arab print media exist on a relatively weak economic base. They suffer from small literate populations and, in most places, limited incomes. Sales are therefore limited and, in addition, the practice of advertising in the media has not developed very extensively. Even as some Arab states and individuals became wealthy during the second half of the twentieth century, advertising remained modest and businesspeople did not see media as a lucrative investment. Although newspapers were no longer an expensive luxury for the middle classes, as they were during the middle of the twentieth century, price and literacy still limited circulations.

Second, Arab media tend to be closely tied to politics in a number of ways. The first newspapers were published by governments with the intent of informing bureaucrats and the public. The first indigenous Egyptian newspapers, *Jurnal al-Khadyu* and *al-Waqaʾi al-Misriyya,* appeared in the 1820s as government publications. The practice also emerged elsewhere. In Algeria the government started publishing *al-Mubashir* in 1847; in Tunisia the government started *al-Raʾid al-Tunis* in 1861, and in Damascus the government started *Suriya* in 1865. In Iraq the government began issuing *Jurnal al-Iraq* in 1816. Private individuals and families did begin to publish newspapers, but in the nineteenth century they appeared only in Syria, Lebanon, Egypt, and Morocco. More private papers emerged later, but after World War II, in the era of Arab nationalism and anticolonialism, Arab governments tended to want to control their own newspapers; government-owned papers still exist in most parts of the region, where they are still seen as important political instruments.

Some newspaper owners have tended to seek financial patronage from domestic and foreign governments or from local political parties. The Arab political parties that emerged after World War II sought to disseminate their views through the press, and party newspapers still exist in a number of Arab countries, although many of them are relatively small circulation weeklies.

Third, from the beginning, Arab newspapers have tended to include a significant amount of cultural content, traditionally publishing short stories, poetry, and serialized novels. Scholars and literary figures often write in the newspapers. At the same time, the profession of journalism, including the habit of aggressive reporting and the presentation of objective, unbiased news, has not been as fully developed in the Arab world as it has in some other parts of the world.

Finally, the structure of Arab print media tends to be fragmented, with most of the readership of individual newspapers confined to the paper's country of origin; many papers have small, specialized audiences. Most newspapers are published in one or two cities in each country because of the concentration of literate readers and because of barriers to distribution.

Organization

Arab print media can be divided for purposes of analysis into four separate organizational categories. One type can be called the "mobilization press." This type of media is under the tightest government control and supervision. Newspapers of this type never criticize or print negative information about senior officials. They avoid criticism of basic government policy, and only occasionally complain about the way lower-level individual government employees manage their responsibilities. There is no significant diversity among newspapers, all of which are owned by the government or by its political agents. The regime in fact controls all essential levers of power in the country, including the press. It sees itself as the vanguard of the people and regards the press as a tool of political mobilization of the public; it is not content with passive acquiescence but expects active editorial support for its policies. This type of print media is found in Syria, Sudan, and Libya. Before 2003 the press structure in Iraq was the clearest example of a mobilization press. The 2003 war in Iraq and the collapse of the regime of Saddam Hussein changed the Iraqi media scene, as genuinely private newspapers emerged for the first time in decades. As of 2003 the Iraqi system was still in transition.

A second press type can be called "loyalist," because although most newspapers are privately owned, their news and commentary loyally support the government in power. They eschew criticism of the top leadership, although they do complain about shortcomings of the government bureaucracy and express occasional mild criticism of government ministers. There is little diversity among the daily papers except in style. This type of print media is found in the conservative monarchies of Saudi Arabia, Bahrain, Qatar, Oman, and the United Arab Emirates, as well as in Palestine. From the final years of the 1990s, however, a more liberal trend began to appear in these countries, initiated by some of the younger leaders who have gained more influence.

The Palestinian press, however, has some unique characteristics. Palestine was ruled by the Ottomans until 1917, then for thirty years by the British, then by Israel and Jordan until 1967, when Israel also occupied the West Bank and Gaza. Palestinian journalism found outlets in several Arab countries, but not in Palestine itself until the middle of the 1990s, when the Palestinian Authority assumed responsibility for some of the territory, and government-sponsored and private print media emerged there. Palestinian publications as of 2003 remained subject to controls of various kinds not only by the Palestinian Authority but also by Israel, since Palestine has not yet achieved independent statehood.

A third type of print media can be called "diverse," because its most distinguishing characteristic is that newspapers represent a considerable diversity in content, style, and political orientation. Essentially all are privately owned, and many but not all are quite critical of the government. The clearest example of this type of press is found in Lebanon, but during the twenty-first century it is found also in Morocco, Kuwait, and Yemen. Behind the press is a political system that includes active political parties and an environment of freer speech than in most other parts of the Arab world.

A fourth type of print media can be called "transitional," because its structure has been undergoing change in recent years; it is the subject of debate and discussion in the country and may change further. Some print media are owned by the government, some by private individuals, and some by political parties. Some freedom of expression exists, but a variety of governmental controls and economic pressures restrict that freedom. Laws on the books allow the government authorities to take action against journalists and editors, and court cases are relatively frequent. This type of press is found in Egypt, Jordan, Tunisia, and Algeria.

Offshore Publishing

Finally, there is an additional and separate category of important Arab newspapers that are primarily based in Europe but published for readers throughout the Arab world. This phenomenon began during the 1970s when the Lebanese civil war forced some Lebanese publishers and journalists to leave their country and set up "offshore" operations in London, Paris, and Rome. Some did not survive, but others did. When the civil war ended, some moved back to Beirut, such as the weekly al-Hawadith; others kept their bases in Europe. The improvements in satellite and computer technology during the 1990s made it possible for these offshore publications to overcome distribution obstacles because they could do the editorial work in Europe and print the paper in various cities in the Arab world for local distribution. Editors were concerned about local censorship and taboos, but they were nevertheless somewhat freer than locally published papers, and some of them varied their content depending on the target country.

By 2003, three major Arab publishing houses in London were producing newspapers and magazines for distribution throughout the Arab world. All were owned by wealthy Saudi nationals. The Saudi Research and Marketing Group, chaired by a Saudi prince, has produced the daily al-Sharq al-Awsat since 1977, and it also produces more than a dozen other publications, including the popular weekly magazine al-Majalla. Another publishing house, founded originally by a Lebanese family but now owned by another Saudi prince, produces the daily al-Hayat plus a weekly magazine, and it has a joint venture with a satellite television company. A third Arab daily that appears in London and is aimed at a pan-Arab audience is al-Quds al-Arabi; it is edited by Palestinians and tends to focus on Palestinian issues.

Non-Arabic and Specialized Publications

Most Arabs read newspapers in Arabic, but there are some important publications that appear in French or English. On the Persian Gulf, where thousands of English-speaking South Asians reside, there are many daily newspapers published in English, aimed primarily at those expatriates. Two of Kuwait's seven dailies are in English. In North Africa, where the French colonial legacy can still be seen, and French is still spoken by many people, Morocco, Tunisia, and Algeria all have important newspapers in French. By 2003, of the eighteen dailies appearing in Algeria, eleven were in French, including five with circulations of more than one hundred thousand. Seven of the nineteen dailies in Morocco were in French. Of the sixteen leading dailies in Lebanon, one was in English and one in French. Even in Egypt, where most readers prefer Arabic, *The Egyptian Gazette* in English (which began publication in 1880) and *Le progrès Egyptien* in French (which started in 1893), are still appearing, although with limited circulations.

Every Arab country produces its own weekly and monthly magazines. Some have political agendas but most are special-interest publications that have no particular political agenda, but rather deal with specialized subjects such as sports or women's issues. The most common type is the weekly pictorial variety and current-events magazine, such as Egypt's *al-Musawwar* and Lebanon's *al-Hawadith*. Scholarly journals such as Egypt's *al-Siyasa al-Dawliyya*, religious magazines such as the Saudi *al-Da'wa*, and literary and intellectual publications such as Kuwait's *al-Arabi* appeal to specialized readers.

Conclusion

In short, print media vary across the Arab world. Government, generally quite strong, influences the media in different ways. In one country there may be uniformity among publications, and the media play an advocacy role in support of the government. In another country, government influence will be more subtle and indirect. In some Arab countries, publications exist that express views in clear opposition to the government. The fundamental factor explaining these differences is the prevailing political system of the particular country in which the media are published.

Bibliography

Alterman, Jon B. *New Media, New Politics?: From Satellite Television to the Internet in the Arab World,* Policy Paper no. 48. Washington DC: The Washington Institute for Near East Policy, 1998.

Kamalipour, Yahya R., and Mowlana, Hamid, eds. *Mass Media in the Middle East: A Comprehensive Handbook.* Westport, CT: Greenwood Press, 1994.

Rugh, William A. *The Arab Press: News Media and the Political Process in the Arab World.* 2d edition. Syracuse, NY: Syracuse University Press, 1987.

WILLIAM A. RUGH

IRAN

Newspapers have been active in Iran since 1850.

The first Iranian government newspaper, *Ruznameh-e vaqa-ye ittifaqiyeh* (Newpaper of current affairs), was founded by the reform-promoting prime minister Amir Kabir (Mirza Mohammad Taqi Khan Farahani) in 1850, and it continued after his downfall (in 1851) as a chronicle of official information. No other newspapers were permitted during the reign of Naser al-Din Shah (1848–1896). Consequently, the most important early Iranian newspapers were published outside the country: *Akhtar,* founded in Istanbul in 1875; *Qanun,* founded in London in 1890; and *Habl al-Matin,* founded in Calcutta in 1893. Following the Constitutional Revolution of 1906, numerous newspapers were published inside Iran. Most papers supported the various ideological factions that emerged after 1906. By 1909 Tehran's largest circulation paper was *Iran-e now* (New Iran), a paper that openly espoused European socialist ideas. Ziya Tabataba'i founded a paper in Shiraz, *Islam,* that backed the constitutional movement. During World War I he moved to Tehran, where his paper *Ra'ad* supported the British. In 1921 he joined with the future shah, Reza Khan (subsequently Reza Shah Pahlavi), in organizing the coup d'état that led less than five years later to the deposition of the Qajar Dynasty. As Reza Shah consolidated his power throughout the 1920s, the independent press was subject to increasing censorship. Press freedom was restored after Britain and the Soviet Union forced Reza Shah's abdication and exile following their joint invasion of Iran in August 1941. During the next twelve years newspapers represented every ideological tendency found in Iran, and papers in Armenian, Azeri, Turkish, Kurdish, and other ethnic minority languages also were founded.

The 1953 coup d'état that enabled Mohammad Reza Shah Pahlavi to assert his authority over the Majles and effectively establish a royal dictatorship ushered in another period of strict press censorship that lasted for twenty-five years. Just after the Iranian Revolution of 1979, there was a new and rapid development of newspapers that reflected a diverse range of opinions and views, but after six months, press restrictions of increasing severity began to be introduced. By the early 1980s censorship prevented publication of material deemed contrary to the official ideology. After 1989 censorship regulations gradually relaxed, and the number of publications again increased. In 1997 the Ministry of Culture began to issue licenses to virtually anyone who applied for a publishing permit, and within a year more than one hundred new dailies—more than one-fifth of them in Tehran—were being printed throughout the country. Many of these newspapers proclaimed their commitment to democracy and criticized political leaders and policies they identified as antidemocratic. The objects of these political barbs used the court system to get several papers banned on grounds of slander and incitement, and in several cases journalists were fined or given prison sentences. Despite these setbacks, many editors and publishers subsequently brought out their former papers under new names. Since April 2000, what could be termed the reformist press has been more careful in its political reporting to minimize conflict with a generally hostile judiciary. Nevertheless, Iran's newspapers and print media in the early 2000s had a larger readership and offered a broader spectrum of views on political ideas than at any other time in the country's modern history.

See also IRANIAN REVOLUTION (1979); NASER AL-DIN SHAH; PAHLAVI, MOHAMMAD REZA; PAHLAVI, REZA; TABATABA'I, ZIYA.

Bibliography

Kamalipour, Yahya R., and Mowlana, Hamid, eds. *Mass Media in the Middle East.* Westport, CT: Greenwood Press, 1994.

ERIC HOOGLUND

ISRAEL

Historical, political and sociological overview of the Israeli printed press.

The Israeli press is a combined product of a nation-building ideology, an elitist-colonial concept of the media, and a more recent industrial market-oriented climate. The Zionist ideology has steered the Hebrew press since its emergence in Palestine in 1863. When the State of Israel was established in 1948, the press was vibrantly partisan. Most newspapers belonged to political parties, and only a few were privately owned. They included sixteen dailies—thirteen in Hebrew, one in English, and two in German—serving a population of 650,000. Newspapers owned by political parties include *Davar* (The Word; labor party MAPAI); *ha-Tzofeh* (The Seer; national religious party), *Kol ha-Am* (Communist party), and others. Private newspapers include *Haaretz* (The Land) and *Yediot Aharonot* (Last News) in Hebrew, *Jerusalem Post* (formerly *Palestine Post*) in English, *Yediot Hadashot* (Recent News) in German, and others. Seven years later, when Israel's population reached 1.7 million, the number of dailies had risen to twenty-five: sixteen in Hebrew, two in German, and one each in English, Arabic, French, Yiddish, Hungarian, Romanian, and Polish, all aimed at the Arabic and new immigrant populations.

The Israeli press inherited from the British Mandate an elitist role of social and cultural educator. Also, the colonial rule determined the legal status of the press, for the Press Ordinance of 1933 has remained the major press-licensing instrument in Israel, and the Emergency Measures of 1945 are still the legal basis of military censorship.

After 1948, due to a general decline in ideology and to political and economic processes, particularly since the 1970s, the large number of nationwide dailies published mostly in Tel Aviv and catering to a politically segmented population became a smaller number of wide circulation newspapers. In 2003 there were twenty dailies in Israel, but only eight in Hebrew. The remaining twelve were English (one); Russian (seven), aimed mostly at new immigrants from the former Soviet Union; Arabic (one), also read in the areas controlled by the Palestinian Authority; and Romanian (two) and Polish (one), aimed at Israel's foreign workers. Since the 1960s a dynamic local press published mostly by the leading nationwide press groups has accompanied the decentralization of the population and the emergence of local leaderships. Also a large number of general-interest and specialized magazines are published.

The replacement of ideological zeal and party subsidies with privatization and industrial professionalism has been expressed in a bolder critical and investigative journalism, professional training and hiring policies, and improved ethics. Concentration and cross-ownership, particularly since the 1980s, have allowed a few Israeli and powerful foreign groups and family enterprises to control the press. In 2003 they included four groups—Yediot Aharonot, Ma'ariv, Haaretz, and Jerusalem Post—and one financial paper, *Globes,* and some low-circulation party newspapers, mostly religious.

Newspapers have always been an integral part of the political process in Israel, first as mouthpieces of the political parties to which they belonged, and later as independent critics and challengers on issues such as war and peace, occupation, socioeconomic justice, democracy, and globalization.

British Mandatory emergency measures that stipulated that all publications must be cleared by a military censor remain part of Israeli law. An agreement among the government, the army, and the press has eased this measure: A list of security-related topics issued by the censor defines the press items that must be cleared, and only a fraction of articles fall under it. Newspapers that refuse or are not allowed to join the agreement, including the Arabic press, are subject to full censorship. Foreign correspondents work under strict control, particularly in the occupied territories.

The Press Council, established in 1963 on a voluntary basis, brings together the National Association of Journalists, publishers, editors, and members of the public. The council aims to protect the freedom of the press, free access to information, and professional ethics.

See also RADIO AND TELEVISION: ISRAEL.

Bibliography

Caspi, Dan, and Limor, Yehiel. *The In/Outsiders: The Mass Media in Israel.* Cresskill, NJ: Hampton Press, 1999.

DOV SHINAR

TURKEY

Newspapers in Turkey emerged during the Ottoman Empire.

The emergence of newspapers and print media in the later Ottoman Empire had a profound impact on sociocultural and political life. Turkish-language works were first printed in Istanbul in 1727 by

Turkey's first newspapers originated in the mid-eighteenth century. Though the Turkish press has long struggled under government restrictions, many of those restrictions have been lifted, and critical and investigative journalism have flourished. © DAVE BARTRUFF/CORBIS. REPRODUCED BY PERMISSION.

Ibrahim Müteferrika, following earlier presses established by Jewish, Armenian, Greek Orthodox, and expatriate Western European communities. The first newspaper, *Takvim-i Vekayi* (1831; Calendar of events), was an official organ, primarily a means for the state to communicate with provinces. In 1840 *Ceride-i Havadis* (Journal of news) was established by Englishman William Churchill, and under Ottoman editors and writers it played a pioneering role in creating an appetite for news of current events. With *Tercüman-ı Ahvâl* (1861; Interpreter of events), edited by Ibrahim Sinasi, and *Tasvir-i Efkâr* (1862; Mirror of opinion), newspapers became instrumental in the appearance of new types of journalism and literary writing (e.g., novels and new poetry). Writers discussed a newspaper's role in the formation of public opinion and educating the citizenry, and contributed to the emergence of a style of written Turkish simpler and more direct than that typical of official discourse and letters.

Following the Young Turk Revolution of 1908, many restrictions on the press were lifted, and there followed a short lived explosion of periodical publications in Istanbul and regional centers such as Salonika and Izmir, by and for communities and interests that had come to think of themselves in corporate terms (e.g., ethnic and religious minorities, women, professionals). With the establishment of the Turkish Republic in 1923 under Mustafa Kemal (Atatürk), the press became subject to the same dramatic centralization as other institutions, and essentially it became an organ of mass mobilization for the Republican People's Party's state. *Hakimiyet-i Milliye* (National sovereignty) in Ankara and *Cumhuriyet* (Republic) in Istanbul were left as the only national papers in 1925, and most regional papers were under government control by the time of a press law in 1931. By 1935 there were thirty-eight dailies in the country (twenty-two in Istanbul, six in Izmir, and two in Ankara). Journals and reviews such as *Ülkü* (Ideal) also tended to reflect the developmentalist-populist nature of the state, presenting articles in a direct language on regional and national culture, folklore, history, social conditions, and new technological developments, with little discussion of "political" topics.

With multiparty politics in 1946 came liberalizing measures, including easing of the press laws, and the emergence of real mass circulation newspapers such as *Vatan*, *Milliyet*, and *Hürriyet*, which saw themselves less as instruments of political mobilization and more as means of information for citizens in a democratic system. Under the Democrat Party a more liberal press law was passed, but by 1953 the ruling party tried to silence political opposition and the press, resorting to closures and jailing critics. The coup of 1960 was followed by a liberalization of the press, and journalists themselves drew up a Code of Ethics that was signed by all the major papers. These liberties were restricted after the coup of 1971, and again after that of 1980, but the public's expectation of an independent press was irreversible. Through the 1990s Turkey was criticized

by several human-rights organizations for imprisoning journalists. With the winding down of the Kurdish separatist insurgency in 1999 and new legislation in line with European Union requirements press restrictions have been lifted gradually, and critical and investigative journalism has become characteristic of some newspapers.

See also RADIO AND TELEVISION: TURKEY.

Bibliography

Groc, Gérard. "Journalists as Champions of Participatory Democracy." In *Politics in the Third Turkish Republic*, edited by Metin Heper and Ahmet Evin. Boulder, CO: Westview Press, 1994.

Heper, Metin, and Demirel, Tanel. "The Press and the Consolidation of Democracy in Turkey." *Middle Eastern Studies* 32, no. 2 (1996): 109–123.

Karpat, Kemal. "The Mass Media: Turkey." In *Political Modernization in Japan and Turkey*, edited by Robert Ward and Dankwart Rustow. Princeton, NJ: Princeton University Press, 1964.

BRIAN SILVERSTEIN

NEW WAFD

Egyptian political party.

The Wafd, outlawed by Gamal Abdel Nasser in 1953, was relaunched in 1977 by its former secretary-general, Fu'ad Sarraj al-Din, as the New Wafd. The New Wafd, again the party of constitutional nationalism, liberalization, and landed and professional interests, was seen as a spent force by President Anwar al-Sadat, who therefore made it the first legal opposition party in 1978. It quickly developed a mass membership and outspoken opposition to his domestic and foreign policies, and alleged the unconstitutionality of presidential rule by referenda rather than regulated election. The government then banned the participation of politicians active before 1952, and the New Wafd disbanded in protest.

The party re-emerged in 1983 after Husni Mubarak's renewed liberalization. In 1984 it contested the elections in alliance with the Muslim Brotherhood and won 15 percent of the vote (58 seats), making it the largest opposition party. The alliance collapsed, and in 1987 the New Wafd fought alone and won 35 seats. In 1990 the New Wafd initiated an election boycott widely credited with defending the political system in the face of emergency laws. Throughout its existence, however, the party has carefully moderated its opposition to the regime, leading to accusations of clientalism and to continuing internal tensions over the legitimate extent of opposition. In the 1995 elections the party turned broadside against the Muslim Brotherhood, and again received criticism for supporting the government line. By contrast, the strengthening of New Wafd opposition to Islamism has also been seen as a product of a deepening secularist-Islamist cleavage. New Wafd secularism also is underpinned by support from Coptic voters.

Serageddin died in 2000 and was replaced as party leader by his deputy, Nuʿman Jumaʿa.

See also EGYPT; WAFD.

Bibliography

Hinnebusch, Raymond. *Egyptian Politics under Sadat.* Cambridge, U.K.: Cambridge University Press, 1985.

Kassem, May. *In the Guise of Democracy: Governance in Contemporary Egypt.* Reading, U.K.: Ithaca Press, 1999.

RAYMOND WILLIAM BAKER
UPDATED BY GEORGE R. WILKES

NEZZAR, KHALED
[1937–]

Algerian general and defense minister.

Born near Biskra, Khaled Nezzar served in the French Army before deserting to join the Armée de Libération Nationale (ALN) in 1958, and from that point he pursued a military career. He was stationed along the Moroccan frontier during the border war of 1963 and commanded a battalion sent to Egypt to demonstrate Algerian solidarity after the Arab–Israel War of 1967. Nezzar's military education included studies in the Soviet Union and France. He was appointed to the central committee of the ruling Front de Libération Nationale (FLN) in 1979 and was promoted to general and assistant chief of staff in 1984. He quelled the destabilizing October 1988 riots, resulting in hundreds of casualties. In 1990 Nezzar received particular publicity when he was appointed Algeria's first minister of defense since 1965—a portfolio usually held by Algeria's authoritarian presidents. Faced with the prospect of a Front Islamique du Salut (FIS) government, Nezzar and

others deposed President Chadli Bendjedid in January 1992 and established the Haut Comité d'Etat (HCE). Nezzar continued to serve as minister of defense as the civil war broke out, escaping assassination in February 1993. He retired in 1994 but continued to play a dominant role in the Pouvoir—the ruling establishment of military and civilian elites. While he was visiting France in 2001, Algerians filed charges against him for crimes of repression, including torture. The lawsuits were eventually dropped because of the duress placed upon the plaintiffs. Concurrently, Nezzar sued Habib Souaidia, a former Algerian officer and author of *La sale guerre* (2001; The dirty war), who had made televised comments accusing the military of massacres and tortures. Nezzar returned to Paris to defend the army, but his defamation suit against Souaidia was dismissed in September 2002.

Nezzar has authored *Mémoires du général Khaled Nezzar* (2000; Memoirs of General Khaled Nezzar) and *Algérie: Échec à une régression programmée* (2001; Algeria: defeat of a regressive program). He is also an entrepreneur, cofounding an Internet company called Soft Link Com. Nezzar remains a most powerful member of the Pouvoir.

See also ALGERIA: POLITICAL PARTIES IN; ARMÉE DE LIBÉRATION NATIONALE (ALN); FRONT DE LIBÉRATION NATIONALE (FLN).

Bibliography

Naylor, Philip C. *The Historical Dictionary of Algeria,* 3d edition. Lanham, MD: Scarecrow Press, 2005.

PHILIP C. NAYLOR

NHAISI, ELIA
[1890–1918]

Zionist pioneer who mobilized the Libyan Jews in Tripoli.

Elia Nhaisi was born in Tripoli, Libya, to a poor Jewish family. He earned his living as a photographer, sold photographic postcards, and was the Tripolitanian correspondent for the Florentine Jewish weekly, *La Settimana Israelitica,* later known as *Israel.* In 1913, he established the Jewish Cultural Club and, in 1914, the Talmud Torah evening school for modern Hebrew. In 1916, he founded the Zionist Club, *Circolo Sion,* which by 1923 evolved into a

Libyan Zionist organization. His movement was supported by the community rabbis but opposed by the "Italianized" president and community council members, who championed Italianized assimilation for the Jews. The Italian Jewish press was his staunch supporter, and his Zionist group prevailed. Nhaisi died after a short illness at the age of twenty-eight.

Bibliography

Roumani, Maurice M. "Zionism and Social Change in Libya at the Turn of the Century." *Studies in Zionism* 8, no. 1 (1987).

MAURICE M. ROUMANI

NIATI, HOURIA
[1948–]

Algerian painter, installation and performance artist, singer, and poet.

Houria Niati was trained in Algeria as well as at the Camden and Croyden art schools in England, where she has lived since the late 1970s. She is best known for her paintings/installations *No to Torture* (1983–1996) and *Bringing Water from the Fountain Has Nothing Romantic about It* (1991). These works critique the romanticized and stereotypical portrayals of Arab women in colonial postcards and orientalist paintings, particularly those of Eugène Delacroix, whose subject was the women of Niati's native Algeria. Through a series of visual commentaries upon those earlier paintings, and through the creation of other pieces that manipulate the imagery and ideas in them, Niati interrogates the objectified orientalist images of the sensuous and secluded Arab/Muslim woman that were propagated through colonialism. For example, she imprisons, mutilates, and disfigures the women in her version of Delacroix's painting, thereby calling specific attention to how the female body was the site of violence under French colonialism and how the romanticism of the orientalists provided a cover for this "torture." In her work, she subverts the male perspective that was central to the colonial project and re-authors the subjectivity of Algerian women, thereby transforming her own experience of being arrested by the colonial authorities for protesting as a young girl. She also critiques the violence against women in contemporary Algeria. Her influences have included post-Impressionism, ancient Algerian rock paintings, and children's art.

Niati is a trained singer in the Andalusian *sha'bi* and *rai* traditions and often does performances to accompany her exhibitions, singing songs and reciting poetry inspired by those musical genres.

See also ART; ALGERIA.

Bibliography

Hassan, Salah. "Nothing Romantic about It! A Critique of Orientalist Representation in the Installations of Houria Niati." In *Gendered Visions: The Art of Contemporary Africana Women Artists,* edited by Salah Hassan. Trenton, NJ: Africa World Press, 1997.

Niati, Houria. "Enacting Vision: A Personal Perspective." In *Displacement and Difference: Contemporary Arab Visual Culture in the Diaspora,* edited by Fran Lloyd. London: Saffron Books, 2001.

Rogers, Sarah. "Houria Niati's *No to Torture*: A Modernist Reconfiguration of Delacroix's *Women of Algiers in Their Apartment.*" *Thresholds* 24 (2002): 36–41.

JESSICA WINEGAR

NILE RIVER

The longest river in Africa and, arguably, the world.

The Nile (*Bahr al-Nil*) dominates the landscape of eastern and northern Africa as well as the lives and livelihood of its people. The Nile traverses 35 degrees of latitude and 4,200 miles in its flow from Burundi in the East African rift valleys through ten riparian countries to Egypt on the Mediterranean. Within this 1.25-million-square-mile drainage area, the Nile Basin encompasses unique wildlife habitats and broad biodiversity. At the same time, Nile Basin countries are home to 300 million people, a number projected to double by 2025.

The Nile Basin is environmentally sensitive. Stretching from the equator to the Mediterranean, the Nile is a principal flyway for migrating birds that nest along its many marshes, lakes, and tributaries. Its wetlands, forests, and open lands are home to a broad array of flora and fauna. Its natural beauty has attracted tourists for centuries. But increasing population and limited water supply have put stress on the people of the basin as well as on the environment. Total water and water availability per capita in the Nile Basin remain low.

Compared to other major river basins, the Nile's disparity in water availability differs sharply among sub-basins. Arid portions (perhaps one-third of the basin) yield negligible flows; in contrast, the highlands of Ethiopia, comprising 10 to 20 percent of the land area of the overall basin, and draining through the Blue Nile and Atbara, yield approximately 120 billion cubic yards, or 60 to 80 percent of the annual flow at Aswan. Flows from the White Nile originating in the region of Lake Victoria are buffered by the great Sudd swamps of southern Sudan, and thus are approximately constant through the year. Flows from the Blue Nile are concentrated in a three-month period of late summer, creating the famous annual inundation of Egypt.

Twelve miles south of Cairo, the Nile divides into the Rosetta and Damietta branches and enters the delta. For Egypt and Sudan, the river is almost the sole source of water, and their inhabitants have always been intensely concerned with the utilization of its waters. The valley of the lower Nile and delta has among the most fertile soils in the world, created by millennia of sediment deposition during the annual inundation. Since the building of the High Dam at Aswan in the 1960s, this felicitous natural process has been much curtailed. As population and industrialization grow along its banks, the quality of Nile waters has become degraded by pollution.

See also ASWAN HIGH DAM; EGYPT.

Bibliography

Howell, P. P., and Allan, J. A. *The Nile: Resource Evaluation, Resource Management, Hydropolitics, and Legal Issues.* London: SOAS/RGS, 1990.

Hurst, H. E. *The Nile A General Account of the River and the Utilization of Its Waters.* London: Constable, 1952.

Said, R. *The River Nile: Geology, Hydrology, and Utilization.* Oxford, U.K.; Pergamon, 1993.

Waterbury, John. *Hydropolitics of the Nile Valley.* Syracuse, NY: Syracuse University Press, 1979.

ARTHUR GOLDSCHMIDT
UPDATED BY GREGORY B. BAECHER

NIMR, FARIS
[1856–1951]

Lebanese Christian intellectual, publisher, and journalist who played an important role in popularizing modern science and Western ideas in the Arab East in the late nineteenth century.

A Greek Orthodox from Hasbeya, Lebanon, Faris Nimr was among the first Lebanese to study at the Syrian Protestant College (later renamed the American University of Beirut). He graduated at eighteen and became a tutor in astronomy and mathematics at the college. In 1876, he and fellow Syrian Protestant College graduate Yaʿqub Sarruf (1852–1927) began publishing in Beirut a scientific-literary journal called *al-Muqtataf* (The selection). In 1882, the two editors became embroiled in a fierce controversy over Darwinism that shook the college, where they were still teaching. Their support of Darwinism, articulated in *al-Muqtataf,* put them at odds with the college authorities, and they were dismissed in 1884. They then moved to Egypt, taking their periodical with them. In Cairo, *al-Muqtataf* rapidly developed into a leading opinion maker. Spurred by their success, the two Lebanese expatriates decided in 1889 to found *al-Muqattam,* a pro-British newspaper that promoted free enterprise. Sarruf retained primary responsibility for *al-Muqtataf,* and Nimr concentrated on *al-Muqattam,* which soon became one of the most influential dailies in Egypt.

Faris Nimr is remembered as one of the most prominent members of the early wave of Western-educated Lebanese intellectuals who played a leading role in introducing modern scientific knowledge and positivist ideas into the Arab East. What distinguished Nimr from most of his peers was his wide range of interests (which cut across the scientific-literary divide), his dual career as an intellectual and a publisher, and the remarkable sense of initiative and entrepreneurship that he demonstrated throughout his life, from his creation of *al-Muqtataf* when he was only twenty to his decision to relocate his business to Egypt and create a newspaper there. His writings and activities as a publisher in Cairo ensured that the impact of his ideas was felt much beyond his country of origin. Through *al-Muqattam* in particular, he inspired an entire generation of Arab intellectuals attracted to Western notions of individualism and laissez-faire economic ideas.

See also NEWSPAPERS AND PRINT MEDIA.

Bibliography

Reid, Donald M. "Syrian Christians, the Rags-to-Riches Story, and Free Enterprise." *International Journal of Middle East Studies* 1 (1970): 358–367.

Sharabi, Hisham. *Arab Intellectuals and the West: The Formative Years, 1875–1914.* Baltimore, MD: Johns Hopkins Press, 1970.

Tibawi, A. L. "The Genesis and Early History of the Syrian Protestant College (Part 2)." *The Middle East Journal* 21, no. 2 (Spring 1967): 199–212.

GUILAIN P. DENOEUX

NISSIM, ISAAC

[1895–1981]

Controversial Sephardic Chief Rabbi of Israel.

Born in Baghdad, Isaac Nissim moved to Jerusalem in 1926. Nissim was elected Sephardic Chief Rabbi of Israel in 1955, a position he held until 1972, although not without controversy. In 1964, he overcame a challenge by those Sephardim who sought to elect Rabbi Ya'acov Moshe Toledano, the politically unaffiliated Chief Rabbi of Tel Aviv. At the time, Nissim was the candidate of the National Religious party.

CHAIM I. WAXMAN

NIXON, RICHARD MILHOUS

[1913–1994]

U.S. president, 1969–1974.

Born in Yorba Linda, California, Richard Milhous Nixon attended Whittier College and Duke University Law School. After serving in World War II, he was elected to Congress (1946–1950), where he was a member of the House Un-American Activities Committee during the McCarthy era of anti-Communism, then to the U.S. Senate (1950–1952), where he continued his strongly anti-Communist stance. He was selected to run as vice president on the Republican ticket with Dwight D. Eisenhower in 1952 and again in 1956. During the Eisenhower administration, Nixon was given substantive foreign policy missions to fifty-six countries, including the USSR. In 1960, he ran for president but lost to John F. Kennedy. Nixon won the presidency in the 1968 election.

Nixon's Middle East policy was marked by crisis abroad and conflict at home. Abroad, the War of Attrition and the Arab-Israel War of 1973 demanded the full attention of the State Department while the U.S. government was still trying to repel the Communists in Vietnam. Nixon's secretary of state, William Rogers, and his national security adviser, Henry Kissinger, pursued separate and often contradictory Middle East policies. With the collapse of the Rogers Plan for Arab-Israeli peace, Kissinger emerged as the dominant adviser, and this was consolidated when he was made secretary of state in 1973.

Under Nixon, the United States sold both Israel and Iran large amounts of miliary equipment, including Phantom jets to Israel. In May 1972, during a visit to Iran, Nixon promised that the United States would sell them an unlimited supply of nonnuclear weapons, and by the end of the Nixon administration, Israel and Iran emerged as the "two pillars" of U.S. policy in the Middle East.

The major crisis of Nixon's administration began with the 1973 Arab-Israel War and the resulting Arab oil embargo by OPEC (the Organization of Petroleum Exporting Countries). This began an escalating spiral of price gouging and inflation that continued into the 1980s in the United States. Nixon attempted to placate the Arab states, especially Saudi Arabia. Until August 1974—when Nixon resigned the presidency—he and Kissinger had to negotiate numerous cease-fires and armistice lines between Israel, Egypt, and Syria. They also visited both Communist China and the USSR, improving relations with both.

In his desire for another term in office, Nixon and his White House staff became involved in a cover-up of their actions involving a break-in at Democratic national headquarters at the Watergate complex. The escalating investigation over this impeachable set of offenses resulted in Nixon's resignation.

See also ARAB–ISRAEL WAR (1973); WAR OF ATTRITION (1969–1970).

Bibliography

Ambrose, Stephen. *Nixon,* Vol. 1: *The Education of a Politician, 1913–1962.* New York: Simon and Schuster, 1987.

Ambrose, Stephen. *Nixon,* Vol. 2: *The Triumph of a Politician, 1962–1972.* New York: Simon and Schuster, 1990.

Spiegel, Steven. *The Other Arab-Israeli Conflict: Making America's Middle East Policy, from Truman to Reagan.* Chicago: University of Chicago Press, 1985.

ZACHARY KARABELL

NIZAM AL-JADID, AL-

Regular Egyptian army of the early nineteenth century, established by Muhammad Ali Pasha, consisting of conscripted men trained in the European style.

In 1805, as soon as Muhammad Ali Pasha gained some independence from the Ottoman Empire and consolidated his position as *wali* (provincial governor) in Cairo, he began conscripting skilled laborers to work on government projects. His model was the conscript armed force instituted by Ottoman Sultan Selim III. The existing Egyptian military force, to which the Mamluks (powerful landlords) sent their own retainers for use by the state, was then replaced by 1822 with a new, drafted, regular army called *al-nizam al-jadid.*

The first four thousand men called up came from Upper Egypt. Those from the region between Manfalut and Qina were assembled at a training camp near Farshut, and those from the region between Qina and Aswan were gathered in Aswan. Their initial tour of duty was set at three years. Their replacements were selected from lists of prospective draftees drawn up by the officers in charge of the training camps as part of a comprehensive system of village census taking. Conscripts were drilled according to European procedures and organized into defined regiments, with a centralized command structure to supervise the distribution of arms, clothing, and other equipment. State officials even orchestrated a propaganda campaign in support of the new army, urging prominent religious scholars to write treatises sanctioning these innovative practices.

Regular infantry and artillery units were complemented by a flotilla of warships built along European lines in government yards. Both the new army and navy played major roles in the Egyptian campaigns in the Aegean Sea and Syria after 1824. Both were also strictly limited by Britain after Muhammad Ali's capitulation to the European powers in 1838. Thus ended this army.

See also MUHAMMAD ALI.

Bibliography

Lawson, Fred H. *The Social Origins of Egyptian Expansionism during the Muhammad Ali Period.* New York: Columbia University Press, 1992.

Marsot, Afaf Lutfi al-Sayyid. *Egypt in the Reign of Muhammad Ali.* Cambridge, U.K., and New York: Cambridge University Press, 1986.

FRED H. LAWSON

NIZAMIYE COURTS

Secular Ottoman courts.

The Nizamiye (or Nizami, meaning regulation) courts were organized in 1869 by Minister of Justice Ahmet Cevdet to decide cases under new criminal and commercial law codes. The new court system extended from the lowest regional level, the *nahiye,* through the *kaza, sanjak,* and *vilayet,* or provincial levels. It was capped by the Council of Judicial Regulations (Divan-i Ahkam-i Adliye) in Constantinople (now Istanbul), which was the final court of appeal. After 1876, the courts were administered by the Court of Cassation (Temyiz Mahkemesi) in the ministry of justice. Under Abdülhamit II, Minister of Justice Küçük Sait Paşa introduced the institution of public defender in the Nizamiye courts and revised the commercial and criminal codes. A law school founded in 1878 produced one hundred graduates a year who staffed the expanding Nizamiye system.

Despite underfunding and overcrowding, the court system was generally considered efficient. Because of this, and the fact that the new law codes were prepared with the counsel of religious legal scholars, the *ulama*'s opposition to the Nizamiye was diminished, even though the new courts challenged the jurisdiction of *shari'a,* or religious, courts.

See also ABDÜLHAMIT II; CEVDET, AHMET.

ELIZABETH THOMPSON

NIZIP, BATTLE OF (1839)

Town, now in southern Turkey, where Egyptian forces defeated the Ottoman army on 24 June 1839, prompting the European powers to take steps to push Egypt out of Syria.

Throughout the spring of 1839, the Ottoman Empire encouraged unrest along the border between Anatolia and its former Syrian provinces, which had been captured in 1831 by the armies of Egypt's

Muhammad Ali Pasha—who named his son Ibrahim Pasha to govern them. Ibrahim at first refrained from responding to Ottoman activities, but was forced to mobilize when the Ottomans struck south across the Euphrates river in June. The two armies clashed at the town of Nizip, resulting in a crushing defeat of the Ottomans. Ibrahim immediately advanced north toward Konya, halting only when his father, who was worried about the impact that this move might have on regional diplomacy, ordered him not to go beyond the Taurus mountains. Meanwhile, an Ottoman fleet that had been sent to attack Alexandria in Egypt voluntarily surrendered to Muhammad Ali.

At the height of the crisis, the Ottoman sultan died. His successor had little choice but to enter negotiations with the victorious Egyptians. Egypt demanded control of the southern Turkish districts of Diyarbakir and Urfa—which commanded the primary trade routes between Syria and northern Iraq. The British government interpreted these demands as a direct threat to British interests in the region. France, on the other hand, signaled that it supported Egypt. Britain eventually persuaded Russia, Austria, and Prussia to agree to cooperate in expelling the Egyptian army from Syria, a commitment which was codified in the London Convention of July 1840. British warships then bombarded the Mediterranean ports of Beirut and Acre, forcing Ibrahim to withdraw his troops from all of Syria. Muhammad Ali returned the captured Ottoman fleet in exchange for recognition as the hereditary ruler of Egypt, which the Ottoman sultan granted on February 13, 1841. France returned to the European concert in July 1841, signing the Straits Convention with the other great powers.

See also LONDON CONVENTION; MUHAMMAD ALI; STRAITS CONVENTION.

Bibliography

Marsot, Afaf Lutfi al-Sayyid. *Egypt in the Reign of Muhammad Ali.* Cambridge, U.K., and New York: Cambridge University Press, 1986.

Rodkey, Frederick S. *The Turco-Egyptian Question in the Relations of England, France, and Russia, 1832–1841.* Urbana: University of Illinois Press, 1924.

FRED H. LAWSON

NOOR AL-HUSSEIN (QUEEN NOOR)
[1951–]

Queen of Jordan and wife of King Hussein ibn Talal.

Noor al-Hussein became queen of Jordan in 1978, after her marriage to King Hussein Ibn Talal, who ruled the Hashimite kingdom from 1953 to 1999. Born Elizabeth Najeeb Halaby, she changed her name to Noor al-Hussein (light of Hussein) in the context of her engagement to the king and her conversion to Islam.

Queen Noor grew up in the United States in a prominent Arab-American family. She was part of the first coeducational class to enter Princeton University, graduating in 1974 with a bachelor of arts in architecture and urban planning. After graduation, she worked on a series of international development projects before concentrating on the design and development of aviation training centers and airports. It was in this capacity that she joined Royal Jordanian Airlines and met King Hussein, himself an avid pilot with a deep personal interest in the kingdom's national airline.

Following her marriage to Hussein in 1978 and her coronation, Noor began work on a series of philanthropic endeavors, with particular emphasis on child welfare and women's empowerment. In 1981, she worked with Yarmuk University to create the now annual Jarash international festival for culture and the arts. The festival has grown annually and become a major tourist attraction for the kingdom. Queen Noor is perhaps best known for the work of her Noor al-Hussein Foundation, which includes many programs supporting education, cultural preservation, health care, and the rights of and opportunities for women and children; however, her patronage extends to many programs across a wide range of activities, including archaeology, business development, environmental conservation, child welfare, and even tennis. During the late 1990s, Noor also added her support to the national campaign to prevent honor crimes (that is, the killing of women by male family members who suspect them of adultery or of otherwise offending "family honor"). Queen Noor pressed for the repeal of legislation that allowed for leniency in sentencing. She also became a high-profile spokesperson for the international campaign to ban land mines.

Her role in Jordan and on the international stage continued after the death of King Hussein in 1999. After a change in the royal succession and the accession of King Abdullah II ibn Hussein, the new king appointed Noor's eldest son, Hamza, crown prince and designated successor to the throne.

See also HUSSEIN IBN TALAL.

Bibliography

Noor, Queen. *Leap of Faith: Memoirs of an Unexpected Life.* New York: Miramax, 2003.

Ryan, Curtis R. *Jordan in Transition: From Hussein to Abdullah.* Boulder, CO: Lynne Rienner, 2002.

CURTIS R. RYAN

NORDAU, MAX
[1849–1923]

Author and Zionist leader.

One of Theodor Herzl's earliest supporters, it was Max Nordau who formulated the goal for the Zionist movement in Basle Program at the First Zionist Congress in 1897: "The creation for the Jewish people of a publicly recognized, legally secured Home in Palestine." Following Herzl's death, Nordau became a close adviser to David Wolffsohn, the second president of the World Zionist Organization. Nordau was a staunch advocate of Herzl's brand of political Zionism and was opposed to Ahad Ha-Am's cultural Zionism and Chaim Weizmann's practical Zionism.

See also AHAD HA-AM; HERZL, THEODOR; WEIZMANN, CHAIM; WORLD ZIONIST ORGANIZATION (WZO).

Bibliography

Hertzberg, Arthur. *The Zionist Idea.* Garden City, NY: Doubleday, 1959.

MARTIN MALIN

NORTH ATLANTIC TREATY ORGANIZATION (NATO)

Post–World War II alliance for the defense of its members against the Soviet Union.

On 4 April 1949 twelve countries—including the United States, France, Great Britain, and Canada—signed the North Atlantic Treaty, establishing the basis for the North Atlantic Treaty Organization. NATO was designed to defend Western Europe in the face of a perceived threat from the Soviet Union and its Communist satellite states, which formed the Warsaw Treaty Organization in 1955.

Turkey applied for NATO membership in 1950, occupying a key strategic position between Europe and the Middle East. Admitted on 18 February 1952, Turkey agreed to provide NATO with secure access to the Straits at Istanbul and to the Black Sea.

With the end of the Cold War, NATO membership was expanded to include the Czech Republic, Hungary, and Poland (1999), and seven more states are due to accede in 2004. In September 2001 NATO invoked Article 5 of the treaty for the first time, declaring the terrorist attacks against the United States an attack against all members. NATO played no formal role in the American war in Iraq in 2003, though it agreed to assure Turkey's security under Article 4 of the treaty.

Bibliography

Lenczowski, George. *The Middle East in World Affairs,* 4th edition. Ithaca, NY: Cornell University Press, 1980.

North Atlantic Treaty Organization. Official homepage. <http://www.nato.int>.

ZACHARY KARABELL
UPDATED BY ANDREW FLIBBERT

NORTHERN TIER

The region comprising the countries of Iran and Turkey in the Middle East and Afghanistan and Pakistan in central Asia; its location on the border of the Soviet Union made it an area of high interest for U.S. defense planners and their allies during the Cold War.

In the early 1950s the Northern Tier assumed strategic significance in Anglo-American plans for defense of the Middle East against an attack that the Western powers assumed the Soviets would launch in a drive toward the Suez Canal. The Western allies intended to arm Turkey and also to prepare Iraq and Syria, neither of which was contiguous with the Soviet Union, to resist invasion. The United States and Britain planned to defer Iran's participation but attempted to convince Egypt to join Western planning for the Middle East Command (1951) and the Middle East Defense Organization (1952).

Egypt's refusal to participate in such regional defense plans brought the schemes to an end; nevertheless, the Western powers still believed that a "Middle East NATO" was possible. In April 1954 the United States signed an arms deal with Iraq and hoped that the bilateral treaty that Turkey and Pakistan signed that month could be expanded to include several Arab states. In 1955 Britain arranged and then joined with Iran, Iraq, Pakistan, and Turkey in the Baghdad Pact, which had the support of the United States.

See also BAGHDAD PACT (1955); CENTRAL TREATY ORGANIZATION (CENTO); MIDDLE EAST DEFENSE ORGANIZATION (MEDO).

Bibliography

Hahn, Peter L. *The United States, Great Britain, and Egypt, 1945–1956: Strategy and Diplomacy in the Early Cold War.* Chapel Hill: University of North Carolina Press, 1991.

Kuniholm, Bruce Robellet. *The Origins of the Cold War in the Near East: Great Power Conflict and Diplomacy in Iran, Turkey, and Greece.* Princeton, NJ: Princeton University Press, 1980.

Louis, William Roger. *The British Empire in the Middle East: 1945–1951: Arab Nationalism, the United States, and Postwar Imperialism.* New York; Oxford, U.K.: Oxford University Press, 1984.

ZACH LEVEY

NOUAKCHOTT

Capital of Mauritania.

Nouakchott is located 4 miles inland from the Atlantic Ocean, just south of central Mauritania. Three years before Mauritania's independence from France in 1960, Nouakchott, then just a village, was selected as the capital of the future independent Mauritania. City architects planned for a potential 15,000 inhabitants. By 1967, 20,000 people had moved to Nouakchott. As a result of Saharan droughts in recent decades, hordes of people have moved to the city, and as of the early twenty-first century more than 800,000 people inhabited Nouakchott, around 25 percent of the Mauritanian population.

Nouakchott, Mauritania's administrative and economic center, is home to all ethnicities. North of Nouakchott, Nouadhibou, a city of 100,000 people, also is a center of trade. Fishing, light industry, and handicraft manufacturing centers are located in Nouakchott and Nouadhibou. Foreign investment remains crucial for increased economic growth as population size and skilled labor are limited.

From any point in Nouakchott, Islamic prayer calls can be heard emanating from the mosques five times a day. Nouakchott has two large markets with men and women vendors lined up selling items such as fabric, electronics, Qur'ans, meats, vegetables, and rice. One of the markets is located in the Cinquième district, where more of the Pulaar population live and sell their products. The other large market, in the Capitale district, is mainly populated with black and white Maure vendors and shoppers. Nouakchott has restaurants of all types, a movie theater, internet cafés, beautiful mosques, a university, and an international airport.

NAOMI ZEFF

NOUIRA, HEDI
[1911–1993]

Tunisian nationalist and politician.

Educated in Tunis and Paris, Hedi Nouira played an important role in shaping and publicizing the nationalism of Habib Bourguiba in the early days of the Neo-Destour political party, largely through his work on the party's French-language newspaper. Following several periods of imprisonment by the French colonial administration (France held a protectorate over Tunisia from 1881), and participation in the negotiations toward independence in the 1950s, Nouira became a leading member of Bourguiba's inner circle.

With independence in 1955–1956, he was appointed minister of finance (1955–1958), then head of the Central Bank of Tunisia (1958–1970). In November 1970, he was appointed to be the new prime minister by Bourguiba, a post he held for seven years; in 1974, during a party congress, he was named heir apparent by Bourguiba. As prime minister, Nouira initiated a period of economic liberalization—by placing new emphasis on the private sector, encouraging trade and foreign investment, and distributing large parts of state farms to small landholders. When these policies led to social and economic dislocation, Nouira (with Bourguiba's support) met the ensuing political turmoil with repression. In early 1980, shortly after the Gafsa Incident (a clash between Libya and Tunisia), Nouira was reported to have fallen seriously ill and was replaced.

See also BOURGUIBA, HABIB; GAFSA INCIDENT (1980).

Bibliography

Perkins, Kenneth. *Tunisia: Crossroads of the Islamic and European Worlds.* Boulder, CO: Westview, 1986.

MATTHEW S. GORDON

NUʿAYMI FAMILY, AL-

The ruling family of the emirate of Ajman in the United Arab Emirates (UAE).

The rulers of Ajman are members of the Nuʿaym tribe, one of the largest in southeastern Arabia, with members spread from Oman to Bahrain. The first ruler of Ajman was Rashid ibn Humayd al-Nuʿaymi (r. 1816–1838), one of the Persian Gulf rulers who signed a peace treaty with the British in 1820. A small emirate with few economic resources, Ajman has been a recipient of financial aid from the ruler of Abu Dhabi, but it has not always followed the larger emirate's political lead. Due to his strong personality and his long tenure as amir (r. 1918–1981), Rashid bin Humayd al-Nuʿaymi, the ruler of Ajman at the time of the UAE's federation, hewed an independent line, often siding with the ruler of Dubai. The ninth and current ruler of Ajman is Humayd bin Rashid al-Nuʿaymi, born in 1931. He has ruled since 1981 and has served on the Supreme Council of the UAE since 1981. He is also the sponsor of the Shaykh Humayd bin Rashid prizes for Culture and Science.

See also AJMAN; UNITED ARAB EMIRATES.

Bibliography

Anthony, John Duke. *Arab States of the Lower Gulf: People, Politics, Petroleum.* Washington, DC: Middle East Institute, 1975.

Peck, Malcolm C. *Historical Dictionary of the Arab Gulf States.* Lanham, MD: Scarecrow Press, 1997.

ANTHONY B. TOTH

NUBAR, BOGHOS
[1851–1930]

Armenian political leader and philanthropist.

Boghos Nubar was born in Alexandria, Egypt. He was the son of Nubar Pasha, the late-nineteenth-century prime minister of Egypt, and nephew and protégé of Boghos Bey Yusufian, his son's namesake and the great minister of Muhammad Ali, the founder of modern Egypt. Boghos Nubar received his training as a civil engineer in France and served as a director of the state railways in Egypt.

In 1906 Boghos Nubar, heir to his father's title and family fortune, took the lead, along with a group of wealthy Armenians in Egypt, to found the Armenian General Benevolent Union (AGBU) in Cairo, Egypt. Growing out of the concern for the tens of thousands of Armenians made destitute by the massive loss of life at Hamidian (1894–1896), the AGBU hoped to support the recovery of the Armenians from the brutalization suffered at the hands of the Ottoman government. Within three years of its founding, the 1909 mass killing of Armenians at Adana precipitated the AGBU to focus its resources in building orphanages, hospitals, and shelters for widows and elderly survivors in the region of Cilicia. The 1915 deportations and killings of Armenians required the AGBU to recommit significant funds to attempt a measure of relief for the entire Ottoman Armenian community now made refugees. The AGBU set up orphanages and clinics all across the Middle East wherever the Armenian refugees concentrated.

Boghos Nubar in Paris headed the Armenian National Delegation to Paris in 1918 to represent the disenfranchised Armenians of the Ottoman Empire with the hope of establishing a national home for them. In France Boghos Nubar was also instrumental in getting the French army to approve the formation under its command of the Legion d'Orient manned mostly by Armenians who saw some fighting in the Allied campaign in Palestine. Though a person of conservative political leanings, with his pedigree Boghos Nubar emerged as the leading spokesman for the Armenians at the Paris Peace Conference.

While the independent Armenian republic was too short-lived to see the AGBU extend its philanthropy to Russian Armenia, in the 1920s the AGBU responded to a disastrous earthquake that struck the city of Leninakan (formerly Alexandropol, currently Gyumri) and stayed to build educational and medical facilities in Soviet Armenia during that decade. Shut out of Armenia after Stalin's rise to power, the AGBU returned to Armenia in December 1988 after another devastating earthquake shattered the same city and the surrounding countryside.

Boghos Nubar died in Paris. Before his death, he had already set the AGBU in a new direction. After the immediate minimum physical needs of the Armenian refugees had been met, he donated funds to the AGBU, and in so doing set an example emulated since by other well-to-do Armenians, for the establishment of educational programs and institutions to begin the moral and intellectual recovery of a generation of Armenians which had known nothing but exile, hunger, and privation. Over the decades the organization founded by Boghos Nubar Pasha grew to become the largest in the Armenian diaspora with chapters around the world supporting schools, orphanages, clinics, libraries, youth centers, theaters, publications, and a host of other activities designed to sustain Armenian culture and identity in diaspora communities.

See also ARMENIAN GENOCIDE; MUHAMMAD ALI; NUBAR PASHA; ORMANIAN, MAGHAKIA; YUSUFIAN, BOGHOS.

Bibliography

Hovannisian, Richard G. *The Republic of Armenia*, Vol. 1: *The First Year 1918–1919*. Berkeley: University of California Press, 1971.

Hovannisian, Richard G. *The Republic of Armenia*, Vol. 2: *From Versailles to London 1919–1920*. Berkeley: University of California Press, 1982.

Walker, Christopher J. *Armenia: The Survival of a Nation*, 2d edition. New York: St. Martin's, 1990.

ROUBEN P. ADALIAN

NUBAR PASHA
[1825–1899]

Legal reformer, cabinet minister, and three-time prime minister of Egypt.

An Armenian born in İzmir, educated in France and Switzerland, Nubar was brought to Egypt by his uncle, who was a translator for Muhammad Ali. Nubar worked for his uncle and his successors. Having learned eleven languages and spent his youth in Europe, he knew how to charm Europeans and often mediated with them on Egypt's behalf, meanwhile making his own fortune. He successfully negotiated with the European powers to gain their consent to set up the mixed courts to try cases between Egyptian and foreign nationals. He presided over the short-lived "European cabinet" set up by Khedive Isma'il in 1878.

Not involved in the Urabi revolution, Nubar returned to power in 1884, at a time when Britain obliged Egypt to give up the Sudan, and led a third cabinet in 1894 and 1895. Clever and subtle as an intermediary between Egypt and Europe, he was both admired and resented by most Egyptians, who accused him (not unjustly) of enriching himself by exploiting his power.

See also ISMA'IL IBN IBRAHIM; MIXED COURTS; MUHAMMAD ALI; URABI, AHMAD.

Bibliography

Bell, C. F. Moberly. *Khedives and Pashas: Sketches of Contemporary Egyptian Rulers and Statesmen*. London: S. Low, 1884.

Hunter, F. Robert. *Egypt under the Khedives, 1805–1979: From Household Government to Modern Bureaucracy*. Pittsburgh, PA: University of Pittsburgh Press, 1984.

Sayyid-Marsot, Afaf Lutfi al-. *Egypt and Cromer: A Study in Anglo–Egyptian Relations*. London: Murray, 1968.

Schölch, Alexander. *Egypt for the Egyptians! The Socio-Political Crisis in Egypt, 1878–1882*. London: Ithaca Press, 1981.

ARTHUR GOLDSCHMIDT

NUBIANS

People of the Nile Valley south of Aswan, at the first cataract extending into the northern Sudan.

Nubia is the land of ancient kingdoms, such as Kush and Meroe, and Christian kingdoms before Islam that rivaled, were controlled by, or entered into peace treaties with Egypt. *Nab* is the ancient Egyptian word for gold, and Nubia was the source of gold for the region. Nubians have been active in trade and politics along the Nile since ancient times. They are renowned boatmen of the Nile River, and were enslavers of people farther south during the eighteenth and nineteenth centuries as well as victims of slavery. Although culturally and linguistically distinct, Nubians' complex history reflects contact with many peoples, including Africans farther south along the Nile, Arabs who conquered North Africa, and Europeans, especially the Greeks who in their early encounter described them as "Aethiopian," or "the people of the burnt faces."

Nubians and their subgroups have a long history linked to the rise of Nile Valley agriculture, states, and urbanism. Nubians straddle the borders of contemporary Egypt and Sudan. Although they speak Arabic, the Nubian language of Rotana and various dialects, such as Kenuz, Sukot, Fadija, Halfawi, and Donglowai, have been retained. Estimates of the number of Nubian speakers range from two hundred thousand to one million; one-quarter live in Egypt and the rest in Sudan. Nubian is generally considered an Eastern Sudanic language, a branch of Nilo-Saharan.

The social status of Nubians varies markedly. In Egypt they are generally identified as Sa'eedi (from the south) and are unskilled laborers, or often doormen, and are considered honest but simple. In Sudan, Arabized Nubians of the north were favored by the British colonialists and are concentrated among the elites. They have held state power since independence in 1956. When the Aswan High Dam was constructed in the 1960s, much of Nubia was flooded, destroying archaeological sites and displacing most Egyptian Nubians, resulting either in their resettlement—in some cases at sites far removed from their historical villages along the Nile—or by moving their homes to higher elevations.

Bibliography

Jennings, Anne. *Nubians of West Aswan.* Boulder, CO: Lynne Rienner, 1995.

"Nubia." In *Historical Dictionary of the Sudan,* edited by Richard A. Lobban, Robert Kramer, and Carolyn Fluehr-Lobban. Lanham, MD: Scarecrow Press, 2002.

ALEYA ROUCHDY
UPDATED BY CAROLYN FLUEHR-LOBBAN

NUCLEAR CAPABILITY AND NUCLEAR ENERGY

Nuclear proliferation in the greater Middle East is a central issue in international affairs.

In the 1990s and into the twenty-first century, the issue of nuclear weapons in the Greater Middle East came to the fore as never before. Several developments played a role in this change: In 1998 nearby India and Pakistan almost simultaneously tested several nuclear weapons each. In 2002 these nations' ongoing conflict over Kashmir brought them close to the nuclear brink. Then came reports of the transfer of nuclear technology and materials from Pakistan to North Korea and perhaps also Iran. Other reports suggested that Pakistan considered its nuclear program to be an "Islamic bomb" enterprise that could provide extended deterrence to Israel's nuclear threat to the Arabs. Israel implied that it would use nuclear weapons if attacked by Iraq with chemical or biological weapons. Also of great concern was the proliferation of various delivery systems—ballistic and cruise missiles, long-range aircraft abetted by aerial refueling—by several states in the region that might be joined to nuclear weapons arsenals. Around the world fears grew that terrorist organizations such as al-Qa'ida might somehow acquire nuclear weapons or materials for a "dirty" nuclear weapon derived from radioactive wastes. There were also increasing fears about Iraq's acquisition of nuclear weapons—a major rationale for the U.S.-led coalition's invasion of Iraq in 2003—and Iran's seemingly imminent development of nuclear weapons.

Israel

Israel was the first of the nations in the region to cross the nuclear threshold. But despite a growing body of writings about the history of its nuclear program, vast gaps remain in what is known about the size of its arsenal, the dates of its initial deployments, and its current command-and-control structure. It appears that the initial decisions to move toward nuclear weapons status were made shortly after the Jewish state was created. Crucial to Israel's nuclear development was its nuclear cooperation with France, which grew out of the two nations' close relations at the time of the 1956 Suez War and continued until 1967–1968. Israel's nuclear development was centered on the French-supplied Dimona reactor, which went into operation around 1961, and continued to produce plutonium despite remonstrances from the Kennedy administration and some limited U.S. inspections.

Israel probably began plutonium separation and the deployment of operational nuclear weapons be-

Patriot antimissile missiles deployed near Israel's nuclear research reactor at Dimona. The Israelis refuse to allow international inspection of the facility, but satellite photographs taken by the Federation of American Scientists in 2000 confirmed that the reactor has the ability to produce 100–200 nuclear warheads. © AP/WIDE WORLD PHOTOS. REPRODUCED BY PERMISSION.

tween the 1967 and 1973 Arab-Israel wars, with the Soviet Union's active involvement in the Suez "war of attrition" (1969–1970) perhaps serving as a final trigger. In 1973 Israel's implicit threats to use nuclear weapons after the initial military setbacks in Sinai and on the Golan Heights appear to have impelled the U.S. arms resupply airlift after initial hesitation.

In 1979 U.S. satellites detected a flash over the southern Indian Ocean that was widely, though not definitively, attributed to an Israeli or joint Israeli-South African nuclear test. In 1986 Mordechai Vanunu, a disaffected Israeli who had worked at the Dimona reactor, leaked voluminous information and photographs that revealed the scope of the Israeli nuclear program. Those disclosures, now widely considered credible, indicated a program consisting of both fission and fusion weapons, involving up to or more than 200 weapons, mounted on de-

livery systems that could cover the entire Middle East. The latter delivery systems included now longer-range Jericho missiles (perhaps up to 1,500 miles), F-16 fighter aircraft with aerial refueling capability, and—perhaps—three diesel submarines purchased from Germany.

Various rationales have been offered for the Israeli nuclear program. The main rationale is that the program serves as a credible deterrent against the threat of an overwhelming Arab conventional force, which some deem inevitable. The size of Israel's program appears to imply the prospective use of tactical nuclear weapons in such a scenario, backed by a threat against cities. Other rationales for the nuclear program are that it offers increased assurance of American arms resupply during crises; it may convince Arab nations of Israel's permanence, thereby nudging them along in the "peace process"; and it may deter involvement in the Arab-

Israeli conflict by powerful peripheral nations such as Iran, Pakistan, and Turkey, the latter semi-allied to Israel.

Iraq

Iraq's initial efforts to become the second Middle Eastern nuclear power were thwarted by Israel's bombing of the Osirak reactor in Baghdad in 1981. During the subsequent decade, Iraq allegedly built a clandestine nuclear infrastructure with the aid of numerous Western suppliers of relevant technologies, most notably that of gas centrifuges. That operation apparently was vastly underestimated by Western intelligence services, and the full scope of the program was revealed only in the wake of Iraq's defeat in the Gulf War of 1991 and its subsequent submission to United Nations inspections, which appear to have resulted in the dismantling of part of Iraq's nuclear infrastructure. In the aftermath of the 2003 invasion, however, the status of the Iraqi nuclear program was unclear. Little evidence was found. Various analysts suggested that intelligence reports had overstated the program; that it was well hidden by the Saddam regime; or that prior to the invasion it had been dismantled or the evidence moved to Syria or elsewhere outside of Iraq.

Iran, Algeria, and Libya

Since the end of the Iran-Iraq War in 1988 and subsequent to the Gulf War, Iran is widely believed to have embarked on an energetic effort to acquire nuclear weapons. That effort is centered on its nuclear research complex at Isfahan. Reports suggest extensive outside assistance, particularly from Pakistan and perhaps from China and Russia. There are reports of work on centrifuge technology, and on plutonium production reactors. Israel in particular dreads the possible advent of an Iranian nuclear weapons program that would include long-range missiles capable of reaching Israel.

During the latter part of the shah's reign, Iran embarked on a program to build several nuclear reactors. One was nearly completed by a West German firm. In 2003 Iran was negotiating with Russia over the building of four new reactors, plans that were fiercely opposed by the United States. One reactor, at Bushehr, is apparently under construction.

Algeria has acquired a small nuclear reactor, causing anxiety in Western Europe over the threat that Islamic fundamentalism could lead to a European-Algerian conflict. Libya reportedly has made efforts to acquire nuclear weapons or technology, but to no avail. In December 2003, Libya announced the cessation of all of its nuclear, chemical, and biological weapons programs.

Conclusion

The vast oil and gas resources of the Middle East presumably render almost superfluous the acquisition of nuclear power reactors for peaceful purposes. Statements about generating electricity appear to provide rhetorical cover for intended nuclear weapons programs.

Nuclear disarmament is unlikely to be achieved in the region in the foreseeable future. Israel clearly sees nuclear deterrence as vital to its survival. It could not conceivably abandon its stockpile unless Pakistan did so as well, which would require India also to disarm, and thus also China, the United States, and Russia. That is a daunting row of dominoes.

See also DIMONA.

Bibliography

Aronson, Shlomo. *The Politics and Strategy of Nuclear Weapons in the Middle East.* Albany: State University of New York Press, 1992.

Burrows, William E., and Windrem, Robert. *Critical Mass: The Dangerous Race for Superweapons in a Fragmenting World.* New York: Simon and Schuster, 1994.

Cohen, Avner. *Israel and the Bomb.* New York: Columbia University Press, 1998.

Cordesman, Anthony. *Weapons of Mass Destruction in the Middle East.* Washington, DC: Center for Strategic and International Studies, 2003.

Feldman, Shai. *Israeli Nuclear Deterrence: A Strategy for the 1980s.* New York: Columbia University Press, 1982.

Hersh, Seymour. *The Samson Option: Israel's Nuclear Arsenal and American Foreign Policy.* New York: Random House, 1991.

Jones, Rodney W., McDonough, Mark G., et al. *Tracking Nuclear Proliferation: A Guide in Maps and Charts, 1998.* Washington, DC: Carnegie Endowment for International Peace, 1998.

Khan, Saira. *Nuclear Proliferation Dynamics in Protracted Conflict Regions: A Comparative Study of South Asia and the Middle East.*

Aldershot, U.K., and Burlington, VT: Ashgate, 2002.

Peimani, Hooman. *Nuclear Proliferation in the Indian Subcontinent: The Self-Exhausting "Superpowers" and Emerging Alliances.* Westport, CT: Praeger, 2000.

Sagan, Scott D., and Waltz, Kenneth N. *The Spread of Nuclear Weapons: A Debate Renewed.* New York: Norton, 2003.

ROBERT E. HARKAVY

NUER

People who live along the Nile in Sudan.

The Nuer, who call themselves the Nath, and their associated subgroup the Atuot are among the most numerous of the southern Sudanese Nilotic peoples. They live in the swamps and open savannas on both sides of the Nile south of Malakal in Sudan but have been seriously disrupted by protracted civil war in southern Sudan, waged most intensively since 1983. Culturally, they have a common origin with the Dinka, with common ties of pastoralism, intermarriage, and cultural borrowings. Periodic rivalries and conflicts have also characterized this relationship, including conflicts related to the resistance of the Sudan's People's Liberation Movement to the national government in Khartoum. The Nuer were the last of the Sudanese people to submit to British rule, and then only after a substantial military campaign in 1930, known as the Nuer Settlement. In more recent times the Nuer, some of whom have become well educated and politically active, have played an aggressive role in the southern Sudanese insurgency movement and remain the dominant military force in Nuerland.

See also DINKA; SUDANESE CIVIL WARS.

Bibliography

Collins, Robert O. *Shadows in the Grass: Britain in Southern Sudan, 1918–1956.* New Haven, CT: Yale University Press, 1983.

"Nuer." In *Historical Dictionary of the Sudan,* edited by Richard A. Lobban, Robert S. Kramer, and Carolyn Fluehr-Lobban. Lanham, MD: Scarecrow Press, 2002.

ROBERT O. COLLINS
UPDATED BY CAROLYN FLUEHR-LOBBAN

NUMEIRI, MUHAMMAD JA'FAR
[1930–]

Military leader; president of Sudan.

Muhammad Ja'far Numeiri (Nimeiri, Numairi, Numayri) was born at Wad Nubaw'i, a suburb of Omdurman, Sudan. After education at the local Qur'anic school, El Hijra Elementary School, the Medani Government School, and the Hantoub Secondary School, he entered military college in 1949 and graduated as a second lieutenant in 1952. Thereafter, Numeiri served in the Western Command and the armored corps stationed at Shendi. He became a great admirer of Gamal Abdel Nasser's pan-Arab revolution, a view reinforced by training in Egypt and by his arrest and suspension from duty (1957–1959) after supporting the abortive coup by Abd al-Rahman Kabediya. He later served in Juba, in southern Sudan, and in Khartoum, where he proved troublesome and consequently was sent on military training courses to Cyprus, Libya, West Germany, and Egypt. Numeiri returned to play an active role in the overthrow of the government of his superior, General Ibrahim Abbud, in October 1964, which resulted in his arrest and transfer to the American Command School at Fort Leavenworth, Kansas. Upon his return to Sudan he was implicated in another abortive coup but once again survived to be given a more sedentary position as commanding officer of the military school in Khartoum.

Stationed in the capital, Numeiri was able to plot and successfully carry out a military coup on 25 May 1969 against the government of Isma'il al-Azhari, whom he replaced with his Revolutionary Command Council (RCC), an imitation of Nasser's revolutionary command council of 1952. The first challenge to his regime came from the Ansar (Mahdists) in March 1970. The Sudan army assaulted the historic sanctuary of the Mahdi and his Ansar at Aba Island, 150 miles south of Khartoum, decisively defeating the rebels and killing the spiritual leader of the Ansar, the Imam al-Hadi.

The second and more serious challenge came from the Communist Party (SCP) of Sudan. The Communists had originally been represented in the RCC and, emboldened by their success, sought to seize control of the government by a coup d'état on 19 July 1971. After a bloody struggle lasting three

Muhammad Ja'far Numeiri (second from right) with Libyan leader Muammar al-Qaddafi in 1970. During Numeiri's presidency, relations between Libya and the Sudan fluctuated, largely due to Sudan's improving relations with Egypt. Diplomatic relations between the two countries were severed for several years in the 1970s, and only began to make steady improvement after Numeiri was out of power. © BETTMANN/CORBIS. REPRODUCED BY PERMISSION.

days, Numeiri prevailed. The Communist leaders were promptly executed, the party prorogued, and its organization in the Sudan dismantled. Having defeated his enemies on both the right and the left, he called for a plebiscite that elected him president of the Sudan, after which he dissolved the RCC and established the Sudanese Socialist Union (SSU) as the single ruling party.

Having consolidated his control in northern Sudan, Numeiri turned to the seventeen-year civil war with the southern Sudanese. He and the respected southerner, Abel Alier, brought the war to a conclusion after negotiations with the Anya-Nya southern insurgents at Addis Ababa on 27 February 1972. The Addis Ababa Accords granted a limited autonomy to southern Sudan, but the means of its implementation and preservation were never clear. At the time it was an extraordinary achieve-

ment whereby one of the most destructive civil wars in Africa seemed to have been peacefully resolved. Numeiri basked in an outpouring of international acclaim for his statesmanship. With Sudan at peace, he enjoyed ten years of complete authority marred, however, by his growing isolation from the Sudanese, whose frustration erupted in several abortive attempts to overthrow him. These halcyon years were accompanied by an economic boom that resulted from Numeiri's encouragement of foreign investment in Sudanese agriculture to transform Sudan into the "breadbasket" of the Middle East. Large tracts of land, much of it marginal, were seized by the state, which displaced Sudanese farmers and herdsmen for Sudanese and Middle Eastern entrepreneurs anxious to reap quick profits from large mechanized agricultural schemes. Numeiri also sought, with little success, to establish a rapprochement and national unity with Sadiq al-

Mahdi and his Ansar, whom he had savagely defeated in 1970.

These initiatives were accompanied by a change in his lifestyle and ideology. Abandoning the habits of a tough soldier, Numeiri in the late 1970s became engrossed in rigorous interpretation of Islam at a time when there were endless political disagreements with the southern Sudanese and a decline in the nation's economic prosperity. He came increasingly under the influence of the Sudanese Islamists led by Hasan al-Turabi who were determined to transform Sudan into an Islamist state from the secular one of Ja'far Numeiri. He misperceived that the increasingly influential National Islamic Front (NIF) were more dependable political allies than the southern Sudanese. In October 1981, after a series of strikes and demonstrations precipitated by the declining economy, he dismissed the National Assembly and the leadership of the SSU. Next, he unilaterally repudiated the Addis Ababa Agreement by dissolving the southern Regional Assembly and imposing his own Council for the Unity of the Southern Sudan.

The rapid deterioration of his popularity was hastened by the introduction in September 1983 of *shari'a* (Islamic law), which would apply to all Sudanese, Muslim and non-Muslim, in its restrictions on individual behavior and its draconian penalties for petty offenses. This led to criticism from both Muslims and non-Muslims, dismay among the northern Sudanese, and the revival of the civil war in southern Sudan in May 1983, led by Colonel John Garang de Mabior and his Sudan People's Liberation Army (SPLA).

Numeiri declared a state of emergency. His adoption of the Islamist religious policies and stringent economic decrees produced serious riots throughout the cities of northern Sudan. He left Khartoum for the United States to seek additional financial assistance. While in Washington, D.C., on 6 April 1985, he was deposed in a bloodless coup d'état led by his chief of staff, Lieutenant General Suwar al-Dhahab, a Muslim Brother. Numeiri traveled from Washington to Cairo, where he was granted asylum and kept in house confinement for eleven years, until President Bashir allowed him to return to Sudan in May 1999. He received a spontaneous reception at the airport but has been told to live in quiet retirement.

See also ABBUD, IBRAHIM; ANSAR, AL-; SUDANESE CIVIL WARS; TURABI, HASAN AL-.

Bibliography

Alier, Abel. *Southern Sudan: Too Many Agreements Dishonoured.* Exeter, U.K.: Ithaca Press, 1990.

Khalid, Mansour. *Nimeiri and the Revolution of Dis-May.* London: Kegan Paul, 1985.

Malwal, Bona. *People and Power in Sudan: The Struggle for National Stability.* London: Ithaca Press, 1981.

ROBERT O. COLLINS

NUMISMATICS

The study of coins and related objects.

Numismatics is an ancillary science to history that seeks to identify coins as to place, date, and government of issue so that the inscriptions, images, and other features of the coins can be used as evidence for political, economic, social, and cultural history. For archaeologists, coins are the most consistently datable evidence. Islamic coins produced in Muslim countries and similar coins sometimes issued by non-Muslims are especially useful for historical research—nearly all were inscribed with their city and date of issue and usually (according to the tradition of Islam) did not have images. This left space for long inscriptions, including the names and titles of the rulers under whom they were issued and something of their religious beliefs.

As a field of study, numismatics began during the European Renaissance as part of the general rediscovery of the classical world. Muslim historians did not use coins as historical evidence, although occasionally an extraordinary issue might be mentioned or described. More often they noted changes in the monetary system of their countries, and some writers, notably al-Baladhuri in the ninth century and al-Maqrizi in the first half of the fifteenth century, wrote brief treatises on monetary history. A few descriptions of mint operation were written as well as a few disquisitions on monetary theory, of which the most interesting is by the great historian Ibn Khaldun of fifteenth-century Egypt.

Some Islamic coins were noted in passing in works on other subjects, but the first study of Islamic numismatics was a twenty-page article in 1759.

The first catalog of an Italian Islamic collection was published by Adler in 1782, followed by Assemani's catalog of a collection in Padua in 1787 and Tychsen's catalog of the Göttingen collection in 1787/88. Catalogs of public and private collections continued to be published throughout the nineteenth century, culminating at the end of the century in the great catalogs of the national collections of England, France, Germany, and Russia. Stanley Lane-Poole's ten-volume set of the British Museum Islamic coins (1875–1890) continues to be a standard reference, partly because of his excellent scholarship and also because it was the only complete catalog of any collection (the British Museum has acquired many more coins since that time). His introductions to the volumes, describing the history and coinage of each Muslim dynasty, are still useful. Lavoix's three massive volumes on the collection of the Bibliothèque Nationale, in Paris, and Nützel's two volumes on the collection of the Königliche Museum, in Berlin, are also standard references. Markov's catalog of the Hermitage collection, in St. Petersburg, is less used because the inscriptions are brief, the work is difficult to find in the West, and it is reproduced directly from his Russian manuscript.

A major impetus to European numismatic research on Islamic coins in the countries from Scandinavia through the Baltic states and into Russia has been the immense quantities of seventh-to-tenth-century Islamic silver coins brought to those countries and buried by the Vikings. Stockholm is one major center for this study, beginning with Tornberg's several catalogs and studies from 1846 to 1870, and culminating with the great *Corpus Nummorum Saeculorum IX–XI,* a collective project to publish (first volume 1975) all the Islamic (and English and German) silver coins of the Viking age that were found in Sweden. The other major center for such study, founded by C. M. Fraehn, was St. Petersburg. His works, beginning in 1808, were important not only for Russian numismatists but for scholars throughout Europe. In particular, he devised a scheme for the arrangement of the Islamic coin-issuing dynasties that was followed, with subsequent modifications, by most Islamic numismatists until recently. Russia's numismatic research was also impelled by Russian interest in the coinage of its newly conquered territories in the Caucasus and central Asia.

Toward the end of the nineteenth century, the leading Russian scholars were Markov, mentioned previously, and Tiesenhausen, who published the only general corpus of Abbasid coins produced to date (a corpus attempts to assemble all known coins of a historical period or place, whereas a catalog is limited to the coins of a single collection or several related collections). Perhaps the most brilliant scholar of the Russian school, Vasmer, was executed in 1938. Numismatic scholarship remained active in the Soviet Union, however, with major centers in Leningrad, Moscow, and the cities of Muslim central Asia.

Islamic numismatics has an early history in Spain, since the coinage of the Arabs there (the Moors) was part of that country's heritage from 711 to 1492. Vives's catalog of all Muslim Spanish issues remains a standard reference. George Miles founded Islamic numismatics at the American Numismatic Society in New York City, which remains one of the principal centers for the field. In 1989, Tübingen University, in Germany, acquired an extremely important collection of Islamic coins and has begun to develop a center for research and training.

The Turks of the Ottoman Empire were the first people of the Middle East to join in numismatic research, publishing in European journals as early as 1862. At the turn of the century, the Müzei Humayun (Imperial Museum) published a series of major catalogs in Ottoman Turkish that rank in importance with the productions of the large European museums. This promising beginning was halted by World War I and the series was never finished. Europeans living in Arab countries produced various works of significance during the first part of the twentieth century, but few Arabs contributed until the demise of the Ottoman Empire and the establishment of some Arab states.

Abd al-Rahman Fahmi produced several important catalogs and studies based on the collection of the Museum of Islamic Art, in Cairo, and Nasir al-Naqshbandi founded a school of numismatists in Baghdad, where the Iraq Museum is a major center for research with a journal devoted to Islamic coins called *al-Maskukat.* The Damascus Museum, in Syria, also has an active collection, and its late curator, Muhammad Abu al-Faraj al-Ush, produced several important works. Recently the Bank al-Maghrib of

Rabat, Morocco, has created a numismatic center and published two major corpora of Moroccan coins by Daniel Eustache. Some public collections were built in Iran in the 1970s, but little has been published there. In Jordan, a center for numismatic research has been established at Yarmuk University with private support; a journal, *Yarmouk Numismatics,* was founded there.

The real explosion in Islamic numismatics began in the 1970s as a result of the new wealth brought by Organization of Petroleum Exporting Countries (OPEC) oil. Many private collectors in the Gulf countries began to bid up the price of Islamic coins, and the interest generated by rising prices led to great collector interest in Europe, the Americas, and Japan. This, as well as the expansion of Islamic studies in the West, has made the field extremely active.

See also ORGANIZATION OF PETROLEUM EXPORTING COUNTRIES (OPEC).

Bibliography

Album, Stephen. *A Checklist of Islamic Coins,* 2d edition. Santa Rosa, CA: Author, 1998.

Bates, Michael L. *Islamic Coins.* ANS Handbook 2. New York, 1982.

Bates, Michael L. "Islamic Numismatics," *Middle East Studies Association Bulletin* 12, no. 2 (May 1978): 1–16; 12, no. 3 (December 1978): 2–18; 13, no. 1 (July 1979): 3–21; 13, no. 2 (December 1979): 1–9.

Broome, Michael. *A Handbook of Islamic Coins.* London: Seaby, 1985.

Krause, Chester L., and Mishler, Clifford. *Standard Catalog of World Coins.* Iola, WI: Krause, annual editions.

Mayer, L. A. *Bibliography of Muslem Numismatics, India Excepted,* 2d edition. London: Royal Asiatic Society, 1954.

Mitchiner, Michael. *Oriental Coins and Their Values.* 3 vols. London: Hawkins, 1977.

MICHAEL L. BATES

NUQRASHI, MAHMUD FAHMI AL-
[1888–1948]

Egyptian educator and politician.

Mahmud Fahmi al-Nuqrashi was educated in Alexandria and at Nottingham University, England. When he returned to Egypt, he taught school, then was promoted in the administration until he became director of public instruction for Asyut. A Wafd supporter, he became vice-governor of Cairo, then deputy interior minister under Sa'd Zaghlul. Implicated in Sir Lee Stack's murder, he was briefly imprisoned and then cleared.

Nuqrashi held ministerial positions in the Wafdist cabinets of 1930 and 1936 but broke with Mustafa al-Nahhas in 1937. With Ahmad Mahir, he formed the Sa'dist Party, which took part in several non-Wafdist coalition governments. After Ahmad Mahir was assassinated in 1945, Nuqrashi became the leader of the Sa'dist Party and headed cabinets in 1945 and 1946 and from 1946 to 1948. He led the 1947 Egyptian delegation to the United Nations (UN) Security Council to demand that Britain withdraw from Sudan and allow it to unite with Egypt, but he did not gain UN support. When the State of Israel was declared in May 1948 and the Arabs attacked Israel, Nuqrashi reportedly tried to delay committing Egyptian troops, but he was overridden by Egypt's King Farouk. As setbacks to the Arab forces led to rising discontent within Egypt, he tried to outlaw the Society of Muslim Brothers (the Muslim Brotherhood). He was assassinated by a student member of that society on 28 December 1948.

See also FAROUK; MAHIR, AHMAD; MUSLIM BROTHERHOOD; NAHHAS, MUSTAFA AL-; STACK, LEE; WAFD; ZAGHLUL, SA'D.

ARTHUR GOLDSCHMIDT

NURCU

See NURSI, SAID

NURI, ABD AL-MALIK
[1921–1992?]

Iraqi author.

Abd al-Malik Nuri, one of the most gifted writers of fiction in modern Iraq, was born in Baghdad. He studied law, graduating in 1944. Concurrently he showed an interest in contemporary fiction, especially that of James Joyce. His first collection of short stories, *Rusul al-Insaniyya* (Baghdad, 1946; Messengers of humanity) contains stories in a naturalist vein, expressing sympathy with the underdogs of

Baghdad society. His second volume, *Nashid al-Ard* (1954; The song of the earth) inaugurated a new phase in the language and techniques of modern fiction in Iraq. Stream-of-consciousness is judiciously employed, and the exterior movement that characterizes earlier stories is replaced by an internal flow of thoughts and emotions.

In 1972, Nuri published a short allegorical play, *Khashab wa Mukhmal* (Wood and velvet); his third and last collection of short stories to date, *Dhuyul al-Kharif* (Autumn's tails), appeared in 1980.

Like many other Iraqi intellectuals, Nuri was attracted to leftist ideas, especially in the 1940s. In subsequent years his political commitment seems to have declined markedly. Like several other Iraqi novelists of his generation (e.g., his close friend Fu'ad Takarli), Nuri wrote the dialogue of his stories in the vernacular of Baghdad rather than in *fusha*, the literary language of Arabic writing. This gave his stories a distinctive local color but made it difficult for readers outside Iraq to understand his works fully. In his drama, however, he used *fusha*.

See also LITERATURE: ARABIC.

Bibliography

Badawi, M. M., ed. *Modern Arabic Literature.* Cambridge, U.K., and New York: Cambridge University Press, 1992.

SASSON SOMEKH

NURI, FAZLOLLAH
[c. 1842–1909]

Iranian religious scholar, important for his objections to Western-style constitutionalism during the revolution of 1906–1909.

After completing his preliminary religious studies in Iran, Nuri traveled to Iraq to study with the great authorities of Shi'ite Islam, such as Mirza Hasan Shirazi. Returning to Iran in 1883, he soon established himself as the most influential religious leader of Tehran, controlling several theological colleges. When the Constitutional Revolution began in 1907, Nuri initially collaborated with his colleagues who favored the cause. He soon began to turn his weight against the movement, however, claiming that its original aim—the implementation

of *shari'a* (Islamic law)—had been subverted by the emergence of unbelievers among the constitutionalists. In protest, in July 1907, Nuri withdrew from Tehran to a nearby shrine where he began publishing broadsheets that denounced constitutionalism as a European import, incompatible with Islam, and he called for a form of constitutional government more in accord with Islam. He objected in particular to concepts such as parliament possessing the right to legislate, the legal equality of Muslims and non-Muslims, and the unqualified freedom of the press. When in June 1908 the parliament was closed down by a royalist coup, Nuri effectively sided with the shah, although he continued to advocate his own concept of an Islamic-style constitution. In July 1909, the parliamentary regime was restored, and Nuri was executed at the end of the month. His violent end caused revulsion even among the constitutionalist religious scholars and contributed heavily to a disillusion with political involvement that was to last several decades.

See also CONSTITUTIONAL REVOLUTION.

Bibliography

Arjomand, S. A. "The Ulama's Traditionalist Opposition to Parliamentarianism: 1907–1909." *Middle Eastern Studies* (1981).

HAMID ALGAR

NURSI, SAID
[1876–1960]

Influential religious writer in Turkey who advocated the compatibility of Islam and modern science.

Said Nursi was born in a Kurdish village, Nurs, in Bitlis province. He had a traditional religious education with different Sufi orders but was primarily self-educated. He worked to revitalize Islamic faith and Muslim society through raising religious consciousness. In 1907 he went to Istanbul to ask Sultan Abdülhamit II to establish a university in Van that would reconcile scientific reasoning with Islam. He was disappointed in the sultan's response and critical of his use of Islam for political purposes. Nursi developed close ties with the Young Turks movement before the 1908 revolution, but its later political agenda disillusioned him, and he joined the radical Islamic Muhammad Union. He was charged with joining the April 1908 counterrevolution but was acquitted, and then returned to eastern Anatolia. Nursi shifted his strategy from political to religious activism and focused on individual consciousness through activist piety. During the World War I occupation of eastern Anatolia he fought against Russian troops and became a prisoner of war, serving two years in Russia. He supported the War of Independence under the leadership of Mustafa Kemal (later Atatürk), but eventually became disenchanted with Atatürk's radical secular agenda and withdrew from politics to contemplative writing. Nursi was charged with complicity in the 1925 Kurdish rebellion and sent to exile to Isparta. In the following years he was arrested many times and tried for his alleged political use of Islam. These trials led to further exiles, to Eskisehir (1935), Kastamonu (1936), Denizli (1943), and Emirdag, near Afyon (1944). Only after the Democrat Party came to power in 1950 did his exile come to an end.

Nursi's collection of essays constitute the *Risale-i Nur* (Epistle of light), which seeks to raise religious consciousness to arm Muslims with new moral and scientific ideas to preserve and expand their Islamic identity in society. His disciples are known in Turkish as *Nurcus,* the followers of Nursi. The *Risale-i Nur* initially was copied by hand for distribution because neither Nursi nor his disciples could afford the printing costs, and before the 1950s they also lacked the freedom to print religious texts. The main concern in his writings is the negative impact of positivist ideas in terms of the "moral and spiritual destruction" of Muslim believers, and of society as a whole. His goal was to rebuild the moral charter of Islamic ethics out of the Qur'an. For Nursi, this moral charter was necessary to control the dangerous appetites of people and to provide for the higher pursuit of human perfection.

See also ABDÜLHAMIT II; ANATOLIA; ATATÜRK, MUSTAFA KEMAL; DEMOCRAT PARTY; QUR'AN; YOUNG TURKS.

Bibliography

Yavuz, M. Hakan. *Islamic Political Identity in Turkey.* Oxford, U.K.: Oxford University Press, 2003.

NICO LANDMAN
UPDATED BY M. HAKAN YAVUZ

NUSAYBA FAMILY

Prominent Palestinian family from Jerusalem that traces its roots in the Old City to ancient times.

According to tradition, the Nusayba family took its name from a woman named Nusayba, who went to the Prophet Muhammad with a delegation of women and complained to him about the unfair treatment they received. Since the Muslim conquest of Jerusalem in the seventh century, the Sunni Muslim Nusayba (also Nuseibeh) family has held the keys of the Church of the Holy Sepulchre. This arrangement emerged during the days of the second Muslim caliph, Umar, who hoped to avoid clashes among rival Christian dominations for control over the church. Although symbolic, the arrangement has provided the Nusayba family a visible role in Christian activities in Jerusalem, which include pilgrimages and visits by Western Christians.

Notable members of the family have included Anwar Nusayba (1913–1986), who received a master's degree from Queen's College in Cambridge. His political career began as a member of the Arab Higher Committee in 1946 and secretary general of the All-Palestine Government in 1948. He was the chief Arab delegate on the Jordan and Israel Mixed Armistice Commission in 1951, and held ministerial posts in Jordan, including defense in 1953 and education in 1954 and 1955. He was made governor of the Jerusalem province from 1961 to 1963 and later served as Jordan's ambassador to the United Kingdom.

Hazem (also Hazim) Nusayba (1922–) studied at the American University of Beirut and later received a Ph.D. from Princeton University in 1945. He became a Jordanian diplomat, serving as foreign minister from 1962 to 1963 and again in 1965, as an ambassador, and as Jordan's longtime ambassador to the United Nations (1976–1985).

Sari Nusayba (1949–) obtained his bachelor's degree from Oxford University in 1971 and his doctorate from Harvard University in 1978. After teaching at Bir Zeit University from 1978 to 1988, he went on to serve as president of al-Quds University in Jerusalem. Sari has also been known for his outspoken and moderate political views. A supporter of al-Fatah, Nusayba helped organize secret talks in 1987 between the Israeli government and

Faysal Husayni, Fatah's leading figure in the West Bank. He has supported the peace process, serving on the steering committee to the Palestinian delegation at the Madrid Conference in 1991 and proposing joint Palestinian-Israeli plans for the future resolution of the conflict.

See also FATAH, AL-; MADRID CONFERENCE.

Bibliography

Fischbach, Michael R. "Nuseibeh Family." In *Encyclopedia of the Palestinians,* edited by Philip Mattar. New York: Facts on File, 2000.

Heller, Mark, and Nusseibeh, Sari. *No Trumpets, No Drums: A Two-State Settlement of the Israeli-Palestinian Conflict.* New York: Hill and Wang, 1991.

Muslih, Muhammad Y. *The Origins of Palestinian Nationalism.* New York: Columbia University Press, 1988.

LAWRENCE TAL
UPDATED BY MICHAEL R. FISCHBACH

NUSEIBEH FAMILY

See NUSAYBA FAMILY

NUTEG-NURI, ALI AKBAR

See NATEQ-NURI, ALI AKBAR

NUUN MAGAZINE

Arabic-language feminist quarterly magazine published in Egypt by the Arab Women's Solidarity Association.

Members of the Arab Women's Solidarity Organization (AWSA) suggested during its 1988 conference the creation of a magazine that would raise public awareness about women's issues. The first issue of *Nuun* (also *Nun*) appeared on 1 May 1989, and was originally distributed only to AWSA members due to limitations imposed by the Egyptian government on the distribution of materials published by nongovernmental organizations.

The magazine was concerned with the promotion of the general goals of AWSA: equality between the sexes, the advancement of women's rights and the promotion of cooperation between women, and the defense of democracy, development, and independence in the Arab world from a progressive feminist standpoint. *Nuun* aimed to serve as a forum in which Arab women could exchange views and experiences, and to promote a new consciousness about the liberation of Arab women. The name originated from the Arabic expression *nun al-nisa,* which refers to the formation of the feminine plural in the Arabic language. Because of its antitraditionalist, feminist, and progressive stance, the magazine confronted numerous attempts to curtail its dissemination. In 1991 the Egyptian government closed down the magazine for opposing Egypt's role as an ally of the United States during the Gulf War.

See also ARAB WOMEN'S SOLIDARITY ASSOCIATION INTERNATIONAL; GENDER: GENDER AND POLITICS; NEWSPAPERS AND PRINT MEDIA: ARAB COUNTRIES.

Bibliography

Sadawi, Nawal. *A Daughter of Isis: The Autobiography of Nawal El Saadawi.* London and New York: Zed Books, 1999.

VANESA CASANOVA-FERNANDEZ

OASIS

See GLOSSARY

OASIS GROUP

Consortium of three U.S. oil companies in Libya.

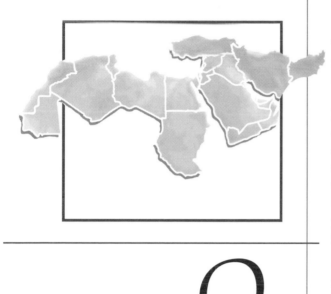

O

The Oasis Group (originally the Conorada Group) is a consortium composed of three U.S. "independent" oil companies: Amerada (now Amerada Hess), Continental (now ConocoPhillips), and Marathon. Bidding independently, the companies won concessions throughout Libya during the first auction of oil rights in 1955. Following the concession awards, the Oasis companies pooled their acquisitions. By 1965, when Libya opened a second round of concession bidding, Oasis was the number two producer of oil in Libya, bringing in more than 300,000 barrels per day.

Beginning in mid-1970, Libya's militant postrevolutionary government threatened to limit or halt oil production in selected concessions unless their owners agreed to higher prices. Two weeks after Occidental Petroleum capitulated to this pressure, the Oasis Group followed suit. The government continued its pressure on foreign oil companies. It nationalized part of Oasis, amounting to 51 percent by 1973.

Meanwhile, U.S. relations with Libya deteriorated steadily, reaching a nadir in 1986 when the United States imposed economic sanctions as part of President Ronald Reagan's declaration of war against terrorism. The Oasis partners were three of only five U.S. oil companies to retain properties in Libya after sanctions were imposed, by that time amounting to only 40.8 percent of Oasis. In 1992 the addition of United Nations sanctions further dimmed prospects for U.S. oil companies hoping to resume operations in Libya.

UN sanctions ended in 1999, following the Libyan government's surrender of suspects in the Lockerbie bombing of Pan Am flight 103. The ending of sanctions brought foreign oil companies back to Libya, but continuing U.S. sanctions prevented U.S. companies from returning. Despite energetic lobbying, Congress passed a five-year extension of U.S. sanctions in August 2001, and Libya remains on the State Department list of countries accused of sponsoring international terror. Oasis companies continue their efforts to be allowed to resume operations in Libya. They face the prospect of losing their properties if the Libyan government decides that progress in negotiations with the United States to end the sanctions is unlikely to bear fruit. A large number of foreign companies are eager to acquire concessions in Libya and could bid on the Oasis properties if and when they are re-tendered by the Libyan government.

See also LIBYA; OCCIDENTAL PETROLEUM; PE-TROLEUM, OIL, AND NATURAL GAS; PETRO-LEUM RESERVES AND PRODUCTION.

Bibliography

Rand, Christopher T. *Making Democracy Safe for Oil: Oilmen and the Islamic East.* Boston: Little, Brown, 1975.

Sampson, Anthony. *The Seven Sisters: The Great Oil Companies and the World They Shaped.* New York: Viking, 1975.

Tétreault, Mary Ann. *Revolution in the World Petroleum Market.* Westport, CT: Greenwood Press, 1985.

Wardell, Simon. "Middle East: Scaling Back Energy Investment." *World Markets in Focus 2002—Energy.* London: World Markets Research Centre, 2002.

MARY ANN TÉTREAULT

OCCIDENTAL PETROLEUM

U.S. firm active in Libya.

Occidental Petroleum was a small, nearly bankrupt company when it was purchased in 1956 by Armand Hammer, a Russian-born American entrepreneur. Occidental won oil concessions in Libya during the 1965 bidding round and struck oil shortly afterward. Within two years, Occidental had become a major shipper of oil to Europe as a result of the abundance and quality of Libya's oil, and the closure of the Suez Canal during the Arab-Israel War of 1967.

Occidental's dependence on Libya made it a prime target for "the Libyan squeeze." The government of Muammar al-Qaddafi, who took over Libya in a bloodless coup in 1969, ordered Occidental to cut back production for refusing to agree to higher oil prices. Within three months, Hammer agreed to pay 30 cents more per barrel as well as a higher rate of taxes. Other companies followed his lead, touching off the oil price revolution of the early 1970s.

Although Occidental produced oil elsewhere, it kept its operations in Libya despite the nationalization in 1973 of 51 percent of its holdings. In 1985 Occidental sold 21 percent of its Libyan equity to the Austrian firm OMV.

In 1986 U.S. economic sanctions against Libya ordered all U.S. firms operating there to halt their activities. These sanctions were augmented in 1992 by U.N. sanctions imposed in retaliation for Libya's refusal to extradite two suspects in the December 1988 bombing of a Pan American flight over Lockerbie, Scotland. In 1999 U.N. sanctions were lifted, but two years later, the U.S. Congress voted to renew U.S. sanctions for five additional years. Despite Occidental's close ties with high-level members of the U.S. presidential administrations of Bill Clinton and George W. Bush, it was unable to have Libya removed from the State Department's list of countries supporting international terrorism. The Clinton administration did allow Occidental to survey its abandoned production facilities in 1999. Despite its success in getting the Bush administration to expand its support for the drug war in Colombia (which, incidentally, protects its operations there), Occidental has been unable to get permission to resume operating in Libya. As the prospects for the return of U.S. oil companies to Libya continue to dim, Occidental risks the loss of its Libyan holdings. Should the Libyan government ever implement its September 2001 ultimatum that Occidental and the other four U.S. companies with oil interests in Libya resume operations there, they would face the revocation of their concessions.

See also ARAB–ISRAEL WAR (1967); LIBYA; PE-TROLEUM, OIL, AND NATURAL GAS; PETRO-LEUM RESERVES AND PRODUCTION; QADDAFI, MUAMMAR AL-; SUEZ CANAL.

Bibliography

Mobbs, Philip M. "The Mineral Industry of Libya—2001." Available from <http://minerals.usgs.gov/minerals.>

Rand, Christopher T. *Making Democracy Safe for Oil: Oilmen and the Islamic East.* Boston: Little, Brown, 1975.

Sampson, Anthony. *The Seven Sisters: The Great Oil Companies and the World They Shaped.* New York: Viking, 1975.

Tétreault, Mary Ann. *Revolution in the World Petroleum Market.* Westport, CT: Greenwood Press, 1985.

MARY ANN TÉTREAULT

OCTOBER

See NEWSPAPERS AND PRINT MEDIA: ARAB COUNTRIES

OGLU

See GLOSSARY

OIL EMBARGO (1973–1974)

Arab nations' reduced oil production in response to the Arab-Israel War of 1973.

Members of the Organization of Arab Petroleum Exporting Countries (OAPEC) decided in late October 1973 to cut oil production by 25 percent until Israel withdrew to the 1949 armistice lines. OAPEC also decided to cut off oil to the United States and the Netherlands to protest U.S. military and Dutch political support for Israel. Exempted from the boycott were France, Spain, Muslim countries, and Great Britain (conditionally). The remaining countries divided whatever oil was left between them. The result was a fourfold increase in the price of oil. The embargo was lifted in March 1974.

See also ORGANIZATION OF ARAB PETROLEUM EXPORTING COUNTRIES (OAPEC).

Bibliography

Yergin, Daniel. *The Prize: The Epic Quest for Oil, Money, and Power.* New York: Simon and Schuster, 1993.

BRYAN DAVES

OLIVES

See FOOD: OLIVES

OMAN

Arabian Peninsula sultanate formerly known as Muscat and Oman.

Oman, officially the Sultanate of Oman since 1970, extends some 1,000 miles along the southeast coast

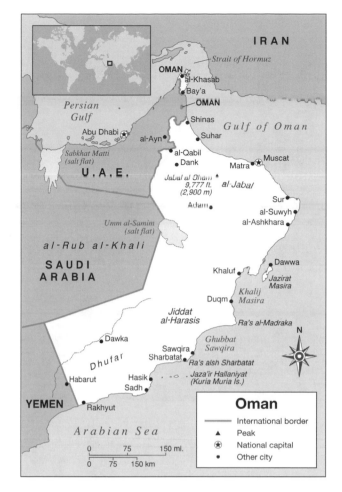

MAP BY XNR PRODUCTIONS, INC. THE GALE GROUP.

of the Arabian Peninsula, on the Arabian Sea and the Gulf of Oman. Approximately 118,000 square miles, it has a population of 2,018,074 (1993 census). Oman's long-disputed southern border with Yemen and its western borders with Saudi Arabia and the United Arab Emirates, and the maritime northern border with Iran in the Strait of Hormuz, have all been largely negotiated and demarcated.

Physically, Oman in divided into three regions: Ru'us al-Jibal, Oman Proper, and Dhufar. The Ru'us al-Jibal exclave is separated from Oman by a 50-mile corridor of United Arab Emirates territory and is the mountainous tip of the Musandam Peninsula. Oman Proper, including Masira and the Daymaniyat Islands, is characterized by a narrow coastal plain (Batina), a parallel mountain chain (Jabal Hajar) anchored by Jabal al-Akhdar, and along its western limits, a dry gravel plain (al-Dhahira) that blends into the Rub al-Khali desert. Additional

Qabus bin Said became the sultan of Oman in 1970 after ousting his father, Sa'id ibn Taymur. Upon assuming leadership of the country, Qabus instituted a program of extensive modernization, opening up the long-isolated Oman to the rest of the world and adopting a moderate, independent foreign policy. © CORBIS SYGMA. REPRODUCED BY PERMISSION.

desert and gravel plains (Sharqiyya and Wusta) extend to the south. Dhufar, including the Halaniyat (Khuriya Muriyah) Islands, also has parallel regions of a coastal plain, the Qara Mountains, and interior desert. The overall climate is hot, with summer temperatures reaching 120° F; dry inland, the coast is extremely humid. The climate of Dhufar is moderated by summer monsoon rains.

Oman's population is 80 percent Omani Arab, plus a significant South Asian expatriate community. Arabic is the predominant language, but English is used widely. Oman is unique because Ibadi Islam, characterized by its adherence to the principle of an elected religious leader called an imam, is the majority faith. Other Muslims include large Sunni and small Shi'ite minorities, and a small Hindu community. The Muscat capital area, an amalgam of several formerly separate coastal towns adjacent to Muscat, is the major urban center, with

550,000 people. Other cities are Salala, Nizwa, and Suhar.

Oman's modern history began in 1749 when Ahmad ibn Sa'id (1749–1783), founder of its present Al Bu Sa'id dynasty, restored Omani independence from Persian invaders and gained election as imam. Ahmad successfully balanced tribal and religious support while encouraging maritime and commercial expansion, but his successors devoted greater attention to external affairs and abandoned claims to the imamate. Sa'id ibn Sultan Al Bu Sa'id (1804–1856) established the antecedent of today's sultanate by utilizing Muscat as the base for expansion in the Persian (Arabian) Gulf and East Africa to form the western Indian Ocean's leading maritime state. But this proto-sultanate was considered illegitimate by Omanis committed to the imamate ideal. Periodic interventions by the Sa'udis aggravated the internal instability, and Sa'id often ran afoul of his British allies' efforts to suppress both the slave trade and piracy, the latter a consequence of Sa'id's expansionism. With his options in Arabia thwarted, Sa'id made Zanzibar his principal residence in the 1830s. Following Sa'id's death in 1856, the British recognized separate Al Bu Sa'id sultanates in Muscat and Zanzibar. Long-simmering Omani opposition to political conditions peaked with the election of Azzan ibn Qays (1868–1871), leader of an Al Bu Sa'id cadet branch, as imam, and the unification of Oman under his rule. The British government utilized gunship diplomacy to overthrow the imamate and restore the sultanate. Muscat became a thinly veiled British protectorate. Support for the imamate remained strong and continued to grow as a consequence of the disruptive influences of economic globalization in the late nineteenth century. In the early twentieth century the imamate reappeared in Oman's interior but failed to overthrow the British-defended sultanate. In 1920 the rival Omani governments signed the so-called Treaty of Sib and regularized the conditions under which they coexisted for the next thirty-five years. Sa'id ibn Taymur Al Bu Sa'id (1932–1970) signaled Muscat's revival by diminishing British influence, suppressing the imamate, and reuniting Oman in 1957, then initiating exploitation of its oil resources. But his opposition to socioeconomic development led to widespread disaffection, a rebellion in Dhufar, and greater de-

Due to the country's 1,700 km of coastline, fishing is a fast-developing commercial industry in Oman. Since the early 1990s, the government has been investing substantially in this sector, building new harbors, granting fishermen subsidies to purchase boats, and constructing cold stores and processing facilities © JON HICKS/CORBIS. REPRODUCED BY PERMISSION.

pendence on the British. In July 1970 Qabus (also Qaboos) ibn Saʿid deposed his father. The new sultan ended Oman's long diplomatic isolation, suppressed the insurgency in Dhufar, and launched political and economic reforms.

Oman's political system has evolved from autocracy to nascent democratic system during the past thirty years. The Basic Law of 1996 defines the political system, which has two consultative bodies—an elected Majlis al-Shura and an appointed Council of State. There are no political parties. The sultan continues to be the source of all law. An independent judiciary system was implemented in 2001. In principle, women have full political rights, and they do serve in both consultative bodies and senior government positions.

Until the early 1970s Omanis subsisted upon an agricultural and fishing economy. Oil exports began in 1967 and funded modest economic development under Saʿid ibn Taymur. Those efforts accelerated greatly under Qabus after 1970. Modernized agriculture, livestock, and fishery practices still support about 50 percent of the population, but service jobs (35%) in both the public and private sector have increased dramatically. Industry and commerce (15%) provide other livelihoods. Production of petroleum products, both crude oil and natural gas, dominates the economy, accounting for 70 percent of state revenues and 90 percent of exports, mostly to East Asia. Oman also exports copper and chromite, some industrial goods (mostly clothing), and food products, and it imports machinery, transport, and consumer goods, mainly from Japan, Britain, the United Arab Emirates, and South Asia. Since 1970 the government has developed a comprehensive communication and transportation infrastructure and provided modern education through university level and healthcare facilities for the Omani people.

See also AL BU SAʿID FAMILY AND TRIBE OF OMAN; AL BU SAʿID, QABUS IBN SAʿID; AL BU SAʿID, SAʿID IBN TAYMUR; DHUFAR; MAJLES AL-SHURA; MUSCAT; SIB, TREATY OF (1920); ZANZIBAR.

Bibliography

Allen, Calvin H., Jr., and Rigsbee, W. Lynn. *Oman under Qaboos: From Coup to Constitution, 1970–1996.* London: Frank Cass, 2000.

Anthony, John Duke. *Historical and Cultural Dictionary of the Sultanate of Oman and the Emirates of Eastern Arabia.* Metuchen, NJ: Scarecrow Press, 1976.

Kechichian, Joseph A. *Oman and the World: The Emergence of an Independent Foreign Policy.* Santa Monica, CA: RAND, 1995.

Landen, Robert G. *Oman since 1856: Disruptive Modernization in a Traditional Arab Society.* Princeton, NJ: Princeton University Press, 1967.

Peterson, J. E. *Oman in the Twentieth Century: Political Foundations of an Emerging State.* London: Croon Helm, 1978.

Wilkinson, John C. *The Imamate Tradition of Oman.* Cambridge, U.K.: Cambridge University Press, 1987.

ROBERT G. LANDEN
UPDATED BY CALVIN H. ALLEN, JR.

OMAR, MUHAMMAD (MULLAH)
[1959–]

Afghani leader of the Taliban Movement that ruled most of Afghanistan between 1996 and 2002.

Muhammad Omar was born of Pashtun ethnic heritage in the village of Singesar, near Kandahar, and attended a religious school. He started teaching before finishing his degree but when the Soviet Union invaded Afghanistan in 1979, he joined the resistance and commanded a small group of *mujahidin* (also *mojahedin*) (fighters), losing an eye in one of the confrontations with the Soviet military. After the withdrawal of the Soviet Union, he went back to teaching in Kandahar but was driven to start in 1994 a small movement called the Taliban in order to end the crimes and abuses of local strongmen during the Afghani civil war.

Benefiting from Pakistani endorsement and help and initial Pashtun grassroots support, he managed to recruit a number of former *mujahidin* trained for the most part in the schools set up in the refugee camps in Pakistan and by 1998 had taken control of most of Afghanistan. Affected by a history of war and foreign oppression and motivated by a strong devotion to Islam, the Taliban's ideology was influenced by the Egyptian Muslim Brotherhood and the Pakistani Jamaati Islami, focusing on fighting Western occupation and intervention, and seeking to establish an Islamic State. Reclusive and autocratic, Omar directed the movement with a small number of associates and adopted an increasingly strict interpretation of his cultural and religious heritage, resorting to a repressive control of Afghan society, restricting the work and education of women, and ordering the destruction of ancient Buddhist statues deemed idolatrous.

Though at first mostly concerned with Afghani issues, the Taliban became more involved with pan-Islamism with the increased presence of non-Afghani Muslims, including Osama bin Ladin, who provided them with funds and support. After the 11 September 2001 attacks on U.S. targets, the Taliban refused U.S. demands for the extradition of bin Ladin. As a result, the United States invaded Afghanistan in 2002 and dispersed the Taliban, whose leaders went into hiding.

See also BIN LADIN, OSAMA; TALIBAN.

Bibliography

Nojumi, Neamotollah. *The Rise of the Taliban in Afghanistan.* New York: Palgrave 2002.

MAYSAM J. AL FARUQI

OMAR MUKHTAR CLUB

Cyrenaican (Libyan) political organization.

The club was founded in 1943 by younger men advocating an independent and unitary Libya. It be-

came increasingly critical of the British military administration and older leaders cooperating with it. By 1949, it had accepted that a federation of the provinces of Cyrenaica, Tripolitania, and Fezzan was an essential feature of Libyan independence.

JOHN L. WRIGHT

OMDURMAN

Historical capital of the Sudan.

Although Khartoum is the official capital of the Sudan, Omdurman is the country's historic, cultural, and spiritual capital. It is also part of a tri-city metropolitan area (with Khartoum and Khartoum North) that forms the country's political, industrial, and commercial heart. Originally an insignificant fishing village on the west bank at the confluence of the Blue Nile and the White Nile, Omdurman became a major city at the end of the nineteenth century when Muhammad Ahmad al-Mahdi made it his military headquarters in 1884. After the Mahdist forces destroyed Khartoum (1885), the Mahdi's successor, Khalifa Abdullah, made Omdurman his capital, and the city grew as the site of the Mahdi's tomb. The Battle of Karari (1898), which took place near Omdurman, marked the defeat of the Mahdist state in Sudan by the Anglo-Egyptian army of Lord Kitchener. Although most of the city was destroyed after the battle, the Mahdi's tomb has been restored and embellished. The Khalifa's former residence is now a museum. Recently, Omdurman has grown rapidly, and has an estimated population of well over two million. The major Sudanese political groups have their headquarters in the city, as do the television and radio networks and the famous soccer and cultural clubs. Although the official headquarters of the army is in Khartoum, the principal military installations are in Omdurman, including those of Sudan's air force.

See also AHMAD, MUHAMMAD; KHARTOUM; KITCHENER, HORATIO HERBERT; *MAHDI*.

Bibliography

Ahmed, Medani Mohammed. *Current Studies on the Sudan.* Omdurman, Sudan: Mohamed Omer Beshir's Center for Sudanese Studies, 1998.

Pollock, John. *Kitchener: Architect of Victory, Artisan of Peace.* New York: Carroll & Graf, 2001.

Woodward, Peter, ed. *Sudan after Nimeiri.* London and New York: Routledge, 1991.

ROBERT O. COLLINS
UPDATED BY KHALID M. EL-HASSAN

OPIUM

Papaver somniferum, the air-dried, milky juice obtained from incisions to the unripe seed pods of the poppy plant.

Opium is a powerful analgesic of mixed blessings. It is one of the richest sources of many useful medicinal alkaloids, such as codeine, morphine, and papaverine. But repeated and extensive use of it and its derivatives—most notoriously heroin—are known to cause severe addiction.

The poppy plant grows wild just about everywhere in the plains of Asia and the Mediterranean, and by the late medieval period there are references to opium use in various parts of the Middle East, as both a medicine and a narcotic. The escalation of opium production and trade seems to have been closely linked to burgeoning European colonial and commercial interests in Asia, and official international controls of opium trafficking, cultivation, and consumption are a twentieth-century phenomenon. The United States spearheaded this effort with an international conference convened by President Theodore Roosevelt in Singapore in 1909. This was followed by a series of conventions held in The Hague, culminating in the convention of 1912.

Despite international initiatives undertaken during the twentieth century, Middle Eastern countries such as Afghanistan, Iran, Pakistan, and Turkey still produce a substantial portion of the world's opium supply. In Afghanistan in particular, precarious living conditions and geopolitical developments caused its production of opium to skyrocket during the 1990s, making it the world's largest opium producer. As of 2003, most of the drug of Afghan origin is reportedly distributed northward through the neighboring countries of Central Asia, with Europe as its final destination.

Bibliography

Observatoire Geopolitique des Drogues. "The World Geopolitics of Drugs: 1998/1999 Annual Report."

April 2000. Available from <http://www.ogd.org/2000>.

KAREN PINTO
UPDATED BY ANA TORRES-GARCIA

ORAN

Largest urban center in western Algeria (estimated pop. 693,000, 1998).

On a bay of the Mediterranean Sea, Oran is the administrative, commercial, and educational hub of the petrochemical complex of Arzew-Bethioua (50 km [30 mi.] to the east).

Oran was founded in 903 C.E. by Muslim merchants from Andalusia searching for an alternative port to Ceuta on the West African gold route. The waters of the Ra's al-Ayn river supported the foundation of a sizable walled city with a citadel (qasaba, or Casbah). Muslim CORSAIRS succeeded the merchants at the end of the fourteenth century, then were ousted in 1509 by Christian Spaniards. The Ottomans fiercely opposed Spain's expansion and incorporated Algeria into their empire, but it was only in 1791 that Turkish troops wrested Oran from the Spanish.

The French entered western Algeria in 1831 and occupied Oran, which had some 3,000 Muslim and Jewish inhabitants. European settlers far outnumbered Muslim rural migrants prior to World War I; it was only after World War II that the indigenous population rose to about 40 percent of a total of 413,000 inhabitants.

In the 1840s a canal system and a safe port with breakwaters were constructed. Administrative, commercial, and cultural functions shifted from the Muslim city to the east, along an east-west axis. The Muslim population was forcibly removed in 1845 to its own quarter in the south, resulting in de facto segregation of European settlers and Muslims well into the twentieth century. An urban streetcar system and a main train depot were in place around the turn of the century, an airport was constructed in the 1920s, and paved streets appeared by the 1930s.

During the colonial period Oran was the leading exporter of agricultural goods (red wine, olive oil, soft wheat, citrus, artichokes, tobacco, esparto,

Oran, Algeria's second largest city, was founded in 937 C.E. and is the birthplace of Nobel prize–winning author Albert Camus. © MARC GARANGER/CORBIS. REPRODUCED BY PERMISSION.

wool, and leather). There was little interest in industrialization; apart from mostly small construction and food-processing enterprises, two steelworks were financed by foreign capital. Trade disruptions during World War II encouraged the establishment of import-substitution industries (bottles, containers, cement, and hardware), but these struggled to survive after the war. The Plan of Constantinople (1958), with which France sought to jump-start industrialization in response to the Algerian War of Independence (1954–1962), created jobs in public works projects but did not enlarge the industrial sector.

After independence Algeria's government embarked on a gigantic program of state industrializa-

tion. In 1967 the Oran region was selected to become the main center for the exportation of hydrocarbons and the production of industrial chemicals. These basic industries were supplemented with factories for agricultural machinery and consumer goods. Private investment went primarily into the textile, plastic, food-processing, metalworking and footwear sectors. By the early 1980s the industrial base had grown to 112 state and 284 private businesses with 10 or more employees and total workforces of 32,000 (state) and 10,000 (private).

When the European settlers left Algeria in 1962, they abandoned close to two-thirds of the housing stock of Oran. By 1970 housing was scarce, however, and during the 1970s and 1980s some 12,000 new apartments (about a quarter of what was needed) were constructed. In spite of the periodic razing of shantytowns and the forced return of the inhabitants to their villages of origin, by the mid-1980s about one-third of the rural population had permanently settled in Oran and the other cities of the industrial region. The rural migrants who flooded the city found jobs primarily in construction, low levels of administration, retail, private industry, and the informal sector. Jobs in state industries typically were open only to qualified older workers.

Given the lack of convenient housing, the commute between residence and workplace often is as far as 30 miles (50 km), mostly by public bus or company van. Nearly half of Oran's industrial workforce works outside the city. The new suburbs require additional trips for shopping and entertainment, given the continued concentration of retail shops, services, and entertainment in the city center. On the other hand, many local and regional administrative offices, a new technical university, and vocational colleges have been moved to the suburbs, evening out the distribution of traffic.

In the center of Oran there has been a proliferation of bars, most of which sell coffee and tea. During the interwar period, they were the birthplace of rai, a music of bedouin immigrants that has become Algeria's rock 'n' roll. Also, the mixture of apartment buildings and small commercial and crafts establishments, typical of European inner cities prior to World War II, is still largely intact. Traditional food, clothing, and kitchenware shops are clustered in downtown Oran, and Medina Jadida (a kilometer to the south).

In downtown Oran, upscale residences, professional practices, airline offices, banks, restaurants, and furniture, jewelry, perfume, leather, and record shops coexist with less expensive apartment buildings, retail businesses, and bars as well as mechanical and electrical repair shops (the latter mostly on the periphery). The inner city is no longer the place where established families and rural migrants are neighbors, as was the case in the 1960s, but they still share the same neighborhoods.

The cancellation of the first national elections in 1992 and the return to de facto military rule slowed the process of devolution. In the struggle between the military and Islamists during the 1990s, Oran experienced less violence and terrorism than did Algiers; yet the paralysis was severe. Security under President Abdelaziz Bouteflika, inaugurated in 1999, has improved.

Bibliography

Thompson, Ian B. *The Commercial Centre of Oran.* Glasgow, 1982.

PETER VON SIVERS

ORDINANCES ON VEILING

Prohibitions on women in Afghanistan.

The pamphlet *Shari'a Ordinances on Veiling (Fatawa-i-Shara'i dar Mawrid-i-Hijab)* was issued in 1994 by the Afghan Supreme Court *(Stera Mahkama)* during the Islamic Government of Burhanuddin Rabbani (1992–1996). The pamphlet was signed by sixteen members of the Bureau of Jurisdiction and Deliberation *(Riyasat-i-Ifta wa al-Mutali'at)* of the Supreme Court. The last paragraph reads in part: "The Afghan nation fought for fourteen years and suffered enormous losses in order to free the country from the hands of the atheist [Communists] and reinstate Divine Ordinances. Now that this objective has been fulfilled by the Grace of the Almighty, . . . we urge that God's ordinances be carried out immediately, particularly those pertaining to the veiling of women. Women should be banned from working in offices and radio and television stations. Girls schools, which are in effect the hub of debauchery and adulterous practices, must be closed down.. . ." The ordinances required women to cover their face outside the home and not to leave their home without having a compelling reason and first obtaining their husband's permission. The wearing of noisy shoes, anklets, perfume, or any other embellishment that might attract a man's attention was prohibited. These ordinances were precursors to similar decrees issued later by the Taliban.

See also AFGHANISTAN; CLOTHING; GENDER: GENDER AND LAW; TALIBAN.

SENZIL NAWID

ORGANISATION ARMÉE SECRÈTE (OAS)

A movement of French colons and renegade army officers that sought to block Algeria's independence.

The Secret Army Organization (Organisation Armée Secrète; OAS) was created in February 1961 under the leadership of Colon activists Pierre Lagaillarde and Jean-Jacques Susini. Its military leadership was provided by Generals Raoul Salan, Marie-André Zeller, Edmond Jouhaud, and—for a short time—Maurice Challe.

In April 1961, under Challe's leadership, the OAS attempted a coup in Algiers that appeared for a short time to threaten the metropolitan government as well. When the coup failed, the movement adopted a policy of undermining government authority by bombings and by assassinations of officials, of liberal intellectuals, and prominent Muslim leaders. As the Evian negotiations proceeded, the organization switched to a campaign of terror against Muslims in general, and finally, after France agreed to independence, to a "scorched earth" policy of massive destruction of infrastructure. On 17 June 1962, the OAS signed a cease-fire with the Front de Libération Nationale (FLN: National Liberation Front).

See also ALGERIAN WAR OF INDEPENDENCE; COLONS.

Bibliography

Horne, Alistair. *A Savage War of Peace: Algeria, 1954–1962,* revised edition. New York: Penguin, 1987.

JOHN RUEDY

ORGANISATION MAROCAINE DES DROITS DE L'HOMME

Moroccan human rights organization.

The Moroccan Human Rights Organization (OMDH) was founded in 1988 by a group of Moroccan professionals to address the problem of human rights violations in the kingdom. Prior to the establishment of the OMDH, the Istiqlal Party had founded the Ligue Marocaine de Défense des Droits de l'Homme (Moroccan League for the Defense of Human Rights) in 1972, and the Union Socialiste des Forces Populaires (Socialist Union of Popular Forces, USFP) had established the Association Marocaine des Droits de l'Homme (Moroccan Association of Human Rights) in 1979. The OMDH planned its first congress for May 1988. Initially banned by the government because of its "extremist" membership, the OMDH was finally allowed to hold its inaugural assembly at Agdal (Rabat), in December 1988. The presidency has been held by Omar Azziman (1988–1989); Khalid Naciri (1990–1991); Ali Oumlil (1991–1992); Abdelaziz Bennani (1992–2000), and Abdellah Oualladi (2000–).

Among the goals of the organization are the diffusion of knowledge about individual and collective human rights at the civil, political, cultural, and socioeconomic levels; the protection of human rights; the reinforcement of the rights of the individual during the judiciary process; the consolidation of an independent judiciary and its impartiality; the consolidation of democracy and the rule of the law; and the promotion of international solidarity in the defense of human rights. The OMDH is a member of the International Federation of Human Rights, based in Paris; the International Commission of Jurists, based in Geneva; the World Organization against Torture, based in Geneva; and the Arab Organization of Human Rights, based in Cairo. The organization periodically cooperates with international and regional organizations, such as the Association Marocaine des Droits Humains, the Ligue Marocaine pour la Défense des Droits de l'Homme, and the Comité de Défense des Droits Humaines.

The OMDH's initial focus on abuses of prisoners' rights led the government to release over one thousand prisoners by the end of 1989. In response to published OMDH reports, King Hassan II founded the Conseil Consultatif des Droits de l'Homme (Consultative Council of Human Rights). The creation of a Ministry of Human Rights in November 1993 was interpreted as a new attempt on the part of the government to neutralize the work of the existing human rights organizations. Disturbances in late 1990 sparked renewed activism on the part of OMDH in 1991, which continued into 1992 and 1993. To its earlier agenda of concern with issues of torture, the disappeared, and prison conditions, the OMDH added passport denials, violations of travel freedom, an independent judiciary, and press controls as points of contention with the government.

The OMDH publishes a magazine, *al-Karama*, and OMDH materials often appear in the publications of other organizations, such as the Rassemblement Nationale des Indépendants (National Rally of Independents), the former Communist paper *al-Bayan* (The clarion), and USFP newspapers.

In February 1993, Mohamed Mikou, secretary-general of the Conseil Consultatif des Droits de l'Homme (CCDH), recommended that the government cooperate with human rights organizations and that King Hassan ratify the U.N. Convention on Torture, to which the king agreed on 14 June 1993; the United Nations acknowledged the Moroccan ratification on 21 July 1993. Amnesty International's April 1993 report on Morocco stated that five hundred people had "disappeared" in Morocco since 1963. It named secret detention centers and provided a list of forty-eight Sahrawi prisoners who had died in detention between 1976 and 1990.

The death of King Hassan II and the enthronement of King Muhammad VI in July 1999 was received with a certain level of hope by the progressive sectors of the country. In 1999, the OMDH called on international human rights organizations to form a fact-finding mission to investigate human rights abuses in the Lahmada refugee camps of Tinduf, stronghold of POLISARIO. In 2001, the OMDH denounced governmental repression against the Moroccan Association National des Diplomés Chômeurs (Association of Unemployed College-Degree Holders). Following a month of street mobilizations, the OMDH joined other Moroccan human rights organizations in denouncing the "disappearance" of individuals suspected of having links with al-Qaʿida in December, 2002. The OMDH has opposed the sentencing to three years of imprisonment of Moroccan journalist Ali Mrabet, director of the French language publication *Demain* and its Arabic counterpart *Duman*, for the publication in a Catalonian newspaper of several cartoons critical of the Moroccan monarch; the organization continues to demand a full investigation of the "disappearances" and during the 1990s and beyond has focused on the abuses in Moroccan prisons. It has also criticized human rights abuses in the Republic of Tunisia under the Zayn al-Abidine Ben Ali government. In January 2003, the OMDH issued a statement condemning the U.S. military attack against Iraq as an action that contravened international law.

See also BEN ALI, ZAYN AL-ABIDINE; ISTIQLAL PARTY: MOROCCO; POLISARIO; RASSEMBLEMENT NATIONAL DES INDÉPENDANTS (RNI); UNION SOCIALISTE DES FORCES POPULAIRES (USFP).

Bibliography

Amnesty International. *Morocco: Amnesty International Briefing.* New York: Amnesty International, 1991.

Dwyer, Kevin. *Arab Voices: The Human Rights Debate in the Middle East.* Berkeley: University of California Press, 1991.

Human Rights Watch: Morocco. Available from <http://www.hrw.org/mideast/morocco.php>.

Organisation Marocaine des Droits Humains. Available from <http://www.omdh.org>.

LARRY A. BARRIE
UPDATED BY VANESA CASANOVA-FERNANDEZ

ORGANIZATION FOR THE LIBERATION OF THE OCCUPIED SOUTH

Yemeni independence group, founded 1965.

Created through a merger of organizations and leading personalities in North and South Yemen (including Muhammad Ahmad Nuʿman, Abdullah Ali Asnaj, and Muhammad Ali Jifri), the Organization for the Liberation of the Occupied South (OLOS) was originally a rival of the National Liberation Front (NLF) but later joined elements of the NLF to create the Front for the Liberation of South Yemen (FLOSY). Not long thereafter, the NLF

insisted on its independence, and the two organizations were again rivals. Members of the al-Jifri family later became prominent in the operations and governance of the Yemeni Socialist Party, until exiled after the Yemeni civil war of 1994.

Bibliography

Carapico, Sheila. *Civil Society in Yemen.* Cambridge, U.K., and New York: Cambridge University Press, 1998.

Dresch, Paul. *A History of Modern Yemen.* Cambridge, U.K., and New York: Cambridge University Press, 2000.

Gause, F. Gregory. *Saudi-Yemeni Relations, 1962–1982.* New York: Columbia University Press, 1990.

Halliday, Fred. *Revolution and Foreign Policy: The Case of South Yemen.* Cambridge, U.K., and New York: Cambridge University Press, 1990.

Mundy, Martha. *Domestic Government; Kinship, Community and Polity in North Yemen.* New York: St. Martin's Press, 1995.

Suwaidi, Jamal al-, ed. *The Yemeni War of 1994.* London: Saqi Books, 1995.

Wenner, Manfred. *The Yemen Arab Republic: Development and Change in an Ancient Land.* Boulder, CO: Westview Press, 1991.

MANFRED W. WENNER

ORGANIZATION OF AFRICAN UNITY (OAU)

An alliance of African states (known as OAU) formed for mutual support in economics, self-government, and security.

In May 1963, the OAU was founded at Addis Ababa, Ethiopia, by thirty-two African states, including Algeria, Tunisia, Morocco, Egypt, Libya, Djibouti, Mauritania, Somalia, and Sudan. Devoted to issues such as colonialism, economic development, and mutual security, the OAU, like most multistate coalitions, has had limited success in transforming its ideals into reality. Although the OAU was an active supporter of liberation movements in Mozambique, Angola, and Zimbabwe, it had difficulty providing more than moral and diplomatic encouragement; in intra-African conflicts, such as that over the Western Sahara, the OAU has found itself in a quandary. The Arab states of the Maghrib (North Africa) have been and continue to be its ardent members.

Egypt's President Gamal Abdel Nasser pressured the OAU to his side in his stand against Israel, so through the 1960s, the OAU moved gradually toward the Arab camp. In 1971, the OAU issued a strong resolution criticizing Israel's handling of the Palestinian issue. By the end of 1973, all but four (Lesotho, Malawi, Swaziland, and Mauritius) of the OAU member states had broken relations with Israel. The Camp David Accords between Egypt and Israel (1979) caused a slow process of renewal of diplomatic relations with Israel—Zaire was first in 1982.

Bibliography

Amate, C. O. C. *Inside the OAU: Pan-Africanism in Practice.* New York: St. Martin's, 1986.

Mansfield, Peter. *The Arabs,* 3d edition. New York: Penguin, 1985.

ZACHARY KARABELL

ORGANIZATION OF ARAB PETROLEUM EXPORTING COUNTRIES (OAPEC)

Organization formed to promote cooperation among Arab oil-producing states.

The Organization of Arab Petroleum Exporting Countries (OAPEC) is a regional organization, established in 1968 by Saudi Arabia, Libya, and Kuwait, and modeled after the older Organization of Petroleum Exporting Countries (OPEC). The other members are Algeria, Bahrain, Egypt, Iraq, Qatar, Syria, and the United Arab Emirates. Egypt was suspended between 1979 and 1987. Tunisia withdrew in 1986. The goals of OAPEC are to promote the oil interests of member countries, to enhance cooperation among them in production, marketing, and associated industries. It aims also to carry out joint ventures to diversify their economies, to participate in stabilizing the oil market, and to provide suitable circumstances for capital and experience to be invested in the member countries. Although OAPEC was not intended as a political instrument, one of the critical decisions taken by member states in 1973, at its Kuwait headquarters, was the oil embargo following the Arab-Israel War. Since that time, OAPEC oil and gas world share has been steady at about 25 percent, with significant increases mainly by Saudi Arabia and Kuwait to compensate

for the two-thirds reduction of Iraq's share since 1990. OAPEC proven oil reserves have not increased. By 2010 OAPEC oil production may increase by 50 percent to 30 million barrels per day, to meet about one-third of world needs. OAPEC capacity utilization, already high at 85 percent, may increase to above 90 percent. As of 2003, OAPEC share of worldwide natural gas production stood at 35 percent; it may double by 2010.

Bibliography

"Organization of Arab Petroleum Exporting Countries." Available from <http://www.oapecorg.org>.

EMILE A. NAKHLEH
UPDATED BY KARIM HAMDY

ORGANIZATION OF PETROLEUM EXPORTING COUNTRIES (OPEC)

Group formed in 1960 to protect economic interests of oil-exporting countries.

In the early 1950s, international oil companies (IOCs) developed the posted price system to help host governments estimate oil revenues in advance. Posted prices were accounting devices that host governments used to calculate the amount of taxes the companies would pay under industrywide fifty-fifty profit-sharing agreements. Despite normal fluctuations in the real prices at which crude oil was traded, posted prices were not adjusted, and fixed posted prices became an industry norm. When competitive pressures forced the IOCs to reduce posted prices unilaterally in February 1959, an immediate outcry arose from the affected host governments.

OPEC's Founding

The first Arab Oil Congress met later that year. Delegates from oil-exporting countries came to plan concerted action against the oil companies. Structural differences among national oil industries made coordination among these countries difficult technically. Conflicts of interest over investment and production shares made coordination difficult politically. Competition between Venezuela and Middle Eastern exporters was heightened by the 1959 posted price cuts. British Petroleum set lower prices in parts of the Middle East than in Venezuela in hope of breaking the As-Is Agreement, a mediated connection between world oil prices and the U.S. market. Venezuelan oil thereby became even less competitive, requiring further downward price adjustments and convincing oil exporters that their responses to the companies had to be closely coordinated.

Political conflicts ended the Oil Consultation Commission, the first producer attempt to institutionalize coordination. But when the IOCs imposed yet another round of price cuts in August 1960, five oil-exporting countries set aside their political differences to salvage their economic interests. Venezuela, Saudi Arabia, Iran, Iraq, and Kuwait formed the Organization of Petroleum Exporting Countries (OPEC) in September 1960. OPEC's first resolutions included calls to restore posted prices to their pre-February 1959 levels and to stabilize oil prices by regulating production.

The U.S. government refused to recognize OPEC, forbade U.S. oil companies to negotiate with it, and imposed trade sanctions on OPEC members to discourage other countries from joining. This suited the IOCs, which saw an advantage in continuing their accustomed practice of dealing with host governments one at a time. OPEC responded creatively, developing joint negotiating positions with the understanding that any member able to gain an additional advantage on its own should do so. Any gains would constitute a new floor for bargaining in the next round. During its first ten years, this "leapfrogging" earned OPEC members incremental gains in oil revenues, which both increased OPEC's international stature and attracted new members to the organization.

Perhaps OPEC's most significant contribution to the oil revolution was its support and implementation of "participation," the gradual nationalization of foreign-owned oil properties. Most members did not follow the participation strategy to the letter, but years of discussion provided an opportunity to prepare for the responsibilities that would come when they became full owners of their oil industries. This accomplishment was overshadowed, however, by OPEC's successful utilization of leapfrogging to achieve rapid oil price increases, by Libya in 1970 and afterward by alternating pressure exerted first by oil-exporting countries in the

Mediterranean and then in the Persian Gulf. This set the stage for OPEC's takeover of crude oil pricing when the 1973 Arab–Israel War, with its well-designed Arab oil embargo, provided the opportunity.

Pricing Strategies

OPEC's success in taking over oil pricing created new problems for the group. Oil-importing countries, led by the United States, demonized OPEC as the primary cause of worldwide economic decline. Inside OPEC, structural differences among member industries led to disagreements over pricing strategies. Low-price-preference members such as Saudi Arabia, with small populations and huge oil reserves, favored moderate oil prices to discourage consumers from seeking alternative fuels. High-price-preference members like Algeria, with large populations, wanted high prices so they could pay for ambitious development programs, while their small reserves offered no incentive to support pricing policies that would sustain the long-term attractiveness of oil as a fuel. Some members with large reserves, like Iran and Libya, also favored high prices. Iran had a large population and an ambitious development program, but Libya's preference was politically motivated by Libya's desire to assert its autonomy among its OPEC peers as well as its independence from western domination.

Price positions could be flexible, however. In 1978, the threat of revolution pushed Mohammad Reza Shah Pahlavi of Iran to seek allies among his neighbors. Iran joined most of the Arab gulf countries in pushing for the adoption of a long-range moderate pricing strategy to replace what had, until then, been an ad hoc method of setting oil prices. The new system became obsolete almost before it was agreed upon, however; it was superseded by pressures that doubled oil prices in one year thanks to panic buying during the Iranian Revolution. Predictably, oil demand fell, but the availability of new, non-OPEC supplies from the North Sea and elsewhere allowed major importers to shift their purchases, making OPEC the marginal supplier of crude oil to the world market.

Market weakness in the early 1980s caused OPEC to focus on oil production sharing as a strategy for controlling oil prices by regulating crude supply. A voluntary production-sharing plan was launched in 1982 but, as had happened to the voluntary oil import quota in the United States during the 1950s, producers ignored it. A mandatory quota system was introduced in March 1983, and crude prices were reduced for the first time since OPEC had assumed its price-setting role in the hope of stimulating consumer demand. An Austrian accounting firm was hired to monitor member production in order to discourage cheating on the quotas.

The quota system had many flaws. Even small producers were required to accept a quota, prompting Ecuador to leave OPEC in 1993 to escape its quota obligations. Saudi Arabia, OPEC's largest producer, refused to accept a formal quota that it said was an unacceptable infringement on its sovereignty. This marginalized Saudi production within OPEC as crude from many sources flooded the market and total demand for OPEC oil declined. Without a quota and its implied entitlement to produce a defined share of OPEC crude, the Saudis had to accept the informal role of swing producer, one which would vary its production to satisfy market demand remaining after other producers had supplied their quota amounts. As OPEC's swing producer, however, Saudi Arabia would have to absorb more than a proportional share of demand reduction. This already unpleasant situation would be complicated in the Saudi case by its heavy dependence on associated natural gas, which led to shortages of fuel for power generation when oil production there fell to below 3 million barrels per day in mid-1985. Shortly afterward, Saudi Arabia decided to produce oil with only its own needs in mind. Global supplies burgeoned and oil prices plummeted, dipping below $10 U.S. per barrel in June 1986. Although oil prices recovered, they have yet to return to pre-1985 highs.

Political Divisions

Political conflicts continued to divide OPEC members during this time. The first Gulf War, between Iran and Iraq (1980–1988), so split the organization that OPEC could not agree on a new secretary-general when it was Iran's turn to nominate one of its nationals. An assistant secretary-general, Fadhil al-Chalabi of Iraq, served as acting secretary-general from 1983 to 1988. Hostility among

members during this period made meetings acrimonious and reduced the usefulness of OPEC as a forum for coordinating policy.

The end of the Iran–Iraq War provided an opportunity to mend intra-OPEC relations, but the second Gulf War, which began when Iraq invaded Kuwait in 1990, brought new turmoil to oil markets and to OPEC itself. Before Iraq invaded Kuwait, world oil prices were depressed and virtually every OPEC member with excess production capacity was producing over its quota. Unfortunately for Kuwait, it was the only country small enough and close enough to suffer Iraq's wrath directly. After Kuwait was liberated in February 1991, U.N. sanctions against Iraq, imposed in retaliation for the invasion, ended legal oil exports from Iraq. Starting in December 1996, Iraqi income from smuggled oil was augmented by earnings from the U.N. Oil-for-Food Program, which supervised the marketing of some 3.4 billion barrels of Iraqi crude between the start of the program and March 2003, when the United States and Britain invaded Iraq. The United Nations also ensured that the Iraqi share of oil-for-food income was spent only to meet humanitarian needs. The rest went for war reparations (25 percent after December 2000, 30 percent before), the cost of U.N. weapons inspections (0.8 percent), and administrative and operational costs for the program (2.2 percent).

Overproduction by OPEC members remains a problem during periods of ample crude supplies, but political turmoil and consequent supply disruptions in member countries, from Venezuela and Nigeria to Iraq and Indonesia, have masked the problem of excess capacity by creating or even merely threatening war-related shortages. Yet members able to do so are expanding production capacity, which will add to conflict over production ceilings and quota allocations as growing supplies from Iraq come to the market.

Overall, OPEC's difficulties in managing and stabilizing the international oil market continue to be beyond member control. Following the collapse of the Soviet Union, the new Central Asian countries offered attractive terms to potential investors in oil and gas exploration and development. Now rising production from this region adds to pressures on the price structure. The need for capital investment is another axis of competition pitting OPEC against Central Asian and non-OPEC African producers, leading many OPEC members to reconsider their positions on nationalization. IOC operations are expanding in virtually every OPEC nation, while the occupation of Iraq could leave a privatized Iraqi oil industry as one of its legacies.

OPEC's gravest failure has been its concentration on oil market conditions rather than on the economy as such. Consequently, it has failed to develop strategies to prepare members for a post-oil world. As long as prices are low and supplies seem secure, oil will remain a competitive fuel in global markets and the deep restructuring necessary to wean member economies from their addiction to oil revenues can be avoided. Yet whether post-Saddam Iraq will be reintegrated into OPEC or not, relying on hydrocarbon revenues as the mainstay of their economies leaves members vulnerable not only to the day-to-day vagaries of the market but also to the impact of long-term structural change. The almost exclusive concentration of governments, press, and public on oil pricing actually prevents OPEC from devoting significant intellectual and financial resources to other aspects of industry development, including research on alternative sources of energy for export and domestic use. Kuwait's early research into solar power, for example, was quickly abandoned as its oil reserves expanded and reliance on oil revenues seemed less risky than devoting substantial resources to bringing a competing energy source to markets where it already had an advantage. Yet with concerns about pollution and global climate change encouraging consumers to shift out of hydrocarbons, OPEC members' acute dependence on oil and gas revenues leaves their economic security as vulnerable to changes in market structure as they are to political conflict.

See also As-Is AGREEMENT; OIL EMBARGO (1973–1974); PETROLEUM, OIL, AND NATURAL GAS.

Bibliography

Mikdashi, Zuhayr. *The Community of Oil Exporting Countries: A Study in Government Cooperation.* Ithaca, NY: Cornell University Press, 1972.

Mitchell, John, et al. *The New Economy of Oil: Impacts on Business, Geopolitics, and Society.* London: Earthscan, 2001.

Skeet, Ian. *OPEC: Twenty-Five Years of Prices and Politics.* Cambridge, U.K.: Cambridge University Press, 1989.

Tétreault, Mary Ann. *Revolution in the World Petroleum Market.* Westport, CT: Quorum Books, 1985.

Weisberg, Richard C. *The Politics of Crude Oil Pricing in the Middle East, 1970–1975.* Berkeley: University of California, 1977.

MARY ANN TÉTREAULT

ORGANIZATION OF THE ISLAMIC CONFERENCE

Organization founded in 1972 by Islamic states to promote their cooperation by coordinating economic, social, scientific, and cultural activities.

As a response to the August 1969 burning of the Aqsa Mosque in Jerusalem, the first Islamic Conference of Kings and Heads of State was convened in Rabat in September of the same year. This summit resolved that Islamic nation states should foster "close cooperation and mutual assistance in the economic, scientific, cultural, and spiritual fields." As a first step toward facilitating such cooperation, the summit established the Islamic Conference of Foreign Ministers, which eventually ratified the charter of the Organization of the Islamic Conference (OIC) at its third meeting in March 1972. Membership in the OIC is based on a commitment to the United Nations and its declarations on human rights, as well as an affirmation of the fundamental principles of mutual equality, respect for sovereignty, and the peaceful settlement of disputes among member states. The charter also enumerates the following principal objectives: the promotion of global Islamic solidarity; the eradication of racial discrimination and colonialism; the liberation of Palestine; support for the struggles of oppressed Muslim peoples everywhere; and a dedication to international peace, security, and justice.

Four specialized institutions have been established within the framework of the OIC: the Islamic Development Bank; the Islamic Educational, Scientific, and Cultural Organization; the Islamic States Broadcasting Organization; and the International Islamic News Agency. The general secretariat of the OIC has permanent observer status at the United Nations and maintains its headquarters in Jidda, Saudi Arabia. The Doha Declaration (November 2000) called for an end to the occupation in Palestine and invited those member states that had established relations with the State of Israel to "put an end to all forms of normalization with Israel until it genuinely and accurately implements U.N. resolutions relevant to the issue of Palestine." The Kuala Lumpur Declaration on International Terrorism, issued during the extraordinary session of the Islamic Conference of Foreign Ministers in April 2002, rejected "any attempt to link Islam and Muslims to terrorism" and condemned acts of international terrorism, emphasizing "the importance of addressing the root causes of international terrorism." The following states were members of the OIC as of August 2003: Afghanistan, Albania, Algeria, Azerbaijan, Bahrain, Bangladesh, Benin, Brunei Dar es Salaam, Burkina Faso, Cameroon, Chad, Comoros, Cote d'Ivoire, Djibouti, Egypt, Gabon, Gambia, Guinea, Guinea-Bissau, Guyana (Republic of), Indonesia, Iran, Iraq, Jordan, Kazakhstan, Kuwait, Kyrgyzstan, Lebanon, Libya, Malaysia, Maldives, Mali, Mauritania, Morocco, Mozambique, Niger, Nigeria, Oman, Pakistan, Palestine, Qatar, Saudi Arabia, Senegal, Sierra Leone, Somalia, Sudan, Surinam, Syria, Tajikistan, Togo, Tunisia, Turkey, Turkmenistan, Uganda, United Arab Emirates, Uzbekistan, Yemen, and Zanzibar. Three countries held observer status: Bosnia and Herzegovina, Central African Republic, and Thailand.

See also JERUSALEM.

Bibliography

Ahsan, Abdullah. *The Organization of the Islamic Conference: An Introduction to an Islamic Political Institution.* Herndon, Va: International Institute of Islamic Thought, 1988.

Selim, Mohammad El Sayed, ed. *The Organization of the Islamic Conference in a Changing World.* Giza, Egypt: Center for Political Research and Studies, Cairo University, 1994.

SCOTT ALEXANDER
VANESA CASANOVA-FERNANDEZ

ORIENTALISM

The study and exploration of the Orient by Occidentals.

The word *orientalism* derives from the Latin *oriens,* which means "east." The idea of a cultural division between East and West, between the Orient and the Occident (from the Latin *occidens,* which means "west"), goes back to Greco-Roman times, where in texts as diverse as Herodotus's *Histories* or Varro's *On the Latin Language* distinctions were made between Asia and Europe, which corresponded to Orient and Occident. Throughout the Middle Ages, there was a growing perception of a distinction between a civilization that was the heir of the Judeo-Christian, Greco-Roman traditions (the West) and one that was the heir of the Indian and Chinese religious traditions (the East). The Islamic civilization of the Middle East fits uncomfortably into this polarity.

Even though the East and West, whatever cultural labels one may assign to them, were in contact through trade, exploration, and cultural and intellectual exchange and military activity from early Roman times, and even though they shared economic, cultural, intellectual, artistic, and religious influence, the idea of orientalism took root during the late Middle Ages, with the Portuguese voyages of discovery during the late fifteenth century, and developed through the nineteenth century. From that point on, Western explorers, scholars, writers, artists, and, ultimately, colonial administrators undertook to study, represent artistically, govern, and economically exploit the East. Traditional orientalism focused on the literary and scholarly results of that enterprise and included grammars, dictionaries, encyclopedias, texts, translations, travel accounts, novels, and paintings. The most important study of this process is that of Raymond Schwab. The artistic extension of orientalism is the school of orientalist painters, a group of nineteenth-century, mostly academic, painters, predominantly French, English, and German, who focused on real and imagined scenes of Middle Eastern exoticism in their work.

The field of orientalism changed radically with the 1978 publication of *Orientalism,* by Edward W. Said. Said, although focusing solely on the Islamic Middle East, exposed orientalism as a colonialist enterprise, "a Western style for dominating, restructuring, and having authority over the Orient" (p. 15). His work has exercised a vast influence over the field of cultural studies and has been applied by scholars in the other fields of traditional orientalist studies, including India, China, Japan and Southeast Asia.

See also NERVAL, GÉRARD DE; SAID, EDWARD.

Bibliography

Benjamin, Roger, ed. *Orientalism: Delacroix to Klee.* Sydney, Australia: Art Gallery of New South Wales, 1997.

Said, Edward W. *Orientalism.* New York; London: Penguin, 1995.

Schwab, Raymond. *The Oriental Renaissance: Europe's Rediscovery of India and the East, 1680–1880,* translated by Gene Patterson-Black and Victor Reinking. New York: Columbia University Press, 1984.

Williams, Patrick, ed. *Edward Said,* 4 volumes. Thousand Oaks, CA; London: Sage, 2001.

JOHN M. LUNDQUIST

ORIENTALISTS, INTERNATIONAL CONGRESS OF

A group whose meetings were devoted to the spread of learning in Oriental subjects.

Initiated in Paris in 1873, these periodic meetings of scholars—dedicated, as one scholar put it, to "the propagation of the knowledge of the History, Languages and Civilizations of Oriental people among Western Nations"—represented the academic profession of Orientalism as it was recognized in nineteenth-century Europe. Few non-Europeans attended the early meetings, and no meetings were held outside Europe until the fourteenth congress was held in Algiers in 1905. Papers on Asian and African topics of all sorts, but primarily focusing on philology and archaeology, were presented in sessions organized by geographical region or language family. The small size of the academic community concerned with Asia and Africa is indicated by the fact that the number of members, on all topics combined, remained in the hundreds throughout the nineteenth century. Some members, however, attended as representatives of national Oriental societies. Congress proceedings were normally published. The work of the International Congress of Orientalists is carried on by the International Congress of Asian and North African Studies.

Bibliography

Said, Edward. *Orientalism.* New York: Pantheon Books, 1978.

RICHARD W. BULLIET
UPDATED BY VANESA CASANOVA-FERNANDEZ

ORMANIAN, MAGHAKIA
[1841–1918]

Armenian clergyman and scholar; Armenian patriarch of Constantinople, 1896–1908.

Born in Istanbul, Ormanian was sent to seminary in Rome (1851) and was subsequently ordained a Roman Catholic priest. In 1877 he left the Roman Catholic Church to join the Armenian Apostolic Church. He was ordained a celibate priest in 1879 by Nerses Vazhapetian, Armenian patriarch of Constantinople, who employed his linguistic skills to prepare appeals to embassies and foreign governments concerning the situation of Armenians in the Ottoman Empire. In 1880 Ormanian was elected primate of Erzurum, and in 1887 he became a teacher of theology at Echmiadzin in Russian Armenia. Banished by the czarist government for his political views, in 1889 Ormanian became the dean of the seminary of Armash, near İzmir.

Ormanian was appointed Armenian patriarch of Constantinople in 1896, just after a series of mass killings attributed to the policies of Sultan Abdülhamit II had been unleashed against the Armenians of the Ottoman Empire. As religious leader of the Armenians, Ormanian steered a cautious course during an era of repression. This brought him much animosity from radical elements in the Armenian community who opposed policies of the sultan. In 1908, during the Young Turk revolution, he was removed from office.

Thereafter, Ormanian devoted his time to writing one of the great works of Armenian historical scholarship. His three-volume *Azgapatum* (National history; 1912 to 1927) is an exhaustive Armenian ecclesiastical history. In 1914 Ormanian entered the Armenian monastery of St. James in Jerusalem. He was exiled to Damascus in 1917 by the Young Turk regime and died a year later in Istanbul.

ROUBEN P. ADALIAN

ORMSBY-GORE, WILLIAM GEORGE ARTHUR
[1885–1964]

British colonial official, also known as Lord Harlech.

In 1918 William George Arthur Ormsby-Gore went to Palestine as assistant political officer for the

Zionist Commission. In April of that year he defended the Balfour Declaration, but urged restrictions on Jewish immigration and land purchases because of growing indigenous impoverishment. In a speech in London in August 1918, however, Ormsby-Gore asserted that the indigenous population west of the Jordan River was not Arab and that the real Arab national movement lay outside of Palestine with Prince Faisal of the Hijaz (now part of Saudi Arabia), who was soon to be named king of Syria.

Ormsby-Gore became the British member of the Permanent Mandates Commission (1921–1922). As Britain's colonial secretary from 1936 to 1938, he rebuffed advocates of the partition of Palestine, and retired from office amid the controversy.

> *See also* BALFOUR DECLARATION (1917); FAISAL I IBN HUSSEIN; PERMANENT MANDATES COMMISSION; ZIONIST COMMISSION FOR PALESTINE.

Bibliography

Abboushi, W. F. *The Unmaking of Palestine.* Wisbech, U.K.: Middle East and North African Studies Press, 1985.

Ingrams, Doreen, ed. *Palestine Papers, 1917–1922: Seeds of Conflict.* London: J. Murray, 1972.

ELIZABETH THOMPSON

ORTAOYUNU

The Ottoman popular theater-in-the-round.

Sometimes described as "karagöz come to life," Ortaoyunu has frequently been compared to the commedia dell'arte because of its improvisational character. An urban entertainment, it was traditionally an open-air presentation performed by an all-male cast in a space encircled by the audience (women separated from men). Performances also were presented in taverns, palaces, and eventually theaters. Scenery was minimal: a chair or table to indicate a shop or booth, and one or two folding screens painted to represent a building, a forest, and so on.

A small group of folk musicians supplied music for dancers who appeared before the main presentation. This was followed by a burlesque dialogue between the two main characters, Pişekâr and Kavuklu, who correspond closely to the shadow play figures Hacivat and Karagöz, respectively. The play might be chosen from the special ortaoyunu repertory or, like karagöz, retell the plot of a well-known romance (Leyla and Mecnun, Ferhat and Şirin, etc.). The presentation was always open in form, however, and rather than a plot, might offer various scenes that entertained while imparting a human or political message.

At the beginning of the twentieth century, the improvisational aspect of ortaoyunu inspired the tuluât theater, but attempts (including the staging of Western plays) failed to preserve the Turkish theater-in-the-round as a viable form of entertainment.

Bibliography

Halman, Talât Sait. *Modern Turkish Drama: An Anthology of Plays in Translation.* Minneapolis, MN: Bibliotheca Islamica, 1976.

KATHLEEN R. F. BURRILL

OSIRAK

A French-produced nuclear reactor sold to Iraq.

Osirak was originally developed in 1964 as a material-testing reactor. The purchase contract was signed on 17 November 1975; on 13 January 1976, Iraq signed a contract with Italy to purchase "hot cells" used to separate plutonium, which would make the reactor capable of producing fissionable material for an atomic bomb. Construction began in the late 1970s on the outskirts of Baghdad and was supposed to be completed by late 1981. Osirak was destroyed by Israel's air force on 7 June 1981; part of a smaller reactor survived.

Bibliography

Timmerman, Kenneth R. *The Death Lobby: How the West Armed Iraq.* Boston: Houghton Mifflin, 1991.

RONEN ZEIDEL

OSLO ACCORD (1993)

Agreement between Israel and the PLO negotiated secretly in Oslo, Norway, and signed at the White House on 13 September 1993.

In 1993 Israel and the Palestine Liberation Organization (PLO) agreed to recognize each other, and signed a Declaration of Principles (DOP) providing for Palestinian self-government in the West Bank and Gaza Strip for five years.

Backdrop to the Accord

The agreement resulted from a convergence of events and trends that created an optimal opportunity for peace between the two parties. The first Intifada (uprising) by the Palestinian population of the West Bank and Gaza against Israel's occupation, which began in December 1987, empowered the PLO, as the Palestinians' representative, to seek a diplomatic settlement with Israel. In 1988 PLO chairman Yasir Arafat recognized Israel, accepted United Nations Security Council Resolution 242, and renounced terrorism. The PLO could not immediately capitalize on these concessions, however, because Israel did not reciprocate. The PLO's position deteriorated due to the collapse of the Soviet Union, which left the PLO without superpower support. Furthermore, the Israeli government of Yitzhak Shamir adamantly refused to deal with the PLO or to make territorial concessions for peace. Believing that Iraq could help the Palestinian cause, Arafat sided with Saddam Husscin during the Gulf Crisis (1990–1991), and thereby lost the financial support of the Gulf states.

The collapse of the Soviet Union, mass Jewish immigration to Israel, and the destruction of Iraq's army in 1991 enhanced Israel's security, but the Intifada convinced the Israeli Labor and left-of-center parties that continued occupation and repression were deemed costly in terms of international isolation and domestic discord, whereas granting self-government to the Palestinians was gradually viewed as less objectionable.

Moreover, more and more Palestinians and Israelis and their leaders concluded that there was no military solution to their conflict. The PLO had galvanized Palestinians and gained international recognition, but its armed struggle against Israel failed to liberate an inch of Palestine. Even though Israel was considered to be the fourth strongest military power in the world, it could not destroy the PLO or subdue a civilian population of two million in the occupied territories. Both sides concluded that mutual recognition and sharing historic Palestine was the only viable option.

U.S. president George H. W. Bush and Secretary of State James Baker III thus had an unprecedented opportunity to broker peace in the Middle East by arranging the Madrid Peace Conference (1991) between Israel and the Arabs, including the Palestinians. When Prime Minister Shamir appeared to be stalling, Bush and Baker withheld a guarantee for a $10 billion loan for Israel. In the next elections in Israel, the public brought to power a moderate coalition, headed by Yitzhak Rabin, with a "territory for peace" policy. But eleven sessions and twenty-two months after Madrid, the negotiations proved unproductive. The PLO regarded the framework for talks as unfair, and did not consider the United States or its middle-range officials to be "honest brokers." Israel realized that Palestinian negotiators from the occupied territories were unwilling or unable to negotiate independently from the PLO.

Norway's foreign ministry arranged for a private, secret channel in Oslo for two Israeli scholars, Yair Hirshfeld and Ron Pundak, who were in touch with Yossi Beilin, Israel's dovish deputy foreign minister, and a PLO economist and aide to Chairman Arafat, Ahmad Sulayman Qurai (Abu Ala). Negotiations began in the winter and spring of 1993. When they progressed, Israel's foreign minister, Shimon Peres, took charge, and convinced security-conscious Prime Minister Rabin to support the agreement. Israel and the PLO initialed two sets of documents in Oslo in late August: an exchange of letters of mutual recognition and the Declaration of Principles on Interim Self-Government Arrangements (DOP).

The Accord and Its Reception

On 9 September 1993 Arafat signed the PLO letter recognizing Israel's right to exist, accepted Security Council Resolution 242, renounced the use of terror and violence, and pledged to remove clauses in the Palestinian Covenant calling for the elimination of Israel. By recognizing Israel, the PLO renounced the Palestinian people's claim to 78 percent of historic Palestine, in which they had lived for centuries. The next day Rabin signed

Pictured left to right are Israeli prime minister Yitzhak Rabin, U.S. president Bill Clinton, and Palestinian leader Yasir Arafat. In 1993, the three leaders met in Washington to sign the Israeli-PLO peace accord. © AP/WIDE WORLD PHOTOS. REPRODUCED BY PERMISSION.

Israel's letter, recognizing the PLO as the representative of the Palestinian people and declaring Israel's intention to negotiate with the PLO. Implicit was Israel's recognition of Palestinian demands for self-determination and independence in the West Bank and Gaza Strip.

The second document, the DOP, which was signed at the White House on 13 September 1993, outlined a five-year plan for Palestinian self-government, starting with Israel's withdrawal of troops from the Gaza Strip and the West Bank town of Jericho, and the transfer of authority over economic development, education and culture, taxes, social welfare, and tourism. This was followed by elections of an interim self-government council. After the second year, negotiations would begin on Jerusalem, refugees of 1948, Jewish settlements, and borders.

Most Israelis and Palestinians were initially approving. Palestinians were disappointed that the most fundamental issues were deferred, but supported the agreement because there was no credible alternative. There were, however, vocal rejectionists in both camps. In Israel, leading figures in the Likud Party such as Ariel Sharon and Benjamin Netanyahu stated that should they come to power, they would not honor the agreement, and Jewish settlers warned of violent resistance to the removal of settlements. Palestinian radicals initiated deadly violence against settlers and soldiers. Negotiations over implementation of the interim agreement dragged on until another was signed in Cairo in May 1994. Then Israel's troops withdrew and Palestinian police took over in Jericho and the Gaza Strip. Violence by both sides and postponements diminished support for the Oslo Agreement, yet the parties managed to reach a number of partial agreements, including Oslo II, signed at the White House on 28 September 1995. Oslo II set the stage for Israel's further withdrawal from the West Bank and for Palestinian elections.

With each new agreement, the opponents of a peaceful settlement intensified their violence. HAMAS and Islamic Jihad conducted a number of deadly terrorist acts against Israelis. In Israel, the Likud Party increased its inciteful rhetoric against Prime Minister Rabin, providing Jewish extremists with the climate that resulted in his assassination in November 1995. The new prime minister, Shimon Peres, moved forward with the peace process, but was defeated in May 1996 by the Likud's Benjamin Netanyahu, who capitalized on popular security anxiety caused by a series of deadly terrorist bombings in Jerusalem and Tel Aviv. Netanyahu initially declined to meet Arafat, and refused to implement the Rabin government's agreement on troop withdrawal. He pursued a hardline policy—much to the disappointment of the administration of U.S. president Bill Clinton—that included the construction of a controversial Jewish settlement at Har Homa (Jamal Abu Ghunaym) on the outskirts of Jerusalem Although Netanyahu signed in October 1998 the Wye River Memorandum, which mandated further Israeli withdrawal, Oslo continued to unravel. The election of Ehud Barak of the Labor Party gave some hope for a peaceful resolution of the conflict, but negotiations between Barak and Arafat, mediated directly by Clinton at Camp David in July 2000, and indirectly elsewhere, broke down.

The failure of diplomacy and the worsening conditions in the territories resulted in the Aqsa Intifada, which began on 29 September 2000, the day after Ariel Sharon and an Israeli security force of 1,000 visited al-Haram al-Sharif, or Temple Mount. Arafat probably acquiesced to, if not encouraged, the violence in the hope of achieving diplomatic gains he could not get at the negotiating table, but by doing so he broke his promise made at Oslo to end the attacks on Israel. Barak was voted out of office in early 2001 and replaced by Sharon, a hardline member of Likud and an opponent of Oslo. The spiral of violence that followed resulted in the collapse of the Oslo peace process.

Both sides blamed the other for the breakdown. Palestinian officials blamed Clinton and Barak, even though Clinton offered far-reaching parameters on 23 December 2000 that moved the process forward, and Barak made groundbreaking concessions to the Palestinians at Taba, Egypt, in January 2001. Israeli and some U.S. officials, especially Barak and Clinton, blamed Arafat, who had championed a two-state solution for three decades but could not accept the offer at Camp David, which would not have led to a viable, contiguous, and independent Palestine state. The media and the public in the Arab world, Israel, and the United States adopted their respective official one-sided versions of the breakdown. Balanced accounts—such as those offered by Deborah Sontag of the *New York Times,* Clinton's advisor Robert Malley, and Charles Enderlin, a French-Israeli television journalist—reveal complex causes and indicate that responsibility for the failure can be shared three ways.

Despite its detractors, the accomplishments of the Oslo Accord are considerable. For the first time in a century, most Arabs and Jews agreed on a solution—a two-state solution. And, after a decade of negotiations from Madrid to Taba, both sides had narrowed their differences on most of the key issues.

See also AQSA INTIFADA, AL-; ARAFAT, YASIR; BAKER, JAMES A.; BARAK, EHUD; BUSH, GEORGE HERBERT WALKER; CAMP DAVID SUMMIT (2000); CLINTON, WILLIAM JEFFERSON; LIKUD; MADRID CONFERENCE (1991); NETANYAHU, BENJAMIN; PALESTINE LIBERATION ORGANIZATION (PLO); PERES, SHIMON; QURAI, AHMAD SULAYMAN; RABIN, YITZHAK.

Bibliography

Abbas, Mahmoud. *Through Secret Channels: The Road to Oslo.* Reading, U.K.: Garnet, 1995.

Ashwari, Hanan. *This Side of Peace: A Personal Account.* New York: Simon and Schuster, 1995.

Enderlin, Charles. *Shattered Dreams: The Failure of the Peace Process in the Middle East, 1995–2002.* New York: Other Press, 2003.

Malley, Robert, and Agha, Hussein. "Camp David: The Tragedy of Errors." *New York Times Review of Books.* 9 August 2001.

Peres, Shimon. *Battling for Peace: A Memoir.* New York: Random House, 1995.

Said, Edward. *End of the Peace Process: Oslo and After.* New York: Pantheon, 2000.

Savir, Uri. *The Process: 1,100 Days that Changed the Middle East.* New York: Vintage, 1999.

Shlaim, Avi. *The Iron Wall: Israel and the Arab World.* New York: W.W. Norton, 2000.

Sontag, Deborah. "Quest for the Mideast Peace: How and Why It Failed." *New York Times.* 26 July 2001.

PHILIP MATTAR

OSMAN, HOUSE OF

The longest ruling dynasty in Islamic history, 1300–1922.

The Osmanli dynasty was named for Osman I, the Turkish leader in whose time (ruled c. 1299–1324) the foundations were laid for a state that later became the Ottoman Empire. The name was corrupted to Othoman, which became Ottoman in European usage. Succession went to the most successful son, often as a result of civil war or at least the threat of it. To prevent further strife, the new sultan was obliged to kill all his brothers and their sons. From the early 1600s, lateral succession became possible; and by the end of the 1600s, seniority had become the rule.

During the reign of the thirty-sixth sultan, Mehmet VI Vahidettin, the Ankara government abolished the sultanate (1 November 1922) and, on 3 March 1924, also the caliphate—the office of the head of Islam—which had been assumed by Ottoman sultans. Abdülmecit II, the last caliph and thirty-seventh ruler, and all members of the dynasty were immediately sent into exile, from which they were to be allowed back into the Republic of Turkey fifty years later—thirty years for female members of the family.

See also ABDÜLMECIT II.

Bibliography

Alderson, A. D. *The Structure of the Ottoman Dynasty.* Oxford: Clarendon Press, 1956.

I. METIN KUNT

OTTOMAN AND TURKISH ART

See ART

OTTOMAN BUREAU OF TRANSLATION

See BUREAU OF TRANSLATION

OTTOMAN EMPIRE

This entry consists of the following articles:

OVERVIEW
CIVIL SERVICE
DEBT

OVERVIEW

Multiethnic, multireligious, monarchical Muslim empire founded by the Ottoman (or Osmanli) Turks in the late thirteenth century; it survived until after World War I, when, as one of the losing Central powers, it was formally dissolved by the peace treaties of 1918–1922. Mustafa Kemal (Atatürk) overthrew the last sultan in 1922.

In the thirteenth century, as the power of the Seljuk Turks declined, the Ottoman Turks began to absorb their small states. In the fourteenth century, the Ottomans took over some of the Byzantine Empire's territories and, late in that century, several Balkan states. Under Selim I and Süleyman I (the Magnificent), the Ottomans brought Hungary and much of the Balkan peninsula, parts of Persia (now Iran), and the Arab lands under their rule. In 1453, they conquered Constantinople (now Istanbul) and made it their capital. During the sixteenth and seventeenth centuries, the Ottoman Empire was at its peak and controlled much of southeastern Europe, the Middle East, and North Africa, comprising some 1.2 million square miles (1.9 million sq. km) with some sixteen million people. That area would today include parts or all of the following: southeast Hungary, Albania, the six republics that were pre-1991 Yugoslavia (Serbia, Montenegro, Croatia, Macedonia, Slovenia, and Bosnia and Herzegovina), Greece, Bulgaria, Romania, southern and Caucasian Russia, Turkey, Syria, Iraq, Lebanon, Israel, Jordan, Egypt, Saudi Arabia, Kuwait, the United Arab Emirates, Libya, Tunisia, and Algeria.

By 1914, only about 11,000 square miles (17,700 sq. km) remained of the Ottoman Empire in Europe of the 232,000 square miles (373,000 sq. km) controlled during the sixteenth century, with 613,000 square miles (986,000 sq. km) remaining overall—about half the territory of the sixteenth century. That greatly reduced territory included only what is now Turkey, the Arab states, and Israel until the empire's official dissolution (1918–1922).

The empire's early capitals included Bursa and Edirne (formerly Adrianople), but Constantinople (Turkish, Konstantiniye) served as its capital from its capture in 1453 until 1923, when the Republic of Turkey declared its new capital at Ankara. Constantinople was by far the largest Ottoman city, with about 400,000 population in 1520 and some 1 million in 1914. Other major Ottoman cities included Belgrade, Aleppo, Cairo, and Damascus. After 1800, cities such as İzmir (Smyrna), Beirut, and Alexandria rose to prominence—products of increasing nineteenth-century economic ties with Europe.

The empire's administrative divisions changed with time. By the nineteenth century, most provinces (*vilayets*) were divided into districts (*sanjaks*) and subdistricts (*kazas*), each of which had a number of village areas (*nahiyes*).

The Sprawling Empire

Geography and climate varied greatly, since the empire ranged over three continents, including much of what is today's Middle East. Mountains of modest height cut by corridor valleys and heavy forests characterized part of the European provinces, while in Anatolia, narrow coastal plains and high interior plateaus with little vegetation rose to rugged snow-capped mountains in the eastern part of the peninsula. In the Syrian province, similarly narrow coastal plains bordering the Mediterranean rose to the mountains of Lebanon. To the east, highlands yielded to desert and, beyond, to the alluvial lowlands of Mesopotamia (now Iraq). A spine of mountains branches south from the Syrian province, just inland—with one range heading into the Sinai peninsula and the other emerging along the western edge of the Arabian peninsula, reaching the greatest height in Yemen. The great rivers of the empire included the Danube, Tigris, Euphrates, and Nile—but navigable rivers were comparatively rare in both the European and Middle Eastern areas of the empire.

Climatic conditions ranged from the cold heights of eastern Anatolia to the heat of the Egyptian, Arabian, and North African deserts, including the sweltering heat and humidity of the coast of the Persian (Arabian) Gulf. Almost everywhere rainfall was sparse—a fact of Ottoman life.

The empire had a wide base of natural resources; and much of its expansion can be understood as an effort to seize and control areas rich in various resources. For example, the Ottoman conquest of Serbia derived, in part, from an interest in its silver mines. As the empire lost territory in the nineteenth and twentieth centuries, it also lost the rich diversity of its resource base. The Ottoman state bent the economy to meet its imperial needs before any others. Edicts directed mineral, agricultural, and industrial products to satisfy both the imperial military and the bureaucracy.

The Empire's Agricultural History

Agriculture was the basic economic activity, providing a livelihood for the majority of Ottoman subjects through the centuries—although the produce varied according to time and place. Some areas were not cultivated during periods of political disorder but were tilled again with the guarantee of political security. During the sixteenth century, the areas under cultivation were so extensive that they remained at peak production until the post-1830 period of increasing governmental recentralization. The fertility of the soil was legendary in some areas, such as the Nile delta or the Aydin river valley in western Anatolia. More commonly, however, the soil was not rich or, when fertile, lacked sufficient rainfall. In many areas, agriculture was a precarious enterprise; crop failures and famines were normal in the cycle of life. Consequently, to survive, many families mixed animal raising and handicraft production with farming. Landholdings were usually small, a pattern preferred by the state, which sought direct relations with the farming families (and fiscal and political control over them). Large estates became more common after 1750, as agriculture became increasingly commercial—particularly on new land being brought into cultivation. Hence, great estates were most common in the eastern Syrian and Iraqi regions that were settled or resettled in the later nineteenth century. Such large holdings grew cereal grains; generally, overall grain output increased because of rising market opportunities. Vineyards and olive orchards flourished in the Mediterranean provinces of the empire, and cotton grew in the Macedonian, Anatolian, Syrian, and Egyptian regions—but their yields fluctuated greatly over time. Forest products were common to the Balkan regions and

The church of Hagia Sophia in Istanbul, late 1800s. Commissioned by the emperor Justinian in the sixth century, the church was built in only five years (532–537 C.E.) and stands as one of the greatest examples of Byzantine architecture. © MICHAEL MASLAN HISTORIC PHOTOGRAPHY/CORBIS. REPRODUCED BY PERMISSION.

along sections of the Anatolian Black Sea coast, while dates were harvested in the Iraqi areas.

Industrial production first served both international and domestic markets but, after about 1800, internal demand predominated. Textiles, leather making, and food processing were of great importance; urban-based enterprises were highly visible, but rural manufactories were extensive and important. Until the nineteenth century, guildlike bodies (esnaf) in the cities and towns played important roles in organizing and controlling production. They worked in an uneasy cooperation with the state, helping it to obtain goods in exchange for government support of esnaf privileges.

Significant economic changes in the Ottoman Empire resulted from the rising economic, political, and military power of Europe in the late eighteenth and nineteenth centuries. Until about 1750, the Ottoman economy was autarkic—that is, relatively self-sufficient—by government design. It imported comparatively little and exported a variety of textiles and other manufactured goods, both to the East and the West. Thereafter, the export of many finished products decreased, but the export of agricultural products and raw materials, such as cereal grains and raw cotton, increased—almost exclusively to Western markets. Ottoman industry received a rude shock from the competition of European manufactured goods. Ottoman textile manufacturers then restructured their enterprises along nonguild lines with unregulated production and lower wages, so most of the craft guilds lost power and ceased functioning. Using machine-made thread and other low-technology imports, many nineteenth-century local textile makers survived and even increased production for the expanding domestic market. In addition, several new international export industries emerged that employed tens of thousands of poorly paid workers, notably in raw-silk reeling and carpet making.

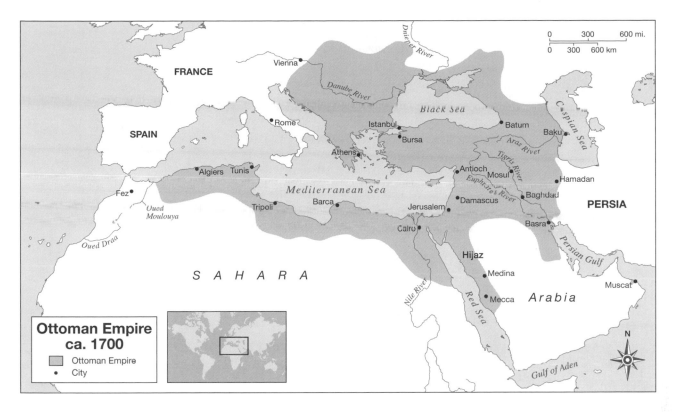

Ottoman Empire ca. 1700

Ottoman Empire
City

MAP BY XNR PRODUCTIONS, INC. THE GALE GROUP.

The Challenges of Ethnic Diversity

The ethnic and religious makeup of the Ottoman Empire was diverse and intermingled. As if to lead by example, the Ottoman ruling family was truly international, counting dozens of ethnic groups among its ancestors. The relative size of the empire's ethnic groups is very difficult to determine, since the pertinent statistics were manipulated for use as weapons by nineteenth-century nationalism. Various ethnic groups sought their own states or attempted to deny the claims of competitors. In the era before territorial shrinkage, speakers of Turkish and of the Slavic languages formed the two largest groups in the empire. The largest ethnic groups were the Turks, Arabs, Greeks, Slovenians, Serbs, Albanians, Ruthenians, Wallachians, Moldavians, Croatians, Armenians, Laz, and Kurds. The official language of the empire was Ottoman Turkish, an administrative language consisting largely of Turkish grammar, with Turkish, Arabic, and some Persian vocabulary. The elite classes spoke and wrote in Ottoman Turkish, exchanging official correspondence and sharing a high culture, which gave the empire a unity that was superimposed over its

diversity. The religious makeup was equally diverse. Until the nineteenth century, when districts with large Christian populations broke away, most Ottoman subjects were Christians of various denominations, usually of the Orthodox church, the descendant of the Byzantine state church. There also were Armenian and Greek Orthodox Catholics, Maronites, and those belonging to smaller Christian denominations; there was as well a diverse but small population of Jews. Within the Ottoman Islamic community, adherents of Sunni Islam slightly out-numbered adherents of Shi'ism. During the nineteenth century, Islam became the predominant religion in the empire, just as Turks became the dominant ethnic group. By 1914, about 83 percent of the population practiced Islam.

During the four centuries before 1850, the Ottoman state had sought to organize the various ethnic and religious communities into a smaller number of religious nations, called millets. Under the leadership of its own religious authority, each millet organized, funded, and administered its own religious and educational institutions. The Greek

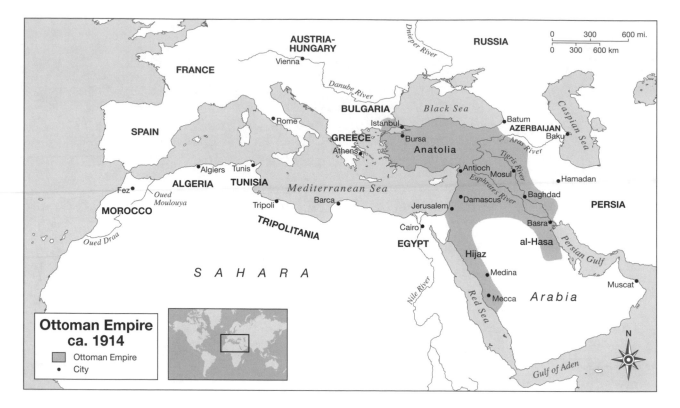

AUSTRIA-HUNGARY

FRANCE

Vienna

Danube River

Dnieper River

RUSSIA

0   300   600 mi.
0   300   600 km

BULGARIA

Black Sea

SPAIN

Rome

Istanbul

GREECE

Bursa

Athens

Anatolia

AZERBAIJAN

Batum

Baku

Caspian Sea

Aras River

Algiers   Tunis

ALGERIA   TUNISIA

Mediterranean Sea

Antioch   Mosul

Tigris River

Hamadan

Fez

Oued Moulouya

Tripoli   Barca

Euphrates River

Baghdad

PERSIA

MOROCCO

Jerusalem

Damascus

Oued Draa

TRIPOLITANIA

Cairo

Basra

Persian Gulf

EGYPT

Hijaz

al-Hasa

S A H A R A

Nile River

Red Sea

Medina

Muscat

Mecca

Arabia

N

Ottoman Empire ca. 1914

Ottoman Empire
• City

Gulf of Aden

Orthodox millet, for example, ran schools and churches for the lay population, as well as seminaries to train its clergy. The sultan, who had descended from Osman, the fourteenth-century founder of the dynasty, ruled the empire throughout its history. Until 1453, the sultans shared power with other important families, as the first among equals. Thereafter, they theoretically were without peer, although power passed from the sultan to members of his government after about 1640. Until the end of the seventeenth century, power rested with the central state in the capital; during the eighteenth century, power became dispersed among provincial notables. A centralized state emerged during the early 1800s—based on internal evolutionary developments, as well as borrowings from Western models. Struggles for control of the state between the reforming sultans and the reforming bureaucrats swung in favor of the bureaucracy between 1839 and 1878 and then back to the sultan until 1908. After the revolution of the Young Turks in July of 1908, the last sultans reigned rather than ruled.

During the nineteenth century, the Ottoman Empire lost its Balkan territories to rising European nationalism and imperialism—especially pan-Slavism as instigated by Russia. Various Balkan ethnic groups—the Serbs, Greeks, and Bulgarians—abandoned, with great-power sponsorship, the Ottoman multicultural formula and opted for nation-statehood, which aspired to ethnic homogeneity but did not achieve it. Government efforts to create a competing Ottoman nationality foundered in the face of exclusivist nation-state identity. Efforts to eradicate differences among its remaining subjects were similarly unsuccessful. Take for example the state program to abolish the millets; fearing a loss of influence, various religious authorities—both Christian and Muslim—as well as many European statesmen opposed the move.

Increased Westernization Shapes the Empire

At the same time, ongoing domestic-reform efforts produced a revitalized, powerful Ottoman state that reasserted its presence in an unprecedented fashion. A series of reform decrees—the Hatt-i Şerif of Gülhane (1839) and the Hatt-i Hümayun (1856)—presented the path that Ottoman leaders intended

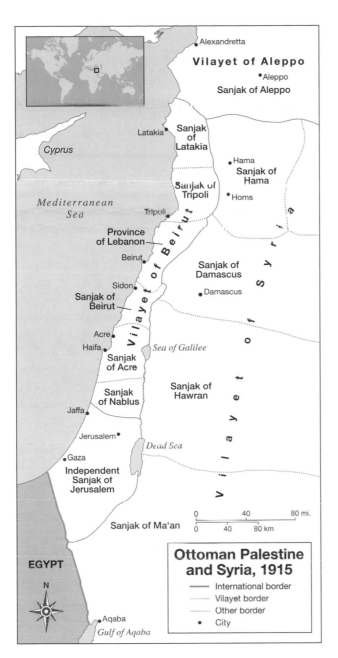

Ottoman Palestine and Syria, 1915

— International border
Vilayet border
Other border
• City

MAP BY XNR PRODUCTIONS, INC. THE GALE GROUP.

vast network of secular, nonsectarian, Westernizing schools to inculcate the new values. In the realm of popular culture, entertainment forms of Western origin—the theater and novels—became increasingly popular, as did European-style clothing and manners. Nineteenth-century Ottoman experiences foreshadowed those of third-world states of the twentieth century in yet other ways. After increasing taxation to finance the expensive civil and military changes, the Ottoman Empire ultimately resorted to borrowing vast sums from abroad, which eventually resulted in virtual bankruptcy and a partial foreign takeover of the Ottoman economy. Toward the end, despite centuries of success, the empire could not compete with the explosion of twentieth-century European economic, military, and political power; after participating as a member of the losing Central powers in World War I, it was partitioned.

See also TANZIMAT; YOUNG TURKS.

Bibliography

Davison, Roderic H. *Turkey.* Englewood Cliffs, NJ: Prentice-Hall, 1968.

Faruqhi, Suraiya. "Agriculture and Rural Life in the Ottoman Empire, ca. 1500–1878." *New Perspectives on Turkey* 1 (1987): 3–34.

Gerber, Haim. *The Social Origins of the Modern Middle East.* Boulder, CO: L. Rienner, 1987.

El-Haj, Rif'at Ali Abou. *Formation of the Ottoman State: The Ottoman Empire, Sixteenth to Eighteenth Centuries.* Albany, NY: 1991.

Inalcik, Halil. "Application of the Tanzimat and Its Social Effects." *Archivum Ottomanicum* (1973): 97–128.

Karpat, Kemal H. *Ottoman Population 1830–1914: Demographic and Social Characteristics.* Madison: University of Wisconsin Press, 1985.

Lewis, Bernard. *The Emergence of Modern Turkey,* 3d edition. New York: Oxford University Press, 2002.

Owen, Roger. *The Middle East in the World Economy, 1800–1914.* London: Methuen, 1981.

Pamuk, Şevket. *The Ottoman Empire and European Capitalism, 1820–1913: Trade, Investment, and Production.* Cambridge, U.K., and New York: Cambridge University Press, 1987.

Pitcher, Donald Edgar. *An Historical Geography of the Ottoman Empire from Earliest Times to the End of the Sixteenth Century.* Leiden, Neth.: Brill, 1968.

to follow. Ottoman military forces successfully adopted Western weapons, strategy, and tactics and crushed local notables, nomadic tribes, and other domestic challenges to the central regime. The state apparatus became marked by increasing centralization, specialization of function, and ever greater size. Knowledge of Western languages, administrative practices, and culture became critical to advancement in the political and, finally, social spheres. The government, for example, founded a

Quataert, Donald. *Social Disintegration and Popular Resistance in the Ottoman Empire, 1881–1908: Reactions to European Economic Penetration.* New York: New York University Press, 1983.

DONALD QUATAERT

OTTOMAN EMPIRE: CIVIL SERVICE

Government administrative service exclusive of the military.

In the sense of an administrative system that recruits and promotes officials on merit and operates by impartially applied rules, civil service is an anachronistic concept almost anywhere (except China) before the mid-nineteenth century. Even after that time, to apply the concept to the Ottoman Empire is questionable, in that the regulatory apparatus, although created, was used to thwart its impartiality.

For centuries, however, the Ottoman Turks had had a branch of the ruling elite whose functions were civil—in the sense of being neither military nor religious. Until the end of the eighteenth century, this group is best understood as scribes. Ottomans referred to them with terms like *kalem efendileri* ("men of the pen" or "of the offices"), or the corresponding abstract noun *kalemiye.* The scribes conducted the government's correspondence and kept its financial accounts and records on land tenure. Nineteenth-century reforms expanded and changed this branch of service into something like the civil services then emerging in Europe. From the late 1830s on, it also was referred to with a different term, *mülkiye,* having implications associated with land tenure and sovereignty. Particularly relevant to local administration, this term came to refer generally to civil officials, *memurin-i mülkiye.*

The state of the late eighteenth-century scribal service shows where this change began. It had a core of fifteen hundred men, serving in Istanbul in the Land Registry *(Defterhane-i Amire),* the grand-vizierial headquarters that Europeans called the Sublime Porte *(Bab-i Ali),* and the Treasury *(Bab-i Defteri).* Considering that scribes also served in military organizations or on provincial governors' staffs, an outside total can be estimated at two thousand. While it may seem odd that so few could suffice for a large empire, the Ottomans did not historically use scribes as administrators. In the years of con-

quest and through the sixteenth century, for example, local administration had been largely in cavalry officers' hands. By the eighteenth century, an able man might rise through scribal ranks to provincial governor, a kind of proto-foreign minister *(reis ül-küttab),* or grand vizier. Such careers were exceptional, and an ordinary scribe's role remained that of secretary *(katib).*

Many traits of the scribal service indicated its obscurity within the ruling elites. It had as yet no recruitment system beyond familial and patronage networks. It lacked its own form of training, other than apprenticeship. Except for those raised to heights that exposed them to elite factional politics, career patterns bore imprints of the guild tradition and the Sufi ethos that permeated it. To serve as a scribe was the chief practical application of the adab-tradition—the worldly, literary aspect of the learned Islamic culture. Building on an ancient Middle Eastern cultural elitism, Ottoman scribes had elaborated their craft to a high point in which mastery of stylistic conventions became more important than clear communication.

The shift from scribal to civil service began under sultans Selim III (1789–1807) and Mahmud II (1808–1839). In response to defeat by Russia during the last quarter of the eighteenth century, Selim's "New Order" *(Nizam-i Cedit),* the first attempt at comprehensive governmental overhaul, included both reform of existing agencies and the first Ottoman attempt to create European-style systems of permanent consular and diplomatic representation. In 1821, Mahmud II created the Translation Office *(Tercüme Odasi)* at the Sublime Porte, which trained young Muslims as translators. Following his abolition of the janissary infantry (1826), administrative reform accelerated. In the 1830s, Mahmud II revived the diplomatic corps and reorganized government departments as ministries. To support his efforts at centralization, he also laid the bases of civil personnel policy by reforming conditions of service. He created a new table of civil ranks, abandoned the practice of annual reappointment *(tevcihat)* to high office, replaced old forms of compensation (such as fee collecting) with salaries, founded the first secular civil schools, and enacted laws eliminating some insecurities inherent in officials' historical status as the sultan's slaves. These reforms climaxed with the Gülhane Decree, which proclaimed "security for life, honor, and property" and equality for all—civil officials included.

Several weak sultans followed Mahmud II. This enabled top civil officials—their position in relation to the ruler now much secured, and their importance increased by their role in negotiating with the European powers on whom the empire was becoming dependent—to run the government until another strong sultan emerged. The period so opened became known as the Tanzimat (the Reforms, 1839–c. 1871). The center of power shifted from the palace to the Sublime Porte. As civil officialdom's Westernizing diplomatic vanguard grew in power, a new line of promotion appeared, running from the Translation Office through the embassies to the post of Foreign Minister and the grand vizierate. Westernizing policy changes followed en masse, as the Ottoman government grew in size and in its impact on people's lives. Civil officials now did take responsibility for local administration. Westernizing legal reform and the creation of secular courts gave them judicial roles. Modern census and population registration systems required Ottomans to face civil officials to get identity papers and passports. The teachers in the new secular schools were civil officials. Out of the Westernist official elite a literary vanguard emerged, too; from it the region's first Western-style political protest movement, the Young Ottomans (Yeni Osmanlilar), in turn arose to exploit the tensions created by rapid change.

Between the death of Grand Vizier Ali Paşa (1871) and Sultan Abdülhamit II's accession (1876), the Tanzimat political configuration broke up. Abdülhamit shifted power back to the palace, making it the hub of a police state. Administrative reform continued along the lines charted during the Tanzimat, however. For example, Abdülhamit's reign became a growth period for education, publishing, and public works, especially railroads. In addition, his reign became the most important since Mahmud II's for the development of personnel policy for civil officials. The process began with creation of the personnel records system (sicill-i ahval, 1877). A decree on promotion and retirement followed, in 1880, introducing the idea of a retirement fund (tekaüd sandiği) financed by salary deductions. Commissions were set up to supervise the appointing of civil officials. With these, the civil personnel system assumed the general outlines of a modern, merit-based civil service, except that Abdülhamit manipulated the system, using it rather as a tool by which to control his officials. Under him, the growth of civil officialdom continued, as he pressured the politically conscious to accept office, in which they would become dependent on him. Ultimately, he had about 35,000 career officials and an equal number of hangers-on in civil service.

With the revolution of the Young Turks (Jön Türkler) in 1908 came a bold start in purging civil officialdom and streamlining administrative agencies. Despite gains like the 1913 provincial administration law, World War I and the dismemberment of the empire overcame these efforts. Still, in terms of elites, legislation, and organization, the Republic of Turkey inherited enough so that the early development of its administrative system has been described as evolutionary, rather than revolutionary.

See also ABDÜLHAMIT II; MAHMUD II; SUBLIME PORTE; TANZIMAT; YOUNG OTTOMANS; YOUNG TURKS.

Bibliography

Findley, Carter Vaughn. Bureaucratic Reform in the Ottoman Empire: The Sublime Porte, 1789–1922. Princeton, NJ: Princeton University Press, 1980.

Findley, Carter Vaughn. Ottoman Civil Officialdom: A Social History. Princeton, NJ: Princeton University Press, 1989.

CARTER V. FINDLEY

OTTOMAN EMPIRE: DEBT

Borrowing in the Ottoman Empire by the government and within the private sector.

Throughout most of its history, from 1300 to 1922, the government of the Ottoman Empire relied on short-term loans from individual lenders as well as currency debasement and short-term notes to resolve fiscal shortfalls. On occasion, the Ottoman government just confiscated the monies needed, either from the lenders or from state officials. In the private sector, individuals, who only sometimes were professional moneylenders, lent their surplus to others. Both public and private borrowers commonly paid interest for the privilege. Both public and private borrowing persisted until the end of the empire—although confiscation became rare after about 1825. Very important changes occurred in the forms of borrowing, within and outside the government, beginning about 1850, when foreign capital became available and assumed an unprecedented role.

In many ways, the international borrowing experiences of the Ottoman Empire during the nineteenth century anticipated those of today's third-world nations. The Ottoman economy was competing in a world dominated by the industrialized nations of the West, which possessed superior military technologies and political and economic power. Ottoman survival strategy required large, modern military forces and state structures. As both were exceedingly expensive, government expenditures mounted accordingly. Unlike the economies of many of the countries with which it was competing—notably Britain and France—the Ottoman economy remained essentially agrarian and incapable of generating the funds needed for increasingly complex and costly military and civilian structures. Thus, the government borrowed to modernize and survive.

Acutely aware of the dangers, Ottoman statesmen resisted international borrowing until the crisis provoked by Ottoman participation in the Crimean War, 1854–1856. International loans then quickly succeeded one another, on decreasingly favorable terms. These loans were private, the creditors being European bankers and financiers who were usually given diplomatic assistance by their own governments. By the early 1870s, Ottoman state borrowing too easily substituted for financial planning; between 1869 and 1875, the government borrowed more than its tax collectors took in. The Ottoman state suspended payments on its accumulated debt in 1875, after crop failures cut revenues between 1873 and 1875 and the global depression of 1873 dried up capital imports.

Perhaps fearing occupation by the European governments of its creditors, the Ottoman government eventually honored its obligations. Prolonged negotiations resulted in a reduction and consolidation of the total Ottoman debt and the formation, in 1881, of the Ottoman Public Debt Administration; this body took control of portions of the economy. The Ottoman Public Debt Administration supervised the collections of various tax revenues, turning the proceeds over to the European creditors—an international consortium representing bond-holders of Ottoman obligations. Residents of France, Great Britain, and Germany held most of the bonds. The ceded revenues came from the richest and most lucrative in the empire—taxes imposed on tobacco, salt, silk, timber, alcohol, and postage stamps.

Although nominally a branch of the Ottoman government, the Debt Administration actually was independent and answerable only to the bondholders. Many scholars consider its founding as the beginning of Ottoman semicolonial status—when the state lost control over parts of its economy. Still worse, perhaps, the state's legitimacy and relevancy also declined in the eyes of subjects who had to pay their taxes to a foreign group rather than their own state. The Debt Administration represented a true loss of Ottoman sovereignty, but, as the government may have hoped, the consortium reassured foreign investors, who provided still more loans to the state, which needed still more cash to finance modernization.

Foreign capital invested in the Ottoman private sector became significant only after 1890. A part of the more general diffusion of European capital into the global economy, these investments also derived from the comforting presence of the Debt Administration, which was involved in many of them. Industrial or agricultural investment was nearly completely absent. Railroads, port facilities, and municipal services absorbed most of these monies, more firmly linking the Ottoman and international economies by facilitating the outward flow of raw materials and the import of finished goods. French financiers were the most important single source of funds, while the British and Germans also were significant providers. Almost all these new loans were administered by the Debt Administration.

By 1914, Ottoman public and private debts to foreign financiers consumed, in roughly equal shares, more than 30 percent of total tax revenues. In one way or another, the Debt Administration administered virtually the entire amount. This pattern of indebtedness makes clear the ongoing subordination of the late Ottoman economy to the European until the demise of the empire after World War I.

Bibliography

Blaisdell, Donald. *European Financial Control in the Ottoman Empire.* New York: Columbia University Press, 1929.

Issawi, Charles. *An Economic History of the Middle East and North Africa.* New York: Columbia University Press, 1982.

DONALD QUATAERT

OTTOMANISM

A supranational and protonationalist political principle that stressed patriotism and the group feeling of all Ottoman citizens.

Political elites used Ottomanism to achieve consensus among different ethnic and religious communities and foster political and social unanimity in allegiance to the sultan. It originated as a response to foreign encroachments and separatist movements during the Tanzimat period and was sustained by enhanced social and political mobilization. While Ottomanism was sufficiently vague and malleable to serve different political platforms, the territorial indivisibility of Ottoman domains was its constant concern. The administrative principle of centralization was integral to Ottomanist policies.

Ottomanism germinated from the Tanzimat recognition of the notion of citizenship. The Young Ottomans infused Ottomanism with constitutionalist ideas, which Sultan Abdülhamit II supplanted with Islamic symbols and solidarity. The Young Turks subscribed to secular and constitutionalist Ottomanism but were divided about the nature of the underlying administrative framework. The centralist position prevailed after the revolution of 1908. The piecemeal dismemberment and secession of non-Muslim parts of the empire compromised the secularist thrust of Ottomanism. Ottomanism was not a coherent ideology but blunted the growth of particular nationalisms, particularly among the Muslim groups.

See also TANZIMAT; YOUNG OTTOMANS; YOUNG TURKS.

Bibliography

Berkes, Niyazi. *The Development of Secularism in Turkey.* Montreal: McGill University Press, 1964; reprint, New York: Routledge, 1998.

HASAN KAYALI

OTTOMAN LIBERAL UNION PARTY

Political party opposed to the Committee for Union and Progress, also known as Osmanh Ahrar Firkasi.

The Liberal Union party was established in 1908 by Riza Nur, as the major opposition party after the 1908 revolution. Rooted in Prince Sabahettin's wing of the Young Turk movement, it espoused a platform that sympathized with the ethnic aspirations of Albanians and Armenians, and thus opposed the Committee for Union and Progress's (CUP) strongly centralist and Turkish leanings. The Liberal Union won only one seat, as against the CUP's 288 seats, in the November 1908 parliamentary elections. In 1909 the party was repressed under the martial law that followed the April counterrevolution.

The Liberal Union was revived in November 1911 as an umbrella opposition group called the Freedom and Accord party (Hürriyet ve Itilaf Firkasi). It won a Constantinople (now Istanbul) by-election in late 1911, but it lost the national elections in April 1912. It then allied with the Group of Liberating Officers who dislodged the CUP from power that summer. The coalition ruled only until January 1913, when the CUP forced Grand Vizier Mustafa Kamil Paşa to resign at gunpoint after losses in the Balkan War. The CUP government dissolved the Liberal Union in June 1913, executing and exiling its leadership after Grand Vizier Mahmut Şevket was assassinated. Damat Mehmet Ferit briefly revived the party in 1919 to replace the CUP, but the party split and its liberal wing joined the Kemalists.

Bibliography

Shaw, Stanford J., and Shaw, *Ezel Kural. History of the Ottoman Empire and Modern Turkey,* Vol. 2: *Reform, Revolution, and Republic: The Rise of Modern Turkey, 1808–1975.* Cambridge, U.K., and New York: Cambridge University Press, 1977.

ELIZABETH THOMPSON

OTTOMAN MILITARY

This entry consists of the following articles:

OTTOMAN ARMY
OTTOMAN NAVY

OTTOMAN ARMY

Military organization that defended the Ottoman Empire and helped establish the Turkish republic.

The origins of the modern Ottoman army date to the destruction of the janissaries by Sultan Mahmud II (June 1826). Mahmud then laid the foundation for a new military organization based on Western models. Its centerpiece was a European-style infantry corps, the Trained Victorious Troops of Muhammad (Muallem Asakir-i Mansure-yi Muhammadiye, Mansure for short). Other military services—cavalry, artillery, and transport—were established mainly by reforming existing military units. Mahmud also created a modern corps of imperial guards out of the Bostanci corps, which had guarded imperial palaces.

There also were attempts to centralize the command structure. The authority of the commander in chief (ser asker) of the Mansure was gradually extended over the other services and branches. Thus his headquarters (Bab-i Ser Asker) gradually came to combine the roles of a ministry of war and general staff, and eventually was in charge of all land forces.

Under Mahmud II the military engineering schools were rejuvenated and reformed. He also established a military medical school (1827) and an officer school (1834). Russia and Britain sent military instructors. Most useful services were rendered by a Prussian military mission that grew from one officer (Helmuth von Moltke) in 1835 to twelve in 1837.

In the 1830s Mahmud sought to strengthen the army. Large permanent units with regular commanding officers and staffs were formed. In 1834 a provincial militia (redif) was established to provide reserve forces. However, the commissary system could not support the rapid increase of the military. Epidemics were rife, and over a quarter of all recruits succumbed to disease. Desertion was very common. Although the army had been successfully employed as an instrument of coercion and centralization, as a military force it remained relatively small and poorly organized, trained, and equipped. By the end of Mahmud's reign there were only some 90,000 men in all the services. The wars with Russia (1828–1829) and with Muhammad Ali's Egypt (1831–1833, 1839) resulted in heavy losses and the disruption of the army's development.

During the Tanzimat period (1839–1876) the army consolidated and built on the shaky founda-

The horsemen of the Ottoman Empire's Imperial Calvary were considered excellent horsemen and skilled warriors, c. 1880s. © MICHAEL MASLAN HISTORIC PHOTOGRAPHS/CORBIS. REPRODUCED BY PERMISSION.

tions laid in the previous era. The Bab-i Ser Asker continued to acquire new departments. The army steadily grew, and recruitment and training improved. In 1843 the army, renamed the Regular Imperial Troops (Asakir-i Nizamiye-yi Şahane, Nizamiye for short), was organized in permanent territorial commands, each consisting of an army corps (ordu) under a field marshal (müşir). The field marshals, directly responsible to the ser asker, had wide jurisdiction in all military matters. This limited the provincial governors' ability to intervene in military affairs, and was intended to centralize further the military organization and strengthen the authority of the ser asker. Five territorial army corps were established, with headquarters in Istanbul, Üsküdar, Monastir, Sivas, and Damascus. In 1848 a sixth corps was established with headquarters in Baghdad. In 1849 the Nizamiye had some 120,000 men and the redif, 50,000. With local and semiregular organizations, the empire's land forces numbered some 250,000 men.

The reign of Abdülaziz (1861–1876) witnessed considerable increases in military appropriations and improvements in the army's equipment and training. Modern weapons were purchased abroad, mainly from Germany, and with them came German military instructors. Since the majority of the officers were poorly educated, in 1855 the army initiated its own network of schools to prepare youths to become soldiers and officers. In 1867 over 8,000 students were enrolled in these schools.

In 1869 the army was reorganized into seven territorial corps, with headquarters in Istanbul, Shumla, Monastir, Erzurum, Damascus, Baghdad, and San'a in Yemen. Each corps was required to have some 26,500 men. During the Russian war of 1877–1878 the Ottoman army had some 500,000 men, of whom some 220,000 took the field. During this period the Ottoman Empire reemerged as an important military power in southeastern Europe and the Middle East. Its army performed well during the Crimean War (1853–1856) and in the early stages of the Russian war of 1877–1878. In the latter conflict, however, the Ottomans were outclassed by the superior Russian army.

Under Abdülhamit II (1876–1909) the army benefited from ever increasing allocations, improved recruitment and training, and modern weaponry (mostly from Germany). It received assistance from a German military mission led by Kolmar von der Goltz (1883–1896). At the same time, however, Abdülhamit weakened the authority of the ser asker and placed military affairs under the supervision of permanent commissions staffed by his confidants. He personally approved the appointment and promotion of officers, and established networks of informers throughout the army.

By the 1890s the officer corps had become rife with discontent and sedition. The great expansion of the military had brought growing numbers of young officers from classes whose loyalty to the regime was not unconditional. Furthermore, the officers were better educated, and many espoused liberal ideals. In addition, officers and men were poorly paid, with salaries usually months in arrears. Finally, throughout most of Abdülhamit's reign the army was employed, with little success, in suppressing national and ethnic uprisings as well as lawlessness, especially in Macedonia and eastern Anatolia. Many officers, frustrated by the growing numbers of casualties, believed that the government was either unwilling or unable to provide the necessary

means to restore order and protect the empire's territorial integrity. This led many officers, especially in the junior and intermediate ranks, to join the Young Turk movement, which called for the overthrow of Abdülhamit. The Young Turk Revolution (July 1908), which restored constitutional government and led, a year later, to Abdülhamid's deposition, began as a mutiny in the Third Army Corps, based in Macedonia.

In the following years, the Young Turk regime provided the army with increased allocations, modern weapons, and another German military mission, led by Gen. Otto Liman von Sanders (November 1913). At the beginning of World War I, the Ottoman army had some 640,000 men. During the war the Ottomans mobilized an estimated total of some 4 million men. Although the army was plagued by problems of logistics and command, it generally fought well and was successful, especially in Gallipoli (1915–1916) and in Iraq (1915–1916), and in defending Anatolia from foreign invasion following the war. In the end, however, the army could not save the empire from final collapse. Nevertheless, as the institution that had benefited more than any other from reform and modernization, it played a crucial role in the rise of the Turkish republic.

See also ABDÜLHAMIT II; CRIMEAN WAR; MAHMUD II; MANSURE ARMY; RUSSIAN–OTTOMAN WARS; TANZIMAT; YOUNG TURKS.

Bibliography

Levy, Avigdor. "The Officer Corps of Sultan Mahmud II's New Ottoman Army, 1826–1839." *International Journal of Middle East Studies* 2 (1971): 21–39.

Ralston, David B. *Importing the European Army: The Introduction of European Military Techniques and Institutions into the Extra-European World, 1600–1914.* Chicago, 1990.

Shaw, Stanford J., and Shaw, Ezel Kural. *History of the Ottoman Empire and Modern Turkey,* Vol. 2: *Reform, Revolution, and Republic: The Rise of Modern Turkey, 1808–1975.* Cambridge, U.K., and New York: Cambridge University Press, 1976–1977.

AVIGDOR LEVY

OTTOMAN NAVY

Military vessels and fleets of the Ottoman Turks.

View of Constantinople Harbor, 1893. Constantinople is often considered, geographically, to link Europe with Asia and is home to the Hagia Sophia mosque. © CORBIS. REPRODUCED BY PERMISSION.

In the fifteenth and sixteenth centuries, sea power played a central role in the expansion of the Ottoman Empire, and Ottoman fleets operated on the high seas in the Atlantic, the Mediterranean, and east into the Indian Ocean. In the seventeenth and eighteenth centuries, the Ottoman navy was generally neglected and its effectiveness declined, but it was revived at times during the nineteenth and early twentieth centuries. The decline of the navy in the seventeenth and eighteenth centuries was largely due to the new geostrategic realities, whereby the main challenges to the empire no longer came from the naval powers of Spain, Portugal, and Venice, but from the land powers of Austria, Poland, Russia, and Persia (now Iran).

The origins of the modern Ottoman navy can be traced to the Russian-Ottoman Wars of 1768–1774. A Russian fleet based in the Baltic circled the European continent and destroyed the Ottoman fleet at Cheshme (July 1770). This led to a massive effort to rejuvenate the navy. During the reigns of Abdülhamit I (1774–1789) and Selim III (1789–1807), scores of modern warships were constructed under the supervision of European shipwrights. The Naval Engineering School (Tersane Mühendishanesi) was founded (1776), and the navy's command structure was modernized and placed under the supervision of the newly established Ministry of the Navy (1805). At the beginning of the nineteenth century, the navy was once again a formidable, though largely untested, force. In 1806, it listed 27 ships of the line and 27 frigates, as well as smaller vessels, armed with 2,156 guns and manned by some 40,000 sailors and marines.

After the fall of Selim III (1807), the navy was again neglected, and its strength declined. During the Greek War of Independence (1821–1830), it suffered many losses at the hands of the Greeks. The heaviest single blow, however, came on 20 October 1827, when a combined British-French-Russian fleet destroyed the Ottoman-Egyptian fleet inside the harbor of Navarino (now in Greece). The Ottomans alone lost thirty-seven vessels and thousands of sailors. It took the navy more than a decade to recover from the disaster at Navarino. By 1838, it had fifteen ships of the line and an equal number of frigates, as well as smaller vessels.

As of 1838, there was growing cooperation between the Ottoman and British navies: Ottoman and British squadrons conducted joint maneuvers; the navy was reorganized on British lines; Ottoman officers were sent to Britain for training; and British naval officers and engineers arrived in Constantinople (now Istanbul), the Ottoman capital, to serve as advisers from time to time.

In July 1839, the Ottoman grand admiral, Ahmet Fevzi Pasha, suddenly sailed the entire fleet to Alexandria and surrendered it to Egypt's ruler, Muhammad Ali, who was trying to become independent from the empire. This extraordinary act was the result of a power struggle within the Ottoman government following the death of Mahmud II. The fleet was returned in the following year as part of a general settlement of Ottoman-Egyptian relations, giving Egypt its autonomy.

During the Tanzimat (reform) era (1839–1876) in the empire, considerable resources were directed toward the further development and modernization of the navy, and sailing vessels were replaced with steamships. On the eve of the Crimean War (1853–1856), the Ottoman navy had 10 ships of the line and 14 frigates, as well as smaller vessels, with a total of 2,080 guns and a staff of more than 20,000 men. On 30 November 1853, Russia's Black Sea squadron, using new shell-firing guns, destroyed an Ottoman wooden fleet at Sinop. This had important political consequences, since it enraged British public opinion against Russia, leading to the Crimean War. It also marked an important milestone in naval history, resulting everywhere in the construction of iron-clad warships. The Ottoman navy also replaced most of its main wooden warships with iron-clads. By 1877, it had thirteen iron-clad frigates in addition to three wooden frigates, four corvettes, and various smaller craft.

During the reign of Abdülhamit II (1876–1909), priority was given to the development of the army, while the navy, because of financial constraints, was neglected, leading to its decline. In 1912, the navy listed four battleships, two cruisers, eight destroyers, three corvettes, and smaller craft. During the Balkan Wars (1912/13), it was outclassed by the Greek navy, which dominated the Aegean Sea.

Following the Balkan Wars, the Ottoman government, led by the Young Turks, placed great emphasis on modernizing and strengthening the navy. A British naval mission led by the Admiral Arthur H. Limpus helped reorganize the navy and its various departments. The navy was to be greatly strengthened by two modern battleships ordered from Britain whose delivery was expected in August 1914. On 3 August, however, the British government announced that with the impending European crisis (that very soon became World War I), the ships would not be delivered. On 11 August, the Ottoman government permitted two powerful German cruisers, *Goeben* and *Breslau,* to enter the Dardanelles; they subsequently announced their purchase by the Ottoman navy as replacement for the British-built warships. The cruisers were given Turkish names, but they remained under the command of their German crews. On 29 October, Ottoman warships, including the two former German cruisers, suddenly attacked Russian ports in the Black Sea, marking the entry of the Ottoman Empire into the war.

See also BALKAN WARS (1912–1913); CRIMEAN WAR; GREEK WAR OF INDEPENDENCE; RUSSIAN–OTTOMAN WARS; TANZIMAT.

Bibliography

Marmont, Duc De Raguse, Marshal. *The Present State of the Ottoman Empire,* translated by Frederic Smith. London, 1839.

Oscanyan, C. *The Sultan and His People.* New York: Derby and Jackson, 1857.

Shaw, Stanford J., and Shaw, Ezel Kural. *History of the Ottoman Empire and Modern Turkey.* 2 vols. Cambridge, U.K., and New York: Cambridge University Press, 1976–1977.

AVIGDOR LEVY

OTTOMAN PARLIAMENT

Attempt at representative government in the empire between 1877 and 1920.

The Ottoman parliament met from 1877 to 1878 and between 1908 and 1920. The constitution of 1876 stipulated a bicameral parliament: a lower Chamber of Deputies elected popularly and a Chamber of Notables nominated by the sultan. The parliament of the First Constitutional period (1876–1878) had two terms that convened March to June, 1877, and December 1877 to 14 February 1878, when Sultan Abdülhamit II abolished parliament. The Young Turk Revolution of 1908 forced Abdülhamit to re-institute it. The three parliaments of the Young Turk period met December 1908 to January 1912, May to August 1912, and May 1914 to December 1918. The last Ottoman parliament that convened in January 1920 dissolved itself after the Allied occupation of Istanbul in March 1920.

For the 1877 to 1878 parliament, previously elected provincial administrative councils selected the deputies according to quotas based on population and proportionate allocations of Muslims and non-Muslims (seventy-one Muslims and forty-eight non-Muslims in the first session; sixty-four Muslims and forty-nine non-Muslims in the second). Due to inaccurate population figures in remoter Asian and African provinces and the political exigency of catering to separatist Christian elements and their European protectors, non-Muslim communities and European provinces received higher quotas.

Abdülhamit intended to legitimate his rule by giving his consent to parliament but stripped it of the authority to legislate independently and to limit the executive. Nevertheless, the deputies, who on the whole represented the provincial elites, were vocal in their criticism of the government. Abdülhamit closed parliament indefinitely on the pretext of the national emergency engendered by the ongoing war with Russia.

Thirty years later, the Young Turk Revolution of 1908 reintroduced the constitution and parliament. Constitutional amendments enhanced parliament's legislative prerogatives vis-à-vis the sultan, provided for ministerial accountability to parliament, and eliminated religious quotas. In the two-tier elections, males above the age of twenty-five voted for secondary electors, who then elected the deputies. Candidates had to be literate males who knew Turkish and were above the age of thirty. The election of one deputy for every 50,000 males produced chambers of around 250 deputies. The Committee for Union and Progress (CUP) managed to dominate the elections due to its revolutionary élan and moral authority in 1908, through electoral manipulation in 1912, and by suppressing opposition and effectively instituting a single-party regime in 1914. Electoral victory did not guarantee CUP's domination of parliament, which was the breeding ground of opposition.

From the dissolution of the body in August 1912, which followed a government crisis and anti-CUP rebellions, to May 1914, parliament remained in suspension. New elections were delayed until the winter of 1913/14 due to the extraordinary circumstances of the Balkan Wars, the forcible CUP takeover in January 1913, and the assassination of Grand Vizier Mahmut Şevket Paşa in June 1913. As World War I began, emergency powers were ceded to the cabinet, and parliament's significance diminished even though it continued to meet with interruptions.

The two-tier election system favored the election of representatives of privileged social groups: *Ulama*, officials, landowners, and professionals. However, party politics produced a more diverse Chamber of Deputies in the Second Constitutional period compared with 1877/78. Parliament always served as a forum where both local and national issues were voiced. Newspapers reported its proceedings on a daily basis. Despite the executive's attempts to control parliament, the Chamber of Deputies served as a check on the sultan, the cabinet, and occasionally on the CUP's extralegal interventions.

See also BALKAN WARS (1912–1913); COMMITTEE FOR UNION AND PROGRESS.

Bibliography

Ahmad, Feroz. *The Young Turks: The Committee of Union and Progress in Turkish Politics, 1908–1914.* Oxford: Clarendon, 1969.

Devereux, Robert. *The First Ottoman Constitutional Period: A Study of the Midhat Constitution and Parliament.* Baltimore, MD: Johns Hopkins Press, 1963.

HASAN KAYALI

OUARY, MALEK
[1916–2001]

Algerian novelist, poet, and journalist.

A Christian born in Ighil Ali, Malek Ouary was educated in his village and became a radio journalist in Algeria. He then worked at the Office de la Radiodiffusion-Télévision Française (ORTF) in Paris. A francophone writer, his works include *Par les chemins d'emigration* (investigative report); *Cahier d'epreuves* (1955); *Poèmes et chants de Kabyle* (1972); and also the novels *Le grain dans la meule* (1956), *La montagne aux chacals* (1981), and *La robe kabyle de Baya* (2000).

PHILLIP C. NAYLOR
UPDATED BY ANA TORRES-GARCIA

OUAZZANI, MOHAMED HASSAN
[1910–1978]

Moroccan nationalist.

In the early 1930s, Mohamed Hassan Ouazzani, a native of Fez, was a leader of the Comité d'Action Marocaine (CAM). He was elected secretary-general of the Bloc d'Action Nationale in October 1936, but the following year founded the Parti Démocratique Constitutionnel (PDC). Ouazzani was imprisoned for nine years (1937–1946) on political charges. Periodically, he cooperated with the Istiqlal, and from 1953 to 1954, he and his followers joined the National Front. Ouazzani was named minister of state without portfolio in King Hassan's 1961 coalition government. He was among those wounded in 1971 in the attempted coup against the king.

See also COMITÉ D'ACTION MAROCAINE (CAM); HASSAN II; ISTIQLAL PARTY: MOROCCO; PARTI DÉMOCRATIQUE CONSTITUTIONNEL (PDC).

BRUCE MADDY-WEITZMAN

OUFKIR, MUHAMMAD
[1918–1972]

Moroccan general and politician.

Muhammad Oufkir was from Middle Atlas Berber stock, from central Morocco. He served with distinction in the French army in Italy and Indochina during World War II and thereafter. When Morocco became independent of French colonialism in 1956, he was promoted to general and, in 1964, was appointed by King Hassan II as minister of the interior. In 1965, he was at the center of the Ben Barka affair and sentenced by a French court to life imprisonment (in absentia). In 1971, Oufkir led the suppression of an army coup attempt against King Hassan and was made minister of defense. In the next year, however, he helped organize a second coup attempt; following its collapse, he committed suicide.

See also BEN BARKA, MEHDI.

Bibliography

Nelson, Harold D., ed. *Morocco: A Country Study.* Washington, DC: U.S. Government Printing Office, 1985.

MATTHEW S. GORDON

OUJDA GROUP

Algerian nationalists instrumental in winning independence and in governing the new nation.

The term *Oujda group* refers to Houari Boumédienne and a circle of colleagues that emerged in Oujda, Morocco, during the later years of the Algerian War of Independence. The best-known members of that circle included Ahmed Kaid, Ahmed Medeghri, Cherif Belkacem, Abdelaziz Bouteflika, Mohamed Tayebi, and Ali Mendjli.

As French repression of Algerian guerrillas intensified during 1957 and 1958, more and more of them were forced across the borders into Tunisia and Morocco. Boumédienne, who had begun his revolutionary career fighting in Wilaya Five, the western Algeria military district, ended up in Oujda, about 7 miles (12 km) from the Algerian border. There he helped to organize the Moroccan branch of the external Armée de Libération Nationale (ALN; National Liberation Army), which he eventually rose to command. When the separate commands of the ALN were unified in December 1959, Boumédienne became chief of its general staff, bringing members of the Oujda group with him.

In 1960 and 1961, factional divisions within the political leadership of the Front de Libération Nationale (FLN; National Liberation Front) began to lessen the effectiveness of the Provisional Government of the Algerian Republic (Gouvernement Provisoir de la République Algérienne; GPRA). The ALN general staff, dominated by the Oujda group, emerged as the most cohesive of the revolutionary institutions. It was frequently in conflict with the civilian leadership. Within days of independence in 1962, Ben Youssef Ben Khedda, president of the GPRA, fired Colonel Boumédienne, and Majors Kaid and Mendjli. The officers refused to recognize the GPRA's authority to take such action and instead entered Algeria to begin building internal support.

At Tlemcen, near the Moroccan border, there coalesced a group hostile to Ben Khedda and the GPRA that was headed by Ahmed Ben Bella. Support for Ben Bella, who had spent most of the war years in French prisons, came from disillusioned liberal politicians, some radical socialists, and especially from Boumédienne and the Oujda group. The latter provided the military support that enabled Ben Bella to take over Algiers and manage his election as Algeria's first president in September 1962.

Ben Bella was to remain in power until June 1965, devoting much of his time to attempts to eliminate political competitors inside the government and the party. By October 1963 he had managed to eliminate many opponents. By then, power was about equally divided between his own followers and those of Boumédienne. Thereafter, he moved gradually to eliminate the latter, until, by early 1965, only Boumédienne in the War Ministry and Bouteflika in the Foreign Ministry survived. During May and June, Ben Bella moved to undercut the authority of Bouteflika, threatening to dismiss both him and Boumédienne, but the latter intervened.

On 19 July 1965, the military overthrew Ben Bella in a bloodless coup engineered in the name of a body called Council of the Revolution. The heart of this council was the Oujda group, which also took over key posts in the cabinet (defense, interior, foreign affairs, finance). Boumédienne headed both the Council of the Revolution and the government. These allies helped him, through the remainder of the decade, to consolidate his own power. But, between 1972 and 1976, as cleavages developed in the inner circle over difficult political choices, Boumédienne eliminated one after another the members of the Oujda group from his government.

See also ALGERIAN WAR OF INDEPENDENCE; ARMÉE DE LIBÉRATION NATIONALE (ALN); BELKACEM, CHERIF; BEN BELLA, AHMED; BEN KHEDDA, BEN YOUSSEF; BOUMÉDIENNE, HOUARI; BOUTEFLIKA, ABDELAZIZ; FRONT DE LIBÉRATION NATIONALE (FLN); KAID, AHMED.

Bibliography

Quandt, William B. *Revolution and Political Leadership*. Cambridge, MA: MIT Press, 1969.

Ruedy, John. *Modern Algeria: The Origins and Development of a Nation*. Bloomington: Indiana University Press, 1992.

JOHN RUEDY

OULD SID'AHMED TAYA, MA'OUIYA
[1941–]

President of Mauritania since 1984.

Born in 1941 in Atar, the capital of the Adrar region, Ma'ouiya Sid Ahmed Taya is the fourth military leader to hold the office of the presidency in Mauritania since its independence from France in 1960.

Taya joined the military in 1961 after Mauritania gained its independence from France. During the latter half of the 1970s Taya served as a military commander in the conflict with Western Sahara. In 1984 Taya led a coup d'état, overthrowing the previous military leader, Mohamed Khouna Ould Haidallah, and appointed himself head of state. Still leader in 1991, Taya drafted a new constitution that legalized political parties and called for a turn toward democracy. Taya, representing the Parti Républicain Démocratique et Social (PRDS), won the January 1992 presidential election, gaining most of his support from the military, members of his Smacid tribe and other white Maure groups, and residents of his native region of the Adrar. Financial scandals and political instability overshadowed much of Taya's democratization efforts in the early 1990s.

In 1991 Mauritania broke ties with the United States and signed agreements with Iraq during the

Gulf War. As the war came to a close, Taya opted for a more moderate position in world affairs, making amends with Senegal, breaking ties with Iraq, and recommending Mauritania's good relations with France and the United States. Despite pressure from Arab states to break ties with Israel, Taya recently accepted a visit from Israeli foreign minister Shimon Peres, and he increasingly thrives from his good relationship with the United States. He also believes that Mauritania's relationships with West African states and with the Arab Maghreb Union are valuable, and he has been working to improve relations with Senegal since the conflict in 1989. Taya faces international pressure to further democratize Mauritania and end human-rights abuses. Since 1999 Taya also evolved his economic policy of central control to one that encourages more privatization of businesses.

Taya won the 1997 presidential election with 90 percent of the vote. In reaction to charges of fraudulent municipal elections in January 1999, Taya issued voting and identity cards to prevent future electoral scandals. Elections are held every five years.

As of 2003 Mauritanian exiles charged Taya with crimes against humanity, arguing that he called for a policy of "denegrification" following the border clashes and ethnic violence along the Senegal River in 1989. He is also blamed for prolonging undemocratic policies such as slavery, extrajudicial incarcerations, and press censorship.

See also MAURITANIA.

NAOMI ZEFF

OULED SIDI CHEIKH

A nineteenth-century tribal confederation/brotherhood of western Algeria.

Because of their location in western Algeria, this powerful group of tribes was often influenced by the sultan of neighboring Morocco. The Ouled (also Awlad Sidi Shaykh) had capricious relations with the authorities of French colonialism. They cooperated with Governor-General Thomas-Robert Bugeaud de la Piconnerie against the renowned Amir Abd al-Qadir. One of the chief collaborators, however, Mohammed ben Abdallah, later turned against the

French. This led to conflicts at Laghaout (1852) and Touggourt (1854). Then, during this campaign, Si Hamza, of the Ouled (Cheraga), joined the French.

A basic lack of French sensibilities toward the confederation's traditions produced a major insurrection in 1864/65. During the Great Kabylia Revolt of 1871, the Ouled were generally restive rather than rebellious—then passive thereafter in relations with the French.

See also KABYLIA.

PHILLIP C. NAYLOR

OUZIEL, BEN ZION MEIR HAI
[1880–1953]

Sephardic chief rabbi.

Ben Zion Meir Hai Ouziel was born in Jerusalem and studied in various yeshivot there. He became chief rabbi of Jaffa in 1914. After serving as rabbi of Salonika from 1921 to 1923, he was selected as Sephardic chief rabbi of Tel Aviv, and in 1939 he became the Sephardic chief rabbi of Palestine, a position he occupied until his death. Ouziel was active in the Mizrahi Movement, served as a delegate to several Zionist congresses, and held several committee positions in the Jewish Agency. He testified before the Anglo-American Committee of Inquiry and the United Nations Special Committee on Palestine. In addition to being active in the political sphere, Ouziel published extensively on practical Jewish religious law (Halakhah) and on Jewish thought.

See also HALAKHAH; JEWISH AGENCY FOR PALESTINE; MIZRAHI MOVEMENT.

CHAIM I. WAXMAN

OYAK (ORDU YARDIMLASMA KURUMU)

Turkish military pension program that became a public conglomerate with political power.

Ordu Yardimlasma Kurumu Army Mutual Assistance Association was founded in Turkey in 1961 as a pension program to protect career military officers from inflation, but it soon became Turkey's largest and most diversified public conglomerate. By 1984, OYAK's assets totaled more than US$300 million, with heavy investments in the automotive, electronics, construction, and food-processing industries, among others.

Since the late 1960s, OYAK's economic clout has enhanced its political influence. It is an example of the Turkish state's use of professional associations and social-insurance programs to implement economic policy. OYAK is nominally attached to the ministry of defense but is run autonomously by civilians and technocrats.

Bibliography

Bianchi, Robert. *Interest Groups and Political Development in Turkey.* Princeton, NJ: Princeton University Press, 1984.

ELIZABETH THOMPSON

ÖZAL, TURGUT
[1927–1993]

Turkish prime minister, later president.

Turgut Özal was born in Malatya, a provincial city in southeast Turkey. His father, trained as a religious teacher, taught in the secular schools of the Turkish republic and later worked as a civil servant; his mother was also a teacher. Özal attended Istanbul's Technical University, graduating in 1950 with a degree in electrical engineering. After studying economics and engineering in the United States, he worked under Süleyman Demirel at the Electric Power Survey Administration, which was responsible for several hydraulic and electrical projects. In 1961, Özal participated in the establishment of the State Planning Organization, which issued five-year development plans, and throughout the 1960s, he was an important economic adviser to Prime Minister Demirel. He was one of the architects of the 1970 stabilization program, but following the 1971 military intervention, he left the State Planning Office to work for the World Bank in Washington, D.C.

Returning to Turkey two years later, he served as managing director of two large private sector companies and, in 1977, entered politics as a candidate for the religiously oriented National Salvation Party from İzmir. Özal failed in this campaign, but in 1979, Demirel made him responsible for developing a solution to Turkey's growing economic

Former Turkish prime minister Turgut Özal, 1988. Özal is perhaps best remembered for bringing a free economy to Turkey and for envisioning the country as a modern, democratic society. © AP/WIDE WORLD PHOTOS. REPRODUCED BY PERMISSION.

crisis. As undersecretary of the State Planning Organization, Özal proposed a series of measures to stabilize and reform the Turkish economy known as the 24 January Measures. Following the September 1980 coup, which removed Demirel from power, the military officers that ruled Turkey asked Özal to remain as deputy prime minster in charge of the economy, a position he held until July 1982, when a banking scandal led to his removal from government. In response, Özal and several close associates established, in May 1983, the Motherland Party (Anavatan Partisi; ANAP), which contested the elections of 1983. Despite opposition from the military leadership that supported the Nationalist Democracy party, Özal's Motherland party won an overwhelming victory.

During his years as prime minister, Özal focused on two major goals: reforming the Turkish economy and enhancing Turkey's position in world affairs. In the economy, he sought to tame triple-digit inflation, modernize industry, increase Turkey's exports in order to put an end to persistent shortages of foreign exchange, and privatize Turkey's large public industrial sector. Under his supervision, the economy grew at a rapid rate, and exports expanded dramatically. In addition, many of his reforms have created an environment more conducive to foreign and domestic private investment. He was less successful, however, in selling off the inefficient state sector and in reducing inflation; these failures and subsequent macroeconomic instability have dampened investment.

In foreign affairs, Özal worked to integrate Turkey into the world economy, a strategy leading to his formal request for admission into the European Community in 1987. In the late 1980s, he initiated a new era in Greek-Turkish relations that would be more conducive to a settlement of their conflict. At the same time, he worked to further links with many Middle Eastern countries that were becoming important markets for Turkish exports. His desire for Turkey to play a leading role in regional affairs led him to strongly support the allied coalition against Saddam Hussein, a policy that sparked domestic opposition.

In the late 1980s, Özal faced a number of political challenges. First, Turkey's persistent economic problems, coupled with rampant rumors about his personal corruption and that of his family, led to a precipitous decline in his personal popularity as well as that of the ANAP. Second, the conservative Islamic wing of the Motherland party, which dominated the party's organization, began to challenge the policies of Özal and the more liberal wing of the party. Finally, the party faced challenges from its competitors, the True Path party on the right and the Social Democratic party on the left. In 1989, seeing the declining political fortunes of the ANAP, he engineered his election to the presidency. In doing this, Özal faced a great deal of opposition, both from his own party and from the opposition parties, and was elected only on the third ballot. As president, Özal sought to transform his office from its traditionally above-politics status to the preeminent political position in the country. As a result, he was accused, even by members of the Motherland

party, of interfering in politics and forcing his will on the government. In addition, many of his policies were extremely controversial, particularly his enthusiastic support for the American-led coalition against Saddam Hussein and his calls for a conciliatory position toward the Kurdish issue. When Süleyman Demirel became prime minister in 1991, he vowed to remove his former protégé from the presidency.

One of Özal's final projects was to project Turkish influence into the newly independent Turkic countries of central Asia. Following an exhaustive tour of the republics in the spring of 1993, he died of a heart attack in Istanbul.

See also MOTHERLAND PARTY; NATIONAL SALVATION PARTY; STATE PLANNING ORGANIZATION (SPO).

Bibliography

Ahmad, Feroz. *The Making of Modern Turkey.* London and New York: Routledge, 1993.

Heper, Metin. *Historical Dictionary of Turkey,* 2nd edition. Lanham, MD: Scarecrow Press, 2002.

Sayari, Sabri. "Turgut Özal." In *Political Leaders of the Contemporary Middle East and North Africa: A Biographical Dictionary,* edited by Bernard Reich. New York: Greenwood Press, 1990.

DAVID WALDNER

OZ, AMOS
[1939–]

Israeli author.

Oz was born Amos Klausner, in Jerusalem. He studied in a religious elementary school and in a secular high school. At the age of thirteen, after the death of his mother, he went to live in kibbutz Hulda, of which he later became a member. He studied literature and philosophy at the Hebrew University of Jerusalem and taught at the kibbutz high school. Oz left the kibbutz in the 1980s. In 1996 he moved to Arad and began teaching at Ben-Gurion University of the Negev in Beersheba, where he is a full professor and holds the Agnon Chair of Hebrew Literature. He has also been a visiting fellow at Oxford University, an author in residence at the Hebrew University, and, in 1997, a visiting writer at the New York State Writers Institute.

Oz's first short story was published in 1961 and his first collection of short stories, *Where the Jackals Howl,* in 1965. He has published eighteen books in Hebrew, including novels, novellas, books of short stories, books of essays, one volume of literary criticism, and close to 500 articles and essays in Israeli and international magazines and newspapers, which have been translated into thirty languages.

The kibbutz is the locus of several stories and novels in which Oz examines the relationship between the individual and the collective in modern Israel. The closed society of the commune may be viewed as a human laboratory where national ideals are measured against personal needs and desires. The enemy, often depicted as lurking outside the geographical enclave, proves to be internal, harbored and suppressed within the protagonist.

Closely associated with that time is Oz's study of the family unit, love and loyalty within the family, obsessions, separations, and dissatisfaction. The tension between fathers and sons as representatives of two generations of Israelis, the founders and the followers, is not resolved by oedipal revolt and independence but, rather, by compromise and surrender. This is in line with Oz's political view, which calls for dialogue and the harnessing of violence.

In *Black Box* (1987), an epistolary novel, a divorced couple is entangled in a passionate concern with their straying teenage son, who is perceived as a possible symbol of Israel's future: The broken family serves as a metaphor for political allegory. In *To Know a Woman* (1989), the hero is a former intelligence officer who withdraws from public service in order to come to terms with private emotions, a crumbling family, and a need for confronting his femininity, translated as the need for nurturing the self and the need for human compassion. Other works include *Israel, Palestine and Peace* (1994), *Don't Call It Night* (1994), *Panther in the Basement* (1995), and *But These Are Two Different Wars* (2000). The first chapter of his unfinished memoirs was published in *The New Yorker* in December 1995.

In 1991 Oz was elected a full member of the Academy of the Hebrew Language. He has received the French Prix Femina, the 1992 Frankfurt Peace Prize, the Brenner Prize, and the Israel Prize. In 1997 he was awarded the French Cross of the Knight of the Légion d'Honneur by President Jacques Chirac. A member of the Peace Now movement since its inception in 1977, Oz frequently appears in the media, voicing his opinions on Palestinian-Israeli relations, the peace process, refusal to serve in the military, and other contemporary political issues.

Bibliography

Balaban, Abraham. *Between God and Beast: On Amos Oz.* University Park: Pennsylvania State University Press, 1991.

Fuchs, Esther. "Amos Oz: The Lack of Conscience." In *Israeli Mythogynies: Women in Contemporary Hebrew Fiction.* Albany: State University of New York Press, 1987.

Hakak, Lev. *Modern Hebrew Literature Made Into Films.* Lanham, MD, and Oxford, U.K.: University Press of America, 2001

Mazor, Yair. *Somber Lust: The Art of Amos Oz,* translated by Marganit Weinberger-Rotman. Albany: State University of New York Press, 2002.

Negev, Eilat, with introduction by Risa Domb. *Close Encounters with Twenty Israeli Writers.* London, U.K., and Portland, OR: Vallentine Mitchell, 2003.

ZVIA GINOR
UPDATED BY ADINA FRIEDMAN

OZANIAN, ANDRANIK

See ANDRANIK OZANIAN

OZ VE SHALOM (NETIVOT SHALOM)

Israeli religious peace movement.

Some members of the National Religious Party, who opposed the tendencies of their party to support Greater Israel policies, formed in the early 1970s an ideological forum that advocated moderation, tolerance, and pluralism in matters involving religion and the state and a compromise solution to the Arab-Israeli conflict. In 1975, in reaction to the founding of Gush Emunim, the extreme settlers' movement, they established themselves as an independent "Fabian Society," seeking influence primarily through ideological, educational, and intellectual work, adopting the name "Oz ve Shalom," a famous line from the Jewish prayer book meaning "strength and peace."

In response to the 1982 Lebanon War and the intensification of the activities of Peace Now, a group of younger Zionist-Orthodox activists established a separate peace movement that aspired to appeal to a religious audience. They named themselves "Netivot Shalom" (Paths of Peace). Peace Now, the main peace movement at the time, was a secular movement, using secular terminology and organizing many of its activities on the Sabbath. To avoid duplication, in 1984 both religious peace groups merged under the name Oz ve Shalom/Netivot Shalom. The movement's main public figure was Avi Ravitzky, a professor of Jewish studies at the Hebrew University. They also gained the support of Rabbis Yehuda Amital and Aharon Lichtenstien, the heads of Yeshivat Har Etzion in Gush Etzion. Yet the movement remained limited in scope and at its peak claimed some 3,000 supporters.

See also GUSH EMUNIM; PEACE NOW.

Bibliography

Bar-On, Mordechai. *In Pursuit of Peace, A History of the Israeli Peace Movement.* Washington DC: U.S. Institute of Peace Press, 1996.

Newman, David. *The Impact of Gush Emunim: Politics and Settlement in the West Bank.* London: Croom Helm, 1985

Ravitzki, Aviezer. *Messianism, Zionism, and Jewish Religious Radicalism,* translated by Michael Swirsky and Jonathan Chipman. Chicago: University of Chicago Press, 1996.

WALTER F. WEIKER
UPDATED BY MORDECHAI BAR-ON

PACHACHI, MUZAHIM AL-
[?–1987]

Iraqi statesman.

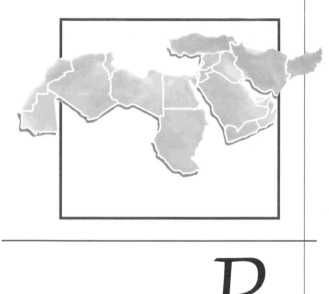

Born in the small town of Bujayla (now al-Nuʿmaniyya), Muzahim al-Pachachi was graduated from the college of Sawr in 1913. He began his active public life in 1924 as a member of the Constituent Assembly. From 1924 to 1925, he was minister of labor and communication and, from 1925 to 1927, the deputy of Hilla province. In 1931, he was appointed permanent representative of Iraq in London, minister of labor and communication, and also minister of the interior. He served as permanent representative of Iraq to the League of Nations from 1934 to 1935, minister plenipotentiary in Rome from 1935 to 1939, and minister plenipotentiary in Paris and Vichy from 1939 to 1942. He was prime minister from 26 June 1948 to 19 January 1949, and deputy prime minister and minister of the interior from 1949 to 1950. He died in Geneva on 23 September 1987. His son, Adnan [1923–], served as an Iraqi diplomat until going into exile in 1969. He returned to Iraq in 2003 and served on the American-created Iraqi Governing Council following the U.S. invasion of the country.

MAMOON A. ZAK
UPDATED BY MICHAEL FISCHBACH

PAGIS, DAN
[1930–1986]

Israeli poet, professor.

Born in Bukovina, Pagis spent three years in a Ukrainian concentration camp, from which he escaped in 1944. Arriving in Palestine after the war, he learned Hebrew and taught on a kibbutz. He obtained his doctorate in medieval Hebrew literature and taught at Hebrew University, the Jewish Theological Seminary of America, and Harvard University. The Holocaust, a formative experience in Pagis's life, had a profound effect on his writings. Like many other Holocaust survivors, however, he was able to let his memory surface only after the capture of Adolf Eichmann in 1960 and the trial in

Jerusalem. It was only in Pagis's third poetry collection, *Gilgul,* published in 1970, that poems which actually turn to the Shoah were first published. Among Pagis's books of poems are *The Shadow Dial* (1959), *Late Leisure* (1964), and *Twelve Faces* (1981). Scholarly works include *Change and Tradition: Hebrew Poetry in Spain and Italy* (1976) and *The Riddle* (1986). *Last Poems* was published posthumously. As the title suggests, the poems center on dying and death.

Bibliography

Pagis, Dan. *Variable Directions: The Selected Poetry of Dan Pagis.* San Francisco, CA: North Point Press, 1989.

Pagis, Dan, with a foreword by Robert Alter. *Hebrew Poetry of the Middle Ages and the Renaissance.* Berkeley: University of California Press, 1991.

Pagis, Dan, with an introduction by Robert Alter. *The Selected Poetry of Dan Pagis (Literature of the Middle East),* translated by Stephen Mitchell. Berkeley: University of California Press, 1996.

JULIE ZUCKERMAN
UPDATED BY ADINA FRIEDMAN

PAHLAVI, MOHAMMAD REZA
[1919–1980]

Shah of Iran, 1941–1979.

Mohammad Reza Pahlavi was born in Tehran on 26 October 1919 to Brigadier Reza Khan (later Reza Shah Pahlavi). He was designated crown prince in April 1926 and graduated from a special primary military school in Tehran in 1931, from Le Rosey secondary school in Switzerland in 1936, and from Tehran Military College in 1938. In 1939, he married Princess Fawzia, the sister of King Farouk of Egypt; they had a daughter, Shahnaz, in 1940 and were divorced in 1948. In 1950, he married Soraya Esfandiari Bakhtiari; this marriage, too, ended in divorce in 1958 because she was not able to produce a male heir. In 1959, he married Farah Diba, who gave birth to Crown Prince Reza in 1961, and three other children thereafter.

Mohammad Reza Shah's thirty-seven-year reign can be divided into five distinct phases: from the 1941 occupation of Iran by the Allied forces to the 1953 coup d'état; the postcoup period (1953–1959); the period of political strife (1960–1963); the period of the shah's increasingly autocratic rule (1963–1976); and the period of revolutionary crisis that ultimately led to the collapse of the Pahlavi dynasty (1977–1979).

From 1941 Occupation to 1953 Coup d'Etat

Mohammad Reza acceded to the throne on 17 September 1941, after Russian and British troops invaded Iran on 25 August, forcing Reza Shah to abdicate. A major crisis in the early years of his reign came in 1945 when the Soviet Union refused to withdraw its forces from northern Iran. Through a combination of international pressures and internal maneuverings by Prime Minister Ahmad Qavam, the Russian force finally left Iran in late 1946, and the pro-Soviet republics of Azerbaijan and Kurdistan collapsed. For much of this period, the shah was forced to conform to the will of the *majles* (parliament), which as a political institution dominated both the young monarch and the cabinet. Following an assassination attempt on 4 February 1949, a Constitutional Assembly was convened on 21 April; it granted him the right to dissolve the *majles.* In March 1951, the British-dominated Anglo-Iranian Oil Company was nationalized by an act of the *majles* under the initiative of Mohammad Mossadegh, the leader of the National Front, who subsequently became prime minister. Although 1951 to 1953 were "the worst years" of the shah's reign, he did not take any initiative to dismiss Mossadegh until he was urged to do so by Prime Minister Winston Churchill and President Dwight Eisenhower, who also urged him to appoint Gen. Fazlollah Zahedi as prime minister. When Mossadegh refused to accept the shah's dismissal order on 16 August, the shah fled the country and went to Rome. On 19 August 1953, he was reinstated to power in a coup conceived by MI-6 (British Military Intelligence) and carried out by the Central Intelligence Agency. The leading *ulama,* the old-guard politicians, the propertied classes, and a core of army generals supported the shah and the coup.

Post-Coup Period

The period 1953 to 1959 began with the repression of members of the intelligentsia who had supported either the National Front or the pro-Soviet Tudeh party, and saw a gradual increase of the shah's power vis-à-vis the old-guard politicians, the propertied classes, and the *ulama.* In this period, the government signed an agreement with a consortium of major Western oil companies in August 1954, joined the Baghdad Pact (later the Central Treaty Organization, CENTO) in October 1955, established an effective intelligence agency (SAVAK) in 1957, and launched the 1954–1962 development plan.

Political Strife (1960–1963)

The period from 1960 to 1963 began with a reactivation of opposition groups and increasing pressures from the administration of John F. Kennedy for reforms. In May 1961, the shah appointed Dr. Ali Amini as prime minister and Hasan Arsanjani as minister of agriculture; the latter became the architect of land reform. The shah, who could not tolerate an independent-minded prime minister, dismissed Amini in July 1962 and asked Amir Asadollah Alam, his closest confidant, to form a new cabinet and continue the reform. The land reform program, which was the centerpiece of the shah's White Revolution, and women's suffrage met with strong resistance from the *ulama,* who joined the opposition forces and instigated urban riots on 5 June 1963 to protest Ayatollah Ruhollah Khomeini's imprisonment. The shah was indecisive in responding to the situation, but Alam took command and gave the shoot-to-kill order to the security forces; more than 100 were killed, and resistance of religious groups was crushed. This event marked the suppression of all opposition forces and the beginning of increasingly autocratic rule by the shah.

Increased Autocratic Rule (1963–1976)

In the period 1963 to 1976, the shah emerged as the sole policymaker; he allocated oil revenues among various agencies and projects and directly supervised the armed forces and security organizations, foreign policy and oil negotiations, nuclear power plants, and huge development projects. In this period, Iran's gross domestic product grew in real terms by an average annual rate of around 10 percent. Meantime, public services substantially expanded and modernized, and the enrollment at all educational levels increased rapidly. The shah also dramatically expanded the military and security forces and equipped them with advanced weapon systems. In the early 1970s he played a key leadership role in the Organization of Petroleum Exporting Countries (OPEC) and helped the organization to raise

President John F. Kennedy meets with the shah of Iran in the White House, 13 April 1962. Supported by the United States, the shah assumed absolute power after a 1953 coup that ousted Prime Minister Mohammed Mossaddeq. © BETTMANN/CORBIS. REPRODUCED BY PERMISSION.

the price of oil sharply. Meanwhile, he emerged as the leading figure in the Persian Gulf after the withdrawal of British forces in 1971. Furthermore, he signed an agreement with the Iraqi leader Saddam Hussein in 1975, ending the two countries' border disputes. By the mid-1970s, the shah managed to establish close ties not only with the United States, Western Europe, and Muslim countries but also with the Communist bloc countries, South Africa, and Israel.

The many diplomatic and economic achievements of the shah led to ostentatious displays of royal hubris. For example, in October 1971 he celebrated the 2,500th anniversary of the foundation of the Persian Empire by Cyrus the Great and formed, in March 1975, a one-party system. Both acts were resented by the intelligentsia and middle classes. He also replaced powerful, independent-minded politicians with more accommodating and submissive aides, a strategy that cost him dearly at times of international and domestic crisis. Concurrently, the shah's White Revolution had undermined the traditional foundation of his authority—the *ulama,* the bazaar merchants, and the landowning classes. They were replaced by the entrepreneurs, the young

Mohammad Reza Shah Pahlavi (1919–1980) ruled as king of Iran from 1941 to 1979. He implemented the "White Revolution" in 1963, the most important aspect of which was the redistribution of half of the privately owned agricultural land to the peasants who share-cropped it. He ruled as a royal dictator until 1979, when the monarchy was overthrown in a popular revolution led by Ayatollah Ruhollah Khomeini. © BETTMANN/CORBIS. REPRODUCED BY PERMISSION.

Western-educated bureaucratic elites, and new middle classes who had developed uneasy relations with the shah. The intelligentsia resented the lack of political freedom and violations of human rights, the rigged elections, corruption, and close ties with the United States. The old religious groups and the bazaar merchants and artisans resented the un-Islamic Western lifestyle promoted by the shah's modernization policies. The entrepreneurial and political elites were discontented with the shah's autocratic rule, and with the lack of their own political power and autonomous organizational base. Under these circumstances the nucleus of an anti-

shah revolutionary coalition was formed by a large group of liberal and radical intelligentsia, and a small group of militant *ulama* and their important followers in the bazaar.

Pahlavi Dynasty Collapse (1977–1979)

The opportunity for the opposition to challenge the shah came after the victory of Jimmy Carter in the U.S. presidential race of November 1976 and the ensuing active support given by his administration to the cause of human rights. When the political upheavals began (1977), the shah's weak and indecisive character contributed to the collapse of the Pahlavi regime and the rise of the Islamic Republic under the leadership of Ayatollah Ruhollah Khomeini, a charismatic figure with a strong will to power. Despite the mass-based nature of the Iranian Revolution, however, not all sectors of the population opposed the shah. The peasantry, for example, constituting over half of the population at the time, continued to support him, though passively. Even labor and the majority of public-sector employees and the middle and lower-middle classes did not join the uprising until the last phases of the revolution, when the shah's regime was on the verge of collapse. After a series of mass demonstrations, mass strikes, and clashes between the shah's security forces and opposition groups in the latter half of 1978, the shah left the country in January 1979; he died of cancer in Cairo on 27 July 1980.

For the shah the ideal model of the imperial persona was the Persian image of the "benevolent autocrat," as exemplified by great Persian monarchs, including his father, Reza Shah. Although this model implied that he should be determined, self-confident, and brave, in reality he was gentle, timid, and indecisive. The shah's inherently fragile character became evident particularly during periods of instability and crisis, whereas his "benevolent autocrat" tendencies came up during periods of stability and success. Furthermore, he was not immune to conspiracy theories. He therefore often saw the secret hands of foreign powers, specifically those of the British, behind virtually every international and domestic incident. He believed, for example, that the Anglophobic Mohammad Mossadegh and the xenophobic Ayatollah Khomeini were British agents. Referring to an Anglo-Russian conspiracy, the shah attributed the Islamic revolution to the "unholy alliance of Red and Black." Belief in conspiracy theories further intensified his inherent vulnerability during periods of crisis. As a result, in the critical periods of 1941 to 1953 and 1960 to 1963, Mohammad Reza showed considerable indecisiveness. On the other hand, in the post-coup period (1953–1959) he began to show more determination, and in the stable period of 1963–1976, he emerged as a "benevolent autocrat," who devoted himself, in his own way, to the welfare of his people. Finally, during the period of revolutionary crisis (1977–1979), the shah, for the third time during his reign, turned indecisive, once again embraced conspiracy theories, and displayed a mood of withdrawal—traits and reactions that may have contributed significantly to his downfall.

See also AMINI, ALI; BAGHDAD PACT (1955); IRAN; IRANIAN REVOLUTION (1979); MOSSADEGH, MOHAMMAD; PAHLAVI, REZA; WHITE REVOLUTION (1961–1963).

Bibliography

Alam, Asadollah. The Shah and I: The Confidential Diary of Iran's Royal Court, 1969–1977, edited and translated by Alinaghi Alikhani. New York: St. Martin's, 1992.

Ashraf, Ahmad. "From the White Revolution to the Islamic Revolution." In Iran After the Revolution: Crisis of an Islamic State, edited by Sohrab Behda and Saeed Rahnema. London and New York: I. B. Tauris, 1995.

Ashraf, Ahmad, and Banuazizi, Ali. "The State, Classes, and Modes of Mobilization in the Iranian Revolution." State, Culture and Society 1, no. 3 (1985): 3–40.

Azimi, Fakhreddin. Iran: The Crisis of Democracy. London: I. B. Tauris, 1989.

Banuazizi, Ali. "Iran: The Making of a Regional Power," in The Middle East: Oil, Conflict, and Hope, edited by A. L. Udovitch. Lexington, MA: Lexington Books, 1976.

Jacqz, Jane, ed. Iran: Past, Present, and Future. New York: Aspen Institute for Humanistic Studies, 1976.

Pahlavi, Mohammad Reza. Answer to History, translated by Michael Joseph Ltd. New York: Stein and Day, 1980.

Pahlavi, Mohammad Reza. Mission for My Country. New York: McGraw-Hill, 1961.

Roosevelt, Kermit. Countercoup: The Struggle for the Control of Iran. New York: McGraw-Hill, 1979.

Wright, Denis. "Ten Years in Iran." Asian Affairs 12 (1991): 259–271.

Zonis, Marvin. Majestic Failure: The Fall of the Shah. Chicago: University of Chicago Press, 1991.

AHMAD ASHRAF

PAHLAVI, REZA
[1878–1944]

Founder of the Pahlavi dynasty in Iran.

Reza Shah Pahlavi was born into the family of a foot soldier in a small village near the Caspian Sea and given the name Reza. A few months after his birth, he lost his father, and he spent most of his childhood with his maternal uncle, an officer in the Cossack Brigade in Tehran. At the age of fifteen, at the behest of his uncle, he enlisted in the Cossack Brigade; on the strength of his personal traits and leadership qualities, he rose to officer rank. Surnames were not common in Iran in the early twentieth century, and his peers called him Reza Khan, the title *khan* being one of respect.

Reza Khan rose to prominence in the early 1920s when Iran was on the verge of economic collapse and political and territorial disintegration. The southward push of the newly established Soviet Union already threatened traditional British strategic and commercial interests in Iran and its colonial rule in India. The creation of a functioning central government capable of holding Iran intact as a buffer state became the main concern of Great Britain. Reza Khan, who aspired to save the country from disintegration, had risen to the rank of brigadier general and replaced the Russian commander of the Cossack Brigade. The commander of British forces in Iran did not oppose the coup d'etat engineered by Ziya Tabataba'i, with the support of Reza Khan, who marched his troops, some 2,500 men, into Tehran on 21 February 1921. The prime minister and cabinet were dismissed and Ahmad Shah, the reigning Qajar monarch, was forced to appoint Tabataba'i prime minister and Reza Khan army commander. Within a few months, however, Reza Khan ousted Tabataba'i and, having become the dominant player on the country's disarrayed political stage, virtually forced the powerless Ahmad Shah first to appoint him minister of war and then to appoint him prime minister. In 1925, Reza Khan masterminded a parliamentary act by which the Qajar dynasty was deposed. He was entrusted with the throne as the founder of the Pahlavi dynasty.

To modernize a debilitated and backward country, Reza Shah began to reorganize and rebuild the army and the bureaucracy practically from scratch. A universal conscription law was passed in 1925 and young army officers were sent to France for military training. He ordered the purchase of a limited supply of weapons, including armored vehicles, fighter planes, and small warships. Administrative and judicial reforms began as early as 1922, when the Iranian *majles* (parliament) enacted a law calling for competitive entrance exams and specific qualifications for prospective civil servants. A new ministry of justice was established in 1925 and charged with drafting and applying a new legal code based on European judicial systems. These legal reforms helped create a secular system of justice that took away much of the clergy's traditional control over the administration of justice.

With the creation of a modern national system of education, the number of pupils in modern schools increased more than tenfold, from approximately 30,000 in 1921 to 370,000 in 1941. In 1935, the University of Tehran was founded; between 1925 and 1940, some 1,500 Iranian students were sent abroad for study in various fields. Concerted efforts were made to revive and propagate Iran's ancient cultural heritage and values in order to strengthen Iranian national identity as the indispensable foundation for a modern nation-state. Reza Shah paid considerable attention to improving the country's communications, transportation, and industrial capacities. An 850-mile-long railway, running from Bandar Shah on the Caspian to Ahvaz near the Persian Gulf, was completed in 1938. The quality of roads was improved and new highways, bridges, and tunnels were constructed. With foreign assistance, the country's postal and telegraph systems were drastically upgraded and a radio transmission system was installed in Tehran. The founding of a national bank in 1927, which replaced the British-controlled Imperial Bank of Persia and was given the right to issue legal tender in 1931, gave the government effective control over the country's financial markets. Bent on asserting Iran's economic independence, Reza Shah expanded Iran's nascent light industries. Although he relied on foreign technical assistance, especially from Germany, for his modernization program, he eliminated virtually all vestiges of foreign, and particularly British, economic and administrative tutelage in Iran.

Reza Shah's modernization policy led to the formation of new urban middle classes and, more specifically, a new professional bureaucratic intelligentsia which became the main support of his regime. He also had the support of the leaders and supporters of the 1905 through 1911 Constitutional Revolution and of the Social Democrats in his efforts to create a modern, independent nation-state. However, his political and social reforms were met with strong resistance from two major traditional forces: tribal chiefs and the clergy. The formation of a centralized bureaucracy and the unification and strengthening of the armed forces undermined the traditional privileges of tribal chiefs and eventually led to the expansion of the central government's authority over tribal areas. The secularization of Iran's judicial and educational systems greatly alarmed the clergy, who had also become concerned about some of Reza Shah's other innovations, such as public dress codes for both men and women, which they saw as undermining traditional Islamic lifestyles and values. Especially controversial was his order that women not appear in public covered in the traditional Iranian chador.

Reza Shah lived the life of a simple soldier. He was known for his parsimony and distaste for luxury. He had a great capacity for work, was often personally involved in minor administrative matters, and had a remarkable memory for the mundane details of governance. However, he also developed an obsession with acquiring large landed estates, mostly through forced gifts from private owners or through outright confiscation. A much more serious character flaw with respect to the sociopolitical development of the country was his highly autocratic and arbitrary leadership style, particularly in the latter half of his reign, in the 1930s. His method of ruling left little room for the development of personal initiative or a genuine parliamentary system of government. Furthermore, his autocratic regime also blocked the formation of a viable political elite that could guarantee the continuation of reforms undertaken during his reign. His mounting fear of disloyalty, rivalry, and sedition led to the banishing or elimination of a number of prominent political figures, most of whom had supported him in his meteoric rise to power and helped him set the country on the path of modernization. Prominent among his victims were the court minister Abdul Hussein Teymurtash; Ali Akbar Davar, the architect of Iran's modern judicial system, state industries, and enterprises, who was driven to suicide; and the chiefs of the Qashqa'i and Bakhtiari tribes. Taqi Arani, the leader of a group of leftist intellectuals, died in prison under suspicious circumstances. Sayyid Hasan Modarres, a leading political cleric, and Farrokhi Yazdi, an acerbic poet and journalist, were also among Reza Shah's victims. By the end of his reign, his authoritarian rule had alienated not only an important group of the professional bureaucratic intelligentsia but also a growing number of the independent intelligentsia, such as Sadeq Hedayat and Malek al-Shoara Bahar; the intelligentsia of the left; and the nationalist figures who rallied around Mohammad Mossadegh in the 1940s.

With the outbreak of World War II in 1939, Iran declared its neutrality. In 1941, after Germany invaded the Soviet Union and Moscow and London became wartime allies, Iran suddenly acquired strategic importance as a potential Allied supply route that circumvented Nazi-controlled Europe. A joint Anglo-Soviet force invaded Iran on 25 August 1941. On 16 September 1941, Reza Shah was forced to abdicate in favor of the crown prince, Mohammad Reza Shah Pahlavi. Reza Shah left Iran on 28 September aboard a British vessel. He remained under de facto house arrest in Mauritius and later in Johannesburg, South Africa, where he died on 26 July 1944.

See also CONSTITUTIONAL REVOLUTION; COSSACK BRIGADE; JANGALI; MILLSPAUGH, ARTHUR; MOSSADEGH, MOHAMMAD; PAHLAVI, MOHAMMAD REZA; SOUTH PERSIA RIFLES; TABATABA'I, ZIYA; TRANS-IRANIAN RAILWAY; UNIVERSITY OF TEHRAN.

Bibliography

Banani, Amin. *The Modernization of Iran, 1921–1941.* Stanford, CA: Stanford University Press. 1961.

Cronin, Stephanie, ed. *The Army and the Creation of the Pahlavi State in Iran, 1910–1926,* London: Tauris Academic Studies, 1997.

Elwell-Sutton, L. P. "Reza Shah the Great: Founder of the Pahlavi Dynasty." In *Iran under the Pahlavis,* edited by George Lenczowski. Stanford, CA: Hoover Institution Press, 1978.

Ghani, Cyrus. *Iran and the Rise of Reza Shah: From Qajar Collapse to Pahlavi Rule.* London: Tauris, 1998.

Wilber, Donald. *Riza Shah Pahlavi: The Resurrection and Reconstruction of Iran, 1878–1944.* Hicksville, NY: Exposition Press, 1975.

Zargar, Ali. *Anglo-Iranian Relations: 1925–1941.* Geneva: Institut Universitaire de Haute Etudes Internationale, 1983.

AHMAD ASHRAF

PAKHTUN

See PUSHTUN

PAKISTAN AND THE MIDDLE EAST

Pakistan's ties to the Middle East are based on history, religion, security, and economics.

Pakistan's historical links with the Middle East go back to the Arab invasion of Sindh in 712 C.E. The Arab–Islamic and Iranian cultures have deeply influenced the civilization of the areas that now comprise Pakistan. Contemporary geopolitical considerations have reinforced Pakistan's interest in the Arab region. For security as well as religious reasons, Pakistan has attached great significance to its relations with the Arab Islamic states.

The perception of a security threat from India and their dispute over Kashmir have impelled Pakistan to look toward the Islamic countries as "natural allies." Nevertheless, Pakistan's use of common Islamic symbols and shared religious identity did not satisfy the countries of the Middle East. Instead, Pakistan's decision to join the U.S.-sponsored security pacts in the 1950s provoked Arab hostility, particularly from Egypt, Syria, and Iraq. Archrival India found the political climate in the radical Arab states more congenial for its diplomacy. Pakistan's relationship with the West brought it closer to Iran, Turkey, and pro-West moderate Arab states.

In response to declining U.S. interest in military alliances, Pakistan's Middle East policy underwent a fundamental transformation in the early

1970s. As an alternative to dwindling Western support, Pakistan began to look toward the Arab oil-producing countries for economic assistance. Under Mohammad Reza Pahlavi, Iran became an important regional ally and also a source of much-needed foreign aid. Saudi Arabia and the Gulf states showed tremendous interest in Pakistan's security and economic development.

With the manifold increase in oil revenues, the Gulf region became more attractive for Pakistan as a market for its surplus manpower. Millions of Pakistanis have worked on developmental projects in the Gulf countries. The Pakistani workers abroad not only have lessened the pressure on unemployment at home but also have earned the country tens of billions of dollars. In the peak years (1980–1988), Pakistani workers remitted about three billion U.S. dollars a year that offset the huge gap in the balance of trade.

While Pakistan has unilaterally and unconditionally supported the Arab states in their disputes with Israel, including a Palestinian homeland, it has not received unanimous political backing of all the Middle Eastern countries in its disputes with India. In pursuit of bilateralism, Pakistan has carefully avoided taking sides in conflicts between the Muslim states. In the Iran–Iraq War in the 1980s, Pakistan remained strictly neutral. Pakistan's participation in Operation Desert Storm against Iraq in 1991 was a different matter. It was launched under the United Nations banner, and the coalition of Western and Arab states enjoyed broader legitimacy in forcing Iraqi invaders from Kuwait.

Over the years, Pakistan has emerged as an important regional actor in the Middle East, although it maintains a low profile. It has security protocols with a large number of Middle Eastern states. Pakistan provides training facilities to the armed forces of Saudi Arabia, Oman, Jordan, United Arab Emirates, Kuwait, and Bahrain. Also, Libya had access to these facilities in the 1970s. Pakistani military personnel serve in various capacities as trainers and advisers for Arab armies. In the 1980s, Pakistan stationed about 10,000 of its troops in Saudi Arabia. As a quid pro quo, Saudi Arabia financed the modernization of Pakistan's air force. In the latter part of the twentieth century, among developing countries, Pakistan had the second largest military presence overseas (after Cuba)—all of it was in the Middle East.

Bibliography

Burke, S. M., and Ziring, Lawrence. *Pakistan's Foreign Policy: An Historical Analysis,* 2d edition. Karachi: Oxford University Press, 1990.

Rizvi, Hasan-Askari. *Pakistan and the Geostrategic Environment: A Study of Foreign Policy.* New York: St. Martin's, 1993.

RASUL BAKHSH RAIS

PALESTINE

Area located on the eastern shore of the Mediterranean south of Lebanon and northeast of Egypt.

The area known as Palestine has taken on different geographic and political connotations over time. The following discussion distinguishes between (a) pre-twentieth-century history of the area; (b) Palestine as a territory under British administration from late 1917 to early 1948; and (c) Palestine as the territory administered by the Palestine National Authority since 1994, also known as the West Bank and Gaza Strip.

Pre-Twentieth-Century History

Palestine has since ancient times been a crossroads between Asia, Europe, and Africa. Its climate is arid. The southern half, the Negev, is desert, but in the north there are several fertile areas. The principal water source is the Jordan River, which flows south through Lake Tiberias into the Dead Sea.

Palestine is of central importance to three monotheistic faiths: Islam, Christianity, and Judaism. For 1,300 of the past 1,400 years, the land was under Muslim rule. Most European and North American Christians and Jews consider Palestine on both sides of the Jordan to be the Holy Land of the Old Testament of the Bible. Although the British initially designated the area of the Palestine Mandate to extend eastward to Mesopotamia (Iraq), by the early twentieth century most people took the Jordan River to be the eastern border of Palestine.

The earliest inhabitants of Palestine were the Canaanites. The land was conquered by numerous invaders, including (in the fourteenth century B.C.E.) the Hebrews and the Philistines, who gave

On Christmas Day, pilgrims flood into the city of Bethlehem, the birthplace of Jesus Christ. © BETTMANN/CORBIS. REPRODUCED BY PERMISSION.

the country its name. The Israelites, a confederation of Hebrew tribes, established a unified kingdom in the area under David and Solomon (c. 1000–922 B.C.E.), which subsequently split into the kingdoms of Israel in the north and Judaea in the south. From 587 B.C.E., Palestine became a province of the Persian Empire, and was later ruled by Jewish kings as part of the Roman empire. The Romans crushed the Jewish revolts of 66–73 and 132–135 C.E., killing and exiling many Jews, and renaming the area *Syria Palaestina*.

In 638 C.E. Arabian Muslim armies captured Jerusalem and replaced the Byzantine rulers of the area, which thereafter became known as *Filastin.* Arab geographers in the tenth century referred to Filastin as one of the provinces of Syria, but by the twelfth and thirteenth centuries the term was no longer used.

From the fifteenth century until the end of World War I, the region was part of the Ottoman Empire. Changing provincial and administrative boundaries within the empire blurred Palestine's separate existence. In an attempt to centralize government administration, the Ottoman Empire was divided into new administrative regions under the Vilayet Law of 1864. Under this arrangement the central and largest part of Palestine, as well as Transjordan, became part of the *vilayet* (province) of Damascus. The northern part of the country, including Acre, Haifa, Tiberias, Safed, Nablus, Jenin, and Tulkarm, was part of the *vilayet* of Beirut. Jerusalem, Gaza, Hebron, and Beersheba became the *sanjak* (district) of Jerusalem, which, because of the city's special religious status and because of European interest, was established as an independent unit governed directly from Constantinople (now Istanbul).

By the mid-nineteenth century the population of Palestine was about 500,000, the vast majority of whom were Muslims. The southern half of the country, later called the Negev, was mostly desert, sparsely inhabited by bedoun tribes. Overall, only about a third of Palestine was suitable for cultivation.

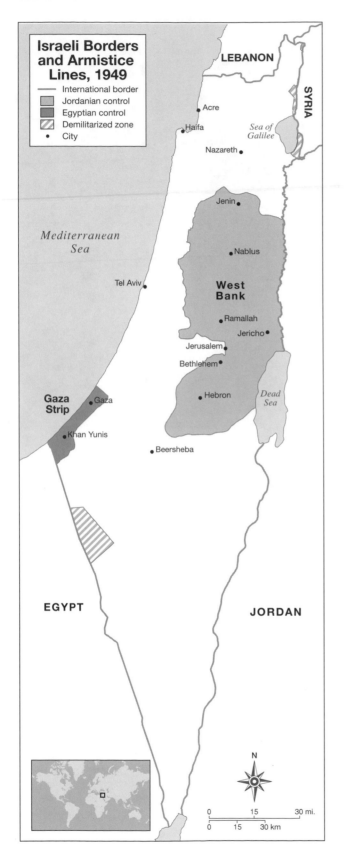

Israeli Borders
and Armistice
Lines, 1949

— International border
Jordanian control
Egyptian control
Demilitarized zone
• City

LEBANON

SYRIA

Acre

Haifa

Sea of Galilee

Nazareth

Mediterranean Sea

Jenin

Nablus

Tel Aviv

West Bank

Ramallah

Jericho

Jerusalem

Bethlehem

Gaza
Strip

Gaza

Hebron

Dead Sea

Khan Yunis

Beersheba

EGYPT

JORDAN

N

0   15   30 mi.
0   15   30 km

By the end of the nineteenth century, a commercial bourgeoisie comprised of Muslims, Christians, Jews, and German Templars played an important role in the incorporation of Palestine's economy into the world economic system. There was a major increase in cultivation of export commodities that included wheat, barley, sesame, olive oil, and oranges. Small-scale industries produced textiles, soap, oil, and religious items.

Palestine as a modern political entity came into existence as a result of the collapse of the Ottoman Empire in World War I. Although the Arabs of the region considered themselves to be a distinctive group, there was no serious conflict between them and the Ottoman Turkish establishment until the early twentieth century. Nineteenth-century Palestinian elites approved of and benefited from the Ottoman reform effort (Tanzimat, from 1839 to 1876), and many of them held influential posts in the ruling establishment in Constantinople. Several served in the parliament; Nablus was reputed to be especially favored by Sultan Abdülhamit II. It was against this backdrop that an Arab "decentralist" movement would emerge before World War I, and within this wider pan-Arab political sentiment the first seeds of a distinct Palestinian nationalism were sown.

Although Jews had been living in Palestine (which they call Eretz Yisrael, the Land of Israel) for millennia, the first politically motivated Jewish immigration came in 1882. At the time, the Jewish population was about 24,000, mostly comprised of Orthodox Jews unaffiliated with the Zionist movement. They were settled mainly in Jerusalem, Hebron, Safed, and Tiberias. There was little friction between these Jews, the "Old Yishuv," and the indigenous Arab population. However, as the number of Zionist settlements increased, quarrels arose between them and neighboring villages over grazing, crops, and land issues. Between 1886 and World War I, there were several armed clashes that resulted from Jewish settlers purchasing land from absentee Arab owners and subsequently dispossessing the peasant cultivators.

Growing opposition to Zionism and emergence of a new pan-Turkish ideology following the Young Turk Revolution in 1908 led to a heightened sense of distinctive Palestinian patriotism. Although most of the Palestinian elite remained loyal to the Ottoman sultan during World War I, a few prominent intellectuals identified with the nascent pan-Arab nationalist movement. During the war, opposition to Ottoman authority increased because of economic disasters (caused by a locust plague, drought, and famine) with which the Ottoman authorities failed to cope, and because of the repressive measures imposed by the Turkish governor, Cemal Paça.

Palestine under British Rule

Before World War I the area that became Palestine was sometimes known as "southern Syria." With the retreat of the Ottoman Army, Palestine was occupied by British forces under General Sir Edmund Allenby in 1917 and 1918, and was placed under a military government administration known as Occupied Enemy Territory Administration South (OETA-S) until 1 July 1920, when the military regime was replaced by a British civil administration. During three decades of British rule, Palestinians further developed their national consciousness and were able to exercise some degree of national-communal political activity.

In London, the British foreign secretary, Arthur J. Balfour, wrote a letter on 2 November 1917 defining His Majesty's Government's new policy favoring the creation of a Jewish national home in Palestine. In April 1918 a Zionist Commission arrived in Jaffa with a mission (despite a local publication ban on the Balfour Declaration) to prepare the Yishuv to enjoy special status and privileges under an expected pro-Zionist British regime that would encourage Jewish immigration, settlement, land purchase, and—eventually—statehood. Rumors about the impending implementation of the Balfour policy alarmed many sectors of the Palestinian population, whose local leadership created, during the first year of the British occupation, a country-wide organization to express its opposition to Zionism. The Muslim-Christian Association (MCA) first appeared in Jaffa early in November 1918, and in Jerusalem later the same month; subsequently it set up branches in various Palestinian towns. The purpose behind creating the MCA was to organize a Palestinian national struggle against the threat of Zionism.

The top leadership of the MCA was drawn largely from the older generation of urban notables who had social standing in Ottoman times. Initially, the

Ashkenazi Jews descend from Poland, Austria, Germany, or Eastern Europe. Traditionally the Ashkenazi Jews speak Yiddish. © HULTON-DEUTSCH COLLECTION/CORBIS. REPRODUCED BY PERMISSION.

MCA, under former Jerusalem mayor Musa Kazim al-Husayni, did not have much political power, and its significance derived from the fact that it embodied the concept of political cooperation between Muslims and Christians in Palestine. Gradually, however, it became a group of leaders and activists who were able to mobilize important segments of Palestinian society around a program of independence and opposition to Zionism. Their main instruments of political action were petitions submitted to the Palestine government and the organizing of demonstrations and other campaigns on instructions from the Jerusalem secretariat, which was headed by Jamal al-Husayni. Yet the notables who led the MCAs were interested in maintaining friendly relations with the new British masters of the country.

As part of its efforts to promote Palestinian national demands, the MCA was instrumental in convening a country-wide congress in Jerusalem from 27 January to 9 February 1919. Called the first

Palestine Arab Congress, it was followed by six more, the last of which was held in 1928. The MCA also initiated the formation of the Arab Executive (AE) Committee that tried to coordinate the national struggle in the 1920s and early 1930s.

Government of Palestine under the Mandate

Following the British takeover, Palestine acquired fixed boundaries, its own government, and a political identity separate from the surrounding countries carved from the Ottoman Empire by Great Britain and France. Its separate identity was given international recognition when Great Britain assumed the Mandate for Palestine under the League of Nations in July 1922. In 1923 the British unilaterally divided the area of the original mandate into

British Mandate for Palestine

— Boundaries, 1923

Area separated and closed to Jewish settlement, 1921

Area ceded by Great Britain to the French Mandate of Syria, 1923

• City

MAP BY XNR PRODUCTIONS, INC. THE GALE GROUP.

Transjordan (east of the Jordan River) and western Palestine, with the Jewish national home provisions of the mandate applying only to the latter territory. The area east of the river became the autonomous emirate (principality) of Transjordan (later the Hashimite Kingdom of Jordan) under the Amir Abdullah, son of the sharif of Mecca.

According to the terms of the Mandate for Palestine, Great Britain was ultimately responsible to the League of Nations for governing the country, which was ruled, in effect, like a colony, under a high commissioner (HC) appointed by the British government. The HC was responsible to the Colonial Office in London rather than to the local population and had authority to make all government appointments, laws, rules, and regulations. He was backed by British military forces and police. Most high commissioners were former British colonial officials or army generals. The government of Palestine created its own courts, postal service, police force, customs, railroad and transportation network, and currency backed by the British pound sterling. Until 1948 the inhabitants of the country, both Arabs and Jews, were legally called Palestinians and considered British subjects.

The British attempted to introduce a limited measure of self-government through establishment of advisory and legislative councils during the 1920s and 1930s. The first, set up in October 1920, was a nominated advisory council (AC) pending the establishment of a legislative body. The AC was composed of ten Palestinian officials: four Muslims, three Christians, and three Jewish members of the Yishuv.

In August 1922 the HC, Sir Herbert Louis Samuel, proposed as a first step toward self-government a constitution that called for the replacement of the AC with a legislative council (LC). The proposed LC was to be composed of twenty-three members: eleven appointed British members, including the high commissioner, and twelve elected Palestinian members, including eight Muslims, two Christians, and two Jews. However, in order to safeguard the Balfour policy of support for the Jewish national home, the HC would retain a veto power and the council's legislative authority would not extend to such central issues as Jewish immigration and land purchase.

The Jews reluctantly accepted, but the Palestinians rejected the proposed constitution and boycotted the elections for the LC in February 1923. Palestinian leaders argued that participation in the council would be tantamount to acceptance of the British Mandate and Balfour policy, which they feared would lead to their subjugation under a Jewish majority in an eventual state. The poor election turnout caused the HC to shelve the LC proposal and revert to the idea of an advisory council. But Samuel failed to convince Palestinian leaders to sit on a revised AC; nor was his subsequent proposal to establish an "Arab Agency" (to be parallel to the "Jewish Agency" recognized under the mandate) any more successful at winning the cooperation of local politicians. Samuel thereupon abandoned the idea of encouraging popular participation in the governing of Palestine. Although the idea of establishing a LC would be revived in 1928 and again in the early 1930s, the British were unable to win both Arab and Jewish support for their proposals. As a result, Palestine was governed, from 1923 until the end of the Mandate in 1948, by a HC in consultation with an AC composed only of British officials.

Britain's Dual Obligation and Intercommunal Rivalry.
The League of Nations Mandate for Palestine incorporated provisions of the Balfour Declaration calling for "establishment in Palestine of a national home for the Jewish people." It also recognized the "historical connexion of the Jewish people with Palestine," promised support of Zionist objectives, and gave preference to Jewish land acquisition and settlement. Although the mandate (like the Balfour Declaration) made no specific reference to the Arab population as possessing national rights (referring to them as the "existing non-Jewish communities"), it prohibited "discrimination of any kind . . . between the inhabitants of Palestine."

As a result of this dual obligation to both foster the establishment of the Jewish national home and ensure "that the rights and position of other sectors of the population are not prejudiced," British policy was ambivalent, and at first seemed destined to arouse unrealizable expectations on the part of both communities. Initial support for Zionist objectives was indicated in the appointment of Herbert Samuel, an Anglo-Jewish leader sympathetic to Zionism, as the first HC to Palestine (1920–1925).

However, opposition by the country's Arab majority to the establishment of a Jewish homeland and to larger imperial interests became a major obstacle to full British cooperation with Zionist leaders who were eager, for their part, to proceed full speed toward their objectives of a Jewish majority and an eventual Jewish state in Palestine.

The dissatisfaction of Palestine's Arab population with Britain's pro-Zionist policy was expressed peacefully in the forms of public demonstrations, protest letters and petitions, and the dispatch of several delegations to London and Geneva. Palestinian leaders, seeking self-determination and the establishment of an Arab state in Palestine, feared Jewish domination (through increasing immigration and land purchases) and the establishment of a Jewish state. Nationalist frustrations led to periodic rioting (April 1920, May 1921, November 1922, August 1929, November 1933) and to a full-scale rebellion known as the Arab Revolt (1936–1939). Local British security forces restored law and order, and the Colonial Office in London issued several policy statements (White Papers) in attempts to redefine or clarify its Palestine policy. But all attempts to bridge the gap between the Arab and Jewish communities were unsuccessful; each community proceeded to develop itself with little, if any, contact with the other. By 1939 Great Britain had retreated from its position on implementing the Balfour provisions of the mandate.

Each community developed its own educational, health, welfare, cultural, political, and labor organizations. Arab schools supported by the Mandatory government's Education Department were conducted in Arabic with their own curriculum. The Yishuv had its own schools, where the language was Hebrew, and its own Hebrew University, founded in 1925. The two communities lived largely separately; contact was only at the peripheries, in government offices, or in a few business enterprises. The Yishuv was mainly urban, concentrated in the coastal region and in the city of Jerusalem, whereas the Arab sector was largely rural, in central Palestine.

By the end of the mandate in 1948, the Palestinian population had doubled, mostly through natural increase, from just over 650,000 (1922 census) to 1.3 million. During the same period the population of the Yishuv increased even more dramatically, largely through immigration, from about 84,000 to approximately 650,000. The increase in the Jewish population from about a tenth to a third of the total population of Palestine was accompanied by extensive expansion of the Yishuv's socioeconomic and politicomilitary infrastructure. The number of rural collectives (*kibbutzim*), cooperatives (*moshavim*), and private farms increased several times; the all-Jewish city of Tel Aviv grew from an adjunct of Jaffa to the second largest municipality in the country. Jewish-owned industry dominated the economy. Despite the growth of its rural sector, the Yishuv was 85 percent urban by the end of the mandate, and Jewish-owned land comprised less than 7 percent of the total, although more than a quarter of the cultivated area was Jewish.

The Yishuv developed its own political parties and self-governing institutions that took responsibility for functions not under jurisdiction of the mandatory government, such as courts, education, and social welfare. The British recognized the World Zionist Organization as the official agency to implement establishment of the Jewish national home. Within Palestine the Yishuv elected its elected assembly (*Assefat ha-Nivharim*), whose national council (*Va'ad Le'umi*) ran the day-to-day affairs of the Jewish community. More than a dozen political parties were divided into four principal categories: labor, general Zionist, Orthodox religious, and Sephardic or Oriental. The strongest political bloc was labor by virtue of its control of the Histadrut, the large labor federation that controlled much of the Yishuv's economy, and of the largest paramilitary group, the Haganah.

Palestinian Political Organization during the Mandate.

The Palestinian community was much less centralized and more loosely organized than the Yishuv. The older politicians, representing the traditional elite and notable families who had been closely associated with the Ottoman establishment, had formed the MCA in 1918 and continued to lead the Palestine Arab Congresses by holding positions on the Arab Executive.

With the defeat of Faisal's Arab kingdom by the French in July 1920, Palestinian leaders who had previously been engaged in the struggle for independent "Greater Syria" focused on local problems, primarily the struggle against the British mandate

and the Jewish national home. Later that year, the third Palestinian Arab Congress convened in Haifa, elected an AE committee, and sent a delegation to plead the Palestinian cause both at the Colonial Office in London and at the League of Nations headquarters in Geneva. Neither the congresses nor the AE were successful in attaining their objective, and both gradually lost credibility. When its chairman, Musa Kazim al-Husayni, died in 1934, the Arab Executive ceased to exist.

Throughout the mandate period serious rivalry for political office and government favor existed between members of the Nashashibi and Husayni families. The most influential Palestinian leader was al-Hajj Muhammad Amin al-Husayni, appointed by the British as mufti of Jerusalem in 1921 and elected president of the Supreme Muslim Council in 1922. By virtue of these positions he commanded extensive financial resources and influence throughout the Palestinian community. Prior to 1936 the mufti pursued a policy of cooperation that aided the High Commissioner in keeping the peace. However, following the outbreak of the Arab Revolt in 1936, al-Hajj Amin al-Husayni became more militantly anti-British. His activities ultimately led the British to seek his arrest, but in mid-1937 he escaped, first to Lebanon, then to Iraq.

Supporters of the mufti, called Councilites (*al-majlisiyyun*), were opposed by "the Opposition" (*al-mu'aridun*) led by the Nashashibi family. Both groups were supported by extensive clan (*hamula*) networks and client relationships. The Husaynis, the larger network, were considered more militant than the Nashashibis, who were willing to compromise with the British. Even though both factions rejected the Jewish national home, these internal rivalries constituted a weakness vis-à-vis the more cohesive Jewish community.

Following demise of the Arab Executive in 1934, younger and more militant elements became active in local Palestinian politics, leading to the creation of the Palestinian branch of the pan-Arab Independence (Istiqlal) Party headed by Awni Abd al-Hadi, who was joined by Akram Zu'aytir and Muhammad Izzat Darwaza. The old MCA and AE forces also regrouped into rival Arab political parties, chiefly the Palestine Arab Party, organized by the Husaynis, and the National Defense Party, headed by the

Nashashibis. The Palestine Arab Party was founded in March 1935 by Jamal al-Husayni, a relative of al-Hajj Amin al-Husayni. Many political activists who had previously supported the AE (1920–1934) joined its ranks. Its leaders maintained close contact with the Roman Catholic community through its officers, Alfred Rock and Emile al-Ghuri, and with the activist scouts' movement and workers' societies in Jerusalem and Haifa. The party endorsed the following set of "national demands," which were later endorsed by an umbrella organization representing all major parties: (a) repudiation of the Balfour Declaration; (b) full stoppage of Jewish immigration and land purchases; and (c) the immediate establishment of Palestine as an independent state under Arab control.

The National Defense Party was formed on 2 December 1934 by the supporters of Raghib al-Nashashibi, the former mayor of Jerusalem. The leaders encompassed most Arab mayors; important politicians from large landowning families; influential middle-class Christians; and the Jaffa branch of the Palestine Arab Workers Society. The party denounced the sale of land to Zionist landholding companies and sought limitations on Jewish immigration. Nonetheless, it was tacitly more cooperative with the British authorities and Zionist leaders, and (unlike the Husaynis) maintained good relations with Amir Abdullah of Transjordan.

General Strike and Revolt, 1936–1939. By April 1936, growing Palestinian concern at the rapid influx of Jewish immigration and the accompanying frustration at British unwillingness to fulfill their national demands led to a general strike against the British authorities and the Yishuv. The strike soon became an uprising, drawing support from the whole Palestinian community and from Arab nationalist circles in the neighboring lands. The Arab Higher Committee (AHC), chaired by the mufti and representing a broad coalition of Arab political organizations, was formed to lead the uprising. Elements of the Palestine Arab Party formed an underground paramilitary force that remained active until suppressed by the British in early 1939.

During a lull in the fighting (1936–1937), the British sent a Royal Commission of Inquiry under William Robert Wellesley, the first Earl Peel, to ascertain the causes of the rebellion and to propose

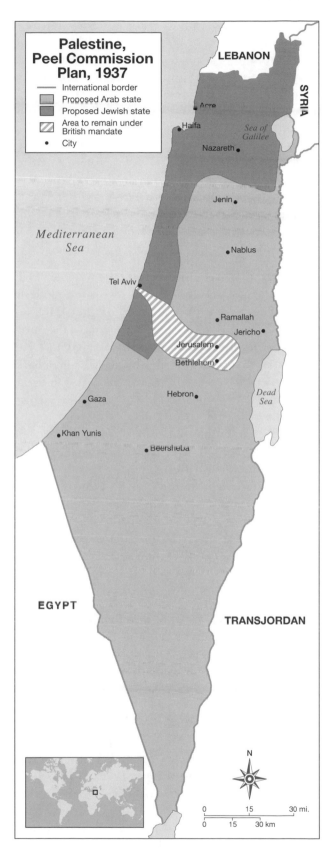

MAP BY XNR PRODUCTIONS, INC. THE GALE GROUP.

solutions. In July 1937 the Peel Commission recommended a form of radical surgery: the partition of Palestine into a small Jewish coastal state, and a larger Arab state to be joined with Transjordan. The Palestine Arab Party denounced the plan, and the revolt resumed, this time with greater support from nationalist groups in Iraq, Syria, and Lebanon. The National Defense Party, for its part, accepted the Peel Commission concept of territorial partition and was not averse to the idea of linking the Arab portion of Mandatory Palestine to Abdullah's Transjordan. The party was criticized by other Palestinian politicians for deviating from the antipartition consensus.

The short-lived unity behind the AHC was broken when the uprising entered its second phase in 1937. The Nashashibi member of the AHC resigned, leaving leadership in the hands of the mufti and his allies. In 1937 the British outlawed the AHC and arrested and deported several of its members. The mufti and several of his associates fled to Syria, Iraq, and Lebanon, from which they attempted to keep the rebellion alive. During 1937 and 1938 a number of assassinations took place as the struggle between followers of the Nashashibis and Husaynis turned violent, contributing to a leadership vacuum in the Palestinian community. By 1939 the rebellion petered out as a result of the conflict within the Palestinian community and the massive use of force by the British. In the end, the Palestinians had suffered staggering losses: more than 3,000 dead, 15,000 to 20,000 wounded, and more than 5,000 leaders and fighters in detention.

In their search for a political formula that would reestablish tranquility in Palestine in light of a looming European war, the British convened a round-table conference of Arab and Zionist representatives at London's St. James's Palace in early 1939. Bickering over who should represent the Palestinians contributed to the ineffectiveness of the small Palestinian delegation (headed by Jamal al-Husayni and George Antonius) that sat through many meetings alongside those of Iraq, Egypt, Transjordan, Saudi Arabia, and Yemen. When the conference broke down without reaching consensus, Colonial Secretary Malcolm MacDonald issued a White Paper in May that retracted the Peel Commission's partition recommendation and proposed instead that, over a period of ten years, self-governing institutions would be developed for an eventual independent Palestinian state that would not be dominated by either Arabs or Jews. At the same time, the White Paper restricted Jewish immigration to 75,000 over five years, with any subsequent immigration dependent on Arab approval. Furthermore, the purchase of land by Jews would be limited in some parts of Palestine and forbidden in others. The White Paper thus limited the expansion of the Jewish community and its territorial holdings, but fell short of the Palestinians' demands for total stoppage of immigration and the immediate granting of independence.

During and after World War II. Overshadowed by the necessities of prosecuting the British war effort after 1939, local political activity in Palestine was quiescent, despite the absence of consensus in support of the new White Paper policy. Within the Yishuv, official Zionist policy was to fight the restrictions of the MacDonald White Paper as if there were no war against Germany, while helping in the fight against the Axis powers as if there were no White Paper. Britain was left to pursue its war effort without official Zionist, Arab, or Palestinian endorsement of the provisions in the White Paper.

Faced with these new directions in British policy, attempts were made to revive the AHC, but these were marred by the continuing rift between the Husaynis and Nashashibis and by the absence of many exiled leaders whom the British had prevented from returning to the country. By 1941 the National Defense Party had become inactive, although Raghib al-Nashashibi continued to issue statements in its name. Some leaders of the Palestine Arab Party were able to return to Palestine and reopen the party's offices in April 1944 and to use its connections with the Arab Bank and the local press to regain substantial influence. A Husayni-dominated AHC was organized in 1945, but it was countered by an opposition Arab Higher Front. When Jamal al-Husayni returned in February 1946 he gained control over the AHC as well as the Palestine Arab Party. Later that year the Arab League intervened, and another AHC was set up.

In the struggle following World War II the AHC rejected various British and Anglo-American compromise proposals and, ultimately, the 1947 United Nations (UN) partition proposal. Paramilitary organizations formed to oppose partition were split between the Husayni al-Futuwwa and the opposition al-Najjada. The 29 November 1947 announcement of the UN General Assembly vote recommending partition led to Palestinian attacks on Jewish quarters in Jerusalem, triggering an intermittent "civil war" that lasted from December 1947 to May 1948. The 14 May proclamation of Israel's independence, immediately upon the official termination of the mandate and the withdrawal of British forces and administration, was followed by the invasion of Palestinian territory by the armies of Transjordan, Egypt, Syria, and Iraq. The first Arab–Israel war, which also involved Lebanese forces and volunteers from Saudi Arabia and Yemen, ended in early 1949 with the defeat of the Arab forces and the signing of armistice agreements between Israel and Egypt, Transjordan, Lebanon, and Syria.

The fighting of 1948 to 1949 displaced more than 700,000 Palestinians (approximately half the Arab population of Palestine) who had fled or been expelled by Jewish (later Israeli) forces. This fragmentation of Palestinian society and the creation of a huge refugee population became known as *al-Nakba* the catastrophe. For many years, controversy has swirled around the question of responsibility for this massive defeat and for the creation and persistence of the Palestinian refugee problem. Blame has been attributed variously to a deliberate Israeli policy of expulsion; disunity, distrust, and disorganization among Palestinian leaders and their supporters in the neighboring Arab countries; and tactical or strategic errors made by the Palestinian leadership—notably their rejection of the UN partition proposal. Recent archival research has unearthed new evidence for the first explanation, and has drawn attention to a fourth contributing factor: the asymmetry or imbalance of forces—throughout the Mandate period, but especially after 1937—between the Yishuv and the Palestinian community. The former was growing, determined, better armed, and highly disciplined, and had enjoyed British protection during its formative years. The Palestinians, on the other hand, were demoralized, disunited, and without effective leaders, many of whom had been killed or exiled during and after the revolt.

Disappearance and Reemergence of Palestine

With the establishment of the Jewish state of Israel in May 1948 and the occupation of the Gaza Strip by Egypt and of the West Bank by Jordan, Palestine ceased to exist as a separate political entity. Yet, during the 1950s, Arab, British, and UN documents continued to refer to the situation "in Palestine" when dealing with Israel, the neighboring Arab states, and areas inhabited by displaced Palestinians. Even without a political territory or government, Palestinians maintained their distinctive national and historic consciousness, and were reluctant to cease identifying with their lost homeland.

Putting their hopes in UN resolutions, the declarations of their own exiled leaders, and the promised support of neighboring Arab regimes, most Palestinians continued to dream of their eventual return to their homes and the establishment of an Arab Palestinian state. As refugees, the Palestinians became the focus of international relief efforts; successive generations of Palestinians were born in exile and in refugee camps of the United Nations Relief and Works Agency for Palestine Refugees in the Near East (UNRWA). Yet, political solutions based on the Palestinians' right to return or compensation (UN General Assembly Resolution 194 of December 1948) eluded generation after generation of Middle Eastern leaders.

Some Palestinians in exile became active in seeking political and military solutions that would result in their return and the eventual creation of an independent Palestinian state. Despairing of the efforts on their behalf of members of the League of Arab States, Palestinians developed their own leadership, known as the Palestine Liberation Organization (PLO). Initially created by Egypt's Gamal Abdel Nasser in 1964, the PLO's first chairman was Ahmad Shuqayri. After 1968 the PLO became an autonomous umbrella organization under the leadership of Yasir Arafat, bringing together many Palestinian groupings. For the next decade, the PLO adopted "armed struggle" as its primary mode of operation, thereafter developing a diplomatic campaign to restore Palestinians to their homeland by replacing the Jewish Israeli state. The boundaries of the future Palestinian state were declared to be those of the former British mandate.

The PLO's quest for international recognition of Palestinian rights was crowned with its first major success in 1974, when the United Nations Gen-

Israel, West Bank, and Gaza Strip, 2000

—— International border

▨ Areas in which the Palestinian Authority exercises various levels of control

☐ Areas under full Israeli control

• City

0   15   30 mi.

0   15   30 km

N

eral Assembly passed Resolution 3236 in support of the "inalienable rights of the Palestinian people in Palestine" to "self-determination without external interference," to "national independence and sovereignty," and "to return to their homes and property from which they have been displaced and uprooted." The following year, the UN created the Committee on the Exercise of the Inalienable Rights of the Palestinian People. Although they provided only moral support, such declarations and activities added much-needed international legitimacy to the Palestinians' quest for recognition of their right to a homeland during a period when both Israel and the United States were defining the PLO as a terrorist organization unworthy of inclusion in diplomatic discussions.

A decade later, in a further effort to open a dialogue with the United States, and hoping to capitalize diplomatically on the intifada against Israeli occupation that had been sparked in December 1987 in the West Bank and Gaza Strip, representatives at the twentieth meeting of the Palestine National Council in Algiers in November 1988 issued a symbolic declaration of Palestinian independence. At the same time, they formally endorsed the land-for-peace and mutual recognition approaches contained in UN Security Council Resolution 242 of November 1967—a resolution whose text makes no mention of the Palestinians or their rights. Afterward, PLO Chairman Yasir Arafat issued several prepared statements denouncing the use of terrorism by all parties, and implying that the future Palestinian state would exist alongside, rather than in place of, the Jewish state of Israel. Arafat's last step resulted in the opening of a PLO dialogue with the United States.

During the 1991 Madrid Conference and subsequent talks at the U.S. State Department, Palestinian leaders were invited to participate (as part of a joint delegation with Jordanians) for the first time in direct negotiations with Israel. Following the historic mutual recognition between the Israeli government and PLO and the signing of the Oslo Accord in September 1993, a process was begun to provide for phased Israeli withdrawals, beginning in Jericho, from occupied Palestinian territories on the West Bank and the Gaza Strip.

In early 1994 a Palestinian National Authority (or Palestine Authority) was created to administer these areas as further interim negotiations continued for additional Israeli pull-backs and other measures toward a final settlement. The Palestine Authority (PA) thus became an embryo government of a still-to-be-created sovereign Palestinian state. Many disappointments and frustrations prevented the scheduled later stages of negotiation from taking place or bearing fruit. This resulted in an untenable situation marked by violence and repression, most dramatically exploding into the second (al-Aqsa) intifada in September 2000. In the course of suppressing this Palestinian intifada, the Israel Defense Forces reoccupied, for varying lengths of time, many parts of the territories that had come under the rule of the weakened PA.

See also ANTONIUS, GEORGE; AQSA INTIFADA, AL-; ARAB–ISRAEL WAR (1948); ARAFAT, YASIR; BALFOUR DECLARATION (1917); DARWAZA, MUHAMMAD IZZAT; GAZA STRIP; HUSAYNI, JAMAL AL-; HUSAYNI, MUHAMMAD AMIN AL-; HUSAYNI, MUSA KAZIM AL-; INTIFADA (1987–1991); ISRAELI SETTLEMENTS; ISTIQLAL PARTY: PALESTINE; LONDON (ROUNDTABLE) CONFERENCE (1939); MACDONALD, MALCOLM; MADRID CONFERENCE (1991); MANDATE SYSTEM; NAJJADA, AL-; NAKBA, AL- (1948–1949); NASHASHIBI FAMILY; OSLO ACCORD (1993); PALESTINE ARAB REVOLT (1936–1939); PALESTINE ECONOMIC CORPORATION; PALESTINE EXPLORATION FUND; PALESTINE LAND DEVELOPMENT COMPANY; PALESTINE LIBERATION ORGANIZATION (PLO); PALESTINE NATIONAL CHARTER (1968); PALESTINE NATIONAL COUNCIL; PALESTINE NATIONAL COVENANT (1964); PALESTINE RESEARCH CENTER; PALESTINIAN ARAB CONGRESSES; PALESTINIAN AUTHORITY; PALESTINIAN CITIZENS OF ISRAEL; PALESTINIANS; PEEL COMMISSION REPORT (1937); SAMUEL, HERBERT LOUIS; SHUQAYRI, AHMAD; TRANSJORDAN FRONTIER FORCE; UNITED NATIONS CONCILIATION COMMISSION FOR PALESTINE (UNCCP); UNITED NATIONS RELIEF AND WORKS AGENCY FOR PALESTINE REFUGEES IN THE NEAR EAST (UNRWA); UNITED NATIONS SPECIAL COMMITTEE ON PALESTINE, 1947 (UNSCOP); VA'AD LE'UMI; WEST BANK; WHITE PAPERS ON PALESTINE; YISHUV; ZIONISM; ZIONIST COMMISSION FOR PALESTINE.

Bibliography

Esco Foundation. *Palestine: A Study of Jewish, Arab, and British Policies.* 2 vols. New Haven, CT: Yale University Press, 1947.

Hurewitz, Jacob C. *The Struggle for Palestine.* Reprint, New York: Schocken Books, 1976.

Ingrams, Doreen. *Palestine Papers, 1917–1922: Seeds of Conflict.* New York: George Braziller, 1973.

Khalaf, Issa. *Politics in Palestine: Arab Factionalism and Social Disintegration, 1939–1948.* Albany: State University of New York Press, 1991.

Khalidi, Rashid. *Palestinian Identity: The Construction of Modern National Consciousness.* New York: Columbia University Press, 1997.

Khalidi, Walid, ed. *From Haven to Conquest.* Reprint, Washington, DC: Institute for Palestine Studies, 1987.

Kimmerling, Baruch, and Migdal, Joel. *The Palestinian People: A History.* Cambridge, MA: Harvard University Press, 2003.

Lesch, Ann M. *Arab Politics in Palestine, 1917–1939: The Frustration of a Nationalist Movement.* Ithaca, NY: Cornell University Press, 1979.

Mattar, Philip. *The Mufti of Jerusalem: Al-Hajj Amin al-Husayni and the Palestinian National Movement,* revised edition. New York: Columbia University Press, 1988/1992.

Morris, Benny. *The Birth of the Palestinian Refugee Problem, 1947–1949.* New York: Cambridge University Press, 1987.

Muslih, Muhammad Y. *The Origins of Palestinian Nationalism.* New York: Columbia University Press, 1988.

Porath, Yehoshua. *The Emergence of the Palestinian-Arab National Movement, 1918–1929.* London: Frank Cass, 1974.

Porath, Yehoshua. *The Palestinian Arab National Movement: From Riots to Rebellion, 1929–1939.* London: Frank Cass, 1977.

Shafir, Gershon. *Land, Labor, and the Origins of the Israeli-Palestinian Conflict, 1882–1914.* Cambridge, U.K.: Cambridge University Press, 1989. Updated ed., Berkeley: University of California Press, 1996.

A Survey of Palestine for the Information of the Anglo-American Committee of Inquiry. 2 vols. Reprint, Washington, DC: Institute for Palestine Studies, 1991.

DON PERETZ
UPDATED BY NEIL CAPLAN,
MUHAMMAD MUSLIH, AND ANN M. LESCH

PALESTINE ARAB REVOLT (1936–1939)

Arab revolt in Palestine to resist British support for a Jewish national home.

The revolt in Palestine (1936–1939) was in many ways the decisive episode in the efforts of the Palestinian Arabs to resist the British mandate's support for a Jewish national home in Palestine. Although it helped force a British policy reassessment, which led to the 1939 white paper curtailing Jewish immigration to Palestine, ultimately the revolt must be judged a failure. At its conclusion in 1939, the Palestinian Arabs were exhausted by more than three years of British repression. Perhaps 5,000 had been killed and 15,000 to 20,000 wounded; 5,600 of their leaders and fighters were in British detention; and most of the rest were scattered outside the country or dead. Such losses, in a population of about 1 million Palestinian Arabs in 1939, meant that more than 10 percent of the adult males were killed, wounded, or detained by the end of the revolt.

Equally important, the Palestinians failed to benefit politically. Their already divided leadership was fragmented further by the events of 1936 to 1939; and with many of its leaders in exile from 1937 on, it was paralyzed by a division between those outside of Palestine and those inside it that persisted for decades thereafter. These divisions contributed to the failure of the Palestinians to capitalize on the potential advantages offered them in the 1939 white paper, which with its limits on immigration and promise of self-government within ten years, held out for the first time the prospect of Arab majority rule in Palestine. In any case, the government of Winston Churchill, which came into office soon after, was resolutely opposed to its implementation. After the war, the impact of the revelation of the Holocaust, the growing strength of the Yishuv in Palestine, and the rising power of the United States in the Middle East combined to render it moot. The Palestinians came out of this ordeal politically weaker than they had gone into it, and unprepared for the struggle for Palestine (1945–1948) that, attendant on the establishment of Israel, resulted in the dispossession of about half the Arab population of the country.

Economically, the revolt was a disaster for the Arabs. It had begun in April 1936 as a spontaneous strike and boycott of the British and of the Jewish economy of Palestine. Effective though it was at the outset, the result was measurably to weaken the Arab sector of the economy, which did not have the resources or the resilience to support the hardships of the revolt, and to strengthen the economy of the Yishuv, which did. The Arab labor boycott, moreover, had the paradoxical effect of furthering the Zionist policy of giving jobs only to Jews—cheaper Arab labor had heretofore been favored by many Jewish businesses—and spurred the economy of the Yishuv to greater self-reliance.

On the military level, the Palestinians lost several thousand of their best fighters and military commanders in combat or to British firing squads, which executed 112 Arabs. Many thousands of others were wounded, detained, or forced into exile. In addition, the British seized over 13,000 weapons and 350,000 rounds of ammunition from Arabs (about 500 guns were seized from Jewish groups in this period), at a time when the British were arming units like the Jewish Settlement Police and cooperating with the Haganah to repulse Arab attacks. All of these losses, particularly in combatants, military leaders, and weapons, were sorely felt when the Palestinians confronted the well-armed and organized forces of the Yishuv during the fighting that started immediately after the partition resolution was passed by the United Nations General Assembly in November 1947. This fighting grew in intensity until May 1948, by which time the Palestinians had been routed in many crucial areas, losing the cities of Jaffa, Haifa, and Tiberias, and scores of villages, towns, and strategic roads and junctions to the advancing forces of the Haganah and its allies. In some sense, the outcome of these decisive battles (1947–1948) was determined by the disastrous political, economic, and military results of the 1936–1939 revolt for the Palestinians.

The revolt was notable for its spontaneous inception, with local committees springing up in April 1936 to organize a general strike and boycott that lasted until October of that year. Among the motives for the revolt was the rapid growth in Jewish immigration to Palestine: From 1932 to 1936 there were 174,000 immigrants, more than the total Jewish population of the country in 1931. The Arab Higher Committee was formed by Palestinian notable leaders soon after the strike began, largely in response to this pressure from below, but never really gained control of events. In the sporadic fighting of 1936 and in the intense battles of the second phase of the revolt, which began in September 1937, local organization was paramount, with minimal coordination between the mainly peasant military bands, which bore the brunt of the fighting. In spite of this lack of coordination, the Palestinians initially had the British on the defensive for much of 1937 and 1938 and took control of most Arab cities, towns, and villages, and much of the countryside. Only the arrival of massive British reinforcements—which brought troop strength to over 20,000 by 1938—and the intensive use of air power were able to break the back of the revolt.

In much Palestinian historiography, the revolt has been glorified as the forerunner of the modern Palestinian "armed struggle" that was launched in 1965. It is commonly linked to the attempts of Shaykh Izz al-Din al-Qassam to organize an armed rebellion against the British, which were aborted when he and some of his comrades were hunted down and killed by British forces in 1935. Qassam's example was very influential, however: Many thousands marched in his funeral cortege, and hundreds of his followers, whom he had organized in clandestine cells in the northern part of the country, played crucial roles during the revolt; they included some of the most senior commanders. Qassam's legacy is a disputed one, however, claimed by al-Fatah and other Palestinian nationalist groups, and more recently by the radical Islamic HAMAS movement, which has named its armed wing for him.

See also ARAB HIGHER COMMITTEE (PALESTINE); ARAB–ISRAEL WAR (1948); CHURCHILL, WINSTON S.; FATAH, AL-; HAGANAH; HAIFA; HAMAS; HOLOCAUST; JAFFA; QASSAM, IZZ AL-DIN AL-; TIBERIAS; YISHUV.

Bibliography

Kayyali, Abdul-Wahhab. *Palestine: A Modern History.* London: Croom Helm, 1978.

Porath, Yehoshua. *The Palestinian Arab National Movement, 1929–1939: From Riots to Rebellion.* London and Totowa, NJ: F. Cass, 1977.

Swedenburg, Theodore. *Memories of Revolt: The 1936–1939 Rebellion and the Palestinian National Past.* Fayetteville: University of Arkansas Press, 2003.

Swedenburg, Theodore. "The Role of the Palestinian Peasantry in the Great Revolt (1936–1939)." In *Islam: Politics and Social Movements,* edited by Edmund Burke III and Ira M. Lapidus. Berkeley: University of California Press, 1988.

RASHID KHALIDI

PALESTINE ECONOMIC CORPORATION

American-funded economic aid program to Jews in Palestine.

Founded in 1926 by a group of prominent American Jews, including Supreme Court Justice Louis D. Brandeis, the Palestine Economic Corporation provided material aid and technical assistance to Jewish business enterprises in Palestine. Funding was usually in the form of loans or equity investments. Subsidiaries to the corporation included the Palestine Mortgage and Savings Bank and the Central Bank of Cooperative Institutions, which provided funds for low-cost housing and credits to kibbutzim, among other social programs.

Through 1946, the corporation had funded more than ninety enterprises and played a key role in establishing such basic industries as chemicals, citrus products, paper, plastics, and tires. The corporation later changed its name to PEC Israel Economic Corporation. By 1967 it had eleven thousand stockholders, mostly in the United States, with assets of more than $28 million in Israel's industrial, construction, and citrus sectors.

Bibliography

Laqueur, Walter. *A History of Zionism.* New York: Schocken, 1989.

ELIZABETH THOMPSON

PALESTINE EXPLORATION FUND

British research group founded under the patronage of Queen Victoria for scientific study of the Holy Land.

Established in 1865 to study biblical sites, the Palestine Exploration Fund began work in Jerusalem in 1867, especially the work of Charles Warren on the Walls of Jerusalem. The fund expanded its scope in the 1870s to conduct a complete survey of the Holy Land. The fund's team of geographers, archaeologists, anthropologists, and orientalists published numerous articles that influenced British public opinion. Its maps, drawn between 1871 and 1877, were used by Sir Edmund Allenby in his victorious cavalry campaign in Palestine in World War I and are invaluable today to historians. The maps designated the historical boundaries of Palestine as extending a few miles east of the Jordan River. Some members of the fund, particularly its director, Claude Reignier Conder, advocated British colonization of Palestine and the restoration of its Jewish population. The group funded the work of archaeologists W. M. F. Petrie and Kathleen Kenyon.

See also ALLENBY, EDMUND HENRY; HOLY LAND.

Bibliography

Elon, Amos. *The Israelis: Founders and Sons.* New York: Holt, Rinehart and Winston, 1971.

Jacobson, Jason M. *Survey of Western Palestine, Including a Survey of Eastern Palestine, 1881.* Slough, U.K.: Archive Editions in association with the Palestine Exploration Fund, 1999.

Moscrop, John James. *Measuring Jerusalem: The Palestine Exploration Fund and British Interests in the Holy Land.* London and New York: Leicester University Press, 2000.

Sanders, Ronald. *The High Walls of Jerusalem.* New York: Holt, Rinehart and Winston, 1983.

Shafir, Gershon. *Land, Labor and the Origins of the Israeli–Palestinian Conflict, 1882–1914,* revised edition. Berkeley: University of California Press, 1996.

ELIZABETH THOMPSON

PALESTINE LAND DEVELOPMENT COMPANY

Land-purchasing company of the World Zionist Organization.

Established in 1908 by Arthur Ruppin, a German Jew, as part of the World Zionist Organization, the Palestine Land Development Company (PLDC) used Jewish National Fund and private monies to purchase and populate tracts of land with Jewish immigrants. It acquired extensive holdings in northern Palestine (Galilee), particularly in the 1920s and 1930s.

The PLDC bought nearly 90 percent of its land from large landowners, rather than individual peasants. Many of the transactions created controversy, such as the PLDC's purchase of 240,000 *dunums* (144,000 acres, 60,000 ha) of fertile land in the Jezreel valley between 1921 and 1925, its purchase of 30,000 *dunums* (18,000 acres, 7,500 ha) at Wadi Hawarith in 1929, and its assumption of the Lake Huleh concession in 1934.

See also JEZREEL VALLEY; RUPPIN, ARTHUR; WORLD ZIONIST ORGANIZATION (WZO).

Bibliography

Laquer, Walter. *A History of Zionism.* New York: Holt, Rinehart, and Winston, 1972.

Shafir, Gershon. *Land, Labor and the Origins of the Israeli–Palestinian Conflict,* revised edition. Berkeley: University of California Press, 1996.

ELIZABETH THOMPSON

PALESTINE LIBERATION ORGANIZATION (PLO)

The institutional structure of the Palestinian national movement and the political representative of about nine million Palestinians.

The Palestine Liberation Organization (PLO; Arabic, *Munazzamat al-Tahrir al-Filastiniyya*) was created at the Arab summit in January 1964 to contain and channel Palestinian nationalism and prevent Palestinian guerrilla groups from taking independent actions to liberate Palestine, from which Palestinians had fled or had been expelled by the Israel Defense Force (IDF) in 1948. The Palestine National Council (PNC), the PLO's parliament, convened with 422 members in Jerusalem in May 1964 and elected a fifteen-member Executive Committee, which chose as its chairman a lawyer, Ahmad Shuqayri. The PNC adopted a national covenant or charter (*al-mithaq al-watani*), which was revised in 1968, calling for the elimination of Israel and the restoration of Palestine to the Palestinians.

When Israel defeated Egypt, Syria, and Jordan in 1967 and occupied the West Bank and the Gaza Strip, both Arab and Palestinian leaders were discredited. Shuqayri was replaced by another lawyer, Yahya Hammuda. The guerrilla groups, the most significant of which was Al-Fatah, expeditiously moved to fill the political vacuum by increasing their attacks on Israel. On 21 March 1968, Israel massively retaliated at Karama, Jordan. The guerrillas' stiff resistance resulted in the deaths of at least 21 Israelis, about 100 Palestinians, and 40 Jordanian soldiers who aided the Palestinians. The guerrillas embellished their own accomplishment, inflated Israel's casualties, and gave little credit to the Jordanians. Karama became a symbol of struggle against Israel, which many had considered invincible. Al-Fatah gained thousands of recruits, Arab admiration, and financial support, primarily from the Gulf Arab states. More important, the guerrilla groups won control over the PLO. They amended the national charter in July 1968 to underscore the rejection of Arab interference in Palestinian affairs, the total liberation of Palestine by Palestinians through armed struggle, and establishment of a democratic secular state of Arabs and Jews.

Groups within the PLO

The battle at Karama propelled Yasir Arafat, head of al-Fatah, into the leadership position. An engineer educated at Cairo University, he was elected at the fourth PNC (February 1969) to replace Hammuda as chair of the Executive Committee. The PLO was transformed from an Arab-controlled organization to an umbrella of disparate military and political groups. Although these groups had a common goal, the liberation of Palestine, they differed considerably on ideology and tactics. The dominant group was al-Fatah, established in Kuwait by Salah Khalaf (Abu Iyad), Khalil al-Wazir (Abu Jihad), and Arafat (Abu Ammar), who became its spokesperson. It owed its broad appeal to Arafat's charismatic personality and to its pragmatic politics, which eschewed ideology for action toward a simple national goal: the liberation of Palestine. Al-Fatah's chief rival in the PLO was the Popular Front for the Liberation of Palestine (PFLP), headed by George Habash, a Christian physician educated at the American University of Beirut. The PFLP is a Marxist group dedicated to the overthrow of conservative Arab governments. Its contempt for the government of Jordan led it to challenge Jordan's sovereignty, triggering the 1970–1971 civil war that resulted in the PLO's defeat and its relocation to Lebanon. An offshoot to the left of the PFLP that espouses Marxism-Leninism is the Democratic Front for the Liberation of Palestine (DFLP), led by a Jordanian Christian, Nayif Hawatma. Another offshoot is the Popular Front for the Liberation of Palestine–General Command (PFLP-GC), led by Ahmad Jibril. Oth-

Yasir Arafat, Palestine Liberation Organization (PLO) chairman, smiles at a child in a Palestinian refugee camp in west Beirut, Lebanon, 15 July 1982. During the height of Israeli occupation, Arafat made several such tours to help boost morale among Palestinians. © AP/WIDE WORLD PHOTOS. REPRODUCED BY PERMISSION.

ers include al-Sa'iqa, controlled by Syria, and the Arab Liberation Front (ALF), controlled by Iraq.

The influence of these groups has been disproportional to their numbers, but some see them as a necessary alternative to the centrist al-Fatah. They have stimulated political debates. They have charged that the lack of a coherent ideology within al-Fatah has led to an absence of vision regarding politics and society in the diaspora and the future state of Palestine; that many of its functionaries are inept and corrupt bureaucrats tolerated by Arafat; that the PLO drifts from crisis to crisis; that Arafat manipulates Palestinian institutions such as the PNC and the Executive Council and has autocratic powers that undermine Palestinian democracy; and that Arafat flirts with almost any nation—Jordan, Egypt, the United States—without a clear policy.

PLO diversity resulted in the groups working at cross-purposes or in costly blunders. For example, the Arab-controlled Sa'iqa and ALF emphasized Arab unity while others insisted on Palestinian self-reliance. Al-Fatah denounced airplane hijackings in 1969 and 1970 by PFLP and PFLP-GC as counterproductive to the Palestinian cause. While al-Fatah sought Arab support and generally avoided Arab problems, the leftist groups involved the PLO in the civil war in Jordan and contributed to PLO involvement in Lebanon's civil war and in the Gulf crisis. Disagreements have led groups to secede from the PLO or to leave it temporarily. These could have brought violent conflict and disunity had it not been for the dominance of al-Fatah and Arafat's mass appeal and political skills. He often appeased or reflected diverse currents and articulated vague and, at times, contradictory positions—which, while damaging his credibility abroad and creating diplomatic immobility, enabled him to maintain the coalition. His leadership allowed the PLO to develop political, military, and socioeconomic institutions in Lebanon until 1982.

Institutions

Foremost among these institutions was the PNC, the PLO parliament, whose membership varied. It represented virtually all ideological tendencies and groups, including the commando organizations and their political branches, ten unions—those, for example, of workers, women, teachers, students, writers, and engineers—and Palestinian communities. It developed a large and complex infrastructure for the estimated 360,000 Palestinians in Lebanon. Its well-trained armed forces numbered about 16,000. Its social and economic institutions served almost half a million Palestinians and poor Lebanese. The Palestine Martyrs Works Society (SAMED) operated businesses and light industry grossing $40 million annually. The Red Crescent Society supervised sixty clinics and eleven hospitals, and the Department of Social Welfare provided financial assistance for the blind, day-care centers, the wounded, and families of "martyrs." By the early 1980s the PLO had gone from an umbrella of guerrilla groups to the institutional embodiment of Palestinian nationalism and a state within a state.

The political and economic institutions enhanced the PLO's prestige and legitimacy. The Arab League recognized the PLO as the sole legitimate representative of the Palestinian people at the Rabat conference (October 1974). A month later, the United Nations invited Arafat to address the General Assembly and awarded the PLO observer status. In 1976 West Bank and Gaza Palestinians voted out pro-Jordan mayors, replacing them with supporters of the PLO. By 1982, over 100 countries had recognized the PLO.

Setbacks

Despite such success, however, the PLO suffered major setbacks. After its expulsion from Jordan, it established a state within a state in Lebanon, thereby undermining Lebanon's sovereignty, incurring Israel's retaliation, and embroiling it in Lebanon's civil war after 1975. In March 1979, at Camp David, Egyptian President Anwar al-Sadat signed a separate peace agreement with Israel that excluded PLO participation and provided for a limited Palestinian autonomy instead of full self-determination. With Egypt neutralized, Israel invaded Lebanon in June 1982 to destroy the PLO but succeeded only in forcing the PLO to move to Tunis; stripped of PLO protection, between 800 and 1,500 Palestinians in the Sabra and Shatila refugee camps were massacred in September by the Israel-allied Phalange. The 1982 Reagan peace plan, based on the Camp David autonomy proposal, once again excluded PLO participation. The following year, dissension within al-Fatah caused a revolt by Sa'id Musa Muragha (Abu Musa), with the help of Syria, which had long sought to control the PLO. When Arafat attempted to reestablish PLO power in Lebanon in 1983, Syria unleashed the forces of Abu Musa, who drove him out of Lebanon again. Israel attempted to undermine the PLO leadership by bombing its headquarters in Tunis in October 1985 but failed to kill Arafat.

Moderation and Diplomacy

Unable to strike at Israel, the PLO relied primarily on diplomacy to achieve a compromise settlement. At the twelfth PNC in 1974 and the thirteenth in 1977, the PLO had moderated its goal of liberating all of Palestine to one of establishing a state in the West Bank and Gaza; it supported the 1982 Fahad Plan that implicitly accepted a two-state solution. Empowered by the intifada, the Palestinian uprising that began against Israel's occupation in December 1987, Arafat in November 1988 led an enlarged PNC that included the DFLP to endorse the establishment of an independent Palestine state. It also endorsed the 1947 United Nations General Assembly Resolution 181. In December 1988, Arafat declared the PLO's acceptance of Israel's right to exist, recognition of Security Council Resolution 242, and the renunciation of terrorism. The United States promptly opened a dialogue with the PLO.

Israel and its supporters, however, refused to acknowledge the change.

Israel's failure to reciprocate largely convinced Arafat to support Saddam Hussein in the 1990–1991 Gulf Crisis. This was a blunder that resulted in loss of financial support from the Gulf states. Without the support of the Soviet Union, short on funds, and fearing irrelevance, the PLO accepted the U.S. peace initiative that led to the 1991 Madrid peace conference between Israel and the Arab states and the Palestinians. However, twenty-two months and ten rounds of negotiations proved fruitless. The PLO regarded the framework for the talks as unfair and did not consider middle-level U.S. officials, especially those associated with pro-Israel lobbies, as "honest brokers." Norway established a secret channel in Oslo through which the PLO and Israel agreed to recognize each other. On 13 September 1993, at the White House, they signed a Declaration of Principles for a five-year Palestinian limited autonomy in the West Bank and Gaza, starting with the Gaza Strip and the town of Jericho, followed by elections for an interim council, Israel's withdrawal from other parts of the West Bank, and transfer of power. Unresolved final status issues—Jerusalem, Jewish settlements, refugees of 1948, and borders—were deferred.

Toward Establishing a State

In May 1994, the IDF withdrew from Jericho and most of the Gaza Strip, and Palestinian police and a civil administration took over. Arafat moved to Jericho in June. Despite a decline in support for the peace process due to the violence and the slow pace of the negotiations, the PLO and Israel reached a number of agreements regarding the interim period, especially Oslo II, signed on 28 September 1995, which set the stage for Israel's further withdrawal from of the West Bank and the establishment of Palestinian Authority (PA) control over this area. The PLO held two PNC meetings in April 1996 and December 1998 to rescind articles in the National Charter that called for the destruction of Israel; the latter vote took place in the presence of U.S. president Bill Clinton. Clinton invited PLO chair Arafat and Israeli prime minister Ehud Barak to Camp David to negotiate final status issues of the West Bank and Gaza Strip. The negotiations took place in July 2000, but failed and were followed by the second Palestinian uprising (Aqsa Intifada) against Israeli occupation. Even though the PLO resumed the negotiations with Israel, especially at Taba in January 2001, the negotiators ran out of time when Clinton left office in January and Prime Minister Ehud Barak was replaced by Ariel Sharon in February 2001. Sharon refused to resume negotiations with the PLO until the Palestinians stopped their violence. He reoccupied Palestinian cities, including Ramallah, where the IDF attacked Arafat's headquarters and placed Arafat under virtual house arrest.

Arafat and many of the leading members of the PLO are also leaders in the PA. Arafat is both the chair of the PLO and the president of the PA. Mahmud Abbas, who was Arafat's deputy in the PLO, became the first prime minister of the PA in 2003. Ahmad Qurai, deputy director of the PLO's department of economic affairs, became the second prime minister of the PA in 2003 and 2004. The PLO still has a primary role: to negotiate with Israel over the future of the West Bank and the Gaza Strip. Yet, with the establishment of the PA, the PLO was increasingly eclipsed by an elected Legislative Council and the many "state" institutions. If a state is established, the organization is likely to decline further, because its goal of establishing a state would have been fulfilled, and its institutions would be replaced by state institutions.

See also ABBAS, MAHMUD; ARAFAT, YASIR; FATAH, AL-; GAZA STRIP; HABASH, GEORGE; PALESTINIAN AUTHORITY; QURAI, AHMAD SULAYMAN; RAMALLAH; WEST BANK.

Bibliography

Cobban, Helena. *The Palestinian Liberation Organization.* New York: Cambridge University Press, 1985.

Gresh, Alain. *The PLO, the Struggle Within: Towards an Independent Palestinian State.* London: Zed, 1986.

Lesch, Ann M. "Palestine Liberation Organization." In *Oxford Companion of Politics of the World,* edited by Joel Krieger. New York: Oxford University Press, 1993.

Miller, Aaron David. *The PLO and the Politics of Survival.* New York: Praeger, 1983.

Nassar, Jamal R. *The Palestine Liberation Organization: From Armed Struggle to the Declaration of Independence.* New York: Praeger, 1991.

Rubin, Barry. *Revolution until Victory? The Politics and History of the PLO.* Cambridge, MA: Harvard University Press, 1994.

Sayigh, Yezid. *Armed Struggle and the Search for State: The Palestinian National Movement, 1949–1993.* Oxford: Clarendon, 1997.

PHILIP MATTAR

PALESTINE NATIONAL CHARTER (1968)

Amended version of the Palestine National Covenant with greater emphasis on armed struggle against Israel.

The fourth Palestine National Council meeting (Cairo, July 1968) amended the 1964 Palestine National Covenant to produce the Palestine National Charter (PNC). Following the Arab defeat of June 1967, the leadership of the Palestine Liberation Organization (PLO) passed to the more action-oriented leaders of al-Fatah, the Popular Front for the Liberation of Palestine (PFLP), the Palestine Liberation Front (PLF), and other commando groups. While these groups continued to strive in principle for the ideals of Arab nationalism, in practice their character and development became increasingly Palestinian. Their focus was on Palestinian nationalism and on armed struggle against Israel.

The 1968 charter incorporated new principles that were supposed to guide Palestinian political action after the 1967 defeat. The charter has thirty-three articles. Article 1 explicitly defines Palestine as the "homeland of the Palestinian Arab people," while Articles 3 and 9 in particular stress the principles of self-determination and Palestinian national sovereignty over Palestine. Reference to these principles is made eight times. Moreover, the concepts of self-determination and sovereignty are defined in explicit Palestinian terms. Although the ethno-cultural links of the Palestinians to the larger Arab homeland are emphasized, they do not predominate over the territorial connection between the Palestinians and their homeland Palestine.

The 1968 charter radicalized the instruments of political action to be employed for the liberation of Palestine. Armed struggle is posited as the "sole road" to liberation (Article 9), and the concept recurs thirteen times in an emphatic, declaratory tone. Armed struggle, however, does not exclude conventional warfare as Article 10 suggests, since the Arab countries are considered partners in the battle for liberation. In this formula, the role of commando action was given primacy and regarded as the "nucleus of the Palestinian popular liberation war" (Article 10).

The principles of the charter were superseded by subsequent Palestine National Council decisions. Above all, they were superseded by the Declaration of Principles concluded between Israel and the PLO in September 1993. The PNC voted in April 1996 to cancel the portions of the charter calling for the destruction of the State of Israel and to draft a new charter within six months.

See also FATAH, AL-; PALESTINE LIBERATION ORGANIZATION (PLO); PALESTINE NATIONAL COUNCIL; PALESTINE NATIONAL COVENANT (1964); POPULAR FRONT FOR THE LIBERATION OF PALESTINE.

Bibliography

Brand, Laurie A. *Palestinians in the Arab World: Institution Building and the Search for State.* New York: Columbia University Press, 1988.

Gresh, Alain. *The PLO, the Struggle Within: Towards an Independent Palestinian State.* London: Zed, 1985.

MUHAMMAD MUSLIH

PALESTINE NATIONAL COUNCIL

Constituent assembly or parliament for the Palestinian people.

The Palestine National Council (PNC) is the highest decision-making body within the Palestine Liberation Organization (PLO) and the supreme representative institution of the Palestinian people. The PNC is the forum where official policies of the PLO are debated and formulated. Its resolutions and declarations represent the evolving consensus within the Palestinian national movement on major internal, regional, and international questions. Thus, PNC resolutions are best understood by comparison to previous resolutions and in relation to their wider political context. Similarly, their interpretation by the PLO leadership is best judged by its subsequent actions.

The Palestine National Council met in 1998 to rescind the Palestinian National Charter that had previously called for the destruction of Israel. U.S. president Bill Clinton was present for the historic vote. © AP/WIDE WORLD PHOTOS. REPRODUCED BY PERMISSION.

The PNC, like the PLO itself, grew out of the first Arab Summit, held in Cairo in January 1964. The summit resolved to enable the Palestinian people "to play a role in the liberation of their country" and empowered the Palestine delegate to the League of Arab States, Ahmad Shuqayri, to hold consultations on the implementation of this decision. A Palestinian General Congress, convening as the National Conference of the Palestine Liberation Organization, met in East Jerusalem in May 1964 to ratify its constitution and other documents that formally established the PLO and its institutions. The 397 invited delegates represented a broad spectrum of Palestinian life. Among the proposed institutions approved was a national assembly, which in 1970s came to be known as the Palestine National Council. Its structure, powers, and procedural rules are set forth in the Fundamental Law appended to the Palestine National Covenant, which survives in amended form.

According to the Fundamental Law, the PNC is the supreme authority for formulating the policies and programs of the PLO and its institutions, and all who operate under the PLO umbrella are accountable to its decisions. It does not sit in permanent session, has no permanent committees, and by force of circumstance has no permanent location. It must convene in regular session once a year (changed from every two years in 1971) and whenever requested by the PLO Executive Committee (the executive branch of the PLO) or PNC membership. In some years the PNC has not convened due to conflict (e.g., during the 1975–1976 Lebanese civil war), but under other circumstances its failure to meet has been the subject of fierce criticism, most recently when the PNC was not called into session to debate the 1993 Israeli–Palestinian Declaration of Principles.

Candidates for the PNC must be nominated by a committee (which since 1971 consists of the PLO Executive Committee, the PNC chairman, and the commander in chief of the Palestine Liberation Army), and then elected by a majority of the entire membership at its next session. It elects its own

PLO leaders Bassam Abou Sharif, Mahmud Darwish, and Harwan Kanafi at a 1991 Palestine National Council meeting. © FRANCOISE DE MULDER/CORBIS. REPRODUCED BY PERMISSION.

presidential office, which consists of a chairman, two vice chairmen, and a secretary. The attendance of two-thirds of its delegates is required for a quorum, and its initial practice of "collective decision-making" was in 1981 defined as majority voting. The PNC met in closed session until 1981, when foreign dignitaries and Palestinian observers were first invited. With few exceptions it publishes its resolutions and other documents, and the media may observe and record most of its proceedings.

Although election procedures remain in place, they have not been practiced since the Palestinian guerrilla organizations took control of the PLO in 1968 to 1969. The PLO's constituent organizations and PLO mass unions and labor syndicates are each assigned a quota of seats, decided through negotiation in accordance with each group's respective size and importance. Representative quotas for Palestinian exile communities, other nonformally organized Palestinians, and delegates resident in Israel and the occupied Palestinian territories are directly selected by the PNC nominating committee. Although the PNC is an integral PLO institution, PNC delegates do not necessarily serve as officials in the PLO or as members of its constituent factions.

The size of the PNC has varied over time. In 1968 its membership was reduced from 466 to 100 and limited to representatives of guerrilla factions (68) and political independents (32) to ensure ef-

fective deliberations and guerrilla control over the PLO. Representatives of PLO unions were admitted in 1971, and membership was expanded to 150. In 1977 the PNC again represented Palestinian exile communities and additional diasporic groups (e.g., deportees), increasing its membership to 293. Active membership has since risen to pre-1968 levels. The PNC's progressive shift from guerrilla tactics to genuine diplomacy and conditional acceptance of the state of Israel's existence is mirrored in its current delegates.

At the beginning of each session of the PNC, the PLO Executive Committee must submit a report on its activities and the status of the PLO. A new Executive Committee, whose size and membership is determined by the PNC, is elected at the end of each session. The new Executive Committee's policy guidelines and other instructions, and PLO proclamations, are set forth in resolutions adopted by the PNC typically drafted in committee.

In 1970 the PNC also established the PLO Central Committee (since 1973 known as the Central Council) as an intermediate body between itself and the Executive Committee. It possesses legislative and executive powers and meets at least once every three months to review the work of the Executive Committee, approve its decisions, clarify PNC guidelines where necessary, and issue supplementary resolutions where relevant. Because it was designed to improve coordination between various represented and nonrepresented guerrilla factions, the Central Council is neither elected by the PNC nor entirely composed of PNC members. In its current form it comprises the Executive Committee, the PNC chairman, the Palestine Liberation Army (PLA) commander in chief, representatives of PLO constituent organizations and institutions, and PNC members selected by the Executive Committee. It elects a general secretariat from among its own members.

The PNC also hears the report of the Palestine National Fund (the PLO treasury), approves its budget, (re-)elects its Board of Directors (which elects its own officers), and considers reports and structures of other PLO institutions. It does not, however, have the right to interfere in the internal affairs of the movements that operate under the PLO umbrella.

Given that regular general elections would be difficult if not impossible to conduct under the fragmented conditions of Palestinian existence, the PNC is a genuine attempt at creating a representative body, and generally it has been very successful. The PLO leadership has encouraged pluralism within the PNC, but the PNC exhibits some clearly undemocratic tendencies. Aside from the lack of elections, criticism of the quota system (practiced in all PLO institutions) claims that it places powers of decision-making and accountability in PLO factions rather than constituencies and encourages hegemony by a dominant group. The increasing appropriation of power by the PLO leadership has also led to a lack of regard for PNC resolutions and procedures as well as its marginalization as the locus of Palestinian decision-making. The PNC is now often eclipsed by the actions of the Palestinian Authority (PA), which was created as an interim governing body in 1994 representing pre-1967 Israeli-occupied territories. The PA was created as steps were being taken to establish a Palestinian state. The PNC would have eventually resumed its function with some restructuring, but al-Aqsa Intifada has made it nearly defunct.

The following is a list of cities where sessions have occurred and highlights important PNC resolutions:

1964: Jerusalem. Establishment of the PLO and drafting of the Palestinian National Charter.

1965: Cairo. Meetings held from 20–24 May. Arab–Israel War breaks out 5 June.

1966: Gaza.

1968: Cairo. Entry of the guerrilla movement, and amendment of the Palestine Charter insisting on total liberation of Palestine through armed struggle. Half of the PNC's seats given to the PLO.

1969: Cairo. Yasir Arafat elected chairman of the Executive Committee.

1970: Cairo. Crisis between guerrilla groups and the Jordanian army.

1971: Cairo. Endorsement of a secular democratic state.

1972: Cairo. PNC rejects Jordanian King Hussein's Palestinian/Jordanian United Kingdom Plan. Most Arab countries reject this plan, and Egypt cuts diplomatic ties with Jordan.

1974: Cairo. First steps toward endorsing a two-state solution, with an independent Palestinian state.

1977: Cairo. Reiteration of previous meeting's proposals. Emergence of a more moderate, mainstream PLO as well as West Bank leadership.

1979: Damascus. Rejection of Camp David Accords.

1981: Damascus. Meetings 11–19 April. In August, Saudi Crown Prince Fahd calls for peace plan and creation of Palestinian state recognizing Israel in its pre-1947 borders.

1983: Algiers. Rejection of the Reagan Plan, which outlined a Palestinian state with central authority in Jordanian, not PLO, control. PNC agreed to a confederation between the Kingdom of Jordan and an independent Palestine led by the PLO, based on the 1982 Fez Plan (based on the Fahd Plan) that called for the establishment of an independent Palestinian state.

1984: Amman. Resolutions give Arafat the authority to cooperate with Jordan and Egypt, and call for improving relations with Syria. First Executive Committee decides to remove PLO institutions from Damascus and transfer PNC headquarters to Amman. Call for free Palestinian state in confederation with Jordan, which leads to the 1985 Amman Agreement in 1985.

1987: Algiers. Meetings held 20–25 April after the issue of the Tunis Document (16 March), which called for a free Palestinian state, accord on the Fez Plan, and rejection of the Amman Agreement. Intifada begins 9 December.

1988: Algiers. Referred to as the "Intifada meeting." Unilateral declaration of the independence of the Arab state of

Palestine. Reconciliation between al-Fatah and other factions that had challenged Arafat's leadership. 103 countries recognize the newly created Palestinian state.

1991: Algiers. Authorized Palestinian participation in negotiations with Israel.

1993: Washington, D.C. Israeli–PLO Declaration of Principles on interim self-government signed.

1994: Establishment of the Palestinian National Authority (PNA), an autonomous entity comprising the territory of Gaza and towns and areas of the West Bank occupied by the Israeli Defense Forces in 1967, for a five-year transitional period to include Palestinian interim self-government and a gradual transfer of powers and territories.

1996: Gaza. After signing the Oslo Accords, PNC votes 504 to 54 to void parts of the Palestinian National Covenant that denied Israel's right to exist. Edward Said, scholar and activist, leaves the PNC because he believes the Oslo Accords undermine Palestinian refugees' right to return to their homes in pre-1967 Israel. Arafat elected president of the PA.

1998: Gaza. PNC meets at the insistence of Israeli prime minister Benjamin Netanyahu. With U.S. president Bill Clinton presiding, it reaffirms its 1996 actions. Discussion of Wye River I and II memoranda for implementation of Oslo II accords.

1999: Discussion of Middle East Peace Summit at Sharm el-Shaykh and memorandum on implementation timeline.

2000: Discussion of implications of the Camp David 2000 Summit. PA negotiations on permanent status of a Palestinian State underway until outbreak of al-Aqsa Intifada in October.

2001: Discussion of the Mitchell Report on Israeli–Palestinian violence and al-Aqsa Intifada.

2002: Discussion of Permanent Status Negotiations.

Since the beginning of the al-Aqsa Intifada, Arafat has been confined to highly restricted movement by the Israeli government, making it extremely difficult to carry out the Palestinian legislative processes of the PNC and the PA. To remain the supreme political institution of the Palestinian people as a whole, the PNC must replace the quota system with democratic selection and become a permanent body if it is ever to become the genuine Palestinian parliament. In 2003 the PNC was chaired by Salim Zaʿnun. It had 669 members; 88 were from the Palestinian Legislative Council (PLC), 98 represented the Palestinians in the occupied territories, and 483 represented people of the Palestinian diaspora.

See also ARAFAT, YASIR; OSLO ACCORD (1993); PALESTINE LIBERATION ORGANIZATION (PLO); PALESTINE NATIONAL COVENANT (1964); PALESTINIAN AUTHORITY; PALESTINIANS; SAID, EDWARD; SHUQAYRI, AHMAD.

Bibliography

Gresh, Alain. *The PLO: The Struggle Within: Towards an Independent Palestinian State,* translated by A. M. Berrett. Revised edition. London: Zed Books, 1988.

Hilal, Jamil. "PLO Institutions: The Challenge Ahead." *Journal of Palestine Studies* 89 (1993): 46–60.

Hiro, Dilip. *Sharing the Promised Land: A Tale of the Israelis and Palestinians.* New York: Olive Branch, 1999.

Khalidi, Walid. "Regiopolitics: Toward a U.S. Policy on the Palestine Problem." *Foreign Affairs* 59 (Summer 1981): 1050–2063.

Lukacs, Yehuda, ed. *The Israeli-Palestinian Conflict: A Documentary Record, 1967–1990.* Cambridge, U.K.: Cambridge University Press, 1992.

Muslih, Muhammad Y. *Toward Coexistence: An Analysis of the Resolutions of the Palestinian National Council.* Washington, DC: The Institute of Palestine Studies Publications, 1990.

Palestinian National Authority. "Palestinian National Council." Available at <http://www.pna.gov.ps/Government/gov/palestinian_national_council.asp>.

"The PNC: Historical Background." *Journal of Palestine Studies* 64 (1987): 149–152.

Rubenberg, Cheryl. *The Palestine Liberation Organization: Its Institutional Infrastructure.* Belmont, MA: Institute of Arab Studies, 1983.

Tessler, Mark. *A History of the Israeli–Palestinian Conflict.* Bloomington: Indiana University Press, 1994.

MOUIN RABBANI
UPDATED BY MARIA F. CURTIS

PALESTINE NATIONAL COVENANT (1964)

A 1964 document adopted by the Palestine Liberation Organization.

The Palestine National Covenant was adopted by the Palestine National Council at its first meeting (May–June 1964) after being drafted by a special charter committee. The covenant reflected the Arab political mood of the time and the political mentality of its framers, who were, on the whole, notables selected from among Palestinian public officials, professionals, and businessmen. Five interrelated ideas constitute the thrust of the covenant. First, it emphasized the total liberation of Palestine, which in effect meant the dismantling of Israel. The concept of liberation recurs sixteen times in the twenty-nine articles of the covenant; all other concepts are subordinate to it. This concept encompasses Arab nationalism, Islam, and culture.

Second, and connected with liberation, came the concept of self-determination. However, it is not clearly articulated whether, after liberation, the Palestinians would exercise self-determination within the context of an independent Palestinian state or a Palestine that is united with one or more Arab states (Articles 4 and 10). The word "state" is absent from the covenant, but the tone of the articles and the political persuasion of the majority of the members of the charter committee suggest that preference was given to a liberated Palestine that would be united to a projected unitary Arab nation.

Third, the covenant offered a definition of who was a Palestinian and whether this definition applied to Jews. In an attempt to emphasize the indissoluble link between Palestinians and their homeland, Palestinians are defined as the Arab nationals who "resided normally in Palestine until 1947," that is until the start of the Palestinian exodus following the United Nations partition resolution of November 1947. In a supplementary article the covenant stipulated that the "Jews who are of Palestinian origin will be considered Palestinians if they are willing to live loyally and peacefully in Palestine" (Article 7).

Fourth, the covenant sanctioned the status quo that existed in the West Bank (under Jordanian control) and Gaza Strip (under Egyptian control) by stipulating that the Palestine Liberation Organization (PLO) would not exercise any sovereignty over those areas (Article 24). At the time, the PLO leadership adopted this position because it lacked the desire and the ability to challenge the system of those Arab states whose political prescriptions rested more on perpetuating the status quo than on disrupting it. Moreover, the principle of territorial sovereignty was overshadowed by the dream of Arab unity, which gripped the imagination of the Palestinian and Arab masses. This explains why Article 16 vaguely linked "national sovereignty" to the abstract idea of "national freedom."

Fifth, the charter did not clearly articulate the means by which the goal of liberation should be achieved. Armed struggle and revolution, both being principles that occupied a central position in the ideology of most national liberation movements, had no place in the covenant. Given the mood of the time, it is not surprising that the framers of the covenant prescribed Arab unity as the principle instrument for liberation.

This 1964 covenant was amended in July 1968 as the Palestine National Charter, and the amended version itself was superseded by subsequent Palestine National Council decisions.

See also PALESTINE LIBERATION ORGANIZATION (PLO); PALESTINE NATIONAL CHARTER (1968); PALESTINE NATIONAL COUNCIL.

Bibliography

Harkabi, Y. *The Palestinian Covenant and Its Meaning.* London: Vallentine, Mitchell, 1979.

MUHAMMAD MUSLIH

PALESTINE RESEARCH CENTER

Research and publication center of the Palestine Liberation Organization.

The Palestine Research Center was founded in Beirut in 1965 by the Palestine Liberation Organization (PLO) to study all aspects of Palestinian life in Israel and the Arab countries, Zionism, and contemporary politics and society in Israel. Its library includes approximately 25,000 volumes, in addition to documents, photographs, and microfilms. Among its many publications is the Arabic-language journal *Shu'un Filastiniyya (Palestinian Affairs).* It was directed for many years, beginning in 1978, by Sabri Jiryis.

Israeli authorities confiscated the center during the Israeli invasion of Lebanon in June 1982. The collection was later returned in December 1983, whereupon the center moved to Cyprus.

See also NEWSPAPERS AND PRINT MEDIA: ARAB COUNTRIES; PALESTINE LIBERATION ORGANIZATION (PLO).

Bibliography

Rubenberg, Cheryl A. *The Palestinian Liberation Organization: Its Institutional Infrastructure.* Belmont, MA: Institute for Arab Studies, 1982.

JENAB TUTUNJI
UPDATED BY MICHAEL R. FISCHBACH

PALESTINIAN ARAB CONGRESSES

Seven congresses convened by Palestinian Arab politicians between 1919 and 1928 to oppose pro-Zionist British policies and gain independence.

The first Palestinian Arab congress (al-Mu'tamar al-Arabi al-Filastini) met in Jerusalem from 27 January to 9 February 1919. Organized by local Muslim and Christian associations, its thirty participants framed a national charter that demanded independence for Palestine, denounced the Balfour Declaration (and its promise of a Jewish national home), and rejected British rule over Palestine. A majority sought the incorporation of Palestine into an independent Syrian state, and the delegates strongly denounced French claims to a mandate over Syria. The congress expressed its request for independence in the language of U.S. president Woodrow Wilson's principles supporting the right of self-determination of subject peoples.

Scholars disagree about the second congress. Muhammad Muslih argues that the British prevented it from being held, but other scholars view the Arab congress held in Damascus in March 1920 as the second congress. It proclaimed Syrian independence under Amir Faisal, son of Sharif Husayn ibn Ali of Mecca.

The third congress was held in Haifa in December 1920. The forty-eight delegates elected an executive committee (the Arab Executive), with a permanent secretariat based in Jerusalem; Musa Kazim al-Husayni headed it. The scion of a leading Jerusalem family, he had been removed by the British as mayor after riots in the spring of 1920. The congress and executive committee were dominated by middle-aged men from ranking Muslim and Christian landowning and merchant families, but younger, more radical politicians also participated—those who had returned home from Damascus in July 1920, after the French had overthrown Amir Faisal and established their mandate over Syria. In Palestine, a civil administration was established under Herbert Samuel, a British Zionist. The congress's resolutions omitted references to unity with Syria, but maintained firm opposition to Zionism, insisting that Palestine gain its independence as an Arab state. The resolutions appealed to the British sense of justice and fair play, in the hope that the pro-Zionist policies could be modified.

The fourth congress met in May 1921 in the wake of widespread riots in Jaffa. It resolved to send a delegation to London, headed by Musa Kazim al-Husayni, to alter British policy. The delegation remained in London through July 1922 and had some impact on British thinking: The Churchill White Paper of June 1922 indicated that the government might place some limits on Jewish immigration and promote a degree of Palestinian self-rule.

At the same time, a special assembly was convened in June 1922. It was more militant than the previous congress, and the participants voted to hold a peaceful two-day demonstration in mid-July against the establishment of the British mandate. That militancy increased in the fifth congress, held in Nablus in August 1922, with more than seventy-five delegates attending. They rejected the Churchill White Paper and launched a boycott of elections for the legislative council. Soon afterward, a second delegation went to Istanbul, Lausanne, and London in a futile effort to persuade the Turkish government not to sign a peace agreement without taking into account the interests of its former Arab provinces, which were being ruled by British and French forces.

The sixth congress met in June 1923 at the insistence of local Muslim and Christian societies who feared that Sharif Husayn ibn Ali of Mecca would sign a treaty with London that would recognize the British mandate over Palestine, rather than demand independence for Palestine. The 115 delegates resolved to send a third delegation to London to monitor the negotiations. Moreover, the resolutions stiffened the Arabs' rejection of representative institutions that did not grant policymaking authority to the Palestinian community, and the delegates even proposed such steps toward noncooperation as withholding taxes. However, the large landowners objected to that step, fearing that the British would seize their property in retaliation, and so action on those proposals was shelved.

The British mandate became effective in 1923, and the seventh congress convened from 20 to 22 June 1928, ending five years of tension and division among the Arab politicians. In the intervening years, the Nashashibi family of Jerusalem had withheld its participation in the institutions associated with the Arab congress, founded the National Party (1923), and contested with the Husaynis and their adherents in elections for the Supreme Muslim Council (1926) and local municipal councils (1927). New groups also had emerged among young educated Muslims and pan-Arab activists. The seventh congress sought to unite such factions behind the demand for a representative council and parliamentary government, which would help them attain their national goals. Since Jewish immigration had dipped in 1926 and 1927, the delegates had become less fearful of the Zionist movement than they had been in the past, and they hoped that a gradualist approach to self-government would attain their ends. Their resolutions also emphasized socioeconomic needs such as reopening the Ottoman-period agricultural banks so that farmers could obtain loans, increasing the allotment to education in the government's budget, and reducing the authority of the Greek priests in the Orthodox Christian community. The congress elected an enlarged Arab Executive whose forty-eight members included twelve Christians. The various factions were balanced: Musa Kazim al-Husayni retained the presidency, but both vice presidents (including a Greek Orthodox) favored the Nashashibi camp. The three secretaries were the young radical Jamal al-Husayni, the pro-Nashashibi Protestant lawyer Mughannam Ilyas al-Mughannam, and the pan-Arab, independent-minded lawyer Awni Abd al-Hadi.

The new Arab Executive immediately pressed the British to grant representative institutions, but its efforts coincided with renewed Arab–Jewish tension centered on conflicting claims to the Western Wall in Jerusalem. The riots of August 1929 undermined the cautious negotiating efforts of the Arab Executive; its members were swept up in the growing militancy of the Arab community. The fourth delegation to London in the spring of 1930 presented maximalist demands, including the immediate formation of a national government in which the Arabs would have the majority. The Arab Executive also supported the demonstrations and protests launched by youthful activists in the fall of 1933, as Jewish immigration and land purchases again escalated.

Following the death of Musa Kazim al-Husayni in March 1934, the Arab Executive held its final meeting in August. That meeting permitted the formation of political parties, but resolved to convene an eighth general congress in 1935. The eighth congress never met: By then, politicians were preoccupied with forming their own parties and contesting municipal council elections. When the Arab general strike began in Palestine in April 1936, a new coordinating body—the Arab Higher Committee—was constituted from the heads of the political parties. The Arab Executive then faded away. Although the Arab Executive had limited effectiveness, it had served as an informal voice for the Palestinian community for more than a decade. The congresses had provided an essential forum for Palestinian Arab politicians to debate fundamental policies and articulate their demands.

See also ARAB HIGHER COMMITTEE (PALESTINE); BALFOUR DECLARATION (1917); CHURCHILL WHITE PAPER (1922); HUSAYNI, JAMAL AL-; HUSAYNI, MUSA KAZIM AL-; MANDATE SYSTEM; NASHASHIBI FAMILY.

Bibliography

Ingrams, Doreen. *Palestine Papers, 1917–1922: Seeds of Conflict.* New York: George Braziller, 1973.

Lesch, Ann Mosely. *Arab Politics in Palestine, 1917–1939: The Frustration of a Nationalist Movement.* Ithaca, NY: Cornell University Press, 1979.

McTague, John J. *British Policy in Palestine, 1917–1922.* Lanham, MD: University Press of America, 1983.

Muslih, Muhammad Y. *The Origins of Palestinian Nationalism.* New York: Columbia University Press, 1988.

Porath, Y. *The Emergence of the Palestinian-Arab National Movement, 1918–1929.* London: Frank Cass, 1974.

Porath, Y. *The Palestinian Arab National Movement: From Riots to Rebellion, 1929–1939.* London: Frank Cass, 1977.

ANN M. LESCH
UPDATED BY PHILIP MATTAR

PALESTINIAN AUTHORITY

Autonomous Palestinian government operating in parts of the West Bank and Gaza starting from 1994.

The September 1993 Oslo Accord between Israel and the Palestine Liberation Organization (PLO) called for the establishment of a Palestinian Interim Self-Governing Authority (PISGA) in those parts of the West Bank and Gaza from which Israeli forces would eventually withdraw. Israel would then cede certain autonomous powers to the PISGA pending a final peace settlement. This concept was actualized by the subsequent May 1994 Gaza-Jericho Agreement that led to an initial Israeli withdrawal from those two areas and that created the Palestinian Authority (PA), which would exercise autonomous powers until an elected Palestinian council could replace it. PLO Chair Yasir Arafat and a body of PLO cadres were allowed to return from exile and form the 24-member council of ministers that made up the PA, which commenced functioning in July 1994.

The September 1995 Interim Agreement between Israel and the PLO laid the basis for further Israeli withdrawals from the West Bank and for an elected Palestinian Council that would wield both legislative and, through its executive authority, executive powers. Following elections, the Palestinian Council and the president of its executive authority would thereafter assume the powers of Palestinian self-government from the PA, although in fact the new governmental structure that emerged continued to use the same name. Elections for the 88-seat council and its president were held in January 1996. Arafat won the presidency decisively. Chief PLO negotiator Ahmad Sulayman Qurai (also Qurei, Quray, Abu Ala) was elected as the first speaker of the council.

After further redeployments of Israeli forces starting in late 1995, the PA exercised different levels of authority in the West Bank and Gaza. By early 1997 it exercised full control over Gaza excluding the areas in and around Israeli settlements. The situation in the West Bank was more complicated. Israeli forces had only withdrawn from about 27 percent of the territory. The PA exercised full civil and security control over Area A, which included all of the major towns except Jerusalem (which remained under total Israeli control). It controlled civil matters in Area B—most other Palestinian villages and inhabited sites—but shared security functions with Israel. Finally, Area C remained under complete Israeli authority. Not only was the total area under full or partial PA control less than a third of the West Bank, it was divided among hundreds of separate Area A and B enclaves that were cut off from one another (and from Gaza) by Israeli-controlled Area C.

A burgeoning bureaucracy grew to enable the PA to govern. By early 1997 PA ministries and departments controlled many aspects of daily life for Palestinians. The PA even issued passports and postage stamps, and dispatched a two-man team to the 1996 Olympic Games. A multitude of competing security and intelligence agencies developed. Security forces comprised former soldiers of the PLO's exile Palestine Liberation Army, other exiles, and locally recruited men. These agencies included the National

Palestinian prime minister Ahmed Qurai (left) and leader Yasir Arafat (right) pray before a meeting of the Palestinian parliament. © AP/WORLD WIDE PHOTOS. REPRODUCED BY PERMISSION.

Security Forces; Civil Police; Border Police; Coastal Police; Civil Defense; University Police; and Arafat's own guard, Force 17/Presidential Guard. Intelligence agencies included the General Security Service; Military Intelligence; Special Security Force; and the powerful Preventative Security Forces, headed in Gaza by Muhammad Dahlan and in the West Bank by Jibril Rajub.

Even after the Palestinian Council began meeting, Arafat continued to rule in an authoritarian fashion through the security and intelligence services and his new twenty-two-member executive council (cabinet). The judiciary was not independent; Arafat's government sometimes simply ignored its rulings, and certain cases were decided by secret military courts. Arafat possessed the authority to veto council legislation. As calls for reform mounted, important legislators such as Haydar Abd al-Shafi resigned, and Marwan Barghuthi introduced a no-confidence motion in the council in April 1997.

Palestinian demands for change combined with outside pressures for reform. Israeli and U.S. anger over terrorist attacks by groups such as HAMAS and Islamic Jihad that were based in the PA led to mounting international pressure on Arafat to crack down on militants and to change PA governance. The second intifada saw Israel reoccupy large areas of the PA and decimate its infrastructure. Yielding to pressure, Arafat in April 2003 created the post of prime minister, which was filled by veteran PLO leader Mahmud Abbas. The PA's ability to function, however, remained hostage to rivalries and wider developments in the peace process.

See also ABBAS, MAHMUD; AQSA INTIFADA, AL-; ARAFAT, YASIR; BARGHUTHI, MARWAN; DAHLAN, MUHAMMAD; GAZA (CITY); HAMAS; ISLAMIC JIHAD; ISRAEL: OVERVIEW; ISRAELI SETTLEMENTS; JERUSALEM; OSLO ACCORD (1993); PALESTINE LIBERATION ORGANIZATION (PLO); QURAI, AHMAD SULAYMAN; RAJUB, JIBRIL; WEST BANK.

Bibliography

Ghanem, As'ad. *The Palestinian Regime: A "Partial Democracy."* Brighton, U.K.: Sussex Academic Press, 2001.

MICHAEL R. FISCHBACH

PALESTINIAN CITIZENS OF ISRAEL

A remnant of the larger Arab community living in the parts of British Mandate Palestine that became the state of Israel in 1948.

Until 1948, both Jewish and Arab residents of Palestine were called Palestinians. After 1948, both Jewish and Arab citizens of Israel were called Israelis. In recent years, many Arab citizens of Israel preferred to be called Palestinians. Of the approximately 900,000 Palestinian Arabs who lived in the area that became Israel in 1948, fewer than 170,000 (about 12.5 percent of Israel's population) remained after the Arab–Israel War of 1948: 119,000 Muslims, 35,000 Christians, and 15,000 Druze. About 32,000 were town dwellers; 120,000, villagers; and 18,000, nomads. Some 30,000 were internal refugees, having fled from one part of Israel to another during the 1948 war. Most of the community leaders and professionals had left the country (only ten Palestinian physicians remained); most institutions were in disarray; and nearly every family had some members in the surrounding enemy countries.

The Palestinian population was separated from the Jewish majority in western, central, and upper Galilee, from Nazareth north. A few thousand remained in the former Arab towns of Ramla, Acre, Jaffa, and the city of Haifa, the Negev, and several score of smaller villages—a distribution that remained basically unchanged. Initially, most areas where the Arab minority of the new Jewish state lived were under the military authorities and subject to restrictive military government emergency regulations, which limited freedom of movement, access to civil courts, and individual ownership of land. The military authorities controlled nearly all aspects of life in the Palestinian community. The military government had to approve the appointments for most positions, from teachers in village schools to mayors of Palestinian towns.

Many in Israel's government considered Palestinian Arab citizens a security risk because of the continuing state of war with the surrounding countries, although the severity of military government restrictions was gradually eased until the Knesset terminated most emergency regulations during 1966. Even so, Palestinians living in Israel continued to be mistrusted by many Israelis even though experience demonstrated that the number who might be a security risk was minute.

From 1948 until the early 1990s, government policy regarding Palestinian citizens of Israel was coordinated by the adviser on Arab affairs, a special office in the bureau of the prime minister. Several ministries—including education, religion, minorities, agriculture, and social welfare—also had special offices for Arab affairs, usually headed by Jewish officials. In the absence of most professionals, such as doctors, after the 1948 war, the government took initial responsibility for rehabilitating the Palestinian community. A social welfare network was introduced in Arab areas and welfare offices were opened. Special courses were organized to train Palestinian personnel, and clinics were established by the ministry of health. Village rehabilitation was organized to restore agricultural production through the replanting of olive groves, the introduction of farm mechanization, and agricultural loans.

Policies emphasizing the security and development of Israel as a Jewish state often vitiated efforts to integrate Israel's Palestinian citizens. This was evident in policies regarding land and other immovable property belonging to Palestinians. Property, including homes and farms, belonging to the 30,000 internal Palestinian refugees and to several thousand other Palestinian citizens was taken over by the custodian of absentee property, who was charged with the administration of possessions belonging to those who left their homes during the 1948 war. Most of those affected by the Absentee Property Law had fled to surrounding countries. However, much of the agricultural land belonging to Israel's Palestinian citizens also was seized by the custodian. Other laws pertaining to the acquisition of land for reasons of security and for development resulted in government sequestration of about 40 percent of the land belonging to the country's Palestinian citizens.

Land requisition policies resulted in a shift in the occupational pattern of the Palestinian community, which before 1948 had been mostly rural and agricultural, to widespread employment in the Jewish urban economy. However, the rural social network, based on traditional *hamulas* (families), remained largely intact. The majority of those in the urban economy traveled from their villages or towns to work in centers of Jewish commerce and industry, where they were employed in unskilled or low-paid jobs at the bottom of the economic ladder. Government land requisition led to the depeasantization of the Palestinian community and to shortages of urban property, which resulted in greatly overcrowded villages and towns. Yet some who retained agricultural land prospered, despite the overall decline in Palestinian farmland. From 1949, with the assistance of the agriculture ministry, modern farming methods, extensive mechanization, and irrigation were introduced; Palestinian agricultural productivity increased several times over. Although the overall economy of the Palestinian community lags behind the Jewish sector, a few of those who pay the highest income tax in Israel are from the minority community.

Initially the MAPAI (Labor Party), which controlled the government from 1948 until 1977, organized Palestinian political parties headed by local notables who were co-opted by the military government. These local parties elected several members to the Knesset, where they usually voted with the MAPAI. Some were led by *hamula* or tribal or clan leaders; some identified with ethnic factions such as the Druze. Other Arab Knesset members were affiliated with the Communist Party and the MAPAM (Left Labor Party).

Government officials charged with policy for the minority communities encouraged each to develop its own institutions and organizations. Thus the system of religious courts established during the Ottoman era, and continued during the British Mandate, was maintained; these included *shari'a* (Islamic religious) courts and separate courts for each of the several recognized Christian denominations. In 1962, the first Druze religious court, separate from the Islamic courts, was organized. The Druze were initially permitted to join Israel's military forces; later they were subject to the draft. A few Bedouin and Christian Palestinians also were permitted to join the armed or security forces, and some attained high rank. Government policy generally exempts Muslims other than Bedouins from serving, which results in the exclusion of most of Israel's Palestinians from certain family and other government allowances and increases the difficulty of finding employment, since prior military service is required for many jobs, especially in government jobs related to national defense.

Between 1948 and the early 1990s, the Palestinian community experienced rapid economic, social, and political development. A new generation of leaders replaced those who had fled before and during the 1948 war or who had been co-opted by Israel's government. By the late 1950s, and in the 1960s and 1970s, the new generation of Israel's Palestinians included many politically active professionals, university-educated in Israel or abroad. They became increasingly dissatisfied with the position of Israel's Palestinian citizens. Many with advanced degrees were unable to find employment in jobs commensurate with their training and skills. Issues that concerned them included the government's land policies; the citizenship law, which gave preference to Jewish immigrants; the lack of Arabs in responsible government posts; the disparities between government resources allocated to the Jewish and Palestinian sectors in education, housing, and other services; and the perception that they were not accepted as full citizens of Israel. Opposition to government policies was evidenced in a shift of Palestinian voting patterns away from Labor and other Jewish parties, initially to the Communist Party of Israel. Attempts to organize Palestinian nationalist parties were blocked by government authorities or by internal dissension among potential Palestinian leaders.

By the 1960s, Palestinian nationalist sentiment had increased, and many Arabs in Israel supported Egypt's President Gamal Abdel Nasser. The rise of this national consciousness was demonstrated in 1965 when Israel's Communist Party split into a Jewish faction and a largely Palestinian nationalist faction, the New Communist List (RAKAH). Although several of RAKAH's leaders were Jewish, most of its votes came from Palestinian Israelis who perceived it as the principal legal vehicle for expressing opposition to government policies. Other groups attempted to organize opposition parties but were either banned by the authorities or failed to galvanize sufficient support. By the 1970s, RAKAH was winning more votes within the Palestinian community than any of the Jewish parties, and it became the principal voice opposing government policies toward what was officially called the Arab sector. Later, RAKAH was joined by organizations, such as the Committee for Defense of Arab Lands and the Committee of Heads of Arab Local Councils, to form HADASH (the Democratic Front for Peace and Equality). Like parties in the Jewish political spectrum, Palestinian parties often split, reformed, and acquired new names and leaders. Thus in the 2003 election, the main Arab parties included BALAD (National Democratic Assembly), HADASH, TA'AL (Arab Movement for Renewal), and the United Arab List. More radical Arab parties included the Organization for Democratic Action and the Progressive National Alliance. All advocated equal rights for Palestinian citizens inside Israel and the establishment of a Palestinian state coexisting with it.

The Arab–Israel War of 1967 and Israel's occupation of the West Bank, East Jerusalem (formerly part of Jordan), and Gaza (formerly occupied by Egypt) constituted a watershed for Israel's Palestinian citizens. For the first time since 1948, they could establish direct contacts with Palestinians in surrounding countries. From 1948 until 1967, only a small number of Christians had been permitted to cross from Israel to Jordan once or twice a year, at Christmas and Easter. After 1967, Israel's Palestinian citizens could visit the West Bank and Gaza, and Palestinians in the occupied areas could visit Israel. Many family relationships were reestablished, Israel's Palestinians were increasingly exposed to new developments in Palestinian national consciousness, and they were no longer regarded by the Arab world at large with suspicion or mistrust. Larger numbers of Israel's Palestinians identified themselves not only as loyal citizens of Israel but also as supporters of the Palestinian national cause. Increasing numbers identified themselves as Palestinians first and as Israelis second.

Significant demographic changes characterized Israel's Palestinian community. It grew from 12.5 percent of Israel's population in 1948 to over 18 percent by 2000, mostly as a result of natural increase. By the 1990s, Sunni Muslims constituted 78 percent of the Arab population; the Druze, approximately 9 percent; and various Christian denominations, about 13 percent. Most Christians were Greek Catholic (32 percent), Greek Orthodox (42 percent), or Roman Catholic (16 percent). At the turn of the century, 1,200,000 Palestinians lived under Israel's jurisdiction, including over 200,000 residents of East Jerusalem (annexed by

Israel in 1967; most nations, including the United States, do not recognize Arab East Jerusalem as part of Israel). Few East Jerusalem residents chose to become Israeli citizens; most retain passports issued by Jordan.

Despite great improvements in infant mortality, average life span, literacy, and similar social indicators by 2002, 92 percent of Palestinian workers were in the bottom half of the country's wage scale, and a third of Palestinian children lived below the poverty line. By 2002, only 5.7 percent of civil servants were Palestinian citizens. Of these, more than half worked in health and social services; few were directly involved in policy-making or decision-making roles. Of Israel's 5,000 college and university lecturers, only about 50 were Arab citizens. These were among the factors contributing to the growing radicalization of Israel's Palestinian community. Palestinian discontent led to increasing demands for full equality, expressed in support for groups such as the Democratic Arab Party, the Progressive List for Peace, and the Islamic Movement. Tensions also grew between the country's Jewish and Arab citizens, caused by wide differences over the peace process and Israel's treatment of Palestinians in the occupied territories. Israel's Palestinian citizens were not consulted or involved in the Oslo talks or the negotiations that followed. Most supported or sympathized with the Palestinian intifadas of 1987 through 1991 and 2000. The brutal response of the Israeli police to nationalist protest demonstrations in October 2000 left thirteen Palestinian Israelis dead and scores more wounded, creating a deep wound among Israel's Palestinian citizens. These tensions were underscored in the election campaign of 2003 when the Central Election Committee attempted to strike BALAD leader Azmi Bishara and TA'AL leader Ahmad Tibi from the ballot. Although Israel's Supreme Court overrode the decision, the key issue in dispute remained: Was Israel to be a Jewish state or a state of all its citizens?

> See also AQSA INTIFADA, AL-; ARAB–ISRAEL WAR (1948); ARAB–ISRAEL WAR (1967); COMMUNISM IN THE MIDDLE EAST; DRUZE; GAZA STRIP; INTIFADA (1987–1991); ISRAEL: POLITICAL PARTIES IN ISRAEL; KNESSET; NASSER, GAMAL ABDEL; OSLO ACCORD (1993); *SHARI'A;* WEST BANK.

Bibliography

Abu Nimer, Mohammed. *Dialogue, Conflict Resolution, and Change: Arab Jewish Encounters in Israel.* Albany: State University of New York Press, 1999.

Cohen, Stanley. *Crime, Justice, and Social Control among the Arab Sector in Israel.* Tel Aviv, 1990.

Firro, Kais M. *The Druzes in the Jewish State: A Brief History.* Leiden, Neth.: Brill, 1999.

Ghanem, As'ad. *The Palestinian-Arab Minority in Israel, 1948–2000: A Political Study.* Albany: State University of New York Press, 2001.

Al-Haj, Majid. *Education, Empowerment, and Control: The Case of the Arabs in Israel.* Albany: State University of New York Press, 2001.

Al-Haj, Majid, and Rosenfeld, Henry. *Arab Local Government in Israel.* Boulder, CO: Westview Press, 1990.

Kretzmer, David. *The Legal Status of the Arabs in Israel.* Boulder, CO: Westview Press, 1990.

Lustick, Ian. *Arabs in the Jewish State.* Austin: University of Texas Press, 1980.

Rouhama, Nadim N. *Palestinian Citizens in an Ethnic Jewish State: Identities in Conflict.* New Haven, CT: Yale University Press, 1997.

Smooha, Sammy. *Arabs and Jews in Israel,* 2 vols. Boulder, CO: Westview Press, 1989–1992.

Wolkinson, Benjamin. *Arab Employment in Israel: The Quest for Equal Employment Opportunity.* Westport, CT: Greenwood Press, 1999.

Yiftachel, Oren, and Meir, Avinoam, eds. *Ethnic Frontiers and Peripheries: Landscapes of Development and Inequality in Israel.* Boulder, CO: Westview Press, 1998.

DON PERETZ

PALESTINIANS

A people who consider themselves descendants of the Canaanites, and other peoples who have settled in Palestine since ancient times.

The name *Palestinian* applies in contemporary times to Muslim and Christian Arabs who inhabited Palestine as a consolidated community until the creation of Israel in May 1948, an event that shattered the community and dispersed about 726,000 Palestinians throughout the Middle East, primarily to Gaza, the West Bank, Jordan, Syria, and Lebanon.

In 2004 the total number of Palestinians was estimated at 8.9 million. Approximately 88 percent are Muslims, and the other 12 percent are Christians. Until the initiation of the Palestinian Authority (PA) in the summer of 1994, the largest concentration of Palestinians lived under Israeli occupation. In 2004 approximately 2.1 million lived in the West Bank, 200,000 in East Jerusalem, and 1.33 million in the Gaza Strip. Approximately 1.3 million lived in pre-1967 Israel as Palestinian citizens of the Jewish state. Other Palestinians lived in other Arab countries, especially Jordan, which had approximately 3 million.

Late Ottoman Period

The politics and culture of the Palestinians from the latter part of the nineteenth century until after the signing of the Declaration of Principles between Israel and the Palestine Liberation Organization (PLO) on 13 September 1993 can be divided into five stages. In the first stage, from 1876 to 1917, the Palestinians shared a common cultural heritage shaped primarily by the values of the Arab and Muslim empires that had ruled the country with few interruptions from 638 C.E. to 1917. Palestinian society in this stage consisted of three major classes: peasants (*fallahin*), commercial bourgeoisie, and urban notables or patricians. The patricians were the ruling class, and their influence ran deep in the countryside and in Palestinian cities and towns.

In 1897 the Basel program of the first Zionist Congress strongly affected the Palestinians. The program fixed the Zionist goal: "To create for the Jewish people a home in Palestine, secured by public law." This ushered in the first phase of a protracted struggle between indigenous Palestinians and Jewish immigrants. Opposition to Zionism was the focus of Palestinian political activities, as well as of Palestinian historiography and other forms of writing.

British Rule

The second stage, from 1917 to 1948, was inaugurated with the collapse of the Ottoman Empire at the end of World War I. By the autumn of 1918 Palestine, Transjordan, and Iraq were under British control. This development made Palestine increasingly vulnerable to Zionist colonization—first, by isolating the country from its wider Arab environment and second, by giving the British a free hand in implementing the Balfour Declaration of 2 November 1917, in which the British promised to support a Jewish National Home in Palestine. With the Balfour Declaration, the stage was set for a long struggle between the Palestinians and the Zionist immigrants. The Palestinians, who constituted approximately 90 percent of Palestine's population by the end of World War I, saw in the Zionists a potential threat to their national existence.

In strategic terms, the Palestinian-Zionist struggle was over the status quo. The Palestinians wanted to preserve the status quo, through political and diplomatic efforts between 1917 and 1936 and through armed rebellion during the Palestine Arab Revolt of 1936 to 1939. In contrast, the Zionists sought to change the status quo through mass immigration and land acquisition. The Jewish population in Palestine rose from 9.7 percent in 1919 to 35.1 percent in 1946, and Jewish-owned land increased from 2.04 percent of the total area of Palestine in 1919 to 7 percent in 1946. Meanwhile, British policy in the military sphere was aimed at disarming the Palestinians and arming the Jews. Thus, by 1947 the overall power equation was decisively in favor of the Zionists.

Palestinian society was also affected by three other factors: Zionist settlement activity, British colonial policies, and the expansion of Palestine's economy. While dominant members of urban notable families continued to control the politics of the country, other social forces were at play. The expansion of trade and the growth of coastal cities and towns enhanced the position of the middle class. Artisans and craftsmen, as well as people engaged in the finance, construction, and service sectors, also benefited from the expansion of trade. However, the peasants, who constituted almost two-thirds of Palestinian society, did not benefit from these economic developments. Their condition worsened in great part because of Zionist settlement and the lack of capital. Although Jewish agricultural settlers had adequate land, the indigenous Palestinian peasantry lacked the space necessary for its growing population. The October 1930 report of Sir John Hope-Simpson acknowledged this problem, noting that there was not room for a substantial number of Jewish settlers on the land.

The depressed state of the peasantry, together with other developments, had produced rebellion within Palestinian society by the mid-1930s. The most notable development was the escalating rate of Jewish immigration. The influx of Jewish immigrants had two major consequences: It produced panic and desperation among the Palestinians, reinforcing their fears of Jewish domination in the future; and it radicalized the Palestinians and convinced them that the British were unwilling or incapable of following an evenhanded policy. Against this background, a revolt erupted in May 1936 and continued unabated until the summer of 1939, with only a short lull between November 1936 and January 1937 while the Peel Commission toured Palestine to ascertain the causes of the revolt.

With the publication of the Peel Commission Report in July 1937, the rebellion exploded again in opposition to the commission's recommendation calling for a tripartite partition: a Jewish state; a Palestinian state to be incorporated by Transjordan; and a British mandate over other areas. There was a Palestinian consensus against partition because the proposed Jewish state would cover about 33 percent of the total area of the country at a time when Jewish ownership of land was roughly 5.6 percent, and because a large portion of Palestinian villages, and a high percentage of Palestinians, would fall inside the Jewish state. The British responded to the Palestinian revolt with the full force of their military power. In terms of the cost in human lives, the revolt was a national calamity for the Palestinians: More than 3,075 were killed, 110 hanged, and 6,000 jailed in 1939 alone. At the same time, the British organized, trained, and armed special Jewish forces, creating in the process a Jewish military infrastructure that gave a decisive edge to the Jewish forces ten years later during the Arab–Israel War of 1948.

When the British realized that partition was not practicable, as indicated by the Woodhead Commission report of November 1938, they convened the unsuccessful London Conference in February and March 1939 to resolve the issue of the future status of Palestine. To break the deadlock, Malcolm MacDonald, colonial secretary of state, issued a white paper on 17 May 1939. Although the white paper fell short of meeting long-standing Palestinian demands, it introduced a number of important modifications concerning immigration and the application of the Balfour Declaration.

British implementation of the white paper proved difficult, partly because of Palestinian and Zionist opposition and partly because of the burdens of World War II. In these circumstances, by the 1940s the British were unable to handle the effects of the Balfour Declaration. The military and political structures of a Jewish national home were already in place in Palestine, in great part because of Britain's generosity. In almost every respect these structures were superior to those of the Palestinians.

Against this background, the United Nations (UN) divided Palestine into Jewish and Arab states in November 1947. The Palestinians rejected partition primarily because the UN proposed to give the Jews 55 percent of Palestine when Jewish ownership in November 1947 did not exceed 7 percent of the country's land. By contrast, the Jews found it in their interest to accept partition. Thus, the door for armed conflict in Palestine was wide open. A civil war between Jews and Palestinians followed the partition resolution. After the British left Palestine in May 1948, war, interspersed with cease-fires, continued until July 1949.

Units of armies and volunteers from neighboring Arab countries came to the aid of the Palestinians, who were losing the civil war and fleeing in large numbers. However, the Arab intervention was to no avail. The Jewish immigrant population was militarily superior to all the Arab soldiers combined. The Jews were also superior in terms of leadership, organization, and institutional links to the Western powers. In the end, the Zionists prevailed. Israel seized 77 percent of Palestine; about 726,000 Palestinians became refugees, many of them forcefully expelled by the Jewish forces while others fled out of fear. The Palestinians call this event al-Nakba, or the catastrophe.

The politics of the national struggle left a deep imprint on the intellectual life of the Palestinians, as is clearly illustrated in Palestinian historiography, art, and literature. There were literary and artistic works written in the romantic tradition, such as those by Khalil Baydas, Khalil al-Sakakini, and Muhammad Is'af al-Nashashibi, that focus on the social responsibility of men of letters and the relationship between culture and civilization. Other works, written in the realist tradition, reflect the philosophies of Ibn Khaldoun, Hegel, Marx, and Darwin.

From *al-Nakba* to the 1967 War

The third stage, which lasted from 1948 to 1967, was characterized by formal armistice agreements between a number of Arab states—Egypt, Syria, Lebanon, and Jordan—and Israel; the disarray among Arab states unsuccessfully attempting to achieve Arab unity; the impact of Cold War politics on the Middle East; the eclipsing of Palestinian nationalism by Arab nationalism; and Israel's refusal to accept any responsibility for what had befallen the Palestinians in 1948. Uprooted, dispersed, and with no state of their own, diaspora Palestinians (60% of the Palestinian population in 1948) came under the guardianship of the host Arab countries in which they lived. Another 30 percent lived in the West Bank and Gaza, and the remaining 10 percent lived in Israel. As a whole, the lives of Palestinians during this stage were marked by national dispersion, occupation, job insecurity, uncertain residency, discrimination, and political repression.

The post-1948 situation had serious consequences. First, it made the Palestinians totally dependent on the Arab states. Second, geographical dispersal made it difficult for the Palestinians to work together within one organizational framework. Thus, some Palestinians identified with the Arab National Movement, others with the Arab Ba'th Party or the Muslim Brotherhood; others acquired senior positions in the bureaucracies of Arab governments, particularly the Jordanian government, or formed independent Palestinian movements that advocated armed struggle against Israel. Life in the diaspora radicalized certain Palestinian groups that embarked on armed struggle against Israel in the mid-1960s in the hope of triggering an Arab–Israel war.

Against a background of inter-Arab rivalries and escalating Arab–Israel tensions, the Arab League created the PLO in 1964. The PLO's leadership was entrusted to Ahmad Shuqayri, a diaspora Palestinian of upper-class origin. In theory, the PLO was to work for the liberation of Palestine, but in practice it provided cover for Arab inaction toward Israel. The PLO charter of 1964 called for the total liberation of Palestine. Arab unity, rather than armed struggle or revolution, was posited as the instrument of liberation. Palestinian authors such as Abd al-Latif Tibawi, Fadwa Tuqan, and Fawaz Turki gave expression to this goal. Many of them romanticized

this goal by infusing it with the sentiment of the Palestinian concept of return. History books, novels, and collections of poems and pictures of Palestine poured forth during this period to express the pain of exile and the overpowering desire to return.

Literary and political themes were expressed by poets such as Mahmud Darwish, Samih al-Qasim, and Tawfiq Zayyad and literary critics such as Salim Jubran, Ihsan Abbas, and Afif Salim. Palestinian and Islamic historiography was produced by Arif al-Arif, Muhammad Izzat Darwaza, and Akram Zu'aytir. Stories of great Arab travelers were written by Iskandar al-Khuri al-Baytjali and Nicola Ziyada.

Reemergence of the Palestinian National Movement

The fourth stage of contemporary Palestinian history, from 1967 to the present, began with the Israeli conquest of the West Bank and Gaza in June 1967, a development that resulted in the displacement of more than 300,000 Palestinian refugees who fled the West Bank and the Golan area. Approximately 120,000 of these people were second-time refugees who had lived in refugee camps under Jordanian or Syrian jurisdiction. The Arab–Israel War of 1967 also resulted in the placement of the West Bank and Gaza under the jurisdiction of the Israeli military government. During its occupation of these territories, Israel undertook settlement and other activities that had a devastating impact on the Palestinians, including the formal annexation of East Jerusalem and the doubling of its surface area; the settlement of more than 120,000 Israelis in the Palestinian sector of the city; the confiscation of more than 55 percent of the West Bank and more than 40 percent of the Gaza Strip; and the deportation of some Palestinians from both areas.

Soon after the 1967 war, the Palestinians arose as an independent political force. They asserted the primacy of Palestinian nationalism and expressed themselves in the idiom of revolution and armed struggle. The PLO charter, revised in 1968 to give expression to this new trend, called for the liberation of all of Palestine, emphasizing that armed struggle was the only way. Aware at the time that the problem of Israeli Jews must be addressed, the PLO articulated the idea of a secular democratic state anchored on nonsectarian principles of coexistence among the Jewish, Christian, and Muslim citizens of a liberated Palestine. In terms of political organizing, the Palestinians used Jordan as their early base of operations against Israel. In an attempt to attract international attention, radical Palestinian groups resorted to acts of violence, including the hijacking of civilian airliners and the murder of members of the Israeli Olympic team in Munich in September 1972.

The unprecedented coincidence between the radicalization of the Palestinians and the emergence of pragmatism and a preference for a diplomatic settlement with Israel on the part of key Arab states led to tensions between revolutionary Palestinians and the new Arab political order. The Jordanian Civil War (1970–1971) epitomized the incongruence between the romanticism of revolutionary Palestinians and the pragmatism of the leaders of Arab states. The Palestinian guerrillas were defeated in Jordan, but they moved to Lebanon, where they reemerged as a strong political force in a country deeply divided by sectarian as well as socioeconomic differences. Their presence in Lebanon served as a catalyst for the civil war that was triggered in April 1975. After the Arab–Israel War of October 1973, a new Palestinian consensus emerged with respect to a diplomatic settlement with Israel. This consensus was reflected in the PLO's political programs of June 1974 and March 1977. Both programs implicitly called for peace with Israel and the establishment of a Palestinian state in the West Bank and Gaza.

Momentous events affected the Palestinians between 1982 and 1990. In June 1982 Israel invaded Lebanon. Thousands of Palestinians were killed, maimed, or taken prisoner by the Israeli invading force. After nearly three months of fighting, the PLO evacuated Lebanon under the protection of a multinational force and set up its new headquarters in Tunisia. While the PLO, led by Yasir Arafat, was trying to recover from the devastating impact of the Israeli invasion of Lebanon, the situation of the Palestinians in the West Bank and Gaza continued to deteriorate under the impact of massive Jewish settlements and the policies of the Likud government, which took power in Israel in 1977. The Palestinian response to this situation was the Intifada (uprising), which erupted in December 1987. The Intifada put the West Bank and Gaza Palestinians in the limelight after several years of neglect by Arab governments whose energies were focused on the Iran-Iraq War.

The Struggle for a State

The intifada also catapulted the priorities of West Bank and Gaza Palestinians to the top of the PLO agenda. Before that, the PLO catered primarily to the preferences of diaspora Palestinians. This led to the further crystallization of the pragmatic trend that had begun to emerge in the previous phase. The intifada forced the PLO to move definitively toward the peaceful pursuit of a state in the West Bank and Gaza, where the overriding priority of the Palestinians living in those territories was to end Israeli occupation. This was the crux of the PLO's political program of November 1988, when the Palestine National Council accepted the UN land for peace Resolution 242 and recognized the State of Israel. Politically and intellectually, this phase witnessed the greater salience of religious activism with the emergence of the Islamic Jihad in 1986 and the Islamic Resistance Movement (HAMAS) in January 1988.

Despite their political difficulties, the Palestinians participated in the Arab national debate over cultural and sociopolitical issues. Hisham Sharabi wrote on Arab intellectuals and their interaction with Western culture. Using anthropological and sociological concepts, he also analyzed patterns of authority in contemporary Arab society. Edward Said, a scholar-critic, wrote on Western literature and authored books and articles on the Palestine question and other Middle Eastern topics. Walid Khalidi wrote on the Palestinians in Palestine before their diaspora. Mahmoud Darwish, the Palestinians' national poet, wrote poems about the Palestine struggle and criticized PLO and Arab leaders. Palestinian women such as Fadwa Tuqan, Sahar Khalifa, and Salma al-Khadra al-Jayyusi used poetry and other genres to express the cause of women's rights in the Arab world. Other women, including Hanan Ashrawi, participated in politics and wrote on social and cultural topics.

Iraq's invasion and occupation of Kuwait in August 1990 set in motion a chain of political developments that led to the mutual recognition of Israel and the PLO and the signing of the historic Declaration of Principles in September 1993 by PLO chairman Arafat and Israeli prime minister Yitzhak Rabin. The PLO's support for Saddam Hussein was to a significant degree responsible for the shattering of the Palestinian community in Kuwait, which totaled approximately 350,000 people working as teachers, civil servants, and industrialists. However, the tragic results of the Gulf Crisis provided a propitious occasion for resolving the cause of the Palestinians. The launching of the Madrid peace process in 1991 opened the way for the Israel-PLO accord of September 1993. This accord was followed by other agreements to implement Palestinian self-rule, including the Taba Accords of September 1995. The Oslo Accord (1993) resulted in the withdrawal of Israeli troops from Gaza and major West Bank towns and the establishment of the Palestinian Legislative Council. With the Palestinians exercising control over some areas of the West Bank and Gaza, the realization of Palestinian self-determination seemed possible.

Yet, Palestinian hope for self-determination was dashed by a number of setbacks. One of the architects of Oslo, Yitzhak Rabin, was assassinated in 1995. The foundation for peace that he and Arafat built was undermined by the policies of a new prime minister, Benjamin Netanyahu, an opponent of the Oslo process, who refused to implement troop withdrawal and continued settlement activity, especially at Har Homa/Jamal Abu Ghunaym in East Jerusalem. By the time the more pragmatic Ehud Barak took over the premiership in Israel, most Palestinians had lost hope in the Oslo peace process. During the decade of the negotiations of the 1990s, confiscation of Palestinian land continued and the number of Jewish settlers doubled in the area in which the Palestinians hoped to establish a state. In addition, their economic conditions worsened. They were humiliated at checkpoints and their lives were disrupted by curfews and blockades. Finally, when the Camp David summit meeting in July 2000 failed, and Ariel Sharon provocatively visited al-Haram al-Sharif with 1,000 Israeli armed police on 28 September 2000, on the following day they initiated a second intifada, or uprising, that many considered to be their war of liberation.

Instead, it proved to be a costly rebellion. Palestinian militants attacked military and civilian Israeli targets. The violence helped to bring to power a

hard-line Israeli prime minister, Ariel Sharon. Sharon, an enemy of Oslo, destroyed a large part of the PA's security system, administrative offices, and economic infrastructure. He placed Arafat under house arrest, assassinated Palestinian militants, and continued his confiscation of Palestinian lands for Jewish settlements. As a result of the suicide bombings by Palestinian radicals against Israeli civilians (which Arafat tolerated despite his promises in 1988 and 1993 to fight terrorism) international support for the Palestinian struggle for a state diminished, especially after 11 September 2001, when the United States and its allies declared war on "international terrorism." By early 2004 some 3,000 Palestinians, including about 500 children, and about 900 Israelis had lost their lives. More than half of those killed on both sides were civilians.

There were unexpected benefits arising from the al-Aqsa Intifada. Some reforms, such as financial accountability, were welcomed by the Palestinian public when they were instituted in the PA areas. The office of prime minister was established in 2003 in an effort to share power outside of President Arafat's narrow circle. The United States announced in a diplomatic initiative, Road Map, to support the creation of a democratic, sovereign state of Palestine within three years. Despite the violence and destruction, both the Palestinian and Israeli publics continued to support a two-state solution, and they seemed closer to resolving the final status issues than ever before. In early 2004 Palestinian realization of a state of Palestine was awaiting the right circumstances and leadership to make it happen.

See also AQSA INTIFADA, AL; ARAB–ISRAEL WAR (1948); ARAB–ISRAEL WAR (1967); ARAB–ISRAEL WAR (1973); ARAFAT, YASIR; ARIF, ARIF AL-; BALFOUR DECLARATION (1917); DARWAZA, MUHAMMAD IZZAT; DARWISH, MAHMUD; GAZA (CITY); HAMAS; HARAM AL-SHARIF; INTIFADA (1987–1991); ISLAMIC JIHAD; ISRAEL: OVERVIEW; JORDANIAN CIVIL WAR (1970–1971); KHALIDI, WALID; LEBANESE CIVIL WAR (1958); LONDON (ROUNDTABLE) CONFERENCE (1939); MADRID CONFERENCE (1991); NAKBA, AL-(1948–1949); OSLO ACCORD (1993); PALESTINE; PALESTINE ARAB REVOLT (1936–1939); PALESTINE LIBERATION ORGANIZATION

(PLO); PEEL COMMISSION REPORT (1937);
SAKAKINI, KHALIL AL-; SHUQAYRI, AHMAD;
TABA NEGOTIATIONS (1995, 2001); TUQAN,
FADWA; TURKI, FAWAZ; UNITED NATIONS
CONCILIATION COMMISSION FOR PALESTINE
(UNCCP); UNITED NATIONS RELIEF AND
WORKS AGENCY FOR PALESTINE REFUGEES IN
THE NEAR EAST (UNRWA); UNITED NATIONS
SPECIAL COMMITTEE ON PALESTINE, 1947
(UNSCOP); WEST BANK; WHITE PAPERS ON
PALESTINE; WOODHEAD COMMISSION (1938);
ZIONISM.

Bibliography

Brand, Laurie A. *Palestinians in the Arab World: Institution Building and the Search for State.* New York: Columbia University Press, 1988.

Brown, Nathan. *Palestinian Politics after the Oslo Accords: Resuming Arab Palestine.* Berkeley: University of California
Press, 2003.

Hurewitz, J. C. *The Struggle for Palestine.* New York:
Schocken Books, 1976.

Khalidi, Rashid. *Palestinian Identity.* New York: Columbia
University Press, 1998

Khalidi, Walid. *Before Their Diaspora: A Photographic History of
the Palestinians, 1876–1948.* Washington, DC: Institute
for Palestine Studies, 1984.

Kimmerling, Baruch, and Migdal, Joel S. *The Palestinian
People: A History.* Cambridge, MA: Harvard University
Press, 2003.

Lesch, Ann M. "Closed Borders, Divided Lives: Palestinian Writings." *Universities Field Staff International Reports, Asia,* no. 28 (1985).

Ma'oz, Moshe. *Palestinian Leadership in the West Bank.* London:
Frank Cass, 1984.

Mattar, Philip. *The Mufti of Jerusalem: Al-Hajj Amin al-Husayni
and the Palestine National Movement.* New York: Columbia
University Press, 1992.

Miller, Aaron David. *The PLO: The Politics of Survival.* New
York: Praeger Publishers, 1983.

Muslih, Muhammad. *The Origins of Palestinian Nationalism.*
New York: Columbia University Press, 1988.

Muslih, Muhammad. *Toward Coexistence: An Analysis of the Resolutions of the Palestine National Council.* Washington, DC:
Institute for Palestine Studies, 1990.

Peretz, Don. *Palestinians, Refugees, and the Middle East Peace
Process.* Washington, DC: United States Institute of
Peace Press, 1993.

Said, Edward. *The Question of Palestine.* New York, 1979.

Schiff, Ze'ev, and Ya'ari, Ehud. *Intifada: The Palestinian
Uprising—Israel's Third Front.* New York: Simon and
Schuster, 1990.

Smith, Charles D. *Palestine and the Arab–Israeli Conflict,* 4th
edition. New York: Bedford/St. Martin's Press, 2004.

Tessler, Mark. *A History of the Israeli-Palestinian Conflict.*
Bloomington: Indiana University Press, 1994.

MUHAMMAD MUSLIH
UPDATED BY PHILIP MATTAR

PALIN COMMISSION REPORT (1920)

*British Foreign Office report on the causes of the Arab
violence in Palestine, April 1920.*

The Palin Commission (formally the Palin Court
of Inquiry) was set up in Palestine in May 1920, in
the wake of violent protests by Arab residents of
Jerusalem against the growing presence and political demands of the Jewish community. In early
1920, Arab protests had been mounted against the
Balfour Declaration, against privileges accorded the
Zionist Commission, and against the denial of Arab
independence. They culminated in violent attacks
on Jews in Jerusalem during the celebration of the
Muslim holiday of Nabi Musa in early April, which
coincided with Passover. Five Jews and four Muslim Arabs died. At that time, Palestine was ruled by
a British military administration, headed by General Louis J. Bols, who sought to reassure the Palestinian Arabs that Britain would observe the status
quo in that territory.

The British Foreign Office appointed a commission composed of three military officers and
headed by Major General P. C. Palin, which filed
its report on 1 July 1920. The report, which was
never made public, argued that the disturbances
were caused by the Arabs' disappointment over unfulfilled promises of independence, which the
British had made during World War I to Sharif
Husayn ibn Ali of Mecca; their belief that the Balfour Declaration implied the denial of their own
right of self-determination; and their fear that the
establishment of a Jewish National Home would lead
to such substantial Jewish immigration that the
Arabs would be subject to the Jewish community.
The report argued that those feelings were aggravated by the proclamation of Sharif Husayn's son

Amir Faisal ibn Hussein as king of Syria, in March 1920, with a potential claim to Palestine, too. Feelings were also aggravated by the actions of the Zionist Commission, which sought a privileged status vis-à-vis the British military administration and asserted the right of the Jewish community to statehood. The report called the Zionist Commission "arrogant, insolent and provocative" and said that its members could "easily precipitate a catastrophe" (McTague, 1983, p. 102). Nonetheless, the report concluded that the British must rule with a firm hand, proving that the policy of the Balfour Declaration would not be reversed but also that the Arabs would be treated fairly.

The report's substantive findings paralleled the views of General Bols, who wanted to reduce the authority of the Zionist Commission and reassure the Arabs. Instead, the British government decided that the Arabs would acquiesce once British pro-Zionist policy was implemented firmly. Therefore, London replaced the military administration with a civilian administration on the day before the Palin Report was submitted; that administration would be guided in its policy by the Balfour Declaration and presided over by a Jewish High Commissioner. The Palin Report's predictions proved accurate concerning mounting Arab-Jewish tension and the difficulty of reconciling their contradictory aims if Zionist aspirations were not moderated. But the report was never published or publicized and, therefore, failed to influence the public debate in London and Jerusalem at a time when British policy and the Arab-Jewish relationship might still have been modified.

See also HUSAYN IBN ALI.

Bibliography

Government of Palestine. *A Survey of Palestine*, vol. I. Jerusalem, 1946. Reprint, Washington, DC: Institute for Palestine Studies, 1991.

McTague, John J. *British Policy in Palestine, 1917–1922.* Lanham, MD: University Press of America, 1983.

ANN M. LESCH

PALMAH

Labor Zionist elite military organization (1941–1948).

The Palmah (Plugot Mahatz, or "shock companies") was the Haganah's elite strike force, founded in May 1941 to help defend the Yishuv against potential German invasion. Its founders were Yitzhak Sadeh and Yigal Allon, Haganah leaders affiliated with the left-wing Kibbutz ha-Meuhad (United Kibbutz) movement. The elite force of pioneer-soldiers was largely recruited from and was based and housed at the movement's kibbutzim. Trained in commando tactics, the Palmah had a strong esprit de corps that stressed military professionalism and socialist values. It became the military vanguard of the Zionist Left, which caused tensions with the MAPAI-affiliated Haganah, to which it was ostensibly subordinate.

In its early years, the Palmah actively cooperated with the British. Palmah units served alongside the British Army in the campaign against the Vichy regime in Syria and later saw service against Iraq's pro-Nazi regime. But after 1945, the Palmah participated along with the other Jewish undergrounds in the armed struggle against the British Mandatory authorities in 1945 and 1946. Specially trained Palmah volunteers played a lead role in "the Saison" of 1944 and 1945 against the renegade Irgun and LEHI underground groups. This internecine operation took on an ideological dimension as left-wing Palmah members captured and sometimes tortured right-wing Irgunists. Political rivalries again came to the fore in June 1948, when a Palmah unit under the command of Yitzhak Rabin was used to destroy the Irgun weapons ship *Altalena*, commanded by Menachem Begin.

The Palmah produced a number of senior officers in the 1948 War, and five Palmah officers later served as chief of staff of the Israel Defense Forces (IDF): Moshe Dayan (1953–1957), Yitzhak Rabin (1963–1967), Haim Bar-Lev (1968–1972), David Elazar (1972–1975), and Mordechai Gur (1975–1978). During the 1948 war, Palmah battalions fought on all fronts (Galilee, central, and south) and played a critical role in defeating the Egyptians in the Negev. Of the more than 4,000 Israeli combatants killed in the war, approximately 1,000 were from the Palmah, about one-fifth of its ranks. Because of its strong ties to the leftist MAPAM party and the United Kibbutz movement, David Ben-Gurion viewed the Palmah with suspicion, and on 7 October 1948, it was formally dissolved as a separate military structure and was blended into the newly established IDF, which incorporated the Palmah's military tactics and professionalism.

Bibliography

Ben-Eliezer, Uri. *The Making of Israeli Militarism.* Bloomington: Indiana University Press, 1998.

Perlmutter, Amos. *Military and Politics in Israel: Nation-Building and Role Expansion.* New York: Praeger; London: Cass, 1969.

Van Creveld, Martin. *The Sword and the Olive: A Critical History of the Israeli Defense Force.* New York: Public Affairs, 1998.

AMOS PERLMUTTER
UPDATED BY PIERRE M. ATLAS

PALMERSTON, LORD HENRY JOHN TEMPLE

[1784–1865]

British statesman, diplomat, and prime minister whose policies in the Middle East curtailed Ottoman power in the mid-nineteenth century.

Henry John Temple was born at Westminster and died at Brocket Hall, England. At the death of his father in 1802, he became third Viscount Palmerston at age seventeen. Palmerston entered politics in 1806 as a member of the House of Commons and served in parliament for an unbroken fifty-nine years.

During his first twenty years in Commons, he did a competent job as secretary of war but held no cabinet rank. His first cabinet appointment was in 1828, during the prime ministership of the Duke of Wellington. In his subsequent distinguished career, Lord Palmerston was foreign secretary from 1830 to 1841 and 1846 to 1852, then prime minister from 1855 to 1858 and 1859 to 1865.

In the Middle East, Palmerston pursued an aggressive policy. When Muhammad Ali, viceroy of Egypt, attempted to seize control of the entire eastern Mediterranean coast, renouncing his fealty to the Ottoman sultan, Palmerston risked war with France (1839–1841), which had supported the viceroy and his son, Ibrahim Pasha, as they concentrated Egyptian troops in Syria. In the end, the French failed to assist their client. Britain bombarded Beirut and Acre, landed troops there, and gave a series of graded ultimatums to Muhammad Ali, offering him greater rewards for immediate retreat. The Egyptians, harboring false expectations of French aid, hesitated too long. The London Conference of 1840 and its follow-up in 1841, inspired by Palmerston, ended by depriving Muhammad Ali of Syria, Lebanon, Palestine, and the Sinai desert, leaving him only the consolatory title Hereditary Viceroy of Egypt. At those conferences, all the great world powers supported Palmerston by declaring that warships, except for small vessels in diplomatic service, were barred from passing the Straits of the Bosporus and Dardanelles while the Ottoman Empire was at peace. Even France, Muhammad Ali's former ally, supported the London Conference of 1841.

In 1850 Palmerston risked losing office when he sent the navy to bombard Piraeus after the Greek government had been desultory in paying damages to a British subject whose property had been destroyed in a riot. He emerged from the crisis enjoying the confidence of the British parliament, stronger and more popular than ever.

Even before Muhammad Ali's retreat from Syria, Palmerston had succeeded in persuading the Ottomans to allow foreign consuls to be stationed in Jerusalem and to allow foreign nationals to reside permanently in the holy city—something not previously tolerated. William Tanner Young, who opened the British consulate in 1838, had full capitulatory rights, including powers of life and death to judge British subjects in Ottoman Jerusalem who were under British law.

When Anthony Ashley Cooper, seventh earl of Shaftesbury, married Lady Palmerston's daughter by her first marriage, Palmerston found himself under personal pressure to back his stepson-in-law's evangelical Christianity. This chiefly meant giving strong support to English and German Protestant missions in Palestine. Jews were the largest single group at whom missionary efforts were directed, as it was illegal in Turkey to convert Muslims to Christianity. Thus, by 1847, Britain was prepared to extend consular protection to Russian and other stateless Jews whose visas had expired. For a brief period, Palmerston contemplated creating a Jewish commonwealth in Palestine, under British protection, but under Ottoman suzerainty. Even after abandoning that idea as premature, Palmerston continued to encourage Consul James Finn in Jerusalem to grant blanket protection not only to Jews without valid passports, but also to such native Ottoman subjects as Druze, Samaritans, and Armenians. He saw no contradiction between the acquisition of willing clients and the primary British goal of saving the Ottoman Empire from partition at the hands of the French or Russians. Because France had become the protector of Roman Catholics in the Middle East and Russia had become the protector of Orthodox Christians, Palmerston regarded it as merely an evening of the contest for Britain to become the protector of Palestinians who were not Catholic, Orthodox, or Muslim.

Palmerston was out of office in 1853 when Britain, France, and Russia blundered into the Crimean War. He became prime minister in 1855, in time to participate in the negotiation of the Treaty of Paris (1857), a settlement that ensured the total removal of all fortifications and warships from the Black Sea.

Throughout his career, Palmerston did everything possible to prevent France from sponsoring the construction of a canal at Suez because he feared that it would become still another source of conflict. He did not live to see the completion of the Suez Canal in 1869, and he certainly could not have predicted that by 1874 Britain would control the waterway. By July 1860 Palmerston was sufficiently comfortable with Napoléon III that Britain became a party to a treaty, negotiated at Paris, permitting France to send 6,000 troops to Lebanon to end the endemic strife there between the religious sects in that Ottoman province.

See also BRITAIN AND THE MIDDLE EAST UP TO 1914.

Bibliography

Bell, Herbert C. F. *Lord Palmerston*, 2 vols. Hamden, CT: Shoestring Press, 1966.

Conwell, Brian. *Regina v. Palmerston: The Correspondence between Queen Victoria and Her Foreign and Prime Minister, 1837–1865.* London: Evans Brothers, 1962.

Southgate, Donald. *"The Most English Minister . . .": The Policies and Politics of Palmerston.* New York: St. Martin's Press; London: Macmillan, 1966.

Webster, Charles. *The Foreign Policy of Palmerston, 1830–1841: Britain, the Liberal Movement, and the Eastern Question,* 2 vols. New York: Humanities Press, 1969.

ARNOLD BLUMBERG
UPDATED BY ERIC HOOGLUND

PALMYRA

Ancient city in an oasis of the northern Syrian desert at the site of present-day Tadmur.

The first mention of Tadmur (or Tamar, city of dates), Palmyra's ancient and modern name, goes back to the nineteenth century B.C.E. It was probably a Caananite town that later came under Aramaic influence. In the third century B.C.E., the city achieved international prominence when the Seleucids made it a transfer point of east-west trade. Through trade contacts, the city absorbed Hellenic culture and the Greek language, which was spoken alongside Aramaic, Arabic, Syriac, and other languages. From the time of the reign of Emperor Tiberius (14–37 C.E.), the city came under Roman control and was renamed Palmyra (city of palms). During the Pax Romana and with the benefit of paved Roman roads, the city's commercial fortunes expanded.

Palmyra's golden age was the third century C.E. Emperor Caracalla (211–217 C.E.) granted Palmyra the status of a Roman colony, exempting it from taxes. The city became the chief way station between Damascus and the Euphrates river. Goods came on caravans of camels from Rome, Egypt, India, the Persian Gulf, and from China along the silk route. Some Palmyran merchants owned ships that sailed the Indian Ocean. Palmyra's busy bazaars and ruling institutions were housed in fine Roman and Mesopotamian stone buildings with Corinthian colonnades, whose ruins remain in good condition today. Palmyra became the seat of the personal empire of Septimius Odaenathus, a member of a local Arab tribe, who gained the title Emperor of the East after saving the Roman Emperor Valerian in 260 from capture by the Sassanian king, Shahpur I.

From 267 to 272 C.E., the city was ruled by Queen Zenobia. Under her vigorous rule, Palmyra in 270 conquered Syria, Egypt, and Anatolia. Zenobia

An amphitheater that stands in the ancient Roman city of Palmyra. © CHRISTINE OSBORNE/CORBIS. REPRODUCED BY PERMISSION.

then declared the empire of Palmyra independent of Rome, but two years later, Roman Emperor Aurelian reconquered all the territory and plundered the city of Palmyra. Zenobia tried to flee by camel toward the Euphrates, but was captured and taken to Rome, where she lived the rest of her days. Palmyra was reduced from a capital to a small frontier city after the destruction caused by Aurelian's reconquest in 273.

Ancient Palmyrenes worshiped the deity Bol (also Baal or Bel) who presided over the movements of the stars. Bol's chief sanctuary, shared with the sun and moon gods Yarhibol and Algibol, still stands. Greek and Roman deities were incorporated into the local belief system. In the second century, the worship of a single unnamed god became important, and by 325, a Palmyra bishop attended the Nicaean Council.

In 634, Khalid ibn al-Walid conquered Palmyra and assimilated it into the expanding Muslim caliphate. The city was destroyed by an earthquake in 1089 and reportedly had a mere two thousand inhabitants in the twelfth century. After the city was sacked by Tamerlane at the end of the fourteenth century, it fell into ruins. In the seventeenth century, Fakhr al-Din of Lebanon used Palmyra as a military training ground and erected a castle on a hill nearby.

The city was first excavated in 1929, and restorations have continued since then. Today, Tadmur is a city of thirty thousand inhabitants, the site of tourist facilities and a prison.

Bibliography

Bulliet, Richard W. *The Camel and the Wheel.* New York: Columbia University Press, 1990.

Starcky, J., and Gawlikowski, M. *Palmyre,* revised edition. Paris: Librairie d'Amérique et d'Orient, 1985.

ELIZABETH THOMPSON

PAMIR MOUNTAINS

Afghan mountain range.

The Pamir mountains run north to south from Tajikistan to northern Pakistan, separating the Oxus drainage from the plains of Kashgar in China. In Afghanistan, the Pamirs extend through the Wakhan corridor, an area inhabited by Kirghiz nomads until the nomads were relocated to Turkey during the war of resistance (1978–1992). This area was annexed to Afghanistan in 1885 by the British, connecting Afghanistan to China so as to keep the British Empire of South Asia separate from the Russian Empire in Central Asia. Given their remote location and difficult terrain, the Pamir Mountains have been a choice place for hiding people or caches of weapons or other contraband. The area was annexed by the Soviet Union in 1980, then returned to Afghanistan when the Soviet Army withdrew a decade later. This corridor also provides a passage to China, albeit over a high and difficult terrain.

See also AFGHANISTAN: OVERVIEW.

Bibliography

Dupress, Louis. *Afghanistan*. Princeton, NJ: Princeton University Press, 1980.

GRANT FARR

PAN-ARABISM

Movement and doctrine for Arab political unity.

Pan-Arabism, the desire or drive for Arab political unity, was largely, albeit not entirely, a product of World War I, when much of the former Ottoman Empire was awarded to British or French mandates by the League of Nations. Arab attention in the ensuing two decades focused on obtaining political independence from European control as opposed to broader discussions of social reform or the adoption of a particular political system. In the process, budding Arab nationalism and vague formulations of Arab unity became increasingly interwoven with support for Palestinians in their opposition to Jewish land purchase and immigration under the British Mandate.

As the Arab leadership organized to resist foreign occupation, it fostered a debate over which elements of the Arab heritage could best be employed as symbols around which to shape the image of Arab states. Some Arab writers continued to assert the primacy of Islamic bonds while others, like the Syrian educator Sati al-Husari, rejected Islamic sentiments in favor of a unified Arab nation bound by ties of Arab culture. Emphasizing the secular components of the Arab heritage, al-Husari envisioned an Arab nation, unified politically, and similar to the nations of Europe.

As late as World War II, pan-Arabism in the sense of a political movement aimed at unifying the Arab nation remained centered on Iraq, Syria, and the Arabian peninsula. The Ba'th Party in the 1940s called for comprehensive Arab unity in the form of a single Arab state stretching from the Atlantic Ocean to the Persian Gulf. Neither Egypt nor the Maghrib, the western Islamic world traditionally comprising Algeria, Morocco, Tunisia, and later Libya, played a significant role in pan-Arab movements until after the end of the war.

In the 1950s Gamal Abdel Nasser and the United Arab Republic (UAR) coopted the pan-Arabism of the Ba'th Party. Nasser argued that the Arab nations enjoyed a unity of language, religion, history, and culture, which they should exploit to create their own system of cooperation and defense. The peak of both Nasser's popularity and pan-Arabism as a political movement occurred between the 1956 Suez crisis and the June 1967 Arab–Israeli war. The collapse of the UAR in 1961 followed by the Arab defeat in 1967 dealt a severe psychological blow to the prestige of Arab leaders and the confidence of the Arab people; it is considered by many to constitute the Waterloo of pan-Arabism.

Over the next two decades, only a few Arab governments, notably Muammar al-Qaddafi's Libya, continued to promote pan-Arabism in terms of practical political union. As other Arab states established themselves and began to define and pursue national interests, their commitment to pan-Arabism was increasingly perfunctory. By the end of the twentieth century, its time as a widely accepted doctrine and political movement had passed; and if pan-Arabism was not dead, it was surely a spent force. By the 1990s, Islamist political movements, inspired in part by the successful Iranian Revolution of 1979, were growing in popularity and strength throughout the Arab and Islamic worlds, often supplanting the earlier enthusiasm for pan-Arabism.

See also BA'TH, AL-; HUSARI, SATI AL-; NASSER, GAMAL ABDEL; QADDAFI, MUAMMAR AL-; UNITED ARAB REPUBLIC (UAR).

Bibliography

Antonius, George. *The Arab Awakening: The Story of the Arab National Movement.* New York: G. P. Putnam's Sons, 1946.

Dawisha, Adeed. *Arab Nationalism in the Twentieth Century: From Triumph to Despair.* Princeton, NJ: Princeton University Press, 2003.

Haim, Sylvia, ed. *Arab Nationalism: An Anthology.* Berkeley: University of California Press, 1962.

Hourani, Albert. *Arabic Thought in the Liberal Age, 1798–1939.* New York; London: Oxford University Press, 1970.

Khalidi, Rashid; Anderson, Lisa; Muhammad Muslih; et al., eds. *The Origins of Arab Nationalism.* New York: Columbia University Press, 1991.

RONALD BRUCE ST JOHN

PAN-SYRIANISM

See SYRIAN SOCIAL NATIONALIST PARTY

PAN-TURKISM

A movement advocating the union of Turkish peoples.

In the second half of the nineteenth century, Turkish-speaking Ottoman intellectuals became familiar with European cultural nationalism. The result was increased awareness of the origins of Turkish peoples, an enhanced consciousness of a distinct Turkish identity, and interest in Turks living outside the Ottoman Empire. Aided by the political interest the Ottoman sultans took in the Muslim Turks of central Asia under the onslaught of Russian imperialism, Turkish consciousness gradually became politicized and led to formulations for political unity of Turkish peoples.

Meanwhile, Eastern European scholars and nationalists fighting Russian expansionism stressed the Asian roots of their peoples and forged the notion of pan-Turanism. "Turan" refers to the Turkish-populated regions east of Iran and extending into the Ural and Altai mountains, also ancient homeland of Finns, Hungarians, and Mongolians. In strict terms "pan-Turanism" refers to a vague union of Ural-Altaic peoples. "Pan-Turkism," often used interchangeably with "Pan-Turanism," refers to a political union of Turkish peoples who in the nineteenth century lived within and beyond Turan.

Pan-Turkish ideas influenced Young Ottoman leaders (particularly Ali Suavi) and found systematic expression in a linguistic movement to simplify literary Turkish. From the 1880s on, Turks in Russia clung to pan-Turkish ideas to resist Russian cultural subjugation. The best-known propagandist was Ismail Gasprinski, a Tatar who published a journal called Interpreter. Emigrés from Russia propagated pan-Turkish ideas in the Ottoman realm. In 1904, Yusuf Akçura, a Kazan Turk educated in Constantinople (now Istanbul), wrote his influential *Three Kinds of Policy,* making a case for pan-Turkism against Ottomanism and Islamism. He also contributed to the foundation of cultural and literary Turkish societies, best known among them the Turkish Society and Turkish Hearth Association. Writers such as Halide Edip, Ömer Seyfettin, and Mehmet Emin Yurdakul joined Russian Turks (including Akçura, Ahmed Ağaoğlu, and Ali Hüseyinzade) in Turkish cultural activity.

In the Ottoman period, contrary to later nationalist contentions in the empire's successor states, pan-Turkism did not become the predominant ideology. Even in the thought of Turkists, such as Ziya Gökalp, Turkism could not be separated from Islamism or Ottomanism. As a political program pan-Turkism remained vague and marginal. Tekin Alp (Moise Cohen), a Jewish journalist, was an ardent propagandist. Pan-Turkish thought did promote nationalist consciousness among certain educated segments of Turks and, with the collapse of the Ottoman Empire, contributed to the crystallization of a Turkish nationalism limited in scope and restricted to Anatolia.

Pan-Turkism flourished at the end of World War I and until the consolidation of the Bolshevik state and the Turkish republic. The simultaneous collapse of the Russian and Ottoman empires stimulated fantastic, ill-conceived, and unrealistic schemes of unifying the Turks of Asia. Enver Paşa and Cemal Paça, who fled Istanbul at war's end, spent their lives in uncoordinated attempts to establish the great Turkish state. The Soviet governments discouraged and systematically undermined pan-Turkism in Central Asia.

Pan-Turkish sentiments briefly surged in Turkey during World War II with the aid of German propaganda and with the expectation that the Soviet Union would crumble. In the Republic of Turkey, pan-Turkish racialist ideas have inspired the ultranationalist right. A pan-Turkish political framework has not emerged as a realistic or popular scheme among the Turkish republics of central Asia since the breakup of the Soviet Union, while cultural and economic interchange among them and with Turkey has intensified.

See also ALI SUAVI; CEMAL PAŞA; ENVER PAŞA; OTTOMANISM.

Bibliography

Berkes, Niyazi. *The Development of Secularism in Turkey.* Montreal: McGill University Press, 1964; reprint, New York: Routledge, 1998.

Kushner, David. *The Rise of Turkish Nationalism, 1876–1908.* London: Cass, 1977.

Landau, Jacob M. *Pan-Turkism: From Irredentism to Cooperation,* 2d revised and updated edition. Bloomington: University of Indiana Press, 1995.

HASAN KAYALI

PARCHAM

Afghan Marxist political faction; also its newspaper.

Parcham (Banner), a faction of the People's Democratic Party of Afghanistan (PDPA), was founded in 1965 as a worker's revolutionary party dedicated to a Marxist revolution in Afghanistan. In 1967, the PDPA split into the Khalq (People's) faction and the Parcham faction. The split was in part the result of rivalries between the two leading personalities of the PDPA. Babrak Karmal was the leader of the Parcham faction, which attracted followers from the Persian-speaking Kabul intelligentsia; the Khalq faction had a predominantly rural and Pakhtun base.

In 1968, the Parcham faction published a newspaper also called *Parcham.* Published by Sulaiman

Layeq and edited by him and Mir Akbar Khaiber, it was closed by the parliament after only six editions for being "anti-Islamic."

In April 1978 the two factions of the PDPA united to stage a successful revolution and took over the government. The Parcham faction was soon purged, however, and its leaders were jailed or sent abroad as diplomats by late 1978. On 25 December 1979 a large Soviet airlift began; two days later a Parcham faction staged a coup with the help of the Soviet Union. Babrak Karmal returned to Kabul, and the Parchamis took over the government. The government of Karmal attempted to move the party toward an ideological center and denounced many of the reforms and actions of the Khalq faction. Karmal and President Najibullah, who succeeded him in 1986, attempted to undo most of the radical reforms of the Khalqis and announced a plan of national reconciliation. They even changed the name of the PDPA to the Hezb-e Watan (Homeland party) in 1989. These changes, however, were unsuccessful in convincing the Afghan mojahedin leaders to put a halt to the war of resistance. The Parcham government collapsed in 1992.

See also KARMAL, BABRAK; PEOPLE'S DEMOCRATIC PARTY OF AFGHANISTAN.

Bibliography

Adamec, Ludwig. *Historical Dictionary of Afghanistan,* 2d edition. Lanham, MD: Scarecrow Press, 1997.

Arnold, Anthony. *Afghanistan's Two Party Communism: Parcham and Khalq.* Stanford, CA: Hoover Institution Press, 1983.

GRANT FARR

PARIS PEACE SETTLEMENTS (1918–1923)

Post–World War I treaties and agreements that reconfigured the Middle East.

The defeat of the Ottoman Empire in 1918 led to its dissolution. In the long term the victorious Allies' partition of the Ottoman territories was less important than their introduction of a new system of political organization based on the European model of the nation-state. The modern Middle East was shaped physically and politically by the peace agreements. At the initial Paris Peace Conference in 1919 Britain and France, the victorious allies, were more concerned with adjusting their differences and harmonizing their territorial appetites than with a just and durable final settlement. Hence they agreed at the San Remo Conference in April 1920 to divide the former Arab provinces of the Ottoman Empire along the lines of the Sykes-Picot Agreement, with some minor modifications. France received the mandates for Syria and Lebanon, which the League of Nations confirmed in 1922. France waived its claims to Mosul in Iraq in exchange for shares in the Turkish Petroleum Company (later the Iraq Petroleum Company). Britain obtained mandates for Iraq, Transjordan (which it created in 1920), and Palestine. The Zionists succeeded at the Paris conference in convincing Britain to incorporate the Balfour Declaration into the preamble of the Palestine mandate.

To the Arab nationalists, the Paris conference was a political disaster; it sowed the seeds of future conflicts in the region. The victorious Allies initially tried to enforce a similar settlement on the defeated Ottoman government in the 1920 Treaty of Sèvres, which was designed to partition Turkey into very small, unviable segments. But unlike their Arab counterparts, the Turkish nationalists, led by Mustafa Kemal (Atatürk), successfully challenged the clauses of the Sèvres settlement related to Anatolia and Thrace, forcing the Allies, after a long, debilitating military campaign, to renegotiate a new settlement at Lausanne in July 1923. The Treaty of Lausanne confirmed Turkish sovereignty over the whole of Anatolia; the Sèvres clauses calling for an independent Armenia and an autonomous Kurdistan were forgotten.

See also ATATÜRK, MUSTAFA KEMAL; SÈVRES, TREATY OF (1920); SYKES–PICOT AGREEMENT (1916).

Bibliography

Hurewitz, J. C., ed. *The Middle East and North Africa in World Politics: A Documentary Record,* Vol. 2: *British-French Supremacy, 1914–1945.* New Haven, CT: Yale University Press, 1979.

Sachar, Howard M. *The Emergence of the Middle East, 1914–1924.* New York: Knopf, 1969.

FAWAZ A. GERGES
UPDATED BY ERIC HOOGLUND

PARIS, TREATY OF (1857)

Anglo-Iranian treaty that forced Iran out of Afghanistan and Muscat, 1857.

After Iran had tried to annex the Afghan city of Herat, British troops occupied Iran's Kharg Island and part of her mainland. Iran then signed this treaty, agreeing to withdraw from Afghanistan and relinquish Iranian claims to Herat, Afghanistan, and parts of Musqat in return for British withdrawal from Iran.

FARHAD SHIRZAD

PARLIAMENTARY DEMOCRATIC FRONT

The members of Kamal Jumblatt's parliamentary bloc in Lebanon.

The Parliamentary Democratic Front was a powerful political group in the 1972 Lebanese election, although it did not have a clear political agenda beyond loyalty to the political leadership of Kamal Jumblatt. It included members from various sects but was predominantly Druze-oriented, given the Druze basis of Jumblatt's leadership.

See also DRUZE; JUMBLATT, KAMAL.

Bibliography

AbuKhalil, As'ad. *Historical Dictionary of Lebanon.* Lanham, MD: Scarecrow Press, 1998.

AS'AD ABUKHALIL
UPDATED BY MICHAEL R. FISCHBACH

PARSIPUR, SHAHRNUSH
[1946–]

Iranian author.

Born and raised in Tehran, Shahrnush Parsipur graduated from Tehran University. Her first short stories (she writes in Persian) were published in the early 1970s. Her first book was the novel *Dog and the Long Winter* (1976). Riots, demonstrations, and the Iranian Revolution in 1978–1979 caused the shah and his family to leave. In 1979, the Islamic Republic of Iran was proclaimed, under the leadership of the Ayatollah Ruhollah Khomeini.

After two volumes of short stories, a second novel came out, *Tuba and the Meaning of Night* (1988), which Parsipur wrote after spending four years in prison for political reasons. In 1990, a slim volume of interconnected stories was published, *Women without Men,* which was banned by the Islamic republic, and her novel *Blue Reason* remained unavailable there as of the mid-1990s.

Parsipur, whose writings exhibit a woman-centered Iranian universe, stands as the leading figure in a fourth generation of Iranian women literary artists. The chief figure in the first generation was the traditionalist poet Parvin E'tesami (1907–1941); in the second, the prominent short-story writer and novelist Simin Daneshvar (born 1921); the third generation saw Iran's most famous woman writer, the poet Forugh Farrokhzad (c. 1934–1967).

Translations of Parsipur's stories appear in *Stories by Iranian Women since the Revolution* (1991) and *Stories from Iran: A Chicago Anthology* (1991). Her career receives treatment in Michael Hillman's *From Durham to Tehran* (1991). English translations of Parsipur's major writings were in print by 1992, when the author toured the United States and participated in the International Writer's Program at the University of Iowa.

See also LITERATURE: PERSIAN.

MICHAEL C. HILLMAN

PARTI DE L'AVANT-GARDE SOCIALISTE (PAGS)

Successor to the Algerian Communist Party.

Created in 1966, the Socialist Vanguard Party (PAGS) succeeded the Algerian Communist Party (PCA), which had been founded in 1936 and banned in November 1962. The PAGS renewed its political activities under Houari Boumédienne's regime (1965–1978). University graduates, students, unionists, and workers made up the majority of the party. PAGS provided support to Boumédienne's progressive agrarian and industrial policies and his anti-imperialist foreign policy. In the 1980s the Front de Libération Nationale (FLN) banned PAGS members from participation in state institutions or in the FLN's mass organizations. PAGS officially restarted its movement following Algeria's liberalization. In 1990 PAGS elected Hachemi Chérif as national coordinator. He succeeded Sadek Hadjerès, who had led the party since the 1950s. PAGS was renamed Ettahadi and later the Social and Democratic Movement (MDS) under the charismatic Chérif, who staunchly opposed Islamist ideology. Chérif contested Abdelaziz Bouteflika's disorderly economic liberalization, which resulted in massive unemployment because many state-owned enterprises were dismantled and sold to private owners without regard to the future of the employees. Chérif also disliked Bouteflika's cozy relationship with Islamists. MDS advocates a total break with the regime and calls for a secular democratic alliance that excludes Islamists whatever their degree of moderation.

See also BOUMÉDIENNE, HOUARI; BOUTEFLIKA, ABDELAZIZ; FRONT DE LIBÉRATION NATIONALE (FLN).

Bibliography

Zoubir, Yahia H. "Stalled Democratization of an Authoritarian Regime: The Case of Algeria." *Democratization* 2, no. 2 (1995): 109–139.

YAHIA ZOUBIR

PARTI DÉMOCRATIQUE CONSTITUTIONNEL (PDC)

Moroccan political party founded in 1937.

The Parti Démocratique Constitutionnel (PDC) was founded by Muhammad Hassan al-Wazzani (Ouezzani) as the result of a split with the Bloc d'Action National owing to personal differences between Allal al-Fasi and Wazzani, as well as disagreements over negotiating strategies with the French authorities. The PDC remained a small group, more of a political club than a party, centered on Wazzani's followers and friends. After World War II, it cooperated periodically with the Istiqlal Party and in 1953 and 1954 joined the National Front, which opposed the continuation of the French protectorate. In 1958, it merged with the Parti Démocratique de l'Indépendance (PDI); in 1963 it operated within the Front pour la Défense des Institutions Constitutionnelles (FDIC).

See also Fasi, Allal al-; Front pour la Défense des Institutions Constitutionelles (FDIC); Istiqlal Party: Morocco: Overview; Parti Démocratique de l'Indépendance (PDI); Wazzani, Muhammad Hassan al-.

Bruce Maddy-Weitzman

PARTI DÉMOCRATIQUE DE L'INDÉPENDANCE (PDI)

Political party in Morocco.

Formed after World War II by a splinter group originating in the Istiqlal Party and led by Muhammad Hassan al-Wazzani, the Parti Démocratique de l'Indépendance (PDI) briefly joined with the Istiqlal and the two nationalist parties in the Spanish zone in 1951 to form the short-lived Moroccan National Front. On its own again, and deriving its support mainly in the predominantly Berber tribal areas, it received six portfolios in the first representative Moroccan government, established in December 1955 after the sultan had returned from exile. Its only clear idea was uniting around the person of the king, as well as opposing the hegemony of the Istiqlal. In 1959, following the defection of a number of party leaders to the Union Nationale des Forces Populaires (UNFP), it renamed itself the Parti Démocratique Constitutionnel (PDC) and competed in the 1963 elections within the framework of the pro-palace Front pour la Défense des Institutions Constitutionelles (FDIC). In recent decades, the party competed in local and national elections with little success, winning no seats in the 1977 and 1984 parliamentary elections. In the 1993 parliamentary elections, again operating under the PDI banner, and headed by one of the original PDI founding members and ex-Moroccan diplomat Thami al-Wazzani, it experienced a revival of sorts, winning nine seats. In the 1997 elections, it dropped to just one seat; in the 2002 elections, it won two seats.

See also Front pour la Défense des Institutions Constitutionelles (FDIC); Istiqlal Party: Morocco; Morocco: Political Parties in; Parti Démocratique Constitutionnel (PDC); Union Nationale des Forces Populaires (UNFP); Wazzani, Muhammad Hassan al-.

Bruce Maddy-Weitzman

PARTI D'UNITÉ POPULAIRE (PUP)

Opposition political party in Tunisia.

The Parti d'Unité Populaire (Party of Popular Unity), one of the six legal opposition parties in Tunisia, was an offshoot of the Mouvement pour l'Unité Populaire (MUP) founded in Paris in 1973 by Ahmed Ben Salah. In 1981 a rift between the Paris-based group and its Tunisian branch was formalized with the creation of a second Movement of Popular Unity (often called MUP-II). In 1985 it was renamed the Parti d'Unité Populaire (PUP). In 1999 Mohamed Bel Haj Amor, PUP secretary general, entered the first presidential elections in Tunisia to allow more than one candidate but lost. In 2000 Amor was succeeded as the head of the PUP by Mohamed Bouchiha.

Bibliography

Murphy, Emma. *Economic and Political Change in Tunisia: From Bourguiba to Ben Ali.* New York: St. Martin's in association with University of Durham, 1999.

Matthew S. Gordon
Updated by Ana Torres-Garcia

PARTI DU PEUPLE ALGÉRIEN (PPA)

Algerian nationalist organization that used direct, often violent, action that led to the war of independence.

The Parti du Peuple Algérien (PPA; Party of the Algerian People) was founded early in 1937 by Messali al-Hadj, widely viewed as the father of the Algerian nationalist movement. An extension onto Algerian soil of the Etoile Nord-Africaine (ENA; Star of North Africa), whose constituency was principally among the émigré community in Paris, it was remarkably successful in mobilizing urban working classes, lower middle-class Algerians, as well as the sons of some of the more affluent Algerians behind the nationalist cause. Messali al-Hadj and five of the PPA's directors were imprisoned in August 1937, and the party itself was banned in September 1939. During World War II, it functioned underground at reduced levels both in Algeria and France.

In 1943, leaders of the party approved the drafting of the Manifesto of the Algerian Muslim People and the more radical *additif* that followed it. When, in March 1944, the moderate Ferhat Abbas decided to organize a coalition of forces called the Amis du Manifeste et de la Liberté (Friends of the Manifesto and of Liberty), members of the underground PPA flocked to it in such numbers that they eventually came to dominate it in all but name. It was PPA elements that helped turn the V-E Day celebrations of 8 May 1945 into a series of bloody confrontations between nationalists and the colonial authorities that are considered a direct precursor of the Algerian revolution.

When he was released from prison in 1946, Messali al-Hadj made an abrupt decision to reenter the political process by creating the Mouvement pour le Triomphe des Libertés Démocratiques (MTLD; Movement for the Triumph of Democratic Liberties) as a front for the outlawed PPA. From then on, until the war of independence, the MTLD ran candidates in most elections. But the PPA continued at a secret level in order to retain within the fold the growing group of militants who favored direct action. The party's detractors considered this dual approach one of its major weaknesses.

See also HADJ, MESSALI AL-; MANIFESTO OF THE ALGERIAN MUSLIM PEOPLE; MOUVEMENT POUR LE TRIOMPHE DES LIBERTÉS DÉMOCRATIQUES; STAR OF NORTH AFRICA.

Bibliography

Ruedy, John. *Modern Algeria: The Origins and Development of a Nation.* Bloomington: Indiana University Press, 1992.

JOHN RUEDY

PARTI NATIONAL

Moroccan political party.

Established in April 1937 by the bulk of Morocco's nationalist leadership (except Muhammad al-Wazzani and his followers) after the French authorities dissolved the Comité d'Action Marocaine (CAM), the Parti National, to show continuity with the CAM, located its headquarters in the same premises, in Fez. Organizationally, it was similar as well, consisting of an executive committee, a national council, local branches, and party cells. Its program was the implementation of a new French protectorate as a step toward full independence. It also campaigned against the power of rural chieftains, especially Glawi Pasha.

The French authorities cracked down on the party in the fall of 1937, arresting many of its leaders, most of whom were exiled. Nevertheless, clandestine party cells continued to function. Following his release in 1938, Ahmad Muhammad Lyazidi assumed leadership of the movement. In 1941, a reorganized supreme council was formed by Ahmad Maqwar and Lyazidi; the establishment of party branches followed the landing of Allied forces in 1942. Ahmad Balfarej was allowed to return from Paris in January 1943, and at the end of the year, together with the exiled Allal al-Fasi, reconstituted the party as the Istiqlal.

See also COMITÉ D'ACTION MAROCAINE (CAM); FASI, ALLAL AL-; ISTIQLAL PARTY: MOROCCO.

BRUCE MADDY-WEITZMAN

PARTI NATIONAL DÉMOCRATIQUE (PND)

Political party in Morocco.

Originally known as the Parti des Indépendants Démocrates, the PND was founded in 1981 by a breakaway faction of the Rassemblement National des Indépendants (RNI). Led by Muhammad Arsalane al-Jadidi and Abdel Hamid Kacemi, it included fifty-seven members of parliament and three cabinet ministers. The group represented large landowning interests who opposed International Monetary Fund recommendations to reduce credit to the agricultural sector, particularly the large commercial farms. Its numbers in parliament declined by more than half in the 1984 parliamentary elections, to twenty-four; it maintained this figure in the 1993 elections, when it ran as part of the pro-palace Entente (Wifaq) bloc. In a government reshuffle in January 1995 the PND received three cabinet posts. In the 1997 elections, it dropped to only ten seats and was left out of the new government. In the 2002 elections it attained twelve seats and remained outside of the government.

See also MOROCCO: POLITICAL PARTIES IN; RASSEMBLEMENT NATIONAL DES INDÉPENDANTS (RNI).

BRUCE MADDY-WEITZMAN

PARTI POPULAIRE SYRIEN (PPS)

See SYRIAN SOCIAL NATIONALIST PARTY

PARTITION PLANS (PALESTINE)

Plans for the territorial division of Palestine that attempted to reconcile the rival claims of the Jewish and Arab communities; first suggested in 1937 by Britain's Peel Commission.

Following the outbreak of the Arab rebellion in 1936, the British government, which had been granted the Palestinian mandate by the League of Nations, appointed Earl Peel to chair a royal commission. The commission learned that Jewish nationalism was as intense and self-centered as Arab nationalism, that both were growing forces, and that the gulf between them was widening. Partition was seen as the only method for dealing with the problem. In its final report (July 1937), the Peel Commission recommended that Palestine be partitioned into a small Jewish state; an Arab state to be united with Transjordan; and an area, including Jerusalem, to remain under a permanent British mandate. The Zionist leadership accepted the principle of partition and prepared to bargain over the details. But the Arab leadership refused to consider partition and reasserted its claims to the whole of Palestine. Although the Peel plan was not acted upon, the principle of partition guided all subsequent exercises in peacemaking (1937–1947).

On 29 November 1947, the United Nations (UN) General Assembly voted in favor of a resolution (no. 181) for replacing the British mandate with two independent states, thereby suggesting that the logic of partition had become inescapable. The UN partition resolution laid down a timetable for the termination of the British mandate and for the establishment of a Jewish state and an Arab state linked by economic union, along with an international regime for Jerusalem. An exceptionally long and winding border separated the Jewish state from the Arab one, with vulnerable crossing points to link three Jewish enclaves—one in eastern Galilee, one on the coastal plain, and one in the Negev. The Jewish state would also contain a substantial Arab minority within its borders.

Despite doubts about the viability of the state as proposed, the Zionist leadership accepted the UN partition plan. Local Arab leaders and the Arab states rejected it vehemently as illegal, immoral, and unworkable. To frustrate this partition, the Palestinian Arabs resorted to arms. The UN partition plan thus provided both an international charter of legitimacy for a Jewish state as well as the signal for the outbreak of war between Arabs and Jews in Palestine.

See also ARAB NATIONALISM; NATIONALISM; PALESTINE ARAB REVOLT (1936–1939); PEEL COMMISSION REPORT (1937).

Bibliography

Katz, Yossi. *Partner to Partition: The Jewish Agency's Partition Plan in the Mandate Era.* London and Portland, OR: Frank Cass, 1998.

Khalidi, Walid, ed. *From Haven to Conquest: Readings in Zionism and the Palestine Problem until 1948.* Beirut: Institute for Palestine Studies, 1971.

Segev, Tom. *One Palestine, Complete: Jews and Arabs under the Mandate,* translated by Haim Watzman. New York: Metropolitan Books, 2000.

Shlaim, Avi. *The Politics of Partition: King Abdullah, the Zionists, and Palestine, 1921–1951.* New York: Columbia University Press, 1990.

AVI SHLAIM

PASHA

See GLOSSARY

PATRIARCH

A leader in an Eastern Christian church.

By the fourth century C.E., the Christian church was divided into five administrative districts: Jerusalem, Antioch, Alexandria, Constantinople (now Istanbul), and Rome. Each of these was headed by a bishop called a patriarch. Today, "patriarch" is the title for the head of an Eastern Christian church, such as the Armenian patriarch or the Greek Orthodox patriarch (who still resides in Istanbul).

Bibliography

Deanesly, Margaret. *A History of the Medieval Church, 590–1500,* 9th edition. London: Methuen, 1969.

Shaw, Stanford J., and Shaw, Ezel Kural. *History of the Ottoman Empire and Modern Turkey,* Vol. 2: *Reform, Revolution,* and Republic: The Rise of Modern Turkey, 1808–1975. Cambridge, U.K., and New York: Cambridge University Press, 1977.

ZACHARY KARABELL

PATRIARCHS, TOMB OF THE

Ancient biblical shrine.

Located in Hebron in the West Bank, the Tomb of the Patriarchs (Cave of the Machpelah) is one of the most ancient biblical shrines. Among the most authentic sites, it is purported to be the burial place of Abraham and Sarah, Isaac and Rebecca, Jacob and Leah, and according to Jewish folklore, Adam and Eve as well. Viewed as one of the holiest shrines by both Jews and Muslims, it has been the focal point of persistent struggles between Palestinian and Jewish nationalists.

See also HEBRON.

CHAIM I. WAXMAN

PATRIOTIC UNION OF KURDISTAN (PUK)

Kurdish political party.

Established in 1977, the Patriotic Union of Kurdistan (PUK) advocated the self-determination of Iraqi Kurds through armed struggle. Led by Jalal Talabani, the PUK claims to be more leftist than the rival Democratic Party of Kurdistan (DPK). In 1987 the PUK put an end to ten years of internecine fighting and joined the Kurdistan Front of Iraq with the KDP and six other smaller organizations. After the Gulf War (1991) the PUK shared power with Mas'ud Barzani's DPK inside the Kurdish Autonomous Zone, in the parliament elected in May 1992, and in the Kurdish Regional Government formed in Irbil in July 1992. In May 1994 internecine fighting resumed and continued until the Washington Agreement of September 1998. The PUK formed its own government in Sulaymaniyya, and the Kurdish Autonomous Zone was de facto split into two regions. It took four more years to implement the Washington Agreement (1998) and to convene the Kurdish Parliament, which met again for the first time in full session on 4 October 2002. Both the DPK and the PUK approved a draft of Federal Constitution for the future Iraq.

See also DEMOCRATIC PARTY OF KURDISTAN (IRAQ); KURDISH AUTONOMOUS ZONE; TALABANI, JALAL.

Bibliography

McDowall, David. *A Modern History of the Kurds.* London: I. B. Tauris, 1996.

CHRIS KUTSCHERA

PEACE AND AMITY, TREATY OF (1805)

Treaty concluded in 1805 between the United States and Tripoli.

This treaty ended the conflict that began in 1801 when Yusuf Karamanli, pasha of Tripoli (in present-day Libya), closed the U.S. consulate, expelled the consul, and declared war on the United States. This conflict ended an uneasy peace in which the U.S. government paid an annual tribute of $18,000 in return for Tripoli's nonbelligerence vis-à-vis U.S. shipping in the Mediterranean. U.S.-Tripoli relations deteriorated in 1801 because Karamanli demanded $250,000 and the Americans refused to pay.

The treaty was concluded on 4 June 1805 and was ratified by the U.S. Senate on 12 April 1806. It was negotiated by Karamanli and Colonel Tobias Lear. The United States agreed to a one-time payment of $60,000 to secure the treaty and to ransom American prisoners of war. It also consented to abandon Derna (a provincial capital in eastern Libya occupied during the war) and not to supply its mercenary allies, who supported the pasha's brother, Ahmad Karamanli, in his claim to be the legitimate ruler of Tripoli. In return, Yusuf Karamanli agreed to release Ahmad's wife and children, whom he was holding hostage. A secret article (dated 5 June 1805), not revealed until 1807, granted Yusuf four years to release Ahmad's family, in return for the Americans' assurance that Ahmad not challenge Yusuf's legitimacy to rule Tripoli. In 1809, Yusuf permitted Ahmad to return to Tripoli as governor of Derna. But in 1811, he again felt threatened by Ahmad, who fled to Egypt.

Under terms of the treaty, prisoners were exchanged. On the American side, they consisted primarily of the 297-man crew of the U.S.S. *Philadelphia.*

Five Americans had died in captivity, and five chose to remain in Tripoli. One week after the Americans were freed, eighty-nine Tripolitan captives were returned, along with the $60,000.

The political and economic effects of the war undermined Yusuf's government. Disorder broke out in the early 1830s, encouraging the Ottoman Empire to reestablish its presence in Tripoli in 1835, thus bringing the Karamanli dynasty to an end.

Bibliography

Dearden, Seton. *A Nest of Corsairs: The Fighting Karamanlis of Tripoli.* London: J. Murray, 1976.

Irwin, Ray W. *The Diplomatic Relations of the United States with the Barbary Powers, 1776–1816.* Chapel Hill: University of North Carolina Press, 1931.

Kitzen, Michael L. S. *Tripoli and the United States at War: A History of American Relations with the Barbary States, 1785–1805.* Jefferson, NC: McFarland, 1993.

LARRY A. BARRIE

PEACE CORPS

U.S. volunteer agency whose goal is to help developing nations share American expertise and to enhance mutual understanding.

The Peace Corps was established by U.S. President John F. Kennedy on 1 March 1961 "to promote world peace and friendship" by providing developing nations with volunteer American personnel. It was hoped that, through daily contact with Americans doing development work, developing nations would better understand the people of the United States and that in turn Americans would better understand other peoples and their situations.

Since its inception, the Peace Corps has sent more than 170,000 American volunteers to over 136 developing countries, including the following countries in the Middle East: Bahrain, Iran, Jordan, Libya, Morocco, Oman, Tunisia, Turkey, and the Yemen Arab Republic. In all of these countries, Peace Corps volunteers were teachers, engineers, designers, and administrators of special programs.

In Iran from 1962 until 1976, Peace Corps volunteers founded kindergartens, taught English, built libraries, designed a new mosque in a Khorasan village after the old one was destroyed in a 1968 earthquake, and planned a college of dentistry in Mashhad. In Morocco, volunteers faced the challenge of learning both Arabic and French; they were employed in activities ranging from irrigation projects to teaching physical education in secondary schools. In addition to teaching, the Peace Corps in Tunisia supplied the Habib Thameur Hospital in Tunis with nurses. In Turkey, some of the over two hundred volunteers founded a home for street boys in Istanbul and others worked at the Middle East Technical University in Ankara. And in the former Yemen Arab Republic, Peace Corps volunteers helped construct a water-pumping station in Hodeida.

Though Peace Corps volunteers are sent only at the invitation of the host country, the program has not been without its critics. A problem that has plagued the Peace Corps in the Middle East and elsewhere has been the failure to train host-country counterparts to replace Peace Corps volunteers once their twenty-seven months of service have ended. Still, although the Peace Corps has not always succeeded as a development organization, its record has been more benign and its effects more beneficial than some other U.S. aid programs developed during the height of the Cold War.

The Peace Corps no longer had any volunteers in the Middle East in late 2003 but was planning to reinstate its programs in Jordan and Morocco in the spring of 2004. According to the Peace Corps Media Office, 68 volunteers served in Bahrain from 1974 to 1979; 1,748 served in Iran from 1962 to 1976; 227 served in Jordan from 1997 to 2003; 295 served in Libya from 1966 to 1969; 3,444 served in Morocco from 1963 to 2003; 160 served in Oman from 1973 to 1983; 2,130 served in Tunisia from 1962 to 1996; 1,460 served in Turkey from 1962 to 1972; and 564 served in North Yemen and, after unification in 1990, all of Yemen from 1973 to 1994.

Bibliography

Coates, Redmon. *Come As You Are: The Peace Corps Story.* San Diego, CA: Harcourt, Brace, Jovanovich, 1986.

Ridinger, Robert Marks. *The Peace Corps: An Annotated Bibliography.* Boston: G.K. Hall, 1989.

ZACHARY KARABELL
UPDATED BY CHRISTOPHER REED STONE

PEACE NOW

Israeli peace protest movement.

Peace Now, the oldest, largest, and at times most effective peace movement in Israel, was founded in the spring of 1978 by a group of reserve officers of the Israel Defense Forces who, in response to Egyptian President Anwar Sadat's dramatic November 1977 visit to Israel, wrote a collective letter to Prime Minister Menachem Begin, imploring him not to miss this opportunity to conclude peace with Egypt. The letter was followed by a number of large demonstrations in the streets of Tel Aviv and Jerusalem. Begin claimed that these demonstrations impressed him sufficiently to persist in his efforts to conclude the Israel-Egypt Peace Treaty the following year.

The Egyptian-Israeli agreements signed at Camp David in September 1978 provided also for further negotiations on the Palestinian question. When these negotiations, which became known as the "autonomy talks," failed—and in reaction to the massive increase of Jewish settlements in the occupied territories—Peace Now decided to focus on the struggle against the occupation in general. This decision put the movement in a direct clash with the Begin government, in opposition to the Israeli invasion of Lebanon in June 1982 and in protest against the involvement of Israeli forces in the massacre perpetrated by Lebanese Phalange militia in the Palestinian refugee camps of Sabra and Shatila in Beirut. The movement organized a number of massive demonstrations, the largest of which assembled over 250,000 demonstrators (some estimates reached 300,000 and 400,000) in the Tel Aviv Municipal Square.

The success of Peace Now in mobilizing sizable parts of the public against the war drew the attention of right-wing extremists, and Peace Now activists became targets of personal attack and abuse. On 10 February 1983, during a demonstration near the prime minister's office calling for the dismissal of Ariel Sharon as minister of defense, a hand grenade was thrown at the demonstrators, killing Peace Now activist Emil Grunzweig and wounding seven others.

Peace Now is not a membership organization. However, counting the number of signatures on recurrent petitions, financial contributions, and participation in demonstrations, the movement reached at its peak more than 200,000 supporters. In order to maintain is broad cross-party support, Peace Now has declined offers to become an established political party and run in Knesset elections. Nevertheless, a number of its leaders have become members of the Knesset and even cabinet ministers (such as Minster of Immigration Absorption Ya'el Tamir, Minister of Industry and Commerce Ran Cohen) while belonging to other parties.

Over the years Peace Now has also been heavily involved in dialogue with Palestinians on every level, from the top leadership to meetings of youth and students, as well as in local initiatives. Peace Now was also involved in defending Palestinians whose rights were encroached on by settlers, especially in Jerusalem, where a special litigation institution called Ir Shalem was established. The well-known human-rights watch group B'Tselem was also started by activists of Peace Now.

After 1993, when the Rabin government followed, through the Oslo process, policies long advocated by Peace Now, the movement seemed to lose much of its raison d'être. But the decay of the peace process after Rabin's assassination, during the tenures of Benjamin Netanyahu and Ehud Barak, revived the movement, whose activities were concentrated during this phase primarily on public monitoring of settlement activity. The outburst of the second Palestinian Intifada after the collapse of the Camp David negotiations in July 2000 left Peace Now discouraged, and reflected a general malaise of the Israeli left. Yet with the continuous financial support of its support organizations abroad it manages to continue its activities and even attract many younger people to the ranks of its leadership. Its most recent initiative was the creation of a broadly based Coalition for Peace in which a number of Palestinian activists, led by Sari Nusayba, the chancellor of al-Quds University in Jerusalem, became active as well.

Bibliography

Aronson, Geoffrey. *Israel, Palestinians and the Intifada: Creating Facts on the West Bank.* New York: Kegan Paul, 1990.

Bar-On, Mordechai. *In Pursuit of Peace: A History of the Israeli Peace Movement.* Washington, DC: U.S. Institute of Peace Press, 1996.

Fernea, Elizabeth Warnock, and Hocking, Mary Evelyn, eds. *The Struggle for Peace: Israelis and Palestinians.* Austin: University of Texas Press, 1992.

Kaminer, Reuven. *The Politics of Protest: The Israeli Peace Movement and the Palestinian Intifada.* Brighton, U.K.: Sussex Academic Press, 1996.

MORDECHAI BAR-ON

PEAKE, FREDERICK GERARD
[1886–1970]

British military officer in Transjordan.

A graduate of Sandhurst, the British Royal Military Academy, Peake served in India from 1908 to 1913. In September 1920, Captain Peake was sent to Transjordan to investigate the condition of the police and gendarmerie. He subsequently received permission to raise two small forces to maintain law and order. The first, the 100-man Mobile Force, guarded the Amman–Palestine road. The other, of fifty men, helped the British official posted in Karak. In April 1921, Peake was appointed one of Amir Abdullah I ibn Hussein's advisers. During the summers of 1921 and 1923, he organized the 150-man Reserve Mobile Force, which became the nucleus of the Arab Legion.

As a result of regional skirmishes, the Reserve Mobile Force was reorganized with 750 officers and men and given additional financing. The reorganized force thwarted Wahhabi raids in 1922 and the Adwan tribal rebellion in 1923.

In September 1923, all forces in Transjordan were merged with the Reserve Mobile Force, put under Peake's command, and renamed the Arab Legion. During the first three years of his command, Peake developed the Arab Legion into a highly effective force that accepted able-bodied volunteers from any Arab country, preferably men from villages and towns. John Bagot Glubb, who arrived in 1930 as Peake's second in command, created the Desert Mobile Force, composed mainly of bedouins, to shore up the Arab Legion, which had been weakened by the creation of the Transjordan Frontier Force in 1926. Peake retired in 1939 and was succeeded by Glubb.

See also ABDULLAH I IBN HUSSEIN; ARAB LEGION; GLUBB, JOHN BAGOT; TRANSJORDAN FRONTIER FORCE.

JENAB TUTUNJI

PEARL DIVING (BAHRAIN)

Before the 1930s, pearling was the major industry in the island nation of Bahrain.

Boats from Manama, Muharraq, al-Hidd, and other towns on the Bahrain coast set out for the main oyster banks in the Persian/Arabian Gulf, to the east of the islands, during a season that lasted from June through September. Representatives of the merchants who financed the operation often accompanied the pearl fishing fleet, purchasing the day's catch on the spot. Profits were distributed among the owners, pilots, divers, and crew at the end of the season according to shares drawn up in advance. Delays in payment and the vagaries of diving usually left divers and crew in perpetual debt to the merchants and captains. Since Bahrain was a British protectorate from 1880 to 1971, British officials attempted to remedy this state of affairs by promulgating a formal code for the industry in 1923, but the risks and hardships of pearling led most divers and crew to take up jobs in the new petroleum and construction sectors that opened in the early 1930s. Respectable fleets continued to set out from Bahrain as late as the mid-1940s, but by the end of World War II, the numbers dwindled so that only a handful of boats took part in the annual pearl harvest.

See also MANAMA; MUHARRAQ.

Bibliography

Rumaihi, Mohammed Ghanim al-. *Bahrain: A Study on Social and Political Changes since the First World War.* Kuwait: University of Kuwait, 1975.

FRED H. LAWSON

PEEL COMMISSION REPORT (1937)

Royal Commission Report that listed the causes of unrest between Arabs and Jews in mandated Palestine and recommended territorial partition.

During the Arab general strike, which began in April 1936, the British decided to send a high-level fact-finding commission to mandated Palestine. In May the colonial secretary stated that the Royal Commission would investigate the causes of unrest after order was restored, but it would not question the terms of the Mandate. After the strike ended in October, the commission sailed to Palestine, headed by William Robert Wellesley, the first earl Peel, former secretary of state for India. In Jerusalem the commission heard the testimony of sixty witnesses in public sessions and of fifty-three more witnesses in forty private sessions. In January 1937 the commissioners returned to London and heard two witnesses in a public session and eight witnesses (including Zionist leader Chaim Weizmann) during the course of seven *in camera* sessions.

The British government issued Command Paper 5479 on 7 July 1937. It concluded that the terms of the Mandate were unworkable and could only be enforced by repressing the Arab population. Both Arabs and Jews demanded political independence. Establishing an Arab state would violate the rights of the Jewish minority, but forming a Jewish state in the entire territory would violate the rights of the Arab majority and arouse international Arab and Muslim opposition. The only feasible solution was partition: two sovereign states? Arab and Jewish? with a British zone encompassing Jerusalem, Bethlehem, and a narrow corridor to the Mediterranean near Jaffa. Britain would temporarily control the strategic ports of Haifa and Aqaba. The Jewish state would cover about 25 percent of the country, north from Tel Aviv along the Mediterranean coast and all of Galilee. The Arab state would lie in the central mountains and the Negev, include Jaffa port, and merge with the Hashimite state in Transjordan.

The Jewish Agency accepted the principle of partition but criticized the proposed boundaries and insisted that all Palestinians be deported from the Jewish state at British expense—at that time, 300,000 Palestinians, a number equal to the Jewish residents in the area. The Palestinians' Arab Higher Committee denounced the plan and insisted that Palestine remain a unitary state because 70 percent of the population was Palestinian and 90 percent of the land was under Palestinian control. Palestinians in Galilee, whom the Jewish Agency wanted expelled, then played leading roles in the rebellion that erupted again in October 1937.

The Woodhead Commission, appointed to recommend partition borders, concluded in Command Paper 5854 (8 November 1938) that partition was not feasible and proposed limited zones of sovereignty within an economic federation. The government's Command Paper 5893 concluded "that the political, administrative and financial difficul-

ties involved in the proposal to create independent Arab and Jewish states inside Palestine are so great that this solution of the problem is impracticable" (*A Survey of Palestine*, vol. 1, p. 47). Maintaining a unitary Palestinian state was reaffirmed in the MacDonald White Paper of May 1939. But the partition idea, first broached by the Peel Commission Report, reemerged as the basis of the majority proposal approved by the United Nations General Assembly in November 1947.

Bibliography

Anglo-American Commission of Inquiry. *A Survey of Palestine*, vol. 1. Jerusalem: Anglo-American Commission of Inquiry, 1946. Reprint, Washington, DC: Institute for Palestine Studies, 1991.

Hurewitz, J. C. *The Struggle for Palestine.* New York: Schocken Books, 1976.

John, Robert, and Hadawi, Sami. *The Palestine Diary: Volume 1, 1914–1945.* New York: New World Press, 1970.

Morris, Benny. *Righteous Victims: A History of the Zionist–Arab Conflict, 1881–1999.* New York: Knopf, 1999.

ANN M. LESCH

PELED, MATTITYAHU
[1923–1995]

Israeli general, scholar, politician, and peace activist.

Born in Haifa, Mattityahu (Matti) Peled served in the Jewish underground military organization as a platoon commander in the Palmah (Haganah's "Crack Troops"). In 1946 he studied law in London. Peled returned to serve in the Arab-Israel War of 1948 as a company commander and was wounded while breaking through the Egyptian lines near al-Majdal. He served for more than twenty years as a career officer in the Israel Defense Force, holding different positions; among them was as the first military governor of the Gaza Strip and of Sharm al-Shaykh from 1956 to 1957. In 1957 he was appointed commander of the Jerusalem area. From 1961 to 1963 Peled studied Arabic literature and Middle East studies at Tel Aviv University. During the Arab-Israel War of June 1967 he served as quartermaster general, holding the rank of major general. In 1969 he retired from active service to complete his Ph.D. in the United States and was appointed lecturer in the Arabic Literature department of Tel Aviv University.

During the mid-1970s Peled became active in politics and joined the Israeli Council for Israeli-Palestinian Peace, which advocated recognition of the Palestine Liberation Organization (PLO) as the sole legitimate representative of the Palestinian people and the creation of a Palestinian state. During the late 1970s and early 1980s Peled was heavily involved in dialogue with Palestinian leaders, prominent among them Isam Sartawi, the PLO representative in Paris, as well as with senior European leaders (such as Bruno Kreisky, Pierre Mendès-France, and Willy Brandt). During 1983 and early 1984, together with a few colleagues from the Israel-Palestine Council, Peled met with Yasir Arafat three times in Tunis and Geneva, in defiance of Israeli law. In 1986 he was elected to the Knesset on behalf of the Progressive List for Peace, an Arab-Jewish party, and served one term (until 1986). Peled died of cancer in March 1995.

See also ARAB–ISRAEL WAR (1948); ARAB–ISRAEL WAR (1967); ARAFAT, YASIR; HAGANAH; KNESSET; PALESTINE LIBERATION ORGANIZATION (PLO); PALMAH; SARTAWI, ISSAM.

Bibliography

Bar-On, Mordechai. *In Pursuit of Peace: A History of the Israeli Peace Movement.* Washington, DC: United States Institute of Peace Press, 1996.

MORDECHAI BAR-ON

PELT, ADRIAN
[1892–1981]

United Nations commissioner for Libya.

In November 1949 the United Nations General Assembly called for the creation by January 1952 of an independent Libyan state, which would include the three historic regions of Cyrenaica, Tripolitania, and Fezzan. In December 1949 the General Assembly appointed Assistant Secretary-General Adrian Pelt UN commissioner for Libya, with a charter to assist the inhabitants of Libya in drawing up a constitution and establishing a state independent of British and French control. Pelt submitted a report to the General Assembly on 17 November 1950, calling for creation of a national assembly no later than 1 January 1951 and of a provisional government by 1 April 1951. Following the creation of the assembly and the proclamation of a Libyan constitution on 7 October 1951, the United Kingdom of Libya declared its independence on 24 December 1951. The most comprehensive and authoritative historical account of the independence of Libya under the auspices of the United Nations is found in Pelt's own book, *Libyan Independence and the United Nations.* Libya was the first African state to achieve independence from European rule and the first and only state created by the UN General Assembly.

See also LIBYA.

Bibliography

Pelt, Adrian. *Libyan Independence and the United Nations: A Case of Planned Decolonization.* New Haven, CT: Yale University Press, 1970.

St John, Ronald Bruce. *Libya and the United States: Two Centuries of Strife.* Philadelphia: University of Pennsylvania Press, 2002.

RONALD BRUCE ST JOHN

PEOPLE'S ASSEMBLY
Egyptian political body.

The dominance of the executive branch of Egypt's government is tempered slightly by a strong tradition of judicial independence. In contrast, the People's Assembly is constitutionally weak. Moreover, rigged elections regularly give the National Democratic Party, an extension of the government, overwhelming parliamentary majorities.

RAYMOND WILLIAM BAKER

PEOPLE'S DEMOCRATIC PARTY OF AFGHANISTAN
Afghan Marxist political party; also called Democratic Party of the People of Afghanistan.

The People's Democratic Party of Afghanistan (PDPA) was formed in the period of constitutional reform in Afghanistan (1963–1973) during which parliamentary elections were held and political parties were allowed to organize. It officially came into being on New Year's Day, 1965, at the home of Nur Mohammad Taraki. Taraki was the first secretary-general of the party's central committee, and Babrak Karmal was its first deputy secretary-general. Although its ideology, judging by the early literature, could be characterized as national democratic and progressive, later, after 1978, the PDPA became openly Marxist, with strong Leninist tendencies.

By 1965, the PDPA had split into two factions, each associated with the name of its newspaper: the Khalq (People) faction, led by Nur Mohammad Taraki and Hafizullah Amin, and the Parcham (Flag) faction, led by Babrak Karmal. The Khalq faction was dominated by Pashto-speaking Afghans from outside of Kabul and had strong ties to the military, whereas the Parcham faction was dominated by Persian-speaking Afghans from Kabul.

On 27 April 1978 the two factions of the PDPA united to stage a coup and take control of Afghanistan. In 1978 and 1979, the PDPA began to institute a series of radical social reforms dealing with land tenure, education, and women's rights. These reforms, coupled with the PDPA's strong antireligious and anticlerical position, proved too progressive for Afghans accustomed to the traditional social system, and by 1979 the Islamic opposition had begun to mount an aggressive guerrilla war against the government. On 23–24 December 1979, a large contingent of Soviet military forces entered Afghanistan and did not leave until 1989.

Calling itself a party of national socialism and having changed its name to Fatherland Party, the PDPA had by 1990 largely abandoned Marxism. It ruled Afghanistan until 1992, when its last president, Najibullah, resigned and Kabul was taken over by Islamic rebels.

See also AMIN, HAFIZULLAH; KARMAL, BABRAK; PARCHAM.

Bibliography

Hammond, Thomas T. *Red Flag over Afghanistan: The Communist Coup, the Soviet Invasion, and the Consequences.* Boulder, CO: Westview Press, 1984.

GRANT FARR

PEOPLE'S DEMOCRATIC REPUBLIC OF YEMEN

The name of South Yemen from late 1970 to May 1990, the first two decades of independence from Britain.

The People's Democratic Republic of Yemen (PDRY) spanned the twenty years between the constitution that ended the People's Democratic Republic of South Yemen and the unification of the two Yemens in May 1990. South Yemen had been created politically on 30 November 1967, when the victorious National Liberation Front (NLF) assumed power upon Britain's departure from Aden colony and the Aden protectorates. Britain had first occupied Aden in 1839. For the next century, Britain was preoccupied with the port of Aden, while neglecting the dozens or so states in the interior with which it signed treaties of protection only in the last quarter of the nineteenth century. As a consequence, no single political entity in modern times except the stillborn South Arabian Federation of the mid-1960s embraced even most of what was to become an independent South Yemen in late 1967. Instead, what existed was the 75-square-mile (194 sq km) Aden colony—a city-state, a partly modern urban enclave, and, by some measures, the world's second or third busiest port in the late 1950s—and the vast, mostly distant, politically fragmented interior states, which were, for the most part, based on subsistence agriculture and traditional sociocultural institutions. Neither the British administration nor the nationalists who first stirred in Aden in the 1940s had much knowledge of, interest in, or impact on these states, despite Britain's adoption of a new "forward policy" during the last decades of imperial rule. As a result, the people of Aden were closer, in more ways than just geographically, to the city of Ta'iz in North Yemen than to the Hadramawt, which lay far to the east of Aden and had its

Old Sultan's Palace located in Yemen's capital city, Seyun, is now a museum. © EARL & NAZIMA KOWALL/CORBIS. REPRODUCED BY PERMISSION.

View of Shibam, Yemen, in the desert valley of Hadhramawt. Hundreds of ancient, tower-like houses of up to nine stories high and built from clay can be seen from far away. UNESCO has declared it a protected world monument. © Earl & Nazima Kowall/Corbis. Reproduced by permission.

strongest business and familial ties with people in the Persian (Arabian) Gulf, India, Indonesia, and East Africa.

The infrastructure barely holding together the major settlement areas of South Yemen at independence in 1967 consisted of dirt tracks, unpaved roads, a number of airstrips, and the telegraph. The country consisted of many microeconomies, most of them agriculturally based and largely self-sufficient; isolated Wadi Hadramawt was an odd case, dependent as it was upon emigration to and remittances from the Gulf and Southeast Asia. What little market economy existed during the British period mostly centered on the port of Aden and its environs, and this in turn was plugged less into the surrounding states than into the international economic system via its sea-lanes. This fragile modern sector was dealt devastating blows near the time of independence when the blockage of the Suez Canal during the Arab–Israel War of 1967 nearly brought port activities to a halt, and Britain's rapid withdrawal ended both subsidies from London and the significant economic activity tied to the large British presence.

The history of South Yemen since independence is distinguished by five major periods: (1)

During the period of political takeover and consolidation (1967–1969), the NLF established control in Aden and over the interior at the same time that the party's balance of power passed from the nationalists led by Qahtan al-Shaʿbi to the party's left wing. (2) The long period of uneasy leftist coleadership of Salim Rabiyya Ali and Abd al-Fattah Ismaʿil (1969–1978) was distinguished by the efforts of these two rivals both to organize the country in terms of their versions of Marxist-Leninist "scientific socialism" and to align the country with the socialist camp and national liberation movements around the world. (3) The Ismaʿil interlude (1978–1980) began with the violent elimination of Salim Rabiyya Ali by Ismaʿil and was notable for the firm establishment of the Yemeni Socialist Party (YSP) and bitter conflict between a militant PDRY and the Yemen Arab Republic (YAR), the other Yemen. (4) During the era of Ali Nasir Muhammad (1980–1986), the consolidation of power in this single leader was paralleled by increasing moderation in both domestic affairs and external relations, especially with the YAR. (5) The final period of collective leadership and political weakness (1985–1990) began with the intraparty bloodbath that ousted Ali Nasir and otherwise decapitated the YSP. It ended with the merger with the YAR to form the Republic of Yemen. During the transition period that followed formal unification in May 1990, the YSP shared power with the ruling party of the YAR, the General People's Congress, under their respective leaders, Ali Salim al-Baydh and Ali Abdallah Salih.

Despite this pattern of bitter and sometimes lethal intraparty conflict, between 1967 and 1990 the PDRY regime did maintain rule and order throughout the country, made progress in bridging the gap between Aden and the rest of the country, pursued social goals with some success, and made good use of limited resources in efforts to develop a very poor country. Despite pressures toward fragmentation, especially urgings from Saudi Arabia that the Hadramawt go its separate way, South Yemen held together during difficult political and economic times. This was largely the result of political will, agitation, and organization. The gap between city and countryside remained a constant concern of the leadership, and progress was made in extending education, medical care, and other social services beyond Aden and the other urban centers. In addition, a campaign was waged to extend women's rights and other progressive ideas and institutions to the countryside. Great differences in wealth and property were eliminated, and the economy was organized along socialist lines, most notably in terms of a variety of agricultural and fishing collectives and cooperatives. In the end, however, the socialist experiment, short of time as well as money, failed; the discovery of of oil, in 1986, simply came several years too late. Moreover, there was nei ther time nor resources to push the modern ideas and institutions into the countryside where entrenched tradition prevailed. Nevertheless, the regime remained relatively committed, egalitarian, and free of corruption.

In many ways, the PDRY of the 1970s and 1980s, like Cuba, became both heavily dependent and a great burden upon the Soviet Union. The sudden collapse of the latter and its socialist bloc in the late 1980s left the PDRY weak and in isolation, shorn of fraternal and material support. This as much as the bloodbath that decapitated the YSP in early 1986 left South Yemen unable to resist North Yemen's call for unification in late 1989.

See also ALI NASIR MUHAMMAD AL-HASANI; ARAB–ISRAEL WAR (1967); BAYDH, ALI SALIM AL-; ISMAʿIL, ABD AL-FATTAH; SALIH, ALI ADULLAH; RABIYYA ALI, SALIM; WADI HADRAMAWT; YEMEN ARAB REPUBLIC; YEMENI SOCIALIST PARTY.

Bibliography

Auchterlonie, Paul, compiler. *Yemen.* Oxford, U.K., and Santa Barbara, CA: Clio Press, 1998.

Ismael, Tareq Y., and Ismael, Jacqueline S. *The People's Democratic Republic of Yemen: Politics, Economics, and Society; The Politics of Socialist Transformation.* London: F. Pinter; Boulder, CO: Lynn Rienner Publishers, 1986.

Long, David E., and Reich, Bernard, eds. *The Government and Politics of the Middle East and North Africa,* 4th edition. Boulder, CO, and Oxford: Westview, 2002.

ROBERT D. BURROWES

PEOPLE'S HOUSES

Institution founded on Atatürk's ideas, designed to strengthen Turkish culture among Turkey's people.

In Turkey, the Republican People's Party (RPP) established the People's Houses (*Halk Evleri*) in 1932,

during the single-party era. Party leaders' conceptualized the People's Houses as a multipurpose institution designed to strengthen Turkish national identity, promote Western scientific thought, and educate the masses in Kemalism—the six principles of republicanism, nationalism, populism, statism, secularism, and reformism—put forth by the first president of the Republic of Turkey, Mustafa Kemal Atatürk.

The People's Houses succeeded the Turkish Hearth Association (*Türk Ocağı*), having acquired the use of its property and its role as an institution of political indoctrination. But unlike the Turkish Hearth, which often promoted pan-Turkism and Islam, the People's Houses advanced secularism and confined their nationalist ideology to Turkey.

The RPP not only controlled the houses, but provided funds for their operation from the state budget. The RPP also held title in its own name to house property. The party central committee had authority to open houses in localities throughout the country. RPP by-laws required deputies to support the houses, and provincial RPP committees managed local house finances. The ministry of education strongly encouraged school administrators and teachers to join the houses and play an active role in their activities. The party provincial chairman appointed the house head; local party officials and teachers usually comprised each house's administrative board. Through direct supervision and frequent reporting requirements, national and local RPP leaders made certain that each house advanced party doctrine.

A house could have as many as nine activity sections: (1) language and literature, (2) fine arts, (3) library and publications, (4) history and museum, (5) drama, (6) sports, (7) social assistance, (8) educational classes, and (9) village development. House leaders encouraged teachers to research local Turkish history and culture and to write up their studies for the house's publication series. They also encouraged students to attend house functions and to use the house library. Hoping to make each house a focus of community activity, leaders invited local residents to utilize house facilities for their weddings, circumcision celebrations, and other special occasions. Despite these efforts, however, few houses became the friendly gathering places of the general public.

The RPP quickly established People's Houses in all of Turkey's provincial capitals and in many of its towns. In 1939, the party decided to extend the house's influence—by establishing People's Rooms (*Halk Odalari*) in small towns and villages. Each room was administratively attached to a local house. By 1950, there were 478 houses and 4,322 rooms spread over much of Turkey. Although house and room membership was open to all citizens, regardless of gender or class, most members were middle- and upper-class males. Of about 100,000 members in 1940, only 18,000 were women and some 27,000 were (male) farmers and workers. The remainder of the men and more than 17,000 of the women were government and party officials, teachers, and professionals. A majority of the workers were employed by state enterprises that encouraged their membership. Many, if not most, of the common people probably viewed the houses as alien institutions associated with the often oppressive RPP, dominated by the urban elite, and allied with antireligious forces. Some critics claimed, without solid foundation, that the People's House—concept had been inspired by the Soviet Union's *Narordi Dom* (People's House).

In the late 1940s, when the RPP allowed multiparty politics in Turkey, the opposition (Democrat Party, DP) openly resented the RPP's attempts at promoting their agendas through the People's Houses at public expense. Shortly after the Democrat Party came to power in the 1950 election, the RPP proposed to preserve the People's Houses as Atatürk's heritage, but to reorganize them in the light of Turkey's new multiparty political structure. The Democrats, who criticized the houses for closely identifying with the RPP—and for failing to serve all the people as originally intended—rejected the RPP proposal. The DP put an end to the houses in 1951 by confiscating the property they occupied, claiming it belonged to the state treasury.

Despite this ignoble end, many members of the RPP continued to regard the People's Houses as an admirable attempt by the political and intellectual elite to advance the Turkish nation along the path set by Atatürk.

See also ATATÜRK, MUSTAFA KEMAL; KEMALISM.

Bibliography

Karpat, Kemal H. "The People's Houses in Turkey: Establishment and Growth." *Middle East Journal* 17 (1963): 55–67.

PAUL J. MAGNARELLA

PEOPLE'S SOCIALIST PARTY

Yemeni political party.

Founded in 1962 by the Aden Trades Union Congress, the People's Socialist party (PSP) was led by Abdullah al-Asnaj (later an important participant in the politics of North Yemen as well). Modeling itself on the Labour Party, it supported political means to accomplish its goals of British withdrawal, independence, and union with North Yemen. Its unwillingness to use political violence to accomplish these objectives resulted in a loss of influence to the rival National Front.

Bibliography

Dresch, Paul. *A History of Modern Yemen.* Cambridge and New York: Cambridge University Press, 2000.

Halliday, Fred. *Revolution and Foreign Policy: The Case of South Yemen.* Cambridge and New York: Cambridge University Press, 1990.

Wenner, Manfred. *The Yemen Arab Republic: Development and Change in an Ancient Land.* Boulder, CO: Westview Press, 1991.

MANFRED W. WENNER

PERA

The most Europeanized district of Istanbul during the last century of Ottoman rule.

Pera (Beyoğlu) comprised the long ridge stretching north above Galata, and its slopes to east and west. Galata, the Genoese and Venetian port concession on the northern shore of the Golden Horn in Byzantine Constantinople, remained such in the Ottoman city but was subject to greater government control. Especially after the arrival of large numbers of western and northern European traders in the seventeenth century, Pera became the site of embassies and merchants' mansions. Its great age of prosperity, power, and prestige came in the second half of the nineteenth century, after trade liberalization and social Europeanization. With tremendous expansion of European trade, the Grande Rue de Pera flourished with shops, restaurants, hotels, banks, and office buildings in the latest European styles; it was populated by foreigners, local non-Muslims, and Muslims in the vanguard of Europeanization. In republican times, though Turkified and much less cosmopolitan, the area managed to maintain, somewhat diminished, its social, cultural, and commercial importance.

Bibliography

Çelik, Zeynep. *The Remaking of Istanbul: Portrait of an Ottoman City in the Nineteenth Century.* Berkeley: University of California Press, 1993.

I. METIN KUNT

PERES, SHIMON

[1923–]

Israeli politician, military leader, and cabinet member; prime minister, 1984–1986, 1995–1996.

Born Shimon Perski in Belorussia in 1923, Peres migrated to Palestine in 1934. In 1947, he joined the Haganah, which was then led by David Ben-Gurion, who became Peres's political mentor. He spent several years in Kibbutz Geva and Kibbutz Alumot. In 1948 Ben-Gurion appointed Peres, then twenty-five, to head Israel's navy. Peres subsequently studied politics and economics in the United States. In 1952 he was appointed deputy director-general of the Israeli Defense Ministry and served as director-general until 1959. As a leading Defense Ministry official, he participated in secret armament negotiations with the French prior to the Sinai campaign of 1956.

Peres advocated military aid (in addition to other aid and exchange programs) for the new states of Africa to help Israel develop influence there. In 1959 he was elected for the first time to the Knesset, and he and his ally Moshe Dayan argued for a change in government policy that shifted government emphasis from pioneering to enhancing state efficiency. From 1959 to 1965 Peres served as deputy defense minister. During this period he helped to develop a "special relationship" with France; he was also responsible for Israel's nuclear program.

Although being a protégé of David Ben-Gurion was advantageous in Peres's early career, it was dis-

Israeli foreign minister Shimon Peres, center, received the 1994 Nobel Peace Prize for his efforts to bring peace between Israel and the Palestinians. Peres shared the honor of the award with Israeli prime minister Yitzhak Rabin and Palestinian leader Yasir Arafat. © PHOTOGRAPH BY YA'ACOV SA'AR. GOVERNMENT PRESS OFFICE (GPO) OF ISRAEL. REPRODUCED BY PERMISSION.

advantageous later when Ben-Gurion's political capital within MAPAI decreased. In 1965 Peres left the Defense Ministry to help Ben-Gurion establish Rafi, a new party, and in 1967 he helped to negotiate a reconciliation between Rafi, MAPAI, and Ahdut ha-Avodah that resulted in the creation of the new Israeli Labor Party.

In 1969 Peres was appointed minister of immigrant absorption; from 1970 to 1974 he served as transport minister in the government of Golda Meir. During 1974 he was minister of information. Although he was one of the contenders to succeed Meir when she resigned in 1974, he lost the Labor leadership race to Yitzhak Rabin. The competition between Peres and Rabin for leadership of the Labor Party would continue until Rabin's assassination in 1995. In 1974 Peres was named defense minister, an office he held until the 1977 election, and he served briefly as acting prime minister in 1977 after Rabin's resignation. After gaining command of the Labor Party in 1977, he led it twice to defeats by Menachem Begin and the Likud Party (1977, 1981). According to many, his losses were due to the public's skepticism about his rapid change from defense hawk to dove in relation to dealing with the Palestinians.

In 1984 both major parties failed to win a majority of seats in the Knesset and a national unity government involving both the Labor and the Likud parties was formed. Shimon Peres served as prime minister and Yitzhak Shamir as foreign minister until 1986, whereupon they switched roles for the remainder of the term of the Knesset.

In the Knesset elections of 1992 the Labor Party recaptured power and Peres became foreign minister in the cabinet of Prime Minister Rabin. As foreign minister he negotiated the later stages of the Oslo Agreement and convinced Rabin to support it. In recognition of his efforts to achieve peace in the region Peres shared a Nobel Peace Prize with Rabin and Yasir Arafat of the Palestine Liberation Organization in October 1994.

Following Rabin's assassination in November 1995 Peres became prime minister for seven months until the elections of May 1996, when he again lost to the Likud, headed by Benyamin Netanyahu. A year later Peres resigned as chair of the Labor Party, and in June 1997 Ehud Barak, former chief of staff and member of the Knesset, was elected to chair the Labor Party.

Barak was elected prime minister in 1999, and Peres served as his minister of regional cooperation from July 1999 to March 2001. After the March 2001 election in which Barak lost to the Likud's Ariel Sharon, Peres was appointed minister of foreign affairs and deputy prime minister in the national unity government led by Sharon. In October 2002 Peres and other members of the Labor Party resigned from the Sharon government.

See also ARAB–ISRAEL WAR (1956); BARAK, EHUD; BEN-GURION, DAVID; NETANYAHU, BENJAMIN; OSLO ACCORD (1993); SHARON, ARIEL.

Bibliography

Golan, Matti. *The Road to Peace: A Biography of Shimon Peres.* New York: Warner Books, 1989.

Golan, Matti. *Shimon Peres: A Biography.* New York: St. Martin's, 1982.

Peres, Shimon. *David's Sling,* reprint edition. New York: Random House, 1995.

Peres, Shimon, and Landau, David. *Battling for Peace: A Memoir.* New York: Random House, 1995.

Peres, Shimon, and Littell, Robert. *For the Future of Israel.* Baltimore, MD: Johns Hopkins University Press, 1998.

Sachar, Howard M. *A History of Israel: From the Rise of Zionism to Our Time.* New York: Knopf, 1981.

GREGORY S. MAHLER

PÉREZ DE CUÉLLAR, JAVIER
[1920–]

Peruvian diplomat; United Nations secretary-general, 1982–1991.

Javier Pérez de Cuéllar received a law degree from the Catholic University in Lima in 1943. He joined Peru's ministry of foreign affairs in 1940 and the Peruvian diplomatic service in 1944; in 1946, he was a member of the Peruvian delegation to the inaugural session of the United Nations (UN) General Assembly. He later served as ambassador to Switzerland, the Soviet Union, Poland, and Venezuela. A scholar as well as a diplomat, he authored the *Manual de derecho diplomático* (Manual of diplomatic law) in 1964.

In 1971 Pérez de Cuéllar was appointed the permanent representative of Peru to the UN, where he served as president of the Group of 77 (1972) and president of the UN Security Council (1973–1974). He was appointed a special representative to UN Secretary-General Kurt Waldheim in 1975, successfully resolving the crisis in Cyprus. After a two-year stint as Peruvian ambassador to Venezuela, he returned to the UN in 1979 as an undersecretary for political affairs; in that position, he dealt with the aftermath of the Soviet invasion of Afghanistan.

In January 1982 Pérez de Cuéllar began the first of two successive terms as UN secretary-general. During his tenure, he negotiated the August 1988 cease fire that ended active hostilities in the Iran–Iraq War. He later led the UN in its confrontation with Iraq after the latter invaded Kuwait in August 1990. Under his leadership, UN peacekeeping forces were awarded the Nobel Peace Prize in 1989. After retiring from the post of UN secretary-general in 1991, he continued to serve in a variety of international organizations, notably the United Nations Educational, Scientific, and Cultural Organization (UNESCO) and the Inter-American Dialogue.

In 1995 Pérez de Cuéllar made an unsuccessful bid for the presidency of Peru. He later served as both prime minister and foreign minister in the interim Peruvian government of Valentín Paniagua (2000–2001). He was then appointed Peruvian ambassador to France. In the course of his career, Pérez de Cuéllar has been decorated by thirty-four countries and honored by more than fifty colleges and universities around the world.

See also UNITED NATIONS AND THE MIDDLE EAST.

Bibliography

Pérez de Cuéllar, Javier. *Pilgrimage for Peace: A Secretary General's Memoir.* New York: St. Martin's Press, 1997.

St John, Ronald Bruce. *The Foreign Policy of Peru.* Boulder, CO: Lynne Rienner, 1992.

BRYAN DAVES
UPDATED BY RONALD BRUCE ST JOHN

PERIM

Yemeni island in the Red Sea.

This small, barren volcanic island with a well-protected harbor is located in the Bab al-Mandab Straits at the lower end of the Red Sea, between Yemen and the coast of Africa at Djibouti, and theoretically should have some strategic value. Seized by the British occupiers of Aden in 1857, Perim (also Barim) Island was used as a coaling station by the British until the 1930s. The island became a part of South Yemen upon independence in 1967; with the unification of the two Yemens in 1990, it became a part of the Republic of Yemen. Despite the presence of a tiny garrison of South Yemeni troops through the 1980s and even rumors of the presence of Israeli observers, Perim was accorded no real strategic or economic significance during the late twentieth century, in contrast to Socotra Island in the Arabian Sea. A poor fishing village exists side by side with the rusting, collapsing remains of its more glorious days as a coaling station.

See also YEMEN; YEMEN CIVIL WAR.

Bibliography

Burrowes, Robert D. *Historical Dictionary of Yemen.* Lanham, MD: Scarecrow Press, 1995.

ROBERT D. BURROWES

PERMANENT MANDATES COMMISSION

Oversight body of the League of Nations.

The Geneva-based commission was established in 1919 under Article 22 of the Covenant of the League

of Nations to supervise the administration under the mandate system of fifteen mandated territories including four in the Middle East—France's Lebanon and Syria and Britain's Palestine and Iraq. It required annual reports from mandatory governments and advised the Council of the League of Nations on policy regarding the mandates. The Commission, however, exercised little supervisory authority, and three of the mandates in the Middle East—Lebanon, Syria, and Palestine—were generally run autonomously, much like colonies.

Most members of the commission were representatives of colonial powers: Great Britain, France, Italy, Portugal, Spain, Belgium, the Netherlands, Germany, and Japan. Only two members were noncolonial states: Switzerland and Norway. Citizens of the mandates could appeal to the commission but only through their mandatory high commissioner. The commission repeatedly rejected Palestinian Arabs' appeals for the right to self-determination and tolerated France's delays in granting autonomy to Syria and Lebanon. However, the commission granted independence to Iraq in 1932. The commission existed until 1946, when the United Nations replaced it with its Trusteeship Council as the Mandate System became the trusteeship system.

See also MANDATE SYSTEM.

Bibliography

Henkin, Louis, et al. *International Law: Cases and Materials,* 2d edition. St. Paul, MN: West Publishing Group, 1987.

Hurewitz, J. C. *The Struggle for Palestine.* New York: Schocken, 1976.

Lesch, Ann M. *Arab Politics in Palestine, 1917–1939: The Frustrations of a Nationalist Movement.* Ithaca, NY: Cornell University Press, 1979.

Moore, John Norton, ed. *The Arab–Israeli Conflict,* Vol. 3. Princeton, NJ: Princeton University Press, 1974.

ELIZABETH THOMPSON

PERSIAN

An Indo-European language related to English, Sanskrit, Kurdish, and Pashto.

Modern Persian arose about the ninth century C.E. It is the national language of Iran, Afghanistan, and

Tajikistan. It is known generally and in Iran as Farsi; in Afghanistan, as Dari; and in Tajikistan, as Tajiki. It has exerted great influence on the Indian subcontinent and in Ottoman Turkey.

Persian has twenty-three consonants and six vowels. It has two consonants lacking in English: *gh* (similar to the French *r*) and *kh* (similar to the *ch* in the German *Buch*). It lacks the *th* sounds (as in *thin* and *this*); the consonant *w*; the vowels in *bit, but,* and *put;* and syllable-initial consonant clusters (as in *strip*). It has neither gender, articles, nor number agreement.

Persian uses a slightly modified Arabic script, written from right to left (except for the numerals). There are seven diacriticals (three seldom used). Seven letters cannot join each other or any following letter. Under Soviet rule, Tajiki briefly used the Latin script, then switched to the Cyrillic. Since the dissolution of the Soviet Union, there has been a movement for the return to the Arabic script. The Persian script's main features are inconsistent representation of certain vowels and alternative spellings of some consonants and vowels. These and other features, causing problems in reading and writing, have since the nineteenth century led some Iranians to advocate the adoption of Latin or some other script.

Persian has changed little in the last thousand years or so: a person who knows Persian can understand tenth-century Persian (except for a few words and phrases). Persian includes an extensive Arabic element, the language of Islam, and was for a time the language of science and scholarship for all Muslims. There are also a number of Turkish and Mongolian loanwords, reflecting Turkish and Mongol rule in Iran. Growing contacts with Europe since the nineteenth century have led to extensive borrowings from French and, since World War II, from English. Greek, Aramaic, and Indian languages also account for a few words. In its turn, Persian is the source of some words in Arabic, large numbers in Turkish and Urdu, and smaller numbers in Western and other languages. Most of these words have found their way into Western languages through classical Greek, Latin, Arabic, and Spanish (for example, the English *tulip, narcissus, khaki, orange, sugar, julep, jasmine, pajamas, magic, arsenic,* and *cushy,* and the names Cyrus and Roxanne).

Bibliography

Jazayery, Mohammad Ali. "Western Loanwords in Persian, with Reference to Westernization." *Islamic Culture* 40 (1966):207–220 and 41 (1967):1–19. London: K. Paul, 1935.

Windfuhr, Gernot L. "Persian." In *The World's Major Languages,* edited by Bernard Comrie. New York: Oxford University Press, 1987.

M. A. JAZAYERY

PERSIAN (ARABIAN) GULF

Arm of the Gulf of Oman and Indian Ocean.

The Persian Gulf is a shallow body of water between the Arabian Peninsula and Iran; it is more than 500 miles long and as wide as 200 miles. Fed on the northwestern end by the confluence of the Tigris and Euphrates rivers (called the Shatt al-Arab), the gulf drains to the southeast through the Strait of Hormuz into the Gulf of Oman and the Indian Ocean. Its maximum depth is only 328 feet. There are numerous islands in the gulf, Bahrain and Qeshm being the largest ones.

Since antiquity the gulf has been a major trade and marine route between East Africa and South Asia. In the nineteenth century British commercial interests supported British military intervention in the gulf. Consequently, all the Arabian Peninsula coastal principalities were forced to conclude protectorate treaties with Britain, while British commercial and naval influence progressively increased in the ports along the Iranian coast of the gulf. In addition to the gulf's economic significance derived from trade and pearling, the British perceived the waterway as having strategic importance as a gateway to their imperial possessions in India. The early-twentieth-century discovery of petroleum deposits throughout the coastal region and even in the seabed of the gulf further enhanced its increasingly intertwined economic and strategic values. By the 1970s and into the twenty-first century, more than 80 percent of Middle East oil exports passed through the gulf. Inevitably, its waters became polluted by oil spills that harmed the local fishing industry and threatened rare sea mammals and other aquatic life.

See also BAHRAIN; PETROLEUM, OIL, AND NATURAL GAS; SHATT AL-ARAB.

Bibliography

Schofield, Richard, ed. *Territorial Foundations of the Gulf States.* London: UCL Press, 1994.

Sick, Gary, and Potter, Lawrence, eds. *The Persian Gulf at the Millennium.* New York: St. Martin's Press, 1997.

ELIZABETH THOMPSON
UPDATED BY ERIC HOOGLUND

PERSIAN CATS

Long-haired cats that were exported from Iran in the nineteenth and early twentieth centuries.

The Persian cat is a stocky domesticated feline with long, silky hair, a large, round face, small ears, and a bushy tail. It is called "Persian" because it was exported from Iran, or ancient Persia. The cat, known as *buraq* in Persian, was first described by European travelers, who observed that some Safavi dynasty princes and high government officials kept the cat as a house pet in seventeenth-century Isfahan, then the capital of Iran. Even though the cat has long been associated with Iran, its exact origins remain unclear. The Kurdistan region of southeastern Turkey, the central plateau area of Iran, and the Bukhara district in modern Uzbekistan all have been cited as probable places of origin. During the nineteenth century, however, the Isfahan region of Iran was the major source for the export of Persian cats to Europe and India. Wealthy Iranians kept them—as well as more common short-haired cats—as pets. Nasir al-Din Shah Qajar (r. 1848–1896) had a reputation for adoring and keeping cats, and his favorite Persian cat, Badri Khan, was assigned human attendants to care for him in royal fashion.

In Europe, the keeping of cats as house pets became common only during the eighteenth century, but by the nineteenth century Europeans who could afford to do so were purchasing cats imported from Iran and the Ottoman Empire. The Persian cat became especially popular beginning in 1871 when Britain's Queen Victoria bought a pair of imported Persian cats at London's first Oriental cat fair. Thereafter, the keeping of Persian cats as desirable—and valuable—house pets spread from England to Europe and North America. The domestic breeding of Persian cats in all the aforementioned places gradually eliminated the need to import them. Although the export of Persian cats from Iran con-

Persian cats were first exported from Iran in the nineteenth and early twentieth centuries. Though long associated with Iran, the Persian cat's origins may actually be from elsewhere in the surrounding region. COURTESY OF PHILIP MATTAR.

tinued during the first decade of the twentieth century, the practice ceased after 1912.

Bibliography

Floor, Willem. "A Note on Persian Cats." *Iranian Studies* 36, no. 1 (March 2003): 27–42.

ERIC HOOGLUND

PERSIAN SCRIPT

Modified Arabic alphabet used for writing Persian.

As a result of Arab expansion, the Middle Persian, or Pahlavi, script (developed from Aramaic) was replaced by the Arabic script during the ninth century. Despite changes in vocabulary and in the script, the Persian language has remained largely intact for centuries. The Persian script, while mainly the same as modern Arabic, contains changes, such as extra markings on the Arabic *ba* (Roman B) to create the Persian *pe* (Roman P), on the Arabic *ghayn* (Roman Gh) to create a Persian *che* (Roman Ch) and on the Arabic *ra* (Roman R) to create the Persian *zhe* (Roman Zh), none of which exist in Arabic. Arabic calligraphy, primarily used to write the Qu'ran, also changed as a result of Persian influence. The Arab styles of *taliq* and *naskh* combined to form the Persian *nastaliq* style. From *nastaliq* comes *shekasteh*, broken script allowing greater speed; with *shifih* the letters are farther apart but conjoined in a "lover's embrace." Persian calligraphy was not confined to the Qu'ran, and became most popular during medieval times through Persian court and mystical poetry.

See also ARABIC; ARABIC SCRIPT; PERSIAN.

Bibliography

"Persian." Omniglot: A Guide to Writing Systems. Available from <http://www.omniglot.com>.

ROXANNE VARZI

PESH MERGA

See GLOSSARY

PETAH TIKVAH

First new Jewish settlement in Eretz Yisrael in the modern era.

Located several miles east of Tel Aviv, Petah Tikvah (also, Petah Tiqva) was founded in 1878 by a group of religious Jews from Jerusalem led by Rabbi Yoel Salomon, David Gutman, and Yehoshua Stampfer, who were active in the goal of redeeming land and liberating the Jewish community in Palestine from the yoke of the Halukka. Petah Tikvah was the first colony founded.

In its first decade, the community was beset with problems: malaria, insecurity, complicated disputes with Arabs living on adjacent lands, and financial shortages. Some of the settlers received financial aid from the Hibbat Zion movement and, eventually, substantial support from Baron Edmond de Rothschild.

When the State of Israel was founded in 1948, the population of Petah Tikvah was about 20,000. By 2000 its population had grown to more than 200,000. Especially because of the land shortage, the city has an increasing number of high-rise buildings.

See also HALUKKA; HIBBAT ZION; ROTHSCHILD, EDMOND DE.

Bibliography

Gvati, Chaim. *A Hundred Years of Settlement: The Story of Jewish Settlement in the Land of Israel.* Jerusalem: Keter, 1985.

CHAIM I. WAXMAN

PETER VII

109th Coptic patriarch of Egypt (1809–1852).

Originally chosen by Mark VIII (1796–1809) as *abuna* (archbishop) of the Ethiopian Orthodox Church, Peter instead became an important bishop close to the patriarch and eventually succeeded him. Peter was a thrifty and judicious administrator whose wise handling of accounts created a fortune that made possible the reforms of his successor, Cyril IV (1854–1861). Peter assembled part of the patriarchal library in Cairo and had new copies of important treatises made from old versions, sometimes participating in the task. He wrote theological treatises clarifying the Coptic Church's position on Communion and Christ's nature. Peter's good relations with the viceroy of Egypt became legendary. In particular, Peter won great favor with Muhammad Ali when he refused an offer from the Russian czar to put the Coptic Orthodox Church under his protection.

See also COPTS; CYRIL IV; MARK VIII.

DONALD SPANEL

PETRA

Ancient city carved from the cliffs in today's Jordan.

In about 500 B.C.E., the Nabatean Arabs established a presence in the region east of the great Jordan–Dead Sea rift. They built their capital and trading center at Petra, in southern Jordan, close to the Wadi Araba and adjacent to the contemporary village of Wadi Musa. In its location and appearance, Petra is a unique city. The only easy access is through a half-mile-long (1 km) narrow passage called the *siq*. At its terminus is the treasury, a large edifice carved into the rock of the rose-colored cliffs. This vista is repeated with additional buildings as well as with simple houses hewed within the stone precipices of the ancient city. They include a huge monastery, a palace, tombs, and an amphitheater, most of which were crafted in a modified Greco–Roman style. For tourism, Petra is one of Jordan's most important archaeological sites and attractions.

Bibliography

Harding, G. Lankester. *The Antiquities of Jordan,* revised edition. New York: Praeger, 1967.

PETER GUBSER

PETROCHEMICALS

Chemicals isolated or derived from petroleum or natural gas.

Petrochemicals include industrial and agricultural chemicals synthesized from refinery products, gases, and natural gas. Research into manufacturing processes was stimulated by the availability of raw materials (most of which would otherwise be waste products) and by foreign demand. The global petrochemicals industry remained relatively small until World War II, when the United States concentrated government investment in petrochemicals into a few large, privately owned plants and in newly constructed state-owned facilities operated by experienced firms. This huge investment in petrochemicals during the war left the U.S. industry in a dominant position for many years, making it very difficult for the national oil companies (NOCs) of Middle Eastern countries to compete. Before the nationalization of their oil industries, the NOCs were hindered by the operating companies' reluctance to supply enough raw materials and process technology to make the NOCs' local ventures competitive internationally. Exports were necessary because Middle Eastern domestic markets for petrochemicals were small. Another disadvantage grew out of the inability of the NOCs to conduct state-of-the-art research on process technology or to fabricate locally the equipment needed to establish and retain a position on the cutting edge of the industry.

These drawbacks decreased in importance after oil prices rose in the early 1970s. Increased costs of drilling for raw material in oil fields gave the NOCs a comparative advantage. Also helpful was the rise in importance of a third class of firms involved in petrochemicals: international contracting firms such as Fluor, Foster Wheeler, and Chiyoda, which were able to design and construct state-of-the-art turnkey facilities and associated infrastructure. During the 1970s and after, Middle Eastern oil-exporting countries found it relatively easy to acquire petrochemicals facilities tailored to their needs.

Persian (Arabian) Gulf petrochemical producers have increased their market share of world petrochemicals from almost 0 percent in 1980 to about 10 percent in 2002. The cost of the feedstock (the raw material, i.e. natural gas or refined oil products) can account for between 40 percent and 70 percent of the final chemical product. Hence the Gulf producers of oil and gas with raw material costs of between $0.50 and $2.00 per barrel of oil have a natural advantage. As a consequence, the large petrochemical manufacturers in the Gulf have taken most of the increase in demand due to the growth of the Far Eastern economies. As of mid-2002, the Gulf countries—mainly Saudi Arabia, Iran, Kuwait, and Qatar—produced a total of 58 million tons of petrochemicals and had plans to start a further 57 million tons within the next five years.

See also NATURAL GAS: ECONOMIC EXPLOITATION OF; PETROLEUM, OIL, AND NATURAL GAS; PETROLEUM RESERVES AND PRODUCTION.

Bibliography

Chapman, Keith. *The International Petrochemical Industry: Evolution and Location.* Oxford: Blackwell, 1991.

Tétreault, Mary Ann. *The Kuwait Petroleum Corporation and the Economics of the New World Order.* Westport, CT: Quorum Books, 1995.

MARY ANN TÉTREAULT
UPDATED BY JEAN-FRANÇOIS SEZNEC

PETROLEUM, OIL, AND NATURAL GAS

Naturally occurring hydrocarbon compounds.

The petroleum industry in the Middle East dates to 3000 B.C.E., when Mesopotamians exploited asphaltic bitumen obtained from seepages and rock asphalt mining to produce construction mortar, mosaic cement, road surfacing, and waterproofing materials. This form of petroleum, called pitch, is the residue left after natural gas and volatile liquid fractions have evaporated from crude oil. Ancient Bahrainis coated pottery and baskets with pitch, and in the biblical story of Noah it is used to caulk the ark. An industry distilling lamp fuel from crude oil began in Alexandria about the second century C.E. About five hundred years later, Byzantine armies began to use "Greek fire," a napalmlike substance distilled from crude oil that was poured or sprayed on enemy troops and ships, and then set afire.

The Modern Oil Industry

The modern oil industry is far more complex and integrated, a continuous process that pivots on the extraction, or production, of petroleum and natural gas from the earth. Upstream from production are exploration (the search for oil-bearing lands), and development (the construction of production infrastructure such as oil wells and natural gas separators in oil fields). Downstream from production are transportation (including pipelines, tankers, trucks, and railroads), refining (turning crude oil into usable products), and marketing (gasoline stations and other outlets). Petroleum and natural gas are both fuel sources as well as the raw material from which petrochemicals, such as fertilizers and the building blocks of plastics, are manufactured.

Looking at the oil industry as a global system lets us identify its choke points, the stages where a powerful firm or government can exert political and economic leverage on the entire process. One potential choke point concerns petroleum reserves and production. In the nations of the Middle East, as in most other nations, mineral rights belong to the state. Firms must negotiate with governments for concessions, or rights, to extract hydrocarbons on their territories. In exchange, they offer lump-sum payments, rents, taxes, and/or royalties (payments per unit of oil or gas produced).

The One Company/One Country Pattern

Before World War II, Middle Eastern countries competed for investment from international oil companies (IOCs). The largest IOCs were more fearful of an oil glut, which would depress prices, than of shortages, which would inconvenience consumers. Under the 1928 Red Line Agreement, the partners in the Iraq Petroleum Company agreed that none of them would explore for or develop new oil in the former Ottoman Empire unless every partner consented to each new project. Countries inside the Red Line had difficulty getting the IOCs to find or develop the oil that could have increased their national incomes because the largest—and richest—Red Line companies were reluctant to add to already excessive oil production capacity.

Oil partnerships and concession patterns also limited the leverage of Middle Eastern governments. Instead of one government hosting several firms that operated on various parts of its territory, the initial pattern of oil industry development in the region was to have a single operating company, often a joint venture or partnership, as the only oil producer in each country. Joint ventures are common in the oil industry because of its capital intensity and high risk. Individual parent companies like Gulf (now part of Chevron) and the Anglo-Persian Oil Company (later Anglo-Iranian Oil Company, then British Petroleum, and now BP Amoco), set up jointly owned operating companies such as the Kuwait Oil Company (KOC) to pool financial resources and risk. Although two separate parents invested in and profited from Kuwait's oil, their business in Kuwait was conducted by a single company, KOC. Such partnerships also offered the IOCs some control over total world oil supplies. They made sharing production information easier (especially for U.S. companies, which were constrained by antitrust laws), dampened competition among partners, and provided a protected environment in which the large IOCs could coordinate their global operations.

Kuwait's ability to choose a concession partner was limited by treaties between its ruler and the British government, which gave Britain the final authority to approve concession agreements. Britain would not allow Kuwait to contract with a non-British company, although Kuwait eventually persuaded Britain to accept a non-British firm as a partner in KOC. The concession further limited

Kuwait's autonomy by giving KOC exclusive rights for ninety years to find and produce oil over the entire land area of Kuwait. Had Kuwait sought better terms from another company during that time, that company would have faced legal challenges from KOC's parents, preventing it from selling Kuwaiti oil in the international market.

Kuwaiti autonomy also was limited by the threat of direct intervention by one or both home governments of KOC's parents, Britain and the United States. In the early 1950s, Iran found itself in exactly this situation. In 1951, the Iranian government under Prime Minister Mohammad Mossadegh nationalized the operations of Iran's oil company following a conflict with its managers. The owner of the oldest oil production facilities in the Middle East, Iran's operating company had only one parent, the Anglo-Iranian Oil Company (AIOC). AIOC obtained court orders enjoining other companies from buying Iranian oil.

Afraid of the example that a successful nationalization might provide to other Middle Eastern governments, the British and American governments worked to destabilize and eventually to overthrow the Mossadegh regime. The restoration of the shah, Mohammad Reza Pahlavi, in 1953, following a brief period of ouster, also reinstated foreign oil companies as managers of the nationalized Iranian oil company. Rather than restoring AIOC to its former position as sole owner, however, the Iranian government sought a "Kuwait solution" and invited non-British participation in the National Iranian Oil Company (NIOC). When NIOC was reorganized, American companies and the French national oil company received 60 percent of the shares, leaving AIOC with only 40 percent.

The one company/one country concession pattern allowed oil companies to treat one or more Middle Eastern host countries as marginal suppliers of oil to the international market despite the cost advantages of their oil over what could be obtained from most other sources. This balancing act was possible because all the major companies whose production holdings stretched across the Middle East were partners in two or more concessions. The way the Iranian crisis was resolved in the 1950s made the management of crude oil supply by the IOCs even easier. The reorganized NIOC was the first op-

An Iranian oil worker at an oil refinery in Iran's capital city, Tehran. Iran's rich petroleum reserve is a major source of revenue for the country; however, as a result, the country struggles with severe air pollution problems. © AP/WIDE WORLD PHOTOS. REPRODUCED BY PERMISSION.

erating consortium in the Middle East to include all of the Seven Sisters—the IOCs dominating the industry from the end of World War II until the oil revolution. Once these companies had estimated the amount of oil needed to balance market demand, they could regulate production by increasing or decreasing offtake in countries whose governments could not retaliate easily.

The End of the One Company/One Country Pattern

The one company/one country pattern in the Middle East unraveled in the 1950s. Following the reorganization of the Iranian concession, which incorporated several independent companies, independents began to compete more vigorously against

---

the majors to win new concessions. When the government of Libya opened bidding for concessions in 1955, it divided its territory into independent parcels, eventually awarding rights covering 55 percent of its land area to fifteen operating companies whose owners included independents from France, Germany, and the United States. At about the same time, older producers with unallocated offshore properties began to auction them off. The independents were innovative bidders for all these properties, offering terms that included higher-than-average lump-sum payments and royalties along with equity shares for host governments. Better terms for new concessions encouraged host governments to demand that prior concession holders relinquish unexploited territories. The new concessions that were signed for relinquished properties included sunset provisions allowing the contracts to lapse if the companies failed to develop promising properties after a predetermined period of time. As more and more independents won concessions and then found oil, markets became glutted and prices weakened.

In what was perhaps the last straw for the IOCs, the U.S. government imposed a quota on U.S. oil imports in 1959. The U.S. market, the largest in the world, was doubly lucrative because the high cost of domestically produced oil gave sellers of lower-cost foreign oil the potential to reap high profits by selling at or slightly under high U.S. product prices. U.S.-based IOCs had long been encouraged by their government to find oil overseas, and access to the protected U.S. domestic market reinforced other incentives to invest abroad. When profits from their international operations were squeezed by higher concession costs and competition from independents, IOCs with marketing outlets in the United States looked toward U.S. oil sales as a source of deliverance. However, cheap imports threatened the domestic price structure, and firms that owned only U.S. production facilities fought oil imports, especially from the low-cost Middle East.

The U.S. government asked oil companies to limit imports voluntarily, but hard-pressed firms were unwilling to forgo profits from crude sales in the United States. Domestic producers, citing national security and the risk of becoming dependent on foreign imports, soon demanded real protection. In 1959, the voluntary quotas became mandatory. Meanwhile, the major companies had begun

to consider reducing per-barrel prices paid to host governments as a way to improve their deteriorating finances. In February 1959, after consulting one another (but not their hosts), the IOCs unilaterally reduced the posted prices of crude oil used to calculate operating-company tax obligations to host countries. Despite the outcry that followed, the IOCs lowered posted prices again in August 1960. In September, Iran, Iraq, Kuwait, Saudi Arabia, and Venezuela formed the Organization of Petroleum Exporting Countries (OPEC).

The OPEC Era

Through OPEC, major oil exporting countries had the same opportunities to coordinate their oil policies that the IOCs had long enjoyed. They used the companies' refusal to engage in joint negotiations with an OPEC representative to ratchet oil prices up in successive negotiations, each taking the best deal made by any other member as its floor for the next round, a tactic called leapfrogging. Following a failed Arab oil embargo imposed after the 1967 Arab–Israel War, OPEC militancy in relation to the IOCs grew. In 1970, the Libyan government used its superior structural position to induce leapfrogging among its own concessionaires, enforcing production cuts on the most vulnerable to make them agree to price increases and then imposing those increases on the rest.

In 1971, OPEC moved toward participation, a concept referring to gradual nationalization, which had originated with Saudi Arabia's oil minister, Ahmad Zaki Yamani. Members that reached participation agreements with their operating companies in the early 1970s later accelerated the timetable to achieve full nationalization more rapidly. Even so, the process allowed each OPEC member to develop a strategic plan for assuming control of its oil industry. After nationalization, most national oil companies (NOCs) managed their new responsibilities far better than predicted, some with the assistance of former concession owners. A few acquired overseas holdings and most added to their hydrocarbon reserves and expanded operations, such as refining, that added value to their exports. Excessive political interference and infrastructure deterioration did not become major problems for most OPEC NOCs until after world oil prices collapsed in the mid-1980s.

As more than one energy analyst has observed, the stone age did not end because the world ran out of stones and the oil age will not end because the world runs out of oil. Middle Eastern oil and gas operations are undergoing a transition. Natural gas has become a highly desirable fuel. New resources have been discovered, including the giant Northern field in Qatar. New technologies allow natural gas to be shipped long distances and off-loaded safely, right at the time when governments in developed countries are tightening antipollution requirements and encouraging consumers to shift to cleaner fuels such as gas. Where air and water quality are high priorities, gas is the hydrocarbon fuel of choice for electrical power generation as well as for direct consumption. Countries with large gas reserves may be better placed economically than those that rely primarily on crude oil sales.

For oil exporters, the future is more ambiguous. Even if oil remains a dominant fuel for some years, supplies are increasing outside the Middle East and competition will keep prices and revenues down. As domestic industries age, new exploration and development will have to be financed out of earnings against which domestic claims are increasing or, as seems increasingly to be the case, foreign investment will make up the difference between what oil exporters can afford to pay and what they need to invest. Strategic investment in overseas oil and gas operations, recreating to varying degrees the multinational vertical integration that had underpinned the old oil regime, has been helpful. Ownership of downstream operations enables OPEC members to guarantee a minimum level of production and sales through their own refining and marketing networks, and also helps them stabilize oil profits because of the inverse relationship between price movements in crude and products—when one falls, the other generally rises.

Overall, however, strategic investment of oil revenues outside of the oil and gas industry is a more pressing need, whether this includes research on alternative energy sources or concentrates on identifying and supporting domestic industries vibrant enough to employ rising generations and satisfy key local needs. A quarter of a century ago, the economist Walter J. Levy deplored "the years that the locust hath eaten," the resources consumed rather than invested to achieve long-term, post–oil age economic security. Since then, the locusts have consumed many more resources, while Middle Eastern governments and populations remain acutely dependent on oil revenues for basic needs. Wisdom suggests anticipating the end of the oil age by adopting new investment policies, but the combination of expediency and their strong positions in hydrocarbons offer more tempting and far easier alternatives to Middle Eastern countries making choices about how to use their petroleum and natural gas resources.

See also ANGLO–IRANIAN OIL COMPANY; IRAQ PETROLEUM COMPANY (IPC); MOSSADEGH, MOHAMMAD; OIL EMBARGO (1973–1974); ORGANIZATION OF PETROLEUM EXPORTING COUNTRIES (OPEC); PETROLEUM RESERVES AND PRODUCTION; RED LINE AGREEMENT; YAMANI, AHMAD ZAKI.

Bibliography

Ahrari, Mohammed E. *OPEC: The Failing Giant.* Lexington: University of Kentucky Press, 1986.

Levy, Walter J. "The Years That the Locust Hath Eaten: Oil Policy and OPEC Development Prospects." *Foreign Affairs* 57 (winter 1978–1979): 287–305.

Mitchell, John, et al. *The New Economy of Oil: Impacts on Business, Geopolitics, and Society.* London: Earthscan, 2001.

Sampson, Anthony. *The Seven Sisters: The Great Oil Companies and the World They Shaped.* New York: Viking, 1975.

Skeet, Ian. *OPEC: Twenty-five Years of Prices and Politics.* Cambridge, U.K.: Cambridge University Press, 1988.

Tétreault, Mary Ann. *The Kuwait Petroleum Corporation and the Economics of the New World Order.* Westport, CT: Quorum Books, 1995.

MARY ANN TÉTREAULT

PETROLEUM RESERVES AND PRODUCTION

An industry based on the distillation of crude oil for the creation of fuel in local and world markets.

In March 2003, the Middle East and North Africa produced 29 percent of all the oil produced worldwide (22.5 million barrels/day out of a total of 76.5 mb/d), and held 69.3 percent of the total world proven crude oil reserves of 1,050 billion barrels. At this rate of production, the Middle East will exhaust its oil reserves by 2030 unless significant new reserves are found. The inflow of cash to the region in 2003 from oil and related products can be estimated at US$215 billion.

Within the Middle East, five countries (Iran, Iraq, Saudi Arabia, Kuwait, and the United Arab Emirates [U.A.E.] control 90.5 percent of all reserves and 67 percent of production. Should Iraq be in a position to resume its pre-war(s) production, this group of five countries would produce 74 percent of the regional production and 29 percent of the world's demand. In 2001 the United States imported an average of 2,775 barrels per day from the Middle East, about 23.8 percent of its imports (BP Statistical Review of World Energy, 2002).

Production and Pricing

The cost of oil production in the Gulf is the lowest in the world. Marginal increases in production cost between $0.50 and $2.00 per barrel. The lower end of this range is most common in Saudi Arabia, the higher in the United Arab Emirates, due to the higher costs of offshore drilling. (For comparison,

incremental costs are $12–$15/b in the North Sea fields, $3–$5/b in Mexico, and $18–$20/b in U.S. offshore wells.)

Most of the oil produced in the Middle East is sold via long-term contracts between national oil companies and direct users, such as ExxonMobil, TotalElfFina, ChevronTexaco, BP-Amoco, or AGIP. The oil producers also sell to large trading companies, such as Mark Rich in Switzerland or Phibro in the United States, which in turn resell to ultimate users. The contracts between the users and producers generally specify that prices be set (often quarterly) by the producer based on a standard benchmark, such as prices of Brent or Dubai light, and adapted to conditions such as distance, sweetness (level of sulfur), and gravity. Some producers also sell contracts to deliver oil through the main oil exchanges, primarily London and New York, but the exchanges are mostly used by the traders. Although the volume of oil traded on the exchanges represents only 20 to 30 percent of the total oil sold worldwide, the market price set on these exchanges is the main source of information used by major producers in setting their prices.

The most common price benchmarks used in long-term contracts between the Gulf state oil companies and their buyers are Dubai Light for shipments to the Far East, Dated Brent (North Sea) for shipments to Europe, and West Texas Intermediate (WTI) grade for shipments to the United States. Prices of the crude oil actually shipped are modified by adding or subtracting a certain amount per barrel to reflect the grade, the quality, the distance to the market served, and the timing of the purchase relative to the benchmark quote.

When a producer is ready to effect a shipment under a given contract, it contacts the user, who in turn arranges to have a tanker ready at the point of sale for loading within forty-eight hours. Shippers and users, who have quite precise expectations on when to expect loading orders, often have tankers waiting nearby the loading facilities. In the case of Gulf shipments, tankers wait near Khor Fakkan on the Gulf of Oman.

API Gravity and Pricing

Crude oil is graded according to gravity, measured by the American Petroleum Institute degree of grav-

Crude oil in the Middle East and North Africa, 2002 average

Country	Oil production (in thousands) b/d*	Population (in thousands)	Bbls/ capita	Reserves in billions of barrels at end 2001**
Saudi Arabia	7,551	21,030	0.36	261.80
Iran	3,470	64,530	0.05	89.70
Iraq	2,014	23,580	0.09	112.50
United Arab Emirates	1,952	2,650	0.74	97.80
Kuwait	1,853	1,970	0.94	96.50
Libya	1,317	5,410	0.24	29.50
Oman	950	2,620	0.36	5.50
Algeria	883	31,840	0.03	9.20
Qatar	640	700	0.91	15.20
Egypt	630	67,890	0.01	2.90
Syria	530	16,720	0.03	2.50
Yemen	470	19,110	0.02	4.00
Turkey	48	68,610	0.00	—
Bahrain	27	650	0.04	—
Tunisia	—	9,670	0.00	0.30
Jordan	—	6,850	0.00	—
Lebanon	—	6,560	0.00	—
Israel	—	6,450	0.00	—
Morocco	—	650	0.00	—
Total	22,335	357,490	0.06	727.40

*SOURCE: *Middle East Economic Survey* 46:11 3/17/03, 46:12 3/24/03.
**SOURCE: *BP Statistical Review of World Energy*, 2002.

TABLE BY GGS INFORMATION SERVICES, THE GALE GROUP.

ity (API): the higher the number, the lighter the grade. Heavier grades require more energy to refine than the lighter grades and are used to produce heavier and cheaper products. The region produces a large range of crudes from the newly developed Saudi ultra-light crude at API 50.4 to the Syrian Souediah Heavy at API 24. Standard light crudes in the Gulf have an average API of 34; Algerian crude is very light at API 44.

Many refineries are unable to use a wide range of API crudes. When refineries are overstocked with light crude, the discount on heavy crudes may decline and sometimes turn into a premium. In general, crudes of different API degrees from the same point of sale will be priced differently. For crude shipped out of Ra's Tanhura in 1991, the average discount on heavier grades amounted to 10.7 percent for an API difference of 7 degrees.

Prices, relative to the benchmark oils, are modified according to the sweetness of the relative crudes, the less sulfur the sweeter. In the Middle East, the light Gulf crudes tend to be relatively sweet, while the Syrian crudes are very sour. Sweet crudes are preferred by refiners because they are cheaper to process and less corrosive on equipment.

Pricing, Distance, and Timing of Sale

The distance and cost of transport between the point of sale and the place of delivery is reflected in prices. At similar API grade, Arabian Light 34 sold on an average of seven years (1988 to 1994) at a discount of about $1.73 from North Sea Brent for shipments to Europe. Arabian Light 34 for the same period sold at a discount of $3.01 from WTI for shipments to the United States. (This last difference also reflects a difference in lightness in favor of WTI.) Even within the Gulf, prices also are adjusted for distance. In 1991 similar-grade oil shipped to Europe—Oman Light 34 (shipped from Oman)—sold at a premium of 2.7 percent over the Saudi Light 34 shipped from Ra's Tanhura approximately 560 miles (900 km) north, and at a premium of 5.1 percent over Iranian Light 34 shipped from Kharg island, 683 miles (1,100 km) north.

Changes in market conditions between shipment announcement and loading is included in the computation of price. For example, Saudi Light 34

Comparison of FOB (free on board) crude oil prices for major grades in 1991*

API Type of Oil	Average $ from Origin Grade	Average $ from Northwest Europe	Average U.S. Gulf	Average from Singapore
Arab Light Saudi Arabia	34	19.8	19.42	19.33
Arab Heavy Saudi Arabia	27	17.68	17.12	16.69
Iran Light Iran	34	19.35	—	19.39
Minhan U.A.E	39	20.92	—	21.58
Kirkuk Iraq	36	20.46	—	—
Kuwait Kuwait	31	17	—	17.99
Sahara Blend Algeria	44	22.01	23.06	—
Zouitina Libya	41	22.43	—	—
Oman Oman	34	20.33	—	—

* In dollars per barrel.

SOURCE: *International Crude Oil Prices, Major Time Series from the 1860s to 1991.* Middle East Petroleum & Economic Publications.

TABLE BY GGS INFORMATION SERVICES, THE GALE GROUP.

---

was adjusted by $1.90 per barrel on shipment to Europe ordered in December 1993 but effected only in January 1994.

Numerous other factors also affect the prices and the above-mentioned adjustments. The availability of tankers at any one time influences the cost of shipping; supply and demand for ships is arranged by numerous ship brokers worldwide. Price terms are quoted in reference to an index of total daily costs called the "Worldscale." Insurance rates also influence prices. At times of turmoil in the Gulf, insurance rates rise significantly and force the producers to absorb most of the increase to entice buyers to continue lifting crude from within the Gulf.

Main Gulf suppliers of crude oil to the United States, 2001

	In thousands of b/d
Saudi Arabia	1,600
Kuwait	275
Iraq	780
Total U.S. Imports From the Gulf	**2,700**

SOURCE: Energy Information Administration. <http://www.eia.doe.gov/emeu/cabs/pgulf.ht>

TABLE BY GGS INFORMATION SERVICES, THE GALE GROUP.

Purchases of Saudi and most other crudes in the region by the oil companies and major traders are usually done using thirty-day sight letters of credit, confirmed by a local bank. However, the original ARAMCO partners are not required to issue such letters of credit and instead buy on open-book basis from ARAMCO. Upon loading of oil, the shipmaster signs the bill of lading. The seller then presents the bill of lading, the insurance documents, and a signed draft to the local bank for payment. Payment is then effected by the local bank within thirty days of the date of the bill of lading.

Pipelines

Pipelines allow producers to bring oil closer to the main users and thereby cut the cost of transport. The main pipelines in the region have been laid to facilitate access to the European markets. Pipelines from the Gulf fields to the Mediterranean, which provide the most efficient transport, are subject to political problems. The tapline opened in 1975 from Saudi Arabia to Lebanon was closed by Syria; the Iraq-Syria pipeline was closed by Syria in 1982, but has been partially reopened by Syria in 2001 and is being tested for use at a rate of about 200,000 barrels per day. The pipeline from Iraq to Turkey is being used for most shipments of Kirkuk oil from Iraq to the Mediteranean. Its present capacity is about 1.5 million barrels per day but could be increased with investments in pumping facilities. The Trans-Arabian pipeline from Iraq to Yanbu on the Red Sea, through Saudi Arabia, was closed in 1990 when Iraq invaded Kuwait and has remained closed since.

The major pipeline presently used in the Gulf is the East West Arabian pipeline (Petroline), which is 745 miles (1,200 km) long and has a capacity of 4.8 million barrels per day. The other major pipeline is the Sumed pipeline in Egypt, which allows oil shipments to bypass the Suez Canal and has a capacity of 2.4 million barrels per day. Algeria exports gas to Europe by two pipelines; one through Tunisia to Italy and one through Morocco to Spain.

Bibliography

British Petroleum, Statistical Index. Available from <http://www.bp.com/centres/energy2002>.

Energy Information Administration. Available from <http://www.eia.doe.gov>.

Hartshorn, J. E. *Oil Trade: Politics and Prospects.* Cambridge and New York: Cambridge University Press, 1993.

International Crude Oil Prices, Major Time Series from the 1860s to 1991. Nicosia, Cyprus: Middle East Petroleum & Economic Publications, 1993.

Middle East Economic Survey. Nicosia, Cyprus: Middle East Petroleum & Economic Publications, 1957–.

Stauffer, Thomas R. *Indicators of Crude-Oil Production Costs: The Gulf versus Non-OPEC Sources.* Occasional Paper, no. 19. Boulder, CO: International Research Center for Energy and Economic Development, 1993.

JEAN-FRANÇOIS SEZNEC

PETROMIN

Catalyst for the Saudi acquisition of ARAMCO.

The General Petroleum and Mineral Organization (PETROMIN) was established by Saudi Arabia in 1962. In 1963, PETROMIN began marketing petroleum products in the kingdom. By 1980 PETROMIN was marketing all the oil produced in the kingdom that was not lifted by the ARAMCO (Arabian American Oil Company) partners, about 20 percent of total production. Under its president, Dr. Abdal Hadi Taher, a U.S.-trained petroleum engineer, PETROMIN developed as a fully integrated oil company. It established a vast number of subsidiaries in refining, transport, and distribution. By the mid-1970s, PETROMIN was able to show the American owners of ARAMCO that the Saudi government, in the long run, could potentially control their oil operations independently from ARAMCO. It is not known if PETROMIN was actually an important factor in the negotiations for the friendly acquisition of the U.S. oil companies' interest in ARAMCO. After ARAMCO was turned over to the Saudis, however, the role of PETROMIN started to decline. In 1994, PETROMIN and its successor company SAMAREC were merged into ARAMCO.

See also ARABIAN AMERICAN OIL COMPANY (ARAMCO).

JEAN-FRANÇOIS SEZNEC

PHALANGE

Political party in Lebanon.

The Phalange (Kata'ib) party was founded in 1936 as a Maronite Catholic paramilitary youth organization by Pierre Jumayyil, who modeled it on the fascist organizations he had observed while in Berlin as an Olympic athlete. It was authoritarian and centralized in organization, and its leader was all-powerful. The Phalange became a major political force in Mount Lebanon. After allying itself with the French Mandate authorities, the Phalange later—just before Lebanese independence—sided with those calling for independence; as a result, the party was dissolved in 1942 by the French high commissioner (it was restored after the French left Lebanon). Despite this dispute, over the years the Phalange has been closely associated with France in particular and the West in general. For many years, the party newspaper, *al-Amal*, was printed in Arabic and French.

Consistent with its authoritarian beginnings, Phalangist ideology has been on the right of the political spectrum. Although it has embraced the need to modernize, it has always favored the preservation of the status quo. The Phalange party motto is "God, the Fatherland, and the Family," and its doctrine emphasizes a free economy and private initiative. It focuses on the primacy of preserving the Lebanese nation, but with a "Phoenician" identity distinct from its Islamic Arab neighbors. Party policies have been uniformly anticommunist and anti-Palestinian, with no place for pan-Arab ideals. The Lebanese Civil War of 1958 and the intensification of sectarian conflict benefited the party; its membership increased from 300 in 1936 to 40,000 in 1958. The power of the party was reflected in parliament; from 1959 through 1968, 61 percent of its candidates were elected. In the 1972 parliament, the Phalange had seven deputies, including Pierre Jumayyil and his son Amin Jumayyil. By the start of the Lebanese Civil War that began in 1975, the party's membership had increased to 65,000, including a militia of nearly 10,000.

Throughout the civil war, the Phalange party was the most formidable Christian force, and its militia bore the brunt of the fighting on the Christian side. Because the party was part of the mostly Christian, right-wing coalition known as the Lebanese Front, the power of the Jumayyil family increased considerably. Ironically, as Pierre Jumayyil's son Bashir Jumayyil was consolidating his power through the integration of all right-wing militias into his Lebanese Forces, the role of the Phalange party diminished. Bashir, a member of the party, marginalized its traditional leadership, which he felt was too moderate.

During the 1980s, the Phalange lost much of its credibility and political stature. In 1982, under military pressure from Israel, which occupied a good deal of Lebanon, Bashir Jumayyil was elected president. He was assassinated before assuming office, and his brother Amin took his place. The corrupt and partisan rule of Amin further harmed the image of the party, and the death of Pierre Jumayyil in 1984 inaugurated a struggle for power within the party. The party was even attacked by the Lebanese Forces, the erstwhile political child of the Phalange, in 1985. George Saade, elected president of the party in 1987, tried to rejuvenate the organization, but the changing political sentiment in the country in favor of Syria did not help his cause. The Phalange was briefly led by Munir al-Hajj after Saade's death in 1998. The race to replace al-Hajj was a rivalry between Amin Jumayyil, who returned to Lebanon in July 2000, and Karim Pakradouni (who was not Maronite, but Armenian). In early 2002, Pakradouni became leader, and Jumayyil was expelled from the party in July 2002.

See also JUMAYYIL, AMIN; JUMAYYIL, BASHIR; JUMAYYIL, PIERRE; LEBANESE CIVIL WAR (1958); LEBANESE CIVIL WAR (1975–1990); LEBANESE FORCES; LEBANESE FRONT; MARONITES; SAADE, GEORGE.

Bibliography

AbuKhalil, As'ad. *Historical Dictionary of Lebanon.* Lanham, MD: Scarecrow, 1998.

AbuKhalil, As'ad. "Lebanon." *Political Parties of the Middle East and North Africa,* edited by Frank Tachau. Westport, CT: Greenwood, 1994.

AS'AD ABUKHALIL
UPDATED BY MICHAEL R. FISCHBACH

PHARAONICISM

An intellectual outlook found particularly in early twentieth-century Egypt.

Intellectuals of a Pharaonicist orientation assumed the existence of a unique Egyptian national character shared by ancient and modern Egypt; their writings attempted to demonstrate the ancient Pharaonic origins of many of the characteristics and traits of contemporary Egyptians. Expounded particularly by those Egyptians who were educated in Europe or who were Westernized intellectuals, Pharaonicism faded as Arab-Muslim nationalist sentiment grew in Egypt.

JAMES JANKOWSKI

PHARAON, RASHAD
[1912–]

Diplomat and physician in Saudi Arabia.

Rashad Pharaon, born and trained in Syria, became the private physician to a succession of Saudi monarchs from 1936 onwards. Enjoying the confidence of the Al Saʿud family, he was appointed their first ambassador to France and Europe (1947–1966); during the same period, he was also the kingdom's first minister of health (1954) and senior delegate to the United Nations (1963–1964), and he was involved in most areas of Saudi foreign relations as the closest adviser to Faisal ibn Abd al-Aziz when he was foreign minister and then king.

LES ORDEMAN
UPDATED BY GEORGE R. WILKES

PHILAE

An island, now submerged, that was the site of an ancient Egyptian temple complex.

The island of Philae was located in the Nile River at the First Cataract, south of the present Aswan dam; it is now totally submerged. Between 1972 and 1980, before the island was submerged into Lake Nasser, the main temples were disassembled and reassembled on the island of Agilkia, under the aegis of the United Nations Educational, Social, and Cultural Organization (UNESCO).

From the Late Period of Egyptian history (304 B.C.E.–30 B.C.E.), Philae served as the frontier between Egypt and Nubia. Philae was approximately 460 feet by 1510 feet (140 m by 460 m) in size. It was paired with another nearby island, Biggeh, as a focal point of the worship of the Egyptian god Osiris. Biggeh housed an *abaton,* one of the purported tombs of Osiris, while Philae was home to a temple to the sister/wife of Osiris, Isis. This tem-

ple, thought to be the single most beautiful preserved ancient Egyptian temple, housed a *mammisi,* or birth house, built to celebrate the birth of Harpocrates to Isis and Osiris.

The Isis temple is of Ptolemaic date (304 B.C.E.–30 B.C.E.). The temple was laid out on the east side of the island, built along two axes, with a roughly south-northeast orientation. A long courtyard flanked by colonnades gave access to the first, 66-foot-tall (20 m) pylon, or entrance gateway. Inside this pylon was a second courtyard with a colonnade on the east and the *mammisi* on the west. A second, 43-foot-tall (13 m) pylon gave access into the Isis temple proper.

There were a number of other notable buildings and structures on the island, particularly a kiosk on the east side dating to the time of Augustus (30 B.C.E.–14 C.E.). This kiosk, perpendicular to the Isis temple, formed a second processional axis. The latest datable inscription in Egyptian hieroglyphic script (24 August 394 C.E.) was found on the island.

Bibliography

Arnold, Dieter. *The Encyclopedia of Ancient Egyptian Architecture,* edited by Nigel and Helen Strudwick, translated by Sabine H. Gardiner and Helen Strudwick. Princeton, NJ: Princeton University Press, 2003.

Vassilika, Eleni. *Ptolemaic Egypt.* Leuven, Belgium: Uitgeverij Peeters, 1989.

DAVID WALDNER
UPDATED BY JOHN M. LUNDQUIST

PHILBY, HARRY ST. JOHN
[1885–1960]

The leading European explorer of Saudi Arabia.

Harry St. John Philby was born in Ceylon (now Sri Lanka) to a family of the Raj (British administration in India) and educated at Cambridge University in England. He joined the Indian civil service after his graduation in 1908, but when his temperament stalled his career, he transferred in 1915 to the Indian expeditionary force in Mesopotamia (now Iraq). Again he ran afoul of his superiors, who sent him to central Arabia in 1917 to negotiate with an unreliable ally. In the course of this mission, which had only limited success, Philby discovered his life's passion—exploration of Arabia—and a patron, the aforementioned unreliable ally, Abd al-Aziz ibn Abd al-Rahman, known in the West as Ibn Saʿud, then ruler of Najd and subsequently, founder of Saudi Arabia.

Although Philby eventually tied his fortunes to Ibn Saʿud, immediately after World War I he was posted to Iraq and Transjordan (now Jordan) where he irritated superiors with his hostility to the Hashimites, the Hijazi family to whom the British entrusted the rule of these states newly carved from the Ottoman Empire. Because the Hashimites were rivals of the Saudis, they became Philby's enemies too.

In 1925 Philby quit the colonial service to become a merchant in Jidda. However, it was not until after his conversion to Islam in 1930 that his fortunes began to improve. In 1932 his plan for a voyage through Rub al-Khali (the Empty Quarter), a feat that had long eluded Europeans, finally gained Ibn Saʿud's approval. To Philby's immense chagrin, a rival Briton, Bertram Thomas, had just preceded him, but Philby did complete a more ambitious course and his explorations of the peninsula continued throughout his life. These constitute the most enduring of his achievements, for he was a meticulous observer of the land, its flora and fauna, and archaeological remains. His precise observations drew the map of Arabia.

In 1933 Philby helped to negotiate the agreement that opened Saudi Arabia to American oil exploration, the first stage in the creation of the Arabian American Oil Company (ARAMCO). He had other business successes, including a concession to sell Ford motor cars in Arabia. His political instincts were less fortunate. Throughout much of his life he waged a constant campaign against what he considered to be the stupidity and immorality of the policies of the British government. On several occasions Philby meddled in Palestinian affairs, consulting with Jewish dissenter Judah Magnes to produce an ill-fated Arab-Zionist peace plan in 1929. In 1939 he proposed to senior Zionist officials in London a scheme under which King Ibn Saʿud might be persuaded to support the creation of a Jewish state in Palestine in exchange for Jewish political influence in London and in Washington, D.C., on behalf of the complete "unity and independence" of the remaining Arab lands, and "extensive financial help" to the Arabs, including a hefty subsidy to the Saudi ruler.

Philby's wartime harangues included praise for Adolf Hitler and disparagement of the British war effort, leading the Foreign Office to consider him a dangerous crackpot. In 1940, during a stopover in India on his way from Arabia to the United States, he was arrested, shipped to England, and imprisoned for nearly a year. After the war he was able to return to Arabia, but the death of Ibn Saʿud in 1953 and Philby's criticism of his successors brought him banishment to Beirut in 1955. He resettled in Riyadh only after abandoning politics.

The charge that Philby was a secret agent is unfounded. However, he enjoyed the company of Western diplomats, to whom he provided much gossip. And his son, Kim Philby (1912–1988), was a high-ranking official in British counterintelligence before being exposed as a Soviet mole.

Bibliography

Caplan, Neil. *Futile Diplomacy*, Vol. 2: *Arab–Zionist Negotiations and the End of the Mandate, 1931–1948.* Totowa, NJ; London: Frank Cass, 1986.

Monroe, Elizabeth. *Philby of Arabia.* London: Faber and Faber, 1973.

BENJAMIN BRAUDE
UPDATED BY NEIL CAPLAN

PHOENICIANISM

A Lebanese nationalist ideology.

Phoenicianism is based on the idea that Lebanon is unique in the Middle East for its location, people, and mission, and therefore should not be bound in any arrangement to neighboring countries, which are seen as inferior. The ideology of Phoenicianism flourished early in the twentieth century, when decentralization parties proliferated in the Arab region of the Ottoman Empire. Many Christians were dedicated Arab nationalists, although some Lebanese Christians believed that their nation should not be associated with the Arab region.

Phoenicianism is based on the belief that the Lebanese political entity is, contrary to historical realities, not the product of the twentieth century. "Lebanese nationalists"—a term that has come to describe the views of the right-wing Maronite Christian establishment and its allies in other sects—believe that Lebanon, both as a political entity and as a people, has been in continuous existence since Phoenician times. The Phoenicians are seen as ancient Lebanese, and Phoenician achievements are exaggerated to the point that the Greek and Roman civilizations are perceived as inferior to the "Lebanese Phoenician civilization." Lebanese nationalists argue that the Phoenician identity defines the Lebanese political identity. Other identities, such as those based on Islam or Arabism, are regarded as alien to the Lebanese historical experience.

The dispute over Phoenicianism is at the root of the Lebanese political problem. There is no consensus on the identity of Lebanon. Although the Maronite establishment has insisted that the Lebanese identity should be defined in purely historical terms (i.e., Phoenician), Lebanese Muslims and others who support their views argue that the Lebanese identity has been shaped by the Islamic Arab legacy. Arab nationalists dismiss the Phoenician claims and compare then to Zionist claims over Palestine. The political arrangement of Lebanon since 1943 has failed to settle this thorny political issue. The National Pact of 1943, for example, tried to please both sides by declaring that Lebanon has "an Arab face," leaving the determination of the identity of the "body" unspecified. For advocates of Phoenicianism, the only linkage between Lebanon and the Arab world rests in Lebanon's membership in the League of Arab States.

Phoenicianism has developed from an ideology into a full-fledged myth. Nobody has contributed to the nourishment of the myth more than Lebanese poet and ultranationalist Sa'id Aql, who traces most of the great discoveries of civilization to the Phoenician people. Even the discovery of America is attributed by Aql—among others in Lebanon—to Phoenician travelers who preceded Columbus. The great Greek thinkers are called Phoenicians. The school curricula in Lebanon reinforce the myths about the Phoenician people among all who accept a version of history promulgated by ideologues who have dominated the Ministry of Education since independence.

See also AQL, SA'ID; LEAGUE OF ARAB STATES; NATIONAL PACT (LEBANON).

Bibliography

Kaufman, Asher. "Phoenicianism: The Formation of an Identity in Lebanon in 1920." *Middle Eastern Studies* 37 (January 2001): 173.

AS'AD ABUKHALIL

PHOENICIANISM

Export of these compounds is vital to the economies of Israel, Jordan, and Morocco.

Natural calcium phosphate deposits occur worldwide in the crust of Earth. Although the global phosphorous content is only 0.1 percent, in economically viable deposits it ranges between 26 percent and 38 percent, measured in phosphorous pentoxide, or P_2O_5. Many Arab countries produce phosphate rock for transformation into phosphoric acid and other complex fertilizers. These include Morocco, Algeria, Tunisia, Egypt, and Jordan, as well as Syria, and Iraq. Some other countries in the region are minor players in phosphate production and export. In 2000, the economic reserves of the main five producers were estimated at 7 billion tons, 1.6 billion tons, 267 million tons, 600 million tons, and 1.27 billion tons, respectively. These five countries provide close to half the world's production, which is mostly processed for use as agricultural fertilizers. Morocco produces the richest phosphate (32% P_2O_5 at Khouribga). Important Moroccan sites are Khouribga, Benguerir, Youssoufia, and Bougraa-Layoune in the Western Sahara. Algeria's phosphate reserves are located in the Constantine region, in the east of the country. At 15 percent P_2O_5, they are not as rich as Moroccan deposits. They were mined early by the colonial French, during the nineteenth century. A number of Algerian sites were abandoned or exhausted, including Djebel Dekna, Djebel Dyr. Four sites are still in production: M'zaita, Tocqueville, Bordj R'dir, and Kouif. Tunisia's phosphates contain 30 percent P_2O_5. Major production in Tunisia is in various sites in the Gafsa province, in the southwest, including Mdilla, Metlaoui, and Moulares. The quality of Egypt's phosphate is similar to Tunisia's. Abu Tartur, located 31 miles (50 kilometers) west of the

Kharga Oasis in the Western Desert, is its major phosphate site. Jordan's phosphate is mined at Eshidyia, al-Hassa, al-Abyad, and al-Rusayfa. In these five countries, phosphate production, processing, and export represent an important component of economic output, and at the same time a serious source of industrial pollution. In 1998, fertilizer production accounted for $8.5 billion of the $13 billion chemical industry output in the Arab region.

Bibliography

Hamdi, Ali, and Ashkar, Shafik. "The Growing Capability of AFA Member Companies to meet Global Ferltilizer Demand." Arab Fertilizer Association, Egypt. Available from <www.fertilizer.org/ifa/publicat/PDF/1999_biblio_84.pdf>.

KARIM HAMDY

PICA

See JEWISH COLONIZATION ASSOCIATION

PILAF

See FOOD

PINSKER, LEO
[1821–1891]

Early Zionist leader.

Born in Russia, Leo Pinsker was active in the Odessa branch of the Society for the Promotion of Enlightenment, which advocated assimilation as the solution to the problem of European Jewry. Following the pogroms of 1881, Pinsker changed his view and began calling for the resettlement of Jews in a country where they would constitute a majority and attain political independence. He proposed the establishment of a national fund based on contributions for the settlement of immigrants with financial needs. He expressed hope that those who oppressed the Jews might aid in their resettlement. He did not advocate any particular location for the Jewish center but suggested the convening of a congress to make such a decision. Pinsker published his ideas in German, in a pamphlet entitled *Autoemancipation: A Warning of a Russian Jew to His Brethren* (1882). The pamphlet made a profound impression on the

Hibbat Zion movement, which adopted it as its manifesto. In 1884, he was made chair of the Central Committee of Hibbat Zion, serving as its head until 1889.

Bibliography

Hertzberg, Arthur, ed. *The Zionist Idea: A Historical Analysis and Reader.* Philadelphia: Jewish Publication Society, 1997.

MARTIN MALIN

PLAGUE

Epidemic disease spread by fleas that infest rats.

Plague is caused by the bacillus *Pasteurella pestis*. Bubonic plague, which affects the lymph nodes, is most commonly identified with major epidemics since the fourteenth century; it can decrease infected populations by as much as one-third. Numerous outbreaks were recorded in the Middle East in the nineteenth century. The most severe bubonic plague epidemic in the twentieth century was in Egypt, some 520 miles south of Cairo, in 1912. Some 237 deaths out of a total of 357 cases were recorded.

Pneumonic plague, which affects the lungs, occurs more commonly during the winter; it is highly infectious, with a mortality rate of almost 100 percent. It is spread through the air from person to person. Septicemic plague, which affects the blood stream, is the rarest form. It is 100 percent fatal, because death occurs within a few hours of infection.

JENAB TUTUNJI

PLUMER, HERBERT CHARLES ONSLOW
[1857–1932]

British career officer who was High Commissioner for Palestine from 1925 to 1928.

Lord Plumer was born in Yorkshire, England, on 13 March 1857, and entered the British army in 1876. He served in the Sudan in 1884 and in South Africa during the Boer War (1899–1902), which led to his promotion to major general. He was a senior general on the European front during World War I and became a field marshal in 1919. Lord Plumer served as governor and commander in chief of Malta from 1919 to 1924, but he is best known for his three years as British high commissioner for Palestine from 1925 through 1928.

As a career officer in the British armed forces, Lord Plumer stressed the importance of maintaining security and stability in the volatile mandated territory. During his three years' rule, Jewish immigration stagnated, and therefore the Arabs became less fearful of eventual Jewish political domination. Lord Plumer, however, resisted requests by Palestinian Arab politicians to hold elections for a legislative council; he preferred to hold elections for municipal councils that would test the feasibility of self-government and provide combined representation for Arabs and Jews. The relative quiet of his years in office persuaded him that he could reduce the number of British troops in Palestine. In reality, tension was simmering below the surface, which led to major riots at the Western (Wailing) Wall in Jerusalem, August 1929.

See also HIGH COMMISSIONERS (PALESTINE); TRANSJORDAN FRONTIER FORCE; WESTERN WALL DISTURBANCES.

Bibliography

Porath, Yehoshua. *The Emergence of the Palestinian–Arab National Movement, 1918–1929.* London: Cass, 1974.

Powell, Geoffrey. *Plumer: The Soldiers' General: A Biography of Field-Marshal Viscount Plumer of Messines.* London: Leo Cooper, 1990.

Wasserstein, Bernard. *The British in Palestine: The Mandatory Government and Arab–Jewish Conflict, 1917–1929.* Cambridge, MA: B. Blackwell, 1991.

ANN M. LESCH

POGROM

An armed riot by one ethnic, tribal, or religious group against another, incited by the government; usually accompanied by looting, mass property destruction, rape, and murder.

The term *pogrom* derives from the Russian *pogromit* (to destroy); Russia was the scene of the first modern pogroms, against its minority Jewish population, beginning in 1881. During the Russian Civil War (1918–1923), armed forces of all sides perpe-

trated atrocities against the Jews, though Vladimir Lenin's government went on record as opposing antisemitic violence.

Bibliography

Laqueur, Walter. *A History of Zionism.* New York: Holt, Rinehart, 1972.

JON JUCOVY

POINT FOUR

U.S. aid program to the Middle East under the Truman Doctrine.

The name refers to the fourth point made in U.S. president Harry Truman's 1949 inaugural speech, wherein he cited the need to support democracy and economic stability where small nations are threatened by outside (that is, Soviet) influence.

Point Four led to unprecedented U.S. military and economic aid to the Middle East, allocated under various programs, expanding aid given to Turkey and Greece under the Marshall Plan since 1947. Of the $2.94 billion in military equipment sent to the region during the 1950s, Turkey received $1.87 billion, with Iran, Iraq, Jordan, Lebanon, Libya, Pakistan, and Saudi Arabia receiving lesser amounts. Aid also went to agricultural projects and to Palestinian refugees.

Bibliography

Bryson, Thomas A. *American Diplomatic Relations with the Middle East, 1784–1975: A Survey.* Metuchen, NJ: Scarecrow Press, 1977.

ELIZABETH THOMPSON

POLISARIO

Acronym of the Frente Popular para la Liberación de Saguia el-Hamra y Rio de Oro (Popular Front for the Liberation of Saguia el-Hamra and Rio de Oro), the movement struggling to establish the independent state of Western Sahara in Spain's former Spanish Sahara colony.

POLISARIO was founded on 10 May 1973 by a combined group of Moroccan students of Sahrawi background studying at Muhammad V University in Rabat, Morocco; a small number of veterans of anticolonial struggles during the late 1950s residing in Mauritania; and youth from within Spanish Sahara. The group evolved out of the earlier, more informal Movement for the Liberation of the Sahara. Its first head was the charismatic Mustapha Sayed al-Ouali. POLISARIO's founding manifesto spoke of a strategy of "revolutionary violence" and "armed struggle" against Spanish colonial rule, but it was not until the second congress, more than a year later, that independence was explicitly declared as POLISARIO's goal.

The notion of a Sahrawi nation was a new one, the combined product of the sedentarization among the formerly nomadic Saharan tribes, socioeconomic changes in Spanish Sahara, and new ideological currents linked to decolonization in Africa and developing nations. POLISARIO was a reflection of these changes as it sought to transcend traditional tribal cleavages and fashion a supratribal Sahrawi national identity, although the majority of the POLISARIO leadership was Reguibat in origin, from the largest of the Sahrawi tribal confederations.

Libya's Muammar al-Qaddafi was the first head of state to provide support and until the early 1980s was an important supplier of arms. Algeria was initially hesitant but by mid-1975 had become POLISARIO's main benefactor and POLISARIO was rendered almost completely dependent on Algiers. The Spanish departure in early 1976 and the entrance of Moroccan and Mauritanian troops inaugurated the Western Sahara War. (By agreement with Spain, Morocco was to occupy the northern two-thirds of the territory and Mauritania the remaining one-third.) One immediate outcome was a large-scale exodus (estimates range from one-third to two-thirds) of the Sahrawi population (about 74,000, according to the 1974 Spanish census) from Western Sahara to the Algerian side of the border, around Tindouf. POLISARIO was granted a great degree of autonomy to run the refugee camps, which served as POLISARIO's military, political, and social base. POLISARIO's military wing, the Sahrawi Popular Liberation Army, numbered between ten thousand and fifteen thousand during the early 1980s, and eight thousand to nine thousand in 1991. The POLISARIO leadership established a formal government-in-exile, SADR (Saharan Arab Democratic Republic). Al-Ouali was killed in fighting in June 1976. His replacement, Muhammad

Abd al-Aziz, was chosen at the third POLISARIO congress and was still head of POLISARIO and president of SADR in 2003.

Morocco gradually gained the upper hand militarily and consolidated its control over the bulk of Western Sahara during the 1980s. Concurrently, Algerian aid decreased. Hence, POLISARIO's diplomatic gains—recognition of SADR by more than seventy countries at its peak, and full membership in the Organization of African Unity—proved to be of limited value. Morocco and POLISARIO formally agreed to a United Nations–sponsored cease-fire in 1991, which was to be followed by a UN-supervised referendum in 1992, giving Sahrawis the option of independence or incorporation into Morocco. The plan was POLISARIO's best hope, but it was also risky. Its winner-take-all formula stipulated that defeat would necessitate POLISARIO's disbanding. As it happened, the vote never took place, owing to the two parties' persistent failure to reach agreement on the list of eligible voters. In 2001, Morocco's unhappiness with the revised voter rolls, and the UN Security Council's unwillingness to impose the referendum by force, led UN mediator James A. Baker to propose delaying the referendum in favor of a five-year period of autonomy for the region, to be followed by a referendum with an expanded voter list. POLISARIO initially resisted the plan. However, in 2003, under the prodding of Algeria, it assented, and the UN Security Council endorsed the plan. Fearing that its claim to sovereignty over the territory, Morocco rejected the plan, and the matter remained unresolved.

See also MOROCCO; SAHARAN ARAB DEMOCRATIC REPUBLIC (SADR); SPANISH MOROCCO; WESTERN SAHARA; WESTERN SAHARA WAR.

Bibliography

Damis, John. *Conflict in Northwest Africa: The Western Sahara Dispute.* Stanford, CA: Hoover Institution Press, 1983.

Hodges, Tony. *Historical Dictionary of Western Sahara.* Metuchen, NJ: Scarecrow Press, 1982.

Hodges, Tony. *Western Sahara: The Roots of a Desert War.* Westport, CT: L. Hill, 1983.

Lawless, Richard, and Monahan, Laila, eds. *War and Refugees: The Western Sahara Conflict.* New York and London: Pinter, 1987.

Zoubir, Yahia H., and Volman, Daniel, eds. *International Dimensions of the Western Sahara Conflict.* Westport, CT: Praeger, 1993.

BRUCE MADDY-WEITZMAN

POLITI, ELIE
[1895–?]

Jewish Egyptian journalist, publisher, and banker.

Elie Politi was born in Cairo to a family of modest income. Though he obtained a rudimentary French education, he was largely self-educated. Politi turned to journalism during the 1920s. He founded and directed the daily *L'informateur financier commercial* in the late 1920s and published a number of economic directories while helping to establish *al-Misri* in Cairo, which became one of the most influential daily newspapers in the Middle East during the 1940s and early 1950s.

From 1914, Politi was also one of the leading businessmen and land developers in Egypt. He directed and managed the Commercial Bank of Egypt, transforming it into a major and respected financial institution, and helped to develop the new city of Muqattam on the eastern hills overlooking Cairo, as well as the beach and urban area of Ma'amura, east of Alexandria. *Al-Misri* was closed when Gamal Abdel Nasser took power in 1954, in spite of its nationalist stance during clashes with Britain the previous year, and the banks were nationalized at the end of the decade. Like most of the Egyptian Jewish economic elite, Politi was a committed Egyptian patriot. In 1965 he published his memoirs, *L'Egypte de 1914 à Suez,* in Paris.

Bibliography

Beinin, Joel. *The Dispersion of Egyptian Jewry.* Berkeley: University of California Press, 1998.

Laskier, Michael M. *The Jews of Egypt 1920–1970.* New York: New York University Press, 1992.

Mizrahi, Maurice. "The Role of the Jews in Economic Development." In *The Jews of Egypt: A Mediterranean Society in Modern Times,* edited by Shimon Shamir. Boulder, CO: Westview Press, 1987.

MICHAEL M. LASKIER
UPDATED BY GEORGE R. WILKES

POLLARD AFFAIR

Israeli espionage against the United States.

Jonathan Pollard, a civilian intelligence analyst with the U.S. Navy, was arrested by the Federal Bureau of Investigation in November 1985 while seeking sanctuary in the Israeli embassy in Washington. A Jew and passionate Zionist, Pollard was recruited to spy for Israel's Bureau for Scientific Liaison (Lekem), which operated independently of the Mossad (Israel's foreign intelligence agency). U.S. officials claimed that Pollard had compromised more than 1,000 classified documents, many of them top secret, during seventeen months of espionage. Material included reports on Soviet arms shipments to Arab states, on missiles, and on chemical weapons.

Pollard, who was sentenced to life imprisonment, claimed to have been motivated not by financial gain but by a desire to help Israel combat terrorism. The affair briefly rocked the most sensitive and secret elements of Israel's relationship with the United States. Pollard himself dismissed Israeli suggestions that his recruitment was a rogue operation by the Lekem chief, Rafi Eitan, and an overzealous air force officer. Two Israeli commissions of inquiry failed to establish precisely where responsibility lay.

No lasting damage was done to military and intelligence links between the two countries. Pollard's supporters, especially those in the Jewish community, continued to seek a presidential pardon, arguing that he had been treated more harshly than others who had spied for the United States's enemies, let alone for one of its most intimate allies.

Bibliography

Black, Ian, and Morris, Benny. *Israel's Secret Wars: A History of Israel's Intelligence Services.* New York: Grove Weidenfeld, 1991.

Blitzer, Wolf. *Territory of Lies: The Exclusive Story of Jonathan Jay Pollard.* New York: Harper and Row, 1989.

IAN BLACK

POLYGAMY

Marriage in which a spouse of either sex may have more than one mate at a time.

Polygamy for men (polygyny) is sanctioned in Islam by direct reference in the Qur'an and is practiced to some extent in all countries with Muslim populations except where prohibited by law. Muslim men may have as many as four wives at a time but are admonished to treat all equally. The *shari'a* warns of the unlikelihood that the wives in a polygamous marriage can, in fact, be treated equally. Therefore, monogamy is the preferred condition.

Polygamy is statistically minimal in Middle Eastern countries that uphold the *shari'a* in family law. This is partly due to legislation that makes polygamy difficult to enter into or to maintain. Economic considerations also make polygamy virtually impossible, since there must be a separate household for each wife. Consequently, those who practice polygamy are often relatively wealthy or influential. Community and political leaders are more likely to practice polygamy as a sign of respect and as a matter of prestige.

In bedouin and tribal cultures, tribal leaders practice polygamy both to enhance their own prestige and to form or strengthen alliances with other tribes.

See also SHARI'A.

JENAB TUTUNJI

POPULAR FRONT

The 1930s French government that was supportive of Arab nationalism.

The Popular Front government came to power in France in June 1936, under the premiership of the socialist Léon Blum, author of the Blum–Viollette Plan. Tension between the French government and Arab nationalism was alleviated by the new government's vision of its commitment in the Middle East, particularly of the French mandate over the Levant. Stalled independence negotiations with nationalists of Syria were rejuvenated, and a Franco–Syrian treaty was signed in September 1936, in which France maintained some major supervisory powers. The treaty was never ratified by France, which by June 1937 had a new government with a more conservative colonial outlook.

Bibliography

Khoury, Philip S. *Syria and the French Mandate: The Politics of Arab Nationalism, 1920–1945.* Princeton, NJ: Princeton University Press, 1987.

CHARLES U. ZENZIE

POPULAR FRONT FOR THE LIBERATION OF PALESTINE

Radical, left-wing Palestinian guerrilla organization.

The Popular Front for the Liberation of Palestine (also known as the PFLP, al-Jabha al-Sha'biyya li-Tahrir Filastin, al-Jabha al-Sha'biyya, and the Red Eagles) is a Marxist-oriented group established by George Habash, a Christian Palestinian, after the June 1967 Arab–Israel War. Habash created the PFLP after successfully uniting three groups: Heroes of the Return, the National Front for the Liberation of Palestine, and the Independent Palestine Liberation Front. In 1968 the group joined the Palestine Liberation Organization (PLO) and was second in importance and influence among the Arab Palestinians only to Arafat's al-Fatah movement.

The group's ideology is based on three principles: Palestinian national sovereignty (*wataniyya*), Arab unity (*qawmiyya*), and Marxist-Leninist ideology. The PFLP has sought to unite Palestinian efforts within a secular governing framework, and it has modeled some of its operative activities and strategies on Cuban leader Fidel Castro's revolutionary guerrilla methods. Central to the group's understanding of *wataniyya* is a strict opposition to the State of Israel, an interest in restoring Arab unity in the region, and criticism of pro-Western Arab states.

In 1970 internal conflict split the PFLP into three separate groups: the PFLP, the Democratic Front for the Liberation of Palestine (DFLP), and the Popular Front for the Liberation of Palestine–General Command (PFLP-GC). Habash remained at the head of the PFLP and forged ties with other leftist groups outside Palestine such as the German Baader-Meinhoff group, the Irish Republican Army (IRA), and the Japanese Red Army. The PFLP began operating in Europe and elsewhere, claiming responsibility for such events as an attack at Lod Airport in 1972 and the hijacking of an Air France airbus to Entebbe in 1976. In the Arab world, they are associated with hijacking and the destruction of four international airplanes in Jordan in 1970. These acts of terrorism led to their being banned in Jordan, where they had originally been based. When Jordan's King Hussein expelled the organization, they relocated in Lebanon.

Although it is a member of the larger umbrella group of the PLO, the PFLP has often opposed al-Fatah's policies, forming splinter groups in opposition to Arafat's concessions in the Middle East peace process. During the first Intifada in 1987, key PFLP members formed a group called the Red Eagles that carried out attacks on Israel in the West Bank, and later formed a coalition with other opposition groups such as the DFLP and the Damascus Ten. In 1993 the group finally separated from the PLO after it signed the Declaration of Principles. At that time, the PFLP elected a new executive body: George Habash, Abu Ali Mustafa (Mustafa Zibri), Abd al-Rahim Lalluh, Abu Ahmad Fuʾad, Sabir Muhi al-Din, Taysir Kubʿa, and Umar Kutaysh.

With the decline of Soviet support after the disintegration of the former U.S.S.R., the PFLP became marginal in comparison to emerging Islamist groups such as HAMAS and Islamic Jihad. Although the group disagreed with the provisions set out in the 1993 Oslo Peace Accord, it renewed its ties with Arafat's al-Fatah group in 1999. This renewal of ties with the PLO signaled a shift in the PFLP's Marxist doctrine, which has become increasingly focused on socialist democracy. Whereas formerly the PFLP did not recognize Israel as a state, it now accepts the possibility of a Palestinian state with Jerusalem as its capital alongside a temporary Israeli state that eventually reverts to an "historic Palestine" after the right of return sees Palestinian refugees repatriated.

Habash retired in 2000 and was succeeded by Abu Ali Mustafa. Mustafa had been a founding member of the PLO and a member of its Executive Committee. After taking over in 2000, he moved PFLP headquarters from Syria to Ramallah in the West Bank and began organizing attacks on Israeli targets there. After learning that Mustafa and the PFLP intended to carry out attacks on Israeli schools and other civilian areas, Israeli authorities bombed his office, killing him and several others. Ahmad Saʿadat then became head of the PFLP; he was as-

sociated with the assassination of Rehavam Zeʾevi, Israel's tourism minister, and in April 2002 was sentenced to one year in prison for taking part in the assassination. Although the courts later ruled in favor of his release, continued PFLP attacks have prevented this.

The PFLP's funding comes from a variety of sources. Financial and military support are said to come from Syria and Libya, and in 1999, Iranian president Mohammad Khatami promised to continue Iran's support of not only the PFLP, but also the PFLP-GC, Islamic Jihad, and HAMAS. In addition to outside support, the PFLP has financed its activities from front companies as well as legitimate business activities.

During the al-Aqsa Intifada, the PFLP claimed responsibility for a number of violent incidents within Israel's pre-1967 border areas. Habash maintained his opposition to Arafat's signed accords with Israel. Saʿadat also stood in strong opposition to the Oslo Accords, although the general language of the PFLP has shifted from Marxist-Leninist revolutionary appeals to a focus on democracy and social justice.

See also FATAH, AL-; HABASH, GEORGE; PALESTINE LIBERATION ORGANIZATION (PLO); POPULAR FRONT FOR THE LIBERATION OF PALESTINE—GENERAL COMMAND.

Bibliography

Abdulhadi, Rabab. "The Palestinian Women's Autonomous Movement: Emergence, Dynamics, and Challenges." *Gender and Society* 12, no. 6 (December 1998): 649–673.

Alexander, Yonah. "Popular Front for the Liberation of Palestine." *Palestinian Secular Terrorism.* Ardsley, NY: Transnational Publishers, 2003.

Andoni, Lamis. "The PLO at the Crossroads." *Journal of Palestine Studies* 21, no. 1 (Autumn 1992): 54–65.

Habash, George, and Soueid, Mahmoud. "Taking Stock: An Interview with George Habash." *Journal of Palestine Studies* 28, no. 1 (Autumn 1998): 86–101.

Salim, Qais. "Resistance and Self-Determination in Palestine." *MERIP Reports* 28 (May 1974): 3–10.

Sayigh, Yezid. "Armed Struggle and State Formation." *Journal of Palestine Studies* 26, no. 4 (Summer 1997): 17–32.

Tessler, Mark. *A History of the Israeli-Palestinian Conflict.* Bloomington, IN: Indiana University Press, 1994.

Usher, Graham; Barghouti, Marwan; and Abu Jiab, Ghazi. "Arafat and the Opposition." *Middle East Report* 191 (November–December 1994): 22–25.

MOUIN RABBANI
UPDATED BY MARIA F. CURTIS

POPULAR FRONT FOR THE LIBERATION OF PALESTINE–GENERAL COMMAND

Radical Palestinian group.

With between 500 and 1,000 members, the Popular Front for the Liberation of Palestine–General Command (PFLP-GC) is one of the smaller Palestinian guerrilla organizations. The PFLP-GC recruits mainly from the Palestinian refugee camps of Lebanon and Syria. Its leadership, under Ahmad Jibril, served in the Syrian military before forming the Palestine Liberation Front (PLF) in 1965. After briefly merging with al-Fatah, in 1967 they were founding members of the Popular Front for the Liberation of Palestine (PFLP), then broke away in October 1968. The PFLP-GC was admitted to the Palestine Liberation Organization (PLO) in late 1969 and acquired a seat on the PLO Executive Committee in June 1974. Based first in Amman and then in Beirut, its headquarters have been in Damascus since 1982. During the late 1960s another, unrelated PFLP splinter group, led by Ahmad Za'rur and eventually known as the Organization of Arab Palestine, also used the name PFLP-GC, but it was usually distinguished as PFLP-GC (B). During this period the original PFLP-GC was therefore often known as PFLP-GC (A) and occasionally operated as the al-Aqsa Fida'iyyun Front.

Nominally Marxist-Leninist, the PFLP-GC has been one of the most uncompromising of the Palestinian "rejectionist" groups. In October 1974 it was a founding member of the Front of Palestinian Forces Rejecting Surrenderist Solutions (the Rejection Front). In 1983 it was one of two PLO factions to rebel after Yasir Arafat hinted at making peace with Israel, and it has since boycotted all PLO institutions, supporting a series of rejectionist coalitions from Damascus.

The PFLP-GC is known for its indiscriminate military actions specializing in the use of small,

Ahmed Jibril, the leader of the Popular Front for the Liberation of Palestine–General Command, a group which opposes the rule of Yasir Arafat. © REZA/WEBISTAN/CORBIS. REPRODUCED BY PERMISSION.

highly trained units for high-profile operations. It was responsible for a suicide raid on an apartment building in the northern Israeli town of Kiryat Shmona in April 1974 that killed eighteen Israeli civilians, and for the November 1987 hang-glider attack on an army camp in northeast Israel that killed six soldiers. It is presumed to be responsible for the February 1970 midair explosion of a Swiss airliner en route to Israel that killed more than forty-five people; the 1978 bombing of a Beirut building that killed more than two hundred PLO personnel; and a series of Syrian-backed attacks in Jordan and Europe, notably the bombing of a civilian airliner over Lockerbie, Scotland in December 1988. Its military positions across Lebanon face regular Israeli attacks, and Jibril's son Jihad, responsible for operations in Lebanon, was killed in 2002 by a car bomb that was widely believed to have been planted by Israel.

The PFLP-GC's close links with Syria (as well as Libya and, more recently, Iran) have reduced its autonomy, undermining its credibility among Palestinians when its other loyalties placed the PFLP-GC in military conflict with the PLO. In 1977 a faction led by Muhammad Zaydan and Tal'at Ya'qub split off to revive the PLF after Jibril justified Syrian military incursions into Palestinian camps in Lebanon. In 1984 Jibril was expelled from the PLO following Syria's 1983 confrontation with the PLO. A decade later, the PFLP-GC was implicated in attempts on Arafat's life. The PFLP-GC's presence in the West Bank and Gaza Strip is consequently small. Nevertheless, its 1985 prisoner exchange with Israel, enabling hundreds to return to the Palestinian territories, infused valuable (if primarily non–PFLP-GC) cadres into these territories. Its 1987 hang glider operation also perceptibly emboldened the Palestinian population on the eve of the Intifada, and from the 1990s, the PFLP-GC trained and smuggled arms to Islamist groups in the territories. Its Syrian-based radio station, Idha'at al-Quds (Radio Jerusalem), established in 1988 to encourage rebellion in the West Bank, was popular, and often jammed by Israel. It publishes *Ila al-Amam* (Forward), first issued in 1963, and *al-Jabha* (The front), which first appeared in 1969.

> See also FATAH, AL-; JIBRIL, AHMAD; PALESTINE LIBERATION ORGANIZATION (PLO); POPULAR FRONT FOR THE LIBERATION OF PALESTINE; REJECTION FRONT.

Bibliography

Cobban, Helena. *The Palestinian Liberation Organization: People, Power and Politics.* Cambridge, U.K.: Cambridge University Press, 1984.

Gresh, Alain. *The PLO—The Struggle Within: Towards an Independent Palestinian State,* revised edition, translated by A. M. Berrett. London: Zed Books, 1988.

Quandt, William B., et al. *The Politics of Palestinian Nationalism.* Berkeley: University of California Press, 1973.

Smith, Charles D. *Palestine and the Arab-Israeli Conflict.* Boston: Bedford/St. Martin's Press, 2004.

MOUIN RABBANI
UPDATED BY GEORGE R. WILKES

POPULAR FRONT FOR THE LIBERATION OF THE OCCUPIED ARABIAN GULF

Marxist, antigovernment organization of southern Oman (1968 to 1971).

The Popular Front for the Liberation of the Occupied Arabian Gulf (PFLOAG) was organized in 1968 as the successor to the Dhufar Liberation Front, a largely tribal group attempting to overthrow the rule of Sa'id ibn Taymur Al Bu Sa'id's dynasty in Oman's southernmost province. PFLOAG not only aimed to enlarge the scope of the rebellion, but gave it a radical, Marxist orientation and tried to impose a collectivist regime where its forces were in control. With financial support and weaponry from Iraq, the People's Republic of China, and the Soviet Union as well as a secure base in neighboring Marxist South Yemen (People's Democratic Republic of Yemen), the front took most of Dhufar from the shaky regime of Sultan Sa'id. The accession of his son, Qabus ibn Sa'id Al Bu Sa'id, by coup in July 1970, turned the situation around, with the considerable foreign military assistance from Great Britain and Iran playing a key role. Well-funded civil action programs helped secure the loyalty of a population little drawn to PFLOAG's anti-Islamic ideology. In December 1971 it absorbed the National Democratic Front for the Liberation of Oman and the Arab Gulf (NDFLOAG) and assumed its second identity as Popular Front for the Liberation of Oman and the Arab Gulf with acronym unchanged. In May 1974, after serious reverses, those favoring continued military action formed the Popular Front for the Liberation of Oman (PFLO). By 1976 Dhufar was completely and securely in government hands.

> See also AL BU SA'ID, QABUS IBN SA'ID; AL BU SA'ID, SA'ID IBN TAYMUR; NATIONAL DEMOCRATIC FRONT FOR THE LIBERATION OF OMAN AND THE ARAB GULF.

Bibliography

Allen, Calvin H., Jr. *Oman: The Modernization of the Sultanate.* Boulder, CO: Westview, 1987.

Peterson, J. E. *Defending Arabia.* New York: St. Martin's, 1986.

MALCOLM C. PECK

POPULATION

Demography is crucial to an understanding of economic, social, and political life in the Middle East.

Until the nineteenth century, the Middle East experienced a typical Malthusian demographic system: high fertility outpaced high mortality, but there was occasional extraordinary mortality from warfare, famine, or epidemic disease, particularly bubonic plague. The population grew slowly until one of these demographic crises occurred, dipped sharply, then

Children attend school in Baghdad, the heterogeneous capital city of Iraq. The population of Baghdad is nearly five million, accounting for approximately 25 percent of the country's total population. © REUTERS NEWMEDIA INC./CORBIS. REPRODUCED BY PERMISSION.

began to grow slowly once again. This pattern ended in much of the Middle East during the nineteenth century. Despite minor outbreaks, truly catastrophic epidemics ended with the cholera epidemic of 1865. The increase in central government control facilitated security, trade, and delivery of food to famine regions. Egypt's population began to grow early in the century, as did that of Anatolia and the coastal provinces of Ottoman Syria during the 1870s. Iraq, Arabia, and Iran took little part in either the improvement in civil conditions or population growth.

The period of World War I (and the wars in Anatolia that followed it) was a demographic watershed in the Middle East, a period of great mortality and forced migration unequalled in the previous millennium. After the war, the Middle East began a new period of population growth, erasing the wartime population losses within a decade. Turkey's population began to expand fairly rapidly, from 14.6 million in 1927 to 18 million in 1940. Egypt's population grew from 13 million inhabitants in 1917 to 16 million in 1937. Other countries grew less quickly, but population increased markedly across the region. Nevertheless, the Middle East can be described as underpopulated before World War II. Large areas of potentially fertile lands were uncultivated. Population density was low, due to high mortality and lack of developed resources. By modern standards, mortality had declined only slowly. In late Ottoman times, mortality had averaged more than 3.5 percent per year. This condition only gradually improved between the two world wars. However, Egypt, Palestine, and Turkey managed to lower mortality through irrigation, public sanitation, and by ending conditions of civil unrest that had diminished the distribution of crops and goods. Medical improvement was a minor factor.

Population of the Middle East, 1800 to 2025, in millions*

Year	Population	Year	Population
1800	32.8	1925	54.7
1825	33.4	1950	79.2
1850	33.8	1975	154.3
1875	36.0	2000	308.6
1900	44.1	2025	449.3

* Including the areas of today's Bahrain, Egypt, Gaza, Iran, Iraq, Israel, Jordan, Kuwait, Lebanon, Oman, Qatar, Saudi Arabia, Syria, Turkey, United Arab Emirates, West Bank, and Yemen.

SOURCE: Projections to 2000 and 2025 from United Nations, *World Population Prospects*, 2000. (medium-fertility variant)

TABLE BY GGS INFORMATION SERVICES, THE GALE GROUP.

After World War II, as in much of the world, the Middle Eastern population began to increase rapidly. Fertility, always high, remained so, while introduction of modern medicine greatly lowered mortality. Modern agricultural techniques and the new crops of the green revolution increased the ability of Middle Eastern economies to feed larger populations. The result was a population boom. From 1950 to 1990 the population of the Middle East increased threefold. By the 1960s the rate of population increase meant that, if the high rates continued, future populations would double every twenty-five years. These rates of increase put great strain on the economies of the region. The results have included rapid and unplanned urbanization

Life expectancy at birth*

	1950	2000		1950	2000
Bahrain	51	73	Yemen**	33	57
Egypt	42	68	Oman	36	74
Iran	46	69	Qatar	48	75
Iraq	44	61	Saudi Arabia	40	73
Israel	65	78	Syria	46	70
Jordan	43	72	Turkey	44	70
Kuwait	56	77	U.A.E.	48	76
Lebanon	56	71			

* "1950" is actually for the years 1950–1955
** 1950 is average for North and South Yemen

SOURCE: United Nations, *World Population Prospects*, 1990; World Bank, *World Development Indicators*, 2002.

TABLE BY GGS INFORMATION SERVICES, THE GALE GROUP.

and unemployment, as well as overuse of fertilizers and poor agricultural techniques that temporarily yield large crop increases but eventually exhaust the soil.

Fertility

The average fertility of Middle Eastern women changed little for centuries. Women who lived through their childbearing years (many did not) could expect to have six to seven children (the total fertility rate). Since the late 1970s fertility decreased in most countries. By 1999 the average woman in Turkey had 2.4 children, in Egypt 3.3, in Iran 2.7. However, in Syria and Saudi Arabia, the average remained very high, at 4.6 per woman. Women in Yemen and Oman had 6.2 children on average. Contraceptive usage varies greatly: in 1999, more than 60 percent of Turkish women used some form of contraception at some time in their lives; in Jordan, 27 percent. In some other countries the figures were much lower. Despite recent reductions, the Middle East remains one of the highest fertility regions in the world.

The history of high fertility has strained the capacity of the Middle Eastern economies. Nearly one-half of the population in Syria, Iraq, and Yemen is children under age fifteen. Even Middle Eastern countries with lower fertility, such as Turkey, have populations in which one-third are under fifteen. (This compares with 21 percent in the United States and 20 percent in Western Europe.)

If present fertility trends continue, future Middle Eastern populations will divide into two very different patterns. Israel is already nearing a European pattern of low fertility. Kuwait, Lebanon, Qatar, the Emirates, and Turkey are approaching that standard. Yemen, Syria, Iraq, Saudi Arabia, and others still retain high fertility. The demographics of the latter countries will in fifty years look very different from those of the former, with very large numbers of children and a fast-growing population. For example, at the beginning of the twenty-first century, Syria, Iraq, Jordan, and Saudi Arabia taken together had a slightly smaller population than Turkey. If trends continue, in fifty years they will together have twice as many people as Turkey.

Fertility and mortality, 1980–1999

	Total fertility rates (births per woman)		Mortality rates (crude death rate/1000 people)	
	1980	1999	1980	1999
Egypt	5.1	3.3	13	7
Iran	6.7	2.7	11	6
Israel	3.2	2.9	7	6
Syria	7.4	3.7	9	5
Saudi Arabia	7.3	5.5	9	4
United Arab Emirates	5.4	3.3	5	3
Yemen	7.9	6.2	19	12

SOURCE: World Bank, *Development Indicators*, 2001.

TABLE BY GGS INFORMATION SERVICES, THE GALE GROUP.

Mortality

In the absence of extraordinary causes, fertility would have always outstripped mortality in the traditional Middle East. The population would have risen at approximately I percent per year. In fact, epidemics, wars, and famines meant that mortality equaled fertility. The most common causes of death were gastrointestinal diseases. Infant mortality was particularly high, with more than 40 percent of children dying before their first birthday, more than half before age five. Epidemics of plague and cholera caused temporary high mortality. In Egypt, for example, cholera took more than 100,000 lives in each of the epidemics of 1855 and 1865 and almost 200,000 in 1831. Bubonic plague took 500,000 lives in 1835 alone.

Warfare also caused great mortality in the nineteenth century. The Ottoman wars with Russia were particularly deadly for both military and civilian populations. From the beginning of the Balkan Wars in 1912 to the end of fighting in the Turkish War of Independence in 1922, the region suffered some of the worst wartime mortality in history. The highest death rates were found in eastern Anatolia—the result of war between the Ottomans and Russians and conflict between Muslims and Armenians in western Anatolia after the Greek invasion and in Palestine. In Anatolia, 3.8 million died (22 percent), and in Palestine 50,000 (6 percent). In all those conflicts, starvation and disease took a higher toll than did actual battle. Lebanon also suffered mass starvation during the war.

After World War II, the rapid introduction of modern medicine, public sanitation techniques, and agricultural improvements reduced mortality rates sharply. In 1950 the Middle East had a high crude death rate (deaths divided by total population) of more than 2.3 percent a year, but by 1999 it had fallen to less than 0.6 percent a year. Some countries, such as Egypt (0.7 percent in 1999) and Yemen (1.2 percent in 1999) lagged behind. A major part of the postwar improvement came in infant mortality. In 1950 one in five Middle Eastern children died before age five; in 1999 only one in nineteen died before age five, compared to a world average of one in thirteen.

The Iran–Iraq War of 1980–1988 resulted in the deaths of hundreds of thousands of Iranian and

Tenement housing in Cairo, Egypt. Estimates of Cairo's population vary from 8 to 12 million as of 2003. A population explosion that began in 1952 has resulted in overcrowding, scarce housing, unemployment, and health concerns. © TOM NEBBIA/CORBIS. REPRODUCED BY PERMISSION.

Istanbul is Turkey's largest city, boasting a population of over ten million as of 2000 and an annual increase of 3.45 percent due to migration from the countryside. One of every six Turks lives in Istanbul, contributing to a population density of 1,700 persons per square kilometer. © YANN ARTHUS-BERTRAND/CORBIS. REPRODUCED BY PERMISSION.

Iraqi soldiers, with consequent effects on the size and gender structure of both populations. In addition, it is estimated that the Baʿthist regime in Iraq killed some three hundred thousand of its own citizens during campaigns against the Kurds in the north of the country and against the Shiʿa in the south.

The United Nations has lowered its projections of the region's population growth to 2025 as a result of the faster than expected decline in fertility. This has translated into slower population growth rates starting in Egypt and spreading east. The absolute increases in population are still growing in many countries because of past fast growth rates, and it will take ten to twenty years for slower growth rates to translate into smaller absolute increases.

Migration

Refugee migrations have been a major demographic factor during the past two centuries. Only the most prominent population transfers can be mentioned here: During the nineteenth and early twentieth centuries, great population movements took place as direct results of Russian imperial expansion in the Crimea and Caucasus and of nationalistic movements among the Christian peoples of the Ottoman Empire. Russia expelled or caused the migration of approximately 1.2 million Circassian, Abhazian, and Laz Muslims from the lands of the Eastern Black Sea. Of these, 800,000 survived and most eventually settled in what today is Turkey, as did the 300,000 Crimean Tatars forced to emigrate during the 1850s and 1860s. A sizable group of the Circassians were settled in the Arab world. Russian expansion also fostered a century-long population exchange, with much attendant mortality, between the Turks and Kurds of Russian Transcaucasia and the Armenians of Ottoman Anatolia and Iran. Between the 1820s and 1920s, 500,000 Armenians and 400,000 Muslims (not including the Circassians and Abhazians) crossed the borders. During World War I, an estimated one million Muslims were internal refugees in Eastern Anatolia; an estimated 275,000 Armenians were deported to or were refugees in the Arab world, and 135,000 were refugees in Europe and the Americas.

Nearly 600,000 Turks (40 percent of its Turkish population) were surviving refugees from the new state of Bulgaria after the Russian–Ottoman Wars of 1877–1878. Greece, Bulgaria, Serbia, and Montenegro expelled to Anatolia and Eastern Thrace 414,000 Turks during and immediately after the Balkan Wars of 1912–1913. During World War I, the Turkish War of Independence, and the Greek-Turkish population exchange that followed, more than one million Greeks from Anatolia and eastern Thrace went to Greece and 360,000 Turks from Greece to Turkey. Up to 1.5 million Turks were internal refugees within Anatolia and eastern Thrace during the Greek-Turkish war.

Before World War II a major immigration of primarily European Jews swelled the Jewish population of Palestine from 60,000 in 1918 to 600,000 in 1946. More than 700,000 Palestinian Arabs were refugees in the Arab-Israel War of 1948. Between 1948 and 1975, 1.6 million Jews came to Israel. Half of these were from the Middle East and North Africa, another third from Eastern Europe, especially the Balkans. Immigration to Israel has continued recently with nearly one million Jews from Russia and successor states.

The only Middle Eastern country to be heavily affected by refugees from the Afghan War was Iran, which accepted more than two million Afghan refugees. Turkey took in 300,000 ethnic Turkish refugees from Bulgaria, as well as Iranian refugees after the Iranian revolution and Kurdish refugees after the Gulf War. Many of the refugees to Iran and Turkey have been repatriated or have moved to other countries. A significant number of the refugees from Afghanistan, Iraq, and Bulgaria have returned home at least once, only to leave once again when economic and political conditions changed.

The quest for employment has been a major cause of migration into and from the Middle East. In Ottoman times, 175,000 Turkish emigrants went to the United States from 1869 to 1914. More recently,

Drought, hunger, and over two decades of war forced over one million Afghan refugees—mostly women and children—to seek shelter in neighboring countries. In 2002, a massive program undertaken by the United Nations High Commissioner for Refugees, the Afghan Ministry of Refugees and Repatriation, and the governments of the affected countries helped relocate some 1.8 million Afghans back to their home country. © REUTERS NEWMEDIA INC./CORBIS. REPRODUCED BY PERMISSION.

the International Labor Organization estimated that 1.8 million Turks were working in Germany, the Netherlands, and Belgium in 1988. During the same year, 20,000 Koreans, 50,000 Indonesians, and 90,000 from the Philippines worked in the Gulf states. Before the Gulf War, up to two million foreign workers, mainly Egyptians, worked in Iraq.

Urbanization has been the most significant factor in internal migration in the modern Middle East. Driven by population pressure in rural areas, the urban population increased from twenty-one million (27 percent urban) in 1950 to 185 million (60 percent urban) in 1999. There is considerable variance between countries: In 1990, Syria's population was only half urban, Egypt's less than half urban, while the populations of Iraq and Turkey were more than 60 percent urban. Istanbul was one of the twenty largest cities in the world. Smaller countries such as Israel and Lebanon were as urbanized as Europe or North America.

Censuses and Population Data

A census by definition registers the entire population at one time. Prior to 1882 no real census was taken in the Middle East. In the place of censuses, the Ottoman and Egyptian governments made compilations of registration data. The registers were lists of inhabitants by household in each village, taken by government officials. These often produced surprisingly accurate counts of the population, especially in areas that were under close governmental control. On occasion, the central governments of Egypt and the Ottoman Empire ordered general updates and compilations of the registers. During the 1860s the Ottoman government began to publish population numbers in the *salnames* (yearbooks) of its provinces. The Ottoman compilations usually listed data by sex and religion only, even though age-specific figures were kept and are available in archives. The 1313 Istatistik-i Umumi ("1895 General Statistics") was the only Ottoman publication to include data by age group. Population data was collected sporadically in Iran, but was not published officially.

The first real census in the Middle East was taken by the khedival government in Egypt just prior to the British occupation in 1882. Under British statistical influence, Egypt published censuses in 1897, 1907, 1917, 1927, and 1937. The British also undertook a limited form of census in Aden (later People's Democratic Republic of Yemen) in 1881, then published other counts of Aden, as part of the censuses of India, in 1891, 1901, 1911, 1921, and 1931. The Turkish republic began a modern census program with censuses in 1927 and 1935, followed by censuses every five years. The British Mandate government in Palestine took fairly accurate and very detailed censuses in 1922 and 1931, and with limited success updated the census data through birth and death records and published the data in the Palestine Blue Books. The French collected data in Syria and Lebanon, but only published brief summaries that indicate poor recording. An incomplete census was taken in Lebanon in 1942–1943.

Modern Middle Eastern censuses have routinely been supplemented by publications of detailed information on marriage, divorce, birth, and death, although these often have been accurate only for urban areas. Sample surveys of the population, often supported by the United Nations or other international bodies, have also been published.

Bibliography

Karpat, Kemal H. *Ottoman Population, 1830–1914: Demographic and Social Characteristics.* Madison: University of Wisconsin Press, 1985.

McCarthy, Justin. *The Arab World, Turkey, and the Balkans (1878–1914): A Handbook of Historical Statistics.* Boston: G. K. Hall, 1982.

United Nations. *Demographic Yearbook.* New York: United Nations Department of Economic and Social Affairs, Statistical Office, 1948–.

United Nations. *World Population Monitoring.* New York: United Nations, Department of International Economic and Social Affairs, 1989–.

United Nations. *World Population Prospects.* New York: United Nations, 1900s–. 2000 edition available from <http://www.un.org/esa/population>.

United Nations Department of Economic and Social Affairs. *Sex and Age Distributions of Population.* New York: United Nations, 1990–1996.

JUSTIN MCCARTHY
UPDATED BY PAUL RIVLIN

Middle Eastern censuses after World War II

Country		Census years
Bahrain	1941,	1950, 1959, 1965, 1971, 1981, 1991, 2001
Egypt	1947,	1960, 1966, 1976, 1986
Iran	1956,	1966, 1976, 1986, 1996
Iraq	1947,	1957, 1965, 1977, 1987, 1997
Israel	1948,	1961, 1972, 1983, 1995
Jordan	1952,	1961, 1979, 1994
Kuwait	1957,	1961, 1965, 1970, 1975, 1980, 1985, 1990, 1995
Lebanon	1970	
N. Yemen	1975,	1986
Oman	1977,	1981, 1993, 2000
Qatar	1970,	1986, 1997
Saudi Arabia	1962/63,	1974, 1992
S. Yemen	1946,	1955, 1973, 1988
Syria	1947,	1960, 1970, 1981, 1994
Turkey	1927,	1935, 1940, 1945, 1950, 1955, 1960, 1965, 1970, 1975, 1980, 1985, 1990, 2000
U.A.E.	1968,	1975, 1980, 1985, 1990, 1995

TABLE BY GGS INFORMATION SERVICES, THE GALE GROUP.

PORT SA'ID

Mediterranean port in Egypt.

Port Sa'id (Bur Sa'id), Egypt, situated on a narrow peninsula on the Mediterranean Sea coast, is located on the west side and at the northern end of the Suez

Canal, which links the Mediterranean and Red Sea. Established in conjunction with canal construction in 1859, it was named for Sa'id Pasha, viceroy of Egypt (1854–1863). Built in nineteenth-century European architectural style to accommodate Europeans working on Ferdinand de Lesseps's Suez Canal Project (1859–1869), it is complemented by a twin city, Port Fouad, located on the eastern side of the canal. The harbor became a maritime fueling station with export industries (especially chemical, tobacco, cotton, and food processing) supplementing sardine fishing and the production of salt from evaporated seawater. In 1904 a railroad link was completed between Port Sa'id and Cairo. As a major trade and business center, Port Sa'id thrived through both world wars. In July 1956 Egypt nationalized the canal after it had been an international waterway for nearly eighty-seven years. The port was strategic during the Arab–Israel wars and was attacked by Israeli forces in 1967 and 1973. The harbor was closed from 1967 to 1975, and most inhabitants evacuated the city. Egypt regained Port Sa'id in 1973, instituted major residential and commercial reconstruction, and established a tax-free industrial zone. Tourism was encouraged, and the city became an important summer resort. In 2003 Port Sa'id was the nation's fourth largest city, with 565,000 inhabitants, and second only to Alexandria as a commercial port.

See also SA'ID PASHA; SUEZ CANAL.

Bibliography

Modelski, Sylvia. *Port Sa'id Revisited.* Washington, DC: Faros, 2000.

DAVID WALDNER
UPDATED BY CHARLES C. KOLB

POSTAGE STAMPS

Government-issued stamps encapsulate the history and culture of the region.

The Islamic states of the Middle East had operated elaborate postal messenger systems since the seventh century, but it was Great Britain in 1840 that issued the world's first postage stamp. It depicted Queen Victoria. Postage stamps quickly spread, with the Ottoman Empire issuing its first stamp in 1863, followed by Egypt in 1866, Persia in 1868, Afghani-

The Ottoman Empire issued its first postage stamp in 1863. Other Middle Eastern nations followed suit. The first stamps to be issued refrained from depicting human figures, but in the late nineteenth century, some nations did begin to issue stamps with portraits of current or past leaders on them. COURTESY OF DONALD M. REID, GEORGIA STATE UNIVERSITY.

stan in 1871, the Hijaz (now part of Saudi Arabia) in 1916, and Yemen in 1926. Elsewhere, British, French, and Italian colonial officials in the Middle East designed the first stamps for their jurisdictions.

Early Middle Eastern stamps, like Islamic coins before them, observed conservative Islamic tradition by rarely portraying human figures. Arabesque designs, calligraphy, or a crescent and star served as symbols instead. In 1876, Persia broke with tradition by showing its ruler on a stamp; the Ottomans did the same in 1913. Egypt, Iraq, and Transjordan followed during the 1920s; then Afghanistan, Syria, and Lebanon during the 1940s. Saudi Arabia, more isolated and conservative, waited until the 1960s.

Rulers appeared variously in traditional dress, in Western coat and tie, or in military uniform. Turkey's Mustafa Kemal Atatürk, who secularized Turkey after the dissolution of the Ottoman Empire by, among other things, outlawing Muslim headwear, wore civilian dress on his stamps from 1926 on, but many soldiers-turned-president preferred military uniforms. After coming to power in 1979, Iraq's President Saddam Hussein appeared variously on stamps in coat and tie, army uniform, and Arab *kafiyya*. Some rulers promoted a cult of the leader on their stamps, with the hero towering above the masses he claimed to embody. Syria's Hafiz al-Asad, Egypt's Anwar al-Sadat, and Iraq's Saddam saturated stamps with their own portraits. Egypt's president Gamal Abdel Nasser was more reticent, and Husni Mubarak followed Nasser's rather than Sadat's example in this regard.

The first stamps of the Ottoman Empire, Egypt, Persia, Afghanistan, Saudi Arabia, and Yemen bore inscriptions in only Arabic script. Although they were not French colonies, they soon added French, long the main language of world diplomacy. All later switched to English as their second language on stamps—except Afghanistan, which kept French, and Turkey, whose adoption of the Latin alphabet in 1928 made its Turkish-only stamps partly accessible to Westerners. French colonial possessions used French, and British possessions English. French Algeria and Italian Libya used no Arabic on their stamps until independence (1962 and 1951, respectively). Hebrew has been the main language on Israel's stamps since independence in 1948, with English and Arabic as secondary languages.

European colonial stamps presented romanticized and orientalist colonial picturesque themes—pre-Islamic ruins, old mosques, colorful landscapes, and folk scenes. European officials first selected the pyramids and sphinx as symbols for Egyptian stamps, but many Egyptians came to identify, at least partially, with these pre-Islamic symbols. Egypt often commemorates ancient pharaonic treasures on stamps; folk costumes are also shown as part of a proud national heritage. Even so, stamps with such themes are often issued with Western tourists and collectors in mind.

Revolutions drastically changed stamp designs. "The people"—symbolic soldiers, peasants, workers, professionals, and women in both traditional and Western dress—celebrate liberation, modernization, and the drive for economic development. Stamps advertise such things as petroleum pipelines, factories, and broadcasting stations. Socialist countries commemorated land reform, the spread of healthcare, and five-year plans. In addition to such symbols of material and social progress, Israel also depicts themes from biblical history, Jewish history, and Zionism.

The stamps of Israel and the Arab states also reflect their respective versions of the Arab–Israel conflict. Stamps commemorate the war dead, advertise the latest aircraft, and boast of specific victories. Most Arab countries have issued stamps deploring the Dayr Yasin massacre (as they describe the event) of 1948, mourn the plight of Palestinian refugees, and celebrate Palestinian resistance to Israel. Since Israel's occupation of East Jerusalem in 1967, the Dome of the Rock (in the Haram al-Sharif) has often appeared on stamps as a symbol of Arab and Islamic claims to Jerusalem. The stamps of Arab countries that depict maps omit the name *Israel,* showing only the borders and sometimes the name of pre-1948 Palestine. With its borders still unsettled and controversial, Israel's stamp designers make it a practice to avoid showing national maps.

During the 1950s and 1960s, pan-Arab themes tended to overshadow symbols of local territorial patriotism. Beginning in the 1970s, Islamic themes became popular—mosques, Qur'ans, hegira dates, and crescents—on stamps honoring the prophet Muhammad's birthday, the Islamic New Year, and the hajj. Islamic themes stand out above all on the stamps of the Islamic Republic of Iran since the 1979 revolution, depicting deceased Shi'ite holy men, martyrs killed in the jihad (holy struggle) against Iraq, and anti-American symbols.

See also ARAB–ISRAEL CONFLICT; COLONIALISM IN THE MIDDLE EAST; DAYR YASIN; ORIENTALISM.

Bibliography

Hazard, Harry W. "Islamic Philately as an Ancillary Discipline." In *The World of Islam: Studies in Honour of Philip K.*

Hitti, edited by James Kritzeck and R. B. Winder. New York: St. Martin's Press; London: Macmillan, 1959.

Reid, Donald Malcolm. "The Postage Stamp: A Window on Saddam Hussein's Iraq." *Middle East Journal* 47 (1993): 77–89.

Reid, Donald Malcolm. "The Symbolism of Postage Stamps: A Source for the Historian." *Journal of Contemporary History* 19 (1984): 223–249.

Scott 2003 Standard Postage Stamp Catalogue, 9 vols. Available from <http://www.scottonline.com>.

DONALD MALCOLM REID

POTASH INDUSTRY

Potash, a potassium or potassium compound, is used in industry and as a component of agricultural fertilizer.

In 1861 Adolph Frank, a German Jew, discovered the benefits of potash, and his work helped create the potash industry. In 1902 Theodor Herzl's utopian work, *Altneuland,* envisioned a modern industry based on the chemical compounds in the Dead Sea. Moshe Novomeysky (1873–1961), a mining engineer and Zionist who immigrated to Palestine from Siberia in 1920, devised a plan to extract the Dead Sea's chemical compounds for industrial use, and approached the British government for concessionary rights. Following ten years of negotiation, he established the Palestine Potash Company, which became a major enterprise in the Middle East. The first plant was established on the northwestern shore of the sea in 1931. In 1937 a second plant was established on the southwestern shore, near Sodom. The Anglo-American Committee of Inquiry (1946) noted the Palestine Potash Works as a positive point of contact between the Arab and Jewish economies.

Much of the company was destroyed during the Arab–Israel War of 1948. Only the southwestern plant remained and, after the establishment of the State of Israel, became a government-controlled company. But production did not resume until 1954, when the road from Beersheba to Sodom was completed. Since then the company, privatized under the name Dead Sea Works Ltd., and its output have grown significantly. By 2000 Dead Sea Works was one of the world's largest producers of potash, producing almost 10 percent of the global output.

During the 1980s Jordan developed its own potash industry with technical and financial assistance from a variety of countries. But by the turn of the century sales were declining, with the Jordan Phosphate Mines Company reporting a loss of $40 million for the year 2000.

Bibliography

Novomeysky, Moses A. *Given to Salt: The Struggle for the Dead Sea Concession.* London: Parrish, 1958.

Novomeysky, Moses A. *My Siberian Life.* London: Parrish, 1956.

CHAIM I. WAXMAN

POTSDAM CONVENTION

Russo–German agreement concerning their involvement in the Middle East.

From its inception, the German-dominated Berlin–Baghdad Railway project aroused the suspicion of the other European powers. On 6 through 9 August, 1911, Germany and Russia concluded an agreement at Potsdam, Germany, whereby Russia acquiesced to continued German involvement in the railway in return for a German affirmation of Russia's position in Persia (now Iran).

See also BERLIN–BAGHDAD RAILWAY.

Bibliography

Anderson, M. S. *The Eastern Question, 1774–1923: A Study in International Relations.* London: Macmillan; and New York: St. Martin's, 1966.

Hurewitz, J. C., ed. *The Middle East and North Africa in World Politics: A Documentary Record,* 2d edition. 2 vols. New Haven, CT: Yale University Press, 1975.

ZACHARY KARABELL

POWELL, COLIN L.
[1937–]

U.S. army officer, diplomat.

Born in New York City to Jamaican immigrant parents, Colin Luther Powell received his B.S. in geology from the City College of New York in 1958, and later received an M.B.A. from George Washington University in Washington, D.C. Powell was commissioned as an officer in the United States army in 1958. He was sent as an adviser to the army of the Republic of Vietnam (South Vietnam) in 1962, returning for a second tour of combat in 1968 to 1969 after the U.S. military entered the conflict in force. His Vietnam service left him with eleven military decorations.

Powell rose thereafter through the army to the rank of general. From October 1989 to September 1993 he was the first African American to serve as chairman of the Joint Chiefs of Staff—the highest military officer in the nation. During that period Powell oversaw the massive deployment of U.S. forces in the Middle East and the Horn of Africa, during the 1991 Gulf War and the intervention in Somalia in 1992. He was the author of the Powell Doctrine, which advocates committing U.S. forces to war only if massive force is used in conjunction with carefully articulated political goals and a defined exit strategy.

After several years of retirement from the military, Powell was appointed secretary of state beginning in January 2001. During his tenure he again was involved with momentous U.S. policy decisions regarding the Middle East and Southwest Asia. While he was secretary of state U.S. forces invaded Afghanistan in October 2001 and Iraq in March 2003. Powell was also active in pushing Israelis and Palestinians to resume negotiations in accordance with the Road Map for peace created by the United States, Russia, the European Union, and the United Nations.

See also AFGHANISTAN: U.S. INTERVENTION IN; BUSH, GEORGE WALKER; GULF CRISIS (1990–1991); GULF WAR (1991); SEPTEMBER 11TH, 2001; WAR IN IRAQ (2003).

Bibliography

Atkinson, Rick. *Crusade: The Untold Story of the Persian Gulf War.* New York: Mariner Books, 1994.

Powell, Colin. *My American Journey.* New York: Random House, 1995.

Trainor, Bernard, and Gordon, Michael R. *The Generals' War: The Inside Story of the Conflict in the Gulf.* New York: Back Bay Books, 1995.

MICHAEL R. FISCHBACH

PRINCESS BASMA WOMEN'S RESOURCE CENTER

Women's resource center for policy makers and women's groups in Jordan.

Prior to the 8 March 1996 celebrations of International Women's Day, the Princess Basma Women's Resource Center was opened in Amman. At the inauguration of the center Princess Basma, sister of the late Jordanian King Hussein ibn Talal, stressed that "the women's movement is undergoing a new stage in Jordan, which is that of implementing and executing strategies," adding that "both the governmental and nongovernmental organizations that deal with women's issues should co-operate, re-examine, and develop ways of implementing strategies." The center is directed by Princess Basma's daughter, Farah Daghestani, and it aims to gather and analyze information and enhance effective policies on women's issues. It also aims to increase the participation of women in development and decision-making processes in addition to organizing seminars and training workshops for women's groups. The center intends to implement mechanisms for the Platform of Action, which was agreed to at the 1995 United Nations Fourth Conference on Women in Beijing. The establishment of the center is perceived by many as an attempt by Princess Basma to take full control of women's issues in Jordan, especially because it came after the 1992 establishment of the Jordanian National Committee for Women and the 1995 establishment of the Jordanian National Women's Forum.

See also BASMA BINT TALAL; GENDER: GENDER AND LAW; GENDER: GENDER AND POLITICS; JORDAN.

Bibliography

Brand, Laurie. *Women, the State, and Political Liberalization: Middle Eastern and North African Experience.* New York: Columbia University Press, 1998.

Princess Basma Women's Resource Center web site. Available from <http://www.nic.gov.jo/jmaw/pbwrc.htm>.

ISIS NUSAIR

PROGRESSIVE SOCIALIST PARTY

Lebanese political party, founded in Beirut in 1949 that played an important role in Lebanon after independence.

The Progressive Socialist Party (PSP) was a major vehicle for the political ambitions of its founder, Kamal Jumblatt. Born in Mukhtara in 1917, Jumblatt belonged to one of the major Druze families, the head of a major Druze family confederation (the Jumblatis) in Lebanon.

The party was originally formed as a multisectarian party with Christians and Muslim intellectuals comprising its leadership, but increasingly it became organized around its president and his electoral calculations and interests. Major policy decisions were undertaken by the president, who is the center of authority. Despite claims to the contrary, the PSP is widely perceived to operate according to the sectarian political interests of the Druze community, as determined by its leader.

The tenets of the party are a mixture of social democratic practices and Arab nationalist thought. Jumblatt believed that industrialization was inevitable but that it had to be reined in because of ecological concerns. The PSP has advocated the abolition of the political confessional system, the creation of civil courts for civil marriages, a unified educational system, the nationalization of important services, and a progressive inheritance taxation system. In foreign policy, the PSP has emphasized Lebanon's Arab identity and role, solidarity with the Palestinian cause, and support for major issues and concerns regarding developing countries.

During the civil war (1975–1976), the PSP under Jumblatt became the linchpin for the Lebanese National Movement and fielded 2,000 fighters. Following the assassination of Jumblatt, his son, Walid Jumblatt, became the president of the PSP in 1977. Walid Jumblatt succeeded in fending off any challenges to his leadership within the Druze community, and in the War of the Mountain (beginning in 1983) he emerged as the undisputed leader of the Druze community. The party has been continuously represented in the parliament since 1972, including in the post-Ta'if parliaments.

See also DRUZE; JUMBLATT, KAMAL; JUMBLATT, WALID; LEBANESE NATIONAL MOVEMENT (LNM).

Bibliography

Suleiman, Michael W. *Political Parties in Lebanon.* Ithaca, NY: Cornell University Press, 1967.

GEORGE E. IRANI
UPDATED BY AS'AD ABUKHALIL

PROTECTORATE STATES

Traditional southern Arabian political entities protected by British treaty from 1839 to 1967 when they united to form South Yemen.

The dozen or so protectorate states to the north and east of the Aden colony occupied a huge area relative to that of the colony. They were viewed primarily as a political-military buffer for that highly valued port and military base. Over the 125 years of British occupation of Aden since 1839, the protectorates were defined and redefined geographically as well as administratively in a largely ad hoc way. Political-military pressure first from the Ottoman Turks and then from the imamate of North Yemen caused the British to become increasingly involved in the governance of the states in Aden's immediate environs during the first six decades of the twentieth century; local political turmoil in the decades after World War I drew the British more directly into the governance of the vast Hadramawt region far to the east of Aden. Out of these "independent," amorphous protectorates, eventually in combination with Aden itself, the British in the 1960s sought to build the South Arabia Federation, the ship of state they hoped would succeed them when they withdrew in 1967. They failed, but Aden and the protectorate states went on to comprise South Yemen, the People's Democratic Republic of Yemen (PDRY).

See also HADRAMAWT; PEOPLE'S DEMOCRATIC REPUBLIC OF YEMEN.

Bibliography

Gavin, R. J. *Aden under British Rule, 1839–1967.* New York: Barnes and Noble Books, 1975.

Pieragostini, Karl. *Britain, Aden, and South Arabia: Abandoning Empire.* New York: St. Martin's, 1991.

ROBERT D. BURROWES

PROTESTANTISM AND PROTESTANT MISSIONS

Protestant missions were active in the Middle East from the nineteenth century.

Protestant denominations based chiefly in the United States and Britain have sponsored missionary activities in the Middle East since the opening of the nineteenth century, leaving a legacy of educational and benevolent institutions whose influence is felt to the present day. Protestantism, one of the three major branches of Christianity, encompasses a large number of denominations with widely differing liturgical and theological structures. What they have in common is that they do not recognize the moral and doctrinal authority of the Roman pontiff, they stress the centrality of the Bible and each individual's interpretation of it, and they share the belief that in the matter of salvation, the relationship between the individual and God is unmediated.

Missions in the Nineteenth Century

The most prominent missionary organization in the United States was the American Board of Commissioners for Foreign Missions (ABCFM), supported by the Congregational Church, which established mission stations in Lebanon in 1823, in Constantinople in 1831, and in Urmia (Iran) in 1834. In 1870 the ABCFM turned over part of its territory of operations, including Lebanon, to the Board of Foreign Missions of the Presbyterian Church. The Arabian Mission, founded as a nondenominational mission under the auspices of the Dutch Reformed Church in America in 1889, established a school in Basra and hospitals in Muscat, Bahrain, and Kuwait. In Britain the leading missionary organization in the Middle East was the Church Missionary Society (CMS), which began work in Smyrna (İzmir) in 1815, in Egypt in 1825, in Julfa (Isfahan) in 1875, and in Damascus in 1860. Among many smaller or short-lived mission societies that attempted work in the Middle East were the Boston Female Society for Promoting Christianity amongst the Jews, founded in 1816, and the London Society for Promoting Christianity amongst the Jews.

The original goal of Protestant missions in the Middle East was to preach the Gospel to Muslims. Both goal and method met immediate obstacles: Despite Muslim respect for the prophethood of Jesus, Christ as deity was and is incompatible with Islamic monotheism; for the person to be converted, leaving one's religious community, whether Christian, Muslim, or Jewish, meant separation from family and social networks; politically, under Ottoman authority missionaries were forbidden to preach among Muslims; and finally, the price of apostasy in Islamic law is death. Lack of familiarity with indigenous languages on the part of missionaries was also a serious obstacle to successful preaching.

Consequently, in a pattern that most missionary societies were to follow, the ABCFM turned its attention to indigenous Christian communities: Nestorian, Armenian, Coptic, Greek, and Syriac. Considered by the ABCFM to be "nominal Christians," unschooled in the Bible and bankrupt of Christian virtues, these Christians were to be reformed from within so as to serve as models of emulation to their Muslim neighbors, and ultimately become the instrument of their evangelization. The method of attracting potential proselytes to the Gospel message was benevolent service, such as establishing schools for children and clinics to offer medical care. Often such evangelizing aroused the resentment and noncooperation of indigenous church leaders whose parishioners began to gravitate to the missions, and with good reason: Protestant missionaries were perceived to be well-connected politically and able to offer protection to minorities; they offered schools and medical care available nowhere else; and, after the creation of a Protestant Millet, becoming Protestant entitled converts to commercial privileges originally afforded only to Europeans.

The outcome was breaking off of separate Protestant congregations from each of the Eastern Orthodox churches, which had already been fractured by the creation of separate Catholic denominations. In Turkey, where Armenians were the primary target, there were 111 Armenian Protestant churches by 1895, and in Egypt, by 1926 there were 150 congregations of Coptic Protestant Christians with 155 Egyptian clergy. As a percentage of the total population, the number of Christians of all denominations declined precipitously in the last decades of the twentieth century, especially in Palestine, but in the mid-1970s there were altogether about 250,000 indigenous Protestants in the Middle East.

Protestant missions have been criticized for bringing about increased sectarianism in a region already fragmented by religious sectarianism. Missionary activity has also been blamed for prompting violence against religious minorities, such as the massacre of Nestorian Assyrian Christians by Kurds in 1843 and the assaults against the Alawi in eastern Turkey later in the century. On the other hand, the benevolent work of Protestant missions brought about positive and lasting change. In order to proselytize, for example, missionaries imported the first printing presses into the region, prepared translations, and helped to expand literacy. Missionary health care institutions, such as the Arabian Mission hospitals in Bahrain and Kuwait, the Edinburgh Medical Mission in Damascus, the CMS medical missions in Baghdad and Mosul, and twelve missionary hospitals in Iran, offered the best medical care available for their time.

The most enduring achievement of the missions lay in founding institutions of higher education, such as the American University of Beirut, established in 1864 as the Syrian Protestant College; Robert College in Constantinople (1863); and the American University in Cairo (1920). The Presbyterian Mission's American Junior College for Women in Beirut, the American College for Girls in Cairo, and Constantinople College for Girls were the first institutions of higher education for women in the Middle East. Around the Persian Gulf and in many rural areas across the region, missionary schools were the only secondary schools offering secular subjects for girls until well after World War I. The British Syrian Mission alone opened fifty-six schools for girls, starting in 1860.

By the end of World War I, missionary work in the Middle East began to decline along with Western enthusiasm for the missionary enterprise worldwide. In the 1930s and 1940s governments of the newly independent states in the Middle East placed increasing limitations on missionary activities, by nationalizing schools, for example, so that many missionary societies consolidated their efforts or ceased operations.

Contemporary Missions

Since about 1980 globalization has brought Protestant missions back onto the world stage in a new burst of activity. Using the Internet and satellite television for fundraising and recruitment, and establishing cooperative links with international agencies, churches, and other mission organizations abroad, mission societies both old and new have a presence in almost every country in the Middle East.

In method, purpose, and constituency, these societies fall into two broadly divergent categories. On the one hand are spiritual and institutional de-

scendants of mainline Protestant denominations who have consolidated mission projects institutionally and partnered their efforts with each other and with indigenous Christian churches. Concerned with Christian benevolent action for the benefit of all, as opposed to proselytizing on behalf of a particular religious doctrine, these mission organizations focus on building community with indigenous religious groups, promoting social justice, and alleviating human suffering. Global Ministries, for example, represents a consolidation of the Division of Overseas Ministries of the Disciples of Christ and Wider Church Ministries of the United Church of Christ, and partners with a wide network of regional and international religious organizations that share their goals and values. These links include Churches for Middle East Peace, which is itself an ecumenical advocacy group of mainline U.S. and Middle Eastern Protestant churches, the Coptic Evangelical Organization for Social Services (CEOSS), Sabeel Ecumenical Liberation Theology Center, the Young Men's Christian Association International, and the Middle East Council of Churches, which is a fellowship of local Christian communions tied to the World Council of Churches (WCC). The WCC maintains its own relief agency in the Middle East, Action of the Churches Together (ACT), which responds to emergencies by joining forces with like-minded international agencies. In anticipation of humanitarian needs resulting from the 2003 U.S.-led war in Iraq, for example, ACT joined with U.K.-based Christian Aid, Norwegian Church Aid, Lutheran World Federation, and the Dutch-based Inter Church Organization for Development Cooperation.

By contrast, U.S. conservative evangelical missionary organizations targeting the Middle East are concerned primarily with evangelizing Muslims through forthright teaching that salvation comes through Jesus Christ alone. For these groups, extending humanitarian aid is a worthy task in its own right, but it is to be given in tandem with a Christian message. The International Mission Board of the Southern Baptist Convention, for example, in anticipation of Iraqi refugees crossing into Jordan in 2003, sent food boxes carrying a quote from John 1:17 translated into Arabic: "For the Law was given through Moses; grace and truth were realized through Jesus Christ." Similarly, the evangelical mission Samaritan's Purse (SP) supports a health clinic in Afghanistan and a hospital, schools, and agricultural and food aid in war-torn Sudan, where mission staff are bound to fulfill SP's statement of faith, which includes the belief that evangelism is a responsibility of the church and of every individual Christian. There are also evangelicals in the Middle East who encourage activities that have the effect of overt evangelism. For example, in 1995, religious associations in Lebanon and in Egypt joined a consortium of European and U.S. evangelical groups to establish a Christian satellite television station, SAT-7.

One outcome of proselytizing among Muslims has been a spate of assaults on evangelical missionaries, including the 2002 killing in southern Lebanon of a U.S. nurse working at a missionary clinic and the shooting death in Yemen two months later of three missionary medical staff and the wounding of a fourth. These assaults, in the viewpoint of mainstream clergy in the Middle East, both Catholic and Protestant, are evidence that direct evangelizing of Muslims is not only counterproductive but puts all missionaries as well as local Christians in jeopardy. Evangelicals counter that their objective is merely to expose people to the truth that Jesus is their savior, and let them decide for themselves. Franklin Graham, head of Samaritan's Purse and politically the most influential evangelical leader in the United States, equates their deaths with martyrdom, and sees them as an inspiration to others who would follow in their footsteps.

Another major source of contention between U.S. evangelical and mainline Protestant missions stems from the evangelicals' stated belief in the Bible as literal word of God, interpreted to sanctify the expansion of Jewish settlement over all of Palestine and beyond. By contrast, mainline Protestant groups seek a peaceful resolution of the conflict that accommodates all the region's peoples.

Bibliography

Robert, Dana L. *American Women in Mission: A Social History of Their Thought and Practice.* Macon, GA: Mercer University Press, 1997.

Stanley, Brian. *The Bible and the Flag: Protestant Missions and British Imperialism in the Nineteenth and Twentieth Centuries.* Leicester, U.K.: Apollos, 1990.

Tejirian, Eleanor H., and Simon, Reeva. *Altrusim and Imperialism: Western Cultural and Religious Missions in the Middle East.* New York: Columbia University Press, 2002.

Tibawi, A. L. *American Interests in Syria, 1800–1901.* Oxford, U.K.: Oxford University Press, 1966.

ELEANOR ABDELLA DOUMATO

PROTOCOLS OF THE ELDERS OF ZION

One of the world's most notorious antisemitic documents, crafted at the end of the nineteenth century by the Tsarist Russian secret police, the Okhrana.

Drawing upon what was originally a German plagiarism of a French novel attacking the French emperor, Napoléon III—and which had nothing whatever to do with Jews, the *Protocols of the Elders of Zion* was brimming with paranoid ruminations of a Jewish lust for world domination, and purported to be the transcript of a conspiratorial meeting of elderly Jewish plotters in the Jewish cemetery in Prague. This delirious fantasy has had the most extraordinarily long life. Intended originally to bolster the sagging fortunes of tsarist rule in Russia, the *Protocols* reached a broad public audience during the Russian Revolution and Civil War, when they were mobilized against the Bolshevik insurgents. They soon became a basic part of the antisemitic canon, helping to form part of the world view of such diverse proponents as Henry Ford and Adolf Hitler. Among many elements that attracted readers were the lurid portrayal of the plotters' mentality, the disparaging picture of modernity, and allusions to modern economic inequities. Although convincingly exposed as a forgery in England in 1921, the *Protocols* have been called the most widely circulated book on the globe, next to the Bible, and have appeared in countless editions and translations.

The *Protocols* have become an important text in anti-Israel and antisemitic propaganda, have been disseminated widely throughout the Middle East, and have benefited from periodic approbation from politicians, academics, and the mass media in the Arab and Muslim world. As recently as November 2002, during Ramadan, the *Protocols* served as a main theme of an Egyptian television series, "A Rider without a Horse," that reached millions of viewers throughout the region.

Bibliography

Cohn, Norman. *Warrant for Genocide: The Myth of the Jewish World Conspiracy and the Protocols of the Elders of Zion.* New York: Harper & Row; London: Eyre & Spottiswoode, 1967.

Institute of Jewish Affairs. *The Post-War Career of the Protocols of Zion.* Research Report. London: Author, 1981.

Joly, Maurice. *The Dialogue in Hell between Machiavelli and Montesquieu: Humanitarian Despotism and the Conditions of Modern Tyranny,* edited and translated by John S. Waggoner. Lanham, MD: Lexington, 2002.

Segel, Binjamin W. *A Lie and a Libel: The History of the Protocols of the Elders of Zion,* translated by Richard S. Levy. Lincoln: University of Nebraska Press, 1995.

MICHAEL R. MARRUS

PUSHTUN

Largest ethnic group in Afghanistan.

The Pushtun, sometimes also referred to as Pathans or Pakhtuns, make up between 38 and 45 percent of the population of Afghanistan, and since the beginning of the nineteenth century have comprised the ruling elite of the country. Although Pushtuns live in most parts of Afghanistan, they are concentrated in the southeast, especially along the border with Pakistan's Northwest Frontier province, where several million more Pushtun also live.

The language spoken by Pushtun, usually called Pushto, is distantly related to Persian and belongs to the Iranian family of languages. Pushto, along with Dari, the Afghan version of Persian, is an official language of Afghanistan. There are no words in Pushto that refer exclusively to a "lineage," in which descent is demonstrated, or a "clan," in which descent is merely assumed; the suffixes -*zai* and -*khel,* added to names of males to imply descent from them, can mean either "lineage" or "clan." The ambiguity is very useful in practice. Instead of allowing genealogy to dictate their behavior, the Pushtun can manipulate their tables of organization so as to change the significance of levels of segmentation, to the extent of incorporating totally alien groups within their genealogical fold. The critical variable in determining whether a group belongs is the exchange of women in marriage.

Durrani, Ghilzai, and Karlanri have been for the last two hundred years the names of the major groups of Pushtun clans. Symbolically, the unity of the Pushtun is expressed through their adherence to Pushtunwali, the ideal code of behavior, stressing honor, hospitality, and revenge; it is also a customary system of mediation that includes provisions for settling disputes ranging from theft to homicide.

Bibliography

Dupree, Louis. *Afghanistan.* Oxford and New York: Oxford University Press, 1997.

ASHRAF GHANI
UPDATED BY ERIC HOOGLUND

PYRAMIDS

Burial monuments for ancient Egyptian kings.

For over a thousand years, from the Step Pyramid of King Djoser (r. 2654–2635 B.C.E.) to the beginning of the New Kingdom with the Eighteenth Dynasty (1549 B.C.E.), Egyptian kings were buried in pyramid tombs. There may be as many as one hundred; remains of some that are mentioned in texts have not yet been discovered. The ruler's pyramid was the center of a pyramid complex, which generally included a mortuary temple on the east side, a causeway leading down to a valley temple on the edge of the flood plain, and subsidiary pyramids for queens. All were plundered long ago. The three major pyramids of Giza (Fourth dynasty, c. 2547–2475 B.C.E.), the largest of which is that of Khufu (Cheops), are the most famous. Easily visible from Cairo, they are central objectives of archaeological research and tourism. Khufu's Great Pyramid is unusual in containing three burial chambers, probably reflecting changes in plan, with the king buried in the uppermost. The interior walls of the pyramid of Unas, the last ruler of the 5th Dynasty (2375–2345 B.C.E), and those of the 6th Dynasty (2345–2181 B.C.E) at Saqqara are elaborately inscribed with religious passages known as Pyramid Texts. After Egyptian rulers stopped building pyramids, nonroyal funerary chapels sometimes included small pyramid-shaped structures. Centuries later in what is now northern Sudan, the Nubian kings of Meroe and Napata built steep-sided pyramids on a smaller scale than those of their Egyptian predecessors. First depicted on postage stamps in 1867 and giving their name to *al-Ahram* (Egypt's leading newspaper), they have become national symbols of Egypt.

See also GIZA.

Bibliography

Edwards, I. E. S. *Pyramids of Egypt.* New York: Penguin Putnam, 1986.

Lehner, Mark. *The Complete Pyramids: Solving the Ancient Mysteries.* London: Thames and Hudson, 1997.

DONALD MALCOLM REID

QABBANI, NIZAR
[1923–1998]

Syrian poet.

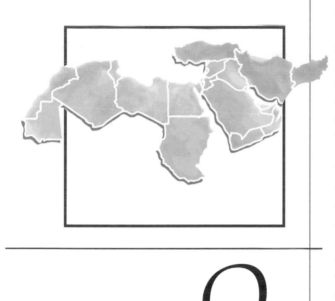

Nizar Qabbani was born in Damascus on 21 March 1923. He completed his study of law at the Syrian University in 1945, and later joined the foreign ministry and served in Cairo, Ankara, London, Madrid, and Beijing, resigning in 1966 to establish in Beirut a publishing house carrying his name and devoted to printing poetry. He began writing at age sixteen and published more than thirty of his own volumes. His major themes involve physical beauty. One poem, "Bread, Hashish, and a Moon" (1954), brought upon him the wrath of the conservatives in the Syrian parliament, who called for his resignation. After the Arab defeat in the Arab–Israel War of 1967, Qabbani wrote a scathing attack on Arab mores and leadership in his poem "Marginal Notes on the Book of the Relapse" (1967), which won him wide popular acclaim. Henceforth, his writings addressed the political and social malaise of Arab society in a poetic diction that was intentionally simplified by the occasional use of Arabic vernacular. Large crowds attended his readings, attesting to his popularity in the Arab world. His works went into several editions and sold in exceptionally large numbers. He resided in London, and died there in May 1998.

Qabbani's published works include *The Brunette Said to Me* (1944), *Childhood of a Breast* (1948), *Samba* (1949), *You Are Mine* (1950), *Poems* (1956), *My Beloved* (1961), *Poetry Is a Green Lamp* (1963), *Drawing in Words* (1966), *The Diary of a Blasé Woman* (1968), *The Book of Love* (1970), *A Hundred Love Letters* (1972), *Outlawed Poems* (1972), *Love Will Remain My Master* (1989), *I Have Married You Freedom* (1989), *The Match Is in My Hand, and Your States Are of Paper* (1989), *No Winner but Love* (1990), *The Secret Papers of a Qarmati Lover* (1990), and *On Entering the Sea: Erotic and Other Poetry of Nizar Qabbani* (1998).

See also LITERATURE: ARABIC.

Bibliography

Boullata, Issa J. *Modern Arab Poets, 1950–1975*. Washington, DC: Three Continents Press, 1976.

Jayyusi, Salma Khadra, et. al., trans. *Entering the Sea: the Erotic and Other Poetry of Nizar Qubbani.* Northampton, MA: Interlink, 1996.

Qabbani, Nizar. *Arabian Love Poems: Full Arabic and English Texts.* Boulder, CO: Lynne Rienner, 1999.

BASSAM NAMANI
UPDATED BY MICHAEL R. FISCHBACH

QABOOS, SULTAN

See AL BU SAʿID, QABUS IBN SAʿID

QADDAFI, MUAMMAR AL-

[c. 1942–]

Ruler of Libya since 1969.

Muammar al-Qaddafi (also spelled Muʿammar al-Qadhdhafi) was born during World War II, probably in the spring of 1942, to a Bedouin family near Sirte in northern Libya. The only surviving son of a poor family, he did not attend school until he was nearly ten, when he was sent to a local mosque school. He was evidently very intelligent, for he went on to secondary school in Sabha (or Sebha), in the southern province of Fezzan, between 1956 and 1961. Like many young people in the Arab world at the time, he was an admirer of Gamal Abdel Nasser, the ruler of Egypt, whose anti-imperialist and Arab nationalist foreign policies and egalitarian domestic reforms were then widely popular.

By 1961, when he was expelled from school in Sabha, Qaddafi's political inclinations were well known. His dismissal is variously attributed to an altercation with the son of the powerful governor of the Fezzan and to demonstrations he organized against the breakup of the union of Syria and Egypt (the United Arab Republic) that year. Qaddafi finished secondary school in coastal Misurata, where he renewed contact with some of his childhood friends, several of whom joined him in entering the Libyan Military Academy. These friends subsequently became members of the group that plotted the successful overthrow of the pro-Western Libyan monarchy in 1969. This lends credence to Qaddafi's claim that he determined very early on that only through a military coup could someone with his humble family background and ambitious political goals exercise power in Libya.

A six-month signals course in Britain followed graduation from the military academy in 1965, and Qaddafi was then posted near Benghazi. From there, he readied his secret network of conspirators for 1 September 1969, when they took advantage of a vacation trip by aging King Muhammad Idris al-Mahdi al-Sanusi to Turkey to topple the monarchy in a bloodless coup. The Free Unionist Officers, as they called themselves, initially constituted themselves as a collective Revolutionary Command Council (RCC) and appointed a number of more senior military and civilian figures to government positions. By December, however, when a countercoup was said to have been foiled, the RCC was given full authority and Qaddafi was revealed as the regime's leading figure. Although he serves as head of state, to this day Qaddafi holds no formal position of authority.

The 1970s

The new regime's initial posture reflected Qaddafi's admiration of Nasser's Arab nationalism as well as his own admiration of Islam. (Indeed, although Qaddafi's politics were often controversial, his reputation for personal integrity has remained virtually untarnished through his tenure in office.) Soon alcohol was outlawed, churches and night clubs closed, the British and American military bases evacuated, foreign-owned banks seized, the remaining Italian residents expelled (Libya had been an Italian colony before World War II), and only the Arabic language permitted in all official and public communications.

By the mid-1970s, Qaddafi was not only disenchanted with Nasser's successor in Egypt, Anwar al-Sadat, but had come into his own as a political visionary. Between 1976 and 1979, he published the three slim volumes of the *Green Book,* in which he expounded his third international theory (also known as third universal theory), an attempt to develop an alternative to capitalism and communism, both of which Qaddafi found unsuitable to the Libyan environment. Disenchanted with both competitive and single-party politics, Qaddafi instituted instead a system of popular congresses and committees—composed of elected members—to run the country on all levels, including local administration, state-owned enterprises, universities, and national policy review and implementation.

Muammar al-Qaddafi (b. 1942) became the leader of Libya in 1969 when he staged a coup that successfully overthrew the country's monarchy. Qaddafi employs socialist philosophies in his dictatorship, and has been linked to various terrorist activities. Pictured are (from left to right) Qaddafi, Yasir Arafat, Gamal Abdel Nasser, and Hussein I. © BETTMANN/CORBIS. REPRODUCED BY PERMISSION.

Contributing to the upheaval precipitated by these political innovations were Qaddafi's parallel economic reforms, which were based on his radically egalitarian precapitalist vision of economic relations. In his view, the exploitation entailed in wage labor, rent, and commerce must be replaced by equal partnerships and by nonprofit state-run distribution of goods and services. Workers were encouraged to take over the enterprises in which they were employed, landlords lost their property to their tenants, and retail trade disappeared. This immediately produced shortages and hoarding of basic commodities, halted housing construction, and increased already widespread economic inefficiency. That the country survived these disruptions was a function of its very large petroleum revenues during the 1970s and the substantial expatriate workforce they subsidized.

By the late 1970s, Qaddafi had grown dissatisfied with the performance of the committees and congresses; their lackluster record resulted partly from inexperience, partly from bad faith, and partly from unrealistic expectations on the part of their founder. To rectify the problems, he introduced watchdog "revolutionary committees." Domestically, these oversight groups did little more than further obscure the lines of authority, but they earned considerable notoriety abroad. Because Qaddafi attributed the failures of his revolution to foreign and domestic subversion, he assigned the revolutionary committees responsibility for "liquidating the enemies of the revolution"—that is, assassinating government opponents at home and abroad.

From the 1980s On

Qaddafi was soon branded one of the world's principal sponsors of terrorism by many Western nations, notably the United States, which initially viewed his coup with tolerance. By the late 1970s, his vitriolic condemnation of the Camp David Accords capped a decade of increasingly hostile relations with the West. Qaddafi's large arms purchases,

Libyan leader Muammar al-Qaddafi attends a meeting of the New Partnership for Africa's Development. © AP/WIDE WORLD PHOTOS. REPRODUCED BY PERMISSION.

his support of national liberation movements—from various Palestinian factions to the Irish Republican Army—and his campaign to assassinate Libyan opponents of the regime outside the country provided justification for the U.S. campaign that culminated in the bombing of Tripoli and Benghazi in April 1986. Qaddafi appeared to have been targeted personally—several of his family were wounded and an adopted daughter was killed in the raid—and his high-profile involvement diminished for some time thereafter.

Severe economic problems in the second half of the 1980s and the implosion of the Soviet Union at the end of the decade also contributed to Qaddafi's quieter demeanor. In response to a fall in oil prices and the imposition of economic sanctions by the United States, Qaddafi reversed some of his domestic reforms. Small-scale retail trade was allowed to resume, and some political prisoners were released. Time and experience thus tempered Qaddafi's methods; however, there was no indication his commitment to a vision of unity, justice, and freedom for the Libyan people and their Arab compatriots had diminished.

As the twentieth century closed, Qaddafi initiated significant changes in the tone, content, and

direction of Libyan foreign policy, and he accelerated this process in the wake of the 11 September 2001 terrorist attacks on the United States. Following the suspension of U.N. sanctions in 1998, he championed a number of new initiatives in Africa, signaling a major shift in emphasis from the Arab world to the African continent. For example, Libya took the lead in establishing the Community of Sahel-Saharan States (COMESSA) in 1998, called for the creation of a United States of Africa in 1999, and became the African candidate for chairman of the U.N. Human Rights Commission in 2002. In tandem with these initiatives, the Qaddafi regime strengthened long-standing commercial and diplomatic ties with key European states, including Britain, Italy, and Russia. Eager to reestablish diplomatic relations with the United States, Qaddafi was an enthusiastic, early supporter of the war on terrorism.

Internally, the Qaddafi regime, by the end of the 1990s, had successfully corralled domestic opposition on a number of fronts, including the army, tribal groups, and militant Islamists. A shopworn economy, adversely affected by low oil prices in the 1990s, was posed in the early twenty-first century to benefit from foreign investment and private enterprise. Finally, even as Libya sought political reform, including the promotion of democracy and human rights, Qaddafi's quixotic personality masked a relatively stable political system in which external policies were often linked to issues of domestic legitimacy.

Qaddafi later took several significant steps on the road to international reintegration. Libyan officials in September 2003 agreed to pay $2.7 billion in compensation to the families of the victims of the 1988 bombing of Pan Am flight 103. In December 2003, Libya renounced its unconventional weapons programs, agreeing to international inspections to verify compliance. And in January 2004, Libya cleared one of the last hurdles in its campaign to rejoin the international community, reaching a settlement in the 1989 bombing of a French airliner over Africa.

See also CAMP DAVID ACCORDS (1978); GREEN BOOK; LIBYA; REVOLUTIONARY COMMAND COUNCIL (LIBYA).

Bibliography

Bianco, Mirella. *Gadafi: Voice from the Desert.* London: Longman Group, 1975.

El-Kikhia, Mansour O. *Libya's Qaddafi: The Politics of Contradiction.* Gainesville: University Press of Florida, 1997.

Qaddafi, Muammar. *Escape to Hell and Other Stories.* New York: Stanké, 1998.

St John, Ronald Bruce. *Libya and the United States: Two Centuries of Strife.* Philadelphia: University of Pennsylvania Press, 2002.

Tremlett, George. *Gadaffi: The Desert Mystic.* New York: Carroll & Graf, 1993.

LISA ANDERSON
UPDATED BY RONALD BRUCE ST JOHN

QADDUMI, FARUQ

[1931–]

Palestinian political activist.

Born in Jinsafut in the northern West Bank, Qaddumi studied economics and political science at Cairo University. In the late 1950s, he helped found al-Fatah, the most significant organization in what became the Palestinian national liberation movement. Known as Abu al-Lutf, Qaddumi has long been a member of al-Fatah's Central Committee. He helped to secure funding from Arab Gulf states and represented the group's aims to Syria, Iraq, and Egypt in the 1960s. Qaddumi has held important positions within the Palestine Liberation Organization (PLO). He was elected to its Executive Committee in February 1969 and has headed the Political Department since July 1974. He was long considered a potential successor to PLO Chairman Yasir Arafat.

Qaddumi's 1967 proposal for establishing a Palestinian state in the West Bank and Gaza was an early step in what became official PLO policy in 1977. Qaddumi has often clashed with Arafat, questioning the wisdom of Arafat's embrace of various diplomatic solutions to the Arab-Israeli conflict. He opposed the Israeli-PLO Oslo Accord of 1993 and increased his attacks on Arafat and his policies thereafter. He refused even to enter the territory of the Palestinian Authority (PA), and was long an opponent of Mahmud Abbas, the Fatah leader, who helped negotiate the Oslo Accord and who served as the PA's first prime minister in 2003. Qaddumi still serves as the "foreign minister" of the PLO, most recently representing the PLO at an Arab League meeting in 2003.

See also ABBAS, MAHMUD; ARAFAT, YASIR; OSLO ACCORD (1993); PALESTINE LIBERATION ORGANIZATION (PLO); PALESTINIAN AUTHORITY; WEST BANK.

Bibliography

Iyad, Abou, with Eric Rouleau. *My Home, My Land: A Narrative of the Palestinian Struggle,* translated by Linda Butler Koseoglu. New York: Times Books, 1980.

MICHAEL R. FISCHBACH

QADI

Islamic judge.

According to Muslim legal doctrine, the *qadi* or judge is a public official whose primary responsibilities entail the administration of justice on the basis of the divinely revealed law of Islam, known in Arabic as the *shariʿa.* Eligibility for this office has been traditionally restricted to male jurists of majority age who have a reasonably comprehensive knowledge of the doctrine of their particular school of law. Because Islamic law construes the qadi as an agent of the legitimate governing authority, the government usually reserves the right to appoint qadis for the towns, cities, or regions under its control. In many historical and cultural contexts, judicial hierarchies have been established with the creation of one or more "chief judges" whose responsibility is to appoint and oversee the conduct of subordinate judges. While in theory, the qadi is empowered to adjudicate cases involving every legal issue—both civil and criminal—addressed by the *shariʿa,* in practice the qadi's authority extends only as far as the *shariʿa* is actually applied as the law of a given Muslim society. In many medieval and modern contexts, government institution and application of far-reaching secular legal codes have limited the jurisdiction of the qadi to areas of personal status (i.e., marriage, divorce, child custody, and inheritance) and the supervision of religious endowments (*waqf*).

See also SHARIʿA.

SCOTT ALEXANDER

QADIRIYYA ORDER

Sufi brotherhood.

The Qadiriyya Order was named for Abd al-Qadir al-Jilani (c. 1077–1166), Sufi teacher and founder of a Hanbali *madrasa* and religious hostel. Biographies of Abd al-Qadir date from more than a century after his death, so not much is known for certain about his life. Many apocryphal stories exist, attributing miracles, sayings, and poems to him.

Adb al-Qadir was born in the Jilan district of modern-day Iran, south of the Caspian Sea. He went to Baghdad at a young age to study philosophy and law and began preaching at about age fifty. The institutions that he founded in Baghdad were perpetuated, in large part by his forty-nine sons and other associates, until Baghdad fell to the Mongols in 1258. Abd al-Qadir is buried in Baghdad, and his tomb is a pilgrimage site.

Surviving works of Abd al-Qadir include *The Resource for Seekers of the Path of Wisdom* (a guidebook to Hanbali belief and practice, with a concluding section on Sufism), *The Divine Beginning* (a collection of sixty-two sermons), and *The Revelation of the Hidden* (a collection of seventy-eight sermons). The main theme of his work is the integration of Hanbali and Sufi thought in Islam.

Some claim that the Qadiriyya was widespread during Abd al-Qadir's lifetime. Although he was unquestionably a charismatic figure with many followers, the founding and spread of a brotherhood with fully developed institutions probably date from well after his death. In any case, the Qadiriyya was one of the earliest and became the most widespread of Sufi brotherhoods, playing a significant role in the spread of Islam.

From Iraq, the Qadiriyya spread first to Syria in the late fourteenth and early fifteenth centuries, with centers in Damascus and Hama. Refugees introduced the Qadiriyya into Morocco after they were expelled from Spain in 1492. The Qadiriyya spread to other parts of the Fertile Crescent and the Maghrib (North Africa), then to central Asia, the Arabian peninsula, India, and Eastern Europe. In the nineteenth century, the Qadiriyya reached sub-Saharan Africa and the Malay Peninsula.

Through his sermons, Abd al-Qadir taught asceticism, peacefulness, generosity, humanitarianism, and submission to the will of Allah. The emphases of the Qadiriyya have varied by time and place. Some brotherhoods venerate the personage of Abd al-Qadir and suggest that he performed miracles; others stress his teachings. Many brotherhoods are also derivative of the Qadiriyya but are named for followers of Abd al-Qadir.

See also HANBALI SCHOOL OF LAW; SUFISM AND THE SUFI ORDERS.

Bibliography

Schimmel, Annemarie. *Mystical Dimensions of Islam.* Chapel Hill: University of North Carolina Press, 1975.

Trimingham, J. Spencer. *The Sufi Orders in Islam.* New York: Oxford University Press, 1998.

LAURENCE MICHALAK

QAFIH, YIHYE BEN SOLOMON
[1850–1932]

Yemenite Jewish scholar.

Yihye ben Solomon Qafih was born in San'a, capital of Yemen, orphaned as a child, and raised by his grandfather. His areas of scholarly expertise included the halakhah (the body of Jewish law supplementing scriptural law and forming the legal part of the Talmud) and the works of both medieval and Enlightenment Jewish thinkers. Unlike other Yemenite scholars, he established communication with foreign contemporaries, among them the rabbis Abraham Isaac Kook and Hillel Zeitlin, with whom he communicated regarding the essence of Kabbalah (a system of Jewish theosophy and mysticism).

Qafih's most important enterprise was the Darda'im movement (named for Darda, one of the four ancient Jewish sages), founded on the eve of World War I, and emulating Haskalah (the Enlightenment) as it appeared among European Jewry during the eighteenth century. Although leading to partial Jewish intellectual revival in San'a, it provoked considerable controversy among local rabbis. Nevertheless, Qafih is considered the most important Jewish reformer of modern-day Yemen.

See also HALAKHAH; HASKALAH; KOOK, ABRAHAM ISAAC HACOHEN.

MICHAEL M. LASKIER

QA'ID

See GLOSSARY

QA'IDA, AL-

Militant organization formed, not necessarily formally as a political party, sometime after 1986 by Osama bin Ladin, who settled in Afghanistan to help in the organization of Muslim Arab volunteers driven by hostility against Soviet communism.

Al-Qaʿida (also Al-Qaeda and Al Qaeda; literally, "the base") was founded by bin Ladin and his lieutenants to take advantage of the religious fundamentalist revival that was spurred by the Iranian Revolution and the Soviet invasion of Afghanistan, and has clearly left its mark on world affairs due to its practice of spectacular and largely indiscriminate violence worldwide. This small organization cannot be separated from the career and fortune, literally, of its founder, Saudi millionaire Osama bin Ladin.

Bin Ladin was born in Saudi Arabia in 1957 to a very wealthy father. He attended King Abd al-Aziz University in Riyadh, and obtained a degree in public administration and management. He fell under the spell of Palestinian fundamentalist advocate Abdullah Azzam, who popularized the cause of the "struggle against the Soviet infidels" after the Soviet invasion of Afghanistan in 1979. Bin Ladin relocated to Pakistan to organize the efforts of Arab volunteers; he quickly distinguished himself with his organizational skills, but was not known as the overall leader. He still served more as an assistant to Azzam, and did not distinguish himself in battle. He used some of his fortune to help in the organization and recruitment efforts. After the death of Azzam, bin Ladin rose in stature, and founded in the mid-1980s (probably in 1986) the highly secretive organization that was later known as al-Qaʿida. It became a vehicle for the declaration of international military struggle against governments and Western representatives and institutions in the Muslim world. It would later carry the blood struggle worldwide. Its ideology is influenced by the fundamentalist worldview and militant piety and dogmatism of seventh-century Kharijites, Wahhabism, and contemporary extremist offshoots of the Egyptian Muslim Brotherhood. The organization benefited from the largesse of oil-rich Arab governments and the CIA during the 1980s. But when Iraq invaded Kuwait, bin Ladin broke with the Saudi royal family after years of a close alliance. He relocated in 1991 to Sudan, where he stayed until 1996. Bin Ladin continued to secretively recruit and form bases and cells in many parts of the Muslim world, and even among Muslim immigrants in Western countries.

After his expulsion from the Sudan in 1996, he sought refuge in Afghanistan, where the militant Taliban government was in power. He influenced the thinking of the Taliban, and joined ranks with the disaffected rejects of the Arab state prison systems. Fundamentalist militants who were wanted in their home countries flocked to Afghanistan to join the new movement. Ayman al-Zawahiri (1951–), a physician and militant fundamentalist from Egypt who served time after the assassination of Egyptian president Sadat, became bin Ladin's deputy; they both announced the formation in 1998 of the Islamic Front for the Combat of Jews and Crusaders. This announcement clearly showed the influence of al-Zawahiri, who was an early advocate of indiscriminate violence in the name of Jihad. Bin Ladin was an enthusiastic partner, and the two complemented one another. Al-Zawahiri was the ideologue, but since he lacked charisma, he left it to bin Ladin to inspire the thousands of young recruits who passed through the training camps of Afghanistan. The agenda of al-Qaʿida was initially centered around the expulsion of all Christians and Jews from Arabia, relying for that on a reported *Sahih* hadith of the Prophet. The organization would later develop an agenda that contained a litany of complaints about Western intervention in the Middle East.

This secretive organization remains mysterious despite the new revelations about it that came out in the Western press after 11 September 2001. It is not structured like a regular political party, and the organization seems to be more horizontal than vertical. Groups are trained in camps, where they receive military training and ideological indoctrination, and are then dispatched to faraway places to either improvise an attack or implement a plan that had been set by bin Ladin and his aides. In 1998, the organization came to international attention with twin suicide bombings against U.S. embassies in Tanzania and Kenya. This was followed by U.S. strikes on al-Qaʿida bases in Afghanistan, intended to kill bin Ladin. Bin Ladin survived, and had most likely been busy with the planning for his most spectacular and violent act yet: 11 September 2001.

Al-Qaʿida has an unusual mix of traditional ideology with an adept utilization of modern technology for its violent ways. Members communicate through e-mails, and computers were found in caves after the eviction of al-Qaʿida from Afghanistan. This technical side perhaps reflects the construction business from which the bin Ladin family came. Bin Ladin has also a very keen sense of the value of propaganda, and the audio and video tapes that are produced by al-Qaʿida (through its affiliated propaganda outfit, Muʾassasat al-Sahhab) are quite sophisticated, although the language is crudely and vulgarly hateful against Jews and Christians (all Jews and all Christians). The organization has not tried to win mass appeal, and bin Ladin's repeated calls for jihad have fallen on deaf Arab and Muslim ears.

The United States went to war against al-Qaʿida after 11 September 2001, but has not succeeded in either capturing or killing bin Ladin and al-Zawahiri, or in eliminating the organization altogether. Al-Qaʿida's chief operational figure, the Egyptian Muhammad Atif (also Alef; 1944–2001), however, was reported killed in November 2001. Bin Ladin continues to issue messages through recorded audiotapes, but the movement suffered severe blows with the overthrow of the Taliban government and the consequent loss of a base of operation and training camps. Many top and middle-rank leader have been killed or captured by U.S. forces. While bin Ladin remains at large, his ability to rejuvenate the movement, or perhaps to strike at the United States at the scale of 11 September remains impaired. Al-Qaʿida's main success, however, has probably been in its war against the House of Al-Saʿud. The Saudi royal family was embarrassed with the revelation that fifteen of the nineteen hijackers of 11 September were Saudi nationals. The image of the royal family in Western countries, which has cost millions of dollars in propaganda expenditure, was probably irreparably damaged. Inside the kingdom, al-Qaʿida clearly has some presence, especially since its fanatical fundamentalist ideology is not that inconsistent with the Wahhabi doctrine, the ruling ideology of the kingdom. The corruption and hypocrisy of the royal family, and the decline of the economic fortunes of the kingdom, have all increased the dissatisfaction of youths, who have been targeted by bin Ladin. Series of bombings in the kingdom took place in 2003, and al-Qaʿida claimed responsibility through a variety of flyers and pamphlets, often disseminated on the Internet. It is unlikely that al-Qaʿida would last without bin Ladin, which explains the efforts of U.S. government to catch him.

See also BIN LADIN, OSAMA; SEPTEMBER 11, 2001.

Bibliography

AbuKhalil, Asʿad. *Bin Ladin, Islam, and America's New "War on Terrorism."* New York: Seven Stories Press, 2002.

AsʿAD ABUKHALIL

QA'IMMAQAM

See GLOSSARY

QAIRAWAN

City in north central Tunisia.

Qairawan (also Kairouan, al-Qayrawan) is located some 100 miles (156 km) south of Tunis. Its population in 2002 was estimated at 162,130. Its economy is based on agriculture, arboriculture, carpets, and leatherwork. Like many North African cities, it has a walled older section and a modern quarter established during colonialism. It was initially a military camp set up by the Arab Muslim invaders spreading Islam during the late seventh century. Gradually a town emerged with the building of mosques, shops, and fortresses; its founding is often associated with Okba (Uqba ibn Nafi), a Muslim general (to whom a mosque is dedicated); others also played a role, however. The city boasts the oldest extant mosque in Africa.

Following upheaval brought on by Kharijite revolts, the town came under Aghlabid rule in the ninth century, and under their patronage it was transformed into an important regional intellectual and religious center, known for its schools and pilgrimage stops. Decline followed, however, as did the pillaging of the city by nomadic groups in the mid-eleventh century. In the early thirteenth century, the capital was moved to Tunis, which became the hub of political and intellectual life in Tunisia. Today, Qairawan is considered a Holy City of Islam, and it is the center of the governorate of the same name.

MATTHEW S. GORDON

QAJAR, ABDULLAH MIRZA

[1849–1908]

Pioneering Persian photographer.

Abdullah Mirza Qajar was the son of Jahangir Mirza, a member of the Qajar family—the rulers of Persia. Photography had been introduced to Persia in the 1860s, and the shah, Naser al-Din, was a keen photographer. Abdullah studied photography in Paris and Vienna and was the official photographer at the Dar al-Fonun, the modern school founded by Mirza Taqi Khan Amir Kabir, the reform-minded minister of the shah.

Abdullah Qajar was appointed chief of the imperial printing press during the reign of the succeeding shah, Mozaffar al-Din, and in 1900, accompanied him to Europe. He photographed public personalities, common people, urban and rural scenes, and buildings, and he signed them *Special photographer to His Imperial Majesty, and His humble servant, Abdullah Qajar.* In 1896, he wrote a short account of the methods he had studied in Europe and about his career.

Bibliography

Afshar, I. "Some Remarks on the Early History of Photography." In *Qajar Iran: Political, Social, and Cultural Change, 1800–1925,* edited by Edmund Bosworth and Carole Hillenbrand. Edinburgh: Edinburgh University Press, 1983.

MANSOUREH ETTEHADIEH

QAJAR, AGHA MOHAMMAD

[1742–1797]

Founder and first monarch of Persia's Qajar dynasty; shah in 1796.

Agha Mohammad Qajar (also Aqa Mohammad Ghadjar) was born the son of Mohammad Hoseyn Khan of the Qovanlu branch of the Qajar family, a Turkic tribe that had settled in and near Astarabad, now in northeastern Iran. The chief of the tribe, Fath Ali Khan, was killed by Nader Shah Afshar, so his son Mohammad Hoseyn Khan took refuge with other Turkomans. After Nader was killed in 1747, his successor Adel Shah took Mohammad Hoseyn Khan's six-year-old son Agha Mohammad Khan and emasculated him. When Adel Shah died, Agha Mohammad joined Karim Khan Zand, who ruled in southern and central Persia, with a capital at Shiraz. Mohammad Hoseyn was killed in battle by Karim Khan Zand in 1758; Zand then took Agha Mohammad and his family as hostages to his capital.

Agha Mohammad was treated well and was trusted by Karim Khan, but when Karim died in 1779, Agha Mohammad escaped and raised the standard of revolt against the descendants of the Zands (Persian dynasty 1750–1794). Gradually, he succeeded in conquering, pacifying, and uniting Persia. Still, he had to contend with Lotf Ali Khan Zand, Karim Khan's successor. After being defeated by Agha Mohammad in Shiraz, Lotf Ali escaped to Kerman in southeast Persia. There he was finally captured by Agha Mohammad in 1794, who proceeded to sack the city and treat the citizens with great cruelty for sheltering Lotf Ali.

In 1796, Agha Mohammad had himself crowned king (becoming Agha Mohammad Shah Qajar), in Tehran, which he chose for his capital. At the time, Tehran was a small and insignificant township selected for its proximity to the seat of Qajar power in the north. Agha Mohammad set about reconquering Georgia, once a tribute state to Persia, but transferred by its ruler, Heracleus, to Russia. During his second expedition to Georgia in 1797, the shah was assassinated outside Shusha, Georgia's capital.

Though Agha Mohammad Shah was harsh and cruel, by his courage, astuteness, and endeavor he reunited his country and founded the dynasty that ruled Persia until 1925.

See also QAJAR DYNASTY.

Bibliography

Curzon, George Nathaniel. *Persia and the Persian Question* (1892). 2 vols. London: Cass, 1966.

Lambton, A. K. S. "Persian Society under the Qajars." *Journal of the Royal Central Asian Society* 48 (1961): 123–138.

Malcolm, Sir John. *The History of Persia, from the Most Early Period to the Present Time.* London: J. Murray, 1815.

Watson, Robert G. *A History of Persia from the Beginning of the Nineteenth Century to the Year 1858.* London: Smith Elder, 1866.

MANSOUREH ETTEHADIEH

QAJAR DYNASTY

Ruling family of Iran, 1796–1925.

The Qajars were a Turkoman tribe that rose to prominence in Iran during the Safavi dynasty (1501–1722). In the turbulent civil wars that broke out after the Safavis were deposed by invading Afghans, the Qajars gradually consolidated power until Agha Mohammad Shah Qajar crowned himself shah at Tehran in 1796. He was killed a year later, and his nephew succeeded him as Fath Ali Shah (r. 1797–1834). During his reign, Russia defeated Iran in two wars (1805–1813, 1827–1828), acquiring territory in the north, while England blocked Iranian aspirations in Afghanistan. Both countries secured favorable treaty rights in Iran and acquired influence in the succession, which went in 1834 to Fath Ali's grandson Mohammad Shah, who ruled the country uneventfully until his death in 1848.

During the long reign of Naser al-Din Shah (r. 1848–1896), Iran had to confront an increasingly powerful European presence. Trade and budget deficits forced Naser al-Din Shah to grant lucrative concessions in the north to Russia for the operation of the Caspian fisheries, and in the south to Britain for telegraphs, tobacco exports, and river navigation. Believing that various economic and so-

Ahmad Shah (center), the last Qajar monarch of Iran, during a visit to London in 1919. Ahmad Shah and the Qajar dynasty were formally deposed by a vote of the Majles (parliament) in 1925. © HULTON-DEUTCH COLLECTION/CORBIS. REPRODUCED BY PERMISSION.

cial reforms would help his government withstand British and Russian influence, Naser al-Din set up European-style educational institutions, brought in Russian advisers to drill his Cossack Brigade, created government printing offices, and tried to establish factories to supply the army. However, he neglected the financial and administrative requirements of the reforms, thus undermining their effectiveness. A serious challenge to his rule arose between 1890 to 1892, when the shah was forced to repeal a monopoly concession for tobacco that he had granted to an English company. In the first mass social movement of the modern period, the entire nation, including Naser al-Din's wives, boycotted tobacco in protest against European economic encroachment and the shah's acquiescence in it.

The aftermath of the Tobacco Revolt was marked by further popular unrest, which culminated in the assassination of Naser al-Din Shah on 1 May 1896. His son, Mozaffar al-Din Shah (r. 1896–1907), faced worsening economic conditions, which the bazaar merchants and *ulama* (Islamic religious leaders) increasingly attributed to the shah's helplessness in confronting foreign pressures. The less numerous Western-trained intelligentsia began to criticize European economic control and Qajar absolutism. In 1905 the beating of four sugar merchants (because of high prices) in the bazaar touched off a series of protests that soon engulfed Tehran and culminated in the summer of 1906 with the bazaar merchants closing their shops en masse and the *ulama* withdrawing from their religious services. Mozaffar al-Din Shah, unable to rely on support from Russia owing to the revolution there, was forced to agree to the formation of a national assembly (the Majles). This body set about in the fall of 1906 to write a constitution, which the shah signed on 30 December 1906, only nine days before his death.

The Constitutional Revolution brought political turmoil upon Iran between 1905 and 1911. The new king, Mohammad Ali Shah (r. 1907–1909), proved to be autocratic, and with Russian support he closed the Majles in June 1908. Constitutional resistance to the shah organized in Tabriz and other cities, and in July 1909, two proconstitution armies converged on Tehran and deposed Mohammad Ali Shah. His eleven-year-old son, Ahmad Shah Qajar, was crowned and ruled under a regent and the watchful eye of the reconstituted Second Majles.

The former shah attempted a comeback, with tribal support, in the summer of 1911, but was defeated by the constitutional forces.

The central government under the figurehead Ahmad Shah looked on helplessly during World War I as Russian and British troops fought against Turkish forces in Iran. Local movements arose in several provinces to challenge Tehran, especially in Gilan. A coup d'état in February 1921 brought to power Reza Khan, commander of the Cossack Brigade. As war minister, Reza Khan repressed the provincial opposition movements; by October 1923 he had become prime minister. Soon thereafter, Ahmad Shah left Iran for Europe on a trip of indefinite duration (in fact, he never would return). Reza Khan used his power base in the army and among the majority parties in the Fifth Majles to bring about the deposition of Ahmad Shah on 31 October 1925. Two months later the Majles vested the monarchy in Reza Khan, who adopted Pahlavi as his family surname. This "legal" transfer of royal authority formally ended the rule of the Qajar dynasty.

See also AHMAD QAJAR; BAZAARS AND BAZAAR MERCHANTS; CONSTITUTIONAL REVOLUTION; FATH ALI SHAH QAJAR; MOZAFFAR AL-DIN QAJAR; MUHAMMAD ALI; NASER AL-DIN SHAH; PAHLAVI, REZA; QAJAR, AGHA MOHAMMAD; TOBACCO REVOLT.

Bibliography

Amanat, Abbas. *Pivot of the Universe: Nasir al-Din Shah Qajar and the Iranian Monarchy, 1831–1896.* Berkeley: University of California Press, 1997.

Foran, John. "The Concept of Dependent Development as a Key to the Political Economy of Qajar Iran (1800–1925)." *Iranian Studies* 22, nos. 2–3 (1989): 5–56.

Lambton, Ann K. S. *Qajar Persia: Eleven Studies.* Austin: University of Texas Press, 1987.

JOHN FORAN
UPDATED BY ERIC HOOGLUND

QALQILIYA

West Bank City.

Qalqiliya, whose origins extend back to Canaanite times, is situated in the northwest corner of the West Bank, close to the Green Line the (boundary with Israel) and 14 miles (23 km) from the Mediter-

ranean Sea. The city's strategic position on the border between Palestine's coastal plain and the mountains made it an important locale in the eyes of caravan merchants and invading armies. By modern times, Qalqiliya was noted for its abundant agricultural produce. Its fertile land produced citrus fruits, vegetables, other fruits, and grain.

The town's history was affected dramatically by the Arab–Israeli conflict. As a result of the Arab–Israel War of 1948 and the subsequent 1949 Rhodes armistice between Jordan and Israel, Qalqiliya ended up as part of the Jordanian-controlled West Bank, although most of its agricultural land came to lie on the Israeli side of the cease-fire line. In October 1956, two weeks before the Arab–Israel War of 1956, the town was the scene of a bloody Israeli retaliatory raid that prompted Jordan's King Hussein ibn Talal to request assistance from the United Kingdom under the terms of his country's defense pact with the British. During the Arab–Israel War of 1967, Israeli forces occupied Qalqiliya, holding the town until they handed it over to the Palestinian Authority in December 1995. The city had a population of 31,753 in of 1997, the year of the last census.

As a result of Palestinian suicide bombings during the al-Aqsa Intifada, which began in September 2000, Israel reoccupied Qalqiliya for a time. It also began constructing a barrier between Jewish population centers and Palestinian territory in the West Bank. The wall had a particularly devastating impact on Qalqiliya, which was not only cut off from much of its remaining agricultural land but also surrounded on three sides by the wall.

See also AQSA INTIFADA, AL-; ARAB–ISRAEL WAR (1948); ARAB–ISRAEL WAR (1956); ARAB–ISRAEL WAR (1967); HUSSEIN IBN TALAL; PALESTINIAN AUTHORITY; WEST BANK.

MICHAEL R. FISCHBACH

QANAT

See GLOSSARY

QANUN

Secular law promulgated by ruler's decree.

Rooted in the legal tradition of *yasa* (a royal edict) in the Turkish and Mongol empires of central Asia, qanun was most fully developed by the sultans of the Ottoman Empire. Qanun (also Kanun) was theoretically restricted to those areas of public life not covered by *shari'a* (Islamic law).

In the fifteenth century, Sultan Mehmed II was the first leader of the Ottoman Empire to codify his decrees into a *kanunname* (book of laws) on the rights of subjects, the organization of the state, taxes, landholding, and economic organization. Later sultans progressively extended the scope of secular law, thereby infringing on what had once been the monopoly of religious law. Qanun underwent extensive reform in the nineteenth century, when French law codes were incorporated into the Ottoman Empire's legal system.

See also SHARI'A.

Bibliography

Shaw, Stanford J., and Shaw, Ezel Kural. *History of the Ottoman Empire and Modern Turkey.* 2 vols. Cambridge, U.K. and New York: Cambridge University Press, 1976–1977.

ELIZABETH THOMPSON

QARADAWI, YUSUF AL-
[1926–]

Egyptian Sunni Muslim scholar.

Yusuf al-Qaradawi was born in Egypt into a poor family of peasants who were devout Muslims. When his father died, his uncle took over the responsibilities for his upbringing and education. Qaradawi memorized the Qur'an when he was barely ten years old. After completing his secondary school education, he joined the famous al-Azhar University in Cairo and had a distinguished educational career in Islamic studies during the 1950s and 1960s. In 1973, at long last, he was able to defend his Ph.D. thesis after the delay caused by President Gamal Abdel Nasser's crackdown on the Muslim Brotherhood.

It was while attending the secondary school of Tanta that he joined Imam Hassan al-Banna's revivalist Muslim Brotherhood organization. Imam al-Banna believed strongly in the virtues of prayer and discipline nurtured within an organization that was dedicated to service for socioreligious welfare and political activism. Qaradawi's al-Azhar education was interrupted several times by detentions in Egyptian jails due to his affiliation with the Muslim Brotherhood. He began to preach in Cairo mosques in the mid-1950s and developed a reputation as a preacher, a teacher, and a writer. In 1962 al-Azhar sent him to Qatar to head the Qatari secondary institute of religious studies. In 1977 he laid the foundation for what was to be the College of *shari'a* and Islamic Studies and also the Center of Sunna and Sirah Studies at the University of Qatar, both of which he heads.

Qaradawi is probably the foremost scholar of the Sunni Muslim world today. Unlike the strict Salafi/Saudi-trained scholars, he is known for taking moderate positions on many religious issues pertaining to what is lawful and unlawful in Islam. He combines well the traditional knowledge of *shari'a* that he obtained from al-Azhari with a contemporary understanding of the issues that Muslims face today. His writings (exceeding forty) are widely read and have been translated into many languages. He has also become a very popular television preacher on the al-Jazeera satellite television station, with an audience said to be in the tens of millions. In recent religious rulings, Qaradawi has been praised for his condemnation of the 11 September 2001 attacks, defense of the right of American Muslim soldiers to fight against other Muslims in Afghanistan, and critique of the October 2002 bombing of two nightclubs on the Indonesian island of Bali as a heinous crime. His account of Palestinian suicide bombers as martyrs engaged in a just struggle against an occupying force and militarized society that targets them has not been as well received.

See also AZHAR, AL-; BANNA, HASAN AL-; MUSLIM BROTHERHOOD; *SHARI'A*; SUNNI ISLAM.

Bibliography

Qaradawi, Yusuf al-. *The Lawful and the Prohibited in Islam.* Kuala Lumpur: Islamic Book Trust, 1985.

ABDIN CHANDE

QARAMANLI DYNASTY

Dynasty of Turkish origin that attained autonomous rule of Tripolitania under Ottoman suzerainty, 1711–1835.

The Qaramanli (also Karamanli) dynasty—Ahmed (1711–1745), Mehmed (1745–1754), Ali (1754–1793,

1795/96), and Yusuf (1796–1835)—directed autonomous Tripolitanian domestic and foreign policies, including the signing of international treaties. Their economy was based on international trade and sea piracy; their pirates were the scourge of the Barbary Coast, known as the Barbary pirates. During Ali's reign the region suffered from epidemics, plague, and famine, as well as from power struggles among Ali's sons. Algerian strongman Ali Burghul (Bulghur) took advantage of the situation and with Ottoman approval ruled Tripoli between 1793 and 1795, causing the population severe hardship.

Under Yusuf, the European powers and the newly independent United States went to war against the Barbary pirates, ending the taking of ships, cargoes, and men (who were often sold into slavery). This forced Yusuf to impose high taxes, which caused a popular revolt. On 27 May 1835 an Ottoman naval force landed in Tripoli following a local request for Ottoman intervention. Its commander was proclaimed governor, and members of the Qaramanli family were arrested or exiled.

Bibliography

Dearden, Seton. A Nest of Corsairs: The Fighting Karamanlis of Tripoli. London: J. Murray, 1976.

Folayan, Kola. Tripoli during the Reign of Yusuf Pasha Qaramanli. Ife, Nigeria: University of Ife Press, 1979.

RACHEL SIMON

QARAWIYYIN, AL-

First university in the Islamic world.

Al-Qarawiyyin was built as a mosque in Fez in 859. The building was enlarged in the tenth century and later under the respective rules of the Almoravid, Almohad, Marinid, Sa'di, and Alawiite dynasties. Its architecture expresses the Arab-Hispanic art that makes the Qarawiyyin one of the most prestigious monuments in Fez and in North Africa.

Since the twelfth century, most of the Moroccan *ulama* (Islamic clergy) received their religious teaching at the Qarawiyyin. Students came from all regions of Morocco and from the Arab world.

Under the Alawite dynasty, the Qarawiyyin was subject to a series of reforms regulating its organization and programs of teaching. The sultan Abd al-Rahman (1822–1859) reorganized the teaching there by *dahir*. This reorganization was oriented toward communicating to students religious disciplines guided by conformism to Islam. Among topics taught were Qur'anic exegesis, astronomy, dialectics, mysticism, lexicography, philology, geography, medicine, and divination.

The teaching was free of charge, and the student could join the university at any time of the year. However, each student had to spend five years in the university to receive an *ijaza* given by his teacher if the student showed regularity and attended courses successfully.

In the nineteenth century, the teachers constituted a body of *ulama* that gave allegiance to the sultan and were consulted by him on different matters. They enjoyed high status in Fez, and *qadis* (judges) were recruited from among them. After the French takeover, the Sultan Mulay Youssef signed a *dahir* (on 19 May 1914) creating a council charged with the task of improving the university's methods of teaching, its administration, and the status of its teachers. In 1918, the university became affiliated with the Ministry of Justice and was led by le Conseil de Direction.

The most important change occurred after two *dahirs* were promulgated by Muhammed V on 1 April 1931 and 10 May 1933. The teaching became organized in cycles: elementary, secondary, and higher. Higher education in Qarawiyyin had two sections: one specialized in religious law, hadith (legends and traditions surrounding the Prophet), and interpretation of the Qur'an; the second specialized in literature, Arabic language, history, and geography. Exams, hours of teaching, holidays, and the status of teachers were also regulated. In 1947, the Qarawiyyin became a state university.

After independence, the Qarawiyyin became affiliated with the Ministry of National Education, having as objectives to teach religious knowledge and to promote scientific research in this field. Three other institutions became linked to the Qarawiyyin: the Faculty of Arabic Language in Marrakech, Faculty of Theology in Tetuan, and Dar al-Hadith al-Hasaniyya in Rabat.

See also YOUSSEF, MULAY.

RAHMA BOURQIA

QASEMLU, ABD AL-RAHMAN

See GHASSEMLOU, ABDUL RAHMAN

QASHQA'I

See TRIBES AND TRIBALISM: QASHQA'I

QASIM, ABD AL-KARIM

[1914–1963]

Leader of the leftist nationalist 1958 revolt in Iraq; president and prime minister of Iraq, 1958–1963.

Abd al-Karim Qasim (also Kassem) was born into a poor Baghdad family. His father, a carpenter, was a Sunni Arab and his mother was a Kurdish Shi'ite.

General Abd al-Karim Qasim (1914–1963) salutes a line of armed forces as they pass the reviewing stand. Qasim, an army officer, overthrew the Iraqi monarchy in 1958, and then became the leader of the Republic of Iran. © BETTMANN/CORBIS. REPRODUCED BY PERMISSION.

After finishing high school, he taught for one year in a primary school before changing careers and joining the military college of Iraq from which he graduated in 1934. As part of an Iraqi military unit, he participated in the first Arab–Israel War, 1948–1949. Like other officers of his generation, he retained a bitterness about the defeat, which he attributed to the weakness and corruption of the Arab monarchies.

In 1952, the Egyptian monarchy was overthrown by nationalist officers and a republic was established. Reverberations from that coup soon reached Baghdad. The Iraqi military was not only disgusted with corruption in the Baghdad regime but was still bitter over the failed anti-British military coup of 1941 and the repression of nationalists that followed.

In Iraq, after the Egyptian revolution, junior officers began to organize underground cells. Qasim joined this clandestine organization in 1955 and, because of his seniority and his respected professional reputation, soon became chairman of the Central Committee of the Free Officers, as they called themselves.

On 14 July 1958 these officers staged a successful coup, which resulted in the killing of the royal family and the Prime Minister Nuri al-Sa'id—and the proclamation of a republic. General Qasim became president and prime minister, and his fellow officer and colleague Abd al-Salam Arif became deputy prime minister. In a very short time, relations between the two men soured over differences relating to Iraq's policy toward Egypt's President Gamal Abdel Nasser. Arif advocated an immediate rapprochement with Nasser and an eventual joining of the United Arab Republic (Egypt and Syria); Qasim wanted to keep his distance from Nasser.

As prime minister, Qasim took several anti-Western steps in foreign policy. He let Iraq's membership in the Baghdad Pact lapse, he restored diplomatic relations with the Soviet Union, and he signed an arms agreement with that country. In domestic policy, he began an agrarian reform program and passed progressive legislation giving women additional rights in matters of divorce and inheritance. In 1961, Qasim issued Law Number 80, which stripped the foreign-owned Iraq Petroleum Company of 99.5 percent of its concessionary territory. For a time, he allowed open activity by political parties; his lenience toward the Communist party, however, led to serious dissatisfaction among the population and the army.

Criticism of his policies toward Nasser and the Communists exacerbated the rift between him and Arif, who was arrested (on charges of attempting to kill Qasim) and imprisoned. In March 1959, Iraqi nationalist officers attempted a coup in Mosul. In response, the Communists and their allies took to the streets in Baghdad and elsewhere, which resulted in mass killings in Mosul and Kirkuk in July 1959 (that Qasim did little to prevent).

Besides facing opposition from Arab nationalists and the Ba'th party, Qasim had to confront a renewal of Kurdish revolts for separatism. After returning to Iraq in 1958, Mustafa Barzani, the renowned Kurdish leader, staged a revolt in 1960 that lasted (off and on) until 1963, further weakening Qasim and his legitimacy. Qasim also had political problems within the Middle East: In May 1961, Britain ended Kuwait's protective status, making that country independent. Relying on vague historical claims, Qasim announced that Kuwait was an integral part of Iraq but sent no troops to back up his claim. British troops were, however, dispatched to Kuwait to defend it, although these were eventually replaced by forces from the League of Arab States. Thus Qasim became isolated from his Arab League neighbors.

During these events, the Arab nationalists and Ba'thists had been organizing and undertook a successful military coup in Baghdad. On 8 February 1963 Qasim was arrested and executed the following day. Arif became president of the republic, with a Ba'thist as prime minister and a civilian government, after annulling the military law that had been in force since 1958.

See also ARAB–ISRAEL WAR (1948); ARIF, ABD AL-SALAM; BAGHDAD PACT (1955); BARZANI FAMILY; BA'TH, AL-; IRAQ PETROLEUM COMPANY (IPC); KURDISH REVOLTS; LEAGUE OF ARAB STATES; NASSER, GAMAL ABDEL.

Bibliography

Dann, Uriel. *Iraq under Qassem: A Political History, 1958–1963.* New York: Praeger, 1969.

Khadduri, Majid. *Republican Iraq: A Study in Iraqi Politics since the Revolution of 1958.* London: Oxford University Press, 1969.

LOUAY BAHRY

QASIMI FAMILY OF RA'S AL-KHAYMA, AL-

Ruling family of Ra's al-Khayma in the United Arab Emirates.

Humayd ibn Abdullah al-Qasimi ruled Ra's al-Khayma between 1869 and 1900, when the emirate rejoined with Sharjah and was ruled by another branch of the family. In 1921 Sultan ibn Salim al-Qasimi seized control of the emirate from his nephew, Muhammad bin Salim al-Qasimi, and Ra's al-Khayma once again separated from Sharjah, causing lingering resentment between the two branches of the family. In the 1940s Muhammad and his relatives charged that the sultan was not distributing revenues from oil companies in an equitable manner. When the sultan was out of the country, Muhammad's second-oldest son, Saqr, captured the amir's fort in the capital and was thereafter recognized by local elites and by the British as ruler. Because of his strength of will and independent-mindedness Saqr ran afoul of British officials and other rulers. In the 1960s he was a strong advocate of Arab nationalist causes and of the involvement of Egypt and other countries in the affairs of the emirates. He also was reluctant at first to bring Ra's al-Khayma into the UAE's federation. The heir apparent is his son Khalid, who was educated in the United States.

See also RA'S AL-KHAYMA; TRUCIAL COAST; UNITED ARAB EMIRATES.

Bibliography

Anthony, John Duke. *Arab States of the Lower Gulf: People, Politics, Petroleum.* Washington, DC: Middle East Institute, 1975.

Peck, Malcolm C. *Historical Dictionary of the Arab Gulf States.* Lanham, MD: Scarecrow Press, 1997.

ANTHONY B. TOTH

QASIMI FAMILY OF SHARJAH, AL-

Ruling family of Sharjah in the United Arab Emirates.

During the seventeenth century the Qawasim tribe possessed the most powerful maritime forces in the waters of the lower Persian Gulf, asserting control even in the face of encroachments by the British. Sharjah and Ra's al-Khayma were the most prominent regional ports. The most notable ruler of the region from 1727 to 1777 was Rashid ibn Mattar bin Rahman al-Qasimi, who claimed descent from the prophet Muhammad. The patriarch of the current rulers of Sharjah is Sultan bin Saqr bin Rashid al-Qasimi, who ruled for fifty years starting in 1804. Sharjah is notable for the political turbulence in modern times among the members of the ruling family. Saqr bin Sultan al-Qasimi ruled from 1951 to 1965. However, he was arrested after attempting to overthrow his successor and nephew, Khalid ibn Muhammad al-Qasimi (r. 1965–1972), who was killed in the process. The current ruler is Sultan bin Muhammad al-Qasimi, who has been in power since 1972. He was born in 1939 and was educated at Cairo University, the University of Exeter, and the University of Durham. He received a doctorate in history and has published several books on the history of the lower Persian Gulf, including *The Myth of Arab Piracy in the Gulf*.

See also SHARJAH; UNITED ARAB EMIRATES.

Bibliography

Anthony, John Duke. *Arab States of the Lower Gulf: People, Politics, Petroleum.* Washington, DC: Middle East Institute, 1975.

Peck, Malcolm C. *Historical Dictionary of the Arab Gulf States.* Lanham, MD: Scarecrow Press, 1997.

Al-Qāsimī, Sultān Muhammad. *The Myth of Arab Piracy in the Gulf.* Dover, NH; London: Croom Helm, 1986.

ANTHONY B. TOTH

QASSAM, IZZ AL-DIN AL-
[c. 1880–1935]

Islamic militant who fought the French in Syria and the British in Palestine.

Izz al-Din al-Qassam was born in Jabla, near Latakia, Syria. He studied in Cairo at al-Azhar University and reportedly came in contact with Rashid Rida, the precursor of Arab nationalism. Following the French occupation of Syria, he participated in guerrilla activities (1919–1920) in the Alawiya region of Jabal Sahyun, for which he was sentenced to death by a French court-martial. After the French suppressed Syrian resistance, Qassam escaped to Pales-

tine. He was hired to teach at an Islamic school in 1921, and a year later was appointed by the Supreme Muslim Council as a preacher at the new Istiqlal mosque in Haifa. He preached a puritanical way of life that alarmed some people enough to seek his dismissal. He was appointed marriage registrar in the *shari'a* court at Haifa in 1929, which enabled him to travel throughout Palestine.

Qassam became convinced that Britain's support for Jewish immigration and land purchases, which ultimately lead to a Jewish state. He therefore began to advocate a popular uprising against the British once the Palestinians were united and organized. In 1928 he was a founder of the Young Men's Muslim association, which with the Boy Scouts, organized military drills and the stockpiling of arms, and initiated violent attacks on Jewish settlements (1931–1933). According to Subhi Yasin, his contemporary (and the source of much of our information about Qassam), Qassam sent a follower to the mufti of Jerusalem, Muhammad Amin al-Husayni, suggesting that he start a revolt in the south while he (Qassam) started one in the north. The mufti reportedly declined, stating that he was seeking a political solution. While Qassam believed that a revolt should take place, with only 200 recruits and insufficient arms and training, he felt the Palestinians were not yet ready. Two factors made him change his mind: the discovery, on 18 October 1935, of an arms shipment destined for Jewish forces, and the immigration that year of the largest number of Jews (almost 62,000) to Palestine. On 21 November he left Haifa with ten of his followers to attack a police arsenal to acquire its arms, but an unplanned clash, in which a police sergeant was killed, alerted the police. Hundreds of police chased and caught up with the group; rather than escape or surrender, Qassam and his men fought it out. He and two of his men were killed.

Qassam became a symbol of martyrdom for Palestinian youth groups such as Ikhwan al-Qassam (Qassamite Brotherhood), which formed resistance cells to take up the mantle of Qassam. The Qassamite attack in which two Jews were killed on 15 April 1936 was a catalyst for the most violent uprising against the British, the Palestine Arab Revolt (1936–1939).

Half a century later, the legacy of Qassam inspired another generation of Palestinians. Shortly after the Intifada began in 1987, an Islamic fundamentalist group, HAMAS (Islamic Resistance Movement), was established to resist Israeli occupation through its military wing, Kata'ib Izz al-Din al-Qassam, which conducted terrorist attacks against Israelis.

See also HAMAS; HUSAYNI, MUHAMMAD AMIN AL-; INTIFADA (1987–1991); PALESTINE ARAB REVOLT (1936–1939); RIDA, RASHID.

Bibliography

Mattar, Philip. *The Mufti of Jerusalem: Al Hajj Amin al-Husayni and the Palestinian National Movement,* revised edition. New York: Columbia University Press, 1991.

Porath, Yehoshua. *The Palestinian Arab National Movement: From Riots to Rebellion, 1929–1939,* Vol. 2. London: Frank Cass, 1977.

PHILIP MATTAR

QAT

See GLOSSARY

QATAR

Nation on the western shore of the Persian Gulf.

Qatar occupies a mitten-shaped peninsula that extends about 105 miles into the Persian Gulf roughly midway along its western coast. About 50 miles across at its widest point, it has an area of 4,400 square miles. Qatar shares a land border with Saudi Arabia and is separated from Bahrain to the west by about 30 miles of water. It consists largely of desert sand and gravel with occasional limestone outcrops and *sabkhas* (salt flats). A lack of water made the establishment of permanent settlements in Qatar's interior impossible until the post-oil era. Summer weather is severe, with temperatures as high as 122°F (50°C) and high humidity along the coasts; winters are pleasant, with temperatures generally around 60°F (17°C), with a continuous north wind. Scant rainfall sustains meager vegetation. Qatar's proven oil reserves were estimated to be 15.2 billion barrels in 2001. More importantly, the country's natural gas reserves amounted to an estimated 21 trillion cubic meters in 2002, most of it in the North Dome field, the world's largest deposit of nonassociated gas.

A degassing station in Dukhan, Qatar's center for oil production and the country's only onshore oil field. Dukhan, which was first drilled in 1939, contains three reservoirs which supply the majority of Qatar's oil. © CHRISTINE OSBORNE/CORBIS. REPRODUCED BY PERMISSION.

Qatar's population was estimated at nearly 800,000 in 2002, having grown rapidly since oil income started to flow after World War II. Even earlier, the population included significant numbers of immigrant Iranians and East Africans originally brought as slaves and freed in the first half of the twentieth century. Oil wealth and the rapid economic development it has generated have brought large numbers of expatriates to Qatar, reducing the indigenous population to about one-fifth of the total. Iranians account for about a sixth, other Arabs for a quarter, and South Asians for a third. The great majority of the population is Sunni Muslim, with Qataris subscribing to the same strict Wahhabi interpretation of Islam as the Saudis; an estimated one-sixth is Shi'ite. About three-fifths of Qatar's population lives in Doha, the capital and principal port, located on the east coast. Other major urban areas include Khawr, located north of Doha, and the industrial complex of Umm Sa'id to its south.

History

In the 1760s the Al Khalifa, one of the Utayba clans from central Arabia that had earlier settled in Kuwait, migrated to Qatar and established its base at Zubara, on the west coast. After they seized the islands of Bahrain from the Iranians in 1783, their hold on Qatar weakened and the Al Thani, a family from central Arabia, established a leading position on the east coast. An 1867 attack by the Al

MAP BY XNR PRODUCTIONS, INC. THE GALE GROUP.

duced in Japan. In 1935 a concession was granted to a subsidiary of the Anglo-Iranian Oil Company (later British Petroleum). The modest concession payments enabled Abdullah ibn Qasim to solidify his position and that of the Al Thani clan, a process completed when the ruling family began to earn oil export income after 1949. Political independence was thrust upon Qatar in 1968, when the United Kingdom decided to end its protective relationships with the lower Gulf states by the end of 1971. It declared its independence on 3 September 1971 after the failure of efforts to join Bahrain and the seven Trucial Emirates in a federation.

Economy

Earnings from oil and natural gas production have given Qataris one of the world's highest per capita incomes and have made dramatic economic development possible. In 1991 Qatar began production of gas from its vast North Field. As part of the second phase of development of the North Field, the country built a liquefied natural gas (LNG) production and export facility at Ra's Laffan, which began exports in 1996. The country's modern physical infrastructure includes excellent roads linking Qatar with the other Gulf states, an international airport, and a large, modern port at Doha. Attempts have been made to diversify the economy by building cement plants and flour mills, and expanding the shrimping industry. Modern techniques in agriculture have made possible vegetable and chicken production sufficient to meet an increasing local demand.

Government and Politics

In 1970, a year before independence, Qatar became the first of the lower Gulf states to adopt a written constitution. It provided for a council of ministers or a cabinet to be appointed by the ruler, and an elected advisory council. Members of the ruling family dominate the cabinet and the advisory council has thus far consisted only of members appointed by the ruler. With perhaps as many as 20,000 members, the Al Thani family is the largest ruling family in the region and has dominated most important areas of government. In June 1995 Shaykh Hamad ibn Khalifa overthrew his father, Shaykh Khalifa ibn Hamad Al Thani. Hamad has attempted to open the country's social and political environment. In

Khalifa and the ruling Banu Yas tribe of Abu Dhabi against Doha and other settlements led to British intervention that established Muhammad ibn Thani as de facto ruler of Qatar. In 1893 his son, Qasim ibn Muhammad Al Thani, defeated superior forces of the occupying Ottoman Turks, who had extended their suzerainty over Qatar in 1871. In 1916 Abdullah ibn Qasim signed a treaty with Great Britain that conferred British protection over the emirate, forbade Qatar to have relations with or cede territory to other states without British agreement, and gave special rights to Great Britain and its subjects in Qatar.

Like the other Persian Gulf Arab states, Qatar's pearling industry, virtually its sole source of income before oil, was devastated in the 1930s due to the influx into the world market of cultured pearls pro-

More than half the population of Qatar resides in Doha, which was founded in the nineteenth century as a fishing and pearling village. Doha grew rapidly after the country began exporting petroleum in 1949 and became Qatar's capital city in 1971. © CHRISTINE OSBORNE/CORBIS. REPRODUCED BY PERMISSION.

1996 he allowed the creation of al-Jazeera, a semi-independent satellite television network that has become world famous for its groundbreaking coverage of Arab issues, including the United States's conflict with Osama bin Ladin and al-Qaʻida. In addition, the ruler oversaw Qatar's first elections, which were held in March 1999 for members of the largely consultative Municipal Council.

Foreign Relations

Apart from its wider oil interests, Qatar has focused its foreign policy largely on Persian Gulf affairs, seeking to maintain close and friendly relations with the other traditional, dynastic Arab states. Two long-standing and contentious border disputes, with Bahrain and Saudi Arabia, were resolved peacefully in 2001. Hamad has pursued a more active and independent foreign policy than did his deposed father. Qatar agreed to the deployment on its soil of U.S. and other non-Arab military forces during the Gulf Crisis in 1990 and 1991, and its troops participated in the fighting to liberate Kuwait. In the wake of increased U.S. military activities in the region after 11 September 2001 and the reluctance of Saudi Arabia to accede to U.S. military requests, Qatar permitted the construction of a large airbase called al-Udayd where U.S. command and control facilities and other assets were transferred from Saudi Arabia in 2002 and 2003 during the U.S. buildup for its war on Iraq.

See also AL KHALIFA FAMILY; AL THANI FAMILY; AL THANI, HAMAD IBN KHALIFA; ANGLO–IRANIAN OIL COMPANY; BAHRAINI–QATARI WARS; DOHA; JAZEERA, AL-; MUWAHHIDUN.

Bibliography

Crystal, Jill. *Oil and Politics in the Gulf: Rulers and Merchants in Kuwait and Qatar.* New York; Cambridge, U.K.: Cambridge University Press, 1990.

Metz, Helen Chapin. *Persian Gulf States: Country Studies,* 3d edition. Washington, DC: Library of Congress, 1994.

Peterson, J. E. *The Arab Gulf States: Steps toward Political Participation.* New York: Praeger, 1988.

Zahlan, Rosemarie Said. *The Creation of Qatar.* New York: Barnes and Noble; London: Croom Helm, 1979.

MALCOLM C. PECK
UPDATED BY ANTHONY B. TOTH

QATAR GENERAL PETROLEUM COMPANY

See QATAR PETROLEUM

QATAR PETROLEUM

Qatar's national oil company, established in 1974, formerly known as Qatar General Petroleum Company.

As they did in other countries in the region, Western companies controlled Qatar's oil production until local leaders insisted on nationalizing this valuable resource. The Qatar General Petroleum Company (QGPC) was established in 1974, with 40 percent of the ownership held by foreign companies. The company was fully nationalized in 1977, after which it began to expand its operations from onshore and offshore oil and natural gas production to refining, petrochemical production, exploration, and development.

A major turning point came in 1991, with the opening of phase one of the North Field natural gas development project. The North Field is the largest natural gas field in the world, and its development has made Qatar a major producer. Abdullah bin Hamad al-Attiya, minister of energy and industry and the company's chairman and managing director, announced in 2001 that his company's name change to Qatar Petroleum (QP), which happened in that year, reflected in part its increased status in world energy markets. Many of QP's projects revolve around developing the field and utilizing its products in domestic and international markets while promoting the hiring of Qatari nationals in the company and maintaining a policy sensitive to the region's natural environment.

See also QATAR.

Bibliography

Economist Intelligence Unit. *Country Profile: Qatar.* London: Author, 2002.

El Mallakh, Ragaei. *Qatar: Energy and Development.* Dover, NH; London: Croom Helm, 1985.

Metz, Helen Chapin, ed. *Persian Gulf States: Country Studies,* 3d edition. Washington: Library of Congress, 1994.

MARY ANN TÉTREAULT
UPDATED BY ANTHONY B. TOTH

QA'WAR, WIDAD
[1932–]

Scholar, collector, and conservator of traditional Palestinian and Jordanian embroidery, costumes, and textiles.

Born to a Christian Palestinian Arab family in Tulkarem, in British Mandate Palestine, Widad Qa'war (*née* Irani) and her brothers were sent to Lebanon for primary school. Because of heightened tensions and uncertainty in Palestine, she was brought home in the mid-1940s to complete her secondary education at the Friends Girls School in Ramallah. The shock, upheaval, and sudden transformations of Palestinian society in 1948 and 1949 initially sparked her desire to collect and preserve examples of traditional Palestinian folk culture.

Qa'war returned to Lebanon and continued her studies at the Beirut College for Women (now the Lebanese American University), receiving a B.A. in history in 1950. She pursued postgraduate studies at the American University of Beirut and there met Kamil Amin Qa'war, her future husband, with whom she settled in Jordan.

Qa'war's unique collection of embroidery (in Arabic, *tatriz*) preserves a fading way of life and the cultural heritage of Palestinian women and village life. Each village is characterized by its own embroidery styles, patterns, and color schemes. From two traditional embroidered dresses that she received as a gift, Qa'war's collection has grown to become the largest and richest collection of Palestinian, Jordanian, and Syrian costumes now extant the Hashimite kingdom of Jordan. Qa'war's interests extend beyond collecting. She has also conducted interviews with village women about the transmission, practice, and innovation of the ancient craft of embroidery, with a special focus on the communal and political dimensions of embroidery from the late 1960s onward.

The June 1967 war prevented Qaʿwar from visiting the villages of her childhood. The hardships of occupation, and the creation of a new group of Palestinian refugees, strengthened her desire to collect as many examples of embroidery as possible.

After 1968, Qaʿwar focused on documenting and researching the history of Palestinian textiles, particularly on the wedding trousseaus of the women in the village of Bayt Dajan, near Jaffa, who were now living in refugee camps in and around Amman. A hand-woven wedding garment was usually part of the trousseau. Each trousseau features six to twelve embroidered garments, including accessories such as scarves and pillowcases.

Embroidery patterns and themes were drawn from daily life and natural surroundings. Trees, houses, flowers, and insects are all found in Palestinian needlework, which uses four types of stitches. *Al-madda* (stretch/extending), was found in the Galilee but also in Nablus and Tulkarm. It is characterized by its simplicity. *Falahi* (meaning "of the peasants") is a cross-stitch found in most Palestinian embroidery. *Tahrira* (to make silky) is a more complicated stitch originating in Jerusalem and Bethlehem. It is made from silk, first imported from Syria. The *wasla* (connecting) stitch is new, appearing after 1967. It depicts images of the Palestinian flag, Jerusalem, and the Dome of the Rock, and has acquired different names in different locales, knows as *swaisiya* or *sabaly* in the Jaffa area, *manaajel* in the areas between Ramallah and Hebron, *aqeedeh* in Gaza, and *tanbeeteh* in Beersheeba.

Qaʿwar's collection of embroidery and textiles has grown to include examples from other Arab countries. She has taken the collection on tour in Europe and is committed to using it as an educational resource on Palestinian culture and history. In 1990, she was a founding member of the Arab Resource Center for the Popular Arts in Beirut.

See also ARAB–ISRAEL WAR (1967); ART; REFUGEES: PALESTINIAN.

Bibliography

Arab Resource Center for the Popular Arts/al-Jana. Available from <http://www.oneworld.org/al-jana>.

Kawar, Amal. *Daughters of Palestine: Leading Women of the Palestinian National Movement.* Albany: State University of New York Press, 1996.

LAURIE KING-IRANI

QAWUQJI, FAWZI AL-
[1890–1974]

Military officer who led Arab nationalist forces against the imperial powers in Palestine.

Born in the late 1880s in Tripoli, Syria (later within Lebanon), Fawzi al-Din al-Qawuqji graduated from the Ottoman military academy in Istanbul and served in the early part of World War I as a captain in the Ottoman cavalry. He switched sides to join the Arab revolt in 1916 and fought the French invasion of Amir Faisal I ibn Hussein's independent Syria in July 1920. Qawuqji commanded a cavalry company of the Syrian legion after the war and used that position to lead a revolt in October 1925, in Hama (Syria), against the French mandate forces. He coordinated with other nationalist forces in the landowning and merchant classes as well as with rural rebels. Qawuqji continued to lead a rebel band in the countryside during 1926/27 but fled to Iraq in April 1927 (where Faisal was king). Qawuqji then served in the Iraqi army, from where he hoped to launch an attack on Syria to free it from French rule. His 200-man guerrilla force was, however, diverted to Palestine from August to November 1936 to assist the Palestinian general strike against British rule and Zionism. Qawuqji's forces were better prepared militarily than the Palestinian guerrilla bands but did not cooperate effectively with the Palestinians. Qawuqji called himself Commander in Chief of the Arab Revolution in Southern Syria and failed to coordinate with Abd al-Qadir al Husayni, leader of the Palestinian guerrillas in the Hebron area.

Qawuqji spent World War II in Iraq and Axis-controlled Europe. Despite his tensions with Palestinian politicians, the League of Arab States requested Qawuqji to return to Palestine in January 1948 to head the Arab Liberation Army, which sought to prevent the partition of Palestine. Once again, Qawuqji failed to cooperate with Abd al-Qadir al-Husayni and other Palestinian guerrilla leaders. He was severely defeated in his few encounters with the Haganah (the prestate armed forces of the Zionist movement). After Israel was established in May 1948 and the Arabs attacked, the Arab Liberation Army was forced out of central Galilee in July 1948 by Israeli forces—and from the rest of northern Galilee in October 1948. Qawuqji had taken a strong stand against the flight of Palestinian Arabs from their homes; he threatened to punish villagers who fled, and his forces even blocked roads to prevent them leaving. Nonetheless, his six-thousand-man force was too small to keep northern Palestine from being seized by Israel and many of its Arab residents being expelled by Israel's forces.

Bibliography

Khoury, Philip S. *Syria and the French Mandate: The Politics of Arab Nationalism, 1920–1945*. Princeton, NJ: Princeton University Press, 1987.

Morris, Benny. *The Birth of the Palestinian Refugee Problem, 1947–1949*. Cambridge, U.K., and New York: Cambridge University Press, 1987.

Porath, Yehoshua. *The Palestinian Arab National Movement: From Riots to Rebellion*. Vol. 2: *1929–1939*. London: Frank Cass, 1977.

El-Qawuqji, Fauzi. "Memoirs, 1948." *Journal of Palestine Studies* 4, 5 (1972): 27–58, 3–33.

ANN M. LESCH

QIRSH

See GLOSSARY

QIRYAT ARBA

See KIRYAT ARBA

QIYOMIJIAN, OHANNES

Early-twentieth-century Ottoman official in Lebanon.

Ohannes Qiyomijian was born in Istanbul to an Armenian Catholic family. After completing his formal education, he was appointed to the Foreign Ministry. He served as a counselor for the embassy of the Ottoman Empire in Rome. He was twice asked to become a *mutasarrif* in Lebanon before he accepted the assignment in January 1912. Among his responsibilities was adding a member from Dayr al-Qamar to the Administrative Council and revising the election laws. Qiyomijian established commer-

cial courts and opened ports in Juniya and Nabi Yunis. He enlarged the army to 1,200 and raised the salaries of the soldiers after their sit-in strike in Ba'abda. In 1913, he imported salt and tobacco directly into Lebanon in return for fees paid to the treasury of Mount Lebanon. Turkish mass killings of Armenians led Cemal Paşa to insist on his dismissal and he tendered his resignation in June 1915.

AS'AD ABUKHALIL

QOM

Shrine town in Iran.

The city of Qom (also Qum), 92 miles (148 km) south of Tehran, is, after Mashhad (the burial place of the eighth Shi'ite imam, Ali Reza), the second most important shrine town in Iran. The sister of Imam Reza, Hazrat-e Fatima, is buried in Qom. The city was a winter capital as well as a royal mausoleum town during medieval times and was strongly patronized when the Shi'ite Safavids came to power during the sixteenth century. In 1920 a religious center of learning *(hauzeh-ye ilmiyeh)* was established in the city by Shaykh Abd al-Karim Ha'eri Yazdi. Through its *madrasas* (religious schools) Qom is one of the main centers of Islamic studies in Iran today. With the accession to power of Reza Shah Pahlavi in 1925 and the modernization reforms undertaken, the town soon became the scene of a struggle between the monarchy and the religious establishment. The first major episode of violence that precipitated the Iranian Revolution of 1979 occurred there. When Ayatollah Ruhollah Khomeini returned to Iran in 1979 as the leader of the revolution, he established his headquarters in the Madrasa-y Faiziyeh in Qom.

See also IRANIAN REVOLUTION (1979).

PARVANEH POURSHARIATI

QOTBZADEH, SADEQ
[1937–1982]

Iranian politician.

Charged with treason and plotting to kill Ayatollah Ruhollah Khomeini, Sadeq Qotbzadeh was executed in 1982 by partisans of the Islamic Republic of Iran, after having spent his entire life bringing about the downfall of the Pahlavi regime. He was born in

Tehran in 1937 (1938 according to some accounts) to a conservative, religious merchant family. In 1958, fearful of being arrested by the government of Mohammad Reza Shah Pahlavi because of his association with the more religious branch of the National Front, he left Iran to attend Georgetown University in Washington, D.C. While in America, he worked in the Islamic Student Association with Ibrahim Yazdi and Mostafa Chamran. His anti-shah activities in the United States led to the cancellation of his visa. He moved to Europe in 1963, where he joined an opposition movement led by Abolhasan Bani Sadr. In 1979, he returned to Iran (on the same plane that was carrying Ayatollah Khomeini back to Iran) and became a member of the Revolutionary Council. In 1980, President Bani Sadr chose him to be foreign minister, but by February 1981, Bani Sadr had fled the country and Qotbzadeh was arrested on charges of conspiracy against the state and plotting to kill Ayatollah Khomeini. Qotbzadeh was not a radical and not a cleric, and as post-1979 Iran moved in both those directions, prodigal sons of the revolutionary movement were no longer favored. Qotbzadeh was, however, by some accounts, one of the key people involved in the disappearance of Imam Musa Sadr, Lebanese Shiʿite leader, in Tripoli in 1978.

See also BANI SADR, ABOLHASAN; CHAMRAN, MOSTAFA; KHOMEINI, RUHOLLAH; NATIONAL FRONT, IRAN; PAHLAVI, MOHAMMAD REZA; YAZDI, IBRAHIM.

Bibliography

Jerome, Carole. *The Man in the Mirror: A True Inside Story of Revolution, Love, and Treachery in Iran.* London: Unwin Hyman, 1988.

NEGUIN YAVARI

QUEEN SURRAYA
[1899–1968]

Afghan queen who fought for women's rights.

Surraya, wife of Amanollah Khan, king of Afghanistan (1919–1929), was the pioneer force behind women's emancipation and education in Afghanistan. She was born in 1899 in Damascus, the daughter of the famous Afghan writer and journalist Mahmud Tarzi, who returned to Afghanistan in 1905 after years of exile in Syria. She married Prince Amanollah in 1916 and used her royal position to promote change in the status of Afghan women. She was responsible for the establishment of the first schools for girls and the first association for the protection of women's rights in Afghanistan. In 1927, she accompanied her husband on an official tour of Europe and the Middle East and was the first Muslim queen to appear unveiled in public in Europe. She was also the only Afghan queen to be introduced in person to the Afghan Grand Assembly (*Loya Jirga*).

Queen Surraya's campaign for the emancipation and unveiling of women was one of the reasons for the outbreak of uprisings instigated by the clergy in 1928. After King Amanollah's abdication in 1929, the royal couple lived in exile in Europe. Surraya died in 1968 in Rome but was permitted by King Zahir Shah to be buried in Afghanistan in recognition of her service to the cause of Afghan women.

See also AMANOLLAH KHAN.

Bibliography

Nawid, Senzil. *Religious Response to Social Change in Afghanistan, 1919–29: King Aman-Allah and the Afghan Ulama.* Costa Mesa, CA: Mazda Publishers, 1999.

SENZIL NAWID

QURAI, AHMAD SULAYMAN
[1937–]

Palestinian economist and statesman, architect of the 1993 Oslo Accord.

Qurai (also Qurei, Quray; nom de guerre: Abu Ala) was born into a wealthy family in Abu Dis, near Jerusalem. In 1968, shortly after Israeli occupation, he left for Jordan and subsequently Saudi Arabia, gaining employment in the banking sector. He now joined the Palestine National Liberation Movement (al-Fatah) and was appointed director of Samid, the institution responsible for Palestine Liberation Organization (PLO) finances in Lebanon. Relocating to Tunis after the PLO's 1982 evacuation from Beirut, he became deputy director of the PLO's Department of Economic Affairs and in 1989 was elected to the Fatah Central Committee. The architect of PLO development plans for the Palestinian territories, he was chief Palestinian delegate at the secret Israeli-Palestinian negotiations in Oslo that produced the

September 1993 Declaration of Principles on Interim Self-Government Arrangements.

In 1994, Qurai became director of the Department of Economic Affairs of the Palestinian Authority, creating the Palestinian Economic Council for Development and Reconstruction as a channel for international investment. He became the first speaker when the Palestinian Legislative Council was established in 1996, took part in the unsuccessful "final status" talks of 2000/01, and, in September 2003, was appointed prime minister, raising the prospect, in spite of the weakness of his popular support, of a renewed accommodation with Israel.

Bibliography

Corbin, Jane. *The Norway Channel: The Secret Talks that Led to the Middle East Peace Accord.* New York: Atlantic Monthly Press, 1994.

Smith, Charles D. *Palestine and the Arab-Israeli Conflict,* 5th edition. New York: Bedford/St. Martins, 2004.

MOUIN RABBANI
UPDATED BY GEORGE R. WILKES

QUR'AN

The sacred scripture in Islam.

The Qur'an (literally, recitation) consists of the ensemble of revelations recited by the prophet Muhammad and considered by the Muslims to be the word of God verbatim. The Qur'an was revealed piecemeal during the prophetic career of Muhammad, starting in 611 C.E. with a vision he experienced during a night known as the Night of Destiny (*laylat al qadr*) and ending with his death in 632. The word *Qur'an* is coined by the revelation itself, which is also designated by other terms such as *kitab* (book), *tanzil* (literally, what is sent down), and *dhikr* (remembrance). The Qur'an, which is shorter than the Christian New Testament, is divided into 114 chapters (*sura,* plural *suwar*) and 6,616 verses (*aya,* plural *ayat*). The word *aya* means literally "sign," and is used also in reference to any natural phenomenon as the expression or sign of God's will.

The Qur'an is not arranged either chronologically or thematically, but rather on the basis of pre-Islamic aesthetic criteria, to which the Qur'an implicitly refers when it challenges doubters to compete with it on literary grounds (2:23, 11:13), and which constitute the basis for the claim of the miraculous nature of the Qur'an expressed as *i'jaz,* or inimitability. The chapters are arranged roughly in order of length, and they all start with the *basmala* (the invocation of God's name). The prophet is reported to have rearranged the text regularly with the onset of new revelations, and Muslim tradition maintains that he made also the final ordering of the text. The first chapter is called *al-fatiha* (the opening), and consists of a prayer addressed to God. In the other chapters, some verses deal with rituals and social and economic regulations, and many others consist of didactic parables and stories about former biblical and Arabian prophets, historical figures, and communities. The largest number of verses, however, is of a hortatory nature, dealing with God's majesty and power and with the various aspects of His creation. The Qur'an uses indifferently the terms *I, We,* and *He* when God addresses His creatures, whether directly or indirectly, through the Prophet.

Themes and Interpretation

The themes of the Qur'an build around the central claim of *tawhid,* or the absolute unity and transcendence of God. God is an omnipotent, all-powerful deity, on whom creation is completely dependent. All of creation was offered to humanity as a trust to allow the latter to carry out its task as God's vicegerent (*khalifa*) on earth. The Qur'an, which is written in powerful rhymed prose with striking imagery, vividly reminds human beings that they will report to God on the Day of Judgment and that the afterlife (paradise and hell) is predicated on one's actions in this life. Parables and moral didactic stories abound, as well as warnings and general advice on how to succeed as God's vicegerent and avoid the failure to which pride and greed lead. Because the Qur'an refers to the human endowment (*fitrah*) that allows people to distinguish good from evil, it calls itself *dhikr* (reminder or remembrance); and it is repeatedly pointed out that similar messages, based on a single divine source of revelation called *umm al-kitab* (13:39), had been sent to all communities over time, and eventually gave rise to different interpretations in the form of different religions. The Qur'an itself is the conclusion of this string of revelations that start with Adam as the first prophet and end with Muhammad.

The Qur'an has given rise to a number of sciences, the most important of which is *asbab al-nuzul* (the study of the historical context of the verses), and to countless commentaries that range from the literalist to the mystical. Modern commentaries such as those of Muhammad Abduh, Abu al-A'la al-Mawdudi, and Sayyid Qutb have shifted from the early traditional atomist approach to a comprehensive approach that integrates the various meanings of the text.

Collection of the Qur'an

Muslim tradition holds that the Prophet relied primarily on the memorization by his disciples of the revelations he taught them, but he did have a number of secretaries transcribe the text of the Qur'an. There is agreement that after his death, these transcriptions were collected by Zayd ibn Thabit, one of his main secretaries, but no official canon or reference was established. By the time of Uthman's reign (644–656), the spread of variant readings of the text (based on the use of synonyms, and on pronunciations found in dialects other than that of the Qur'an), and the proliferation of manuscripts (*mushaf*, plural *masahif*) made without reference to the original recitation, caused alarm amongst the Companions of the Prophet. Consequently, Uthman ordered Zayd to establish an official canon in the Quraysh dialect based on the original collection, and to get confirmation and approval of his work from the Companions. All other existing manuscripts and personal copies (which often contained personal annotations, or omitted some passages, or followed a different order of the chapters) were ordered destroyed, and all new copies of the Qur'an were made from the new canon. However, differences persisted. Muslim tradition identifies and accepts as part of the original text of the Qur'an seven dialects (*ahruf*) in which the text is said to be revealed, though the standardization of the Uthman canon, which emphasized the Quraysh dialect, made these obsolete. In addition, different readings or styles of recitation (*qira'a*) arose based on different possible orthographic forms and pronunciations. The Qur'an had been recited aloud from its inception; eventually, ten different readings were accepted as legitimate, based on the authenticity of the oral traditions that transmitted them and on evidence that the original reader's recitation had been tolerated by the Prophet. Further standardization came with the development of diacritical dots and marks in the written text.

Contemporary Orientalist views of the collection of the Qur'an diverge widely, ranging from the claim that it is a late forgery to near-total endorsement of traditional Muslim claims. However, with very few exceptions, there is general agreement that the current text of the Qur'an is in accordance with Uthman's canon (as there are no traditions referring to other canons), and that the variations that prompted codification of the Qur'an were mostly minor divergences of pronunciation and orthography and omissions in some personal copies of some chapters or insertions of prayer formulas external to the text. More importantly, it seems that the early Muslim community accepted the Uthman canon: There were no attempts made by the early dissenting political groups (Shi'ite and Khawarij) to claim a divergent text; instead, they insisted on a divergent interpretation of it.

Place in Islam

The Qur'an is the ultimate reference for the Muslim who reveres it as the only expression of the sacred on earth. Besides providing the central worldview from which Muslim culture and civilization springs, it directly affects a number of disciplines and arts. Thus grammar, syntax, lexicography, law, and literary criticism are all based on the Qur'anic text. Calligraphy, the most sophisticated of Islamic art forms, was developed to celebrate the holy text, and the chanting of the Qur'an, based on abstract modular improvisation that organizes musical motifs in complex patterns, provides the core structure of the various genres of Islamic music.

See also ABDUH, MUHAMMAD; ISLAM; MAWDUDI, ABU AL A'LA AL-; MUHAMMAD; QUTB, SAYYID.

Bibliography

Faruqi, Lois L al-. *Islam and Art.* Islamabad, Pakistan: National Hijrah Council, 1985.

Rahman, Fazlur. *The Major Themes of the Qur'an.* Minneapolis, MN: Bibliotheca Islamica, 1980.

Said, Labib al-. *The Recited Koran.* Princeton, NJ: Darwin Press, 1975.

Watt, M. W. *Bell's Introduction to the Qur'an.* Edinburgh, U.K.: Edinburgh University Press, 1970

MAYSAM J. AL-FARUQI

QURAYSH TRIBE

See TRIBES AND TRIBALISM: QURAYSH TRIBE

QUSAYR, AL-

Historic Egyptian port on the Red Sea.

The town al-Qusayr in Egypt on the Red Sea is located slightly north of the twenty-sixth parallel, and linked to the Nile by a trade route to Qina. The site has been in use since pharaonic times and served as a port of embarkation for Muslim pilgrims to Mecca. It was a major commercial center in Mamluk and early Ottoman Empire times and experienced a revival under Muhammad Ali, but the pilgrimage traffic was diverted to Suez after the canal was built (1859-1869), eclipsing its importance.

Bibliography

Garcin, J. "Kusayr." *Encyclopedia of Islam,* new edition, Vol. V, edited by C. E. Bosworth, B. Lewis, E. van Donzel, and C. Pellat. Leiden, Netherlands: Brill, 1979.

Meyer, Carol. *Glass from Quseir Al-Qadim and the Indian Ocean Trade.* Chicago: University of Chicago Press, 1992.

ARTHUR GOLDSCHMIDT
UPDATED BY DONALD MALCOLM REID

QUTB, SAYYID

[1906–1966]

Radical ideologue of the Muslim Brotherhood.

Born in Asyut, south of Cairo, to a family of impoverished rural notables, Sayyid Qutb was trained as a teacher at Dar al-Ulum. Until 1942, he was an inspector in the Ministry of Public Instruction; he also wrote Wafdist political opinions in the popular press and published poetry, short stories, and literary criticism. From 1945 to 1948, he wrote a series of articles critical of Egyptian politics and several books on literary figures and issues. He was highly critical of the government in his writings, and this earned him de facto exile to the United States, where he was sent by the ministry to study the education system. During his three-year stay in the United States, disturbed by what he considered to be U.S. sexual permissiveness, materialism, and racism, he rediscovered his deep Muslim roots. Upon his return to Egypt in 1951, he was recruited by the Society of the Muslim Brethren, or Muslim Brotherhood. He became a member of the Guidance Council and head of the propaganda section. In 1953, he was appointed editor-in-chief of the society's newspaper *al-Ikhwan al-Muslimin* (the Muslim brethren).

In the months before and after the July 1952 Egyptian revolution, Qutb and Gamal Abdel Nasser met regularly. Nonetheless, in the wake of a 1954 assassination attempt on Nasser by a Muslim Brother, Qutb was imprisoned. He was released in 1964 but was arrested again in 1965. After being tortured and tried by a military court for conspiracy against Nasser, Qutb was hanged on 29 August 1966.

In prison, Qutb converted from moderate to radical Islamism. It was there that Qutb indoctrinated some of the future radical leaders, including Shukri Mustafa. During his incarceration, from 1954 to 1964, Qutb wrote, and circulated outside prison, numerous books, including one of his most influential, *Maʿalim fi al-Tariq* (Signposts on the road). An account and interpretation of events in Nasser's concentration camps, it is a seminal work and served as the basis for the reconstituted Islamist movement in the early 1960s. *Maʿalim* describes both the words and the actions that are needed for the destruction of the secular regime and the creation of a Muslim state.

Qutb's theoretical writings, addressing the political, economic, and social organization of the Islamic state, vividly expressed the unity of *din* (religion) and *dawla* (state), in distinct contrast to the post-Enlightenment separation of church and state prevalent in the West. Focusing on the intersection of *shariʿa* (Islamic law) and modern society, he maintained that the former was imbued with an inherent sense of *tajdid* (renewal). As such, it offered the principles necessary for progress through action. Moreover, Qutb held that laws and statutes were only one of Islam's two pillars; the other was education, which alone could provide Muslims with an Islamic theory of life.

Through his writings, Qutb established the theoretical foundations for radical Islamist organizations. His books, which upheld the doctrines of divine governance *(hakimiyya)* and insisted on attacking worldly unbelief or paganism *(jahiliyya)* through violent revolutionary means, have become the gospels of Islamic radicals, including the Arabs who during the 1980s fought the Soviet invasion of Afghanistan.

See also MUSLIM BROTHERHOOD; NASSER, GAMAL ABDEL; WAFD.

Bibliography

Abu Rabi, Ibrahim M. *Intellectual Origins of Islamic Resurgence in the Modern Arab World.* Albany: State University of New York Press, 1996.

Moussalli, Ahmad S. *Radical Islamic Fundamentalism: The Ideological and Political Discourse of Sayyid Qutb.* Beirut: American University of Beirut, 1992.

JEAN-MARC R. OPPENHEIM
UPDATED BY AHMAD S. MOUSSALLI

QUWATLI, SHUKRI AL-
[1891–1967]

Three-time Syrian president; Arab nationalist.

Shukri al-Quwatli was born in Damascus to a Sunni Muslim family of prosperous landowners and bureaucrats who made their fortune through agriculture and trade with Abd al-Aziz ibn Abd al-Rahman Al Sa'ud in the Arabian Peninsula. He was one of the most important figures in the political life of modern Syria. He received his education in the elite schools of Damascus and his public administration training in Constantinople (now Istanbul). Having no stake in the Ottoman Empire, he joined the secret Arab nationalist society al-Fatat and then the Hashimite-led Arab Revolt in 1916. His underground activities on behalf of the cause of Arab independence during World War I enabled him to emerge as a nationalist hero.

Although al-Quwatli served in the local administration of the Hashimite Prince Faisal I ibn Hussein's Arab government, which was set up in Damascus after the defeat of the Ottoman state, he belonged to a group of avowed anti-Hashimite pan-Arabists who devoted most of their time to the Istiqlal Party (Arab Independence party). Forced to flee Syria after the French invasion of July 1920, al-Quwatli spent the next ten years in exile first in Cairo, which he used as a base for his activities on behalf of the Hashimite-leaning Syrian–Palestine Congress, and then in Europe, primarily Berlin, where he collaborated with other exiled Syrians in anti-French propaganda campaigns. He was

The inauguration ceremony of Syrian president Shukri al-Quwatli (1892-1967), shown seated in the House of Parliament, in Damascus. Quwatli succeeded Hashem al-Atassi (1875-1960), in 1940. © BETTMANN/CORBIS. REPRODUCED BY PERMISSION.

active in supporting the Great Syrian Revolt of 1925–1927.

With the French amnesty of 1930, al-Quwatli returned to Damascus. Initially he maintained a low political profile devoting much of his time and energy to business ventures, primarily the processing and exporting of fruits and vegetables. The Syrian Conserves Company, which he founded in 1932, vaulted him into the limelight as an industrialist who promoted Syria's economic interests during a critical phase of its fight for independence.

Following the election of a Syrian parliament in 1932, al-Quwatli joined the National Bloc, Syria's principal nationalist organization from 1927 until the end of the French mandate era. An uncompromising pan-Arabist devoted to the cause of Arab independence, al-Quwatli was soon disenchanted with the bloc's ineffectiveness and its policy of "honorable cooperation" with the French, and he became a leading instigator of the general strike that erupted in Syria on 27 January 1936, and brought commercial and educational life to a standstill for thirty-six days. When the all-bloc government was formed in Damascus in 1936, al-Quwatli served as minister of defense and of finance only to resign two years later. Although he was the leading nationalist politician in Syria during World War II, his anti-French activities forced him to go into exile in Iraq. His connections with Ibn Saʿud, however, made the British apply pressure on the French to accept his return. In the Syrian elections of 1943, he was elected to the presidency of a "formally" independent Syria. His nationalist sentiment, which was beyond reproach, enabled him to remain in office despite the factionalism and scandals that plagued his administration.

In March 1949, al-Quwatli was deposed as president by Colonel Husni al-Zaʿim's successful coup and once again he went into exile, but this time in Egypt, a country on which he came to depend during the rest of his political life. Thanks to Egyptian and Saudi support, he returned to Syria in 1954 after the overthrow of the military regime of Colonel Adib Shishakli. In August 1955, he was elected president of Syria for a third time. By that time, the political landscape in Syria had changed. The class of urban notables from which he hailed and that controlled Syrian politics from the latter part of the nineteenth century through the early years of independence was under attack by new political forces, including al-Baʿth and the communists. Syria's domestic politics was also weak and unstable, and the country itself was at the heart of a struggle for dominance between Hashimite Iraq and republican Egypt on the one hand, and the big powers on the other hand.

Al-Quwatli strongly supported the ideas of an Egyptian–Syrian union in 1957 and 1958. With the consummation of the union and emergence of the United Arab Republic (UAR) in 1958, al-Quwatli's active participation in Syrian politics came to an end. He resigned his post as president to allow Gamal Abdel Nasser, Egypt's charismatic president, to take over the presidency of the UAR. Before his death in 1967, al-Quwatli witnessed the collapse of the UAR in 1961 and the coming to power of a factionalized group of Baʿthist military officers who came in the main from rural Alawi, Druze, and Ismaʿili backgrounds significantly different from the landowning, scholarly, and mercantile Sunni families from which his generation of leaders hailed. The advent of these new groups to power brought with it the reorientation of Syrian politics, both domestically as well as in the area of foreign relations.

See also ABD AL-AZIZ IBN SAʿUD AL SAʿUD; ARAB REVOLT (1916); BAʿTH, AL-; FAISAL I IBN HUSSEIN; FATAT, AL-; ISTIQLAL PARTY: SYRIA; NASSER, GAMAL ABDEL; NATIONAL BLOC; UNITED ARAB REPUBLIC (UAR); ZAʿIM, HUSNI AL-.

MUHAMMAD MUSLIH

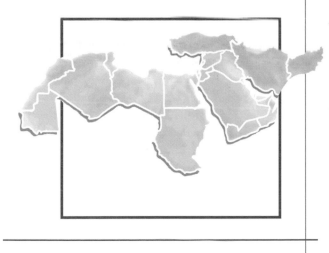

R

RAAB, ESTHER

[1894–1981]

The first Palestinian-born woman poet in the modern era to write and publish in Hebrew.

Esther Raab's childhood in the early years of the first Jewish settlement of Petah Tikvah shaped an intimate connection between her and the wild and primary landscape of Eretz Yisrael (Palestine). This emotional relationship is expressed throughout her poems. In 1923 Raab's first poem, "Ani Tahat ha-Atad" (I am underneath the bramble bush), was published in the new Hebrew literary periodical *Hedim,* but it was only in 1930 that her first book, *Kimshonim* (Thistles)—containing thirty-two poems written between 1920 and 1930—was published.

Raab was a pioneer in her poetics. As early as the 1920s, Raab's poems differed markedly from those of her mainstream male contemporaries and from those of other women poets of the time. Her early poetry is striking in its sensuous descriptions of the landscape of Eretz Yisrael and in its rebellious female voice. Moreover, this early work is notable for its rejection of the stanza and meter in favour of free verse and idiosyncratic syntax and word order. These elements of form and content, which set Raab's poetry apart from the poetic and thematic conventions of her time, may have contributed to her fate as a poet. After the cool and sometimes openly hostile reception of her book, Raab fell into a two-decade-long silence. She started to publish again in the late 1950s.

Raab died in Tiveon and was buried in the city of her birth, Petah Tikvah. She requested that a few lines from her poem be engraved on her tombstone: "Your earth-clods were sweet to me/Homeland—just as the clouds of your sky/Were sweet to me."

Among Raab's books of poetry are *The Poetry of Esther Raab* (1963), *As Last Prayer,* (1976), *Root's Sound* (an anthology; 1976), and *Esther Raab, Collected Poems* (1988). A second, enlarged edition of her collected poems was published in 1994, the one-hundredth anniversary of her birth.

See also ERETZ YISRAEL; LITERATURE: HEBREW.

SHIBOLET ZAIT

RAAD, IN'AM
[1929–1998]

Lebanese politician.

In'am Raad (also Ra'd) was born to a Greek Orthodox family in Ayn Zhalta. His father, Tawfiq, a graduate of the American University of Beirut (AUB), was a pharmacist who emigrated for a few years to Australia. In 1949 the younger Raad obtained his degree in political science at AUB. Until 1957 he taught Arabic, English, geography, and history at Broummana High School and other schools in Lebanon. In 1944 he had joined the Parti Populaire Syrien (later called the Syrian Social Nationalist Party) and was elected several times to its politburo. Between 1958 and 1961 he was chief editor of the party's publications, *al-Bina* and *Sabah al-Khayr*. In 1961, following an attempted coup mounted by the party against the Lebanese government, Raad and his followers were condemned to death; Raad's sentence later was commuted to a life sentence. In 1969 President Charles Hilu announced an amnesty for the civilian party members implicated in the coup. In 1992 Raad was elected president of the party. He died in 1998.

See also AMERICAN UNIVERSITY OF BEIRUT (AUB); HILU, CHARLES; SYRIAN SOCIAL NATIONALIST PARTY.

GEORGE E. IRANI
UPDATED BY MICHAEL R. FISCHBACH

RABAT

One of the four imperial cities of Morocco; national capital since 1912.

Since being named capital by the French in 1912, Rabat (also Ribat al-Fath) has grown in size and prestige as the new administrative, educational, and cultural center of Morocco. It is bordered by the Atlantic Ocean and the Bou Regreg River, which separates it from its rival sister city to the north, Salé.

Rabat takes its name from a small tenth-century *ribat* (monastery-citadel) manned by Muslim holy warriors *(murabits)*. The Almohad Sultan Ya'qub al-Mansur constructed a city on the site and named it Ribat al-Fath (Monastery of Conquest), in honor of a victory over Spain in 1195. Rabat's historical significance, along with its neighboring rival, Salé, stemmed from commercial trade and piracy in the seventeenth and eighteenth centuries. Spanish Muslims expelled from Spain in 1610 formed the core of Rabat's population.

At the beginning of the French protectorate in 1912, the French decision to relocate Morocco's capital to Rabat opened it to extensive development outside the original Arab city *(madina)* to the south and west. French colonial administrator General Louis-Hubert Gonzalve Lyautey, in laying out the plan for Rabat, saw it as an opportunity to design an exemplary modern city. The major national university, Muhammad V, is located in Rabat, as are various national research institutes. Rabat and Salé together form an administrative prefecture that has grown at a rate of more than 5 percent annually since the late 1960s. The population of Rabat-Salé and environs numbers 1,386,000 (1994 figures).

See also LYAUTEY, LOUIS-HUBERT GONZALVE; MOROCCO.

Bibliography

Abu-Lughod, Janet L. *Rabat: Urban Apartheid in Morocco.* Princeton, NJ: Princeton University Press, 1980.

DONNA LEE BOWEN

RABAT ARAB SUMMIT

See ARAB LEAGUE SUMMITS

RABBANI, BURHANUDDIN
[1940–]

President of Afghanistan, 1993–1996.

Burhanuddin Rabbani was the president of Afghanistan from 1992 to 1996. He was born in Faizabad, Badakhshan province, to a Tajik family and educated in Islamic studies at Kabul University and al-Azhar University in Cairo, where he received a master of arts degree (1968). He returned to Kabul to teach in the faculty of Islamic law at Kabul University (1970) and was a leader of the Islamist movement in Afghanistan. In 1971 he joined the Jami'at-e Islami and became its leader. In 1974 he fled Afghanistan, first traveling to Saudi Arabia and then to Pakistan, where he reorganized the Jami'at-e Islami as a guerrilla militia to fight against the Kabul government.

As he was Tajik, Rabbani's political party drew most of its followers from the non-Pushtun Afghans, especially in the northern and western regions of Afghanistan.

With the collapse of the People's Democratic Party of Afghanistan (PDPA) government in 1992, Rabbani returned to Kabul and became president of Afghanistan. Driven from Kabul by the Taliban in 1996, Rabbani sought refuge in northern Afghanistan, where he formed the United National and Islamic Front for the Salvation of Afghanistan (UNIFSA), also known as the Northern Alliance, to fight against the Taliban government. When the Taliban fell in late November 2001, UNIFSA forces captured Kabul. Although Rabbani was still seen as the president of Afghanistan by some of his followers, he was forced to relinquish control to the new government of Hamid Karzai.

See also JAMI'AT-E ISLAMI; PEOPLE'S DEMOCRATIC PARTY OF AFGHANISTAN.

Bibliography

Roy, Olivier. *Islam and Resistance in Afghanistan.* Cambridge, U.K.: Cambridge University Press, 1986.

Rubin, Barnett. *The Fragmentation of Afghanistan.* New Haven, CT: Yale University Press, 2002.

GRANT FARR

RABBI

Title derived from rav, *which in Hebrew denotes a master.*

In its Talmudic origins, the mastery to which *rabbi* referred was a knowledge of both Scripture and Jewish oral tradition, including competence in interpreting law and recalling legends. Although at first the title was honorific, it evolved into something more formal. Always connected with a level of superior scholarship and familiarity with sacred Jewish texts, it has in contemporary times also come to signify general religious leadership.

Although the requirements for acquiring the title are not stipulated in Jewish law, *semikha* or ordination—in which another rabbi attests to the scholarship and learning of the initiate—has become an assumed prerequisite of being called rabbi. Throughout much of Jewish history, this process occurred in the con-

A rabbi holds a photograph of Jerusalem's Temple Mount, or Old City Mosque, at a gathering of Israel's chief rabbinate, August 2000. They discussed building a synagogue on the area that is thought to be the Jewish Second Temple, ruined by the Romans in 70 C.E. © AFP/CORBIS. REPRODUCED BY PERMISSION.

text of yeshivas; currently, it also takes place in theological seminaries.

Generally, civil authorities have recognized the right of the Jews to decide for themselves who may be called rabbi. This became more complicated after Jews ceased to speak with a single communal voice in the modern period, with the consequence that different groups of Jews set various criteria for deciding who would be entitled to be called rabbi. Thus in the modern period in the United States, for example, there are four types of rabbis being ordained, to represent the four different denominations: Reformed, Reconstructionist, Conservative, and Orthodox. The Orthodox denomination, although it represents a minority of world Jewry, produces the most rabbis. Throughout Jewish history, the title has been granted only to men, but in the late twentieth century, non-Orthodox Jews began to ordain women as well. In Israel, only Orthodox rabbis are officially recognized, even though Reformed and Conservative rabbis are also there.

Two general categories of rabbis evolved in modern times: those who were primarily teachers, scholars, or issuers of legal decisions and remained in the academy of Jewish learning or sometimes served on a religious court, and those who ministered in the community and the synagogue. Rabbis have also become ratifiers of changes in personal status by officiating at weddings, funerals, and other rites of passage.

The rabbinate in modern Israel is unique in several important respects. Because there is no strict separation of religion and state in Israel, Halakhah is the governing law in all matters of personal status. Accordingly, the Orthodox rabbinical interpretation of Jewish law is dominant. In Israel, many rabbis exert their authority as officials of the state Ministry of Religion and the office of the Chief Rabbinate. Headed by two national chief rabbis elected by a board of fellow rabbis for a term of ten years, the Chief Rabbinate is divided into Ashkenazic and Sephardic wings. Ostensibly empowered to make all ultimate religious decisions, it also provides parish rabbis and chief rabbis for major municipal regions.

There are other rabbis in Israel, particularly within Hasidic and yeshiva circles. Unlike the state rabbis whose authority is official, these rabbis dominate by virtue of their charisma or perceived scholarship. The relatively few non-Orthodox rabbis in Israel have a limited following. During the last few decades, the chief rabbis and their subordinates have steadily lost moral authority. Today the majority of secular Israelis consider them irrelevant, and the minority of ultra-Orthodox Jews guide themselves by their own sages whom they endow with greater rabbinic authority. This leaves only a narrow band of Orthodox Jews—primarily religious Zionists—who recognize the moral preeminence of the Chief Rabbinate. Nevertheless, the Chief Rabbinate is assured of influence as long as it continues to control matters of personal status and religious certification in the state.

See also HALAKHAH.

Bibliography

Heilman, Samuel C. "Jewish Unity and Diversity: A Survey of American Rabbis and Rabbinical Students." In Encyclopedia Judaica, Vol. 13. New York: Macmillan, 1973.

SAMUEL C. HEILMAN

RABI, MUBARAK
[1935–]

Moroccan novelist and short-story writer.

Mubarak Rabi was born in Benmaʿashu, near Casablanca, Morocco. He received a degree in philosophy from the Faculty of Arts in Rabat and has a master's degree in psychology. He is at present dean of the College of Arts and Sciences at Ben Msik in Casablanca and teaches psychology at Mohammad V University in Rabat. Rabi is a member of the Union of Arab Writers and writes in Arabic. After unsuccessful efforts at poetry, he has concentrated on fiction. He received the Maghribi Prize for the novel and the short story in 1971.

Rabi is primarily concerned with Moroccan life and the role of magic and traditional beliefs in people's lives. This is best illustrated in his collection of short stories, *Sayyidna Qadr* (1969; Saint destiny). His books reveal a clear interest in human nature and a desire to discover the factors that shape it, producing good and bad. He is preoccupied with the loss of values in modern times and the ensuing conflicts among people. His fiction remains detached from the political turmoil in Morocco.

Rabi is also deeply interested in the education of children, as is obvious from his novel *Badr Zamanihi* (1983; The full moon of his time) and his collection of essays, *Awatif al-Tifl* (1984; The child's emotions). His later works include a novel, *Burj al-Suʿud* (1990; The lucky zodiac), a collection of short stories, *al-Balluri al-maksur* (1996; The broken crystalline), and a trilogy, *Darb al-Sultan* (1999–2000; The sultan's way). His concern remains humans evil and good inclinations seen with the eyes of a psychologist.

See also LITERATURE: ARABIC, NORTH AFRICAN.

Bibliography

Williams, Malcolm, and Watterson, Gavin, trans. An Anthology of Moroccan Short Stories. Tangier, Morocco: King Fahd School of Translation, 1995.

AIDA A. BAMIA

RABIN, YITZHAK
[1922–1995]

Israeli military leader and politician; member of the Knesset; prime minister, 1974–1977 and 1989–1995.

Born in Jerusalem, Yitzhak Rabin received part of his early education at an agricultural school; later, he became active in the Ahdut ha-Avodah (socialist labor) movement in the Galilee. In 1941 he joined the Palmah, the Haganah's elite commando unit. Rabin's early military experience included fighting against Vichy French forces in Syria and Lebanon. In the Israeli War of Independence (1948) he fought against the Egyptians in the Negev campaign and also in Jerusalem. After the war he studied in Britain at the army staff college, from which he graduated in 1953.

Rabin, whose first career was in the military, was appointed chief of staff of Israel's armed forces in 1964; at the time of the June 1967 war he was Israel's commander in chief. In 1968 he retired from the army and became Israel's ambassador to the United States. He was very successful in that capacity, and the diplomatic experience combined with his military career gave him the leverage to start a second career, in politics, at the age of fifty-one.

Rabin returned to Israel from Washington, D.C., in March 1973; in the same year, he was elected to the Knesset for the first time and also served as minister of labor in the government of Prime Minister Golda Meir. In April 1974, when Meir resigned because of intense criticism of her government's handling of the 1973 war, the Labor Party's Central Committee sought her successor from among a field of candidates that included Shimon Peres, Moshe Dayan, Yigal Allon, Pinhas Sapir, and Abba Eban, as well as Rabin. Rabin was selected in June 1974 primarily because of his reputation as a war hero and because he was not associated with the government's unpreparedness for the Yom Kippur War.

In creating his coalition, Rabin, who was Israel's first *sabra* (native-born) prime minister, refused to give in to the extremist demands of members of the National Religious Party for greater Orthodox (Jewish) religious influence on public policy. He consequently achieved only a bare majority, with the help of the new and small Citizens' Rights movement, and this left his government vulnerable to periodic attacks in the Knesset. From 1974 to 1975 Rabin worked closely with U.S. Secretary of State Henry Kissinger, who was involved in the shuttle diplomacy that led to disengagement agreements with Egypt and Syria.

Rabin's first term as prime minister was marked by continuous intraparty bickering, primarily be-

Former military leader Yitzhak Rabin served as prime minister of Israel for two terms, the first beginning in 1974 and the second in 1989. Rabin made notable strides towards peace with other Middle Eastern countries and with Palestinians, which led to his assassination in 1995 by Yigal Amir, a disillusioned young Israeli who claimed he killed Rabin to halt this process. © PHOTOGRAPH BY YA'ACOV SA'AR. GOVERNMENT PRESS OFFICE (GPO) OF ISRAEL. REPRODUCED BY PERMISSION.

cause Defense Minister Shimon Peres attempted to take over leadership of the party and become the prime minister. Domestic economic problems, chiefly inflation, continuing criticism of the Labor Party's performance in the Yom Kippur War, and increased ethnic tensions between Ashkenazic and Sephardic Jews all contributed to a gradual decline in the Labor Party's popularity and the rise of the Likud Party under Menachem Begin. Rabin resigned from the party leadership and from his post as prime minister in May 1977 because of a financial scandal involving his own and his wife's bank accounts in the United States. Shimon Peres replaced him as party leader.

After twelve years, during which the Labor Party, led by Shimon Peres, was the opposition party in a shared-power arrangement with the Likud, Rabin again became party leader and prime minister in 1989. Over intense opposition from conservative forces in Israel, he pressed hard for a peace treaty with the Palestinians and Israel's Arab neighbors. In September 1993 he signed an Agreement on Principles on Interim Self-Government with Yasir Arafat of the Palestine Liberation Organization, and an Accord to Implement Self-Rule for the Palestinians was signed in May 1994. In October 1994 Rabin signed a full peace treaty with King Hussein of Jordan. In the same year, he shared a Nobel Peace Prize with Foreign Minister Peres and Chairman Arafat.

On 4 November 1995, while he was speaking at a peace rally in Tel Aviv, Rabin was assassinated by a Jewish right-wing extremist who opposed his overtures to Palestinians and other Arab leaders working toward peace in the Middle East. "The Rabin legacy" is often cited, but there is disagreement about its substance. For some it is associated specifically with the Oslo peace accords. For others it refers generally to the quest for peace. Critics have observed that those who allude to "the Rabin ideology" or "the Rabin legacy" mistake their own views for those of Rabin; these critics argue that Rabin did not have an ideology or a legacy—what he had was a sense of responsibility for the state and a willingness to pragmatically consider new ideas in order to pursue peace.

See also AHDUT HA-AVODAH; ASHKENAZIM; ISRAEL: POLITICAL PARTIES IN; KISSINGER, HENRY; MEIR, GOLDA; PALMAH.

Bibliography

Inbar, Efraim. *Rabin and Israel's National Security.* Washington, DC: Woodrow Wilson Center Press; Baltimore, MD: Johns Hopkins University Press, 1999.

Kurzman, Dan. *Soldier of Peace: The Life of Yitzhak Rabin, 1922–1995.* New York: HarperCollins, 1998.

Makovsky, David. *Making Peace with the PLO: The Rabin Government's Road to the Oslo Accord.* Boulder, CO: Westview Press, 1996.

Rabin, Yitzhak. *The Rabin Memoirs.* Boston: Little, Brown, 1979.

Rabin, Leah. *Rabin: Our Life, His Legacy.* New York: Putnam, 1997.

"The Rabin Legacy." *Jerusalem Post.* 30 October 2001.

Sachar, Howard M. *A History of Israel: From the Rise of Zionism to Our Time.* New York: Random House, 1981.

GREGORY S. MAHLER

RABIYYA ALI, SALIM
[c.1935–1978]

Politician and government leader of South Yemen.

Salim Rabiyya Ali (or Rubiyya Salim Ali, or Salmine) came from the up-country of South Yemen, northeast of Aden, and first made his name fighting in the national liberation struggle against the British and their feudalist allies in the Radfan region during the mid-1960s. He was president of the People's Democratic Republic of Yemen (PDRY) throughout most of the 1970s. He and his colleague and rival Abd al-Fattah Isma'il were founders of the National Liberation Front (NLF), early leaders of its left wing, and allies in the successful effort to rout its right wing in 1969; they were essentially co-rulers of the PDRY for the next decade, with Rabiyya Ali serving as president and Isma'il as secretary-general of the NLF. At the same time, they were bitter rivals and represented different perspectives on South Yemen's Marxist revolution: Rabiyya Ali, the Maoist, was identified with populist, grass-roots organizing as well as state institutions, whereas Isma'il, inspired by the Soviet model, was identified with the ruling party and its cadres. Their intraparty struggle for control of the revolution intensified and in mid-1978 erupted into armed conflict triggered by Rabiyya Ali's continuing efforts to improve previously hostile relations with North Yemen, Saudi Arabia, and the other Arab Gulf states, and more immediately by mutual accusations about responsibility for the assassination of North Yemen's president, Ahmad Husayn Ghashmi. Forces loyal to Rabiyya Ali lost the fight and he and two of his senior colleagues were summarily tried and executed.

See also ISMA'IL, ABD AL-FATTAH; PEOPLE'S DEMOCRATIC REPUBLIC OF YEMEN.

Bibliography

Bidwell, Robin Leonard. *The Two Yemens.* Boulder, CO: Westview; Harlow, U.K.: Longman, 1983.

Lackner, Helen. *P.D.R. Yemen: Outpost of Socialist Development in Arabia.* London: Ithaca Press, 1985.

ROBERT D. BURROWES

RADIO AND TELEVISION

This entry consists of the following articles:

ARAB COUNTRIES
ISRAEL
TURKEY

ARAB COUNTRIES

Origins and development of radio and television broadcasting in the Arab world.

Most Arab radio and television systems are government-owned, for several reasons. First, Arab governments regard radio and television as potent domestic political instruments because they reach most of the population regardless of literacy and income levels. Moreover, Arab broadcasting underwent its first major expansion during the period after World War II when Arab nationalism and anticolonialism were strong, and governments were very eager to use them for purposes of political nation building and national defense. Governments justified controls on the basis of the alleged need to protect the country against its enemies, old and new. By the same token, radio and television facilities have been prime targets of revolutions seeking to take power, and therefore the governments took special measures to protect them. Third, broadcasting is not a lucrative source of income for commercial investors because commercial advertising in the Arab world, and especially in the electronic media, is relatively limited, and generally advertising revenues do not cover costs. Fourth, governments are concerned about their image as conveyed in other countries through broadcasting so they want to control the programs. There are a few exceptions, especially in Lebanon and among the new satellite television companies, but the norm is government control of electronic broadcasting.

Arab Radio Broadcasting Development

Arab radio broadcasting began in the 1920s, but only a few Arab countries had their own broadcasting stations before World War II. After 1945, most Arab states began to create their own radio broadcasting systems, although it was not until 1970, when Oman opened its radio transmissions, that every one of them had its own radio station.

Egypt's Radio and Television Building in Cairo, which produces the bulk of the country's media programming, contains recording studios, hundreds of offices, an information center, a press center, and a broadcasting museum. On 31 May 2003, Egypt's annual Media Day, President Husni Mubarak inaugurated a new ten-story extension to the building which houses eight digital studios and a 1,200-seat auditorium. © DAVE BARTRUFF/CORBIS. REPRODUCED BY PERMISSION.

Among Arab countries, Egypt has been a leader in radio broadcasting from the beginning. Broadcasting began in Egypt in the 1920s with private commercial radio, and in 1934 the government gave the Marconi Company the exclusive right to broadcast. In 1947, however, the Egyptian government declared radio a government monopoly and began investing in its expansion.

By the 1970s, Egyptian radio had fourteen different broadcast services, including six for foreign audiences, staffed by more than 4,500 employees. With a total air time of 1,200 hours per week, Egypt

Qatar-based television network al-Jazeera has increasingly been referred to as the "Arab CNN." The network has one of the world's largest audience bases, with some 45 million subscribers. © AFP/CORBIS. REPRODUCED BY PERMISSION.

ranked third in the world among radio broadcasters, The programs were all government controlled, and much of the motivation for the government's investment in radio was due to the aspirations of President Gamal Abdel Nasser to be the recognized leader of the Arab world. Egypt's "Voice of the Arabs" station, which targeted other Arab countries with a constant stream of news and political features and commentaries, became the most widely heard station in the region. Only after the June 1967 war, when it was revealed that this station had misinformed the public about what was happening, did it lose some credibility; nevertheless it retained a sizable listenership.

On the Arabian Peninsula, radio was slower to develop. In Saudi Arabia, radio broadcasts started in the Jidda-Mecca area in 1948, but they did not start in the central or eastern provinces until the 1960s. Neighboring Bahrain had radio by 1955, but Qatar, Abu Dhabi, and Oman did not start indige-

nous radio broadcasting until nearly a quarter century later.

Arab Television Development

As for television, indigenous television broadcasting in the Arab world first began during the late 1950s, in Iraq and Lebanon. Thirteen other Arab countries followed during the 1960s, but it was not until 1975, when North Yemen inaugurated its television station, that all Arab states had television stations.

Before that, some Arab audiences had begun to be exposed to television from foreign sources. In the North African countries of Morocco, Tunisia, and Algeria, where knowledge of the French language was widespread, some of the population was able to watch television broadcast across the Mediterranean from France. In Libya, Arabs living near the U.S. military base at Wheelus were able to watch U.S. television transmitted by the U.S. armed forces, until the base was shut down after the revolution of 1969. In eastern Saudi Arabia some Arabs were able to watch U.S. TV programs broadcast by the U.S.-run Arabian American Oil Company (ARAMCO) located there.

Audiences

Audiences for Arab radio and television have expanded considerably over the years. All Arab countries have passed the United Nations Educational, Scientific, and Cultural Organization (UNESCO) minimum standard of fifty radio receivers per thousand population, and nearly all of them have passed the UNESCO minimum standard for television receivers of 100 per thousand population, as shown in the table below (worldbank.org and unesco.org, March 2003; data is for 2000, except 1997 for Oman, UAE, Bahrain, and Qatar).

When compared with other less developed areas of the world, these audience rates are roughly equivalent for radio, and they are substantially higher for television. Because multiple listeners and viewers use each radio and television receiver, it is assumed that radio listening is nearly universal among the almost three hundred million Arabs, and that television reaches more than one hundred million of them.

Ownership and Control

When Arab television developed, it was a government monopoly almost everywhere except in Lebanon. During the 1950s, the Lebanese government gave television licenses to two groups of private businesspeople. During the civil war in the 1970s, several private groups and parties started their own unauthorized television stations, but by the 1990s the government had limited the television companies to four, each more or less representing one of the major Lebanese political-religious groups.

During the 1990s, Arab satellite television broadcasting emerged, and it has become the most powerful of all media instruments in the Arab world. In 1990 and 1991, during the Gulf crisis and Gulf War that resulted from Iraq's occupation of Kuwait, the U.S. satellite broadcaster CNN was very widely watched in the Arab world because it provided news and images of developments in the crisis quickly when everyone was eager to know what was happening. Yet CNN's broadcast was in English, and its

Electronic media density			
	Population in millions	Radios per 1000	TVs per 1000
Algeria	30	244	110
Bahrain	0.7	580	472
Egypt	64	399	189
Iraq	23	222	83
Jordan	4.9	372	84
Kuwait	2.0	624	486
Lebanon	4.3	687	335
Libya	5.0	273	137
Morocco	29	243	166
Oman	2.4	621	563
Qatar	0.6	450	404
Saudi Arabia	20	319	260
Sudan	31	464	273
Syria	16	276	67
Tunisia	10	158	198
U.A.E.	2.9	318	292
Yemen	18	65	283

TABLE BY GGS INFORMATION SERVICES, THE GALE GROUP.

reporting and editorial judgments presented from a U.S. point of view, and many Arabs wished they had such a service that presented news and events from an Arab point of view and in Arabic. Also, the cost of satellite dishes was becoming lower and therefore within reach of more people. A few wealthy Arabs therefore decided to invest in the creation of Arab satellite television systems; they were willing to invest large sums and to lose money for the prestige and political influence of the new media.

In 1991 Saudi Arabian investors established Middle East Broadcasting (MBC). It was the first private Arab satellite TV station that aimed primarily at a pan-Arab audience. It offered news and entertainment, and soon other investors started to imitate its success. In 1994 two other groups of Saudi investors established two other Arab satellite companies, the Arab Radio and Television Network (ART) and Orbit. MBC, like most of the others, was a free-to-air broadcaster that carried advertising to cover at least part of its costs, but ART and Orbit are fee-based broadcasters that used a coded system accessible only to subscribers. During the next three years, two groups of Lebanese private investors started the satellite stations named Future and Lebanese Broadcasting Company, respectively, and Syrian private investors started Arab News Network. During the same period, the Government of Qatar subsidized the start of a satellite station in

An Iranian reporter broadcasts live during the February 2000 elections. State-run Iranian television was broadcast from twenty-eight stations as of the late 1990s, reaching 4.61 million television sets across the country. In 1997 Iran also launched a satellite channel that covered Europe, parts of Asia, and other regions in the Middle East. © TOUHIG SION/CORBIS SYGMA. REPRODUCED BY PERMISSION.

that country that was nominally private, called al-Jazeera, which became controversial and popular because its programming broke many Arab taboos. Al-Jazeera's discussions and call-in programs frequently include, for example, direct criticism of the policies and specific personalities of several Arab governments, to an extent not heard before in Arab media. In addition, the programs discuss religion and gender in ways rarely dealt with in public.

In the twenty-first century, eight more private satellite television stations have been created, including two owned by Lebanese, three by Egyptians, and one each by Tunisians, Algerians, and Saudis. Meanwhile, most Arab governments got into the act, creating their own satellite television systems alongside their existing terrestrial ones. Even the new satellite companies, although nominally private, tended to operate under some government influence because of legal reasons, financial necessity, and personal connections between owners and government officials.

Palestinian-controlled broadcasting is a special case. For years, Palestinian broadcasters only had access to transmitters outside Palestine and located in other Arab countries, using the government-owned and -controlled transmitters of those countries. During the 1990s, after the Palestinian-Israeli Oslo Accords, radio and television began under the auspices of the Palestinian Authority (PA) and by private individuals. Nevertheless, the PA often restricted the latter, and Israel restricted both.

See also COMMUNICATION.

Bibliography

Alterman, Jon. *New Media, New Politics?: From Satellite Television to the Internet in the Arab World.* Washington, DC: Washington Institute for Near East Policy, 1998.

Boyd, Douglas A. *Broadcasting in the Arab World: A Survey of the Electronic Media in the Middle East,* 3d edition. Ames: Iowa State University Press, 1999.

El-Nawawy, Mohammed, and Iskander, Adel. *Al Jazeera: How the Free Arab News Network Scooped the World and Changed the Middle East.* Cambridge, MA: Westview Press, 2002.

Ghareeb, Edmund. "New Media and the Information Revolution in the Arab World." *Middle East Journal* 54, no. 3 (summer 2000): 402–409.

Rugh, William A. *The Arab Press: News Media and Political Process in the Arab World,* 2d edition. Syracuse, NY: Syracuse University Press, 1987.

Sakr, Naomi. *Satellite Realms: Transnational Television, Globalization and the Middle East.* New York and London: I. B. Taurus, 2001.

WILLIAM A. RUGH

ISRAEL

History of radio and television in Israel.

Broadcasting in Israel has accompanied the gradual weakening of state hegemony, the transition from a "melting pot" philosophy to a multicultural orientation, and the growth of privatization and market control. After its introduction by the British, broadcasting was a full government monopoly for some thirty years. The first radio station, the *Voice of Jerusalem,* went on the air in 1936 under the Palestine Broadcasting Service. Following a traditional British colonial policy of curbing nationalist content while allowing for some carefully monitored cultural expression, the government controlled the news tightly. Other programming was produced by the Jewish and Arab communities.

Renamed *Kol Yisrael* (the voice of Israel) when Israel was established in 1948, radio came under the direct control of the Ministry of the Interior, and later of the Prime Minister's office. Most programming was in Hebrew, some in Arabic and in the languages spoken by new immigrants. For many years, Israel's broadcasting system was monolithic and government-controlled, including *Kol Yisrael* and *Galei Tzahal,* the army station opened in 1950. Direct official control was justified by security challenges and by the need to stabilize the nation and to achieve immigrant acculturation. The government monopoly was abolished in 1965 in response to popular and political criticism and in an effort at satisfying increasing media needs. The Israel Broadcasting Authority (IBA) Law was enacted in the same year, introducing the IBA as a public, nongovernmental body broadcasting in Hebrew and Arabic.

Israel Television became part of the IBA shortly after its establishment in 1968. An educational television service set up in 1966 by the Rothschild Foundation was transferred to the Ministry of Education. Although formally modeled on the BBC, the IBA has never been entirely free from governmental influence. In the 1980s an "open skies" philosophy emerged, producing demands to increase the number of news channels and to upgrade cultural creativity. The broadcasting system underwent remarkable growth: Private cable TV appeared in 1989 and satellite services in 2002, two commercial television channels went on the air in 1992 and 2002, and regional private commercial radio stations started transmissions in 1996.

Media concentration, privatization, and incorporation reduced competition for entrance into and access to the market. Economic interests and government pressures have enhanced media conformism that favors government policies and powerful economic groups. Nevertheless, technological progress helped to empower some "voiceless" groups through a large number of pirate radio stations, such as the now defunct left-wing *Voice of Peace* and right-wing *Channel Seven*; low-powered ultraorthodox religious stations called "holy channels"; pirate radio and cable TV in Russian and Arabic; and an illegal industry of homemade audio- and videocassettes operated by Israeli-Palestinian partnerships. Also activist groups of the elderly, feminists, gays, greens, and others have gained access to community radio and television outlets, and to radio stations in schools and colleges.

Radio and television have always been important components of the political scene. In addition to their use for electoral purposes, they have served both to support the government and to criticize its policies and actions on issues such as war, occupation, peacemaking efforts, economic crises, and social integration.

The procedures that govern press censorship also apply to broadcasting. According to Israeli law, all broadcast materials must be submitted to the military censor, in a fashion similar to press censorship. Adopted from British Mandatory emergency measures, these laws have been adapted to the changing circumstances. Thus, an agreement between the government, the army, and the media provides a list of security-related topics that must be cleared, allowing for only a fraction to be submitted. Foreign correspondents work under strict control, particularly in the occupied territories.

See also NEWSPAPERS AND PRINT MEDIA: ISRAEL.

Bibliography

Caspi, Dan, and Limor, Yehiel. *The In/Outsiders: The Mass Media in Israel.* Cresskill, NJ: Hampton Press, 1999.

DOV SHINAR

TURKEY

Outline of Turkish state- and independent-media broadcasting developments.

Radio broadcasting in Turkey began in Istanbul in 1927, when there were roughly 5,000 radios in the country, and a few months later in the same year Ankara Radio began broadcasting. The value of radio as a vehicle for mass mobilization and education was immediately realized by the new Republican authorities, and programming consisted mainly of news bulletins, concerts, weather, and programs such as *Radio Gazete* (Radio Journal), presenting news summaries; *Evin Saati* (Home Hour), a homemaking show; and *Ziraat Takvimi Saati* (Calendar Hour on Agriculture), appreciated in rural areas. In 1942 around 60 percent of programming was musical, another 35 percent consisted of speeches and discussions, and the number of radios in the country had risen to more than 100,000, or around 4.1 per thousand people, with half concentrated in Ankara and Istanbul.

With multiparty politics in 1946 the Democrat Party came to power in 1950. Frustrated by newspapers' general support for the opposition, it began to pressure the radio to reflect its party views. In the wake of the coup of 1960 regional stations were established in İzmir, Adana, Antalya, Erzurum, Gaziantep, and Kars. With the expansion of radio and demand for television, the state Turkish Radio and Television (TRT) Corporation was established in 1964. In 1969 a radio station was established in Diyarbakir.

Television broadcasting began in 1968, transmitting from Ankara, then from İzmir in 1970 and Istanbul in 1971. Following the coup of 1971 the autonomy of the TRT was curbed, neutralizing its treatment of social and political issues; the 1980 coup temporarily narrowed again the range of discussion on TRT. By 1977 television transmissions reached about 60 percent of the population, and in 1981 selected programs began to be broadcast in color. TRT 2 (culture and art) was established in 1986, and 1989 saw the creation of GAP-TV, directed toward the southeast, and TRT 3. In 1990 the stations began broadcasting via satellite, greatly extending coverage, including TRT-INT for the Turkish population in Europe.

Satellite dishes became popular in the late 1980s for watching "pirate" channels broadcasting from Europe, including Turkish-language ones, and in the early 1990s for watching private stations in Turkey. The wider range and frankness of discussion, as well as the perceived drabness of TRT, combined with agreements to carry soccer matches on the new channels, led to their instant success. In 1993 the government closed all pirate radio and TV stations, to the public's strong objection, and then officially ended its monopoly of TV and radio broadcasting in 1994 and set up a High Council for Radio and Television (RTÜK) to handle licensing and infrastructure, but also to monitor broadcasts and mete out fines and suspensions.

In the late 1990s Turkey launched its own satellites, greatly expanding broadcast areas in Europe, the Middle East, and Central Asia. According to a 1996 survey, more Turkish households had television sets than had telephones, an indication of how profoundly TV has become a part of social life in the country. TV, and to a lesser extent radio, are now major economic sectors subject to market pressures, and play major roles in the formation of public opinion and popular culture.

See also NEWSPAPERS AND PRINT MEDIA: TURKEY.

Bibliography

Aksoy, Asu, and Robins, Kevin. "Peripheral Vision: Cultural Industries and Cultural Identities in Turkey." *Environment and Planning A* 29 (1997): 1937–1952.

Creatonic Media Research. "A Brief History of Television in Turkey." Available from <http://www.creatonic.com/tv/>.

Idil, Esra. "Political Changes Reflected in Turkey's Radio System." *Turkish Daily News Electronic Edition.* Available from <http://www.turkishdailynews.com/old_editions/05_07_98/feature.htm>.

Sahin, Haluk, and Aksoy, Asu. "Global Media and Cultural Identity in Turkey." *Journal of Communication* 43, no. 2 (1993): 31–41.

BRIAN SILVERSTEIN

RAFI PARTY

See ISRAEL: POLITICAL PARTIES IN

RAFSANJANI, ALI AKBAR HASHEMI
[1935–]

President of Iran, 1989–1997.

Born in the southeast Iranian city of Rafsanjan, Ali Akbar Hashemi Rafsanjani began his religious education at the early age of fourteen in Qom (Qum), where from 1958 onward he was a leading figure among the younger disciples of Ayatollah Ruhollah Khomeini. His first arrest for political activities against the regime of Mohammad Reza Shah Pahlavi came in 1964; he succeeded in escaping after undergoing two months of torture. He thereupon joined the ranks of the Allied Islamic Associations, and in January 1965, after the assassination of Prime Minister Hasan Ali Mansur by four members of this organization, he was jailed for four and a half months.

Resuming his clandestine organizational work in Qom, Rafsanjani next was jailed in 1967 for publicly opposing the shah's extravagant coronation ceremonies. In 1973 he was sentenced to eight years in prison on charges of collaboration with the Mojahedin-e Khalq guerrilla organization; he served four years of this sentence.

After the triumph of the Iranian Revolution in February 1979, Rafsanjani was appointed to the Council of Islamic Revolution, and when the government of Mehdi Bazargan resigned in November of that year, he was also appointed acting minister of the interior. A founding member of the Islamic Republican Party (IRP), he was elected chairman of Iran's legislature, the Majles al-Shura—which was dominated by that party and its allies—on 20 July 1980. Through the skillful use of this office, he swiftly became one of the most visible and influential politicians in the country, a process that was accelerated when his senior colleagues in the IRP became victims of assassination. Also important in the growth of his popular appeal were the nationally televised sermons he frequently delivered for the Friday prayers at Tehran University. After the death of Ayatollah Khomeini on 3 June 1989, President Ali Khamenehi was elevated to the position of leader (*rahbar*) of the Islamic Republic, and Rafsanjani was elected the next president in August 1989. On 11 June 1993 he was elected to a second term with 63.2 percent of a turnout that represented 57.6 percent of the electorate. Once reputed to favor radical socioeconomic reform, Rafsanjani as president enjoyed the reputation of a pragmatist concerned above all with the reconstruction of the Iranian economy. After the end of his second term as president in 1997, Rafsanjani was appointed as chair of the influential Expediency Council, which has authority to revoke vetoes by the Council of Guardians.

See also BAZARGAN, MEHDI; IRANIAN REVOLUTION (1979); KHOMEINI, RUHOLLAH; MAJLES AL-SHURA; MOJAHEDIN-E KHALQ; PAHLAVI, MOHAMMAD REZA.

Bibliography

Moslem, Mehdi. *Factional Politics in Post-Khomeini Iran.* Syracuse, NY: Syracuse University Press, 2002.

HAMID ALGAR
UPDATED BY ERIC HOOGLUND

RAHNAVARD, ZAHRA

[c. 1947–]

Iranian artist and writer.

Zahra Rahnavard was born into a religious family in Tehran. After graduating from high school, she attended the Tehran Teachers' College, where she obtained a teaching certificate. In the late 1960s, she met Mir-Hosain Musavi, who opposed the regime of Mohammad Reza Shah Pahlavi, as she did, and who shared her Islamic values; they married in 1969. Subsequently, she studied at and obtained a master's degree from Tehran University's department of arts. In the early 1970s, she joined the study circle around the Islamist philosopher Ali Shariʿati. In 1976, After Shariʿati was arrested, Rahnavard fled with her two children to the United States, where she became affiliated with the Confederation of Iranian Students, especially with its Islamist faction. She returned to Iran just before the success of the Iranian Revolution and became one of the influential women promoting the cultural, economic, and political programs of the new Islamic Republic, especially during her husband's tenure as prime minister, from 1981 to 1988.

Rahnavard is the author of a number of publications on art, literature, poetry, religion, and politics. Her writings have been translated into Turkish, Arabic, Urdu, and English. Her essays include "The Uprising of Moses," "The Colonial Motives for the Unveiling of Women," "The Beauty of the Veil, and the Veil of Beauty," and "Women, Islam, and Feminism in Imam Khomeini's Thought." Rahnavard has also held several exhibits of her art. Her large sculpture "Mother" is situated prominently in the middle of a busy Tehran square. In the first decade of the revolution, she used her considerable oratorical skills and her talent as a writer to propagate Islamist values in Iran and abroad. She was a founder of the Women's Society of the Islamic Republic and the Islamist Women's Society and editor of *Rah-i Zaynab,* a popular women's journal. In 1997, Rahnavard joined the reformist camp of President Mohammad Khatami and in 1999 she became president of the influential al-Zahra Women's College in Tehran.

See also CONFEDERATION OF IRANIAN STUDENTS; IRANIAN REVOLUTION (1979); KHATAMI, MOHAMMAD; MUSAVI, MIR-

HOSAIN; PAHLAVI, MOHAMMAD REZA; SHARIʿATI, ALI.

Bibliography

Afary, Janet. "Portraits of two Islamist Women: Escape from Freedom or from Tradition?" *Critique* 19 (fall 2001): 47–77.

JANET AFARY

RAJAVI, MASUD
[1947–]

Leader of the Iranian Mojahedin-e Khalq since 1979.

Masud Rajavi was born in Tabas, in central Khorasan. He completed secondary school in Mashhad and studied political science at Tehran University. Because of his activities with the Mojahedin-e Khalq, he was arrested in 1971 and condemned to death, but the sentence was commuted to life imprisonment. He remained in jail until the Iranian Revolution of 1979. Following the revolution, Rajavi rebuilt the Mojahedin, attracting hundreds of thousands of supporters. Since a 1981 government crackdown, Rajavi has led the Mojahedin from exile. In 1985 he married Maryam Azodanlou, who took on Rajavi's family name. Maryam Rajavi was declared not only the co-leader of the Mojahedin but also the future president of Iran.

See also IRANIAN REVOLUTION (1979); MOJAHEDIN-E KHALQ.

Bibliography

Abrahamian, Ervand. *The Iranian Mojahedin.* New Haven, CT: Yale University Press, 1989.

ERVAND ABRAHAMIAN

RAJUB, JIBRIL
[1953–]

Palestinian activist and senior security official in the Palestinian Authority.

Born in the West Bank village of Dura, Jibril Rajub joined al-Fatah as a youth. Imprisoned by Israel soon thereafter in 1968, he was released in a 1985 Israeli-Palestinian prisoner exchange. He had become one of al-Fatah's most senior figures in the West Bank when Israel deported him during the first intifada. In Tunis he served as an advisor to Palestine Liberation Organization chair Yasir Arafat, and helped to coordinate the first intifada as deputy to al-Fatah security chief Khalil al-Wazir (Abu Jihad).

With the establishment of the Palestinian Authority (PA) in 1994, Rajub returned from exile to head the Preventative Security Forces (PSF) in the West Bank. Along with Gaza PSF chief Muhammad Dahlan, Rajub was one of the two most important security officials in the PA. He eventually ran afoul of Arafat, who dismissed him in April 2002. As part of the feud between Arafat and PA prime minister Mahmud Abbas in the summer of 2003, Arafat mended fences with Rajub and appointed him as his national security adviser, pitting him against his rival Dahlan, Abbas's minister of state for security affairs.

See also ABBAS, MAHMUD; ARAFAT, YASIR; DAHLAN, MUHAMMAD; FATAH, AL-; INTIFADA (1987–1991); PALESTINIAN AUTHORITY; WAZIR, KHALIL AL-; WEST BANK.

MICHAEL R. FISCHBACH

RAMADAN, TAHA YASIN
[1938–]

Iraqi politician.

Taha Yasin Ramadan, also known as Taha al-Jazrawi, was born in Mosul to a working-class Arabized Kurdish family. In 1959 he was dismissed from the army by the regime of Abd al-Karim Qasim, because of his leanings toward the Baʿth party. In 1966, he became a member of the Baʿth party's regional (Iraqi) leadership, and after the Baʿthist takeover in 1968, he supervised the purging of the army. Starting in 1969, Ramadan became a member of the Revolutionary Command Council and, starting in 1972, he commanded the Baʿthist militia. He was one of the ideological hard-liners among Saddam Hussein's entourage, always toeing Hussein's line. Between 1979 and 1991 he was first deputy prime minister, following which he was appointed vice president. Ramadan emerged from the Gulf Crisis of 1990 and 1991 as one of the most powerful individuals in Iraq outside of Hussein's own family, with his power base resting in the city of Mosul and in the party apparatus.

Following the U.S. occupation of Iraq starting in March 2003, Ramadan became a wanted figure. He was eventually captured in Mosul by Kurdish forces in August 2003, whereupon he was handed over to the U.S. forces.

See also Baʿth, al-; Gulf Crisis (1990–1991); Hussein, Saddam.

Bibliography

Baram, Amatzia. "The Ruling Political Elite in Baʿthi Iraq, 1968–1986." *International Journal of Middle East Studies* 21 (1989): 447–493.

Batatu, Hanna. *The Old Social Classes and the Revolutionary Movements of Iraq: A Study of Iraq's Old Landed and Commercial Classes and of its Communists, Baʿthists, and Free Officers.* Princeton, NJ: Princeton University Press, 1978.

AMATZIA BARAM
UPDATED BY MICHAEL R. FISCHBACH

RAMALLAH

Palestinian city in the West Bank.

Located about 6.5 miles north of Jerusalem on the western side of the Nablus–Jerusalem road, Ramallah was an important urban center under the British Mandate. After Jordan annexed the West Bank in 1950, Ramallah became part of the Jerusalem governorate. In the Arab-Israeli War of 1967, Ramallah was occupied by Israel. It was the site of many clashes between Israel's military authorities and Palestinians between June 1967 and December 1995, when Israel withdrew and the Palestinian Authority (PA) assumed control. The city underwent an economic boom during the mid-1990s when the PA established the town, unofficially, as its main West Bank administrative center. Many PA offices were built, as well as villas for returning emigres.

Ramallah was occupied by the Israelis several times after the start of the al-Aqsa Intifada in late 2000. It is noteworthy among Palestinian towns for its strong educational and professional heritage. U.S. Quakers established a girls' school in Ramallah in 1889, and nearby Bir Zeit University is one of the best Palestinian universities in the West Bank. In the last official census of 1997, the city's population stood at 17,851.

See also Arab–Israel War (1967); Bir Zeit University; Palestinian Authority; West Bank.

Bibliography

Fischbach, Michael R. "Ramallah." In *Encyclopedia of the Palestinians,* edited by Philip Mattar. New York: Facts On File, 2000.

LAWRENCE TAL
UPDATED BY MICHAEL R. FISCHBACH

RAMGAVAR AZADAGAN PARTY

Armenian political party of Lebanon.

The ultimate goal of the Ramgavar Azadagan party, founded in 1921, was the liberation of Armenia. It has oriented its activities toward preserving Armenian culture among Armenian communities throughout the world. After a period of dormancy, the party was revived in the 1950s, in the wake of the increasing conflicts between the Dashnak party and the Hunchak Party. The Ramgavar party presented itself as an alternative that avoided issues divisive to the Armenian community. During the Lebanese civil war of 1975, the Ramgavar party opposed what it considered to be the right-wing policies of the Dashnak party.

See also Dashnak Party; Hunchak Party.

AS'AD ABUKHALIL

RAMLA

Also called Er Ramleh; a town in Israel 12 miles southeast of Tel Aviv.

Ramla was founded in 717 C.E. to replace nearby Lydda as the region's capital under the Arab caliphate. It soon outstripped its neighbor in size and prosperity, thriving on trade and industry, particularly soap and olive oil. More than three-quarters of Ramla's 1946 population of 16,380 were Palestinian. In the 1948 Arab–Israel War, Israeli troops occupied the area and forced the evacuation of thousands of the town's Palestinian residents. The town grew again after the war with the arrival of Jewish immigrants. As of 1994, its population of 62,000 included fewer than 12,000 Arabs (similar to the nationwide balance between the two populations), half of whom lived in mixed neighborhoods and the other half in two rundown all-Arab sections. In 1993 Yoel Lavi, the newly elected mayor from the right-wing Likud Party and a son of Holocaust survivors, undertook a program to improve the educational opportunities available to the town's Arab children, in cooperation with several Israeli-Arab town councilors.

See also ARAB–ISRAEL WAR (1948); LIKUD.

ELIZABETH THOMPSON
UPDATED BY YEHUDA GRADUS

RAMSES COLLEGE FOR GIRLS

An Egyptian school for girls from kindergarten through twelfth grade.

Ramses College for Girls (founded as the American College for Girls), located at Ramses Square in Cairo, Egypt, originated as a trilingual (English, Arabic, and French) missionary school of the United Presbyterian Church of North America. Founded by Ella Kyle, its first building was inaugurated in 1910 by former U.S. president Theodore Roosevelt. The student body included girls of various ethnicities—Armenian, Greek, Jewish, Abyssinian (Ethiopian), Egyptian, Syrian, and Lebanese, as well as girls from the Gulf states—many of whom attended as boarders. Dr. Helen T. Martin served as principal from 1923 to 1956. In 1960, with the nationalization of private schooling, its ownership was transferred to the Evangelical Synod of the Nile, an Egyptian Protestant organization. The school's cosmopolitan community gradually dwindled until it became entirely Egyptian. In 1967, following the Arab–Israel War and subsequent strained relations with the United States, the school's name was changed to Ramses College for Girls. From 1967 to 1992 the school's principal was Reda Salama of the legendary Salama sisters (her sister Mary was principal of Port Said School), who established an Institute of Secretarial Studies and a Department for Girls with Special Needs. The school's graduates include leading figures in social development, aviation, diplomacy, government, and education, such as Aziza Hussein, Lutfia Nady, Aida Guindi, and Nawal al-Tatawi. By 2003, more than two thousand girls were enrolled in the school.

LINDA HERRERA

RANIA AL-ABDULLAH (QUEEN RANIA)

[1970–]

Queen of Jordan and wife of King Abdullah II ibn Hussein.

Rania al-Abdullah became queen of Jordan in 1999, following the succession in the Jordanian Hashimite monarchy from her father-in-law, King Hussein ibn Talal, to her husband, Abdullah II ibn Hussein. Abdullah was the eldest son of Hussein, who had served as Jordan's monarch since 1953.

Born Rania al-Yasin, Queen Rania grew up in Kuwait in a well-known and well-to-do Palestinian family. She was educated in Kuwait and then went to Egypt to attend university, graduating in 1991 with a bachelor's degree in business administration from the American University in Cairo. She married then-Prince Abdullah in 1993. For some Jordanians, their Jordanian-Palestinian marriage symbolized hope for greater unity and opportunity for both groups within Jordanian society.

Since joining the Hashimite royal family, Rania has used her position to patronize causes of particular interest to her, including support for emerging small businesses. She shares with her husband an interest in economic development, in particular with developing information technology in the kingdom. She has also patronized programs supporting tourism and historic preservation. Her greatest interest, however, is supporting programs protecting women and children from domestic violence. She joined the campaign to prevent "honor crimes," or killings of women by male family members who suspect them of committing adultery or otherwise compromising "family honor." Queen Rania has called for the repeal of laws allowing leniency in sentencing the offenders. Her public role in Jordanian domestic politics and foreign relations steadily increased after she became queen in 1999. She serves on numerous boards and committees dedicated to supporting women, children, and family life, and her role in public life extends beyond Jordan. In 2002 she became a member of the board of the powerful World Economic Forum, the only board member from an Arab country. In 2003 and 2004, she served as president of the Arab Women's Summit, a forum of Arab first ladies, activists, and other professionals.

See also ABDULLAH II IBN HUSSEIN; JORDAN.

Bibliography

Ryan, Curtis R. *Jordan in Transition: From Hussein to Abdullah.* Boulder, CO: Lynne Rienner, 2002.

CURTIS R. RYAN

RASAFI, MA'RUF AL-

[1875–1945]

Most prominent poet in Iraq between the world wars.

Ma'ruf al-Rasafi was born in Baghdad into a family of Kurdish origin, and studied at the Rashidiyya school there. His knowledge of classical Arabic sources enabled him to teach Arabic language and literature in higher institutes of learning in Baghdad, Jerusalem, and Constantinople (now Istanbul). He represented Baghdad in the Chamber of Deputies in Constantinople, and after the establishment of the kingdom of Iraq, he was elected to parliament.

Although his poetry was composed in a classical language, Rasafi was regarded as a voice of the people who fearlessly attacked Iraq's social and political maladies.

A first edition of Rasafi's *Diwan* was published in Beirut in 1910. Subsequent editions in his lifetime appeared in 1925 in Cairo and in 1931 in Beirut. A five-volume annotated edition was published in Baghdad in 1986.

Rasafi published works on Arabic language and literature, including an important study on the modern dialect of Baghdad (serialized in al-Karmali's *Lughat al-Arab* in 1926–1928).

See also LITERATURE: ARABIC.

Bibliography

Badawi, M. M. *A Critical Introduction to Modern Arabic Poetry.* Cambridge, U.K., and New York: Cambridge University Press, 1975.

Badawi, M. M., ed. *Modern Arabic Literature.* Cambridge, U.K., and New York: Cambridge University Press, 1992.

Jayyusi, Salma Khadra. *Trends and Movements in Modern Arabic Poetry.* Leiden: Brill, 1977.

SASSON SOMEKH

RA'S AL-KHAYMA

Northernmost of the United Arab Emirates.

Ra's al-Khayma's two separate territories cover some 650 square miles and have coastlines on both the Persian (Arabian) Gulf and the Gulf of Oman. The emirate has greater topographical diversity than the other emirates, and its slightly greater rainfall makes significant agriculture possible. Ra's al-Khayma has the largest oil and natural gas reserves of the small emirates north of Sharjah (the Northern Emirates). In addition, it utilizes the mineral resources of the Hajjar Mountains, exporting aggregate stones and producing cement, asphalt, and lime. Fishing is also important for the emirate's economy.

According to a 1997 estimate the emirate had 153,000 inhabitants, most of whom lived in the capital city of the same name. Nearly 90 percent of the population is indigenous.

In the eighteenth and early nineteenth centuries Ra's al-Khayma's Qasimi rulers held sway along the shores of the lower Persian (Arabian) Gulf and the northern Indian Ocean until attacks on British shipping to India elicited a massive British campaign that resulted in the almost total destruction of the tribe's capital and fleet. The Qasimi rulers never regained formal power; this has given rise to resentment in modern times over the preeminence of the ruler of Abu Dhabi.

Upon its independence in 1971, Ra's al Khayma's ruler, Shaykh Saqr ibn Muhammad, angered by his state's limited political role in the new federation and expecting imminent discovery of oil in his territory, remained outside the U.A.E. federation for six weeks after its formation on 2 December 1971. (Modest oil deposits were not discovered until 1983.) At the same time, Iran seized the Tunb Islands from Ra's al-Khayma, and it continues to occupy them, a circumstance that contributes to current strains between Iran and Persian (Arabian) Gulf Arab states.

See also QASIMI FAMILY OF RAS AL-KHAYMA, AL-; TUNB ISLANDS; UNITED ARAB EMIRATES.

Bibliography

Anthony, John Duke. *Arab States of the Lower Gulf: People, Politics, Petroleum.* Washington, DC: Middle East Institute, 1975.

Heard-Bey, Frauke. *From Trucial States to United Arab Emirates: A Society in Transition.* New York; London: Longman, 1982.

Metz, Helen Chapin, ed. *Persian Gulf States: Country Studies,* 3d edition. Washington, DC: Library of Congress, 1994.

Peck, Malcolm C. *The United Arab Emirates: A Venture in Unity.* Boulder, CO: Westview Press; London: Croon Helm, 1986.

MALCOLM C. PECK
UPDATED BY ANTHONY B. TOTH

RASSEMBLEMENT NATIONAL DÉMOCRATIQUE (RND)

Political party of Algerian president Liamine Zeroual.

The Rassemblement National Démocratique (RND) was created on February 1997, a few months before the June legislative elections. It received its official approval on April 1997. Called the "political party of President Zeroual," it is also the party of the Algerian administration. Since its creation, it has been directed by three men: Abdelkader Bensalah, former member of the National Council of Transition; Tahar Benbaibèche, former leader of the Organization of Martyrs' children; and Ahmed Ouyahia, the current prime minister and former minister of justice. According to analysts and diplomats in Algeria, the RND was founded by some defectors from the FLN (the National Liberation Front, once Algeria's sole party) who were opposed to its willingness to enter into a dialogue with Islamists. It was created as a vehicle to support President Zeroual's policies, to win the 1997 elections, and to punish the FLN for its involvement, two years before, in the Sant Egidio agreement.

In the legislative elections of June 1997, which were tarnished by massive irregularities, the RND arrived at the head of the list with 155 elected deputies (46.5% of the vote), gaining 80 seats of the 96 in the upper house. During the provincial and municipal elections of October 1997, it won 896 seats (of 1,779 seats) in the Provincial Popular Assembly (APW) and more than the half of 13,126 seats in the communal assemblies.

In the 2002 legislative elections the FLN won 199 seats at the National Popular Assembly (APN) and the RND lost its majority at all levels.

See also SANT EGIDIO PLATFORM.

Bibliography

Arsala, Deane. *Algeria's June 5, 1997, Parliamentary Election.* Washington, DC: National Democratic Institute for International Affairs, 1997.

Salah Tahi, M. "Algeria's Legislative and Local Elections: Democracy Denied" In *Mediterranean Politics,* Vol. 2, no. 3, 1997, pp. 123–133.

Sammakia, Nejla. *Algeria: Elections in the Shadow of Violence and Repression.* New York: Human Rights Watch/Middle East, 1999.

AZZEDINE G. MANSOUR

RASSEMBLEMENT NATIONAL DES INDÉPENDANTS (RNI)

Parliamentary grouping of independent supporters of Morocco's monarchy.

The Rassemblement National des Indépendants (RNI), founded in October 1978, projected a centrist liberal image representing landowners, senior civil servants, technocrats, industrialists, and businessmen, many from old established families. Initially, it held 141 seats in parliament, making it the largest single group there. It was led by King Hassan II's brother-in-law, Ahmed Osman (prime minister 1972–1979), and the king's cousin, Ahmed Alawi. In 1981 a breakaway group led by former trade union leader and labor minister Muhammad Arslane Jadidi and Abdel Hamid Kacemi, representing a group of rural landholding notables, formed the Parti des Indépendants Démocrates, later renamed the Parti National Démocratique (PND). Following the 1981 government reshuffle, the RNI was left out of the government in order to create a "loyal opposition." In the 1984 parliamentary elections the RNI lost 80 seats and was replaced by the newly formed Union Constitutionelle (UC) as the single largest party in parliament, although it subsequently was part of the governing coalition, and Osman was named speaker of parliament. In 1993 the party refrained from affiliating with the pro-palace Entente bloc, preferring to run alone in parliamentary elections. It suffered a further loss of 20 seats in the 1993 parliamentary elections and was left out of the newly formed government of technocrats. In 1997 it won 46 seats and joined the government led by the Union Socialiste des Forces Populaires (USFP) as a junior partner with six cabinet posts. In the 2002 elections it won 41 seats and again received six cabinet posts in the new government headed by the nonparty king's loyalist Driss Jettou.

See also MOROCCO: POLITICAL PARTIES IN; PARTI NATIONAL DÉMOCRATIQUE (PND);

Union Socialiste des Forces Populaires (USFP).

Bibliography

Pennell, C. R. *Morocco Since 1830.* New York: New York University Press, 2000.

Waterbury, John. *The Commander of the Faithful.* London: Weidenfeld and Nicolson, 1970.

BRUCE MADDY-WEITZMAN

RASSEMBLEMENT POUR LA CULTURE ET LA DÉMOCRATIE (RCD)

The unique secular party in Algeria.

The Rassemblement pour la Culture et la Démocratie (RCD) was born from a split within the FFS (Socialist Forces Front), the traditional Kabyle political party headed by Hocine Aït Ahmed. This secular party was created in February 1989 during a meeting of the Amazigh Cultural Movement. Its aims include political pluralism, the abolition of the Family Code of 1984 that limits women's freedom, an official redefinition of the Algerian identity in its triple dimension (Amazigh, Arabic, and Muslim), social justice, modernization of the Algerian economy to include free enterprise, and the separation of politics from religion. Opposed to the country's forced Arabization, it also considers the use of the French language in Algeria a matter of cultural enrichment.

During the municipal elections of June 1990, the RCD won only 87 communes, mainly in Kabylia (as compared to the 900 won by the FIS). During the first round of legislative elections held in December 1991, it did not win a single Islamist seat in the Popular National Assembly (APN, the Algerian parliament). With the overwhelming FIS victory, Saïd Sadi, head of the RCD, supported the interruption of the electoral process that drove the country into civil war. A strong supporter of "eradication" policy, the RCD preferred to see the Algerian army rule Algeria rather than the Islamists. It organized resistance to Islamists in Kabylia and called for the formation of defensive groups against terrorism.

The RCD participated in the 1995 and subsequent elections and took part in different coalition governments. In the summer of 2000, however, it pulled out of the government in protest against the regime's policies toward the Kabyles. It boycotted the 2002 legislative elections.

Bibliography

Malley, Robert. *The Call from Algeria: Third Worldism, Revolution, and the Turn to Islam.* Los Angeles: University of California Press, 1996.

Willis, Michael. *The Islamist Challenge in Algeri: A Political History.* New York: New York University Press, 1996.

AZZEDINE G. MANSOUR

RATEB, AISHA
[1928–]

Egyptian diplomat, lawyer, and law professor.

Aisha Rateb (also A'isha Ratib) was educated in Cairo and Paris. At twenty-one, she applied for a position as judge on Egypt's highest administrative court, the State Council. After being rejected, she sued the government. One of its members later filed an opinion confirming that Egyptian law—and Islamic jurisprudence—did not prevent women from serving in the judiciary. The judge concluded the problem was societal. Rateb's struggle was supported by the media, the people, and by feminist leader Huda al-Sha'rawi.

Rateb was the first professor of international law at Cairo University, and in 1971 she was the second woman to hold the post of minister of social affairs, where she remained until 1977. She was the first person responsible for two ministries—in her case, social insurance and social affairs. In 1978 she became the Egyptian minister of foreign affairs. She was the first Egyptian woman to be appointed ambassador for Egypt, serving in Denmark from 1979 to 1981 and in Germany from 1981 to 1984. Despite Egypt's history of women's participation in civil society since the turn of the twentieth century, it has been slow to open the doors of its judiciary to women. Rateb's efforts have helped to open this door to other women. Egypt appointed its first female judge to the Supreme Constitutional Court, Tahani al-Gebali (al-Jabali), in January 2003.

See also EGYPT; GENDER: GENDER AND LAW; GENDER: GENDER AND POLITICS; SHA'RAWI, HUDA AL-.

Bibliography

Apiku, Simon. "Women Win Reform in Egypt's Judiciary: Her Honor Is Historic." *World Press,* 10 March 2003.

Khalil, Ashraf. "Egypt's First Female Judge May Remain 'The Only.'" *Women's eNews.* 23 September 2003. Available from <http://www.wcwonline.org>.

Negus, Steve. "Splash in the Glass: The Appointment of Egypt's First Female Judge Is an Important Step That Needs to Be Followed Up." *Cairo Times.* 16–22 January 2003.

MARIA F. CURTIS

RATEBZAD, ANAHITA
[1930–]

First Afghan female physician; Marxist politician.

Anahita Ratebzad was deputy head of state in the People's Democratic Party of Afghanistan (PDPA) government from 1980 to 1986. She was the first Afghan woman to play an active role in government and one of the few Afghan women to become a medical doctor. Born in Guldara in Kabul province, Anahita Ratebzad attended the Malalai Lycée in Kabul. She received a degree in nursing from the Chicago School of Nursing and an M.D. degree from Kabul University. She became involved in leftist politics and was elected to parliament in 1965. A founder of the PDPA, she was active in the Parcham wing of that party. She served as ambassador to Belgrade (1978–1980), minister of social affairs (1978–1979), and minister of education (1979–1980). In 1986 President Najibullah replaced the Parcham government and Ratebzad fled to Moscow with her companion Babrak Karmal. They returned to Kabul in 1989, but were forced to flee to Moscow again in 1992 when the Najibullah government fell. After the fall of the Taliban government in 2001, they did not return to Kabul.

See also PEOPLE'S DEMOCRATIC PARTY OF AFGHANISTAN.

Bibliography

Arnold, Anthony. *Afghanistan's Two-Party Communism: Parcham and Khalq.* Stanford, CA: Hoover Institution Press, 1983.

GRANT FARR

RATOSH, YONATAN
[1908–1981]

Hebrew-language poet and journalist.

Born in Russia as Uriel Halperin, Yonatan Ratosh was raised in a completely Hebrew-speaking environment. In 1921, he moved to Palestine, where he worked as a journalist for *Haaretz* and *ha-Yarden* and where he also wrote many books of poetry.

Ratosh is known for his belief in the existence of a Hebrew people who are distinguishable from the people living in Israel and from the people of many different cultures who follow the Jewish religion. According to his belief, the distinctive Hebrew people, who are the descendants of the Canaanite nation, developed a new national identity based on Hebrew culture.

See also LITERATURE: HEBREW; NEWSPAPERS AND PRINT MEDIA: ISRAEL.

Bibliography

Diamond, James S. *Homeland or Holy Land? The "Canaanite" Critique of Israel.* Indianapolis: Indiana University Press, 1986.

Shavit, Yaacov. *New Hebrew Nation: A Study in Israeli Heresy and Fantasy.* London and Totowa, NJ: F. Cass, 1987.

BRYAN DAVES

RAUF EZZAT, HEBA
[1965–]

Egyptian political scientist and Islamic thinker and activist.

Heba Rauf Ezzat (also Hiba Ra'uf Izzat) was educated in German Catholic schools and is at the point of receiving a Ph.D. in political science from Cairo University. Rauf has become a prominent spokesperson on gender issues in Egypt and on the Internet. From 1992 to 1997 she wrote a weekly column, "Women's Voice," for *al-Sha'b,* the Islamist-leaning newspaper of the Egyptian Labor Party. She supports change from within to counter what she sees as secularization of the (Muslim) family. Conceptualizing the Muslim family as outside of history, she criticizes Western feminists for analyzing it within the framework of the rise of bourgeois and patriarchal social structures. Yet she gives more centrality to gender than do many Islamic activists, such as her mentors,

Zaynab al-Ghazali and Safinaz Kazim. Arguing from central texts of Islamic jurisprudence, she finds strong precedent for women's participation as leaders in public life as long as they are Islamically qualified. Although knowledgeable about Western political philosophy, in her polemics Rauf nevertheless expresses common misperceptions about European and American society. She tends to support monolithic notions of "Islamic" and "Western" societies as inevitably dichotomized. She rejects the label of "feminist" and sees feminism as a diversionary and unnecessary practice, irrelevant to those who work within an Islamic framework.

See also GENDER: GENDER AND EDUCATION; GENDER: GENDER AND LAW; GENDER: GENDER AND POLITICS; GHAZALI, ZAYNAB AL-; SHARI'A.

Bibliography

Rauf Ezzat, Heba. "Women and the Interpretation of Islamic Sources." In *Islam 21.* Available at <http://www.islam21.net/pages/keyissues/key2-6.htm>.

Gawhary, Karim, el-. "An Interview with Heba Ra'uf Ezzat." *Middle East Report* 191 (Nov.–Dec. 1994): 26–27.

Karam, Azza. *Women, Islamisms and the State: Contemporary Feminisms in Egypt.* London: Macmillan, 1998.

MARILYN BOOTH

RAVIKOVITCH, DAHLIA
[1936–]

Israeli poet.

Dahlia Ravikovitch was born near Tel Aviv. Her father was killed by a drunken driver when she was six, a trauma that she describes in her collection of autobiographical stories, *Death in the Family* (1976), and that reappears in various guises throughout her work. Raised on a kibbutz and in Haifa, she studied at the Hebrew University of Jerusalem and in England, and then worked as a teacher and as a journalist. The author of eight volumes of poetry and the recipient of several awards, among them the prestigious Israel Prize for Literature (1998), Ravikovitch also has published short stories, children's books, and Hebrew translations of English poetry.

Ravikovitch's poems are predominantly personal and written in high diction, finicky form, and idiosyncratic vocabulary, at times mythological or archaic. These properties merge, in her highly charged poems, with simple, almost childlike syntax, tone, and point of view, creating a unique simultaneity of dreamlike beauty and lurking danger, a perfect aesthetic expression of struggle. This tension is dominant in *A Love of an Orange,* Ravikovitch's first collection (1959), and is recognizable in works such as *The Third Book* (1969). Later volumes manifest a tendency toward simpler expression.

During the 1980s, the war in Lebanon sparked a poetic-political protest in which Ravikovitch took part. The voice of her poetry identifies with the vulnerable and speaks frequently of the feminine condition. Her retrospective collection, *The Complete Poems So Far* (1995), confirms her status as one of Israel's leading poets and its foremost woman poet.

See also LITERATURE: HEBREW.

Bibliography

Pincas, Israel. "Leaving Traces." *Modern Hebrew Literature* 1 (1988): 36–39.

Ravikovitch, Dahlia. *A Dress of Fire,* translated by Chana Bloch. New York: Sheep Meadow Press; London: The Menard Press, 1976.

Ravikovitch, Dahlia. *The Window: New and Selected Poems,* translated by Chana Bloch and Ariel Bloch. Riverdale-on-Hudson, NY: Sheep Meadow Press, 1989.

Weis.eltier, Meir. "Real Love Is Not What It Seems to Be." *Modern Hebrew Literature* 17 (1996): 15–19.

NILI GOLD
UPDATED BY ZAFRIRA LIDOVSKY COHEN

REAGAN PLAN (1982)

Plan for Arab–Israeli peace.

On 1 September 1982, U.S. president Ronald Reagan issued a policy statement in the wake of Israel's June 1982 invasion of Lebanon and the successful expulsion of the Palestine Liberation Organization (PLO) and its estimated 15,000 fighters from that country, following extensive mediation by U.S. special envoy Philip Habib. In his speech Reagan expressed satisfaction that Lebanon's troubles were over and turned his attention to the Palestinian-Israeli conflict. Citing the Camp David Accords as its basis, the Reagan plan called for Arab recognition of Israel and negotiations over control of an undivided Jerusalem. The plan ruled out Israeli sovereignty or permanent control of the West Bank and Gaza, as well as an independent Palestinian state, favoring instead a confederation between Jordan and the West Bank and Gaza. Israeli prime minister Menachem Begin rejected the plan and reiterated Israel's claim to the West Bank; Arab leaders were less categorical but hardly enthusiastic. The assassination of Lebanese president-elect Bashir Jumayyil two weeks later, the massacre of Palestinian civilians at Sabra and Shatila, the hasty return of U.S. Marines to Beirut, and an ongoing deterioration of the Lebanese situation refocused U.S. attention on Lebanon, however, and the Reagan Plan for Palestinian-Israeli peace fell by the wayside.

See also CAMP DAVID ACCORDS (1978); HABIB, PHILIP CHARLES; REAGAN, RONALD; SABRA AND SHATILA MASSACRES.

Bibliography

Eisenberg, Laura Zittrain, and Caplan, Neil. *Negotiating Arab-Israeli Peace: Patterns, Problems, and Possibilities.* Bloomington: Indiana University Press, 1998.

Quandt, William B. *Peace Process: American Diplomacy and the Arab-Israeli Conflict since 1967.* Berkeley: University of California Press, 2001.

Shultz, George. P. *Turmoil and Triumph: My Years As Secretary of State.* New York: Scribner's, 1993.

LAURA ZITTRAIN EISENBERG

REAGAN, RONALD
[1911–]

President of the United States, 1981–1989.

Born in Illinois, Reagan graduated from Eureka College. Beginning in 1937, he was a film and television actor in Hollywood. Reagan entered politics in 1966 when he was elected governor of California; he was reelected in 1970. He later served two terms as president of the United States, surviving a gunshot wound he received in an assassination attempt in March 1981.

Reagan's two terms in office saw him grappling with some important issues in the Middle East and Southwest Asia, and engaging in policies that would affect future American involvement in the region

tremendously. The most openly pro-Israeli U.S. president to that time, he announced a plan for Arab-Israeli peace on 1 September 1982, following Israel's invasion of Lebanon and the evacuation of Palestine Liberation Organization (PLO) forces from Beirut. The Reagan Plan called for establishment of Palestinian self-government in the West Bank and Gaza Strip, in association with Jordan, on the basis of the Camp David Accords of 1978. Israel rejected the Reagan Plan, and the Arab states announced their own proposal, the Fez Plan, several days later. Reagan also ordered U.S. forces to Lebanon from 1982 to 1983, both to supervise the PLO withdrawal and to bolster the Lebanese government. In 1983, bombings destroyed both the U.S. embassy and the U.S. marine barracks in Beirut, leading to the ignominious withdrawal of American forces. Reagan was also plagued by the long captivity of several American hostages in Lebanon. As with the bombings, Hizbullah is generally considered to have been behind the kidnappings. The circuitous exchange of arms to Iran, via Israel, in return for the release of the hostages, led Reagan into the worst scandal of his presidency.

Reagan was also president during the bulk of the Soviet occupation of Afghanistan (1979–1988). His administration provided massive support to Islamic guerrillas fighting the Soviets, laying the basis for the country to become a haven for Islamic militants worldwide. Finally, his government's support for Iraq and Saddam Hussein during the long Iran–Iraq war (1980–1988) helped stem a possible Iranian victory and bolster Saddam to face the U.S. in later years.

See also CAMP DAVID ACCORDS (1978); GAZA (CITY); HIZBULLAH; HUSSEIN, SADDAM; PALESTINE LIBERATION ORGANIZATION (PLO); WEST BANK.

Bibliography

Jentleson, Bruce W. *With Friends Like These: Reagan, Bush, and Saddam, 1982–1990.* New York: W.W. Norton, 1995.

Lesch, David W. *The Middle East and the United States: A Historical and Political Reassessment.* Boulder, CO: Westview, 2003.

MICHAEL R. FISCHBACH

RE'AYA
See GLOSSARY

RECAIZADE MAHMUD EKREM
[c. 1846–c. 1913]

Ottoman Turkish poet and literary reformer.

Mahmud Ekrem Recaizade was born in Istanbul during the Ottoman Empire and enrolled in the military academy. He later transferred to the Civil Service School where he met and became a disciple of Namik Kemal. He worked for many years as Kemal's assistant on the newspaper *Tasvir-i Efkar;* in 1867, after Kemal's flight to Paris, Recaizade became chief editor of the newspaper.

Recaizade was a member of the second generation of Tanzimat writers who created the New Literature school, which sought literary inspiration in everyday life. Recaizade also contributed to the *Servet-i Fünun* (Wealth of sciences) movement, which focused on the problems of the individual under the oppressive regime of Sultan Abdülhamit II. He is considered a transitional figure between the romanticism of Namik Kemal and the realism of Ömer Sayfettin. In addition to his poetry, his novels, and his plays, he published theoretical studies of literature that criticized traditional forms of artistic expression and created an environment for greater artistic experimentation.

See also NAMIK KEMAL.

Bibliography

Ertop, Konur. "Trends and Characteristics of Modern Turkish Literature." In *The Transformation of Turkish Culture: The Atatürk Legacy,* edited by Günsel Renda and C. Max Kortepeter. Princeton, NJ: Kingston Press, 1986.

Lewis, Bernard. *The Emergence of Modern Turkey,* 3d edition. New York: Oxford University Press, 2002.

Mitler, Louis. *Ottoman Turkish Writers: A Bibliographical Dictionary of Significant Figures in Pre-Republican Turkish Literature.* New York: P. Lang, 1988.

DAVID WALDNER

RED CRESCENT SOCIETY

Name of the International Red Cross in Muslim countries.

A humanitarian organization that maintains neutrality, the International Red Cross was established in 1864 at the behest of Jean-Henri Dunant, a Swiss citizen who had organized emergency medical aid for French and Austrian victims at the Battle of Solferino in 1859. In 1876, Ottoman officials requested that a red crescent, instead of a red cross, be used to mark their ambulances. The symbol, later accepted by other Muslim nations, was formally accepted by the society in 1929.

The Red Crescent Society is part of the International Federation of Red Cross and Red Crescent Societies. National societies have traditionally concentrated on natural disasters, while the International Committee of the Red Cross has concentrated on situations of conflict and warfare. Red Crescent societies have made an important contribution to the international organization, developing policies that are inclusive of non-Western traditions.

Bibliography

Benthall, Jonathan. "The Red Cross and Red Crescent Movement and Islamic Societies, with Special Reference to Jordan." *British Journal of Middle Eastern Studies* 24, no. 2 (1997): 157–177.

Haug, Hans. *Humanity for All: The International Red Cross and Red Crescent Movement.* Berne: P. Haupt, 1993.

VANESA CASANOVA-FERNANDEZ

RED LINE AGREEMENT

Part of the post–World War I reorganization of the Turkish Petroleum Company (TPC) as the Iraq Petroleum Company (IPC).

TPC was formed in 1914, shortly before the outbreak of World War I. Fifty percent of TPC was owned by the Anglo-Persian Oil Company (later British Petroleum). A 5 percent beneficial interest was owned by the Armenian entrepreneur Calouste Gülbenkian, who had put together the TPC consortium. The remainder was split between the Deutsche Bank and a subsidiary of Royal Dutch Shell. The original TPC agreement included a clause pledging the principals to refrain from seeking additional concessions in the Ottoman Empire except through TPC.

At the San Remo Conference in 1919, the German share of TPC was transferred to France. The Americans, also victors in the war, demanded a share as part of their spoils and accepted 20 percent in 1922 (later enlarged to 23.7 percent). However, this did not end the disputes impeding the company's reorganization. Gülbenkian insisted that the "self-denying clause" be retained in any new agreement. The French, with their 23.7 percent share, supported Gülbenkian; the other participants did not.

The final agreement establishing IPC was signed in July 1928 at Ostend, Belgium. It included the self-denying clause. However, the principals declared themselves unsure of the actual boundaries of the Ottoman Empire. Legend has it that Gülbenkian, then and there, took a red pencil and drew a line around what he meant by "Ottoman Empire"—the Red Line. With the exception of Kuwait and Iran, the Red Line encompassed most of what would become the great oil-producing areas of the region.

The Red Line, along with the As-Is Agreement, shaped the structure of foreign ownership and the tempo of development of Middle Eastern oil. For example, Gulf Oil (now owned by Chevron), an original party to the IPC agreement (it later dropped out), became an active contender for a share of the Kuwait concession, in part because its participation in IPC prevented it from seeking promising concessions elsewhere in the Gulf. Gulf's success in winning a share thwarted expectations that Anglo-Persian (APOC) would be able to monopolize Kuwait, then a British protectorate. The Red Line prevented APOC and the U.S. partners in IPC, chiefly Standard Oil of New Jersey (now Exxon) and Standard Oil of New York (now Mobil), from seeking concessions in Saudi Arabia. The rich fields in the eastern part of Saudi Arabia were discovered by Casoc, a subsidiary of Standard Oil of California (now Chevron). Texaco purchased half of Casoc in 1936. Neither was a Red Line company.

The need for additional capital to develop the oil fields of Saudi Arabia led to the end of the Red Line. Once again, a world war provided the opportunity to reorganize oil concessions in the Middle East. After the Germans occupied France in 1940, the IPC holdings of Gülbenkian and the French were sequestered under British law. The IPC board in London was notified that the IPC agreement might have been invalidated by having become a contract with an enemy power. The IPC principals chose not to pursue this possibility during the war, but afterward, Standard of New Jersey's legal counsel brought the issue before U.S. officials, who joined

the corporation in pressing for a revision of the IPC agreement to eliminate the self-denying clause. The successful conclusion of these maneuvers in 1947 ended the Red Line and allowed Standard of New Jersey and of New York to take shares in ARAMCO while retaining their shares in IPC.

See also AS-IS AGREEMENT; GÜLBENKIAN, CALOUSTE; ROYAL DUTCH SHELL.

Bibliography

Anderson, Irvine H. *Aramco, the United States, and Saudi Arabia: A Study of the Dynamics of Foreign Oil Policy, 1933–1950.* Princeton, NJ: Princeton University Press, 1981.

Sampson, Anthony. *The Seven Sisters: The Great Oil Companies and the World They Shaped.* New York: Viking, 1975.

MARY ANN TÉTREAULT

REFAH PARTISI

Main Islamic-oriented political party in Turkey, 1984–1998.

The emergence of pro-Islamic parties in Turkey can be traced back to 1969, when a group of dissident parliamentarians in the Justice Party attempted to establish a new party focusing on their program called Milli Gorus (National Vision).

The National Order Party (NOP) was set up in January 1970 under the leadership of Necmeddin Erbakan, a mechanical engineer, former university professor, and former president of the Turkish Industry Chambers Union. The major aim of the party was to strengthen national industry and to restore Islamic teaching and morality. Following a military memorandum in 1971, the Constitutional Court investigated the party's antisecular program and closed it in 1972, and Erbakan left for Switzerland. At the end of the same year, a new party, the National Salvation Party (NSP) was founded by lawyer Süleyman Arif Emre.

The NSP, which Erbakan assumed leadership of, participated in several coalition goverments between 1974 and 1980, when a military coup led to the banning of all political parties. After the reopening of political life in 1983, the third pro-Islamic party, Refah Partisi (RP), was established in March 1984 under the leadership of Ahmet Tekdal. Following a referendum the same year, the restitution of political rights to party leaders was accepted. This encouraged Erbakan, who once more assumed the leadership of RP. RP took positions against multinational corporations and European Union membership. The empowering factors were the new urban groups, Muslim intellectuals, and grass roots organizations in the large cities. The party targeted distinct social groups such as youth, women, workers, civil servants, professional cadres, retired persons, and disabled people. The Ladies Commission brought dynamism to the party. The intense activism that took place within the elaborate RP structure was carried out predominantly by religiously mobilized, very dedicated, industrious women. The female party members constantly stressed that they worked "for God's sake," meaning that they did not expect any rewards such as elective or appointive offices in return. In the rural areas of central and southeast Turkey the party included peripheral forces of local merchants and manufacturers, a majority of whom were practicing Muslims and Turkish nationalists. The party succeeded in obtaining the support of Kurds, who seemed to be searching for a political organization that was not part of the political establishment. RP opted to highlight Islamic solidarity more than ethnic or class distinction. RP's transnational character was crucial in securing financial contributions to the party. The large network of migrant associations in Germany supportive of the "National Vision" contributed large membership donations.

The municipal elections of March 1994, the national elections of 1995, and the local elections of June 1996 in which the RP took 33.5 percent of the vote, secured the mayorship of metropolitan cities such as Ankara and Istanbul, as well as the leadership of twenty-two provinces. Erbakan became prime minister in 1996. However, his controversial visits to Libya, Indonesia, Malaysia, and Iran led the military to exert pressure for the resignation of the RP coalition government in June 1997. The Constitutional Court banned the party in February 1998 on grounds of antisecular policies.

The RP leadership immediately established a new party, the Virtue Party (VP), under the leadership of Erbakan's closest collaborator, Recai Kutan. All the deputies of the dissolved RP joined the VP. The new party participated in the 1999 general elections but lost its previous leading position. With 21.3 percent

of the general vote and 111 seats out of 550 in the parliament, it became the main opposition party. The Constitutional Court ruled that the VP was solely a continuation of the RP and dissolved it in June 2001.

Subsequently, the conservative wing of the dissolved VP founded the Felicity Party (FP) under the leadership of Recai Kutan. Claiming to be the only representative of the National Vision, the FP received only 2.49 percent of the vote in the general elections of 2002.

Following the dissolution of the Virtue Party, the reformist wing founded under the leadership of the former mayor of Istanbul, Tayyip Erdoğan, the Justice and Development Party (JDP). Although a novice among the competing eighteen parties, the JDP received 34.6 percent of the general vote and 363 seats in parliament. The JDP denied being an Islamist party and used moderate, rather than secular, discourse during the electoral campaign. The JDP does not emphasize the primacy of culture, as did the RP and VP; instead, it claims to represent the true essence and will of society and defines itself as a democratic conservative party.

See also ERBAKAN, NECMEDDIN; MILLI GÖRÜŞ HAREKETI; NATIONAL SALVATION PARTY.

Bibliography

Arat, Yeşim. *Political Islam in Turkey and Women's Organizations.* Istanbul: Turkish Economic and Social Studies Foundation (TESEV), 1999.

Gülalp, Haldun. "The Poverty of Democracy in Turkey: The Refah Party Episode." *New Perspectives on Turkey* 21, no. 2 (1999): 35–59.

Yeşilada, Birol A. "Realignment and Party Adaptation: The Case of the Refah and Fazilet Parties." In *Politics, Parties, and Elections in Turkey,* edited by Sabri Sayari and Yilmaz Esmer. Boulder, CO: Lynne Rienner, 2002.

NERMIN ABADAN-UNAT

REFUGEES

This entry consists of the following articles:

AFGHAN
BALKAN MUSLIM
JEWISH
KURDISH
PALESTINIAN

AFGHAN

Afghans who fled civil war in their country during the 1980s and 1990s.

The flight of refugees from Afghanistan began in 1978, driven by internal conflict caused by the takeover of Afghanistan by the Marxist-Leninist People's Democratic Party of Afghanistan and later by the Soviet invasion in December 1979. By the early 1980s, a large-scale resistance war was being waged and more than six million refugees had fled Afghanistan, most settling in the neighboring countries of Pakistan and Iran, but many thousands also fleeing to India, Turkey, the United States, and Western Europe.

The Afghan refugees referred to themselves as *muhajarin,* from the Arabic root *hijra,* referring to the flight of the prophet Mohammed from Mecca to Medina, thus giving the refugees a religious status. Afghan refugee camps were established in Pakistan and Iran, assisted by the United Nations High Commission for Refugees and other world relief agencies. Areas of Pakistan near the Afghan border, especially the Northwest Frontier Province and Baluchistan, became crowded with Afghan refugees, creating local hostility among the Pakistanis. In Pakistan, most of the refugees were ethnic Pushtun from the southeastern provinces of Afghanistan, although some Persian-speaking refugees, especially Hazara, fled from central Afghanistan to the area around Quetta in Baluchistan. Most of the two million Afghan refugees who fled to Iran were Persian speakers from the western provinces of Afghanistan. These large refugee camps became centers of political activity and recruiting grounds for young men to fight in the Islamic insurgencies in Afghanistan.

Attempts at large-scale refugee repatriations occurred several times, beginning in 1992, only to be halted by renewed instability and the outflow of even more refugees. The first repatriation attempt occurred in 1992, after the mojahedin succeeded in ousting the Soviet-supported government in Kabul. (The Soviet Union had withdrawn its troops in 1990). More than 1.4 million refugees were repatriated in 1992 and 1993. However, the mojahedin, which was split into several antagonistic groups, was unable to develop a viable government, leading to internecine warfare and increased insta-

bility in Afghanistan. As a result, hundreds of thousands of refugees again fled Afghanistan in the mid-1990s.

In the midst of this chaos, the Taliban, a religious movement from the Kandahar region, gained control of most of Afghanistan. The Taliban government's strict Islamic codes, human-rights abuses, and bias against non-Pushtuns led to a steady refugee flight throughout the 1990s.

In addition to the political and economic instability in Afghanistan during the 1990s, Afghanistan also experienced a severe drought beginning in 2000, which created harsh conditions for millions of Afghans. In the year 2000 alone, over 172,000 Afghans fled to Pakistan because of the drought conditions or the political instability. Hundreds of thousands were displaced internally.

After the events of 11 September 2001, coalition forces began bombing the Taliban government in Kabul, and by November 2001 an interim government headed by Hamid Karzai had replaced it. Although this presented opportunities for refugees to repatriate, the immediate consequence of the allied bombing and the change in government was an increase in refugees. Even though Pakistan had closed its borders, over 160,000 Afghans crossed into Pakistan between 11 September 2001 and the end of the year. At the same time—the fall of 2001—the Iranian government, fearing a large exodus of Afghans into Iran, established two refugee camps just inside Afghanistan, which housed over 11,000 refugees.

By the spring of 2002, the refugees' situation began to change as the Karzai government brought some stability to Afghanistan. In addition, the United Nations and other relief agencies began large-scale repatriation efforts, which gave refugees who were willing to return grain and help with transportation. In total, 1.8 million refugees were repatriated during 2002. By 2003, the repatriation rate had slowed, in large part because most of those who wanted to return had already done so. Even with the massive number of refugees who returned, four million Afghans still lived outside of their home country as of the early twenty-first century. Many, maybe most, of these remaining refugees may never return.

See also AFGHANISTAN: OVERVIEW; BALUCHIS-
TAN; HAZARA; KARZAI, HAMID; PUSHTUN;
TALIBAN.

Bibliography

"Afghanistan: Displaced in a Devastated Country." In
*Caught between Borders: Response Strategies of the Internally Dis-
placed,* edited by Marc Vincent and Brigitte Refslund
Sorensen. Sterling, VA; London: Pluto Press,
2001.

GRANT FARR

BALKAN MUSLIM

*People who have migrated and relocated from Bosnia,
Bulgaria, Montenegro, Serbia, and other Balkan countries.*

The Balkans—the area including parts of Albania,
Bosnia, Bulgaria, Croatia, Kosovo, Macedonia, Montenegro, Romania, Serbia, and Slovenia—have been
home to nations whose boundaries have been drawn
and redrawn since Hellenistic times. The Balkans
have been the site of significant and continued upheaval at least since the Ottoman conquest during
the fourteenth century, which caused mass migrations
of Muslims. As a result of the Russian–Ottoman
War of 1877–1878, Muslims were forced from conquered areas in Bulgaria, Montenegro, and Serbia.
Later, the Balkan allies either exiled or caused the
deaths of a majority of the Muslims from territories
they conquered during the Balkan War of 1912–1913.
Other Balkan Muslims became refugees in regions
taken by Greece after World War I. Some 400,000
refugees came to Turkey during the Greco-Turkish
population exchange of the 1920s. The collapse of
the Soviet Union prompted several "breakaway" republics in southeastern Europe and sparked or
reignited varied political, cultural, and religious
clashes. The 1990s proved to be a difficult time,
especially with the disintegration of Yugoslavia.
Roughly 800,000 Muslims left Bosnia after it declared independence from Yugoslavia and conflict
with Serbia escalated in 1991. Significant numbers
of Bosnian Muslims (around 50,000 at least) fled
to Croatia, a predominantly Christian country.
Continued fighting between Serbian government
forces (Christian, led by Slobodan Milosevic) and
the Kosovo Liberation Army (Muslim, generally
ethnic Albanian) in the predominantly Muslim republic of Kosovo prompted a continued refugee situation as well, especially when fighting escalated in
1998. Despite ongoing international mediation, the
Balkan Muslim refugee crisis is far from resolved.

See also RUSSIAN–OTTOMAN WARS.

Bibliography

Crampton, R. J. *The Balkans Since the Second World War.* New
York: Longman; London: Pearson, 2002.

Hupchick, Dennis P. *The Balkans: From Constantinople to Communism.* New York and Basingstoke, U.K.: Palgrave,
2002.

JUSTIN MCCARTHY
UPDATED BY NOAH BUTLER

JEWISH

*Jews who fled from Arab and Muslim countries to Israel
after 1948.*

Following the 29 November 1947 United Nations
resolution to partition Palestine, the establishment
of Israel on 14 May 1948, and its subsequent victory
over the armies of five neighboring Arab countries
in the 1948 war, an estimated 800,000 Jews living
in Arab and Muslim countries were subjected to anti-
Jewish violence, abuse, and persecution, which led
most of them to seek refuge in Israel. The government of Israel, working through the Mossad le-Aliyah
Bet (a clandestine state institution for immigration)
and the Jewish Agency, mounted airlift operations
funded by the United Jewish Appeal through its subsidiary body, the American Jewish Joint Distribution
Committee.

In 1949 and 1950, 48,315 Jews were airlifted
from Yemen and Aden in the Magic Carpet Operation, flying directly from Aden to Tel Aviv on chartered U.S. planes. In 1950, the Iraqi government
permitted its 160,000 Jews to emigrate provided
they renounced their Iraqi nationality and whatever
properties and assets they could not sell. Iraq demanded total secrecy and insisted that the planes
flying the Jews make a landing in Cyprus en route
to Israel. Between 1950 and 1951, 123,370 Iraqi
Jews were airlifted to Israel in Operation Ezra and
Nehemiah (also known as Operation Ali Baba).
Each was allowed 50 dinars on departure.

In 1948, some 100,000 Jews lived in Egypt;
16,000 fled to Israel between 1948 and 1951;

The Jewish community in Ethiopia, frequently referred to as Beta Israel, or the falashas (the alien ones), have been emigrating to Israel by the thousands since the late 1970s. By early 2003, eighty thousand Ethiopian Jews were living in Israel, frequently in the poorest sections of the country. © GIDEON MENDEL/CORBIS. REPRODUCED BY PERMISSION.

17,500 settled in Israel between 1952 and 1956; and the majority came after the 1956 Arab–Israel War. Following the 1967 Arab–Israel War, 2,500 Egyptian Jews fled, the majority settling in Israel. Some 33,000 Jews from Libya settled in Israel between 1948 and 1960, the rest going to Italy; 2,678 Jews fled from Syria and 235 from Lebanon to Israel between 1948 and 1951, many of them walking across the border. An additional 2,700 came from those countries between 1952 and 1960. In 1991, on the intercession of U.S. president George H. W. Bush, Syria allowed 1,400 Jews to leave for Israel.

In 1948, some 600,000 Jews lived in French-controlled Morocco, Algeria, and Tunisia. As the struggle for independence from France intensified, the situation of the Jews deteriorated and Israel began to evacuate them, mainly by sea via France. Between 1948 and 1971, some 235,000 out of 400,000 Moroccan Jews emigrated to Israel. The rest went to France and other countries. Most of Algeria's Jews fled after that country gained its independence from France in 1962. The majority went to France, as they were considered French nationals; 20,000 immigrated into Israel between 1948 and 1971. During the same period, some 54,000 Tunisian Jews fled to Israel.

In recent years, the World Organization of Jews from Arab Countries has been registering Jewish-owned properties left behind in Arab countries in order, possibly, to make future demands for restitution or to offset Palestinian Arab demands for property left behind in Israel in 1948.

See also ARAB–ISRAEL WAR (1948); ARAB–ISRAEL WAR (1967).

Bibliography

Hillel, Shlomo. *Operation Babylon,* translated by Ina Friedman. Garden City, NY: Doubleday; London: Collins, 1987.

Laskier, Michael. *North African Jewry in the Twentieth Century: The Jews of Morocco, Tunisia, and Algeria.* New York: New York University Press, 1994.

Schechtman, Joseph B. *On Wings of Eagles: The Plight, Exodus, and Homecoming of Oriental Jewry.* New York: T. Yoseloff, 1961.

Sicron, Moshe. *Immigration to Israel 1948–1953.* Jerusalem: Falk Project for Economic Research in Israel, 1957.

Statistical Abstract of Israel. Jerusalem: Central Bureau of Statistics, annual since 1949/50 edition.

MICHAEL M. LASKIER
UPDATED BY MERON MEDZINI

KURDISH

People of Kurdistan, a territory inhabited mainly by the Kurds of five countries, who fled to escape repression and possible death.

In September 1925, more than 20,000 Assyrian Christians (Nestorians) and Kurds arrived in northern Iraq, fleeing the repression that came after the end of the Kurdish revolt in Turkey (1922–1925). This was the first time the international media mentioned the problem of Kurdish refugees.

More recently, thousands of Kurds sought asylum in Iran after the collapse of General (Mullah Mustafa) Barzani's independence movement in 1975. Kurds also fled to Iran and Turkey after the Iraqi Kurdish resistance in the aftermath of the Iran–Iraq War (1988). These were small flights compared to the huge refugee crisis caused in April 1991 by Saddam Hussein's attacks toward the end of the Gulf War (January–April 1991). Fearing for their safety after the failure of their uprising in March 1991, about 2 million Iraqi Kurds fled toward the Turkish and Iranian borders. The arrival of such a huge number of refugees, thousands of whom died of hunger and cold, internationalized the Kurdish problem and forced unwilling Western governments to extend their protection to the Kurds. While those who went to the Turkish border came back to Iraq after the creation of a safe haven, dozens of thousands of Kurdish refugees stayed for years in Iran, living in the cities or in camps. Most of them came back in the late 1990s after the stabilization of the Kurdish region. A small number of Kurdish refugees from Iran and Turkey live in camps in Iraq.

See also BARZANI FAMILY; HUSSEIN, SADDAM; IRAN–IRAQ WAR (1980–1988).

Bibliography

Bruinessen, Martin van. *Aghas, Shaikhs, and States: The Social and Political Structures of Kurdistan.* London: Zed Books, 1992.

Graham-Brown, Sarah. *Sanctioning Saddam: The Politics of Intervention in Iraq.* London: I. B. Tauris, 1999

CHRIS KUTSCHERA

PALESTINIAN

People of Palestine who fled or were driven out in 1948 and 1967; their repatriation remains a controversial issue.

A major consequence of the Arab–Israel War (1948) was the flight of approximately 700,000 members of the indigenous Arab population from their homes in those parts of Mandatory Palestine that became the new state of Israel, 30 percent of whose territory lay beyond the borders of the UN partition plan. Since 1948, the Palestine refugee problem has been one of the most important and controversial issues in the continuing conflict. It has appeared

Refugees from Palestine travel to Gaza after being evacuated by the UN, 31 March 1949. The question of Palestinian refugees has been a core issue in the Arab–Israeli conflict since 1948. © HULTON-DEUTSCH COLLECTION/CORBIS. REPRODUCED BY PERMISSION.

on the agenda of every UN session since 1948 and has been the subject of numerous UN resolutions calling for repatriation or compensation to the refugees, or sometimes both.

Whereas the Palestinians, the Arab states, their supporters, and many Israelis assert that the refugees were forced by Israeli military or paramilitary units to leave their homes and property, the government of Israel has disclaimed responsibility, placing blame for the flight on Palestinian leaders and the surrounding Arab countries, which, Israel states, urged the refugees to leave. In recent years, several Israeli revisionist accounts have produced evidence that in many instances the Israeli military did force Palestinians to depart. Another cause of the flight was the breakdown of Palestinian Arab society during the war in Palestine, followed by chaos and the total disruption of civil society. The number of original Palestinian refugees is based on estimates rather than an accurate census. The UN estimated in 1949 that more than 700,000 of Palestine's 1948 Arab population could be classified as refugees.

A second major exodus occurred following the June 1967 war, when over 300,000 Palestinians left the West Bank and the Golan area in Syria, many of them second-time refugees who had lived in camps since 1948. By 2003, those classified as refugees by the UN Relief and Works Agency for Palestine Refugees in the Near East (UNRWA) had increased to more than 2.4 million. UNRWA considers as refugees individuals and their direct descendants who lived in Palestine a minimum of two years preceding the 1948 conflict, who lost homes and means of livelihood, and who reside in areas where UNRWA services are available. According to this definition, nearly half the total number of Palestinians in the world were refugees in the 1990s.

The largest concentration is in Jordan, with over 1.5 million in the occupied West Bank and Gaza. More than 700,000 live in Jordan, more than 390,000 in Lebanon, and 400,000 in Syria. Initially most refugees lived in camps established by the UN. However, by 2003, 2.7 million lived in other places but received education, health care, and other social services from UNRWA. More than half of UNRWA expenditures were for education. Although the educational and social services provided by UNRWA are of relatively high quality, the area occupied by the refugee camps has not been greatly extended despite the rapid population increase. Thus the camps have become extremely overcrowded, and housing and other public facilities have become greatly overburdened.

In most areas, the internal affairs of the camps are run by the Palestinians themselves. Refugee frustration with low wages, poor living conditions, and their inability to return to their original homes has caused social and political unrest, with the result that some camps in Lebanon have become bases for Palestinian guerrilla activity. Political life in the camps is intense, and refugees are active in nearly every Palestinian political faction and paramilitary organization. On some occasions, the camps have become targets of non-Palestinian military forces—of the Israeli army and various local militias in Lebanon and of the royal army in Jordan—resulting in thousands of Palestinian casualties.

The refugee question has long been a focus of attempts to resolve the Arab–Israel conflict, beginning in December 1948 with UN General Assembly Resolution 194(III), stating "that the refugees wishing to return to their homes and live at peace with their neighbors should be permitted to do so at the earliest practicable date, and that compensation should be paid for the property of those choosing not to return."

The refugees and the Arab states have emphasized the right to return as fundamental in any peace settlement. However, Israel has opposed any large-scale repatriation, instead emphasizing resettlement in the surrounding Arab countries. Attempts at refugee resettlement have not been successful, largely because of refugee insistence on the right of return. By the 1990s, the right to return was interpreted by many refugees and some Arab states as return to a Palestinian state in the West Bank and Gaza rather than within the borders of Israel. Following the 1991 Madrid Middle East peace conference, one of the five multilateral groups established to deal with functional problems dealt with the refugee issue.

See also ARAB–ISRAEL CONFLICT; ARAB–ISRAEL WAR (1948); ARAB–ISRAEL WAR (1967); MADRID CONFERENCE (1991); UNITED NATIONS AND THE MIDDLE EAST; UNITED NATIONS RELIEF AND WORKS AGENCY FOR PALESTINE REFUGEES IN THE NEAR EAST (UNRWA).

Bibliography

Arzt, Donna E. *Refugees into Citizens: Palestinians and the End of the Arab-Israeli Conflict.* New York: Council on Foreign Relations, 1997.

Peretz, Don. *Palestinians, Refugees, and the Middle East Peace Process.* Washington, DC: United States Institute of Peace Press, 1993.

Schiff, Benjamin N. *Refugees unto the Third Generation: UN Aid to Palestinians.* Syracuse, NY: Syracuse University Press, 1995.

Takkenberg, Lex. *The Status of Palestinian Refugees in International Law.* Oxford, U.K.: Clarendon, 1998.

Viorst, Milton. *Reaching for the Olive Branch: UNRWA and Peace in the Middle East.* Bloomington: Indiana University Press, 1989.

DON PERETZ

REJECTION FRONT

Grouping of Palestinian organizations (1974–1980) that opposed a diplomatic solution to the Arab–Israeli conflict.

The Rejection Front was formed in 1974 by Palestinian organizations opposed to the strategy under discussion within the Palestine Liberation Organization (PLO) that envisioned a negotiated, two-state solution to the Arab–Israeli conflict. The Rejection Front proposed instead to continue the armed struggle for the liberation of all Palestine. Led by the Popular Front for the Liberation of Palestine, the front eventually included as well the Popular Front for the Liberation of Palestine–General Command, the Arab Liberation Front, the Palestine Liberation Front, and the Palestinian Popular Struggle Front. The front ceased functioning within the rubric of the PLO and was backed by the Baʿthist government of Iraq.

As the PLO's strategy changed after the 1978 Camp David Accords, and as Iraq reconciled with the PLO, the front's activities waned and had stopped altogether by 1980.

See also PALESTINE LIBERATION ORGANIZATION (PLO); POPULAR FRONT FOR THE LIBERATION OF PALESTINE; POPULAR FRONT FOR THE LIBERATION OF PALESTINE–GENERAL COMMAND.

Bibliography

Fischbach, Michael R. "Rejection Front." In *Encyclopedia of the Palestinians,* edited by Philip Mattar. New York: Facts On File, 2000.

Seale, Patrick. *Abu Nidal: A Gun for Hire.* New York: Random House, 1992.

ELIZABETH THOMPSON
UPDATED BY MICHAEL R. FISCHBACH

RENAISSANCE PARTY

See NAHDA, AL-

REPUBLICAN BROTHERHOOD

The Republican Brotherhood is one of the earliest examples of a reformist movement in Islamic societies that addressed issues of the status of women and non-Muslims in Islamic states.

The Jamhuriyin, as the Republican Brothers are known in Sudan, were founded by Mahmud Muhammad Taha in 1945 as the Republican Party, one of many parties struggling for independence from Great Britain. Although the party favored independence, it scored no electoral victories when independence was achieved in 1956. In 1958, Taha began campaigning for Islamic reform, after the 1964 broadly democratic popular October Revolution that overthrew the first military regime of Abboud. From its origins it has acted less like a party and more like a movement, and grew over the next two decades. Its youthful followers, female as well as male, engaged in public teaching and proselytizing on the streets of Khartoum and Omdurman, and at the universities. A parallel Republican Sisters branch was formed specifically for education and outreach to women, although Taha's seminars in his home were famous for being coeducational, with lively participation on the part of women.

The movement was unique in Islamic Africa and the Middle East at the time. Taha wrote a number of books and several hundred pamphlets dealing with the theological and philosophical bases of his reform program, which came to be known as the Second Message of Islam. The Republican Brotherhood was the popular name for what Taha called the New Islamic Mission, which was intended to develop a new Muslim consciousness with a modern vision of the faith of Islam and Islamic law, *shariʿa.* Taha's analysis was based upon historical and contextual analysis of the Qurʾanic texts revealed to the prophet Muhammad between 610 and 632 C.E. at Mecca and Medina. The earlier Meccan texts deal with religious belief and practice and are meant as a universal message for all humankind, whereas the later Medinan texts he saw as intended to reform Arab society through the newly enlightened community of Muslims. Taha argued that *shariʿa* and Muslim practice should be based upon the primary Meccan texts. His writings and teachings were circulated through more than 200 pamphlets, which ranged from the basic theological points of the Second Message to the reform of specific aspects of the *shariʿa* and the status of women. The Republican Brothers specifically called for reform of Islamic law in regard to women and Muslim marriage, seeking to reduce or eliminate expensive dower (*mahr*) and equalize the status of women and men in marriage. For example, they argued for marriage contracts that pledged monogamy on the part of the husband and gave both partners equal rights to divorce. Republican egalitarianism extended to non-Muslims as well; their religious rights and freedoms would be protected equally with those of Muslims.

While the movement generally abjured direct involvement in politics, it nonetheless opposed the Sudan government's Islamization of law. In September 1983, General Muhammad Ja'far Numeiri declared that *shari'a* would be comprehensively applied as state law, despite the fact that one-third of the population, especially in the south, is animist or Christian. This precipitated a resumption of civil war over the issues of autonomy and religious freedom, which had been negotiated in the Addis Ababa Peace Accords of 1972. The Republican Brotherhood launched a major campaign against this imposition of *shari'a.* With the divisive effect of Islamic law apparent, the movement intensified its criticism of the regime in a leaflet of protest issued symbolically on 25 December 1984. In response, the government arrested five Republican leaders, including Taha, charging them with sedition, undermining the constitution, and inciting unlawful opposition to the government. By January 1985, all had been found guilty of apostasy and sentenced to death. All repented and received reprieves except Mahmud Taha, who, then in his mid-seventies, was executed by hanging. Within two months, a popular uprising overthrew the Numeiri regime; many of its opponents had been galvanized into action by Taha's death.

See also NUMEIRI, MUHAMMAD JA'FAR; SHARI'A; SUDAN; SUDANESE CIVIL WARS; TAHA, MAHMUD MUHAMMAD.

Bibliography

Howard, Stephen. "Republican Brotherhood." In *Historical Dictionary of the Sudan,* 3d edition, edited by Richard A. Lobban, Robert Kramer, and Carolyn Fluehr-Lobban. Lanham, MD: Scarecrow Press. 2002.

Magnarella, Paul J. "The Republican Brothers: A Reformist Movement in the Sudan." *Muslim World* 72 (1982): 14–21.

Taha, Mahmoud Mohamed. *The Second Message of Islam,* translated by Abdullahi Ahmed An-Na'im. Syracuse, NY: Syracuse University Press, 1987.

CAROLYN FLUEHR-LOBBAN

REPUBLICAN PEOPLE'S PARTY (RPP)

The Republic of Turkey's first political party, founded in 1923.

The Republican People's Party (Cumhuriyet Halk Partisi), was founded by its first president, Mustafa Kemal (Atatürk), and its first vice president, Ismet Inönü Its major goal was the establishment of a national-territorial Turkish state. Until the late 1920s the RPP was ideologically eclectic, attempting to reconcile the views of conservatives and the supporters of progress. During its first years, the leadership focused on modernization. Denying social cleavages, the party refused to identify with any particular class. Kemalism was first proclaimed as a political doctrine at the second party congress in October 1927, when Mustafa Kemal delivered a six-day speech outlining the RPP goals: republicanism, meaning rejection of monarchy and dictatorship; nationalism, or the rejection of any dynastic, religious, or racial bases for statehood; secularism, or the separation of religion from the state; and popularism. After the economic crisis of 1929 the party added etatism (state economic enterprises) to its principles. At the third party congress in May 1931 the six principles of Kemalism were symbolized in the form of six arrows. The 1931 convention was a turning point for the RPP and for Turkey itself. With the strong emphasis on nationalism and secularism, the state was made arbiter of religious affairs, and the new definition of nationalism attempted to raise the Turkish nation to the highest level of civilization.

In 1935 the RPP merged with the bureaucracy. The minister of interior became, ex officio, the general secretary of the party. In 1937 the six principles of Kemalism were incorporated into the constitution. In 1938, after Mustafa Kemal's death, his successor, Ismet Inönü, became the national leader. The one-party regime lasted through six elections. Two efforts to form competing parties (in 1925 and 1930) ended in failure. In 1941 some democratic processes were permitted, including fielding independent candidates and nominating more candidates than available parliamentary seats. The end of one-party rule came in 1946, when the newly founded Democrat Party (DP) won all seats where its candidates were placed on the ballot. The opposition forced the government to change the existing electoral law. The new law in 1949 introduced secret balloting, open counting, and judicial supervision. On 14 May 1950 the Democrats won 53.3 percent of the popular vote and 83.8 percent of the parliamentary seats. After a peaceful transfer of power, the two-party format lasted until 1960. However, relations between the government and the opposition deteriorated after 1953. The DP supported the more liberally inclined demands of business and catered to the peasant voters. Toward the end of the 1950s the DP became more authoritarian. In April 1960 the DP set up a parliamentary investigating committee that charged the opposition with subversive activities. The ensuing unrest lead to the military coup of 27 May 1960 and the dissolution of the Democrat Party.

In the framework of the Constituent Assembly, the RPP played a determining role in shaping the new constitution. However, the RPP did not obtain a majority in the 1961 elections, and their participation in coalition governments lasted only until 1963. The turning point in the history of the RPP occurred on the eve of the 1965 elections, when Inönü set forth the maxim "left of center" to describe the party's position. Bülent Ecevit was elected the party's general secretary in 1967. The new image of the party tried to provide a moderate-left alternative for the masses of underprivileged voters, with a strong emphasis on a liberal-pluralist social order, a mixed economy, land reform, and a strong cooperative movement. This required a realignment of Turkey's party system, by which the old center-periphery cleavage was replaced by a new functional cleavage. However, the election of 1973 brought the RPP only 33.3 percent of the vote, and the coalition governments headed by Ecevit did not last. The election of 1977 made the party, with 41.4 percent of the vote, the largest in the assembly, but the deadlock between the RPP and the main opposition party paralyzed the government. Civil strife, violence, and poor performance of coalition governments led to the third military coup, in September 1980.

The RPP was disbanded on 16 October 1981 by Turkey's National Security Council. The new constitution of 1982 brought a ten-year ban on all former politicians, but political parties were allowed to reopen under their traditional names. In 1993 the successor of the dissolved RPP, the Social Democratic Populist Party (SHP), merged with the revived RPP. In the 1995 election the RPP, under a new leader, Deniz Baykal, won 10.8 percent of the vote. The fragmentation of the leftist vote had led to a new polarization between the nationalist and Islamic parties. In the 1999 election the RPP received only 8.6 percent of the vote and remained out of parliament. Although Baykal resigned from the party leadership in 1999, he was reelected in 2000 and was able to obtain 19.3 percent of the vote in the 2002 election.

The post-1993 ideological debate within the party has concerned the nature of secularization, the nature of state-society relationships, the role of the nation-state, the approach of the party to globalization, and minority rights and liberties. A new interpretation of secularism has been triggered by the debate around the Anatolian Left. This concept, initiated by Baykal in 2000, draws parallels between the two Muslim groups (Alevi and Sunni) as well as non-Muslims. Baykal argues that the RPP has to have a deeper and more correct analysis of Turkish culture and history. By returning to the Anatolian roots and claiming a nationally authentic flavor, the dichotomy between the elite and masses can be overcome. This implies a move away from a class analysis to a human-centered analysis. The RPP maintains good relations with some organized interest groups, such as trade unions, small business organizations, and secular women's associations. The RPP indicated its sympathy for the identity search among people of Kurdish origin, but maintains a clear distinction between ethnic separatism and identity politics. With regard to human rights, the RPP has made this issue its primary focus. During the 2002 electoral campaign, accountability of parliamentarians and transparency of the administration dominated its political rhetoric. On basic issues of a welfare state, the RPP proposes universal education, healthcare, and social security reforms. In the realm of economics, the RPP defends the role of the market economy but wants to control it with organized labor and consumer groups. The RPP actively supports Turkey's admission to the European Union and is a member of the Socialist International. The major weaknesses of the party are the domination of factionalism and the increasingly fierce intraparty competition due to the shrinking of the party.

See also ATATÜRK, MUSTAFA KEMAL; ECEVIT, BÜLENT; İNÖNÜ, İSMET; KEMALISM.

Bibliography

Çarkoğlu, Ali. "The Turkish Party System in Transition: Party Performance and Agenda Transformation." *Political Studies* 46, no. 3 (1998): 544–571.

Güneş-Ayata, Ayşe. "The Republican People's Party." *Turkish Studies* 3, no. 1 (2002): 102–121.

Heper, Metin, and Landau, Jacob M., eds. *Political Parties and Democracy in Turkey.* New York: I. B. Tauris, 1991.

NERMIN ABADAN-UNAT

REUTER CONCESSION

See GLOSSARY

REVISIONIST MOVEMENT

See ZIONIST REVISIONIST MOVEMENT

REVOLUTIONARY ASSOCIATION OF THE WOMEN OF AFGHANISTAN (RAWA)

Activist organization formed to advocate women's rights in Afghanistan.

The Revolutionary Afghan Women's Association (Anjoman-i-Enqilabi-i-Zanan-i-Afghanistan), known as RAWA, was founded in 1977 in Kabul by Meena Keshwar Kamal and a small group of close associates in opposition to the pro-Soviet Democratic Organization of Afghan Women (DOAW). RAWA opposed the fundamentalism of the radical Islamic groups as well as the pro-Soviet People's Democratic Party of Afghanistan (PDPA), which had been the dominant political forces in Afghanistan since the mid-1960s. Despite deep ideological differences, the radical Islamists and the members of the PDPA both rejected RAWA as a Maoist organization. Due to violent threats from radical Islamists, RAWA was forced to operate underground. Working clandestinely, RAWA members were active in rallying female student protests in Kabul against the December 1979 occupation of the city by Soviet troops.

RAWA eventually moved its headquarters to Quetta, the border city inside Pakistan, where it became openly involved in the anti-Soviet movement and provided health care and education to refugee Afghan women and children. Its member-ship grew rapidly as many newly arrived educated, professional Afghan women joined its ranks. In 1981, Keshwar Kamal started the monthly *Payam-i-Zan* (Women's message) to encourage exiled women to fight for freedom, democracy, and social justice for all. After Kamal's assassination on 4 February 1987 in Quetta, RAWA once again became a clandestine organization. Rather than choose a single leader, the members elected a rotating governing council of twelve and continued to fight for freedom and social justice and to provide relief for women refugees.

After the fall of the pro-Soviet regime in 1992, RAWA protested the seizure of power by radical Islamic forces. It declared the day the fundamentalists entered into Kabul (28 April 1992) "the Black Day" in Afghan history, and condemned Pakistan and the United States for backing the fundamentalists. On 28 April 2002, the eighth anniversary of the rule by Islamic fundamentalist regimes in Afghanistan, RAWA organized protest rallies in Pakistan and in Washington D. C., demanding a free and democratic Afghanistan. The gathering in Washington was sponsored by the Feminist Majority Foundation and the National Committee of Women for a Democratic Iran.

Since 1997, RAWA has used the Internet to share its message with a global audience and has succeeded in bringing to world attention the plight of Afghan women, but its exceedingly harsh language and personal attacks drove away some of its early sympathizers.

> *See also* AFGHANISTAN: SOVIET INTERVENTION IN; GENDER: GENDER AND LAW; GENDER: GENDER AND POLITICS; KASHWAR KAMAL, MEENA; SAMAR, SIMA; TALIBAN.

Bibliography

Brodsky, Anne E. *With All Our Strength: The Revolutionary Association of the Women of Afghanistan.* New York: Routledge, 2003.

Emadi, Hafizullah. *Repression, Resistance, and Women in Afghanistan.* Westport, CT: Praeger, 2002.

Revolutionary Association of the Women of Afghanistan (RAWA). Available from <http://rawa.false.net/index.html>.

SENZIL NAWID

REVOLUTIONARY COMMAND COUNCIL (EGYPT)

Egyptian political body formed in the summer of 1952.

The Free Officers movement formed the RCC following its overthrow of King Farouk (July 1952) and establishment of a military junta. Led by Colonel Gamal Abdel Nasser, the members of the RCC included Colonel Anwar al-Sadat, Major Abd al-Hakim Amir, Major Salah Salam, Major Khalid Muhyi al-Din, and other high-ranking officers. General Muhammad Naguib, an older and widely respected officer, was brought in as prime minister and, in June 1953, president of the newly declared Republic of Egypt. The RCC faced a series of challenges in consolidating power, that from the Muslim Brotherhood probably the most significant. A power struggle between Nasser and Naguib led to Naguib's ouster in November 1955 and was an important step in Nasser's rise to power. The RCC was officially dissolved in 1956.

See also FREE OFFICERS, EGYPT; MUSLIM BROTHERHOOD.

Bibliography

Harris, Christina. *Nationalism and Revolution in Egypt: The Role of the Muslim Brotherhood.* The Hague: Mouton, 1964.

Vatikiotis, P. J. *The History of Modern Egypt: From Muhammad Ali to Mubarak,* 4th edition. Baltimore: Johns Hopkins University Press, 1991.

MATTHEW S. GORDON

REVOLUTIONARY COMMAND COUNCIL (LIBYA)

Leaders of Libya's 1969 revolution and subsequent government until 1977.

Following the overthrow of the Libyan monarchy on 1 September 1969, the central committee of the Free Unionist Officers movement designated itself the Revolutionary Command Council (RCC) in a December 1969 constitutional proclamation. Initially exercising both executive and legislative functions, the RCC took whatever measures it deemed necessary to protect the revolution. Even when the RCC later appointed outsiders to a council of ministers, it reserved supreme authority in all fields to itself.

The twelve members of the RCC shared similar backgrounds, motivations, and worldviews. Largely drawn from the lower middle class and minor tribes, most of its members graduated from the military academy in Benghazi at a time when a military career offered opportunities for upward socioeconomic mobility. The language of the RCC was the language of Arab nationalism, guided by precepts from the Qur'an and strengthened by the conviction that the revolutionary government spoke for the masses.

Members of the RCC constituted the cabinet of the Libyan government until 2 March 1977, when the Declaration of the Establishment of the People's Authority stated that direct popular authority would be the basis for a new Libyan political system. At that point, Muammar al-Qaddafi was designated general secretary of the newly formed General People's Congress and the remaining four members of the now defunct RCC composed its general secretariat.

See also JAMAHIRIYYA; LIBYA; QADDAFI, MUAMMAR AL-.

RONALD BRUCE ST JOHN

REVOLUTIONARY GUARDS

Iranian military organization created in 1979 to protect the Islamic revolution.

The Islamic Revolutionary Guards Corps, or *Sepah-e Pasdaran-e Enqelab-e Islami,* was formed in May 1979 as an ideologically committed force entrusted with protecting the political success of the Iranian Revolution from external and internal enemies. Initially, it comprised the several unofficial militias that had been organized spontaneously during the final weeks of the revolution in Tehran and other cities to protect demonstrators from the shah's security forces. These militias continued to grow after the revolution, taking on security functions and tracking down suspected counterrevolutionaries. Even though Iran's armed forces had declared political neutrality in February 1979, deep suspicions about military officers' loyalty to the revolution existed among the new revolutionary leaders. Consequently, the provisional government of Mehdi Bazargan accepted the argument that the various militias should be organized into a centralized force, the Revolutionary Guards, that could counter a potential military coup.

The Revolutionary Guards assumed a primary role in suppressing the armed autonomy movements among ethnic Baluchis, Kurds, and Turkmen in 1979 to 1980, the antigovernment demonstrations in Tabriz in December 1979, and the armed uprising by the Mojahedin-e Khalq that began in June 1981. They also had a central role in prosecuting the Iran-Iraq War, which Iraq initiated in September 1980 by launching an invasion of western Iran. Throughout the eight-year war, the Revolutionary Guards remained a separate and rival military force to the army, but after Ali Akbar Hashemi Rafsanjani became Iran's president in 1989, he implemented a policy of integrating the militaries as co-equal units of a National Defense Force with a unified command. In 2004 the Revolutionary Guards was a force of 120,000 men, the overwhelming majority of whom had elected to serve their compulsory 18-month military service in this branch of the armed forces.

The Revolutionary Guards has overall authority for the 40,000 volunteers of the paramilitary force known as the *Sepah-e Basij,* which was formed in November 1979. The impetus for organizing the Basij was a perceived need for a mobilized and armed population to confront a possible attack by the United States. At the time, there was widespread fear that the United States might attempt to overthrow the revolution and restore Mohammad Reza Shah Pahlavi, as it had done in 1953. Any Iranian sixteen years and older could join the Basij and receive training in the use of small arms. Some women joined, and the Basij organized several women's units. The majority of volunteers, however, were young men from the lower urban classes or from rural backgrounds, and they constituted an important source of recruits—hundreds of thousands—during the war with Iraq. Since 1989, the Revolutionary Guards generally, and its Basij militia specifically, have seen their mission to be maintaining the ideological purity of the revolution. Given the lack of consensus among the political elite with respect to what policies are consistent or inconsistent with revolutionary ideals, these guardian organizations of the revolution risk becoming entangled partisans in the intense factional politics that have characterized Iran since the early 1990s.

See also BALUCHIS; BAZARGAN, MEHDI; HOSTAGE CRISES; IRANIAN REVOLUTION (1979); IRAN–IRAQ WAR (1980–1988); KURDS; MOJAHEDIN-E KHALQ; PAHLAVI, MOHAMMAD REZA; RAFSANJANI, ALI AKBAR HASHEMI; TABRIZ.

Bibliography

Katzman, Kenneth. *Warriors of Islam: Iran's Revolutionary Guards.* Boulder, CO: Westview Press, 1993.

ERIC HOOGLUND

RICHMOND, ERNEST T.
[1874–1974]

Archaeologist and architect in Egypt during World War I.

Ernest T. Richmond served the Mission to Palestine as consulting architect for the Dome of the Rock Mosque in Jerusalem (1918–1919). As assistant to chief secretary Wyndham Deedes and then to Gilbert Clayton (1920–1924), he was given control of the Political Department of the Secretariat as a result of high commissioner Herbert Samuel's desire to protect Arab interests and to restrain Zionist excesses. Members of the Arab Executive saw Richmond as virtually their only friend in the British administration of Palestine. He was strongly disliked by the Zionists for his sympathies with the Arabs of Palestine and his opposition to Zionism.

Richmond helped secure the appointment of al-Hajj Amin al-Husayni as mufti of Jerusalem and president of the Supreme Muslim Council (SMC). He sought to expand the powers of the mufti and the jurisdiction of the SMC and to promote the latter as a partial counterweight to the Jewish Agency. Richmond became chief adviser to the high commissioner on Muslim affairs. When he resigned, he was appointed to the nonpolitical position of director of antiquities, in which capacity he served until 1937.

JENAB TUTUNJI

RIDA, RASHID
[1865–1935]

Disciple and biographer of Egyptian religious reformer Muhammad Abduh; editor of the Islamic modernist magazine al-Manar.

Rashid Rida was born in the village of Qalamun, near Tripoli, in what was then the Ottoman Empire and is now Lebanon. Rida came from a family of local prominence and piety. He attended the local Qur'an school and continued his education in Tripoli at an Ottoman state school and an Islamic school run by Shaykh Husayn al-Jisr. Although exposed to the Turkish and French languages, as well as to mathematics and Western science, Rida considered languages other than Arabic unnecessary for a scholar of Islam like himself. Inspired by the classic *Revival of the Religious Sciences* by Ahmad Abdullah al Ghazali, Rida joined the Naqshbandi Sufi order. An encounter with the dance of Mevlevi dervishes, however, shocked him into publicly denouncing what he took to be the excesses of Sufism.

Al-Urwa al-Wuthqa (The indissoluble bond), the magazine that Jamal al-Din al-Afghani and his disciple Muhammad Abduh issued from Parisian exile in the 1880s, awakened Rida to his life mission of reviving Islam. He hoped to join al-Afghani, who was then residing in Istanbul under Sultan Abdülhamit II's surveillance and never received Rida's letter. Afghani died in 1897; Rida went instead to Cairo to join Afghani's erstwhile disciple Muhammad Abduh—whom he had met twice before. Rida became Abduh's inseparable disciple, founding the magazine *al-Manar* in 1898 to spread Abduh's reformist Islamic, or Salafiyya, message.

For thirty seven years, until his death, Rida wrote much of *al-Manar* himself and published other religious works on the *al-Manar* press. His books in Arabic, usually serialized in *al-Manar* first, include the *Biography of the Master Imam Shaykh Muhammad Abduh* (3 vols.), *The Caliphate or Supreme Imamate, The Muhammadun Revelation,* biographies of the Prophet Muhammad and the caliphs Umar and Ali; with Abduh, an unfinished twelve-volume *Commentary on the Qur'an.*

Like Afghani and Abduh, Rida made the Islamic *umma* (community) his central concern, asking why it had declined relative to the modern West and blaming the decline on medieval additions to Islam—such as the reverence for Sufi saints—which obscured the pure religion of the ancestors (*salaf,* from which comes the name for the Salafiyya movement). He urged reformist *ulama* (Islamic leaders) to follow Abduh and himself in returning to the Qur'an and the *sunna* (body of customs) and interpreting them

afresh for the modern age. At first *al-Manar* concentrated its fire on the conservative *ulama* entrenched in the mosque-university of al-Azhar in Cairo. Rida blamed them for succumbing to the blandishments of the state, tolerating folk superstitions, and failing to mount a vigorous defense of Islam; by the 1920s, however, Rida had grown more conservative and came to see Western-inspired secularism and liberal nationalism as greater dangers. He drew nearer to the strict literalism of the Hanbali Law School, its fourteenth-century juridical theologian Ibn Taymiya, and their Muwahhidun proponents in Arabia. King Ibn Sa'ud of Arabia responded with financial support for Rida's activities.

After his early years with Afghani, Abduh had retreated from overt politics, but Rida made frequent forays into Ottoman, Syrian, Arab, and caliphal politics. He saw Sultan Abdülhamit II's rule in Syria as repressive, and *al-Manar* published the attack of Abd al-Rahman al-Kawakibi on Abdülhamit II and his call for restoring the caliphate (held by the Ottoman Turks) to the Arabs. Hoping that changed circumstances after the Young Turk Revolution of 1908 would allow him to open a school for Islamic propaganda and guidance, Rida spent a year in Istanbul. The authorities changed their minds, however, and Rida opened his school in Cairo in 1912, only to have it fall victim to World War I. Meanwhile, as a member of the Ottoman Decentralization Society, he protested the Young Turks' tightening grip on the Arab provinces. After the war, when Mustafa Kemal (Atatürk) abolished first the Ottoman sultanate and then the caliphate, *al-Manar* published a series of studies on the caliphate and the possibility of its revival by an Arab ruler. Rida had a hand in the rival caliphal congresses in Mecca and Cairo in 1926, which unsuccessfully advanced the claims of King Ibn Sa'ud of Arabia and King Fu'ad of Egypt for the office. In the mid-1920s, when Ali Abd al-Raziq denied the caliphate's Islamic legitimacy and Taha Husayn declared pre-Islamic Arabic poetry a later forgery, Rida found himself agreeing with the Azhari *ulama* in defending revered traditions. Rida had a final try at congress politics as a participant in the 1931 Islamic Congress in Jerusalem.

As a Syrian, Rida felt the tug of emerging Arab nationalism more than Iranian-born Afghani or Abduh, an Egyptian. *Al-Manar's* publication of Kawakibi and Rida's Decentralization Society activities had Arabist implications, and he was even chosen president of the Syrian Congress, which in 1920 declared the independence of the short-lived Syrian Arab kingdom under Faisal I ibn Hussein. After the French mandate over Syria was effected in 1921, Rida went to Geneva as vice president of a delegation to the League of Nations protesting the mandates granted to Britain and France in the Middle East as part of the peace settlements of World War I.

Rida's influence waned in the later years, and his death in 1935 attracted little notice. His most direct heir was Hasan al-Banna, who founded the Muslim Brotherhood in Egypt in 1928/29 and admired Rida's Islamic activism and his strict interpretation of the *shari'a* (Islamic law). Banna put out a few issues of *al-Manar* after Rida's death, but it disappeared in 1940.

Rida displayed an unusual blend of timidity and combativeness. He lacked the charisma of Afghani and Abduh before him and Hasan al-Banna after him. Rida's works are not widely read today; nevertheless, he was an essential link in the chain of Islamic activism running from Afghani and Abduh to Banna and Sayyid Qutb—and the present-day Muslim Brethren and their more radical Islamist offshoots.

See also ABDUH, MUHAMMAD; AFGHANI, JAMAL AL-DIN AL-.

Bibliography

Adams, C. C. *Islam and Modernism in Egypt.* London: Oxford University Press, 1933; reprint, New York: Routledge, 2000.

Haim, Sylvia, ed. *Arab Nationalism: An Anthology.* Berkeley: University of California Press, 1976.

Hourani, Albert. *Arabic Thought in the Liberal Age, 1798–1939.* Cambridge, U.K., and New York: Cambridge University Press, 1983.

Kerr, Malcolm H. *Islamic Reform: The Political and Legal Theories of Muhammad Abduh and Rashid Rida.* Berkeley: University of California Press, 1966.

Kramer, Martin. *Islam Assembled: The Advent of the Muslim Congresses.* New York: Columbia University Press, 1986.

Safran, Nadav. *Egypt in Search of Political Community: An Analysis of the Intellectual and Political Evolution of Egypt, 1804–1952.* Cambridge, MA: Harvard University Press, 1961.

DONALD MALCOLM REID

RIF

Moroccan mountain chain.

Contiguous with the Jibala massif at the western end, the Rif mountains run along the Mediterranean coast of Morocco for a distance of nearly 200 miles (300 km) but are nowhere more than 50 miles (80 km) wide. Some peaks rise to a height of 6,600 feet (2,000 m). Heavily wooded until clearance began in the seventeenth century, the region now suffers from environmental degradation and drought, and its largely Berber-speaking inhabitants have a history of labor migration.

Bibliography

McNeill, J. R. *The Mountains of the Mediterranean World: An Environmental History.* Cambridge, U.K., and New York: Cambridge University Press, 1992.

Mikesell, Marvin. *Northern Morocco: A Cultural Geography.* Berkeley: University of California Press, 1961.

C. R. PENNELL

RIFAAT, ALIFA
[1930–]

Egyptian fiction writer.

Alifa Rifaat (also Rif'at) was born in Cairo. She began her literary career under a pseudonym in 1955 with the publication of short stories in the magazine *al-Risala.* Her husband's opposition to her writing brought her literary career to a halt for over a decade. In 1972, she began publishing again, under her own name. A number of the stories Rifaat published in the 1970s and 1980s focus on women's fantasies and thoughts, exploring women's emotional lives and the psychological damage done to them by men, and also a system of social mores that does not take into account women's need for personal, sexual, and emotional fulfillment. Rifaat and other women writers who began publishing in the 1960s and 1970s were among the first to express feminist concerns in fictional form.

Deeply influenced by the Qur'an and other religious texts, Rifaat couches her social critique within an Islamic framework. Echoes of her concern for women's emotional and sexual well-being are found in the works of prominent writers of the 1970s generation, including Salwa Bakr and Ni'mat al-Bihayri. In 1981, Rifaat published her short story collection *Man yakun al-Rajul?* (Who will be the man?) and since then she has published four other collections in Arabic. A fifth collection, *Distant View of a Minaret,* was translated into English and published in 1983. Her first novel, *Jawharat Fir'awn* (Pharoah's jewel) was published in 1991.

See also BAKR, SALWA; GENDER: GENDER AND EDUCATION.

Bibliography

Al-Ali, Nadje Sadig. *Gender Writing/Writing Gender: The Representation of Women in a Selection of Modern Egyptian Literature.* Cairo: The American University in Cairo Press, 1994.

Booth, Marilyn. "Introduction." In *My Grandmother's Cactus.* London: Quartet Books, 1991.

Rifaat, Alifa. *Distant View of a Minaret,* translated by Denys Johnson-Davies. Oxford: Heinemann International, 1983.

CAROLINE SEYMOUR-JORN

RIFA'I, SAMIR AL-
[1899–1965]

Prime minister of Jordan during the period 1944 to 1963.

Born in Safed in Mandatory Palestine, Samir al-Rifa'i was noted for his resourcefulness, subtlety, and intelligence. As prime minister in 1944 and 1945, he participated in negotiations to establish the League of Arab States and signed the charter on behalf of Jordan. As prime minister when King Abdullah I ibn Hussein was assassinated, he handed power over to the veteran Tawfiq Abu al-Huda in July 1951.

Al-Rifa'i was asked to form a government on 9 January 1956, in the aftermath of anti-Baghdad Pact protests. He proclaimed martial law and decisively rejected the Baghdad Pact, refusing to sign "any new pacts." This allowed him to reject the Covenant of Arab Union at the same time. To prevent a rupture in ties with the United Kingdom and subsequent loss of British subsidies, al-Rifa'i favored renegotiating rather than abrogating the 1948 Anglo–Jordanian treaty. But this stand was very controversial. He remained in office this time until October 1956, when Sulayman al-Nabulsi, who opposed the relationship with Britain, was asked to form a government.

Following the "royal coup" of 25 April 1957, which ousted al-Nabulsi's cabinet, Rifa'i served as deputy premier and effective leader of the government in the cabinet of Ibrahim Hashim. He guided negotiations for Jordan's federation with Iraq, headed the regional cabinet in Amman during the federation, then continued as prime minister of Jordan after its breakup in 1958. Al-Rifa'i steered King Hussein ibn Talal through that difficult period and helped him survive plots by Colonel Abd al-Hammid Sarraj, the interior minister of Syria, when it was the "northern region" of the United Arab Republic (UAR). Al-Rifa'i also helped engineer Jordan's friendly ties with the United States and secured American subsidies, although Jordan never officially accepted the Eisenhower Doctrine. Unfortunately, al-Rifa'i became too closely identified with Jordan's quarrels with President Gamal Abdel Nasser of the UAR. A break in ties with the UAR followed, and al-Rifa'i resigned on 5 May 1959.

Al-Rifa'i formed his sixth and last cabinet on 27 March 1963, with a mandate to improve relations with Syria, Egypt, and Iraq. When the three countries agreed to form an expanded United Arab Republic, however, public demonstrations favoring Jordan's participation in the union led to clashes with the army, notably in the West Bank. Al-Rifa'i was on the verge of being denied a vote of confidence when he tendered his resignation. He went on to serve as president of the upper house of parliament, or Senate.

See also ABDULLAH I IBN HUSSEIN; ABU AL-HUDA, TAWFIQ; BAGHDAD PACT (1955); HASHIM, IBRAHIM; HUSSEIN IBN TALAL; LEAGUE OF ARAB STATES; NABULSI, SULAYMAN AL-; NASSER, GAMAL ABDEL; UNITED ARAB REPUBLIC (UAR).

Bibliography

Abidi, Aqil Hyder Hasan. *Jordan: A Political Study, 1948–1957.* New York: Asia Publishing House, 1965.

Dann, Uriel. *King Hussein and the Challenge of Arab Radicalism: Jordan, 1955–1967.* New York: Oxford University Press, 1989.

JENAB TUTUNJI

RIFA'I, ZAID AL-
[1936–]

Jordanian politician.

Son of the prominent Jordanian politician Samir al-Rifa'i, who was of Palestinian origin, Zaid (also Zayd) al-Rifa'i was known as a boyhood friend and loyal confidant of Jordan's King Hussein ibn Talal. He held numerous positions in the Foreign Ministry before beginning service to the king in 1964, where he eventually rose to chief of the royal court (1969), political adviser to the king (1972–1973), prime minister/defense minister/foreign minister (1973–1976), and prime minister/foreign minister (1985–1989).

Jordan suffered a series of setbacks in the early 1980s as the effects of petroleum pricing in the Gulf states battered its once-booming economy. Jordan became more dependent on loans and struggled with high inflation. The al-Rifa'i government introduced a series of austerity measures in November 1986 and March 1989, the latter in consultation with the International Monetary Fund. New taxes and sharp increases in consumer prices led to rioting in traditionally pro-regime districts, such as Ma'an and al-Karak, along with denunciations of corruption in the al-Rifa'i government and calls for his resignation. After al-Rifa'i quickly resigned, King Hussein announced that general parliamentary elections would be held in November 1989, for the first time since 1967. Al-Rifa'i was later appointed to the Jordanian senate, and served as president.

See also HUSSEIN IBN TALAL; KARAK, AL-; RIFA'I, SAMIR AL-.

Bibliography

The Middle East and North Africa, 37th edition. London: Europa Publications, 1991.

Piro, Timothy J. *The Political Economy of Market Reform in Jordan.* Lanham, MD, and Oxford: Rowman & Littlefield, 1998.

MICHAEL R. FISCHBACH

RIF WAR

One of the most successful Moroccan attempts to resist an initial European invasion, 1921–1926.

The Treaty of Fes (1912), imposing a French protectorate over Morocco, assigned northern and

Led by Muhammad ibn Abd al Karim al-Khattabi, Moroccan tribesmen rebelled against Spanish rule in 1912. They inflicted many defeats on the Spanish before finally being overwhelmed by combined French and Spanish forces in 1926. Here, Moroccans man artillery in 1923. © HULTON-DEUTSCH COLLECTION/CORBIS. REPRODUCED BY PERMISSION.

southern zones to Spain. Until the end of World War I, the Spanish army and economy were not strong enough to take advantage of this. But, in 1919, the Spanish army began to push westward from Melilla into the Rif mountains, and a loosely organized coalition was formed to oppose it. In 1920 Muhammad ibn Abd al-Karim al-Khattabi took over leadership of the coalition and set about creating unity based on the strict imposition of the *shari'a,* allied with European military techniques.

By June 1921 Spanish military intelligence was warning that Abd al-Karim's supporters could resist further Spanish advances, despite the 25,000 troops in the eastern zone. The warnings were ignored, new advance garrisons set up, and on 2 June the Rifis attacked a post at Dahar Abarran. The garrison was withdrawn, but other posts came under attack. On 22 July, the main Spanish forward base at Anwal withdrew with heavy casualties. The retreat became a rout, and by 9 August all Spanish positions outside Melilla were lost and over 13,000 soldiers killed. Melilla was not occupied because Abd al-Karim, concerned that he might lose control, wanted to avoid the slaughter of civilians.

In little more than a year, Spanish forces had almost regained their old lines, but Abd al-Karim used the supplies they had abandoned to equip a regular army. He capitalized on the prestige of his victory to institutionalize a bureaucratic government in the central Rif, staffed largely by members of his own family. He emphasized the *shari'a*, both for ideological reasons and to ensure order. An infrastructure—roads and a telegraph system—was built to maintain control and better fight the Spanish. In February 1923 he received formal *bay'as* (declarations of allegiance) from the central Rif tribes and established a Rifi state.

Abd al-Karim overcame such local opponents as Ahmad ibn Muhammad al Raysuni, a sharif of the Jibala mountains, and Abd al-Rahman al Darqawi, head of the Darqawiyya *tariqa* whose headquarters at Amjutt were just over the figurative border of the French zone. Both of the local chiefs resented Abd al-Karim's growing authority, but in doing so came into conflict with the French and Spanish. The attack on isolated Spanish outposts in the Jibala began in August 1925, and in November Spanish forces withdrew from the town of Shawin. The Spanish army lost around 10,000 men.

Abd al-Karim was reluctant to attack the French zone. He did not want to have to fight two European armies. He agreed because he needed to secure food supplies and deal with the Darqawiyya and because of pressure from some of his commanders. The attack on Amjutt in April 1925 succeeded, and Rifi forces moved on Fez, overrunning many French positions. The French army held the Rifi attack, and in June 1925 a conference in Madrid agreed on a joint Franco-Spanish campaign to crush the Rifis.

In September 1925 Spanish landings at Alhucemas and French advances from the south were coordinated. By the winter, the Rif was surrounded and running out of food. The following April, brief peace negotiations at Oujda, in eastern Morocco, failed and Rifi resistance collapsed. On 15 May 1926, Abd al-Karim surrendered to the French.

See also KHATTABI, MUHAMMAD IBN ABD AL-KARIM AL-; *SHARI'A*.

Bibliography

Pennell, C. R. *A Country with a Government and a Flag: The Rif War in Morocco, 1921–1926*. Wisbech, U.K.: Middle East and North African Studies Press, 1986.

Woolman, David. *Rebels in the Rif, Abd el-Krim and the Rif Rebellion*. Stanford, CA: Stanford University Press, 1969.

C. R. PENNELL

RISHON LE-ZION

Town in central Israel, seven miles southeast of Tel Aviv, stretching to the Mediterranean coastline.

Formerly known as Ayun Qara, Rishon le-Zion was founded in 1882 by ten Zionist settlers from Russia under the leadership of Zalman Levontin. They were soon joined by 100 additional pioneers. They experienced severe difficulties in the early years, including lack of funds and water resources, but financial support provided by Baron Edmond de Rothschild, who bought back the land from them and provided monthly stipends and funds to plant vineyards, culminated in 1889 in the opening of Carmel wine cellars. The first Hebrew kindergarten and elementary school opened in Rishon le-Zion during the 1880s; the first agricultural workers' association was founded there in 1887.

At the beginning of the twentieth century, Rishon le-Zion became a cultural and social center, with its own orchestra and choir. The lyrics of the national anthem were written there by Naphtali Imber. The Jewish National Fund was founded there and the first telephone system and electrical generator were installed in Rishon. The town's urbanization began in the 1950s and by the 1970s Rishon had become a densely populated urban center. By the end of 2002, the population had surpassed 211,500 and the town was considered part of the Tel Aviv metropolitan area.

See also LEVONTIN, ZALMAN; ROTHSCHILD, EDMOND DE; TEL AVIV.

BRYAN DAVES
UPDATED BY YEHUDA GRADUS

RIYADH

Saudi Arabia's capital and largest city.

Riyadh is located in the southern Najd region. More correctly transliterated as *al-Riyad* ("the gardens"), the city is also the capital of a large province of the same name. Nearby are the ruins of al-Dir'iyya, the original seat of the Al Sa'ud family until an invading Egyptian army destroyed the village in 1818 and put an end to the first Saudi state. The Al Sa'ud thereupon relocated at Riyadh, which became the capital of the second Saudi state of the mid-nineteenth century. With a second decline in

Saudi fortunes, Riyadh was lost to the rival Al Rashid dynasty of Haʾil in 1891. But in 1902, Abd al-Aziz ibn Abd al-Rahman (also known as Ibn Saʿud) infiltrated the town with a small band of followers. Launching a surprise attack on al-Musmak fortress, Abd al-Aziz succeeded in capturing the Al Rashid governor and restoring Saudi control over Riyadh.

Over the next two decades, the Al Saʿud used Riyadh as their base to extend their authority once again over all of Najd. From the late 1920s, Saudi Arabia had two capitals, with the king resident in Riyadh, the capital of Najd, but most of the ministries and embassies located in al-Hijaz. By 1955 most government ministries and head offices had moved to Riyadh. The Foreign Ministry and foreign embassies remained in Jiddah until 1985, when they too were required to move to the capital. Riyadh's population was estimated at only 169,000 in 1962, but the oil boom (beginning in 1974) dramatically transformed the city and caused its population to increase to over 1.5 million. By 2003 the capital's population was estimated at nearly 4.5 million. The skyline has been enhanced in recent years by two skyscrapers, the thirty-story al-Faysaliyya Center and the Kingdom Tower.

Very little of the old city remains intact; the old mud-brick fort of al-Musmak has been preserved and Ibn Saʿud's al-Murabbi Palace was restored during the country's centennial celebrations in 1999. Many buildings in the new diplomatic quarter, which is known as al-Dirʿiyya because of its proximity to the old village, imitate the traditional mud-brick architecture. Near this quarter are located the new King's Office Complex (al-Yamama Palace) and the headquarters of the Gulf Cooperation Council. Also nearby is the campus of King Saʿud University; founded in 1957, it is the country's oldest university. Imam Muhmmad ibn Saʿud University, one of the kingdom's three Islamic universities, is located in Riyadh as well. The city is the inland terminus of a railroad from al-Dammam on the Persian Gulf coast, and the previous international airport has become a major air force base. The government is the largest employer in Riyadh, although light industry and retail firms are also important.

See also AL SAʿUD FAMILY.

Bibliography

Facey, William. *Riyadh: The Old City from Its Origins until the 1950s.* London: Immel, 1992.

J. E. PETERSON

RIYADH ARAB SUMMIT

See ARAB LEAGUE SUMMITS

RIYAD, MAHMUD
[1917–1992]

Egyptian diplomat and former secretary-general of the League of Arab States.

In 1939, Mahmud Riyad enrolled in the Egyptian Military Academy and obtained a master's degree in military sciences. In 1948, he headed the Egyptian delegation to the armistice talks with the Israelis in Rhodes. In 1955, he was appointed ambassador to Syria, and two years later he participated in the Syria–Egyptian unity talks. On 1 June 1972, he was elected secretary-general of the League of Arab States. As secretary-general he played an important role in mediating the conflict between the two Yemens (1972), the border conflict between Iraq and Kuwait (1973), and the Palestine Liberation Organization–Lebanese government clashes in 1973.

GEORGE E. IRANI

RIYAD, MUSTAFA AL-
[1834–1911]

Egyptian official, cabinet minister, and three-time premier.

The origins of Mustafa al-Riyad, usually known as Riyaz Pasha during his lifetime, are obscure; he may have been Jewish. In Egypt, he began his career as a clerk in the foreign ministry and then in the army. Aide-de-camp for Abbas Hilmi I, he then held a succession of provincial governorships. Khedive Ismaʿil entrusted various ministerial portfolios to him. He contributed to Egypt's intellectual life by inviting Jamal al-Din al-Afghani and the editors of *al-Muqtataf* to settle there and also provided an endowment for the newly founded National Library. He backed Egypt's foreign creditors against Khedive Ismaʿil and helped write the 1880 liquidation law, which reduced Egyptian government indebtedness by strictly limiting expenditures.

Riyad underestimated the strength of the Egyptian officers in his first term as head of Egypt's government. Having acceded to their demand to dismiss his war minister in February 1881, he had to resign after their Abdin demonstration in September of that year. He stayed in Europe as long as the followers of Ahmad Urabi held sway. He served again as head of Egypt's government from 1888 to 1891 and from 1894 to 1895. He was widely thought to oppose the British occupation and to support the establishment of Cairo's first Muslim-owned daily, al-Mu'ayyad. He favored bringing in Western technology but resisted the growing power of Europeans over Egyptian finances, justice, and government.

Bibliography

Hunter, F. Robert. *Egypt under the Khedives, 1805–1879: From Household Government to Modern Bureaucracy.* Pittsburgh: University of Pittsburgh Press, 1984.

Moberly-Bell, C. F. *Khedives and Pashas.* London: S. Low, 1884.

Sayyid-Marsot, Afaf Lutfi. *Egypt and Cromer: A Study in Anglo-Egyptian Relations.* London: Murray, 1968.

Schölch, Alexander. *Egypt for the Egyptians! The Socio-Political Crisis in Egypt, 1878–1882.* London: Ithaca Press, 1981.

ARTHUR GOLDSCHMIDT

RIYAL

See GLOSSARY

ROCKEFELLER MUSEUM

Name popularly given to the Palestine Archaeological Museum in Jerusalem.

The museum, which opened in 1938, was funded by $2 million pledged by John D. Rockefeller, Jr., to match an endowment fund. The building, designed by Austen St. Barbe. Harrison, stands on ten acres facing the Old City walls. In addition to exhibition space, there are study galleries, record offices, a library, an auditorium, and offices. An ancient cemetery, dating from the sixth and fifth centuries B.C.E., was discovered on the site and excavated.

Before the termination of Britain's Palestine Mandate in 1948, the building was turned over to an international board. In November 1966, Jordan nationalized the museum and took possession of the building and its contents. After capturing Jerusalem during the Arab-Israel War of 1967, Israel took over the museum, claiming it as captured Jordanian state property. It entrusted the museum to the Israeli Department of Antiquities, which invited the Israel Museum to operate the exhibition galleries. This move created controversy. For example, when the Israel Museum tried to include some items from the Rockefeller Museum in an exhibition in the United States entitled "Treasures from the Holy Land: Ancient Art from the Israel Museum" in 1985, the Metropolitan Museum of Art in New York City challenged Israel's acquisition of some of the items. The U.S. Smithsonian Institution then agreed to host the exhibit the following year, but objected to the inclusion of eleven artifacts from the Rockefeller Museum. Israel refused to change the exhibition, which consequently was not shown.

See also ARAB–ISRAEL WAR (1967); ARCHAEOLOGY IN THE MIDDLE EAST.

Bibliography

Reed, Stephen A. *The Dead Sea Scrolls Catalogue: Documents, Photographs and Museum Inventory Numbers.* Atlanta: Scholars Press, 1994.

MIA BLOOM
UPDATED BY MICHAEL R. FISCHBACH

ROGERS, WILLIAM PIERCE
[1913–2001]

American secretary of state, 1969 to 1973.

William Pierce Rogers was born in June 1913 in Norfolk, New York. He graduated from Colgate University in 1934 and received a law degree from Cornell University in 1937. He served three Republican presidents in a public career that lasted nearly fifty years: He was Dwight Eisenhower's attorney general (1957–1961) and Richard M. Nixon's secretary of state (1969–1973) and in 1986, under Ronald Reagan, he headed the investigation into the *Challenger* space shuttle disaster.

As secretary of state, Rogers promoted a ceasefire in the Middle East that lasted from 1970 until the 1973 war. His 1970 Rogers Peace Initiative was an effort to implement the 1967 UN Security Council Resolution 242, which put forth principles for peace negotiations between Arabs and Israelis, including the principle of land for peace. Rogers's objective was "to encourage the parties to move to a just and lasting peace." The initiative was one of the key efforts that contributed to peace between Egypt and Israel in 1979.

Rogers was a 1973 recipient of the U.S. Presidential Medal of Freedom, the nation's highest civilian honor, and he received several honorary doctorates, including one his alma mater, Colgate. He died of congestive heart disease in January 2001.

See also UNITED NATIONS AND THE MIDDLE EAST; UNITED STATES OF AMERICA AND THE MIDDLE EAST.

Bibliography

Nixon, Richard M. *RN: The Memoirs of Richard Nixon.* New York: Simon and Schuster, 1990.

ZACHARY KARABELL
UPDATED BY AHMED H. IBRAHIM

ROLO FAMILY

Sephardic Jewish family of businessmen who had settled in Alexandria by the mid-nineteenth century.

The Rolo family produced a number of well-known and influential businessmen, among them Ruben (b. 1820), and his sons Simon, Giacomo (1847–1917), Robert S. (b. 1869), and Robert J. (b. 1876).

Robert S. Rolo gained the strongest influence in Egypt's economy among the family's members, since he served as a legal advisor to Crown Prince Fu'ad and was later regarded as a close confidant of the king, serving as an indispensable intermediary between the royal court and the British residency. He also served as director of the Egypt National Bank for many years. Ruben, Simon, and Giacomo Rolo joined forces with other Sephardic families, notably the Suarès and Cattaoui, in promoting such economic enterprises as the Helwan Railway and in creating Kum Ombo, Egypt's well-known agricultural company. Robert J. Rolo served as the president of Alexandria's Jewish community between 1934 and 1948.

Bibliography

Krämer, Gudrun. *The Jews in Modern Egypt: 1914–1952.* Seattle: University of Washington Press, 1989.

Landau, Jacob M. *Jews in Nineteenth Century Egypt.* New York: New York University Press, 1969.

Mizrahi, Maurice. "The Role of the Jews in Economic Development." In *The Jews of Egypt: A Mediterranean Society in Modern Times,* edited by Shimon Shamir. Boulder, CO: Westview Press, 1987.

MICHAEL M. LASKIER

ROMAN CATHOLICISM AND ROMAN CATHOLIC MISSIONS

Native Middle Eastern groups or individuals or those who established religious institutions there to convert people to Roman Catholicism.

The term *Catholic* is ambiguous in the Middle East. In Arabic, it refers to the Melkites; in English, it refers to Christians of the Latin rite, usually called Roman Catholics in the United States.

Since the Christian Church evolved in the Middle East, differences in theology and ritual that had existed for centuries between the eastern and western parts of the Roman Empire led to a schism in 1054. In the West (Europe) the Latin rite became basic to the Roman Catholic church. In the East (Byzantium) the Byzantine state church prevailed until the rise of Islam in the seventh century C.E. The expansion of Islam was rapid, with Muslims conquering North Africa and the Iberian peninsula by the eighth century and ruling until the fifteenth century. In 1009 Muslims destroyed the Holy Sepulchre in Jerusalem; in 1095 Pope Urban II called for a holy war to "rescue the Holy Land from the Muslim infidels." To do this, the First Crusade was organized in 1096. The Crusaders, under Godfrey of Bouillon, succeeded in conquering Jerusalem in 1099. Seven more Crusades followed, with successes and failures, until the Mamluks of Egypt conquered Acre in 1291, evicting the Crusaders.

The Roman Catholic Church was reestablished in the Middle East in 1099, when a hierarchy under a Latin partriarchate at Jerusalem was established. By the end of the thirteenth century, however, after the Crusaders were evicted from the region, only the Franciscan Brothers stayed on as custodians of the shrines. As the Crusader venture collapsed, the pope's contacts with the Mongols in central Asia inspired the Franciscan and Dominican orders to work among them, in the Ilkhanate of Persia, during the thirteenth and fourteenth centuries. Then after the fall of Constantinople (now Istanbul) to the Ottoman Turks in 1453—which ended the Byzantine Empire—Franciscan, Capuchin, Dominican, Carmelite, and later, Jesuit missionaries went to the provinces of the Ottoman Empire under the protection of European powers to try to convert Eastern Christians to Roman Catholicism.

In the nineteenth century the Latin-rite presence in North Africa increased because of the French occupation of Algeria. The ancient see of Carthage was restored in 1876. Cardinal Lavigerie was named primate of Africa, with more than one million Catholics in Morocco, Algeria, and Tunisia—where he founded the White Fathers and White Sisters to work in the region.

In 1847 the Latin patriarchate of Jerusalem had been reestablished and numerous missionaries, engaged in education and nursing, had been sent to Ottoman Palestine. During the twentieth century, however, with the dismantling of the Ottoman Empire by the Allies after World War I and the post–World War II independence of Israel, Tunisia, Algeria, and Morocco, the Roman Catholic presence dwindled both in North Africa and in Palestine.

In 1990 the number of Latin-rite Roman Catholics throughout the Middle East was estimated to be 1.3 million (about 35 percent are migrant workers from Sri Lanka, India, and the Philippines). Some 566,000 Roman Catholics are indigenous to Sudan and more than 60,000 live in the West Bank and Jordan. These discrete communities are unusual for the region; most of the other Catholics form small communities or are family groups who left other local Christian churches, especially one of the Eastern Orthodox (which include the Nestorian and the Monophysite churches—the Coptic, Ethiopian, Armenian, and the Mar Thoma of India) or Uniate churches.

Arabia and the Gulf

The jurisdiction of the apostolic vicar for Arabia extends to the countries of the Arabian peninsula and the Gulf, excluding Kuwait, which has its own vicar. There are few local Catholics, but there are large

Students study theology at the Camboni School in Khartoum, the capital city of Sudan. © GILBERT LIZ/CORBIS SYGMA. REPRODUCED BY PERMISSION.

numbers of Palestinian, Indian, Sri Lankan, and Filipino workers in the region. The *Annuario Pontificio* counts 470,000 for 1990. There are parishes in the United Arab Emirates (U.A.E.) and Bahrain and Catholic schools in the U.A.E. and in Kuwait. In Saudi Arabia chaplains for foreign workers are allowed to operate "clandestinely," although this provokes occasional troubles. In North Yemen the government has called in nursing sisters to staff hospitals, and there are a few priests to care for expatriate Catholics.

Egypt

The three vicariates in Egypt had been reduced to one at Alexandria. While the official count of Latin Catholics is only 8,000, there are some 200 men and 1,000 women members of Latin orders and congregations, mostly engaged in education.

Syria

Syria, with a vicariate at Aleppo, lists 12,000 Latin Catholics, with about 250 men and women engaged in social and apostolic work since Catholic schools were closed in 1967.

Iraq

Baghdad is an episcopal see with an archbishop, but Latins number only a few thousand, and since

Catholic schools were closed in Iraq, only a few Latin-rite religious orders remain, staffing a seminary, a parish, and a hospital.

Lebanon

Lebanon has a large number of Latin-rite religious orders and congregations, with about 250 men and over 1,000 women working in 150 Catholic schools, a university, several hospitals, and numerous social ministries. The community numbers about 20,000.

West Bank and Jordan

In the West Bank and Jordan a substantial Palestinian community of 60,000 Roman Catholics has its own patriarch and diocesan clergy (about 60) who celebrate the Latin rite in Arabic. There is a Catholic University at Bethlehem and over 270 educational establishments. As this region is the Holy Land, it is a center for several Catholic religious orders.

Sudan

The largest Middle Eastern indigenous Roman Catholic community is found in Sudan. Some 217,000 Roman Catholics are in Juba and some 348,000 are in Khartoum. Each city has its local ordinary with a growing diocesan clergy aided by a few hundred men and women in non-Sudanese orders. The famine in the south has caused the displacement of many Sudanese Catholics.

North Africa

Morocco has two residential sees, one in Tangiers and one in Rabat, caring for some 40,000 Catholics, including over 200 men and women in religious orders engaged in a variety of social and educational works.

Algeria has a metropolitan see at Algiers with suffragan bishops in Oran and Constantine ministering to over 40,000 Catholics. Men and women in religious orders number about 350, many engaged in secular roles. In both Morocco and Algeria the diocesan clergy is substantial (about 50 in each) but of European origin.

There has been a prelature in Tunis since 1964, when a Vatican accord with the government suppressed the see of Carthage and closed all but 7 of its 100 churches. Catholics number over 15,000, cared for by 15 priests. Over 200 men and women in religious orders work in a variety of apostolates, including the research institute and library of the White Fathers.

Libya has a vicar apostolic and about 30 women in religious orders working in hospitals. Four religious men and one diocesan priest care for the spiritual needs of the 30,000 or so expatriate Catholics.

Iran and Turkey

Iran has a bishopric at Isfahan and a few priests and nuns caring for the Latin-rite community of 2,000. Turkey has an episcopal see in İzmir and a vicariate in Istanbul for some 7,000 Catholics. The number of Roman Catholic expatriates fluctuates with economic conditions; still, their presence in the Middle East, which had been relatively stable, is now in decline. Missionary vocations are sparse, and the need for educational and social help from expatriates is narrowing. At the same time, the Vatican is concerned about the increased emigration from indigenous Latin communities that has been provoked by political constraint and the resurgence of pan-Islamic sentiment.

Bibliography

Atiya, Aziz S. *A History of Eastern Christianity,* enlarged and updated edition. Millwood, NY: Kraus Reprint, 1980.

Betts, Robert Brenton. *Christians in the Arab East: A Political Study,* revised edition. Atlanta: John Knox Press, 1978.

JOHN J. DONOHUE

ROMANIZATION

Writing the Turkish language in the Latin alphabet.

Turkic peoples have used a variety of scripts in the course of their history, the earliest being the Orkhon script known through eighth-century inscriptions found in Mongolia. With conversion to Islam, the Turks adopted the Arabic script and used it over the centuries. On 9 August 1928, Mustafa Kemal (Atatürk), president of the new Republic of Turkey, announced its replacement by a Latin alphabet—essentially phonetic, omitting q, w, and x; adding ç

($=ch$), ğ ("soft" g), and ş ($=sh$); and including eight vowels: a, e, i, ı, o, ö, u, and ü.

Dissatisfaction with the Arabic script was not new. Discussion of and experimentation in modifying it date from the Tanzimat. The script, ill-suited to the Turkish phonetic system and hard to read and write (or print), was thus a prime cause of illiteracy. It symbolized adherence to Islam and Arab–Persian culture, and at a time when he was leading Turkey toward a new, Western-oriented way of life, Atatürk considered it a major obstacle to progress.

As for the Latin script, Namik Kemal was among the first to mention it as a suitable alternative (1879). Articles favoring it appeared in the early twentieth century, and Atatürk himself demonstrated its possibilities in Turkish sections of letters (otherwise in French) sent to a friend after becoming military attaché in Sofia (1913). During World War I, however, Enver Paşa devised a modified Arabic script for the military, but this had little effect.

Discussion continued under the republic, but a proposal for Latin letters was rejected at the 1923 İzmir Economic Congress. Interest increased, however, with the announcement of a romanization policy for the USSR's Turkic languages (a policy later reversed in favor of Cyrillic). On 24 May 1928 the Grand National Assembly legislated the introduction of international numerals, and Atatürk determined to proceed with the alphabet. A commission studying the plan submitted its proposed alphabet on 1 August 1928. Eight days later Atatürk announced its adoption, admonishing everyone to learn it as a patriotic duty.

Atatürk also demanded a speedy transition, and on 3 November 1928 the Grand National Assembly approved the new script. Turks were required to prove ability to use it in place of the Arabic script by the beginning of 1929, passing an examination or attending "national schools" set up across the country. The assembly also decreed that printing in the old script was illegal, and by the middle of 1929 all publications were being printed in the new script.

Romanization coupled with language reform affected many aspects of Turkish life. By breaking with traditions of the Ottoman-Islamic past, it stimulated Turkish nationalism and secularization. It facilitated dissemination of information, improved education and the literacy level, speeded modernization and technology through increased interaction with the West, and helped lead Turks to ever greater social and political awareness.

See also ARABIC SCRIPT; İZMIR ECONOMIC CONGRESS; TURKISH LANGUAGE.

Bibliography

Feyzioğlu, Turhan. "Secularism: Cornerstone of the Turkish Revolution." In *Atatürk's Way*. Istanbul, 1982.

Levonian, Lutfi, ed. and trans. *The Turkish Press: Selections from the Turkish Press Showing Events and Opinions, 1925–1932*. Athens: School of Religion, 1932.

Lewis, Bernard. *The Emergence of Modern Turkey*, 3d edition. New York: Oxford University Press, 2002.

Sperco, Willy. *Moustapha Kemal Atatürk, 1882–1938*. Paris: Nouvelles Editions Latine, 1958.

KATHLEEN R. F. BURRILL

ROME, TREATY OF

French–Italian pact in which some Middle Eastern territory changed hands.

In an effort to obtain Italy's support against Nazi Germany, France's foreign minister Pierre Laval signed the Treaty of Rome with Italy's dictator Benito Mussolini on 7 January 1935. France conceded small amounts of land in North and East Africa to Italy and, according to some accounts, the negotiations involved an unwritten pledge by Laval to support Italian claims in Ethiopia. When World War II began in 1939, Italy was allied with Germany, and Germany occupied France, so prewar agreements were negated or renegotiated.

Bibliography

Hurewitz, J. C., ed. *The Middle East and North Africa in World Politics: A Documentary Record*, 2d edition. 2 vols. New Haven, CT: Yale University Press, 1975–1979.

Taylor, A. J. P. *The Origins of the Second World War*. New York: Atheneum, 1961.

ZACHARY KARABELL

ROMMEL, ERWIN
[1891–1944]

German general (field marshal) in World War II.

Erwin Rommel (1891–1944), shown with a German officer in a car during inspection of German troops sent to aid the Italian army in Libya, North Africa, in 1941. Rommel, a German general, was called the "Desert Fox" for his brilliant military acts in World War II battles in North Africa. © AP/WIDE WORLD PHOTOS. REPRODUCED BY PERMISSION.

Erwin Rommel, the Desert Fox, is best known as the commander of the Afrika Korps, which took North Africa during the early years of World War II. Assuming command in February 1941, Rommel reversed Italian setbacks and crossed North Africa from west to east, driving the British into Egypt by May 1942. Hitler ordered a drive on Cairo and the Suez Canal, which led to the defeat of the Afrika Korps at al-Alamayn in November 1942, while Rommel was on sick leave in Germany. With his troops in retreat from the British Eighth Army, Rommel retired to Germany in March 1943, disenchanted with war and Hitler's politics. Implicated in a plot on Hitler's life, he committed suicide by poison in October 1944.

See also ALAMAYN, AL-.

Bibliography

Young, Desmond. *Rommel: The Desert Fox.* New York: Harper, 1950.

DANIEL E. SPECTOR

ROOSEVELT, FRANKLIN DELANO
[1882–1945]

Thirty-second president of the United States.

Franklin Delano Roosevelt was born at Hyde Park, New York; he died of a cerebral hemorrhage at Warm Springs, Georgia. Born into a wealthy family (a distant cousin of President Theodore Roosevelt), he attended Groton, Harvard, and Columbia Law. In 1905, he married Anna Eleanor Roosevelt (another distant cousin), and in 1907 began a law practice in New York City.

Early Career

His political career began in 1910, with his election to the New York State Senate. An opponent of the Democratic party's machine in New York City called Tammany Hall, he soon gained a reputation for independence and progressivism within the Democratic party. He worked for Woodrow Wilson's presidential campaign and was made assistant secretary of the Navy in Wilson's administration from 1913 to 1920, becoming the Democratic nominee for vice president in 1920. When the Cox/Roosevelt ticket lost to the Republican Harding/Coolidge ticket, he returned to his law practice. In August 1921, infantile paralysis left his legs and lower abdomen paralyzed.

Through exercise and treatment, Roosevelt recovered some movement of his lower limbs and was able to continue his law practice and civic affairs. He supported the popular New York City Democrat Alfred E. Smith in the presidential races of 1924 and 1928, then reentered elective politics himself to win the governorship of New York State in 1928 and 1930. In 1932, during the worst of the Great Depression, he won the first of his four presidential elections. His New Deal helped him remain in office throughout the Depression and World War II—one of the most pivotal periods of the nation's history.

Presidential Career—Foreign Policy and World War II

During the 1930s, Roosevelt's foreign policy reflected the isolationist mood of the nation. Relations with Germany, Italy, and Japan cooled; neutrality prevailed after Italy's attacks in North Africa and Germany's on Poland (1939); and the Lend-Lease Program of March 1941 provided matériel to Britain and other nations at war before the United States formally entered World War II in December 1941, after Japan's attack on Pearl Harbor.

During World War II, Roosevelt cooperated closely with the Allies, including the Soviet Union.

He traveled to hold a series of conferences with the heads of state of the major Allied powers, in which he agreed that Europe would be the first priority, with a second front opened against Germany and Italy (the Axis) at the earliest time. This began with the invasion of North Africa by U.S. and British forces in November 1942 (against German and Italian troops), followed by landings on Sicily (a German-occupied Italian island in the Mediterranean) in July 1943, and culminating with the invasion of German-held Normandy (northern France) in June 1944. Crucial to the European theater was the support of Middle Eastern countries. During the December 1943 Tehran Conference, Roosevelt sponsored a communiqué recognizing Iran's contributions to the war effort and expressing support for Iran's independence and territorial integrity. Shortly thereafter, Roosevelt and Britain's Prime Minister Winston Churchill met in Cairo and requested that Turkey enter the war, a goal that had been pursued by the British since late 1942. Turkey agreed in principle, in exchange for arms support, but a British mission in early 1944 was unable to achieve much; Turkey finally declared war on Germany in February 1945.

Japan's forces were being steadily conquered in the Pacific islands and nations under their occupation and control, and Roosevelt insisted on a policy of unconditional surrender, with the formation of a United Nations to guide world peace in the postwar years. Although he did not live to see either, his vice president, Harry S. Truman, became president on his death, 12 April 1945; Truman had two atomic bombs (developed during the Roosevelt Administration) dropped on Japan in August 1945 and received Japan's unconditional surrender 14 August 1945; Germany had already surrendered in May 1945. Truman also appointed Roosevelt's widow, Eleanor, to join the U.S. delegation at the United Nations; there she headed the UN Commission on Human Rights and was influential in helping to settle the Palestine partition in 1947/48 that resulted in the formation of the State of Israel (1948), which Truman was the first to recognize and back with diplomatic relations.

Wartime Policies toward Refugee Jews and the Middle East

During the war years, victory had been Roosevelt's primary objective. By 1942, although it was clear

U.S. president Franklin Delano Roosevelt met with Winston Churchill in Casablanca, Morocco, in 1943. Here they announced that they would accept only an unconditional surrender by the Axis nations. This conference set the basis and direction for the rest of the war. COURTESY OF THE FRANKLIN DELANO ROOSEVELT LIBRARY. REPRODUCED BY PERMISSION.

that Hitler's program aimed at territorial conquest, it was also clear that total destruction of Europe's Jews was part of the Nazi plan. Advised by members of his administration that any increase in U.S. immigration would meet strong opposition and might affect a successful war effort, Roosevelt did not pursue that route of relief. He also declined to overcome the objections of the U.S. Department of State to ransoming Jews from Nazi-occupied Romania, Bulgaria, and France. He was told that using war matériel to move Jews to Palestine and/or North Africa might incite the Arabs or even cause vindictive action by the Nazis. As the war progressed, the role of petroleum-rich Saudi Arabia increased in importance to the United States.

Before 1940, the United States had no diplomatic representation in Saudi Arabia. The primary U.S. presence was the Arabian American Oil Company (ARAMCO), which had been operating a sixty-year oil concession since 1933. With the beginning of war, ARAMCO activities were curtailed and Muslim pilgrims ceased their pilgrimages to Mecca and Medina—both of which caused an economic crisis for Saudi Arabia. Although Germany and Japan would have welcomed the chance to provide assistance and gain an influential oil-rich ally, Saudi King Ibn Saʿud preferred to continue his alliance with the United States; in early 1941, he requested a loan of thirty million U.S. dollars from ARAMCO to cover lost royalties and, when ARAMCO could not do this, applied to the U.S. government for assistance. Roosevelt was reluctant at first—he had no legislative authority to do this—but he soon managed to have loan monies that had gone to Britain partially diverted to Saudi Arabia, thereby averting that country's bankruptcy. By 1945, Britain had in this way provided some 2.5 million pounds sterling to Saudi Arabia (although after 1943 Lend-Lease was extended and included Saudi Arabia).

Roosevelt's policy on victims of Nazi oppression reflected the general mood of the United States. Fearing that immigration would bring foreign agents (who would cause trouble from within the U.S.) as well as an increase of unemployment (during what was still the Depression, before war work increased necessary jobs nationwide), his administration strictly enforced the very limited quotas of the National Origins Act of 1924. In 1939, he allowed some 27,000 German and Austrian refugees into the United States; this was after the *Anschluss* (German annexation of Austria), when 190,000 Jews were being expelled from Austria, most into countries that were soon to be occupied by Nazi troops. In 1939, Roosevelt also sponsored a conference of thirty-two nations to discuss the refugee problem—the conference was not able to achieve anything of substance, and Britain refused to discuss the possibility of immigration to Palestine. U.S. immigration actually decreased in 1939 to below the level allowed by the quotas, but this decline was attributed to the transfer of the U.S. Immigration and Naturalization Service from the Department of Labor to the Department of Justice.

With regard to Jewish immigration to Palestine, Roosevelt was balancing an inclination to support Zionism with the realities of World War II and the consequent pressures from both his Arab and British allies. In 1943, he assured Abdullah I Ibn Hussein, amir of Transjordan, that the United States would not make decisions about Jewish immigration to Palestine that would be hostile to the Arabs. Meeting with King Ibn Saʿud after the Yalta Conference in February 1945, Roosevelt gave him similar assurances, recapping them in a letter on April 5th. At the same time, Roosevelt had also been expressing support for Zionism; in February 1944 a joint

resolution was put before Congress (1) to support unrestricted Jewish immigration to Palestine and (2) for the development of Palestine as a Jewish commonwealth. The vote on this was postponed after General George C. Marshall expressed concern over the impact it might have in the Arab world. Instead, Roosevelt made a public statement in favor of Zionism.

A month earlier, in January of 1944, Roosevelt had agreed to a proactive policy toward refugees from Nazi Europe, including the Jews. This had been the result of a report by Secretary of the Treasury Henry Morgenthau, Jr., "On Acquiescence of This Government to the Murder of the Jews." Roosevelt established the War Refugee Board, with its charter to rescue those singled out for destruction. The board avoided the problem of U.S. immigration quotas by establishing emergency rescue shelters to house the refugees temporarily. The change in policy was too late for most of Europe's Jews, and it was not accompanied by a change in bombing policies—which might have been aimed at disrupting the rail lines and ancillary activities that led to the concentration camps.

Roosevelt's strength began to fail during the last year of the war, although his charisma and charm continued to be felt by his people, who championed his efforts with his allies and against his enemies. His personal leadership during the war was recorded on news film and broadcast on radio. Only many years after his death was his administration criticized with respect to its handling of the Middle East situation.

Bibliography

Dallek, Robert. *Franklin D. Roosevelt and American Foreign Policy, 1932–1945.* New York: Oxford University Press, 1979.

Lenczowski, George. *The Middle East in World Affairs,* 4th edition. Ithaca, NY: Cornell University Press, 1980.

Schlesinger, Arthur M., Jr. *The Coming of the New Deal.* Boston: Houghton Mifflin, 1988.

Schlesinger, Arthur M., Jr. *The Crisis of the Old Order, 1919–1933.* Boston: Houghton Mifflin, 1988.

Schlesinger, Arthur M., Jr. *The Politics of Upheaval.* Boston: Houghton Mifflin, 1988.

DANIEL E. SPECTOR

ROOSEVELT, KERMIT
[1916–2000]

Theodore Roosevelt's grandson, who, as a CIA agent, became involved in Middle Eastern affairs.

Born in Argentina, Kermit Roosevelt graduated from Harvard University and, after a short teaching career, joined the Office of Strategic Services and, following World War II, its successor, the Central Intelligence Agency (CIA). Roosevelt confirmed rumors that the 1953 coup in Iran that led to the downfall of the nationalist government of Mohammad Mossadegh and the restoration of the Pahlavi dynasty was staged by the CIA and, in his account of the events, supported by the U.S. government. Roosevelt was also deeply involved in the Suez Crisis of 1956, and some sources hold him responsible for the failure of the U.S. secretary of state, John Foster Dulles, to convince Egyptian president Gamal Abdel Nasser to cancel an arms deal with the Soviet Union. They moreover accuse Roosevelt, and the CIA, of undermining the State Department by counseling Nasser to ignore Dulles. Roosevelt resigned from the CIA during the Eisenhower administration and, after working in the oil business, founded his own corporation in 1964. In 1975 the Senate Foreign Relations subcommittee reported that Roosevelt had used his CIA contacts in Iran and Saudi Arabia to win government contracts for the Northrop Corporation, a major U.S. aircraft manufacturer.

In 2000 the *New York Times* obtained a copy of the CIA's secret history of the coup, which by most accounts was written by Donald Wilber, an Iranist and part-time CIA operative. The account expanded significantly on what Roosevelt had volunteered about the U.S. government's role in overthrowing the government of Mossadegh.

See also CENTRAL INTELLIGENCE AGENCY (CIA); DULLES, JOHN FOSTER; MOSSADEGH, MOHAMMAD.

Bibliography

Abrahamian, Ervand. "The 1953 Coup in Iran." *Science and Society* 65, no. 2 (2001): 181–215.

Gasirowski, Mark. "The 1953 Coup d'Etat in Iran." *International Journal of Middle East Studies* 19, no. 3 (1987): 261–286.

Risen, James. "How a Plot Convulsed Iran in '53 (and in '79)." *New York Times,* 16 April 2000.

Roosevelt, Kermit. *Countercoup: The Struggle for the Control of Iran.* New York: McGraw-Hill, 1979.

NEGUIN YAVARI

ROSHANFEKR

See GLOSSARY

ROTHSCHILD, EDMOND DE
[1845–1935]

Jewish philanthropist active in Palestine.

Known as the Benefactor (*ha-Nadiv*), Edmond James de Rothschild, scion of the Rothschild banking family, was born in Paris. His concern in 1882 to give sanctuary to Eastern European pogrom victims was translated into a commitment for the development of a self-supporting Jewish homeland and finally a state. His assistance to the Jewish settlements of Rishon le-Zion and Zikhron Ya'akov in Palestine (1883–1884) rescued them from financial collapse. Rothschild purchased land and equipped the colonies he established. He also supported the development of cash crops and industry. For example, after establishing a winepress at Rishon le-Zion in the early 1890s, he formed a company that began to market its wines in 1896.

Insisting that his support not be purely charitable, Rothschild was determined that the colonies be self-supporting. When the Jewish immigrants could not make them succeed, he appointed his own managers and staff, hired workers, and underwrote agricultural experimentation, to the chagrin of the Zionist socialists who, after the start of the twentieth century, began to dominate the Zionist enterprise.

Acceding to the wishes of the leadership of Hovevei Zion, Rothschild transferred the administration of his settlements to the Jewish Colonization Association, which had been established to administer philanthropic monies to Jews in need of economic support. In 1924, under the auspices of his son, James Armand de Rothschild, who had arrived in Palestine as a British soldier with General Edmund Allenby, the Palestine Jewish Colonization Association (PICA) was established. It supported kibbutzim, moshavim, and Jewish settlements; swamp drainage; stabilization of sand dunes; agricultural research; and educational and cultural institutions. PICA encouraged the development of industrial enterprises, and after 1948 bought and modernized flour mills, saltworks, and chemical enterprises, many of which were turned over to the State of Israel after the death of James de Rothschild and the termination of PICA (both in 1957).

Rothschild visited Palestine often, touring his settlements and assessing their progress. In 1929, he was made honorary president of the Jewish Agency. Rothschild is buried in Israel overlooking the colonies Zikhron Ya'akov (named after his father) and Binyamina (named after himself; his Hebrew name was Avraham Binyamin), and the area near Caesarea where he had funded clearing of malarial swamps.

See also ALLENBY, EDMUND HENRY; JEWISH AGENCY FOR PALESTINE; JEWISH COLONIZATION ASSOCIATION; RISHON LE-ZION; ZIKHRON YA'AKOV.

Bibliography

Schama, Simon. *Two Rothschilds and the Land of Israel.* New York: Knopf, 1978.

REEVA S. SIMON

ROYAL DUTCH SHELL

An Anglo-Dutch petroleum conglomerate.

The Royal Dutch Shell group of companies was created in 1907 from the merger of the Royal Dutch and Shell oil companies. More commonly known as Shell, the group is one of the largest oil companies in the world and is one of the Seven Sisters. Though headquartered in London, the company's main interests were in Iraq, Iran, Kuwait, and Turkey until nationalization of oil resources by the Gulf countries. It had no sizable role in the oil industry of Saudi Arabia. In 2001, the company had 91,000 employees worldwide, sales of $135 billion, and net assets of $56 billion.

JEAN-FRANÇOIS SEZNEC

RUB AL-KHALI

Sand desert with an area of 200,000 square miles (518,000 sq. km) shared by Saudi Arabia, the United Arab Emirates, Oman, and Yemen; one of the largest sand deserts in the world.

Rub al-Khali (the Empty Quarter) has no permanent settlements and is separated from populated areas by wide gravel plains devoid of vegetation. The northern part is watered by occasional winter rains, while the southern part is sometimes watered by spillover of monsoon rains from the Indian Ocean. Al-Murra and al-Dawasir bedouin frequent the northern parts of the Empty Quarter, where their camels feed on bushes and grasses that grow in the sand. Al-Manasir (of Abu Dhabi) and al-Duru (of Oman) tribes roam the eastern regions while the al-Kathir and al-Rawashid of Oman and the al-Manahil and Sa'ar of Yemen use the southern and western reaches. The Rub al-Khali's boundaries have been mostly demarcated. In 1974 the borders between Saudi Arabia and the U.A.E. (Abu Dhabi) were agreed; in 1990 Saudi Arabia and Oman signed a border treaty; in 1992 Oman and the new Republic of Yemen reached an agreement; and in 2000 Saudi Arabia and Yemen finalized their land boundaries.

Bibliography

Schofield, Richard, ed. *Territorial Foundations of the Gulf States.* New York: St. Martin's, 1994.

ELEANOR ABDELLA DOUMATO
UPDATED BY J. E. PETERSON

RUBINSTEIN, AMNON
[1931–]

Israeli law professor and political leader.

Born in Tel Aviv, Amnon Rubinstein studied at the Hebrew University and became a member of the bar in 1963. He earned a Ph.D. in law from the London School of Economics in 1966 and served as a professor (1961–1975) and dean (1968–1973) of the law faculty at Tel Aviv University. In 1974 he founded the centrist Shinui Party, which advocated free enterprise, electoral reform, and the formulation of a written constitution. In 1977 Shinui was part of the Democratic Movement for Change Party, but it broke away in 1978 and Rubinstein became its chair. In 1992 Shinui joined Ratz (Citizens' Rights Movement) and MAPAM (United Workers Party) to form Meretz (Vigor), and won twelve seats in the Knesset.

Rubinstein has served on many key Knesset committees, serving as chair of the Knesset Economic Committee and the Knesset Constitution, Law, and Justice Committee. From 1984 to 1988 Rubinstein was communications minister in a national unity government; from 1992 to 1996 he was minister of education and culture. Rubenstein is one of the best-known scholars in the Knesset, having written several books and many articles in the popular press and in academic periodicals on political and legal topics.

See also ISRAEL: POLITICAL PARTIES IN.

Bibliography

American-Israeli Cooperative Enterprise. "Amnon Rubinstein." In *Jewish Virtual Library.* Available from <http://www.us-israel.org/jsource/biography>.

Rubinstein, Amnon. *From Herzl to Rabin: The Changing Image of Zionism.* New York: Holmes and Meier, 2000.

Rubinstein, Amnon. *Jurisdiction and Illegality: A Study in Public Law.* Oxford, U.K.: Clarendon Press, 1965.

Rubinstein, Amnon. *The Zionist Dream Revisited: From Herzl to Gush Emunim and Back.* New York: Schocken Books, 1984.

State of Israel Ministry of Foreign Affairs. "Amnon Rubinstein, MK." In *Personalities.* Available from <http://www.mfa.gov.il/mfa>.

BRYAN DAVES
UPDATED BY GREGORY S. MAHLER

RUMELIA

The European part of the Ottoman Empire, in particular the Balkan peninsula.

Formerly written as *Rum-ili*, the word *Rumelia* has its origins in the medieval Muslim practice of referring to the Byzantine as Rum and their territory as Bilad al-Rum. With the arrival of the Turks in Anatolia and, in particular, with the advancement of the Ottoman Empire, the use of Rum to designate Western Anatolia survived and evolved eventually into Rumelia or Rumeli.

During the reign of the Ottoman sultan Murat I (1362–1389), Rumelia emerged as a name to designate Ottoman territories in Europe, governed as a separate military-administrative region under the rule of a beylerbeyi, the first such governorate of its kind in the Ottoman Empire. It was around this time, too, that the empire was officially divided into two large administrative regions straddling the Sea of Marmara: Rumelia and Anadolu (Anatolia). At first, each successive territorial conquest in Europe, up to the Danube, was added to the beylerbeyi of Rumelia. After 1541, with the establishment of the governorate of Budin and Bosnia, the number of beylerbeyis began to proliferate. In the nineteenth century, during the Tanzimat, the administrative divisions of Rumelia underwent further changes. Finally, in 1894, Rumelia was officially subdivided into the *vilayets* (provinces) of Edirne, Selanik, Qoskova, Yanya, Ishqodra, and Manastir.

Currently the word is generally understood to refer to the triangular region between Istanbul and Edirne and the peninsula of Gallipoli—all that remains of Turkish Europe. The word is, however, no longer used in official documents or atlases; rather Trakya, a Turkish variant of Thrace, is used instead. The last official recorded use of Rumelia was during the Turkish War of Independence in 1919.

Today it is used most commonly by the residents of Istanbul to distinguish the European side of the city from the Anatolian. It forms an integral part of many a place name on the European side, such as Rumelihisari and Rumelifenerai.

Bibliography

Birnbaum, Henrik, and Vryonis, Speros, Jr., eds. *Aspects of the Balkans: Continuity and Change.* The Hague: Mouton, 1972.

Inalcik, Halil. *The Middle East and the Balkans under the Ottoman Empire: Essays on Economy and Society.* Bloomington: Indiana Turkish University Studies, 1993.

KAREN PINTO

RUPPIN, ARTHUR
[1876–1943]
Sociologist and Zionist official.

Born in the Prussian province of Posen (now Poznan in western Poland), Arthur Ruppin became head of the Palestine office of the World Zionist Organization in 1908. Ruppin's leadership opened a new epoch of Zionist settlement in Ottoman Palestine. The restoration of constitutionalism in the Ottoman Empire after the Young Turk Revolution of 1908 created some opportunities for Jewish settlers. Ruppin, a technician and social theorist, negotiated the purchase of large tracts of land in the Jezreel valley and mobilized funds to add to Jewish neighborhoods in Haifa, Tel Aviv, and Jerusalem. Through his official position and personal influence, he provided financial support for young Jewish pioneers, who developed the kibbutz and moshav as new types of collective agricultural communities.

Ruppin grew up in Europe during a period of rapid economic change that brought ruin to his family, forcing him to leave school at fifteen. Apprenticed to a grain merchant, Ruppin was quickly promoted to office manager. After completing secondary school, he studied law and economics at the universities of Berlin and Halle. A scholar and a man of action, Ruppin's *The Jews in the Modern World* (1904) laid the foundation for the study of the sociology of Jewry. He lectured in Palestine, in sociology at the Hebrew University, and directed Palestine's Institute for Economic Research. On behalf of the Jewish Agency (the liaison between Palestinian Jews and the British mandate authorities), he promoted policies to develop Jewish industry and agriculture. During World War I, he saved Palestine's Jews from starvation by supervising the distribution of American funds, even after he was exiled in 1916 to Istanbul. In the last decade of his life, he aided the absorption of German Jews fleeing the Nazis. A founder of Brit Shalom in 1925, Ruppin advocated, for a short time, the establishment of Palestine as a binational state. While he modified this view, he stressed the importance of Palestinian Jews reaching an agreement with Palestinian Arabs that would not compromise Zionist goals. He died in Jerusalem in 1943.

See also BINATIONALISM; JEWISH AGENCY FOR PALESTINE; JEZREEL VALLEY; KIBBUTZ; MOSHAV; PALESTINE LAND DEVELOPMENT COMPANY; WORLD ZIONIST ORGANIZATION (WZO); YOUNG TURKS.

Bibliography

Bein, Alex. "Arthur Ruppin: The Man and His Work." *Leo Baeck Institute Year Book* 17 (1972):71–89.

DONNA ROBINSON DIVINE

RUŞDIYE SCHOOLS
Ottoman secular primary schools.

The first *ruşdiye* primary schools were established in 1838 at the Süleymaniye and Sultan Ahmet mosques in Istanbul by Sultan Mahmud II, to prepare young men to attend his new technical schools. These schools slowly became an alternative to the religious education system, numbering sixty by 1853. Their graduates staffed the Ottoman Empire's expanding administration and military during the Tanzimat era and beyond. In the early years, students aged ten to fifteen years (and later even younger) studied languages, mathematics, science, history, and religion for four years. By the late nineteenth century, nearly every provincial town had a ruşdiye school. In 1895, more than thirty-five thousand students, about four thousand of them non-Muslim, attended the state-run ruşdiye schools. The first ruşdiye for girls was founded in 1858.

The military built its own system of schools beginning in 1855, and its ruşdiye schools enrolled eight thousand boys in 1895. İdadi (middle) Schools were added in the late nineteenth century. In addition, in 1895 a separate system of millet ruşdiye schools, run by various religious groups, enrolled seventy-six thousand non-Muslim students.

See also İDADI SCHOOLS; TANZIMAT.

Bibliography

Kazamias, Andreas M. *Education and the Quest for Modernity in Turkey.* Chicago: University of Chicago Press, 1966.

Shaw, Stanford J., and Shaw, Ezel Kural. *History of the Ottoman Empire and Modern Turkey,* Vol. 2: *Reform, Revolution, and Republic: The Rise of Modern Turkey, 1808–1975.* Cambridge, U.K., and New York: Cambridge University Press, 1977.

ELIZABETH THOMPSON

RUSK, DEAN
[1909–1994]

American secretary of state.

David Dean Rusk was born in Georgia. A Rhodes Scholar, he studied at Saint John's College, Oxford, and later at the University of California Law School in Berkeley. During World War II, Rusk served in the army in the China-Burma-India theater, rising to the rank of colonel. He held key positions in the Department of State (1946–1952) and helped implement the Marshall Plan and U.S. Far East policy. From 1952 to 1961, he was president of the Rockefeller Foundation. He served as secretary of state (1961–1969) in the Kennedy and Johnson administrations.

He was a hawkish steward of American foreign policy during the Cold War, believing in the use of military action to combat communism. Rusk emphasized diplomatic efforts during the Cuban missile crisis and North Korea's seizure of the USS *Pueblo*, but advocated military escalation in the Vietnam War (1955–1975). On the Palestinian refugee issue, Rusk followed former Secretary of State John Foster Dulles in hoping (in vain) that the U.S. administration would apply pressure on Israel to make a generous gesture regarding compensation and return. He cautioned against acceding to Israel's requests for a security guarantee on the grounds that it would harm American interests in the region without appreciably enhancing Israeli security. In the build-up to the Middle East crisis of 1967, he strongly endorsed plans for sending a U.S.-led multinational flotilla through the Strait of Tiran to challenge Egypt's blockade of Israel's southern port of Eilat, but he advised against President Johnson's giving the Israelis a yellow (or amber) light to proceed cautiously with a preemptive attack on Egypt. His post-1967 behind-the-scenes diplomatic efforts paved the way for the 1969 Rogers Plan. Ending his years of government service, Rusk taught international law at the University of Georgia from 1970 to 1984.

See also ARAB–ISRAEL WAR (1967); REFUGEES: PALESTINIAN.

Bibliography

Ben-Zvi, Abraham. *Decade of Decisions: Eisenhower, Kennedy, and the Origins of the American-Israeli Alliance.* New York: Columbia University Press, 1998.

Quandt, William B. *Peace Process: American Diplomacy and the Arab–Israeli Conflict since 1967,* revised edition. Washington, DC: Brookings Institution, 2001.

Rusk, Dean. *As I Saw It.* New York: Norton, 1990.

Who Was Who in America. New Providence, NJ: Marquis, 1998.

CHARLES C. KOLB

RUSSIA AND THE MIDDLE EAST

From Catherine the Great's 1774 victory against the Ottoman Empire until the late twentieth century, Russian/Soviet policy was to rule the Black Sea and the lands around it.

In the late eighteenth and early nineteenth centuries, Russia increased pressure on the Ottoman and Persian empires in an attempt to capture parts of the Black and Caspian seacoasts, as well as of the Caucasian interior. Persia's refusal to recognize Russia's 1801 annexation of Georgia led to a war (1804–1813) and a Russian victory. According to the Treaty of Golestan (1813), Persia lost a large part of the Caucasus, including Georgia, as well as parts of the western Caspian coast. Persia also recognized Russian naval preeminence in the Caspian Sea.

The next round for the control of the central Caucasus was fought between 1826 and 1828. It, too, ended in a Russian victory. Under the terms of the Treaty of Turkmanchai (1828), Persia relinquished to Russia part of Armenia and recognized the Aras River as the Transcaucasian boundary between the two states. In addition, Persia granted Russia important commercial concessions and extraterritorial privileges, enabling Saint Petersburg to establish a strong political and economic position in the Persian Empire. In the late 1850s Russia turned its attention to Transcaspian Muslim central Asia, conquering the Khanate of Khiva in 1873 and Kokand and Bokhara in 1876. The process was completed in the mid-1880s with the annexation of Merv and Panjdeh, situated near the Afghan border. In 1881 Persia agreed to the Atrek River as the Transcaspian boundary with Russia.

Russia's southward expansion alarmed Great Britain, for Russian control of the Turkish Straits would threaten part of the maritime lifeline of the British Empire. London was also alarmed at the steady Russian encroachment into Persia and, later, Afghanistan. If unchecked, these advances would ultimately bring the Russians to the border of India, the crown jewel of the British Empire. Hence, throughout the nineteenth century, London attempted to prevent Russia from overrunning the Ottoman and Persian empires and from making major inroads into Afghanistan. In the early twentieth century, however, fear of imperial Germany prompted Britain and Russia to reconcile their dif-

A meeting at the Kremlin in Moscow at which Egyptian president Gamal Abdel Nasser, pictured at right, sits across from Soviet leaders Leonid Brezhnev, Alexei Kosygin, and Anastas Mikoyan, pictured from left to right. Both the Russian and Middle Eastern leaders were critical of U.S. attacks on North Vietnam. © BETTMANN/CORBIS. REPRODUCED BY PERMISSION.

ferences in Asia. According to their 1907 treaty, Afghanistan became a British sphere of influence and Persia was split into three zones: Russia dominated the northern and Great Britain the southern parts of the country; separating them was a third, or neutral, zone. After the outbreak of World War I, the two allies concluded the Constantinople Agreement (1915), stipulating that after the war Russia would occupy the Turkish Straits. This dramatic reversal of long-standing British policy was dictated by the necessity of keeping Russia in the allied coalition.

Tsarist Russia did not survive to enjoy the fruits of victory over the Central powers. The communist regime, in power after November 1917, renounced the concessions secured by its predecessor, proclaimed itself an ally of the exploited masses, and, in 1921, concluded treaties of friendship and neutrality with Turkey, Persia, and Afghanistan. Nonaggression treaties with Turkey and Afghanistan were signed in 1925 and 1926, respectively.

The Soviet Union and the Middle East, 1945 to 1991

During World War II, after Germany invaded the U.S.S.R. in 1941, Soviet and British troops occupied Iran to secure a safe supply route for the flow of Allied war matériel to the Soviet Union. The treaty of alliance concluded between Iran, Great Britain, and the U.S.S.R. in 1942 provided for the withdrawal of foreign forces not later than six months after the end of the war. By early 1946 the British had pulled out, but the Soviets remained. They left later in the year, after Tehran had signed an agreement permitting Soviet oil exploration in northern Iran (it was never implemented). More significantly, Washington exerted pressure on Moscow to abide by the 1942 agreement.

Stalin's refusal to leave Iran was but one of the perceived indications of his aggressiveness. As seen in the West, his ambitions in the Middle East complemented Soviet expansion in Eastern Europe and the Far East. In 1945 Stalin renounced the Soviet-Turkish nonaggression treaty and renewed tsarist claims to Turkish territory, including the Straits. He was also held responsible for efforts by Greek communists to topple that country's pro-Western government. Washington responded by promulgating the Truman Doctrine (1947), which assumed responsibility for the defense of Greece and Turkey. The U.S. Sixth Fleet was deployed in the Mediterranean in 1946 and its presence was later augmented by Strategic Air Command bombers based in Morocco, Libya, Turkey, and Saudi Arabia. Jupiter missiles followed in the 1950s and Polaris submarines in the 1960s. By means of the Eisenhower Doctrine (1955), Washington pledged to defend the Middle East against Soviet aggression, and the Baghdad Pact, consisting of Turkey, Iran, Iraq, Pakistan, and Great Britain, was formed during the same year.

The vast accumulation of U.S. power in and near the Mediterranean was seen in Moscow as a threat to its security. Hence, for much of the post-Stalin period the U.S.S.R. worked hard to neutralize the U.S. military presence in the vicinity of its southern border. As part of the general superpower competition, the Soviets made a major effort to establish a viable naval and air presence in the Middle East. A naval squadron was permanently deployed in the Mediterranean in 1964, but naval and air bases became available in Egypt only in 1970. Cairo withdrew these privileges later in the decade, but by then the Middle East had ceased to represent a major strategic threat to the U.S.S.R. Ironically, this was due not to Soviet countermeasures but to technological advances: Washington came to rely on land-based and submarine-launched intercontinental ballistic missiles. Until 1991 the U.S.S.R., mainly for political reasons, maintained its Mediterranean squadron and had access to facilities in Syria, Algeria, Libya, and Yemen. The most dramatic projection of Soviet power in the post-1945 Middle East occurred in Afghanistan. To preserve a faltering communist regime, Soviet troops entered the country in 1979. They were withdrawn in 1989, leaving Afghanistan stalemated militarily and politically.

An early Soviet political objective was to undermine Western positions in the Middle East. The trend was set by Stalin's support of the partition of Palestine and of the State of Israel (1947–1948), and it lasted into the Gorbachev period. Western influence has declined from the peak reached in 1945, but this process was initiated by local actors, pursuing their own (not Soviet) interests. The U.S.S.R. played a part by lending moral and material support to regional leaders who were refused Western assistance or arms, but its role was facilitative and, therefore, secondary.

In addition, especially during the Khrushchev and Brezhnev periods, the U.S.S.R. attempted to strengthen its own position and to gain U.S. recognition as a political equal in the Middle East. Efforts to improve Moscow's standing were crowned with some short-term successes. In the 1950s the Soviet Union established working relations with Iraq, Syria, Egypt, and Algeria. Later, treaties of friendship and cooperation were signed with Egypt (1971), Iraq (1974), and Syria (1980). However, these apparent gains did not net the U.S.S.R. any permanent, long-term benefits.

Egypt abrogated its treaty in 1976. In 1980 Iraq attacked Iran without consulting the Kremlin. Moscow's ensuing attempts to maintain evenhanded relations with the combatants during their eight-year war led ultimately to a deterioration of both sets of relationships. Gorbachev's realization of the cost-ineffectiveness of the Kremlin's political involvement in the Middle East was partly responsible for his decision to disengage from the Soviet commitment to the Arabs in their conflict with Israel, an obligation that Moscow had maintained through the Khrushchev and Brezhnev periods. Lastly, efforts to gain U.S. recognition of Moscow's political parity in the Middle East had also been unsuccessful.

One of the regional problems that the U.S.S.R. had used to advance its political interests in the Middle East was the Arab–Israel conflict. In 1953, in a major about-face, the Soviets abandoned Stalin's policy of support for the Zionist cause and sided with the Arabs. In the ensuing years Moscow extended Egypt and Syria large-scale military and economic assistance and adopted a strong pro-Arab and anti-Israeli position. With some modifications, this attitude was maintained well into the 1980s. Among other things, the U.S.S.R. recognized the Palestine Liberation Organization as the official representative of the Palestinian Arabs and backed the Arab states in the Arab–Israel wars of 1956, 1967, and 1973. In 1967 Moscow broke diplomatic relations with Israel. As noted, a major change in the Soviet position occurred in the late 1980s when "new thinking" in Gorbachev's foreign policy led the Kremlin to improve relations with Israel. Large-scale Jewish emigration from the U.S.S.R. to Israel was accompanied by the restoration of diplomatic relations between the two states in 1991. As Moscow's policy became "evenhanded," to the chagrin of the Arabs, the U.S.S.R. ceased to play an important role in the Arab-Israel conflict.

Before 1970 the U.S.S.R. had no important economic interests in the Middle East. In the 1970s and 1980s the Soviets became heavily involved in selling arms to Iraq, Syria, Libya, Egypt, and Iran. These transactions, worth tens of billions of dollars, ranked second to petroleum sales as the U.S.S.R.'s main earner of foreign currency. (The stunning superiority of Western arms over the Soviet weapons in the hands of the Iraqi military during Operation Desert Storm in 1991 has seriously eroded the market value of such Russian-made armaments for the foreseeable future.) In addition, the U.S.S.R. bartered various types of goods and services for Iraqi, Libyan, and Algerian oil and Iranian gas. Until its dissolution, the U.S.S.R. looked at the oil-rich Persian Gulf states as sources of capital in restructuring the Soviet economy.

On balance, between 1945 and 1991 the U.S.S.R. can be said to have improved its military position vis-à-vis the Middle East in the sense that no strategic threat to Soviet security emanated from the region. But the U.S.S.R. also suffered disappointments and setbacks, and its military and political gains usually proved temporary. In the 1990s the U.S.S.R.'s position was further weakened by the collapse of the Soviet economy and

Gorbachev's frantic efforts to revive it by normalizing relations with the Western powers, especially the United States. Given these priorities, the continuation of superpower competition in the Middle East made little sense from the new Soviet perspective. As contiguous states with a large Muslim population, however, Russia and the various independent republics that were formed from the Soviet Union in 1992 will inevitably remain interested parties in the regional affairs of the Middle East.

Relations with the Russian Federation States, 1991 to the Present

Following the collapse of the Soviet Union in December 1991, a weakened Russian Federation, no longer following the "anti-imperialist" foreign policy of the U.S.S.R. and increasingly concerned with economic development and protecting Russia's southern borders, focused its Middle East policy primarily on four countries: Iran, Israel, Turkey, and Iraq. Iran was the closest Middle East ally of post-Soviet Russia. Moscow was Iran's primary supplier of military equipment; the two countries cooperated diplomatically in a number of areas including Tajikistan, where they jointly arranged a cease-fire; TransCaucasia, where until 2001 they worked together against Azerbaijan; and Afghanistan, where they both opposed the Taliban. The centerpiece of the relationship was the nuclear reactor that Russia, despite strong U.S. opposition, was constructing for Iran at Bushehr. The one major area of disagreement was the demarcation of the Caspian Sea.

Economics also was a major factor in the Israeli-Russian relationship, with trade rising to over a billion dollars per year by 2002. The relationship was also marked by extensive cultural cooperation and the joint development and sale of military equipment. The major problem in the relationship was Russia's supply of the nuclear reactor to Iran, which Israel saw as a major enemy. Similarly, economics played an increasingly important role in the Turkish-Russian relationship. With trade rising to over $10 billion annually before the Russian economic collapse in 1998, Turkey became Russia's leading trading partner in the Middle East. There had been a rivalry between Turkey and Russia in Central Asia in the 1990s, as well as serious disagreements over ethnic issues, with Russia alleging Turkish aid to the Chechen rebellions, and Turkey alleging Russian assistance to the terrorist Kurdish Workers Party. But by 2000, with the Blue Stream natural gas pipeline being built to carry Russian natural gas to Turkey, Russian Prime Minister Mikhail Kasyanov could state that the Turkish-Russian relationship had moved from rivalry to partnership. Finally, in its relations with Iraq, Russia hoped to recover as much as possible of the $8 billion in debt owed to Moscow by the regime of Saddam Hussein, as well as obtain business opportunities for Russian companies such as LUKOIL. Despite opposing the Anglo-American attack on Iraq in 2003 that ousted the Hussein regime, and the subsequent military occupation of the country, Russia pursued business opportunities with the Iraqi Governing Council that was appointed by the United States, and Moscow held out the possibility of reducing the Iraqi debt in return for contracts for Russian companies.

See also AFGHANISTAN: SOVIET INTERVENTION IN; BAGHDAD PACT (1955); BREZHNEV, LEONID ILYICH; COMMUNISM IN THE MIDDLE EAST; TURKMANCHAI, TREATY OF (1828).

Bibliography

Freedman, Robert O. *Moscow and the Middle East: Soviet Policy since the Invasion of Afghanistan.* New York: Cambridge University Press, 1991.

Freedman, Robert O. *Russian Policy toward the Middle East Since the Collapse of the Soviet Union: The Yeltsin Legacy and the Challenge for Putin.* Seattle: The Jackson School of International Studies, University of Washington, 2001.

Kuniholm, Bruce R. *The Origins of the Cold War in the Near East: Great Power Conflict.* Princeton, NJ: Princeton University Press, 1980.

Lenczowski, George. *The Middle East in World Affairs,* 4th edition. Ithaca, NY: Cornell University Press, 1980.

Ro'i, Yaacov. *From Encroachment to Involvement: A Documentary Study of Soviet Policy in the Middle East.* London: Croom Helm, 1974.

Rubinstein, Alvin Z. *Red Star on the Nile: The Soviet-Egyptian Influence Relationship.* Princeton, NJ: Princeton University Press, 1977.

Smolansky, Oles M. *The U.S.S.R. and Iraq: The Soviet Quest for Influence.* Durham, NC: Duke University Press, 1991.

OLES M. SMOLANSKY
UPDATED BY ROBERT O. FREEDMAN

RUSSIAN–OTTOMAN WARS

Wars between the Russian and Ottoman empires over opposing expansionist policies.

During the nineteenth century, Russia's approach to the Ottoman Empire was governed by several distinct but interrelated considerations. In terms of military strategy, the Black Sea provided access to the rich Ukrainian plain, which became regarded as Russia's "soft underbelly," and entry into the Black Sea was possible only through the Turkish Straits, the gateway to and from the Mediterranean. Hence, control of the straits became an important Russian objective. As the European powers awakened to Russian ambitions, Russia modified its quest for annexation of Ottoman territory and attempted to establish protectorates in such regions as the principalities (Wallachia and Moldavia) and Bulgaria. Other Slavic nationalities struggling against Ottoman control also represented a political interest. Economically, trade in and beyond the Black Sea became an important concern, especially after the fertile lands along the northern shore were opened to cultivation. Reinforcing these interests, Russia's role as protector of Greek Orthodoxy in the Ottoman Empire added yet another dimension to the quest for dominance in the Black Sea region.

Europe's preoccupation with Napoléon Bonaparte early in the century enabled Russia to consolidate its position in the Black Sea area. The Treaty of Bucharest (1812) ended a six-year war by ceding to Russia Bessarabia and territory in the western Caucasus and extending privileges in the principalities. In 1829 Tsar Nicholas I (r. 1825–1855) used the Greek War of Independence as reason to declare a war against the Ottoman Empire. The Ottomans lost and in the Treaty of Adrianople (1829) ceded to Russia the mouth of the Danube and additional territory in the Caucasus. The treaty also conferred autonomy upon the principalities, placed them under Russian protection, and, for the first time, guaranteed Russian merchant ships free passage through the straits.

In 1833 Russia and the Ottoman Empire signed the Treaty of Hunkar-Iskelesi, one of only two treaties of mutual assistance entered into by the two states. (The first, directed against Napoléon, had been signed in 1805.) This unusual treaty resulted not from a war but from Russian assistance to Sultan

The Treaty of San Stefano was signed in 1878 between Russia and the Ottoman Empire. The Ottomans ceded to Russia parts of Armenia and the Dorbuja; agreed to pay a substantial indemnity; recognized the independence of Romania, Serbia, and Montenegro; and increased the territories of Serbia and Montenegro. © CORBIS. REPRODUCED BY PERMISSION.

Mahmud II, whose reign (1808–1839) was being threatened by Muhammad Ali, the rebellious pasha of Egypt. Once the Russian troops arrived, at the Sultan's invitation, they were, for the first and only time, in control of the straits area and Istanbul. They left later in the year after Mahmud II signed the Treaty of Hunkar-Iskelesi, which closed the straits to warships of all foreign nations. The establishment of a Russian protectorate over the Ottoman Empire proved unacceptable to Great Britain and Austria. The ensuing Treaty of London (1840), which sent Muhammad Ali back to Egypt, and the Straits Convention (1841) made the independence and territorial integrity of the Ottoman Empire a common concern of Europe's great powers acting in concert.

As an outgrowth of Tsar Nicholas I's inability to resolve the Eastern (i.e., Ottoman) question to his satisfaction, the Crimean War (1854–1855) pitted Russia against the Ottoman Empire, which was allied with Great Britain, France, and the Kingdom of Sardinia. Russia capitulated after the allied troops landed in the Crimea and Tsar Nicholas died. Under the terms of the Treaty of Paris (1856) the Ottoman Empire regained the mouth of the Danube and southern Bessarabia and agreed to the demilitarization of the Black Sea; the principalities became a protectorate of the victorious European allies; and an international commission was established to assure free navigation on the Danube. Russia also abandoned its claim to the protectorate of the Greek Orthodox Church in the Ottoman Empire. In 1871, using the diplomatic upheaval caused by the Franco-Prussian War, Russia unilaterally renounced the Treaty of Paris.

The war of 1877 to 1878 grew out of the local disturbances in the Balkans. The Turks' brutal suppression of the Balkans, followed by the declaration of war on the Ottoman Empire by Serbia and Montenegro (1876), provided Russia with a pretext to intervene on their behalf. The defeat of the forces of Sultan Abdülhamit II (r. 1876–1909) prompted harsh terms in the 1878 Treaty of San Stefano. The last armed confrontation between the two empires occurred during World War I. The Russians had made some headway in the Transcaucasus, but the Communists, who had seized power in 1917, took Russia out of the war and renounced all imperial claims to Ottoman territory.

See also BUCHAREST, TREATY OF (1812); HUNKAR-ISKELESI, TREATY OF (1833); SAN STEFANO, TREATY OF (1878); STRAITS CONVENTION.

Bibliography

Anderson, M. S. *The Eastern Question, 1774–1923: A Study in International Relations.* New York: St. Martin's Press, 1966.

Jelavich, Barbara. *A Century of Russian Foreign Policy, 1814–1914.* Philadelphia: Lippincott, 1964.

Shaw, Stanford J. *History of the Ottoman Empire and Modern Turkey,* Vol. 1: *Empire of the Gazis: The Rise and Decline of the Ottoman Empire, 1280–1808.* New York and Cambridge, U.K.: Cambridge University Press, 1977.

OLES M. SMOLANSKY
UPDATED BY ERIC HOOGLUND

RUTENBERG, PINHAS

[1879–1942]

Engineer and Yishuv leader; pioneer of hydroelectricity in Palestine.

Born in Romny, Ukraine, Pinhas Rutenberg became active in the Russian revolutionary movement and participated in the "Bloody Sunday" march—the start of the 1905 Revolution. From 1907 to 1915 he worked as an engineer in Italy. During this period he became interested in Jewish affairs and wrote a pamphlet titled "The National Revival of the Jewish People."

During World War I Rutenberg went to London to try to influence the Zionist leadership to establish Jewish military units to liberate Palestine from the Ottoman Empire. When he discovered that Vladimir Ze'ev Jabotinsky had similar interests, he contacted him to coordinate their efforts and traveled to the United States to spread the idea.

After Aleksandr Kerensky's March Revolution of 1917 overthrew the tsarist government of Russia, Rutenberg returned there to be appointed deputy governor of Saint Petersburg, in charge of civilian affairs. In November 1917, with the Bolshevik takeover, Rutenberg was arrested, spent six months in prison, and escaped to rejoin anti-Bolshevik groups. By 1919, perceiving antisemitism in the revolutionary movement, Rutenberg saw no future for himself in the new Soviet state and left for Palestine, where he joined a British team surveying Palestine's water resources, particularly the Jordan River.

Rutenberg drew up a far-reaching plan for creating a hydroelectric scheme to supply both sides of the Jordan with power and water for irrigation. From 1920 to 1923, Rutenberg worked to influence the British authorities to grant him a preliminary concession for his Palestine Electric Corporation Limited. In 1926 he was awarded the full concession over the use of the Jordan and Yarmuk rivers for supplying hydroelectricity to Palestine. He raised the money for the company mainly from Jews in the United States and Great Britain. In 1932 the first Jordan power station was opened in Naharayim, at the confluence of the Jordan and Yarmuk rivers. The station functioned until it was destroyed during the 1948 Arab–Israel War.

Rutenberg was an active Zionist and headed the Va'ad Le'umi (National Council) in the crisis year of 1929. During the 1936 disturbances, he joined with four other Yishuv leaders to propose a plan for Arab-Jewish coexistence. His water-development plans had already brought him into friendly contact with Abdullah ibn Hussein, the amir of Transjordan, but nothing came of these efforts. Strongly concerned about infighting among Jews, Rutenberg also attempted unsuccessfully to mediate between David Ben-Gurion's MAPAI Party and Jabotinsky's Revisionists, who were constantly at odds. In 1939 Rutenberg again became the head of the Vaʿad Leʾumi, and served until he died in 1942. In secret wartime conversations with British officials in London, he discussed plans for assassinating the exiled mufti of Jerusalem, Hajj Amin al-Husayni.

See also JABOTINSKY, VLADIMIR ZEʾEV.

Bibliography

Lipsky, Louis. *Gallery of Zionist Profiles.* New York: Farrar, Straus and Cudahy, 1956.

Sachar, Howard. *Zionist Portraits and Other Essays.* London: Blond, 1959.

SARA REGUER
UPDATED BY NEIL CAPLAN

RUZNAME

See GLOSSARY

SA'ADA, ANTUN
[1904–1949]

Founder and leader of the Syrian Social Nationalist Party.

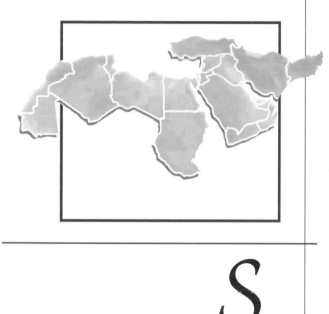

Antun Sa'ada was a charismatic leader and a revolutionary Arab thinker who in 1932 founded, and then headed the Syrian Social Nationalist Party (SSNP) until his death in 1949. He was born in Shuwayr, Mount Lebanon, on 1 March 1904 to Eastern Orthodox Lebanese parents. His father, Khalil Sa'ada, a product of the late-nineteenth-century Arab Renaissance, was a well-known physician, novelist, linguist, publicist, and political activist. Sa'ada joined his father in Brazil in 1921. He was strongly affected by his father's modern views while they worked together publishing a newspaper and a journal throughout most of the 1920s. During this period, Sa'ada's intellectual formation was solidified by his mastery of several languages and his involvement in political activism. In 1930 Sa'ada returned to Lebanon determined to bring about change, and he secretly founded the SSNP in 1932. The party was initially called the Syrian National Party; Sa'ada added the word *social* to the party's name in the 1940s to emphasize the social dimension of nationalism. Sa'ada was accused of fascist leanings, but this continues to be debatable.

The secret organization, whose membership in its early days drew mainly on students from the American University of Beirut, where Sa'ada was tutoring in German, mushroomed to more than 1,000 members in two years. French colonial authorities uncovered the party on 16 November 1935; Sa'ada was arrested along with other party leaders and put in jail for six months. During his imprisonment, Sa'ada finished his seminal work, *The Genesis of Nations.* The party continued to grow in size and influence, although Sa'ada was detained again in 1936 and 1937 for a total of seven months. The oppression of Sa'ada and the party by the French, rekindled by an arrest warrant in 1938, played a role in shifting his activities overseas, where his main goals were to organize Syrian emigrants and to promote his cause in international circles. But World War II and the French measures taken against him blocked his return home, and he was exiled, mainly to Argentina, for several years.

Sa'ada was received as a hero upon his return to Beirut on 2 March 1947. The newly independent Lebanese state quickly moved to curb his increasing influence, to no avail. Meanwhile, he succeeded in consolidating his power in the party and in solidifying the party's growth in Lebanon, Syria, Palestine, and Jordan. An attack on the SSNP by the proestablishment Phalange Party in June 1949 in Beirut was followed by an aggressive government campaign. As a result, Sa'ada mounted a rebellion against the Lebanese state on 4 July 1949. The Syrian president, Husni al-Za'im, to whom Sa'ada turned for help, betrayed Sa'ada's trust and turned him over to his foes. Sa'ada was summarily tried without due process in Beirut and executed on 8 July 1949.

Sa'ada saw the SSNP as an agent of change and progress. The party's goals included the revival, independence, sovereignty, and development of the "Syrian Nation" as part of the Arab World. This nation was partitioned by British and French colonial powers into new political entities after the collapse of the Ottoman Empire in 1918. According to Sa'ada, the Syrian Nation included Lebanon, Syria, Palestine, Jordan, Iraq, Kuwait, and Cyprus. The reform principles emphasized the abolition of feudalism and sectarianism and promoted secularism. The SSNP is historically characterized as well-disciplined and staunchly secular, with multiethnic and multiconfessional membership.

See also GREATER SYRIA; PHALANGE; SYRIAN SOCIAL NATIONALIST PARTY; ZA'IM, HUSNI AL-.

Bibliography

Kader, Haytham. *The Syrian Social Nationalist Party: Its Ideology and Early History.* Beirut: n.p., 1990.

Saadeh, Sofia A. *Antun Saadeh and Democracy in Geographic Syria.* London: Folios, 2000.

Zuwiyya Yamak, Labib. *The Syrian Social Nationalist Party: An Ideological Analysis.* Cambridge, MA: Harvard University Press, 1966.

CHARLES U. ZENZIE
UPDATED BY SAMI A. OFEISH

SAADAWI, NAWAL AL-
[1931–]

Egyptian feminist, writer, and doctor.

Nawal al-Saadawi (also spelled Nawal al-Sa'dawi or Nawal el-Saadawi) was born in the village of Kafar Tahla in Egypt. She graduated from the faculty of medicine at Cairo University in 1955 and practiced medicine for ten years, becoming a vigorous opponent of the exploitation of women in Egypt and the Arab world. She was dismissed from her position as Egypt's general director of health education for having written *Woman and Sex* (1972), which discussed the sexual exploitation of women, including prostitution, clitoridectomy, incest, and sexually transmitted diseases. For instance, she discussed in detail the female sexual anatomy, especially the variation in hymen types. She also discussed the epistemology of psychological, physical, and social epidemics affecting sexual roles and relationships. She openly discussed taboos such as rape, women's submissive roles in the family and society, sexual repression, and inconsistent social and religious values. Between 1979 and 1980, she became the United Nations advisor for the Women's Program in Africa and the Middle East. Her literary and scientific writings resulted in her imprisonment in 1981. Upon her release in 1982, she founded the Arab Women's Solidarity Association International, which was closed down in 1991 by the Egyptian government. She and Dr. Sherif Hetata, her second husband, were members of the Commission of Inquiry for the International War Crimes Tribunal (1992), which investigated war crimes against Iraq. She also served on a mission to bring medical aid to Iraq in defiance of U.S. sanctions. In 2001, an Egyptian court dismissed a lawsuit filed against her by a religious extremist for having "scorned Islam."

The candor with which she has approached health, economic, political, and social problems has made her a radical and progressive activist, working against social injustice exercised in the name of religion, morals, and love. She has written more than thirty books, which have been translated into thirty languages and have reached both a popular and an academic audience worldwide. Her books in English include *Searching* (1991), *My Travels around the World* (1992), *Memoirs from the Women's Prison* (1994), *Woman at Point Zero* (1997), *The Nawal El Saadawi Reader* (1997), *Hidden Face of Eve: Women in the Arab World* (1997), *The Innocence of the Devil* (1998), *Daughter of Isis: The Autobiography of Nawal El Saadawi* (1999), and *Walking through Fire: A Life of Nawal al Saadawi* (2002).

See also ARAB WOMEN'S SOLIDARITY ASSOCIATION INTERNATIONAL; SANCTIONS, IRAQI.

Bibliography

Al Ali, Nadje Sadig. *Gender Writing/Writing Gender: The Representation of Women in a Selection of Modern Egyptian Literature.* Cairo: The American University in Cairo Press, 1994.

Badran, Margot, and Cooke, Miriam, eds. *Opening the Gates: A Century of Arab Feminist Writing.* Bloomington: Indiana University Press, 1990.

Malti-Douglas, Fedwa. *Men, Women, and God(s): Nawal El Saadawi and Arab Feminist Poetics.* Berkeley: University of California Press, 1995.

"Nawal El Saadawi, Sherif Hetata." Available from <http://www.nawalsaadawi.net/>.

DAVID WALDNER
UPDATED BY RITA STEPHAN

SAADE, GEORGE
[1930–1998]

Lebanese politician.

Born to a Maronite Catholic family, George Saade completed his schooling in Lebanon. In 1955 he left for Spain, where he enrolled as a student at Madrid's Central University and completed degrees in literature and philosophy and Semitic languages. Elected to the Lebanese parliament in 1968, Saade was also appointed as minister in several governments. In 1945, while a student, he joined the Phalange Party (Hizb al-Kata'ib), in which he played important roles, including adviser for educational matters to the party founder, Pierre Jumayyil. In 1969, following clashes between the Lebanese army and the Palestine Liberation Organization (PLO), Saade was appointed to a joint dialogue group with the Palestinians. In the 1970s he played a key role in the Phalange Party's relationships with the Arab countries. In 1986 he was elected president of al-Kata'ib. In 1991 and 1992 Saade was a member of the Lebanese government until his resignation in September 1992. He died in November 1998.

See also JUMAYYIL, PIERRE; PALESTINE LIBERATION ORGANIZATION (PLO); PHALANGE.

GEORGE E. IRANI
UPDATED BY MICHAEL R. FISCHBACH

SABA FAMILY

Prominent Palestinian/Lebanese business family.

The Sabas, Christians originally from Shafa Amr in Palestine, achieved prominence in the twentieth century through the extraordinary business and political career of Fu'ad Saba. In the 1920s, Fu'ad [1902–] founded the now-huge accounting firm of Saba & Co. In the 1930s, he helped establish the Palestinian National Fund and acted as secretary to the Arab Higher Committee. He was briefly exiled by the British in the late 1930s for his political activities.

Fu'ad relocated Saba & Co. to Beirut before the 1948 Arab-Israel War and started other enterprises there, including the al-Mashriq Financial Investment Company (1963), the Arabia Insurance Company, and the Middle East Society of Associated Accountants. His business boomed after signing contracts with the American oil firm of J. Paul Getty and a top American accounting firm, Arthur Andersen and Company. He lived in Beirut until his death in the late 1980s.

Fu'ad's son Fawzi, born in 1931 in Jerusalem, attended the American University of Beirut, as his father did. He became a partner in Saba & Co. and has been living in Saudi Arabia and Dubai. (The family is of no known relation to Elias Saba, the 1970s Lebanese finance minister from northern Lebanon.)

Bibliography

Khalaf, Issa. *Politics in Palestine: Arab Factionalism and Social Disintegration, 1939–1948.* Albany: State University of New York Press, 1991.

Smith, Pamela Ann. *Palestine and the Palestinians, 1876–1983.* New York: St. Martin's, 1984.

ELIZABETH THOMPSON

SABAH, RASHA AL-
[1950–]

Advocate for women's rights in Kuwait.

Rasha al-Sabah, a member of Kuwait's ruling family, was born 18 November 1950. She received a bachelor's degree from the University of Birmingham (U.K.) in 1972, and a master's degree and doctorate from Yale University in 1974 and 1977 respectively.

At Kuwait University she became the head of the University Language Center in 1977, a dean in 1982, and a vice rector for community service and information in 1985. Rasha is well-known as a champion of women's rights at home and as a spokeswoman for her country abroad. A cousin of Amir Jabir al-Ahmad, she is among his most trusted advisors. Currently she holds the position of undersecretary of higher education. She also served as Kuwait's deputy ambassador to the United Nations from 1990 to 1994. She was a prominent supporter of the amir's controversial May 1999 initiative to confer full political rights on Kuwaiti women and was openly disappointed when the National Assembly voted it down twice in November 1999. An innovative advocate of women's interests, she opened the first mixed-sex *diwaniyya* in Kuwait, where both women and men participate weekly in conversations at her home about the issues of the day. Rasha is the recipient of a number of honors, including a Doctor of Laws conferred in 1997 by Richmond University in London.

See also GENDER: GENDER AND EDUCATION; KUWAIT.

Bibliography

Rush, Alan de Lacy. *Al-Sabah: Genealogy and History of Kuwait's Ruling Family, 1752–1986.* London and Atlantic Highlands, NJ: Ithaca Press, 1987.

MARY ANN TÉTREAULT

SABAH, SUAD AL-
[1942–]

Poet, economist, publisher, activist in social change affecting women and children.

Suad Muhammad al-Sabah (also spelled Souad al-Sabah or Suʿad al-Sabah) was born in 1942 in Kuwait as a member of the ruling family. She graduated from the Faculty of Economics and Political Sciences at Cairo University in 1973. She obtained a doctorate in economics from Sari Guilford University in the United Kingdom in 1981. She later returned to Kuwait and established the Suad al-Sabah Publishing and Distribution House. She has published several books of poetry and established a literary prize that carries her name. She also has written hundreds of economic and political essays as well as popular articles in several Arabic local and international newspapers and magazines. Her poetry has been translated into many languages, including English.

Upon the 1990 Iraqi invasion of Kuwait, al-Sabah campaigned against the war, writing newspaper articles and hosting radio programs, attempting to persuade Arab organizations to adopt firm stands against Iraq's aggression. In 1991 she published an anthology of ironic and bitter poetry on the Gulf War entitled *Will You Let Me Love My Country?* The poems delve into the spiritual crisis experienced by most Arab intellectuals in the new world order.

Al-Sabah is the director of Kuwait Stock Exchange and a member of the Higher Council for Education, the executive committee of the World Muslim Women Organization for South East Asia, and the board of trustees and the executive committee of the Arab Intellect Forum. She is also a founding member of the Arab Cultural Establishment, the executive committee of the Arab Human Rights Organization, and the Arab Council for Childhood and Development. Her poetry has captured the attention of popular artists as well as university researchers in many countries. Her literary publications include *Wamdatt Bakira* (Early blinks) and *Lahathat min Umri* (Moments of my life, 1961). Her scientific works in English include *Development Planning in an Oil Economy and the Role of the Woman* (1983) and *Kuwait: Anatomy of a Crisis Economy* (1984).

Bibliography

Cooke, Mariam. *Women Claim Islam: Creating Islamic Feminism through Literature.* New York: Routledge, 2000.

RITA STEPHAN

SABBAGH, HASIB
[1920–]

Palestinian entrepreneur and philanthropist.

Hasib Sabbagh came from a Christian family in Safed in British Mandate Palestine, although he was born in Tiberias. He graduated from the Arab College of Jerusalem in 1938, and in 1941 gained a civil engineering degree from the American University of Beirut.

In 1943, with four other contractors, he established the Consolidated Contractors Company (CCC) in Haifa. Sabbagh left Palestine in April 1948 and moved to Lebanon. CCC was reestablished there in 1950, becoming the region's largest multinational and one of the largest contractors worldwide.

A longtime member of both the Palestine National Council and of its central council, Sabbagh provided crucial international contacts for Yasir Arafat during the 1970s and 1980s. Most controversially, his 1978 meeting with the Phalange, first agreed to and then denounced by Arafat, provoked condemnation from the Lebanese and Syrian governments as well as from Palestinian opposition groups. In 1988, his active support encouraged Arafat to steer the Palestine Liberation Organization firmly toward a renewed peace initiative.

Through the Diana Sabbagh Foundation, one of the largest Arab charitable foundations, Sabbagh has supported institutions of higher education across the Arab world and the West, and has influenced a range of dialogue initiatives, notably in the United States at the Council on Foreign Relations, the Carter Center, and the Center for Muslim–Christian Encounter, and in Palestine within the Palestinian Initiative for the Promotion of Global Dialogue and Democracy (MIFTAH), under Hanan Ashrawi. He also cofounded the Welfare Association for Palestinians, chaired the Palestinian Students Fund, and has been on the boards of the Arab Bank and of many academic institutions and pro-Palestinian think tanks, such as the Institute of Palestine Studies.

See also ARAFAT, YASIR; PALESTINE LIBERATION ORGANIZATION (PLO); PALESTINE NATIONAL COUNCIL.

Bibliography

Brynen, Rex. *Sanctuary and Survival: The PLO in Lebanon.* Boulder, CO: Westview, 1990.

Hindley, Angus. "Profile-CCC: Arab Giant Achieves Global Reach." *Middle East Economic Digest* 38 (29 July 1994): 30.

King, Mary, and Deeb, Mary, eds. *Hassib Sabbagh.* Lanham, MD: Middle East Institute of University Press of America, 1996.

MOUIN RABBANI
UPDATED BY GEORGE R. WILKES

SABBAGH, SALAH AL-DIN AL-
[1889–1945]

Arab nationalist; Iraqi army officer who headed the Golden Square group that opposed the government and influenced politics from 1939 to 1941.

Born in Mosul of a Lebanese father and an Iraqi mother, Salah al-Din al-Sabbagh was educated in Mosul and the Ottoman Military College in Istanbul, graduating as an officer in 1915. During World War I, he served in Palestine and Macedonia and was taken prisoner, ultimately joining Amir Faisal I ibn Hussein, who became king of Iraq, to return to Iraq in 1921 to a position in the Iraqi army. His military education also included courses in Belgium and in Britain. Sabbagh became an instructor at the Baghdad Military College in 1924 and later taught at the Staff College. By 1940 he was assistant chief of staff of the Iraqi army.

Al-Sabbagh was an Arab nationalist and the head of the Golden Square, the group of army officers that from 1939 to 1941 influenced Iraqi politics from behind the scenes. An admirer of the Jerusalem mufti (chief Muslim jurist) Hajj Muhammad Amin al-Husayni, al-Sabbagh worked with him and with Rashid Ali al-Kaylani in their negotiations with the Axis powers for support of their pan-Arab goals. Al-Sabbagh backed Rashid Ali as prime minister in 1941 and was a major advocate of war with Britain in April and May. After the Iraqi defeat in the Anglo–Iraqi War of 1941, Sabbagh fled to Iran and then to Turkey, where he was extradited to Iraq and executed in 1945. His book *Fursan al-Uruba fi al-Iraq* (The knights of Arabism in Iraq), an autobiographical account of his pan-Arabism, was published posthumously in Baghdad in 1956.

See also FAISAL I IBN HUSSEIN; GOLDEN SQUARE; HUSAYNI, MUHAMMAD AMIN AL-; KAYLANI, RASHID ALI AL-.

Bibliography

Simon, Reeva S. *Iraq between the Two World Wars: The Creation and Implementation of a Nationalist Ideology.* New York: Columbia University Press, 1986.

REEVA S. SIMON

SABBATH

The seventh day of the week; the day of religiously mandated rest.

In Judaism, the Sabbath (in Hebrew, *Shabbat*, or rest) was and is the holiest day of the week. Historically, no work of any kind could be done; hence, fire could not be made and, by extension, nothing that runs electrically or mechanically can be started up by observant Jews. Food is prepared in advance and special customs ensure rest and reflection on the past week, and thereby restoration of the soul for the coming week.

The Jewish Sabbath begins at sundown Friday and lasts twenty-five hours, until nightfall Saturday; the Christian Sabbath is usually celebrated on Sunday. In Israel on the Sabbath, public facilities are closed. Outside of Haifa, buses of the state cooperatives do not run, no El Al (Israeli) airliners take off or land, and no Hebrew newspapers are published.

Public observance of the Sabbath has been the source of some tension within Israeli society. Since the formation of the state, Orthodox and, in particular, *haredi* (ultra-Orthodox) Jews have been insistent that restaurants, movie theatres, and other "profane" public establishments remain closed in observance of the Sabbath. Although such closings have been common, increasing numbers of businesses are remaining open on the Sabbath.

There is no ban in Israel on the driving of private cars on the Sabbath, but *haredi* Jews, in an effort to enforce the religious prohibitions of the Sabbath, have periodically clashed with local authorities and drivers by demanding the closure to automobile traffic of public thoroughfares that pass near or through their enclaves on the holy day of rest. This has occasionally led to violent demonstrations, stone-throwing, and mass protests by Orthodox Jews against "desecration of the Sabbath." Although most of these demonstrations ultimately have led to the limitation or eventual halt of the flow of traffic on these thoroughfares during the Sabbath, the protests have also led to increased tensions between Orthodox and secular Israelis and often hostile debates about religious coercion in Israeli society.

SAMUEL C. HEILMAN

SABRA

Word ultimately derived from the Arabic for a variety of prickly pear found in Israel; also the name for a native-born Israeli.

Native-born Israelis are described as Sabras because their personality is often thought to be similar to the fruit of the plant: tough and prickly on the outside, sweet on the inside.

BRYAN DAVES

SABRA AND SHATILA MASSACRES

Mass killing of hundreds of Palestinians in refugee camps, 16–18 September 1982.

Shortly after Israel invaded Lebanon on 6 June 1982, the Israel Defense Force (IDF) laid siege to Beirut. A cease-fire accord reached in August allowed the entry into West Beirut of a multilateral force, including a contingent of U.S. Marines. Following a U.S. pledge to protect Palestinian civilians, Palestine Liberation Organization (PLO) fighters and officials departed the city, as did the multinational force. The day after the president of Lebanon, Bashir Jumayyil, was assassinated (14 September), Israel sent troops into West Beirut, where they surrounded two Palestinian refugee camps in violation of the cease-fire agreement. Defense Minister Ariel Sharon and Chief of Staff Rafael Eitan arranged for the Israel-supported Phalange militia to enter the camps to clear out what Sharon described as "2,000–3,000 terrorists who remained behind. We even have their names." The Phalange murdered hundreds of Palestinians, mostly women, children, and older men. Israel put the figure at 800; other sources estimated it at 1,500.

The international community condemned Israel's role in the mass killing, and up to 400,000 Israelis (8 percent of the population) demonstrated against the government of Menachem Begin and demanded a judicial inquiry. A three-man Israeli commission, headed by the president of the Supreme Court, Yitzhak Kahan, found that Israeli officials were "indirectly responsible" because they arranged for the Phalange, mortal enemies of the Palestinians, to enter the camps and, even though Israeli officers and government officials received reports about the atrocities, they ignored them and allowed the Phalange to extend their stay in the camps. The International Commission, chaired by Sean MacBride, former assistant secretary general of the United Nations, charged that under international law, Israel was directly responsible because the camps were under its jurisdiction as an occupying power and because the IDF planned and facilitated its ally's entry into and activities in the camps, prevented survivors from leaving the camps, and did not stop the mass killing after hearing about it. Despite the findings of both commissions, no one was prosecuted. In 2001, Human Rights Watch and Amnesty International called for an investigation of Ariel Sharon for his role in the Sabra and Shatila massacres.

See also ARAB–ISRAEL WAR (1982); EITAN, RAFAEL; KAHAN COMMISSION (1983); PHALANGE; SHARON, ARIEL.

Bibliography

Government of Israel. The Kahan Commission Report. Jerusalem: Author, 1982.

Smithe, Charles D. Palestine and the Arab–Israeli Conflict. New York: St. Martin's Press, 1988.

Tessler, Mark. A History of the Israeli–Palestinian Conflict. Bloomington: Indiana University Press, 1994.

PHILIP MATTAR

SABRA AND SHATILA REFUGEE CAMPUS

See SABRA AND SHATILA MASSACRES

SABRI, ALI
[1920–1991]

Egyptian military officer and politician.

Ali Sabri was educated at the Military Academy, taught at the Air Force Academy in 1949, and served as an air force officer. Though not a member of the Free Officers, he supported their movement and acted as liason to the U.S. embassy prior to the 1952 revolution in which the Free Officers overthrew King Farouk. Between 1957 and 1962, Sabri was minister of presidential affairs, giving him access to President Gamal Abdel Nasser, who appointed him to the Supreme Executive of the Arab Socialist Union (ASU) in 1962, a position he held through 1965, at which time he was appointed secretary-general of the union. Sabri is well known in Egyptian politics as perhaps the most influential leftist. His tenure in the ASU is closely associated with Nasser's shift to the left in the early 1960s. As head of the ASU, Sabri sought to make it the leading political body in Egypt by subordinating the public

sector, the bureaucracy, labor unions, and professional syndicates to its control. On the death of Nasser, Sabri was one of the most powerful men in Egypt. He was responsible for naming Anwar al-Sadat president, under the mistaken assumption that he could control Sadat. In May of 1971, Sabri and his supporters publicly broke with Sadat. Sadat responded by arresting Sabri for plotting a coup. Sabri was sentenced to death, but this was commuted to twenty-five years in prison. Sabri was released from prison in 1981.

See also ARAB SOCIALIST UNION; FREE OFFICERS, EGYPT.

Bibliography

Hinnebusch, Raymond A., Jr. Egyptian Politics under Sadat: The Post-Populist Development of an Authoritarian-Modernizing State. Cambridge, U.K., and New York: Cambridge University Press, 1985.

Waterbury, John. The Egypt of Nasser and Sadat: The Political Economy of Two Regimes. Princeton, NJ: Princeton University Press, 1983.

Wucher King, Joan. Historical Dictionary of Egypt. Metuchen, NJ: Scarecrow Press, 1984.

DAVID WALDNER

SADAT, ANWAR AL-
[1918–1981]

President of Egypt from 1970 until his assassination in 1981.

Anwar al-Sadat was born 25 December 1918 in the village of Mit Abu al-Kum in the Lower Egyptian province of Minufiyya. His father, a mid-level government official, arranged for him to enroll in primary and secondary school in Cairo, from which he was graduated in 1936. That same year, admission in the national military academy was opened to young men from nonaristocratic families, and Sadat seized the opportunity to pursue a career as a military officer. He was graduated in 1938 and was posted to Manqabad in Upper Egypt, where he became friends with another ambitious young officer, Gamal Abdel Nasser. Transferred to the outskirts of Cairo in 1939, he immediately made contact with a range of underground political organizations working against the monarchy of King Farouk. They included the Muslim Brotherhood (al-Ikhwan al-Muslimin) and a cell based in the signal corps

Anwar al-Sadat (1918–1981) was an Egyptian political leader and president (1970–1981). Muslim extremists, who were against his peace initiatives with Israel, assassinated him. THE LIBRARY OF CONGRESS. REPRODUCED BY PERMISSION.

sympathetic to Nazi Germany. Since World War II was raging in North Africa, his association with this cell led to his arrest in 1942 for conspiring against the British war effort (Britain maintained a protectorate over the Suez Canal and Egypt). Upon his escape from prison in 1945, he revived his contacts with the Muslim Brotherhood, taking part in a January 1946 plot to assassinate a prominent pro-British politician. He was arrested again in connection with this incident and spent two more years in prison awaiting trial. His longstanding connections with high-ranking but anti-British members of the armed forces won him reinstatement in the officers' corps in 1950.

Toward the end of 1951, Sadat was asked by Nasser to join the inner circle of the clandestine Free Officers movement. He played little direct part in the coup d'état headed by General Muhammad Naguib that overthrew the monarchy and brought the movement to power in July 1952, but he was chosen to broadcast the first announcement of the coup on the morning it occurred. He was thereafter editor of the newspaper al-Jumhuriyya, a member of the ruling revolutionary command council, and a minister of state.

As secretary-general of the ruling political party, the Arab Socialist Union (ASU), Sadat assumed the role of faithful subordinate to Nasser, assisting him in moving first against the Muslim Brotherhood and then against his rivals within the Free Officers. When Nasser overcame Naguib to lead the ruling junta, he repaid Sadat's loyalty by appointing him first speaker of the reconfigured national assembly in 1962, one of four vice presidents in 1964, and then, in December 1969, vice president of the republic.

Nasser's unexpected death by heart attack in September 1970 precipitated eight months of intense jockeying for power at the highest echelons of the Egyptian regime. Proponents of continuing the government's socialist economic policies—led by the secretary-general of the ASU, Ali Sabri—faced firm opposition from advocates of a more liberal order, such as the editor of the semiofficial al-Ahram newspaper, Muhammad Hasanayn Haykal. Sadat, who had been appointed provisional president by the cabinet shortly after Nasser's death, took advantage of his relatively insulated position in the national assembly to play these factions against one another, emerging as the regime's key figure when the cabinet of ministers tendered its resignation to the assembly in May 1971. He immediately charged the powerful minister of the interior with plotting to set up a police state and replaced him with a trusted ally, Mamduh Salim. He then moved to cultivate public approval by commissioning the national assembly to formulate a permanent constitution, pardoning most of the country's political prisoners and returning properties sequestered during the socialist era of the early 1960s to their original owners. At the same time, he attempted to undermine leftist influence by catering to those sympathetic to the Muslim Brotherhood through carefully choreographed displays of his own religiosity in the mass media and by tolerating the spread of Islamist political groups on university campuses.

These moves precipitated a wave of unrest among university students in January 1972 that persuaded

Sadat to initiate major shifts in Egypt's foreign policy as a way of consolidating his position at home. That July he ordered all Soviet military advisers out of the country and began planning for a campaign to recapture the Sinai peninsula, which Israel had occupied during the Arab–Israel War of 1967. While preparing to attack Israel's forces in the Sinai, Sadat effected a rapprochement with Saudi Arabia and created a working alliance with Syria as well, which enabled the Egyptian armed forces to strike across the Suez Canal on 6 October 1973. Although the attack was, in the end, repelled and Israeli units drove deep into the Egyptian delta before a ceasefire was arranged on 23 October, the comparatively good showing made by Egyptian troops led Sadat to claim the honorific "the hero of the crossing" and invite U.S. Secretary of State Henry Kissinger to mediate an interim settlement with Israel. Two disengagement agreements negotiated under U.S. auspices in January 1974 and September 1975 laid the foundation for Sadat's 9 November 1977 surprise announcement that he intended to travel to Jerusalem to initiate peace talks with Israel's government. Ten days later he addressed the Israeli parliament, smashing what he called "the psychological barrier" to peace between the two states. He then took part in a series of face-to-face negotiations with Israeli Prime Minister Menachem Begin that culminated in the September 1978 Camp David Accords, which in turn led to the signing of an Egyptian–Israeli peace treaty in March 1979. This document resulted in the withdrawal of Israeli forces from the Sinai in April 1982.

Sadat's unprecedented trip to Jerusalem was prompted by internal as well as external developments. In June 1974, the regime implemented an economic program designed to attract greater amounts of foreign investment into the country and provide new opportunities for local entrepreneurs, which came to be known as the policy of *infitah* (opening up). At the same time, competing factions within the ASU were encouraged to organize into separate political groupings (*manabir*), which by 1976 had become established as autonomous parties; the largest of these, the centrist National Democratic Party, continued to dominate the national assembly, while smaller rightist and leftist parties, the Social Democratic Party and the National Progressive Unionist Party, played the role of loyal opposition

to the government. It was in these circumstances at the beginning of 1977 that the regime agreed to implement austerity measures demanded by the International Monetary Fund and cut state subsidies on a wide range of basic foodstuffs and other necessities. This decision sparked large scale riots in Cairo, Alexandria, and other Egyptian cities, forcing the government to restore the subsidies. President Sadat immediately castigated the rioters as "thieves" and ordered wholesale revisions to the Parties Law of 1977 that substantially limited the activities in which political associations were permitted to engage. The subsequent electoral successes of the main prerevolutionary party, the Wafd, added to Sadat's displeasure with the new political order he had helped to create. In June 1978, he ordered the arrest of the Wafd's leadership; he supervised the de facto rigging of parliamentary elections a year later; and in September 1981, he issued new regulations that led to the imprisonment of virtually all opposition activists.

These measures added fuel to the smoldering popular discontent generated by Egypt's persistent economic difficulties and Sadat's unilateral peace treaty with Israel. The Camp David Accords failed to bring appreciably greater levels of U.S. assistance into the country, even as the policies associated with *infitah* steadily increased the gap between rich and poor. They did little better in persuading Israel to proceed with the direct talks concerning the future of the occupied territories that were envisaged as the second stage of the agreement. Furthermore, the very image affected by Sadat to win popular support in the United States—that of a benevolent patriarch, complete with sweater and pipe—grated on dissidents at home. Militant Islamist cells proliferated in poor neighborhoods, in the provinces of Upper Egypt and, most notably, within the armed forces. Members of one of these cells, al-Jihad, assassinated Sadat on 6 October 1981 as he reviewed a military parade commemorating the eighth anniversary of the attack across the Suez Canal. He was succeeded by his vice president, Husni Mubarak.

See also ARAB–ISRAEL WAR (1967); ARAB SOCIALIST UNION; BEGIN, MENACHEM; CAMP DAVID ACCORDS (1978); EGYPTIAN–ISRAELI PEACE TREATY (1979); FAROUK; FREE OFFICERS, EGYPT; HAYKAL, MUHAMMAD HASANAYN; INTERNATIONAL MONETARY

FUND; KISSINGER, HENRY; MUBARAK, HUSNI; MUSLIM BROTHERHOOD; NAGUIB, MUHAMMAD; NASSER, GAMAL ABDEL; NATIONAL PROGRESSIVE UNIONIST PARTY; NEWSPAPERS AND PRINT MEDIA: ARAB COUNTRIES; SABRI, ALI; WAFD.

Bibliography

Baker, Raymond William. *Sadat and After: Struggles for Egypt's Political Soul.* Cambridge, MA: Harvard University Press, 1990.

Beattie, Kirk J. *Egypt during the Sadat Years.* New York: St. Martin's, 2000.

Cooper, Mark N. *The Transformation of Egypt.* Baltimore, MD: Johns Hopkins University Press, 1982.

Hirst, David, and Beeson, Irene. *Sadat.* London: Faber and Faber, 1981.

Sadat, Anwar El-. *In Search of Identity: An Autobiography.* New York: Harper and Row, 1978.

Waterbury, John. *The Egypt of Nasser and Sadat: The Political Economy of Two Regimes.* Princeton, NJ: Princeton University Press, 1983.

FRED H. LAWSON

SADAT, JIHAN AL-
[1933–]

Egyptian feminist and political activist.

Jihan al-Sadat was born on Rawda Island in Cairo. Her father, Safwat Ra'uf, was Muslim and a civil servant in the Ministry of Health, and her mother was British. Although raised as a Muslim, Jihan attended a Christian missionary school. In 1949 she married Anwar al-Sadat, the future president of Egypt. Known as the First Lady of Egypt during her husband's presidency, she was an outspoken supporter of women's rights and peace with Israel. She founded the Talla Society, a cooperative that taught women various handicrafts so that they could support themselves, and *al-Wafa wa al-Amal* (Faith and Hope), which built the Middle East's largest hospital complex for disabled war veterans and their families. She represented Egypt at the International Women's Year Conference held in Mexico City in 1975. Two years later she founded SOS Children's Villages International for orphans. She later led the fundraising drive for the rehabilitation of Qasr al-Ayni Hospital. She earned B.A., M.A., and Ph.D.

degrees in Arabic Literature at Cairo University. Along with other prominent feminists, she helped to draft what became known as Jihan's Laws, which gave women the right to divorce, custody of children, and the right to the family home if their husbands took second wives (portions of this legislation were abrogated in 1985). Soon after President Sadat was assassinated in 1981, Jihan moved to the United States, where she lectures on women in developing countries and on Islamic culture. She has taught at the University of South Carolina, Radford University, American University, and the University of Maryland, where she has been an associate of its Center for International Development and Conflict Management since 1988 and has promoted the Anwar Sadat Chair for Population, Development, and International Peace. She has received at least eighteen honorary doctorates and numerous awards.

See also GENDER: GENDER AND POLITICS; SADAT, ANWAR AL-.

Bibliography

Davis, Nedda. "Jehan Sadat." *The World and I,* v. 15, no. 3 (March 2000): 325.

Fay, Mary Ann, ed. *Auto/biography and the Construction of Identity and Community in the Middle East.* New York: Palgrave, 2002.

Goldschmidt, Arthur. "Al-Sadat, Jihan." In *A Biographical Dictionary of Modern Egypt,* edited by Arthur Goldschmidt. Boulder, CO: Lynne Rienner Publishers, 2000.

Sadat, Jihan. *A Woman of Egypt.* New York: Simon and Schuster, 1987.

Selle, Robert. "Woman of Peace and Patriotism." *The World and I,* v. 14, no. 7 (July 1999): 64.

Sullivan, Earl L. *Women in Egyptian Public Life.* Syracuse, NY: Syracuse University Press, 1986.

Talhami, Ghada Hashem. *The Mobilization of Muslim Women in Egypt.* Gainesville: Florida Universities Press, 1996.

ARTHUR GOLDSCHMIDT

SADAWI, BASHIR
[c. 1882–1957]

Libyan (Tripolitanian) politician.

Associated with the Tripolitanian republic after World War I, Bashir Sadawi was in exile for many years, during which he acted as adviser to the Saudi

Arabian monarchy of Ibn Sa'ud. In 1947, with Arab League support, he founded the National Council for the Liberation of Libya in Cairo to promote the unity of the regions of Tripolitania and Cyrenaica. In 1949, popular protests against Anglo-Italian trusteeship proposals for Libya prompted several political groups to form the Tripolitanian National Congress party under Sadawi's leadership. During the many years of international debate on Libya's future (1945–1949) and the subsequent preparations for independence under UN supervision (1949–1951), Sadawi emerged as Tripolitania's leading politician, consistently supporting a unitary Libyan state and Amir Idris al-Sayyid Muhammad al-Sanusi as the sole leader capable of uniting the country.

Sadawi's political hopes were dashed, first by the decision that independent Libya was to be a federal kingdom under Idris, then with the failure of his National Congress party to win as many seats as expected in the first postindependence elections in February 1952. The government used postelection riots as an excuse to deport Sadawi, who returned to Saudi royal service.

See also IDRIS AL-SAYYID MUHAMMAD AL-SANUSI.

Bibliography

Pelt, Adrian. *Libyan Independence and the United Nations: A Case of Planned Decolonization.* New Haven, CT: Yale University Press, 1970.

JOHN L. WRIGHT

SADIQI COLLEGE

Secondary school in Tunis.

Sadiqi College was founded in 1875 and 1876 by Khayr al-Din. Its curriculum, which included modern sciences and languages, was taught in Arabic and French. In an effort to modernize the college, subjects such as translation, administrative law, and Islamic jurisprudence were added to the curriculum. During the French protectorate, French replaced Arabic as the language of teaching for most subjects. In 1892 the school acquired a French director.

Sadiqi attracted few students at first, but its enrollment increased steadily. As its popularity grew,

it became very selective in the choice of its students, in contrast to Zaytuna University. Sadiqi graduated seventy-eight students in 1954.

The graduates of Sadiqi usually went to France for their higher education. As a result, they were criticized by those who considered the college an institution for bourgeois children and were accused of maintaining strong links with France and its culture.

Although Sadiqi was a model for many of the Franco–Arabic schools that arose in Tunisia during the French protectorate, it was only in 1911 that its diploma was officially recognized.

See also KHAYR AL-DIN; ZAYTUNA UNIVERSITY.

Bibliography

Abun-Nasr, M. Jamil. *A History of the Maghrib.* Cambridge, U.K.: Cambridge University Press, 1971.

Gordon, David. *North Africa's French Legacy.* Cambridge, U.K.: Cambridge University Press, 1962.

Hourani, Albert. *A History of the Arab Peoples.* New York: Warner Books, 1992.

AIDA A. BAMIA

SADI, SAID
[1947–]

Leader of the Algerian political party Rally for Culture and Democracy.

Said Sadi was born into a poor family in Aghrib in Kabylia. A charismatic psychiatrist, he began his militant activities for cultural and workers' rights while a student and joined the clandestine opposition party Front des Forces Socialistes (FFS; Socialist Forces Front). He strongly opposed single-party rule and called for Berber cultural rights. One of the leaders of the 1980 Berber Spring uprising, he demanded recognition of the Berber language and culture within a democratic state. He was jailed five times in the 1980s. He subsequently broke with the FFS and joined a group of militants devoted to human rights and to cultural and women's issues. In 1985 they founded the Human Rights League. In 1989 Sadi founded and headed the Rassemblement pour la Culture et la Démocratie (RCD; Rally for Culture and Democracy), an outgrowth of the Berber movement. Sadi has been a staunch critic of both the regime and Algeria's Islamists. The RCD boycotted the 1991 legislative elections but participated actively in the November 1995 presidential election and the June 1997 legislative vote. Sadi obtained 10 percent of the votes in 1995. The RCD obtained 19 seats at the assembly in 1997. Sadi has equated Islamism with terrorism, which explains his support for the military against radical Islamism. Although he boycotted the 1999 presidential election, Sadi supported President Abdelaziz Bouteflika's program to reform the economy, justice and educational systems, and administration. Two members of the RCD served as ministers in the government. Sadi withdrew the RCD from the government because of the Kabylia crisis, triggered in April 2001 following the killing in Tizi-Ouzou of a youngster by the National Gendarmerie. The demonstrations and violence that developed following that incident revealed the regime's inability to provide adequate democratic institutions to represent the nation's diverse interests. Because of the acute crisis, the RCD boycotted the legislative and municipal elections in May and October 2002, respectively. Sadi has sided with the *aruch* (tribal councils) and called repeatedly for the end of repression.

> *See also* ALGERIA; BERBER SPRING; BLACK SPRING; KABYLIA; RASSEMBLEMENT POUR LA CULTURE ET LA DÉMOCRATIE (RCD).

> YAHIA ZOUBIR

SADR, MUHAMMAD BAQIR AL-
[1931–1980]

Iraqi Shiʿite religious leader whose writings inspired and influenced the Islamic movement in Iraq.

Born in the Shiʿite district of Kazimiyya, Baghdad, to an Arab family from Lebanon, Muhammad Baqir al-Sadr studied in Baghdad and al-Najaf. Among his teachers was Muhsin al-Hakim, the highest Shiʿite *Marja al-Taqlid* of the time. Sadr rose in the Shiʿite clerical hierarchy to the rank of ayatullah, becoming the only Arab of eight living *marja al-Taqlids*. He was placed under house arrest in June 1979, following the Shiʿite riots in al-Najaf and Karbala. On 8 April 1980 he was hanged, following assassination attempts on several officials earlier that month. He was accused of being the leader of the outlawed al-Daʿwa party, being the mastermind behind the assassinations, and plotting with

Iran against Iraq's government. A prolific writer, Sadr published more than twenty books dealing with various subjects, including Islamic government and economy.

> *See also* MARJA AL-TAQLID.

Bibliography

Wiley, Joyce N. *The Islamic Movement of Iraqi Shiʿas.* Boulder, CO: Lynne Rienner, 1992.

> AYAD AL-QAZZAZ

SADR, MUHSIN
[1871–1963]

Iranian politician.

Born to a clerical family from Mahallat, Muhsin Sadr entered the bureaucracy in 1907 as a clerk at the Ministry of Justice during the reign of Naser al-Din Shah Qajar. During the Constitutional Revolution, he sided with Mohammad Ali Shah and became chief interrogator after the bombardment of the *majles*. An opportunist, Sadr exploited his links to the Iranian aristocracy after the restoration of the Constitutionalists and resumed his service at the Ministry of Justice. He was appointed minister of justice five times, speaker of the senate twice, governor of Khorasan once, and prime minister once. Reza Shah Pahlavi removed him from the Ministry of Justice in 1936.

> *See also* CONSTITUTIONAL REVOLUTION; MOHAMMAD ALI SHAH QAJAR; NASER AL-DIN SHAH; PAHLAVI, REZA.

Bibliography

Bamdad, Mehdi. *Biographies of Iranian Notables in the Twelfth, Thirteenth, and Fourteenth Centuries,* Vol. 3. Tehran, 1979.

> NEGUIN YAVARI

SADR, SITT RABAB AL- (CHARAFEDDINE)
[1946–]

A social and human-rights activist and Shiʿite philanthropist.

Born in Iran, Sitt Rabab al-Sadr moved to Lebanon at the age of fifteen. She adopted and promoted the social vision of her brother, Imam Musa al-Sadr, who encouraged her to join the Imam al-Sadr Foundation in Lebanon around 1960 and devote herself to social work and humanitarian aid. Meanwhile, she completed a B.A. in arts and an M.A. in philosophy in Lebanon. After the disappearance of Imam Musa in 1978 during a visit to Libya, Rabab became the president of the Imam al-Sadr Foundation, which consists today of six vocational schools and an orphanage. Al-Sadr oversees the girls' section of the foundation, providing much-needed economic assistance and social guidance to orphaned and dependent girls, regardless of their religious background. The foundation faced particular financial and organizational challenges after the dramatic increase in orphans due to the Lebanese war (1975–1991), the Israeli occupation of South Lebanon, and brutal attacks on civilians. She helped obtain a license for the foundation as a nonprofit organization in the U.S. in order to help gather contributions for widows, orphans, and poor children, mostly from South Lebanon. The schools sponsored by the foundation use modern technology and advanced educational methods and equipment.

Al-Sadr remains critical of the Lebanese government for abandoning South Lebanon and marginalizing it in state development policies. Following the Israeli withdrawal from South Lebanon in May 2001, the foundation launched two mobile medical clinics, which traveled to remote villages with no health facilities in order to offer preventive and curative medical services. Nearly 10,000 people benefited from these services. The foundation works to increase the attendance of orphans at primary schools, trains women for jobs, and runs day-long health centers. Al-Sadr strongly believes in the central role of education for women as a means for social change and personal growth. During numerous regional and international conferences on women's issues, she called on policymakers to acknowledge the need for gender equality and cooperation between men and women in the pursuit of a harmonious society. Her admirers and supporters urged her to run in parliamentary elections in Lebanon but she expressed her aversion to politics due to the restrictions it placed on social and family life.

See also AMAL; GENDER: GENDER AND EDUCATION; LEBANESE CIVIL WAR (1958); LEBANESE CIVIL WAR (1975–1990); LEBANON; SHI'ISM.

Bibliography

Al-Sadr Foundation. Available from <http://www.sadr-foundation.org.lb/>.

"Exclusive Interviews with Rabab al-Sadr." *Middle East News and World Report* (11 December 2002).

Sadr, Sitt Rabab al-. "Islam and Peace in the Fifteenth/Twenty-first Century." *Center for Global Peace and Nonviolence International,* The American University Center, Washington, D.C., 6–7 February 1998.

"Sadr on Southern Lebanon." *Washington Report on Middle East Affairs* 20, no. 4 (May/June 2001): 90–91.

RULA JURDI ABISAAB

SA'DUN, ABD AL-MUHSIN AL-
[1879–1907]

Leader of the Muntafiq tribe and Iraqi politician.

Son of Fahd Pasha al-Sa'dun, Abd al-Muhsin al Sa'dun was head of one of the two major branches of the ruling house of the Muntafiq tribe. He was graduated from the Ottoman Military College in 1905, became aide-de-camp to the sultan, but resigned his commission in 1909 and returned to Iraq. In 1910 and 1912 he was elected to represent the Muntafiq district in the Ottoman parliament. During the British mandate in Iraq, he headed al-Taqaddum (Progressive) party, which advocated termination of the mandate and independence through conciliation. President of the Constituent Assembly and twice president of parliament, Abd al-Muhsin held numerous cabinet portfolios and was four times prime minister. As principal Iraqi negotiator of the 1926 Anglo–Iraqi Treaty, he obtained important amendments regarding oil, military, and finance and shepherded its ratification. He was knighted in 1926.

See also ANGLO–IRAQI TREATIES; SA'DUN FAMILY, AL ; TRIBES AND TRIBALISM.

Bibliography

Ireland, Philip Willard. *Iraq: A Study in Political Development.* London: J. Cape, 1937.

ALBERTINE JWAIDEH

SA'DUN FAMILY, AL-

Ruling family of the Muntafiq in southern Iraq.

These are descendants of Mani, a sharif of Mecca who fled to the Euphrates around 1600 to escape a feud; won influence over the Muntafiq tribes by adjudicating their disputes; and was finally acknowledged as their ruler. The family name derives from Sa'dun, a great leader who led numerous raids against the Turks before being captured and beheaded in 1741. As rulers of the powerful Muntafiq, the Sa'dun were almost independent of Turkish rule until 1870 when the Ottomans made an attempt at regular land settlement. At the behest of their shaykh, Nasir Pasha, who founded the town of Nasiriyya and accepted high government office, the Sa'dun converted from tribute-receiving chiefs into regular landlords under Ottoman auspices. As a result of this "betrayal" to the Turks, the Sa'dun chiefs rapidly lost power over their tribes, whom they had reduced from landowners to tenants.

See also TRIBES AND TRIBALISM.

Bibliography

Longrigg, Stephen Hemsley. *Four Centuries of Modern Iraq.* Oxford: Clarendon Press, 1925.

ALBERTINE JWAIDEH

SA'EDI, GHOLAMHOSSEIN
[1935–1985]

Iranian novelist, playwright, short-story writer, and scriptwriter.

Gholamhossein Sa'edi, who used the pen name Gowhar Morad, was born in Tabriz and was graduated from the medical school at Tehran University with a specialty in psychiatry. He was the first Iranian who seriously engaged in writing "village literature," representing a village and its population not as a romantic entity but showing its deprived and actual face. One of the most popular Iranian writers of the 1960s and 1970s in Iran, he produced several plays and collections of short stories. Sa'edi left Iran in the late 1970s for Paris, where he died. Much of his work is available in English.

See also LITERATURE: PERSIAN.

Bibliography

Moayyad, Heshmat, ed. *Stories from Iran: A Chicago Anthology, 1921–1991.* Washington, DC: Mage, 1991.

PARDIS MINUCHEHR

SAFED

City located in the upper Galilee region of Israel.

Situated atop a mountain at an elevation of 2,780 feet (848 m), Safed (Hebrew, *Tzfat;* Arabic, *Safad*) is 25 miles (40 km) north of Tiberias and 30 miles (48 km) east of Acre. Safed is not mentioned in the Bible but was cited by the Roman historian Flavius Josephus as one of the cities he fortified. The Crusaders built a fortress in Safed, and the Mamluks made it an administrative center. Safed was one of the hills from which fires were built to signal the beginning of the lunar cycle and festivals. In the sixteenth century Joseph Karo, the author of the legal rabbinical work *Shulhan Arukh* (The set table), and Isaac Luria, founder of practical kabbala, turned Safed into a center for Jewish mysticism. In the late eighteenth century two large groups of Jews emigrated to Safed: Hasidim and their detractors, the followers of Rabbi Elijah, the Gaon of Vilnius. In 1837 an earthquake struck the area, killing 5,000.

In 1929, at a time when riots were breaking out throughout Palestine, Arabs attacked and destroyed the Jewish quarter of Safed; it was rebuilt in the 1930s. At the outbreak of the Arab–Israel War of 1948, the Jewish population in the city numbered only 2,000 out of a total of 12,000 inhabitants. When the British evacuated their position in Safed in April 1948, Arab forces attacked. Divisions of the Palmah counterattacked on 10 May 1948, putting to rout the Arab military units and the Arab population. Today the city is a center for artists and mystics.

See also ARAB–ISRAEL WAR (1948); HASIDIM; PALMAH.

Bibliography

Rossoff, Dovid. *Safed: The Mystical City.* Spring Valley, NY, 1991.

BRYAN DAVES

SAFVETI ZIYA
[1875–1929]

Ottoman Turkish writer.

Born in Istanbul, Safveti Ziya attended the Galatasaray Lycée. He held various government posts, and in the early years of the republic, he became chief of protocol in the Foreign Ministry. In 1896 he joined the French-influenced Servet-i Fünün literary movement. Safveti Ziya is best known for his novel *Salon Köşelerinde* (1910), a portrait of the cosmopolitan social life of Istanbul.

ELIZABETH THOMPSON

SAGUES, ALBERT
[1883–c. 1950]

Educator employed by Alliance Israélite Universelle.

Albert Sagues, born in İzmir, Turkey, was one of the most effective architects of the Alliance Israélite Universelle (AIU) schools, bolstering French cultural influence in Morocco and Tunisia. His efforts proved crucial for the spread of French language and culture among urban Jews. Sagues was a school principal for the AIU in Casablanca (1909–1912), Tunis (1912–1924), and Tangier (ca. 1925–post 1945). A firm advocate of the preservation of French colonial influence in the Maghrib, Sagues opposed political Zionism while favoring a modern Hebrew cultural renaissance.

See also ALLIANCE ISRAÉLITE UNIVERSELLE (AIU).

Bibliography

Laskier, Michael M. *The Alliance Israélite Universelle and the Jewish Communities of Morocco: 1862–1962.* Albany: State University of New York Press, 1983.

MICHAEL M. LASKIER

SAHARA

World's largest desert.

The Sahara (in Arabic, desert) encompasses an area of 3.32 million square miles (8.6 million sq km), stretching across eleven countries and Western Sahara, and covering nearly the entire northern region of Africa from the Atlantic Ocean to the Red Sea hills. Parts of the Sahara reach all the way north to the Mediterranean; to the south, it extends nearly 1,500 miles (2,400 km). The two countries with the highest percentage of desert are Libya (99 percent) and Egypt (98 percent). Fifteen percent of the Sahara consists of sand "seas"; the rest is a mixture of *hammada* (barren rocky plateaus), coarse gravel, two mountain chains in the central regions (with the

Hills and valleys of the El Oued Dunes, located in the Algerian Sahara Desert, Algeria. © ADAM WOOLFITT/CORBIS. REPRODUCED BY PERMISSION.

highest point being 11,204 feet [3,417 m] at the peak of Emi Koussi in Chad), lowlands, depressions (the lowest point being 436 feet [133 m] below sea level at the Qattara depression in western Egypt), oases, and transition zones.

The Nile and Niger are its only two permanent rivers. Transition zones receive between 5 and 10 inches (12.7 and 25.4 cm) of rain per year; most of the rest receives fewer than 5 inches (12.7 cm). Large portions of the area receive no rainfall for years at a time. Its climate is among the most inhospitable—the highest evaporation rates, highest temperatures, and lowest humidity (a life-threatening 2.5 percent) have all been registered there. Extreme wind velocities and massive drops in nighttime temperatures, sometimes to subfreezing level, are also a regular feature of the Sahara.

Desertification has slowly encroached upon previous transition zones, such as the *sahel* belt of vegetation covering fossil sand dunes that separate the Sahara from Equatorial Africa; some also occurs in Arab North African countries. The reasons for the Sahara's continuing expansion range from climatic changes to some direct human influence, such as overgrazing by sheep herds and wood gathering for fuel. The most important minerals found in the Sahara include petroleum and natural gas fields, uranium, phosphates, iron ore, and a long list of other metals.

The four main ethnic groups of the Sahara are all predominantly Berber in origin: the Arabo-Berbers in the north; the Moors (Maures), a mixture of Arab, Berber, and black African groups in the southwestern regions (encompassing parts of present-day Mauritania, Mali, and Western Sahara); the distinctive Twaregs, the most numerous of the four, of the south-central area; and the Tibu of the Tibesti area of Chad, who are also of Berber and black African mixture. Apart from livestock grazing, the old traditional economy included a profitable trade in gold and slaves from West Africa, salt from the desert, and cloth and other products from the Mediterranean coast. The camel, probably introduced in the second century B.C.E., was the backbone of trans-Saharan trade.

Before the prolonged droughts of the 1970s and 1980s, best estimates of the Sahara's population were approximately 2 million persons; about two-thirds were concentrated in oases; the rest engaged in seasonal movements and some were purely nomadic. In Arab North Africa, sedentarization had become almost complete, owing to the erosion of the pastoral economic base. Both "push" and "pull" factors were at work: desertification, which reduced livestock herds; displacement stemming from anticolonial struggles; the exploitation of oil and gas fields, which provided employment; and the extension of governmental authority, resulting in increased enclosure of land for farming, as well as expanded health and education services.

Historically, the Sahara was a large barrier to aspiring conquerors—Egyptians, Romans, Carthaginians, and Arabs. Islam spread steadily, however, in part from the activities of Muslim traders and scholars. Explorers from Britain and France began to penetrate the Sahara in the early part of the nineteenth century. French conquests began in 1830. Political boundaries in the Sahara were defined only in the late nineteenth and the twentieth centuries. Much was left imprecise by the French, who ruled over most of the region, resulting in a number of border disputes after decolonization, including those between Morocco and Algeria over the Tindouf area, and Libya and Chad with regard to the Aozou strip.

See also AOZOU STRIP; BERBER; DESERTS; TINDOUF; TWAREG; WESTERN SAHARA.

BRUCE MADDY-WEITZMAN

SAHARAN ARAB DEMOCRATIC REPUBLIC (SADR)

The official government-in-exile of POLISARIO.

The founding of the Saharan Arab Democratic Republic (SADR) was proclaimed at Bir Lehlou, a town in northwestern Western Sahara, on 27 February 1976, one day after the departure of Spain's authorities from the territory, by a previously established Provisional Sahrawi National Council. Its constitution, adopted at the third POLISARIO (Popular Front for the Liberation of Saguia El-Hamra and Rio de Oro, a politico-military organization formed in 1973 to secure the independence of Western Sahara) congress in August 1976, proclaimed SADR to be a "democratic Arab republic," with a "republican political system." SADR was declared part of the Arab nation and Islam the state religion. Fundamental objectives included socialism, social justice, and the attainment of Maghrib unity as a step toward Arab and African unity. POLISARIO's executive committee was charged with presiding over SADR's executive organ until independence and sovereignty were attained. POLISARIO's August 1991 Congress adopted a new draft constitution for the future Saharan state, including provisions for a multiparty system, a free enterprise economy (with strategic resources controlled by the state), universal suffrage, a free press, and cooperative relations with Morocco. POLISARIO head Muhammad Abd al-Aziz was the first, and thus far the only, president of SADR. He was re-elected secretary-general, receiving 92 percent of the vote, at POLISARIO's 11th congress, held in October 2003 in Tifariti, the POLISARIO-controlled territory of Western Sahara.

SADR's main value for POLISARIO has been in the diplomatic sphere: At its peak, it attained recognition from more than seventy countries (the number had dropped to around sixty by 2003), and, after years of struggle, assumed its seat in 1984 as a full member of the Organization of African Unity (OAU), triggering a Moroccan walkout. In contrast to the OAU, the League of Arab States (Arab League) kept SADR and POLISARIO at arm's length.

See also LEAGUE OF ARAB STATES; MAGHRIB; ORGANIZATION OF AFRICAN UNITY (OAU); POLISARIO; WESTERN SAHARA.

Bibliography

Damis, John. *Conflict in Northwest Africa: The Western Sahara Dispute.* Stanford, CA: Hoover Institution Press, 1983.

Hodges, Tony. *Western Sahara: The Roots of a Desert War.* Westport, CT: Lawrence Hill, 1983.

Pazzanita, Anthony G., and Hodges, Tony. *Historical Dictionary of Western Sahara.* Metuchen, NJ: Scarecrow Press, 1982.

BRUCE MADDY-WEITZMAN

SAHNOUN, AHMED
[1907–2003]

Islamic religious scholar and leader in Algeria.

Shaykh Ahmed Sahnoun, born in 1907 in Biskra, northeast of Algiers, was a highly respected religious figure and scholar viewed as the spiritual leader of the Islamists in Algeria. He was closely associated with the Islamic reformer Abdelhamid Ibn Badis (1889–1940) and the Association of Algerian Scholars, which was established in 1931 to resist the assimilationist policies of the French and reassert the Algerian Arabo-Islamic identity. During the struggle for Algerian independence, Sahnoun was imprisoned several times by the French for his anticolonial stance.

After independence, he refused to be associated with the state-controlled religious institutions, and continued preaching, promoting religious education, and establishing independent associations. In the 1960s he cofounded al-Qiyam (Values) Association to reassert Arab and Islamic identity in independent Algeria. Following violent clashes between Islamist and leftist students at the main campus at the University of Algiers in 1982, Sahnoun, along with Abbasi Madani and Shaykh Abdellatif Soltani, cosigned a fourteen-point statement that criticized the secular policies of the state and demanded the promotion of Islam in government and society. Due to his advanced age he was placed under house arrest rather than imprisoned, then released in 1984.

President Chadli Bendjedid met with Sahnoun, Ali Belhadj, and Mahfoud Nahnah following the massive riots of October 1988 and urged them to assist in restoring order. Sahnoun established the Association of the Islamic Call in 1989 to unite all the Islamic movements in the country, coordinate

their activities, and prevent escalations of violence with the regime. Throughout the Algerian civil war, which began in 1992. Sahnoun refused to engage in dialogue with the military regime and demanded the release of the imprisoned leaders of the Front Islamique du Salut, Abbasi Madani and Ali Belhadj. Sahnoun suffered from health problems, and died in early 2003 at the age of 96.

See also ALGERIA; BENDJEDID, CHADLI; BOUYALI, MOUSTAFA; FRONT DE LIBERATION NATIONALE (FLN); FRONT ISLAMIQUE DU SALUT (FIS); SOLTANI, ABDELLATIF.

Bibliography

Shahin, Emad Eldin. *Political Ascent: Contemporary Islamic Movements in North Africa.* Boulder, CO: Westview Press, 1998.

EMAD ELDIN SHAHIN

SA'ID, AMINA AL-
[1914–1995]

Leading Egyptian feminist.

Amina al-Sa'id was born in Asyut and raised in Cairo. She is known as a leading feminist, journalist, writer, and activist in the period before and following the 1952 Egyptian revolution. In 1931 she was among the first women to enroll in Fu'ad I University, founded in 1908 and renamed Cairo University in 1952. As a protégé of Huda Sha'rawi, she removed the veil early on and also advanced the cause of women's sports by daring to play tennis on the university campus. She enjoyed success as the author of novels, social tracts, biography, and travel writing. An avid pan-Arabist, she helped create the Pan-Arab Feminist Union and was also active in the Egyptian Feminist Union. Throughout her career she pressed for the reform of Islamic personal status laws. In the 1940s she became the first paid woman journalist to work for a mainstream publishing house, Dar al-Hilal, and became vice president of the Board of Press Syndicate in 1956. She wrote for *al-Musawwar* and founded and edited the pan-Arab journal *Hawa*. The burgeoning feminist movement underwent severe state repression following 1952, but al-Sa'id endured as the only major feminist from the previous generation to be supported by the government.

See also EGYPTIAN FEMINIST UNION; GENDER: GENDER AND EDUCATION; *HIJAB*.

Bibliography

Badran, Margot. *Feminists, Islam, and Nation: Gender and the Making of Modern Egypt.* Princeton, NJ: Princeton University Press, 1995.

Nelson, Cynthia. *Doria Shafik, Egyptian Feminist: A Woman Apart.* Cairo: American University in Cairo Press, 2000.

LINDA HERRERA

SAID, EDWARD
[1935–2003]

Author, educator, and scholar.

Edward Said was one of the greatest public intellectuals, scholars, and writers of the twentieth century. He almost single-handedly created the fields of cultural studies and post-colonial studies with the publication of his book *Orientalism* (1978), which ranks as one of the most influential books of the twentieth century. He was a brilliant, multitalented thinker, speaker, writer, and musician, publishing widely in the fields of literature, Middle Eastern politics, orientalism, and music. In the latter field, for example, Said was an accomplished pianist, served as music critic for the *Nation* magazine, and with conductor and pianist Daniel Barenboim published *Parallels and Paradoxes: Explorations in Music and Society* (2002). He and Barenboim also co-founded East West Divan, an orchestra comprised of Arab and Israeli musicians.

Said was born in British Mandate Jerusalem to affluent Palestinian Christian parents. The family moved to Cairo early in his life and he attended Victoria College in Cairo, where his classmates included the future King Hussein ibn Talal of Jordan and the actor Omar Sharif. In 1951, Said was sent by his parents to the United States, where he attended Mount Hermon School in Massachusetts, and then Princeton University and Harvard University, where he received his Ph.D. in English in 1964 with a dissertation, *Joseph Conrad and the Fiction of Autobiography* (published by Harvard University Press in 1966). Said became an instructor at Columbia University the year before he received his Ph.D. degree and became a full professor there in 1970. In 1977, he was appointed to an endowed chair at Columbia

as the Parr Professor of English and Comparative Literature. There followed appointments as the Old Dominion Foundation Professor of Humanities and finally University Professor, Columbia's highest honor for a faculty member. Said died in New York City at the age of sixty-seven.

Said was deeply involved in the politics of the Middle East, particularly the Israel-Palestinian crisis, as well in as the politics of colonialism—the way that centuries of Western scholars, artists, administrators, explorers, and writers have used Western military, economic, and cultural dominance to stereotype, dominate, and subjugate Eastern (particularly Islamic Middle Eastern) peoples, all in the name of what was presented as an objective, nonintrusive, nonjudgmental process: orientalism. Said was for years a member of the Palestine National Council and helped write the Palestinian constitution in 1988. He broke with Yasir Arafat following the Oslo Accords of 1993 both because he felt that the Palestinians got a very bad deal out of the accords and because he came to favor a single Jewish-Palestinian state rather than the two separate states that the leaders on both sides continued to pursue.

Said was the author or editor of at least twenty-eight books, as well as countless scholarly articles, newspaper articles, and editorials. In addition to the books mentioned above, he will be remembered particularly for *Culture and Imperialism* (1993), which extends the themes whose exploration he began in *Orientalism; The Politics of Dispossession: The Struggle for Palestinian Self-Determination, 1969–1994* (1994); *Covering Islam: How the Media and the Experts Determine How We See the Rest of the World* (1997); and *Out of Place: A Memoir* (1999).

Said served as president of the prestigious Modern Language Association during 1999. At that time, Richard Poirier, president of the Library of America, stated that Said "is certainly the most influential critic in anything touching upon the cultural criticism of literature."

Throughout his career, Said served as a lightning rod for criticism from all sides, owing on the one hand to his fierce and unwavering support for the freedom and independence of the Palestinian people—which led him to withering denunciations of Israel and of what he viewed as imperialist American support for Israel and projection of U.S. power in the Middle East—but also, in his later years, to his equally harsh denunciations of the violence, duplicity, and tyranny of Middle Eastern rulers and of their journalistic and intellectual supporters.

See also ARAB–ISRAEL CONFLICT; ARAFAT, YASIR; ORIENTALISM; ORIENTALISTS, INTERNATIONAL CONGRESS OF; OSLO ACCORD (1993); PALESTINIAN NATIONAL COUNCIL.

Bibliography

Kennedy, Valerie. *Edward Said: A Critical Introduction.* Malden, MA: Blackwell; Cambridge, U.K.: Polity Press, 2000.

Said, Edward W. *Edward Said: A Critical Reader,* edited by Michael Sprinker. Cambridge, MA, and Oxford, U.K.: Blackwell, 1992.

Said, Edward W. *The Edward Said Reader,* edited by Moustafa Bayoumi and Andrew Rubin. New York: Vintage Books, 2000.

Williams, Patrick, ed. *Edward Said,* 4 volumes. London and Thousand Oaks, CA: Sage, 2001.

JOHN M. LUNDQUIST

SA'ID, NURI AL-
[1888–1958]

Frequent minister or prime minister of Iraq and one of Iraq's leading statesmen from 1921 to 1958.

Nuri al-Sa'id was born in Baghdad during the Ottoman Empire into a middle-class Sunni Islamic family of Arab Turkish stock. At an early age he was enrolled in primary religious school before going to the Ottoman military secondary school. Later he attended the military college in Istanbul, and was graduated an officer in 1906. He returned to Baghdad, where he worked in an army unit responsible for collecting taxes from tribesmen, a position that enabled him to travel, to gain intimate knowledge of the country, and to establish contacts with *shaykhs* (tribal leaders), which he later used to his political advantage. In 1910, Nuri returned to Istanbul to attend the Ottoman staff college. In 1912, the year he graduated, he saw action against Bulgaria in the Balkan Wars.

In his youth, Nuri believed in Arab nationalism and the modernization of the Ottoman Empire (along the lines of the principles of the Young Turks, who seized power in Istanbul in 1909). He was, however, disillusioned by their anti-Arab policy and in 1913 joined al-Ahd (the Covenant), a secret society supporting self-determination for Arabs. When the Turks became suspicious of his activities, Nuri, fearing arrest, fled to Cairo, Egypt, in the spring of 1914. From there he went to Basra (Iraq), where he aligned himself with Sayyid Talib Pasha al-Naqib, a well-known leader of the Arab cause and the head of a local important family.

Nuri was in a Basra hospital, recovering from an illness, when the British seized the city at the beginning of World War I. They arrested him as an Ottoman officer and sent him to India, where he was put under loose house arrest. Nuri was released in 1915 and left India for Cairo where, encouraged by the British, he joined the movement of Sharif Husayn ibn Ali of Mecca, who had called for Arab independence from the Turks. Nuri played a major military role in the revolt (which Sharif Husayn finally proclaimed) against the Turks on 5 June 1916.

With the collapse of the Ottoman Empire at the end of World War I, Nuri became chief of staff for Prince Faisal I ibn Hussein, one of the sons of Sharif Husayn. He went with Faisal to Paris and London as an adviser during the peace talks.

In 1920, the British were awarded a mandate over Iraq by the League of Nations and established an indigenous Iraqi government. Ja'far al-Askari, Nuri's brother-in-law, became minister of defense and called Nuri to Iraq, where he was nominated chief of staff of the army. The following year, Faisal became king of Iraq, an objective toward which Nuri had worked hard. In the years that followed, Nuri was active in building the Iraqi army and police.

In 1929, Nuri assumed the first of his many prime ministries. It was he who negotiated the Anglo–Iraqi treaty of 1930, which officially ended the British mandate over Iraq, but which allowed Britain military bases and an assured influence in Iraq until 1955. His ability to secure its passage through parliament led the British to appreciate Nuri's skills and personality. This act inaugurated his long career as Iraq's dominant politician and demonstrated his strong belief in collaboration with the British.

These British leanings met with strong opposition from nationalists, however, who wanted complete independence. In dealing with the opposition, Nuri used tactics for which he later became famous—censorship of the press, proroguing parliament, and manipulating elections.

In 1936, Ja'far al-Askari was killed in a military coup, and a number of the pro-British politicians were removed. Nuri left Baghdad for Cairo in self-imposed exile and did not return until October 1937.

King Ghazi ibn Faisal of Iraq, who inherited the throne in 1933, died in a 1939 automobile accident. His infant son Faisal II ibn Ghazi was declared king, and his uncle Abd al-Ilah ibn Ali became regent, with Nuri's blessing.

After his return to Iraq, Nuri began to associate with a group of rising Arab nationalist military officers, who became prominent after the 1936 coup. They frequently intervened in politics, with Nuri's connivance. The harmony between Nuri and these officers slowly dissipated, however, after the beginning of World War II. While Nuri advocated a pro-British stand during the war, the officers slowly shifted to a pro-Axis one. The tension between the two camps rose when the British, fearing direct intervention by Nazi Germany, landed troops in southern Iraq. The nationalist officers staged a coup in May 1941, and the regent and Nuri fled the country. After encountering some resistance, the British were able to quell the nationalist movement and gain control of Baghdad.

The regent then returned to Baghdad, and a pro-British government headed by Jamil al-Midfa'i was formed. Nuri chose to stay in Cairo as ambassador but was called back in October 1941 to head a new cabinet as prime minister, a post he held until 1944. During that period Nuri worked closely with the British in prosecuting both nationalist officers and civilians; they were arrested, tried, and in some cases executed. These measures left a deep wound among Iraqis, who had considerable sympathy toward the nationalists. Soon, most of the Iraqis lost faith in Nuri and became critical of both his policies and his leadership.

Nuri kept Iraq quiet for the remainder of the war, but the war left its imprint on Iraq. A high in-flation rate and the widening gap between poor and rich allowed the leftists, a small but aggressive group, to gain strength. They became a target of suppression by Nuri and his successors.

Nuri was the first to advocate a council or league of Arab States, even before the end of the war. He was successful in launching his idea when a protocol for the foundation of the Arab League (as it is also called) was signed in Alexandria, in 1944.

In the postwar period, Nuri's influence over Iraq was unchallenged; even when he did not hold office he was able to steer the body politic in the direction he desired. A pro-Nuri majority was assured in parliament—especially among rich landlords and shaykhs. Nuri used this position to gain support among the Shi'a and the Kurds. When the Kurdish leader Mulla Mustafa al-Barzani revolted in 1945, Nuri—with the backing of the British—crushed the revolt and compelled him to take refuge outside Iraq.

With the rise of petroleum prices and Iraq's increased oil income, Nuri turned part of his attention to the establishment of an economic development program. In 1950, he engineered the passage of a law establishing a development board, composed of Iraqi and foreign experts, to lay down a five-year development plan. Between 1950 and 1958, four such plans were passed, and some 70 percent of oil revenue was devoted to Iraq's long-term development.

In 1952, Nuri negotiated a 50–50 split of oil revenues with the Iraq Petroleum Company (IPC). Between 1951 and 1958, Iraq's oil revenues rose dramatically from 32 million to US$237 million. Iraq's dependence on oil revenues rose, too. By 1958, oil revenues accounted for 28 percent of gross national product and 60 percent of the budget. Increased oil revenues were not accompanied by a change in social structure; rich landlords and tribal shaykhs gained title to much of the arable land, while urban merchants grew increasingly wealthy on government contracts.

The development of Iraq's human resources also lagged behind its needs. Between 1950 and 1958, although higher-education institutions expanded, by 1958 they still graduated only a few thousand students a year, and secondary education remained concentrated in urban areas. Opposition to the regime increasingly erupted in street violence. In 1952, when a riot broke out at the College of Pharmacy in Baghdad, it quickly spread throughout Iraq, so a military government was appointed to maintain order.

Between 1952 and 1958, regional Arab issues played a dominant role in internal politics. In 1952 a coup d'état in Egypt brought to power a group of Arab nationalist military officers, led by Gamal Abdel Nasser. The fall of King Farouk's monarchy in Egypt and the anti-Western tone taken by the new Egyptian regime had broad effects in the Arab world—particularly in Iraq, where the regime was pro-West. These events helped to destabilize Iraq's regime and eventually led to its fall.

The 1930 Anglo-Iraqi treaty was due to expire in 1955, and Nuri was searching for a vehicle to replace it. Britain proposed what became known as the Baghdad Pact, which would include the northern tier of the Middle East—Iran, Turkey, and Pakistan—as a new shield against Communism. Nuri wanted to include Kuwait and even Egypt, but Nasser would have nothing to do with any instrument tied to the West. Nuri's most significant impact on Iraq was in foreign policy, since he tied Iraq to the Western alliance and the Baghdad Pact. This provided for a shield against encroachment from the Soviet Union but seriously isolated Iraq from its Arab neighbors. The group of agreements that constituted the Baghdad Pact was signed in 1955—among Iraq, Turkey, Britain, Iran, and Pakistan.

The Iraqi people virtually rejected the pact. Eventually, Nuri dissolved parliament and fostered the election of a majority that favored his policies. Thus was the pact effected. In 1956, Egypt's President Nasser nationalized the Suez Canal, and England, France, and Israel attacked Egypt, taking the canal. Iraqi popular opposition to Nuri's regime then intensified and, faced with uprisings, he imposed martial law to bring about control.

In February 1958, Egypt and Syria announced the formation of the United Arab Republic. Popular support for this union was strong in Iraq and Jordan, but the governments of these two countries saw it as a serious threat to their regimes; a federation between Iraq and Jordan was then announced. Nuri's last post was that of the federation's prime minister—and one of his last political acts was an attempt to bring Kuwait into the federation.

In 1957, while Nuri was involved in foreign policy, four opposition parties—the Istiqlal (Independence), National Democratic, Ba'th, and Communist parties—joined together as a national front against the Iraqi government. Far more serious opposition to the regime came from the army, where junior officers were busy organizing military cells to topple the monarchy. Nuri downplayed as insignificant warnings of trouble in the army.

In May 1958, civil war broke out in Lebanon. The Jordanian government, fearing the war might spill over, asked its federation partner, Iraq, to send troops to Jordan. On 14 July 1958, they complied. Nevertheless, under the command of the Free Officers, Iraqi troops also occupied strategic points in Baghdad—the ministry of defense, the radio station, and the king's palace. The monarchy was abolished, and the Republic of Iraq was declared. The king and the regent were killed, and Nuri escaped from his residence—but the following day, fleeing in the streets disguised as a woman, he was shot dead. His only son, Sabah, was also killed during the coup.

The new Iraqi government under Prime Minister Abd al-Karim Qasim dismantled much of Nuri's work, dissolved the federation with Jordan, and allowed Iraq's membership in the Baghdad Pact to lapse. Political ties with the Soviet Union, severed in 1954, were reestablished, and Iraq turned to the Soviet bloc for arms. Rapprochement with Egypt's Nasser was brief, and the revolution failed to eliminate the most lasting contributions of Nuri and the British—the Iraqi state and its two foundations, the army and the bureaucracy.

Bibliography

Batatu, Hanna. *The Old Social Classes and the Revolutionary Movements of Iraq.* Princeton, NJ: Princeton University Press, 1978.

Birdwood, Christopher Bromhead, baron. *Nuri as-Said: A Study in Arab Leadership.* London: Cassell, 1959.

Gallman, Waldemar J. *Iraq under General Nuri: My Recollections of Nuri al Said, 1954–1958.* Baltimore, MD: Johns Hopkins Press, 1964.

Khadduri, Majid. *Independent Iraq, 1932–1958: A Study of Iraqi Politics.* London: Oxford University Press, 1960.

Longrigg, Stephen. *Iraq, 1900–1950: A Political, Social, and Economic History.* London: Oxford University Press, 1953.

Marr, Phebe. *A Modern History of Iraq,* 2d edition. Boulder, CO: Westview Press, 2003.

LOUAY BAHRY

Landes, David S. *Bankers and Pashas: International Finance and Economic Imperialism in Egypt.* Cambridge, MA: Harvard University Press, 1979.

Toledano, Ehud R. *State and Society in Mid-Nineteenth-Century Egypt.* New York and Cambridge, U.K.: Cambridge University Press, 1990.

DONALD MALCOLM REID

SA'ID PASHA
[1822–1863]

Son of Muhammad Ali; viceroy of the semiautonomous province of Ottoman Egypt, 1854–1863.

Prince Sa'id commanded the Egyptian navy during the last years of the reign of his father, Muhammad Ali, and through the short reign of his nephew Abbas Hilmi I. Sa'id's childhood friendship with the French consul, Ferdinand de Lesseps, paved the way for the French concession to build the Suez Canal despite the opposition of the British and the viceroy's Ottoman overlord. European fortune-seekers flooded into the country under the Francophile Sa'id, who started Egypt down the road to ruinous foreign debt. Egypt's contribution of 20,000 troops to the Ottoman Crimean War effort also strained its resources. Sa'id rehabilitated Rifa'a al-Tahtawi and other officials who had fallen into disfavor under Abbas. Sa'id's Land Law of 1858 attempted to extend central authority in economic affairs, and in 1858 he appointed Auguste Mariette head of what became the Egyptian Antiquities Service, but his capricious decisions and increasing European interference made institution building difficult. The viceroy gave more power to indigenous Egyptians in provincial administration and promoted them into the junior ranks of the officer corps at the expense of the Turkish-speaking elite. Port Sa'id, at the Mediterranean entrance to the Suez Canal, bears Sa'id Pasha's name. Historians have devoted relatively little attention to the reigns of Abbas Hilmi I and Sa'id compared to those of their flamboyant predecessor Muhammad Ali and their successor Khedive Isma'il.

See also CRIMEAN WAR; EGYPT; LESSEPS, FERDINAND DE; OTTOMAN EMPIRE; SUEZ CANAL.

Bibliography

Hunter, F. Robert. *Egypt under the Khedives, 1805–1879: From Household Government to Modern Bureaucracy.* Pittsburgh, PA: University of Pittsburgh Press, 1984.

SA'IDZADEH, SEYYED MOHSEN
[1958–]

Iranian legal scholar, writer, and outspoken clerical proponent of gender equality.

Seyyed Mohsen Sa'idzadeh was born in Qa'en, Khorasan, Iran. He began his religious studies at age ten at the seminary in Qa'en. In 1973 he moved to Mashhad to continue his studies, and in 1976 he moved to Qom. He was among the first graduates of the Qom Law School, set up in 1979 to train judges for the revolutionary courts. After graduation in 1983, he served as a judge in Kermanshah until 1986, when he resigned and returned to Qom to pursue advanced studies. He has certificates from fifteen ayatollahs attesting to his proficiency in Qur'anic exegesis and *hadith* literature. In 1988, he began researching women's issues in Islamic jurisprudence and developing premises for the construction of equal rights for women within a *shari'a* framework. He has written extensively on women's rights in Islamic law and tradition, but little of his work has been published so far; what has appeared in print is mainly in the feminist journal *Zanan,* sometimes appearing under pseudonyms. His unconventional views and his critique of patriarchal interpretations of the *shari'a* dismayed traditionalists within the clerical establishment. In June 1998, following publication in the independent reformist newspaper *Jame'eh* of an article in which he criticized misogynist traditions, Sa'idzadeh was arrested and tried in camera by the Special Clergy Court. He was released after three months but defrocked and banned from publishing.

See also GENDER: GENDER AND LAW; GENDER: GENDER AND POLITICS; IRANIAN REVOLUTION (1979); QOM.

Bibliography

Ghanea Bassiri, Kambiz. "Hujjat Al-Islam Mohsen Sa'idzadeh: A Contemporary Iranian Cleric on *Fiqh,*

Women, and Civil Society." *UCLA Journal of Islamic and Near Eastern Law* I, no. 2 (2002): 229–237.

Mir-Hosseini, Ziba. "Hojjat al-Eslam Sa'idzadeh–Iran." In *Dossier (Women Living under Muslim Laws).* Combaillaux (Montpellier), France: WLUML (Women Living under Muslim Laws), 1998.

Mir-Hosseini, Ziba. *Islam and Gender: The Religious Debate in Contemporary Iran.* Princeton, NJ: Princeton University Press, 1999.

ZIBA MIR-HOSSEINI

SAINT CATHERINE'S MONASTERY

Monastic complex in the Sinai Peninsula begun in the fourth century.

Saint Catherine's monastery sits near the foot of "God-trodden" Mount Sinai (Jabal Musa) in the middle of Egypt's southern Sinai Peninsula. In the mid-200s Christian hermits began to gather around the place where they believed God had spoken to Moses in the burning bush (Exodus 3:2–6). In 337 Helena, mother of Byzantine Emperor Constantine I, ordered the building of a small church and tower on that spot.

In 551 Emperor Justinian commissioned his favorite architect Stephanus of Ailae to erect high enclosure walls and to build a large church with monks' dwellings and gardens. In the 800s the "monastery of the bush" was renamed after Saint Catherine. The legend was that after her martyrdom in 305 in Alexandria, angels had borne her body to Mt. Sinai; five centuries later the monks discovered the holy relics.

This strong tradition was based on extant inscriptions (the debate about the dating being unresolved) that Muhammad himself protected the complex by an immunity decree. Guided by this tradition, later Muslim rulers in Egypt arranged for a tribe of bedouin mountaineers to protect—not always successfully—the monks from marauding nomads. The Frankish crusading Knights of the Sinai (from 1099 to 1270) and Napoleon (in 1798) also provided protection to the monks.

The monastery's library of more than 4,500 manuscripts (mostly Greek, but also Arabic, Syriac, Egyptian, and Slavonic) and its collections of more than 2,000 icons are uniquely precious. The iso-

lation of the monastery preserved the earliest icons from being smashed by the imperial iconoclastic decrees of Leo III (726) and his successor Constantine V.

Foreign grants and the expertise of foreign scholars have ensured that the icon collections are catalogued, displayed, and safeguarded. Because Jewish, Muslim, and Christian pilgrims and tourists climb Mt. Sinai in ever increasing numbers, daily access to Saint Catherine's is limited to a few morning hours, except for those who stay in a well-managed, modest guest house.

Bibliography

Kamil, Jill. *The Monastery of Saint Catherine in Sinai: History and Guide.* Cairo: American University in Cairo Press, 1991.

Paliouras, Athanasios D. *The Monastery of St. Catherine on Mount Sinai.* Sinai: St. Catherine Press, 1985.

Weitzmann, Kurt. *The Monastery of Saint Catherine: Icons.* Princeton, NJ: Princeton University Press, 1976.

THOMAS STRANSKY

SAINT JOSEPH UNIVERSITY

Jesuit university in Lebanon.

Saint Joseph University, established in 1875, was administered by the Society of Jesus (Jesuits) and had strong ties to the University of Lyons in France. It had branches in Tripoli, Sidon, and Zahla. French is the primary language of instruction, although some courses are offered in English and in Arabic. The Department of Arabic and Oriental Studies is considered very strong. Faculties in 1994 included theology, medicine, pharmacy, dentistry, engineering, law and political science, economics and business administration, and letters and humanities.

AS'AD ABUKHALIL

SAINT MARK'S CATHEDRAL

Seat of the Coptic patriarchate.

Built in the 1970s, Saint Mark's Cathedral provided a new seat of the Coptic patriarchate and a cultural and religious focal point for Egypt's Copts, one of the largest and most important Christian minorities in the Middle East. On 2 June 1968, the relics of Saint Mark were returned to the Coptic church by Pope Paul VI with great fanfare. They are now interred beneath the main altar of Saint Mark's and lend the cathedral an enhanced importance and venerability. Located in the once-fashionable Abbassiya district of greater Cairo, the cathedral offers Coptic rite services in Arabic, English, and French.

See also COPTS.

RAYMOND WILLIAM BAKER

SA'IQA, AL-

Pan-Arabist Palestinian guerrilla organization.

The Organization of the Vanguards of the Popular Liberation War—Forces of the Thunderbolt or al-Sa'iqa (Thunderbolt) was founded by pro-Syrian Palestinian Ba'thists in 1968, following a 1966 Ba'th Party resolution to create a Palestinian chapter. (The rival, pro-Iraqi Ba'thists later established the Arab Liberation Front.) Sa'iqa joined the Palestine Liberation Organization (PLO) in February 1969, but relations with the PLO mainstream deteriorated after Syria's 1976 intervention in Lebanon, with Sa'iqa openly involved in Syrian attacks on the PLO. Sa'iqa was one of two factions that rebelled against Yasir Arafat in 1983, and it has since boycotted all PLO institutions in favor of a series of Syrian-sponsored anti-Arafat alliances (the National Alliance in 1984, the Palestinian National Salvation Front in 1985, and subsequently the Group of Ten).

A number of Sa'iqa's founders, including its first secretary-general, Dafi Jumani, were ousted in 1970 by the new Syrian regime of Hafiz al-Asad after Sa'iqa backed the losing side in a struggle for power within Syria. At Syrian insistence, Jumani was replaced by Mahmud Mu'ayita and, in 1971, by Zuhayr Muhsin. Muhsin was assassinated in 1979 under circumstances that remain unclear, and was succeeded by Isam al-Qadi. The organization's publications include the weekly *al-Tali* (The Vanguards), first published in 1969, and an internal bulletin, *al-Sa'iqa*.

Throughout its existence, Sa'iqa has received political, military, and financial support from Syria, whose Palestinian refugee camps and whose own military provide most of the group's recruits. Sa'iqa's policies have been either dictated by Damascus or

calculated to serve Syrian interests within the Palestinian movement. Syrian patronage once made Sa'iqa the second largest constituent member of the PLO, giving it a generous quota of seats in the Palestine National Council and the PLO Executive Committee. However, its presence in the Palestinian territories and other areas beyond Syrian control has been weak, and its role as a Syrian instrument is widely resented there. Sa'iqa contributions to the 1973 Arab-Israel War were confined to a supporting role in the Syrian Golan. Its support of Syria's intervention in Lebanon in 1976 led to mass defections and its total elimination from areas under PLO control. Sa'iqa's absence during the 1982 siege of Beirut and its open collusion with Syria in the latter's efforts to impose its hegemony over the PLO and Lebanon during the 1980s have strained its credibility further. In January 2003 an attempt at bringing Sa'iqa into the Cairo reconciliation process between the PLO and Palestinian opposition groups failed, despite insistence on their inclusion by HAMAS and Islamic Jihad.

Syria has also operated a distinct "Sa'iqa" force, which was particularly active in the 1970s and early 1980s in targeting U.S., Israeli, Jordanian, and Egyptian embassies, Jewish institutions, and other civilian groups around the region and across Europe.

See also MUHSIN, ZUHAYR; PALESTINE LIBERATION ORGANIZATION (PLO); SYRIA.

Bibliography

Cobban, Helena. *The Palestinian Liberation Organisation: People, Power, and Politics.* Cambridge, U.K.: Cambridge University Press, 1984.

Gresh, Alain. *The PLO—the Struggle Within: Towards an Independent Palestinian State,* revised edition, translated by A. M. Berrett. London: Zed Books, 1988.

MOUIN RABBANI
UPDATED BY GEORGE R. WILKES

SAISON

Crackdown against Zionist dissident organizations by mainstream Zionist underground in British Mandatory Palestine.

The Saison, or "hunting season," was an operation authorized by David Ben-Gurion from November

1944 to March 1945 against dissident Jewish underground groups. In February 1944 the Irgun Zva'i Le'umi, led by Menachem Begin, initiated an armed revolt against the British authorities in Palestine in an attempt to secure Jewish independence. Their violent activities ran counter to the official policy of the Yishuv (the Jewish community in Palestine) at the time and would not be tolerated. On 31 October, Begin was issued an ultimatum by Haganah leaders to cease and desist, which he rejected. On 6 November, Walter Edward Guinness, Lord Moyne, the senior British official in the Middle East, was assassinated in Cairo by LEHI, an Irgun splinter group. This provided an opportunity to conduct a sweeping crackdown on both extremist groups. Special units of Palmah and Haganah volunteers arrested and handed over approximately 1,000 suspected Irgun and LEHI members to the British, some of whom were tortured beforehand. Many religious Zionists and General Zionists opposed the operation, and the bitter rivalry between Labor Zionism and Revisionist Zionism gave the Saison political and ideological overtones. Begin ordered his forces not to retaliate, fearing a Jewish civil war. Irgun activities against the British ceased until after the end of World War II.

See also BEGIN, MENACHEM; BEN-GURION, DAVID; GUINNESS, WALTER EDWARD; HAGANAH; IRGUN ZVA'I LE'UMI (IZL); LOHAMEI HERUT YISRAEL.

Bibliography

Bell, J. Bowyer. *Terror out of Zion: The Fight for Israeli Independence.* New Brunswick, NJ: Transaction, 1996.

Sprinzak, Ehud. *Brother against Brother: Violence and Extremism in Israeli Politics from Altalena to the Rabin Assassination.* New York: Free Press, 1999.

PIERRE M. ATLAS

SAKAKINI, KHALIL AL-
[1878–1953]

Palestinian writer and educator.

Khalil al-Sakakini was born in Jerusalem to a Greek Orthodox family. His early life was devoted to Arab letters. In 1909, he founded the Dusturiyya school in Jerusalem, which developed an influential model for a secular, Arab curriculum. Also before World War I, he played a leading role in the Nahda Urthuduksiyya (Orthodox Revival) movement. During the mandate period in Palestine, Sakakini continued his advocacy of public education and became principal of the Dar al-Mu'allimin (Teacher's College) in Jerusalem. He is perhaps best remembered for his books on teaching Arabic to beginners, some of which are still used in the Arab world.

Sakakini also participated in the early Palestinian national movement, and his diaries are an important source for scholars of the period. He argued that Jewish immigration threatened to disrupt the unity of Arabic culture. An ardent pan-Arabist, he admired Faisal I ibn Hussayn, who led the Arab revolt of 1916 and, from 1921 to 1933, was King of Iraq. In 1923, Sakakini became secretary for the Arab Executive Committee in Jerusalem. He and his family fled to Cairo in early 1948, during the Arab-Israel War. His best-known book is *Kadha Ana Ya Dunya: Yawmiyyat Khalil Sakakini* (Such am I, O world).

Bibliography

Kedourie, Elie. "Religion and Politics: The Diaries of Khalil Sakakini." *St. Antony's Papers* 4 (1970s): 77–94.

Mandel, Neville J. *The Arabs and Zionism before World War I.* Berkeley: University of California Press, 1976.

Ziadeh, Farhat J. *A Reader in Modern Literary Arabic.* Seattle: University of Washington Press, 1981.

ELIZABETH THOMPSON

SALAFIYYA MOVEMENT

Modernist Islamic intellectual movement of the nineteenth and twentieth centuries, which had some following among Sunni elites living in the Ottoman Empire.

The Salafiyya movement sought to engineer a religious revival and reform that would incorporate Western conceptions of modernity and assert the religious and cultural identity of Islam at the same time. The most prominent spokesmen of the movement were Jamal al-Din al-Afghani (1838–1897), Muhammad Abduh (1849–1905) and Rashid Rida (1865–1935). The members of the movement (*salafis*) took the line that the values of early Islam were compatible with those of modern Europe. In so doing, they attributed to Islam mainly secular virtues such as rationalism, the encouragement of sciences, political power, and democracy. In this way they were able to place blame for the relative decline of Islamic societies and power vis-à-vis the West on Muslims who over time had diverged from Islam's original teachings. For this trend, the *salaf* or "forefathers," had in fact two complementary meanings. One was the early companions of the Prophet Muhammad, who were perceived to have abided by the Qur'an and the sunna (deed and/or utterance of the Prophet) as closely as possible. Using this conception of the salaf, the Salafiyya emphasized the return to the scriptures. The second meaning of the salaf denoted reverence for the founders of the Islamic schools of law and for particular medieval jurists, such as al-Ghazali, who influenced the Salafiyya in one way or another.

The central part of the Salafiyya program consisted of legal reform through reinterpreting Islamic law (the *shari'a*) to make it compatible with Western and modern values. In fact, the Salafiyya became caught between two opposing trends: (1) a Westernizing trend, which wanted to adopt Western secular codes and legislate completely outside Islamic law, and (2) a traditional trend, which was perceived as adhering to rigid and premodern interpretations of the four jurisprudence schools of Sunni Islam. Striving to pursue a third alternative, the Salafiyya renounced the widespread nineteenth- and twentieth-century belief in Sunni circles that the gate of reinterpretation of Islamic law (*ijtihad*) had been closed at some point between the tenth and twelfth centuries. For the Salafiyya, *ijtihad* should be permissible in all aspects of transactions (*mu'amalat*), except where there is an explicit text (*nass*) in the Qur'an or in an authentic sunna. The Salafiyya also called for unifying the interpretation of the *shari'a* by employing two general principles. The first was the principle of public interest (*maslaha*), which was treated as one of the sources of Islamic law. The second principle was a combination (*talfiq*), whereby, for the interpretation of a religious precept in the field of transactions, the judge would not be confined to the opinion of one Islamic school of law but could make use of the interpretations of any school. The Salafiyya movement may also be regarded as a forerunner of Arab nationalism, since it emphasized Arab-based Islam and the Arabic language, albeit concurrent with modern sciences.

Politically, the Salafiyya produced two trends. One was the trend of Jamal al-Din al-Afghani, which emphasized fighting the advance of Western imperialism into the East, in general, and in Muslim lands, in particular. This made al-Afghani validate several lines of political approach to mobilize various Muslim and non-Muslim groups against the West. He thus spoke in terms of both religious and secular nationalism. He called for healing the divisions between the Sunnis and Shi'ites by concentrating on the common religious basics among these two largest of Muslim sects.

The second trend was that of Muhammad Abduh. After working closely with al-Afghani for a short period, Abduh dissociated himself from his friend's politics, shunned political activism, and concentrated on the issues of Islamic religious reform through education and jurisprudence.

As for Rashid Rida, generally speaking, he followed Abduh's political line during the period preceding World War I; however, he shifted his position and adopted an anti-Western activist political line, akin to that of al-Afghani, after the war—as a reaction to the establishment of direct European rule in most of the core Arab-Islamic areas, namely Syria and Iraq.

In Morocco, as in the Arab East, the Salafiyya movement condemned the doctrines and practices of popular Sufi orders, which it regarded as having no textual basis in Islamic thought. Politically, the Moroccan Salafiyya championed the nationalist liberal anticolonial cause and gained popularity thereby, especially because the rival Sufi orders cooperated with the French, in one way or another, after France proclaimed Morocco a protectorate in 1912. As an intellectual reformist movement, however, the Salafiyya of Morocco, and especially one of its leaders, Allal al-Fasi, emphasized the need for internal reform in Muslim society and to that end pursued a social line of self-help.

See also ABDUH, MUHAMMAD; AFGHANI, JAMAL AL-DIN AL-; RIDA, RASHID; *SHARI'A*.

Bibliography

Abun-Nasr, Jamil. "The Salafiyya Movement in Morocco: The Religious Basis of the Moroccan Nationalist Movement." *Middle Eastern Affairs*, no. 3, *St. Antony's Papers*, no. 16, edited by Albert Hourani (1963).

Commins, David Dean. *Islamic Reform: Politics and Social Change in Late Ottoman Syria.* New York: Oxford University Press, 1990.

Gibb, H. A. R. *Modern Trends in Islam.* Chicago: University of Chicago Press, 1947.

MAHMOUD HADDAD

SALAM FAMILY

Prominent Lebanese family involved in education, phil anthropy, and politics.

Salim Ali (1869–1938). One of the major Sunni Muslim figures in Beirut during the late Ottoman period. In addition to his activities as a merchant, he served as mayor of Beirut and was a member of the Ottoman parliament.

Anbara (1897–1986). Daughter of Salim Ali. She was born in Beirut and became a leading author, translator, and feminist. She married Palestinian educator Ahmad al-Samih al-Khalidi and in 1929 moved first to Jaffa and then to Jerusalem. She participated in a women's political meeting that same year that marched to the British high commissioner to present their grievances.

Salim (1922–). Businessman. After completing his studies at the American University of Beirut in 1947, he worked for Middle East Airlines. He was chairman and chief executive officer from 1982 to 1992.

Tammam (1945–). Son of Sa'ib Salam. He went into business in 1968. In 1974, he formed the Ruwwad al-Islah movement. As the heir to the Salam family's political leadership, he was first elected to the parliament in 1996.

Hala Salaam Maksoud (1943–2002). Granddaughter of Salim Ali. She studied at the American University of Beirut and earned a Ph.D. in political theory from Georgetown University. She taught at both Georgetown University and George Mason University. A leading personality in the Arab-American community, she served as president of the Association of Arab-American University Graduates, the Arab Women's Council, and the American-Arab Anti-Discrimination Committee. She married Clovis Maksoud, former ambassador for the League of Arab States to the United Nations.

Ghida (1963–). Married Prince Talal bin Muhammad of Jordan, nephew of King Hussein ibn Talal, in 1991.

See also AMERICAN UNIVERSITY OF BEIRUT (AUB); HUSSEIN IBN TALAL; KHALIDI, AHMAD AL-SAMIH AL-; SALAM, SA'IB.

MICHAEL R. FISCHBACH

SALAM, SA'IB
[1905–2000]

Major Sunni politician in Lebanon.

Sa'ib (also Saeb) Salam was born in Beirut to Sa'id Ali Salam, of the wealthy Salam Family. He attended the American University of Beirut and the University of London but received a degree from neither. Salam was first elected to parliament in 1943, shortly before Lebanon's independence from France. He later came to political prominence during the Lebanese Civil War of 1958, when he championed the cause of those who opposed the government of Camille Chamoun. Salam articulated the sentiments of "the Beiruti street" by emphasizing Sunni political support for Gamal Abdel Nasser. He was identified with the Wasat (center) political bloc during the 1960s and criticized the government of Fu'ad Chehab. In 1970, after the election of Wasat member Sulayman Franjiyya as president, he was appointed prime minister. He resigned in 1973 to protest the refusal of Franjiyya to dismiss the Maronite commander in chief of the Lebanese army, whom Salam held responsible for Israel's raid on Beirut that resulted in the assassination of three top Palestine Liberation Organization (PLO) leaders. Salam's views became consistently pro-Saudi, and his educational enterprises (such as al-Maqasid) received funding from the Saudi government. Salam opposed the right-wing militias during the war but was more opposed to the leftist coalition. In the summer of 1982, he arranged indirect talks between PLO Chairman Yasir Arafat and U.S. envoy Philip Habib, talks that led to the PLO's withdrawal from Beirut. Salam also helped formulate the 1989 Ta'if Accord that ended Lebanon's lengthy civil strife.

Salam is also noted for establishing Middle East Airlines, Lebanon's national carrier, in 1945. Following two assassination attempts, he left Lebanon and lived in Geneva, Switzerland, from 1985 to

1994. He died on 21 January 2000, four days after celebrating his ninety-fifth birthday.

See also AMERICAN UNIVERSITY OF BEIRUT (AUB); ARAFAT, YASIR; CHAMOUN, CAMILLE; CHEHAB, FU'AD; FRANJIYYA, SULAYMAN; HABIB, PHILIP CHARLES; NASSER, GAMAL ABDEL; PALESTINE LIBERATION ORGANIZATION (PLO); SALAM FAMILY; TA'IF ACCORD.

Bibliography

Hudson, Michael C. *The Precarious Republic: Political Modernization in Lebanon.* Boulder, CO: Westview, 1985.

Salibi, Kamal S. *Crossroads to Civil War: Lebanon, 1958–1976.* Delmar, NY: Caravan Books, 1976.

AS'AD ABUKHALIL
UPDATED BY MICHAEL R. FISCHBACH

SALANT, SAMUEL
[1816–1909]

Renowned scholar of traditional Jewish law and chief rabbi of Jerusalem.

Samuel Salant was born in Bialystok and studied in a number of yeshivas (Jewish religious schools) in Eastern Europe. He arrived in Jerusalem in 1841 and was soon appointed rabbi of the Ashkenazic community; he became Jerusalem's chief rabbi in 1878. In Palestine, Salant led the development of a vast network of Ashkenazic educational, medical, and social institutions. With Sir Moses Montefiore, he advocated the growth of the Jewish community in Jerusalem's Old City and in new areas beyond its walls.

CHAIM I. WAXMAN

SALIH, ALI ABDULLAH
[1942–]

President of the Yemen Arab Republic, then of Yemen, since 1978.

Salih became a public figure in the mid-1970s as a military commander and a supporter of the reform policies of Ibrahim al-Hamdi (assassinated in 1977). Hamdi's successor, Ahmad Husayn Ghashmi, was also assassinated shortly thereafter (1978). A four-man presidential council was then formed, one of whose members was Salih. After intense political maneuvering, he was elected president by the People's Constituent Assembly (created by Ghashmi).

Salih's origins did not augur well for his success: he is a member of the Sanhan tribe, a minor element of the Hashid tribal confederation. Though this made him a part of one of the major political forces in the country, he was not able to draw immediately upon the support of any of its major constituent elements, and it was widely assumed that his tenure would be brief. He undertook no radical policy shifts and moved to develop his own basis of support within the military and in civilian society. By shrewdly exploiting North Yemen's very limited room to maneuver in the international arena (in view of Saudi Arabia's strong position and more developed international associations), and promoting economic development programs and the exploitation of Yemen's limited oil resources, Salih grew in stature and popularity.

Developing a broader basis of support and legitimacy for his rule required dealing with several foreign and domestic policy issues. In foreign policy, the two most important areas were relations with South Yemen (PDRY) and Saudi Arabia. Frictions with the government and personnel of the PDRY led to two wars in less than a decade (1972 and 1979). However, the demise of the Soviet Union, and some mutual issues that required resolution (e.g., borders, oil resources) led to the unification of North and South Yemen in 1990; Salih became president of the unified state. Tensions between Yemen and Saudi Arabia have remained high throughout Salih's regime, but increased at the time of the first Gulf War due to Saudi Arabia's fear of the power of the unified state of Yemen.

In the domestic arena, Salih tried to move away from his reliance on the military: after a series of organizations designed to provide a greater civilian role in government, Salih promoted the creation of a National Legislature, in which his own political party, the General People's Congress (GPC), played the major role.

Perhaps the greatest threat to his government was the outbreak of a civil war between the North and South, in 1994, in which the North decisively defeated the South. In its aftermath, some significant changes were made to the institutions of government. Tentative steps toward more democratic rule had begun with multiparty elections in 1993. However, the 1997 elections were boycotted by the representatives of the South, allowing Salih's party and its allies to dominate the new legislature. In 1994 parliament abolished the old presidential council and replaced it with a one-man presidency. Under the new rules, it elected Salih to a five-year term. Then, in 1999, Yemen held its first direct elections to the presidency; Salih won with 96.3 percent of the vote. In 2000 several other changes to the constitution were approved; among them, the president's term was extended to seven years and he was granted several new powers. The next round of parliamentary elections was held on schedule in 2003. Once again, Salih's party, the GPC, completely dominated the outcome (winning 238 of 301 seats).

Most observers regard Salih's role in all these developments as crucial. Although it is clear that he enjoys genuine popular support, there are many critics (both secular and Islamist) of his policies, and there is little doubt that his regime is characterized by personalism, corruption, and nepotism (an example being the important role of his eldest son, Ahmad). But, there is also no doubt that his innate political shrewdness and ability to deal with the multitude of political, economic, and social interests found in (and around) the country are important reasons for the fact that he is among the longest-serving Arab rulers.

Bibliography

Carapico, Sheila. *Civil Society in Yemen.* Cambridge and New York: Cambridge University Press, 1998.

Dresch, Paul. *A History of Modern Yemen.* Cambridge and New York: Cambridge University Press, 2000.

Wenner, Manfred. *The Yemen Arab Republic: Development and Change in an Ancient Land.* Boulder, CO: Westview Press, 1991.

MANFRED W. WENNER

SALIH, TEYIB
[1929–]

The most famous Sudanese novelist.

Teyib (also Tayyib) Salih was born in 1929 in the Northern Province of Sudan to an ethnic group known for the propagation of Islamic scholarship in the region. His primary education was religious, and he was a precocious scholar. By the time he en-

tered secondary school in Khartoum, he had already studied prominent Arab authors such as Taha Husayn. He studied at Khartoum and London universities and has spent most of his life outside of his homeland. He studied in England before working at the British Broadcasting Corporation as head of drama in the Arabic Service. On his return to Sudan, he became the director of Sudanese National Radio. He later worked as a director-general of information in Qatar in the Persian Gulf; with the United Nations Educational, Scientific, and Cultural Organization (UNESCO) in Paris; and as UNESCO representative in Qatar.

Salih's major publications are the anthology *The Wedding of Zein and Other Sudanese Stories* (1969) and the novel *Season of Migration to the North* (1969). He has also written many short stories, which are among the best to be found in modern Arabic literature. Salih's novels have gained worldwide attention, especially *Season of Migration to the North.* His writing is drawn from his experience of communal village life and centers on people and their complex relationships. At various levels and with varying degrees of psychoanalytic emphasis, he deals with the themes of reality and illusion, the cultural dissonance between the West and the Orient, the harmony and conflict of brotherhood, and the individual's responsibility to find a fusion among his or her contradictions. These motifs and their contexts derive from both his Islamic background and the experience of modern Africa. He constructs an impervious unity of the social, religious, and political essence of the African or African Arab, holding that a harmony of existence is possible for individuals in a society of values and ethics. His books have been translated into several languages and *The Wedding of Zein* was made into an Arabic film that won an award at the Cannes Film Festival in 1976.

See also FILM; HUSAYN, TAHA; LITERATURE: ARABIC.

KHALID M. EL-HASSAN

SALIM, ALI
[1936–]

Egyptian dramatist.

After a successful career as a comic actor, Ali Salim turned to writing and became one of the major comic dramatists in Egypt; he is well known for his satiric wit. His early plays are full of farcical situations and telling criticism of the idiocies of bureaucracy and the phobias of the common man; notable among these are *al-Nas Illi fi al-Sama al-Thamina* (1966; People in eighth heaven) and *Bi'r al-Qamh* (1967; The wheat well). *Madrasat al-Mushaghibin* (1971; School of troublemakers), in which a kind teacher reforms a class of rowdy teens, was one of his great popular successes. Salim has written several more serious works, of which *al-Buffeh* (1968; The buffet) and *Kumidiya Udib: Int Illi Qatalt al-Wahsh* (1970; The comedy of Oedipus: You're the one who killed the beast) have had considerable success on stage. The latter, which transports the Oedipus legend to Egyptian Thebes, provides Egyptian audiences contemplating the consequences of the Arab–Israel War of 1967 with a telling view of a nation ruled by an idealistic leader whose bold plans divert his attention from the fact that his security forces are terrorizing the nation.

Retired from the Ministry of Culture, he is also known for traveling to Israel after the Oslo peace talks. His best-selling account of the trip (*Rihla ila Isra'il*, 1994) takes to task those fearful of cultural invasion, rues the mental state of war besieging many of his compatriots, insists that the real battle is one of civil rights, and answers the curiosity of many Egyptians toward their Israeli neighbors. Salim was expelled from the Egyptian Writers Union for publishing the book. He continues to work for peace, and he has also returned to his first love, puppet theater.

See also LITERATURE: ARABIC.

Bibliography

Badawi, Muhammad Mustafá. *Modern Arabic Drama in Egypt.* Cambridge, U.K.: Cambridge University Press, 1987.

Salim, Ali. *A Drive to Israel: An Egyptian Meets His Neighbors.* Syracuse, NY: Syracuse University Press, 2001.

ROGER ALLEN
UPDATED BY NANCY BERG

SALIM HASAN
[1888–1961]

Egyptian Egyptologist.

The second Egyptian Egyptologist of note after Ahmad Kamal, Salim Hasan was educated in Cairo and Paris. He taught at Cairo University and reached the second highest post in the Egyptian Antiquities department, under its French director. Salim Hasan excavated extensively at Giza, site of the Sphinx and the great pyramids, worked at Saqqara, and published voluminously in Arabic, English, and French.

DONALD MALCOLM REID

SALIM, JAWAD
[1919–1962]

Iraqi sculptor and painter.

Jawad Salim, one of the two best-known sculptors in modern Iraq (the other is Khalid al-Rahhal), was born in Baghdad into a middle-class family. His father, his two brothers (Sa'ud and Nizar), and his sister (Naziha) were avid painters. Jawad Salim's talents became apparent early in his life, and in 1938 he was sent by the government to study art in Paris. He moved to Rome in 1939, and toward the end of that year he returned to Baghdad, where he was appointed instructor of sculpture at the newly established School of Fine Arts. He was also employed by the Iraqi Museum in the restoration of Mesopotamian artifacts.

During World War II, Salim met a group of Polish artists who had fled to Iraq. Paris-trained post-Expressionists, they encouraged him to pursue an "Iraqi path" in his painting and sculpture but also awakened his enthusiasm for such artists as Cézanne, Renoir, and Goya. Around 1944, Salim befriended a British artist, Kenneth Wood, who was a diplomat in Baghdad. According to Salim's diary, Wood exerted significant influence on his development. During that period, Salim produced such sculptures as *al-Usta* (The master builder), which portrayed modern Iraqi masons but drew inspiration from Ibsen's play of the same title.

In 1946, Salim went to London to study at the Slade School of Art; he returned to Iraq some five years later. He was much impressed by such modern British artists as Henry Moore. In Baghdad, he both painted and sculpted, and established the Baghdad Group for Modern Art. After the fall of the monarchy in 1958, he was commissioned by the regime of Abd al-Karim Qasim to design and execute a massive monument titled *al-Hurriyya* (Freedom), consisting of fourteen bronze units. This work, placed in one of the main squares of Baghdad, consumed the last two years of his life.

See also ART; QASIM, ABD AL-KARIM.

Bibliography

Inati, Shams, ed. *Iraq: Its History, People, and Politics.* Amherst, NY: Humanity Books, 2003.

SASSON SOMEKH

SALLAL, ABDULLAH AL-
[1919–1994]

First president of the Yemen Arab Republic.

Abdullah al-Sallal was born in 1919 on the northern highlands of Yemen; he was from the lower class of barbers and butchers. He became a soldier and was one of the very important group of young soldiers sent by Imam Yahya to Iraq for training during the mid-1930s. He returned after about one year abroad and became a politically active officer. He was involved in planning the 1962 coup against the monarchy and became president of the Yemen Arab Republic from 1962 until 1967. Al-Sallal was coarse in manner and appearance, neither thoughtful nor visionary, and came to be seen as a puppet of President Gamal Abdel Nasser of Egypt; he was ousted and exiled in 1967 by a combination of factions opposing both the long civil war between the republicans and the royalists and the dependence of republican Yemen on Egypt. In 1982, the regime invited al-Sallal to return from exile. He died in Yemen in 1994, at the age of seventy-four, having enjoyed the role of elder statesman for more than a decade.

See also NASSER, GAMAL ABDEL; YAHYA IBN MUHAMMAD HAMID AL-DIN; YEMEN ARAB REPUBLIC.

Bibliography

Burrowes, Robert D. *The Yemen Arab Republic: The Politics of Development, 1962–1986.* Boulder, CO: Westview; London: Croon Helm, 1987.

Dresch, Paul. *A History of Modern Yemen.* New York and Cambridge, U.K.: Cambridge University Press, 2000.

ROBERT D. BURROWES

SALNAME

See GLOSSARY

SALONIKA

A principal city in the Ottoman Empire that has belonged to Greece since 1912.

Located at the head of the Gulf of Salonika, Salonika (also known as Salonica or Thessalonika) was captured by the Ottoman sultan Murad I in the late fourteenth century. The city flourished as a trade and cultural center through the seventeenth century and revived in the nineteenth century, becoming an industrial center and the seat of the political and cultural wings of the Young Turk movement. The founder of the Republic of Turkey, Mustafa Kemal Atatürk, was born in the city in 1881 and attended its military *rüşdiye* school from 1893 to 1895. In 1901 the modern port was opened, and in 1908 the Committee of Union and Progress launched its revolution there.

Greece captured Salonika from the Ottomans in November 1912, during the First Balkan War. Five years later, a fire destroyed much of the city. Its Jewish community was wiped out under German occupation (1941–1944). It is the second largest city in contemporary Greece.

Bibliography

Shaw, Stanford J., and Shaw, Ezel Kural. *History of the Ottoman Empire and Modern Turkey*, vol. 2. Cambridge, U.K.: Cambridge University Press, 1977.

ELIZABETH THOMPSON
UPDATED BY ERIC HOOGLUND

SALT, AL-

A small, picturesque town in Jordan.

Al-Salt is located about 20 miles (29 km) northwest of Jordan's capital, Amman, in the hills overlooking the Jordan valley to the west. It contains some beautiful examples of Islamic residential architecture. The archaeological evidence shows that Salt has been inhabited since about 3000 B.C.E. It was the principal town in Transjordan in the 1920s and one of the gateways from Palestine to Transjordan and countries further east and south. Salt suffered a steady decline, as other population centers flourished in Jordan and routes to Palestine moved south or north. It has never fully recovered from this decline, although it is a regional capital (Balqa district) and boasts several "firsts": the first hospital and the first secondary school in Jordan. The latter lays claim to having educated many of Jordan's prime ministers, most of its ministers, and a large number of prominent members of Jordanian society. Salt also has a substantial Christian minority that enjoys cordial relations with the Muslim community. The population of al-Salt in 1994 was about 56,000.

Bibliography

Gubser, Peter. *Jordan: Crossroads of Middle Eastern Events.* Boulder, CO: Westview, 1983.

JENAB TUTUNJI

SAMARITANS

People claiming descent from the ancient Kingdom of Israel.

In the fourth and fifth centuries C.E., the Samaritans numbered about 1,200,000 persons dwelling in many cities and villages in the biblical Land of Israel (from southern Syria to northern Egypt). By 1917, centuries of harsh religious decrees, forced conversions to Islam and Christianity, slaughter, and persecution had thinned the Samaritan community to a bare 146 persons. During the 1930s, however, the community began to increase, and it has been gradually developing in all areas of life. By January 2003 its numbers increased to 654: 349 in Holon, near Tel Aviv, and 305 in the Kiryat Luza neighborhood, on the peak of Mount Gerizim overlooking Nablus.

Throughout their history, the Samaritans never lost their uniqueness as a people. They have their own writing, the ancient Hebrew script; they speak their own language, the ancient Hebrew dialect spoken by Jews until the beginning of the first millennium C.E.; and they are brought up in accordance with a unique, millennia-old tradition, dating back to the return of the people of Israel under Joshua, son of Nun, to its homeland.

The Samaritans are guided by four principles of faith: (1) one God, who is the God of Israel; (2) one

prophet, Moses, son of Amram; (3) one holy book, the Pentateuch (the Torah handed down by Moses); and (4) one holy place, Mount Gerizim.

The Samaritans celebrate only those holidays mentioned in the Torah: Passover, the Feast of Unleavened Bread; the Feast of Weeks (Shavuot); the First Day of the Seventh Month; the Day of Atonement (Yom Kippur); the Feast of Tabernacles (Sukkot); and the Eighth Day of Assembly and Rejoicing of the Torah (Shemini Atzeret, Simhat Torah). Unlike that of mainstream Judaism, the Samaritan New Year is celebrated fourteen days before Passover, and the eve of their Passover is marked by a sacrifice of lambs and male goats on Mount Gerizim.

Samaritans adhere to four symbols of identification: (1) living in the Land of Israel, (2) compulsory participation in the animal sacrifice on Mount Gerizim at Passover, (3) keeping the Sabbath as written in the Pentateuch, and (4) adhering to the laws of purity and impurity as written in the Pentateuch.

The Samaritans perform circumcision on the eighth day following a male birth. A boy or a girl who completes the reading of the Pentateuch is considered "Concluder of the Law." The attachment between a couple proceeds in three stages: consent, engagement, and marriage. Marriage with Jews outside the community is acceptable. Divorces are rare. Funerals take place on Mount Gerizim, or in the Samaritan section of the Kiryat Sha'ul cemetery in Tel Aviv.

The peace process between the government of Israel and the Palestinians, bringing Nablus under Palestinian administration, has led to a separation between the Samaritan communities in Holon and on Mount Gerizim.

Bibliography

The Israelite Samaritans. Available from <http://www .mystae.com/samaritans.html>.

BENYAMIM TSEDAKA

SAMARRA

One of the oldest cities in Iraq, situated 65 miles (104 km) north of Baghdad.

There is evidence of a prehistoric Chalcolithic culture around Samarra, but the site was only sparsely populated in ancient times. The present city was founded on the east side of the Tigris River by the Abbasid caliph al-Muʿtasim in 835 C.E.; it was divided into quarters, based on business and profession. It served as the capital of eight Abbasid caliphs from 836 to 892, when Caliph al-Muʿtamid moved the capital back to Baghdad. During the Abbasid period, the caliphs were eager to make Samarra a beautiful city, with new palaces, lakes, and wide squares, and they brought in many types of plants from all over the Islamic world.

With its rich Islamic history, Samarra has many sites of historic and architectural interest. The most important is the al-Malwiyya Mosque with its spiral minaret, which is 171 feet (52 m) in height with a round room at the summit that is 19.6 feet (6 m) high. It was begun in 1443 by the Caliph al-Mutawakkil. Also of interest are the House of the Caliph, which contains three monumental staterooms, large residential complexes, and outdoor recreation facilities; the mosque of Abu Dulaf, with its spiral minaret; al-Mankur Palace; and many walls, especially al-Qadissiyya, Isa, Ashnas, and Shaykh Wali. A museum was established in Samarra for the artifacts found during excavations in the area.

Two apostolic imams, Ali al-Hadi and his son Hasan al-Askari, were buried in Samarra; therefore it is a holy city of Shiʿism, one of four in Iraq. The imams' shrine is visited by Shiʿa from all over the Islamic world. Part of the mosque marks the spot where, according to the Shiʿa, the twelfth and last apostolic imam, al-Mahdi, disappeared.

The majority of contemporary Samarra's population is composed of members of tribes from the surrounding countryside, who follow Sunni Islam. In 1992, the population was estimated at 150,000. Clan and political links tend to unite Samarra with the cities to its north and south, Tikrit and Baghdad. A road links it with both major centers. Under the republican regime, the city was governed by the *qaʾimmaqam* (chief of the administrative unit), who reported to the *muhafidh* (the representative of the central government in Baghdad). With the creation of the Coalition Provisional Authority, following the 2003 invasion of Iraq, Samarra came under the authority of a military commander directly appointed by occupation forces in late April 2003. It soon became a center of opposition to American forces in the region.

Samarra has a desert climate, with great temperature differences between day and night and between summer and winter. The high reaches 110°F (43°C), and the low is just above freezing. Annual relative humidity is 18 to 30 percent; annual rainfall ranges from 4 to 16 inches (10–40 cm). The area grows cereal crops, citrus fruits, apples, and many types of vegetables. The major industries are a pharmaceutical plant and an electrical power plant. Strong tribal connections to the governing authorities during the Baʿathist period contributed to the city's prosperity.

One vital project nearby is the al-Tharthar Dam, opened in 1956, which prevents the flooding of Baghdad by shifting the flow of the Tigris during its rise to the al-Tharthar Valley, a depression between Samarra on the Tigris and Hit on the nearby Euphrates.

See also BAGHDAD; SHIʿISM; TIGRIS AND EUPHRATES RIVERS; TIKRIT.

Bibliography

Marr, Phebe. *The Modern History of Iraq,* 2d edition. Boulder, CO: Westview Press, 2003.

"The Monuments of Samarra." Available at <http://www.www.dur.ac.uk/derek.kennet/monuments.htm>.

Nakash, Yitzhak. *The Shiʿis of Iraq.* Princeton, NJ: Princeton University Press, 1994.

NAZAR AL-KHALAF
UPDATED BY PAUL S. ROWE

SAMAR, SIMA
[1957–]

Physician, advocate for democracy and women's rights in Afghanistan, and Afganistan's Minister for Women's Affairs.

Sima Samar was born in Ghazni, Afghanistan. She received a medical degree from Kabul University in 1982. After the arrest and disappearance of her husband, she went to Quetta, Pakistan, and became a humanitarian relief worker and supporter of the Revolutionary Association of the Women of Afghanistan (RAWA). In 1987, she received funding from the Church World Service and several other organizations to establish a women's hospital in Quetta. In 1988, she organized the Shuhada Foundation to provide medical care and education for Afghan women refugees and their children in Pakistan. She received the Ramon Magsaysay Award for Community Leadership in 1989 and the John Humphrey Freedom Award in 2001 for her efforts to protect the rights of women in Afghanistan.

In late December 2001, she became minister for women's affairs in Hamid Karzai's interim government. She resigned in June 2002, when conservatives threatened her with a death penalty for allegedly questioning the relevance of Islamic law in an interview during a visit to Canada. She was acquitted of the charge of blasphemy by the high court of Afghanistan and given a new position as chair of Afghanistan's Independent Human Rights Commission.

See also AFGHANISTAN; GENDER: GENDER AND LAW; GENDER: GENDER AND POLITICS; KASHWAR KAMAL, MEENA; REVOLUTIONARY ASSOCIATION OF THE WOMEN OF AFGHANISTAN (RAWA); TALIBAN.

Bibliography

Emadi, Hafizullah. *Repression, Resistance, and Women in Afghanistan.* Westport, CT: Praeger, 2002.

SENZIL NAWID

SAMMAN, GHADA
[1942–]

Syrian-Lebanese writer.

Ghada Samman was born and raised in Syria, moved to Lebanon in the 1960s, and has been living in France since 1984. She is one of the Arab world's most prolific female authors, having published more than thirty books in a variety of genres. Her work has been translated into many languages. She studied English literature at Damascus University and the American University of Beirut and began her career as a journalist. She writes a weekly column for the London-based *al-Hawadith* magazine. Among her books is *al-Raghif Yanbud ka al-Qalb* (1975), which exposes political corruption in the Arab world and attacks social inequality, especially the mistreatment of women. Her *al-Amal Ghayr al-Kamila* (1979)

is a multivolume collection of fiction and nonfiction on her travels to various Arab and European capitals, with insightful comparisons on culture, society, and politics.

Samman is also known for her fiction. Her novel *Beirut '75* (1974) is a gripping urban narrative that touches upon class divisions, gender inequality, and the selfish rich. It prophetically anticipated the outbreak of violence in Lebanon the following year. *Beirut Nightmares* (1976) draws from the author's own experiences during the first year of the Civil War, when she was trapped for a week near the Beirut hotel district. A sequence of nightmares, from the mundane to the surreal, are told in a wrenching first-person voice. One of her collections of short stories, *The Square Moon* (1999), is set mostly in Paris and focuses on cultural conflict and the perspectives of exile.

For decades, she has given voice to Arab women: "The liberated woman is not that modern doll who wears make-up and tasteless clothes. . . . The liberated woman is a person who believes that she is as human as a man. The liberated woman does not insist on her freedom so as to abuse it," she wrote in 1961. In her many works of fiction and nonfiction, Samman has been a staunch supporter of Arab nationalism and has criticized Zionist and imperialist policies, but she has not shied away from critiquing repressive aspects of her own culture.

See also GENDER: GENDER AND EDUCATION; LEBANESE CIVIL WAR (1958); LEBANESE CIVIL WAR (1975–1990); LITERATURE: ARABIC.

Bibliography

Cooke, Miriam. *War's Other Voices: Women Writers on the Lebanese Civil War.* Cambridge, U.K.: Cambridge University Press, 1988.

Zeidan, Joseph. *Arab Women Novelists: The Formative Years and Beyond.* Albany: State University of New York Press, 1995.

ELISE SALEM

SAMUEL, HERBERT LOUIS
[1870–1963]

First high commissioner in Palestine under the British Mandate, 1920–1925.

Herbert Louis Samuel was born to a Jewish banking family in Liverpool, England, in 1870. Educated at Balliol College, Oxford, he entered parliament as a Liberal in 1902 and in 1909 became the first practicing Jew to serve in a British cabinet. He rose to be home secretary in 1916 (and again in 1931–1932). During the First World War Samuel was the first person to raise with the cabinet the idea of British sponsorship of Zionism. In 1920 he was knighted and sent to Palestine as first head (high commissioner) of the British civil administration under a League of Nations mandate. His appointment was greeted with enthusiasm by Zionists but he disappointed them by his suspension of Jewish immigration in response to Arab anti-Jewish riots in May 1921 and by his appointment of an Arab nationalist leader, Muhammad Amin al-Husayni, as mufti of Jerusalem. Samuel was responsible for extending the border of the Mandate eastward to include Transjordan. He was the principal author of the Churchill White Paper of 1922, which established the criterion of "economic absorptive capacity" as the basis for limiting Jewish immigration.

Although Samuel's efforts to establish an elected legislative council proved abortive, he restored a measure of political calm from 1922 to 1925. His recognition of the Palestine Zionist Executive as the Jewish Agency, defined in article 4 of the Mandate, and his creation of the Supreme Moslem Council, headed by the mufti, laid the basis for the institutional partition of Palestine between Jews and Arabs. In the late 1930s, however, Samuel strongly opposed proposals for territorial partition. But his alternative proposals for an Arab-Jewish settlement, formulated with a Conservative MP, Earl Winterton, found little support. He was created Viscount Samuel of Mount Carmel and Toxteth in 1937.

See also HUSAYNI, MUHAMMAD AMIN AL-; JEWISH AGENCY FOR PALESTINE; WHITE PAPERS ON PALESTINE.

Bibliography

Samuel, Herbert Louis, Viscount. *Memoirs.* London: Cresset Press, 1945.

Wasserstein, Bernard. *Herbert Samuel: A Political Life.* Oxford, U.K.: Clarendon Press, 1992.

BERNARD WASSERSTEIN

SAN'A

Capital of the Republic of Yemen.

One of the world's oldest continuously inhabited sites, San'a was the capital of the Yemen Arab Republic from 1962 to 1990, at which time it became the capital of the new Republic of Yemen. Over earlier centuries it had been the capital and chief city of a succession of political entities: the Hamid al-Din Zaydi imamate from the end of World War I to 1962; the two Ottoman occupation regimes during the sixteenth and nineteenth centuries; earlier Zaydi imams before and after the Ottoman occupation; and numerous other regimes, major and minor. Regardless of ruler, San'a was for centuries the great Zaydi urban center in the highlands of North Yemen, surrounded by tribes that accepted and defended Zaydism. The city has been Islamic since the earliest days of Islam, and its major mosque is said to be built on the ruins of one that was built before the death of the prophet Mohammad. In recent decades, the city has been the stage for much of Yemen's highest political drama: the sacking of San'a by the tribes as punishment for its role in the aborted 1948 revolution and the heroics of its citizens and republican defenders during the seventy-day siege of San'a in early 1968.

San'a is located at an altitude of about 7,500 feet in the geographical center of modern North Yemen, northeast of the port of Hodeida (al-Hudayda) and north of Ta'iz. Its barren setting conveys an austere, almost monastic aura, but it has a dry, temperate climate, marred seasonally by lip-cracking dryness and dust-filled winds. Wells and erratic rains in the spring and late summer allow for both irrigated and dry farming as well as extensive animal husbandry in the city's environs. San'a is not a green place; people and factories have won out decisively over trees, grass, and flowers in the competition for water.

Guarded by the small, bald mountain of Jabal Nuqum, San'a stretches across a wide, flat plain from the mountain's western flank. Before the 1962 revolution, San'a had an hourglass configuration: the Jewish quarter (Qa al-Yahud) to the east separated by a half mile of gardens and the usually dry watercourse from the much larger, walled Islamic city at the foot of the mountain. This configuration was largely erased by the unplanned growth of the

A skyline view of Yemen's capital city, San'a. © ABBIE ENOCK; TRAVEL INK/CORBIS. REPRODUCED BY PERMISSION.

1960s and 1970s and, even more so, by the urban sprawl of the 1980s. Still, the old Islamic city remains one of the urban architectural treasures of the world. It was declared a World Heritage Site by the United Nations Educational, Scientific, and Cultural Organization (UNESCO) in the early 1980s and has been the object of considerable restoration and preservation campaigns since then. In addition to its main gate, restored portions of thick wall, and dozens of slender minarets, the city is distinguished by the dense concentration of houses, many of them several stories tall, made of cut stone and of baked and sun-dried bricks. The domestic architecture of San'a dates back at least two millennia and is a triumph of art and engineering. The city's ancient marketplaces still thrive; the most famous of these is at the core of the old city. These marketplaces house shops selling goods from all over the world and are also home to artisans and traditional manufacturers. In recent years, the new city and the outskirts have become the locale for modern stores, distribution centers, showrooms, and light industry. San'a has also become a city of schools, most notably the San'a University.

During the 1960s and 1970s, San'a boasted handsome stone government offices and other public buildings, old and new, as well as many mosques, schools, and fine homes, but Ta'iz claimed to be the commercial and business center of North Yemen—the more modern city, more open to the ideas and practices of the outside world. By the 1980s, however, with a population of more than 500,000 and growing rapidly, San'a had emerged as the undis-

puted center of political, cultural, and economic life in North Yemen. With Yemeni unification in 1990, government officials and supplicants flooded from Aden to San'a, the political capital, and the preeminence of San'a became even more apparent; it remains to be seen what ranking and division of labor will ultimately prevail between San'a and Aden, the designated economic capital of unified Yemen. The cities, while similar in size, are wildly different in appearance and lifestyle, making them a complementary pairing. As they grow, both must cope with traffic congestion, water and electricity shortages, limited sewage facilities, great housing needs, and the inadequacy of other urban services. The great challenges of becoming a livable modern city in a poor, developing country were compounded in San'a after 1990 by the deluge of unemployed workers expelled suddenly from Saudi Arabia at the beginning of the 1991 Gulf War. By the mid-1990s, San'a's population had reached almost one million. For the first time rimmed by slums and replete with beggars, San'a is nonetheless beginning to meet some of these challenges, and the old city survives as an urban treasure.

See also HAMID AL-DIN FAMILY; YEMEN; YEMEN ARAB REPUBLIC; YEMEN CIVIL WAR; ZAYDISM.

Bibliography

Bonnenfant, Paul, ed. *Sanaa: Architecture domestique et société.* Paris: CNRS Editions, 1995.

Serjeant, R. B., and Lewcock, Ronald, eds. *San'a: An Arabian Islamic City.* London: World of Islam Festival Trust, 1983.

ROBERT D. BURROWES

SAN'A UNIVERSITY

One of two universities in the Republic of Yemen.

For a long time San'a University was the only university in the former Yemen Arab Republic. Since its founding in 1970, San'a University has grown dramatically in the number of students and faculty, become diversified in the degrees and programs it offers, and improved the quality of its educational offerings. The university began on a modest, ad hoc basis with a teachers' college and a law school; the first external aid for the university was secured from

Kuwait during its first year, and Kuwait remained its biggest benefactor throughout the 1970s and 1980s. Its arts and science faculties underwent rapid growth during its first decade, and among the departments created during the 1980s were engineering, agriculture, and medicine. By 1990 it occupied two large, modern campuses in the city. Since San'a University was funded over the years largely by Kuwait, modeled on and guided by Kuwait University, and staffed through the 1980s mostly by Egyptians, it tended for a long time to be something of a pale carbon copy of Kuwait University's carbon copy of Cairo University. Consequently, a theme at least since the beginning of the 1980s has been the struggle to make the university relevant to the nature and needs of Yemen through the Yemenization of its program, faculty, and administration. In addition, classes have been coeducational from the outset, making it a battleground between secular modernists and resurgent Islamic conservatives.

By the 1990s, San'a University, while continuing to grow, was merely the flagship of a national university system that had smaller units in all major cities; indeed, with Yemeni unification in 1990, it had to share top billing with the large, long-established Aden University. More significantly, the failure of Yemen to join the international coalition during the crisis and war in the Persian Gulf during 1990 and 1991 led to the total loss of Kuwaiti funding, a loss that has not been made up since from other sources. The continuing growth in the demand for higher education and a regime that has not made meeting the need for higher education a top priority have led to an erosion of the quality of education at San'a University and throughout the university system generally since the early 1990s. Class size increases, the need for new offerings goes largely unmet, and many current and potential faculty members are seeking employment in other countries and professions. Higher education in Yemen is in crisis, and not only at San'a University.

See also CAIRO UNIVERSITY; GULF CRISIS (1990–1991); KUWAIT UNIVERSITY; SAN'A; YEMEN.

ROBERT D. BURROWES

SANCTIONS, IRAQI

Trade and financial restrictions imposed by the United Nations on Iraq between 1990 and 2003.

The nature and effects of the United Nations sanctions on Iraq are more complex than has often been supposed. In brief, the UN, largely at the instigation of Britain and the United States, declared comprehensive trade and financial sanctions against Iraq under UN Resolution 661, passed on 6 August 1990, four days after Iraq invaded Kuwait. That Iraq was in a position to attack Kuwait at all was largely due to the almost unanimous support, both material and moral, that it had received from the international community in the course of its war with the Islamic Republic of Iran between 1980 and 1988, a war Iraq had started with the tacit encouragement of the United States.

Early Sanctions

The Gulf War, whose stated and rapidly achieved objective was to remove Iraq from Kuwait, was launched under UN auspices on 17 January 1991 and ended with Iraq's surrender on 24 February of the same year. In the course of this period, Iraqi cities were repeatedly bombed and damage was done not only to military installations but also to the civil infrastructure. The damage included the destruction of water purification and pumping plants, much of the electrical system, and many oil installations.

In April 1991, UN Resolution 687 allowed Iraq to import foodstuffs and materials for "essential civilian needs," although oil exports were not allowed. All restrictions would be lifted if Iraq complied with four principal conditions: the identification and elimination of its weapons of mass destruction; the demarcation of its frontier with Kuwait, to be accompanied by acceptance of Kuwaiti sovereignty; the release of Kuwaiti and other nationals held in Iraq; and the establishment of a compensation commission, which would assess war damage and pay for it by a levy on Iraqi oil revenues. Until the U.S. invasion of Iraq in the spring of 2003, Iraq only complied fully with one of these conditions: the recognition, in November 1994, of the frontier with and the sovereignty of Kuwait.

It had never been envisaged that the sanctions would still be in place some twelve years after their imposition. In fact, their severity was considerably reduced by the provisions of UN Resolutions 986 (14 April 1995; accepted by Iraq in January 1996) and 1153 (20 February 1998), which permitted Iraq,

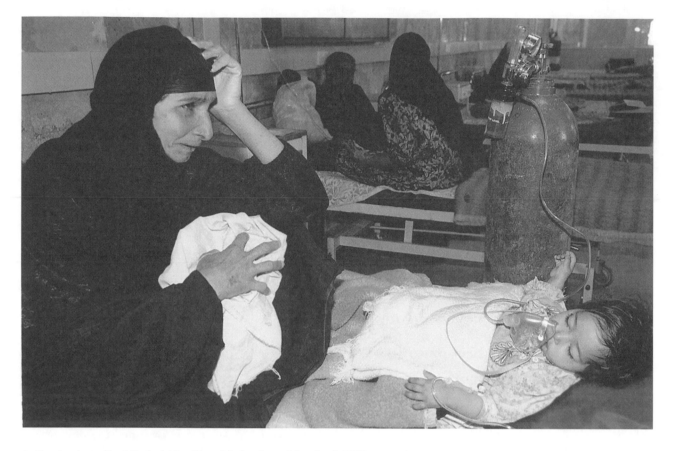

An Iraqi woman sits at the bedside of her sick daughter. After the Gulf War, sanctions were eased regarding the amount of oil that Iraq could export, as well as what products could be imported under the enacted dual use restrictions, the flow of goods and money began to ease. Sanctions were lifted from Iraq in 2003. © AP/WIDEWORLD PHOTOS. REPRODUCED BY PERMISSION.

under UN supervision, to sell first $2 billion (Resolution 986) and then $3.55 billion (Resolution 1153) net worth of oil in exchange for food every six months; in October 1999, the UN Security Council raised the revenue cap to $8.3 billion.

Oil for Food

Attempts to introduce oil-for-food arrangements had begun on the UN side as early as 1991 but had been continually rejected by Iraq as an intrusion on its sovereignty. These earlier efforts had insisted on a considerable degree of on-site monitoring and also required Iraqi acceptance of the presence of the UN Special Commission (UNSCOM, the UN weapons inspectorate), set up in May 1991. What Iraq held out for before January 1996 (when it reluctantly accepted Resolution 986), but could not obtain, was the comprehensive lifting of sanctions. This was not made more likely by continuing revelations of the extent of Iraq's nuclear, chemical, and con-

ventional weapons arsenals. The regime apparently felt this capacity was important enough to sacrifice the well-being of its people in order to maintain it.

The overriding argument against these and other sanctions—that their indiscriminate nature punishes the innocent and has little effect on the guilty (that is, the regime itself)—is persuasive. Various international organizations wrote heartrending reports on the effects of shortages of basic foodstuffs and medicines: The monthly food ration was reduced by 40 percent in October 1994, and severe malnutrition among young children was widely reported from 1991 by both internal and external observers. The provision of both education and health care deteriorated noticeably. In education, large numbers of teachers left the profession, with the result that fewer children went to school, while diseases associated with poverty, such as kwashiorkor, tuberculosis, and respiratory and digestive illnesses, reappeared after 1991 after having been virtually eliminated over the previous decades. However shocking these developments may have been, allocating all blame for them on the sanctions is not entirely justified; at least equal blame must be placed at the door of the regime for not taking the necessary steps to ensure that they would be lifted. Historian Pierre-Jean Luizard, in his book *La question irakienne*, put it thus: "The regime . . . used the embargo to move Western politicians and intellectuals, as if it were not itself responsible for the tragic situation of the Iraqi population, and as if the embargo was not linked to its remaining in power" (p. 270).

The sanctions acted as a major obstacle to Iraq's economic recovery after 1991, but again it is certain from the evidence of both defectors and UNSCOM itself that the regime had been developing biological and chemical weapons in the late 1980s and was working toward the capacity to operate nuclear missiles. There is little doubt that it was no longer able to do so after the early 1990s, and it is not unreasonable to assume that the sanctions played a major role in this. Modification of the sanctions regime in such a way as to make it less onerous to the civilian population was certainly an option, but the oil-for-food arrangements, proposed five years before they were accepted, were intended to ease that particular burden. All in all, however, sanctions both in Iraq and elsewhere have often proved a blunt instrument, whose effect has sometimes been to rally the population around an offensive regime rather than to stimulate the population to overthrow it. In the case of Iraq after the brutal repression of Kurdish and Shi'ite resistance in 1991, a popular rising against the regime was never a realistic option in any case.

In the wake of the U.S. invasion of Iraq, the UN Security Council voted to lift the sanctions via Security Council Resolution 1483 of 22 May 2003.

See also GULF WAR (1991).

Bibliography

Farouk-Sluglett, Marion, and Sluglett, Peter. *Iraq since 1958: From Revolution to Dictatorship,* revised edition. New York; London: I.B. Tauris, 2001.

Graham-Brown, Sarah. *Sanctioning Saddam: The Politics of Intervention in Iraq.* New York; London: I.B. Tauris, in association with MERIP, 1999.

Tripp, Charles. *A History of Iraq.* Cambridge, U.K.: Cambridge University Press, 2000.

PETER SLUGLETT

SANE'I, YUSEF

[1927–]

Iranian reformist cleric.

Ayatollah Yusef Sane'i was born in 1927 to a clerical family in Neekabad, Isfahan Province. He entered an Isfahan religious seminary in 1946 and upon completion of preliminary studies entered a Qom seminary in 1951. In 1955 he became a student of Ayatollah Ruhollah Khomeini and obtained the degree of *ijtihad* (interpretation) in 1959, at the age of thirty-two. He started his teaching career in 1975 at the Haghani school, where he taught until 1994. His opposition activities under the shah were mainly sermons, lectures, statements, and participation in demonstrations. In 1980 Khomeini appointed Sane'i a member of the Council of Guardians. He resigned in 1982 to become a (successful) candidate for the Assembly of Experts from Tehran. Khomeini then appointed him public prosecutor, but he resigned this post in 1985. He was also Khomeini's representative at the High Council of Reconstruction of War Zones. Contrary to common belief, it is not Yusef Sane'i but his brother Hassan Sane'i who is the head of the Fifteenth of Khordad Foundation that offers a bounty for the killing of British author Salman Rushdie.

Ayatollah Sane'i is a reformist cleric who maintains that Islam and democracy are compatible, has warned against limitations of women's rights in the name of religion, and has criticized the misinterpretation of the Qur'an. In his declarations and interviews with the women's press he has argued that Islam does not prohibit women from becoming judges (*mujtahids*), or political leaders, and that blood money should be the same for men and women. (Blood money is money paid by one who who has caused loss of life to the family of the victim. By law, this is a permissible alternative to imposing capital punishment. The blood money paid for women is half of that paid for men.) He argues that the women's struggle, continuation of the process of institutionalization of the rule of law, and the legitimacy of the public will lead to the strengthening of women's rights.

See also IRANIAN REVOLUTION (1979); KHOMEINI, RUHOLLAH.

Bibliography

Mir-Hosseini, Ziba. *Islam and Gender: The Religious Debate in Contemporary Iran.* Princeton, NJ: Princeton University Press, 1999.

AZADEH KIAN-THIÉBAUT

SANJAK

See GLOSSARY

SAN REMO CONFERENCE (1920)

Post–World War I talks at which Great Britain and France were awarded mandates over Middle East countries.

In April 1920, the victorious World War I allies, with the exception of the United States, met in San Remo, Italy. At the conference, Britain was awarded mandates over Palestine and Iraq, and France was awarded mandates over Syria and Lebanon. Tech-

A group photo of the leaders at the League of Nations Peace Treaty Conference in San Remo, Italy, 13 May 1920. The League of Nations was founded on the principles of universal peace based on social justice. © BETTMANN/CORBIS. REPRODUCED BY PERMISSION.

nically, a mandate held the territories in trusteeship for the League of Nations until the political systems of these territories were developed enough to warrant independence and admission to the League of Nations.

The San Remo Conference also discussed petroleum in Mesopotamia (now Iraq). France agreed to renounce its claims to the province of Mosul in return for a 25 percent share in the Turkish Petroleum Company. Italy was also promised access to this oil; but the issue of Mosul—whether it was to be an autonomous region of Kurds or a province of Iraq—was not decided until 1926, when it was officially incorporated into Faisal I ibn Hussein's new kingdom of Iraq.

Bibliography

Yergin, Daniel. *The Prize: The Epic Quest for Oil, Money, and Power.* New York: Simon and Schuster. New York, 1991.

ZACHARY KARABELL

SAN STEFANO, TREATY OF (1878)

Signed on 3 March 1878, this treaty concluded one of the major wars fought between Russia and the Ottoman Empire (1877–1878).

Among the provisions of the Treaty of San Stefano were the following:

1. Serbia and Montenegro received their independence from the Ottoman Empire and were granted additional territory.

2. Independence was also gained by Romania, which lost southern Bessarabia to Russia but was compensated by the acquisition of the Black Sea province of Dobrudja.

3. Bosnia and Herzegovina were granted autonomy and were promised reforms, to be supervised jointly by Russia and Austria.

4. In addition to southern Bessarabia, Russia also acquired a substantial part of northeastern Anatolia, including the provinces of Batum, Kars, and Ardahan.

5. Unexpectedly, the treaty also called for the creation of Greater Bulgaria. Its territory extended from the Danube and the Black Sea

to the Aegean Sea in the south and included much of Macedonia. Nominally a part of the Ottoman Empire, Greater Bulgaria was to be ruled by a Christian government and to possess a national militia. For the next two years, it was also to remain under Russian occupation—a clear indication of the direction in which Russia was moving: Bulgaria guards the northern access to the Turkish Straits.

It soon became obvious that the Treaty of San Stefano—a major gain in Russia's contest with the Ottoman Empire for supremacy in the Balkan-Black Sea region—would not be allowed to stand. Among the great powers, early concern was expressed by Great Britain and Austria-Hungary. Britain had long opposed Russia's aggrandizement at the expense of the Ottoman Empire and particularly the Russian drive toward the Turkish Straits. Austria-Hungary shared British apprehensions and was also perturbed by the creation of the Russian puppet state of Greater Bulgaria. Bowing to the British, Austro-Hungarian, and later German pressure, Russia agreed to submit the terms of the treaty of San Stefano to a great power congress—the Congress of Berlin.

The resulting Treaty of Berlin (1878) endorsed many of the provisions negotiated at San Stefano. Russia and Romania kept their territorial gains. Romania, Serbia, and Montenegro retained their independence, and the latter two retained much of the territory allocated to them. Bosnia and Herzegovina were, however, placed under Austrian control, and England was permitted to occupy Cyprus. Finally, despite Russian objections, the Congress of Berlin dismantled Greater Bulgaria. The latter was split into three parts: Bulgaria proper, located north of the Balkan mountains; East Rumelia, situated south of them; and Macedonia. All remained under Ottoman suzerainty but were granted autonomy and were promised reforms.

Great Britain was the main beneficiary of the Congress of Berlin. Supported by Austria-Hungary, Britain denied Russia the opportunity to become the sole arbiter of the affairs of the Ottoman Empire. The congress also prevented Russia from becoming the patron of Greater Bulgaria. Great Britain also acquired Cyprus; strategically located in the eastern Mediterranean, the island was used four years later to effect the British occupation of Egypt.

Bibliography

Langer, William L. *European Alliances and Alignments, 1871–1890,* 2d edition. New York: Knopf, 1950.

Sumner, Benedict H. *Russia and the Balkans, 1870–1880.* Oxford: Clarendon, 1937.

OLES M. SMOLANSKY

SANT EGIDIO PLATFORM

An attempt to defuse the bloody conflict between Islamists and the Algerian government through political dialogue; also known as the Rome Platform.

In 1994, members of the Algerian opposition approached the Roman Catholic lay movement Sant Egidio in Rome, suggesting that it attempt to broker a peace settlement on the model of the successful accord it had helped establish in Mozambique. A first meeting in November demonstrated the gulf between the government, represented by General Betchine, and the opposition parties, which for the first time since the breakdown of the Algerian democratic process in 1992 included the Islamic Salvation Front (FIS) in a multiparty forum. A wide range of opposition parties, representing some 80 percent of the votes cast in the 1991 elections, attended a second meeting in January 1995 and signed a national pact on 13 January, committing them to respect for both democracy and the Islamic traditions of the country and demonstrating the strength of a middle ground marginalized in the armed combat between the army and the Armed Islamic Group (GIA). Although the government immediately attacked the document as an attempt at "outside interference" with the government's efforts at drawing Islamists into the democratic process, the opposition parties claimed the agreement was proof that the government and not the Islamic parties had been responsible for obstructing the democratic dialogue. Hope briefly grew after 26 January, when the government announced presidential elections, but the spiral of violence thereafter demonstrated the powerlessness of the political opposition in the face of the intransigence of key forces in the security establishment and the extremist wing of the Islamist movement.

See also ALGERIA: OVERVIEW; ALGERIA: POLITICAL PARTIES IN; FRONT ISLAMIQUE DU SALUT (FIS).

Bibliography

Riccardi, Andrea. *Sant-Egidio: Rome and the World.* London: St. Pauls, 1999.

GEORGE R. WILKES

SANUSI, MUHAMMAD IBN ALI AL-
[1787–1859]

Muslim scholar and founder of the Sanusi order, 1837.

Muhammad ibn Ali al-Sanusi studied Arabic and Islam in Algeria, Morocco, Egypt, and the Hijaz of western Arabia. He quarreled with leading ulama, (Muslim scholars), became active in Sufi circles, and was successful among Muslim nomads. A follower of Sidi Ahmad al-Fasi, he moved to Cyrenaica, Libya, in 1838, which became the base for the spread of the Sanusi order.

Bibliography

Evans-Pritchard, E. E. *The Sanusi of Cyrenaica.* Oxford: Clarendon, 1949.

Simon, Rachel. *Libya between Ottomanism and Nationalism: The Ottoman Involvement in Libya during the War with Italy (1911–1919).* Berlin: K. Schwarz, 1987.

Ziadeh, Nicola. *Sanusiyah.* Leiden, Neth.: Brill, 1958.

RACHEL SIMON

SANUSI ORDER

Islamic order founded in 1837 by Muhammad ibn Ali al-Sanusi (died 1859); followed by Muhammad al-Mahdi (1859–1902), Ahmad al-Sharif (1902–1917), and Idris al-Sanusi.

Combining orthodoxy and Sufism, the Sanusi order aimed to unite all religious orders by returning to the sources. It called for closeness to the prophet Muhammad through study, training, and intention, but rejected ecstasy. It advocated a modest lifestyle and refraining from daily pleasures. Its main support was tribal (in Cyrenaica and central Africa). The Sanusi organization was based on a network of zawiyas (religious compounds), which were strategically located and served as centers of study and trade, to which neighboring affiliates contributed their ushr (tithe) and manpower. The Sanusi political power was recognized by the Ottoman Empire and by central African kingdoms. The order was a key factor in the resistance to Italian rule (1911–1933), which caused the death and exile of many Sanusi leaders and followers, the confiscation of zawiyas, and the de facto collapse of the order.

See also IDRIS AL-SAYYID MUHAMMAD AL-SANUSI; SANUSI, MUHAMMAD IBN ALI AL-; SUFISM AND THE SUFI ORDERS.

Bibliography

Ahmida, Ali Abdullatif. *The Making of Modern Libya: State Formation, Colonization, and Resistance, 1830–1932.* Albany: State University of New York Press, 1994.

Cordell, D. D. "Eastern Libya, Wadai and the Sanusiya: A Tariqa and a Trade Route." *Journal of African History* 18 (1977):21–36.

Evans-Pritchard, E. E. *The Sanusi of Cyrenaica.* Oxford: Clarendon Press, 1949.

Ziadeh, Nicola A. *Sanusiyah.* Leiden, Netherlands: E.J. Brill, 1958.

RACHEL SIMON

SANU, YA'QUB
[1839–1912]

Egyptian nationalist playwright and satirical journalist.

Born into a Jewish family in Alexandria, Ya'qub Sanu, also known as James Sanu, is considered the father of modern Arabic satire. He organized the first popular theater in Egypt, which presented plays in colloquial Arabic. Influenced by the Muslim reformer Jamal al-Din al-Afghani, Sanu established a political newspaper, *Abu Nazzara Zarqa* (The man with the blue glasses). In 1877 or 1878, the royal court deemed his writings offensive and expelled him from Egypt. Settling in Paris, Sanu continued his campaign of attacking the members of Egypt's political establishment for collaborating with the colonial powers and betraying Egypt.

See also AFGHANI, JAMAL AL-DIN AL-; THEATER.

Bibliography

Gendzier, Irene. *The Practical Visions of Ya'qub Sanu'.* Cambridge, MA: Harvard University Press, 1966.

Goldschmidt, Arthur, Jr. *Modern Egypt: The Formation of a Nation-State.* Boulder, CO: Westview Press, 1988.

DAVID WALDNER

SAPIR, PINHAS
[1907–1975]

Israeli Labor party leader, minister of finance.

Pinhas Sapir, born in Poland as Koslovsky, received a religious education as a child and later became a leader in the ha-Halutz movement.

In 1929 he immigrated to Palestine. From 1937 to 1947 Pinhas Sapir was Levi Eshkol's deputy at Mekorot Water Company. Later Pinhas Sapir served in a number of high government and cabinet positions including director general of the Ministry of Defense (1948–1953) and director general of the Ministry of Finance (1953–1955). He was minister of commerce and industry from 1955 to 1964 and again from 1970 to 1972. He also served as minister of finance from 1963 to 1968 and again from 1969 to 1974.

He was known to be a power broker within the Labor party and played an active role in uncovering the details of the Lavon affair (1960–1961). As finance minister after the Arab–Israel War of 1967, he expressed reservations about Moshe Dayan's proposals for integrating the occupied territories with Israel. He was suggested as a successor to Golda Meir, after her resignation as prime minister in 1974, but he refused the offer. He left the government in 1974 to become chairman of the Jewish Agency executive.

MARTIN MALIN

SARID, YOSSI
[1940]

Israeli political leader and government minister.

Yossi Sarid, the son of a prominent educator, was born in Palestine. After a brief career as a columnist for *Haaretz*, Sarid became active in the Labor Party. He was close to Pinhas Sapir, the powerful, dovish minister of finance, and was responsible for the party's information drives in four election campaigns. In 1974, after the Arab–Israel War the previous year (also known as the October War), Sarid

was elected to the Knesset, and has remained a member ever since. In 1982 Sarid was the only Labor member of the Knesset who opposed Israel's invasion of Lebanon. In 1984, in protest of the formation of the Peres-Shamir Unity Government, Sarid resigned from the party and joined Shulamit Aloni's Movement for Civil Rights and Peace (RATZ). In 1988 Sarid was one of the founders of Meretz, the left-wing party espousing social welfare policies and peace with the Palestinians, based on the principle of "two states for two nations." In 1992 Meretz joined the coalition government, formed by Yitzhak Rabin. Sarid was appointed minister of the environment. He strongly supported the Oslo Accord and was a member of the team of three senior ministers who negotiated its details.

In 1996 Sarid replaced Aloni as chairman of the party. When Ehud Barak formed his coalition government in 1999, Meretz joined once more and Sarid was appointed minister of education. He initiated many reforms in Israel's educational system, but could not complete them; Meretz had to quit the coalition to avoid its breakup during the dramatic negotiations with the Palestinian Authority on the "Final Status" arrangements, which eventually collapsed at the July 2000 Camp David Conference. In the 2002 elections, Meretz suffered the severe drawback of losing four of their ten Knesset members. Sarid took responsibility for the defeat and resigned from his position as head of the party, but remained in the Knesset as a veteran member of its Foreign and Security Committee. Sarid published hundreds of articles and two poetry volumes.

See also ISRAEL: POLITICAL PARTIES IN; OSLO ACCORD (1993).

BRYAN DAVES
UPDATED BY MORDECHAI BAR-ON

SARKIS, ILYAS
[1924–1985]

President of Lebanon, 1976 to 1982.

Ilyas Sarkis studied law at the Université Saint Joseph, then joined the audit office as a magistrate in Lebanon. His integrity and discipline brought him to the attention of Lebanon's President Fu'ad Chehab, who appointed him legal adviser in 1959 and director general of his cabinet in 1962. Chehab's successor, Charles Hilu, appointed him chairman of the Banking Control Commission and, in June 1968, governor of the Central Bank.

As the major Chehabist contender in the presidential election of 1970, Sarkis lost by one vote to Sulayman Franjiyya, whose tenure developed into one of the contentious issues in the Lebanese Civil War (1975). The legislature then specifically amended the constitution to allow early presidential elections to permit the accession of Sarkis in May 1976. Considering him Syria's candidate, Kamal Jumblatt, the leader of the leftist forces and ally of the Palestine Liberation Organization (PLO), tried unsuccessfully to disrupt the parliamentary session in favor of the candidacy of Raymond Eddé.

As prescribed by the Arab summit conferences at Riyadh and Cairo, Sarkis attempted, using a neo-Chehabist team, to disarm all the Lebanese militias with the help of the Syrian-dominated Arab Deterrent Forces (ADF). He was blocked in doing so by the Phalange and the National Liberal Party (NLP), who insisted that the PLO disarm first. Since Israel would not allow Syrian troops to descend south of the Litani River, PLO guerrillas remained in southern Lebanon, where raids and counterraids across the border finally led to Israel's invasion of the area in March 1978. Although United Nations peacekeeping troops were deployed in the wake of Israel's withdrawal, Israel would not allow Sarkis to send Lebanese army units to the southern border area, propping up instead the local Christian militias under Major Sa'd Haddad. In September 1978, tensions between the Maronite Christian militias and the Syrian troops of the ADF culminated in the bombardment of the Ashrafiyya quarter in east Beirut, bringing the president close to resignation.

Henceforth, all that Sarkis could do was maintain the status quo among the disparate armed groups and try to manage the crisis. In 1980, the rise of Bashir Jumayyil as the charismatic militia leader of the Maronite community forced Sarkis to mend fences. He ultimately persuaded the young Jumayyil to steer his course more toward the United States instead of relying exclusively on Israel. Toward the end of his term, Sarkis increasingly believed in the desirability of electing the strong Bashir to office. Sarkis refused suggestions that he remain for two more years as an extraordinary measure—even in the wake of Israel's 1982 invasion and after Bashir Jumayyil's assassination while president-elect.

Although accused by critics in the Maronite and leftist camps of being weak and vacillating, Sarkis was an honest and moderate president. He insisted that he had transferred power to his successor, Amin Jumayyil (Bashir's brother), with the government's apparatus still united and the economy strong despite the intermittent civil war. In retrospect, these were by no means negligible accomplishments.

See also CHEHAB, FU'AD; EDDÉ, RAYMOND; FRANJIYYA, SULAYMAN; HADDAD, SA'D; HILU, CHARLES; JUMAYYIL, AMIN; JUMAYYIL, BASHIR; JUMBLATT, KAMAL; LEBANESE CIVIL WAR (1975–1990); NATIONAL LIBERAL PARTY; PALESTINE LIBERATION ORGANIZATION (PLO); PHALANGE.

Bibliography

Cobban, Helena. *The Making of Modern Lebanon.* London: Hutchinson, 1985.

BASSAM NAMANI

SARTAWI, ISSAM

[1935–1983]

Palestinian doctor and political activist.

Issam Sartawi was born in 1935 in Acre during the British mandate over Palestine, received his university and medical education in Iraq, and then went to Ohio University in the early 1960s to specialize in heart surgery. In 1968, he returned to the Middle East and joined his family in Amman, Jordan. That year he formed the Organization of Action for the Liberation of Palestine, which carried out clandestine attacks against Israel from Jordan. In 1970, after King Hussein's forces fought to keep the armed Palestinian guerrilla groups in Jordan from overthrowing the government that had given them sanctuary, Sartawi disbanded his small force and joined al-Fatah, the armed Palestinian group led by Yasir Arafat.

Later, he became an advocate of recognizing Israel and seeking Israeli-Palestinian peace on the basis of a directly negotiated two-state solution. He frequently advised Arafat, who was by then Palestine Liberation Organization (PLO) chairman, and was roving representative for the PLO, although not a member of the PLO Executive Committee. In addition, Sartawi served as informal liaison between

Arafat and the Israeli doves and Western leaders. Sartawi had to contend with mounting criticism within the PLO. This led to his resignation from the Palestine National Council in 1981, though Arafat refused to accept it.

In April 1983, against a background of failed negotiations between Arafat and King Hussein on whether the latter would take part in U.S.-sponsored negotiations representing the Palestinians, Sartawi attended a meeting of the Socialist International in Portugal. On 10 April, he was assassinated there by a gunman. Sabri al-Banna's (Abu Nidal) al-Fatah (Revolutionary Council), which had broken away from the PLO nine years earlier, took responsibility for the shooting.

See also ARAFAT, YASIR; BANNA, SABRI AL-; PALESTINE LIBERATION ORGANIZATION (PLO).

Bibliography

Sartawi, Issam. "Dr. Sartawi Speaks His Mind." *New Outlook* (March 1982).

Tessler, Mark. *A History of the Israeli–Palestinian Conflict.* Bloomington: Indiana University Press, 1994.

BENJAMIN JOSEPH

SASSON, ELIYAHU
[1902–1978]

Israeli senior official, diplomat, and cabinet minister.

Eliyahu (Elias) Sasson was born in Damascus to a middle-class Jewish family that emigrated to Palestine in 1919. He followed in 1927, after immersing himself in the life and politics of Damascus, including its Arab nationalist activities. This provided the basis for a wide network of contacts, which he put to full use once he became head of the Arab section of the Jewish Agency's Political Department in 1934. When the Israeli state was established, in May 1948, he was appointed director of its Foreign Ministry's Middle East Department.

Both before and after 1948, Sasson played major roles in Zionist–Arab and Israel–Arab diplomacy, seeking to promote understanding and agreement. His history placed him in a unique position as a Zionist who had a genuine rapport with Arab nationalists. During the 1940s, he held secret meetings with Amir (later King) Abdullah and members of his entourage. In December 1947, he wrote to the secretary-general of the Arab League hoping to find a way to prevent the outbreak of hostilities. After the first Arab–Israel War, he was part of the Israeli negotiating team in the armistice talks with the Egyptians at Rhodes.

In the bureaucratic politics of the young Israeli state, he was identified with the accommodationist line of Moshe Sharett. But Sharett was no match for David Ben-Gurion, and the softer policies of Sharett's school were defeated by the harsh realities of Arab-Israeli relations. Sasson found himself removed from the center of policy making when he was appointed Israel's first head of mission (as minister) in Turkey in 1949. After 1952, he took up the post of Israel's ambassador to Italy yet continued to advise his colleagues in the Foreign Ministry about Arab affairs from his station in Rome. From 1961 to 1969, he served in various Labor-led cabinets as minister of posts and minister of police, representing the Mizrahi/Sephardic component of Israel's population.

See also ARAB–ISRAEL WAR (1948); BEN-GURION, DAVID; SHARETT, MOSHE.

Bibliography

Caplan, Neil. *Futile Diplomacy*; Vol. 2: *Early Arab–Zionist Negotiation Attempts, 1913–1931*; and Vol. 3: *Arab–Zionist Negotiations and the End of the Mandate.* London: Frank Cass, 1983, 1986.

Shlaim, Avi. *Collusion across the Jordan: King Abdullah, the Zionist Movement, and the Partition of Palestine.* Oxford: Clarendon Press, 1988.

NEIL CAPLAN
ITAMAR RABINOVICH

SASSOON FAMILY

Family of international renown, which originated in the Jewish community of Baghdad.

Sassoon ben Salih (1750–1830) was a banker to the *vali* (provincial governor) of Baghdad. His son David (1792–1864) fled from a new and unfriendly *vali*, going first to the Gulf port of Bushehr in 1828 and then to Bombay, India, in 1832, with his large family. In Bombay, he built the international business called David S. Sassoon, with the policy of staffing it with people brought from Baghdad. They filled the functions of the various branches of his business in India, Burma, Malay, and east Asia. In each branch, he maintained a rabbi. His wealth and munificence were proverbial, and his business extended to China and then to England.

His eight sons also branched out into many directions. Elias David (1820–1880), his son by his first wife, left the firm to establish E. D. Sassoon. Three of his other sons became prominent in England and were great friends of the Prince of Wales, later Edward VII. Of those who settled in England, Sir Edward Albert Sassoon (1856–1912) was a Conservative member of Parliament from 1899 until his death, and the seat was inherited by his son Sir Philip Sassoon (1888–1939) from 1912 until his death. Sir Philip served in World War I as military secretary to Field Marshal Sir Douglas Haig and, during the 1920s and 1930s, as Britain's undersecretary of state for air. The English poet Siegfried Sassoon (1886–1967) is David's great-grandson. Intermarriage in England has caused the general loss of Judaism within this branch.

The branch that carried on the ancestral tradition has been represented by Rabbi Solomon David Sassoon (1915–1985), who moved from Letchworth to London and then to Jerusalem in 1970. He was the son of the David Sassoon who collected Jewish books and manuscripts and who catalogued them in *Ohel David*, in two volumes. This David was the son of Flora Abraham, who had moved from India to England in 1901 and established a famous salon in her London home.

SYLVIA G. HAIM

SATELLITE CITIES DEVELOPMENT

Egyptian satellite cities built on the outskirts of Cairo to reduce overpopulation.

Cairo is overwhelmed by a population estimated at 16 million, with some 90 percent of Egypt's 60 million inhabitants residing on only 4 percent of the country's territory. In 1976, as part of Anwar Sadat's "Open Door Policy," his government started building fourteen new cities to draw people away from Cairo to redirect urban growth toward the desert and away from the limited arable land. The plan encouraged foreign investment in Egypt largely banned since the country's 1952 socialist revolution under Gamel Abdel Nasser.

Bearing names that honor events in recent Egyptian history, the new cities have drawn industry away from the capital through tax exemptions for private investors, but have done little to alleviate Cairo's overpopulation. By the late 1990s, only 500,000 people had relocated to the new cities due to the poor quality of housing, lack of water and electricity, and their remoteness, characterized in the 1997 novel *Irtihalat al-Lu'lu* (The movement of pearls), by Ni'imat al-Bihayri.

The original plan focused on human habitability and an improvement in the quality of life. As the government was unable to fund the needs of these cities, their futures and the provision of human services fell on the shoulders of investors. Therefore, some towns have flourished, while others are virtual ghost towns. Greater Cairo's market in luxury housing absorbs a large portion of available investment capital and makes little contribution to needed housing for the general populace. Investors who choose to do so make infrastructural improvements to their developments; other developments are built under subpar conditions. The wealthy rim of Cairo's infrastructure is being rebuilt, while the city's center, and the poor populations who remain there, are neglected. In an attempt to reduce illegal squatting, the government has relocated some poor families to sites that function as public housing; some of these sites lack basic services such as water, electricity, and sewerage.

The satellite cities can be broken down into two general groups: residential, and a combination of industrial and residential. The residential areas invest in infrastructure that leads back into Cairo, while the idea behind the industry-based sites is to develop self-sufficient cities. While the following is not an exhaustive list, it provides an overview of development and success.

Residential

Madinat Nasr, or "Victory City," one of the largest and earliest of the desert development areas of the 1970s, is now a vast residential quarter. Approximately 50 percent of its residents are high-ranking diplomats. Other luxurious residential areas (some gated communities), evoking Sadat's fascination with American cities like Los Angeles and Houston, are named Beverly Hills, Gardenia Park, Dreamland, and Hayy al-Ashgar (Treeville). Another area that is under private development in the northeast is called New Cairo.

Residential/Industrial

Sadat City relies on approximately 180 heavy industrial enterprises. It now has a new fee-paying primary school, built by its businessmen, who claim it is the most modern and well-equipped school in the country. Investors in Sadat City are funding a rail link that they estimate could be running by 2005. Sixth of October City is experiencing the fastest expansion rate. There are over 1,300 factories, as well as sports stadiums and cinemas. It has greatly benefited by the Twenty-sixth of July Overpass connecting it to Cairo. It is the home of the private October 6 University. Tenth of Ramadan City has thousands of small and micro enterprises, making products aimed at a range of markets, from tourists to heavy industry. It suffers from environmental waste problems despite laws passed in 1994 to protect the environment. Its problems provide a negative example of the free reign investors have had in the development.

Fifteenth of May City began as commuter city serving nearby factories. It is now showing some signs of development, although it is not developing as rapidly as other cities. Madinat al-Salam has had virtually no major investors show interest and remains underdeveloped.

A 1989 government report estimated the population in all the satellite cities at one-fifth of the original plan. New tax incentives, in some cases "twenty-year tax holidays," have caught the attention of investors. By 1996 many of Egypt's 400 state-owned companies had been sold to private investors, and the government has paved the legal and regulatory way for entrepreneurs. Taking Sadat's idea one step further, Husni Mubarak has pledged nearly $9 billion to build 18 new cities in remote desert regions of the Sinai, the Red Sea, and the New Delta, estimating the settlements will house 3.3 million Egyptians, create 70,000 new jobs, and support 75,000 acres of farmland.

Bibliography

Dennis, Eric. "Urban Planning and Growth in Cairo." *Middle East Research & Information Project* 202, vol. 27. no. 1 (1997): 7–12.

Doughty, Dick. "Inside the Mega City." *Aramco World Magazine.* March–April 1996.

Fernea, Elizabeth Warnock, and Fernea, Robert A. "Egypt." In *The Arab World: Forty Years of Change.* New York: Doubleday, 1997.

Ghannam, Farha. *Remaking the Modern: Space, Relocation, and the Politics of Identity.* Berkeley: University of California Press, 1997.

HANI FAKHOURI
UPDATED BY MARIA F. CURTIS

SAUDI ARABIA

Country in the Arabian Peninsula.

The Kingdom of Saudi Arabia occupies the greater part of the Arabian Peninsula, with a size of approximately 830,000 square miles (2,150,000 sq. km) and a population in 2002 of approximately 22 million. The country is bounded on the west by the Red Sea; on the north by Jordan and Iraq; on the east by the Gulf (also known as the Persian or Arabian Gulf) and the small states of Kuwait, the island state of Bahrain just off the Saudi shore, Qatar, and the United Arab Emirates; and on the south by Oman and Yemen. The country forms a rough triangle, tilting from west to east. Al-Hijaz, the westernmost of the three principal regions, rises from a low, barren coastal plain to a craggy, mountainous spine before leveling out into a gravel plateau. As the birthplace of Islam, al-Hijaz contains Islam's holiest cities, Makka (Mecca) and al-Madina (Medina). It also contains Saudi Arabia's second-largest city, Jidda (Jedda), with the country's biggest port. The center of the country is occupied by the Najd, the historic center of modern Saudi Arabia and the location of its capital, Riyadh. The Eastern Province, lying between Riyadh and the Gulf, contains nearly all of the kingdom's massive oil deposits. Besides the conurbation of al-Zahran (Dhahran), al-Dammam, and al-Khubar (Khobar), the province also embraces the extensive and ancient oases of al-Ahsa (Hasa) and al-Qatif. Along the southeastern border, Saudi Arabia shares with Oman and Yemen the world's largest sand desert, al-Rub al-Khali (The empty quarter). In the southwest, the mountains of

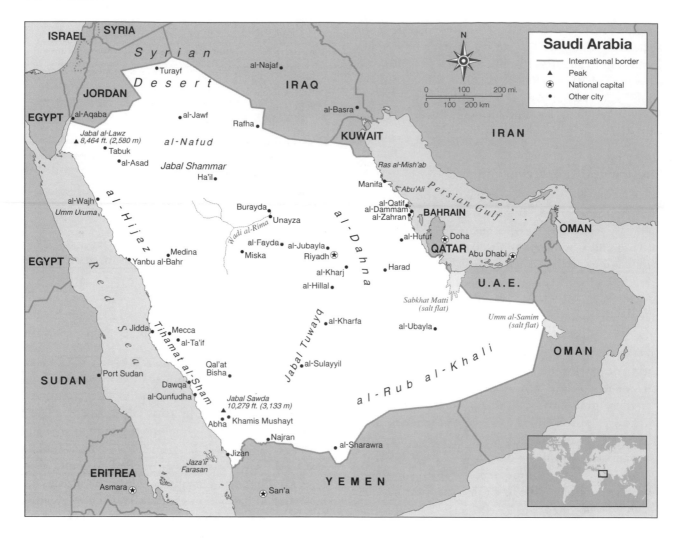

MAP BY XNR PRODUCTIONS, INC. THE GALE GROUP.

al-Hijaz grow higher as they proceed south across Asir into Yemen. The country is divided into thirteen provinces.

Nearly all of the country is desert, and the climate is generally very hot in the summer and humid along the seashores. Although the coastal plains are mild in winter, the interior desert can be cold. Small juniper forests exist only in several spots in the western mountains. There are no rivers or permanent bodies of water. Rainfall is sparse.

Economy

Traditionally, the majority of the people were engaged in pastoral nomadism, herding camels, goats, and sheep. Subsistence agriculture was practiced in the extensive oases of al-Ahsa (Hasa) and al-Qatif in the Eastern Province, as well as in other smaller

oases across the country. Cultivation was also intense in the southwest highlands, and fishing was a feature along both the Red Sea and Gulf coasts, The west, particularly Mecca, Jidda, and Medina, relied on the hajj (the annual Muslim pilgrimage) for income. Trade was important throughout the country, but especially for the small ports along the coastlines and for transshipment centers such as Burayda and Unayza in the Najd.

Oil exploration began in the Eastern Province in the 1930s, and commercially exploitable reserves were discovered in 1938. The advent of the Second World War delayed large-scale production until the late 1940s. Production levels reached 0.5 million barrels per day in 1949, doubling by 1955, and rising to 3.5 million barrels per day by 1968. By the beginning of the 1980s, Saudi Arabia was producing about 10 million barrels per day. This declined to less than 4 million barrels per day as a result of the decline in world demand for oil, but at the beginning of the twenty-first century the kingdom was again producing over 8 million barrels per day and had become the world's largest crude oil exporter. Total reserves were estimated at 262 billion barrels in 2002, giving Saudi Arabia about 25 percent of the world's total. Other natural resources are negligible, although several small gold mines were put into operation in the early 1990s.

Oil completely transformed the Saudi economy. Prior to oil, the nascent Saudi kingdom was a poor state, highly dependent on hajj revenues for the government's income. Since then, Saudi Arabia has become a highly developed social welfare state. In the 1980s, it also embarked on a large-scale program of industrialization, emphasizing petrochemical industries and other energy-intensive industrial programs that could make effective use of locally refined oil or gas for fuel. The small ports of al-Jubayl on the Gulf and Yanbu on the Red Sea were selected as complementary sites for new industrial cities. Other industrial efforts have gone into import substitution and highly subsidized agricultural programs.

Language, Religion, and Education

Nearly all Saudi citizens are Arab, although there has been considerable ethnic mixing in al-Hijaz as a result of centuries of immigration connected with the hajj. Arabic is the sole indigenous language, but English is widely spoken. All Saudis are Muslims and most are Sunni. The Hanbali school of Islamic jurisprudence predominates because of Wahhabism, a movement within Sunni Islam, founded in eighteenth-century Najd by Muhammad Abd al-Wahhab, emphasizing the ascetic values of early Islam and widely followed within the kingdom (its adherents prefer to be known as Muwahhidun, or Unitarians). Saudi Arabia also perceives itself as having a special responsibility for the protection of the Islamic holy places. As many as 500,000 inhabitants of al-Qatif and al-Ahsa oases are Jaʿfari (or Twelver) Shiʿa, and small Shiʿite communities are to be found in Medina and Najran.

Great strides were made in education over the last half of the twentieth century, and about 62 per-

The Kaʿaba Stone is located in the Haram mosque in Mecca, Saudi Arabia. Millions of Muslim pilgrims walk around the Kaʿaba Stone each year at the end of the Hajj, which is a pilgrimage to Mecca. © CORBIS. REPRODUCED BY PERMISSION.

cent of Saudi citizens are literate. The country has eight universities, the oldest of which dates from 1957. Three universities specialize in Islamic disciplines and the other five offer broader curricula. Several hundred thousand Saudis have received a university education abroad, notably in the United States and the United Kingdom.

Political Structure

Saudi Arabia is a monarchy, headed by a king drawn from the Al Saʿud royal family. The country's four monarchs since 1953 all have been sons of King Abd al-Aziz ibn Abd al-Rahman (r. 1902–1953): Saʿud (r. 1953–1964), Faisal (r. 1964–1975), Khalid (r. 1975–1982), and Fahd (r. 1982–). King Fahd also holds the title of prime minister. His half-brother Abdullah is heir apparent and first deputy prime minister. Because of King Fahd's poor health, Abdullah serves as the de facto head of government. Although the king holds enormous power, he is not

King Faisal ibn Abd al-Aziz Al Saʿud (1904–1975) is welcomed to the White House by President Richard Nixon and his wife Pat, during a 27 May 1971 state visit. During the 1960s and 1970s King Faisal positioned Saudi Arabia as the powerful supporter of the United States among the Middle East's Islamic nations. NATIONAL ARCHIVES, NLNP-WHPO-MPF-C6399(32A). REPRODUCED BY PERMISSION.

an absolute monarch, being required to rule according to Islamic precepts and tribal tradition. Important decisions are made only after gaining the consensus of an inner circle of male members of the royal family. Generally, the process of consensus-building also includes the rest of the family, other key families (such as collateral branches of the Al Saʿud and the Al al-Shaykh, descendants of Muhammad Abd al-Wahhab), the religious establishment, tribal shaykhs, senior government officials, and prominent merchant families.

The Council of Ministers was established in 1953 and its ranks have expanded so that the majority is made up of commoners, in addition to members of the Al Saʿud. The family continues to hold the key portfolios of defense, interior, and foreign affairs. The armed forces are divided into four services: army, air force, air defense, and navy. There is also a large national guard, which serves as

a counterbalance to the regular armed forces and is said to be particularly loyal to the Al Saʿud. Saudi Arabia's orientation in foreign policy traditionally has been first to the Arab states and then to the Islamic world. Since the 1940s, the United States has been a key partner in oil exploitation, socioeconomic development, trade, and military and security matters. Staunchly anti-Communist, the kingdom established diplomatic relations with the Soviet Union only in 1990 (earlier relations in the 1920s and 1930s were allowed to lapse).

History

The present kingdom is the third Saudi state established since an alliance was struck in 1744 between Islamic reformer Muhammad Abd al-Wahhab and Muhammad ibn Saʿud Al Saʿud, then the head of the small town of al-Dirʿiyya in Najd. Imbued with the religious fervor of Wahhabism, Muhammad ibn

Al-Mamlika center is a complex in Riyadh, Saudi Arabia, that houses retail, offices, and a five-star hotel. The center is an illustration of the country's modernization and prosperity due to oil revenues. © AP/WIDEWORLD PHOTOS. REPRODUCED BY PERMISSION.

(1979) and Iran-Iraq War (1980–1988) had refocused both Saudi and Western assessments of the principal threat to the kingdom away from the Soviet Union to a resurgent Iran. Saudi-Iranian relations remained troubled through the 1980s but improved through the 1990s. An even more serious threat emerged in August 1990, when Iraq invaded Kuwait and raised fears that it had designs on Saudi oil fields as well. Riyadh invited Arab and Western governments to participate in a coalition to drive the invading forces out of Kuwait. Operation Desert Storm was launched from Saudi territory in early 1991 and accomplished the liberation of Kuwait and the destruction of much of Iraq's military and industrial capability. The kingdom participated fully in the subsequent economic sanctions

against Iraq, although popular opinion increasingly turned against them.

The kingdom has relied heavily on its "special relationship" with the United States for more than fifty years. But ties were severely strained after the terrorist attacks on the United States of 11 September 2001. Al-Qaʿida, a radical Islamist network established by a Saudi national, Osama bin Ladin, apparently orchestrated the attacks and recruited fifteen Saudis to be among the nineteen hijackers. In the following years, many in the United States claimed that the kingdom was not doing enough to stop the flow of funding to terrorist groups and that the country encouraged anti-American beliefs. The Saudi government strenuously denied these allegations and the Saudi and U.S. governments continued to have close official relations. A May 2003 terrorist attack on residential areas in Riyadh sparked a Saudi campaign to eradicate extremists in the kingdom, and a number of arrests and shootouts occurred over the succeeding months.

Riyadh's refusal to allow the United States to use military facilities in the kingdom during the 2003 war against Iraq prompted Washington to establish alternative bases in Qatar. By the end of that summer, all U.S. military detachments (apart from elements involved in training Saudi forces) were removed from the kingdom; this had been a key al-Qaʿida demand.

See also AL AL-SHAYKH FAMILY; AL SAʿUD FAMILY; BIN LADEN, OSAMA; MECCA; MEDINA; MUWAHHIDUN; PETROLEUM, OIL, AND NATURAL GAS; PETROLEUM RESERVES AND PRODUCTION; QAʿIDA, AL-; SHIʿISM.

Bibliography

Fandy, Mamoun. *Saudi Arabia and the Politics of Dissent.* New York: St. Martin's Press, 1999.

Helms, Christine Moss. *The Cohesion of Saudi Arabia: Evolution of Political Identity.* Baltimore, MD: Johns Hopkins University Press, 1981.

Holden, David, and Johns, Richard, with Buchan, James. *The House of Saud: The Rise and Rule of the Most Powerful Dynasty in the Arab World.* New York: Holt, Rinehart, and Winston, 1982.

Kechichian, Joseph A. *Succession in Saudi Arabia.* New York: Palgrave, 2001.

Niblock, Tim, ed. *State, Society, and Economy in Saudi Arabia.* London: Croon Helm, for the University of Exeter Centre for Arab Gulf Studies, 1982.

Rasheed, Madawi Al-. *A History of Saudi Arabia.* Cambridge, U.K.: Cambridge University Press, 2002.

J. E. PETERSON

SAUDI, MONA
[1945–]

Jordanian sculptor and poet.

Mona Saudi (also Muna Saʿudi), born in Jordan, is one of the few Arab women artists to work primarily in stone, and especially to execute large-scale stone sculptures. Her sculptures have been produced in marble, granite, limestone, and other materials, and she has also done etchings to accompany them. She was educated at the Ecole Supérieure des Beaux Arts in Paris and was influenced by Brancusi, but her work also reflects an engagement with Islamic and ancient Middle Eastern artistic traditions. For example, many of her works are refined, abstract forms taken from Arabic calligraphy and Arabic words, or are done in the spirit of ancient Egyptian and Sumerian art. Saudi describes her pieces as already formed within the piece of stone and says her work is to draw them out through sculpting. Her work is also inspired by her reading and writing of poetry, and her poems have been translated in her collection *An Ocean of Dreams* (1999). Saudi is also an arts activist. She has published the drawings of Palestinian refugee children and organized arts exhibitions to support the Palestinian cause. She lives and works in Beirut, and her large-scale public sculptures can be found there, as well as in Jordan and at the Institut du Monde Arabe in Paris.

See also ART; GENDER: GENDER AND EDUCATION.

Bibliography

Mona Saudi. Available at <http://www.monasaudi.com>.

JESSICA WINEGAR

SAUNDERS, HAROLD
[1927–]

Senior U.S. official who helped to negotiate peace between Egypt and Israel, then launched a nongovernmental peace-through-dialogue program.

Harold H. (Hal) Saunders earned a Ph.D. in political history at Yale University before joining the U.S. Air Force and then the CIA as an analyst. He joined the National Security Council staff of the Kennedy administration in 1961, was involved in U.S. Mideast policy during the 1967 and 1973 Arab-Israel wars, witnessed the 1970 crisis in Jordan, and in 1974 joined the U.S. State Department as deputy assistant for the Near East and North Africa. From 1973 to 1975 he worked with Secretary of State Henry Kissinger on scores of Mideast missions: in response to the oil embargo and the outbreak of civil war in Lebanon; helping to mediate three interim Egyptian-Israeli peace agreements; and restating U.S. policy to the Palestinians (in what was later known as the Saunders document of 1975). As assistant secretary of state for the Near East and South Asia, Saunders advised President Jimmy Carter at the Camp David talks of 1978, attracting criticism from both Israeli president Menachem Begin and some Palestinian leaders over U.S. policy regarding Israeli settlements in Gaza and the West Bank. He also helped to draft the Egyptian–Israeli peace treaty of 1979, and, following the revolution in Iran, coordinated efforts to secure the release of U.S. embassy staff there.

Drawing on the early concept of a "peace process" that he helped to develop while working under Kissinger, Saunders became a leading advocate of "sustained" nongovernmental dialogues as an instrument of conflict resolution.

See also CAMP DAVID ACCORDS (1978); KISSINGER, HENRY.

Bibliography

Kissinger, Henry. *Years of Upheaval.* London: Phoenix, 1982.

Saunders, Harold H. *The Other Walls: The Arab–Israeli Peace Process in a Global Perspective,* revised edition. Princeton, NJ: Princeton University Press, 1991.

Saunders, Harold H. *Public Peace Process: Sustained Dialogue to Transform Racial and Ethnic Conflicts.* New York: St. Martin's Press, 1999.

GEORGE R. WILKES

SAVAK

See GLOSSARY

The science and technology systems in most Middle Eastern countries are, with two exceptions, similar to those in other developing countries. Israel, whose system is akin to that of industrial countries, is the major exception. The other is Afghanistan, which has not yet established a scientific infrastructure.

Most Middle Eastern countries are primarily interested in applying science and technology for development. Some have sought to acquire capabilities in defense technologies but have been only partially successful. Israel alone has succeeded in applying technology for developmental and military purposes.

With the exception of Israel, information on professional manpower and science-related institutions in all countries is limited.

Manpower Development

Governments of the region have long recognized the importance of professional manpower to national development and have consequently devoted considerable efforts and resources to the provision of higher education. During the early 1950s, most countries except for Egypt and Israel suffered from shortages of professional manpower. These shortages have today been overcome everywhere in the region except Afghanistan.

Substantial numbers of engineers and scientists are now available. The Arab countries are in the lead, with a total of some 600,000 engineers. The figures on research and development (R&D) scientific manpower, though incomplete and fragmentary, are as follows: Egypt (1986), 21,000; Iran (1985), 3,200; Israel (1984), 20,000; Turkey (1985), 11,300. These countries also had a substantial number of university professors: Egypt (1988), 33,000; Algeria (1988), 14,000; Morocco (1989), 7,000; Iraq (1986), 4,600; Saudi Arabia (1988), 10,000; Syria (1986), 5,000; Iran (1988), 14,000; Turkey (1989), 31,000.

Graduate level education and postdoctoral specialization in the basic and applied sciences are still dependent on foreign study.

Despite large numbers of scientists and engineers, the science and technology systems in most countries suffer from a lack of articulation: higher education is not integrated with demand. Moreover, continuing and distance education is still underdeveloped. Consequently, there is an inability to adapt and upgrade manpower skills in an efficient and cost-effective manner.

Israel, by contrast, depends heavily on educated immigrants. Its universities are of high quality, and effective systems of continuing and distance education have been introduced.

Research & Development

R&D in Israel is at the same level as those of leading industrial countries. It publishes about 10,000 papers a year in refereed journals surveyed by the Institute of Scientific Information (ISI) in Philadelphia. Its per capita publication output compares favorably with that of the United States, and the profile of its publications is similar to that of other industrial countries.

Israeli researchers circulate in and receive funding and support from European and American research establishments. A considerable proportion of Israeli R&D is directed toward weapons systems; but Israel also has strong research programs in most scientific and technological fields of relevance to its economy. It devotes about 3 percent of its gross national product (GNP) to R&D, and currently has about 50,000 research scientists. Its heavy emphasis on military technology is, however, causing serious economic problems as a result of the current collapse of the world demand for weaponry.

The scientific output of the Arab countries can be compared favorably with that of Brazil and India, the leading developing countries. During the 1980s, the number of scientific publications per million inhabitants was 18 (Brazil), 16 (India), and 15 (the Arab world). The per capita output of the Arab countries is some 2 percent that of industrial countries. In 1990, there were more than 5,000 publications from 700 Arab institutions. Half of these were from 12 institutions, 11 of which were universities. Other institutions involved in publishing were hospitals and agricultural research stations.

R&D in the Arab countries is overwhelmingly of an applied nature. Thirty-eight percent of publications are in medicine; 20 percent in agriculture;

17 percent in engineering; 17 percent in the basic sciences; and 8 percent in economics and management. Even work that is classified as basic science is often of an applied nature. The three leading countries in order of research output are Egypt (37 percent), Saudi Arabia (20 percent), and Kuwait (12 percent). In 1990, Kuwaiti output had started to approach that of European countries.

Publications from Iran and Turkey are on a more limited scale; their output in 1990 was 161 and 1,300, respectively. The number of publishing institutions was 80 (Iran) and 155 (Turkey).

The profile of publications from Iran and Turkey, like that in the Arab countries, emphasizes traditional and applied fields such as medicine and agriculture; the proportion of publications in the basic sciences, molecular biology, information sciences, and other advanced areas is far below international levels.

The exact funding of R&D in the Arab world, Iran, and Turkey is not accurately known; it is estimated, however, to be below 1.0 percent (probably closer to 0.5 percent) of GNP throughout the region.

Institutional Framework

The capacity to apply science and technology is dependent on the prevailing institutional framework rather than on the actual number of professionals. Most of the countries have some form of institution to manage science and technology: ministries of science and technology or directorates, attached to the ministry of higher education, of planning, or to the prime minister, which are responsible for different aspects of science and technology.

But the pervasive nature of science and technology is still not recognized, and these institutions are generally bureaucratic and inflexible; they tend to regard science and technology as being restricted to R&D and manpower.

Once again, Israel is the exception; it has established an effective and comprehensive system of science policy planning and management.

The Application of Science and Technology

Some of the instruments through which science and technology are developed and applied are: consult-

ing and contracting organizations, agricultural research stations, extension programs, hospitals, industrial firms, testing laboratories, information services, and others.

Most countries have organizations to provide these services that vary in competence and efficiency. A brief description follows of two strategic types of organizations.

Consulting organizations are critical instruments for planning and designing new projects and for adapting and transferring technology. A substantial number of state-run and private consulting firms have been established throughout the region. In fact, one of the largest international consulting firms in developing countries is Lebanese (Dar al-Hanadasa [Shair & Partners]). Large public-sector consulting firms are found in most countries of the region.

Consulting firms are heavily oriented toward civil engineering technologies, with the result that the region is still dependent on the importation of consulting services in industrial technology.

Contracting organizations bring together ideas, plans, materials, equipment, labor, and financing to produce the desired products within an agreed schedule and cost. The largest contracting firms in the region are in Turkey, whose government has provided them with the necessary financial, risk cover, and diplomatic support.

There are around 100,000 Arab contracting firms, but the Arab countries still depend on foreign firms for 50 percent of their requirements. This is largely due to the absence of appropriate public policies. The leading Arab contracting companies are privately owned and based in Lebanon and Saudi Arabia.

National Science Policies

Israel is the only country in the region with the capacity to design and implement science and technology policies. In the rest of the region, national, regional, and international organizations have sought to promote the development of capabilities in science policy formation, but the results have been limited. This is due to the prevalence of preindustrial political cultures, which have made science policy formation difficult, if not impossible.

a medical degree in the Soviet Union and was promoted to the rank of military general by the Marxist regime of Babrak Karmal (1980–1986) in recognition of her service as a surgeon during the fighting between the Karmal regime and the mojahedin (Afghan freedom fighters). Although she received her medical training in the Soviet Union and worked closely with Soviet doctors in the military hospital in Kabul, there is no evidence to suggest that she joined the Afghan communist party (the People's Democratic Party of Afghanistan). She was director of the Women and Children's Hospital in Kabul under the Taliban and an advocate for the protection of women, but she opposed the campaign in support of Afghan women led by Western feminists and Afghan women activists in exile; in her opinion, they were inadequately informed about conditions inside Afghanistan and attempted to use the plight of Afghan women to promote a Western feminist agenda. She is highly regarded by educated women inside Afghanistan.

SENZIL NAWID

SEFARETNAME

See GLOSSARY

SEFRIOUI, AHMED

[1915–]

Moroccan novelist and short-story writer.

Ahmed Sefrioui was born in Fez, Morocco. He studied at the Mulay Idris College in Fez, where he received a predominantly French education. He subsequently held posts at the Moroccan Office of Arts and Crafts, the Batha Museum in Fez, and the Office of Historic Monuments in Rabat.

Sefrioui's writings show his great interest in his country's folklore. *Le jardin des sortilèges ou le parfum des légendes* (1989; The garden of sorcery or the perfume of legends) is essentially a book of folktales. Other works, such as *Le chapelet d'ambre* (1949; The amber rosary) and *La boîte à merveille* (1954; The magic box), portray traditional Moroccan life and customs, which Sefrioui cherishes. Although they were written while Morocco was a French colony, Sefrioui's books ignore the foreign presence. His portrayals of his country's traditions are an affirmation of a threatened identity.

Sefrioui's approach is that of an ethnologist describing his society's customs and traditions and his religion's (Islam's) dictates. His novel *La maison de servitude* (1973; The house of slavery) provides a glimpse of traditional life in the city of Fez and of the teaching at the *qarawiyyin* (mosque university), paying special attention to details and using many Arabic terms to add an element of local color. Sefrioui's concern for the preservation of his culture is not unconditional and blind, however: He believes in the evolution of societies and the inevitability—and benefit—of change.

See also LITERATURE: ARABIC, NORTH AFRICAN.

Bibliography

Jack, Belinda. *Francophone Literatures: An Introductory Survey.* New York: Oxford University Press, 1996.

Marx-Scouras, Danielle. "North African Literature in French." *Encyclopedia of African Literature,* edited by Simon Gikandi. London and New York: Routledge, 2003.

AIDA A. BAMIA

ŞEKER AHMET

[1841–1907]

Ottoman Turkish painter.

Ahmet Ali Paşa, known as Şeker Ahmet Paşa, was born and educated in the Uskudar district of Istanbul. While a student at the medical school, his talent for painting drew the attention of Sultan Abdülaziz, who sent him to Paris where he studied the academic painting of the period with French artists Boulanger and Gérôme. In 1870, he displayed his work in a Parisian exhibition, and in 1871, he returned to Istanbul. Şeker Ahmet Paşa organized and participated in a number of exhibitions in Istanbul and won many Ottoman and foreign awards for his work. The highly finished quality of his paints and the static linearity of his renderings call to mind French academic painters such as Daubigny and Courbet. His series of landscapes of the gardens and parks of Istanbul, as well as a variety of still lifes, reflects the conscious efforts of Turkish artists to develop Western techniques of painting.

Bibliography

Renda, Günsel, and Kortepeter, C. Max, eds. *The Transformation of Turkish Culture: The Atatürk Legacy.* Princeton, NJ: Kingston Press, 1986.

DAVID WALDNER

SELÇUK, MUNIR NURETTIN
[1899–1981]

Turkish singer and composer.

One of the most skillful and famous Turkish singers of the twentieth century, Munir Nurettin Selçuk was born in Istanbul during the Ottoman Empire, the son of an official in the Imperial Council. His aptitude for music and his beautiful voice became apparent when he was still a child, and he then began to take music lessons from the foremost teachers of the time.

He gave his first public concert at the age of eighteen. Throughout the 1920s, he continued to study music, including a period of piano study in Paris, and his first recordings date from this decade. Beginning in 1942, he served on the board of directors of the Istanbul Conservatory and became its chief in 1953. He composed more than one hundred pieces and was a founder of the Eastern Music Group, which was led by Ali Rifat Çagetay.

See also MUSIC.

DAVID WALDNER

SELIM III
[1761–1808]

Twenty-eighth Ottoman sultan, 1789–1807.

The son of Mustafa III, Selim was allowed by his uncle Abdülhamit I an unusually free and liberal upbringing, on the assumption that he would succeed to the throne. Wars against Russia during the reigns of his father and uncle convinced Selim of the need to modernize the Ottoman army, and while still a prince he sought advice and assistance from King Louis XVI of France for this purpose.

When Selim succeeded his uncle in April 1789, the Ottoman Empire was again at war with Russia and Austria. Selim's first act, in May, was to convene a special assembly of leading statesmen to discuss the empire's military and financial problems,

A 1798 engraving of Selim III (1761–1808), sultan of the Ottoman Empire from 1789 to 1807. Selim's attempts to reform the empire angered conservatives and the Janissaries, who overthrew him in 1807 and then had him strangled. © MICHAEL NICHOLSON/CORBIS. REPRODUCED BY PERMISSION.

and to request detailed reports on how to proceed with reforms. The resulting New Order program accelerated and formalized the piecemeal military and educational Europeanization started earlier. A new army corps was formed, with a separate financial bureau to administer earmarked revenues to support the effort. Schools to train officers for the army and navy in the European manner were given new impetus. Another extension of a process begun earlier was in diplomatic relations with European powers. Ambassadors had been sent to leading

United Airlines flight 175 was the second hijacked plane flown into the World Trade Center in New York City on 11 September 2001. These attacks, which have been linked to the al-Qaʿida terrorist network, prompted the United States to military action against Afghanistan's Taliban leadership as part of its "War on Terrorism." © AP/WIDE WORLD PHOTOS. REPRODUCED BY PERMISSION.

to the 11 September attacks. More than half of them were convicted on traffic or visa violations and were deported out of the United States. Around the world, 11 September signaled a new era of international relations with the inauguration of the Bush Doctrine, according to which the United States would claim the right to attack other countries, and to overthrow their governments, if those governments were perceived to pose a threat to the United States. The aggressive response of the United States, through the wars in Afghanistan and Iraq, and the presence of U.S. troops in more than 120 countries, alarmed world public opinion, although Americans remained by and large supportive of U.S. efforts. In the Middle East, antipathy to the U.S. government seems to have increased after 11 September following the statements and actions of the White House, which remains convinced that its problem with the Muslim world is one of public relations, not politics. Toward that effort, the U.S. government has been spending millions to influ-

ence the opinions and politics of the Muslim world. It is certain that the events of 11 September (the subject of hundreds of books in many languages) will influence world affairs for years, if not decades, to come.

See also BUSH, GEORGE W.; QAʿIDA, AL-.

AS'AD ABUKHALIL

SERASKER

See GLOSSARY

SERI, DAN-BENAYA
[1935–]

Israeli author.

Seri was born in Jerusalem. His first novel, *Grandma Sultana's Salty Biscuits* (1980), was acclaimed for its originality in weaving folk motifs, psychological depth, and surrealism into a poetic prose rich in language and detail. His second book, *Birds of Shade* (1987), includes four novellas, one of which, "Siman-Tov's Thousand Wives," was made into a film.

Seri's works are set in Jerusalem and focus on its Sephardic (Mizrahi) Jewish communities. He creates bizarre plots of sexual perversion stemming from cultural mores, customs, and taboos, as well as individual eccentricity. The fictitious community featured in these works is oblivious to the surrounding world, lives by its folk traditions and lusts, and is controlled by the intensity of a pseudological progression of events. The gallery of characters created by Seri appears in all of his books, forming a fantastic-realistic world of consistent anomalies. His prose style is saturated with biblical and Talmudic references, often used out of their original context and meaning, thus producing a cunning modernistic irony.

Mishael, the protagonist of Seri's novel *Mishael* (1992), is a lonely widower who discovers that he is pregnant. As his body grotesquely transforms to that of a woman, Mishael sets out to find himself a new wife, all the while confronting his own sexual identity and the harassment of his community. The novel suggests childhood traumas and guilt as the grounds for this predicament, yet the hero's acceptance of the unnatural as reality is its main strength.

ZVIA GINOR

SETIF

City southwest of Constantine in northeastern Algeria.

Setif is located at the site of the ancient Roman city of Sitifis. Near Setif in 1152 the Almohads defeated the Banu Hilal tribe. The city declined during the Ottoman Empire. During France's colonial administration, the city was the site of bloody riots and retributions (the Setif Revolt) in May 1945, which galvanized Algerian nationalism. The estimated population in 1998 was 212,000.

Bibliography

Abun-Nasr, Jamil M. *A History of the Maghrib in the Islamic Period.* Cambridge: Cambridge University Press, 1987.

PHILLIP C. NAYLOR

SETIF REVOLT (1945)

One of the most violent incidents in the history of French colonialism in Algeria.

The May 1945 revolt in the city of Setif, Algeria, was caused by the deportation proceedings of Messali Hadj, the rising expectations for reform, and the agitations of nationalists. After the start of a parade celebrating Europe's victory over fascism, Muslims demonstrated carrying nationalist placards. This provoked the police, leading to rioting and the deaths of 103 Europeans. French retribution probably caused between 5,000 and 10,000 Muslim deaths (although some contend that the fatalities were in the tens of thousands).

This event convinced many younger nationalists that violence was the only recourse to French colonialism as disclosed by the 1947 formation of the Organisation Spéciale (OS) and in 1954 the Front de Libération Nationale (FLN).

See also FRONT DE LIBÉRATION NATIONALE (FLN); HADJ, MESSALI AL-.

PHILLIP C. NAYLOR

SETTLEMENT POLICY (ISRAEL)

See ISRAELI SETTLEMENT POLICY (ISRAEL)

SEVEN SISTERS

See GLOSSARY

ŞEVKET, MAHMUT
[1856–1913]

Ottoman general and grand vizier.

Born in Baghdad the son of a provincial government official, Mahmut Şevket, known as Şevket Paşa, completed his studies in Constantinople (now Istanbul), where he entered military service. As part of a special commission for military purchases and training, he was sent to Germany for nine years. He was promoted to the rank of general in 1901. Between 1905 and 1909, he held several posts in Rumelia, achieving minor successes in easing tension in the region.

A year after the Young Turk revolution, Şevket Paşa achieved new prominence as commander of the Hareket Ordusu (operations army) that marched on Constantinople in April 1909, putting down the counterrevolution. In the new post of inspector general of Constantinople, he led the brutal represssion and punishment of the rebels under martial law for the next two years. In 1910, he became minister of war and advocated withdrawal of the military from politics. When the Committee for Union and Progress (CUP) seized power in January 1913, it appointed him grand vizier. Six months later, he was assassinated by CUP opponents. His murder introduced a new period of violent repression by the CUP.

See also COMMITTEE FOR UNION AND PROGRESS.

Bibliography

Lewis, Bernard. *The Emergence of Modern Turkey,* 3d edition. New York: Oxford University Press, 2002.

Shaw, Stanford J., and Shaw, Ezel Kural. *History of the Ottoman Empire and Modern Turkey,* Vol. 2: *Reform, Revolution, and Republic: The Rise of Modern Turkey, 1808–1975.* Cambridge, U.K., and New York: Cambridge University Press, 1977.

ELIZABETH THOMPSON

SÈVRES PROTOCOL (1956)

Secret Israeli-British-French agreement.

The Sèvres Protocol was the product of secret negotiations among British, French, and Israeli leaders

From an aristocratic family of Tunis, Bashir Sfar was one of four editors of Tunisia's news periodical *Al-Hadira* (The capital). Sfar was a leader of the reformist Young Tunisian movement, which brought together classically trained Tunisians from the Zaytuna mosque and modernly trained Tunisians from Sadiqi College in the middle years of the French protectorate. This was a precursor to the movement for independence from France.

LAURENCE MICHALAK

SFAR, TAHAR
[1903–]

Tunisian nationalist.

One of the early and most vocal leaders of the nationalist Destour movement, Sfar was educated at the Tunisian Sadiqi College and in France. Sfar became adjunct secretary-general of the Neo-Destour Party in 1934, during the Ksar Hellal Congress that consecrated the rupture between the Neo and Archeo sectors of the independence movement and delineated new guidelines in the struggle toward independence under the leadership of Mahmoud Materi, with Habib Bourguiba as secretary-general. In the late 1930s, faced with increasingly repressive measures by the French colonial administration and disillusioned with the militant stance adopted by Bourguiba and others, Sfar effectively withdrew from politics.

See also BOURGUIBA, HABIB; TUNISIA: OVERVIEW; TUNISIA: POLITICAL PARTIES IN.

Bibliography

Moore, Clement Henry. *Tunisia since Independence: The Dynamics of One-Party Government.* Berkeley: University of California Press, 1965.

MATTHEW S. GORDON
UPDATED BY VANESA CASANOVA-FERNANDEZ

SFAX

Tunisian seaport on the northeast coast of the Gulf of Gabès.

Sfax (also Sfaqes or Safaqis) was a Phoenician trading center before it was settled in the eighth century by Arab invaders spreading Islam; they built a mosque in the mid-ninth century. It continued as an important seaport for the Mediterranean olive oil trade and was one of the few Tunisian towns to resist the French occupation after the protectorate of 1881, thus suffering bombardment. After Tunisia became independent in 1956, Sfax became the center of a governorate and the second-largest Tunisian city, with a population of some 232,000 (as of 1984).

Today it has a medical school, one of three appellate courts, a large prison, the regional radio station, an international airport and an air-force base, and a busy port that handles mainly phosphates and olive oil.

Bibliography

Nelson, Harold D., ed. *Tunisia: A Country Study.* Washington, DC: U.S. Government Printing Office, 1986.

MATTHEW S. GORDON

SFEIR, NASRALLAH
[1920–]

Lebanese Maronite patriarch.

Nasrallah Sfeir (Sufayr) was born in Rayfun, Lebanon, in 1920, and was ordained a priest in 1950. After a service as auxiliary Bishop of Antioch, he was ordained bishop in 1961. He was appointed and confirmed as a Maronite patriarch in 1986, and was elevated to cardinal in 1994. The intra-Maronite civil war in East Beirut and Kisrawan in the late 1980s affected Sfeir's leadership. In 1990 followers of General Michel Aoun chased the Maronite and publicly humiliated him before television cameras. Aoun was later ousted, and he sought refuge in France. The arrest and trial of Samir Geagea, the former commander of the Lebanese Forces), left the Maronite community eager for leadership and guidance, which was promptly provided by Sfeir. Sfeir's political role and influence expanded in the 1990s and in the early twenty-first century. He was largely quiet about the Israeli occupation of Lebanon, but became very vocal against the Syrian military presence in Lebanon after 2000. He also criticized what he saw as the misapplication of the Ta'if Accord, and he has never visited the Syrian capital in recent years despite several invitations. He chaired the Maronite bishop council and released overtly political statements on a monthly basis. His political influence within the Maronite community is supreme, and he receives a wide range of visitors every day.

See also AOUN, MICHEL; MARONITES; TA'IF
ACCORD.

As'ad AbuKhalil

SHAB'A FARMS

*A group of farms near the convergence of Syrian,
Lebanese, and (due to Israel's occupation of Syrian territory since 1967) Israeli territories.*

Shab'a Farms became a focus of international conflict in the summer of 2000, after Israel withdrew
its forces from South Lebanon, ending a costly occupation that began in 1976. The fourteen farms
that make up Shab'a Farms are named after the village of Shab'a, on the western slopes of Mount Hermon (in Arabic, Jabal al-Shaykh). The area of
Shab'a Farms encompasses approximately 6.5 square
miles. Israel maintains that the farms are Syrian territory and thus argues that it should have rights over
them. The Syrian government insists that the farms
are part of Lebanese territory. Since the border in
this area is not clearly demarcated, the United Nations has asked the Syrian government for docu-
mentation to back up its claim that the farms are
not part of its territory. Hizbullah, which led the
successful resistance movement against Israel's occupation of South Lebanon, argues that Israel's
withdrawal from Lebanon will not be complete unless and until Israel withdraws from the farms. The
Lebanese government supports this position. Israel
has established a military post on one of the hills
overlooking the area and has exchanged fire with
Hizbullah forces. It is unlikely that the status of the
farms will be settled before the issue of Israel's occupation of Syrian territories—that is to say, the
Golan Heights—is resolved. UN Secretary-General
Kofi Annan has recommended that all sides recognize the demarcation line drawn after the 1973
Arab–Israel war as a temporary measure. But Israel
does not seem ready to leave the farms, and some
reports have mentioned the settlement of Ethiopian
Jews there.

Syria and Hizbullah may also be interested in
keeping the issue of Shib'a Farms alive as it grant
them a reason, or excuse, to escalate or de-escalate,
the level of tensions with Israel. However, there is
certainly a nationalist basis for both Syria and
Lebanon, which explains why every piece of land becomes important.

See also ANNAN, KOFI A.; GOLAN HEIGHTS;
HIZBULLAH.

As'ad AbuKhalil

SHABBI, ABU AL-QASIM AL-
[1909–1934]

Noted Tunisian poet.

Born in the southern Tunisian oasis town of Tozeur,
Abu al-Qasim al-Shabbi had a mobile childhood
because of his father's judicial career. The constant
traveling familiarized him with the Tunisian countryside and people and induced in him a profound
and lifelong infatuation with both that permeated
his later poetry. Studies at Tunis's eminent Zaytuna
Mosque university and law school also influenced
al-Shabbi, but they clashed with his penchant for
European and Arabic literature and with his budding rebellion against the French colonial system
and the restrictions of the Arab poetic tradition. His
entire poetic career was compressed in a seven-year
period that occurred between age eighteen, when he
began publishing his poetry, and age twenty-five,
when he succumbed to heart disease. The pressures
of family obligations caused by his father's untimely
death in 1929 and the additional responsibilities occasioned by his marriage are thought to have contributed to his early demise in October 1934.

New currents in Arab poetry from the Middle
East and North America stirred al-Shabbi's imagination, as did the European Romantics. Al-Shabbi
sought to break the bonds of convention and tradition and to revolutionize both poetry and society.
Although he opposed the French colonial regime, he
also castigated traditional Tunisian mores and called
for social transformation, freedom, and progress.
For this imaginative poet, the city contrasted unfa-
vorably with nature, where he felt he could escape
into a solitary utopia and indulge in his pursuit of
idealized womanhood.

Al-Shabbi's revolutionary stance appealed to a
later generation of Tunisian and Arab nationalists.
Along with other Tunisians of his generation, al-
Shabbi contributed to the literary renaissance of his
country, at the same time that other Tunisians heralded a social renaissance (for example, Tahir al-
Haddad in his epochal work on Tunisian women)
and a political renaissance (for example, Habib

in Beirut before moving to Paris, where he received most of his secondary education and all of his university training. After obtaining a French *licence* (bachelor of arts degree) in law, he returned to Beirut, where he first worked first as cultural attaché at the French embassy. He later became a professor and then the secretary-general at the Ecole Supérieure des Lettres, which had emerged as a center for the promotion of French avant-garde poetry in the region.

His first collection of poems, *Poésies I,* published in Paris in 1938, showed very clearly the influence of surrealism on his work and gained him the attention of French and international critics. Repeated stays in Paris enabled him to maintain a close friendship with André Breton, a leader in the surrealist movement, whom he had met during his student days. He also developed friendships with Jean Cocteau, Paul Eluard, St.-John Perse (pseudonym for Marie-René-Auguste-Aléxis St. Léger), Jules Supervielle, and other leading French intellectuals. By the early 1950s, Shahada already had established himself as one of the leading neosurrealist poets and the foremost representative of Lebanese poets writing in the French language. It was then that he started writing plays, which soon brought him more recognition than his poetry and indeed established him as the best-known French-language dramatist outside France.

During the 1950s and 1960s, Shahada wrote more than a half-dozen important plays; the best-known of these are *Monsieur Bob'le* (1951), *La soirée des proverbes* (1954; The evening of proverbs), *Le voyage* (1961; The voyage), and *L'emigré de Brisbane* (1965; The emigré from Brisbane). Although Shahada always wrote in French and spent a great part of his life in France, his work reflects his emotional attachment to his native land and an unmistakable Eastern influence. Its emphasis on magic and fantasy has even led some critics to compare it to Middle Eastern fairy tales and to describe Shahada as a storyteller in the tradition of Sheherazade. His heroes (for instance, M. Bob'le and Vasco) are usually good-natured, naive figures who were able to preserve a childlike innocence and the ability to wonder at the marvels of nature and life. They identify mysteries behind the appearance of the ordinary and are usually led from banal, everyday situations into increasingly unexpected, odd, and captivating adventures.

Far less preoccupied with understanding the world than with experiencing its beauty, they are sometimes shown communicating not only with other human beings, but also with the animals and objects that surround them.

By placing such strange but charming characters at the center of his humorous plays, Shahada seeks to evoke the harmony that men and women can find with nature and each other. He invites the members of his audience to look for the mysteries of life, and to listen to their intuitions and dreams instead of being driven by their intellects. Shahada's plays thus constitute a plea for feeling before understanding, and they exhibit an unmistakable Middle Eastern sensitivity to the wonders of nature.

Although Shahada's suspenseful, funny plays highlight the comical, incongruous, and tragic aspects of the human condition and draw on technical devices that were used in the avant-garde theater of the 1950s, they nevertheless differ from the so-called Theater of the Absurd. Unlike plays by Eugène Ionesco or Samuel Beckett, for instance, they betray an optimistic outlook on life. Beckett's characters tend to feel helpless, frustrated, and bitter, and live only in their minds, whereas Shahada's heroes are spontaneous individuals who still display the simple happiness and purity of childhood. In sharp contrast to the way Beckett emphasizes the chaotic and meaningless aspects of life, Shahada invites his audience to appreciate what he sees as the intrinsic harmony and beauty of the world and to look at one's surroundings with the innocent, uncorrupted eyes of a child.

In 1973, Shahada returned to poetry. In December 1986—a year after his last collection of poems, *Le nageur d'un seul amour* (The swimmer of an only love) was published in Paris—the Académie Française awarded him the Grand Prix de la Francophonie during a summit of French-speaking countries held in Paris. By becoming the first recipient of this prestigious honor three years before his death, Shahada obtained well-deserved recognition of his unique place in the world of Francophone literature. He is remembered as the twentieth-century author who best blended Western surrealist literature and avant-garde dramatic techniques with the Eastern tradition of storytelling.

See also LITERATURE: ARABIC.

Bibliography

Berndt, Barbara Ann. "The Franciful World of Georges Schehadé." Ph.D. dissertation, University of Wisconsin-Madison, 1979.

GUILAIN P. DENOEUX
UPDATED BY MICHAEL R. FISCHBACH

SHAHBANDAR, ABD AL-RAHMAN
[1880–1940]

Syrian politician

Born in Damascus, Abd al-Rahman Shahbandar attended the Syrian Protestant College (later the American University of Beirut). He received his medical degree in 1906 and became a professor of medicine. He was one of the most prominent nationalists in Damascus after World War I, serving Amir Faisal I ibn Hussein as chief liaison with Britain, and as an interpreter for the King-Crane Commission in 1919. Shahbandar was appointed minister of foreign affairs in 1920 by the newly crowned King Faisal. The French promptly disbanded this government, and Shahbandar fled to Egypt. He returned to Damascus under French amnesty in 1921 and founded the first nationalist organization in Syria, the Iron Hand. Shahbandar was arrested and sentenced to twenty years in prison for nationalist activities in 1922. The sentence was changed to exile, and after seeking support for Syria's independence in the West, with the help of his friend Charles R. Crane, he returned to Damascus in 1924.

In 1925, Shahbandar organized and led the People's Party, which played a central role in the revolt (1925–1927). He spent ten years in Cairo, then returned to Damascus in April 1937. His pro-Hashimite stance put him in direct confrontation with the ruling National Bloc, and he was placed under house arrest in 1938. Shahbandar's quest for Britain's support for a confederation of Syria, Transjordan, Palestine, and Lebanon under Amir Abdullah I ibn Hussein, and his denunications of his more hard-line nationalist rivals, led to his assassination in Damascus (June 1940). Ultimate responsibility for the assassination was never fixed, though National Bloc members may have been involved.

Bibliography

Khoury, Philip S. *Syria and the French Mandate: The Politics of Arab Nationalism, 1920–1945.* Princeton, NJ: Princeton University Press, 1987.

CHARLES U. ZENZIE

SHAHIN, TANYOS
[1815–1895]

Leader of the Lebanese peasant revolt.

Tanyos Shahin was born into the Saʿada family in Rayfun, Kisrawan. When peasant protests against the feudal landlords swept parts of Mount Lebanon in 1858, Shahin was approached by armed peasants and asked to become a local leader in Rayfun; his influence quickly spread through the Kisrawan region. He succeeded Salil Sfayr, who feared the consequence of his role and resigned. Shahin articulated the grievances of the peasants to the Mashayikh (heads of Maronite landowning families) and was not reluctant to use violence to achieve his aims. The Maronite patriarch Bulus Masʿad accused Shahin of intensifying the conflict between the peasants and the landlords. When the landlords tried to ignore the demands of the peasants, Shahin made clear his willingness to use force. At one point he tried to arrest leading landlords who were meeting in a monastery, but the presence of clerics stopped him. Shahin called for the confiscation of property and crops owned by the landlords and in 1859 seized silk and wheat belonging to landlords and put it in his own house. His power allowed him to punish and reward individuals. By the spring of 1859, he had expelled all members of the Khazin family from Kisrawan. At the end of the year, the Maronite peasant rebellion had become interwined with the Maronite-Druze conflict, which led to the civil war of 1860. The appointment of a Mutasarrif in 1861 led to the defeat of Shahin, although he was allowed to remain in Kisrawan as local leader.

ASʿAD ABUKHALIL

SHAHIN, YUSUF
[1926–]

Egyptian film director.

Born in Alexandria, Egypt, to a middle-class Christian family, Yusuf Shahin studied at Alexandria

period are unclear. In November 1992, Shamikh returned to the GPC as secretary of utilities, tourism, and communications, surviving a cabinet reshuffle in April 1993 in which he was designated secretary of utilities, public works, transport, and communications. The GPC was again reshuffled in December 1995, and Shamikh became the secretary of utilities and housing, a post he held until early 2000.

On 2 March 2000 Shamikh was named GPC secretary (prime minister) in a new Libyan minigovernment after the General People's Congress (parliament) labeled the previous government of Muhammad Ahmad al-Manghusha a failure, dismantling most of its ministries and transferring their functions to municipal councils. He was replaced as GPC secretary by Shukri Ghanim, secretary of economy and foreign trade, on 14 June 2003 in an effort to promote a policy of greater economic openness. Since June 2003 Shamikh has served the Qaddafi regime as head of the general planning council.

See also LIBYA; QADDAFI, MUAMMAR AL-.

Bibliography

St John, Ronald Bruce. *Historical Dictionary of Libya,* 3d edition. Lanham, MD: Scarecrow Press, 1998.

RONALD BRUCE ST JOHN

SHAMI, MUHAMMAD ABDULLAH AL-
[c.1890 –c.1964]

Senior administrator for Imams Yahya and Ahmad from the 1940s through the early 1960s.

Muhammad Abdullah al-Shami came from a prominent traditional family of judges, administrators, and teachers (a *qadi* family) from the town of Kawkaban, near San'a. After a career as senior administrator in many large towns, he served Imam Ahmad as governor and frontier officer in the eastern border town of al-Baydha during the 1950s, a time when the British were pushing north from Aden into the hinterland and Yemen was resisting this push. He conducted repeated border negotiations with his British counterpart, Basil Seager, and he repeatedly encouraged tribal forays into territory disputed with the British and subverted South Yemeni tribes in those territories with money and arms. Later, when

he was already more than seventy years of age, al-Shami successfully negotiated for the ailing Imam Ahmad a tentative end to the tribal revolt of 1960; he was senior administrator of San'a at the time of the overthrow of the imamate in 1962. In the wake of the 1962 revolution, al-Shami was imprisoned, tried, and convicted. He was released after several months and retired to Kawkaban, where he died in about 1964.

Bibliography

Bidwell, Robin. *The Two Yemens.* Boulder, CO: Westview; Essex, U.K.: Longman, 1983.

ROBERT D. BURROWES

SHAMIR, MOSHE
[1921–]

Israeli writer and political activist.

Moshe Shamir was born in Mandatory Palestine, in Safed, and raised in Tel Aviv. From 1941 to 1947 he was a member of Kibbutz Mishmar ha-Emek. In 1944 he joined the Palmah, and he fought in the Arab-Israel War (1948). Shamir is a leader of the first generation of native Israeli writers and best known for his novels of the 1940s and 1950s, which depict in rich detail and glowing terms the development of the new state and the sabra character. *Hu Halakh Ba-Sadot* (1947; *He Walked through the Fields* [1959]), *Ad Elat* (1950; Until Elat), and *Kilometer 56* (1949) were all written in this vein. This adulatory attitude toward Israeli society metamorphosed into a critical one in the novels *ha-Gevul* (1966; The border) and *Yonah Be-Hazer Zarah* (1975; Pigeon in a strange yard). Shamir's early embrace of Marxism influenced the underlying themes of class conflict in many of his historical novels, such as *Melekh Basar Va-Dam* (1954; *The King of Flesh and Blood* [1958]) and *Kivsat ha-Rash* (1956; *David's Stranger* [1964]).

Following the 1967 Arab–Israel War, Shamir helped found the Greater Land of Israel movement, advocating the retention of all captured land west of the Jordan River. In 1973 he joined the Likud Party under Menachem Begin but then switched to the right-wing Tehiyah Party to protest the conclusion of a peace treaty with Egypt. He served as a member of the ninth Knesset (Israel's parliament) from 1977 to 1981.

While continuing to publish novels (*Playboys* [1986], *To the End* [1991], and *Ya'ir Avraham Shtern* [2000]), Shamir in recent years has also written critiques of Israeli literature (*Personal View* [1987], *The Seed Carriers* [1989], *For and Against* [1989], and *Filling the Gap* [1999]), of Israeli politics (*The Red Thread* [1987]), studies of Jewish identity (*Searchlight to the Depth* [1996]) and one book calling for a Zionist renaissance (*The Green Place* [1991]).

Bibliography

Almog, Oz. *The Sabra: The Creation of the New Jew*, translated by Haim Watzman. Berkeley: University of California Press, 2000.

Shaked, Gershon. *Modern Hebrew Fiction*, translated by Yael Lotan. Bloomington: University of Indiana Press, 2000.

Shamir, Moshe. *The King of Flesh and Blood*, translated by David Patterson. New York: Vanguard, 1958.

Shamir, Moshe. *With His Own Hands*, translated by Joseph Shachter. Jerusalem: Institute for the Translation of Hebrew Literature, 1970.

ANN KAHN
UPDATED BY DONNA ROBINSON DIVINE

SHAMIR, YITZHAK
[1915–]

Israeli prime minister, 1983–1984, 1986–1992.

Shamir, whose name means "hard stone," was born Yitzhak Yzernitsky in 1915 in Rozhnoï, eastern Poland, to leftist parents. He emigrated in 1935 to Mandatory Palestine, where he studied briefly at the Hebrew University. In 1937 he joined the Irgun Zva'i Le'umi (IZL) in Tel Aviv, where, under the code name "Nissan," he participated in terrorist attacks and reprisals against the Arab population and British interests. In 1940, after the IZL decided to stop all operations against the British and join them in their fight against Nazi Germany, Shamir joined the "IZL in Israel" (Hebrew: Etzel be-Yisrael; acronym: IZL Beth), a splinter group headed by Abraham Stern that rejected any cease-fire with the British occupation forces in Palestine. During that time, the group also tried unsuccessfully to establish relations with the Third Reich.

Shamir was captured by the British police in December 1941 and incarcerated in the Mazra prison

A former member of the Lohamei Herut Yisrael and the Mossad, Yitzhak Shamir became Israel's prime minister after the retirement of Menachem Begin in 1983. Shamir served a second term from 1986 until 1992, when his Likud Party was defeated in the general elections. © BETTMANN/CORBIS. REPRODUCED BY PERMISSION.

camp, from which he escaped in August 1942. With the remnants of the IZL Beth, he created the Fighters for the Freedom of Israel (Hebrew: Lohamei Herut Yisrael; acronym: LEHI) which he led with Natan Yellin-Mor and Israel Eldad. As chief of operations, Shamir organized several major terrorist attacks against British targets, notably, in September 1944 in Cairo, the assassination of Walter Edward Guinness, Lord Moyne, the British minister of state. Arrested again in June 1946, he was deported to a prison camp in Asmara, Eritrea, and a year later escaped to the colony of French Somaliland (now Djibouti), where he became a political refugee.

In May 1948 Shamir returned to the newly proclaimed State of Israel where, with the disbanded

Middle East, Political

International boundary
Disputed boundary
⊛ Capital city
• Other city

ATLANTIC
OCEAN

PORTUGAL

SPAIN

FRANCE

BELGIUM
LUXEMBOURG

GERMANY

SWITZERLAND

CZECH
REPUBLIC

POLAND

SLOVAKIA

AUSTRIA

HUNGARY

SLOVENIA

ROMANIA

CROATIA

BOSNIA AND
HERZEGOVINA

SERBIA
AND
MONTENEGRO

BULGAR

ITALY

MACEDONIA

ALBANIA

GREECE

Mediterranean Sea

⊛ Algiers

Tunis ⊛

⊛ Tripoli

Benghazi

Rabat ⊛
Casablanca

Fez

MOROCCO

Marrakech

Ouargla

TUNISIA

ALGERIA

Adrar

LIBYA

Sabha

El Aaiún

Djanet

al-Jawf

Western
Sahara

Fdérik

Atar

MAURITANIA

MALI

NIGER

CHAD

⊛ Nouakchott

SENEGAL

GAMBIA

BURKINA FASO

GUINEA-
BISSAU

GUINEA

BENIN

NIGERIA

SIERRA
LEONE

CÔTE
D'IVOIRE

GHANA

TOGO

CENTRAL AFRICAN
REPUBLIC

LIBERIA

CAMEROON

EQUATORIAL
GUINEA

SÃO TOMÉ
AND PRÍNCIPE

REPUBLIC
OF THE
CONGO

GABON

DEMOCRATIC
REPUBLIC
OF THE CONGO

ATLANTIC
OCEAN

ANGOLA

45°N

30°N

15°N

0°

15°E